LATIN LITERATURE

Gian Biagio Conte

Latin Literature

A HISTORY

Translated by Joseph B. Solodow

Revised by Don Fowler and Glenn W. Most

THE JOHNS HOPKINS UNIVERSITY PRESS
BALTIMORE AND LONDON

Original Italian-language edition, *Letteratura latina: Manuale storico dalle origini alla fine dell'impero romano,* published by Casa Editrice Felice Le Monnier.
Copyright © 1987 by Le Monnier, Firenze

© 1994 The Johns Hopkins University Press
All rights reserved
Printed in the United States of America on acid-free paper

Johns Hopkins Paperbacks edition, 1999
9 8 7 6 5 4 3 2 1

The Johns Hopkins University Press
2715 North Charles Street
Baltimore, Maryland 21218-4363
www.press.jhu.edu

Library of Congress Cataloging-in-Publication Data
can be found at the end of this book.

A catalog record for this book is available from the British Library.

ISBN 0-8018-6253-1 (pbk.)

Contents

PART FIVE   **The Late Empire**

Detailed Contents

PART FIVE

The Late Empire

Foreword

The book you are holding in your hand is an extraordinary achievement. If you care at all about Rome and its literature, pagan and Christian, this book will soon become your friend, and before long you will wonder how you ever managed without it.

Three notable ingredients have been combined in this encyclopedic history of Latin literature: Gian Biagio Conte's exceptional distinction as an interpreter and literary critic; the careful planning he and his team of colleagues put into the design of the first and second Italian editions; and the enthusiasm and good judgment the editors of the Johns Hopkins University Press applied to enlist the most sympathetic and perceptive scholars from Europe, Britain, and the United States to cooperate with Professor Conte in redesigning the book for American and British readers. If the author had been less humane, or the publisher less enterprising, this might have ended up as another standard literary handbook, telling you both too much and too little, supplying raw dates, titles, and summaries without critical exegesis. Or again, it might have resembled the recent Roman volume of the *Cambridge History of Classical Literature,* providing a series of interpretive essays varying in approach and critical acumen from one contributor to another, while presupposing the reader's command of all the elementary facts.

Many of us are unable to read Italian with ease, and it is a regrettable aspect of Anglo-American culture that until recently very few works of literary criticism were translated from other European languages for student use. None of Gian Biagio Conte's critical interpretation or theory was available in English before 1987, twenty years after the publication of his first articles on Lucretius and Lucan, poets distant from each other in time, technique, and, many would claim, genre. The best critics reach their major achievement in large-scale interpretation only after carefully testing their methods on detailed analysis of controversial texts, and this has been the pattern of Conte's achievement. His major critical studies *Memoria dei poeti e sistema letterario* (1974) and *Il genere e i suoi confini: Cinque studi sulla poesia di Virgilio* (1980) are firmly based on earlier criticism of complex and allusive Latin texts. Fortunately the greater part of these two books has recently been translated by Charles Segal, with the addition of a special introduction by Conte himself, as *The Rhetoric of Imitation: Genre and Poetic Memory in Virgil and Other Latin Poets* (1987).

Conte's criticism is always stimulating, often demanding, but never without the highest consideration for the art of the ancient writer and the needs of the modern reader. This is not the place to go into the relationship of his critical theories to traditional German philology (for which he shows detailed appreciation and respect), Russian formalism, reader-response theory, or the Italian structuralist tradition. But some of the principles he maintains are so important to our understanding of ancient literature that they deserve to be recalled in this foreword, not least as an acknowledgment of my own debt to his writing.

From the beginning Conte has concerned himself with reexamining the major concepts that articulate all literary history and theory: canons, genres, the imitative processes of emulation and allusion, and context in its fullest sense. Most literary historians implicitly or explicitly accept certain authors as canonical, unwittingly doing an injustice to both the subordinated and the privileged texts. For the new reader the affirmation that the text before him or her is by a great poet (or prose author) can be as oppressive as it is discouraging to approach the marginalized work of a "minor" author (or poet). (Horace has perhaps suffered more than any other Roman from this canonization, which interposes itself between the student and his unprejudiced enjoyment of a text.) Conte rightly insists that writers be treated without prejudice, and this inclusive approach is apparent in his willingness to explore the thought of Pliny the Elder, in his encyclopaedic *Natural History*—ostensibly an extreme instance of the nonliterary work— in search of the author's organizing principles and ideology.

Many of Conte's early studies explore texts that stand poised at the boundaries of genres—between bucolic and elegy, between didactic and epic, or between elegy and didactic. In his investigation of Virgilian poetry in "Genre and Its Boundaries" (*The Rhetoric of Imitation,* 100–208) Conte shows how genre and literary artist interact. The expectations established by the genre challenge the artist to create both within its code and beyond it, so that the work that is his response itself contributes to redefining the nature of the genre for future writers and their audience.

Most classicists study their Greek and Latin texts as students of Shakespeare read his plays—with commentaries stocked with parallels and precedents for the author's usage. Some of these are useful to explain a point of language or clarify an argument, but most are included as demonstrations of the artist's inherited forms (or content), implicitly detracting from his uniqueness and originality. More recently we have been taught to appreciate two aspects of the dialogue between the young artist and his predecessors: the attitude of emulation and the technique of allusion. But emulation alone does not make an orator or a poet, and allusion is something more than erudite name-dropping, the incorporation of tags from approved classical and Hellenistic Greek poets. Scholars in the United States and Britain have greatly refined our understanding of the nature and art of allusion in the last few years, and many of us now share Conte's concern to show how deeply allusive reference can enrich the new text with significance from the (unquoted) original context; indeed, an artist such as Virgil often simultaneously evokes by a single resonant phrase the treatment of the same (or another) theme in exemplary passages from both Greek and Latin models. Not to recognize such allusion is to enjoy only a part of the poet's meaning or his art. At the same time, Conte has taught us that the relationship between a poet and his predecessors includes both intended and, as it were, spontaneous assimilation of elements from previous traditions: Cicero and Quintilian acknowledged that even imitation of style alone will produce a new style compounded of the chosen features of the model and the innate personality of the successor, and Seneca in turn compared the relationship between model and emulator to that between father and son, where there is individuality as well as resemblance.

Finally, context is all-important both in the work of art and in its model. And context extends to historical setting, requiring a full understanding of the intellectual, social, and political circumstances of the artist and the individual creation. The Augustan context changed between the creative years of Horace, Virgil, Tibullus, and Propertius and the early years of Ovid, and Ovid's own circumstances underwent an extreme change with his relegation to the Black Sea outpost of Tomis. It makes a difference to the appreciation of Senecan tragedy or Tacitus's *Dialogue on Orators* whether we believe they were composed in exile or in Rome, during or after the reign of terror of Domitian.

All this Gian Biagio Conte himself will explain better and more subtly than I can hope to in the new introduction that he has composed for this English-language edition of *Letteratura latina*. So let me pass on to the book itself.

Even in a country where histories of Latin literature are published by almost every major scholar and are in constant demand for *licei classici* and universities, *Letteratura latina* has been a landmark. Conte and his colleagues have been able to cover the history of Latin literature from the hymns of the Salii and Saturnian accentual verse to the founding fathers of medieval poetry and history. More than a hundred pages discuss literature after the death of Apuleius, with substantial treatment of Augustine and the other church fathers, the poetry of Ausonius, the philosophy of Boethius, and the histories of Bede and Gregory of Tours. Poetry and creative writing have not been privileged over prose or nonfiction genres such as oratory, letter writing, and philosophy. Both Cicero and Seneca are treated at length, and technical writers receive separate chapters in parts 3 and 4, as do the jurists and the history of the legal corpus.

For each generation or significant cultural phase there is a separate preliminary discussion, as there is for all the authors. Horace, for example, is treated at several levels. His relationships with Virgil, Maecenas, and Augustus are considered in the introduction to the literary period (carefully delimited by events of literary rather than political history, from 43 B.C. and the death of Cicero to the death of Ovid in A.D. 17). Then the entry for Horace (as for each author) begins with the known details of his career and introduces his *Epodes, Satires, Odes,* and *Epistles* with brief analyses of the content of each poetry book. Then the reader is ready to follow the interpretive discussion of each book within its generic tradition—Horace's Epicureanism, his debt to Alcaeus or Sappho, Anacreon or Pindar, or his relationship to Hellenistic critics. After the generic and roughly chronological treatment of Horace's works comes a brief account of his posthumous influence, rounded off by a bibliography of editions and critical studies.

The supporting materials that follow the main body of the text are no less useful: an appendix of Roman political, social, and ideological terms (e.g. *clientela, fides, senatus*) complements the extended appendix of rhetorical, metrical, and literary terminology. The separate list of Greek authors and texts, Appendix 2, meets an urgent need of which I complained when reviewing the *Cambridge History.* (It more than passes my five-*P* test, identifying and documenting Polybius, Panaetius, Poseidonius, Philodemus, and Parthenius.) Each writer is again listed in the extensive index including every named individual or anonymous work. Appendix 1, the chronological table, sets Roman cultural history year by year opposite political history and Greek culture up to A.D. 300 (when Greek culture and history are subsumed under Roman). Thus the entry for 65 B.C. lists Horace's birth, Caesar's aedileship, and Atticus's return to Rome; A.D. 65 reports the deaths of Seneca and Lucan and the exile of Cornutus (with the failure of the Pisonian conspiracy in political history); and in the entry for 565 Venantius Fortunatus leaves Italy to begin his pilgrimage, while Justinian's death is followed by the succession of Justin II as emperor in the East.

Many of us have longed to be able to refer our students to just such a comprehensive and sophisticated literary history, and the Johns Hopkins University Press is to be warmly congratulated (and heartily thanked) for the initiative that has made this international enterprise possible. But the story does not end with an unmodified translation of the most recent Italian edition: The translator, Joseph Solodow, himself an author of important work on Roman poetry, was consulted for his expertise in literary criticism. Author and publisher have sought out scholars from America and Britain to advise on the special needs and interests of English-speaking readers, many of whom meet Latin literature at a later age, and hence with more maturity and sophistication, than most young Italian students. Sections on posthumous influence have been reoriented towards American and British cultural history, and the bibliographies have been updated and reconsidered to focus primarily on scholarship in English. (As an "Anglo-American" educated in England, who has since taught in Scotland, Canada, and three American universities, I particularly appreciate the need for this bilateral approach.) Finally Gian Biagio Conte himself, with typical concern for his readership, has written a completely new introduction to the history and added to the introductory account of Augustan literature an important section on Roman selective redefinition of genres from the hybrid multigeneric poetry of Alexandria. Responding to recent major advances in scholarship, he has also expanded or rewritten the discussions of Lucretius, Catullus, Varro, Horace, Ovid, Statius, Silius Italicus, Martial, Apuleius, and Martianus Capella.

Readers will find that the aims of an informative history are not incompatible with sophisticated (and lucid) literary criticism and that criticism itself does not preempt the reader's opinions but merely sharpens his or her alertness and enjoyment of the text. It is my belief that professional classicists will be as stimulated by this work as students or teachers in other fields. I have learnt much from it and look forward to continued pleasure in its use, if I can prevent my copy from being borrowed or stolen as soon as I let it be seen.

ELAINE FANTHAM

Preface

THE TRANSMISSION OF LATIN LITERATURE

In order to deepen our understanding of Roman literature, we should keep in mind the nature of the documents we use as source material. These documents are to a large extent literary texts and have reached us by way of manuscript tradition. Modern printed editions take up this long tradition and try to improve it still further. We call *critical editions* those that adopt scientific principles and rules and take into consideration the entire manuscript tradition of a work, in the most complete and direct way possible. (The information needs to be complete because no ancient literary text has come down to us in autograph and because the manuscripts we have do not show the same degree of uniformity among themselves to which printed texts have accustomed us.) The principles and procedures that guide these editions cannot be cited here. Let it suffice for the moment to say that the witnesses to a text can vary considerably in quality and quantity. A text of a Roman author might be transmitted to us solely by a papyrus of the first century B.C. (this is very rare in Latin literature, unlike in Greek) or solely by an edition printed in the sixteenth century (obviously in the case where the other, earlier materials have been physically lost). Far more often, the text has reached us through manuscripts of the late ancient or medieval or humanist eras: a single manuscript (e.g., the first six books of Tacitus's *Annals* and an important part of Petronius's *Satyricon*) or many (more than two hundred in the case of Ovid's *Heroides*). Whatever the particular character of an author's manuscript tradition, our relation with these texts can be called direct in the sense that they have been reproduced for their own sake, on account of the interest they aroused. This does not cure the physical injuries, errors, omissions, interpolations, and other injuries they have suffered, but a direct tradition at least proposes the goal of literally transmitting the words of the author.

Nonetheless, Latin literature is not made up solely of texts that we can read directly. An enormous quantity of it was lost already at the threshold of the Middle Ages. The reasons for this loss are intrinsically interesting and worth analyzing: changes in taste and esthetic criteria or more general cultural transformations led certain works to be discarded; others were, so to speak, replaced, by reworking, abridgment, or simplification; material factors also had a large role—fire, plunder, destruction of books and libraries, lack of writing material, all these in an age of crisis. This unknown Latin literature remains important for us, nonetheless. The extant texts intersect constantly with the lost texts. Latin literature would be much less substantial if we did not attempt to take into account these fragmentary, half-hidden texts.

Authors crucial for the development of Roman culture, such as Naevius, Ennius, and Lucilius, are known to us exclusively by indirect means, and only in this way do we know some important authors' works that fate has not preserved, such as the *Origines* of Cato or the *Hortensius* of Cicero. What is meant by *indirect tradition?* Using terms that are vague but as precise as possible, we call *indirect* a tradition in which a text is reported by means of an extraneous, nonoriginal context. The typical form in which these secondary texts present themselves is the fragment; the typical function guiding the indirect tradition is quotation. The existence of a quotation implies both the disappearance of the original context and the formation of a new context. Scholars need to devote much attention to this second aspect: the loss of the original context causes a loss of information, and the new context for its part may create confusions. For that reason the texts transmitted in fragments are particularly tricky and controversial, as well as especially fascinating for philologists.

It seems worthwhile to clear up several possible misunderstandings. First, the term *fragment* is also applied in cases of direct tradition, for instance, in cases in which material difficulties have intervened: papyrus fragments, manuscripts that are paged incorrectly, mutilated, or partially illegible, palimpsests, and so on. The distinction between direct and indirect tradition, therefore, is not quantitative but depends only on the manner and the context in which a text has been transmitted to us. There are fragmentary texts of direct tradition and complete texts (generally, of course, not very long!) of indirect tradition. Second, there is no true qualitative opposition between these two modes: direct tradition is not necessarily good and faithful, and indirect tradition is not necessarily inaccurate. The problem needs to be evaluated case by case, author by author, passage by passage. Finally, texts can be transmitted by both direct and indirect tradition (as when Virgil is quoted by Gellius, Macrobius, Servius, or other authors), and there is a direct tradition of those texts that also transmit to us part of other texts. The Latin grammarians, for example, have preserved for us a valuable collection of fragments from texts that are lost to us; but because these fragments are quoted by grammarians, they are subject to the tradition, which obviously is direct, of those grammarians. For this reason too, no fragment can be properly evaluated if it is abstracted from the context that preserves it for us.

Let me conclude this brief notice with a fresh exhortation to caution, which ought to be applied especially to the use of textbooks of literary history. A considerable part of the literature dealt with here is known to us only indirectly. Consider the case of an author such as Lucilius, who was regarded by the Latins themselves as a figure of the first importance in the development of their literature. Only fragments and indirect notices of him are left to us, and on these alone do we base our picture of him. This picture has a wide margin of uncertainty, and it would not be honest to conceal this from those who begin to study him from a textbook, and not only because, as is inevitable, the fragments pose greater problems than the texts preserved entire. It is also necessary to recall that the fragments are the result of a selection that has been made for its own purposes. Those who quote fragments of Lucilius, mostly ancient grammarians, have their own particular linguistic interests: they attach importance to what seems to them difficult, on any of various grounds, especially the unusual individual word or construction, the archaism, the neologism, the Grecism, the linguistic experiment. It is evident that Lucilius was a great experimental poet, but our picture of his experimentation is based largely on examples previously chosen by the grammarians, and we do not know, within the totality of his work, the actual density of these features, the frequency with which they were found. In relying on what remains, therefore, we must always take into account the means of transmission as well as the limits of our information—an interesting reminder of the relativity that every literary study contains.

REFERENCE WORKS ON LATIN LITERATURE

At a scholarly level, Latin studies are still admirably international, and contributions appear in all the major languages of Europe. This causes obvious problems at the school and college level, however, where knowledge of more than English should not be presumed, and the bibliographies in this volume concentrate on scholarship in English. The bibliographies to the original Italian edition of this manual were intended for an Italian-speaking audience, and some of the references have been left in: to leave them out would be to encourage the existing neglect of Italian scholarly work by English-speaking scholars. As in the original edition, major works in French and German, and occasionally other languages, have also been cited, but there is no attempt at systematic coverage.

Useful first ports of call for information on authors are the *Oxford Classical Dictionary* (ed. 2 Oxford 1970, ed. 3 in preparation) and especially the multivolume German *Realenzyclopädie der classischen Altertumswissenschaft* (known as *RE* or Pauly-Wissowa from its first editors) and its smaller and more up-to-date companion *Der kleine Pauly* (5 vols. Munich 1979). The *Reallexikon für Antike und Christentum (RAC)* is another large-scale German enterprise still in progress: its articles are usually more up-to-date than those in *RE,* and it has of course a wider coverage. The standard German history of Latin literature by M. Schanz and C. Hosius (Munich 1914–35) is being updated by R. Herzog and others (only vol. 5 published to date, Munich 1989). The nearest English equivalent, the *Cambridge History of*

Latin Literature, which forms the second part of the *Cambridge History of Classical Literature* (*CHCL,* Cambridge 1982), contains good bibliographies by M. Drury.

Further bibliography may be obtained from the comprehensive analytical listings in the annual *L'Année philologique,* published in Paris, usually several years in arrears; for very recent work the lists in the periodicals *Gnomon* and *Bolletino di studi latini* (which also publishes systematic surveys) are invaluable. *L'Année philologique* also contains the definitive list of abbreviations for periodical titles. There is a useful guide to further bibliographical aids at the end of *The Oxford Classical Dictionary,* 1151–53. The periodical *Lustrum* is exclusively devoted to bibliographical surveys of authors and topics, and similar surveys are a particular feature of *Classical World* and *Anzeiger für die Altertumswissenschaft;* many older surveys appeared in the volumes of the *Jahresbericht über die Fortschritte der klassischen Altertumswissenschaft,* founded by Conrad Bursian, which ceased publication in 1955. The massive volumes of *Aufstieg und Niedergang der römischen Welt* (*ANRW,* Berlin 1972–) also contain many surveys, of variable quality. Finally, the volumes of the series Wege der Forschung, published by the Wissenschaftliche Buchgesellschaft, of Darmstadt, contain selections of important articles (usually translated into German) with bibliographies, and the bibliographies in the *Dizionario degli scrittori greci e latini,* ed. F. della Corte (Milan 1987), are often excellent. There is an excellent survey of bibliographies published between 1945 and 1979 by J. H. Dee in *Classical World* 73 (1979–80) 275–90.

Acknowledgments

Non possum reticere. Like Catullus, I cannot leave unmentioned how much the completion of this book owes to the perceptive collaboration of friends and colleagues, especially of Alessandro Barchiesi, Emanuele Narducci, Giovanni Polara, Giuliano Ranucci, and Gianpiero Rosati. Several others, my familiar working associates, have freely given me the support of their attentive and considerate criticism: Mario Labate, Alessandro Schiesaro, Rolando Ferri. As a teacher I make sure that I often hear the criticism of my victims; in fact I have often gained from them valuable suggestions and various improvements of detail. Most deserving of mention are Ernesto Stagni, Sergio Casali, and Andrea Cucchiarelli. To all of them I offer my warmest gratitude.

But my acknowledgments cannot stop here: the English edition has put me in the debt of still more friends. Elaine Fantham has contributed a generous foreword that notices only the merits of my work. Joseph Solodow has gallantly translated a cumbersome book with exceptional fluency and versatility. Don Fowler, with his customary learning and discernment, has provided a bibliography at once selective and academically satisfying; in a sense he has helped to direct the whole editorial enterprise. Glenn Most, a scholar deeply versed in comparative literature, has entirely rewritten the sections covering the posthumous history of the major authors, giving particular attention to literature composed in English, and following the varying reception or adaptations of Latin literature by successive generations of medieval and modern readers and writers. The assistance of such friends, old and new, has made the task of producing this book a very great personal pleasure.

LATIN LITERATURE

Introduction: Literary History and Historiography

The traditional manual of literary history is easily justified by its practical usefulness. The author of such a work may not be able to invent or reinvent very much, nor does he need to begin with a justification. All one can do is indicate certain small corrections and expedients, certain minute changes made to a device that has long since assumed a tried and tested form.

I think it is worthwhile, however, to ask whether there are good reasons for writing literary history and whether it can actually be written. Some scholars have concluded that it cannot be done. For them, writing a history of literature is an activity that goes beyond the elementary necessity of setting the individual literary texts in a historical context. As they constantly remind us, every text is an entity that fuses together into a single structure elements of historical experience and expressive codes; the former are continuously variable, the latter more stable, conventional, and slow to change. It is the syntagmatic relation between these elements of varying historicity that produces meaning. Hence, tracing the development of any one element of the text, whether it belongs to the sphere of expression or the sphere of content, has the result of throwing into disorder the structural unity of the individual texts and so robbing them of their specifically literary values. A truly literary history is therefore regarded as impossible, because it could not be genuinely literary.

The problem is real, though not necessarily insoluble. It is important not to overestimate this danger but instead openly to acknowledge the fact that every literary historical judgment can claim only an approximate value. Every history, and hence every literary history, because it organizes events and characters in a narrative succession, must necessarily be a *story*. In the case of a literary history, the events and the facts to be narrated are the lives and the literary programs of authors, their association together in schools, their reciprocal thematic and formal influences, the continual emergence of new rhetorical features besides the traditional ones, and the location of the individual texts within the system of genres. This narrative framework leads one to say of a certain author that he or she "derives" a particular feature from another author; or, similarly, someone may be said to "anticipate" an innovation that develops fully only later or to "rediscover" old veins of poetry long since abandoned. Such a story must have some authors who play a major role, the ones who animate whole episodes of the culture, and others to whom we can assign only a limited role. In this way, currents of taste, poetic theories, literary genres, and ideologies become part of the narrated action, as though they too functioned as characters moving against a backdrop of historical events. It is the responsibility of the historian-critic to keep a watchful eye upon all the events, the vicissitudes, and the characters of this story, for it is he who narrates and who, as the occasion permits, can take advantage of the procedures proper to narrative—delays and surprises, complications and resolutions.

This is the organization the study of literature inherited from the culture of Romanticism when it left behind the erudite history of the eighteenth century. It was this narrative model that realized the ideological model of historicism: the primary interest lay in reconstructing the genesis of the facts presented and in considering those facts in the light of a scheme of teleological development. Literature was investigated as the product of a variety of external factors. It became a kind of repository of disparate items of historical information (biographical, sociological, psychological). Literary history thus came to concentrate above all on individual works and on the contingent conditions that brought them into being, conditions that were seen as substantially "external" to the texts.

The twentieth century, however, has seen many attacks on historicism and on the prevailing historical method. As a result, a new model has begun to appear, one that holds out the promise of a more secure foundation for literary study. The factors that caused this model to emerge were the (to some extent convergent) experiences of phenomenology, formalism, stylistic criticism, thematic and symbolic criticism, the New Criticism, and also the more recent developments in structuralism and its successors. This new critical approach focuses upon the individual works as manifestations of a specifically literary language: literariness, understood as the feature that is relevant and distinctive of texts, has become the center of attention. Literary works are seen as forming a historical sequence proper to themselves. Because every work is formed and finds meaning in relation to other literary works, every text is viewed as conditioned by other texts, through similarity or differentiation. Thus modern literary historical investigation has increasingly directed its attention to intertextuality, to precisely those relations that, like a network of signification, connect one text to another within the body of literature.

On this model, literature can be studied as a system in continuous evolution, containing both constants and variables, and the latter are as important as the former. Literary history as practiced according to the model of genetic historicism largely denied an internal development to literature itself and took into account only the external influences, with the result that, as I have already said, literary texts were reduced to documents, to evidence for the reconstruction of history. Now, however, each text has come to be seen as the product of two forces, the internal dynamic of the literary system and the external impulses, which are undeniable.

Obviously, the crisis of historicism, and therefore the crisis of the genetic and teleological model of literary history that I have described, cannot free us from our obligation to reintegrate the works within the historical context in which they were conceived and within the culture that supplied them with an expressive language. Indeed, the enormous historical distance that separates us from these texts makes this reintegration all the more urgent. Only a painstaking and rigorously disciplined philological criticism that fully recognizes the distance separating us from the language of that culture can hope to restore to us the meaning of that distant world, a world, moreover, that we know only by means of a discontinuous tradition and a few fragmentary survivals. Certainly it will be difficult, in some cases very difficult, to rediscover the true intention of the texts. But without the tension that drives us to seek an original intention in the literary work, our very relation to these works loses any real interest. I see no other protection from the arbitrary incursions of many modern interpreters, who may be eager readers but whose views are often unconsciously alien to the original historical contexts and cultural codes.

These new techniques of literary criticism and historical research, the refinement of philology in its broadest sense and of its ancillary disciplines, make it easier to evaluate and control our attempts at interpretation today. To reconstruct the expectations that were the original cultural context of distant texts, modern interpreters must become reader-historians. Every literary text is constructed in such a way as to determine the intended manner of its reception. To identify by philological means the intended addressee within the text itself means to rediscover the cultural and expressive codes that originally enabled that addressee to understand the text. But this historicization, in order to produce the results it can, must keep a firm grasp upon the philological reading of those texts. They may be archetypal monuments of our culture, yet they always remain distant from us in conception and expression.

Besides the continuity that binds those texts to us, their substantial cultural otherness must always be acknowledged too. There is only one way for the modern interpreter to grasp the value and the meaning of ancient literature, and that is precisely to forget that it is called *classical,* a term that all too readily induces in the modern reader the complacent belief of easy accessibility (this is the familiar humanistic illusion that imagines it is rendering past literature more up-to-date by seeking within it the direct confirmation of a contemporary interest). Only if we acknowledge the otherness of ancient culture will we stand a chance of reliably reconstructing the expectations of the audience for whom the texts of Greek and Latin literature were originally composed. Within the form of the text the "form" of its addressee, that is, the form of its culture, is inscribed. This is both the limit within which modern interpreters must stay and their only guide along the difficult path of interpretation. To clarify the contrast between the expectations of the ancient addressees and our own expectations invites us to reflect upon the otherness of function and meaning inherent within the texts of Latin literature and mediates our correct understanding of it.

Even within a culture such as that of Rome, the corpus of literary texts has its own specific elements, since each of the texts that make up that corpus has within it qualities and functions originally different from those of nonliterary texts. Yet we all know that between literary and nonliterary texts there is a wide band of intermediate forms, and indeed it is a particular feature of ancient culture that it does not make sharp distinctions between these categories. Moreover, literariness itself, however problematic its definition may be, comprises a complex of characteristics that can be found in the most disparate verbal products. Indeed, it is precisely the continual shifting of the institutional boundaries of the Latin literary system that seems to be one of its most powerful dynamic factors, a fruitful opening outwards that continually assures new vitality. Texts that were not originally intended for the literary corpus but seemed susceptible to esthetic evaluation and were in some way marked by rhetorical characteristics often received a generous and honorable welcome within the official literature. This happened, for instance, with many religious and legal texts. Almost every natural genre of discourse tends to correspond to some codified literary genre: one thinks most obviously of the letter or of Caesar's war diaries. And yet, Latin literature, like almost every other major literature, can reproduce within itself, even if only through stylized features, any register or level of language, including the special languages that are most distant from any hint of literariness. In this way Latin literature opens up its own boundaries.

In itself, literature is only one of the means by which the imagination of a culture can be represented. To produce these representations, literature makes use of rhetoric, that great reservoir of ideas, symbols, forms, and languages. Through rhetoric the different models of discourse, complexes of metaphors, strategies of communication, and techniques of style that traditionally mark the various literary genres and subgenres are differentiated from each other and given a dynamic organization. These conventions of expression provide history and events, ideologies and cultural projections, with the possibility of becoming literary discourse, of being "spoken" literarily. In this sense, the various literary genres are languages that interpret the empirical world: genres select and emphasize certain features of the world in preference to others, thereby offering the representation of various forms of the world, different models of life and culture. It is the literary genre, in fact, that suggests the general meaning of the individual texts and the audience to whom they are directed.

Genre constitutes a field of reference within which, by means of comparisons and contrasts, the author can direct the specificity of his texts and the addressee can recognize it. However, the historian of literature knows that the constantly shifting and overlapping nature of the genres makes it impossible to define them in too rigidly schematic a way. Even if, hypothetically, a genre could be imagined in its pure state, its realization in individual texts is subject to many possible deformations: it can be combined, reduced, amplified, transposed, and reversed; it may suffer various types of functional mutations and adaptations; the content and expression of one genre may become associated with another. But it remains true that in the ancient literary system any combination of literary forms and structures, however complex and disparate it may be, always respects a single discursive project (this we would call a *genre*). A single genre predominates and thus subordinates to itself all the elements that come together to make up the text.

It is from this perspective that the unending process of textual generation we have learned to call intertextuality becomes so important. Classical scholars have always known about this phenomenon. The ancient grammarians and commentators already knew that poets read one another and that they imitate one another by stealing bits of texts and individual stylistic features; scholars could engage in heated discussions about whether these were actually thefts or episodes of creative emulation. But collections of *loci similes* usually remain a static register of more or less clandestine, more or less voluntary debts and loans. Whether *loci similes* are inert reminiscences or allusions fraught with significance, the relation among the various texts is reconstructed in such a way as to offer a static frame that reproduces chance coincidences and juxtaposes isolated fragments. Such a static model is even implicit in some classical structuralism, despite its emphatic attention to the phenomenon of intertextuality. An excessive preoccupation with the organic structure of individual texts ends up immobilizing their meaning and function, as if literary works were not also mechanisms able to provoke questions, answers, or reactions, as if there were not a constant dialogue between texts. If we instead see every text as an interlocutor of some other text, the frame becomes animated and starts to move. Every new text enters into a dialogue with other texts; it uses dialogue as a necessary form of its own construction, since it tries not only to hear other voices but somehow to respond to them in such a way as to define its own.

Precisely because of the typological stability of the classical literary system, intertextuality does not connect bare episodes, scattered occurrences, or casual encounters within the body of texts; instead, it sets in motion long chains of significance, mobilizes whole blocks of the literary tradition. Every interdiscursive phenomenon suggests more general relationships and for the most part involves not only particular texts but also the rhetorical classes to which it belongs. Thus intertextuality, while pursuing the paths marked out by the genres, produces a complex set of effects: it displaces, frees, and shifts spaces occupied by other discourses and often contrasts them polemically. The dialogue begun with other voices becomes a way to measure the difference between them and to propose new rhetorical projects.

If literary genres were merely closed structures, obedient to the inviolable rules laid down by Hellenistic theorists, then this dialogue between texts would only take the form of direct patrilineal succession: in each instance, the patriarch, the author-inventor, would stand at the beginning of the family, and after him would follow a pure-blooded genealogy. But in reality, voices of various origins are continuously superimposed in the memory of the poets. A genre, in fact, often continues to live by diffusing itself through other forms of discourse: even if it abandons its characteristic trappings, it will survive if it can preserve some of the features that animated it in the beginning and that adhere to it by connotation and accompany it, still recognizable, in new literary panoramas. I have no wish to hypostasize the category of genre: my perspective is purely empirical. Just as genres were of service to authors as means of projecting a discourse, and of projecting it in such a way as to be understood, so they serve the critic as a scheme to explain the processes of intertextual derivation as simulacra of meaning still recognizable behind the various transformations of the original model. Often the factor that serves to distinguish a line of descent in a new context is merely a residual feature of the original model, but it is still enough to orient the reader and to produce meaning.

Let me give an example. The didactic genre as it had been recreated by Lucretius seems not to have found an authentic continuation; it did not escape from the intense, sublime experience of the *De Rerum Natura.* But traces of it may be discerned in a number of important later developments in Latin literature. These traces are often implicit and not easily visible. The genre survives only as a function, or, rather, as an attitude of discourse, a way of talking. In the Augustan and post-Augustan periods, a didactic literature takes shape that refers back to the experience of Lucretius but diminishes its specific demands in contexts that are various and increasingly distant, to the point of entirely denying them. I am thinking here not so much of the special case of Virgil's *Georgics* as of Horace and the satiric tradition.

In the *Epistles* (a different genre from didactic, based on the colloquial form of conversation, the *sermo*) Horace enters into a dialogue with Lucretius's great codification of didactic poetry and transfers its features into the context of modern Augustan culture, thereby modifying them. But one important feature of the Lucretian model remains: that literary attitude which projects the teacher towards the possible disciple, the friend to whom the affectionate epistolary message is directed. Horace invites his addressee to attain to a philosophical refuge that reproduces the sublime *templa serena* of Lucretius's poem in the more modest existential *angulus* that Horace can offer. He transfers the same pedagogical gesture into a substantially different genre, and the intertextual dialogue that he thereby sets up with the *De Rerum Natura* produces a revision in the missionary element Lucretius had embedded in didactic. In the *Epistles,* however, this revision, while establishing its distance, intends only to reduce the model's enthusiasm, its way of pressing against its readers, upsetting them, elevating them to grandeur of spirit. Horace does not have the radically polemical, negative intentions that are evident in Persius's *Satires,* the next stage of this implicit didactic tradition. Persius has lost any hope of finding an attentive and docile addressee, and the contrast between his own didactic gesture and the combative and agonistic model of Lucretian didactic is acute. In the new satiric form, the original teacher is reduced to the figure of a disappointed monologist, enclosed within a bitter solipsism, and forced to attack the many, who are weak, rather than seek out someone who might be strong. Thus the Lucretian model moves through different forms and genres, from Horace's *Epistles* to Persius's *Satires:* the didactic idea leaves behind its institutional boundaries and explores new possibilities of adaptation and persistence.

Such an analysis could be further expanded to reveal literary interdiscursiveness as the index of large-scale cultural choices. Intertextuality is similarly central, for example, to the works of the archaic Roman poets (Livius Andronicus, Naevius, Ennius): Latin literature, which is born with them, is marked from its very beginning by the perceived need for dialogue. This is the historical outcome of an original bilingualism. The Greek matrix resides in the very geography of those authors and produces in Rome the first literature based upon textual—and cultural—translation. But once we come to see the memory of the poets as a necessary structural factor in every literary communication, the ancient prejudice that viewed Latin literature as devoid of originality loses all support. It would not even be worth mentioning the terms of this old debate (born from the ideologies of Romanticism and practically obsolete by the turn of this century) if it did not offer an opportunity for literary historical considerations of some importance. Nowadays no one would wish to deny the profoundly innovative character of those early poets, who constructed a new national poetry, not from primitive folklore, but from the sophisticated culture of Hellenism, the innate reflexivity of which it takes over. Hence the inclination towards polemics from the beginnings of Roman literature, and its basic conception of literature as difficult.

The practice of these poets reveals their awareness that a literary phenomenon takes form chiefly when its expressive rules and its very legitimacy are called into question. To a large extent, it is the experience of the Greek artistic tradition that refines in them the sense of what is specifically literary: passing through different linguistic codes permits them to compare alternative possibilities of verbal rendering, opens writing to the effect of expressive connotations, emphasizes cultural differences, establishes rhetoric as a substantial science, and predisposes authors towards the creation of novelty. This is why the lesson of Hellenism seems the deepest one in archaic Latin poetry, however mediated by the Roman context. And when Latin literature, with the Augustans, goes on to choose a modern and different originality, the polemics it directs against the ancients of the Roman tradition (who are now seen as insufficiently accurate mediators of Greek form and style) will aim, paradoxically, at establishing contact with the true ancients, those distant Greeks who seemed to be the creators of the very first literature of all: Homer, Hesiod, Alcaeus, Archilochus, Pindar, and the other great lyric poets.

Thus the ambition of originality becomes, as it were, a search for origins. The great Augustan poets strive to secure for themselves the status of classics, and to find it they look directly (and no longer only by mediated forms) to the canonical figures who had marked the origins of the Greek literary tradition: now at Rome too a Homer, a Hesiod, an Alcaeus comes to seem possible. A literary history conceived in this way—a history of literary codifications and their transformations—seems to me not only possible but even legitimate and effective.

I said before that the author of a handbook can attempt but minor improvements in a tool that is intended for study and for consultation and has developed, with use, a form that serves these purposes. My changes are chiefly the result of new concerns; they derive from my experiences and from an interest in methods like those that I have attempted to explain above. To reveal myself candidly to the reader, I give here the particular features that characterize the work.

1. Dimensions have been altered. Today it is no longer necessary for works such as this to respect unnatural hierarchies of scale by continuing to give relatively more space to school authors precisely because they are school authors, at the expense of others who, for various reasons, are read less frequently in school. Now that we have decisively left behind all fetishes—the timeless value of classical culture, the worth of certain classical texts for moral training, and so on—we can no longer exclude very large texts, such as Plautus or Petronius, on grounds of literary value (not to speak of the prejudices against all late Latin authors). I have thus reassigned space within the book, without, I hope, having done serious harm to the treatments of Terence, Caesar, and Cornelius Nepos. On the same principle of fairness, readers will find the treatment of the late ancient period more full and detailed than usual; here it seemed important to "recount" the texts somewhat more than is customary, because in this field textbooks often take the place of a direct meeting with the texts. A careful textbook treatment of this field is as new as it is traditional.

2. Periodization is notoriously the crucial operation in any historical enterprise. We recognize that dividing the facts into periods enables the reader to grasp them, if not to comprehend them. But we recognize also that this division is subjective and culturally bound. In any event, accepting the traditional framework and its references to political history does not necessarily mean obscuring the continuity of the transitions or abstractly regularizing the changing rhythms of the development. In this matter we have been utterly traditional, except for the necessary adjustments in the dating of the texts: for instance, scholarship today makes it impossible to go on treating the *Appendix Vergiliana* among Virgil's works and not among the poetic genres of the first century A.D.

3. We have in no way intended to challenge the biographical framework that is typical of handbooks and remains central in teaching Latin literature: from a certain point of view the authors may also appear as the (real)

characters of a story that is the very story of the culture and its literature. It did seem necessary, however, to distinguish clearly between the lives of the authors and their works (in part for convenience of study). Given the nature of our sources, we attempted to avoid the danger of providing biographical fantasies where it was possible at least to describe the texts with a certain objectivity. (We are not speaking here only of clearly false and invented biographical notices, which, as is well known, form part of the ancient history of a text: our Plautus gladly gives up his wearisome mill.) In fact, even where there are consistent and reliable biographies, the confusion between life and texts is always a risk. All the better forms of literary and philological criticism practiced in the twentieth century, even the ones most distant and most hostile to one another, have at least this much in common: they have taught us to be cautious in tracing relationships between biographical information and the analysis of literary texts. It should be added that only rarely are the biographical notices truly independent from the texts: they have often been derived from the texts themselves, conjectures drawn from their words in order to fill in a vacuum of information. One must beware the vicious cycle that may lie behind biographical interpretations.

For this reason, we have incorporated into the biographical treatments a certain sense of their problematic nature. Where necessary, and to the extent allowed by considerations of clarity and space, we have emphasized in which points the biography is based on deductions and reconstructions and from which texts, which combinations of evidence, and what indirect (more or less reliable) source we derive our knowledge. Anyone may memorize the dates pure and simple, or go a bit deeper into the problems connected with them and see how little we really know about such figures as Lucretius or Petronius. We realize that there is little appeal in presenting things this way (in many authoritative literary histories authors' lives are given a special importance and a lively, concrete attractiveness), but we would prefer not to superimpose on the direct fascination of the texts the fascination of our projections.

4. Many of the devices modern literary histories esteem highly—literary sociology, geography, the material nature of the texts, statistics, study of oral communication, microhistories, and so on—have only a limited application to our field of work (because of the limits of our information and sources). Nonetheless, we have, so far as we were able, taken into account these concerns too, at least by posing the relevant problems, and this especially when our ideas on the public to whom the texts were addressed have a direct importance for understanding the texts themselves and the various kinds of conventions that govern and shape them.

5. This brings us to the difficult matter of the authors' literary success. Some reference must be made to their later fame, but how should this be conceived? If the idea is to contribute to the students' general culture, we have grave doubts about the practicability of the matter. Take the case of Ovid, for instance. The ideal, of course, would be a monograph of twenty, thirty, forty, or more pages. The alternative of a mere list of the salient

points would create more confusion than cultural enrichment: in a few lines one would jump hastily from medieval poetry and Flemish painting to Ariosto, Shakespeare, and neo-classicism.

Certain information must be provided, however, and we have no formula for resolving the dilemma. As a stimulus to greater knowledge, though, we should like to indicate a guiding principle we have followed: to regard the literary success as a form of the text's existence, or rather as a history of its reception by classes of the public not intended or foreseen by the author. Thus the modern artists who refer to the ancient text are to be viewed as readers just like the others; and the work's fate is interpreted as a dialectic between the text's original qualities and the changing expectations of the reading public. If the study of the literary success of the texts does not become a study of their reception, we, for our part, see no reason to take much interest in it.

6. Now we come to the question of the genres. Here we are on firmer ground, since no one now appears to question the usefulness of this. Naturally, we too see no reason for setting the literary genres in competition with the individual people. It is necessary only that the genre operate as a literary program inscribed in the work, as a model of meaning and of form that can be recognized behind the discursive structure of the text. If genre is the point of reference by which each new text locates itself, it becomes possible to follow the dialectic between tradition and innovation as the main highway; and here each artistic personality has its natural room.

The importance accorded to the literary genres does not, therefore, contradict the structure of the sketches that is traditional in literary histories. It is enough that in the different historical segments we be quite clear about the working of these institutions of communication, these modes already prepared to construct the discourse, that are the genres. Above all, it must always be kept in mind (and here periodization can do its greatest harm) that each genre has its different tempos, stubborn perseverance or varying rhythms of development.

It has thus been possible to respect absolute chronology, with some natural adjustments. Figures who for various reasons are minor have often been incorporated in the clarifying framework of a genre. In one particular case, the archaic period, we have provided a chapter on institutions, which sets the scene for and facilitates the treatment of the dramatists from Livius Andronicus to the age of the Gracchi. For the history of philology too, which is so important and not always given its due, and for the history of legal literature we have practiced an almost monographic concentration, with the result that some small repetitions with the diachronic sequence were inevitable.

We have gone on too long, and may have allowed some personal idiosyncrasy to show itself here and there. Yet even the authors of "objective" textbooks have their inevitable obsessions, likes, and dislikes. It is not a bad idea, before assuming the detached voice of the expert, to admit them and put them on record.

ONE

The Early and Middle Republics

The Origins

*Birth of Latin
literature*

The question how artistic works originated in the Latin language was posed by the Romans themselves in quite simple terms. The prevailing opinion was that the precise date of birth could be fixed: 240 B.C., the year in which Livius Andronicus put on the stage a drama he had written, presumably a tragedy. On the far side of this historic threshold lay a long period, perhaps four centuries, during which literature was silent.

*Artistic works and
forms of communica-
tion*

This notion of the origins may appear simplistic, but it makes sense in relation to its own presuppositions: if literature is limited to works of art fixed with the aid of writing, then a precise date of birth can be accepted. Yet the Romans of the classical period were fully conscious themselves that the origins of literature do not coincide with the origins of the forms of communication in which a culture finds expression. The history of these forms of communication is complex; it is not limited to written communication nor to anticipating and preparing the development of literature.

The Romans themselves were fully aware that the origins of Greek literature provided an analogy that aided the understanding of their own. The splendid Greek theater of the fifth century must have had a prehistory: simpler dramatic actions, not fixed in written texts and closely related to rural rites and festivals. Homeric poetry presupposes as background a rich tradition of epic songs entrusted to wandering bards. Thus the Romans, too, became curious about their literary prehistory. Yet the Greek example could be not only a stimulus but also a source of deception. Some Roman reconstructions of their origins, of their epic and theater, for instance, seem too closely tied to the Greeks' reconstructions of their own literary past. The Greeks, in having Homer, had an undeniable advantage: a great poem and cultural document standing astride the very beginnings of literature, a text the layers of which revealed a long prior tradition. No Roman literary text occupied a similarly privileged position. The theatrical works of Andronicus, which for the Romans were the threshold of their literary chronology, are in fact secondary texts, translations made from an already mature literary genre, the Greek tragedy of the classical and Hellenistic periods.

I will limit myself here to a separate treatment of some questions that are indispensable to the discussion of literary origins: (*a*) chronology and spread of writing; (*b*) nonliterary forms of communication; and (*c*) preliterary forms: the *carmina*. It is important to keep in mind that the evidence we rely on is varied in nature. We have information drawn from Roman literary sources. These are notices derived from sources far later than the time they refer to: historians, antiquarians, jurists, literary men, grammarians, and others. They must be evaluated critically, their limits and true importance studied. Then, too, we have the contributions of modern scholarship, based on historical, archaeological, linguistic, epigraphic, and other material. These data, combinations of data, and hypotheses are useful for the reconstruction of Roman culture in its preliterary phase.

I. THE CHRONOLOGY AND SPREAD OF WRITING

First instances of written Latin

From the remotest times, at least the seventh century, Latin-speaking inhabitants of Latium recorded in writing the simplest messages: an invitation to drink, upon a wine cup; an artisan's signature, on an artistic vessel ("Novius Plautius made me in Rome"); a religious prohibition, on a gravestone; and others as well. The use of writing therefore is connected with occasions of daily life. The distinctions between languages are still fluctuating, and in the territory of the earliest Rome people are found who speak and write in Greek, Oscan, and Etruscan. We have Latin inscriptions in the Greek alphabet and boustrophedon writings, which go from right to left and then from left to right. The alphabetic signs are still very much prone to variation.

There is no reason to believe that the Romans of the first centuries wrote only upon durable materials: the conditions of our records for archaic Latium—different from those in Egypt, for example—are responsible for the failure of perishable writings to be preserved. Consequently we have only graffiti and inscriptions, and we lack funerary documents, which ordinarily, as in Greece, are important sources. What is left shows the existence of a melting pot of peoples and languages. Only gradually does the use of Latin and the Latin alphabet assert itself. The Latin alphabet itself, in fact, gives clear testimony of the situation in early Rome. In substance, it is derived from a particular West Greek alphabet, the one used in the powerful Campanian city of Cumae, but it is also somewhat influenced by Etruria. (This explains, for example, how the letter *C* serves as the abbreviation for the name *Gaius:* Etruscan had a single sign for the two velar consonants, voiceless and voiced.)

Literacy and the diffusion of books in archaic Rome

The presence of inscriptions on objects of daily, domestic use seems to prove that already in earliest Rome a certain capacity for writing was found even among persons of middling social position. It is natural in any event to suppose that writing was more widely diffused in the higher classes of society, among the priests and those likely to hold public office. The use of writing is indispensable for a number of public functions: preservation of oracles, religious formulas and prescriptions, lists of magistrates and priests, statutes, laws, treaties. And it was certainly important for the nobility, which began very early to record genealogies, family traditions, and the commemorative inscriptions of their ancestors. In this period, however, before the appearance of the first figures of literary history, such as Andronicus, or of prehistory, such as Appius Claudius, there is no evidence of a genuine circulation of books, such as is presupposed by written literary communication. Characteristically, the most ancient books of which we have any notice, the famous Sibylline books that were said to be introduced at Rome in the days of Tarquin the Proud, are religious texts and were, as far as we can tell, written in Greek.

Already by the middle years of the Roman Republic, in the times of Livius Andronicus and Plautus, literacy seems to be quite extensive. In parallel to the rise of true literary texts, the ability to read and write is notably more extensive. First of all, a large number of citizens, those engaged in civil, priestly, or military affairs, are accustomed to possessing written records of their activity, even records of their personal activity (*commentarii*). But it is credible that many common people as well had at least the rudiments of literacy. At the end of the third century, moreover, a guild of scribes (*scribae*) is recognized by the state. At first their social position, like that of writers, is not very high; they are simple artisans of writing, manual laborers. The middle and upper classes of society are already thoroughly literate.

2. NONLITERARY FORMS OF COMMUNICATION

Literature and non-literary communication

It is appropriate now to review briefly forms of communication that presuppose the use of writing but, at least in the mind of the writer and of the recipient, do not constitute literature, however uncertain and variable the boundaries of that category may seem. Each of these forms of communication undoubtedly played a role also in preparing the ground for a true literary culture in Latin. For example, the use of Latin as the official language of the Roman people, employed in laws, treaties, religious formulas, public inscriptions, and oratory, gave an invaluable impulse to the development of Latin, continuously enhancing its expressive abilities. But looking ahead also to the development of the literary culture, it is possible to identify a specific inheritance from these nonliterary forms, which we may rather call preliterary. The characteristic traditionalism of Roman culture during the Republic favored the perpetuation of certain formulas and structures of thought. Traces of them exist even in authors who are imbued with the new Hellenizing culture, and not only in Naevius or Plautus but in the Latin of Catullus and Virgil as well. We will see this aspect of formal continuity better in the section on the *carmina*.

Greek influences on archaic Rome

A preliminary observation is in order. If we consider the legacy from these forms of communication to much later literary texts, in an author such as Plautus, for example, or Virgil, it is easy to set up a neat opposition: on the one hand, an original and autonomous Italian-Roman ground, on the other, superimposed Greek influence; on the one hand, the rigid formulas of law and religion, on the other, the plastic forms of the language of Homer, Menander, and Callimachus. But this opposition should not be exaggerated. Historical, especially archaeological, research shows that in the history of Rome a Greek influence, however variable in degree and intensity and however liable to change, was always present. Rome in the sixth century, for example, appears increasingly to be a crossroads of trade and of cultures; and long before Roman writers consciously follow Greek literary models, Greek influence is already present in many aspects of Roman life. It is a gradual process, without sudden changes. The Roman writers themselves tend to exaggerate the qualitative change with respect to the tradition. Ennius, for instance, in the name of the new poetic principles that are open to Hellenistic taste, attacks his "primitive" predecessors, who stood for an unrefined, obscure poetry. But among these "primitives," we know, was Naevius, a writer nourished on Greek culture and engaged in a great effort to fuse the different cultures. As we will see shortly, even the Saturnian, the most ancient Roman meter, which the Romans themselves considered their only refined native verse, may have been affected very early by contacts with the Greek world. In studying the origins of Rome a recurring theme is the necessity not to draw excessively sharp boundaries between different cultures.

Laws and Treaties

From the earliest days of the Roman city-state the use of writing was linked to the need for precise official records, of treaties, international pacts, and laws. These needs also exercised a strong influence on the shaping of Latin prose.

Of treaties (*foedera*) from archaic times we have only indirect attestation, no actual fragments: one example is the treaty made between Rome and Carthage in 509 B.C., about which the Greek historian Polybius (second century B.C.) informs us.

Laws of the kings

The historic, social, and cultural importance of the first laws of Rome was immense. We have, to begin with, remains of ancient *leges regiae,* which must go back to the monarchic period of the city's first centuries. They were dominated, as far as we can tell, by a rigidly sacral approach, as in this: "A concubine must not touch the altar of Juno. If she will do so, she must make expiation by sacrificing a lamb to Juno, with her hair unbound." The earliest law naturally must have been based chiefly on customary regulations.

Laws of the Twelve Tables

A great civil and political achievement was marked by the composition of the Laws of the Twelve Tables, so called because they were engraved on twelve bronze tablets displayed in the Roman Forum. The weaker segments of the population especially found in these laws, once written and made public, a bulwark against the excessive power of the great families. The laws are said to have been written by a special commission from 451 to 450. The version we have is undoubtedly recast, but it still preserves a clear trace of archaic language.

The Romans of the classical period saw in the Laws of the Twelve Tables the truest foundation of their cultural identity. According to Livy (3.34.6), they were always *fons omnis publici privatique iuris;* for Cicero they surpassed all the books of the Greek philosophers, at least in usefulness and seriousness (*De Oratore* 1.195). Boys learned them by heart; scholars continued to comment on them and analyze them.

In their monumental assonances and alliterations, in the staccato rhythms of their parallel *cola,* these laws unfailingly produce the effect of a judgment against which there can be no appeal, for instance: *Si nox furtum faxsit, si im occisit, iure caesus esto,* "If by night he shall have committed a theft, if he shall have killed him, he shall have been killed in accordance with law." (Note the ellipse of the subject, which occurs repeatedly even though there are obviously different subjects, the thief and his killer.)

The *Fasti* and the *Annales*

The calendar

Another very ancient use of writing, also connected to the informational needs of public life, was for the calendar. The Roman community had developed an official calendar, regulated and sanctioned by the religious authorities. The days of the year were divided into *fasti* and *nefasti,* according to whether the conduct of public affairs was permitted or forbidden. The pontiffs were responsible for the regulation of this. Soon the term *fasti* began to designate not only the annual calendar but also the lists of magistrates elected year by year (*fasti consulares, fasti pontificales*) and the record of military triumphs won by magistrates in office (*fasti triumphales*).

The amount of information stored in the *fasti* increased over time. The magistrates used them to record their official acts. Another important step was the use of the *tabula dealbata:* the supreme pontiff used to set up in public a "white tablet," which announced, in addition to the names of the magistrates for the current year, events of public concern, such as treaties, declarations of war, prodigies, or natural catastrophes. These official records, deposited year by year, took the collective name *annales* and began to form a true collective memory of the Roman state. In the time of the Gracchi the pontiff Publius Mucius Scaevola undertook to collect on rolls the *annales* of the previous 280 years; the collection was called the *Annales Maximi.*

It is obvious that these bare collections of facts, set down in chronological order, possessed great potential as historical documents. The historians concerned with Rome's first centuries, Cato or Dionysius of Halicarnassus, for example, would later refer to this record to buttress the authority of their own accounts. More generally, these official *annales* of the pontiffs exercised an enormous influence upon the structure of Latin historical works: the chronological framework of the *annales* tended to yield a narrative of Roman history that was arranged according to a year-by-year scheme. Thus the tradition of the pontifical *annales* contributed an original element, one free from Greek influence, to the development of a characteristically Roman historiography; and traces of it still remain in Livy and Tacitus.

The year-by-year scheme

The *Commentarii*

Alongside the official tradition of the *annales* we find the use of *commentarii,* more personal and not necessarily public writings. The term has a wide range of applications in classical Latin: by itself it may denote nothing more than "notes," "memoirs," "observations," of a private character.

Private memoirs

The term would later be used, for instance, by Julius Caesar for his narratives of the Gallic War and the war against Pompey. These works have a high literary finish and a deliberate political stance, but by calling them *commentarii* Caesar wanted to emphasize that they were not so much literary historiography as firsthand recollections. Already before Julius Caesar, Lucius Cornelius Sulla had written at least twenty-two books of *Memoirs* (according to some, the title was probably *Commentarii Rerum Gestarum*). The *commentarii* thus present themselves as nonprofessional works, merely supplying information and personal recollections. Whether they actually were so is a separate question.

Public memoirs

The origin of this meaning lies in a practice of the republican magistrates. An important magistrate, a consul, for example, tended to collect in a kind of diary the principal actions and events of his term of office. These *commentarii* might take on the character of official records and be deposited with the priestly colleges: later on, the pontiffs themselves preserved records of their own activity in the *libri pontificum.* We possess, however, only indirect notices of these works.

The use of *commentarii* presumably favored the development of a prose writing that was connected to contemporary politics and not far removed from the composition of proper memoirs. This tradition of Latin prose remained distinct from the tradition of judicial and public oratory, which was always more liable to rhetorical literary elaboration.

The Dawn of Oratory: Appius Claudius Caecus

Before Roman culture was decisively Hellenized, which took place during the century between the war against Tarentum (280–272 B.C.) and the invasion of Greece, writing was considered a technique, and unquestionably a very useful one, but speaking well was much more important: the Romans considered oratorical ability a form of power and a key to success. It is not an accident that the first name we meet in the history of Latin literature belongs to a man of eloquence, a semi-legendary figure who was

Oratory as the basis of public life

regarded as the founder of oratory: Appius Claudius Caecus. Henceforth, at least until the age of the Scipios, oratory is considered the only intellectual activity truly worthy of a distinguished citizen. Whereas poets for a long time, until Accius and Lucilius, were freedmen or non-Roman Italians of low status, oratory was from the start the domain of noble citizens. The ability to persuade was the indispensable basis of a political career, and the Romans had no need, as they did in the case of poetry, to import from outside an interest in rhetoric; they needed the assistance of *rhetores,* Greek-trained "professors of eloquence," solely to refine their own natural aptitudes as *oratores.* Unlike true literature, which belongs to a man's *otium,* the "free time" he may choose to dedicate to pleasurable pursuits, oratory is considered an integral and essential part of the active life.

Appius Claudius Caecus

Appius Claudius Caecus, who came from a very noble family, was consul in 307 and 296, censor in 312, and dictator. The ancients attached his almost legendary name to a large number of important undertakings in war and in peace. He fought against Etruscans and Sabines and was victorious over the Samnites in the Third Samnite War. He permitted plebeians to enter the Senate. During his censorship he promoted fundamental public works: from him the *aqua Claudia* or *Appia,* the first Roman aqueduct, takes its name, as does the *Via Appia,* the first of the great roads built by the Romans, which upon its completion would link Rome with Brundisium.

In certain features Appius Claudius appears to be a forerunner of Cato. He is remembered for his forcefulness and oratorical ability: in a famous oration he opposed Pyrrhus's peace proposals, and Cicero refers to this as the first official speech ever published in Rome. We do not know whether the text that circulated in Cicero's day was genuine, but the notice is interesting regardless, since it demonstrates already in that early period a lively interest in the ability to speak. Appius Claudius was, moreover, an expert in law and was concerned, it seems, with scholarly questions of language: the replacement of intervocalic *s* with *r* (rhotacism) is traditionally attributed to him. Under his name there circulated a collection of maxims *(Sententiae)* of a moral and philosophizing character, which was held to be a repository of archaic wisdom (a famous *sententia* is "Each man is the artisan of his own destiny"). In this too Appius seems to herald the personality of Cato. We do not know whether his expressive abilities were already fostered by contacts with Hellenistic culture, as would be the case with Cato; certain of his moral maxims suggest Greek Pythagorean sources.

It is significant that Cicero mentions *(Tusculanae Disputationes* 4.4) the existence of a *carmen* by Appius, who was, we have seen, the father of prose at Rome. This does not mean that Appius was really, properly speaking, a poet. We will understand this better in the following section.

3. PRELITERARY FORMS: THE *CARMINA*

Form in nonliterary texts

Even though all the forms of communication we have been concerned with up to this point had a practical aim, each one of them, in its own way, may have contributed to the formation of literary Latin. It ought not to be thought that the formal elements of a text are solely those directed to an artistic purpose. The effects produced by certain formal devices have an importance even outside what we call literature. The laws, for example, are authoritative texts par excellence: in archaic Rome the style of the laws is deliberately solemn, vigorous, monumental. Alliteration, rhyme, the *figura etymologica,* parallelism, chiasmus, and other similar effects were probably far more common in such texts than in the spontaneous language of daily life or private communications, including written ones. The same is true for prayers and ritual formulas, the message of which should imitate a certain order in the world, imposing upon the words of the phrase a structure that is perceived as ordered, or even lead to certain patterns of behavior. The form should also, naturally, aid the memory in learning to repeat the phrase exactly: like rhythm and rhyme, it should create artificial links among the words so that the whole can be memorized. And of course magic formulas, medical prescriptions, wise saws, and rules for agriculture ought to be viewed in the same light. As for political communication, the importance attached to public speeches and commemorative inscriptions points up the necessity of certain forms. There is, then, a large field in which certain cultural manifestations appear together that we would group very differently and that the Romans themselves kept clearly separate. This shared field is defined by formal character and has to do with the unusual range of possible meanings for the word *carmen.* The most common meaning of *carmen,* which derives from *cano,* "sing, sound," is "poem." Yet a poet like Ennius does not seem fond of the term, since he denominates his work with a Greek word, *poema.* There are two reasons for this. First, Ennius wanted to stress his own novel inclination for writing poetry in the Greek style. Second, he underscored his rejection of a certain ancient tradition. In this tradition *carmen* means far more than "verses" or "poem." The Augustan poets would be the first to narrow the meaning of the term, which had an aura of national antiquity about it, and to apply it to their own works in verse. In archaic Rome, by contrast, *carmen* is an oddly ill-defined term; for this reason Ennius does not like it.

Cicero, in speaking of the Twelve Tables, calls them a *carmen.* In speaking of magic formulas, the Twelve Tables refer to them as *carmina.* For Livy the text of a very ancient treaty is a *carmen.* The same word is applied to prayers, oaths, prophecies, judicial judgments, and lullabies for babies. A *carmen* therefore is not a *carmen* by virtue of its content or its use; to characterize it we must look at its form.

We can establish now an important point about the relations between poetry and prose in archaic Rome. The boundary between these two is much less sharp than in our culture or, still more, than in Roman culture of the classical period. The earliest Roman prose, on one side, is characterized by a strong stylization, as we have seen. It has an intensely marked, perceptible *rhythmic* texture, on account of its phonetic and morphological repetitions, and particularly the correspondences it shows among the members *(cola)* of the phrase, which are constructed so as to have equal length and matching syntactic structure—in short, on account of its strong effects of verbal parallelism. Archaic poetry, on the other side, has a peculiarly feeble *metrical* structure, since it exists in a loose framework and is subject to rules with large loopholes (at least so it seems to us, but also to an educated Roman of Cicero's time!). As a result, prose and poetry seem to draw close to one another: "weak" verses and "strong" prose practically touch and meet.

Among classical meters no other verse is so unpredictable as the Saturnian (see p. 25), except perhaps, to some extent, Plautus's iambic senarius. Nor is there in classical prose the same tendency towards a highly formalized construction, based on parallelism, homoeoteleuton, alliteration, and brief symmetrical *cola*. A single stylistic matrix unites the extremely various manifestations and employments of *carmina* such as the following:

uti tu morbos	visos invisosque
viduertatem	vastitudinemque
calamitates	intemperiasque
prohibessis	defendas averruncesque

(a private prayer for the ritual purification of the fields, recorded, without attribution, by Cato in *De Agri Cultura* 141.3: "that you, o Mars, prevent, fend off, and avert diseases seen and unseen, sterility and desolation, catastrophes and storms");

novum vetus	vinum bibo
novo veteri	morbo medeor

(an incantation to be uttered when drinking the new wine, in order to restore its medicinal powers, in harmony with the cycle of nature—a disputed interpretation: "I drink the new, the old wine, I heal the new, the old disease" [?]);

summum ius	summa crux

("extreme justice, extreme torment": an ancient and popular variant, recorded in Columella 1.7.2, of the more familiar *summum ius summa iniuria,* "extreme justice, extreme injustice");

magna sapientia	multasque virtutes
aetate quom parva	posidet hoc saxsum

("great wisdom, many virtues, but a brief life this rock contains," from the epitaph of one of the Scipios, second century B.C.);

male perdat, male exset, male disperdat. Mandes, tradas nei possit
amplius ullum mensem aspicere, videre, contemplare

(from a curse formula of the late Republic, requesting that a certain person not survive beyond February: "may he be terribly ruined, terribly consumed, terribly destroyed; order, command that he not be able to look upon, see, behold a single month more." The Latin is vulgar yet stylized).

There is, undoubtedly, something arbitrary in collecting popular sayings, magic formulas, prayers, and sophisticated metrical epitaphs of illustrious persons all in one place. And yet if we include items solely on the basis of certain recurring formal features, the collection becomes larger still and reaches into regular literature: for the attuned ear, certain cadences or rhythms in Plautus and Ennius, and even in Catullus and Virgil, may still recall the tradition of the *carmina*.

The stylistic tradition of the *carmina* is the most important element of continuity linking the period of its origins to the rest of Roman literary history. While Greek influences accumulate and become stronger and deeper, the tradition of the *carmina* never completely disappears: it has left a lasting mark on Latin literary style, a mark that distinguishes it even from those Greek models that are the most carefully imitated. It is a manner of writing for effect, without observing sharp distinctions between poetry and prose; it stands in opposition to the casual, informal style of ordinary conversation; it represents a stylistic attitude unknown to literary Greek but ingrained in the expressiveness of the Romans (and perhaps of other Italic peoples as well). Catullus and Virgil, when they echo this manner, are closer to rustic proverbs and religious litanies than to Homer and Callimachus.

Sacral Poetry

The most ancient forms of *carmina* to come down to us, except for funereal inscriptions, which we will take up below, are of a religious and ritual nature. Rituals are by nature conservative and inviolable, and they evolve more slowly than religious sensibility; and the Romans are a people noted for conservatism. And so we possess remains and traces of religious songs that were bound up with the performance of annual public rituals. The chief pieces of evidence we have refer to two important ritual *carmina*, the Salian and the Arval.

The first was the chant of a venerable priestly college, the Salii, which is said to have been founded by Numa Pompilius. The Romans connected the name etymologically with *salio,* "leap." The college consisted of twelve priests of the god Mars, who in March of every year carried in procession the twelve sacred shields, the *ancilia;* one of the shields was the famous shield that fell from the sky as a pledge of divine protection for Rome. The Salii must have had several different *carmina.* They pronounced them while advancing in a kind of ritual ballet, moving to a triple beat—the movement was called *tripudium* because they beat the ground three times rhythmically with the foot—and accompanied by percussion, as they struck the shields with lances. The language of the Salii was incomprehensible to the Romans of the historical period, and the remains of the hymn that we have are very obscure to us. We do know that a fundamental concern was to invoke, individually and collectively, all the divine powers, in order to avoid potentially disturbing omissions.

Early Roman religion worshipped a complicated set of *numina,* in which Hellenized divinities were found alongside what might be called functional powers, who were tied to the minute, discrete forces of everyday life; thus, *Sator* presided over sowing and *Sterculinius* over manuring. The invocations, then, we should suppose, were found in litanies of great length.

The *Carmen Arvale,* or *Carmen Fratrum Arvalium,* "Chant of the Arval Brethren," is a little less shadowy for us. In May the *fratres Arvales,* a college of twelve priests created, according to legend, by no less a personage than Romulus, sang a hymn for the purification of the fields (*arva* in Latin); they implored the protection of Mars and of the *Lares,* ancestors regarded as the propitious spirits of the dead. We have a fairly reliable version of the text, though the interpretation is difficult. The insistent triple rhythm is notable here too, as in the *tripudium* of the Salii: the *carmen* began, for instance, with a triply repeated request for aid, *enos Lases iuvate* (*nos, Lares, iuvate* in classical Latin, "aid us, o Lares"). In religious folklore and in magic, triple words and acts are widely considered to guarantee efficacy. Despite the archaic language, the chant must be the work of a real artist, a vatic bard not untouched by Greek literature and culture.

Some characteristics of these hymns, such as expressive fullness, repetition, and certain rhetorical figures, must have had lasting influence on nonreligious Latin literature. Yet Rome in the historical period did not possess a true religious literature. There were but a few scattered exceptions: during the Second Punic War, Andronicus was commissioned to write a hymn to Queen Juno; Horace's later *Centennial Ode* is, more than anything else, a work for a particular occasion, propagandistic in intent, and marked by Hellenistic influence. Similarly, Rome did not possess a true distinct priestly class. Greek religion and mythology therefore could penetrate all the more thoroughly, bringing with it all its weight of literary creativity and, still more important, figurative imagination.

Popular Poetry

We have already noticed in passing, when speaking of the *carmina,* certain manifestations that belong here: proverbs, curses, spells, rustic precepts, and healing formulas. The freedmen who appear in Petronius's *Satyricon* seem still immersed in this oral culture. It is obvious that a vast legacy has been lost to us here—work songs, love songs, and the lullabies that Catullus, Horace, and many another heard from their nurse.

The fullest evidence we have pertains to oral, improvised poetry of a mocking and comical character, the most common defined type being that of the Fescennine verses. According to the ancients, the etymology derives either from Fescennia, a small town in southern Etruria, or from *fascinum,* "the evil eye" and also "penis," the indecency of which had power to cast a spell. The term would be, then, either a trace of Etruscan influence or the expression of an apotropaic function (i.e., keeping the evil eye at a distance), which these songs were thought to have. It seems that the home of the *fescennini* was the rustic festivals. According to Horace (*Epistles* 2.1.139 ff.), out of this developed a tradition of biting mockery, which might even become a kind of public defamation. Horace connects this trend to the characteristic cursing of the earliest Attic comedy.

Fescennine verses came into play on many social occasions in ancient Rome: the jests traditional at weddings (see Catullus, poem 61); "popular justice," a form of public defamation (again see Catullus, poem 17); also the *carmina triumphalia.* At a triumph the soldiers improvised songs that mingled praise for the conqueror with mockery and pasquinade; perhaps here too an apotropaic function can be discerned by which the exaltation attendant on success was moderated and tempered by laughter, in order not to bring down the consequences of sacrilegious arrogance.

It is clear that this popular feeling for the comic had a considerable influence on certain comic elements in literary works, namely, Plautine comedy and the development of satire and the satiric epigram. But there is no proof that the "fescennine spirit" was transformed directly into proper literary genres. The chief impulse to the creation of the comic theater undoubtedly came from contact with the Greek theater of Magna Graecia and from the circulation of Attic and Hellenistic literary texts. The origin of satire should also be looked on in this light (for Livy's notices about "Etruscan" spectacles and "dramatic *satura*" see pp. 30 and 113). Italic popular comedy found more immediate reflexes in the success of the Atellan farce (see p. 36).

Heroic Poetry

Analogy with other Mediterranean cultures might lead us to think that at Rome too a celebratory poetry was in use: verse accounts of heroic deeds, conceived orally and performed at private gatherings, such as parties and funeral banquets. These heroic songs, or ballads, could have had a notable influence on the development of a native Latin epic poetry and would have been the ideal vehicles for transmitting myths and legends of earliest Rome, tied, as they would have been, to the ancestral traditions of the great Roman families.

Small importance of heroic songs in early Rome

This reconstruction is appealing but quite hypothetical. The analogy with other cultures could be a mirage, and in fact the significance of these *carmina* was played up especially in the Romantic period, as if in reaction to the excessively learned and literary character of the extant Latin epic poetry. Such a reconstruction romanticized at least the prehistory of Latin epic, which thus could become a heroic poetry that one might imagine was spontaneous, as if it were the natural, original product of mythopoetic inclinations working in the service of national pride. Moreover, the analogies with Greek epic affected the Romans of the classical period themselves, who may under this influence have harbored hazy notions of primitive epic composition.

The words of Cato, as reported by Cicero and Varro, are our principal evidence about these *carmina convivalia.* Not even Cato, who was born before the Second Punic War, seems to have ever heard them directly: he cites them by indirect tradition. If, as it might seem, there really were songs of praise for the deeds of ancestors, it is conceivable that the historians of the second century B.C. made use of them. We do not have, however, any indications of written versions of such poetry, and the historians do not customarily refer to any poetic sources.

It is a striking fact, moreover, that no trace whatever has been left of

Hellenization of Rome and decline of heroic poetry

professional singers—bards, poets, balladeers, or what you will. It is difficult to imagine that a truly literary form could evolve without such figures. If, however, this poetry found performers and audience in the (rather restricted) circle of the great families, as might be implied by the term *carmina convivalia,* which suggests banquets and private gatherings, then it becomes clear why already at the end of the third century we no longer hear any echoes of it. The great families of the city are precisely the social groups among whom a Hellenizing culture takes hold most rapidly, from the third to the second century, between the war against Tarentum and Roman expansion eastward. The aristocratic circles were clearly the first to reject certain traditions and to assimilate instead the fruits of the great artistic and literary culture of Greece. Only now, in the shadow of these great families, do professional writers appear, but from Livius Andronicus onwards they employ literary forms that are learned and profoundly shaped by Greek influence. A comparison with other branches of writing is instructive. The evolution of popular genres was somewhat different: farce, for instance, retained its original Italic character for a much longer time. Yet it should be observed that already at the beginning of the second century Plautus achieves success even among the lower classes, with a literary form such as the *palliata,* which is based on the artistic principles of regular Attic comedy. It is clear, in short, that the celebratory, laudatory function of poetry did not disappear during this new phase; on the contrary, through such Hellenizers as Livius, Ennius, and Accius poetry increasingly becomes a means of securing and perpetuating the glory of distinguished men and families, both in the immediate present and reaching back to the example of the ancestors. The ever greater care over form that is seen in poetry begins to rival the care shown in the Greek models, always the criterion of excellence, and this care becomes a means of vouching for the message of glorification, transforming thereby the literary artifact into a lasting monument. And the poet, by taking on the role of dispenser and guarantor of fame, in which capacity he is valued, affirms his own social usefulness.

Into the discussion of the *carmina convivalia* it is usual to bring two works that are quite nebulous for us, the *Carmen Nelei* and the *Carmen Priami;* but any connection is improbable. Since the *Carmen Nelei,* of which we have very few fragments, was in iambic meter, it was not, as far as we can tell, a proper epic poem. The *Carmen Priami,* of which we have a single verse, a Saturnian, presents itself as an epic but does not have the feel of being genuinely archaic. It is likely to be, rather, a later forgery, connected to an archaizing taste; its *terminus ante quem* is the time of Varro, who cites the fragment. Thus it is impossible to use this evidence in conjunction with the *carmina convivalia.* The motive for such a use could only be to lend substance to some intuition of primitive preliterary epic composition.

The Problem of the Saturnian

Apart from the mysterious rhythmic cadences of the religious songs, the most ancient evidence we have about Roman poetry bears on a particular verse, the Saturnian. The first two Roman epics, Livius Andronicus's translation of the *Odyssey* and Naevius's *Bellum Poenicum,* are composed in Saturnians. Also in Saturnians are perhaps even older texts, the funeral elogia found upon the tombs of two illustrious persons from the family of the Scipios. The two most ancient elogia refer to Lucius Cornelius Scipio, consul in 259, and his father, of the same name, who was consul in 298. The texts are the products of fine literary craftsmanship and reveal a certain familiarity with Greek culture and the traditions of Greek funerary poetry. One of the epitaphs, for instance, praises not only the military but also the intellectual virtues of the deceased and associates, in characteristic fashion, physical attractiveness and personal valor:

> fortis vir sapiensque
> quoius forma virtutei parisuma fuit.

"He was a brave man and a wise one, and his looks were equal to his courage"—a harmonious fusion of courage, handsomeness, and intelligence that recalls the Greek ideal of *kalokagathia,* or "nobleness."

The Saturnian poses complex problems for the students of early Rome. The very etymology of the name suggests something indigenous, purely Italic—the god Saturn, for example—but all the instances we have bear the stamp of a period that is already imbued with Greek culture. The epitaphs of the Scipios presuppose a cultivated, Hellenizing environment. Even the *Carmen Arvale,* several centuries older, is not immune from Greek influences, and it seems possible to find Saturnian cadences in it. Andronicus and Naevius do not write exclusively in Saturnians: in their works for the theater the same authors show a complete mastery of meters that follow the principles of Greek dramatic poetry. Thus it is not possible to situate the Saturnian in a pure, indigenous period free from Greek interference.

The metrical interpretation of this verse poses severe problems: its remarkably fluid structure does not permit a derivation from any regular verse of Greek poetry; indeed, some scholars even doubt whether the principles of the Saturnian's structure are the same as those of classical Greek and Latin meters, that is, whether they are based on alternation in length. As a result, radically different interpretations have been proposed. The debate is important for another reason too, because it involves our ideas about the development of a "prehistory" in Latin literary culture.

Whatever the exact solution to the problem of the meter, it is important to realize that the Saturnian cannot be situated entirely outside of the Greco-Roman world. It is difficult to accept that Andronicus and Naevius could compose poetry simultaneously in accordance with mutually incompatible sets of principles. Less drastic solutions exist: for instance, to see in the Saturnian the transformation of certain *cola,* certain metrical units, that can be found in Greek poetry; or to hold that a decisive role was played by the number of syllables or by the grouping of words.

However its genesis is judged, the Saturnian remains the only truly original contribution made by the Romans in the field of metrical forms. Evidently, it was precisely its conspicuous irregularity with respect to the principles of Greek literature that was responsible in the end for its disappearance. Yet there exist other metrical forms that, though traceable to a precise Greek model, seem to enjoy an autonomous and not exactly literary vitality. This is the case with the *versus quadratus,* a trochaic septenarius stylized in a particular way, which is attested for the classical period in popular, anonymous uses: riddles, children's ditties, banter, pasquinades from the people, as in *pòstquam Cràssus càrbo fàctus, Càrbo cràssus fàctus èst,* "ever since Crassus became carbon, Carbo became fat" (Carbo was notoriously an opponent of Crassus).

This *versus quadratus* seems to have been firmly planted among the Romans before their writers adopted, in a learned way, metrical forms from Greek literature: it represents a subliterary, popular diffusion, brought about perhaps by the first contacts with Magna Graecia. At the present time the chronology is quite hypothetical, and given our uncertainty about the Saturnian's origins (see above), we can say nothing further about the relative chronology of the various types of popular verse at Rome.

The history of the *versus quadratus* is but one aspect of a more general phenomenon: Roman literature, right from its recorded beginnings, knows both a "pure" Hellenizing metric (e.g., the hexameter of Ennius, imported bodily from Greek epic poetry) and "impure," adapted forms (e.g., the majority of the verses used by Plautus and the other comic writers), which, though they have exact counterparts in Greek, nonetheless follow a number of altogether new principles. A fundamental characteristic of early Roman poetry is precisely the coexistence of these two different metrical bases. In the end, the "pure" metric naturally wins out, and already in the first century B.C. the Romans have to labor to understand the structural rules of the Plautine senarius. It is clear, then, that the two different tendencies presuppose different times of adaptation and different paths of transmission, on the one hand, the simple imitation of the regular forms, and on the other, a more gradual and more complex process of acclimatization. Once again the state of our tradition suggests the existence of a long prehistory, now almost completely lost, that came to maturity in the fertile crucible of cultural fusion that was ancient Italy. This is necessarily presupposed by the abrupt "creation" of a national literature in the days of Andronicus, Livius, and Plautus.

BIBLIOGRAPHY

On the origins of Latin and its position within the Indo-European family, see W. M. Lindsay, *The Latin Language* (Oxford 1894, reprint New York 1963), and L. R. Palmer, *The Latin Language* (ed. 3 London 1961); however, there is no satisfactory up-to-date English work comparable to those available in other languages: A. Meillet, *Introduction à l'étude comparative des langues indoeuropéennes* (ed. 8 Paris 1937), G. Devoto, *Origini indoeuropee* (Florence 1962), *Il linguaggio d'Italia* (Milan 1964), *Geschichte der Sprache Roms,* trans. I. Opelt (Heidelberg 1966, with good bibliography), O Szemerényi, *Einführung in die vergleichende Sprachwissenschaft* (Darmstadt 1970).

A work unique in its field, combining structural anthropology and comparative linguistics, is E. Benveniste, *Indo-European Language and Society,* trans. J. Lallot and E. Palmer (London 1973).

On early literacy, see W. V. Harris, *Ancient Literacy* (Cambridge, Mass. 1989) 149–74; on the alphabet, see A. E. Gordon, "On the Origins of the Latin Alphabet: Modern Views," *California Studies in Classical Antiquity* 2 (1969) 157–70.

There is a useful but unreliable collection of archaic Latin texts with English translation by E. H. Warmington, *Remains of Old Latin,* in the Loeb series (4 vols. London 1935–40; vol. 4 contains inscriptions). More scholarly collections include A. Ernout, *Recueil de textes latins archaiques* (ed. 2 Paris 1957, with linguistic commentary in French), E. Diehl, *Altlateinische Inschriften* (ed. 5 Berlin 1959), and E. Pasoli, *Acta fratrum Arvalium* (Bologna 1950).

Among studies on the oldest *carmina* and on rhythmical prose, note C. Thulin, *Italische sakrale Poesie und Prosa* (Berlin 1906), E. Norden, *Aus altrömischen Priesterbüchern* (Lund 1941, an extremely important work dealing especially with the *carmen Arvale* and religious formulae), and B. Luiselli, *Il problema della più antica prosa latina* (Cagliari 1969). In English there is a brief treatment by Gordon Williams in *CHCL* II, 53–55; see also A. Momigliano, "Perizonius, Niebuhr, and the Character of Early Roman Tradition," *Journal of Roman Studies* 44 (1957) 104–14.

There is an extensive bibliography on the problems of the Saturnian meter, which are bound up with broader questions of the relations between Greece and Rome in the archaic period, the persistence of an accentual element in archaic meter, and comparison with Celtic and Germanic metrics. There is a survey by T. Cole, "The Saturnian Verse," *Yale Classical Studies* 21 (1972) 3–73.

The rhythmical/accentual hypothesis was championed especially by W. M. Lindsay, *Early Latin Verse* (Oxford 1922, reprint 1968), the quantitative by F. Leo, *Der saturnische Vers* (Berlin 1905), and G. Pasquali, *Preistoria della poesia romana* (Florence 1936; reprint with important preface by S. Timpanaro, Florence 1981). Pasquali's work is especially important because of its awareness of the historical and archaeological context. Two important studies that take the middle ground are A. W. de Groot, "Le Vers saturnien littéraire," *Révue des études latines* 12 (1934) 284–312, and M. Barchiesi, *Nevio epico: Storia interpretazione edizione critica dei frammenti del primo epos latino* (Padua 1962) 310–27, with detailed bibliography. See also B. Luiselli, *Il verso saturnio* (Rome 1967), G. Erasmi, "The Saturnian and Livius Andronicus," *Glotta* 57 (1979) 125–49, and B. Gentili in *Giorgio Pasquali e la filologia classica del novecento,* ed. F. Bornmann (Florence 1988) 87–99.

The thesis of a dynamic intensive *ictus* is championed in a number of acute and interesting studies, including E. Fraenkel, *Iktus und Akzent im lateinischen Sprechvers* (Berlin 1928), W. F. Jackson Knight, *Accentual Symmetry in Vergil* (Oxford 1939), and H. Drexler, *Einführung in die römischen Metrik* (Darmstadt 1967); see also W. S. Allen, *Accent and Rhythm* (Cambridge 1973) 153–54, 276–78. But although this theory has dominated Anglo-German accounts, there is much to be said for the rival theory of the nonexistence of *ictus:* see the excellent summary by L. E. Rossi, "Sul problema dell'ictus," *Annali Scuola Normale di Pisa* (1964) 119–34, and in English, W. Beare, *Latin Verse and European Song* (London 1957). This view was anticipated in a paper of 1870–71 by the young Friedrich Nietzsche: see the translation of his "On the Theory of Quantitative Rhythm" by J. W. Halporn in *Arion* 6 (1967) 233–43. For a recent and controversial attempt at a new synthesis, see A. S. Gratwick in *CHCL* II, 86–93, and in his edition of Terence's *The Brothers* (Warminster 1987) 276–83.

The Early Roman Theater

I. THE STAGE

Extent of theatrical activity in early Rome

During the century between 240 B.C., when the first regular dramatic performance is said to have been given (of a work by Livius Andronicus), and the time of the Gracchi, Roman culture experiences an extraordinary flourishing of theatrical representations and works for the stage. All the Roman poets of the period who are known to us write for the stage, frequently shifting among the various established genres. The performances involve the authorities of the state, who organize the dramatic festivals, the nobility, who are often the patrons of the artists, and the lower classes, who are the chief ones to enjoy certain genres, for instance, the *palliata* of Plautus. The popularity of this kind of artistic work in Roman society is enormous, comparable or even superior to that of figurative art and certainly greater than the popularity of written literature, which is a more restricted phenomenon. Popular success is accompanied by the flourishing of professional guilds for authors and actors and by literary controversies and declarations of poetic stance; these latter presuppose public discussions of problems, occasionally quite subtle ones, having to do with literary criticism and dramaturgy.

Characteristics and genres of the Roman theater

Before distinguishing the individual genres and the principal authors, it is necessary to take up the general and institutional features of this drama. In order to grasp the background that is common to all early theatrical works, we need to combine the evidence presented by the texts we have, entire or in fragments, with historical, antiquarian, archaeological, and literary information.

All the principal Roman dramatic genres are in origin the results of importation. Of Greek origin are (*a*) the principal comic genre, the *palliata,* so called from the *pallium,* which was the typical clothing of the Greeks (Plautus, Caecilius Status, and Terence wrote *palliatae*); and (*b*) the principal tragic genre, the *cothurnata,* named for *cothurni,* the high footwear of the Greek tragic actors.

The authors of *palliatae* and *cothurnatae* regularly present their works not only as set in Greece but also as derived from specific, acknowledged Greek models (we pass over for the moment the question of the extent of originality and transformation). This is presupposed also in the relations of the works to the educated public, who can more readily catch the subtleties of the adaptation and compare the work with its Greek originals.

Dramas with a Roman plot and their Greek models

There is no contradiction between this tendency and the development of a Roman *palliata* and a Roman *cothurnata,* which are called, respectively, *togata* (since the toga took the place of the *pallium*) and *trabeata* or *praetexta* (from the clothing of the Roman magistrates: Roman tragedies obviously brought figures of high rank on to the stage [see "Roman Terminology for the Theatrical Genres," below]). These are Roman revivals of the corresponding Greek genres, governed by the same dramaturgic principles and following the same stylistic tendencies. On the basis of the extant fragments it is easy to imagine that a tragedy with a Roman plot could be novel in its events, substituting historical facts for the myths of Attic tragedy, and yet at the same time could be inspired by the style and the conventions of the tragedies of Sophocles and Euripides.

The question of the specifically Roman and Italic element, which must have been present in the drama, is not yet answered. It is impossible to discuss it, however, without first explaining the external origin of the early Roman theater.

Etruscans as intermediaries between the Greek and the Roman theaters

Even the technical terms of dramaturgy are all in origin Greek or Etruscan—*histrio,* for instance, the word for "actor." In a famous, though obscure and difficult passage the historian Livy says explicitly that the origin of the Roman spectacles was Etruscan. The most sensible explanation of this notice is that he has in mind public spectacles, not what we in the modern West mean by "theater." Let us accept then the notion that Etruria was the agent for the introduction of spectacles to Rome. It is a debated question whether the Etruscans had a proper theatrical life; if even among them the spectacles were of Greek origin, then the picture becomes more coherent. It is certain that the Etruscans could provide spectacles of music and drama; we have no clear evidence of theatrical texts passing through their hands.

Roman theater and public festivities

The establishment of public spectacles organized by the Roman state was, in any event, a first step of great significance. The occasion of which Livy speaks was marked by public religious ceremonies, and this association is also significant. During the whole period of the Republic the recurring religious festivals and rites are represented as the regular setting for Latin drama. This forms a clear parallel to the situation of Greek tragedy, which is also, and far more profoundly, connected to recurring public festivals. At Rome, however, it seems that from the beginning the link was more external, more institutional. The holidays were certainly an occasion for people to come together, but Latin drama does not appear to have a strong *internal* connection with religious sensibility or with the content of the individual festal celebrations. The public performance of religious formulas and hymns is known at Rome, but these literary forms of worship do not seem to be tied in any way to the birth of the theater.

The ludi

The earliest theatrical event is the one connected with the celebration of the Ludi Romani in honor of Jupiter Optimus Maximus. It was at the Ludi Romani of 240 that Livius Andronicus presented the first regular drama, a tragedy based on a Greek model. The Romans of the classical period regarded this date as the start of their national drama. In the time of Plautus and Terence, about which we are far better informed, four annual occasions are given over to the performance of *ludi scaenici:* the Ludi Romani, already mentioned, in September; the Ludi Megalenses, in honor of the Magna Mater, in April; the Ludi Apollinares, in July; and the Ludi Plebeii, dedicated to Jupiter Optimus Maximus, in November. The organizing of the *ludi* was always in the hands of the magistrates in office, or the urban praetors. The *ludi* were occasions not only for theatrical spectacles but also, for instance, for gladiatorial games, which gives us some idea of the extent to which the theater was a collective entertainment.

Influence of those who commission theatrical works

The official character of the organizing has two important consequences. First, those who commission the theatrical works are identical with the authorities. In an era when public offices are held by the *nobiles,* the importance of certain noble clans in furthering the development of the theater is evident. The nature of the commissioning explains, in the case of historical tragedies, the choice of particular plots, for example, celebrations of the heroic deeds or the illustrious ancestors of particular families. Often, then, the *praetexta* is likely not only to have a national and nationalistic theme but also to refer to politically influential individuals. This relation between content and commission is not observable, however, in the case of comedy, the sphere of which is different and narrower. And in general the importance of those who commissioned works could not eliminate the importance of the audience, which was drawn from the whole of Roman society.

Politics and Latin comedy

The second consequence has to do with comedy. The Latin comedy we know, including that of Terence, who strives in his own way to touch upon problems felt by Roman society, does not really practice social or moral criticism. Still less admissible are direct personal attacks of the type so common in Aristophanes or declarations of political stance. Comedy may be realistic, after its own fashion, but it does not touch the sphere of contemporary politics. We do not know whether there were exceptions. The poet Naevius is famous for his attacks on the noble family of the Metelli, and he was even jailed, it seems, for political reasons; but we no longer have anything from Naevius's comedies and cannot, unfortunately, form even a hazy notion of them.

The guild of authors and actors

Another important date for the Latin theater is 207, when the guild of authors and actors *(collegium scribarum histrionumque)* was established. The societal recognition of these activities is of undoubted historical importance, but the recognition was rather limited: notice the association of the writers, who are identified as *theatrical* writers, with the actors, whose activity no Roman of free birth would have undertaken; notice, too, the use of *scriba,* which in later Latin means "scribe" and not "writer." The subsequent taking over of the term *poeta* from the Greek would indicate a loftier sense of self-esteem: Ennius would lead a movement in society towards setting a high value on literary activity. Social recognition would continue to rise along with popular success, and especially with the strengthening of ties between authors and the aristocracy. In this ascent Ennius would be the key figure for serious literature, as Terence would be for the comic stage.

Organization

How were theatrical works put on? We have mentioned that the financial burdens were assumed by the state, represented by the magistrates who organized the *ludi.* The magistrates had to deal with the authors and with another important figure, the manager *(dominus gregis),* who directed the company, produced the work, and sometimes collaborated with the authors whom he had chosen. The actor-producer Lucius Ambivius Turpio is well known, since he had a large part in Terence's hard-won success.

The stage

The first theater made of stone at Rome was constructed only in 55 B.C.; previously there were only temporary structures of wood. This does not mean that the stage structure and the accommodations for the public were rudimentary and poorly executed. We ought to imagine the performances of the *palliata,* which was modeled on Athenian New Comedy, as more or less reproducing the staging of the Greek theater. The actions always took place out of doors, in front of two or three houses (with the very rare exception of a setting outside the city), upon a street that by convention led on one side towards the center of the city—the forum, the *agora* of the Greek originals—and on the other outwards, towards the country or the harbor.

Masks and characters

A fundamental aspect of the staging was the use of masks. (That masks were used is certain at least from the middle of the second century B.C. onwards, whereas for the age of Plautus the evidence is somewhat more controversial.) These masks were fixed for certain types of characters, who appeared in practically every comic plot: the old man, the young man in love, the matron, the courtesan, the pimp, the slave, the parasite, the soldier, and others. The masks did not altogether exclude communication by means of facial expression, since they were movable and had large spaces for the eyes; but their purpose was to make clear immediately the type of the individual character. It is not accidental that Plautus's prologues, which inform the audience about the plot, refer to the characters by their general type (the old man, the young man, the pimp, etc.) and do not dwell on their names: to sort out the names and remember them would have been a chore for the audience. The use of these types or masks undoubtedly had a strong influence on the poetics of Latin comic writers. This is evident especially in Plautus, who often employs stereotyped, generic psychological character types in order to be able to direct all his attention to the humor of the individual situations and to verbal invention. Terence, on the contrary, it might be said, struggles against this tendency, seeking to deepen the psychology of his characters without relying too much on the traditional repertory of masks or on the traditions of Italic farce.

The use of masks must have had a practical consequence too. One actor, by changing mask and costume, could play more than one part. Thus even an action-filled comedy, with dialogues among three or even four actors who were on the stage simultaneously, could be performed with four, or at most five, players. It is clear that the actors had different degrees of ability and specialization: some characters, usually one or two in a comedy, had very demanding parts, including *cantica,* "arias," which required particular virtuosity in performance.

2. THE FORMS

This leads us from questions of the Roman stage to questions of the dramatic texts. Certain general matters can be treated here first, before we come to the authors individually. The information about the *palliata* is more reliable than that about tragedy, for the obvious reason that we have only fragments of early tragedy. But some general aspects are valid for both.

Comedy: metrical forms of the Latin palliata

The author of *palliatae* whom we know best, Titus Maccius Plautus, writes comedies that (1) are not divided into acts and (2) are composed of parts recited and sung. More exactly, Plautine works included at least three different modes of performance, three different metrical forms: the parts recited without musical accompaniment, written in iambic senarii, the Roman equivalent to the Greek iambic trimeter; the recitatives, for which there was a musical accompaniment, in trochaic septenarii, equivalent to the trochaic tetrameter catalectic; and the sung parts, composed in an extraordinary variety of meters. All these types of verse, unlike the obscure Saturnian, have precise equivalents in the classical Greek metrical system; yet each one shows, in a different way, that it has undergone subtle and profound adaptations. To give but one example, the Plautine iambic senarius, in comparison with the iambic trimeter, is far more free, since it admits a large number of substitutions, which in Greek would be highly irregular, and at the same time is far more fixed, since its apparently anarchic form is shaped by a subtle web of metrical-verbal laws, which regulate the relations between words and metrical units. More generally, the metrical structure of the *palliata* gives a striking impression of richness and musicality. In every work the author could switch about among those three large registers, the third of which itself permitted a vast range of possibilities; this in turn, of course, significantly influenced the plot of the work and its dramaturgy. The differences in the formal structure were great between these works and their models, which were, as we shall see below, the plays of the New Comedy that flourished at Athens in the fourth century B.C.

Metrical forms of Greek New Comedy

These works, by Menander, for instance, normally (1) were divided into acts, (2) were composed almost exclusively of recited parts, or recitatives, and so, in terms of verses, were composed of iambic trimeters or trochaic tetrameters catalectic. The structure of the play was thus more nearly unchanging and more uniform. It is hardly surprising that a verse such as the iambic trimeter was regarded as most apt for imitating the plain, colloquial style of ordinary conversation. It was from this metrical restriction that New Comedy derived its typical effect of "bourgeois realism." This effect was congruent with the choice of a restrained and realistic style and with the handling of the characters and the plot. New Comedy thus distinguished itself from the lively rhythmic creativity of Aristophanes' Old Comedy and from the rich musicality of the tragic theater, which was characterized by frequent, complex choral passages with strophic responsion. Because of the far from lyrical nature of New Comedy, the use of musical passages was confined to a formal, external device: the intermezzi, the pauses marking the divisions between one act and the other, which consisted of musical performances.

Diversity in form and transformations of substance

The *palliata* of Naevius and Plautus dispensed with this usage and also with the sharp division into five acts; but with its sung passages it recovered a substantial element of dramatic presentation. The consequences were decisive for the development of an original Latin comic drama. From a technical point of view, the rewriting of the Attic originals became a process of shifting to new principles of expression (we leave aside, for the sake of the present argument, all the other possible and imaginable reasons for change). To rewrite a character's monologue as an aria, a polymetric *canticum,* involved more than technical changes to the rhythm: it involved the structure of the discourse, the choice of words and concepts, and, ultimately, the very shape of the character and the manner in which he was conceived. The realistic poetry of New Comedy began to alter thereby. And authors did not simply rewrite and reshape situations that lent themselves to rhythmic transposition; they also felt the desire to create new situations and created suitable spaces and pauses for them in the smooth course of the original drama. We will see shortly some original characteristics of Plautine comedy that ought to be related to these transformations: what we will term "comic lyricism" (see pp. 58 ff.) is a more complex phenomenon but certainly parallel to these metrical-expressive tendencies.

Tragedy: importance of the chorus in Greek tragedy

Our understanding of early Roman tragedy is less clear and organic. By use of the fragments and by comparison with Attic tragedy of the fifth century, which remained the model at all times, it is possible to present a couple of impressions. Attic tragedy consisted of an alternation of passages of dialogue, which were recited, with lyric passages. Undoubtedly the most distinctive aspect of the latter was the large strophic constructions, the choruses, with their complicated architecture and internal responsions. The choruses were a fusion of text and choreography: they were musical and were danced to; they were performed by groups of actors who within the dramatic structure generally had a limited or passive function. The usual function of the choral parts within the plot was to comment on the action. The style used to the full the abundant resources of the Greek literary language and was clearly separate from that of the passages where the characters spoke.

Absence of the chorus from Latin tragedy and its structural consequences

Since Latin writers of tragedies did not, it seems, have at their disposal the necessary elements—of stage, dance, or music—to reproduce in the Roman drama the choral insertions of the Attic, profound changes were required in the rewriting of Attic plots. On the one hand, the Latin tragedians needed to reabsorb into their new theatrical presentations whatever of the choral passages seemed to them indispensable or worthwhile. On the other hand, the disappearance of choral lyric left a void of style and imagery in the tragedies, for on their choral passages the Greek tragedians had lavished their boldest images, their most impressive and loftiest figures of style. Tragedy, by contrast with other, lower, more ordinary genres, was very much based on this gap between the languages of dialogue and of lyric.

The style of Latin tragedy

The Latin tragedians filled this void by raising the *entire* stylistic level of their plays. Latin tragedy is characterized by a style that appears uniform in its loftiness and that contrasts clearly with everyday language. The Latin tragic poets, not possessing long-amassed riches in the storehouse of their artistic language, made use of every resource they could: calques from Greek poetic language, bold neologisms, borrowings from the solemn official language of politics, religion, and law. In this way they succeeded in endowing tragedy with an identifiable language of its own, even to the point of excess: Plautus and Lucilius parody the exaggerated style of Ennius and Accius, and the parodies hit the mark, with great comic success.

Metrical variety in Latin tragedy

In its metrical composition too, so far as we can tell, tragedy strove to rise above everyday style and the metrical composition of the other literary genres. Whereas in Attic tragedy, especially Euripides, who is the Romans' favorite model, the greater part of the drama is carried by the "colloquial" iambic trimeter, the equivalent verse in Roman tragedy, the senarius, is in the minority; considerably more space is occupied by verses in a much higher stylistic and emotional register, such as the recitatives in trochaic septenarii and the various kinds of *cantica*. This comprehensive elevation of style served, as has been mentioned, to compensate for the loss of the choral intervals, but its consequences obviously did not stop there. This transformation is linked to certain unusual features of Roman tragedy. First of all, pathos increases, at the expense of a more rational psychological analysis. As for the verse itself, the iambic trimeter, which in Greek tragedy was the vehicle of rational communications—exposition of situations, analysis, and debate, as opposed to lyric comment or emotional outburst—in the new scheme falls into disfavor. The use of its Latin equivalent, the senarius, is greatly reduced: during the Republic it would increasingly become the typical, prosaic, irregular verse of the comic writers.

Structural deficiencies in Latin drama

Before making a broad historical assessment of early Roman tragedy, let us remember once again the caution with which we must proceed in this field where evidence is not abundant. For all we know, the general characteristics we have discussed were already found in Livius Andronicus and Naevius. It is likely that a greater knowledge of dramatic poetry in the Hellenistic age would provide some further missing links, making clearer the passage from choral lyric to the Roman *cantica*. Still, we may fairly conclude that after intense activity, which must have been rapid and even feverish, Roman culture found itself in possession of its own Greek-style drama. Certain solutions were, in a sense, hasty and provisional. The Attic drama of the fourth century was based on a clear division of styles. In order to separate itself from the "realism" of comic language, Greek tragedy, whose subject was the famous figures of myth, drew upon the great reserves of the epic and lyric language and upon the traditions of non-Attic dialects.

From this derived its unbounded capacity for a distancing effect and a natural artfulness. But all this was quite inimitable for the youthful poetry of the Romans. Their new drama did not have a literary past rich enough to permit deep distinctions between the various genres and levels of style. The quest would continue, with alternate experiments, for nearly two centuries, down to the age of Augustus.

3. A DRAMATIC SUBGENRE: THE ATELLAN

Alongside the grand phenomenon of the regular drama—*palliata, togata, tabernaria,* etc.—continues a successful popular genre, the Atellan, which has been likened to the Italian *commedia dell'arte* (a perceptive comparison, possibly wrong, but appealing). The arrival of the Atellan at Rome—the name comes from the city of Atella, in the Oscan-speaking region of Campania—must have already taken place before the establishment of regular literary drama. These preliterary spectacles, probably performed at first *ex tempore,* by improvisation, did not call for a professional structure and were based on rudimentary plots: a dramatic story line that included plays on words, incidents of farcical action, quarrels and wrangling, and ribald exchanges in the spirit of the Fescennine verses (see p. 23). But perhaps the most important characteristic we know of in the Atellan is that the improvisations involved fixed, recurring masks (hence *Fixed masks* the parallel with *commedia dell'arte*): figures such as Bucco, the braggart and gossip, and Dossennus, the evil hunchback. One of these names, Maccus, seems to have been adapted and adopted as a part of Plautus's name (see p. 49).

The use of fixed masks is important for understanding certain aspects of Plautus's drama that are far removed from their Greek literary models (see pp. 56 f.). It is quite likely that the Atellan influenced the regular, Hellenizing drama: the audience must have been the same, and the Atellan itself had certainly assimilated elements of tradition from Greece and Magna Graecia. The *commedia dell'arte,* too, as is well known, influenced high, literary drama.

These are influences that we can reconstruct only indirectly, from the literary dramas of Plautus and Caecilius. Italic farce will experience a renaissance at the beginning of the first century B.C., when it acquires more traditional literary characteristics (see p. 126 f., on Pomponius and Novius), without, however, giving up the unrestrained language of the people.

ROMAN TERMINOLOGY FOR THE THEATRICAL GENRES

For the sake of clarity we summarize here the principal classical Latin terms for the different theatrical genres and specialties.

Fabula. The most general term, which can refer to any type of text for the theater. All the designations listed below are, properly speaking, adjectives modifying and specifying this comprehensive term.

Palliata. A comedy with a Greek setting, that is, as far as we can tell, an adaptation of an original belonging to Attic New Comedy. The characters wore a typically Greek item of clothing, the *pallium,* which contrasts with the distinctive toga of the Romans.

Togata. In a general sense, any theatrical work with a Roman setting. By contrast with the *praetexta,* it is most often a *comedy* with a Roman setting, usually distinct from the more popular comic genres, such as the Atellan (see p. 36) and the mime (see pp. 127 ff.).

Tabernaria. A comic work with a Roman setting. The term is not sharply distinguished from *togata* but seems to have a connotation of greater lowness. *Taberna* is used in Latin for "hut, shack" or "shop, tavern, hostel."

Trabeata. A neologism indicating an occasional experiment. The term is formed on the model of *togata* and derives from *trabea,* the name for the typical garb of the equestrian class at Rome. A freedman of Maecenas, Gaius Melissus, attempted to write "middle-class" plays, to which the novel term was applied.

Crepidata (?), Cothurnata. Little-used terms that identify, by contrast with *praetexta,* tragedies in a Greek setting. The cothurnus was the high footwear typical of the Greek tragic actors; *crepidata* derives from *crepida,* "Greek-style sandal." It is not altogether clear how *crepidata* could refer to the footwear of a tragic actor; hence some think that *crepidata* ought to refer instead to the Greek-style comic genre of the *palliatae.*

Praetexta or *Praetextata.* A tragedy with a Roman setting. The *toga praetexta* was the toga worn by Roman magistrates and marked by a band of purple.

One may represent this division of terms schematically as follows:

	Comedy	Tragedy
Greek setting	*palliata*	*cothurnata/crepidata*
Roman setting	*togata*	*praetexta*

BIBLIOGRAPHY

On the Roman stage in general, see in English W. Beare, *The Roman Stage* (ed. 3 London 1964), R. C. Beacham, *The Roman Theatre and Its Audience* (London 1991), and A. S. Gratwick, *Drama,* in CHCL II, 77–137. On Roman tragedy, see H. D. Jocelyn, *The Tragedies of Ennius* (Cambridge 1967) 3–43; for the details of the plots and the Greek models, O. Ribbeck, *Die römischen Tragödie im Zeitalter der Republik* (Leipzig 1870, reprint Hildesheim 1968), is still invaluable. Ribbeck's collection of the tragic fragments also remains fundamental: *Scaenicae Romanorum Poesis Fragmenta,* vol. 1 (ed. 2 Leipzig 1871–73, reprint Hildesheim 1962; ed. 3 of 1897–98 lacks the *indices verborum*). See also A. Klotz, *Tragicorum fragmenta* (Munich 1953). For editions of individual authors, see below.

On comedy in general, see G. E. Duckworth, *The Nature of Roman Comedy: A Study in Popular Entertainment* (Princeton 1952), F. H. Sandbach, *The Comic Theatre of Greece and Rome* (London 1977), J. Wright, *Dancing in Chains: The Stylistic Unity of the Comoedia Palliata* (Rome 1974), E. Segal, *Roman Laughter,* ed. 2 (New York 1987), and R. L. Hunter, *The New Comedy of Greece and Rome* (Cambridge 1985). For the fragments, see Ribbeck, *Scaenicae Romanorum Poesis Fragmenta,* vol. 2 (Leipzig 1898).

The view taken here of the archaic Latin meters of drama is best represented by C. Questa's fundamental *Introduzione alla metrica di Plauto* (Bologna 1967). English treatments are usually based on the *ictus* theory (see E. Fraenkel, *Iktus und Akzent im lateinischen Sprechvers* [Berlin 1928], W. F. Jackson Knight, *Accentual Symmetry in Vergil* [Oxford 1939], and H. Drexler, *Einführung in die römischen Metrik* [Darmstadt 1967]); see, e.g., D. S. Raven, *Latin Metre* (London 1965) 41–89, and in greater detail, W. M. Lindsay's *Early Latin Verse* (Oxford 1922, reprint 1968) and his commentary on Plautus, *Captivi* (ed. 2 Oxford 1930) 56–102. Closer to the French and Italian traditions, however, is the recent work of A. S. Gratwick in *CHCL* II, 86–93.

Livius Andronicus

LIFE

We do not know Livius's dates of birth and death. He came to Rome at the end of the war between Rome and Tarentum (272 B.C.), probably from Tarentum and, according to some, in the entourage of Livius Salinator. This would explain his Roman praenomen, Livius. Andronicus was to all intents and purposes a Greek, and he assumed the praenomen of his patron, Livius Salinator, whose freedman he was. He was active at Rome as a *grammaticus,* a "teacher" of Greek and Latin, as the author of texts for the stage, and as an actor in the staging of some of his own works. Two important, clearly attested turning points in his literary career came in 240, when a work of his was the first dramatic text put on at Rome, and in 207, when he composed a *partheneion,* "girls' song," in honor of Juno, a work to be performed in public as part of religious ceremonies. After this significant achievement Livius received public honors, and his professional association, the *collegium scribarum histrionumque,* was installed in a public building, the temple of Minerva on the Aventine. This recognition, which for the first time in Rome's history granted an official status to literary activity, is also the last notice we have about the life of Livius.

WORKS

All that has come down to us amounts to no more than sixty fragments, which we owe to quotations in the works of republican authors and of grammarians. We have the titles of eight tragedies: *Achilles, Aegisthus, Aiax Mastigophorus* ("Ajax with the Whip"), and *Equos Troianus* ("The Trojan Horse"), *Hermiona,* all connected with the cycle of the Trojan War, and *Andromeda, Danaë,* and *Tereus*—in all, slightly more than twenty fragments of forty verses total. He also composed *palliatae,* which evidently aroused less interest than the tragedies; we have six fragments of a single verse apiece, sometimes an incomplete verse, and the very titles are unreliably transmitted. Only one is securely attested: *Gladiolus* ("Little Saber"). Nothing is preserved of the *partheneion* for Juno.

SOURCES

The data on his life that are accepted here, along with the two dates of 240 and 207, are based essentially on Cicero (*Brutus* 72 f.) and Livy (27.37.7). The passage of Cicero testifies to an ancient controversy over the life of Livius. It appears that Accius, the tragic poet and philologist of the second century B.C., fixed the date of Andronicus's arrival in Rome as 209 B.C., the date of the capture of Tarentum during the Second Punic War. This would shift the high point of Livius's activity to the first years of the second century B.C., but it is quite difficult to regard him as a contemporary of Plautus and Ennius. Accius's date is to be dismissed, even though the life of Andronicus remains nebulous. It also seems extremely unlikely that the date for Livius's coming to Rome should be set as early as 272, as some have claimed. Only the dates 240 (first performance) and 207 (*partheneion* for Juno) appear exempt from all controversy.

THE BIRTH OF VERSE TRANSLATION

The great Roman classical writers of the first century B.C., Varro, Cicero, and Horace, agree in presenting Livius as the originator of Latin literature. It is obvious that foundation stories of this sort may contain distortions, but what we know of Livius makes it difficult to underestimate his historical importance.

The written translation of a literary work

The enterprise of translating Homer's *Odyssey* into Latin and into Italic meter (the Saturnian) had an immense historical importance. The phenomenon of written translation is hardly a complete novelty, of course: before the Romans and even before the Greeks, the civilizations of Mesopotamia and Egypt practiced translation, of judicial and religious texts, for example. But even a literary culture of the highest refinement and inquisitiveness such as the Greek did not succeed, until the period of the Roman Empire, in conceiving of the translation of a literary work written in a foreign language. Livius's project had purposes that were both literary and, more generally, cultural. Let us take the latter first. Livius made accessible to the Romans a fundamental text of Greek culture. The Hellenized Roman elite naturally read Homer in the original; but the *Odusia* succeeded as a school text, and we know from Horace (*Epistles* 2.1.69 ff.) that already in the first century schoolboys had trouble with Andronicus's difficult, archaic language. Andronicus himself was a schoolmaster and through his work succeeded both in spreading Greek culture at Rome and in advancing literary culture in Latin.

Artistic translation

The *Odusia* seems in fact not to have been conceived only as a school text. Livius's importance in literary history consists in having conceived of translation as an *artistic* process: the creation of a text to stand beside the original, a text that can be enjoyed as an autonomous work and yet strives to preserve, through new means of expression, not only the bare contents but also the artistic quality of the original. The problems Livius confronted must have been enormous, and many of the solutions he found had a lasting influence on the development of Latin literature. Not having behind him an epic tradition, Livius tried by other means to confer solemnity and intensity upon his literary language. Forms such as the genitive in -*as* or the imperative *insece,* "tell me," a translation of Homer's *ennepe* in the first line of the poem, are shown to be, when scrutinized, not only archaic in Hor-

ace's day but also deliberately archaizing for the language used in Andronicus's day. Thus, in response to the artificial and literary quality of Homeric
Greek, that archaizing, conservative tendency begins that will take on such
importance in the history of Latin poetry. The literary language is cut off
from the everyday language. For this reason Andronicus resorts to terms
from the religious tradition, which give loftiness and resonance to his language: he renders the Homeric "Muse" *Camena,* the ancient name of an
Italic water divinity, relying on the etymology then current, according to
which *Camena* comes from *Casmena/Carmena* and thus from *carmen,* "poem."

*Alteration of what is
untranslatable*

The meager fragments reveal a notable desire to stick close to the original and be clear: translating means both preserving what can be assimilated
and altering what proves to be untranslatable, either because of the limits
of the linguistic medium or because of differences of culture and mind.
Homer speaks of a hero "equal to the gods," but this notion is unacceptable
to the Roman mind: Andronicus changes this, without loss of gravity, and
translates *summus adprimus,* "greatest and of first rank." In other cases one
has the impression that Andronicus modifies Homer for specifically artistic
reasons. He is after all a contemporary of the Alexandrian poets: this author, whom Horace would regard as primitive, is himself far removed
in time from the poetry of Homer and has a taste and a poetics of his

*Translation and
dramatization*

own. Unlike its Greek models, early Roman poetry is characterized by the
pursuit of pathos, of expressive force and dramatic tension. In Homer the
swineherd Eumaios speaks to the disguised Odysseus and says: "Grief for
Odysseus, who is no more, takes hold of me" (*Odyssey* 14.144). The situation is fraught with emotion and also with irony, since Odysseus is there
listening but not yet able to reveal himself. Andronicus translates, or rather
interprets: *neque tamen te oblitus sum, Laertie noster,* "yet I have not forgotten
you, dear son of Laërtes." "I have not forgotten you" is more emphatic than
"grief takes hold of me." Moreover, Eumaios here addresses Odysseus *in the
second person:* his grief leads him to apostrophize as if present a person who
is far away but who, as the readers know, is present to hear him.

*Theatrical works of
Livius Andronicus*

This ability to dramatize the Homeric narrative reminds us that Andronicus was also a significant playwright. Andronicus's dramatic works,
too, such as the *Odusia,* had definite Greek models. But in the field of theater the Romans from the beginning were more free to change their originals: they were, at most, adapters, but not translators, properly speaking.
One of the very few fragments we can check against the Greek original—
Sophocles' *Ajax,* the model of the *Aiax Mastigophorus*—includes an embittered utterance: "courage wins praise, but the praise melts more rapidly
than ice in springtime"; the Sophoclean character said merely "as quickly
as favor vanishes among mortals." Already in this passage, as we will find
so often in the history of Roman literature, the *differences* between the Latin
poets and their originals provide a valuable measure of the new culture's
distinctive characteristics. The pursuit of the pathetic, for instance, is a
constant in virtually all archaic Latin poetry and is best seen where we have
the Greek model to contrast it with.

One can believe that nearly all the characteristics of Roman Republican theater that we saw in the previous chapter were already a legacy from Andronicus. The tragic models he followed were in all likelihood Attic texts of the fifth century, Sophocles and Euripides by preference; later on, the same would almost always be true of Naevius, Ennius, Pacuvius, and Accius.

On account of the rapid literary development that followed upon his work, Andronicus very soon fell out of fashion: not only do Cicero and Horace find his art primitive but even Ennius appears to polemicize against his predecessor. The reading of Andronicus in school probably lasted longer than his literary success: all that was left, so to speak, was the bust of a fore-father.

BIBLIOGRAPHY

The epic fragments have been edited by W. Morel, *Fragmenta poetarum latinorum epicorum et lyricorum praeter Ennium et Lucilium* (Leipzig 1927, reprint 1963; see also the much-criticized revision by K. Büchner, Leipzig 1982, with bibliography), the tragic by O. Ribbeck (*Scaenicae Romanorum Poesis Fragmenta,* vol. 1 [ed. 2 Leipzig 1871–73, reprint Hildesheim 1962; ed. 3 of 1897–98 lacks the *indices verborum*]). For an English translation, see volume 2 of E. H. Warmington's *Remains of Old Latin* (Loeb series, 4 vols. London 1935–40).

Much of the work on Livius is in Italian: the fundamental study is Scevola Mariotti, *Livio Andronico e la traduzione artistica* (Urbino 1950, rev. ed. 1986), and see also the valuable analyses in A. Traina, *Vortit barbare: Le traduzioni poetiche da Livio Andronico a Cicerone* (Rome 1970) 11–28. There have been a number of recent monographs, notably by R. Perna (Bari 1978) and U. Carratello (Rome 1979); W. Suerbaum, *Untersuchungen zur Selbstdarstellung älterer römischen Dichter: Livius Andronicus, Naevius, Ennius* (Hildesheim 1968) contains much of importance. In English, Livius benefits from coming first in Martin Drury's appendix to *CHCL* II, 799–802; see also W. Beare, *The Roman Stage* (ed. 3 London 1964) 25–32, and J. Wright, *Dancing in Chains: The Stylistic Unity of the Comoedia Palliata* (Rome 1974) 15–32. On the epic fragments, the best account is in D. C. Feeney, *The Gods in Epic* (Oxford 1991). For the biographical problems, see H. B. Mattingly, *Gnomon* 43 (1971) 680–87. There is a survey in German by J. H. Waszink, "Zum Anfangstadium der römischen Literatur," *ANRW* 1.2 (Berlin 1972) 869–902.

Naevius

Gnaeus Naevius, a Roman citizen of Campanian origin, fought in the First Punic War (264–241), probably the last years of the war. He seems to have been a plebeian by birth, and this would be unusual: in early Rome writers coming from a plebeian background are few. His life bears traces of polemic against the nobility, and we have no indications that he relied on aristocratic patrons, as Livius Andronicus did on Livius Salinator, or Ennius on Fulvius Nobilior and the Scipios, Terence on the Scipios, or Pacuvius on Lucius Aemilius Paullus. The story is told that he attacked in verse the powerful noble family of the Metelli, who replied with threats; it is also suggested that he was imprisoned for certain allusions contained in his plays (see below). He died, perhaps an exile, at Utica in Africa in 204 or 201, leaving behind a large literary reputation. The date of his death is uncertain; many, for sound reasons, place it later, in the first decade of the second century.

Naevius wrote many tragedies (including at least two *praetextae, Romulus* and *Clastidium*) and comedies. A text of his was performed as early as 235 B.C. Of the tragedies with a Greek plot we have seven titles and fifty fragments, consisting of seventy verses; of *Romulus* and *Clastidium* we have in total two very brief fragments. Of the comedies, however, we know of twenty-eight titles and possess eighty fragments, consisting of about 125 verses, not a few of them incomplete.

His principal work is the *Bellum Poenicum,* in Saturnians. Relatively brief, in accord with Hellenistic poetic doctrine, the poem must have contained four thousand to five thousand verses: of these scarcely sixty remain, transmitted chiefly by grammarians. The work had no book divisions, but later it was arranged in seven books by the grammarian Lampadio, a contemporary of Accius. The poem narrated the story of Aeneas, who arrives in Latium from Troy, and in its main section the story of the First Punic War, which Naevius had experienced; the problem of the narrative link between these two sections is not easily solved on the basis of the fragments we have. Since the poem was composed during the years of the war with

Hannibal (i.e., after 218), its content had great contemporary relevance for the Roman public.

Casual notices about Naevius come to us especially from Cicero and St. Jerome. A tantalizing hint is suggested by an allusion in Plautus: in the *Miles Gloriosus* (210 ff.) mention is made of a poet who is imprisoned and forced to keep silent; according to some, the reference is to Naevius. The conclusion is not completely certain.

The notice of Naevius's attacks on the powerful clan of the Metelli (Gellius 3.3.15; cf. Cicero, *In Verrem* 1.10.29) and of his imprisonment is of contested authenticity. From what we know of his personality, it is possible that Naevius gave autobiographical information in his work; however, the extant fragments are of no help in this matter.

BETWEEN MYTH AND HISTORY

Naevius's engagement with politics

If Livius Andronicus is in absolute terms the first Latin writer, the Campanian Naevius is the first Latin writer who is of Roman nationality. And if the biographical traditions and certain of his own fragments do not mislead us, he also appears to us as the first Roman writer vigorously caught up in contemporary affairs, a participant in historical and political events by virtue of his personal experience as much as his literary choice. Naevius is the only Roman writer in the whole period of the middle Republic who takes an active, independent part in the political disputes of the day; this remains true even if the story of his exile is not well founded.

Naevius's engagement with the political life of Rome is evident in the new and distinctive characteristics of his work: the *Bellum Poenicum* is the first Latin epic with a Roman theme (in this sense Naevius is as much a trailblazer as Andronicus); *Romulus* and *Clastidium* are the first titles we have of *praetextae,* that is, tragedies with a Roman plot (see p. 37). *Romulus* treated the dramatic story of Rome's foundation; one of the characters in the play must have been the tyrant Amulius. *Clastidium,* to judge from its title, must have been a celebration of the victory won at the town of that name over the Insubrian Gauls (222 B.C.); the victor, Marcus Claudius Marcellus, died in 208, but we do not know when exactly the tragedy was composed. In any case, a story set so close in time represents a considerable innovation.

The mythical account of Rome's origins

The *Bellum Poenicum* shows such strikingly novel features that its loss must be reckoned particularly unfortunate. The choice of a nearly contemporary historical subject is not its only novelty. Naevius did not limit himself to dealing in verse with the First Punic War, and this at a moment when Rome was once again facing the tremendous threat posed by Carthage; his version, making a bold leap in time, was rooted in Rome's prehistory. From the fragments, we know for certain that Naevius narrated on a rather ample scale, in about one book, the legend of Aeneas, the hero who brings the *penates* of Troy to Rome and, many generations before Romulus, begins the Roman race. We have thus in Naevius a "Homeric" stratum, so to speak: the foundation of Rome was linked to the fall of Troy, and the voyages of Aeneas were in some ways parallel to the wanderings of Odysseus. In this section Naevius must have given considerable play to divine intervention. The gods of Olympus were vital in the Homeric epic, but now, in the new Roman national poem, the traditional divine apparatus took on a historical mission as well and, through large-scale conflicts, gave its sanction to the foundation of Rome. This bold fusion of myth and national history set the rise of Rome within a cosmic perspective, which naturally was fostered by Greek culture.

Rome and Carthage

Yet the poem also had, as its supporting structure, a historical stratum, the account of the war against Carthage. Unfortunately we do not know for certain how these two strata were connected. It is certain that there was no kind of continuous narration; foundation myth and contemporary history came together as separate masses. It is possible that Naevius found a way of inserting among the voyages Aeneas's meeting with Dido; if so, a great arc of dramatic tension would have fused the destinies of the two peoples—and Naevius would be far closer to the *Aeneid* than Ennius's *Annals* are.

Naevius and his Greek models

It is appropriate to emphasize the poem's national inspiration and originality of structure, but one must not for those reasons detach Naevius too much from the Greek literary tradition or make him a kind of opposite number to the "translator" Livius Andronicus. Naevius must have had a profound knowledge of Greek poetry, and his native Campania, like Andronicus's Tarentum, was a region of Greek language and culture. The *Bellum Poenicum* presupposes not only Homer but also the Hellenistic tradition of the celebratory historical poem, in which the poet sings, according to Homeric principles, some historical events of contemporary interest. The idea of weaving together a story of voyages and a story of war (the voyage of Aeneas, the war between Rome and Carthage) points to a crossing of the *Iliad* (the Trojan War) and the *Odyssey* (the voyages of a hero). It is interesting to note that the greatest epic poet of the third century B.C., Apollonius of Rhodes, had similarly combined the models of the two Homeric texts in his *Argonautica*.

Style:
a) The figures of sound

Certain stylistic features also reveal in Naevius an original mixture of Hellenistic poetic culture and national inspiration. The few fragments suffice to show notable variations in tone and diction. A characteristic of all archaic poetic language is the importance of the figures of sound: repetitions, alliterations, and assonances tend to create the supporting structure of the verse. We saw this clearly in the remains of the sacral *carmina,* in proverbs, in the fragments of Andronicus, and also in the earliest prose. The Saturnian, in particular, this verse with the structure that was so "weak" and so irregular in the eyes of Roman writers beginning with Ennius, found its formal framework precisely in the repetitions of sound. Naevius expands the artistic use of this formal device. Consider the following Saturnian:

superbiter contemptim   conterit legiones

("with arrogance, with disdain, he crushes the legions"), the portrait of an aristocratic commander who harries his humble foot soldiers. The harshness of the behavior—and of Naevius's judgment—finds full expression in the alliterating echo *contemptim / conterit*.

b) *Comparison with Greek epic language*

Experimentation with a new poetic language developed in two principal directions; and of course they could also be combined. The mythic section of the poem presented Naevius with the challenge of Greek poetic language, with its inexhaustible store of precious epithets. Take a fragment such as the following:

> deinde pollens sagittis   inclutus arquitenens
> sanctus Iove prognatus   Pythius Apollo

("and then, powerful with arrows, the famed bowman, the holy offspring of Jupiter, Pythian Apollo"), where Naevius actually outdoes the lexical and formulaic richness of Homeric diction, trying out new compounds (*arquitenens*) and new syntactic combinations (*pollens sagittis*) in order to match the richness of Greek poetry's compound epithets, and yet not presenting a mere mechanical reproduction, or calque.

c) *Creation of a historiographic language*

The historical section of the poem posed equally difficult problems, though of a different sort. Naevius adapts his poetic style to a long, unbroken narrative, the model for which was more likely found in historical writings than in works of poetry. Mundane subjects not yet sung of in poetry find a new style, one sometimes monumental and nearly always marked by a striving for form:

> onerariae onustae   stabant in flustris

("laden, the ships lay at anchor upon the sluggish sea"): the language is simple and concrete, the word order linear; yet the first half-verse is bound together by etymology and assonance, and in the second the unmoving quality of the heavy ships makes an elegant contrast to the motion of the waves. Naevius introduces into poetry many technical terms—*flustra* here comes from sailors' language—and does not eschew even prosaic terms, which classical poetry would avoid.

The Bellum Poenicum *as an experimental work*

The *Bellum Poenicum* as a whole seems to be a work of bold experimentation in which the different stylistic components may not have achieved a stable balance. After the decline of the Saturnian the poem's fame would be increasingly overshadowed by Ennius's *Annals*. Linguistically obsolete, Naevius as a writer of epic would nonetheless have his clear influence upon the inspiration of the *Aeneid* and would long retain his prestige as an example of civilized poetry. Certain of his verses give lapidary expression to the earliest ideology of the Roman Republic: "these prefer to die standing at their post rather than return home stained in the esteem of their fellow citizens; but if they had to abandon those courageous soldiers, then there is a great blot upon our people before the nations of the world." That heroic ideology, which would often be evoked in the history of Rome, sometimes in distorted or insincere form, finds in Naevius's work one of its most authentic expressions.

The cothurnatae *of Naevius*

In addition to the *praetextae,* Naevius also composed mythological tragedies, some connected to the Trojan Cycle, which Andronicus too was fond of; perhaps the spread of the Aeneas legend in Latium aided the success of these subjects. Two titles, *Equos Troianus* and *Danaë,* already cropped up in Livius; also belonging to the Trojan Cycle were *Hector Proficiscens* (Hector departing for his final duel with Achilles) and *Iphigenia.* We have in addition fragments from a historically significant tragedy, *Lycurgus:* the myth dealt with the cult of Dionysus, which was beginning to take hold at Rome too, especially among the lower classes.

Naevius as comic writer and the birth of the togata

Naevius's comic works seem to be far more important; they make him Plautus's most distinguished predecessor and suggest an unusually versatile literary talent: the great comic writers of the second century do not work in serious genres, and Ennius's comedies have left few traces. Of Naevius's comedies there remain titles in Greek and Latin, such as *Colax,* "The Flatterer," from Menander; *Guminasticus = Gymnasticus,* "The Teacher of Gymnastics"; *Dolus,* "The Trick"; *Corollaria,* "The Comedy of Wreaths"; and so on. Among them *Tarentilla* stands out, since we have a lively fragment from it, the picture of a coquettish girl.

The fragments give the impression of a colorful verbal inventiveness that looks forward to Plautus. Naevius seems to have composed *palliatae* based on Greek originals, since Terence in one of his prologues (see p. 99) observes that Naevius already used to "contaminate" his models; but several titles might very well point to works in a Roman setting, in the manner of the *togata.* The success of Plautus and Terence would soon eclipse Naevius's comedies.

It is virtually certain that Naevius's drama was more engaged than that of the following century. His work contained personal attacks on political figures, a phenomenon that recalls the Attic comedy of the time of Aristophanes and that would have but a brief existence. Naevius himself paid for his nonconformity, and the Roman comic theater remained definitely outside the political life of Rome (see pp. 125 f.).

BIBLIOGRAPHY

For the epic and tragic fragments, see W. Morel, *Fragmenta poetarum latinorum epicorum et lyricorum praeter Ennium et Lucilium* (Leipzig 1927, reprint 1963; there is a much-criticized revision by K. Büchner, Leipzig 1982, with bibliography), and O. Ribbeck, *Scaenicae Romanorum Poesis Fragmenta* (ed. 2 Leipzig 1871–73, reprint Hildesheim 1962; ed. 3 of 1897–98 lacks the *indices verborum*), respectively; there is an English translation in E. H. Warmington, *Remains of Old Latin* (Loeb series, 4 vols. London 1935–40), vol. 2. There is a Teubner text of the *Bellum Punicum* with bibliography by W. Strzelecki (Leipzig 1964, based on his earlier *editio maior,* Warsaw 1959).

Much work has again been done in Italian. For the *Bellum Punicum,* see the major edition with commentary, history of the work's *fortuna,* and metrical analyses by M. Barchiesi, *Nevio epico: Storia interpretazione edizione critica dei frammenti del primo epos latino*

(Padua 1962), and Scevola Mariotti, *Il "Bellum Punicum" e l'arte di Nevio* (Rome 1955). There is nothing comparable in English, but see Drury, *CHCL* II, 802–4, and on the problems of Naevius's life, H. D. Jocelyn, "The Poet Cn. Naevius, P. Cornelius Scipio and Q. Caecilius Metellus," *Anticthon* 3 (1969) 32–47. The discussion in D. C. Feeney, *The Gods in Epic* (Oxford 1991), is the most helpful introduction. M. Wigodsky, *Vergil and Early Latin Poetry* (Wiesbaden 1972) 22–39, in assessing the reception of the *Bellum Punicum* in the *Aeneid* refers to many of the major issues in its interpretation: see on this also V. Buchheit, *Vergil über die Sendung Roms: Untersuchungen zum Bellum Punicum und zur Aeneis* (Heidelberg 1963).

On the comic fragments, see W. Beare, *The Roman Stage* (ed. 3 London 1964) 33–44, and J. Wright, *Dancing in Chains: The Stylistic Unity of the Comoedia Palliata* (Rome 1974) 33–59. The *Tarentilla* has been much discussed, but not in English: see M. von Albrecht, "Zur Tarentilla des Naevius," *Museum Helveticum* 32 (1975) 230–39, and esp. M. Barchiesi, *La "Tarentilla" rivisitata* (Pisa 1978).

Plautus

The poet's name, at least in its full form, is uncertain. The ancients usually cite him as *Plautus,* the Romanized form of an Umbrian cognomen *Plotus,* the original meaning of which is dubious: either "big-eared" or "flat-footed." This element of his name is at least certain. In modern editions up to the nineteenth century the full name is given as *M.* (abbreviation of the praenomen *Marcus*) *Accius* (also written *Attius*) *Plautus.* Historical considerations cast suspicion on this form itself: the *tria nomina*—praenomen (e.g., Marcus), gentilician name (e.g., Tullius), and cognomen (e.g., Cicero)—are used for a person who has Roman citizenship, and we do not know whether Plautus ever did have it. A very old manuscript of Plautus, the Ambrosian palimpsest, which was discovered at the beginning of the nineteenth century by Cardinal Angelo Mai, shed new light on the problem. The full name of the poet as transmitted in the palimpsest is in its most reliable version *Titus* (abbreviated *T.*) *Maccius Plautus:* by misdivision of the letters, *Maccius* had become the traditional *M. Accius,* which looked plausible because of the influence of *L. Accius,* the name of the famous tragedian. The name *Maccius* suggests interesting conclusions. It is definitely not a true gentilician name, like *Aemilius* or *Iulius,* for instance, and there is no reason why Plautus should have borne one. Instead it is derived from *Maccus,* the name of a typical character from the Italian popular farce, the Atellan (on which see pp. 36 and 126 f.). This derivation must have some link with Plautus's personality and activity. Influences of the Atellan upon Plautus have been noticed ever since the time of Horace. It is thus a likely and appealing hypothesis that the Umbrian dramatic poet Titus Plotus, or Plautus, received at Rome a pseudonym clearly referring to the world of the comic stage and that he thereby preserved in the regular *tria nomina* a peculiar trace of his career as a comic actor.

Various ancient sources explain that Plautus was a native of Sarsina, a small Appenine city of Umbria, today in Romagna; this is confirmed by a punning allusion in *Mostellaria* 769–70. Plautus, then, like nearly all the republican writers of whom we know, was not of Roman origin. Unlike Livius Andronicus and Ennius, however, he did not belong to an Italian cultural region that had already been fully Hellenized. It should be noted as well that Plautus was certainly a free citizen, not a slave or a freedman. The notice that he performed servile tasks in a mill is a biographical invention based on an assimilation of Plautus to the rascally slaves of his comedies, who are often threatened with this punishment.

The date of his death, 184 B.C, is secure. The date of his birth is obtained indirectly from a notice of Cicero (*Cato Maior* 50), according to which Plautus wrote his comedy *Pseudolus* as an old man. Now, the *Pseudolus* was performed in 191, and for the Romans old age began at sixty years. He is thus likely to have been born between 255 and 250 B.C. The notices that fix the poet's literary *floruit* around 200 fit well with these indications. We should imagine a literary activity that falls between the Second Punic War (218–201) and the poet's last years; the *Casina* clearly refers to the suppression of the Bacchanalia in 186.

<table>
<tr><td>WORKS AND
SOURCES</td><td>

Plautus had an immense success, at once and later, and was extremely prolific. In the theatrical world, moreover, because of its very nature, revisions, interpolations, and spurious works are not unknown. It appears that during the second century approximately 130 comedies attached to the name of Plautus were in circulation: we do not know how many were authentic, but the question was the subject of lively debate.

In the same period, towards the middle of the second century, what we might call editorial activity began, which was very important for the future of Plautus's text. True editions of Plautus were made, inspired by the standards of Alexandrian philology. The beneficial effects of this activity are reflected in the manuscripts that have come down to us: the comedies were equipped with *didascalia,* "production notices," and lists of the characters; Plautus's verses were laid out on the page by experts in such a way that their metrical nature could be recognized—and this in a period that still had good, direct information on the matter.

The critical phase in the transmission of the Plautine corpus was marked by the intervention of Varro, who in his *De Comoediis Plautinis* selected a certain number of comedies—the twenty-one that have reached us—about whose authenticity there was general consensus: *Amphitruo, Asinaria* ("The Comedy of Asses"), *Aulularia* ("The Comedy of the Pot"), *Captivi* ("The Prisoners"), *Curculio, Casina, Cistellaria* ("The Comedy of the Chest"), *Epidicus, Bacchides, Mostellaria* ("The Comedy of the Ghost"), *Menaechmi, Miles Gloriosus* ("The Braggart Warrior"), *Mercator* ("The Merchant"), *Pseudolus, Poenulus* ("The Man from Carthage"), *Persa* ("The Persian"), *Rudens* ("The Cable"), *Stichus, Trinummus* ("The Three Coins"), *Truculentus, Vidularia* ("The Comedy of the Satchel"). This is the sequence of the comedies in the manuscripts, not the sequence of composition. The end position of the *Vidularia* exposed it to damage during its manuscript transmission, and we have only fragments of it.

These were the works accepted by Varro as totally and certainly genuine. Many other comedies, among them some that Varro himself considered Plautine but that he did not add to the group of twenty-one because judg-
</td></tr>
</table>

ment about them was more uncertain, continued to be performed and read in ancient Rome. We have only the titles and brief fragments of these, thanks to quotations from the indirect tradition. These texts were lost in late antiquity, in the third and fourth centuries A.D., whereas the selection of the twenty-one was perpetuated in the manuscript tradition until it was fully recovered in the Renaissance.

The chronology of the individual comedies has some firm points: the *Stichus* was staged for the first time in 200, the *Pseudolus* in 191, and the *Casina,* as has been said, presupposes events of 186. Several comedies contain historical allusions that have suggested hypothetical datings too tenuous and controversial to be taken up here. It is very difficult to form an idea of the evolution of Plautus's poetic practice such as would permit us to regard certain comedies as later than others. It is reasonable, however, to hold that the comedies richest in varied and unusual rhythms are later than those that are simpler in their rhythmic texture.

1. TYPICAL FEATURES OF THE PLOTS AND THE CHARACTERS

A cursory glance at the plots of the twenty complete comedies that have reached us—more than 21,000 verses altogether: the longest comedy is *Miles Gloriosus,* with 1,437, the shortest *Curculio,* with 729—is worthwhile, even if it may give a quite partial and even misleading impression. It is unanimously agreed that Plautus's great strength lies in the humor that arises from the individual situations, taken one by one in sequence, and from the verbal creativity each situation can unleash. But only a first-hand reading can give an adequate impression of all this; and if Plautus's comic art by its very nature eludes excessively neat formulation, a greater regularity emerges from considering the plots in the basic outline of their construction.

Amphitruo. Jupiter arrives at Thebes to conquer the beautiful Alcmena. The god impersonates Amphitryon, lord of the city and the woman's husband. Aided by the cunning Mercury, Jupiter takes advantage of the absence of Amphitryon, who is at war, in order to enter the bed of his unwitting wife. Mercury in the meantime impersonates Sosia, Amphitryon's slave. But the two impersonated characters return home unexpectedly. After a brilliant series of misunderstandings Amphitryon is placated, honored to have had a god for a rival. The comedy occupies a special place in Plautus's drama, since it is the only one with a mythological subject.

Asinaria. The play concerns the machinations of a young man to ransom his beloved beauty, a courtesan. The plan succeeds, thanks to the aid of clever slaves and also—something quite rare in this type of plot—thanks to the help of the father of the young man in love. Then a rivalry in love arises between father and son, which is finally resolved, of course, in favor of the young man.

Aulularia. The pot, which is full of gold, has been hidden by the old man Euclio, who has an obsessive fear of being robbed. What with the miser's pointless worrying about one thing and another, the pot in the end disappears for real: it will be used by the young lover, aided by the slave, to win the hand of the girl he loves, who turns out to be Euclio's daughter.

Bacchides. The plural of the title refers to twin sisters, both courtesans. The plot has a complex development and a frantic rhythm: let us say only that the normal situation of the conquest of the woman is not merely doubled here—there are, of course, two young men in love, with a twofold problem over money, and so on— but also complicated by misunderstandings about the identity of the women who are loved. The original of this comedy was the *Dis Exapaton* ("The Double Deception") by Menander. The recent discovery of parts of the Greek original makes it possible finally, at least in one case, to compare Plautus directly with his Greek models.

Captivi. An old man has lost two sons: one was stolen from him when still a boy; the other, Philepolemus, has been taken prisoner of war by the Eleans. The old man obtains two Elean slaves who are war booty in order to attempt an exchange. In the end he not only recovers Philepolemus but discovers that one of the two Elean prisoners is in fact the other, long-lost son. Within the entire Plautine corpus the play is distinctive because of the toning down of the comic element and because of the hints of a gloomy view of human existence; one notes immediately the (exceptional) absence of any erotic background to the plot. For this reason the play has enjoyed a special success of its own, even in periods when little was thought of Plautus's "trivial" comedy.

Casina. An old man and his son both desire a foundling whom they have in their house. They concoct parallel schemes: each one wants to marry her to his own "straw man." The immoral old man, who is married, of course, is tricked and finds in his bed a man instead of the Casina he yearns for. Casina, it is ultimately discovered, is a girl of free birth and can therefore properly marry her young suitor.

Cistellaria. A young man would like to marry a girl of illegitimate birth, while his father intends for him another girl, of legitimate parentage. Fate removes every obstacle, revealing a true and acceptable identity for the beloved and permitting a lawful marriage.

Curculio. The word means "weevil," a voracious insect that is a parasite on grain, a fitting name for a parasite. Curculio is the parasite of a young man who is in love with a courtesan; to help him he swindles both the pimp who holds her and a boastful soldier, Terapontigonus, who has already started to purchase her. In the end it is discovered that the courtesan is really of free birth and can therefore marry the young man. The pimp forgives the debt. Nor does Terapontigonus have grounds for complaint: the girl, it is discovered, is in fact his own sister.

Epidicus. This is a classic "slave's comedy," with an urgent rhythm. The unstoppable series of machinations carried out by the slave Epidicus is set in motion by a restless young master. The latter falls in love successively with two different girls, hence a double demand for money, a double raid on his old father's pocketbook, and the expected difficulties. When Epidicus is nearly suffocating in the webs he has woven, a recognition saves the day: one of the two girls is none other than the young man's sister. The other is still available, and finally a pair of lovers is securely united.

Menaechmi. This play is the successful prototype of all comedies of errors (including Shakespeare's). Menaechmus has a brother Menaechmus, utterly identical to him. The two do not know one another because they were separated as infants. When they are adults, one arrives at the city of the other and, unaware of the deceptive likeness, unleashes a tremendous confusion. The comedy consists entirely of the tangled exchanges of identity, which go on until the simultaneous mutual recognition of the two at the end.

Mercator. In a plot quite close to that of the *Casina,* we see a young man, the merchant of the title, and his aged father meet in a love rivalry. After a series of moves and countermoves the young man thwarts the aims of the old man, who has a battle-axe of a wife, and wins the courtesan he loves.

Miles Gloriosus. The comedy, which is recognized as one of Plautus's masterpieces, brings on to the stage a clever slave, Palaestrio, and a hilarious swaggering soldier, Pyrgopolynices. The basic plot is the usual one—a young man puts himself into the hands of the slave in order to steal the girl he loves from someone—but the execution of it provides for a large number of brilliant variations.

Mostellaria. Is there a ghost in the house of old Theopropides? The cunning slave Tranio, to conceal somehow the love affair of his young master, leads people to believe so. The deception is amusing but cannot last long: thanks to the intercession of a friend, the matter comes to an end with a general pardon for the debauched young man and for the slave.

Persa. Another hoax is played on a pimp in this work, except this time the one in love is a slave himself. Another slave acts as his assistant. The trick, which succeeds, involves a hoax with masks, in which the slave-assistant impersonates an implausible Persian.

Poenulus. Here the title character really is a stranger, a Carthaginian; the action takes place, as usual, in Greece. We witness the complicated events that befall a family of Carthaginian origin, ending in a recognition and the reuniting of the lovers, who, it turns out, are cousins—all this at the expense of a pimp.

Pseudolus. Along with the *Miles,* this play is one of the high points of Plautine drama. The slave of the title is a veritable mine of tricks, the champion among Plautus's clever slaves. Pseudolus succeeds in cheating his adversary Ballio, a pimp of exceptional dramatic force, depriving him of the girl his young master loves and of his money as well. The hoax is so successful that Ballio, without realizing that he has already lost the woman, bets a goodly sum that Pseudolus will never be able to succeed with his plan!

Rudens. A *rudens* is a cable, a natural prop to find in a comedy set on the beach. In an unusual prologue the star Arcturus foretells the shipwreck of a wicked person, the pimp Labrax. Labrax illegally has with him a girl of free parentage. Fate causes a storm to cast the shipwrecked people onto a beach where both the girl's father and her beloved are. Everything conspires to injure the wicked pimp, and a chest, fished out of the sea with the cable of the title, plays a decisive role in the final recognition.

Stichus. This plot has an unusually modest development and but little tension. A man has two daughters, married to two young men who for some time have been traveling on business. He would like to force them to divorce, but the arrival of the husbands resolves the matter, amidst lengthy celebrations.

Trinummus. A young spendthrift, who in the absence of his father has nearly ruined himself, is saved by an old friend of his father through a well-intentioned swindle. The plot and tone are far more exemplary than usual, with elements that for once suggest the humanity of Terence.

Truculentus. Here for the only time we have a courtesan who is not a passive element, a mere prize in the action: Phronesium is an inventor of tricks, who exploits and cheats her three lovers. The exchange of the traditional roles causes the protagonist to be treated more grimly than the average Plautine villain, as if it were worse to be the villain outside the usual roles. It is certainly an isolated experiment, an attempt by Plautus to lengthen the already long list of his successes. It is not a coincidence that the play is dated to the later period.

Predictability of the plots

A comprehensive view must first of all accept as a fundamental fact the marked predictability of the plots and of the human types embodied in the characters. It is obvious that Plautus actually seeks this predictability; he does not want to raise problems about the character of his characters, nor is he especially interested in ethics or psychology. As if that were not enough, Plautus also tends to provide expository prologues that furnish information essential for the development of the plot and that eliminate any surprise or *coup de théâtre* (for the question of the prologues, see also pp. 97 ff., on Terence).

The character types

The characters can be reduced to a limited number of types that in general contain few surprises: the clever slave, the old man, the young lover, the pimp, the parasite, the braggart soldier. These types are revealed in the prologues, where in fact it is not their proper names that are emphasized, but rather their typological terms (*senex, adulescens,* etc.); thus right from the beginning the audience has a track along which its understanding of the stage events may run.

But whereas the use of typical figures is a very common device in playwriting, still more characteristic of Plautus is the predictability of the plots. Nearly all the plays summarized above can be reduced to a contest between two antagonists over the possession of a property, generally a woman and/or a sum of money needed to secure her (the equivalence is itself suggestive!), more rarely money and nothing else. The contest is decided, of course, with one party winning and the other losing.

It is an appropriate norm that the young man is victorious and that the loser contains within himself the reasons for his being the loser: he is an old man or a married man or a pimp, a rich slave-dealer. Thus the final victory of one party over the other corresponds perfectly to the cultural norms that the audience already has and satisfies their legitimate expectations.

The slave's comedy

Once he adopts this very simple scheme, which, as we will soon see, derives from the conventions of New Comedy, Plautus is then free to direct his main interest to particular forms of plot. (These forms are particular realizations of the general scheme, those that are preferred to the many other possible realizations.) The form preferred far ahead of all others—

and undoubtedly the most amusing!—is the one that is frequently termed the "slave's comedy." The formula runs like this: the task of winning the property that is at stake is delegated by the young man who desires the prize to an ingenious slave. With time, however, Plautus's slaves grow in intellectual stature and imaginative freedom; they not only create deceptions but even theorize about them. In the maturest works the center of the action is occupied by a true demiurge, an artist of fraud, a poet who stages the event before everyone's eyes: Epidicus in the comedy of the same name, Chrysalus in the *Bacchides,* Palaestrio in the *Miles,* and even more, Pseudolus, the poet-slave who indulges in a self-referential dialogue with the audience, and also Tranio in the *Mostellaria,* who is distinguished by a lightning-quick illusionism and a kind of taste for the absurd. It is hardly surprising that Molière learned more from these two scripts than from any

The slave as deviser of the stage action

others. Here is Pseudolus, for instance, freely engaging in dialogue with the spectators and justifying his creative role: he is at a loss how to begin drafting his new plan, but "just as the poet, when he has taken up his tablets, is looking for something that doesn't exist anywhere, and yet he finds it and makes a lie credible, I'll make myself a poet now: the twenty *minae,* which now don't exist anywhere—I'll find them anyhow" (vv. 401 ff.). And a little further on: "I suspect that now you are suspecting that I promise these great projects to entertain you until I finish acting the play, and that I won't do what I'd said I would do. But I won't change a bit. And yet surely, as far as I know, I don't know how I'll do it. Look, whoever comes on stage ought to bring some new invention in a new way; if he can't do that, let him give way to others who can" (vv. 562 ff.).

The pairing of the eager youth and the tricky slave is thus the most usual thematic constant in Plautus's drama. Numerous variants are possible, but they touch merely some external features, not the heart of the plot: it is obvious that the trickster can also be a parasite (as in the *Curculio*) or that, for once, the slave can be the young man in love (as in the *Persa*). The slave's inventions can be multiplied by two (*Epidicus, Miles*) or by three (*Bacchides*), but the scheme still works wonderfully. The division of the action into three distinct stages is also well marked: the slave plans the trick, he acts, and in the end he triumphs.

The comedy of Fortune

To complete our schematic picture, only a single element is missing, which is not a character, however: the omnipresent force, Fortune, *Tyche,* the undisputed queen of the Hellenistic theater. The presence of Fortune has a great stabilizing value. The slave needs an ally and also an opponent on his own level; otherwise, he would sometimes run the risk of dominating the plot too thoroughly, as if he were manipulating a mechanical toy theater. And the comic plot often needs a burst of the irrational, its quotient of the unpredictable. But this is not the only value of Fortune in Plautus's drama.

The comedy of recognition

Besides the slave's comedy, and together with it (we will soon see that these two types are not mutually exclusive), Plautus shows another marked preference: comedies that turn completely on a recognition, an identity hidden at first, or lied about, or accidentally lost, and then happily revealed to all. These comedies may include a long period of errors and confusions on the part of people—in this case it is right to speak of a "comedy of errors," as in the *Menaechmi*—or, quite often, the problem of identity turns up only at the end, yet they all have in common the happy surprise of the concluding recognition, which dissolves all difficulties. Courtesans and female slaves become free women; sons, daughters, brothers, or sisters are discovered; illegitimate children become legitimate; foundlings exist only for the sake of the dénouement.

Initial and final realities

In nearly all of these comedies a clever slave is at work. The work is immoral, perhaps, but directed at acceptable goals and destined to succeed. The slave, for his part, works upon a preexisting reality, and it is his "dirty" job to falsify, confound, and alter appearances. The contrast between pretense and reality, however amusing, cannot last forever, and precisely here Fortune comes into play. Thanks to Fortune we discover that there exists, as it were, a reality more authentic and more genuine than the initial reality, the one upon which, with little morality, the slave was working his tricks. The initial reality, after all, was not much more true and stable than the deceptions of Epidicus and Curculio.

Comedies of Fortune and slave's comedies thus find an interesting center of balance, and these two trends, which are dear to Plautus, come together in a vision of the world that has inexhaustible comic possibilities.

2. THE GREEK MODELS

The numeri innumeri

Plautus's comic greatness is easier for us to grasp than another aspect of his works, his mastery of rhythm, which nevertheless must have had enormous importance for their quality. The *numeri innumeri* ("numberless meters," according to a definition that Varro and Gellius assure us goes back to Plautus himself; moderns are skeptical) are an integral part of his art, but we catch only a feeble trace of them. This is a feature in which Plautus clearly parts company from his Greek models; or rather, the preference Plautus shows (and let us not forget his predecessor Naevius) for sung forms, a preference that is foreign to the drama of his model Menander, is precisely one of the principal forces shaping the translation, shaping the recreation in Latin of the Greek originals. To rewrite the content of a scene while switching from rather flat, prosaic Greek trimeters to the lively harmonies of the *cantica* is obviously an operation of high artistic independence.

Plautus's Greek models

What do we really know about the relation between *palliata* and Greek models? Let us look first at the detailed information Plautus himself provides. Unlike later authors, such as Terence (see p. 99), Plautus shows very little concern for giving out the name and the ancestry of the Greek comedy from which he takes his start. It is clear that, again unlike Terence, he does not presuppose an audience Hellenized enough to enjoy in detail the reference to well-known originals. Plautus's titles are in virtually no case transparent translations of Greek titles. Furthermore, the use of slaves' names as titles—Psuedolus, for instance, or Epidicus—has very little to do with Greek practice (we have already seen what new preference guides Plautus in making these choices).

Freedom from the models

About several models we are quite well informed: *Cistellaria, Stichus,* and *Bacchides* are based on three Menandrian comedies; *Rudens, Casina,* and *Vidularia* depend on Diphilus, the *Poenulus* on Alexis; the *Asinaria* reworks the *Onagos* ("Ass-Driver") of a certain Demophilus. It is evident that Plautus, though drawing especially on the great masters of Attic comedy, does not have a marked preference for any one of them, and he even relies, at least occasionally, on authors not of the first rank. From this an important consequence follows: the style of Plautus is intrinsically varied and polyphonic, but it varies rather little from comedy to comedy, and in a comparison of his various works the consistency of style and manner is pronounced. This strong consistency of style would be hard to explain if Plautus allowed himself to be much influenced by the style of his various Attic models. Even though we have but fragments of Menander and Diphilus, it is clear that Plautus does not depend heavily on the style of either of them, and even less does he make his comedies from his models in some simple one-to-one relation.

Originality of Plautus:
a) Linguistic

The constant and dominant features of Plautus's style have very little in them that is Attic. These features do not involve the plot of the individual comedies—in this Plautus was more willing to stick to his models—but they are found throughout all of them: plays on words, puns, metaphors and similes, wacky mythological comparisons, riddles, double entendres, neologisms, jesting allusions to Roman military institutions and language. This dense style is undoubtedly a Plautine innovation.

b) Structural

The changes are less profound in regard to the general lines of the plot, though still significant: these start with metrical rearrangement and abolition of act divisions and go on to the complete transformation of the system of names. As far as we know, Plautus almost never gives a character the name he had in the original, and he introduces a large number of personal names not attested on the Attic stage. Moreover, very few names reappear from one play to another in Plautus himself. It is clear that Plautus wanted to propose his own autonomous "civil state": Greek names but not the same as the models, and ever new names, not the established names that went with the masks of Italian farce. Many other alterations, in his technique and stage conventions, for instance, cannot be examined in detail here. The recent discovery of fragments from Menander's *Dis Exapaton,* which for the first time set extensive passages of Plautus beside the corresponding passages of his direct model, has confirmed how intensely Plautus reworked his sources.

The "destruction" of the model

To judge by the results, the transformation of the models almost gives an impression of destruction. Plautus has worked hard to assimilate both the individual Attic models and the entire set of principles that shape them: conventions, modes of thought, typical characters, dramaturgy, ex-

pressiveness. But then he has toiled intensely to destroy many of the fundamental qualities of the models he had chosen: dramatic consistency, psychological development, linguistic realism, motivation, characterization,
serious analysis, feeling for nuance and for suitable limits—just the qualities that define the originality and value of New Comedy. The problem, as
we shall soon see, is to understand not only how but also why Plautus
worked in this way.

3. "COMIC LYRICISM"

An objective evaluation of Plautus's art has always posed grave problems
for the critics and even for literary theorists. Comparison with the Greek
models is, as we have seen, an important and indispensable tool of analysis
and evaluation. Although a valuable tool, it has nevertheless led to serious
mistakes when it has been used by itself and without supplementary tools
and correctives. When, as in Plautus's case, the originals are lost, interpretation is liable to follow a circular path: from the text of Plautus one creates
an idea of the model and then uses this idea to calculate the original element that Plautus has added in transforming his Greek model. The most
delicate point in such analyses is always the formation of this idea of the
model: very often one relies on inconsistencies and difficulties in the dramatic action and presupposes that the features of the Greek original can be
recovered by simply subtracting the difficulties and attributing them all
to the Roman imitator. It is clear that equally often the interpreters let
themselves be guided by a subjective value judgment or by a reductive,
mechanical idea of originality.

To counterbalance these tendencies of "analytic" criticism, which were
developed largely by German philology in the nineteenth and twentieth
centuries, an attempt has been made, especially by Italians, to substitute
quite mechanical, mistaken formulations: for example, to identify as Plautine every feature of Plautus's text (forms, contents, style, plot), taking it
as an axiom that each work of art is a unique, inimitable entity; or to seek
what is original and specific to Plautus's art in an "Italian comic sense" (the
Horatian formula of *Italum acetum*, "Italian vinegar," has often been invoked
mechanically). This pure, popular feeling for the comic would be the mark
of authenticity that stamps Plautus as an independent artist, quite distinct
from his Greek models.

And yet analytic criticism, if employed prudently and with a sense of its
limitations, has been able to render excellent service to the understanding
of Plautus's poetics. To attain to a better understanding, one only needs to
detach these analyses from the esthetic prejudices that have often implicitly
guided them. One should thus be in a position to restore dignity and intrinsic interest to those aspects that analytic criticism tends to disregard,
since it considers them external, extemporaneous additions to the pure
lines of the original action.

The comparative analyses show that Plautus transforms his models in accordance with tendencies and preferences that one may or may not approve of but that give pleasure and are consistent in themselves and directed at a precise goal. Plautus tends to neglect strict consistency of the dramatic action and subtle nuances in the personality of his characters. But drama should not be reduced to unity of action and psychology: Plautus simply prefers, and constructs, a different kind of drama. The "defects" that criticism often recognizes in Plautus—the lack of dramatic continuity and consistency, the scattered nature of the action, the schematic quality of the psychology, the conventionality of the sentiments—are rather to be viewed as sacrifices: Plautus gives up certain good qualities of his Greek originals in order to shift the emphasis to other concerns.

The character of the slave and meta-theater

The construction of the characters, a typical "defect" of Plautine drama, offers a key to this matter. Among all the characters of New Comedy, Plautus clearly has a favorite: the slave, who is a rascal, an amoral figure, the creator of tricks and resolver of situations. This typical figure of comedy plays in Plautus a quite exceptional role. It is nearly always the clever slave who directs the development of the plot; it is he alone who, present on the stage, can supervise, influence, and comment, with irony and lucidity, on the development of events. The slave is at the same time a typical figure, not very individualized in psychological terms. He enters into the action generally as a creator of tricks and thus as the source of the comedy: his is the plan of deception that will give the young master the girl he desires.

The position of the clever slave who shapes the lines of the plot is often equivalent to that of the dramatic poet, as if Plautine drama found in this figure an opportunity for mirroring itself, a way of playing with itself (this is what some properly call "meta-theater"). Not surprisingly, the slave is the character who plays with words more than anyone else: he is a great creator of images, metaphors, double entendres, allusions, and sharp exchanges and is therefore the truest vehicle of Plautus's highly original verbal creativity. Although socially the weakest character, he is the central figure on the stage and the point of attraction, both for the audience and for the other characters. It has been noticed in fact that Plautus not only enlarges as much as possible the role of the slave but even assimilates other characters to this role and this importance: in Plautus some characters who in New Comedy or in Terence, for instance, enjoy a certain respectability are often drawn into the comic sphere that is typically the slave's: old and young masters are outwitted by the slave, but they too play wittily with their roles, just as the rascally slave does.

Ironic distance from the models and "comic lyricism"

In his best moments, then, Plautus uses the plots of his originals as material that possesses significance in itself but is also available for new, unpredictable significations. Some lovers, for example, declare their love in accordance with reason (little) and sentiment (much). This is the role intended for them in the original plot, but while they develop their intended role, the lovers work variations on themselves: they sing, and hear themselves singing, with unexpected, lively emphasis; they play their part and at the same time steal the scene from themselves; they give themselves

shamelessly to brilliant verbal variations, and yet at times they seem un-
done by themselves, as if an access of indifference now and then made them
ironic and self-ironic. The miracle of Plautus lies in the balance with which
this playing (which could, if carried too far, dissolve the dramatic action or
render it too intellectual) is in fact developed in a smooth and unbroken
manner. In "reality" the lover, the old gentleman, or the pimp is himself,
but he also takes part in the unpredictable, ludic reality of the slave, who
is the key character of Plautus's comedy. The originality of Plautine comedy
lies precisely in the intersection of the material of the plot, which Plautus,
with greater or lesser fidelity, takes over from the Greeks, with the opening
up of opportunities in which the action becomes free creative play, becomes, to use the happy phrase of M. Barchiesi, "comic lyricism."

4. THE STRUCTURES OF THE PLOT AND THE RECEPTION OF PLAUTINE DRAMA

Plautine plots:
a) Reversal of values

Looking at the plays in this way does not prevent one from also grasping
the authentic, historically determined intentions in the typical structures
of the plot, the feature in which Plautus is closest to his sources. The preference for a certain type of plot, even though the type can be traced back to
already existing models, is in itself a significant clue. We have already seen
how fundamentally unvarying is the basic scheme to which the deceptively
numerous varieties of individual plots can be reduced. It has been observed
that the putting into play of a property (which may be a woman and/or the
money needed to purchase her) nearly always becomes a critical moment,
in which recognized social and family values can waver: free persons are
treated like slaves, fathers make attempts on the women loved by their
sons, married men instead of bachelors court the women as if they were
rakes. At this stage of the narrative structure the comedies threaten to sub-
vert everything the audience accepts as normal and natural: it is normal
that unmarried sons court a woman and that the old men remain in their
station; it is necessary that a free man not be treated like a slave. In Roman
society it is also normal and natural that the sons be firmly subject to the
authority of the head of household. Conflicts may arise here in which legitimate values and expectations clash, for example, when a son plots against
paternal authority while the father uses his economic power and his power
over the family for an immoral purpose, as in the *Casina.* Plautine comedy
deals with these conflicts on the comic plane of the plot, without ever becoming, as Terence's comedy would, a critical reflection upon them or a
revision of traditional thinking. On occasion the crisis mixes up and con-
fuses even more fundamental values, such as personal identity, as in the
comedies of errors, or the distinction between gods and men, as in the
unique *Amphitruo.*

b) Reordering of
values

Comedy's typical dénouement is the returning of things to the way they
were. The punishment of the pimp, the thwarting of the foolish old libertine or of the soldier, the destined reuniting of a pair of lovers, the rectify-

ing of the error, the restoration of the correct personal identity, are only different ways of carrying out this obligatory scheme. It is clear that the audience finds a particular pleasure in this movement from disorder to order, all the more so in that the social and economic picture evoked by the comedy, even though it is taken over with but light changes from the tradition of the fourth-century Attic stage, is perfectly compatible with the experience of the Roman audience. Except for exotic details, which Plautus consciously takes over unadapted—distancing conventions that are very important in many literary genres and especially in literature for the masses—the body of the plot touches real, everyday problems, such as the availability of women and the use of money in the family. The names of characters and places are Greek, as are also certain legal niceties, political institutions, and historical allusions. These details guarantee that the comedy resides elsewhere, and due to this location "elsewhere" only occasionally are lively, anachronistic gestures made in the direction of Roman reality. But these Roman details merely punctuate and color situations in which the audience, without making any real effort to translate and to relativize, easily feels at home.

Thus the Roman audience participates very concretely in the precipitation of the crisis and in the final establishment of a more reasonable, more reassuring order. No pretense of instruction or moralization, however, governs these typical events. To demonstrate this we need only refer again to the indisputable primacy of the clever slave, who is the engine driving the plot and often the final reordering as well. The centrality of this character is quite incompatible with the conveyance of a serious moral or cultural message. He is the chief source of the fun and even, not surprisingly, the most imaginative character in the cast, the character in whom the audience can least of all recognize a realistic basis and a plausibly ordinary tone, the character, in short, who most often marks the departure of Plautus from his models.

The action of this creative, unrealistic character appears once again as a characterizing trait of the Plautine *palliata*. Beneath the frenzied movement of the plot, a hard-won, disarming sense of balance is noticeable, which is another key to Plautus's unequaled success. Oriented towards the reinforcement of a social order and a behavioral norm, Plautine comedy has very little that is subversive about it, and even the prominence of the slave does not of course mean that the dogmas of social life are brought into question or eroded; on the contrary, the clever slave's unpredictable, amoral action introduces into the plot a certain amount of disorder and irreverence, which leads to the "suspension" of the normality of everyday life. The slave for the most part pursues a legitimate aim—in fact, the solution that will finally prove victorious and acceptable to all—but equally often he does so by illegitimate, fraudulent means. From this fundamental contradiction (interminable discord between ends and means) is born the paradox of an art that eludes our traditional definitions (conformity, nonconformity). Above all, Plautus does not offer, and does not mean to offer, to his audience a clear choice between realism and fiction. His characters are so prone to playing with their own roles and to casting doubt on the verisimilitude of their own creation that they forbid the audience any stable identification. Precisely in this literary genre, with its roots in realistic, everyday life, the Romans learn from Plautus to recognize the inexhaustible ambiguities inherent in a poetic fiction.

5. LITERARY SUCCESS

Antiquity

Plautus's success on stage during his lifetime continued unbroken in the generations after his death. In republican Rome, his plays circulated not as literary works or as school editions but as acting scripts, often performed and hence frequently adapted. Furthermore, his name became attached to many other anonymous plays of his genre and period, sometimes as a guarantee of quality, sometimes perhaps as a guess. Actors' and producers' changes on the one hand and questions of authenticity on the other meant that Plautus was the author who posed the most serious problems to the Roman scholars faced with the task of editing his works. Some responded conservatively, keeping everything, including what was genuine; others attempted to hack a path through the jungle. At the time of Aulus Gellius (3.3.11), in the second half of the second century A.D., 130 plays were attributed to Plautus; but already around 100 B.C. L. Aelius Stilo, Varro's teacher, had recognized only 25 as authentic. Varro himself established a canon of 21 genuine works, and it is his selection that lies at the basis of all extant manuscripts of Plautus; these go back to a school edition, perhaps dating from the fourth century, that was organized alphabetically and in cases of textual doubt probably presented both variant lines or texts, marking with a critical sign the one considered spurious.

Middle Ages

This codex, like many others, became mutilated at its end: the last Varronian play, the *Vidularia,* fell out and was lost until 1815, when Angelo Mai rediscovered (and severely damaged) parts of it in a fifth-century palimpsest in Milan. Of the other plays, the first eight (*Amphitruo, Asinaria, Aulularia, Captivi, Casina, Cistellaria, Curculio, Epidicus;* in one ancient edition the *Bacchides,* which refers at one point to the *Epidicus,* was placed after it, violating the alphabetical order) circulated in the Middle Ages, while the other twelve were virtually unknown until 1429, when Nicholas of Cusa brought an eleventh-century manuscript from Germany (whence the three oldest surviving Palatine manuscripts of Plautus all originated) to Cardinal Orsini in Italy. In general, Plautus was far less read during the Middle Ages than Terence was. Unlike Terence, he was apparently unknown to Dante and his contemporaries, and he never became a medieval school author (although a few writers, such as Aimeric in the eleventh century, suggested that he should be added to the curriculum).

Renaissance

Plautus's popularity started to increase with Petrarch, who quotes from two plays and summarizes a third one. And during the Renaissance he was one of the most influential of all Latin authors (though he was almost always ranked behind Terence). To be sure, he was still banned from the classroom, despite the recommendations of Erasmus and Melancthon: his language, style, and meter, to say nothing of his exuberant immorality, might corrupt the young. But precisely these same features attracted the humanists, who subjected his difficult and corrupt texts to erudite philological study (e.g., Camerarius and Lambinus in the sixteenth century). At the same time, they rediscovered his theatrical vitality. Stage productions in Latin were performed already in the fifteenth century by Pomponius Laetus at the Roman Academy under Pope Julius II and in the early sixteenth century at the school of Lis in Louvain and helped contribute to a brief fashion in humanistic comedies in Latin (e.g., one *Chrysis* by Piccolomini, another by Konrad Celtis). Of greater importance for world literature was the first production, in 1486 at the court of Ferrara, of one of his comedies *(Menaechmi)* in translation. The result was Renaissance vernacular comedy, beginning in Italy with Ariosto (whose *Cassaria*, heavily influenced by Plautus, was the first Italian comedy, written in 1498 and performed in Ferrara in 1508) and Macchiavelli *(The Mandrake)* and spreading after the mid-sixteenth century to England (*Jack Juggler*, based upon the *Amphitruo; Ralph Roister-Doister*, based upon the *Miles Gloriosus;* and Shakespeare's *Comedy of Errors*, largely derived from the *Menaechmi* with an admixture of the *Amphitruo*), Spain (Calderón), Portugal (Camões), and France (Corneille, Molière).

Modern period   Starting in the seventeenth century, Plautus's fortunes took a turn for the worse: there was no way whatsoever in which even the most strenuous critical exertions could reconcile his reckless vitality with neo-classical literary theory. But he was rediscovered in the eighteenth century by Lessing, who translated the *Captivi*, adapted the *Trinummus (Der Schatz)*, and wrote a treatise on Plautus's life and works; and in the same century he influenced such popular authors as Goldoni and Da Ponte. Thereafter he seems to have interested lay readers less and philologists, especially German ones, more—Wilhelm Studemund, for one, lost his sight transcribing Angelo Mai's palimpsest. But he remains the Latin author whose plays are performed by far the most often on stage; and Richard Lester's uproarious film *A Funny Thing Happened on the Way to the Forum* (1965), based on a successful Broadway musical, showed that Plautus, cleverly adapted, could still appeal to millions of people.

BIBLIOGRAPHY

The principal critical editions of the entire extant corpus are those of F. Leo (2 vols., Berlin 1895–96) and W. M. Lindsay (2 vols., ed. 2 Oxford 1910 and frequently reprinted). The text with English translation by P. Nixon in the Loeb Classical Library (5 vols., London 1916–38) is accurate and reliable.

On comedy in general, see G. E. Duckworth, *The Nature of Roman Comedy: A Study in Popular Entertainment* (Princeton 1952), F. H. Sandbach, *The Comic Theatre of Greece and Rome* (London 1977), J. Wright, *Dancing in Chains: The Stylistic Unity of the Comoedia*

Palliata (Rome 1974), E. Segal, *Roman Laughter*, ed. 2 (New York 1987), and R. L. Hunter, *The New Comedy of Greece and Rome* (Cambridge 1985). See also the brief survey by W. G. Arnott, *Menander, Plautus, Terence* (Oxford 1968), with D. Konstan, *Roman Comedy* (Ithaca 1983), and N. W. Slater, *Plautus in Performance* (Princeton 1985), both of which concentrate on Plautus as a poet of the theater. The question of the relation of Plautus's plays to their Greek models has dominated criticism; the fundamental work is E. Fraenkel, *Elementi plautini in Plauto* (Florence 1960, a translation with additional notes of the German edition, Berlin 1922), but see more recently H. W. Prescott, "Criteria of Originality in Plautus," *TAPA* 63 (1932) 103–24, E. W. Handley, *Menander and Plautus: A Study in Comparison* (London 1968), V. Pöschl, *Die neueren Menanderpapyri und die Originalität des Plautus* (Heidelberg 1973), D. Bain, "Plautus vortit barbare: Plautus *Bacchides* 526–61 and Menander *Dis Exapaton* 102–12," in *Creative Imitation in Latin Literature*, ed. D. West and A. J. Woodman (Cambridge 1979) 17–34, and N. Zagagi, *Tradition and Originality in Plautus* (Göttingen 1980). A different approach is championed by O. Zwierlein, *Zur Kritik und Exegese des Plautus I, Poenulus und Curculio* (Stuttgart 1990 and later volumes), who believes the extant texts to be heavily interpolated. There is much of interest in E. Fantham, *Comparative Studies in Republican Latin Imagery* (Toronto 1972), esp. chap. 4, "Plautus and the Imagery of Fantasy." There has been much important work in Italian; see F. della Corte, *Da Sarsina a Roma* (ed. 2 Florence 1967: biography and historical context), A. Traina, *Forma e Suono* (Rome 1977: style), M. Barchiesi, "Plauto e il 'metateatro' antico," in *I moderni alla ricerca di Enea* (Rome 1980: Plautus as poet of the theater), M. Bettini, "Verso un'antropologia dell'intreccio: Le strutture semplici della trama nelle commedie di Plauto," and C. Questa, "Maschere e funzioni nelle commedie di Plauto," in *Materiali e discussioni per l'analisi dei testi classici* 7 (1981) 39–101 and 8 (1982) 9–64, respectively (plot structure, typology and functions of the characters). On Plautus's later *fortuna* there is a brief survey in English in Duckworth, *Nature of Roman Comedy,* 396–433.

Commentaries on individual plays include those on *Amphitruo* by W. B. Sedgwick (Manchester 1950), *Aulularia* by C. Questa (Milan 1972, Italian) and W. Stockert (Stuttgart 1983, German), *Bacchides* by C. Questa (ed. 2 Florence 1975, Italian, including the new Menander fragments and an important discussion) and J. Barsby (Warminster 1986), *Captivi* by W. M. Lindsay (ed. 2 Oxford 1930), *Casina* by W. T. MacCary and M. M. Willcock (Cambridge 1976), *Curculio* by G. Monaco (Palermo 1969, Italian), *Epidicus* by G. E. Duckworth (Princeton 1940), *Mercator* by P. J. Enk (ed. 2 Leiden 1966, 2 vols., Latin), *Mostellaria* by A. Sonnenschein (ed. 2 Oxford 1927), *Persa* by E. Woytek (Vienna 1982), *Pseudolus* by M. M. Willcock (Bristol 1987), *Rudens* by F. Marx (ed. 2 rev. A. Thierfelder, Heidelberg 1962, German), *Stichus* by H. Petersmann (Heidelberg 1973, German), and *Truculentus* by P. J. Enk (Leiden 1953, 2 vols., Latin). The Italian prefaces by C. Questa to the editions with translation published in the series Biblioteca Universale Rizzoli contain both an excellent general introduction to Plautus and specific remarks on the individual plays.

On the meter, see esp. C. Questa's *Introduzione alla metrica di Plauto* (Bologna 1967) and the papers collected in *Numeri innumeri, ricerche sui cantica e la tradizione manoscritta di Plauto* (Rome 1984). For English works, see D. S. Raven, *Latin Metre* (London 1965) 41–89, and in greater detail, W. M. Lindsay's *Early Latin Verse* (Oxford 1922, reprint 1968) and his commentary on Plautus, *Captivi* (ed. 2 Oxford 1930) 56–102.

Caecilius Statius

LIFE   Like Andronicus and Terence, Caecilius Statius was a freedman of foreign origin. He came from Milan, it seems, and was an Insubrian Gaul. Since the height of his activity is placed at around 180 B.C., it is likely that he was brought to Rome after the battle of Clastidium in 222. His date of birth could fall between 230 and 220; his literary activity makes Caecilius a contemporary first of Plautus, then of Ennius. He was also a close friend of Ennius; he died a year after him, in 168, and the two poets were buried near one another.

The notice that the young Terence read his first work, the *Andria,* to the aged Caecilius is probably a fiction intended to connect Plautus's two most admired successors with one another. We know that the *Andria* was staged only in 166. In any event, Caecilius, like Terence, had close relations with the influential actor and theatrical impresario Ambivius Turpio (on whom see p. 32).

WORKS   About forty titles are extant, all of *palliatae,* and about three hundred verses of fragments. By far his best-known comedy is the *Plocium* ("The Necklace"). The titles have both Greek forms, for instance, *Ex hautou hestos* ("He Stands on His Own"), *Gamos* ("The Marriage"), *Epicleros* ("The Heiress"), *Synaristosae* ("Ladies' Luncheon"), *Synephebi* ("The Companions of Youth"), and Latin forms, for instance, *Epistula* ("The Letter"), *Pugil* ("The Boxer"), as well as double forms, such as *Obolostates / Faenerator* ("The Usurer").

SOURCES   Biographical information comes from St. Jerome's *Chronicon* and ultimately goes back to Varro's *De Poetis.* Among the most important judgments one can cite Cicero, *De Optimo Genere Oratorum* 1.2; Horace, *Epistles* 2.1.159; Velleius Paterculus 1.17.1; Quintilian 10.1.99; Gellius 2.23 and 15.24. Caecilius is read and appreciated during the entire Republic and under the Empire at least to the second century.

*Caecilius's literary
success among the
ancients*

The reasons for Caecilius Statius's being treated in our literary histories as a minor figure are altogether accidental and have to do with the loss of his writings. Great intellectuals and men with a deep knowledge of literature such as Varro, Cicero, and Horace regard Caecilius as an author of the first rank, not a whit inferior to Plautus or Terence. Horace praises him for the gravity of his feelings, and Varro approves of his plots, and only about the purity of his Latin does Cicero have any reservations. The canon of the comic poets most valued at Rome, drawn up around 100 B.C. by the learned Volcacius Sedigitus, puts Caecilius first on the list, ahead of Plautus. The loss of Caecilius's writings is not due, then, to disrepute or manifest inferiority to other classical authors.

Respect for his models

Caecilius's historical location suggests a sort of intermediate position between Plautus and Terence. Several indications confirm this. A large number of the fragments we have remind us of Plautine drama: great variety of meters, lively comic imagination, robust taste for the farcical. Compared with Plautus, however, Caecilius seems in a sense closer to the model of Attic New Comedy. The titles we have, at least, are faithful reproductions of the titles of the Greek originals, sometimes literal reproductions, for example, *Plocium* from Menander's *Plokion.* The figure of the slave, moreover, is absent from the titles; in Plautus the enthusiasm for this character prevailed even in the titles *(Pseudolus)* and frequently altered the shape of the Greek original to give itself more room. We have, then, the impression that Caecilius respected the originals somewhat more. He seems, furthermore, to have a decided preference for Menander: for about half the attested titles a Menandrian origin is possible.

*Similarities between
Caecilius and
Terence*

An interest in Menander and a closer adherence to the Greek model adopted, the latter in step with a more educated and Hellenizing phase of Roman culture, are features that link Caecilius and Terence together and separate them from Plautus. We do not have any evidence, however, that Caecilius anticipated basic features that are typical of Terence's manner, such as the rejection of certain varieties of meter, the reduction of coarse farcical effects, and the greater psychological penetration. We know, moreover, that Terence remained a special case in the tradition of the *palliata.*

*Caecilius as transla-
tor: a comparison
with his original*

The most interesting remnant of Caecilius's work comes from a chapter of Gellius's *Attic Nights,* 2.23. Gellius makes a careful comparison between a passage of the *Plocium* and its equivalent in Caecilius's original, the *Plokion* of Menander. Until the recent discovery of a papyrus containing a fragment of Menander's *Dis Exapaton* that can be compared with passages of Plautus's *Bacchides,* this was the only opportunity we had to compare a fairly substantial passage of a *palliata* with its Greek original. We should note clearly how free the reworking is that the Romans term *vertere,* "to turn, translate." The innovations introduced by Caecilius into the fabric of his source are judged rather severely by Gellius and undoubtedly point to an independent notion of comedy. In Menander we have a husband who complains that his peevish wife has thrown the young servant girl out of the house: "She has thrown out of the house, as she wanted, the girl who cast her into shadow, so that all would turn their faces to her and it would be clear that she is my mistress." Caecilius in his treatment takes this merely as a point of departure. Characteristically, he adds a general maxim here: "That man is unfortunate indeed who cannot hide his own suffering"; and he conveys the husband's frustration by having him imagine a lively scene with gossiping women in which his ugly, old wife boasts of her triumph. More generally, the calm Menandrian monologue has been converted into a farcical aria, a *canticum*. From other comparisons we know that Caecilius did not refrain from even stronger writing, giving jokes and coarse humor to Menander's restrained couples: "As soon as I return home, my wife immediately kisses me, with her stomach empty. . . . She doesn't do it by mistake: she wants you to vomit what you've drunk outside the house." In short, Caecilius, like Plautus, strove not so much to repeat the plot that had succeeded for Menander or Diphilus as to reimagine the stories of the original in accordance with a new, independent theatrical stance.

BIBLIOGRAPHY

For the fragments, see O. Ribbeck, *Scaenicae Romanorum Poesis Fragmenta* (ed. 2 Leipzig 1871–73, reprint Hildesheim 1962; ed. 3 of 1897–98 lacks the *indices verborum*), and with English translation E. H. Warmington, *Remains of Old Latin* (Loeb series, 4 vols. London 1935–40), vol. 1; there is also a separate edition by T. Guardi (Palermo 1974). For English discussion see W. Beare, *The Roman Stage* (ed. 3 London 1964) 86–90, and J. Wright, *Dancing in Chains: The Stylistic Unity of the Comoedia Palliata* (Rome 1974) 87–126. On Gellius's comparison of Caecilius and Menander, see L. Holford-Strevens, *Aulus Gellius* (London 1988) 145–48.

Oratory and Historiography in the Archaic Period

1. ORATORY

In the *Brutus,* which is undoubtedly the best history of Roman eloquence ever written, Cicero emphasizes repeatedly the connection between oratory and political life. Like historiography, but even more so, oratory is an intellectual product of the ruling class: in both genres the author expresses his own interpretation of the past and the present, bringing to bear his own ethical and political concerns. The most important orators of the archaic period are prominent politicians: in this regard the difference is evident between oratory and the writing of annals or historical works, since the latter is done by members of the ruling class but, except for Cato, not by persons at the very highest level. The explanation lies in the far more immediate relation of oratory to political activity. According to Cicero, the first Roman whose eloquence was securely attested was Marcus Cornelius Cethegus, consul in 204 (the year of Cato's quaestorship), a man praised by Ennius in the *Annals.* Among Cato's contemporaries, Scipio Africanus Maior, Quintus Fabius Maximus Cunctator, and Lucius Aemilius Paullus distinguished themselves as orators. The scanty evidence we have of their speeches does not allow us to form a satisfactory picture of their style. We are far better informed about the oratory of Cato, who is undoubtedly the greatest orator of the second century (see pp. 89 f.), and we can glimpse something of his political opponent, Servius Sulpicius Galba, even though not a word is extant from the latter's speeches. Cicero says of him that he was remarkable for his use of digressions, but his oratorical greatness lay wholly in the vehemence of his *actio;* naturally, very little of this was to be found in the written versions of those speeches that one could still read in the late Republic.

2. THE ANNALS OF FABIUS PICTOR

The use of Greek in the earliest annals

Just as he stands out among the orators of his day, so Cato is also the most notable among the historians of the archaic period, or rather, he is responsible for the creation of historical writing in Latin (see p. 86). Previously there had not been even a genuine historiography, but only annals written in Greek by members of the Roman ruling class. The use of Greek signified originally a break with the tradition of the pontifical chronicles, from which the nascent historiography drew its materials and whose annalistic structure it inherited. Fabius Pictor, as far as we know, introduced the use of Greek, and the innovation has been plausibly explained by the need to reach not just educated Romans but also a non-Latin public, a Mediterranean public; the chief motive was to counteract the influence of Greek historical writing favorable to the Carthaginians.

The work of Fabius Pictor

Quintus Fabius Pictor, bearing the cognomen because an ancestor of his had been a painter, belonged to the *gens Fabia,* one of the noblest Roman families. A senator and magistrate, he had fought against the Insubrian Gauls between 225 and 222. His historical work extended from the foundation of Rome to the end of the Second Punic War. Aristocratic origin explains in large part the proud interest in the great families, his own in particular, that must have characterized his historical writing. It is likely that he also introduced autobiographical elements: he is probably the source for Livy's detailed account, in books 22 and 23, of the mission to Delphi of Fabius himself, who in 216 B.C., after the defeat at Cannae, was sent by the Senate to consult the oracle.

Governing class and antiquarian taste

In Fabius Pictor's work antiquarian enthusiasm must have played a large role: some of the preserved fragments show how he researched the origins of institutions and ceremonies, which he described with affection and sparkle. He probably had a special interest in the origins of Rome, the period of the monarchy, and the beginning of the Republic, since many institutions and customs, as well as many religious and civil practices, were traced back to those periods. As a member of the senatorial elite, Fabius must have felt himself to be a guardian of the cultural richness of Roman traditions, in which the governing class instinctively saw the base of its own power and upon whose preservation, in its eyes, Rome's success against external enemies depended. It was an interest that, understandably, was destined to remain alive in early Roman historical writing.

Fabius Pictor and the conflict between Rome and Carthage

At the same time, Fabius Pictor was also broadly interested in the greatest political question of the day, the clash between Rome and Carthage, on which he took a decidedly pro-Roman stance. We know this from Polybius, who criticizes his lack of objectivity; Fabius Pictor's distortion, according to Polybius, went in the diametrically opposite direction from that of the pro-Carthaginian Philinus.

3. CINCIUS ALIMENTUS AND THE OTHER ANNALISTS

Like Fabius Pictor and the later annalists, Lucius Cincius Alimentus, although he was a senator and magistrate (praetor in 210 B.C.), of plebeian family, was not a political figure of the highest level either. He fought in the Second Punic War, was taken prisoner, and may have known Hannibal personally. He, too, wrote, in Greek and in annalistic form, a history of Rome from its origins; Polybius and Dionysius of Halicarnassus acknowledged his objectivity and insight. He should not be confused with the historian Cincius Alimentus, a later writer on antiquarian subjects, who is mentioned with the single name Cincius and is presumed to have lived in the age of Augustus.

A short time later we have two other annalists who continue to write in Greek, Gaius Acilius and Aulus Postumius Albinus. The former, a senator, was the interpreter in the Senate for the embassy of the three Greek philosophers—the Academic Carneades, the Stoic Diogenes, and the Peripatetic Critolaus—who came to Rome in 155 and soon afterwards were hastily sent back home. Acilius, too, as far as one can tell from the few fragments preserved, lingered at length over the origins of Rome, since he had strong aetiological interests; the narration became more detailed probably with the First Punic War. Aulus Postumius Albinus, of a patrician family, who was consul in 151, was mocked by Cato because after choosing to write in Greek, he apologized in his preface for possible imperfections due to his using a language not his own. The remark does not surprise us, since Cato was fiercely opposed to the introduction of Greek usages. Far from being the result of a stubborn provincialism, his cutting irony was the sign of a new era: Rome, the undisputed conqueror of the Mediterranean and now the greatest power in it, could proudly assert the use of its own language, even to foreign nations. Cato himself had already begun to write the first historical work in Latin.

BIBLIOGRAPHY

For the remains of the oldest orators, see *Oratorum Romanorum Fragmenta,* ed. E. Malcovati (ed. 4 Turin 1976). There is a good discussion in A. D. Leeman, *Orationis Ratio: The Stylistic Theories and Practice of the Roman Orators, Historians, and Philosophers* (Amsterdam 1963) 19–88.

For the fragments of the early annalists, see vol. 1 of H. Peter, *Historicorum Romanorum Reliquiae* (ed. 2 Leipzig 1914) and volume 3.c of F. Jacoby, *Die Fragmente der griechischen Historiker* (Leiden 1958). Fabius Pictor is also said to have written *Annales* in Latin, but the fragments that we have of these are probably translations or later reworkings of the Greek original. For discussion, see Leeman, *Orationis Ratio,* 67–88, E. Badian, "The Early Historians," in *Latin Historians,* ed. T. A. Dorey (London 1966) 1–38, esp. 2–7, B. W. Frier, *Libri annales pontificum maximorum: The Origins of the Annalistic Tradition* (Rome 1979) with R. M. Ogilvie's review in *JRS* 71 (1981) 199–201, C. W. Fornara, *The Nature of History in Ancient Greece and Rome* (Berkeley 1983) 23–28, and E. Rawson, "The First Latin Annalists," in *Roman Culture and Society* (Oxford 1991) 245–71.

Literature and Culture in the Period of the Conquests

The period of the conquests

The end of the Second Punic War, in 201, had freed Rome from the only opponent capable of seriously contesting her domination over the Mediterranean. The next fifty years were a period of continuous expansion, which was resisted in vain: the Second and Third Macedonian Wars, the conflict with Antiochus, and the defeat of Perseus at Pydna mark the principal stages of Rome's ascent to being the foremost power in the world. The process lasted at least until 133, when Numantia, the last stronghold of a heroic Spanish resistance to Rome, was captured, but it could be said to have ended symbolically in 146, when the armies of the Republic had razed Carthage to the ground at the end of the Third Punic War and had sacked Corinth, pillaging its artistic treasures.

The weakening of the ancient virtues

The cruelty and greed shown by Rome in 146 have been interpreted by ancient and modern historians as the sign of the beginning of its falling away from the austere, noble morality that in the previous period had brought about its greatness. In such a judgment there is a large element of moralism but also a certain amount of truth. Rome's growth from a small city-state to the possessor of hegemony over Italy to the sovereign mistress of the Mediterranean lands could not fail to lead to a profound change in its social-economic and cultural system; this change is described by moralizing historians, not altogether inappropriately, in terms of a perversion of ancient ideals. Contemporaries already recorded the phenomenon with deep concern: the theme of moral degeneration, of the corrupting effects of wealth and extravagance, of the loss of ancient virtues, which was to become a commonplace later, dates more or less from this period.

Social changes: the emergence of the agrarian question

What we find in effect is a split in the citizen body: the ruling class grows immensely wealthy on the spoils of the wars, and the middle class, which shares in the accumulation, takes advantage of the possibilities for rapid social rise; at the same time, the old class of small landholders, who were the basis of Roman expansion in Italy, begins to become a proletariat, chiefly because obligatory military service abroad, on campaigns that lasted for years, had caused them to abandon their farms. The land becomes concentrated in the hands of a few, and this in turn makes it easier to work it intensively with the vast numbers of slaves brought onto the market by the wars. The old landholders and their descendants, now a proletariat, swell the numbers of the urban plebs considerably and constitute henceforth a lasting source of social instability and a mass that can be manipulated to serve the ambitions of the powerful. The unresolved agrarian question would present itself again and again in Roman public life.

Relations with Greece

On this view it is only to be expected that beginning with the end of the Second Punic War, Roman culture and literature show the arising, or rather explosion, of new demands and new conflicts. One of the central problems is the relation to the Greek cultural model, the importation of which is interpreted by traditionalists as one of the factors that unleash moral corruption. The process is set off by Rome's progressive domination of Greece, beginning at the start of the second century. This intensifies cultural as well as political contacts: let us recall the many embassies entrusted to Greek intellectuals or the presence of a person such as Polybius among the hostages brought to Rome after the Third Macedonian War. Nor should we underestimate the importance of the fact that during their sacking of cities the Romans more than once gained possession of entire Greek libraries, the most famous being the library of Perseus, king of Macedon, which Aemilius Paullus transferred to Rome after defeating him in 168: in this way a number of new books circulated and were available to the general public.

The true meaning of Cato's cultural battle

Modern historiography has sometimes dwelt on the polarization of Roman cultural life in this period between the phil-Hellenic party and the anti-Hellenic party, the latter represented by the wing of the aristocracy led by Cato the Censor. For about fifty years both the cultural and the political scene are dominated by the figure of Cato and by his battle to uphold the *mos maiorum* against the ethically "corrupting" elements of Greek intellectual life and against the notion, also Greek, of the "charismatic" politician, who seemed to threaten the solidarity of the aristocracy (see p. 89).

Despite the Horatian tag *Graecia capta ferum victorem cepit,* the tendency today is to view Cato's struggle as victorious, at least on the cultural level. Despite the vehemence of some of his polemics, Cato in fact did not propose to the Romans a complete rejection of Greek culture, but rather a careful selection; he especially wanted to check the most radical pressures of enlightenment, which threatened to undermine the traditional morality. Ennius had created some of these pressures by boldly presenting the theory of Euhemerus to the Roman public (see p. 77); in another respect, the same Ennius's *Annals,* which were in harmony with the Catonian ideal in that they celebrated the *mores antiqui* as the basis of the Republic, nonetheless ceased to be so in that they left room for a heroic view of history, for the exaltation of great personalities. Ennius's separation from his "discoverer" Cato and his drawing near to the Scipionic circle may perhaps be understood in this light too. Furthermore, in a more innocent way, a work such as the *Hedyphagetica,* fitting in with the desire for luxurious, refined articles of consumption, flew completely in the face of the Catonian ideal.

Ennius in his tragedies, and even more Pacuvius, gave room to ethical debates that, through imitating Euripidean models, sometimes breathed the atmosphere of the ancient sophistic antilogies, or "opposing discourses." The Catonian party must have sensed the danger in making morality relative, which in the end, by undercutting the ethical and religious bases of the Republic, might also have had political and social consequences. As it was, other antilogies aroused immediate concerns in Cato, namely, Carneades' antilogies on justice. Before a large Roman audience the philosopher insinuated that Rome's domination over the other peoples, which Rome claimed as just, was maintained instead by violence and rapine. There was no waiting for a reaction, but the embassy to which Carneades belonged was quickly sent back to Greece.

The debate over ethical models continues in the drama of Terence, who brings before the Roman public once again the Menandrian ideals of *philanthropia.* But in the period when Terence writes, the conflict over the value of Greek culture seems to start moving towards a resolution that will be decisive for the future of Roman culture. Terence's patron, with whom he shared ideals and cultural struggles that he may partially have inspired, was Scipio Aemilianus, adoptive grandson of Africanus Maior (he was named Aemilianus because he was actually the son of Aemilius Paullus, victor over Perseus at Pydna). It is important at this point to note that the prospects for cultural renewal that were found in Scipio's entourage were not radically opposed to the Catonian ideal of preserving the ancient Roman virtues.

In the past, scholars used to speak of a true circle of intellectuals gathered around Scipio Aemilianus and sharing a cultural program, rather like the circles of the eighteenth century. Put in these terms, the description is probably a distortion. But Aemilianus was nourished by the classical works of Greece, which his father had made available by leaving to his sons the royal library of Macedonia (this had been brought to Rome with the booty from Pydna), and he undoubtedly did have close relations with the most eminent cultural figures of his time. In his youth he was a friend of Polybius, who, having come to Rome as a hostage, in his historical works investigated the reasons why Rome was superior to other nations. Later Scipio was on intimate terms with Panaetius, the Stoic who in his treatise *On Duty* furnished a model of behavior to the members of the Roman aristocracy. Nevertheless, the "circle of the Scipios" is a term of convenience created by modern scholars and not solidly based on ancient evidence; for that reason it is going too far to concede historical basis, as if it were an organization with a genuine cultural and political program, to what was rather a community of Hellenizing interests and tendencies among some eminent Roman aristocrats. Nonetheless, the importance of these persons in sustaining and promoting some important figures of the contemporary culture would prove to be decisive for the subsequent development of Latin literature and thought. No doubt Cicero's idealization of these men, and of Scipio Aemilianus in particular, in some of his most important works contributed to giving a historical basis to this "circle": in the *De Republica*, the *De Amicitia*, and the *De Senectute* he made these persons the central figures—brilliant representatives of their own ideals of civic and cultural life.

The opening to Hellenistic culture: Panaetius and Polybius

The Scipionic group saw in the opening to Hellenistic culture a decisive factor in rendering the Roman ruling class less provincial and in placing it thereby in a position to carry out its imperial vocation worthily. Panaetius provided an important cultural support for this project by working out, among other things, a theory that justified the Romans in their encounters with other peoples—the complete opposite to Carneades's threatening antilogies on the subject of justice, with which Panaetius may have intended to contrast himself. Not even the rationalism that Polybius introduced into the evaluation of historical events represented a serious threat to the traditional ethical-political values. The theory of the mixed constitution that he used to explain the Roman constitution came down in practice to a justification of the aristocratic regime, and the rationalistic interpretation of the traditional Roman religion as a tool of governance should be understood, not as a criticism of it, but as the recognition of an ethical-political force that was of the highest importance for the preservation of the state. Moreover, the far from revolutionary character of Polybius's historiography and Panaetius's philosophy is shown by their attitude towards the agrarian question: both were opposed to the Spartan revolution of the third century and to the Gracchi's attempts at reform.

Lucilius and the Scipionic circle

Frequently connected with the Scipionic circle are, in addition to the persons already mentioned, not only other minor figures and Aemilianus's inseparable friend Gaius Laelius (see p. 119) but also the poet Lucilius (see pp. 112 ff.). Lucilius is doubly odd in his day: not only is he the first writer to come from the aristocracy but he is the first urban aristocrat to eschew the usual concerns and public activity in general. Lucilius is still tied to the aristocratic style, but he proposes potent new models of behavior. He rejects social rising based on false values such as money, and he equally rejects a political career that avails itself of the same methods. Sometimes one may sense in Lucilius's verses the surfacing of Catonian tones and ideals. But the Censor, in his polemic against moral degeneration and the private abuse of wealth, set himself above all the task of safeguarding the foundations of political life, as embodied in the virtually sacred *mos maiorum*. What emerges in Lucilius is the problem of a personal taste, the desire not to have to involve oneself in a mundane world full of ambitious, corrupt, and vulgar people. In Lucilius we see the first attempt at a new synthesis of refined taste with traditional morality; this, too, is a reflection of the ethical-political crisis and a harbinger of the new times.

Ennius

Quintus Ennius was born in 239 B.C. at Rudiae, a small city near Lecce, in the region the Romans called Calabria—not the present-day Calabria, but Apulia south of Tarentum. The region was occupied historically by the civilization of the Messapians, who were perhaps of Illyrian origin, but it was thoroughly steeped in Greek culture. Suetonius terms Ennius a *semigraecus,* an Italo-Greek, and the poet himself liked to emphasize his trilingual nature—Latin, the language in which he would become a great literary figure; Greek, the language of his cultural upbringing; and Oscan, the language most spoken in the part of southern Italy not colonized by the Greeks.

It is likely that Ennius was educated in the cultivated ambience of Tarentum, the economic and cultural center closest to Rudiae and the city from which Livius Andronicus had come. Ennius arrived at Rome at a mature age, about seventy years after Andronicus: we are in the year 204 B.C., in the midst of the Second Punic War. Cato, according to tradition, was the one who brought him to Rome, after making his acquaintance in Sardinia. Cato in 204 was quaestor in Sicily and Africa and must have met Ennius on his return voyage, when passing through Sardinia. Why Cato was in Sardinia is not altogether clear. In any event, during the next thirty years Cato, who became "the Censor" in 184 B.C., sometimes held cultural views very different from the poet's and was politically hostile to some of his illustrious patrons.

At Rome Ennius was active as a teacher, but soon, by 190, he made a name for himself as a playwright. Allusions to Ennius's tragedies can already be found in the later comedies of Plautus. As a writer of tragedies Ennius occupied the lofty position left vacant by Andronicus and Naevius. In the years 189 to 187 he accompanied the Roman general Marcus Fulvius Nobilior to Greece and was charged with depicting in his verses the military campaign that culminated in the battle of Ambracia. Ennius dedicated a work, quite probably a *praetexta,* to this victory (189 B.C.). The propagandistic move of bringing an author along in the train of the Roman army would be harshly criticized by Cato. In the course of his life Ennius was favored and protected by the family of Nobilior and by the great house of the Scipios; among other things, he received a handsome recompense that also marked the public recognition of his services—the grant of Roman citizenship. The sources assure us, perhaps on the basis of autobiographical references from Ennius himself, that the poet maintained a modest, reserved style of life. In the last part of his life—he died in 169, during the Ludi Apollinares—he dedicated himself to the enormous task of composing the *Annals,* the epic poem that would win him eternal fame at Rome. He did not marry and did not leave any children, but his nephew Pacuvius would be his heir as the leading figure in Roman dramatic poetry.

WORKS

The chronology is naturally rather uncertain: from all his works we have only indirectly transmitted fragments, even though Ennius is, not accidentally, the archaic writer from whom we have the most quotations. It is certain that he began early to write and produce very successful tragedies and continued to do so to his final years, the last being the *Thyestes,* which premiered in 169. We have about twenty titles of *cothurnatae* and an unusually large number of brief quotations, a certain number of them found in Cicero, who rated Ennius high as a tragedian—altogether nearly two hundred fragments comprising around four hundred verses. A trace, six verses, is left of two *praetextae,* the *Ambracia,* already mentioned, and the *Sabinae,* one a contemporary subject, the other related to the legend of the founding of Rome (the rape of the Sabine women, launched by Romulus). This two-sidedness recalls the work of Naevius, who both celebrated recent victories *(Clastidium)* and touched on Rome's early days *(Romulus)* within the dramatic genre of the *praetexta.*

From the comedies, which must not have been the most successful among his works, we have two titles that are fairly certain (*Caupuncula,* "The Innkeeper's Wife," and *Pancratiastes,* "The Wrestler") and a very few verses.

But Ennius's masterpiece, the work that made its author the most prominent figure of early Latin literature in the eyes of the Romans, was the *Annals,* an epic poem in hexameters that narrated the story of Rome in eighteen books; we have 437 fragments and a total of about six hundred verses, quite a few incomplete.

A large variety of minor works is also attested, including:

1. *Hedyphagetica* ("Eating Well"), a didactic work on gastronomy, inspired by a brief Greek poem by Archestratus of Gela (ca. 350 B.C.). If, as everything suggests, it was composed before the *Annals,* it is the first attested Latin poem in hexameters. We have eleven verses from it, preserved by Apuleius in his *Apologia.*

2. *Sota,* a true literary curiosity, a text in verses (we have five, incomplete) that are called "sotadeans," for their inventor, Sotades of Maronea (ca. 280 B.C.). This verse was traditionally used for a parodic or often for an obscene work.

3. Four books (or six) of *Saturae,* in different meters, the loss of which is especially unfortunate in view of the importance of the satiric genre in the

development of Roman literature (see p. 114). Eighteen fragments are left, comprising thirty-four verses.

4. The *Scipio,* a work honoring the victor of Zama, undoubtedly a celebratory poem, about which we can draw few certain conclusions.

5. Several texts that belong together because of their quasi-philosophical content: the *Euhemerus,* perhaps written in prose, a narrative that popularized the thought of Euhemerus of Messina (fourth–third century B.C.), who was known principally for the theory that belief in the gods originated from traditions about deeds of ancient heroes and benefactors of mankind, who were later honored and promoted to the rank of gods; the *Epicharmus,* in trochaic septenarii, referring to the poet Epicharmus (early fifth century), a comic writer who had also become famous as a thinker; the *Protrepticus* ("Speech of Exhortation"), a work whose nature is difficult to determine but whose title suggests a collection of moral precepts (works of the same name go back to Aristotle and various other Greek philosophers).

It is also known that Ennius composed epigrams, in elegiac couplets. We have four, two honoring himself and two honoring Scipio Africanus. These, too, are important for the future development of this poetic genre at Rome, especially in the following century and later.

SOURCES

During much of Roman literary history Ennius is the most notable of the archaic poets, the most quoted, admired, criticized, and revived. This explains why we have far more notices of his life and works than for the other early writers; for the most part these are casual pieces of information, which we cannot collect here. Very interesting is the likelihood that many notices found in later authors are autobiographical. We have no evidence that Andronicus in his own writings left notices of this kind; for Naevius, a very engaged person, this is a likely hypothesis but not firmly grounded. It is certain, however, that Ennius in many of his works allowed a direct, personal voice to be heard. We know that he boasted in the *Annals* of being a citizen of Rome after having been a citizen of Rudiae (an arrogant contrast, given the insignificance of his town of origin) and that he openly carried on controversies with his predecessors; and it is evident that other notices of his life as well may be derived from autobiographical references. It is significant that for him, as later, with greater certainty, for Terence, there also exists a tradition of visual representation: we have evidence of statues or paintings that depicted him. Portraits of a poet are an absolute novelty in early Rome and are the sign of a cultural climate different from the one that prevailed during the Punic Wars.

1. THE DRAMA

Ennius was a prolific playwright whose production extends up to his death: the tragedy *Thyestes,* as was said, is from the year 169. He was the last Latin poet to cultivate both tragedy and comedy. His mediocrity as a comic poet was already noted by the ancients: the canon of Volcacius Sedigitus (see p. 66) ranks him last, and that only on account of his earliness *(causa antiquitatis)*. The extant comic fragments are too meager to confirm or refute the judgment of the ancients, but the genre of comedy was certainly not congenial to him. In his works for the theater Ennius was essentially a tragic poet; one feels it in the stylistic tension of his verses and the strong tendency towards the pathetic. Not by chance was his preferred model Euripides, the most modern of the great fifth-century Attic tragedians, the one most open to psychological introspection and to situations of heightened passion. Ennius translated many tragedies from Euripides, naturally allowing himself great liberty and independence, in accordance with the principles of literary translation, which is essentially a competition with the model *(aemulatio)*. He favored tragedies of the Trojan Cycle: *Alexander, Andromacha Aechmalotis* ("Andromache Prisoner of War"), *Hecuba, Iphigenia,* and so on. From Aeschylus, the first of the great Attic tragedians, was derived the *Eumenides,* the last and most spectacular of the three tragedies making up the *Oresteia* trilogy (the first two are the *Agamemnon* and the *Choephorae*), and perhaps the *Hectoris Lutra* ("The Ransoming of Hector"); from Sophocles was derived, probably, the *Ajax.* It is certain, moreover, that Ennius also imitated originals by other authors, minor tragedians outside the great Attic triad.

Ennius as tragic poet

2. THE *ANNALS:* STRUCTURE AND COMPOSITION

It is natural to focus our view of Ennius on the *Annals,* the most famous Roman epic up to the age of Augustus and one of the very few poetic works from the middle Republic, save for comedies, of which we can form some idea, one that may be fragmentary but is substantial and clear.

Ennius as author of celebratory poetry

A celebratory function must have been fundamental in all of Ennius's works. We have seen that he composed straightforward celebrations for contemporary warriors and politicians: the *Scipio* and the two epigrams for Scipio Africanus (Ennius also wrote epigrams for himself, and the parallel says much about his self-regard); and the *Ambracia,* a *praetexta* dedicated to Nobilior's campaign against the Aetolians. The case of the *Ambracia* is revealing and in a way marked a new epoch. The Hellenistic age had witnessed an extensive development of court poetry. At the courts of the Hellenistic sovereigns, at Alexandria, Antioch, and Pergamum, resided poets who celebrated the deeds of the sovereigns, often in epic narratives. A well-known epic poet, Choerilus of Iasus, had accompanied the first and grandest ruler, Alexander the Great, and had paid him poetic tribute. Poetry and panegyric were thenceforth wedded to one another. Ennius, joining Nobilior's campaign as a poet in his entourage (not poet-soldier: remember Naevius), seems to have introduced this model to Rome. Cato protested vigorously: this innovation was in effect an act of personal propaganda, in behalf of a commander who was also an influential member of the nobility. A close link was thereby established between literary and political power; Andronicus, and to a certain degree Naevius too, had been connected to influential persons, but not so directly.

Ennius saw his poem as celebrating heroic deeds and thus following in the paths both of Homer and of the newer Hellenistic epic, with its historical subject and celebratory content. In the later part of his career he approached the grandiose project of celebrating *all* Roman history in a single mammoth epic poem, the *Annals.* The work differed from the celebratory works of the Alexandrian period in amplitude and extent. The treatment was developed in eighteen books, certainly many thousands of hexameters; the extant fragments amount to several hundred verses.

The closest precedent in richness of structure was Naevius's already classic *Bellum Poenicum,* which, however, as we have seen, did not consist of continuous narration "from the fall of Troy to our days." Ennius decided instead to narrate without breaks and in chronological order, even if, to judge from the evidence we have, some historical periods clearly were more prominent than others and some were treated in summary fashion. Not by accident was the First Punic War in particular sacrificed, since here Ennius was competing directly with his predecessor Naevius. In comparison with Naevius, the division of whose *Bellum Poenicum* into books did not originate with the author, as we saw, another important innovation was the articulation of the account into books, each one conceived as a narrative unit within an overall architecture. Alexandrian epic was structured in books, and the text of Homer himself, from the third century onwards, circulated with book divisions. Ennius recovered this poetic strategy, which continued to be dominant in the whole history of Latin poetry and then in the European tradition.

Our present-day reconstructions envision in general the following distribution of the material in books:

Books 1–3. After an ample proem, Aeneas's arrival in Italy, the founding of the city, with the dramatic episodes surrounding Romulus and Remus, and the period of the kings.

Books 4–6. The wars with the peoples of Italy and the great war against Pyrrhus.

Books 7–10. The Punic Wars, the first of which, already sung by Naevius, must have been treated with great concision, and the second with great emphasis.

Books 10–12. Chiefly the campaigns in Greece after the victory over Hannibal.

Books 13–16. The wars in Syria and also, in book 15, Fulvius Nobilior's triumph over the Aetolians.

Books 16–18. The most recent military campaigns, perhaps even coming down to the time of the poet's death (169 B.C.).

The title *Annals* refers to the *Annales Maximi* (see p. 17), the public records of events year by year. Ennius's work was also done in chronological order, "from the origins to our days." We should not think that Ennius treated all the periods with the same rhythm and the same concentration. He is much more selective than a historian and is concerned, to judge from the fragments remaining, almost exclusively with military events, rarely with domestic politics.

The *Annals* extensively employ historiographic sources, the nature of which, however, we cannot determine. The one certainty is that Ennius knew the historical work of Fabius Pictor. Among the poetic sources, first place is held by Homer, whom Ennius boldly wishes to equal (see below), even though his poetic style shows the clear influences of certain Hellenistic poetry. His great predecessor Naevius is a presence, but also an object of criticism. The ideas behind Ennius's poetic practice were enunciated programmatically in the proems, which are perhaps the most notable feature in the structure of the *Annals.*

3. ENNIUS AND THE MUSE: HIS POETICS

Original plan of the Annals *and subsequent modifications*

Ennius seems to have originally planned a narrative in fifteen books, which must mean the first fifteen. Thus the work would have ended with the triumph of his patron Fulvius Nobilior (187 B.C.), which was told in the fifteenth book, and with his dedication of a temple to the Muses, the Greek goddesses of song and poetry. The triumph of Nobilior was already referred to, as we saw, in the tragedy *Ambracia.*

For reasons not altogether clear, probably in order to update his work with the celebration of other Roman victories, Ennius later added three books to the original plan. His work was still punctuated by the two great proems, to book 1 and to book 7, the latter close to the middle of the original fifteen-book scheme. These two moments, standing out clearly in the architecture of the story, are the ones in which the poet speaks most directly and reveals the inspiration and the motives of his poetic activity.

The first proem: Ennius as reincarnation of Homer

In the first proem the poet told of a dream of his. The motif comes from the proems to Hesiod's *Theogony* and to Callimachus's *Aitia.* It was customary for the poet to derive his song from a meeting with the Muses, the dispensers of poetic gifts. Ennius, however, who held the Muses in respect, conceived something far bolder: in his dream there appeared the shade of Homer, the greatest of all the epic poets, and he not only granted Ennius revelations but also promised that he, Homer, would be reincarnated—in accordance with Pythagorean teachings about metempsychosis, that is, the continuous, cyclical reincarnation of the soul—and would be reincarnated in him, the poet Ennius. Ennius thus presented himself, in the most direct way imaginable, as the reincarnation, the living replacement, of the greatest Greek poet of all time. This scene of poetic initiation would remain famous in all Roman literature, and for good reason: for the Roman poets' desire to appropriate their Greek models a more impressive symbol could not be found than the incarnation of those models in their Latin successors.

The proem in the middle: Ennius as poet-philologist

In the proem to book 7, the proem in the middle of the *Annals,* Ennius gave more space to the divinities who symbolized all his poetry, the Muses, who through him and through Nobilior, triumphator over the Greeks, acquired full citizenship at Rome. The poet emphasized that these were the Muses of the great Greek poets, no longer the Camenae of the early, now old-fashioned Andronicus (see p. 41); and he polemicized against Naevius too, who had composed in Saturnians, the verse that, according to Ennius, had been sung by *Fauni vatesque,* the verse of the age before civilization, one suitable for country divinities and ancient prophets. Ennius himself, by contrast, is represented as the first poet *dicti studiosus,* that is, with an exact linguistic calque of the Greek, the first poet-philologist, or "cherisher of the word"—in other words, the first one who can be put on a level with the refined culture of Alexandria and contemporary Greek poetry. The Alexandrian poets of the third and second centuries presented themselves as poets and at the same time as critics, as writers of poetry and at the same time scholars and theoreticians of literature. And surely Ennius, in proudly affirming his priority among the Romans, may have mentioned the importance of having been the first to adopt the dactylic hexameter, the regular meter of the great Greek poetry.

4. EXPERIMENTATION: LANGUAGE, STYLE, METER

From what the fragments indicate, this proud claim was fully justified by the facts, even though it would be absurd to think of Ennius as an isolated figure and not take into account the ample learning and refined bilingual culture already found in an Andronicus and a Naevius, not to mention the writers of comedy.

Ennius as experimental poet

The fragments we have paint a picture of a profoundly and boldly experimental poet. In some cases our impression could be exaggerated and in part distorted by the fact that a good number of the fragments are cited by later grammarians precisely because of their peculiarities, be they morphological, grammatical, metrical, or lexical, that is, because of the presence of individual features that are uncommon or unclassical.

Ennius allowed numerous Grecisms in his text, not only Greek words or constructions but even Greek endings. He invented, for instance, a genitive in *-oeo* to reproduce the Homeric genitive in *-oio,* an exclusively poetic form. He shortened to *do* the accusative of *domus,* again calquing Homer, who has a form *do* for *doma,* "house." He often wrote hexameters completely in dactyls or completely in spondees: *lābĭtŭr ūnctă cărīnă, vŏlāt sŭpĕr īmpĕtŭs ūndās,* for example, or *ōllī rēspōndīt rēx Ālbāī Lōngāī,* in both of which a stylistic reason for the choice of rhythm is evident. He wrote hexameters with syntactic pauses at practically any point in the line, even where a character begins to speak. He created verses that are completely alliterating, and alliterating with the same phoneme: *o Tite, tute, Tati, tibi tanta, tyranne, tulisti,* "o Titus Tatius, tyrant, you brought upon yourself such great misfortunes!" He invented words such as *taratantara,* to reproduce the sound of a bugle.

The introduction of alliteration into a meter of Greek origin

This last point, the alliteration and the distribution of sounds within the verse, is especially interesting. Ennius abounds in such sound figures; consider, for example, the marvelous speech of Ilia, a model of pathetic style:

haec ecfatus pater, germana, *repente recessit*
nec sese dedit in *c*onspectum *c*orde *c*upitus,
quamquam *m*ulta *m*anus ad *cae*li *cae*rula *t*empla
*t*endebam lacrumans et blanda *voce vocabam*.
vix aegro *c*um *c*orde *meo me* somnus reliquit.

("Thus spoke the father, o sister, and disappeared at once, and did not present himself to my sight, even though I desired it in my heart, however often I stretched my hands towards the blue regions of the sky, weeping and calling him with tender voice. Only now has sleep left me, with my heart suffering" [*Annals* 46–50 Sk.]). Here, in one of the richest examples, the alliterating style goes along with the pathos of the situation and emphasizes the disturbance produced by a disquieting dream.

This alliterating style, typical of the earliest *carmina,* was native to Latin. We find it in the proverbs, laws, and sacral formulas, and it passes into Naevius's Saturnians and into the verses of comedies by Naevius, Plautus, or Caecilius. Ennius imported it into the hexameter, imposing thus upon a Greek verse the effects of a specifically Roman style (in Greek poetry alliteration plays no appreciable role).

The construction of the Latin hexameter

Many innovations that resulted from Ennius's experimentation had a great future in Roman literature. The use of the Greek hexameter was a historic achievement, but it was not Ennius's only achievement. He toiled to adapt the Latin language to the hexameter, and the hexameter to the Latin language. He worked out precise rules for the placement of words in the verse, for the juncture of vowels (synaloephe, hiatus), and for the use of caesura. If his hexameters seem anarchic and arbitrary, it is because they suffer by contrast with the smooth, mannered verses of Catullus or Ovid; but these poets can count on a long hexameter tradition.

Alliteration after Ennius

The most archaic feature of Ennius's style, which to later poets would seem foreign and obsolete, lies precisely in the conjunction of the hexameter and the alliterating style. This repetitive style is, so to speak, native to verses such as the senarii of Plautus or the Saturnian of Naevius, verses that metrically are very free, with numberless possible forms. In such verses alliteration lent a kind of regularity, a kind of rhythmic armature. But the hexameter, because of its nature and structure, was a far more uniform, regular verse. The alliterating style, when applied to the hexameter, thus sounded monotonous and heavily cadenced. Later poets for that reason would use the figures of sound more selectively and with greater restraint in their hexameters, striving to employ them only for particular expressive purposes. But the evolution was gradual and progressive. An author such as Lucretius is still closely tied to the Ennian style, and the threshold of the change is located between him and the stylistic revolution of the *poetae novi.* At the culminating point of this evolution, Virgil alliterates far less than Ennius, and when he does alliterate, often it is precisely because, for the moment, he wants to sound Ennian, to give to his verses the ring of a poetry more ancient and traditional, now far away.

5. ENNIUS AND THE PERIOD OF THE CONQUESTS

The celebration of aristocratic virtus

In its moral content and its ideals the *Annals* accentuates a tendency that must already have been operative in Naevius: to set down in the epic not only accounts of deeds but also values, examples of behavior, cultural models. Greece had made Homer its own basic text: the first Roman epic poets, following them, try to meet the need for a poetry that trains men. The view of the world Ennius conveys in his poem represents, as far as we can tell, the triumph of the aristocratic ideology. The *Annals* celebrates the history of Rome as the sum total of heroic exploits proceeding from the *virtus* of the individuals—of the outstanding individuals, the great nobles and magistrates who had led disciplined armies to victory. From the fragments we have, portraits of the great commanders and politicians emerge rather than anonymous, collective celebrations, such as we sometimes infer for Naevius. (Let us also recall that around 170 Cato wrote a Roman history without giving the names of the individual magistrates and commanders, not to mention his polemic against the Ambracian expedition.) Ennius is thus the greatest poet of an aristocratic circle that rereads the history of Rome in terms of its own values and interests.

The pursuit of a cultivated and humanistic notion of *virtus* is characteristic of this period, and in fact Ennius does not praise solely the warrior virtues, in Homeric fashion, but also, and perhaps especially, the peacetime virtues—wisdom, moderation, the abilities to think and to speak. This feature of the *Annals* recalls the generation of Terence and its attempt to meld traditional aristocratic values with Greek culture, developing both individualism and a sense of social relations in a modern synthesis. The large role that Ennius granted to literature, as we know from various pieces of evidence, is altogether congruent with this humanistic, Hellenizing tendency: it is poetry that must civilize men.

The Annals *and the later development of Roman imperialism*

For centuries Ennius remained *the* Roman national poet, only Virgil his rival in this category. This posthumous view can distort him. The *Annals* could not contain a complete summary of Roman imperialism, for the simple reason that Ennius did not live long enough. In the period when the poem was composed, great military successes and great expansionist movements, chiefly towards Greece and the East, are bringing about a crucial change in point of view: in the first half of the second century Rome completely evolves from a provincial power (though one strong in military might) to a force that dominates the Mediterranean. It is worth remembering that Ennius died about a year before the most important stage of this process, the battle of Pydna. His work certainly gave evidence of a change, but Ennius, who had a philosophical nature and the passion of a historian, could hardly have drawn up a full balance sheet. The first true balance sheet on Roman imperialism would be drawn up in the next generation, by Polybius, the greatest Greek intellectual of what, on the Roman side, is usually called "the age of the Scipios."

BIBLIOGRAPHY

The fundamental collection of all the fragments of Ennius remains J. Vahlen, *Ennianae Poesis Reliquiae* (ed. 3 Leipzig 1903, reprint Amsterdam 1963), with a lengthy Latin introduction. This is now complemented by the editions with full English commentary of the tragedies by H. D. Jocelyn (Cambridge 1967) and the *Annales* by O. Skutsch (Oxford 1985). For the minor poems, see E. Courtney, *The Fragmentary Latin Poets* (Oxford 1993).

There is an English translation in the first volume of the Loeb *Remains of Old Latin*, by E. H. Warmington (4 vols. London 1935–40).

Much of the scholarly work on the fragments has been concerned with points of detail; see, e.g., the collection by O. Skutsch, *Studia Enniana* (London 1968, English and Latin) and the papers in *Ennius* (Entretiens sur l'antiquité classique XVII, Geneva 1972). The paper there by E. Badian, "Ennius and His Friends" (151–208), discusses the biographical problems. There is a comprehensive survey in English by H. D. Jocelyn, "The Poems of Quintus Ennius," *ANRW* 1.2 (Berlin 1972) 987–1026. For some stimulating discussion of individual fragments see G. Williams, *Tradition and Originality in Roman Literature* (Oxford 1968) 359–63 (Ennius and Euripides), 684–99 *(Annales)*. The discussion of Ennius in D. C. Feeney, *The Gods in Epic* (Oxford 1991), is again useful. On the tragedies, see H. D. Jocelyn, "Ennius as a Dramatic Poet," in the Geneva *Ennius* volume, 45–95, and R. A. Brooks, *Ennius and Roman Tragedy* (New York 1981).

There are few studies of the minor works, but the *Saturae* merit a chapter in most surveys of Roman satire: see, e.g., E. Knoche, *Roman Satire*, trans. E. S. Ramage (Bloomington 1975) 17–30, and M. Coffey, *Roman Satire* (ed. 2 Bristol 1989) 24–32 (with bibliography 282). The fragment of the *Hedyphagetica* is reedited by H. Lloyd-Jones and P. J. Parsons, *Supplementum Hellenisticum* (Berlin 1983) 74–75. In general see Jocelyn's *ANRW* survey mentioned above, 1022–26.

Most of the works cited devote some space to the reception of Ennius's works in later Latin literature; see esp. the introduction to Skutsch's edition of the *Annales,* with E. Norden, *Ennius und Vergilius* (Leipzig 1915, reprint Darmstadt 1966), S. Stabryla, *Latin Tragedy in Virgil's Poetry* (Warsaw 1970), and M. Wigodsky, *Vergil and Early Latin Poetry* (Wiesbaden 1972).

Cato

Marcus Porcius Cato was born in 234 at Tusculum, near what is today Frascati, to a plebeian family of prosperous farmers. He fought in the war against Hannibal, and in 214 he was military tribune in Sicily. The aristocrat Lucius Valerius Flaccus aided him in his political career. In 204 Cato was quaestor, accompanying Scipio to Sicily and Africa, in 199 plebeian aedile, and in 198 praetor in charge of governing Sardinia. In 195 the *homo novus* Cato was consul with Valerius Flaccus. While in office he opposed revoking the *lex Oppia,* a sumptuary law that limited the expenditures particularly of women from wealthy families. Spain was assigned as his province, where he acted harshly towards the Spanish tribes and enhanced his own reputation for efficiency and frugality.

In 191 B.C., as military tribune with Valerius Flaccus under the command of the consul Acilius Glabrio, he fought at Thermopylae and carried out an important diplomatic mission at Athens and other Greek cities. From 190 onwards he was prosecutor in a series of political trials against members of the dominant faction of the Scipios. In 184 he was censor along with Valerius Flaccus. In that office he presented himself as the champion of the ancient Roman virtues against moral degeneration and against the spread of a tendency towards individualism that was influenced in part by Hellenistic culture. In addition, and in parallel to his polemic against the extravagance of private citizens, Cato glorified the wealth and power of the state, as must have been evident to all: as censor, he promoted a vast program of public construction. The censorship of Cato remained famous on account of the intransigence with which he performed his duties, giving vent to his moral rigor. Afterwards, too, his attitude won him many enemies, and he was often involved in trials, as accuser as well as defendant. In 181 he opposed the revoking of another sumptuary law, the *lex Orchia,* and in 169 supported the *lex Voconia,* which limited women's rights of inheritance. In 167 he opposed the war against Rhodes (fragments remain of his *Oratio pro Rhodiensibus,* which Cato himself had reported in his *Origines*): before the Third Punic War he, along with a part of the ruling class, may have been thinking of the possibility of a balance among the Mediterranean powers, and for this reason he may have opposed ending Rhodian independence and favored the independence of Macedon.

In 155 Cato spoke against the philosophers whom Athens had sent to Rome as ambassadors (see p. 73), and he secured their expulsion. Probably his conservative nature caused him to fear that they, in particular Carneades, with his antilogies on justice, might lead educated Romans to entertain doubts about the validity of the traditional ethics. In 153, on a visit to Carthage, which after its defeat in the Second Punic War was beginning to flourish again, Cato became persuaded that Rome's survival depended on the destruction of its ancient rival. He therefore urged the Third Punic War, but, dying in 149, did not live to see the destruction of the enemy city.

WORKS

Speeches: Cicero knew more than 150 speeches of Cato. Today we know the titles and the circumstances of about 80 of them, about 20 of which go back to the year of his censorship. We also possess various fragments.

Origines, a historical work in seven books, written in old age; some fragments survive.

A treatise *De Agri Cultura,* which is preserved, the earliest Latin prose text that has come down to us entire; it consists of a preface and 170 short chapters.

Carmen de Moribus, probably a work in prose; the term *carmen* would seem to indicate rhythmic prose.

Apophthegmata, a collection of memorable sayings or anecdotes that went under Cato's name, some of which are cited by such authors as Cicero or Plutarch.

SOURCES

Plutarch's *Life of Cato;* Cornelius Nepos's *Life of Cato;* Cicero's *Cato Maior de Senectute;* sections of Livy, books 29, 32, 34, 36, 38–39, 43, and 45.

1. THE BEGINNINGS OF SENATORIAL HISTORIOGRAPHY

Cato's engaged historiography

Cato wrote the *Origines* in old age, thus starting historiography in Latin; he scorned and derided Roman annals in Greek, such as those of Aulus Postumius Albinus (see p. 70). From its beginning, as we saw, Roman historical writing had felt the effects of being produced primarily by members of the senatorial elite, even though often not by the politically most eminent figures. The case of Cato, a politician of the first rank who wrote history, was fated to remain practically unique in Latin culture; autobiographical *commentarii* such as those of Sulla or Caesar are evidently different.

Its being produced by members of the ruling class, which sees in it a dignified way of filling its own *otium,* lends to the nascent Roman historiography a robust political engagement. In Cato's historical work much space is given to his own concerns over the rampant moral corruption and to his personal battles, waged in the name of public solidarity, against the emergence of notable figures with marked tendencies towards individualism and the cult of personality; some such individuals were found in the

Scipionic circle, chief among them Africanus Maior. For this reason Cato allowed his political polemics a place in the *Origines* and reported his own speeches, for example, those in behalf of the Rhodians or against Sulpicius Galba; indeed, it has been thought, and it is not unlikely, that a part of Cato's historical work was a sort of self-celebration. Moreover, he tended to privilege contemporary history, to which he dedicated about half (three books out of seven) of a work that reached far back, to the very origins of Rome.

Summary of the Origines

The first book of the *Origines* was devoted to the founding of Rome, the second and third to the origins of the Italian cities. The title of the work properly applied only to these first three books. The fourth book told of the First Punic War, the fifth of the Second, the sixth and seventh of events down to the praetorship of Servius Sulpicius Galba, in 152 B.C. The proportions of the individual book grew as the work approached the present: the last two books covered a period of less than fifty years and were a detailed contemporary history.

The history of Rome as the collective work of a people

In attempting to kill at birth the charismatic cult of the great personalities, Cato worked out a conception of Roman history that emphasized above all the gradual formation of the state and its institutions over the generations and the centuries, a conception that would be partially taken up by Cicero in the *De Re Publica*: the creation of the Roman state was seen as the collective work of the *populus Romanus* around the senatorial ruling class. Thus Cato, probably breaking with the traditional annals often composed by members of the noble families, did not give the names of commanders, neither Romans nor foreigners; Hannibal himself, as we see from a preserved fragment, was called *dictator Carthaginiensium*. The *novus homo* from Tusculum probably aimed at dimming the renown of the *gentes* in favor of the *res publica*. In their stead Cato seems to have brought into the light of history the names of rather obscure persons, heroes of less elevated rank, who precisely for this reason deserved to be hailed as symbols of the collective heroism of the Roman people; thus Cato dedicated a certain amount of space to the account of the valiant deeds of a certain Quintus Caedicius.

The high valuation of Italians and foreigners

In other directions, the *Origines* showed a notable broadening of horizons. Perhaps the origins of the *novus homo* Cato outside the city helped give him a lively interest, shown in books 2 and 3, in the history of the Italian populations, emphasizing their contributions to the greatness of Rome and to the creation of the traditional ethical model. He boasted, for example, of the moral uprightness of his own people, the Sabines, and their parsimony, which were due in the first place to their alleged Spartan origins and strengthened by their strong relation to the land. But Cato also showed an almost ethnographic interest in foreign peoples, for instance, in certain customs of the African and Spanish peoples; the particulars that he furnished probably went back to direct observations, since in the course of his political and military career he had been in direct contact with these peoples.

2. THE TREATISE ON AGRICULTURE

The De Agri Cultura *as a practical tool*

The *De Agri Cultura* has no place for literary ornaments or for philosophical reflections on the farmer's life and fate of the sort found in a large number of the subsequent Latin treatises on agriculture; the work consists mostly of a series of precepts laid down in dry, schematic fashion, but sometimes very effectively. The tone of the sententious precepts must have been especially dear to Cato, since it shaped such works as the *Praecepta ad Filium* (on various subjects, but the title and structure are uncertain) and the *Carmen de Moribus,* a collection of lapidary sayings on moral subjects. For grasping the purpose and intended audience of the *De Agri Cultura* the proem is important, in which Cato shows that agriculture is more than anything an acquisitive activity; various social considerations make it preferable to others, for instance, to lending money at interest, which is immoral, or to trading by sea, which is too risky. Agriculture is more secure and more honorable; moreover, it is by farmwork that good citizens and good soldiers are formed.

The De Agri Cultura *and the birth of the latifundium*

The type of farm that Cato describes probably represents the passage from the small family holding to the much vaster estates that were based upon the concentration and intense exploitation of slaves, whom overseas conquests had begun to make available to the Romans in large numbers. Cato, the *homo novus* who had absorbed the aristocracy's values, strives to set the aristocracy's domination upon sturdier economic and ideological bases. In the period when farming by slaves was expanding, he demonstrates to the nobility and the sectors dominated by them how to find great profits in those landholdings that were the traditional inheritance of the ruling class, without needing to resort to more dynamic, but also more dangerous, forms of investment—which, to be sure, Cato did not eschew: we know of an involvement of his in maritime commerce. Remaining attached to the land, the ruling class remained attached also to the ethical-political values which formed the ideological foundation of their power.

The pragmatic ideology of the De Agri Cultura

The *De Agri Cultura* is a collection of general precepts on how the landowner should behave. In the role of *pater familias* he, in accordance with the patriarchal tradition, should be present on his own estate as much as possible, in order to supervise the punctual carrying out of all tasks. The style is spare and concise but enlivened by bits of rustic folk wisdom, which find ready expression in figurative proverbial formulations. The patina of archaism contributes to the effect: alliteration, homoeoteleuton, and repetition are found in abundance in the *De Agri Cultura.* Yet it would be a mistake to imagine that one is dealing with a kindhearted, patriarchal agricultural civilization. The brutality of slave exploitation is manifest in several passages: Cato recommends selling, like scrap metal, a slave who is old or ill and thus incapable of work. It should also be kept in mind that in the *De Agri Cultura* farming is regarded as an enterprise conducted on a vast scale: the landowner ought to have huge storehouses in which to keep the produce while waiting for prices to rise, and he ought to buy as little as possible and sell as much as possible; that is, he ought to have the outlook of a producer, not a consumer. Hence one can infer the salient features of the Catonian ethic, which are the same ones that the late Republic would come to regard as making up the *mos maiorum:* virtues such as *parsimonia, duritia, industria,* the disdain for riches, and resistance to the seductiveness of pleasure show how Catonian severity is not the practical wisdom of an ingenuous, uncorrupted peasant, but represents rather the ideological implication of a genuinely practical requirement: deriving economic advantage from farming, or rather increasing the productivity of the slave labor employed in it.

3. CATO'S POLITICAL-CULTURAL BATTLE

Cato as orator: the ideological rejection of Greek culture

Cato's oratorical style, as far as we can gather from the fragments of his speeches, was lively and full of movement, certainly much less reserved and archaizing than the style of the treatise on agriculture. A famous maxim, transmitted as part of the *Praecepta ad Filium,* seems to express concisely Cato's notions about rhetoric: *rem tene, verba sequentur* ("have the contents clear, and the words will come of themselves"), an ostentatious rejection of *ars,* the Greek rhetorical *techne,* which is also attested in several anecdotes about the Censor. This rejection of stylistic elaboration needs to be interpreted in the light of Cato's unceasing polemic against the penetration of Greek morals and culture, in their various forms, at Rome. In fact Cato was not so ignorant of Greek literature as he is made out to have been by the traditional account, according to which only in advanced age did he approach the study of that language. The *De Agri Cultura* avails itself frequently of Greek agricultural science; the influence of the Greek historian Timaeus upon the *Origines* can perhaps be felt; and even in the speeches Greek rhetorical technique is not so much absent as cleverly concealed, so as to give the audience the impression of lively immediacy and not the scent of midnight oil.

Anti-Greek polemic and defense of the aristocracy

Personally imbued with Greek culture, Cato fought not so much that culture itself as certain of its enlightened features, in particular its criticism of traditional social values and relations, which had been the inheritance of sophistic thought. The enlightened elements of Greek culture may have been for Cato a corrosive agent working upon the ethical-political basis of the Republic and the aristocratic regime. These concerns probably explain the successive expulsions of Greek philosophers and intellectuals from Rome, beginning perhaps in 173. At the same time there was the risk that imitating certain Hellenizing customs could endanger the unity and internal cohesion of the aristocracy by elevating the status of charismatic personalities above the others. From this point of view one can understand Cato's battle in favor of the sumptuary laws, which limited consumption by the wealthy aristocrats and also the pomp and ostentation on the part of individual families. Moreover, by trying to prevent inherited family wealth from being dissipated in such displays of status, the sumptuary laws were also concerned to prevent excessive economic imbalances within the ruling class, which were dangerous since they could undermine its stability.

The apt fusion of Greek and Roman

In his literary work Cato probably aimed at creating a culture that could maintain firm roots in the Roman tradition but also accept Greek contributions, yet without openly propagandizing on their behalf. We know that Cato, who had fought Scipio Africanus, was on good terms with him; this notice is nearly a presage of the destiny of Latin culture. Through the intellectuals of Aemilianus's circle Greek culture, penetrating into Rome, would henceforth go beyond the bounds that the Roman aristocracy wanted to set for it. It would allow a little rationalism to enter, perhaps more than Cato would have tolerated, but still it would stay within the limits of political-social conservatism. It would lead to a new synthesis of the *mos maiorum* with the mitigated forces of enlightenment, which in its turn would become the basis of Cicero's ethical and political thought.

4. LITERARY SUCCESS

Cato the Censor: the name freezes him in his function as censor and declares his transformation from a person into a symbol, a symbol of the rigid custodian of tradition and conservatism. And as a figure who summarizes in himself the fundamental virtues of the Rome of the past—austerity, parsimony, devotion to work, moral rigor—he was idealized by Cicero in the *De Re Publica* and then especially in the famous dialogue *Cato Maior de Senectute.* Cicero, however, attempting to restore unity to the ideological contrasts of the past, mitigated the harsher aspects of his character and the more intransigent features of his aversion to the phil-Hellenic nobility.

The figure of Cato would be honored with various biographies, those of Cornelius Nepos (age of Caesar) and Plutarch (first–second centuries A.D.) and the one contained in the anonymous work *De Viris Illustribus* (fourth century A.D.).

Livy appreciated his gifts but did not refrain from criticizing the intransigent uprightness of a man who seemed to him "a ferocious mastiff set upon the nobility." The highest estimation of his qualities as a writer came from the archaizers of the second century, Gellius, Fronto, and the emperor Hadrian, the last two putting him ahead of Cicero himself. But after the fourth century the firsthand knowledge of his works begins to disappear (a collection of moral maxims in verse circulated under his name, the so-called *Disticha* or *Dicta Catonis*). Only the *De Agri Cultura* would survive in its entirety, on account of its technical nature and utility.

BIBLIOGRAPHY

For the fragments of the speeches, see E. Malcovati, ed., *Oratorum Romanorum Fragmenta* (ed. 4 Turin 1976), and M. T. Sblendorio Cugusi, *M. Porci Catonis Orationum*

Reliquiae (Turin 1982); there is a separate Italian edition with commentary of the *Oratio pro Rhodiensibus* by G. Calboli (Bologna 1978). The fragments of the *Origines* may be found in H. Peter's *Historicorum Romanorum Reliquiae* (ed. 2 Leipzig 1914); see also M. Chassignet, *Caton, Les Origines* (Paris 1986, with French translation and commentary), and W. A. Schneider, *M. Porcius Cato, Das Erste Buch der Origines* (Meissenheim am Glan 1971). There are scholarly editions of the *De Agricultura* by H. Keil (Leipzig 1882–1902, with brief Latin commentary and *index verborum*), G. Goetz (Leipzig 1922), and A. Mazzarino (ed. 2 Leipzig 1982) and a useful Loeb with English translation by W. D. Hooper and H. B. Ash (Cambridge, Mass. 1934). There are editions with translations and notes in German by P. Thielscher (Berlin 1963) and in French by R. Goujard (Paris 1975). For the other works, see H. Jordan, *M. Catonis praeter librum de re rustica quae extant* (Leipzig 1860); there is also a complete edition with German translation by O. Schoenberger (Munich 1980). A few fragments are translated and discussed, with Cornelius Nepos's biography, in N. Horsfall, *Cornelius Nepos: A Selection* (Oxford 1989).

There is a major English biography by A. E. Astin, *Cato the Censor* (Oxford 1978). The best English treatment of the style is in M. von Albrecht, *Masters of Roman Prose from Cato to Apuleius,* trans. N. Adkin (Leeds 1989) 1–32; see also A. D. Leeman, *Orationis Ratio: The Stylistic Theories and Practice of the Roman Orators, Historians, and Philosophers* (Amsterdam 1963) 43–49. R. Till's *Die Sprache Catos* (Leipzig 1936) has been translated into Italian with extra notes by C. de Meo, *La lingua di Catone* (Rome 1968).

Terence

A native of Carthage, Terence is said to have been born in 185/184, but the notice is suspect. A date about ten years earlier is more likely. He is said to have come to Rome as the slave of a certain Terentius Lucanus. The event lies at some distance from the Second Punic War, and it is not clear precisely what the occasion might have been. All the ancient sources emphasize his close relations with Scipio Aemilianus and Laelius. These nobles were certainly his patrons, and Terence in his comedies also makes several references to the support received from illustrious friends (*Heautontimoroumenos* 23 ff., *Adelphoe* 15 ff.). Various hostile rumors, both sexual and literary, circulated about these relations: the real author of Terence's works, according to rumor, was Scipio or Laelius (this type of inference, as is well known, has parallels in the life of Shakespeare). It is clear that these rumors fit into the climate of a fierce controversy, as much literary as political, which is characteristic of this period.

Terence is said to have died in 159, or in any event before the Third Punic War, in the course of a voyage to Greece for cultural purposes. The date, if it is genuine, is interesting, because these cultural tours of Greece would later become traditional in the education of cultivated Romans. A similar story is recounted about the death of Virgil. The details of the circumstances of Terence's death, by drowning, are scarcely credible: they recall the attempt at suicide through drowning by the great comic writer Menander, Terence's acknowledged inspiration.

The visual tradition, because of his Punic origins and his cognomen Afer, presents a typically Carthaginian image of Terence, but this has no real value as a biographical source.

The chronology of the works is precisely attested, even though some particulars remain open to discussion, in the didascalia that the manuscripts prefix to the individual comedies; they are the results of the philological work and the learned researches of the ancient grammarians. There are six comedies, transmitted to us in their entirety: *Andria,* performed with modest success, in 166; *Hecyra* ("The Mother-in-Law"), first performed in 165, when it was a total failure despite the skill of Ambivius

Turpio, the actor and theatrical producer of all Terence's comedies, then given without success along with the *Adelphoe,* and finally done successfully, on the third try, in 160; *Heautontimoroumenos* ("The Self-Punisher"), performed with excellent results in 163; *Eunuchus,* done in 161, Terence's biggest hit with the public and his greatest commercial success; *Phormio,* performed successfully in 161; *Adelphoe* ("The Brothers"), presented in 160. The comedies, which contain about 6,000 verses altogether, vary in size from 880 verses *(Hecyra)* to 1,094 *(Eunuchus).*

The Greek models employed by Terence and declared in the prologues all belong to Attic New Comedy: Menander, Diphilus, and the less well-known Apollodorus of Carystus. Terence's poetic practice in utilizing Greek models is discussed below.

SOURCES

The principal source is the *Vita Terenti* contained in Suetonius's *De Viris Illustribus,* which was composed around A.D. 100 and transmitted to us as an introduction to Aelius Donatus's commentary on Terence, from the fourth century. Suetonius made extensive use of the scholars of the Republic, but the quality of the notices is controversial, since, beginning in Terence's own day (see above), many details of his life were the objects of contradictory and polemical rumors. Donatus's commentary is one of the best works of its kind to have reached us and contains good information on questions of theatrical technique and the staging of the plays.

Terence's date of birth itself is doubtful, since 184 is also attested as the year of Plautus's death: it was customary in ancient biographies to synchronize the births and deaths of authors who in some way succeeded one another in distinction within a particular literary genre. The anecdote that has Terence reading his first work, the *Andria,* to the great comic writer Caecilus Statius and receiving warm encouragement from him might also have been created on purpose to link two different literary generations.

I. HISTORICAL BACKGROUND

The battle of Pydna: a) The opening of a period of peace

The controversial ancient biographical notices place Terence at the center of what modern historians are wont to call "the age of the Scipios." Terence's debut in the theater comes two years after the battle of Pydna, which, as the decisive victory over the Macedonians, became a crucial moment in the evolution of Roman power and in Rome's relations with the Greek East. Henceforth for about twenty years—in any event, well beyond Terence's death—there is a period of peace, in which Rome consolidates her position as an imperial power.

b) Penetration of Greece in Rome

The date of Pydna, 168, is a watershed also from a second point of view. The triumph of Lucius Aemilius Paullus, behind whose chariot the treasures of the Macedonian court were carried in procession, was virtually a symbol of the appropriation of a world. As a consequence of the victory one thousand Achaean hostages were deported to Rome, among them intellectuals such as the historian Polybius, the first Greek to think in a mature, developed way about the causes of Rome's success as a dominant power. The appropriation of the Greek world thus developed on several distinct levels: changes in taste and cast of mind, an increase in the consumption of luxury items and art, and interests in new cultural and ideological models. This last aspect gained strength through new types of cultural contact. A great noble clan, the house of the Scipios, became a center of Hellenizing culture, which was no longer imported passively or transmitted at a popular level but was carried on at the highest level of society. Thus the presence of the great Stoic philosopher Panaetius of Rhodes among the Scipios, like the presence of Polybius himself, is significant. At the same time the teaching of Crates, who was active in Rome in 168, promulgates a new type of eloquence and rhetorical theory.

Innovation in comedy: emphasis on meanings

The new direction led to innovations also in dramatic poetry, beginning with Terence. The comic genre in Plautus's hands had been a great popular entertainment. From this point of view, the extent of refinement in Plautus's art, with its unpredictable rhythmic and verbal imagination, is of small importance. In fact Plautus's comedies succeeded with the vast public as no other literary work ever would. Plautus no doubt entertained and excited even those who were not at all aware of the cultural problems contained in the Menandrian originals. In its content Plautine drama does not require from the audience any efforts of thought and contemplation: everything is absorbed and consumed in the fire of comic invention. The plots offer the audience a conventional frame of reference, without probing too deeply into the psychology of the characters.

Terence's drama accepts the conventional, repetitious framework of these plots, without making any effort at originality. But it does not do this in order to sacrifice everything to an overriding concern for verbal comedy; on the contrary, Terence's principal interest is in meanings, in the human material that is brought into play by the plots of the comedy. Terence attempts the difficult feat of using a basically popular genre to convey new sensibilities and interests that have arisen in the restricted circle of a social and cultural elite. The grave difficulties Terence meets in his relation to the audience (and in relation to certain colleagues in the theater) can be traced back to this new tension.

Failures of the Hecyra

One of the comedies, the *Hecyra* ("The Mother-in-Law"), had a particularly unhappy fate: at the first performance, in 165, the audience preferred a show of tightrope walkers to it; at the second, in 160, everyone left when, right in the middle of the performance, word went around that a show of gladiators was starting just then; only at the third performance, again in 160, could the end be reached.

Cultural change enacted: the interest in psychology

The vicissitudes of Terence's comedies are symptomatic of the decline of Roman popular drama (which would accelerate rapidly in the following period) and of the increasing split between the taste of the mass audience and the taste of the educated elite, which had been brought up on refined Greek culture. Terence's drama, in effect, enacts the ideals of the cultural revival of the Scipionic aristocracy (see p. 73). The author is interested above all in the psychological understanding of the characters (meant in a sense that we will attempt to specify shortly), and for this reason he rejects the comic exuberance of imagination that had contributed so much to Plautus's success. It is convenient at this point to indicate briefly the plots of the individual comedies.

Andria. Menander's *Andria* is the Greek model, "contaminated" with the same author's *Perinthia.* The girl from Andros from whom the play takes its title is Glycerium, abandoned in childhood and brought up by a courtesan. Pamphilus, who is already betrothed to Philumena, daughter of Chremes, falls in love with her. Chremes, informed of Pamphilus's infatuation with Glycerium, flies into a rage and calls off the young man's marriage to Philumena, despite the attempts by Pamphilus's father to save the marriage, which had been planned some time before. The situation is complicated by the rather awkward attempts made by Davus, Pamphilus's servant, to help his master. The plot is resolved with the final recognition: it is discovered that Glycerium is also a daughter of Chremes, so he has no trouble in marrying her instead of Philumena to Pamphilus.

Hecyra. The comedy, as stated above, had an especially troubled history. Terence reworks a comedy of the same name, which means "The Mother-in-Law," by Apollodorus of Carystus, "contaminating" it with the *Epitrepontes* ("The Arbiters") by Menander. The play turns about Sostrata, mother of Philumena and mother-in-law of Pamphilus. Sostrata is completely different from the stereotyped figure of the mother who is jealous of her son and hostile to her daughter-in-law; instead, she does her best to set right the misunderstandings between the two. It is discovered that Philumena, before her marriage, had been made pregnant by an unknown man during a nighttime festival; Pamphilus would like to abandon her, but in the end it turns out that Pamphilus himself is the unknown man who had made Philumena pregnant. Won over by the sweet, compliant character of his wife, Pamphilus is reconciled with her and gives up his love for the courtesan Bacchides, who also does her best to encourage reconciliation between husband and wife.

Heautontimoroumenos. The Greek title—Terence reworks a comedy of the same name by Menander—means "The Self-Punisher." The one who behaves thus is the old man Menedemus, who had driven his son Clinia to enlist in Asia by blocking the son's marriage to a girl of humble origins and now, in order to punish himself, has condemned himself to toil laboriously on the land with his own hands until Clinia returns. When he does return, the father can welcome him with a more intense and more mature affection. After a series of confusions, Clinia succeeds in marrying the girl whom he has long loved, who in the meantime has been revealed to be the daughter of Clinia's friend Chremes.

Eunuchus. This is the reworking of a comedy of the same name by Menander, and it also draws some situations from Menander's *Kolax* ("The Flatterer"). The hetaera Thais, the concubine of the soldier Thraso, is really in love with the young man Phaedria. Thraso brings back to Thais the young girl Pamphila, who had grown up with her like a sister and then been sold. Phaedria's brother Chaerea, who is in love with Pamphila, disguises himself as a eunuch in order to be put in charge of the girl. Thraso, jealous of Phaedria, would like to take back Pamphila by force from Thais but is forced to let her go. The false eunuch is unmasked, but Pamphila is discovered to be an Athenian citizen, and he can marry her. Thais keeps Phaedria as a dear friend.

Phormio. The original is the *Epidikazomenos* ("The Claimant") by Apollodorus of Carystus, a Greek comic writer of the third century B.C. The parasite Phormio, after many vicissitudes, succeeds in helping two cousins, Phaedria and Antiphon, to marry the girls they love. Here, too, recognition plays a part, since towards the end of the play it is discovered that Phanium, the girl Antiphon is in love with, who until now has been thought an orphan, is in fact the illegitimate daughter of Chremes, the father of Phaedria and uncle of Antiphon himself.

Adelphoe. This reworks the comedy of the same title ("The Brothers") by Menander but takes a scene also from Diphilus's *Synapothneskontes* (*Commorientes* in Latin, "Partners in Death"). The comedy compares two different systems of upbringing. Demea has raised his son Ctesiphon with great rigor, while giving his other son, Aeschinus, in adoption to his brother Micio, who has raised him with the greatest freedom. Demea considers Aeschinus a profligate corrupted by the laxity of Micio, and his opinion is confirmed when he learns that Aeschinus has carried off a girl. But Aeschinus has really carried off the girl in behalf of his brother, whom Demea believes to be irreproachable. After various vicissitudes, all is set right; but the comedy has a finale that is difficult to interpret, in which Demea seems to accept, more out of annoyance than sincerity, his brother's proposal to adopt permissive ways (easy, but perilous) and to show himself thenceforth as indulgent towards all.

Nonconformist character typing

The plots of Terence, as can be seen, are the ones usual in New Comedy and the *palliata:* young lovers, fathers who oppose them, slaves busy attempting to satisfy the desires of their young masters, and almost always, at the end, the recognition that resolves the situation. Within the framework of overall fidelity to the traditional plots, Terence's profound innovation lies in choosing, as we have indicated, to get at the psychology of the character. More precisely, Terence often seems interested in the psychological portrayal more of the type than of the individual: the young man in love, the girl tenderly devoted to him, the traditional father concerned for his son's happiness, the prostitute capable of noble sentiments and genuine altruism. Some interpreters, forcing things somewhat, have compared Terence's drama to the *Characters* of Theophrastus. But even though typed, even though frequently not endowed with strong individual personalities, Terence's characters are often the very opposite of conventional: the mother-in-law who is not at all shrewish, but rather strives for the happiness of her daughter-in-law, and the prostitute morally superior to many "respectable" people were very novel characters in relation to audience expectations. Psychological understanding entailed a notable diminution in comic quality, which without doubt contributed to Terence's scant success with the mass audience: it would certainly have been easier to extract laughter from the representation of a sullen, grumpy mother-in-law or a greedy courtesan.

2. STYLE AND LANGUAGE

The apparently smooth style

In view of this, it is easy to understand how Terence's style of expression, precisely because he does not aim at making a display of it, is in general the aspect of his work most neglected by critics and readers. The first, superficial impression is of a smooth uniformity, especially for those who, as is almost always the case, compare it with Plautus's verbal fireworks. Still, a more attentive consideration of the style has much to tell us about Terence's poetics and purposes.

Censored language

In six comedies entirely centered upon love affairs the word "kiss," as Alfonso Traina has observed, does not appear more than twice all told. In Terence lovers do not kiss, normally, and in general there is little talk about bodies, about eating and drinking, or, of course, about sex. The characters do not usually exchange coarse insults, neither those of ordinary speech nor those invented by the poet's creativity (as happens in Aristophanes and in Plautus). The low characters of the *palliata*—the slave, the hetaera, the parasite—appear here too, but they do not bring their particular language onto the stage. If one looks at Terence's language in the light of Plautus, the linguistic material seems to have been carefully selected, even censored. But, significantly, the abstract words that make psychological analysis possible and interesting become more numerous.

Realistic language

This restriction or censorship of the language, as we will soon see, serves to ensure the prominence of certain of the plays' contents. But here one may ask what effect this sort of language had upon the Roman public of the time. It is clear that in a certain sense Terence's calm, intermediate style is more ordinary than Plautus's. The characters do not launch into unpredictable tirades in which literary parodies are mixed with puns, metaphors, and allusions of every sort; rather, their language seems closer to that of an ordinary conversation. The feature that most distinguishes Terence in Latin comedy (and in Latin drama in general, we may add) is his constant, careful concern for verisimilitude, a concept that had taken on greater importance in the Greek literature and esthetics of the Hellenistic period.

Urbane language and restriction of meter

This does not mean that Terence, in order to be lifelike, reproduces the ordinary speech of the day realistically. He does, to be sure, conform to a language in some ways real and really spoken, but it is the language of only a segment of society, that spoken by the educated, cultured urban classes. For the tastes of the Roman public the effect must have been rather idealized. The best-known, and most often cited, critical judgment on Terence, from the pen of Julius Caesar, emphasizes just this idealizing tendency in his style: Terence is termed *puri sermonis amator,* "a lover of pure diction." The restriction and selection of vocabulary corresponds to the great reduction in metrical variety from Plautus's *numeri innumeri:* the truly lyric parts are few, and the proportion of the *cantica* (the parts sung or declaimed with musical accompaniment) to the *deverbia* (the recitatives) is much reduced.

3. THE PROLOGUES: TERENCE'S POETICS AND HIS RELATION TO HIS MODELS

The relations between style and contents

Although his success as a school author has affected his literary image, it would be a mistake to think of Terence as a sort of preacher on education. His interest in moral and cultural content does not come at the expense of dramaturgic technique. On the contrary, Terence is one of the most professional Latin writers, most conscious of the technical aspects of his work. His interest in Attic New Comedy and in Menander particularly demonstrates the coexistence of these two aspects: Menander not only offered both a literary and a cultural model, the latter connected to Terence's interest in values such as *humanitas* (see p. 100); he was also a refined example of style and dramatic technique. Precisely while working thoroughly with Greek models, Terence finds a way to express both his own intellectual position and his own literary vocation.

The rejection of meta-theater

Menander's comedies, as we saw, had been an important model for Plautus too. But Plautus was not particularly close to Menandrian poetics: verisimilitude, the foundation of Menandrian poetics, is not an absolute value for Plautus. In the Plautine *palliata* the play on the stage ends up mirroring itself, calling into question the effect of reality upon the stage plot—this we have called Plautus's meta-theater (see p. 59).

Terence cares much more for the consistency and seamlessness of the dramatic illusion. The action never allows meta-theatrical developments; Terence even rigorously eliminates those exchanges between characters that do not have a direct internal effect upon the plot development but freely address the audience, those exchanges that break the dramatic illusion and thus reveal, like a comment external to the action, the dramatic mechanism that creates and controls the comic invention. In practice Terence's *palliata* opens no space for self-consciousness within itself. All such moments of reflection are concentrated in the prologue. The importance he gives to the prologue as a literary institution is Terence's principal technical innovation in the Plautine tradition.

The prologue as author's space

In the tradition going back to New Comedy, the prologue was generally conceived as a place for exposition, for information necessary for the understanding of the plot. It not only gave the antecedent facts of the action but also anticipated a part of the development and hinted at the resolution, in a final recognition scene or similar *coups de théâtre.* This gave the audience a panorama, making it more attentive to the development of the action and capable of appreciating those ironic effects that arose little by little from the situation on the stage—double meanings, mistaken perspectives, and so on. Terence rejects this informing function of the prologue, even though to do so leads to some obscurities in the movement of the plot. Instead, he uses his prologues as declarations of the author's personal stance: he explains the relation to the Greek originals he has used and responds to criticisms by his opponents on questions of his poetics. It is evident that this new type of prologue presupposes an audience that is more advanced and attuned to problems of taste and technique, an audience that is certainly smaller and more select.

Terence as poet-philologist

This use of the prologue brings Terence closer to such figures as Ennius, Accius, and Lucilius, who in their practice of literature always give more room to moments of critical and poetic reflection, approximating thus to the Alexandrian ideal of the poet-philologist. Not by chance does Terence tend to emphasize his distance from the "old" literary generation, which includes the comic poets around Plautus and Caecilius Statius. The principal opponent, whom Terence refers to indirectly in his prologues, is known to us from other sources to be a minor comic poet, Luscius of Lanuvium.

Contaminatio

In the prologue to the *Andria* Terence rebuts the charge of *contaminare fabulas* (v. 16), that is, so it seems, of ruining his Greek originals by creating inappropriate mixtures, hybrids made up from different texts (hence modern scholars have adopted the term "contamination" to indicate in general the technique of crossing different literary models in a single text). He emphasizes that even the respected Naevius, Plautus, and Ennius did the same with their Greek originals. Thus, for instance, the first scene of the *Andria* is drawn from another comedy of Menander, the *Perinthia,* where in fact, as we learn from Donatus, Terence replaced a dialogue between husband and wife with a dialogue between master and slave. One can see here how contamination was not a mechanical transposition.

The fabula stataria

The notion comes up again in the prologue of the *Heautontimoroumenos,* where Terence contrasts a kind of static comedy *(stataria)* with a comedy full of effects and lively with action (called *motoria* in Donatus's commentary). What is rejected is essentially the popular farce of the Plautine kind, its scenes enlivened with pursuits and quarrels and figures who amount to caricatures—the runaway slave, the capricious slave, the voracious parasite. It is clear that Terence contrasted with this animated style an ideal of an art that was more thoughtful and sensitive to nuance and also more realistic, the sort that based its dramatic action on dialogue, not on stage activity and uproar.

The originality of Terence

It is difficult for us to check Terence's programmatic statements about his use of the Greek models (adaptations, contaminations, etc.) against his practice, since only meager, accidental fragments have come down to us from his originals, for example, the texts of Menander cited as sources in his own prologues. It is thus difficult to analyze the problem of originality definitively. What we can tell is that Terence sticks quite faithfully to the line of the Menandrian plots, without ever failing to amplify the interests that touch him most. This brings us to the contents of his art: the characters and the problems of a "bourgeois" humanity.

4. THEMES AND LITERARY SUCCESS OF TERENCE'S COMEDIES

Greek philanthropia *and Roman* humanitas

We have seen that the principal defects of which Terence stands accused—his *virtus comica* lacks *vis* ("spirit" or "energy"), according to Julius Caesar's epigram—depend on a conscious choice that the poet made. Terence sacrifices the richness of verbal invention and the impromptu comic brilliance that were traditional in the *palliata.* Instead, his characters are deeper and are revealed as such in the course of the plot; the *Hecyra,* for example, brings on stage a courtesan who is unusually generous and self-sacrificing; the *Heautontimoroumenos* tells of a man who punishes himself and removes himself from society on account of the misunderstandings between himself and his son (we find in this comedy the famous remark *homo sum: humani nihil a me alienum puto,* "I am a man; nothing pertaining to mankind do I regard as foreign to me," which came to embody the classical ideal of *humanitas*); the *Adelphoe* explores the father-son relationship through the contrast between two educators, the liberal Micio and the severe Demea. The Latin *palliata,* by its very nature, had always been anchored in family situations; its fixed types were the dissolute young man in love and the old father who is tricked. But in Terence these relations become truly human relations, viewed in their full complexity and taken seriously. This understanding on Terence's part results both from a close adherence to his Menandrian model and from the currency of Greek humanistic ideals in the advanced circles of contemporary Rome. Hence the appearance of a key concept like *humanitas,* which is influenced by the Greek *philanthropia,* and which obviously does not represent some isolated idea of Terence's own but rather is in harmony with the culture of the Scipionic age. In short, various strands of Greek thought meet in the concept of *humanitas*—"to recognize and respect the man in every man," as Alfonso Traina has put it—but what is typically Roman is the constructive and optimistic synthesis of this ideal, inspired by an energetic, pragmatic attitude.

"Plautinizing" Terence

It is surely no accident that the comedy by Terence that had the greatest immediate success, the *Eunuchus,* is the one in which these psychological and humanistic themes are dealt with the least. At the same time the play is Terence's most successful attempt at Plautine comedy: it includes a disguise (a young man pretends to be a eunuch in order to have charge of his beloved) and a burlesque, Plautine braggart soldier. The remarkable nature of this text shows that Terence too had purely comic and dramaturgic goals, which criticism has often undervalued.

Antiquity

Among his contemporaries, to be sure, Terence was less than entirely successful as a playwright. His *Hecyra* was certainly a failure on the stage, and in the second century B.C. Volcacius Sedigitus ranked him only in sixth place after such minor authors as Licinius Imbrex and Marcus Atilius. Later, however, his educational tendencies, his enlightened humanism, his restrained moderation, and his lucid Latin made him one of the most consistently popular and influential school authors in the whole Western literary tradition.

At least four of Terence's comedies (*Andria, Eunuchus, Heautontimoroumenos,* and *Phormio*) were staged a second time between 146 and 134 B.C., and Varro and Horace testify that he was still being performed in theaters of the late Republic. But his vitality as a stage author is not likely to have survived for too much longer: the stage directions in ancient commentaries attest school recitations rather than theatrical productions, and the illustrations in one family of manuscripts dating to the fifth century are probably based upon the scene headings in the manuscripts themselves. It was as the author of a schoolbook, rather than on stage, that Terence survived and flourished. His style, the language of urbane, cultured circles, was appreciated both by Cicero, who admired his lexical refinement *(lecto sermone)*, his sophistication *(come loquens)*, and the pleasure his speeches inspired *(omnia dulcia dicens)*, and by Caesar, who praised him as a lover of linguistic purity *(puri sermonis amator)* but criticized his lack of comic vitality *(vis)* and called him a "pint-sized Menander" *(dimidiatus Menander)*. At the end of the first century A.D., Quintilian recommended the study of his *scripta elegantissima* to the aspiring orator. Like all school authors, Terence attracted many ancient scholars. We know of an edition by Probus in the first century A.D. and of three or four commentaries (Aemilius Asper, Helenius Acron, perhaps Arruntius Celsus, Euanthius) before Aelius Donatus compiled his great literary commentary around the middle of the fourth century (this is preserved, as is another, rhetorical one by Eugraphius). In late antiquity, at the same time that pagan scholars were explaining Terence's language to students who found it ever more difficult, Christian authors were recommending Terence for his humane content. Liberius, bishop of Rome in the mid-fourth century, quoted the *Heautontimoroumenos* in a speech delivered to Ambrose's sister on her becoming a nun; and a generation later Augustine praised Terence for his ethical values. At the end of antiquity an otherwise unknown Calliopius revised and corrected his text.

Terence and the schools

Terence's central role in school curricula helps explain his extraordinarily wide dissemination in late antiquity (one complete manuscript from the fourth–fifth centuries and fragments of three more survive) and the Middle Ages (there are 650 manuscripts written after 800, and numerous medieval commentaries were devoted to him). In the ninth century he seems to have been most read in France; Corbie is likely to have been an important center. A century later, Roswitha, a nun in the German monastery of Gandersheim, wrote six comedies in rhythmic prose, modeled on Terence's comedies and designed to replace him for a Christian audience. She provided edifying plots in which virtue always triumphed in a happy but nonetheless thoroughly moral ending. In the twelfth century, a genre of pseudo-Terentian satirical dramas (e.g., the *Pamphilus*) became popular. Dante quotes him, but perhaps through the mediation of Cicero. While the Middle Ages were quite interested in the sentiments Terence's characters expressed, they ignored or misunderstood the meters in which those sentiments were couched. Towards the end of the thirteenth century, Hugo of Tremberg, like most medieval scribes apparently, thought Terence wrote in prose (although Rufinus and Priscian had explained his meters long ago). It was not until the next century that attempts to analyze the true nature of Terence's meters began.

Renaissance

Petrarch studied Terence and wrote a biography of him. And starting with Boccaccio, whose annotated manuscript of Terence is preserved in Florence, the playwright became enormously popular and was not only widely copied but also widely understood. The first generations of humanists may have enjoyed Plautus's robust vitality, but at least explicitly, they much preferred Terence's fine diction and pedagogical earnestness, and they used the *Andria* as the central example for dramatic theory until Aristotle's *Poetics* came to dominate the field. For several generations, translations and poetic adaptations brought Terence's works back to the stage, for the first time after a lapse of perhaps fifteen centuries. The *Andria* was produced in Florence in 1476—the first production of any play of Terence's since antiquity. Ariosto's translations of some of the comedies for the theater of the Estense family have been lost, but Machiavelli's translation of the *Andria* has been preserved. As early as 1499, Grüninger's complete translation into German prose appeared. (The first translation of any work of Terence's into German, Hans Nythart's version of the *Eunuchus,* had appeared in 1486; by comparison, the earliest German translation of Plautus was not published until 1511.) In the course of the next century Terence's works became widely available in French, English, and Spanish. In the fifteenth century, most humanists who wrote comedies in Latin, such as Reuchlin's *Henno* (1497), took as a model Terence rather than Plautus. In the sixteenth century, the *Phormio* was performed in Italy with a prologue written by Muretus. In the seventeenth century, Molière was one of Terence's most devoted admirers and imitators. Nevertheless, the school was still Terence's natural home. The emphasis, of course, was usually upon Terence's *sermo purus.* Already at the end of the fifteenth century a phrase book, entitled *Vulgaria Terentii,* was compiled from Terence's plays; and in 1566 the rules of the Görlitz school required the students to imitate Cicero when they wrote and Terence when they spoke. But Luther and others emphasized the formative moral effect of Terence's comedies upon the child. Nevertheless, even in the schools his fortunes were not entirely untroubled. In the mid-sixteenth century his plays were banned from Jesuit schools because of their emphasis upon illicit love, after a compromise solution, in which they were rewritten so as to revolve around pure conjugal love, was rejected as not being drastic enough.

Modern period   Despite—or because of—his popularity as a school author, Terence's linguistic clarity meant that few major Renaissance scholars, with the exception of Erasmus, bothered to edit him. A milestone in the scholarly study of Terence was set by Richard Bentley's edition (1726), which paved the way for the modern understanding of the poet's meters and corrected the text, mainly for metrical reasons, in more than a thousand passages. Since then, in comparison with Plautus he has languished both on stage and in scholarship—but not in the classroom, where he continued to teach European children manners and Latin through the nineteenth century.

BIBLIOGRAPHY

The standard editions are those of R. Kauer and W. M. Lindsay (Oxford 1926, ed. 2 rev. O. Skutsch 1958) and J. Marouzeau (3 vols., Paris 1942–49, with French translation). There is a Loeb edition with English translation by J. Sargeaunt (Cambridge, Mass. 1912).

Terence is well served by English commentaries, notably those on *Andria* by G. P. Shipp (Melbourne 1960), on *Heautontimoroumenos* by A. J. Brothers (Warmington 1988), on *Phormio* by R. M. Martin (London 1959), on *Hecyra* by T. F. Carney (Pretoria 1963) and S. Ireland (Warminster 1990), and on *Adelphoe* by R. M. Martin (Cambridge 1976) and A. S. Gratwick (Warminster 1987). In German, see K. I. Lietzmann's commentary on *Heautontimoroumenos* (Münster 1974) and the older but still useful commentaries on *Phormio* by K. Dziatzko and E. Hauler (Berlin 1913) and on *Adelphoe* by K. Dziatzko and R. Kauer (Berlin 1921). There is no modern commentary on *Eunuchus,* but one is in preparation by P.G.McM. Brown; at present there is only the older French edition by P. Fabia (Paris 1895).

There is a very basic but useful introduction by W. G. Forehand, *Terence* (Boston 1985). Other studies in English include G. Norwood, *The Art of Terence* (Oxford 1923), and S. M. Goldberg, *Understanding Terence* (Princeton 1986, with bibliography). On comedy in general, see G. E. Duckworth, *The Nature of Roman Comedy: A Study in Popular Entertainment* (Princeton 1952), F. H. Sandbach, *The Comic Theatre of Greece and Rome* (London 1977), J. Wright, *Dancing in Chains: The Stylistic Unity of the Comoedia Palliata* (Rome 1974), E. Segal, *Roman Laughter,* ed. 2 (New York, 1987), and R. L. Hunter, *The New Comedy of Greece and Rome* (Cambridge 1985); see also W. Ludwig, "The Originality of Terence and His Greek Models," *GRBS* 9 (1968) 169–82. In other languages, note esp. H. Haffter, *Terenz und seine künstlerische Eigenart* (Darmstadt 1967), translated into Italian with additional notes by D. Nardo as *Terenzio e la sua personalità artistica* (Rome 1969), B. A. Taladoire, *Térence: Un Théâtre de la jeunesse* (Paris 1972), K. Büchner, *Das Theater des Terenz* (Heidelberg 1974), and the discussion of Terentian style in A. Traina, *Vortit barbare: Le traduzioni poetiche da Livio Andronico a Cicerone* (Rome 1970) 167–79 and *Forma e Suono* (Rome 1977) 181–200. A comprehensive bibliography is G. Cupaiuolo, *Bibliografia terenziana (1470–1983)* (Naples 1985).

The important ancient commentary of Aelius Donatus was edited by P. Wessner in three volumes (Leipzig 1902–8): see G. B. Waldrop, "Donatus, the Interpreter of Virgil and Terence," *HSCP* 35 (1927) 75–142, and L. Holtz, *Donat et la tradition de l'enseignement grammatical* (Paris 1981) 15–36. See also *Scholia Terentiana,* ed. F. Schlee (Leipzig 1893), and *The Scholia Bembina in Terentium,* ed. J. F. Mountford (Liverpool 1934). On Terence's later *fortuna* there is again a short survey in G. E. Duckworth, *The Nature of Roman Comedy: A Study in Popular Entertainment* (Princeton 1952) 396–433.

The Development of Tragedy: Pacuvius and Accius

I. PACUVIUS

Son of a sister of Ennius, Marcus Pacuvius was born in 220 B.C. at Brundisium, therefore in a Greco-Oscan cultural area. A citizen of free birth and a relative of Rome's most illustrious poet, he lived a life of social respectability at Rome. He was also known as a painter, one of the first Roman men of rank to practice this art (we have seen, on p. 69, how Fabius Pictor owed his cognomen to the painting activity of one of his ancestors). He was certainly in contact with persons from the Scipionic circle, though we do not know how close this connection was. He died at Tarentum in 130 B.C. or slightly before.

Pacuvius's works were exclusively tragic (we have vague notices that he composed satiric works). He wrote relatively little, if his longevity is taken into account and if his activity is compared with that of Ennius or Accius. We have 12 certain titles of *cothurnatae* and 365 fragments comprising about 450 verses.

The following are the tragedies most well documented and well known in antiquity:

Antiope, the myth of Antiope, the mother saved by Amphion and Zethus, the twin boys she had by Jupiter.

Armorum Iudicium, the contest between Ajax and Ulysses over the arms of Achilles.

Chryses, named for the famous priest of Apollo in the *Iliad.* In this tragedy Orestes and Pylades held a contest to determine which would show greater nobility in the face of death.

Dulorestes, "Orestes the Slave," that is, Orestes disguised as a slave in order to avenge his father Agamemnon the more easily, which he does by slaying his father's assassins, his mother Clytemestra and Aegisthus.

Hermiona, the drama of Hermione, daughter of Helen and Menelaus, given in marriage to Neoptolemus after having been betrothed, or already married, to Orestes (the myth is retold by Ovid in the eighteenth of the *Heroides,* the letter of Hermione to Orestes).

Iliona, in which Ilione, Priam's eldest daughter, married to Polymestor, the fierce king of Thrace, exchanges her brother Polydorus, who had been entrusted to her as an infant by her father Priam, and Diphilus, the son she had by Polymestor. Polymestor, bribed by the Greeks, kills his own son thinking he is killing Priam's.

Niptra, "The Bath." As in book 19 of the *Odyssey,* the old nurse washes the feet of Ulysses, who has returned to Ithaca as an unknown stranger. Telegonus, the son of Ulysses and Circe, having come to Ithaca in search of his father, wounds him mortally before recognizing him.

Teucer, in which Teucer is punished with exile by his father Telamon for having returned home to Salamis (an island opposite Athens) without his brother Ajax.

The other titles are *Atalanta, Medus, Pentheus,* and *Periboea.*

Pacuvius also wrote a *praetexta,* the *Paullus,* which celebrated Lucius Aemilius Paullus, the victor of Pydna, in 168 B.C. The date of performance is unknown, and only four verses remain.

SOURCES   Notices scattered in authors of the Republic and the Empire. In general Pacuvius is regarded as holding first place, or second after Accius, among the Roman tragedians. His style was heavily criticized by the satiric poet Lucilius (see p. 115) and later too: he was branded as contorted, bombastic, and reckless with neologisms. Cicero, however, judged him the greatest of the Latin tragic poets.

2. ACCIUS

LIFE   Born at Pesaro (Pisaurum) in 170 B.C. to freedmen parents, Accius made his mark at Rome as a tragic author beginning in 140 or 139, and thus was for a short while in competition with the aged Pacuvius. Around 135 he made an educational trip to Pergamum in Asia. From 120 he is an eminent figure in the *collegium poetarum* and is at the height of his fame as an author. He was vehemently attacked by the satiric poet Lucilius, his contemporary. He died between 90 and 80. Anecdotes portray him as a proud old man who, among other things, although he was not particularly tall, expected a large statue to be erected in the *collegium poetarum.*

WORKS   Accius is distinguished as the most prolific Latin writer of tragedies: we have more than forty titles of *cothurnatae* and around seven hundred lines of fragments. Some of the titles are: *Armorum Iudicium* (attested for Pacuvius too), *Astyanax, Atreus, Bacchae* ("The Bacchants"), *Epinausimache* ("The Battle on the Ships"), *Hecuba, Medea, Melanippus, Myrmidones, Nyctegresia* ("The Night Watch," from an episode of the *Iliad*), *Philocteta, Phoenissae, Telephus, Tereus, Thebes, Troades* ("The Trojan Women"). There are in addition two *praetextae.* The *Brutus,* it seems, told the story of Junius Brutus, head of the revolt against the tyrannical Tarquins. As is typical of the *praetexta,* this remote story had a celebratory connection with the present: a descendant of Brutus, Decimus Junius Brutus, triumphed over the Callaeci, a Spanish people, in 136 B.C. The *Decius* or *Aeneadae* probably dealt with the noble sacrifice of Publius Decius Mus in the battle of Sentinum (295 B.C.). The title *Aeneadae* is important, since it stresses the descent of the Romans from Aeneas, the myth of Aeneas being ever popular.

Unlike Pacuvius, who, to be sure, may also have written satires, Accius was not solely a tragic poet. His remaining works make him resemble rather the figure of the poet-philologist of which we spoke in connection with Ennius (see p. 81).

Little is known about Accius's learned works, but some notices appear particularly interesting. The *Didascalica,* for instance, in at least nine books, seem to have been composed in a mixture of prose and verse, like the Menippean satires of Varro, who in fact dedicated to the aged Accius his first grammatical work, the *De Antiquitate Litterarum.* It was probably in the *Didascalica* that Accius proposed a series of spelling reforms based on the principles of analogy (see p. 124).

We also have notice of other works by Accius and other interests: a *Sota-dicorum Liber* of his is referred to, which would once again link him to Ennius, as would his *Annales* (at least twenty-seven books, in hexameters of course), even if that was perhaps not so much an epic poem as a poetic calendar of the sort that Ovid's *Fasti* was to be.

One can only guess about the contents of the *Pragmatica,* in at least two books. We have a trochaic septenarius from it; perhaps it too dealt with literary critical questions. The *Parerga,* in iambic senarii, is probably a georgic inspired by Hesiod's *Erga,* and perhaps the *Praxidicus* referred to by Pliny the Elder also dealt with agriculture.

SOURCES

The situation is similar to that of Pacuvius, with whom he is often linked. His philological activity left considerable traces, in Varro, for example.

3. THE DEVELOPMENT OF TRAGEDY

Pacuvius and Accius as continuators of Ennius

Our presentation of Ennius spotlights the *Annals* at the expense of what was responsible, almost at once, for his greatest claim to literary distinction, namely, his development of a tragic poetry that increasingly deserved to be put beside the Greek classics. The example of Ennius as tragedian was picked up and developed by the two major tragedians of the second century B.C., Pacuvius and Accius. The "flourishings" of the two are placed, respectively, in the Scipionic age and in the age of the Gracchi and Marius. The period covered by the theatrical activity of these two writers was extensive; born fifty years apart, both were quite long-lived. Pacuvius, born in 220, could have known Andronicus and Naevius, and Accius, still alive after 90, had among his listeners the young Cicero! The tragedies of Pacuvius and Accius aroused interest at once and continued to be performed at least to the end of the Augustan age; and their influence is felt in poets of very different taste and tendency, such as Virgil, Ovid, and even Seneca the Younger.

The titles of the tragedies confirm that still in this period Roman tragedy always has Greek originals to which it can be referred explicitly. (There are a few possible exceptions; for example, some think that Accius's *Epinausimache* was based directly on Homer, as Greek models had been in the time of Aeschylus. Moreover, in this period Latin models are superimposed upon Greek, since tragedy by now has its own native tradition; and the *praetexta* continues to treat specifically Roman themes and events in tragic language.) Nonetheless, it becomes clear, in studying the remaining fragments, that Pacuvius and Accius rework the chosen original with complete independence. We see this better when we can compare the preserved Greek originals, for example, the fragments of Accius's *Bacchae* with Euripides' *Bacchae*. It is natural to think that the practice of *contaminatio* applied to this literary genre as well; the obvious literary critical self-consciousness shown by Terence in his prologues (see pp. 98 f.) should surely have had its equivalent in these sophisticated tragedies. But Pacuvius and Accius add something quite different to their reworkings. When these poets deal with religious, political, moral, or philosophical themes, they use the tragic myths freely and touch upon themes and problems felt in contemporary Roman society. In this regard they are no longer bound by the Greek models, even though the work of Euripides, the most frequent model in early Roman tragedy, would have furnished them with an example of how one might modernize the world of tragedy.

These authors live in a society full of contrasts and new ideological and cultural ferments. When the old myths of Attic tragedy are brought into contact with this environment, they offer new possibilities and take on contemporary meanings. For instance, the theme of tyrannicide, which is frequent in Attic tragedy, became current again in republican Rome, which was riven by deep contrasts between political factions and by the growth of increasingly uncontrollable personal powers. Another instance of revitalization is provided by religious subjects and philosophical debates. The Roman culture of the day had become richly layered, embracing the religious cults of the state, the traditions of Italian popular religion, the new cults from Greece and the Orient (some permitted, some suppressed), and finally the spread of new forms of thought and morality, as seen, for instance, in the increasing influence of Stoicism and Epicureanism. Here, too, tragedy lent itself to enacting ideological contradictions and debates over ideas.

The richness of intellectual content goes along with an increasing taste for pathos and for the novelistic, which certainly contributed to the popular success of the tragedies. Their plots often dwell upon novelistic episodes: shipwrecks, ghosts, dreams, prodigies, madness, deceptions and ambiguities, cruelty of every type, betrayals, and portentous incidents. The fragments we have display a particular taste for the picturesque and the horrible. In this sense Pacuvius and Accius are the principal exponents of a line of anti-classicism that runs through Roman literature and will continue to surface down through Augustan classicism. Blood and obsession, some what as in Elizabethan drama, are among the most fashionable elements in the taste for spectacles. Pacuvius, who was also a painter, is particularly distinguished for the visual quality of his descriptions.

The contribution of rhetoric

Another feature in which second-century tragedy is tied to the contemporary culture is the increasing importance of rhetoric. Roman eloquence in this period undergoes an unprecedented development; the refinements of contemporary Greek rhetoric are constantly becoming better assimilated. In particular, the Asianic school of rhetoric (see p. 120) becomes more and more important. Accius, who visited Pergamum, must have been especially influenced by it. The tragedies, woven out of speeches, which are aimed at arousing and persuading or which are opposed in true debates, offered ample room to the influence of this technique of discourse.

Linguistic experimentation

On the level of style both Pacuvius and Accius are often criticized for their "impure" Latin: strained constructions, bold neologisms, plays on words. These impurities of style, regarded as such from the classical point of view of Cicero or Horace, are the result, not of negligence, of course, but of a tendency towards experimentation that extends back to Ennius. Accius was, even more than Ennius, a poet-philologist, interested in contemporary linguistics and rhetoric. Many *recherché* features and linguistic oddities have led to the preservation of the fragments we have, which are cited by grammarians precisely because of the presence of singular forms and words; this may falsify our picture of these authors. A typical example of linguistic experimentation is the Pacuvian fragment *Nerei repandirostrum incurvicervicum pecus,* a description of dolphins, "the herd of Nereus, bent-snouted and curved-neck." The two compounds, which will not be repeated in the Latin literary tradition, are a tryout of a linguistic structure with few parallels in Latin: {verbal root + noun}, {adjective + noun}. We can document, moreover, linguistic innovations of Pacuvius and Accius that later did enter into the large pool of poetic language in the periods of Caesar and Augustus. These two poets, too, contributed to the development of an increasingly rich and specialized poetic language such as could compete better with the resources of Greek.

The social elevation of the tragedian

The most important consequence of the careers of Pacuvius and Accius may have been that tragedy rose in class and tone. While the genre enjoyed popular success, it became more and more an activity for gentlemen. Accius, for example, is not a mere actor such as Plautus had been, a man living exclusively from his scripts: he is a grammarian, a theoretician of literature, the respected president of a society of select writers. Not surprisingly, in the history of literature between the Gracchi and Augustus the writing of tragedies will become a typical private occupation for educated men, often illustrious politicians. Tragedies will be composed by persons such as Julius Caesar Strabo, Caesar's great-uncle, Varius Rufus, Asinius Pollio, and even, though apparently with very modest success, Augustus himself. It is not fortuitous that Julius Caesar Strabo and his contemporary Gaius Titius are mentioned by Cicero in the *Brutus* as excellent orators and, at the same time, powerful authors of tragedies. Cicero's brother, an officer in the Gallic campaign of 54 B.C., writes a tragedy during a two-week leave. The living relation with the stage is breaking down.

Decline of the tragic genre

In the meantime, after Lucilius's polemics against Accius and Pacuvius, the avant-garde poets abandon the tragic genre. In the period of Catullus and the *Bucolics* poetic genres which are less thundering, more intimate and personal, come to be preferred. Not until Seneca, or rather not until Ovid, whose *Medea* seems to have been a masterpiece, will Roman tragedy again have moments of great inspiration, though it still continues to be performed. Meanwhile, the stage will be busy more and more with successful farces, mimes, and pantomimes.

BIBLIOGRAPHY

For the fragments of Pacuvius and Accius, see O. Ribbeck, *Scaenicae Romanorum Poesis Fragmenta,* 2 vols. (ed. 2 Leipzig 1871–73, reprint Hildesheim 1962; ed. 3 1897–98), supplemented by W. Morel, *Fragmenta poetarum latinorum epicorum et lyricorum praeter Ennium et Lucilium* (Leipzig 1927, reprint 1963, rev. K. Büchner, Leipzig 1982, with bibliography), for the nondramatic fragments of Accius. They are both included in volume 2 of E. H. Warmington's *Remains of Old Latin* (4 vols. London 1935–40). There are recent Italian editions of Pacuvius by G. D'Anna (Rome 1967) and of Accius by V. D'Antò (Lecce 1980).

Although there has been considerable work on points of detail, there is no comprehensive modern treatment of either Pacuvius or Accius. In English there is almost nothing beyond W. Beare, *The Roman Stage* (ed. 3 London 1964) 79–84, 119–27. For recent work in other languages see A. de Rosalia in *BollStudLat* 19 (1989) 119–44.

The Development of Epic Poetry: From Ennius to Virgil

Feeble survival of epic after Ennius

In the period that extends from the age of the Scipios to the age of Caesar, epic writing appears, on the basis of the very few fragments left, to be completely dominated by the example of Ennius. The influence of the *Annals* must have been felt at once. Shortly after Ennius, someone recast in hexameters the *Odyssey* of Livius Andronicus. In the wake of Ennius's achievements and his polemics against his predecessors, the Saturnian is now definitely out of date. Accius gives the title *Annales* to a hexameter poem of his; the subject is completely obscure to us, but the title has a clear programmatic link to Ennius. *Annales* is again the title chosen by Aulus Furius Antias, from the first half of the first century, who seems to have sung Rome's wars against the Cimbri, and Catullus would fiercely attack the *Annales* of a certain Volusius (36.1, 95.7–8). It is clear that the title indicated a type of historical epic that celebrated military events: the narration often may well have been less extensive than Ennius's, limited to particular periods, to military campaigns in which the triumphator was from time to time celebrated as protagonist. (Annalistic historiography appears to have had a very similar development.) This tendency was already shared by the *Bellum Histricum* composed by a certain Hostius, who appears to be a contemporary of Accius: in the title a certain Naevian influence clearly persists. The genre would continue to be practiced without interruption. Historical poems would be composed by Cicero (*De Consulatu Suo,* an unusual instance of epic self-celebration), by Furius Bibaculus, and, if he is a person different from the preceding, by the Furius who wrote a poem on Caesar's feats in Gaul, as well as by Varro of Atax, author of, among other things, a *Bellum Sequanicum.* Following the evidence of indirect testimony, it would be possible to reconstruct a continuous series of epic poems on historical subjects extending from Ennius to Lucan. This celebratory epic genre is often known to us from polemics and parodies: Catullus attacks Volusius, Horace ridicules a certain Alpinus (*Satires* 1.10.36).

The epic and Varro of Atax

The exponents of the new schools of poetry regard this genre as a static survival, dusty and empty. Still, we ought not to think that the historical epic continued the old Ennian formula without ever giving it fresh life. A poet such as Varro of Atax, for example, is a refined stylist, close to the circle of neoterics and versed in Alexandrian models. He certainly must have brought to the writing of historical epic new requirements of taste and a greater concern for form. The genre continued to live—and survived even into the *Aeneid,* which struck out in a completely different direction—because it was sustained by precise needs.

The epic genre as cele-
bratory poetry

Many Romans thought that poetry was nothing but the celebration of heroic deeds in verse; the many illustrious patrons must have encouraged these exercises, which narrated the recent undertakings of generals who were also political leaders—all in Homeric-Ennian style. (One wonders how these poets resolved the problem of the divine apparatus, which was traditional from Homer on. We have the impression that Naevius and Ennius tended to concentrate these divine interventions in the historically most remote part of their account. The reason is obvious: up to what point would the readers have accepted a supernatural dimension in the telling of recent or contemporary events? Silius Italicus, for instance, who is far removed from the facts he describes, would not hesitate to create such a scene. This poetic problem would become current again in the period of Lucan and Silius Italicus; Eumolpus discusses it in Petronius's *Satyricon,* chaps. 118 ff.) However that may be, historical epic by an easy transition would adapt itself to the exploits of the emperors: the battle of Actium, the deeds of Domitian, which Statius exalted, and so forth. In the meantime the style was adjusted to the literary models that prevailed at different moments, from Ennius to Virgil and on to Ovid and Statius. Historical epic poetry continues to be the strongest link between literature and propaganda, between literature and power.

Lucilius

The date of Lucilius's death is certain, 102 B.C., but the date of his birth is a thorny problem. Jerome, our source, says that Lucilius died at the age of forty-six. But if Lucilius was born in 148, it becomes difficult to accept other details that are known of his biography: when working in the headquarters of Scipio Aemilianus during the siege of Numantia, he would have been barely fifteen years old, and his literary precocity would have been extraordinary; moreover, it is incomprehensible how Horace could refer to Lucilius as an "old man" (senex, in Satires 2.1.34). A plausible alternative explanation is that Jerome, misled by nearly homonymous consuls in office in 148 and 180 B.C., has confused 180 with 148; this would make Lucilius nearly a contemporary of Terence. Others, on the basis of creditable arguments, propose an intermediate date, 168/167 B.C., which in the abstract would seem more probable.

Lucilius belonged to a distinguished, prosperous family originally from Suessa Aurunca in northern Campania. The years of his youth are certainly linked to the Scipionic circle. We are ill-informed about the latter period of his life. He is the first man of letters of good family to lead the life of a writer, deliberately removed from public offices and public life.

Thirty books of satires, of which we possess fragments, almost all short, amounting to around thirteen hundred verses.

The edition of Lucilius circulating in the first century B.C., which is attributed to the grammarian Valerius Cato, included: books 1–21, all in dactylic hexameters; 22–25, perhaps in elegiac couplets; 26–30, in iambic and trochaic meters (the meter of Latin comedy) as well as hexameters. This order was metrical and did not coincide with the chronological order of composition. It is generally assumed that Lucilius around 130 B.C. published a first collection of five books, the ones we know, in their transmission through the grammarians, as 26–30.

In that case Lucilius turned more and more towards the hexameter; this is probably the sign of an ironic challenge, in that everyday material and colloquial, often popular diction needed to be adapted to the heroic meter. From Horace onwards the hexameter would become the sole verse pre-

scribed for satire. The books may have consisted either of single compositions or of shorter poetic units. It is not certain that the title *Saturae* goes
back to Lucilius himself, but Horace uses the term *satura* in a programmatic context to designate the genre of poetry begun by Lucilius. In the
fragments that are left Lucilius calls his compositions *poemata* or *sermones*
(rather, *ludus ac sermones,* "joking chats"), and it has been reasonably supposed that the original title of Lucilius's work was Greek, *schedia* ("improvisations").

SOURCES   There are many citations in grammarians, metricians, and late commentators, especially in Nonius Marcellus, a grammarian of the fourth century
A.D., author of the *De Compendiosa Doctrina,* a lexicon of republican Latin.
There are prominent references in the works of Horace (see esp. *Satires*
1.4.1 ff., 1.10.53 ff., 2.1.62 ff.).

Lucilius was read with avid interest even under the Empire (Quintilian
10.1.93). The survival of numerous fragments is explained by the large
number of very rare and difficult words in his work, which provided much
material for grammarians from the second to fifth centuries A.D.

LUCILIUS AND SATIRE

Lucilius's relation to
the Scipionic circle

The work of Lucilius has its roots in the cultural background that had
been Terence's: the great figures of the Scipionic party, Scipio Aemilianus
and Laelius, whom Terence had known as young men, became in their maturity the patrons of the satiric poet. Lucilius's social position, however, is
quite different from that of the African freedman Terence, as is the patronage the Scipionic setting provides for him. Independence of judgment, zeal
in controversy, and curiosity about contemporary life—qualities that the
tradition recognizes in him—suit the image of a cultivated, prosperous
eques who does not live from his own literary work. His belonging to the
rich provincial aristocracy and his position in the Scipionic circle make it
possible for him to launch attacks freely against some of the most distinguished men in contemporary Rome.

Etymology of satura:
the pursuit of variety

The origins of the genre the Romans call *satura* are uncertain and were
mysterious even for the learned. The connection with Greek *satyros,* "satyr,"
is utterly false, even though ancient: satire in origin seems to have nothing
to do either with satyrs or with the Greek comic theater, in which the satyrs
play an important role. It is certain that *satura lanx* indicated in early Rome
a mixed dish of first offerings that was presented to the gods; hence a gastronomic specialty, such as a "mixed salad," and a form of judicial procedure called *lex per saturam,* when laws on different subjects were joined in
a single legislative enactment. (The evidence of Livy on the existence of a
dramatic genre called *satura* in the third century is puzzling and perhaps
misleading [see p. 24].) On the basis of this evidence it is likely that the
sense of "mixture and variety" was the original one and that it was felt also
in the literary employment of the term. The name, then, is not Greek (as

the Atellan also is not, whereas nearly all the other literary genres at Rome have Greek names). Quintilian contrasts satire with the other genres: *satura quidem tota nostra est* (10.1.93), "satire is a completely Roman genre." The attempts of the satiric poets themselves, especially Horace, to create a retrospective genealogy in Greece, for example, referring to the mordant quality of fifth-century Attic comedy (Aristophanes) or drawing inspiration from Callimachus's *Iambs*, do not affect this basic fact. However many Greek cultural contributions satire had received along the way—and the open structure of the genre itself encouraged grafting and mixing—the original impulse is specifically Roman.

Satire as personal space

This impulse may perhaps be understood, here at the beginnings of satire, as the search for a literary genre suitable for conveying the author's personal voice. If we compare the period of Ennius, Latin literature does seem already quite developed by then, but we notice that none of the standard poetic genres—epic, tragedy, comedy—provides a space for direct expression, in which the poet can reflect his relation to himself and to contemporary reality. Yet the example of the Alexandrians, Callimachus in particular, had shown how one could create a poetry outside the epic and dramatic canons. Callimachus throws into confusion the traditional divisions of the literary genres: he talks of poetry and poetics (especially his own), of popular traditions and vignettes from daily life, and at the same time he pursues an increasingly polished and refined poetic form. The esthetic principle of variety *(poikilia)* excluded the high-sounding uniformity of epic narrative.

The satires of Ennius

Variety, personal voice, and realistic thrust are characteristics that to some degree we discern also in the fragments of Ennius's satire. It comprised four or six books, each one made up of several parts in varying meter (the meters are chiefly comic iambo-trochaics but also hexameters and perhaps sotadeans). Especially varied are the subjects that we can reconstruct: a little tale of a country man and a skylark, the satiric portrait of a parasite, dialogues, a debate between Life and Death, and, especially, appearances of the poet in the first person and touches of self-portrait. It is likely that various points in the biographical tradition about Ennius derive from the autobiographical references in his own *Satires*. In this regard, too, Ennius has an important place in the development of poetic self-consciousness. We do not know, however, whether his satire already contained hints of polemic and real attacks on contemporary people. We would be inclined to look for this aggressive side of satire in Naevius, who was known for his attacks on a certain noble family, but it is not even certain that Naevius composed satires, and we know nothing about Pacuvius's satire.

The specialization of the satiric genre and the growth of a new audience

However that may be, this form of poetry, varying in meter and subject and personal in nature, that is, open to the poet's voice and to everyday realism, presented itself to Lucilius as an ideal means of expression to develop. The great historic importance of Lucilius lies in his having concentrated exclusively on the genre of satire. (Ennius, let us remember, had practiced satire as a minor genre among many other genres, subordinate to epic and drama.) The development of satire signifies also the growth of a new audience, one interested in written poetry, culturally aware, and eager for a literature that stayed close to contemporary reality. Lucilius said he desired for himself readers who were neither too much learned (*docti*) nor too little.

Themes of Lucilian satire:
a) *The parody of the* Concilium Deorum

A work in thirty books cannot be reconstructed with certainty on the basis of brief fragments cited mostly on account of their grammatical oddities. As far as we know, Lucilius dealt with a wide range of subjects. The first book contained a large-scale composition known as the *Concilium Deorum.* By means of a parody of the divine councils, which were typical of epic (as in Homer and Ennius), Lucilius attacked a certain Lentulus Lupus, a person disliked by the Scipios: the gods decided to have him die of indigestion. The mixture of literary parody and slanderous content recalls a work such as Seneca's later *Apocolocyntosis* would be. The parody, precisely because it was a joke at the expense of other, well-known literary texts, also carried implications for literary criticism. When the poet represented the gods, who were assembled to discuss wretched human affairs, as behaving according to the protocol and procedures of the Roman Senate, then the *Concilium Deorum,* once it was compared to contemporary reality, was revealed for what it was: nothing other than a common motif, a topos, belonging to high-style poetry, that is, a stylized convention of the epic manner. Lucilius's realistic poetry was intended to be an ironic response to the notion of literature as hollow conventionality.

b) *Description of a journey; gastronomy*

The third book contained the lively narrative of a journey to Sicily. (We will meet the theme of the journey again in Horace's *Satires* 1.5.) In more than one satire culinary advice was offered, just as in Horace's *Satires* 2.4 (it should not be forgotten that Ennius, the first Latin author who certainly wrote satires, was also the author of *Hedyphagetica* [see p. 76]). In book 30 a sordid banquet was described. More generally, references to gastronomy connected with the polemical theme of luxury in food recur in a number of books. In book 30 Lucilius told of a banquet organized by a parvenu, Granius, who is the literary ancestor of the more famous Nasidienus (see Horace, *Satires* 2.8) and Trimalchio.

c) *Love; literary questions*

Book 16 seems to have been dedicated to his ladylove. Lucilius thus is also a precursor of personal love poetry, a tendency we will come upon again, with increasing importance, in Catullus's epigrams and Augustan elegy. Then, too, Lucilius's disquisitions on literary problems are amply attested: judgments on questions of rhetoric and poetics and genuine literary critical and grammatical analyses. In this regard Lucilius recalls the rhetorical-grammatical culture of Accius; but Lucilius mocks the emphatic, declamatory style of Accius, and also of Pacuvius and other lofty poets. The criticism of these lofty literary genres is another important point of convergence between Lucilius and Callimachean taste and another link connecting Lucilius to neoteric poetry.

Lucilius's stylistic realism

We cannot say to what extent Lucilius's satires, in their broad chronological development, were tied to a unified program, and in any event it is dangerous to regard this poet as a sort of reformer. Even Lucilius's political engagement may have been discontinuous and changeable: his relation with the Scipionic group is evident in the first satire, but the poet survived his political patrons by many years. There can be no doubt, however, about the existence of a decidedly unified, innovative literary program, sustained by a personality with a lively nonconformity. His poetry rejects a single stylistic level and is open on all sides. It amalgamates the elevated language of epic, relived as parody; the specialized vocabularies that until then had been excluded from Latin poetry, such as technical terms from rhetoric, science, medicine, sex, gastronomy, law, and politics; and forms of everyday language, drawn from the different social strata and including an enormous number of Grecisms. From this point of view Lucilius, like Petronius, is as close to modern realism as Latin literature ever gets; he even tends to feign improvisation. The poet's criticism, with its lively humor, hits at the most diverse aspects of daily life, which are taken up in their physical and linguistic concreteness, brought to life in the light of philosophical ideals, and viewed in their contrast with reality. In this sense the satire has a certain commitment to education, intimately bound up with social criticism and nonconformity. The disharmony of Lucilius's style is certainly a deliberate choice, going back to a precise program of expression that blends together life and art.

The literary success of Lucilius
As a personal voice of the satiric genre—*ex praecordiis ecfero versum,* says a famous fragment of his, "from my heart I bring forth my poetry"—Lucilius would remain a model for all the Latin satiric poets, from Varro onwards. Against the background of early Latin poetry, his capacity for having a grasp on reality would sound especially bold and new. Horace criticizes Lucilius as a poet of his own time, on the grounds of his torrential way of writing and his lack of formal polish. He thus turns against Lucilius the precepts of the Callimachean school, which Lucilius himself had accepted, though to a different degree. Yet Horace also reveres him as the inventor of satire. At least one feature of Lucilius's legacy was inevitably lost. A certain tone of lively personal polemic, including political polemic, was linked to precise social and institutional conditions; in Rome of the Empire satire will need to find other targets. Horace feels Lucilius to be distant from him in this regard, almost as distant as the comedy of Aristophanes.

BIBLIOGRAPHY

The fundamental edition is still that of F. Marx (2 vols., Leipzig 1904–5), with Latin commentary; this is not superseded by W. Krenkel's more recent German edition (2 vols., Berlin 1969). There is a text with English translation in volume 3 of the Loeb *Remains of Old Latin,* by E. H. Warmington (4 vols. London 1935–40); the most recent text is that of F. Charpin (2 vols., Paris 1978–79), with French translation and notes.

The best English introductions are again those in general books on satire, such U. Knoche, *Roman Satire,* trans. E. S. Ramage (Bloomington 1975) 17–30, and M. Coffey, *Roman Satire* (ed. 2 Bristol 1989) 24–32 (with bibliography 282). G. C. Fiske's *Lucilius and Horace: A Study in the Classical Art of Imitation* (Madison 1920) provides much information but is fanciful in its reconstructions. On the historical context, see A. E. Astin,

Scipio Aemilianus (Oxford 1967) 294–306. In other languages, see esp. C. Cichorius, *Untersuchungen zu Lucilius* (Berlin 1908); see also W. A. Krenkel, "Zur Biographie des Lucilius," in *ANRW* 2.1 (Berlin 1972) 1240–59, W. J. Raschke, "Arma pro amico— Lucilian Satire at the Crisis of the Roman Republic," *Hermes* 115 (1987) 299–318, M. Puelma Piwonka, *Lucilius und Kallimachos* (Frankfurt am Main 1949), and I. Mariotti, *Studi luciliani* (Florence 1961). There is a German survey of scholarship by J. Christen in *ANRW* 2.1 (see above).

Politics and Culture between the Era of the Gracchi and the Sullan Restoration

I. ORATORY AND POLITICAL TENSIONS

The Gracchi

The period from the Gracchan disturbances to Sulla's domination marks the beginning of the crisis that would lead, nearly a century later, to the definitive collapse of the republican aristocracy. In 133, the year when Scipio Aemilianus took Numantia, a relative of his, Tiberius Gracchus, proposed a new agrarian law. Tiberius's intentions were basically conservative: he was moved by the shortage of men he had noticed in various parts of Italy and by the widespread poverty, and he was convinced that under such conditions it would be impossible to maintain the social order that was the backbone of the army, so he proposed to restore a part of the class of small landholders by means of new land distributions. The senatorial aristocracy, which saw in the maintenance of the great estates one of the bases of its own power, took refuge in a short-sighted defense of its own particular interests and moved to block Tiberius, to the point of bringing about his death. This was repeated in 123, when Tiberius's brother Gaius, who had also been elected to the tribunate, proposed his program again, in a broader framework. Despite the death of the Gracchi, the agrarian question was destined to remain at the center of the political and social life of the late Republic. Yet the Gracchan revolution had been shown to be powerless in the face of the political and economic difficulties. Henceforth, the solution was to be imposed by the great military commanders, leading armies of proletarians for whom the distribution of lands represented the reward for long military campaigns.

The dictatorship of Sulla

The importance of what had become almost private armies emerged in the conflicts between Marians and Sullans, which followed soon after the calamitous Social War. The Social War in turn had been triggered by the ruling class's stubborn resistance to pressure from the most influential members of the peninsula's aristocracy for participation in the government of Rome. After the repeated bloodbaths of the Social War and the civil wars, Sulla assumed the dictatorship at the end of 82, only to lay it down in 79. In between he launched a successful constitutional reform that aimed at eliminating the institutional causes of the aristocracy's weakness and that, at least in part, would endure until Caesar. It did not, however, eliminate the deeper causes of the political and social crisis that shook the Republic.

In a period marked by such bitter conflicts, oratory was, in the nature of things, destined to bloom and flourish. Unfortunately, the reputation of Cicero as the supreme Roman orator has brought about the loss of the earlier orators, except for some fragments. And yet it is to Cicero, to his *Brutus* in particular, that we owe a successful sketch of the evolution of Roman eloquence. For ease of presentation and in order to keep to reasonably intelligible chronological divisions, we mentioned the so-called "Scipionic circle" in an earlier section. But from the political point of view, resistance to the Gracchan projects was a motive behind the action of Scipio Aemilianus and his circle: the oratory of Scipio and his friend Gaius Laelius, whom Cicero celebrates in the *De Amicitia,* cannot be considered apart from the oratory of the Gracchi.

a) *Scipio, Laelius,* **and the Gracchi**

In Aemilianus's oratory Cicero recognized a *gravitas,* "solemnity," which he contrasted with the *lenitas,* the agreeably calm style, of Laelius; and yet the latter gave on the whole the impression of being more austere and old-fashioned than his friend Scipio. The social *misericordia* of the Gracchi must have introduced new notes into Roman eloquence. Nothing remains of Tiberius's speeches, but we are better informed about Gaius, the first "classic" of Roman oratory. Both brothers had received a solid education from the best Greek teachers in the house of their mother Cornelia, the daughter of Africanus Maior. Cicero notes Gaius's *ubertas,* the florid exuberance of his style, which was perhaps influenced by the Asianic manner (see below), as well as the vehemence of his delivery, which was marked by an almost Demosthenic forcefulness. In Cicero's words:

> Gaius Gracchus, a man of the highest intelligence, inflamed passion, and precocious learning. No one, Brutus, possessed a fuller and richer eloquence. . . . Roman society and literature suffered a grave loss in his untimely death. If only he had not wished to be more loyal to his brother than to his country! It would have been easy for him, with his talent, to match the glory of his father or grandfather. In eloquence I don't know that he would have had rivals, for there is grandeur in his words, wisdom in his thoughts, and weightiness in the whole of his discourse. The final touch was lacking to his works, which are begun with great mastery but not perfectly brought to completion—an orator whom the young should read before any other, I tell you, my dear Brutus, since he can not only refine their ability but also enhance it. (*Brutus* 125 f.)

b) *Antonius and* **Crassus**

The greatest orators of the following generation were Marcus Antonius and Lucius Licinius Crassus. Cicero, who had heard both in his youth, made them the protagonists of the *De Oratore,* since he judged that with them Roman eloquence had reached maturity. Antonius and Crassus belonged to the aristocratic party (Crassus, who at first had sided with the *populus,* did an abrupt about-face in 106). The former fell victim to the Marians in 87; the latter died a natural death just before the Social War flared up. Antonius's oratory appealed especially to the emotions, whereas Crassus's was more varied and contained skillfully graduated tones and effects, from the arousal of pathos to a lighter mood with a fine sense of humor, all of which it was capable of blending in an inimitable manner: his witticisms, Cicero says, could not be detached from his *gravitas*.

c) *The school of Plot-
ius Gallus and the*
Rhetorica ad Heren-
nium

In 92 Crassus held the censorship together with Gnaeus Domitius Ahenobarbus. Although relations between them were not good, the two censors agreed on an edict that ordered the closing of the school of rhetoric at Rome that had been opened by Plotius Gallus, a client of Marius. The school had democratic, pro-Gracchan tendencies: it did not demand of its students a knowledge of Greek or the payment of high fees, and thus it was accessible to young men who were not well-to-do. By closing it the censors succeeded in eliminating a center from which popular leaders well versed in the art of speaking might have come forth, and they made eloquence a monopoly of the aristocracy, which was able to afford the expensive Greek teachers of rhetoric. The teaching of Plotius Gallus's school seems to be reflected in the *Rhetorica ad Herennium,* a textbook written by an unknown author probably in the eighties (the Middle Ages attributed it to Cicero). In the work, which was to influence the young Cicero, the Gracchan and Marian tendencies are manifest. Greek textbooks provided the basis, but the academic schematization is considerably diminished by the insertion of much material drawn from Roman culture and oratory.

Asianism and Atticism

*The two types of
Asianism*

In the generation before Cicero's, the conflict of tastes and styles between Asianists and Atticists begins to take shape in Roman eloquence. Asianic eloquence was so called because it originated, so it appears, at Pergamum in Asia Minor, between the end of the fourth and the beginnings of the third century B.C. It aimed above all at pathos and musicality, relying on a florid, redundant style and on a histrionic, affected *actio*. Cicero distinguished two types of Asianism: the first seemed to aim at an uninterrupted series of pretty, refined phrases, full of metaphors and plays with words and constructed according to artificial rhythmic schemes; the second type was characterized by a swelling superabundance of colorful words. The two types obviously could be combined and were in fact combined by the rhetorician Hegesias of Magnesia. It has been claimed, as we saw, that mildly Asianic tendencies can be recognized in the oratory of Gaius Gracchus. They were more marked in Publius Sulpicius Rufus (died 88 B.C.), whom Cicero introduces among the minor figures of the *De Oratore*. But Roman Asianism was developed above all by Quintus Hortensius Hortalus, who was only nineteen years old at the time of his first display and died in 50 B.C., after a life entirely devoted to oratory. Hortensius was a rival, and later a friend, of Cicero's, on whose youthful style he exercised a profound influence.

*The Atticist reaction
and Licinius Calvus*

Only later does the Atticist current make itself known at Rome: it is the reaction of a group of young men who take sides against Cicero, the leading orator of the day, and accuse him, without too much justification, of Asianism. The Atticists were so called because they attached great value to the simple, discursive, bare style of the Attic orator Lysias. The ideal they strove for in eloquence was a clear, concise sentence structure. Among the Atticists, apart from Marcus Brutus, the future tyrannicide, Gaius Licinius Calvus (82–47 B.C.) was outstanding. The friend of Catullus, he was for a while Cicero's most threatening rival in the Forum. His eloquence was vibrant and impetuous, yet also very controlled. Quintilian praises its austere purity, which he terms *sanctitas*. Calvus carefully avoided grandiose pathos, which in Cicero's probably one-sided judgment was the symptom of excessive self-control, and this in turn was the source of the overrefined and unpopular character of Calvus's oratory.

2. THE DEVELOPMENT OF HISTORIOGRAPHY

The new historical method:
a) Sempronius Asellio

After oratory, history is the literary genre in which the political-social crisis of the Gracchan era finds its chief expression. The interest in contemporary events is joined to the attempt to establish a new historical method, one that rejects the dryness of the annalistic chronicles and prefers a rational understanding of the events, that is, a causal explanation of them that gives appropriate space to political debates as well as military campaigns. In this way the influence of Polybian rationalism begins to make itself felt upon the Romans who write history. This is particularly clear in the fragments of the proem to the history by Sempronius Asellio, a figure of the Scipionic group who took part in the war of Numantia. Asellio explicitly takes a position against annalistic historical writing: to write in which year a war began or ended and give other information of this sort is, he claims, the equivalent of writing children's stories, not a work of history. For this reason Asellio, breaking with the annalistic tradition, proposes to narrate only the events at which he was personally present and to show why and how (*demonstrare quo consilio quaque ratione*) they came about. A fragment from book 4 of Asellio's history refers to 137 B.C., and another, from book 14 (the last we know of), to 91 B.C., by which time the author must have been quite old.

b) Coelius Antipater

Some years before Asellio, Coelius Antipater had already broken with tradition, in a different way. Of plebeian origin, refined in taste, a jurist and master of eloquence, he had written sometime after 120 B.C. a historical work in seven books, which rather than repeating things *ab urbe condita* limited itself to a monographic treatment of the Second Punic War. Another important difference between Coelius Antipater and the annalists was that the former, appealing to an audience that expected pleasure as well as instruction from the narrative, did not confine himself to the dry exposition of the facts, but included fantastic and miraculous elements, tragic pathos, stories involving dreams and apparitions; the careful elaboration of his style was probably also directed at the reader's pleasure. Cicero, as can be imagined, would greatly admire Coelius Antipater, while criticizing harshly the unadorned style of Sempronius Asellio. His views were partially responsible for the success of the one, from whom we have about seventy fragments, and the near oblivion of the other.

Still, in the age of the Gracchi we also find notable historians who kept to the strictly annalistic method: Lucius Cassius Hemina, whose *Annales,* in at least four books, reached the events of 146 and seem to have found greater favor among the antiquarians than the pure historians; Lucius Calpurnius Piso Frugi, consul in 133, enemy of the Gracchi, implacable chastiser of morals (whence the name Frugi), whose *Annales,* in at least seven books, had great literary success with subsequent historians, including Livy and Dionysius of Halicarnassus; Gaius Fannius, son-in-law of Laelius and consul in 122; Sempronius Tuditanus, consul in 129, another enemy of the Gracchi, author of the ponderous *Libri Magistratuum;* Gnaeus Gellius, successful author of *Annales,* in at least thirty-three books; and Vennonius, whose name alone is left to us.

In the Sullan age annalistic writing in the strict sense (i.e., year-by-year narrative of Rome's history from its beginnings) continues with Licinius Macer, the father of the Atticist Licinius Calvus, and with Valerius Antias. The latter's *Annales* extended through at least seventy-five books, but two-thirds of it seems to have been devoted to the events of the latest decades, from Tiberius Gracchus onwards. Quintus Claudius Quadrigarius was probably a more interesting figure. Although he followed the annalistic method, he began his account of Roman history, in at least twenty-three books, not with the origins of the city, but with the Gallic burning of it and continued down to his own day. He was a lively narrator, but his syntax was monotonous in its avoidance of subordination. Perhaps for this very reason he was admired by writers of archaizing taste such as Gellius and Fronto.

Sisenna and "Tragic" Historiography

The most notable historian of the Sullan age was undoubtedly Lucius Cornelius Sisenna (ca. 120–67 B.C.). A politician of decidedly aristocratic bent, Sisenna wrote *Historiae* that dealt exclusively with contemporary events, from the Social War to the death of Sulla, devoting only a brief introduction to earlier history. In Sisenna's historical writing the figure of Sulla stood out almost like a hero; his qualities as a charismatic leader were probably also emphasized. Sisenna was keen on political events, yet in his narrative fabulous, novelistic details must have played an important role: Sisenna followed the method of "tragic" history (i.e., history full of dramatic elements), for which he went back to Clitarchus, one of the historians of Alexander the Great. Roman history from the era of the Gracchi to the era of Marius and Sulla offered abundant materials for a lively, novelistic

narrative, full of *coups de théâtre* and reversals of fortune. Sisenna's style must have matched the contents of the narrative: a bold Asianism, marked by an abundance of archaisms, the pursuit of lexical rarities, and a tendency towards overloaded colors. Cicero, who valued Sisenna, found "something puerile" in his style and mocked his frequent lexical preciosities, calling him *emendator sermonis usitati,* "improver of everyday speech." From Cicero, too, we know that Sisenna was esteemed as an orator also, but nothing is left of his speeches. A few fragments do remain, though, of his *Fabulae Milesiae,* "Milesian Tales," so called because they reworked a text by Aristides of Miletus. These were short stories of licentious character, composed in a flat but lively style, and destined to be one of the models for the tales contained in the novels of Petronius and Apuleius.

The Beginnings of Autobiography

We have already seen (see pp. 68 f.) how Latin historical writing was in general developed by members of the ruling class, but, with the exception of Cato, not by persons of high political rank, who probably looked upon the requirements of historical research and stylistic elaboration as so much time subtracted from real political action. In the age of Sulla, nonetheless, one witnesses the phenomenon of important politicians writing *commentarii* on their own life and their own political activity. These *commentarii,* perhaps sometimes little more than collections of notes, did not demand particular attention to style, and they could also serve as material for genuine historians. The authors belong to the aristocracy: we know of autobiographical *commentarii* by Aemilius Scaurus (consul in 115), Rutilius Rufus (also consul, in 105), Lutatius Catulus, and (in Greek) by Sulla himself. The rise of these forms of autobiography has been shrewdly connected to the birth of portraiture in Roman figurative art; this connection is based on a widely held, but still controversial, view that sees the origin of republican portraiture in an aristocratic setting and locates its inspiration in aristocratic ideology.

Some autobiographies, such as Rutilius Rufus's, must have been a kind of political self-defense. In others, especially Sulla's, the presence of charismatic qualities seems to have been notable: the author glorified himself as invested with a divine mission (let us recall the epithet *Felix,* "Lucky," which Sulla gave himself as a favorite of the gods), and in order to emphasize his own "investiture," he probably gave a certain amount of room to the mention of miraculous signs, such as premonitory dreams, which were clear proof of his divine "designation." The example of Sulla will have been continued by Lucullus and in all likelihood by Augustus, who, besides the official account in the *Res Gestae,* also wrote an autobiography in which, as it seems, he told of miracles that had preceded his birth and so forth.

3. ANTIQUARIAN, LINGUISTIC, AND PHILOLOGICAL STUDIES

By "antiquarianism" is meant the science that traces the remote origins of usages, customs, and juridical and social institutions, in short, the civilization, of a given people. Antiquarianism is naturally linked with historical writing (for Fabius Pictor's antiquarian interests, see p. 69), but it avails itself also of contributions from other sciences, for instance, philological-linguistic research and archaeology. It is easily understandable how this science, which stirred the national pride, developed at Rome and won wide credit, especially from the period of the conquests onwards.

*Split between histori-
cal writing and anti-
quarianism*

From the antiquarianism of this period we have only the names of a few scholars. We confine ourselves to mentioning, from the first half of the second century, Fulvius Nobilior, the patron of Ennius, the author of *Fasti,* and, from the following generation, Junius Gracchanus, who owed his cognomen to his warm sympathy for the party of the Gracchi. It is likely, in any event, that in antiquarianism there already began to make itself felt the consciousness of the contributions that the different Italic cultures made to the formation of Roman civilization, a consciousness that would come into its full maturity with Varro in the next century. Nonetheless, historiography and antiquarianism split apart from one another. Although the interest in antiquities is strong in the first annalists, it grows successively weaker in the writers of history, perhaps because it is overwhelmed by the pursuit of style and by the desire for a pragmatic understanding of events. Towards the end of the Republic the historian and the antiquarian would become profoundly different types of scholars.

*The birth of philol-
ogy: Aelius Stilo*

In this period, too, Latin philology is born as a specialized discipline, a clear sign of cultural maturity and conscious critical demands. In poets such as Accius and Lucilius philological and grammatical activity was still wedded to the activity of literary creation, as in the Alexandrian tradition. Lucius Aelius Stilo Praeconinus, who would be the teacher of Varro and Cicero, started the critical task of publishing and commenting on literary texts. Stilo, born at Lanuvium around 150, was a knight linked to the aristocratic party. He was concerned with problems about the authenticity of the Plautine comedies (in this field his work was continued and completed by his pupil Varro), and he commented on the *Carmen Saliare* and, probably, the Laws of the Twelve Tables. Octavius Lampadio prepared an edition of Naevius; Vettius Philocomus, one of Lucilius. The compilation of encyclopedic works such as Aurelius Opillus's *Musarum Libri IX* began to respond to the growing demand for erudition.

Analogy and Anomaly in the Use of Language

Around this time Roman grammatical studies begin to echo the disputes that pitted the philological schools of Alexandria and Pergamum against one another. The latter saw language as the free creation of usage *(consuetudo),* accepting as a necessary phenomenon the deviations, or anomalies (irregularities with respect to the established models), that were usual in the *sermo cotidianus.* The school of Alexandria, by contrast, represented a purist, conservative tendency. Appealing to the authority of the classics, it viewed language as based on the norm *(ratio)* and on analogy, the regularity that comes from respecting the recognized models; consequently, it rejected neologisms. Tyrannio the Elder was the resolute supporter of analogism; Alexander Polyhistor, a freedman of Sulla and the author of learned compilations and popular works, defended the cause of anomaly. Aelius Stilo started out from the anomalist views of Crates of Mallus, who was the authoritative exponent of the Pergamene school, and he had heard at

Rhodes the lectures of Dionysius Thrax, an analogist. In his own studies of language he tried to reconcile analogist tendencies with anomalist, and in this he would be followed by Varro. At the same time Julius Caesar would profess himself an ardent analogist and would compose a (lost) treatise *De Analogia*.

4. COMEDY AFTER TERENCE: THE *FABULA PALLIATA* AND THE *FABULA TOGATA*

The palliata *after Terence: Turpilius and the other authors*

It would be a mistake to think that after the great flourishing of Plautus and Terence (and also of the lost Caecilius Statius, whom the ancients regarded as a master of the same rank), the *palliata,* the comedy in Greek setting, experienced an abrupt decline. For one thing, the great classics continued to be performed, at least until the age of Cicero (obviously, they were also read and imitated a great deal, but this has nothing to do with their properly theatrical success). Moreover, for the whole second century we have names of authors and titles of works: Licinius Imbrex, Trabea, Atilius, Terence's enemy Luscius, and also a slightly later author (died in 103) from whom we have several fragments, Turpilius. Of Turpilius we can say that like Plautus and Terence, he continued to imitate Menander, but he also wrote some mythological comedies (after the important experiment of Plautus's *Amphitruo*). The style that appears in the fragments is antiquated, not only archaic but archaizing.

The decline of the palliata

This is a revealing feature. The *palliata* was increasingly felt to be an old-fashioned genre. In the time of Caesar and Cicero the traditional style of the Plautine comedy sounds archaic; the metrical scheme of the *cantica* remains but becomes less enjoyable as it becomes less intelligible; and the meters of the recited parts seem absurdly irregular, nearly anarchic. In the course of the first century B.C., the space of comedy was gradually invaded by alternative genres, such as the Atellan and the mime (see pp. 36 and 126 f.). In comparison with the *palliata,* which was governed by rigid theatrical-literary conventions and linked to a Greek background, these genres met the demand for a greater realism and a flexible structure.

The togata: *Titinius and Afranius*

Similar demands are already reflected in the success of the *togata,* that is, comedy with Roman or Italian settings and usages, which develops in the course of the second century. The first author is Titinius, whose date is uncertain but is perhaps to be put a little before Terence. Lucius Afranius is an approximate contemporary of Lucilius. Of a third author, Atta, it is known that he died in 77 B.C. Unfortunately, we have only titles and meager fragments (15 titles and about 180 verses for Titinius; about 40 titles and a little more than 400 verses for Afranius, the best preserved of the three; only a very few verses and 12 titles for Atta), which do not give a clear idea of the plots and the styles. The *togata* seems to present itself as a *palliata* in Roman setting (the toga was the typical Roman clothing), but it is not easy to say to what extent the authors distanced themselves from the conventions of Plautine comedy. We do not know for sure about any author that he composed both *palliatae* and *togatae* (even though the versatile Naevius might seem a good candidate). Unfortunately, however, the exact lines of demarcation between the two comic genres escape us. We have titles of *togatae* that could belong to Plautus and Terence but also titles that refer directly to Italian and Roman realities: "The Girl from Velletri" (*Veliterna*), "The Cleaner's" (*Fullonia*), "The Divorce," "The Young Soldier's Departure" (*Tiro Proficiscens*), "The Comedy of the Aediles" (Roman magistrates: *Aedilicia*).

It is easy to suppose that the *togata* met the need for a dramaturgy closer to local, everyday realities. One need think only of the *fabula tabernaria*, a particular species of *togata* (if not just another name for it), in which the characters were Roman or Italian and the scene was set in a *taberna*, a shop or tavern (see also p. 37). And yet we must guard against going too far in that direction. It does not appear that the authors of *togatae* waged any programmatic battle for realism. Afranius declared that he admired Terence's elegance, and he imitated not only the Latin playwrights but also the great Greek master, Menander. The few remaining fragments lead one to think that the poets of the *togata* used polymetric *cantica* and that in this, neglecting Terence's experiment, they returned to the practice of Naevius, Plautus, and Caecilius. We ought then to imagine a theater strengthened by Greek influences, even though more likely to be set among the lower classes: not only the typical slaves of the *palliata* but also artisans and common people who were more realistic and less timeless. An important conse-

quence of the setting chosen for the *togata* was a certain moderation in tone. As we saw, the freedom of imagination of the Plautine comedy was linked to the decision to stay outside Roman social reality, except for occasional exchanges of wit. A drama that directly brought onto the stage Roman characters needed to be still more controlled and prudent. The grammarian Donatus, in his commentary on Terence (*Eunuchus* 57), says that whereas in the *palliata* it was possible to bring on stage slaves more able and more intelligent than their masters, in the *togata* this was not permitted. Seneca tells us that the *togatae* kept near the middle between comedy and tragedy. From Afranius we have noble maxims of a philosophical cast, for example, "The wise man loves, everyone else desires." This dampening of the comic tone certainly did not contribute to the popular success of the *togata*, which always remained a genre in a lower key, distant from both the great literary experiments of a Plautus and the commercial success of the more obviously plebeian genres of spectacle.

5. THE ATELLAN AT ROME IN THE LATE REPUBLIC: POMPONIUS AND NOVIUS

In the first half of the first century, more or less in the Sullan period, the popular, subliterary genre of farce that had been the Atellan (see p. 36) returned to favor, but with a change in its cultural level. The Atellan had long been employed as a kind of comic finale (*exodium*), accompanying spectacles of a different level. Now, as a consequence of the maturing of the Roman audience's taste, this type of farce, once it had won independent performance, could be regularized in a way and given over to scripts that were more elaborate and more detailed than the simple plots and familiar exchanges of earlier periods. At the same time, the Atellan kept certain of its popular features and its broad humor, which always responded to audience desires—and not necessarily only the popular audience: compare the modern success of certain comic genres even among the cultured classes.

The Atellan in the age of Sulla: Pomponius and Novius

Thus it is easily explicable that in the age of Sulla authors of literary Atellans achieved renown. We have only titles and fragments of their works: seventy titles and about two hundred verses of Pomponius, forty-four titles and about one hundred verses of Novius. Of Lucius Pomponius we know that he was a native of Bologna and flourished in 89. Of his contemporary Novius we know still less. Perhaps most significant is that Pomponius wrote not only Atellans but also texts of a higher class, such as *palliatae* and even tragedies. This demonstrates the change of level in the fortunes of the Atellan. Another interesting indication is that the titles we have clearly preserve the mark of a repertory of masks ("Bucco the Gladiator," "Maccus the Soldier," "Pappus the Peasant," "Pappus Rejected at the Polls," etc.), but they sometimes include titles typical of the *palliata* (e.g., *Adelphoe,* "The Brothers"). We also know of higher, more solemn titles, even Greek titles, which suggest situations parodying tragedy or myth (*Armorum Iudicium, Andromacha, Hercules Coactor,* "Hercules the Tax-Collector").

The *palliata* had been influenced in origin by the popular Italic farce. Now, in all likelihood, the times were right for an influence in the opposite direction, all the more so in that the *palliata* remained the dominant comic genre under the Republic.

The Atellan under the Empire

The Atellan survives into the Empire, but it is certainly used less extensively. Its style begins to be felt as archaic in an era that experiences a renewal both in literary style and in the tastes of the public.

The success of the mime as a popular form of entertainment, from the age of Caesar onwards, created a new center of interest, to the disadvantage of the traditional comic genres.

6. THE MIME: LABERIUS AND SYRUS

The prehistory of the Roman mime is somewhat complicated, which is always the case with the genres of popular spectacle in the ancient world.

The various forms of the mime genre

The Greek term indicates the *imitatio* of real life, but this label covers not only forms of rather sophisticated literature, which are not always intended for acting (the influence of the mime can be felt even in so refined and elite a poet as Theocritus), but also genres of spectacle more like a variety act or a music-hall performance. The latter tendency is manifested in "numbers" that are unconnected to one another and not always based on real texts, elements of improvisation, and much space given to music, dance, and what we today call mime. The imitation of scenes from daily life turned into either grotesque effects of crude realism or parodies of more elevated, regular literary genres.

The demand for realism and the success of mime

Originally the performance of mimes was linked almost exclusively to the Ludi Florales, near the end of April; afterwards the mime became a spectacle quite in demand. The growing vogue for these spectacles in the age of Caesar is linked to the growing taste for realism, which parts company with the archaic traditions. All Roman art in this period shows this change in style and taste, as a result of which Plautus and Ennius no longer seem up-to-date. Realistic features—use of everyday speech, attention to the ordinary as a source of inspiration—are present even in a sophisticated, difficult writer such as Catullus. The mime is also realistic, and this is noticeable even in its stage conventions, which are distinctive for being different from those of comedy. The actors always acted without masks. This gave great room for facial expressiveness and greater realism in acting, and women's roles were performed on the stage by women, unlike in the theater of Plautus and Terence. The mimes (*mimi,* significantly, indicates the professional performers as well as the spectacles enacted by them) did not wear raised shoes, as the actors in serious plays did; they were therefore called *planipedes,* "flat-foots," because they performed directly on the ground.

Spontaneous mime and literary mime

From fragments and contemporary sources we know about two important authors of mime in the age of Caesar: Decimus Laberius and Publilius Syrus. The picture of mime presented by these two writers is a very partial one. Not all the "authors" of mime were literary figures as Laberius and Syrus were. The success of mime in the Republic and the early Empire continued to be based on schematic plots, improvisations, songs, capers, and even, no doubt to great acclaim, stripteases derived from the mimes. It seems that the basic situations were independent vignettes, with risqué plays on words, ribald love scenes, or noisy quarrels; the spectacle often had an abrupt and surprising ending, with a concluding comic episode and a general free-for-all. In the imperial period the mime became more and more separate from comedy, evolving towards forms of ballet and dumb-show; this was the great success of pantomime.

The literary mime: a) Laberius

Laberius's work was regarded as on a higher level, and so we have some remnants of it: 43 titles and 106 fragments for a total of 176 verses. The author was a Roman knight. He lived, it seems, from 106 to 43, an exact contemporary of Cicero. His works often have titles from Greek comedy or mime ("The Comedy of the Pot," "The Twins," "The Fisherman," etc.) and must have been written with care, since they had literary, and not only theatrical, success. An interesting feature of Laberius is that his work must have abounded in contemporary political allusions, something that, as far as we know, was absent from the comic theater in Plautus's day. In fact, Laberius had the unfortunate idea of attacking the great Julius Caesar. Once he had become dictator, Caesar took his revenge by compelling Laberius to act in one of his own texts; to act in a mime was a degrading activity for a Roman knight, and Laberius sententiously complained of it in a prologue.

b) Publilius Syrus

Publilius Syrus was Laberius's rival and another author of literary mimes. He was younger and not of free birth, and so he personally acted in his own works, as part of a genuine acting company. Publilius seems to have been proverbial for his ability to coin *sententiae,* sayings and maxims of general character; in this sense his work was akin to contemporary rhetoric. Publilius's posthumous fame is represented by an anthology of moralizing maxims; from his mimes we have, apart from such maxims, only two titles and four or five verses. The collection has come down to us under his name, but the consensus is that it has been recast and interpolated. These maxims, in any event, do not give an adequate idea of his theatrical ability. (A parallel phenomenon of anthologization took place for the work of the Athenian comic writer Menander, from whom a collection of *sententiae,* maxims of moral content, was prepared.) It is nevertheless probable that Publilius, like Laberius, was an author of the first rank, remote from the more trivial and commercial aspects of mime production.

Split in taste and decline of the traditional theater

The fact that forms of spectacle such as the Atellan and the mime were preferred by the public shows to what extent the traditional forms of the Latin theater, tragic and comic, had declined. There was lacking, it is true, the capacity on the part of the theater to renew itself; lacking, too, were new authors for the theater. But there was another reason: gradually a split had taken place in the tastes of the public. On the one hand, the cultivated elite began to demand a literary expression more elaborate and refined, more challenging, a demand that would have been satisfied especially by literature for private consumption. On the other hand, the urban mass, which had grown out of all proportion, had undergone a process of cultural degradation, which rendered it open almost exclusively to simple and rather vulgar forms of spectacle. Latin popular theater had also been exhausted because its language was no longer shared by its audience; it had lost its capability for cultural cohesion. For the elite, the popular theater's view of the world was too schematic, too elementary and inflexible for the complexity of present-day experiences and concerns. Yet it contained little truth for those who made up the immense, heterogeneous mass of the Roman people. The latter wanted spectacles that could reproduce directly, without all the conventional dramaturgic elaborations, the simplest manifestations of daily life, the numerous lively situations of little people affected by material needs and capable only of simple, primitive, immediately satisfied emotions.

The death of the popular theater

A new literature would come about for those looking for a poetry to read or recite, since new languages would be created to interpret new models of sensibility, and they would give expression to new ideals and new aspirations of the cultivated classes. But there would never again be a new, truly popular theater, alive and vital, despite all the programmatic earnestness with which official Augustan culture would try to foster its rebirth.

BIBLIOGRAPHY

For the remains of the orators of the period, see E. Malcovati, ed., *Oratorum Romanorum Fragmenta* (ed. 4 Turin 1976). There is a good Loeb text of the *Rhetorica ad Herennium* with translation and notes by H. Caplan (London 1954), and there is an invaluable Italian text and commentary by G. Calboli (Bologna 1969). The standard text remains that of F. Marx (rev. W. Trillitsch, Leipzig 1964). The historians are to be found in H. Peter, *Historicorum Romanorum Reliquiae* (ed. 2 Leipzig 1914), the grammarians in G. Funaiuoli, *Grammaticae Romanae Fragmenta* (Leipzig 1907). For the fragments of comedy, Atellan farce, and mime, see O. Ribbeck, *Scaenicae Romanorum Poesis Fragmenta* (2 vols., ed. 2 Leipzig 1871–73, reprint Hildesheim 1962; ed. 3 1897–98), to be supplemented for Atellan farce by P. Frassinetti, *Fabularum Atellanarum Fragmenta* (Turin 1955), and for mime by O. Friedrich and M. Bonaria, *Mimorum Romanorum Fragmenta* (2 vols., Genoa 1955) and *Romani Mimi* (Rome 1965). The fragments of the *comoedia togata* have been reedited with French translation and commentary by A. Daviault (Paris 1981).

For the orators of the period, A. D. Leeman, *Orationis Ratio: The Stylistic Theories and Practice of the Roman Orators, Historians, and Philosophers* (Amsterdam 1963), is again fundamental; for the historians, see again E. Badian, "The Early Historians," in *Latin Historians,* ed. T. A. Dorey (London 1966) 1–38. On Atellan farce and mime, see W. Beare, *The Roman Stage* (ed. 3 London 1964) 137–58, and A. Nicoll, *Masks, Mimes, and Miracles* (London 1931). The major studies are those of P. Frassinetti, *Fabula Atellana: Saggio sul teatro populare latino* (Genoa 1953), H. Reich, *Der Mimus* (Berlin 1903), and F. Giancotti, *Mimo e Gnome: Studi su Decimo Laberio e Publico Siro* (Messina 1967). There is no English equivalent to F. Della Corte, *La filologia latina dalle origini a Varrone* (ed. 2 Florence 1981), but for the later figures, E. Rawson's *Intellectual Life in the Late Roman Republic* (London 1985) begins to become useful; she also deals with some orators and historians, for example, Cornelius Sisenna, 221–22. See also *CQ* 29 (1979) 327–46, reprinted in Rawson, *Roman Culture and Society* (Oxford 1991) 363–88.

TWO

The Late Republic

The Age of Caesar (78–44 B.C.)

Sulla and Caesar and the crisis of institutions

In the study of Latin culture the final period of the republic has its own marked characteristics and for that reason deserves consideration as an independent era. As chronological boundaries—conveniences, of course, without any objective reality and having only practical value—it is customary to use the deaths of two great figures, Sulla (78 B.C.) and Caesar (44 B.C.). They are not, of course, the only great figures of their generations, and yet we recall them rather than, say, Marius and Pompey. The reason is simple: throughout their lives, Sulla and Caesar are linked each to a great political experiment. Sulla's dictatorship and Caesar's principate (even though the latter had little time to consolidate his power) mark two key moments in the crisis of the republic's institutions and two critical phases in which new solutions visibly ripen. It is hardly by chance that the experiences of Sulla and Caesar would be carefully noted by the man who was to dominate the following, far more enduring political revolution: Octavian Augustus. By separating off the period between the death of Sulla and the death of Caesar and by calling it "the age of Caesar," we aim to give priority to Roman political history and to see the development of Latin literature in relation to it.

Personalities and genres in the age of Caesar:
a) Neoteric poetry

The division into periods seems apt even in regard to simple literary chronology. Cicero, the dominant figure in the cultural life of this generation, begins his public activity under Sulla, a few years before our starting date, and continues it until a few months after Caesar's death. Cicero's violent death in December of 43, even more than Caesar's, seems to symbolize the end of an era. If we focus on the development of poetry, the period 78–44 has a satisfying unity: it includes the entire development of neoteric poetry, which has predecessors in the age of Sulla, comes to full maturity with Catullus, Parthenius, and the *poetae novi,* and declines in the period of the civil wars. Moreover, just in the period 44–43 lie the literary debuts of the founders of the new school, Cornelius Gallus, the one most closely linked to the neoteric milieu, and Virgil, the most innovative and original. The isolated flourishing of Lucretian Epicureanism, which is connected to the contemporary culture by tenuous though not negligible threads, also falls within the age of Caesar.

b) *The development
of all the literary
genres*

Our period witnesses great theoretical, political, and ideological debates, as evidenced by the work of Cicero; the fullest flowering of judicial and political oratory; the powerful impetus of Roman philosophical thought (Cicero again, but also the Pythagoreanism of Nigidius Figulus and the spread of Epicureanism); and the growth of antiquarianism, linguistics, biography, and other forms of cultural diffusion (Varro, but also Atticus, Nigidius Figulus, and Cornelius Nepos). It can be said that no other generation in the history of Rome experienced so varied and complex a cultural development. Among the various literary genres and currents only the theater remained behind. As for historical writing, a retrospective genre par excellence, which requires delay and distance from the events, it is clear that Sallust's work must be located in the Caesarian cultural ambience. Although he wrote in the years following the death of Caesar, Sallust directed all his historical thought at the phase just ended, the long political struggle begun by Marius and Sulla and culminating in the murder of Caesar.

If we regard the period of Caesar and Cicero in very general terms, the phenomenon that strikes us most is the importance acquired by philosophical-political thought. Its new centrality also signifies its independence. Philosophical ideas are more and more fostered by classical Greek thought—Plato, Aristotle and his school, Epicurus, and the Stoics are the chief figures—but increasingly they also have direct consequences in the political-social sphere. Rome thus develops a true modern philosophy that can stand comparison with Greek thought and seeks to acquire the latter's ability to synthesize and interpret reality but also seeks, of course, to adapt itself to specifically Roman traditions and interests. The great thinkers of this era are no longer, as before, exclusively authors writing in Greek; Cicero, Varro, and Nigidius Figulus claim a place of their own alongside Posidonius and Philodemus. Roman culture interprets and questions the great texts of Greek thought with immediate reference to the needs of the present. The role of religion is discussed, not only in the private cults but especially in the life of the state and in political decisions. In a time of collapsing traditions, the question which is the best constitution is considered theoretically. The social behavior of man is analyzed in ethical terms. The culture in the end questions itself about itself, seeking to establish its own proper role in public life and in the training of the ruling class. More concretely, the ideas of the intellectuals, even the most theoretical, shed light on the great players in the struggle for power: the generals Caesar and Pompey, the Senate, the plebs, the city and the provinces. Finally, one may suspect a closer relation in some cases, a direct interweaving of intellectual views and political action. Here, however, the overall picture appears much more uneven and irregular. In the long phase of the struggle for power that began with the death of Sulla, both principal protagonists, Caesar and Pompey, distinguish themselves for their unscrupulousness and cynical tactics. The parties gradually group themselves around the great political-military leaders without too much concern for shared intellectual values.

The fact that many Caesarians can be described culturally as pro-Epicurean should not be pushed too far. It is natural to hear Epicurean echoes in the marked anti-traditionalism of certain representatives of the Caesarian party; but some of Caesar's murderers could also claim Epicurean inspiration, since the Epicurean tradition included distinct anti-tyrannical tendencies.

The independence of the intellectual

In reality this period is not characterized by a particular consistency between political action and ideological inspiration: a true Epicurean would have had to refrain from any political responsibility and certainly would not have embroiled himself in a contest for power. The real characteristic is the intense circulation of ideas and ideals that have a basis in philosophy, as well as the sturdy independence that intellectuals begin to claim in social life. They are no longer advisers or counselors in the service of enlightened aristocrats. Throughout his life and career Cicero illustrates the aspirations of intellectuals to take an active part in society and the state; we will see shortly, in the chapter about him, what the possibilities and the limits of this notion are. But even when they are on the losing side, as Cicero and Sallust were, these intellectuals always claim a proud independence for themselves and seek to legitimize their work.

The independence of the poet:
a) From the models

Independence could also be the watchword of the great poets of this period, who in this regard depart from the traditions of early Roman literature. The poetry of both Catullus and Lucretius, if we leave aside for a moment the enormous differences between them, sees itself as independent from its Greek models. Fostered more than ever by Greek culture, this poetry nonetheless proclaims itself new, the result of free emulation, and in direct contact with the demands of contemporary life—"modern," we would say, substituting our terminology for theirs. Of course, they are more than independent from the archaic literary tradition. But unlike the leading figures in philosophy and oratory, these poets are also independent in social life. Unlike the early writers, they do not have and do not display real patrons: among their predecessors only Lucilius resembles them somewhat. The real audience for poetry in the Caesarian period is the intellectual circle, the coterie united by affinity of taste, poetics, and ideology. The purity of their goals, however, keeps Catullus and Lucretius far from the centers of power.

b) From the patrons

The Augustan age: the poet victorious and the intellectual defeated

By contrast, the great innovation of the Augustan age will be to make the poet more central at the expense of the intellectual. Virgil and Horace, unlike Catullus and Lucretius, are firmly located at the center of a cultural order that is also an ideology and a system of power. By contrast, Cicero's ambition to claim an independent function for intellectuals would find no continuators. The struggle for power and ideological supremacy has been resolved by this time and is destined, in any event, to move along other paths.

Neoteric Poetry and Catullus

Cicero and the
poetae novi

Poetae novi (*neoteroi* in Greek) is the scornful term with which Cicero refers to the innovative tendencies of his day, the modern poetic taste that develops and becomes prominent in the first century B.C. and that marks a decisive turn in the history of Latin literature. Cicero's disdain for those whom he lumped together as "modern poets"—the disdain of a mature Cicero, now remote from his own youthful poetic experiments in a Hellenizing style—is revealed in another celebrated denomination of his: *cantores Euphorionis,* "singers of Euphorion." With this term he intends to stigmatize the new leading lights of the literary scene on the grounds that they have irreverently rejected national tradition, as personified by Ennius, in order to pursue an avant-garde poetic ideal. He takes this term from the name of the poet from Chalcis (third century), who was celebrated for the affected density and precious erudition of his verses and had become a symbol of the notorious Alexandrian poetic ideal; he had been made known around the middle of the first century B.C. by Parthenius of Nicaea, "the prophet of the Callimachean school" at Rome.

*Conquests in the
East and moderniza-
tion of taste*

The reforming of literary taste promoted by the *poetae novi* is only an aspect of the general Hellenization of manners, the transformation of styles of life that followed upon the great conquests of the second century B.C. These conquests had opened the eastern part of the Mediterranean to Roman power and had brought the archaic society of peasant-soldiers into contact with peoples accustomed to more refined forms of life. This vast, complex phenomenon of the civilizing of Rome, which meets unrelenting hostility from the guardians of tradition, the Catonian party, obviously manifests its influence in the field of literature, where we see both a mild yet progressive weakening of literary values and traditions in those literary genres that are politically and morally engaged, such as epic and drama, and at the same time the emergence of new demands dictated by a refinement in taste and sensibility. These ethical and esthetic reforms and this more open attitude towards Greek culture had found expression particularly in the Scipionic circle; and in literature they had shown themselves, for example, in the development of new poetic forms by a poet such as Lucilius, even if some of his other verses still bear the archaic features of the national tradition.

A more conspicuous manifestation of the attention paid to Greek culture in order to satisfy the demands of a more refined taste is the appearance among the cultivated Roman elite of a new type of poetry, light in tone and small in scale, such as epigram, intended for private consumption, and devoted to the expression of personal sentiments (although Lucilius had already introduced his own life into his satires). The playful character of such compositions was implicit in the Greek term for them: *paignia* ("jests"); in Latin they are called *nugae*, "trifles," to indicate their unserious nature as simple entertainment and their lack of pretense. The rise of this nugatory poetry at Rome during the last decades of the second century B.C. in the intellectual circle at the center of which stood Quintus Lutatius Catulus is the most obvious sign of the ferments taking place and forms a prelude to the neoteric revolution. This revolution is the product of *otium*, of time withdrawn from civil duties and devoted instead to reading and intelligent conversation. The claim made by individual needs (now recognized alongside social obligations) is also disclosed in the interest shown in private feelings such as love. And more than anything, the attention paid to form—lexical, metrical, compositional, and others—reveals a taste educated by contact with Alexandrian culture and poetry.

Despite the elements of continuity between nugatory poetry and properly neoteric poetry, the consciousness of the latter is much higher and its rejection of the Latin literary tradition is much clearer. The often mannered elegance and the artificial experiments with the Greek models on the part of Lutatius Catulus's circle give way to a poetry that does not merely grant limited room to *otium* and its pleasures but places them at the very center of its existence and turns them into absolute values and exclusive motives, as with Catullus. Whereas for a Catulus poetry was marginal, an occasional diversion from a life still centered on the duties of the citizen—it is not a coincidence that the same Catulus is also a writer of historical works—neoteric poetry marks the culmination in literature of a tendency perceptible for a while already in Latin culture: decreasing interest in a life spent in the service of the state, in the venerable values of the tradition, in the role of Roman citizen, replaced by a taste for *otium*, for free time devoted to literature and pleasure, to the satisfaction of private, personal needs. The revolution in literary taste, that is, is accompanied by a more general ethical revolt which fosters it, and it reveals the crisis in the values of the *mos maiorum*. The rejection of a life committed to the service of the community and of the paradigm of the citizen-soldier is reflected in, and at the same time fostered by, the spread of Epicureanism, a philosophy that renounces political-military *negotia* for a remote and tranquil life led in intimate contact with friends. The convergence of Epicurean principles and the tendencies of the neoteric poets is evident, but an important difference should also be noted: for the Epicureans, whose goal is *ataraxia*, pleasure without disturbances, eros is an insidious disease, to be shunned as a source of anxiety and pain (one need only think of the fourth book of Lucretius), whereas for the neoterics, especially Catullus, love is the central emotion of life, its essence and raison d'être. Love becomes, accordingly, the special theme of their poetry and aids in giving form to a new style of life, one inspired by the cult of eros and the passions and by the devotion to poetry that feeds on them.

The affinities of taste:
a) *The concern for form*

The neoteric poets do not constitute a circle or a school, nor are they united in a comprehensive program (though the fact that the majority come from Gallia Cisalpina may explain their closeness and friendship). They are united, rather, by affinity of taste, which gets translated into shared contacts, meetings, discussions, and readings—into a critical-philological activity that accompanies their proper poetic activity and serves to support and justify it. The concern for form, the scrupulous care in composition, and the patient polishing of their verses are the chief distinctive traits of the new Callimachean poetics. Just as Callimachus had bitterly attacked the followers of Homeric epic, mocking the sloppiness and prolixity of the long poem, and had championed a new poetic style that aspired to *brevitas* (i.e., poems on a small scale) and *ars* (the meticulous labor of refinement), so Catullus and the neoterics mock the tired imitators of Ennius, the pompous cultivators of traditional epics such as those of Volusius, Suffenus, and Hortensius, which celebrated the nation's glories but were alien to contemporary taste on account of both their carelessness of form and their obsolete content. Callimachean poetics would value other genres, subjecting them to the careful work of the file, the *labor limae:* short genres, such as the epigram, or others, such as the epyllion (the mythological poem in miniature), which give the poet the opportunity to display his precious erudition (as with ancient myths on erotic themes, which are close to modern sensibility) and to employ sophisticated compositional plans (such as embedded stories or narratives strung together that reflect one another).

b) *New literary genres: epigram and epyllion*

The renewal in poetic language

The Callimachean school allows for various experiments. It includes authors such as Furius Bibaculus and Varro Atacinus, who take a conciliatory stance and write works of a more traditional character too, along with Catullus and his friends Cinna and Calvus, whose Callimacheanism is more consistent. These, the chief inspirers of the Callimachean poetics, whatever their differences, work out a new poetic language and, more generally, mark a decisive turn in the history of literary taste at Rome. Neotericism henceforth would become a boundary of modernity, consigning previous literature definitively to the past. Even the practitioners of the more traditional forms would have to take into account the imperatives of the new taste.

1. THE PRE-NEOTERIC POETS

Lutatius Catulus and his circle

A prominent figure in the cultural landscape of the period from the Gracchi to Sulla is Quintus Lutatius Catulus. Born around 150 B.C., of a noble family, he was Marius's colleague as consul in 102 and shared with him the victory over the Cimbri in 101. He later fell victim to the Marian persecution and committed suicide in 87. In addition to being an author of historical and autobiographical works *(De Consulatu et de Rebus Gestis Suis)*, he was an orator of elegance and refined diction (Cicero would celebrate him in the *De Oratore*), sharing the ideals of the Scipionic taste, to which he may be considered heir. A man of wide culture, open to philosophy, he was above all a poet. He introduced into Latin poetry epigrams of Greek type, which he adapted from Hellenistic models; a couple of them have come down to us. Around him gathered a group of writers who shared this new taste for light, entertaining poetry, who were commonly called the "circle of Lutatius Catulus." It is likely, however, that it was not a true circle, with a consistent attitude and a single purpose: too much emphasis has been placed on this group's "democratic" character and its commitment to opposition towards the nobles, when in fact it was made up of writers who differed from one another in social position and political tendency. The various members must have been united only by shared tastes and literary ideals.

Valerius Aedituus, Porcius Licinus, Volcacius Sedigitus

The poets Valerius Aedituus and Porcius Licinus surely belonged to this group, since like their friend and protector, they experimented with the new poetic form. From Valerius Aedituus we have two love epigrams, mannered in the Alexandrian style. From Porcius Licinus we have one epigram and also two fragments, in trochaic septenarii, from an interesting poem on a literary-historical subject, the origins of Latin poetry and Terence's relation with the Scipios. Literary criticism in verse, a genre cultivated by the Alexandrians, must have had its place also in a work such as Volcacius Sedigitus's *De Poetis*, a fragment of which, in iambic senarii, provides us with the canon of the best Latin comic writers: Caecilius Statius first, Plautus second, Naevius third, Terence only sixth.

Laevius

The same taste for light poetry, a taste carried still further by linguistic and metrical experimentation, is shown by a poet who probably lived at the beginning of the first century B.C., Laevius. He wrote a work in six or more books, *Erotopaegnia* ("Love Jests"), from which we have about twenty-five fragments and about fifty verses; it dealt with the myths that were familiar from the epic and tragic tradition and were sometimes reworked in Alexandrian poetry, such as those of Adonis, Helen, Hector, the Sirens, Circe, Protesilaus and Laodamia, and so on. The playful character implied in the new nugatory poetry becomes more marked in Laevius. Charm becomes artifice and affected preciosity, with occasional touches of morbid sensuality. The play is evident in the imaginative pursuit of bold new forms of expression, in the whimsical use of the most disparate meters, in the display of precious lexical oddities, and in the creation of unusual compounds, as in such titles as *Protesilaudamia* and *Sirenocirca*.

Matius

We should place two of Laevius's contemporaries, Matius and Sueius, in this atmosphere of literary and linguistic experimentation, even though their chronology is in part controversial. Matius wrote a translation in hexameters of the *Iliad*, of which some fragments are left, of no great literary value. The same Matius ventured upon a literary genre that was new to the Latins, mimiambs, mimes composed in iambic or, more precisely, choliambic meter ("scazons," or limping iambics); in Greek literature the genre had been practiced by Herodas in the Hellenistic age. Unlike the mimes of Laberius and Syrus (on which see pp. 127 ff.), Matius's mimiambs were intended for private reading, not performance. Several verses are extant, having a light and lively content: someone complains because he broke a water jug; a fig seller cries up his wares ("In so many thousands of figs you won't find a useless one"); two lovers kiss, joining their lips *columbulatim,* "like two tender doves," where we once again meet the linguistic experimentation that was typical of Laevius and would be typical of the neoterics.

Sueius
Sueius is the author of a *Moretum* that Macrobius would call an "idyll" (the name refers to a rustic dish; a poem of the *Appendix Vergiliana* would have the same title [see p. 432 f.]). From the few verses, in hexameter, that Macrobius reports, one gets not so much the picture of a precursor of the bucolic genre, which is what we would expect from its being called an "idyll" (see p. 264), as the impression of a learned pedant who, following Alexandrian models, discourses on the names of the different varieties of nuts. The same linguistic delight in neologisms, preciosity, and artificiality of expression is found in the fragments of the *Pulli* ("The Chicks"), a poem in trochaic septenarii. Small fragments of an epic poem locate Sueius close to Matius and show how these poets, anticipating such neoterics as Furius Bibaculus and Varro Atacinus, did not feel the epic genre to be in conflict with literary activity in an Alexandrian mode.

2. THE NEOTERIC POETS

Laevius between pre-neoterics and neoterics
Despite its extremes of artificiality, the poetry of Laevius marks progress beyond the earliest nugatory poetry, which was still closely dependent on Hellenistic models. He elaborates his models with greater originality, preferring those erotic-mythological subjects that would become so popular in later Latin literature, and he tries out new possibilities of expression. It is thus fair to regard him as an intermediate link, a more direct predecessor of truly neoteric poetry.

The neoterics:
a) Valerius Cato
A prominent figure in the new poetic tendencies, almost a founder, is Valerius Cato. A native of Cisalpine Gaul, as Suetonius tells us in the *De Grammaticis,* he was born probably at the start of the first century B.C. He came to Rome, where he lived as a grammarian and teacher of poetry until he reached an advanced old age, made gloomy by poverty. A reader and formidable critic of poetry, and also a poet himself, he restores in Rome the great tradition of the Alexandrian critic-philologist: he was compared to Zenodotus and to Crates of Pergamum. An epigram about him written within his circle reveals the prestige he enjoyed as a writer and an instructor in taste: *Cato grammaticus, Latina siren, / qui solus legit ac facit poetas,* "Cato the grammarian, the Latin Siren, who alone reads and makes poets." In addition to philological works—he may have edited Lucilius—he wrote poetic works, perhaps epyllia, which were much praised by contemporaries: we hear of a *Dictynna,* or *Diana,* of his, on the Cretan myth of the goddess,

and a *Lydia,* which shows in its title the Alexandrianizing character of the poetry produced by this devoted practitioner of the form.

b) *Furius Bibaculus*   Close to Valerius Cato was Marcus Furius Bibaculus, from Cremona, born about ten years after his friend and teacher and, like him, long-lived. Tacitus and Quintilian record that he wrote harsh epigrams against Augustus, in the neoteric manner. We have extant two affectionately ironic epigrams on Valerius Cato and a biting fragment directed against Orbilius, Horace's pugnacious teacher. His historical epic *Pragmatia Belli Gallici,* if the attribution is secure, must have taken a very different attitude towards Caesar; we have but few verses of this, one of them ridiculed by Horace for its clumsy pomposity. Horace himself refers critically to another poem, the *Ethiopid:* he speaks of a *Furius Alpinus,* which could be a satiric epithet connected to the verse mentioned a moment ago, but doubts persist about the identity of the poet. The mythological subject of this poem goes back to the Trojan Cycle. Another work, *Lucubrationes,* a wittily learned work in prose, must have been closer to the neoteric taste (although the epic-historical poem is taken up by Varro Atacinus also).

c) *Varro Atacinus*   Publius Terentius Varro Atacinus (i.e., from Atax, in Gallia Narbonensis, where he was probably born ca. 82 B.C.) shows several parallels with the contradictory figure of the poet from Cremona. He continued the Ennian style of poetry, composing a historical poem, the *Bellum Sequanicum,* on Caesar's campaign against Ariovistus in 58 B.C.; but he followed the new taste in poetry with a work entitled *Leucadia* (from the name of his beloved), which the elegiac poets would regard as one of the earliest instances of Latin erotic poetry. He also wrote satires (Horace speaks of them critically) and didactic poems; in this too the influence of the Ennian and Lucilian tradition is evident. We hear of a *Chorographia* of his, a geographical work, and of an *Ephemeris* (but even the title is uncertain), a poem on weather signs, in the manner of Aratus. But special mention must be given to his epic, *Argonautae,* a free translation in Latin hexameters, or perhaps rather a rewriting, of the *Argonautica* by Apollonius of Rhodes. Thus, he continues the tradition of the poet-translators, which, following the great Greek models, did so much to develop a new poetic language for Latin, and yet at the same time he shows such a preference for the kind of epic that gave much play to eros and its psychological complications that he attracted the interest of the new poets.

d) *Cinna*   Two other notable poets in the neoteric circle, known to us especially through the poems of their friend Catullus, are Cinna and Calvus, who along with Catullus form virtually a group within the group, since they are very much like one another in the rigor of their poetic stance. Gaius Helvius Cinna, also a native of Gallia Cisalpina (from Brescia), took part with Catullus in the expedition to Bithynia in 57 B.C. Some identify him with the Cinna who is said to have brought the poet Parthenius of Nicaea to Rome in his train; as a freedman, however, Parthenius more probably had already been brought to Rome in 73 B.C. Regardless of such an identification, it is undeniable that the Greek poet, whose presence in Rome acted as stimulus and point of reference for neoteric poetry, influenced Cinna too. Cinna's resolute adherence to the principles of the new taste, learning combined with meticulous *labor limae,* is evident in the dedicatory epigram accompanying the poem of Aratus (the choice itself is significant) that he brought back from Bithynia as a gift for a friend. This adherence also inspires his most famous poem, the *Zmyrna,* which is almost completely lost. This small-scale poem, which with typical Alexandrian taste narrated the incestuous love of Myrrha for her father Cinyras, was praised by Catullus (poem 95) when it was published after nine years of patient work with the file. The brevity of style and the density of learning, which secured for it a reputation for impenetrable obscurity, must have made this poem an exemplar of Callimachean poetics. And if Cinna's artistic aim was to rival in preciosity of erudition and difficulty of style the highly esteemed Euphorion, who was the most Callimachean and most abstruse of the learned poets dear to the neoterics, then one may readily believe that he succeeded in his aim. We know from Suetonius (*De Grammaticis* 18) that the *Zmyrna* required the explanatory notes of a grammarian, and the employment of the form *Zmyrna* for the title instead of the usual *Myrrha* is the first sign of this pursuit of preciosity. Cinna in addition wrote epigrams and a *Propempticon,* a poem of salutation to one starting a journey, addressed to Asinius Pollio in 56.

e) *Calvus*

Licinius Calvus (82–ca. 47 B.C.), born in Rome of an illustrious plebeian family—he was the son of the historian Licinius Macer—was a famous orator; his speeches against Caesar's henchman Vatinius were particularly celebrated (there is a playful reference in Catullus's poem 53). Calvus was a follower of the Atticist movement, which, pursuing an ideal of clear, concise spareness and opposed to emphasis and prolixity, was more congruent with neoteric taste. But he was above all a poet, among the greatest of the new tendency, though very few verses survive. In addition to epigrams of political invective like those Catullus and Bibaculus also composed, he wrote epithalamia and other poems on love themes, among them a grief-filled epicedion over the untimely death of his wife Quintilia. He also wrote an epyllion entitled *Io,* from the name of the heroine who was loved by Jupiter and persecuted by Juno, in which we notice the theme of metamorphosis, so dear to Alexandrian literature.

3. CATULLUS

LIFE

Gaius Valerius Catullus was born at Verona, in Gallia Cisalpina, to a family that was well-to-do (Caesar was a guest in his house). The date of his birth is not certain. Jerome, who relies on Suetonius, places it in 87 B.C. and places his death thirty years later, in 57; but the poet was certainly still alive in 55 B.C., as is proved by his references to events of that year. Thus along with the date of death the date of birth, too, needs to be lowered, so that we get something like 84–54 B.C., if the notice that he died at age thirty is true; otherwise we must suppose that he lived several years more than Jerome says. At Rome—we do not know when Catullus arrived there—he knew and associated with people eminent in politics and literature, from the famous orator Hortensius Hortalus to the poets Cinna and Calvus, from Lucius Manlius Torquatus to the jurist and future consul Alfenus Varus, from Cornelius Nepos to Gaius Memmius. He also had a love relationship with Clodia, the Lesbia of his poetry, who was almost certainly the half-sister of the tribune Publius Clodius Pulcher and the wife of Quintus Caecilius Metellus, consul in 60. Probably in 57 he went to Bithynia for a year as a member of the entourage of the governor Gaius Memmius. During this trip he visited the tomb of his brother, who had died and been buried in the Troad (see the famous poem 101). Of his death, at the age of thirty or a little more, we have already spoken.

WORKS

We have 116 poems of Catullus. (More exactly the number is 113, but the numeration reaches 116 because three Priapean poems, numbered 18–20, were inserted against the manuscript evidence by Muretus, a great French humanist of the sixteenth century, and they formed a part of the text of Catullus until in the nineteenth century Lachmann banished them; the numeration of the individual poems was not changed, however. The three poems can be read among the *Priapea* of the *Appendix Vergiliana,* on which see p. 433.) Totaling nearly twenty-three hundred verses, Catullus's poems were collected in a *liber* that is customarily divided, on the basis of meter, into three sections. The first group (1–60) is made up of generally brief poems of a light nature, known also as *nugae,* "bagatelles," "diversions." These are in various meters, especially phalaecean hendecasyllables but also iambic trimeters, scazons, and Sapphics, for which reason they are called polymetrics (the elegiac couplet, in any event, does not appear). The second group (61–68), quite heterogeneous, includes a limited number of poems, but ones of greater extent and stylistic effort. The meters are various, including the unusual galliambic, glyconics and pherecreteans, hexameters and pentameters. These are the so-called *carmina docta,* "learned poems." The third section (69–116) consists of generally short poems in elegiac couplets, the so-called epigrams. The question of the composition of the Catullan *liber* is controversial: although some attribute the ordering of the collection to the poet himself, the majority tend to believe, rightly, that this ordering, which is not by chronology or content but only by meter, that is, by a criterion of philologists, is rather the work of others, carried out after the poet's death, when a posthumous edition of his poems was prepared. (Some of the poems, however, must have been omitted, since the indirect tradition cites verses attributed to Catullus that do not appear among the poems collected in the *liber.*) It is necessary, then, to suppose that the *libellus* dedicated by Catullus to Cornelius Nepos (see poem 1) did not correspond exactly to the extant *liber* but made up only a part of it.

SOURCES

Details of Catullus's life come to us chiefly from his poems, although the biographical material based on Catullus's *liber* is often elusive and blurred.

About the relations of the poet's family with Caesar we are informed by Suetonius in the biography of Julius Caesar (sec. 73) contained in his *De Vita Caesarum.* We know from Apuleius (*Apology* 10) that Lesbia was a pseudonym for Clodia, and about the Clodia with whom she is regularly identified we learn much from Cicero, who draws a dark portrait of her in the *Pro Caelio,* the speech he gave in defense of Marcus Caelius Rufus, the woman's former lover, who was later accused by her of poisoning.

The Short Poems

Catullus and the neo-teric revolution

Catullus's name and poetry are traditionally associated with the neoteric revolution; indeed, they are the most important document of it. It is a revolution in literary taste but also a revolution in ethics. While at a time of acute crisis for the Republic the old moral and political values of the *civitas* are crumbling, personal *otium* becomes the attractive alternative to communal life, the space in which to devote oneself to culture, poetry, friendship, and love. The small universe of the individual, with its joys and dramas, is identified with the very horizon of existence, and literary activity no longer turns towards epic and tragedy, the genres that speak for the state and its values, but rather towards lyric, towards personal poetry, which is introverted and suitable for embracing and expressing the small events of private life.

The short poems and intimate space

This aim of recovering intimate space and private feelings is met most evidently by the part of Catullus's poetry that is usually referred to as the short poems, that is, the polymetrics together with the epigrams. In these the brief compass itself reveals the modesty of the contents—situations and events of daily life—and at the same time favors the patient work of the file, the striving for perfection of form. Affections, friendships, hatreds, passions, the small, even the minute, aspects of life are the objects of Catullus's poetry: a jesting invitation to dinner (*carmen* 13), a welcome for a friend returning from Spain (*carmen* 9), protests against a far from urbane act (*carmen* 12) or against a malicious gift received by the poet (*carmen* 14). These produce an impression of immediacy, of a life reflected in them, that in the history of criticism has led to a persistent misunderstanding, that the poetry is artless and spontaneous and that the poet is a "child" who freely gives vent to his feelings, without the bonds of morality and the filters of culture. In fact, Catullus's celebrated spontaneity is the cloak that this poetry wears, but it is an appearance deliberately sought and achieved through affluent learning. Even the poems that seem the most casual, an immediate reflection of reality, have their literary antecedents, as for instance, in many cases, the Greek epigram, whose influence is noticeable above all in the elegiac poems. The tie to a precise occasion secures for the Catullan poems a freshness that is utterly incomparable.

The educated recipient

But one should not forget that the recipient of each poem, whose presence before the poet's mind has direct and important consequences for the formal organization of the poem itself, generally belongs to a refined and educated circle. He thus expects a literary product whose style and form reach a certain level—rather, this is his due. Thus one element of the complex stylistic mixture is the precise literary echoes, which almost never have a purely ornamental value but are concealed, more or less skillfully, in an appearance of passionate outburst or playful immediacy, as if they were the unmediated reflexes of an emotion and nothing more. Moreover, solid formal structures constitute the web on which is woven the (to all appearances) entirely free play of the poet. There may be, as in poem 2, a harmonious framework that supports an emotionally lively surface movement and guides it into a simple, refined structure:

> Passer, deliciae meae puellae,
> quicum ludere, quem in sinu tenere,
> cui primum digitum dare appetenti,
> et acris solet incitare morsus,
> cum desiderio meo nitenti
> carum nescioquid libet iocari,
> credo, ut, cum gravis acquiescet ardor,
> sit solaciolum sui doloris:
> tecum ludere sicut ipsa possem
> et tristis animi levare curas!

("Sparrow, pet of my darling, with whom she often plays, whom she holds in her lap, to whom she gives the tip of her finger to peck, and whom she provokes to sharp bites, whenever she, the shining object of my desires, wants to enjoy some pretty play, in order that, as I think, when her fierce passion abates, it may be a small relief from her pain: if only I could play with you as she does and lift the gloomy cares from my heart!"). What appears to be a sigh escaped from the poet is in fact a poem delicately constructed on precise formal relations: the pointed close, consisting of two verses, caps the body of the poem, which is articulated as two symmetrical halves, each of four verses.

Effects of spontaneity and structure of the discourse

One may thus discover, without the effect being destroyed thereby, that a balanced play of antitheses or symmetrical echoes is hidden behind those words that appear to be dictated by the most immediate passion, for instance, in the more well-known of the "kiss poems" (poem 5):

> Vivamus, mea Lesbia, atque amemus
> rumoresque senum severiorum
> omnes unius aestimemus assis.
> soles occidere et redire possunt:
> nobis, cum semel occidit brevis lux,
> nox est perpetua una dormienda.
> da mi basia mille, deinde centum,
> dein mille altera, dein secunda centum,
> deinde usque altera mille, deinde centum.
> dein, cum milia multa fecerimus,
> conturbabimus illa, ne sciamus,

aut ne quis malus invidere possit,
cum tantum sciat esse basiorum.

("Let us live, my Lesbia, and let us love, and let us value at one penny all
the talk of censorious old men. Suns can set and rise again, but once the
brief light has set for us, we must sleep one unbroken night. Give me a
thousand kisses, then a hundred, then a second thousand, then a second
hundred, then still another thousand, then a hundred. Then, when we have
made up many thousands, we will confuse the counting, so that we do not
know it, and so that no wicked person be able to cast an evil eye upon us,
when he knows the number of our kisses"). The reflective and sententious
pause in verses 4–6 creates its meaning on the basis of a contrast, which it
enhances with phono-symbolic effects. Note the opposition between *brevis*
and *perpetua* and the conspicuous collocation of the two assonant monosyl-
lables *lux* and *nox,* one at the end, the other at the beginning of a verse, so
that the antithesis acquires an irresistible pathetic force. To be sure, after
this meditative pause the burst of the "invitation to kisses" seems, at first
sight, to stand out like the happy cry of one who wants to break out of his
dread of death. But analysis reveals the careful construction of what looks
like the spontaneous, unchecked expression of an existential rebellion.
Even the symmetry in the alternation of *deinde* (1), *dein/dein* (2), *deinde/
deinde* (2), *dein* (1) in verses 7–10 shows clearly how none of the effects
is casual.

Thus the intentional circularity of certain structures, despite their fiery
emotional content, can give a strong, peremptory form to what might
appear, at first sight, to be pure affective "gush." Consider, for example, the
unforgettable rhythm of poem 8, with its carefully calculated play of musical tempi:

Miser Catulle, desinas ineptire,
et quod vides perisse perditum ducas.
fulsere quondam candidi tibi soles,
cum ventitabas quo puella ducebat
amata nobis quantum amabitur nulla.
ibi illa multa tum iocosa fiebant,
quae tu volebas nec puella nolebat.
fulsere quondam candidi tibi soles

("Poor Catullus, you should cease to play the fool, and regard as lost what
you see is lost. Once the sun shone bright upon you, when you used to go
where your girlfriend led you, she who was loved as no other will ever be
loved. Then those many delights occurred there, which you wanted and to
which your girlfriend was not opposed. Truly the sun once shone bright
upon you" [vv. 1–8]). In the compass of a few verses we find the force of
the imperious invitation to resign oneself, the pause like the storyteller's
(*quondam*) that recalls the *candidi soles* (marked by rhyme and the phonic
effects of repetition), the reaffirmation in a harsher tone of a will bent on
saving itself, the unexpected bursting of this ostentatious certainty in an

anxious series of short, urgent questions, until the lapidary final verse repeats the opening vocative and the thematic center of the poem—*at tu, Catulle, destinatus obdura*—and at the same time closes the poem in a strong circular form, which manages to convey at the same time anxiety and the effort made to check it.

It is necessary therefore to avoid the risks of a biographical reading—some have in fact believed that on the basis of Catullus's poems they could faithfully reconstruct the story of his affair with Lesbia—and instead to probe in every case the complex origin of this poetry that is pervaded by learning. It is not a question of denying the presence of "real life," the truly unusual importance that biographical experience takes on in Catullus; rather it is one of seeing how it shapes itself within the forms of the tradition.

The world of the short poems

The background of Catullus's poetry is the fashionable, literary milieu of the capital, part of which is formed by his circle of neoteric friends, who are united by the same tastes, by the same language, by an ideal of charm and brilliance of spirit. *Lepos* ("grace"), *venustas* ("charm"), and *urbanitas* ("urbanity") are the principles forming the basis of this ethical and esthetic code, which governs behavior and mutual relations yet also inspires literary and artistic taste. Against this background the figure of Lesbia stands out, the incarnation of the devastating power of eros, the unquestioned protagonist of Catullus's poetry. Her very pseudonym, which recalls Sappho, the poetess of Lesbos, is enough to create an idealizing halo around the woman. In addition to grace and an unusual beauty, she has the intelligence, cultivation, brilliance of spirit, and refinement of manners to bewitch and to stimulate Catullus's passion.

The centrality of love

Joys, sufferings, betrayals, abandonments, regrets, hopes, and disillusionments articulate the events of this love, which is lived by Catullus as the principal experience of his life, an experience capable of filling and giving meaning to it. Love is no longer confined to the marginal space to which traditional morality had consigned it, as if it were a weakness of youth, tolerable provided that it did not go beyond certain limits and social conventions. Now it becomes the center of existence and a primary value, the only one able to compensate for the fleetingness of human life: poem 5, *Vivamus, mea Lesbia, atque amemus . . .*, "Let us live, my Lesbia, and let us love . . . ," is famous in this connection. Catullus transfers all his energies to love and the life of the feelings, withdrawing from the duties and concerns proper to a Roman citizen. Politics and the events of public life remain foreign to him, as do the power conflicts that are tearing apart late republican society; he does no more than express a general disdainful disgust towards the new protagonists of the political scene, who are arrogant and corrupt. The relation with Lesbia, which began essentially as adultery, as free love based on eros, by becoming the exclusive object of the poet's moral commitment tends, paradoxically, to become thereby like a powerful matrimonial bond in Catullus's hopes: the theme of marriage, of conjugal fidelity, recurs insistently, especially in the *carmina docta*.

The violated pact

Recriminations for the love pact violated by Lesbia are an insistent theme in the poet, who emphasizes the sacred character of the concept by appealing to two cardinal values in the Roman social order and ideology: *fides,* which by binding the two parties morally guarantees the pact agreed to, and *pietas,* the virtue proper to the person who carries out his duties towards others, especially blood relations, as well as towards the gods. He tries to make this irregular relationship an *aeternum . . . sanctae foedus amicitiae,* "an everlasting pact of holy friendship" (109.6), and he ennobles it with the tenderness of family affection (*pater ut gnatos diligit et generos,* "as a father loves his children and his children-in-law" [72.4]), but the repeated offense of Lesbia's betrayal produces in him a painful split between sensuality (*amare*) and affection (*bene velle*). The famous instance of this inner conflict is poem 72, which analyzes with lucid bitterness the disappearance of any esteem or affection for that woman who still, even more intensely, inflames the lover's passion: *iniuria talis / cogit amare magis, sed bene velle minus,* "such an injury forces him to love more but to respect less." Especially well known is poem 85, which condenses into an oxymoron the painful sensation of the poet astonished at the split feelings that lacerate him:

Odi et amo. Quare id faciam, fortasse requiris.
Nescio sed fieri sentio et excrucior.

("I love and I hate. You ask perhaps why I do so. I do not know, but I feel it happening and am tormented").

The pleasure of recollection

The ever-frustrated hope for a love that is faithfully repaid accompanies Catullus's consciousness that he never failed to keep the *foedus* of love with Lesbia, the pleasing certainty of his own blamelessness. At one time it was believed that in poem 76 we could glimpse a trust in a recompense in the next world; in fact, however, the poem is the most well-known expression of that consolation that lies in good conscience, of a pleasure in recollection that is assured for the rest of mortal life by the consciousness of having kept faith with a moral commitment. This is the sole sure satisfaction that his love for Lesbia can have given him.

The *Carmina Docta*

The new poetics and the epyllion

Lepidus, novus, expolitus ("charming, new, polished"): presenting his *libellus* thus in the dedicatory poem, Catullus defines not only its material, external features but also, indirectly, its internal features, the criteria of a new poetics inspired by brilliance of wit and refinement in form. This poetics openly reveals its Alexandrian, or rather, Callimachean, ancestry, especially in the sort of manifesto for the new literary taste that we find in poem 95, the announcement of the publication of his friend Cinna's poem. Brevity, elegance, and learning are the principles of a taste to which Catullus adheres without reservation, and he opposes polemically the verbose superficiality of those late representatives of the Ennian school over whom the incompetent public raves. The true connoisseurs, by contrast, will appreciate the new epic developed by the neoteric poets, the epyllion, the brief poem (of a few hundred verses): by its very scale it encourages the patient work of stylistic refinement that is conducive to terseness and pregnant expression, and, as for content, it permits the poet to display his precious learning (for the most part the subjects are exotic mythological events and their pathologically passionate consequences).

Poem 64: fides projected onto myth

Learning and stylistic effort, not to mention a greater amplitude in the compositions, are particularly evident in the section of the poems that for this reason are known as "learned," in which Catullus also tries out new forms of composition in which he displays a refined understanding of structure. Like other neoteric poets—Cinna with his *Zmyrna*, Valerius Cato with the *Dictynna*, Calvus with the *Io*, Caecilius, a poet mentioned by Catullus, with the *Magna Mater*—he ventures upon the new epic genre, the epyllion. Poem 64 would be virtually the model example of it for Latin culture. This very famous poem, in 408 hexameters, recounts the myth of the marriage of Peleus and Thetis, but in the central episode it contains another story, embedded within it by means of the Alexandrian technique of *ekphrasis* and digression, in the form of a scene embroidered on the nuptial bedcover. This is the story of Theseus's abandonment of Ariadne on Naxos, a theme widespread in Greek and Latin literature (the heroine's lament would be the model for Ovid's *Heroides*). The interweaving of the two love stories, the unhappy love of Ariadne and the happy love of Peleus and Thetis, establishes between them a series of relations that all bear on the theme of *fides,* the cardinal virtue in the Catullan ethical world— that *fides* of which the gods themselves were guarantors in the distant heroic era and which in the corrupt present is violated and despised along with the other religious and moral values. The myth, that is to say, becomes the symbolic projection of the poet's aspirations, of his perpetually unsatisfied need to fasten so precarious a love with a firmer bond, a lasting *foedus.*

Poem 63

Poem 63 is also an epyllion. It is inspired by the act of the young Phrygian Attis, who in a religious frenzy castrates himself in order to become a priest of Cybele, the great mother of the gods (her orgiastic cult with its obsessive music and bloody dances was introduced to Rome in 205–204 B.C.), and then, once he is free from his rage, regrets the mad gesture. Poem 63, however, does not have the usual meter of the epyllion, the hexameter; instead it is written in galliambics, an Alexandrian lyric meter used to express the orgiastic frenzy of the cult of Cybele.

The two epithalamia: a) Poem 61

Poems 61 and 62 are epithalamia, that is, nuptial songs (we have already referred to the importance of the theme of marriage in the *carmina docta*). The first is composed for the marriage of Lucius Manlius Torquatus and Vinia (or Junia) Aurunculeia, and it is conceived as sung during the *deductio,* the procession that accompanies the bride: after the hymn to Hymenaeus, god of weddings, follows the invitation to the bride to leave her father's house and to go in procession, amid Fescennine songs, to the house of her husband, who receives her in the bridal chamber. The poem consists of forty-seven strophes and combines the eminently Greek form of this literary genre, which flourished from Sappho to the Alexandrian period, with the typically Italian-Roman elements of the nuptial rite and its ethical and social implications.

b) *Poem 62*

The other epithalamium, poem 62, is made up of a series of strophes, in hexameters, sung alternatively and competitively by two choruses of boys and girls on the theme of marriage and virginity. It is not, however, composed for the real occasion of a marriage. Touches of Roman sensibility are not lacking, but in general the poem has a more marked literary character and adheres more closely to the formal features of the genre. In the structure and topoi the influence of Sappho is especially evident.

Poem 66, the translation from Callimachus

The cycle of the *carmina docta* also contains a poem that is an act of homage to the chief poet of Alexandrianism, Callimachus. This poem, number 66, is the translation into Latin verses of a famous elegy by the Greek poet known as the *Lock of Berenice,* which seems to have occupied the final part of the fourth book of the *Aitia* and which has come down to us in a mutilated, fragmentary form. In this poem Callimachus celebrated in verse the courtly invention of Conon, the court astronomer of Ptolemy III Euergetes, king of Egypt, in which he had identified a new constellation discovered by him as the lock of hair that Queen Berenice had made a votive offering for her husband's return from war and that had subsequently disappeared. In freely translating the catasterism, that is, the transformation of Berenice's lock into a constellation, Catullus introduces or emphasizes themes that are central to his ideology and particularly insistent in the larger poems: glorification of *fides* and *pietas,* condemnation of adultery, and celebration of the heroic virtues, the traditional values. Poem 67 also operates with these themes: in it a door recounts the far from edifying events of the family living in that house.

Poem 65

Poem 65 is closely connected to poem 66. It is a letter, in elegiac couplets, to Catullus's friend Hortensius Hortalus, accompanying the translation from Callimachus. Catullus justifies sending the simple translation instead of the poem he had promised by his desperation over the death of his brother, which has dried up his creative vein.

Poem 68: love and mythic archetype

Poem 68 is particularly complex. The unresolved question of its unity makes interpretation difficult: should this poem, transmitted as a single poem in the manuscripts, really be separated into two, and in that case, what is the relation between the two? The poem, in any event, takes up the principal themes of Catullus's poetry—friendship, love, poetic activity and its connection with Rome, grief over the death of his brother. The recollection of his first, furtive love episodes with Lesbia shades off into myth, into the story of Protesilaus and Laodamia (who were joined in love before marriage and were therefore punished with the death of Protesilaus when he had barely disembarked at Troy); this becomes the archetype of the affair between Catullus and Lesbia, another imperfect and precarious

Towards Latin elegy

union. Poem 68 deserves special mention because of its place in Latin literary history: the large space given to recollection and to a mythically projected real life in a poem that far exceeds the dimensions of the epigram must have made it appear as the ancestor of the Latin subjective elegy.

Style

Elegance and Catul-lan expressiveness

Catullus's literary culture, as has been said, is rich and complex. Beside the dominant influence of Alexandrian literature, with its precious elegance, one feels that of archaic Greek literature too, the intense affectivity of Archilochus and Sappho. Catullus's language is a novel combination of literary language with everyday speech: the vocabulary and the movements of the spoken language are absorbed and filtered by an aristocratic taste that makes it fine and precious without paralyzing its expressive capacities. The filter of Callimachean taste, that is to say, does not produce a lifeless elegance, and it allows, for instance, the crude expressiveness of certain vulgarisms. These should not be understood as a touch of authentically popular language; rather, they should be traced back to the snobbish pleasure of a cultivated elite that loves to display foul language along with more refined erudition. Among the features of *sermo familiaris* the diminutives are particularly frequent. In their very softness of sound and form (*flosculus, labella, turgiduli ocelli, molliculus, pallidulus, tenellulus,* etc.) they seem to reveal that adherence to the esthetic of *lepos,* "charm," that unites the circle of Catullus's friends, shapes their modes of expression, and redefines the hierarchy of their ethical values.

Unity and diversity between nugae *and* carmina docta

The style, in short, is composite and always lively, with a wide range of expressive means extending from mocking disdain and scathing, scurrilous invective to the tenderness of the language of love, from youthful self-assurance as it expands images into hyperbole to light gracefulness, calm melancholy, and, especially in the later poems, the abandon of certain elegiac moments. The vitality of the affective language and the intensity of the pathos are not absent from the *carmina docta* either. For some time now, criticism has rightly reacted against the idea of a sharp distinction between, on the one hand, the short poems, which are more expressive in a lively fashion and in which the affective and autobiographical element is prominent, and, on the other hand, the larger compositions, in which the learning and stylistic care are more in evidence. But the distinction, if it should not be exaggerated, should not be eliminated either, since various elements conspire to give to the *carmina docta* a more obviously literary character in the form of a generally more affected diction and stylistic traits and movements from high poetry, that is, the Ennian tradition, such as archaisms, compounds, alliterative clausulae, and so on.

Literary Success

Antiquity

Individually and in groups, Catullus's poems circulated among his friends during his lifetime, but the collection that has reached us was probably published posthumously and may also reflect an editor's arrangement and divisions. It achieved a vast and immediate success among cultivated Latin readers. In particular, it exercised a profound influence upon the Augustan poets (with the exception of Horace). Not only the elegists, who regard Catullus as one of their most important literary ancestors, but also the Virgil of the *Eclogues* and the Dido episode slip irresistibly into the language of Catullus (especially that of Ariadne) when they combine erotic passion with refined diction and baroque style. At some point, perhaps shortly after Catullus's death, a witty parodist transformed poem 4 into a biting satire on a parvenu, which has survived as *Catalepton* 8 in the *Appendix Vergiliana.* In the imperial period, Catullus is quoted or referred to by the elder and younger Pliny, by Quintilian, and by Apuleius. But among surviving authors it is Martial who most often takes Catullus as his point of reference, though Catullus is for him no longer the poet of turbulent passion, but of wittily pointed malice. Even in late antiquity Catullus is studied by grammarians, lexicographers, and metricians such as Aulus Gellius and continues to fascinate poets—in Gaul, Ausonius, Paulinus, and Sidonius Apollinaris; in Africa, Corippus.

Middle Ages   In the Middle Ages, on the other hand, Catullus seems to have been known scarcely, if at all. The echoes that have been noticed in writers from the eighth through the twelfth century, such as Paulus Diaconus, Heiric of Auxerre, and William of Malmesbury, are rare, faint, and probably indirect. Isidore of Seville quotes him in the seventh century, but then he is not mentioned again until 966, when Bishop Rather of Catullus's own hometown of Verona discovered a manuscript that contained his poems and reproached himself for occupying himself day and night with Catullus's poetry, which he had not known before. Bishop Rather's manuscript promptly vanished again for another three and a half centuries and did not reappear until shortly after 1300, still in Verona. Benvenuto de Campesanis celebrated the discovery as the poet's resurrection from the dead, and in fact the Veronese codex is the sole source of all surviving manuscripts. Had it been lost, the only poem of Catullus's that might have survived to give us some idea of his qualities is poem 62, which was also preserved in the *florilegium Thuaneum,* a ninth-century French miscellany.

Once the Verona manuscript resurfaced, Catullus's survival was assured. In 1329 an anonymous Veronese anthologizer included verses from Catullus in his *Flores moralium auctoritatum.* In 1375 Coluccio Salutati obtained a transcript, and at least 150 late manuscripts descended from it are extant. Catullus became a favorite poet in the Renaissance and a central model for neo-Latin love elegy. Already by 1347 Petrarch read him in the Verona codex and admired and imitated him (though his explicit references are sparing and he does not include Catullus among the *libri peculiares* he constantly reread); so did later humanist poets such as Panormita, Pontano, and Marullus. And in Venice in 1472 appeared the *editio princeps,* together with Tibullus, Propertius, and Statius's *Silvae.*

Renaissance and   Although Martial's epigrammatic Catullus became popular in the
after   Renaissance and in the seventeenth century, it is the elegists' passionate Catullus who has tended most to fascinate modern readers. In the Romantic period, Byron referred several times to Catullus as a poet of love, while Foscolo translated his translation (*carmen* 66) of Callimachus's poem on the Lock of Berenice (already Pope had had it in mind when he had written his

Rape of the Lock) and was inspired by poem 101 in his sonnet on the death of his own brother. More recently Catullus's short poems inspired Pascoli's Latin "Catullocalvos," while his masterpiece, poem 64, was brilliantly adapted by Hugo von Hofmannsthal and Richard Strauss in the opera *Ariadne auf Naxos*. No other Latin poet appeals so directly and immediately to most modern readers.

BIBLIOGRAPHY

For the fragments of the pre-neoteric and neoteric poets, see W. Morel, *Fragmenta poetarum latinorum epicorum et lyricorum praeter Ennium et Lucilium* (Leipzig 1927, reprint 1963), K. Büchner's revision (Leipzig 1982, with bibliography), and E. Courtney, *The Fragmentary Latin Poets* (Oxford 1993), as well as A. Traglia *Poetae Novi* (Rome 1974). The most convenient English account of the pre-neoterics is in D. O. Ross, *Style and Tradition in Catullus* (Cambridge, Mass. 1969) 139–60, though his interpretation is controversial; see also J. Granarolo, *D'Ennius à Catulle* (Paris 1971), and E. Zaffagno, *Espressionismo latino tardo-repubblicano* (Genoa 1987). On the neoterics, see esp. T. P. Wiseman, *Cinna the Poet and Other Essays* (Leicester 1974) 44–58, C. Tuplin, "Cantores Euphorionis," *PLLS* 1 (1977) 1–23, R.O.A.M. Lyne, "The Neoteric Poets," *CQ* 28 (1978) 168–87, E. Castorina, *Questioni Neoteriche* (Florence 1968), and N. B. Crowther, "Parthenius and Roman Poetry," *Mnemosyne* 29 (1976) 65–71. Among studies of individual neoterics may be mentioned N. B. Crowther, "Valerius Cato, Furius Bibaculus, and Ticidas," *CPh* 66 (1971) 108–9 (skeptical); on Cinna and Calvus, the introduction to R.O.A.M. Lyne's edition of the *Ciris* (Cambridge 1978) 39–45, as well as R. F. Thomas, "Cinna, Calvus, and the *Ciris*," *CQ* 31 (1981) 371–74, and L. C. Watson, "Cinna and Euphorion," *SIFC* 54 (1982) 93–110; and on Varro of Atax, M. Bonvincini, "Per un commento a Varrone Atacino," *BollStudLat* 11 (1981) 224–31.

The standard edition of Catullus is the Oxford text by R.A.B. Mynors (Oxford 1958). There is more information on the manuscripts in the edition by D.F.S. Thomson (Chapel Hill 1978), but see D. S. McKie in *Studies in Latin Literature and Its Influence*, ed. J. Diggle, J. B. Hall, and H. D. Jocelyn (Cambridge 1989) 66–86. More readable but more speculative texts are in the editions with commentary of G. P. Goold (London 1983) and G. Lee (Oxford 1990). There are also Teubner texts by H. Bardon (Stuttgart 1973) and W. Eisenhut (Leipzig 1983). The most helpful commentaries in English are those of R. Ellis (ed. 2 Oxford 1889) and C. J. Fordyce (Oxford 1961, omitting the "obscene" poems); more elementary but also useful are those of K. Quinn (London 1970), P. Y. Forsyth (Lanham, N.Y.), and D. H. Garrison (Norman, Okla., 1989). In other languages, note esp. the commentaries of A. Baehrens (Leipzig 1876, Latin), G. Friedrich (Leipzig 1908, German), M. Lenchantin de Gubernatis (Turin 1933, Italian), W. Kroll (ed. 3 Stuttgart 1959, German), and H.-P. Syndikus (3 vols., Darmstadt 1984–90, German, without text). There are separate commentaries on poem 61 by P. Fedeli (trans. M. Nardella, Amsterdam 1983, a poor translation of the Italian original, Fribourg 1972, but incorporating corrections and additions) and on 66 by N. Marinone, *Berenice da Callimaco a Catullo* (Rome 1984).

There are many studies of Catullus in English; note esp. A. L. Wheeler, *Catullus and the Traditions of Ancient Poetry* (Berkeley 1934), C. L. Neudling, *A Prosopography to Catullus* (Oxford 1955), K. Quinn, *The Catullan Revolution* (Melbourne 1972) and *Catullus: An Interpretation* (London 1972), Ross, *Style and Tradition in Catullus,* and T. P. Wiseman, *Catullan Questions* (Leicester 1969) and *Catullus and His World* (Cambridge 1985, speculative, includes the fullest edition of the "fragments" of Catullus). There is a detailed bibliography to 1972 by J. P. Holoka (New York 1985). Note also the collection of mostly English articles edited by K. Quinn, *Approaches to Catullus* (Cambridge 1972), and the German collection by R. Heine in the Wege der Forschung series (Darmstadt 1975).

Lucretius

The most extensive biographical notice about Lucretius appears in the translation of Eusebius's *Chronicon* made by Jerome, who also inserted notices from Suetonius's *De Poetis* about various Latin writers: *Titus Lucretius poeta nascitur: qui postea amatorio poculo in furorem versus, cum aliquot libros per intervalla insaniae conscripsisset, quos postea Cicero emendavit, propria se manu interfecit anno aetatis XLIV* ("The poet Titus Lucretius is born. Subsequently driven to madness by a love-philter, after having written several books in the intervals of lucidity that his madness allowed him, which books were later revised by Cicero, he died by his own hand at the age of 43"). It is not easy to date this notice or to harmonize it with information given by Donatus in his *Vita Vergili*. One can say for certain only that the poet was born in the nineties and died around the mid-fifties.

Some manuscripts of Jerome place his birth in 96, others in 94. The date of death varies accordingly between 53 and 51. But the grammarian Aelius Donatus claims that Lucretius died when Virgil, at the age of seventeen, put on the *toga virilis* and the consuls were Pompey and Crassus, the same as in 70, the year of Virgil's birth. These men, however, were consuls for the second time in 55, not 53, so it has been suspected that the indication of Virgil's age—he would have been fifteen, not seventeen—is corrupt. The date thus obtained (15 October 55) could fit with Jerome's notice if we allow that he has confused the names of the consuls for 94 and 98, the year in which Lucretius's birth ought to be set. Today, 98 and 55 are generally regarded as the most likely dates, but considerable uncertainties remain.

In all likelihood Jerome's notice on the madness of Lucretius ought to be rejected. It is never recorded earlier, not even by Lactantius, although he metaphorically accused the poet of "being delirious" and would not have missed the opportunity to refer to so important an episode had he known of it. The accusation must have first been made in a Christian setting in the fourth century in order to discredit Lucretius's polemic against religion. Still, even today some critics attach importance to the accusation in order to support the improbable notion that Lucretius, as a pathological depressive, was a man without hope; with this they attempt to contrast certain pessimistic traits in Lucretius with the optimism of Epicurus.

Nothing concrete can be asserted about the poet's origin. It has been thought that he was a Campanian, on the grounds that an Epicurean school was flourishing at Naples and that the *Venus physica* worshipped at Pompeii has features similar to the Venus to whom Lucretius devotes the proem of his work. But it must be admitted that this hypothesis lacks any convincing basis, as does the hypothesis that, on the basis of a few references to precise places in Rome, has the poet born there. It would be interesting to determine the social class from which Lucretius comes, but from the tone of the words he addresses to the aristocrat Memmius in the course of the work it is not possible to tell whether he put himself on the same level or was instead a freedman. The breadth of his learning, in any event, is beyond question. Several more penetrating notices on these subjects are actually present in the *Vita Borgiana,* a succinct biography put together by the humanist Gerolamo Borgia and discovered in 1894. The *Vita* claims that the poet lived "in close intimacy" with Cicero, from whom he is said to have received stylistic suggestions, and with Atticus, Marcus Brutus, and Gaius Cassius, that is, with the most outstanding persons of the first half of the first century B.C. The majority of modern scholars, however, hold the *Vita* to be a forgery of the humanist period. The only reference to Lucretius in the works of Cicero comes in a letter to his younger brother Quintus, in February of 54 (*Ad Quintum Fratrem* 2.9.3): *Lucreti poemata, ut scribis, ita sunt, multis luminibus ingeni, multae tamen artis,* which probably means, "In the poems of Lucretius, as you write to me, there are indeed the flashes of genius, but also the signs of great literary art." (The precise sense is difficult to recover, and no definitive consensus has yet emerged among interpreters.) From the tone of the phrase some deduce that the poet had died recently, perhaps in October of 55, and that Cicero was reading for the first time the manuscript that had been entrusted to him for publication (the *emendavit* of Jerome); but the supposition is weak.

WORKS

The *De Rerum Natura,* in hexameters, consists of six books, each containing anywhere from about 1,100 verses to a maximum of about 1,500, giving a total of 7,415. It may be unfinished, or at any rate lacking final revision. It is dedicated to the aristocrat Memmius, probably to be identified with the Gaius Memmius who was the friend and patron of Catullus and Cinna. Jerome, in the same passage of the *Chronicon* in which he reports the biographical notices about Lucretius, asserts that the *De Rerum Natura* was revised and published by Cicero after the poet's death.

The text of the *De Rerum Natura* is transmitted in its entirety by two ninth-century manuscripts, called, on account of their shape, *Oblongus* and *Quadratus* (abbreviated O and Q), and now preserved at Leiden. Some parts are also found in *schedae,* manuscript sheets, preserved at Copenhagen and Vienna. A number of humanist manuscripts reproduce the text that was derived from the manuscript that Poggio Bracciolini rediscovered in 1418, during a trip to Germany. The first printed edition was produced in 1473 by Ferrando of Brescia.

I. LUCRETIUS AND ROMAN EPICUREANISM

Anti-Epicureanism of the Roman governing class

Leaving aside the rigid intolerance of Cato the Censor (see p. 89), the stance of the Roman governing class towards the penetration of Greek thought was that of a careful filtering, which eliminated the elements potentially threatening to the institutional order of the Republic or potentially corrosive of the *mos maiorum*. This was the path taken by the Scipionic elite and later by Cicero. It is not accidental that the latter's sensible philosophical eclecticism raises an insurmountable barrier to Epicureanism (see pp. 193 f.); it is seen as the dissolver of the moral tradition, chiefly because by positing pleasure as the highest good and urging the pursuit of tranquillity, it tends to withdraw the citizens from political engagement on behalf of the institutions. The Epicurean position on the gods presented dangers that were no smaller. Denying their intervention in human affairs, it tended to disturb a governing class that was accustomed to using the official religion as a tool of power.

Penetration of Epicureanism at Rome in the first century B.C.

Although in the second century B.C. steps had been taken to expel two Epicurean philosophers, Alcaeus and Philiscus, who wanted to spread their doctrine at Rome, in the first century Epicureanism had succeeded in spreading itself discreetly within the higher levels of Roman society. A man of consular rank, Calpurnius Piso Caesoninus, offered himself as the patron of Epicurean philosophers, and Philodemus of Gadara gave lessons in his villa at Herculaneum. Another Epicurean group arose in Naples, where young men of varying social origins studied under the direction of Siro, among them the offspring of noble families as well as future poets, such as Virgil and probably Horace. We also know of the Epicurean leanings of Atticus, Cicero's friend, of Caesar, and of the tyrannicide Cassius. This suffices to show how Epicureanism recruited its adherents from both the factions that opposed one another in public life.

Epicureanism among the lower classes

We know less about the penetration of Epicurean doctrines among the lower classes. However, an interesting passage in Cicero's *Tusculan Disputations* (4.7) informs us that popularizations of Epicureanism, written in bad Latin prose by Amafinius (period uncertain, perhaps end of the second, beginning of the first century B.C.) and by Catius (first century B.C.), were in circulation among the plebs, who were attracted by the ease with which they could understand these texts and by the invitations to pleasure that they disseminated. Epicurus himself in fact recommended utter clarity and simplicity of expression. Without yielding to unhistoric distortions about "democracy," we ought to recall the universality of the Epicurean message, which addressed itself not to a rigidly selected elite but to persons of every social rank and even—something unheard of in antiquity—to women.

Epicureanism and poetry

Lucretius nonetheless followed a path radically different from that of an Amafinius or a Catius. In order to popularize the Epicurean doctrine, he chose the form of the epic-didactic poem. This must have aroused wonder, for Epicurus had condemned poetry, above all Homeric poetry, the basis of Greek education, on account of its close connection with myth, on account of the world of beautiful inventions in which it ensnared the readers, keeping them from a rational understanding of reality. Later Epicureans held scrupulously to the master's strictures, cultivating all the more, as Philodemus did, playful poetry or poetry of a purely entertaining sort. Lucretius was probably guided in his choice by the desire to reach the upper levels of society with a message that lacked literary appeal, that outward beauty in which the other philosophies of the day were clothed. Almost at the beginning of the poem Lucretius states explicitly that his purpose is "to spread with the honey of the Muses" an apparently bitter doctrine, just as for children one spreads with honey the lips of a cup containing bitter wormwood in order to make them well. Thus it is not an accident that Lucretius, departing radically from his master Epicurus, displays admiration for Homer. Yet he also found important models in the whole epic-didactic tradition, particularly in Empedocles, the poet-philosopher of the fifth century, who in Lucretius's own day was experiencing a revival of interest at Rome. Lucretius certainly rejected Empedocles' mystical philosophical inspiration, but he was probably fascinated by his missionary zeal and his prophetic stance as revealer of the truth.

It has been thought that Cicero's puzzling attitude is to be explained by the poetic form that Lucretius chose for spreading his message. We have already referred to Jerome's notice that makes Cicero the editor of the *De Rerum Natura.* It is obvious that Cicero could not share Lucretius's philosophical ideals, and ten years after the presumed publication of the *De Rerum Natura,* that is, between 46 and 44, when he undertakes a fierce attack on Epicureanism in his philosophical essays, Cicero makes no further reference to Lucretius's poem, although he mentions in a disparaging way the works of Amafinius and Catius. Perhaps the very unusualness of the poetic form, which makes the work unique in Epicurean literature, urged Cicero to disregard Lucretius—he preferred to go directly to the Greek sources of Epicureanism—but the principal reason for so unusual a silence must have been Cicero's desire not to give space and credibility, by making him an interlocutor in the dialogues, to one who had written a work that tended so strongly to undo the bonds of the society Cicero was addressing.

2. THE DIDACTIC POEM

The title of Lucretius's poem *De Rerum Natura* faithfully translates the title of Epicurus's most important work, the lost *Peri Physeos,* in thirty-seven books. From this had been derived a *Small Epitome,* which may be the preserved *Letter to Herodotus,* and a *Large Epitome,* now lost, which was probably the chief outline followed by Lucretius, who must also have had at hand other texts by Epicurus himself. The date of the poem's composition is not certain. At 1.41 the author declares that Memmius cannot withdraw from his concern for the commonweal "at a difficult moment for the country." The entire first half of the century is ravaged by wars, but there is a tendency to believe that the reference is to the internal discord of the years

Lucretius's choice: motives and models

Cicero and Lucretius

Title and date of Lucretius's poem

after 59, in part because Memmius was praetor in 58. It is not impossible, however, to think of earlier dates.

Summary of the
Poem

The *De Rerum Natura* is clearly articulated into three groups of two books apiece, three dyads. After the overture of the poem, which is formed by the hymn to Venus, the personification of Nature's generative force, the first book sets forth the principles of Epicurean physics: the atoms, those indestructible, immutable, infinite minimal parts of matter, moving about in the infinite void, join together in different ways and give rise to all the realities that exist; the atoms also separate from one another. Birth and death are constituted by this continuous process of aggregation and disintegration. At the end of the book Lucretius reviews critically the doctrines of the other natural philosophers, Heraclitus, Empedocles, and Anaxagoras. In the second book (vv. 216–93) the theory of *clinamen* is illustrated, which is Epicurus's most original feature in relation to Democritus: a minimal swerve interferes with the movement of the atoms, permitting a great variety of aggregations and accounting for human free will. There is an infinite number of worlds, and they are all subject to the cycle of birth and death.

Books 3 and 4 constitute a second pair, which sets forth Epicurean anthropology. Book 3 explains how body and soul are both constituted of aggregated atoms but are different in form. Those making up the soul are lighter and smoother. The soul for that reason cannot escape from the process of disintegration that attacks all realities that consist of atoms. It therefore dies along with the body, and there is no expectation of heavenly reward or punishment. The fourth book investigates the faculty of mind and deals with the theory of *simulacra,* which are thin membranes, made of atoms, that preserve the form of the bodies to which they belong. They detach themselves from the bodies and reach the sense organs. The testimony of the senses is always truthful, and error can derive only from a mistaken interpretation of it. The wandering *simulacra* also explain the images we see in our dreams; equally, they are the origin of sleepers' reactions to the images of the objects of their desires. At this point Lucretius introduces a famous digression on the passion of love and, in verses dripping with sarcasm, points to physical attraction as the sole cause of this passion.

The third pair of books is devoted to cosmology. Book 5 demonstrates the mortality of our world, which is one of innumerable existing worlds, by analyzing the process of its formation. It also examines the problem of the movement of the stars and its causes. A famous section treats of the brutish origin of mankind. The sixth book attempts to provide absolutely natural explanations of various physical phenomena, such as thunderbolts and earthquakes, eliminating any divine will from them. The description of various catastrophic events is followed by the narrative of the terrible plague at Athens in 430, which had already been told by the Greek historian Thucydides. With this the work comes to a rather abrupt end.

The ending

It has already been said that the *De Rerum Natura* probably did not receive the final revision from the author. This is shown by some repetitions of verses and certain inconsistencies. The ending of the poem has given rise to particular problems. Since Lucretius in book 5 announces that he will describe the blessed abode of the gods but does not keep his promise, it has been thought that this description, and not the description of the plague at Athens, was the intended ending of the *De Rerum Natura.* If one were to accept this hypothesis, the poem would have had to end on a tranquil note, which would have been a pendant to the joyous hymn to Venus at the opening, rather than with the terrifying picture of the plague. But it is probably more in line with Lucretius's true intentions to suppose that the intended ending of the poem was indeed the plague and nothing else. According to this view, Lucretius would have wanted to contrast the opening and the close as a sort of "triumph of life" and "triumph of death," in order to show how there is no reconciling the eternal contrast between these two powers.

The didactic genre in Rome and Greece

Until the *De Rerum Natura*, Latin literature had not produced fully serious works of didactic poetry. Ennius (see p. 77) wrote his *Epicharmus* in septenarii (the *Euhemerus* was probably in prose). Accius employed the same meter in his *Pragmatia*, whereas he set forth the historical-literary subjects of the *Didascalica* in a mixture of prose and verse. Hellenistic literature, on the contrary, following the authoritative example of Hesiod, Parmenides, and Empedocles, had used the typical verse of epic, the hexameter. In this meter Aratus of Soli (ca. 320–250 B.C.) wrote the *Phenomena and Weather-Signs*, a treatise on astronomy and the techniques of forecasting the weather, and in the same meter Nicander (second century B.C.) wrote the *Alexipharmaca* and *Theriaca*. All these works were translated more than once at Rome, and even the young Cicero during the eighties produced a version of the *Aratea* in Latin hexameters that Lucretius gives signs of knowing. It is not possible to place very precisely a certain Egnatius, author of a *De Rerum Natura* from which Macrobius cites several verses; it is supposed that he was the same person mocked by Catullus in poem 39, but nothing is known about his work or his life. The *Empedoclea* of Sallustius (who is unlikely to be the historian [see p. 235]), now unfortunately lost, went back to earlier Greek models.

Empedocles and Lucretius

The Latin tradition thus did not provide examples of ambitious didactic poetry. Yet at the same time Lucretius clearly differs from the Hellenistic poets mentioned in that he is eager to describe, and especially to explain, every important aspect of the life of the world and of mankind and to convince the reader of the validity of Epicurean doctrine through logical arguments and proofs. The Hellenistic tradition, by contrast, which revives in Virgil's *Georgics,* seeks its inspiration in subjects that are technical, though detached from their original practical setting and almost idealized, and that to a large extent lack philosophical implications. Not surprisingly, the model Lucretius looks to with express sympathy is Empedocles' *Peri Physeos,* which, on account of its content, organization, and certain formal features, such as the use of the hexameter, is very close to the *De Rerum Natura:* at the end of the first book (vv. 705 f.) the poet pays fervent homage to Empedocles, although his positions are distant from Epicurus's.

The relation with the addressee

Lucretius's consciousness of the importance of his material determines the relation he establishes with the reader-pupil, who is constantly exhorted, sometimes with threats, to follow diligently the course of instruction that the author offers him. This is an ulterior, fundamental difference from Hellenistic didactic poetry, which for the most part limits itself to describing phenomena. Lucretius's poetry, by contrast, investigates the causes of the phenomena and lays before the reader a truth, a rational system in accord with which he is obliged to give a clear judgment of agreement or rejection.

The ethos of Hellenistic didactic (i.e., the intention that governed that didactic poetry) had been an eminently encomiastic ethos: it praised things and suggested that the object of the description was marvelous in itself. In Lucretius, by contrast, *non est mirandum* and *nec mirum* are the formulas that often articulate the argument: "there is nothing to marvel at" in this phenomenon or that, because it is *necessarily* connected with this or that objective rule, and the one who has understood the principles of things and their links with one another cannot be astonished at it. Lucretius replaces the "rhetoric of the marvelous" ("Admire and be astonished, you who hear") with the "rhetoric of the necessary," which is in fact the opposite of the marvelous. In the same way, *necesse est* is another of the most frequent formulas in Lucretius's argument. The recipient, who is made directly responsible, reacts to the instruction and becomes conscious of his own intellectual greatness. This is the root of the sublime in Lucretius. For the author

The sublime style constructing the text, the sublime becomes a stylistic form in which a form of interpreting the world is condensed; at the same time, symmetrically, for the reader who is set before the grand spectacle of the universe and its laws, it becomes a form of perceiving things. The sublime involves the one who is the reader of the text and thus the spectator of the great and moving Lucretian description, and it elevates him to *megalopsychia:* it suggests a moral need to the reader and advances him to greatness of soul.

And so it is that the sublime functions for the recipient also as an invitation to action. By representing the sublime, the poet anxiously conveys an exhortation to the reader, that he too should choose for himself a lofty, strong model of life. The entire *De Rerum Natura* then appears as a *protreptikos logos,* an instruction containing dramatic advice: You yourself, reader, should become like the mirror of this majestic and terrible sublimity of the universe, which I am trying to represent adequately with this sublime style of mine. You yourself should become transformed into a "sublime reader," let yourself be moved, and find within yourself the strength to accept and adapt. Hence derives the great frequency of appeals to the reader to be attentive, ready and receptive, and strong in the face of a poetry of strength.

The sublime reader In Lucretius's didactic project, in short, the genre itself becomes a problematic form. The text expects a reader who is ready to engage in a virtual struggle with an instruction that is hard and harsh, an agonistic reader able to make himself and his reactions into the content of the poem. The poem becomes nearly a dramatic spectacle enacted by the text. (Lucretius seems to want, by means of the difficult experience of the sublime, to free his audience from the slavery of easy pleasure: "I follow paths never trodden before, and which are uphill in any event," "I speak truths too bitter, which cause unprepared people to retreat in horror.") The new form that the didactic genre takes on in Lucretius finds its necessary correlative in the creation of an audience that can adapt itself to the sublime force of an overwhelming experience. The doctrine of the atoms is described in itself, but it is also seen in the reactions of giddiness that it can produce in the audience. We may say, then, that the sublime form of the text and the sublime form of the audience (i.e., the image that the text makes of its ideal reader) are the signs of the transformation that the didactic genre needed to undergo when it chose to become the means of communicating a moral *iter,* a wager between the poet-teacher and the recipient-pupil, a wager that may fail. What in the traditional didactic genre is a framework—the teacher-student relation—becomes in the *De Rerum Natura* a center of tension and a problematic theme. The transposition of the genre into didactic discourse is constantly dogged by doubt as to whether it can be realized; thus the reader is often urged, with various repeated formulas, to commit himself and not give way (*illud in his rebus vereor, ne forte rearis* [1.180]; *ne qua forte tamen coeptes diffidere dictis* [1.267]; *ne leviter credas . . .* [4.435], etc.). And in order to realize how novel this is, it suffices to recall how tranquil and lacking in tension, by contrast, was the didactic structure of the Hellenistic poems on snake poisons, constellations, or gastronomy.

Rhetorical procedures in the De Rerum Natura

From this in turn derive some of the essential characteristics of the poem, the chief of them being the frequent apostrophes to the reader and the rigorous structure of the argument. Among the procedures of proof Lucretius does not neglect the syllogism, a principal tool of philosophical argument, which in the form in which the poet generally uses it serves to demonstrate by *reductio ad absurdum* the falsity of theories held by opponents or possible objections from them. A quite considerable role is also given to analogy, through which the attempt is made to refer to the known and the visible that which is too small or too distant to be observed directly, such as, for instance, astronomical phenomena (book 6) or the existence of atoms and the void they move in (books 1 and 2).

Structure of book 3

The book that perhaps more than any other demonstrates Lucretius's skill at argumentation is the third, which is devoted to refuting the fear of death. Its overall structure is simple. After the introduction (vv. 1–93), which opens with a hymn to Epicurus, there follows the central part of the treatment (vv. 94–829), subdivided into two sections. First, it demonstrates that the soul is material; that is, the soul, like every body, is composed of atoms, extremely fine and thus very mobile, and of void (vv. 94–416). Then the key problem is faced: if the soul is material, it must also be mortal, subject to the cycle of birth and death that is a property of all bodies (vv. 417–829). In these four hundred verses Lucretius presents twenty-nine different proofs, of varying weight and not all equally solid, to defend his position. But the sheer accumulation of them, the deployment of rhetorical devices, and the care shown in the choice of the examples and the images all create a whole of undeniable persuasive force.

Although he has demonstrated scientifically the mortality of the soul and the fact that with death every form of feeling ceases, positive or negative, Lucretius realizes that this is not enough to free man from grief over having to leave life. To convince him, then, he has Nature herself speak at the end of the book (vv. 830–1094), addressing herself directly to mankind (vv. 940 f.): If the life gone by has been full of joy, a person may withdraw as if he were a guest satiated and content after a banquet. If, however, it has been marked by grief and sadness, why desire it to continue? Only fools wish to continue living at any cost, even though nothing new awaits them there, since *eadem sunt omnia semper*, "all things are always the same" (3.945).

The De Rerum Natura *and the literary diatribe*

A last characteristic of the work is particularly clear in this book, namely, its contact with literary diatribe. The diatribe had developed in Greece in the Hellenistic age, and its most well-known representative had been Bion of Borysthenes (ca. 325–255 B.C.), a wandering philosopher who propounded philosophical-moral arguments to the people in the street. Even though his philosophical orientation was predominantly Cynic, he had helped develop a semi-dramatic presentation of his material, which included frequent, lively satiric thrusts and brought together fictitious characters who had distinguished but distant predecessors in the participants in Platonic dialogues. This kind of presentation was then later used independent of its original content.

3. THE STUDY OF NATURE AND THE SERENITY OF MAN

The refutation of religion

Immediately after the proem, with its invocation to Venus, and after a summary description of the work's plan, Lucretius addresses the reader and invites him not to regard the doctrine he is about to present as impious but to reflect instead on the cruelty and impiousness of traditional religion, which, for example, had ordered Agamemnon to sacrifice his daughter Iphigenia in order to assure the departure of the Greek fleet for Troy. One of the most elaborate scenes of the poem is devoted to the killing of the girl (1.80–101), to which Lucretius deliberately gives a tone of great pathos. In this way, he continues, is religion prone to crush human life beneath its weight, to cast a shadow over every human joy through fear. But if men knew that there was nothing after death, they would become insensitive to the threats of eternal punishment made by soothsayers and would cease to be slaves to religious superstition and the fears it brings. What is needed for this purpose is a sure knowledge, made possible by the poem, of the laws governing the universe, which reveal the material and mortal nature of the world, of man, and of the soul itself.

Revolutionary potential of Lucretius's message

Right from the first verses, Lucretius describes clearly the nexus of religious superstition, fear of death, and the need for scientific speculation. His message in fact would be ignored not only on account of the work's intrinsic difficulty but also, one must suppose, because it could have called into question the cultural—and indirectly, the social and political—foundations of the Roman state, which had made religion an essential element of cohesion.

The gods in Epicurus and Lucretius

Lucretius's emphasis on the "terrifying utterances" (1.103) of the soothsayers is probably a polemic inspired by the cultural climate of his day. For the rest he remains faithful to Epicurus's theories about religion. The Greek philosopher had been the first man who "dared to lift up his eyes against the religion which loomed up threatening from the sky" (1.66). The imagery used for Epicurus is noteworthy. Apart from some scattered suggestions of Prometheus, which depict Epicurus as the champion of human freedom from the poem's beginning on (1.62–79), the image of the philosopher armed with *vivida vis animi* ("lively force of spirit") and brave in his *ratio naturae* ("understanding of nature") is obviously modeled on the features of the Homeric warrior engaged in a heroic duel. The ritual of the challenge as codified in the *Iliad*, with its various movements preliminary to the meeting between warriors (looking the enemy in the eyes, taking a firm stance before him, etc.), is the model implicit in Lucretius's description of how his champion takes on that fearful adversary, the monster of superstition (*mortales tollere contra / est oculos ausus, primusque obsistere contra*, "He was the first who dared to lift up mortal's eyes in opposition, the first to take an opposing stance"). This illustrates the epic-heroic tone that Lucretius wanted to add to the didactic enthusiasm of his sublime poem. Epicurus, because of his defiance, can even be worshipped as a god, since he has freed men from enormous moral sufferings. Indeed, all books of the poem except the second and fourth open with an impassioned celebration of Epicurus's merits. He believed that the gods were figures endowed with eternal life, perfect and happy in the peace of the *intermundia* (the region between earth and heaven where they resided), unconcerned with the affairs of the earth and mankind; they could receive the *pietas* of earthly men and could constitute an ideal point of reference. But he utterly rejected the notion that man was subject to the gods in a dependent relation and that he could expect from them, his masters, either favor or punishment. Lucretius also possesses this deep sense of religiosity, which here means the ability to live serenely and contemplate every thing with a mind freed from prejudice (5.1203).

The historic origin of religion

Within book 5 a section of the story of mankind (vv. 1161–1240) is devoted to the birth of religious fear, which arises spontaneously because of ignorance of the mechanical laws that govern, for instance, the perfectly regular course of the stars or because of the terror caused by the thunderbolt and by storms. These are wrongly considered signs of divine punishment; in fact they strike the guilty and the innocent alike, since they are due to physical phenomena, which it is the task of Epicurean physics to explain. It is mistaken to see in these verses a different attitude on Lucretius's part towards religion, a yielding to those fears and terrors that he is trying to combat. Instead, his aim is to delineate the historical origin of a phenomenon the causes of which are not difficult to reconstruct but which nonetheless at the present time need to be combated and eliminated.

4. THE COURSE OF HISTORY

The origins of the world and of mankind

Lucretius's effort, as we have already indicated, is to see to it that in matters of such importance the reader is not led to accept the traditional explanations of mythology and superstition by the *egestas rationis,* the lack of rational explanations in Epicurean terms. In addition to subjects of natural philosophy, such as the nature of matter and the formation of compounds, and other ethical and moral subjects, such as religion, the fear of death, friendship, and love, Lucretius devotes a not inconsiderable part of his work to the history of the world. Above all, he makes clear its mortal nature, how it originated from a casual agglomeration of atoms and is destined for destruction (2.1024–1174). The entire second half of book 5 (vv. 772–1457) deals with the origin of life on earth and the history of mankind. Neither animals nor human beings were created by a god. They were formed because of particular circumstances: moist soil and heat spontaneously generated the first living beings (vv. 797 ff.). Special attention is paid to refuting the traditions about mythical beings that are said to have populated the earth in its first days (vv. 878 f.). To such fantasies Lucretius opposes the solidity of the natural laws of Epicurean physics, which demonstrate the impossibility of two different natures (e.g., man and horse) joining and producing, say, a centaur. This is one of the basic teachings of Epicurus, whose doctrine has shown "what can be born, what cannot, and on the basis of what principle each thing has a limited power and a completely fixed boundary" (1.75–77). Yet it is possible for nature, which is not ruled by higher powers, to make "mistakes" and give birth to men lacking vital body parts (vv. 837 f.). The first men led a rustic life, outside any social bond, and nature supplied the little they truly needed. They were not on that account free from danger: wild beasts tore many of them to pieces (vv. 925 f.).

Human progress

Among the stages of human progress that Lucretius treats next (vv. 1010–1457), the positive ones—the discovery of language, fire, metals, weaving, agriculture—alternate with negative ones, such as the beginning and the progress of warfare or the emergence of religious fear. Nature has often shown men by accident how to act; for instance, metal heated by a chance fire and collected in a hole in the ground may have indicated the technique of casting. But the necessity of communicating pushed mankind to create the first forms of language. Accident and material need are thus the factors responsible for the advance of civilization.

Negative effects of progress and limitation of the desires

Everywhere in the work it is clear that the poet wants to counter the teleological views of human progress that were widespread in the culture of the day. Nature follows its own laws; no god shapes it to mankind's needs. Obviously Lucretius could not believe in a mythical happy age when man lived in an earthly paradise from which the degeneration of the races, according to the famous Hesiodic myth, has inexorably removed him. Material progress, as long as it aimed at satisfying primary needs, is evaluated positively, and Lucretius's reservations are concentrated on the moral decadence that progress has brought along with itself: the rise of unnatural needs, of war, personal ambition, and covetousness, has corrupted human life. Yet Lucretius's vision is not disconsolate and pessimistic. Epicureanism can respond to these problems by inviting men to rediscover that "the nature of the body truly needs but few things" (2.20). Epicurus had enjoined man to avoid desires that were not natural and not necessary and to concentrate on those that were natural and necessary: "The flesh cries out: do not be hungry, do not be thirsty, do not be cold. He who has these things and expects to have them (in the future) can vie even with Zeus in happiness" (*Gnomologium Vaticanum* 33).

The social project of the Epicurean wise man

It is understandable how Epicureanism was often mistakenly regarded, already in antiquity, as a form of unbridled hedonism by those who failed to grasp the spirit of its fundamental precepts, all of which aim at limiting needs and pursuing natural, simple pleasures. The social project of Epicurus and Lucretius is congruent with these premises. The wise man should give up useless wealth, keep his distance from the tensions of political life (Epicurus advised: *lathe biosas,* "live unnoticed"), and devote himself instead to the study of nature in the company of his most trustworthy friends, who are the greatest riches of human life: "Of all those goods that wisdom wins for the complete happiness of life, the greatest of all is the acquisition of friendship" (*Sententiae Capitales* 27).

In the proem to the second book (vv. 1–61) the wise men who pass their lives practicing Epicurus's precepts are compared to those who, standing securely on *terra firma,* observe with detachment the sea in a storm, the perils of another man. Lucretius wants to teach all men how to reach "the high, serene regions fortified by the knowledge of the wise" (2.7–8).

5. THE INTERPRETATION OF THE WORK

The narrative voice of the De Rerum Natura

The confusion between the historical figure of the author and the image of the narrator who speaks within the poem continues to trouble the literary criticism of the *De Rerum Natura.* The two figures should not be automatically identified with one another. No one, for example, would dream of identifying in some simple way the Dante figure of the *Divine Comedy* with the man Alighieri, since the narrator, though he takes on many features of the author, is in fact but one persona among the others, playing his role within the poem's set of values and themes. This alone would be reason enough to reject the theory of those who have anxiously searched the *De Rerum Natura* for traces of a mental imbalance in Lucretius, sometimes in the form of manic-depressive crises, sometimes as generic existential angst. Such readings, of course, have attached great weight to Jerome's notorious notice, the ideological motivations for which are not difficult to grasp. Similarly, a more recent theory, which is still popular, a theory that envisages a skeptical anti-Lucretius whom the "official" Lucretius is above all eager to persuade in the first place, was first formulated in 1868 by the French scholar Patin, a critic profoundly hostile to the poet's materialist credo and bent on demonstrating the intrinsic weakness of his message.

The effort towards enlightenment in Lucretius

An unprejudiced reading of the work leads to the recognition that the author's effort, which can justifiably be called enlightened, is always directed at rationally convincing his reader and transmitting to him the precepts of a doctrine of moral liberation in which he himself deeply believes. Within the poem he does undoubtedly paint dark, violently dramatic pictures, and yet the contextual motives can often be discovered. The impassioned rejection of the Stoic notion of a providential nature, for instance, explains why Lucretius dwells at length on the idea that nature is utterly unconcerned about mankind's needs: "Nature is not prepared for us by divine will: in fact it is burdened by a great defect" (5.198–99). This defect is evident in the harshness of the land, in the difficulty of work, in the hardness of the weather, in the large number of animals harmful to man that the earth feeds (5.200 ff.). And then, too, "why does the turning of the year bring illnesses? why is there premature death?" (vv. 220–21).

The condemnation of the passion of love

When, however, at the end of book 4 Lucretius makes his harsh attack against the folly of the passion of love, he probably wants to clinch the argument that the Epicurean sage, the model to which the reader-pupil is compared, must keep himself removed from an irrational passion that has no justification in the dictates of nature (the poet's condemnation does not involve sex). In this particular case, moreover, different cultural impulses may also have been at work, such as the desire to oppose the erotic ideology of the neoterics, such as Catullus, and the tendency of traditional morality to condemn severely lovers who thoughtlessly wasted their substance on gifts and luxuries ("And thereby the estate is dissolved, transformed into Babylonian carpets; duties are neglected, reputation wavers and suffers" [4.1123–34]). More generally, these powerfully expressive pictures are rooted in the poem's tendency to seek out an elevated, effective stylistic register, which, as we have seen, gathers and fuses in the grandeur of a sublime style elements that belong to diatribe and satire.

Exaltation of reason

The problem of Lucretius's pessimism, of the gap that sometimes appears to separate him from the serenity of Epicurus's credo, nevertheless continues to play a central role in much criticism, and it is not easy to reach a balanced evaluation that takes into account all the nuances and the tones that sometimes vary from one part of the poem to another. On one hand, as we have had occasion to note, we must certainly reject the attempts to find in many places the traces of obvious, systematic contradictions with Epicurus, excessively dark, pessimistic tones, the fruits of an insane mind. Lucretius often repeats that the *ratio* he expounds heralds, for the person who truly assimilates it, inner serenity and freedom, which originate in the rational understanding of the mechanisms of birth, life, and death of man and the cosmos. Lucretius offers his reader the possibility of looking upon all around him with an unblinking gaze and urges him to consciously accept all that exists—life with its eternal appeal and death constantly at hand:

> sic rerum summa novatur
> semper, et inter se mortales mutua vivunt.
> augescunt aliae gentes, aliae minuuntur,
> inque brevi spatio mutantur saecla animantum
> et quasi cursores vitai lampada tradunt.

("Thus the sum of things always renews itself, and mortals live of mutual exchange. Some species increase, others decline, and in a short time the generations of the living change, and like relay runners they pass on the torch of life" [2.75–79]). And compare these lines:

nunc hic nunc illic superant vitalia rerum
et superantur item. miscetur funere vagor
quem pueri tollunt visentes luminis oras;
nec nox ulla diem neque noctem aurora secutast
quae non audierit mixtos vagitibus aegris
ploratus mortis comites et funeris atri.

("Now here, now there, the forces of life are victorious; then they are vanquished in their turn. With funereal groans are mixed the wailings of the newborn scarcely come to the shores of light; no night has followed day, no dawn has followed night, without hearing, mixed with grievous wailings, groans and laments, the companions of death and dark funerals" [2.575–80]).

The limits of rationalism

But this same rationalism shows its limits at times. In the third book, for example, the author insists that death *nihil est ad nos neque pertinet hilum,* "is nothing to us and makes not a whit of difference" (830), because our feeling is lost with death, and forever; it would be foolish to fear a hereafter that does not exist and that in any event we could not experience. All this, however, is not sufficient to eliminate man's anxiety at the idea that his life must have a limit, and it is precisely here that Lucretius becomes very firm. If the life gone by has been pleasant—Nature herself addresses man in these terms—nothing different can be experienced in the future (*eadem sunt omnia semper,* "all things are always the same" [945]), and in that case it is appropriate to depart in the manner of a satisfied guest, willingly (*aequo animo* [39], a typically Epicurean expression that we will come upon again in Horace); otherwise, it is better to conclude an experience that is rich only in grief. Precisely this firmness of his, the paradoxical supposition that never to have been born would not have been a bad thing for man (*quidve mali fuerat nobis non esse creatis?* "What harm would there have been for us in not being born?" [5.174]), the emphasis on the idea that to prolong life does not subtract even a day from the death that awaits us, and the Epicurean exhortation *carpe diem,* "seize the day" (957)—these all form a vivid contrast to the precise, thoroughgoing description of man as prey to the irrational anxiety that Lucretius himself presents us with near the end of the book.

The unresolved contradictions in Lucretius

Some critics, exaggerating perhaps the bearing of this difference in tone, have not hesitated to propose the picture of a Lucretius inwardly dissenting from a philosophical system that is excessively serene and linear but is powerless in the face of primordial anxieties. It has sometimes been but a short step from here to a crypto-religious Lucretius, hungering for faith or worse. Even without espousing such a theory, however, one cannot fail to notice that examples such as the one just cited serve to enrich the text. To Lucretius's poetic personality, to his passionate energy as a prophet, which becomes enthusiasm, it adds a dimension of bitter dissatisfaction, the objective sign of a tormented inner life. And perhaps it is precisely by the marks of the blows that the various unresolved contradictions have dealt to the body of the doctrine that we may recognize the most eloquent passages of the work.

6. LANGUAGE AND STYLE

Lucretius and Virgil

The brief judgment on the *De Rerum Natura* contained in Cicero's letter to his brother Quintus, quoted above, demonstrates that he admired not only Lucretius's acuteness as a thinker but also his abilities in artistic elaboration. Modern criticism has long hesitated to subscribe to the latter, since it judges the poet's style, especially when compared with that of Virgil, the classic model par excellence, to be prosaic and repetitious in stretches and thus too rough and too close to the archaic. For some time scholars have been modifying this view, situating both Lucretius and Virgil in their appropriate historical dimension and appreciating fully the fundamental differences of approach between the *De Rerum Natura* and even the work of Virgil's that is closest to it, the *Georgics*.

*Expository require-
ments and Lucretian
style:
a) Repetitions*

The style, too, as well as the overall organization of the material, had to be shaped to the purpose of persuading the reader. This explains the frequent repetitions, which have long been seen as a sign of Lucretius's stylistic immaturity. Some concepts were summed up in brief, easily memorable formulas, as Epicurus recommended, and were repeated at key points in the poem. Thus, for instance, the essential principle that "every thing that goes out, changed, from its own borders constitutes at once the death of that which was before," that is, that the incessant becoming of the aggregations is made possible only by their continual dissolution, is repeated four times (1.670, 1.792, 2.753, 3.519). The bidding for the reader's attention also needed to be repeated often; and not only some technical terms of Epicurean physics but also the oft-used logical links, such as the formulas of transition between different arguments, such as *adde quod, quod superest, praeterea,* or *denique,* needed to remain fixed and unvarying as far as possible, in order to allow the reader to become familiar with a language that certainly is not easy.

*b) Formulas of
transition*

c) Technical terms

Latin lacked the ability to express certain philosophical concepts, and thus Lucretius found himself obliged to have recourse to new periphrases (e.g., *semina,* "seeds," or *primordia,* "primary things," or *corpora prima,* "first bodies," to designate the atoms) and to coinages of his own, which were sometimes direct calques from the Greek (e.g., *homoeomeria,* "homogeneity"). It is in this circumstance that he complains of "the poverty of the ancestral vocabulary" (*patrii sermonis egestas* [1.832]).

Lucretius's archaisms

The poverty of language, however, did not extend beyond the strictly technical vocabulary. Lucretius utilizes a great mass of poetic words provided for him by the archaic tradition (above all the Ennian), especially compound adjectives (e.g., *suaviloquens,* "sweet-speaking," *altivolans,* "high-flying," *navigerum,* "ship-carrying," *frugiferens,* "fruit-bearing"). He also creates many of these himself, showing a marked propensity for novel adverbs (*filatim,* "thread by thread," *moderatim,* "gradually," *praemetuenter,* "with anticipatory fear") and periphrases (*natura animi,* "nature of the soul," for *animus,* "soul"; *equi vis,* "strength of the horse," for *equus,* "horse," this on a Homeric model). Lucretius draws his most characteristic forms of expression from the Ennian tradition and from the inheritance of elevated Roman poetry in general rather than from the contemporary Alexandrizing style; hence his intense use of alliteration, assonance, archaic constructions, and in general sound effects that belong to the expressive-pathetic taste of Rome's earliest poets.

In grammar the two most conspicuous phenomena are the great number of passive infinitives in *-ier* (more archaic than *-i*) and the prevalence of the disyllabic ending *-ai* (instead of *-ae*) in the genitive singular of the first declension. By Lucretius's day the latter was banished from ordinary language and was regarded as an archaism that contributed to the elevation of the tone of the discourse.

The Lucretian hexameter is clearly different from the archaic Ennian hexameter in that it prefers an opening dactyl, which would become usual in Augustan poetry. Its tendency to compose the verse of two nearly equivalent parts has often been viewed as a sign of the poet's limited ability at exploiting the expressive possibilities for word order; for example, *et magis in promptu / primaque in fronte locata* (1.879), *tangere enim non quit / quod tangi non licet ipsum* (5.152), *dissoluunt nodos omnis / et vincla relaxant* (6.356). According to this view, he ought to have sought a closed word order (*nec calidae citius decedunt corpore febres* [2.34]) or a chiastic one (of the type *a b b a*), such as we find commonly in Virgil and Ovid. But such a word order and the moderate use of enjambment (which is common, however, in the sections where pathos is emphasized) have the effect of lessening the tension created within the verse and between one verse and the other, especially in the technical and argumentative parts. They permit a calmer and more linear understanding of the contents and accentuate the feeling of convincing facts and proofs being accumulated.

Lucretius and Greek literature

Lucretius shows that he possesses a wide knowledge of Greek literature, as evidenced by the echoes of Homer, Plato, Aeschylus (the picture of Iphigenia), and Euripides (lines 2.991–1001, for instance, translate a fragment of the *Chrysippus*); the whole description of the plague at Athens in book 6 is based, of course, on the Thucydidean account. Nor are signs lacking of familiarity with the most sophisticated Hellenistic poets (Callimachus, Antipater). In the proem to book 4 (the same verses are repeated also at 1.925 f.), when Lucretius presents himself as the poet who is the first to arrive at "the trackless lands of the Pierian Muses" in order to reach a new source of poetry and to win glory, he is reproducing the gesture of self-consciousness that Callimachus had made a commonplace in Hellenistic poetry.

Patrii sermonis
egestas *and the
impulse to poetic
creation*

But the most distinctive feature of Lucretian style is concreteness of expression. Plainness and liveliness of description, the visible, perceptible quality of the things discussed, the corporeality of the imaginary—these features of the presentation are, as the poet himself several times declares, effects almost entailed by the lack of a preexisting abstract language for expressing ideas and giving philosophical form to his discourse. Paradoxically, the expression, as if compensating for that poverty, derives from this an advantage: it comes alive to fill the verbal vacuums by recourse to a vast range of explanatory images and examples. But the images of things that are evoked in order to explain thoughts and ideas, and thus the similes too, which by analogy with known things ought to explain the workings of things unknown or hidden, do not remain merely the means of illustrating the abstract argument in an intelligible fashion. The images and the examples become the emotional aspect of an intellectual discourse that aims at becoming, above all else, a description of great poetic potency. At one time it is close up and curious, at another it marvels from a distance; sometimes a contemplation of great matters, sometimes of what is very small; enchantment at the majesty of inanimate nature yet also dismay over the powerful forces that move nature (the "sublime dynamic"). The contrast between things humble and things great, between the static and the dynamic, corresponds to the contrast between a lively, colloquial language, which speaks of ordinary things, and a grand, sublime style. Even if the levels of this style are many and different, running from the energy of spoken discourse to the preciosity of epic-tragic diction, the register that unifies them is a single, continuous one: poetic *enthousiasmos* in the service of a didactic mission that is lived with exceptional ardor. The result is a severe style, capable of harshness and elegance, disposed to emotion and wonder but also to prophetic invective, yet always grandiose, without ever losing itself in pomposity and empty magniloquence.

Poetic "enthusiasm"

7. LITERARY SUCCESS

Antiquity

Lucretius's sporadic and mostly superficial influence upon later Latin literature stands in odd contrast to the high poetic and philosophical quality of his work. It can only partially be explained as being due to the general ill repute of Epicureanism among cultured circles in Rome after the late Republic. Cicero's philosophical works, which often attack Epicurean positions at length, ignore him completely (and perhaps deliberately). Authors of the first century B.C. such as Horace and Ovid occasionally borrow motifs from him or praise him but show few traces of careful study of his poetry. Only Virgil in his *Georgics* seems to have taken Lucretius seriously as a fellow poet, one to be understood, rivaled, and surpassed, and his judgment upon Lucretius—*felix qui potuit rerum cognoscere causas* (*Georg.* 2.490 ff.)—delicately combines admiration with reserve. Later writers such as Manilius, the author of the *Aetna,* the younger Seneca, Persius, Quintilian, and Pliny read him occasionally. Statius characterized finely the "sublime frenzy of erudite Lucretius" (*docti furor arduus Lucreti* [*Silv.* 2.7.76]). Grammarians, starting with Verrius Flaccus, studied his language, and Valerius Probus published a critical edition. But it was only in the second century A.D. that the archaizers excerpted his poems and that some readers could even be said to prefer him to Virgil. In late antiquity his fortunes declined once again: although his criticism of ancient religion provided welcome ammunition to the apologists of Christianity, his atheism and materialism came under heavy attack by such polemicists as Arnobius, Lactantius, and Jerome. Even so, he was imitated in the third century by Commodian, frequently quoted in the seventh century by Isidore of Seville for his explanations of natural phenomena, and perhaps read in the eighth century by the Venerable Bede (unless all of his apparent borrowings from Lucretius are indirect).

Middle Ages   The lone archetype of all later manuscripts emerged around the end of the eighth century and was copied soon after 800 in Charlemagne's palace school. The copy, which survives, was corrected by Dungal, one of the foremost Carolingian scholars. Alcuin himself was apparently unfamiliar with Epicureanism, but his successor, Hrabanus Maurus, used Lucretius to explain both the Bible and physics. From there the text spread westwards to Holland and northern France and southwards along the Rhine. But after that, perhaps because of religious scruples, Lucretius vanishes from view, with very few exceptions, until the fifteenth century; most of the few quotations during this period are derived from Isidore or Priscian—even Petrarch seems to cite him through the mediation of Macrobius.

Renaissance   In 1417, while Poggio Bracciolini was attending the Council of Constance, he discovered a manuscript of Lucretius's in Alsace and sent a copy to Niccolò Niccoli, in Florence, for transcription. From the manuscript derive more than fifty surviving Italian manuscripts (the *editio princeps* appeared in Brescia in 1473) and all of Lucretius's modern fame (which was, however, somewhat delayed by Niccoli's refusal for decades to return Poggio's manuscript to him). Perhaps in part because of his atheistic sensualism, he became a favorite author of such humanists as Marullus (a copy of Lucretius was found upon him at his death), Avancius, Pontano, and especially Lambinus (who even claimed that of all Latin poets, Lucretius was *elegantissimus et purissimus, gravissimus atque ornatissimus*). Through Politian's *Stanze,* Lucretius's depiction of Venus in the opening of the *De Rerum Natura* may even have inspired Botticelli's *Primavera*. Perhaps the most striking proof of Lucretius's fascination for the Renaissance were the "confutations of Lucretius," starting in the fifteenth century, poems written in *Modern period*   Lucretius's language and style but intended to refute his materialism. But the high point of Lucretius's fortunes came in the seventeenth century, when Pierre Gassendi combined Lucretian materialism with a creator God in his *Syntagma philosophiae Epicuri* (1658), Molière translated part of book 4 when dilating upon the defects of women in the *Misanthrope,* and in England he found such translators as John Evelyn, Lucy Hutchinson (who hated him), and Thomas Creech. For the Enlightenment, Lucretius's anti-religious sentiment was exemplary. As late as 1747 Cardinal de Polignac could still consider him a dangerous enough opponent to feel obliged to write an *Anti-Lucretius, sive de Deo et Natura,* and Kant cites Lucretius at least eight times. He remained a source of inspiration for some didactically minded Romantic poets—Wordsworth, Shelley, Goethe, Chénier (who planned a didactic poem called *Hermes* to embody the teachings of the *Encyclopédie* in the style of Lucretius), perhaps Leopardi—and for the late Romantic Tennyson, whose *Lucretius* analyzes the destructive psychology of sexual passion in the wake of book 4.

In 1850 the German scholar Lachmann provided the most celebrated modern contribution to the study of Lucretius by using the textual transmission of this author as a model to demonstrate modern philological method. The basic relations among the manuscripts of Lucretius had been indicated already in 1847 by Bernays, but it was Lachmann's brilliantly imaginative and closely reasoned conjuring up of the lost archetype of all our surviving manuscripts that long remained a touchstone for the application of stemmatic theory to a closed tradition. Generations of classics students became more familiar with Lachmann's reconstructed archetype, down to the shape of its letters and the number of lines on its pages, than with Lucretius's closely reasoned poetry and his powerfully imagined philosophy.

BIBLIOGRAPHY

The text of Lucretius has a central importance in the development of modern textual criticism, for it was in the course of work on it that J. Bernays and K. Lachmann became the first classical scholars to reconstruct a family tree ("stemma") of manuscripts and to use it to choose between readings. The classic account is that of S. Timpanaro, *La genesi del metodo del Lachmann* (ed. 3 Padua 1985). In English, see L. D. Reynolds and N. G. Wilson, *Scribes and Scholars* (ed. 3 Oxford 1991) 187–89. Lachmann's commentary (Berlin 1850) remains useful. The most convenient edition is the Loeb of W.H.D. Rouse revised by M. F. Smith (Cambridge, Mass. 1975), with English translation and brief notes. C. Bailey's Oxford text of 1922 has deficiencies in the apparatus (that in his three-volume edition of 1947 is better), and the Teubner of J. Martin (ed. 5 Leipzig 1963) is excessively conservative. K. Müller's deluxe edition (Zurich 1975) is of importance for the history of the text.

Among English commentaries, note those of H.A.J. Munro (3 vols., ed. 4 Cambridge 1886), W. A. Merrill (New York 1907), W. E. Leonard and S. B. Smith (Madison 1942), and esp. C. Bailey (3 vols., Oxford 1947); Munro and Bailey include translations. In other languages, the most important commentaries are those of C. Giussani (3 vols., Turin 1896–98, Italian) and A. Ernout and L. Robin (3 vols., Paris 1925–28, French, without a text). The older Latin commentary of G. Wakefield (London 1796–97) contains much information neglected by later scholars. There are separate editions in English of book 1 by P. M. Brown (Bristol 1985), book 3 by E. J. Kenney (Cambridge 1971), book 4 by J. Godwin (Warminster 1986; see also the very full commentary on the end by R. Brown, Leiden 1987), book 5 by C.D.N. Costa (Oxford 1984), and book 6 by J. Godwin (Warminster 1992). Note also R. Heinze's German edition of book 3 (Leipzig 1897) and the Italian selections by H. Paratore and H. Pizzani (Rome 1960) and A. Barigazzi (Turin 1974).

A brief but helpful introductory survey of Lucretian studies is E. J. Kenney, *Lucretius,* Greece and Rome: New Surveys in the Classics 11 (Oxford 1977). Other studies in English include J. Masson, *Lucretius, Epicurean and Poet* (2 vols., London 1907–9, dated but not to be neglected), D. West, *The Imagery and Poetry of Lucretius* (Edinburgh 1969), D. Clay, *Lucretius and Epicurus* (Ithaca 1983), and C. Segal, *Lucretius on Death and Anxiety* (Princeton 1990). In French see P. Boyancé, *Lucrèce et l'Épicurisme* (Paris 1963), and P. H. Schrijvers, *Horror ac Divina Voluptas: Études sur la poétique et la poésie de Lucrèce* (Amsterdam 1970), both with good bibliographies. Three collections include material in English: *Lucretius,* ed. D. R. Dudley (London 1965), *Lucrèce,* Fondation Hardt Entretiens 24 (Geneva 1978), and *Probleme der Lukrezforschung,* ed. C. J. Classen (Hildesheim 1986), the latter two of which also contain pieces in French, German, and Italian; see also the Italian collection of L. Perelli (Milan 1977). For the view expressed above in the text, see esp. G. B. Conte, "Hypsos e diatriba nello stile di Lucrezio," *Maia* 18 (1966) 338–68, and *Genres and Readers,* trans. Glenn W. Most (Baltimore 1994) 1–34.

The standard edition of the fragments of Epicurus is that of H. Usener, *Epicurea* (Leipzig 1887, reprint Rome 1963), supplemented by that of G. Arrighetti (ed. 2 Turin 1963, with Italian translation and commentary). For many of the papyrus fragments there are more recent editions; see the annual periodical *Cronache Ercolanesi* for details. The principal fragments with English translation and commentary may be found in C. Bailey, *Epicurus: The Extant Remains* (Oxford 1926); a handy text of the letters and sayings is the Teubner text of P. von der Muehll (Leipzig 1922). Studies include C. Bailey, *The Greek Atomists and Epicurus* (Oxford 1925), A. J. Festugière, *Epicurus and His Gods* (trans. C. W. Chilton, Oxford 1955), J. M. Rist, *Epicurus: An Introduction* (Cambridge 1972), and E. Asmis, *Epicurus' Scientific Method* (Ithaca 1984). Among work in other languages, W. Schmid's article *Epikur* in vol. 5 of the *Reallexikon für Antike und Christentum* (Stuttgart 1962) may be singled out. Rist, Asmis, and Schmid have good bibliographies.

On the *fortuna* of Lucretius, see conveniently in English G. D. Hadzits, *Lucretius and His Influence* (New York 1935).

Cicero

Marcus Tullius Cicero was born in 106 B.C. at Arpinum of a well-to-do equestrian family. He finished with distinction his studies in rhetoric and philosophy at Rome and began to frequent the Forum under the guidance of the great orator Lucius Licinius Crassus and the two Scaevolas, the Augur and the Pontiff. He formed a friendship with Titus Pomponius Atticus that would last all his life. In 89 he saw military service in the Social War under the command of Pompeius Strabo, the father of Pompey the Great. In 81, or perhaps even earlier, he made his debut as a pleader. In 80 he defended the case of Sextus Roscius, which brought him into conflict with important members of the Sullan regime. Between 79 and 77 he made a long voyage to Greece and Asia, during which he studied philosophy and, under Molon of Rhodes, rhetoric. On his return he married Terentia, who gave birth to Tullia in 76 and Marcus in 65. In 75 he was quaestor in Sicily. In 70 he undertook the prosecution brought by the Sicilians against their ex-governor Verres, and by his triumph won for himself the reputation of being Rome's leading orator. In 69 he was aedile. In 66, while praetor, he supported the proposal to grant Pompey exceptional powers for the struggle against Mithridates, king of Pontus. He was consul in 63 and suppressed the conspiracy of Catiline. The first triumvirate troubled him: the alliance between the military power of Pompey, the great wealth of Crassus, and the growing popularity of Caesar, precisely because it was a private agreement, appeared to him to threaten the Senate's authority. After its formation his star was on the wane. In 58, accused of having put to death without trial Catiline's accomplices, he had to go into exile; his house was razed to the ground. Recalled to Rome in 57, he returned in triumph. Between 56 and 51 he attempted, with difficulty, to collaborate with the triumvirs and continued his forensic activity. He composed the *De Oratore* and the *De Republica* and began work on the *De Legibus*. In 51 he was governor of Cilicia but accepted with reluctance the absence from Rome. When civil war broke out in 49, he somewhat tardily joined the cause of Pompey. He went to Epirus with the other senators but was not present at the battle of Pharsalus. After Pompey's defeat he obtained pardon from Caesar. In 46 he wrote the *Brutus* and the *Orator,* and he divorced

Terentia to marry his young ward Publilia, whom he would divorce after a few months. In 45 his daughter Tullia died. While Caesar's domination kept him removed from public affairs, he began to compose a long series of philosophical works. In 44, after the murder of Caesar, he returned to political life and at the end of the summer began his fight against Antony (the *Philippics*). After the about-face of Octavian, who, abandoning the Senate's cause, joined Antony and Lepidus in a second triumvirate, Cicero's name was added to the proscriptions. He was slain by Antony's assassins on 7 December 43.

WORKS

Speeches: *Pro Quinctio* (81), *Pro Roscio Amerino* (80), *Pro Roscio Comoedo* (77?), *Pro Tullio* (72 or 71), *Divinatio in Q. Caecilium* and *Verrines* (70), *Pro Fonteio* (69), *Pro Caecina* (69 or 68), *Pro Cluentio* (66), *De Imperio Cn. Pompei* or *Pro Lege Manilia* (66), *De Lege Agraria* (63), *Pro Rabirio Perduellionis Reo* (63), *Pro Murena* (63), *Catilinarians* (63), *Pro Sulla* (62), *Pro Archia Poeta* (62), *Pro Flacco* (59), *Cum Senatui Gratias Egit* (57), *Cum Populo Gratias Egit* (57), *De Domo Sua* (57), *De Haruspicum Responso* (56), *Pro Sestio* (56), *In Vatinium* (56), *Pro Caelio* (56), *De Provinciis Consularibus* (56), *Pro Balbo* (56), *In Pisonem* (55), *Pro Plancio* (54), *Pro Scauro* (54), *Pro Rabirio Postumo* (54), *Pro Milone* (52), *Pro Marcello* (46), *Pro Ligario* (46), *Pro Rege Deiotaro* (45), *Philippics* (44–43). These are the speeches that have come down to us by direct tradition, some of which are incomplete. We have, moreover, about thirty titles and various fragments of lost speeches, among them the *Pro Cornelio* (from 65) and the *In Toga Candida* (from 64, the year of Cicero's candidacy for the consulship), which we can reconstruct from the commentary of Asconius Pedianus (see below).

Rhetorical works: *De Inventione* (ca. 54), *De Oratore* (54), *Partitiones Oratoriae* (ca. 54), *De Optimo Genere Oratorum* (52), *Brutus* (46), *Orator* (46), *Topica* (44).

Political works: *De Republica* (54–51), *De Legibus* (52–?).

Philosophical works: *Paradoxa Stoicorum* (46), *Academica* (45), *De Finibus Bonorum et Malorum* (45), *Tusculan Disputations* (45), *De Natura Deorum* (45), *De Divinatione* (44), *De Fato* (44), *Cato Maior de Senectute* (44), *Laelius de Amicitia* (44), *De Officiis* (44).

Correspondence: *Ad Familiares* (16 books), *Ad Atticum* (16 books), *Ad Quintum Fratrem* (27 letters), *Ad M. Brutum* (2 books, of disputed authenticity).

Poetic works (only fragments): *Juvenilia, Aratea, De Consulatu Suo, Marius, Limon.*

Lost prose works: *Consolatio* (45), *Hortensius* (45), *Laus Catonis* (45), *De Gloria* (44), *De Virtutibus, De Auguriis, De Consiliis Suis*. We also have notices of a geographical work *(Chorographia?)* and a work of curiosities *(Admiranda)*.

Translations: of Plato's *Timaeus* (preserved in part), of his *Protagoras*, of Xenophon's *Economicus* (a few fragments).

For knowledge of Cicero's life and works the chief sources are his own works, especially the correspondence, the *Brutus,* the proems of several dialogues and treatises, and a number of the speeches (to some of which Asconius Pedianus, in the age of Nero, devoted a historical commentary [see p. 578]). The biography of Cicero by Plutarch is also important.

I. TRADITION AND INNOVATION IN ROMAN CULTURE

Cicero and the crisis of the Republic

Cicero, it has been said, is the person of the ancient world whom we know best, because of the variety of his works in different genres (speeches and rhetorical, political, and philosophical essays) but also because of his rich correspondence, which often allows us to trace the connections between his personal experiences, which sometimes are confided in full sincerity to his friends, and the reworking of them in the writings intended for a wider public. This would still not be much were Cicero not a particularly interesting person on account of the position he occupies in Roman culture and the extraordinary value of his intellectual experience. Protagonist in and witness of the crisis that brings on the decline of the Republic, he develops an ethical-political program in a vain attempt to remedy the situation. His own view, of course, remains a partial one, tied as it is to the striving for dominance of a social group, basically the landowning classes. It is a view that, in order to become accepted by the community as a whole, must be able to employ the most effective stratagems that the techniques of communication can provide. Cicero, the great advocate, the superb manipulator of words for the purpose of persuasion, utilizes such stratagems in his speeches and theorizes about them in his rhetorical treatises. Set in its own time, his art of speaking loses the qualities of vain pomposity with which scholastic and humanistic Ciceronianism had invested it, and it reveals itself, among other things, as a prudent and productive technique, useful for mastering the audience and governing its passions. (This reflects a basic condition of Roman culture, for which oratory constituted the fundamental model not only of high education but also, to a notable extent, of literary expression itself.)

Rhetoric as political instrument

Oratory and philosophy in the service of Cicero's program

Cicero attempted to give substance to his political-social program through practical applications that might be adapted, sometimes opportunistically, to the contingencies of the situation; several speeches give evidence of this. But as his years and his disappointments mounted up, he felt the increasing need to reflect on the bases of politics and morality and went back to Hellenistic thought. The aim of his philosophical works is the same one that inspires some of his most important speeches: to provide a solid intellectual, ethical, political base for a dominant class whose need for order would not be translated into obtuse isolation and whose respect for the national tradition (*mos maiorum*) would not hinder the absorption of Greek culture, a dominant class that, though it performed the duties owed to the state, would not become insensitive either to the pleasures of an *otium* filled with art and literature or to the pleasures of that courteously refined style of life that is summed up in the term *humanitas,* that consciousness of culture that is the fruit of civilization, the capacity to distinguish and to appreciate what is beautiful and fitting.

Contrasting drives in Cicero's thought

In this sense a great part of Cicero's work can be read as the search for a difficult balance between modernization and the necessity of preserving traditional values. Behind the intellectual activity of Cicero one perceives a society pervaded by contrasting drives that are often destructive: the influx of wealth from the conquered countries long ago made the rigid morality of the early days a hopeless anachronism, yet the swift abandonment of the virtues and values that had brought about Rome's greatness was now calling into question the very survival of the republican state.

2. THE SUPREMACY OF THE WORD: POLITICAL CAREER AND PRACTICAL ORATORY

Cicero's oratorical activity is indissolubly bound up with the political events at Rome during the last half-century of the Republic. It is necessary therefore for our treatment to follow a chronological sequence, which, without being too detailed, makes clear the historical setting in which he operated and the circumstances by which he had to measure himself.

First Successes and the Trial of Verres

The Pro Roscio Amerino

Cicero already had several cases to his credit when, in 80, he took up the defense in a case that, because of its political implications, had great reverberations in Roman society (the *Pro Roscio Amerino*). The father of Sextus Roscius had been slain on the orders of two of his own relatives who were in league with Lucius Cornelius Chrysogonus, a powerful favorite and freedman of Sulla, who then had had the name of the slain man inserted in the proscription lists so that he could acquire his considerable estates at auction for a ridiculous price. The murderers, in order to have a free hand, tried to get rid of the son of the slain man too and resorted to accusing him of the murder.

To succeed, the defense could not pass over the responsibility of Chrysogonus, who had been the real director of the entire affair. Yet obvious motives of prudence and political expediency urged the young pleader to involve Sulla as little as possible: he was dictator at the time and held nearly absolute power, and he was Chrysogonus's most influential protector. However much disgust Cicero probably felt at the more repugnant aspects of the Sullan regime, such as the proscriptions and other kinds of arbitrary action, he could not but heap praise upon Sulla. In fact he made himself the spokesman for those members of the nobility who, though they appreciated Sulla's action in suppressing the democratic and popular part, regretted having had to pay for it by placing power in the hands of a single man and by witnessing the social rise of characters such as Chrysogonus.

The oratorical style of the *Pro Roscio Amerino* is not yet that of the mature

Cicero. The orator shows that he is still tied to the Asianism then in fashion: the phrases race by swift and sonorous, with a lively cadence, full of neologisms, and nearly as rich in metaphors as poetry. In later years Cicero would make great efforts to polish his style. Already wholly Ciceronian, by contrast, is the skill at portraiture, at depicting persons and settings in pictures full of color and often containing a happy streak of satire. The portrait of Chrysogonus stands out above all: the man whom Sulla had bought as a slave in the market of Delos now has hair pomaded and curled in ringlets; he often appears in the Forum amidst a large entourage; he lives on the Palatine, the most elegant quarter in Rome, in a luxurious house decorated with Corinthian vases, statues, and carpets; at night one can hear from far away the uproar of his parties, which are sumptuous, though lacking in real elegance. His is the first in a long series of satiric pictures, which continues down to the picture, in the *Philippics,* of Antony and his train of dissolute characters.

The Verrines   After the success of his defense of Roscius Cicero left Rome for a couple of years, for reasons of health or perhaps because he feared the revenge of Sulla and Chrysogonus. He made a voyage of study to Greece and Asia, which helped him to improve his eloquence. Returning to Rome after the death of Sulla, he held the quaestorship in Sicily in 75. He won the reputation of being an honest and scrupulous governor, to such an extent that a few years later, in 70, the Sicilians asked him to handle the prosecution in a case they were going to bring against the ex-governor Verres, who had plundered the province with incredible rapacity. Cicero very energetically gathered the evidence in a short time. This made it possible for him to advance the dates of the trial, which otherwise would have taken place in conditions politically far more favorable to Verres (one of the consuls designate for 69, Quintus Hortensius Hortalus, the famous orator of the Asianic school, was in fact Verres' defender in the trial). At the actual trial Cicero did not have a chance to display in its entirety the immense mass of evidence and proofs he had collected and organized, and he was able to deliver only the first of his *actiones in Verrem,* since after only a few days Verres, overwhelmed by the accusations, fled from Italy and was sentenced by default.

Cicero subsequently published, in the form of a speech of prosecution, the *Actio Secunda in Verrem,* divided into five books, which is, among other things, a historical document of the highest importance for understanding the methods of Roman provincial administration (Verres' was certainly a sensational case, but thoroughgoing exploitation was the rule). The Roman aristocrats needed huge sums of money to finance the forms of "liberality" (i.e., the corruption of individuals and groups) that were necessary to advance their political careers; in addition, they needed to increase their own consumption and private use in order to keep up with the new standards of behavior that had been imposed since the period of the conquests. The governorship of a rich province was therefore an opportunity from which it was easy to profit.

The victory over Hortensius, Verres' defender, was also a victory in the field of literature. In comparison with the naturalness with which the young rival commanded all the nuances of the language, the exaggerated Asianic mannerism of Hortensius must have seemed somewhat cloying. The style of the *Verrines* is already fully mature. Cicero has eliminated some of the exuberance and redundance without thereby approaching the dry, lifeless eloquence of the Atticists. The formation of the periods is harmonious for the most part and structurally complex. The syntax is extremely flexible, and Cicero does not eschew, when it is appropriate, the concise, punchy phrase. The range of registers is controlled with complete sureness, from the simple, plain narration to the colorful anecdote, from withering irony to tragic pathos. Here, too, Cicero shows himself a master in the art of portraiture. He gives us several more or less wretched characters in the governor's entourage, but above all Verres himself, depicted as a despot eager for the property and blood of his subjects and at the same time a dissolute figure, languorously lolling in his litter, always sniffing a bouquet of roses.

The Program of Concord among the Affluent Classes

Having entered the Senate after his quaestorship, Cicero in 66, the year of his praetorship, spoke in favor of the legislative program proposed by the tribune Manilius, which granted Pompey extraordinary powers throughout the East. The grant was made necessary by the urgent need to meet decisively the threat posed by Mithridates, king of Pontus, who was gravely harming Rome's economic interests in the eastern regions (*Pro Lege Manilia* or *De Imperio Cn. Pompei*).

Speaking before the people in favor of the tribune's proposal and thus supporting Pompey, to whom Manilius asked that operations against Mithridates be entrusted, Cicero insisted above all on the importance of the taxes that flowed in from the eastern provinces: the population of Rome would be deprived of the benefit of these taxes if Mithridates continued undisturbed in his behavior. In the *De Imperio Cn. Pompei*, which Cicero himself later repudiated, scholars have wanted to see Cicero coming as close as he ever did to the politics of the *populares*, which were directed at gratifying and corrupting the urban masses with donations and also at infringing upon the Senate's authority. The aristocracy for its part viewed the concentration of enormous powers in the hands of a single individual who was one of its own members as extremely dangerous to its stability. Cicero was defending not so much the interests of the people as those of the publicans, the proprietors of the companies that contracted for the taxes, whose very lucrative activities in the eastern provinces were greatly hindered by Mithridates. The publicans constituted a leading group within the equestrian order, from which Cicero himself came. But it is not right on that account to see Cicero as the representative of the big equestrian businessmen within the Roman Senate. The truth is that he needed their support to cement that concord among the affluent classes (senators and knights) in which he was starting to discern the salvation from the crisis threatening the Republic. To realize his program, he also needed to reach the highest office of the state, and for this reason, too, the support of the equestrian class was vital for the *novus homo,* upon whom the nobility surely did not look with favor. The connection with Pompey is explained by the fact that in this period he, too, was looking for the support of the knights. But if Pompey was inclined to court the tribunes of the plebs, who sometimes expressed the aspirations of the poorest classes, Cicero was not, since he was always openly opposed to agrarian laws or programs for debt relief.

Cicero's consulship and the conspiracy of Catiline

Relying on Cicero's fundamentally moderate nature ("moderate" in a political sense), a part of the nobility decided to join together with the equestrian class and support the brilliant *homo novus* from Arpinum as a candidate for the consulship. Meanwhile, the needs of the proletarian masses in Rome and other regions of Italy found a doubtful champion in an aristocrat of Sullan origin, Catiline, who also aspired to the supreme magistracy. As consul in 63, Cicero suppressed the conspiracy of Catiline. From then on he would be the theoretician of that *concordia ordinum,* "concord of the orders," that had brought him to power.

In the year of his consulship Cicero delivered before the Senate and the people four speeches, of which three are extant, in which he opposed the agrarian law proposed by the tribune Rullus, who may have been a tool of Caesar (the *De Lege Agraria*), and once again took a stand against the popular party, this time in defense of Gaius Rabirius *(Pro Rabirio Perduellionis Reo),* an aged knight on whom revenge was being taken for deeds of thirty-seven years before, connected to the murder of the seditious tribune Saturninus.

The Catilinarians

But the most famous among Cicero's consular speeches are, of course, the four *Catilinarians,* in which he exposed the subversive plans that the decadent nobleman had formed after being defeated in the election, compelled him to flee from Rome, and justified his own decision to have Catiline's accomplices executed without trial. Artistically, perhaps the first *Catilinarian,* in which Cicero attacked Catiline before the assembled Senate, stands out. The tones are vehement, threatening, and full of pathos. Cicero had recourse to a rhetorical device he had never employed before, the *prosopopoeia* ("personification") of the Country, which is imagined as addressing Catiline in words of harsh reproach. Nor can one forget the portrait of Catiline and his followers, corrupted by luxury and vice, which is drawn in the second *Catilinarian.*

The Pro Murena

In the days between the first and second *Catilinarians,* when the outcome of the conflict was as yet undecided, Cicero found himself obliged to defend Lucius Licinius Murena, consul designate for the new year, on a charge of electoral corruption *(Pro Murena).* Cicero hoped to find in Murena a sturdy continuer of his own policy of resisting revolution, the policy that joined the senatorial and equestrian orders in a defensive alliance. The charge of corruption intervened, however, and it had been made by the defeated candidate, Servius Sulpicius Rufus, and supported by the prestige of a descendant of Cato the Censor, Cato the Younger (later called Cato of Utica). The latter also did harm in other ways to the policy of *concordia ordinum:* with his moral rigidity, inspired by the principles of Stoicism, he took a particularly intransigent position on questions of the relation between the state and private economic interests, which often brought him into conflict with the publicans and the equestrian class.

In defending Murena, Cicero chose the path of irony and jest. He made fun of the empty juridical formulary that was the basis of Servius's intellectual formation and maintained that Murena's military successes constituted a far better claim to the consulship. He wittily mocked Cato's anachronistic Stoic rigor. The *Pro Murena* is one of Cicero's most amusing speeches. Despite his sincere esteem for both Servius and Cato, he was able to find here the tones of a light, witty satire, which never falls into mere derision or vulgar mockery. But the speech is interesting for other reasons too: by taking a stand against Cato's archaic morality, Cicero in fact begins to sketch the lines of a new ethical model the definition of which would occupy him to his last years, a model in which respect for the *mos maiorum* is tempered by a softening of customs, by a receptiveness to the joys of life, which the new standards of society now permit.

Cicero in exile

In the following years Cicero did not cease to glorify the historical importance of his consulship (which he also celebrated in a poetic work [see p. 201]) and his fight against Catiline. He regarded himself as a "father of his country," a title that was indeed decreed for him, and as a second founder, after Romulus. Nonetheless, the formation of the first triumvirate by Caesar, Pompey, and Crassus signaled a rapid decline in Cicero's political fortunes. A tribune of the people, Clodius, who also had personal grudges against Cicero, proposed in 58 a law that would condemn to exile anyone who had put Roman citizens to death without a trial. The law aimed at avenging Cicero's action in suppressing the Catilinarian conspirators. No longer supported by the nobility, who could do without him once the danger from Catiline was removed, and abandoned by Pompey as well, who had to pay attention to the demands of his fellow triumvirs, Cicero was forced to give way before Clodius's attack. When he was recalled from exile in 57, Cicero found Rome a prey to anarchy. There were continual street fights between the opposing gangs of Clodius and of Milo, the latter of whom, defending the cause of the optimates, was a personal friend of Cicero's.

The Pro Sestio: *from the* concordia ordinum *to the* consensus omnium bonorum

In this climate when in 56 he found himself defending Sestius, a tribune accused by Clodius of acts of violence *(Pro Sestio),* Cicero expounded a new version of his theory about the concord of the well-to-do classes. As a simple understanding between the senatorial class and the equestrian, the *concordia ordinum* was shown to be a failure. Cicero now expands the concept to *consensus omnium bonorum,* that is, the active agreement of all who were well-to-do, landholding persons, loyal to the political and social order, and disposed to carry out their own duties towards their country and their family. The *boni,* a category that cuts vertically through the existing social strata without being identified with any one in particular, henceforth would be the principal intended audience for Cicero's ethical-political preaching. The enemies of order are identified as those whom poverty or debt drives to desire subversion and overthrow.

The duty of the boni   The duty of the *boni* would be, not to take selfish refuge in the pursuit of their own private interests, but to lend active support to the politicians representing their cause. The generally acknowledged need for a more authoritative government at Rome nonetheless drives Cicero to desire that the Senate and the *boni,* in order to surmount their disagreements, entrust themselves to the guidance of eminent persons of great authority; this theory would be explored in the *De Republica* (see pp. 189 f.). In this light probably we ought to explain Cicero's stance towards the triumvirs during these years. He hoped to influence their action and to bring it about that their power not infringe upon that of the Senate but keep within the limits of republican institutions; the stance does not signify a betrayal of the *nobilitas.*

The period of collaboration with the triumvirs is nonetheless a period of great uncertainty and political vacillation for Cicero. On the one hand, he continues to attack Clodius and the popular party, as in the *In Pisonem,* a violent invective against Caesar's father-in-law. On the other, he supports the policy of the triumvirs: in 56 he speaks in favor of renewing Caesar's command in Gaul *(De Provinciis Consularibus),* and he also defends various people linked to Caesar *(Pro Balbo* in 56, *Pro Rabirio Postumo* in 54, etc.).

The Defense of Marcus Caelius: Cicero and Roman Youth

The Pro Caelio   Among the anti-Clodian speeches a special place is occupied by the one in defense of Marcus Caelius Rufus, a brilliant young man and personal friend of Cicero (*Pro Caelio,* 56 B.C.). Caelius had been the lover of Clodia, sister of the tribune (and Catullus's Lesbia), one of the elegant, corrupt ladies in whom aristocratic Rome abounded at the time. A heap of accusations had been made against Caelius, among them an attempt at poisoning Clodia. It was a trial in which the personal animosities of all the parties involved were closely entwined with political questions of far more general importance. Attacking Clodia, whom he identified as the single director of all the machinations against Caelius, provided Cicero with a way to' discharge his resentment towards her brother: the woman is depicted as a common whore and even accused of incestuous relations with Clodius. On account of its picturesque variety of tones, which range from the cynicism of a man of the world to a funereal pathos, the speech is among Cicero's most successful. Not only the fertile vein of satire but also the maturing of the new ethical models proposed brings the *Pro Caelio* close to the *Pro Murena.* In reviewing the stages of Caelius's life Cicero can give a cross section of Roman society in his day, and he strives to justify to the judges the new customs that the youth have recently adopted, which can give rise to scandal only in the eyes of gloomy moralists too attached to the past. The virtues that once made the Roman state great are no longer found even in books. It is time now to slacken the reins on the young, lest they lose sight of fundamental principles; the moment will come when, with glowing eagerness, they will return to the noble path of the *mos maiorum*. If the split between archaic rigidity and the new opportunities presented by an affluent society should become too deep, society would run the risk of its ideological fabric being loosened. The young would move towards a complete overthrow of values, which would end up substituting the pursuit of pleasure for service to the community. The cultural model Cicero proposes aims at bringing the new behavior back within the scale of values that are still dominated by the traditional virtues but stripped of their excessive rigidity and rendered more responsive to the needs of a world in transformation.

Real Speeches and Written Speeches: The Defense of Milo

The Pro Milone

The clashes between the gangs of Clodius and of Milo continued for a long time. Then in 52 Clodius was killed. Cicero undertook the defense of Milo *(Pro Milone)*. The speech is considered one of his masterpieces because of the balance among its parts and his skill in handling the arguments, which are based on the notion of legitimate defense and on the glorification of what he depicted as tyrannicide. But in the form in which it is preserved for us it is a radical reworking carried out after the trial. Before the judges Cicero was a colossal disaster (and Milo had to flee into exile): his nerves gave way on account of the extreme tension in the city, which was prey to raids by Clodius's partisans, while Pompey's troops tried to impose order.

From the Civil War to the Dictatorship of Caesar

The Caesarian speeches

In 49, upon the outbreak of the civil war, Cicero adhered to Pompey's cause without enthusiasm. He was conscious that whatever the outcome, the Senate would be weakened in relation to the overwhelming power of the victor. After Caesar's victory Cicero obtained his pardon. In the hope of helping to make the regime less authoritarian, at first he sought means of collaborating with it and accepted the task of making several speeches before the dictator that pleaded the case of repentant Pompeians. The Caesarian speeches—the *Pro Marcello*, the *Pro Ligario*, the *Pro Rege Deiotaro*, the last a tetrarch of Galatia suspected of an attempt on Caesar's life—are from 46 and 45. Although he was working in a not ignoble cause, the pardoning of Pompeians who had laid down their arms some while before, Cicero probably fell short of his full dignity; it is rather difficult to accept the sincerity of the Caesarian speeches, which abound in praise for Caesar. The *Pro Marcello* nonetheless strives to expound to Caesar a political program of reforming republican government and the prerogatives of the Senate. Even then, in all likelihood Cicero had few illusions, and Caesar's move to perpetual dictatorship would have very quickly disabused him of them.

The Struggle against Antony

The Philippics *and the hopes placed in Octavian*

After Caesar's murder, which he greeted with joy, Cicero returned to being a leading politician. The dangers for the Republic were not over: Caesar's closest collaborator, Antony, was aiming at taking up his role, while the young Octavian, Caesar's heir, with an army at his command, was emerging onto the Roman political scene. Cicero's political maneuvering attempted to detach Octavian from Antony and bring him under the protection of the Senate. In order to induce the Senate to declare war on Antony and proclaim him a public enemy, Cicero, beginning in the summer of 44, delivered the *Philippic* speeches against him, perhaps eighteen in number. Fourteen of them are extant. The title refers to the very famous speeches of Demosthenes against Philip of Macedon. Whether it originated with Cicero is a debated question; some ancient writers call them the *Antonianae,* whereas *Philippics* is in fact used by Cicero in his private correspondence, though in a joking sense. On account of the vehemence of its attack and its tones of indignant denunciation, the second *Philippic* stands out especially. The only one that was not actually delivered, but circulated privately in a written version, the speech simply breathes hatred: with a satiric force matched only by certain passages of the *In Pisonem,* it presents Antony as a dissolute tyrant, a thief of public money, a drunkard who "vomits gobs of food stinking of wine all over the tribunal."

The second triumvirate and the murder of Cicero

Cicero's political maneuvering was destined to fail. In an abrupt about-face Octavian withdrew from the Senate's protection and formed an agreement with Antony and another Caesarian leader, Lepidus, who together made up the second triumvirate. The three became absolute masters of Rome. Antony expected and was given the head of Cicero, whose name was added to the lists of the proscribed. After giving up an attempted flight, he was found by the assassins at Formiae in the first days of December of 43.

The Significance of Cicero's Political Program

Consistency of Cicero's program

Despite the many fluctuations, Cicero's political career followed a consistent line. In the context of a general rapprochement between Senate and *equites* the *homo novus* supported the *nobilitas,* and even afterwards he remained faithful to the idea of concord and to the senatorial cause. His attempt at collaboration with the triumvirs was a response to the need for an authoritative government, and here, too, Cicero was concerned to preserve the prestige and the prerogatives of the Senate. Even the temporary rapprochement with Caesar, after the civil war, was dictated by his desire to mitigate Caesar's autocratic tendencies and to maintain power within the familiar framework of republican traditions.

The failure of Cicero's program

The program of concord among the well-to-do classes (*concordia ordinum,* later *consensus omnium bonorum*) was in each case an embryonic attempt to overcome the struggles between dominant political groups and factions in the name of the higher interest of the community, or what Cicero regarded as the healthy part of it. There were a number of reasons for its failure. On the one hand, the conditions did not exist for Cicero to secure a following of clients or of soldiers sufficient to make his political view triumphant. On the other hand, like many of his contemporaries, he underestimated the importance private armies would have in the solution to the crisis. He may also have had too many expectations of the *boni.* At the time of the civil war the landholding classes for the most part considered that their needs were best met by Caesar's policy. Even after Cicero's death they did not hesitate to consent to Augustus's domination, which definitively marked the death of the republican institutions.

3. THE SUPREMACY OF THE WORD: THE RHETORICAL WORKS

A response to the crisis

Nearly all Cicero's rhetorical works were written from 55, a couple of years after his return from exile, onwards. Like the *De Republica* and the subsequent philosophical works, they are produced by the need for a political and cultural response to the crisis.

Eloquence and Philosophy

The De Inventione

Whether the orator ought to be content with the knowledge of a certain number of rhetorical rules or whether he needed a broad education in law, philosophy, and history had long been debated in Greece. Cicero in his youth had begun, but not completed, a small treatise on rhetoric, the *De Inventione* — *inventio* is the discovery of material by the orator—for which he had drawn extensively on the nearly contemporary *Rhetorica ad Herennium* (see p. 120). Particularly interesting is the proem, where the young lawyer declares in favor of a synthesis of eloquence and *sapientia* (i.e., philosophical education), since he regards the latter as necessary to the formation of the orator's moral conscience; eloquence without *sapientia,* the eloquence of demagogues and popular agitators, has ruined a state more than once. Cicero's solution is worked out explicitly for Roman society. Many years later he will return to the same themes in the *De Oratore.*

Summary of the De Oratore

The *De Oratore* was composed in 55, during a period of withdrawal from the political scene, while Rome was thrown into turmoil by the gangs of Clodius and Milo. In the form of a dialogue, it is set in 91, in Cicero's youth. The participants are some of the most distinguished orators of the day, among whom the most prominent are Marcus Antonius (143–87 B.C.), grandfather of the triumvir, and Lucius Licinius Crassus, who is in effect Cicero's own spokesman. In the first book Crassus argues for the orator's need for a very broad education. Antonius opposes to this the ideal of a more instinctive, self-taught orator, whose art is based on confidence in his own natural powers, on practice in the Forum, and on familiarity with the example of previous orators. In book 2 they take up more analytic questions, and Antonius sets forth the problems concerning *inventio, dispositio,* and *memoria.* A witty, caustic figure also appears, Caesar Strabo, who is given a long, delightful digression on witticisms and clever sayings. In the third book Crassus discusses the questions having to do with *elocutio* and *pronuntiatio,* that is, with the orator's *actio* in general ("delivery," pretty much), and also confirms the need for a very broad general culture and philosophical training.

The setting of the De Oratore: *the imminence of catastrophe*

The choice of the year 91 for the setting of the dialogue has a precise significance. It is the very year of Crassus's death, which happened a few days after the days on which the dialogue is imagined to have taken place; and Crassus's death precedes by only a little the Social War and the long civil conflicts between Marius and Sulla, in the course of which several other of the principal interlocutors, including Antonius himself, would die cruelly. The crisis of the state is an obsession besetting all the participants in the dialogue and deliberately clashes with the serene, refined setting in which they meet to hold their conversations, the Tusculan villa of Crassus. Awareness of the terrible end of all the participants in the dialogue gives a tragic note to the proems that precede the individual books.

Platonic model and Roman contents

In trying to preserve verisimilitude in the characterization of the individuals, Cicero is obliged to re-create the atmosphere of the last days of peace under the old Republic. The model inspiring him is essentially the Platonic dialogue. With a sovereign gesture, the streets and squares of Athens are replaced by the garden of a Roman nobleman's country villa.

The reuse of the Platonic model for a rhetorical work was a notable departure from the arid Greek manuals of the day and from those produced by the school of Latin rhetors, who limited themselves to enunciating rules. Cicero, by contrast, was able to produce a lively and interesting work, which, however much it is based on a perfect familiarity with the specialist literature in Greek, is nourished by Roman experience and maintains close ties with forensic practice; almost all the examples illustrating Greek theories are drawn from Roman life and the Forum. A saying of Sulpicius, one of the participants in the dialogue, may serve as a summary of the work's principal thesis: "Eloquence is not born from rhetorical theory, but rhetorical theory from eloquence" (1.146).

The orator as a good man

According to this view, talent, the technique of word and gesture, and the knowledge of the rules of rhetoric cannot be considered adequate for the training of the orator; a broad cultural education is required. This is the theory of Crassus, who closely links the orator's cultural education (above all philosophy, especially moral philosophy) to his ethical-political trustworthiness. The orator's versatility, his ability to defend the *pro* and the *contra* in any argument, by which he is able to convince and to sway his audience, may be a grave danger if it is not counterbalanced by the virtues that anchor him to the system of traditional values, wherein respectable people recognize themselves. Crassus demands that *probitas* and *prudentia* be firmly rooted in the soul of anyone who is to learn the art of the word; to entrust the art to one who lacked these virtues would be like putting arms into the hands of madmen (3.55).

Coincidence between rhetorical and political training

The training of the orator thus comes to coincide with that of the politician of the ruling class. He should not be a man of specialized education—men of the ruling class should not practice any profession: for this free men of lower status, as well as slaves, exist—rather, he should be a man of broad general culture, able to master the art of the word and persuade his listeners. He should make use of his ability, not to cajole the people with demagogic suggestions, but to harness it to the will of the *boni*. In the *De Oratore* Cicero has in fact revealed the ambiguous status of an art that oscillates constantly between ethical-political wisdom and the technique of naked domination.

The Orator

Having composed for his son in 54 a kind of textbook on rhetoric, the

Partitiones Oratoriae, cast in a question-and-answer format, Cicero in 46 takes up again the themes of the *De Oratore* in a shorter treatise, the *Orator,* adding to it a section on the characteristics of rhythmical prose. While drawing the portrait of the ideal orator, Cicero stresses the three goals his art should aim at: *probare* (to put forward the thesis with strong arguments), *delectare* (to produce a pleasant esthetic impression with the words), and *flectere* (to arouse the emotions by means of pathos). Corresponding to the three goals are the three stylistic registers that the orator must be able to display by turns: low, intermediate, and elevated or "pathetic" (the last especially suitable in the closing peroration).

The History of Eloquence and Controversies about Style

Beyond Asianism and Atticism

The definition of the orator's highest task as the ability to move the feelings originated in the controversy with the Atticist tendency, whose supporters reproached Cicero with not having distanced himself sufficiently from Asianism. The charges referred to the redundancy of his oratorical style, the frequent use of figures, the accentuation of the rhythmical element, and the abuse of witticisms. Cicero's opponents esteemed instead the simple, lean style, the models for which were found in the Attic orators, principally Lysias. In this dispute Cicero took his stance, in the same year 46, in the dialogue *Brutus,* which not by chance is dedicated, as is the *Orator,* to Marcus Brutus, one of the chief representatives of Atticism.

The Brutus

In the *Brutus* Cicero, who takes the role of principal interlocutor—the other two are Brutus himself and Atticus—sketches a history of Greek and Roman eloquence and therein shows his gifts as a historian of culture and a fine literary critic. Given the fundamentally self-defensive character of the *Brutus,* it is understandable that the history of eloquence culminates in a recollection of the stages of Cicero's own oratorical career, from the rejection of his youthful Asianism to his achievement of full maturity after his quaestorship in Sicily.

Cicero's view of the history of oratory represents a break with the traditional schemes that opposed to one another the stylistic categories to which Asianists and Atticists were strongly attached. The break reflects a basic tendency of Cicero's oratorical practice: different situations demand an alternation among different registers, and the orator's success before his audience is the fundamental criterion by which to gauge the success of his style. The Atticists are criticized for the excessively cold and intellectual character of their eloquence, which rarely succeeds in being effective: they are ignorant of the art of swaying their listeners. Great oratory "without systems" has its chief model in Demosthenes, who is also an "Attic" writer, but of a very different sort from Lysias or Hyperides.

The De Optimo Genere Oratorum

Contemporary with the *Brutus* and, in a sense, complementary to it is another short treatise on a rhetorical subject, the *De Optimo Genere Oratorum.* This was intended to be the introduction to the Latin version of two famous opposing speeches, Demosthenes' *On the Crown* and Aeschines' *Against Ctesiphon,* delivered in the same trial, which was held in Athens in 330. We do not know whether Cicero actually translated the two speeches. In the work he defends the excellence of the two orators, especially Demosthenes: one recognizes in him the most perfect model of Attic eloquence.

The Topica

In 44 Cicero composes the last of his works of rhetorical theory, the *Topica,* which is inspired by Aristotle's work of the same name. It treats the topoi, the commonplaces to which the orator may have recourse when seeking arguments to develop in his speech. But as is easily understandable, the topoi are not useful in oratory alone. They can serve the philosopher, the historian, and the jurist (considerable space is reserved for juridical arguments in the *Topica*); even the poet ought to learn to make use of them. Written in a few days and for the sake of popularization, the work does not have great literary claims.

4. A PROJECT OF STATE

The De Republica: *a projection into the past*

The model of the Platonic dialogue reappears more evidently in the *De Republica,* on which Cicero worked extensively between 54 and 51. He did not attempt, however, to construct the picture of an ideal state, as Plato had done in the *Republic:* in a move that would become increasingly habitual with him, he projects himself into the past, in order to identify the Roman constitution in the time of the Scipios as the best form of state.

Summary of the *De Republica*

The dialogue unfolds in 129 at the suburban villa of Scipio Aemilianus, who along with his friend and collaborator Laelius is one of the principal speakers. Unfortunately, the reconstruction of the course of the work, especially in certain sections, is quite hypothetical because of the extremely fragmentary way in which the dialogue has been preserved. A considerable part was discovered at the beginning of the nineteenth century in a Vatican palimpsest by the future cardinal Angelo Mai; certain pieces of other sections have been transmitted through quotations by ancient writers such as Augustine; and the final section of the work, the *Somnium Scipionis,* has come down to us independently. In the first book Scipio starts from the Aristotelian doctrine of the three fundamental forms of government (monarchy, aristocracy, democracy) and their necessary degeneration into their extreme forms (respectively, tyranny, oligarchy, and ochlocracy, or government by the "dregs" of the people). Taking up a theory of the Greek historian Polybius, Scipio shows how the Roman state of their ancestors was saved from that necessary degeneration by tempering the three basic forms: the monarchic element is reflected in the consulship, the aristocracy in the Senate, the democracy in the *comitia,* or "assemblies." Book 2 was concerned with the development of the Roman constitution. The third book treated justice and was in large part devoted to an attempt at refuting the sharp criticism that the Academic philosopher Carneades had leveled at Roman imperialism. The criticism centered principally on the notion of the "just war," a notion that the Romans, on the pretext of aiding their own "allies" (i.e., subjects) in difficulty, had employed to justify the gradual extension of their dominion and the enlargement of their sphere of influence. The fourth book was concerned with the education of the citizens and of the leaders who must regulate their relations. In books 4 and 5 Cicero introduced the figure of the *rector et gubernator rei publicae,* or the princeps (this part of the work is especially full of gaps). In the sixth book the dialogue concluded with Scipio Aemilianus's recollection of the dream in which, some time earlier, his grandfather Scipio Africanus had appeared to him in order to demonstrate to him, from the height of heaven, the smallness and insignificance of all human things, including earthly glory, and to reveal to him the blessedness that awaits the souls of great statesmen on the far side.

The mixed government

The theory of the mixed government went back, through Polybius, to the Peripatetic philosopher Dicaearchus and to Aristotle himself. In Scipio's version, the tempering of the three basic forms does not take place in equal proportions. Scipio looks upon the democratic element with evident antipathy, regarding it chiefly as a "safety valve" to ventilate and dissipate the people's irrational passions. The praise for the mixed government thus becomes an exaltation of the republican aristocracy of Scipio's day.

The figure of the princeps

Given the lacunose condition in which the relevant part of the work has reached us, it is difficult to spell out how the figure of the princeps was portrayed and how he fit into the organism of the state. Several points can nonetheless be regarded as assured. The singular noun *princeps* refers to the type of the eminent politician, not to his uniqueness. In other words, Cicero seems to be thinking of an elite of eminent persons that guides the Senate and the *boni,* and the role of the princeps is probably modeled on the role that Scipio Aemilianus himself had played in the Roman Republic. This means that Cicero does not prefigure what happened in the Augustan period (though there have been interpretations along this line), but aims at keeping the role of the princeps within the limits of the republican form of government. He is thinking, not of a constitutional reform, but of the consolidation of political consensus around prestigious leaders. The authority of the princeps is not an alternative to that of the Senate but the support it needs to save the Republic.

The ascetic utopia of the princeps

Since his authority does not exceed constitutional limits, the princeps will need to steel his soul against all selfish passions, chiefly against the desire for power and wealth. This is the disdain for all human things that the *Somnium Scipionis* enjoins upon the rulers of the state. (Cicero would return to this question in the *De Officiis* when treating of *magnitudo animi* [see p. 197].) Cicero thus paints the picture of an ascetic ruler, the representative on earth of the divine will, reinforced in his dedication to the service of the state by his disdain for human passions. The Ciceronian ideal could be realized only with difficulty. As we have seen (pp. 180 f.), it is likely that both his own conviction that a more authoritative government was needed and, at the same time, his awareness of the dangers accompanying the concentration of enormous powers in the hands of a few leaders impelled Cicero to attempt a rapprochement with Pompey and the triumvirs, since he hoped to keep their action under the control of the Senate. But the same historical forces that raised up the warriors would rapidly lead to the dissolution of the Republic.

The De Legibus

Inspired again by the model of Plato, who had followed the *Republic* with the *Laws,* Cicero complemented the dialogue on the state with the *De Legibus,* begun in 52 and probably not published during his lifetime. The first three books are preserved, and fragments of books 4 and 5. The action this time is not placed in a bygone era, but in the present, and the interlocutors are Cicero himself, his brother Quintus, and his friend Atticus. It is set in Cicero's villa at Arpinum and in the nearby woods and countryside, which are depicted in a variant form of the motif of the *locus amoenus.* This in turn goes back especially to Plato's *Phaedrus.* The speakers are characterized with naturalness and realism; thus Quintus is depicted as an extreme optimate, Cicero as a moderate conservative, and Atticus as an Epicurean who is almost embarrassed by his own philosophical choices. In book 1 Cicero expounds the Stoic theory according to which law did not arise by convention, but is based on the reason innate in all men and is, therefore, given by god. In the next book, Cicero bases the exposition of the laws that ought to be in effect in the best state—herein lies the chief difference from Plato—not on a utopian legislation, but on the Roman legislative tradition, the guiding principles of which are to be found in pontifical and sacral law. In book 3 Cicero gives the text of the laws concerning magistrates and their competence.

5. A MORALITY FOR ROMAN SOCIETY

The incentives to philosophy

In his youth Cicero had attended the lectures of the most diverse philosophers, and he continued to be interested in philosophy practically throughout his life. Yet he began to write philosophy only in 46, with the small work *Paradoxes of the Stoics,* dedicated to Marcus Brutus, which expounds the Stoic theories most contrary to ordinary opinion. Then in 45 philosophical works come from him one after the other, at an almost incredible rate of production, and this at the same time as the most grievous events in Cicero's life. In February of that year his daughter Tullia died, and to relieve his intense grief he wrote a *Consolatio,* which is lost. But private events were not the only ones pushing him towards philosophy: the dictatorship of Caesar had deprived him of any possibility of participating in public affairs. Now almost indifferent to political events, Cicero lived in isolation and buried himself completely in composing his philosophical works.

The Hortensius *and the* Academica

The *Hortensius,* now lost, was an exhortation to philosophy, on the model of Aristotle's *Protrepticus.* The *Academica,* which treated problems of epistemology, was written in two stages: the first, the *Academica Priora,* in two books, and the *Academica Posteriora,* in four. We have book 2 of the first part, entitled *Lucullus* because in it Lucullus is Cicero's interlocutor, and book 1 of the second part, the *Varro,* in which Varro expounds his own theories, having Atticus and Cicero as interlocutors (this book is lacking its conclusion).

The De Finibus Bonorum et Malorum

The *De Finibus Bonorum et Malorum,* dedicated to Brutus, is considered by some to be Cicero's masterpiece in philosophy. It is certainly one of his most elegant, most harmoniously constructed works. It deals with ethical questions, that is, the problem of the highest good and the highest evil, as the title indicates. This problem is addressed in three dialogues, in five books. In the first dialogue, books 1 and 2, the theory of the Epicureans is set forth, followed by Cicero's refutation. In the second, books 3 and 4, the Stoic theory is compared with the Academic and Peripatetic theories. The third dialogue, book 5, expounds the eclectic theory of Antiochus of Ascalon (Cicero's teacher and Varro's), which is closest to the author's own thought.

The Tusculan Disputations

Another treatment of ethical questions, the *Tusculan Disputations,* is also one of Cicero's greatest philosophical works and certainly the most passionate of them. It, too, is dedicated to Brutus and set in Cicero's villa at Tusculum, whence the title. The work, which marks Cicero's closest approach to the theories of the most rigorous Stoicism, is conducted in the form of a dialogue between Cicero and an anonymous interlocutor and so becomes almost an interior monologue. The five individual books deal, respectively, with the themes of death, grief, sadness, spiritual disturbances, and virtue as the guarantee of happiness. We thus have here a great *summa* of ancient ethics, a vast essay on the subject of happiness. In the *Tusculans* Cicero seeks an answer to his own personal questions too, a solution for his doubts; hence the author's profound emotional participation in the subjects treated, which gives the style a passionate solemnity and bestows on certain pages a lyrical intensity but rarely equaled in Latin prose.

The De Natura Deorum, *the* De Divinatione, *and the* De Fato

Three dialogues deal with religious and theological matters: the *De Natura Deorum,* in three books, also dedicated to Brutus; the *De Divinatione,* in two books; and the *De Fato,* which has come down to us incomplete. The last two are explicitly presented by the author as integral with the first and complementary to it.

The Cato Maior *and the* Laelius

The *Cato Maior de Senectute* and the *Laelius de Amicitia* are two brief dialogues in which philosophical precepts are embodied in two figures of the Roman tradition (they are discussed below). Other works, such as the *De Gloria,* the *De Virtutibus,* and the *De Auguriis,* are lost. In the fall of 44 Cicero begins writing the *De Officiis,* which is virtually his philosophical testament.

Compilation and originality in Cicero the philosopher

Cicero's effort, generally speaking, is towards rethinking the entire body of methods, ideas, and theories that had arisen in the Hellenistic philosophical schools, in order to recompose it in a solid edifice of common sense. He means in this way to offer the Roman ruling class a point of reference, with a view to reestablishing its dominance over society. He does not take up only immediate problems; he poses questions regarding the very roots of the social, political, and moral crisis in Roman society and tries to devise long-term solutions. It is unnecessary to inquire into Cicero's philosophical originality. Even the rapid rate at which he composed his philosophical works shows that they are more than anything compilations from Greek sources. But Cicero is original in the choice of subject and in the shaping of the arguments, since the problems posed by society are new and original and the questions that he puts to society are new. Cicero knits together the torn limbs of Hellenistic thought in order to extract from it an ideal structure that will operate effectively in regard to Roman society.

The Theory of Knowledge

The theory of knowledge in Cicero's philosophical method

For a theory of knowledge Cicero in his mature years held to the probabilism of the Academics, a sort of pragmatic Skepticism that, though it did not deny the existence of a truth beyond the phenomena, was chiefly concerned to guarantee the possibility of a probable knowledge that would be useful for orienting action. In book 2 of the *Academica* Lucullus reproaches Cicero for destroying the very possibility of knowledge by refusing to admit the existence of sure criteria of our perceptions. If everything is but a matter of opinion, Lucullus says, there will no longer be either certainty or truth. Cicero replies that even a general doubt does not entail the negation of truth; he does not even think, as the Skeptics do, that there exist multiple truths. He and his Academic (and in part Peripatetic) sources have grasped the need to avoid opposite errors, both the radical dogmatism that refuses to doubt certain appearances and the radical Skepticism that pushes doubt to the point of bringing into question the very possibility of any knowledge. Wiser is the method that strives to define the real conditions of human experience and to approach the truth through appearances and probability. This also defines the method adopted by Cicero in regard to the most serious philosophical problems, including ethics.

Ethical Systems in Conflict: Cicero's Philosophical Eclecticism

Eclecticism and humanitas

In a famous passage of the *Tusculans* (5.83) Cicero defines the method he follows in dealing with the most important problems: by refusing to formulate a firm opinion, he strives to set forth the different possible opinions and to compare them in order to see whether some are more consistent and more probable than others. Cicero's philosophical eclecticism meets the need for a rigorous method that strives to create among the different doctrines a dialogue from which any polemic spirit is excluded. The same ideology of *humanitas,* to the development of which Cicero made a notable contribution, urged a person to adopt an intellectual attitude of open tolerance. This is manifested even in the conduct of Cicero's philosophical dialogues, which reflect the behavior of good Roman society. The softening of polemical force, the rejection of any harshness in contradiction, the tendency to present one's theories merely as personal opinions, the constant use of polite formulas, the care shown not to interrupt another's reasoning—all these traits reveal the usages of an elite social circle concerned to develop a suitable code of good manners.

Cicero's anti-Epicureanism

But there is one case in which contradiction and refutation, though not descending to the fray, do sometimes become more violent and indignant: Cicero's eclecticism is very far from including Epicureanism, to whose explanation and refutation are dedicated, for example, the first two books of the dialogue *De Finibus Bonorum et Malorum.* There are two principal grounds for Cicero's aversion to Epicureanism, closely linked to one another. First, the Epicurean philosophy leads to a lack of interest in politics, whereas the *boni* ought to participate actively in public life.

Second, Epicureanism excludes the divinity's providential function (to the extent that it does not deny its existence) and thus weakens the links with traditional religion, which remains the fundamental basis of ethics for Cicero.

The dialogues on religious subjects

These considerations explain, at least in part, the point of the dialogues on religious and theological subjects. In book 1 of the *De Natura Deorum* the Epicurean theory of divine indifference to human affairs is expounded and refuted. In book 2 the Stoic theory of providential pantheism is examined, and then in book 3, which has lacunae, Cicero seems to take the side of Academic Skepticism. What is more interesting, because more directly related to the Roman setting, is the *De Divinatione,* a dialogue in two books between Cicero and his brother Quintus, in which the author shows himself as hesitating between the denunciation of the falsity of traditional religion and the necessity of maintaining it in order to preserve domination over the lower social classes, which are easily taken advantage of because of their credulity; the declaration of unfavorable auspices, for instance, could serve to interrupt or adjourn political assemblies.

The De Finibus

The comparison between the different philosophical systems is carried on throughout the entire corpus of Ciceronian dialogues, but it is developed especially extensively in the *De Finibus Bonorum et Malorum.* After the Epicurean theories have been refuted, Cato the Younger takes up, in the third book, the defense of traditional Stoicism, before which Cicero's position was always one of substantial perplexity (let us recall *Pro Murena* [see p. 182]). Cicero recognized that Stoicism furnished the most solid moral basis for the citizens' commitment to the community. Yet by virtue of his taste and culture he felt himself remote from an intransigent Stoic such as Cato or from an Academic of rigid morality such as Brutus. Their ethical rigidity seemed anachronistic to him, scarcely practicable in a society that had undergone radical transformations after the period of the great conquests. Cicero's eclecticism also signifies openness and sympathy for philosophies that were moderately open to pleasure, such as the Peripatetic philosophy, and his Academic probabilism furnished the theoretical basis for his attempt to reconcile diverse tendencies. The *De Finibus* can be seen as an aporetic dialogue. Near the conclusion Cicero, when considering the problem of the highest good, seems to hesitate between the theories of Antiochus of Ascalon (an Academic who had reacted vigorously to the Skepticism of his teachers and returned to dogmatic positions) and a more critical attitude.

Old Age and Friendship

The Cato Maior *and the idealization of Cato*

The two brief dialogues *Cato Maior de Senectute* and *Laelius de Amicitia,* both composed in 44 and dedicated to Atticus, occupy a special place among Cicero's philosophical works. In both the author brings on stage familiar figures of the Roman tradition. Cicero is working on the *Cato Maior* during the first months of 44, shortly before the murder of Caesar, in a period of forced political inactivity. In the person of Cato the Elder, whom he selects as his spokesman, Cicero transforms the bitterness he feels over an old age that, in addition to physical decline and the imminence of death, seems to fear above all the loss of the possibility of political participation. The action is set in 150, the year before Cato's death. In projecting himself into the figure of an old man who preserves intact his authority and prestige, Cicero finds a way of taking refuge in an ideal past, of escaping from his own inactivity by imagining himself in the clothing of the old censor. In portraying him he has taken many liberties with the historically verifiable picture (see p. 89). His Cato appears softened and gentled. The rough Sabine farmer stubbornly attached to his profits has given way to a refined cultivator of *humanitas* and sociability who, with a touch of estheticism, even prefers the beautiful to the useful. In his old age the taste for *otium* is perfectly harmonized with the tenacity of political engagement, two opposing demands that Cicero had in vain attempted to reconcile throughout his life.

The Laelius *and the new basis of friendship*

The atmosphere is different, more combative, in the *Laelius,* which accompanies Cicero's return to the political scene immediately after the murder of Caesar. The dialogue is imagined as taking place in 129, the same year as the *De Republica,* a few days after Scipio's mysterious death during the Gracchan disturbances. Recalling his departed friend, Laelius converses with his interlocutors on the nature and value of friendship itself. *Amicitia,* for the Romans, was above all the forming of personal ties for the purpose of political support. Starting from the attempt to get beyond the clientship and faction that traditionally belong to the aristocratic state, the dialogue follows the Greek philosophical schools in seeking the ethical bases of society in a relation that binds together the will of friends. The novelty of Cicero's approach consists in the effort to enlarge the social basis of friendship beyond the restricted circle of the *nobilitas.* Such values as *virtus* and *probitas,* which are recognized by large segments of the population, are established as the foundation of friendship. Cicero writes for those respectable people to whose political-social centrality he long ago entrusted the fate of his program for the renewal of the state (let us recall the fundamental *Pro Sestio* [see p. 182 f.]). Trust in a renewed value system in which friendship plays a central role should cement the unity of the *boni.* But the friendship promoted by the *Laelius* is not only a political friendship: throughout the work one notes a desperate need for sincere relations, which Cicero, who was caught in the grip of conventions imposed by public life, may have been able to enjoy only with Atticus. There remains, nonetheless, a vast gulf between an elevated notion of morality and virtue and the inescapable reality of political practice. *Amicitia* reveals a degree of ambiguity in that it presents itself simultaneously as the ideal of a life gladdened by brotherly affections and as a system of more or less veiled forms of connivance among the supporters of the social order.

The Duties of the Ruling Class

The De Officiis *and the Stoicism of Panaetius*

The writing of the *De Officiis* was probably begun in the fall of 44. It is a treatise, not a dialogue, dedicated to Cicero's son Marcus, then a student of philosophy in Athens. The work was produced rapidly, for the most part at the same time as several of the *Philippics* (see p. 184 f.). While battling with a man who in his eyes is bringing the country to utter ruin, Cicero seeks in philosophy the bases for a program of vast scope, directed at the formulation of a morality of daily life that will allow the Roman aristocracy to regain control over society. The philosophical basis is provided by the modern Stoicism of Panaetius. Established on clear, firm principles, resolute in its rejection of Epicurean hedonism and the resulting ethic of disengagement, respectful of tradition and the political-social order, but without fanaticism and old-fashioned roughness, the philosophy of Panaetius provides the detailed casuistry necessary for regulating the daily behavior of members of the ruling classes.

The reconciliation between philosophical theory and political practice

In the *De Officiis* Cicero claims to be addressing the young in the first place, which confirms the pedagogic function that he generally attributes to his work of philosophical popularization. To have his program accepted he needed to overcome much resistance. Roman culture was traditionally averse to philosophical, speculative thought, in which it saw an undue avoidance of duties towards the state and the community. The task Cicero took on was precisely that of demonstrating how, in profoundly altered times, the performance of those duties was not possible unless the philosophical thought of the Greeks had first been absorbed and reflected upon. In Panaetius, who had been able to furnish the Roman aristocrats with a model of life firmly rooted in their national usages, he was able to find a stable point of reference for a discourse that could move easily between theoretical thought and the enunciation of precepts valid for everyday life.

Summary of the De Officiis

The three books into which the *De Officiis* is divided deal, respectively, with the honorable, the useful, and the conflict between them. For the first two books the source is the treatise *On Duty (Peri tou Kathekontos)* by Panaetius of Rhodes; the third is a rather eclectic compilation from various sources. Panaetius, who had been part of the circle of Scipio Aemilianus, had given Stoic doctrine a markedly aristocratic stamp. It is likely that the intended audience for his treatise was the Roman governing classes. He tried to free the doctrine from its rough, plebeian features (such as its injunction to "call things by their proper names," that is, not to avoid obscene terms) and especially to soften its moral rigidity, so as to render it practicable for a wealthy, educated, and refined ruling class. Panaetius's teaching was distinguished from the early Stoa chiefly by a positive judgment on the instincts: they should not be oppressed by reason, but rather corrected and disciplined by it. The traditional cardinal virtues of Stoicism— justice, wisdom, courage, and moderation—were reinterpreted so as to be seen as an organic development of these fundamental instincts.

The System of the Virtues

Beneficence

For Panaetius the fundamental virtue was "sociability," a kind of societal fellowship in which the traditional cardinal virtue of justice was joined to beneficence: if the former aims at "giving to each his own," the latter has the task of collaborating in a positive way for the well-being of the community and of placing the person and the possessions of the individual at the disposal of his fellow citizens. The beneficence theorized about by Panaetius corresponded perfectly to the life of the Roman aristocrats, who, by their *officia* and donations to their fellow citizens, were able to attract a political following that could raise them to the highest offices of state. *Beneficentia* naturally posed serious problems for Panaetius, and still graver problems in the time of Cicero. It had been seen too often how *largitio,* or in general the corruption of the masses through demagogic proposals, could be a dangerous tool in the hands of unscrupulous individuals who were resolved to turn the state into their private possession. As examples of "unjust" beneficence Cicero cites the agrarian laws and the proposals for debt relief. For this reason Cicero emphasizes that beneficence must not be put in the service of personal ambition.

Greatness of soul   Panaetius had replaced the cardinal virtue of courage with *magnitudo animi,* "greatness of soul," a gentlemanly virtue that springs from a natural instinct to outdo others and shows itself in the ability to impose one's own domination, an ability the Roman people had already displayed before the world. (Within the Roman people itself, greatness of soul is preeminently a virtue of its governing classes.) One observes, however, a kind of paradox: at the base of *magnitudo animi* the *De Officiis* places an almost ascetic disdain for worldly goods such as honors, wealth, and power. To secure advantages for one's friends or for the state presupposes in the one who secures them a firm control over personal desire. Manifest in this view is the desire to confine with strong bonds a virtue that, if not adequately held in check, can become the passion of the tyrannicide or turn against the Republic and senatorial domination (while Cicero was writing, the example of Caesar was still in everyone's mind).

Instinct guided by   The example of *magnitudo animi* clearly shows the relation that, in Panae-
reason   tius's thought and especially in its reworking by Cicero, links *logos,* "reason," to the natural instincts, and it illustrates the social program into which such a theory fits. The task of reason is to control the instincts, to transform them into virtues, emptying them of whatever is egoistic and of dishonest tendency (let us recall the *Somnium Scipionis* [see p. 190]). Once transformed into virtue, instinct can be placed at the service of the community and the state and can contribute actively to rendering the country still greater and more glorious; if there is no transformation, the path is open to anarchy and tyranny. The dialectic of reason and instinct also expresses the contradiction between, on the one hand, the aggressiveness that the *populus Romanus* should display towards the conquered nations, an aggressiveness that in a civil, refined period is also capable of disguising itself as tolerance and humanity, and, on the other hand, the necessity of not allowing such aggressive tendencies to prevail internally, since they would necessarily have self-destructive results.

The Origins of Etiquette

Decorum   In the ethical system of the *De Officiis* the general regulator of the instincts and virtues, which permits them to be integrated into a harmonious whole, is the final virtue, moderation. Externally, to the eyes of others, it is manifested in a suitable harmony of thoughts, gestures, and words that is called *decorum.* This signifies an ideal of *aequabilitas,* almost of uniformity, which is possible only for the man who has been able to submit his instincts to the firm control of reason. The self-control that Cicero favors pursues a certain goal: the approval of others, which *decorum* allows to be reconciled with order, consistency, and just measure in words and actions. The constant attention to what others may think and the concern not to hurt their feelings are a result of the dense web of social obligations in which the members of the upper classes at Rome find themselves enmeshed.

An etiquette before the letter

Cicero does not eschew entering into detailed rules for the behavior to be adopted in daily life and the usual intercourse with others. In a long section of the *De Officiis* (1.126–140) the author, starting from the modesty with which "obscene" parts of the body need to be treated, lingers in detail over the gestures and attitudes in which *decorum* is or is not shown. He gives advice on toilette and clothing and then provides a long series of rules for conversation, partially suggested by the rules already codified for oratory. Finally, he describes what the Roman aristocrat's house should be like—large and elegant enough to enhance its owner's prestige but without pomp and excessive luxury. With these rules Cicero began a tradition of etiquette that was destined to have a long history in Western culture. Yet in Cicero's day the description of etiquette had not yet become a literary genre in its own right: Cicero's rules are but one of the sections of a treatise that aims at constructing, on solid philosophical bases, a model of the *vir bonus* that includes the most varied aspects of his existence.

Flexibility and the Pluralism of Values

The plurality of possible life choices

One of the most interesting innovations in the ethical model proposed in the *De Officiis* is that the concept of decorum permits a plurality of attitudes and life choices. The appropriateness of the actions and behavior expected of the individual is rooted in each man's personal qualities and intellectual and moral disposition. Like actors in the theater, each one must play in life the part best suited to his talent; hence the legitimation of choices of life other than the traditional one of pursuing a public career, provided that the person who so undertakes does not forget his duties to the community. In this way there comes about a revaluation in the choices of life that were most suspect in Roman society, such as devoting oneself exclusively to economic matters or to one's own property or following an intellectual or scientific vocation. The archaic aristocratic model, which saw in politics and service to the state the only activity worthy of a Roman,

Flexibility of philosophy

is thereby shown to be no longer valid. The new demands of society have conferred a previously unthinkable dignity on a number of social figures. The pluralism in models of life accepted by the late Cicero obviously reflects the different vocations and activities of those *boni* from all Italy of whom he had begun to speak in the *Pro Sestio* (see p. 182 f.): in part actively engaged in politics, in part, to the extent that they are absorbed in other activities, the secure supporters of politicians who work to assure the social order. Philosophy cannot but take note of the changes that have occurred. Its specific task remains to reweave the web of values and to transform and make more pliable the ancient model in such a way that the new, emerging figures are not excluded but are absorbed and can be readily integrated.

6. CICERO AS PROSE WRITER: LANGUAGE AND STYLE

Linguistic purism and neologisms

When preparing to write his poem, Lucretius had to complain of the inadequacy of the Roman language for rendering the philosophical terminology of the Greeks (see p. 169). Cicero encountered analogous problems in his philosophical works, and in his rhetorical works, too, he needed to work out a suitable literary terminology. Cicero's decision, like Lucretius's, was basically purist: to avoid Grecisms. Hence a constant, dogged lexical experimentation in the translation of Greek terms, some evidence of which remains in Cicero's correspondence with Atticus. One may mention, for instance, the long period of perplexity after which Cicero decided to translate the Greek *kathekon* by *officium,* or, in rhetorical terminology, his various attempts to find a Latin equivalent of the technical term *periodos.* The result of this experimentation was the introduction of many new words into Latin. Cicero thus laid the foundation for the abstract vocabulary that was to become the inheritance of the European cultural tradition: for example, *qualitas (poiotes), quantitas (posotes), essentia (ousia),* and so on.

Cicero as model for Western prose

The careful choice of words was of the utmost importance for achieving clarity of expression. But Cicero's most notable contribution to the evolution of European prose lay in the creation of a complex and harmonious kind of period, based on perfect balance and response among the parts, the model for which, beginning with his speeches, he found in Isocrates and Demosthenes. Given the ever-present oratorical model, the demands of the ear and of the rhythm are often prominent, but the Ciceronian period also has in general a rigorous logical structure. The creation of such a period involved the elimination of inconsistencies in construction, of anacolutha, of constructions "according to sense," and of the many other forms of incongruence that archaic Latin prose had inherited from the colloquial

Logical structure and hypotaxis

language. Next came the organization of the phrases in large units that would show an accurate and explicit subordination of the various parts to the leading notion, in other words, the replacement of parataxis (coordination) by hypotaxis (subordination). A perfect capacity for controlling the syntax makes it possible to organize the long and complex, yet always lucid and coherent, periods in which Cicero's pages abound.

Variety of the Ciceronian style

If these are the features that best define the outward appearance of the structure of Cicero's discourse, what most strikes the reader is certainly the variety of tones and stylistic registers that come into play, with a great ease of movement among the different stylistic effects. Each of the three degrees of style (simple, moderate, and sublime) can be used suitably in accordance with the corresponding needs of the discourse: *probare, delectare,* and *movere.* (It is, of course, a question of knowing where and when to use each, according to the canonic Greek principle of *to prepon,* "what is fitting.") To each level of style and each expressive register corresponds a suitable collocation of words, an appropriate sonority made of harmony and eurhythmy; the *ornatus suavis et adfluens* works through the very form and the sound of the words. In particular the disposition of the words must be such as to follow the *numerus.*

The numerus *and rhythmic prose*

In practice the *numerus* acts like a system of metrical rules adapted to prose, so that weighty thoughts are given a solemn, steady movement and plain speech is given a familiar intonation. (As a theoretician Cicero legitimately claimed to have devoted more attention to this aspect of discourse than Greek theoreticians had.) The locale for these metrical-rhythmical effects is the clausula, that final part of the period in which the listener's ear should be impressed by the effects produced by the succession of feet, for example, the dactyl and paeon for the steady tone, or the iambic sequence for the discursive, familiar tone. Here we cannot treat in detail the effective, skillful variety of Cicero's clausulae. It is enough to know that in periodic prose Cicero, an original interpreter of the Greeks, was able to avoid the Asianic excesses of a Hortensius and more nearly approached, in the final analysis, the model of Isocrates, who had been able to combine the use of brief metrical clauses in series with the art of writing periods of ample construction.

7. THE POETIC WORKS

Ancient judgments on Cicero as poet

"With the passage of time," wrote Plutarch in his *Life of Cicero,* "he believed he was not only the greatest orator but also the greatest poet of Rome . . . but as for his poetry, since many great poets came after him, it has remained completely unknown, completely disdained." Cicero alone was deceived about himself and about his fate as a poet. His contemporaries already showed little appreciation; following generations showed none at all. Martial would make him a paradigm of deluded vain ambition: "You will make verses without any inspiration of the Muses, without any assistance from Apollo. Bravo! You share this virtue with Cicero" (*Epigrams* 2.89.3–4). He began very early and continued writing verses for nearly all his life.

Cicero's poems

In his youth Cicero composed short poems on mythological subjects in an Alexandrianizing style: *Glaucus,* in trochaic tetrameters, *Alcyones,* and so on. The *Limon,* probably a miscellaneous work (cf. Suetonius's *Prata,* on which see p. 546), contained among other things a collection of judgments on poets made in verse; one on Terence is preserved, in a fragment. Cicero's most successful poetic work was probably the *Aratea,* a hexameter translation of Aratus's *Phaenomena,* of which considerable portions are extant. Cicero also translated the second section of Aratus's poem under the title *Prognostica.*

There were also epic poems: the *Marius,* which sang of the deeds of the other great man from Arpinum (a youthful work, hardly belonging to his mature period), and the *De Consulatu Suo,* in three books, composed around 60 to celebrate the year of his glorious battle against Catiline; a large section of the latter has been preserved by Cicero himself in the *De Divinatione.* Of Cicero's works this was the one most ridiculed, already by his contemporaries and then by the literary critics of the first century A.D., not only because of its small poetic value but also because of the tiresome praises the author heaps on himself. Two verses in particular became the targets of criticism: *cedant arma togae, concedat laurea laudi,* and *o fortunatam natam me consule Romam!* The *De Temporibus Suis,* to which Cicero refers in several letters, must have been different but equally self-praising.

The two periods of Cicero's poetry writing

Based on what we can tell from the remains of his youthful verse, Cicero's first attempts at poetry, various in meter and subject, would make him a precursor of the neoterics: inclined towards a certain artistic experimentation though not, properly speaking, Callimachean, a poet of a Hellenistic type but not far removed from the poetics of a Lucilius. His tastes must have quickly made him more of a traditionalist, tied in particular to the archaic model of Ennius, to the point where he was more or less bitterly hostile towards the "modern poets," the *neoteroi* or *poetae novi,* as he himself with some disdain termed the representatives of the new poetry that was making a name for itself. Two periods can perhaps be distinguished: the period of his first works, with a taste and manner that was substantially Alexandrian, since it was devoted to short poems of a learned or didactic character; and the period of the epic-historical poems in an Ennian, or at least archaizing, manner. Between these two phases should be placed, in all likelihood, the translation of Aratus's erudite *Phaenomena.* His influence as a versifier, however, must not have been insignificant, at least in the technical-artistic aspects. He contributed not a little to regularizing the Latin hexameter: the position of the caesuras in the verse, for example, and the specialization of certain metrical-verbal forms in clausula. Indeed, the Latin hexameter emerged from his poetic exercises more elegant, certainly more flexible and lively in rhythm, and already in certain regards very close to the structure that it would acquire in the Augustan age. Echoes, especially of the *Aratea,* are to be heard in Lucretius, in Virgil's *Georgics,* and even in Horace and Ovid. If Cicero was a precursor in the technique of the hexameter, his example was probably decisive in attaining greater freedom of expression with word arrangement and in pushing the discourse beyond the rigid confines of the verse. The master of the large, articulated prose period fostered in poetry the development of enjambment and interlocking word order.

Cicero's influence on the Latin hexameter

Enjambment and movement in Cicero's verse

By means of enjambment the logical-syntactic completion of the thought is put off until the following verse; thus some words are artfully thrust forward or held back, and as a result the breathing time needed for the phrase is lengthened. Once the static coincidence is overcome between metrical unit (the six feet of the hexameter) and unit of sense (the completed phrase), the sequence of thoughts can overflow the closed measure of the verse, making a new start and, as it were, invading the space of the next verse. Another effect of stylistic intensification is created by the inter-locking word order, in which two closely linked words are separated by the interposition of other words. The most complex and most elegant case is found in verses such as "aestiferos *validis erumpit flatibus* ignes" or "extremas *medio contingens corpore* terras" or even "corniger *est valido conixus corpore* Tau-rus," in which the arrangement of the adjective at the beginning of the verse and the noun at the end creates a perceptible, tense split between linked words and at the same time frames the whole verse. This artificial structure, an Alexandrian technique, is destined to find favor with Virgil, too. The force of Cicero's stylistic model can be seen in the fact that all three verses just cited are good examples of that special artificial arrangement of words, Alexandrian in origin, that would be dear to the verse technique of the Augustan age: two adjectives in the first part of the verse, the two corresponding nouns in the last part, and in the middle the verb that acts as hinge, according to the scheme *a b c b a.* (Some philologists call this a "silver verse," reserving the term "golden verse" for the scheme *a b c a b.*) Thus, without yet achieving the expressive effects of the very fluid Augus-tan hexameter, the Ciceronian hexameter did succeed in creating a metri-cal-syntactic structure far less static than that created by the archaic hex-ameter.

Cicero as translator   The best proofs of Cicero's poetic art are his translations from the Greek poets, despite the fact that he often proves to be more magniloquent than capable of true pathos. Still, even in this case, apart from certain defects of emphasis, Cicero persisted and succeeded in realizing his constant program of Latinizing Greek culture; and this too must be accounted a valuable service of his.

8. THE CORRESPONDENCE

Survey of Cicero's correspondence   For understanding Cicero's personality we have at our disposal a tool of incomparable value: a considerable number of the letters he wrote to friends and acquaintances is preserved, along with some letters of reply from them. Cicero's correspondence, in the form in which it has been trans-mitted to us, comprises sixteen books *Ad Familiares* (to relatives and friends; the letters date from 62 to 43 B.C.), sixteen books *Ad Atticum* (to Atticus, Cicero's best friend throughout his life; the correspondence covers the period from 68 to 44), three books *Ad Quintum Fratrem* (from 60 to 54), and two books *Ad Marcum Brutum* (of disputed authenticity; the letters are all from 43), for a total of around nine hundred letters. These run from 68 to July of 43 (there are none from the year of his consulship) and were published at an unknown date after Cicero's death, edited perhaps, at least the *Ad Familiares,* by his faithful freedman Tiro.

Variety of contents and tones   Cicero's correspondence is rich and varied, its contents ranging from notes scribbled in haste to lively accounts of political events to elaborate letters that resemble short essays; examples of the last include the letter to his brother Quintus on the good governance of a province (*Ad Quintum*

Fratrem 1.1) and the one to Lucceius on the way to write history, an invitation to celebrate Cicero's struggle against Catiline (*Ad Familiares* 5.12). The variety of contents, occasions, and addressees is reflected in the variety of tone: Cicero is now playful, now concerned over political affairs and personal problems to the point of anxiety, now reserved and committed.

A real correspondence It should be emphasized that these are real letters. When Cicero wrote them, he was not thinking of their publication, as will later be the case with Seneca's correspondence. Thus they show us an unofficial Cicero, who in private confidences reveals openly his sometimes far from edifying behind-the-scenes political moves, his doubts, his frequent uncertainties and hesitations, the highs and lows of his spirits. The character of genuine correspondence is reflected also in the style, which is very different from that of the works intended for publication: Cicero does not avoid periodic constructions, which are often elliptical, slangy, thick with allusions that are occasionally in a kind of code (hence grave problems of interpretation for modern critics), abounding in Grecisms and colloquialisms; the syntax includes much parataxis and many parentheses; the vocabulary is studded with picturesque words, such as diminutives (*aedificatiuncula, ambulatiuncula, diecula, vulticulus, bellus, integellus,* etc.) and Greco-Latin hybrids (*tocullio,* "usurer," from Greek *tokos,* "interest"). It is a language that reflects quite faithfully the everyday speech of the Roman upper classes.

Historical value of the correspondence The exceptional historical value of Cicero's correspondence should not be forgotten. At times approaching what we would regard as a daily newspaper, it allows us to follow day by day the development of political events. Thanks to Cicero's correspondence, the era in which he lived is the one in all of ancient history that we know in greatest detail. Cornelius Nepos (*Life of Atticus* 16) was right to speak of that correspondence as a true and genuine *historia contexta eorum temporum.*

9. CICERO'S LITERARY SUCCESS

Varying judgments of antiquity Cicero saw himself more as a politician and statesman than as a writer and thinker. So too did most of his contemporaries, who would surely have been surprised, if not perplexed, by his subsequent canonization as the greatest writer of Latin prose and one of the founding authors of the Western literary tradition. This may be why many of the contemporary reactions we can discern to Cicero as a writer are distinctly negative. His style was opposed by the Atticist orators as being too ornate, was criticized by Asinius Pollio for carelessness, lack of pure *Latinitas,* and overabundant metaphors, and was rejected by Sallust, who preferred archaic vocabulary and nervous, brief phrases to Cicero's rotund diction and stately periods. But already Velleius Paterculus foretells that his fame will last forever (2.66.5), and Seneca the Elder says the he rivals the Greek orators (*Contr.* 1 *praef.* 6).

An anti-Ciceronian alternative was perfected later in the first century A.D. in the paratactic, pointed style of Seneca the Younger, but the same century saw the beginning of Cicero's canonization as a prose author in the schools (when exactly Cicero first became a school author is uncertain). In the middle of that century, Q. Asconius Pedianus wrote a commentary on Cicero's speeches, putting them into chronological order and attacking one traditional dating as false. And by the end of the century Quintilian could oppose the fashion for Seneca by establishing Cicero as the infallible master of rhetorical theory and the unsurpassable practitioner of oratorical eloquence. As Quintilian puts it, "For posterity the name of Cicero has come to be regarded not as the name of a man, but as the name of eloquence itself. Let us therefore fix our eyes on him, take him as our pattern, and let the student realise that he has made real progress if he is a passionate admirer of Cicero" (*Institutio Oratoria* 10.1.112, trans. Butler). A compelling negative proof of Cicero's canonical status at this time is provided by Larcius Licinus's polemical treatise "Ciceromastix," a title otherwise reserved only for Homer and Virgil. In the next generation, Pliny the Younger explicitly took him as his model (*Epistles* 4.8.4), and Tacitus imitated his style in his *Dialogus;* and in the second century even such archaizers as Aulus Gellius and Fronto continue at least to pay lip service to Cicero as a master of style, even if their own tastes in fact inclined towards greater austerity and less grandiloquence.

Through the rest of antiquity he remained a standard author in the schools. The speeches were read far more than the theoretical texts, and among the speeches the *Catilinarians* and the *Verrines* were the most popular. The scholarly commentaries that had begun at least as early as Asconius Pedianus continued throughout late antiquity. In the fourth century C. Marius Victorinus wrote commentaries to the philosophical and rhetorical treatises, Macrobius and Eulogius wrote on the *Somnium Scipionis,* and Boethius wrote on the *Topics.* As the example of Boethius suggests, Cicero's prestige was scarcely if at all diminished by the advent of Christianity. Lactantius was called the Christian Cicero, Jerome could dream with horror that he was not a Christian but a Ciceronian, and Augustine could take him as a model for style, for public oratory, and for philosophy. More identifiable Latin papyri of Cicero survive than of any other Latin author except Virgil—there are three papyri of the *Catilinarians* alone, including two used to teach Latin to Greek speakers—and surviving manuscripts of Cicero include three palimpsest fragments from the fifth century.

Middle Ages   From the very beginning of the Middle Ages, Cicero was one of the most important mediators of ancient ideas and values and a teacher of philosophy and rhetoric. Already Bede collected his famous sayings, Alcuin based a short rhetorical treatise upon the *De Inventione,* and Einhard quoted the *Tusculan Disputations* and imitated several speeches; and Cicero remained a school author throughout the Middle Ages. The Cicero of the Middle Ages, unlike that of pagan antiquity, is above all the philosopher, especially the political philosopher. To be sure, in the Middle Ages Cicero was revered as "king of eloquence," and the speeches were, at least to a small extent, in circulation (unlike the letters to Atticus, which were completely unknown), but they survived only in small groups in medieval manuscripts that did not start to be put together until the end of the eleventh century (and as late as about 1150 Wibald of Corvey's large collection of Cicero's speeches, philosophical and rhetorical treatises, and letters *ad familiares* seems never to have been copied). But despite the relative popularity of certain speeches (again the *Catilinarians* and the *Verrines,* now with the addition of the *Philippics*), on the whole the speeches tended to circulate more in the form of excerpts in *florilegia* than intact and in their own right. With the collapse of the ideal of pagan eloquence, for the first time Cicero's philosophical writings began to exert more influence than his speeches: Chaucer bases the *Parliament of Fowls* upon the *Somnium Scipionis* but otherwise shows no trace of acquaintance with Cicero's works; Dante neglects Cicero's speeches and letters and does not include Cicero among the best prose authors but is familiar with the *Laelius* (with which he consoles himself when Beatrice dies), *Cato, De Officiis,* and *De Finibus.*

Renaissance   Petrarch's fascination with Cicero both as a writer and as a man paved the way for the Renaissance's canonization of Cicero as ideal thinker, stylist, and statesman and led to Cicero's replacement of Virgil as the dominant Latin author among the humanists. Petrarch, who preferred Cicero to Aristotle as ethic to logic, saw enacted in Cicero's career the fundamental oppositions between *vita activa* and *vita contemplativa* and between politics and philosophy, and he was followed in this by such humanists as Coluccio Salutati and Leonardo Bruni, who found in Cicero's ideal of *urbanitas* an ancient model for the republican culture of the Renaissance city-state. One consequence was that Petrarch was the first to separate systematically the speeches from the other works. But Petrarch also rediscovered Cicero's *Pro Archia,* in 1333 at Liège, and, above all, his letters to Atticus, Quintus, and Brutus, in 1345 at the chapter library in Verona, whereupon he immediately wrote a letter to Cicero to tell him of the discovery (this is the first of Petrarch's letters to dead authors). Such discoveries inaugurated the febrile humanist search for further writings of the master. In 1355 Boccaccio unearthed the *Pro Cluentio;* in 1389 Colluccio Salutati rediscovered the letters *ad familiares* (which Petrarch never knew); in 1415 Poggio Bracciolini found the *Pro Murena* and the *Pro Roscio Amerino* in Cluny and five other speeches in Langres, Cologne, and other cities; and in 1421 Landriani found a manuscript with the *De Oratore,* the *Orator,* and the *Brutus* at the cathedral library of Lodi (after which these works, not widely known in the Middle Ages, started to overshadow such other previously dominant rhetorical treatises as the *De Inventione* and the spurious *Ad Herennium*). But despite the humanist interest in Cicero's person (expressed often in the form of severe criticisms), which led to his letters becoming among his most frequently read and quoted works, the philosophical treatises remained extremely popular. The Renaissance was especially fond of the *Cato,* of which about 350 fourteenth- and fifteenth-century manuscripts have been found (this text was also a favorite of the Middle Ages: about 50 medieval manuscripts have survived), but the *Laelius* was also widely read (Theodorus Gaza translated both treatises into Greek during the fifteenth century). The *Somnium Scipionis,* understood as a program for a renaissance of ancient ideals, became the object of frequent commentaries (so by Vives), and the *De Officiis* was the first classical text to be printed, at Mainz in 1465, followed soon after by the rhetorical treatises.

Cicero as statesman and stylist

Cicero has played an important role in modern history and political thought as a symbol of moderatism and a martyr to tyranny; yet his tendency to privilege liberty over equality and democracy, and the cultured upper classes over the plebs, has exerted an influence that has not always been beneficent. In stylistics, Cicero triggered a Renaissance controversy about the proper prose style to be adopted by the modern writer, which may strike us nowadays as trivial but which permitted the articulation of fundamental oppositions between changeless taste and historical evolution, between imitation and creativity, between past and present—the controversy between, on the one hand, the Ciceronians, who considered only Cicero himself a model worthy to be followed and attacked the usage of words and constructions exemplified only from other authors (so Poggio Bracciolini and Pietro Bembo), and, on the other hand, the anti-Ciceronians, who admitted many models (so Lorenzo Valla, Pico della Mirandola, and Politian). As late as 1528 Erasmus, who in the preface to his edition of the *Tusculan Disputations* of 1523 had declared that Cicero had been saved as a Christian, published an anti-Ciceronian *Ciceronianus,* which was attacked three years later by J. C. Scaliger; and indeed the issues involved continued to be debated wherever Latin prose composition was taught, until even recent times. Even when Latin ceased to be the sole language for learned public discourse in Europe, Cicero remained a powerful model for vernacular eloquence, not least because his writings continued to be held up as a model to many generations of schoolchildren. Thus, in the seventeenth and eighteenth centuries many neo-Ciceronian writers, such as Bossuet, Swift, Addison, Dr. Johnson, Burke, and Gibbon, favored a periodic, Latinate style, while in the late eighteenth and nineteenth centuries political oratory in a self-consciously Ciceronian mode enjoyed a renaissance in England (Pitt, Burke, Fox, and Sheridan), France (Robespierre), and America (Webster).

The nineteenth and twentieth centuries

But with Romanticism's preference for Greek over Latin and for *Volk* over elites, Cicero's fortunes began a decline from which they have never fully recovered. Their nadir was reached in the nineteenth century with Theodor Mommsen's stinging attack upon Cicero as an unprincipled opportunist, a mere rhetorician, in his treatises a flabby journalist and in his speeches a shifty lawyer. Since then scholars have worked to rescue Cicero's reputation in many particulars; his gradual disappearance from the schools has at least permitted his creative style and his inventive rhetorical strategies to be newly rediscovered; and the experience of recent times of convulsion and crisis has made his own achievements under comparably difficult circumstances seem less facile and more worthy of respect. So Cicero has once again won the respect he deserves— but not the love he once enjoyed. It is hard to imagine that he will ever again achieve the cultural centrality he possessed in the generations following Petrarch.

BIBLIOGRAPHY

There are complete editions of the works of Cicero in the Teubner, Loeb, and Budé (Les Belles Lettres) series. The Oxford Classical Texts series at present lacks the philosophical works, though editions are in preparation. See also the Italian series published by Mondadori. The fragments of lost works are conveniently found in the edition of C.F.W. Mueller (vol. 3 of the collected works, Leipzig 1898). For the lost speeches, see also the editions of F. Schoell (vol. 8 of the collected works, Leipzig 1918) and G. Puccioni (Milan 1963), as well as J. W. Crawford, M. *Tullius Cicero: The Lost and Unpublished Orations* (Göttingen 1984); for the philosophical works, the edition of J. Garbarino (Milan 1984) with separate editions of the *Consolatio* by C. Vitelli (Milan 1979) and *Hortensius* by A. Grilli (Milan 1962; see also the edition of M. Ruch, Paris 1958); and for the poetry, the editions of A. Traglia (Milan 1963) and J. Soubiran (Paris 1972). The major edition of the *Letters* is that of D. R. Shackleton Bailey: *Ad Atticum* (7 vols., Cambridge 1965–70, with translation and commentary), *Ad Familiares* (2 vols., Cambridge 1977, with commentary), and *Ad Q. Fratrem* and *Ad Brutum* (Cambridge 1980, with commentary); see also his Teubner text of *Ad Atticum* (2 vols., Stuttgart 1987).

English editions and commentaries relating to individual speeches include R.G. Nisbet, *De Domo Sua* (Oxford 1939), J. O. Lenaghan, *De Haruspicum Responso* (The Hague 1969), E. J. Jonkers, *De Lege Agraria* (Leiden 1963), R.G.M. Nisbet, *In Pisonem* (Oxford 1961), L. L. Pocock, *In Vatinium* (London 1926), T. N. Mitchell, *Verrines II. 1* (Warmington 1980), D. R. Shackleton Bailey, *Philippics* (Chapel Hill 1986), H. C. Gotoff, *Pro Archia* (Urbana 1979), R. G. Austin, *Pro Caelio* (ed. 3 Oxford 1960), W. Yorke Fausset, *Pro Cluentio* (ed. 4 London 1901), E. J. Jonkers, *De Imperio Gn. Pompei* (Leiden 1979), A. C. Clarke, *Pro Milone* (Oxford 1895), H. A. Holden, *Pro Plancio* (ed. 3 Cambridge 1891), J. C. Kinsey, *Pro Quinctio* (Sydney 1971), and W. E. Heitland, *Pro Rabirio* (Cambridge 1882; see also that of W. M. Blake Tyrrell, Amsterdam 1978). On the philosophical works, see esp. the commentaries of J. S. Reid on the *Academica* (London 1885) and *De Finibus* 1–2 (Cambridge 1925; new commentary in preparation by P. Mitsis); of A. S. Pease on *De Divinatione* (2 vols., Urbana 1920–23) and *De Natura Deorum* (Cambridge, Mass. 1925), both massive compilations; of H. A. Holden on *De Officiis* (Cambridge 1899; see also the translation by M. Griffin and M. E. Atkins, Cambridge 1991); of J. C. Powell on *De Senectute* (Cambridge 1988); of R. W. Sharples on *On Fate* (Warminster 1991); and of T. W. Dougan and R. M. Henry on the *Tusculan Disputations* (2 vols., Cambridge 1905–34; see also the smaller editions of A. E. Douglas, book 1 [Warminster 1985], books 2–5, partly in summary [Warminster 1991]). Among the rhetorical works, see esp. the commentaries of A. E. Douglas on *Brutus* (Oxford 1966), A. S. Wilkins on *De Oratore* (Oxford 1892), and J. E. Sandys on *Orator* (Cambridge 1885).

There is an introductory survey by A. E. Douglas (Greece and Rome: New Surveys in the Classics 2, Oxford 1968); see also his survey on the *Rhetorica* in *ANRW* 1.3 (Berlin 1973) 95–138. Biographies and general studies include those of R. E. Smith (Cambridge 1966), D. Stockton (Oxford 1971), E. Rawson (London 1975), D. R. Shackleton Bailey (London 1971), and T. N. Mitchell (New Haven 1979). There is a collection of essays by T. A. Dorey (London 1965). Plutarch's *Life of Cicero* has recently been edited by J. L. Moles (Warminster 1987). On the philosophical works, which have attracted increasingly serious attention from philosophers in recent years, see also H.A.K. Hunt, *The Humanism of Cicero* (Melbourne 1954), and P. Mackendrick, *The*

Philosophical Books of Cicero (London 1989). On the speeches, see W. R. Johnson, *Luxuriance and Economy: Cicero and the Plain Style* (Berkeley 1971), E. W. Wooten, *Cicero's Philippics and Their Demosthenic Model* (Chapel Hill 1983), and J. M. May, *Trials of Character* (Chapel Hill 1988); on the *rhetorica,* see A. E. Douglas, "The Intellectual Background of Cicero's *Rhetorica:* A Study in Method," *ANRW* 1.3: 96–138. Many general works on rhetoric naturally devote much space to Cicero; see, e.g., G. A. Kennedy, *The Art of Rhetoric in the Roman World* (Princeton 1972). The literature in languages other than English is extensive, but the following might be singled out: on the speeches, W. Stroh, *Taxis und Taktik* (Stuttgart 1975), and C. J. Classen, *Recht, Rhetorik, Politik* (Darmstadt 1985); on the rhetorical works, A. Michel, *Rhétorique et philosophie chez Cicéron* (Paris 1960); and on the philosophical works, R. Hirzel's monumental *Untersuchungen zu Ciceros philosophischen Schriften* (3 vols., Leipzig 1877–83), as well as W. Süss, *Cicero: Eine Einführung in seine philosophischen Schriften* (Mainz 1965).

Philology, Biography, and Antiquarianism at the End of the Republic

1. STUDIES OF ANTIQUITY AND NOSTALGIA FOR THE ROMAN PAST

Birth and flourishing of philological-antiquarian studies

Studies of history and antiquarianism were begun towards the end of the second century B.C., availing themselves occasionally of the contribution made by the Latin philology then taking shape (see p. 124). Latin philology, though in its methods it obviously went back to Greek philology, nevertheless directed its interests chiefly to the national culture. Research into etymologies was at the same time research into the origins of customs and institutions; study of the language aimed at reconstructing early Roman antiquities.

Nevertheless, it is only in the last century of the Republic that philological-antiquarian studies enter their first period of great flowering. The contributing factors are various and convergent. The rapid transformation of customs and the consequent general crisis of values lead to the desire, sometimes tinged with nostalgia, for a confrontation with the past, with the Roman tradition, and also with the institutions and customs of foreign civilizations, especially that of the Greeks; and this leads in certain cases to at least an incipient notion about the relativism of values, that is, their historically contingent character. Moreover, the emergence of new groups, who may lack a deep intellectual background but are destined to assume political responsibilities, gives impetus to the composition of works of popularization that a new ruling class may draw on for a rapid orientation towards the culture.

Devotion to the past and foreign contributions

In the late Republic, antiquarian research in its various forms exhibits partially contradictory characteristics. Veneration of the national past is prominent enough to constitute an obstacle to the development of a truly critical historiographic sense; and yet, at least in the case of Varro, the devotion to antiquity does not signify ignorance of the foreign contributions by which Roman civilization was nourished. These considerations must be kept in mind in order to understand what at first sight seems paradoxical: in the biographies of Cornelius Nepos veneration for the traditional values is intertwined with a moderate cultural relativism, at least that small amount of cultural relativism that is implicit in the very fact that the most outstanding Romans and the most outstanding representatives of foreign cultures are compared with one another in their specific categories of excellence.

2. TITUS POMPONIUS ATTICUS, ANTIQUARIAN SCHOLAR AND ORGANIZER OF CULTURE

The circle of Atticus

Our sources allow us to glimpse the important role played by the house of Cicero's friend Atticus on the Quirinal hill, which was a meeting place for the leaders of historical-antiquarian research in this period. In it gathered Cicero himself, Varro, and probably Cornelius Nepos, among others. Titus Pomponius Atticus (110–32 B.C.), of the equestrian class, had left Rome at the time of the Sullan proscriptions for reasons of safety and had remained at Athens for more than twenty years. Returning to Rome in 65, he still continued to reside abroad for long periods, especially in Epirus. He always rejected direct political engagement—and so was satisfied with his status as an *eques*—and spent his life in concern for his own affairs and for art, literature, and antiquarianism. He took a hand in, among other things, the publication of some of Cicero's works, including various speeches. He wrote a historical handbook, the *Liber Annalis,* published in 47, which included all Roman history to the year 49. He carried out general researches on several families of the aristocracy. And he published, probably in imitation of an analytic work by Varro (see below), a kind of album of great Romans, in which each portrait was accompanied by an epigram of four or five verses. Atticus, as far as we know, was an Epicurean. Yet it is revealing that Cicero (*De Finibus* 2.67) composes an elogium of his friend as a scrupulous collector of *memorabilia* (undertakings and achievements of persons of the Roman tradition) to be presented to the reader for his imitation, and he does this in the context of an anti-Epicurean polemic, thus uncoupling his friend from the philosophy of hedonism in order to ascribe to him a cultural mission in the opposite direction, a mission consistent with the exaltation of *virtus,* with political commitment, and with the restoration of the morality of their ancestors. Atticus may have succeeded in reconciling a moderate Epicureanism, removed from all ostentation, with devotion to Roman antiquities. In the years following the death of Cicero the aged knight's dedication to the *mos maiorum* would be a point of contact with Octavian, the new princeps who was eager to present himself as restorer of the traditional values.

The Liber Annalis *and other works*

Atticus's Epicureanism

3. VARRO

LIFE

Marcus Terentius Varro was born in 116 B.C., almost certainly at Rieti. He was a pupil of the antiquarian Lucius Aelius Stilo and the philosopher Antiochus of Ascalon. He was quaestor probably in 85, and subsequently, at unknown dates, tribune of the plebs and praetor. In 78–77 he fought in the Dalmatian campaign. He was in Pompey's entourage during the war against Sertorius (76–71) and the war against the pirates (from 67 on). In

59 he was part of the twenty-man commission charged with the distribution of lands. During the civil war he was Pompey's legate in Spain; he caught up with the Pompeian army at Dyrrhacium and returned to Italy after the catastrophe at Pharsalus. He was lucky enough to recover his estates. In 46 Caesar entrusted him with the task of creating a large library. He was proscribed in 43 but saved by Fufius Calenus. He died at an advanced age in 27 B.C.

In the course of his long life Varro wrote an incredible number of works; some sources speak of six hundred books. A partial list, including the most important titles, follows.

Preserved works: *De Lingua Latina,* of which six damaged books remain from twenty-five, completed after July of 45 and before the death of Cicero, to whom all but the first four books were dedicated; *De Re Rustica* (more precisely, *Rerum Rusticarum Libri Tres*), in three books, completed in 37 but perhaps written in stages over the preceding twenty years.

Works of which we possess only fragments or ones entirely lost:

In verse or prosimetron (i.e., mixed verse and prose): *Saturae Menippeae,* in 150 books (we have about 90 titles and 600 fragments), composed in relative youth; also books of short poems, satires, and tragedies.

In prose:

a) History, geography, antiquarianism: *Antiquitates,* divided into twenty-five books, *Rerum Humanarum,* written first, and sixteen books, *Rerum Divinarum,* the whole work completed and dedicated to Caesar as pontifex maximus in 47; *De Vita Populi Romani,* in four books, dedicated to Atticus; *De Gente Populi Romani,* in four books (between 43 and 42 B.C.); *De Familiis Troianis;* two autobiographical works, *De Vita Sua* and *Legationes,* each in three books; *Annales; Ephemeris Navalis ad Pompeium,* probably from 77; *De Ora Maritima.*

b) Language and literary history: *De Antiquitate Litterarum ad L. Accium; De Origine Linguae Latinae; De Similitudine Verborum; De Sermone Latino,* in five books, after 46 B.C.; *Quaestiones Plautinae,* in five books; *De Comoediis Plautinis; De Scaenicis Originibus,* in three books; *De Actionibus Scaenicis,* in three books; *De Poematis,* in three books; *De Poetis,* a fundamental literary chronology; *Hebdomades vel de Imaginibus,* in fifteen books, probably finished in 39.

c) Rhetoric and law: twelve books of *Orationes; Laudationes; De Iure Civili,* in fifteen books.

d) Philosophy and science: *De Philosophia; De Forma Philosophiae;* seventy-six books of *Logistorici,* dialogues on philosophical and historical subjects, with double titles (we know eleven titles complete, plus eight titles that are fragmentary), composed at an advanced age; nine books of *Disciplinae,* written perhaps from 34 to 33.

The chief sources for the life and works of Varro are, besides Jerome's *Chronicle,* Varro himself and his contemporaries: Cicero (in the published work and the correspondence), Caesar, and others. Details are also given by later writers such as the historian Appian and the learned Aulus Gellius.

Antiquarian Learning, Philology, and Linguistic Studies

Varro's response to the crisis

Philological and antiquarian interests accompanied Varro from his youth on. The *De Antiquitate Litterarum,* dealing with problems of the history of the Latin alphabet, because it is dedicated to Accius, must have been published before his death in the eighties, and nothing prevents us from setting the date several years earlier. Nevertheless, the most important works of this type, such as the *Antiquitates Rerum Humanarum et Divinarum* and the *De Lingua Latina,* were composed after his sixtieth year. There is reason to believe that before then Varro's time for learned studies was limited by political activity and engagement in literary matters.

Varro's devotion to the past

The composition of Varro's antiquarian works falls, as can be seen, more or less in the same years in which Cicero was devoting himself to writing his rhetorical and philosophical works. Thus the hypothesis that, like Cicero, Varro too set himself the task of giving an intelligent and cultivated response to the crisis Rome was passing through, seems persuasive. His love for the past was profoundly tinged with nostalgia. Varro sees the Roman history of the previous century as a decline and regards the growth of consumption as a dangerous corrupting factor. (This is so despite the fact that his hostility to contemporary excess in luxury is to be traced back to a common cultural attitude exalting the moral and political value of simplicity rather than to a conservative devotion to the past. Varro's model of life is that of a country gentleman who can derive good returns from his vast estates and derive pleasure from a style of life.) In any event, attachment to the Roman traditions is very strong in him, perhaps even stronger than in Cicero. Yet Cicero, who made one of the most important contribu-

Evaluation of cultural contributions from abroad

tions to Hellenizing Roman culture, was in other ways far more reluctant than Varro to admit the importance of foreign contributions (Greek, Italian, Etruscan) to the formation of Roman civilization. It seems that in stressing the cultural amalgamation carried out by Rome, Varro aligned himself with the Greek philosopher Posidonius of Apamea, who is said to have singled out as the reason for the Romans' superiority their ability to assimilate the best of the foreign civilizations with which they came into contact. This idea was already widespread in the times of Polybius and Cato, but Varro, rehabilitating a time-honored interpretation of Roman civilization on which Greek and Roman intellectuals had collaborated, probably gave the idea greater clarity and a more organic character.

The Antiquitates

In Varro's work, the *Antiquitates* in particular, which was hailed as a revelation by Cicero, nearly the whole inheritance of Latin civilization was illustrated and given order: the purpose was a systematic review of Roman life in its connections with the past, as evidenced by language, literature, and customs. Understandably, the Varronian legacy was very valuable for

Augustan culture and for all subsequent antiquarian and learned research among the Romans.

The *Antiquitates,* the structure of which is preserved for us by Augustine in the *De Civitate Dei,* was articulated according to a plan that consisted of four hexads (groups of six books) in the first part, devoted to *Res Humanae,* and five triads (groups of three books) in the second part, devoted to *Res Divinae.* Both the first and the second part were preceded by an introductory book. The four sections of the *Res Humanae* dealt with men, places, times, and things, respectively. The same subdivision was maintained in the first four sections of the second part, the *Res Divinae,* in the sense that religious ceremonies are celebrated by men, in certain places and times. The fifth and last section concerned the gods themselves.

The Res Humanae

The *Res Humanae* met with remarkable success among contemporaries, who for the first time saw certain key points about Rome's origins established authoritatively, the date of the city's foundation, for instance, which from Varro onwards is set definitively in 754 B.C. Cicero praises it enthusiastically in the proem to the *Academica Posteriora,* and Virgil himself, whose *Georgics* already owed much to Varro, certainly used it in creating the legend of the *Aeneid.*

The Res Divinae

We can form a better idea of the *Res Divinae* because of the enormous success the work had among the fathers of the church, especially Augustine, who made it a target for polemic, taking it somewhat as the basic text of pagan theology. In it Varro distinguished three ways of conceiving of divinity: a fabulous theology, including the stories of mythology and their elaboration at the hands of the poets; a natural theology, that is, the philosophers' theories on divinity, which must remain exclusively in the possession of the intellectuals of the ruling class and not be spread among the people, for fear that it would threaten the idea of the sacredness of the state institutions; and finally, the civil theology, which conceives of divinity in relation to a political need and thus is useful to the state. Varro took this arrangement of religion from Stoic theology but adapted it to contemporary concerns: the political necessity of preserving the cultural inheritance of Roman religion, even without accepting its credo. The very structure of the *Antiquitates,* which puts *Res Humanae* before *Res Divinae,* shows how for Varro religion, with its cults and rituals, was a creation of men. A few years after the publication of the *Antiquitates Rerum Divinarum,* Cicero in the *De Divinatione* would deal with problems that were in part similar.

History in Varro

History, as conceived in the *Antiquitates* and later in the *De Vita Populi Romani,* is above all the history of customs, institutions, even sets of mind. It is the collective history of the Roman people felt as a unitary organism in evolution. Only in the framework of these collective events do the *magni viri,* the individual heroes of Roman history, find their place and have a claim on the memory of later generations. This view has been referred to the influence of organic conceptions of history found in Greek culture, particularly in the work of Dicaearchus. But this influence, even if it made itself felt on Varro, remains secondary to the centuries-long experience of the Roman people, who were accustomed to regard themselves as a unitary organism gathered around the senatorial elite. That the Roman state was the creation of the Roman people through the ages was, moreover, Cicero's view in the *De Republica,* an idea that ultimately goes back to Cato (see p. 87).

Biography in Varro

This does not prevent Varro from devoting himself to biographical research also. In addition to brief biographies of Roman poets, he wrote a collection of *Imagines,* which are also called *Hebdomades,* since the work was articulated into groups of seven *imagines* (the choice of the number seven and its multiples is owed to Pythagorean influences, which are present in all Varro's work). In this collection seven hundred visual portraits of famous men of every sort, both Roman and Greek—statesmen, poets, and philosophers, but also dancers and priests—were each accompanied by an epigram that characterized the person. It is possible that in addition learned comments in prose were found alongside the poetic text. In the *Hebdomades,* completed around 39, Varro transformed in a revolutionary way the tradition of the *imagines* and the *tituli* of one's forebears, in which tradition he meant to locate himself, typologically speaking. Thanks to his works, the *imagines* ceased to be the privilege of a limited aristocracy; Greeks and Romans who had been distinguished in any activity had equal right to them.

Varro as philologist

Varro accompanied his antiquarian studies with philological studies. In his day there was not a sharp division between these two types of research. He studied archaic drama with great care, and particularly the drama of Plautus, which he treated in two works: the *Quaestiones Plautinae,* which must have been a kind of linguistic-grammatical commentary on the Plautine comedies, and the *De Comoediis Plautinis,* in which he deals with the very numerous comedies (130) that were attributed to Plautus. Aelius Stilo had already reduced to 25 the number of comedies that were of certain Plautine origin; Varro compiled a more systematic catalogue, which divided the plays transmitted under Plautus's name into three groups: the certainly spurious (90), the uncertain (19), and the 21 that were certainly Plautine, the ones that have come down to us. In making the attributions Varro seems to have relied chiefly on his feeling for the language and style of Plautus. His archaizing taste perhaps encouraged the predilection of later critics for poetry with an archaic flavor, a taste against which Horace would struggle. Other works devoted to the early theater were the *De Scaenicis Originibus,* the *De Actionibus Scaenicis,* the *De Personis,* on masks, and the *De Descriptionibus,* a work on the characteristics of the theatrical figures.

The De Lingua Latina

A feeling for style and interest in linguistics led Varro to take an interest in the history of the Latin language too, often starting from problems and methods of Hellenistic culture. The *De Lingua Latina* was an exhaustive systematic treatise that moved from problems of the origin of language and etymology on to questions of morphology, syntax, and stylistics. We know that Varro paid much attention to the assimilation of foreign elements in the formation of the Latin language, following a principle that was of cardinal importance in antiquarian research also. Of the books remaining, books 5–10, three are devoted to etymology and three to the question of analogy and anomaly. Varro's etymologies are frequently bizarre and fantastic because they are based on the idea, Stoic in origin, that the names of things contain in themselves a hidden truth, that is, that linguistic signs are not arbitrary, imposed by convention, but rather are motivated: the word contains in itself the meaning of what it designates, on account of which the apparent form of the signifier resembles that which is its significance. At the time a lively controversy was raging between analogists, who expected a rational regularity from language (and who counted among their adherents Caesar, who wrote an essay *De Analogia* in defense of linguistic purism), and anomalists, who accepted the many irregularities of usage (see p. 231). In this controversy Varro aimed at a balanced conciliation, based on the notion that analogy and anomaly were complementary and upholding the ideal of a language cautious in accepting innovations but free from petty puristic reservations.

Literary and Philosophical Works

The Menippeans *and the decline of morals*

The composition of the *Menippean Satires,* a mixture of prose and verse on various subjects, in 150 books, must have begun quite early, around 80 B.C., and extended over a long period. But the references to contemporary events are not numerous or explicit enough to permit a secure dating. The last certain allusion is to events of 67 B.C., but the *Trikaranos* ("Three-headed Monster"), a pamphlet directed against the first triumvirate, would refer to 60, if it were certain that it was a Menippean. Only fragments of the *Menippeans* are left to us, unfortunately often very short ones, for a total of about six hundred verses and about ninety titles, from which we can form an approximate idea of the subjects treated by Varro. The *Eumenides* was aimed against the fashionable philosophers; *Marcipor* may have been the description of a voyage, following a literary fashion begun by Lucilius; *Marcopolis* contained the description of a utopian city; in the *Sexagesis* Varro told of a person who, having fallen asleep in childhood, awakened at the age of sixty to realize that everything at Rome had changed for the worse. The titles of the Menippean satires, as one can see, are often imaginative and enigmatic (cf. the many interpretations that have been given of *apocolocyntosis,* the title of the Menippean satire written by Seneca); many are proverbial expressions, some in Greek. Moreover, we frequently come across paratragic titles, which suit the whole collection's ethos of burlesque and parody: *Oedipothyestes, Ajax Stramenticius, Pseudaeneas, Catamitus.*

Models and themes of the Menippeans

The theme of the gloominess of the times and the decline of Roman morals must have been found throughout the *Menippeans;* the sharp satire on the vices of contemporaries was the other side of the nostalgic view the antiquarian Varro took of the Roman past. Thus Varro, though certainly not a Cynic—the rejection of social conventions would have repelled him—came unexpectedly close to some themes of the popular preaching by Hellenistic philosophers. He found a model in Menippus of Gadara, in Syria, a wandering philosopher, who in the third century B.C. had composed satires of a Cynic stamp that broke violently with the aristocratic traditions of Greek culture. Varro of course had other, closer models in the *Saturae* of Ennius and Lucilius. The latter is referred to through eloquent formal analogies, linguistic and lexical coincidences that often look like exact quotations, and important starting points for subjects; the *Periplous*, for example, was probably based on Lucilius's *Iter Siculum.* Then, too, the influence of comedy is very strong. Many fragments recall the structure of the Plautine prologues, and many names and colorful expressions may come from Plautus (who is the author most quoted in the *Menippeae*), a familiarity that is hardly surprising in the philologist Varro. But it must have been from Menippus more than anyone else that he derived the mixture of crude realism and fantastic imagination, as well as the bitter, biting tone of popular preaching. The subjects must have been very varied, extending from mythology to contemporary Roman realities, and the variety of subjects was matched by the variety of the registers and tonalities of the style. The language was colorful and rich in creativity, full of plays on words, archaisms, and vulgarisms; following the example of Menippus, prose parts alternated with verse, the latter written in a very rich variety of meters—hendecasyllabics, sotadeans, glyconics, scazons, and others. In Latin literature the *Menippeans* inaugurated the literary genre with which Petronius's *Satyricon* would be associated and, even closer, Seneca's *Apocolocyntosis.*

The genre of the
Menippean satire

If the title of the *Saturae Menippeae* goes back directly to Varro, the label of the literary genre belongs solely to the moderns, and it is almost completely excluded from ancient theoretical discussions (it is referred to in Gellius, Cicero, and Quintilian). Thus Quintilian, who views satire as *tota nostra*, ignored any Greek precedent for Varro (such as Menippus) and, going back beyond Horace and Lucilius, identified in Ennius's satire (composed in various meters and on various subjects) that Latin model that Varro merely enhanced with a few touches: *alterum illud etiam prius saturae genus, sed non sola carminum varietate mixtum, condidit Terentius Varro,* "Varro wrote that other, even older type of satire that includes not only a variety of meters but prose as well" (*Institutio Oratoria* 10.1.95). In fact, the recurrence of markedly Greek features certainly refers to a literary form and a genre quite different from those of the classical tradition of Roman satire. Quintilian took no account of this, but our evidence (if we consider carefully the lexical distinctions of ancient literary criticism) in fact announces the relationship of imitation and emulation between Varro and Menippus: *in illis veteribus nostris quae Menippum imitati, non interpretati, quadam hilaritate conspersimus,* "in those early Roman writings that I dealt with rather light-heartedly when I was imitating—not translating—Menippus" (Varro in Cicero's *Academica* 1.8); *{Menippi} libros M. Varro in saturis aemulatus est, quas alii "cynicas," ipse "menippeas" appellat,* "Varro emulated the works of Menippus in his satires, which others called cynical but he himself called Menippean" (Gellius, *Noctes Atticae* 2.18.7). Under the rubric Menippean, which comes close to the Greek notion of *spoudogeloion,* one might place a series of texts that, because of similarities in form and theme, seem to reflect a single basic model. Thus, for example, one might identify as "Menippean" a certain recurrence of fantastic, celestial themes in Lucilius, Varro, and the *Apocolocyntosis* of Seneca: the council of the gods and the descent to the Underworld.

The prosimetric structure

The most important identifying feature seems to be the technique of the prosimetron, that irregular succession of prose and verse within the narrative that is altogether foreign to the usual practice of Latin. It produces an effect of great distancing, a fact of which the authors show themselves conscious; thus Lucian (*Bis Accusatus* 33) would reproach Menippus, the genre's eponym, with inventing a monstrous hippocentaur, a paradoxical form of dialogue. What chiefly distinguishes the Menippean from other prosimetric forms occasionally (and diffusely) found in classical literature—the novel, for instance, or certain philosophical dialogues with many poetic quotations—is the substantial integration of the verse into the narrative context of the *fabula;* the metrical episode, that is to say, is not confined to commenting lyrically upon the development of the events narrated. Precisely this structural feature allowed the genre to experiment with a wide range of stylistic registers and levels and with every type of mixture and dissonance. If Seneca's satire, in very general terms, gives the impression of a more constant colloquial background, Varro's linguistic mixture appears truly various and irreducible, sometimes seeming to perform a kind of tightrope walk; the same is true for the very intricate style of his late followers Fulgentius and Martianus Capella. Varro's virtuosity translates into an inexhaustible verbal creativity of Plautine type (this is evidenced by the *hapax legomena,* especially fanciful adjectives and high-toned and bizarre compounds), in which the interpreter recognizes the code of the literary genre. An authentic genre sign, and also a residual inheritance from originally Hellenistic baggage, is the recourse to a large number of elements of Greek style, which conventionally connote the form of an apparently extemporaneous speech; hence a rich vocabulary of technical or legal terms, the purpose of which is always parody. The comic pursuit of the Menippean, in fact, continually produces a meta-literary effect: the satiric text, with critical consciousness and detached malice, casts an ironic eye upon the models of grand poetry and the rules by which they are constructed. From Varro to Seneca, the *spoudogeloion genos* turns "serious" literature into a repertory for itself, a repertory that is constant and of unfailing impact, announced by numerous quotations and explicit allusions. The phrases *ut ait Ennius, ut ait Horatius,* and *Homerus dicit* are some of the many signals of ironic authentication; they are constantly suspect references—used for parody, pushed to the point of being absurd and nonsensical—that involve author, characters, and readers. Balancing on the edge between the form of the satiric book and the tradition of the moral-allegorical fable, Menippean satire often treats subjects of lively, contemporary Roman life, from literary polemic to political criticism.

The Logistorici

The *Logistorici* were entirely in prose. They developed for the most part moral themes, illustrating them with examples drawn from myth. The titles were double and indicated the chief person, by whom the exposition was carried out, and the subject of his competence: *Marius de Fortuna, Catus de Liberis Educandis, Orestes de Insania, Curio de Cultu Deorum, Atticus de Numeris* ("On Chronology"), *Pius de Pace.* The double titles have suggested a kinship in literary genre with the late dialogues of Cicero—the *Cato Maior de Senectute* and the *Laelius de Amicitia*—who might have aimed at imitating Varro. But Varro, it seems, usually introduced contemporary persons or ones but recently dead, not figures such as Cato and Laelius, hallowed by a long tradition.

The Disciplinae   In the final decade of his life, Varro, in the nine books of the *Disciplinae,* organized all the knowledge of ancient science in a form that affected the future arrangement of studies in western Europe. In fact he prefigured the distinction of the liberal arts into what would become in the medieval schools the trivium (grammar, dialectic, rhetoric) and the quadrivium (geometry, arithmetic, astronomy, music). In the last two books he treated medicine and architecture, the two most technical arts, which were excluded from the liberal arts.

Agriculture and the Expansion of Consumption

The De Re Rustica   Written in 37, the *De Re Rustica* is a work of Varro's old age. Its three books have the form of a dialogue. The first book, which deals with agriculture in general, is dedicated to Fundania, Varro's wife, who has bought an estate and asked her husband to advise her in running it. The second book, dedicated to a cattle raiser, Turranius Niger, deals with livestock. The third book, dedicated to a country neighbor, Quintinus Pinnius, deals with raising barnyard animals, bees, and fish *(de villatica pastione).* Various persons take part in the dialogue, among them Varro himself and Titus Pomponius Atticus.

Varro's notion of agricultural production emphasizes tendencies already present in Cato, comparison with whose treatise on agriculture (see pp. 88 f.) lies close to hand; it is not by accident that we owe the preservation of both works to the same manuscript. Varro, whose work presupposes the concentration of land ownership, has in mind villas and latifundia of larger dimensions, which are exploited through the intensive use of slave labor. The Varronian villa reserves a certain amount of space for luxurious, elegant forms of production, such as aviaries and fish ponds, which meet the demands of the urban market; the remainder is employed for large-scale production and raising, which are more traditional paths to wealth. In Varro's villa utility and pleasure, the *utilitas* and *voluptas* of agriculture, meet. Such a convergence expresses the self-consciousness of a landowning class that is open to the dynamic of economics and commerce and to the new needs that it creates. Understandably, the true purpose of the work is to present a satisfying picture of himself to the country gentleman, who is eager to behold a dignified, comfortable model of life well realized rather than to learn the minute techniques that are necessary to work the land productively and to look after the raising of animals; the slaves and their superintendents are there to deal with the mud of the fields and the oppressive fumes of the stalls. Thus, not intended (except superficially) for the practical instruction of the steward, but written rather to foster and gratify the ideology of the rich landowner, the *De Re Rustica* in a way estheticizes the farmer's life. And the true intention of the work is echoed significantly in the form of the discourse, which frequently allows digressions, and in the style, which appears more artificial and less casual than, for instance, the style of the *De Lingua Latina*. From time to time the pursuit of ornament shows itself, and traces of liveliness are not lacking, in the form of a witty anecdote or a clever bit of wisdom.

Literary Success

Contemporary judgments

Little remains of Varro's voluminous production, and that little is written in a dry and often obscure style. Indeed, reading him, it is easy to forget that Varro counted among his contemporaries such masters of Latin style as Cicero, Caesar, Virgil and Horace. But already during his lifetime his works were hailed as insuperable masterpieces of erudition, and he continued to enjoy enormous and unbroken popularity throughout antiquity, rivaled in this regard only by Cicero and Virgil. In the public library founded by Asinius Pollio, Varro was the only living author honored by the display of his bust. Cicero greeted the publication of the *Antiquitates* with enthusiastic praise:

> We were wandering and straying about like visitors in our own city, and your books led us, so to speak, right home, and enabled us at last to realize who and where we were. You have revealed the age of our native city, the chronology of its history, the laws of its religion and its priesthood, its civil and its military institutions, the topography of its districts and its sites, the terminology, classification and moral and rational basis of all our religious and secular institutions, and you have likewise shed a flood of light upon our poets and generally on Latin literature and the Latin language, and you have yourself composed graceful poetry of various styles in almost every metre, and have sketched an outline of philosophy in many departments. (*Acad. post.* 1.3.9, trans. H. Rackham)

Virgil based the structure of his *Georgics* to a large extent upon Varro's work on agriculture, and he used him for the *Aeneid* as an authority on the peoples of ancient Italy.

Later antiquity

Varro's stature among his contemporaries may be due, in part at least, to nationalist and political considerations—satisfaction at finally being able to rival the Greeks not only in power and law but in scholarship as well and a concern to find scientifically legitimated historical bases for social consensus at a time of dangerous internal conflict. But for the rest of antiquity as well, Varro remained the paradigm of Latin erudition. On the one hand, pagan scholars—Verrius Flaccus, the elder Pliny, Suetonius, Aulus

Gellius, Censorinus, Macrobius, and Servius, but even a later Christian scholar such as Isidore of Seville as well—took Varro as a model for emulation and a standard of probity and knowledge and passed on to later generations some of the fruits of his labors. On the other hand, church fathers such as Jerome and Augustine found in his works a fully elaborated theory of pagan religion perfectly adapted to serve as a target for Christian polemic, as well as a gold mine, often exploited but not always acknowledged, of information about the ancient world. A collection of proverbs circulated under his name as a warrant for wisdom and erudition. But Varro suffered the fate of all successful ancient scholarly writers: he soon ceased to be read directly by all but the fewest authors and instead was cited indirectly, from compilations. Already Isidore of Seville seems to have had available to him only those writings of Varro's that have reached us.

Modern period Understandably, Varro never became a school author in the Middle Ages. In modern times, he inspired several generations of antiquarians in the sixteenth and seventeenth centuries, but otherwise familiarity with his works has hardly ever passed the bounds of a minority of classical scholars. One curious exception is Petrarch, to whom Boccaccio sent a manuscript of the *De Lingua Latina* in 1355 and who called Varro "the third great Roman light" after Cicero and Virgil.

4. NIGIDIUS FIGULUS

Nigidius and Varro The authors of the Empire admiringly set beside Varro the other great scholar of Caesar's time, Publius Nigidius Figulus. The two figures can be likened in more than one regard, given the community of scientific interests. One of Nigidius's most celebrated works was his *Commentarii Grammatici,* an imposing work in at least twenty-nine books, which was characterized by the juxtaposition of grammatical and antiquarian subjects, a feature typical of Varro's writings.

But unlike Varro, Nigidius Figulus had strong interests in philosophy, cosmology, and natural history. The origin of his cognomen—*figulus* in Latin means "potter"—is one evidence of this: returning from a voyage to Greece, which must have been fundamental for his training, Nigidius declared that the world turned on its own axis at the speed of a potter's wheel.

Nigidius as philosopher Nigidius is commonly classified among the neo-Pythagorean philosophers. The subjects of his researches were already considered abstruse by contemporaries. Let it suffice to cite some transmitted titles of his works: *De Sphaera Graecanica, De Sphaera Barbarica; De Diis, De Augurio Privato, De Extis, De Somniis, De Vento, De Terris, De Animalibus,* and so on.

These were not the sort of interests his contemporaries found easy to understand, and Nigidius Figulus was soon spoken of as a magician. Politically, moreover, Nigidius, who was praetor in 58, was always opposed to the Caesarian party. In 63 he had been close to Cicero during the suppression of the Catilinarian conspiracy. Caesar exiled him, and he died in exile in 45.

Lucan at the end of the first book of the *Bellum Civile* portrays Nigidius as uttering dark prophecies at the beginning of the civil war. In later times, the figure of Nigidius lost some of its dark air, but the vastness and especially the obscurity of the works were responsible in his case, even more than in Varro's, for the fact that the number of his fragments that has come down to us does not correspond to the general admiration felt by posterity for this interesting scholar-philosopher-scientist-magician.

5 · CORNELIUS NEPOS

LIFE

Cornelius Nepos was born in Gallia Cisalpina—scholars make the locale either Ostiglia or Pavia—probably around 100 B.C. He settled quite soon at Rome but did not pursue political office, preferring to devote himself to a life of study. Titus Pomponius Atticus was probably the one to open the doors of good society to him. He had connections with Cicero: in antiquity two books of letters from Cicero to Cornelius Nepos were known, probably a correspondence in large part intellectual. Before 32 B.C. Nepos published the first edition of his chief work, the *De Viris Illustribus.* He died under Augustus's principate, perhaps after 27.

WORKS

A number of his works have been lost: a work of chronography, in three books, the *Chronica;* a collection of *Exempla* in at least five books; perhaps a geographical work, which some would identify with the *Exempla;* also a biography of Cato the Censor and one of Cicero.

A part of Cornelius Nepos's largest work, the *De Viris Illustribus,* has been preserved. Sometimes called *Vitae,* it is a collection of biographies that must have comprised at least sixteen books. We have the book on foreign military leaders *(De Excellentibus Ducibus Exterarum Gentium),* also the biographies of Cato and Atticus, drawn from the book on Latin historians; the life of Cato is the rather brief summary of a larger biography, which has been lost. The dedication to Atticus supposes a publication before 32 B.C., the year of Atticus's death; but in the biography of Atticus the author mentions the addition of several chapters to the part already published while Atticus was alive, thus one assumes a second edition after 32.

SOURCES

Cornelius Nepos's date of birth is obtained from several indirect notices. Jerome, in his *Chronicle,* places the height of Nepos's literary fame in 40 B.C., probably in his middle rather than late years. Nepos, moreover, must have enjoyed an established reputation as a historian when Catullus dedicated a collection of poems to him, certainly before 54, the year of Catullus's death, but perhaps some years earlier. For the date of death, one generally relies on Pliny the Elder, who in two places (*Naturalis Historia* 9.137, 10.60) declares that Cornelius Nepos died "under the principate of Augustus," certainly then after 31, the year of the battle of Actium, and perhaps even after 27, because only after the constitutional changes of that year could the regime truly be called a "principate."

Traditional Values and Cultural Relativism in the Biographies of Cornelius Nepos

The antiquarian interests in Atticus's circle must have encouraged Nepos in his vast historical-anecdotal compilations.

The Chronica

Nepos must have first come to people's notice with the *Chronica,* a systematic exposition of universal chronography, with particular attention to synchronism among events of Greece, Rome, and the Orient. Similar Greek compilations, which had already existed for some while, were not extensively interested in Roman history: the innovation is probably due to Cornelius Nepos. It is not a far-fetched hypothesis that the arrangement of the *Chronica* points to the necessity of comparing Roman civilization with others, which would become explicit in the *Vitae.* Few fragments survive from the collection of *Exempla,* which may have been conceived as a repertory for orators, in which presumably remarkable notices and curiosities of every sort were found in abundance. But quite soon Nepos's principal interests must have turned towards biography.

Biography as a means for comparing civilizations

What remains to us of the *De Viris Illustribus* is but a small part of what must have been Cornelius Nepos's largest and most ambitious project: a great collection of biographies constructed for the purpose of making this literary genre the vehicle of a systematic comparison between Greek civilization and Roman. In this way he was developing the ideas of biography that already characterized Varro's *Imagines* (see p. 214). Cornelius Nepos grouped his persons in professional categories (kings, commanders, philosophers, historians, orators, grammarians, etc.); each category was supposed to fill two books, one treating foreign representatives of the category (Greeks especially) and one treating Roman representatives. Even though the grouping of persons into categories was well attested in Hellenistic biography, the systematic comparison between Romans and foreigners seems to be the significant original contribution of Cornelius Nepos.

It has been thought that the fundamental purpose of such a comparison was to suggest the superiority of the Romans in every field. But what remains of Cornelius Nepos's work does not appear to be shadowed by nationalistic prejudices. Among all Latin writers he is the one, for instance, who portrays Hannibal, the most terrible enemy Rome had ever faced, in the best light.

Cultural relativism

Nepos's project is symptomatic of an era in which the Romans began to ask what was distinctive about their civilization and to open themselves to appreciating the values of different traditions. One can even speak of a moderate form of cultural relativism in connection with the brief preface Cornelius Nepos writes to the book about foreign generals. The notions "morally honorable" and "morally disgraceful," he makes clear, are not the same for Greeks and Romans; the distinction depends on the *maiorum instituta,* "the national traditions," of each people. To the biography of Epaminondas is prefixed a warning not to judge the customs of other peoples by one's own: music and dance, unbecoming for a Roman princeps, or eminent citizen, are not equally so for a person of rank in a Greek city, where in fact they win favor and reputation. It is thus a rather banal relativism that certainly does not aim at eroding the ideological bases of Roman society: the difference between the *maiorum instituta* of individual peoples serves to justify divergent usages, not to argue for an unconditional adherence to foreign practices. Moreover, the relativism of the preface is hardly operative at all in the biographies, where the persons are often judged by absolute values, which are the same for Greece and Rome: *pietas, abstinentia, industria, diligentia, prudentia,* and so on.

Nepos as writer

Cornelius Nepos, taken all together, is a mediocre writer. Although the innovation in his biographical collection is recognized more fully today, the quality of the execution cannot be considered equal to the conception (which might be owed more to Atticus or some other member of his circle than to Nepos). His greatest merit certainly is his influence on Plutarch's *Parallel Lives*. For breadth of intellectual horizons Nepos cannot be compared to Varro or Cicero. It may also be the case that he addressed an audience less prepared culturally. This is implied by the relative simplicity of the style, sometimes almost careless, sometimes allowing itself preciosities, which are, however, more annoying than effective, and especially by the extremely summary character of some biographies, which seems to presuppose readers with limited knowledge. Moreover, he himself was fully conscious that his work was addressed, not to historians, but to people of an ordinary cultural level (see, e.g., *De Viris Illustribus* 16.1.1), an audience that needed a somewhat simplified presentation and was more motivated by an eagerness for anecdotes than concerned for accuracy of information or considered critical judgments.

The biography of Atticus

The most original and probably most successful among Cornelius Nepos's biographies is without doubt the one he devoted to his friend and patron Atticus. The subject was stimulating and different, since it involved, not a figure from bygone eras, but a man of the present day, a man, moreover, whose life choices, especially his abstention from politics, could arouse puzzlement. In telling the episodes of Atticus's life Nepos wanted to show to his readers the example of a conciliation, as happy as it was difficult, between old-fashioned virtues and modern values, between the demands of loyalty to the Roman tradition and the pursuit of personal tranquillity. In creating the character of Atticus, Cornelius Nepos indicates to the generations that were to live under the principate a new ethical model, one that strives to lend dignity to life choices no longer based on participation in political activity.

BIBLIOGRAPHY

Varro

There is an edition containing Varro's *De Lingua Latina,* the *De Re Rustica,* and grammatical fragments by A. Traglia (Turin 1974); the best separate edition of the *De Lingua Latina* is that of G. Goetz and F. Schoell (Leipzig 1910), of the *De Re Rustica* those of

H. Keil (3 vols., Leipzig 1891–1902, with Cato) and G. Goetz (Leipzig 1910). There are Loeb editions by R. C. Kent (Cambridge, Mass. 1938) and H. B. Ash and W. D. Hooper (Cambridge, Mass. 1934, with Cato). Budé editions with French translation and commentary are in progress: see *Res Rusticae,* book 1, ed. J. Heurgon (Paris 1978), and book 2, ed. C. Guiraud (Paris 1985), and *De Lingua Latina,* book 6, ed. P. Flobert (Paris 1989; see also the Italian edition with commentary by E. Riganti, Bologna 1978). A useful selection from the *Res Rusticae* with English commentary is B. Tilly, *Varro the Farmer* (London 1973). The fragments of Menippean satire have traditionally been referred to from the collection in the edition of Petronius by F. Buecheler and W. Heraeus (Berlin 1922, pp. 177–250), but there is a modern Teubner by R. Astbury (Leipzig 1985, with bibliography), and a massive but diffuse French commentary by J.-P. Cèbe is in progress (Rome 1972–). There is no collected edition of the fragments of the prose works, and reference has to be made to a large number of monographs and smaller collections (lists in *CHCL* II, 844, and *Dizionario degli scrittori greci e latini* s.v. "Varrone").

There is no convenient English summary of Varro's vast output, but there is much of interest in Elizabeth Rawson's *Intellectual Life in the Late Roman Republic* (London 1985) despite the deliberate exclusion of a systematic treatment. See also A. D. Leeman, *Orationis Ratio: The Stylistic Theories and Practice of the Roman Orators, Historians, and Philosophers* (Amsterdam 1963) 178, 214–15, and in other languages, G. Boissier, *Études sur la vie et les ouvrages de M. Terentius Varron* (Paris 1861), F. Della Corte, *Varrone, il terzo gran lume romano* (Florence 1970), H. Dahlmann, "Varroniana," *ANRW* 1.3 (Berlin 1973) 3–25 (German; see also the survey of the Menippean satires by L. Alfonsi in the same volume, 26–60), and B. Cardauns, *Stand und Aufgabe der Varroforschung (mit einer Bibliographie der Jahre 1935–1980)* (Mainz 1983). Volume 9 *(Varron)* of the Entretiens sur l'antiquité classique of the Fondation Hardt is devoted to Varro (Geneva 1962) but contains only one piece in English (C. O. Brink, "Horace and Varro"). In Italian note esp. the publications of the Centro di Studi Varroniani at Rieti, including the *Atti del Congresso internazionale di studi varroniani* (Rieti 1976) and G. Galimberto Biffino, *Rassegna di studi varroniani dal 1974 al 1980* (Rieti 1981). Note also two Festschriften, those for J. Collart (Paris 1978) and B. Riposati (Milan 1979).

Nepos

The standard edition of Nepos is now that of P. K. Marshall (Leipzig 1977); there are also texts in the Oxford (ed. E. O. Winstedt, Oxford 1904), Budé (ed. A.-M. Guillemin, Paris 1961), and Loeb (J. C. Rolfe, Cambridge, Mass. 1929) series, the last containing an English translation. There is no comprehensive commentary in English to match that in German by K. Nipperdey and K. Witte (Berlin 1913), but there is a selection in translation with brief commentary by N. Horsfall (Oxford 1989).

The introduction to the last volume gives an account of Nepos's life and work. See also J. Geiger, *Cornelius Nepos and Ancient Political Biography* (Stuttgart 1985), E. Jenkinson, "Nepos: An Introduction to Latin Biography," in *Latin Biography,* ed. T. A. Dorey (London 1967) 1–15, and "Cornelius Nepos and Biography at Rome," *ANRW* 1.3 (Berlin 1973) 703–19, A. D. Momigliano, *The Development of Greek Biography* (Cambridge, Mass. 1971) 97–99, and esp. F. Millar, "Cornelius Nepos 'Atticus' and the Roman Revolution," *G&R* 35 (1988) 40–55, and C. Dionisotti, "Nepos and the Generals," *JRS* 68 (1968) 35–49. E. Rawson, *Intellectual Life in the Late Roman Republic* (London 1985) 227–32 is again invaluable in setting Nepos's works in their intellectual context.

Caesar

LIFE

Gaius Julius Caesar was born at Rome on 13 July 100 B.C. to a patrician family of ancient nobility. Since he was related nonetheless to Marius and Cinna, he was persecuted in his youth by the Sullans. After Sulla's death, in 78 B.C., he returned to Rome from Asia, where he had served in the army, and began his forensic and political career. He was quaestor in 68, aedile in 65, pontifex maximus in 63, praetor in 62, and propraetor in Further Spain in 61. In 60 he entered into a secret agreement with Pompey and Crassus, called the first triumvirate, which divided power among the three. He held the consulship for the first time in 59, acting energetically and disregarding his colleague Bibulus. Beginning in the next year Caesar held the proconsulship of Illyria and Romanized Gaul (Cisalpine and Narbonensis). Using as a pretext alleged provocations and border violations committed in the Gallic area under his jurisdiction by tribes engaged in vast migrations, he undertook the conquest of the entire Celtic world, presenting it as a defensive, preventive operation. The conquest of the Gauls took seven years, and with it Caesar acquired the basis for a vast personal power. Blocked through legal quibbles by his opponents, who tried to prevent him from passing directly from the proconsulship in Gaul to his second consulship, Caesar invaded Italy at the head of two legions, thus starting the civil war (10 January 49). In August of 48 he defeated the senatorial army led by Pompey at Pharsalus in Thessaly; afterwards he suppressed other hotbeds of Pompeian resistance in Africa (battle of Thapsus, 46 B.C.) and in Spain (battle of Munda, 45 B.C.). In the meantime, having become absolute master of Rome, he had held, at times simultaneously, the dictatorship and consulship from 49 on. On 15 March 44 he was assassinated by a group of aristocrats who were firm in their loyalty to the Republic and were troubled by the autocratic, regal tendencies Caesar had been showing.

WORKS

Preserved works: *Commentarii de Bello Gallico,* in seven books, plus an eighth book written probably by Caesar's lieutenant, Aulus Hirtius, to complete the account of the Gallic campaigns; *Commentarii de Bello Civili,* in three books; a verse epigram on Terence (fragment 9 in Morel's *Fragmenta Poetarum Latinorum*).

Lost works: various speeches (in one of them, the funeral elogium over his aunt Julia, he asserted the descent of the *gens Iulia* from Iulus-Ascanius and so from Aeneas and Venus); a treatise on problems of language and style, *De Analogia,* finished in the summer of 54; various youthful verse compositions (a poem, *Laudes Herculis,* and a tragedy, *Oedipus,* as well as a collection of memorable sayings, the *Dicta Collectanea*) and a poem *(Iter)* on the expedition to Spain in 45; and a pamphlet in two books against the memory of Cato of Utica *(Anticato),* written as a reply to the elogium of Cato written by Cicero (*Laus Catonis* [see p. 176]).

Spurious works: besides the eighth book of the *De Bello Gallico,* we have three works of the so-called *Corpus Caesarianum,* namely, the *Belllum Alexandrinum,* the *Bellum Africum,* and the *Bellum Hispaniense,* accounts of the last events of the civil war, actually composed by unknown officers of Caesar's.

SOURCES

The authentic and spurious works of Caesar; the *Life of Caesar* by Suetonius and the one by Plutarch; speeches and letters of Cicero; Appian, *Bella Civilia;* Cassius Dio, books 36–44.

I. THE *COMMENTARIUS* AS A HISTORIOGRAPHIC GENRE

Authors of commentarii

The term *commentarius,* a calque on the Greek *hypomnema,* indicated a type of narration intermediate between the collection of raw materials (in Caesar's case, the personal notes, the reports to the Senate on the course of the Gallic campaigns, etc.) and their elaboration in the artistic form typical of true historiography, that is to say, enriched with stylistic and rhetorical embellishments. We have already referred to the composition of *commentarii* by important politicians, such as Scaurus and Sulla (see p. 123); and Cicero also wrote various *commentarii,* both in Latin and in Greek, on his own consulship, with the aim of offering to some historian—whom in fact he never succeeded in finding—the material, to be shaped and organized into a proper historical narrative in the sense we have seen.

Character of Caesar's Commentarii

Caesar without doubt aimed at placing himself in this tradition. Both Cicero (*Brutus* 262) and Hirtius in the preface to the eighth book of the *De Bello Gallico* speak of Caesar's *Commentarii* as a work written to offer to other historians the material out of which to construct their own narrative. As in the case of Cicero, but for different reasons, these historians were never found. Cicero and Hirtius himself emphasize that no one would have dared to attempt to rewrite what Caesar had already said with incomparable simplicity. In fact Caesar's attitude may have concealed a certain trickery: beneath the humble clothing, the *commentarius* as he conceived and practiced it probably came close to *historia.* This is evidenced by his dramatization of certain scenes and by his recourse to direct speeches in certain passages. But Caesar is admirably restrained in giving dramatic effect to his narrative, avoiding gross, vulgar effects and especially clumsy rhetorical frills. The use of the third person also tends in this direction, detaching the protagonist from the emotionality of the *ego* and setting him in the drama of history as an independent character.

2. THE GALLIC CAMPAIGNS IN CAESAR'S NARRATION

The work commonly referred to as *De Bello Gallico* was probably originally *C. Iulii Caesaris Commentarii Rerum Gestarum.* The subtitle with the reference to the Gallic campaign was probably added after the death of the author, in order to distinguish these *commentarii* from the ones on the civil war and from the others that made their way into the *Corpus Caesarianum.*

Summary of the De Bello Gallico

The seven books of the work cover the period from 58 to 52, during which Caesar systematically subjugated Gaul. The conquest developed in phases, successes alternating with serious setbacks, which Caesar's account diminishes or justifies but does not conceal. The first book, about the events of 58, deals with the campaign against the Helvetii, whose migratory movements had given Caesar the pretext for launching the war, and against the German leader Ariovistus. The second book tells of the revolt of the Gallic tribes, the third of the campaign against the peoples on the Atlantic coast. The fourth book recounts operations against the infiltrating German peoples, who had crossed the Rhine (Usipeti and Tencteri, pitilessly massacred), and against the rebel Gallic leaders, Indutiomarus and Ambiorix. Also in the fourth book and then in the fifth Caesar gives an account of his two expeditions against the Britons, in 55 and 54, who were accused of aiding the Gallic rebels. Yet the conquest of Gaul is not utterly secure: in particular the peoples of Gallia Belgica offer vigorous resistance, which Caesar succeeds in crushing only through a campaign of extermination and devastation, narrated in books 5 and 6. With this revolt scarcely suppressed, a general insurrection breaks out in 52, headed by Vercingetorix, king of the Arverni. After a new campaign of devastation and massacre on the part of the Romans, the Gallic resistance comes to an end with the storming of Alesia, where Vercingetorix is captured (book 7).

Date of composition and style of the De Bello Gallico

There is disagreement among scholars over the dates of the composition of the *De Bello Gallico.* According to some, it was written straight off in the winter of 52/51; others prefer to think of a year-by-year composition during the winters, when military operations were suspended. This second hypothesis is favored by the existence of certain contradictions within the work, which in part have been exaggerated but which nonetheless remain difficult to explain if one supposes a composition that was carried out in a short stretch of time; this hypothesis, moreover, more than the other, seems to make sense of the perceptible stylistic evolution that has been detected in the *Commentarii.* Such an evolution seems to advance from the bare, unadorned style of the true *commentarius* towards a style that increasingly allows the typical ornaments of *historia;* thus in the second half of the work one finds more frequent use of direct discourse and recourse to a greater variety of synonyms, which denotes a certain expansion of the traditional vocabulary. In the first half of the *De Bello Gallico,* by contrast, Caesar is indifferent to using the same words, repeated more than once and at a short interval. Some have wanted to explain this on the grounds that Caesar the linguist adhered to the analogists' theories (on which see below), which would have led him towards a rigorous terminological propriety according to which each thing should be designated by a single name.

3. THE NARRATION OF THE CIVIL WAR

The De Bello Civili:
a) *Date of composition*

The *De Bello Civili* is divided into three books, the first two of which narrate the events of 49 and the third, those of 48, without quite covering entirely the events of the latter year. The times of composition and publication are even more uncertain than for the *De Bello Gallico;* indeed it has been questioned whether the account of the civil war was published by Caesar while he was alive or by someone else only after his death. The latter hypothesis, even if it seems unacceptable, may gain strength from the fact that the work appears unfinished: the narrative leaves the outcome of the war in Alexandria in suspense. Apart from this and other minor difficulties, it is generally believed that the *De Bello Civili* was written in the second half of 47 and 46 and then published in the same year, 46.

b) *Political tendencies*

Caesar's political tendencies come to light, of course, in the work. He does not let the opportunity go by to aim a blow at the old ruling class, represented by a clique of corrupt men. Caesar has recourse to a sober satire—a stylistic innovation in respect to the *De Bello Gallico*—in order to unmask the base ambitions and the petty intrigues of his adversaries, men such as, for instance, Cato or Lentulus Crus, off whose tongues roll words such as "justice," "honesty," and "liberty" but who are motivated by personal rancor or eagerness for profit. The satiric representation culminates in the picture of the Pompeian camp before the battle of Pharsalus: certain of the imminent defeat of Caesar, his opponents decide the punishments that are to be inflicted, divide up the possessions of those who are to be proscribed, and fight over the political offices, sometimes even coming to blows.

c) *Reassurance of the traditionalists*

Nonetheless, one does not find in the *De Bello Civili* the precise points of a program of political reform for the Roman state. Caesar's chief aspiration is to dissolve the image of him that the aristocratic propaganda had created before the public, presenting him as a revolutionary, a continuator of the Gracchi or, still worse, of Catiline. He wants to reveal himself as the man who has always kept within the limits of the law and defended them against the abuses of his enemies. The audience for his propaganda is the moderate, "right-thinking" stratum of Roman and Italian public opinion (the same audience that Cicero would address in the *De Officiis* [see pp. 195 f.]), which sees in the Pompeians the defenders of the republican constitution and of legality and which fears social upheavals. It is a stratum on which aristocratic propaganda had a strong influence, but one that might also be detached from the aristocratic party, the very goal at which Caesar aimed. This explains the tendency in more than one passage to reassure the landowning classes, in regard, for instance, to a burning question such as the debts that weighed upon both the plebs and the dissolute members of the aristocracy. Caesar justifies some of his emergency measures but at the same time emphasizes how there should be no expectation from him of *tabulae novae,* that is, provisions for the cancellation of debts of the sort Catiline had proposed in his day. The desire to reassure creditors is also made clear by Caesar's dwelling upon the suppression of the movement that sought far more drastic measures in favor of the debtors, a movement stirred up by Caelius Rufus, the person Cicero had defended in the *Pro Caelio* (see pp. 183 f.).

d) Pax *and* clementia

By emphasizing that he always kept within the limits of the law of the Republic, Caesar also insists on his own constant desire for peace; the unleashing of the civil war is owed only to the Pompeians' repeated rejection of serious negotiations. Another basic theme of the work is Caesar's clemency towards the defeated, which is contrasted with the cruelty of his opponents. After Marius and Sulla many expected new proscriptions, new bloodbaths. Caesar is careful to reassure the people, and at the same time to disarm the hatred of his enemies. Finally, one cannot forget the true monument that Caesar erects in these *commentarii,* as well as in the *commentarii* on the Gallic War, to the loyalty and bravery of his own soldiers, whose attachment he repays with sincere affection. The praise Caesar gives to the members of his army probably cannot be separated from the process of social advancement, including admission into the Senate, of the *homines novi* of military origin, but Caesar is also thinking of posterity when in his work he preserves the names of centurions or plain soldiers who distinguished themselves in acts of particular heroism.

e) *Glorification of the soldiers*

4. CAESAR'S TRUTHFULNESS AND THE PROBLEM OF HISTORICAL DISTORTION

Objectivity and tendentiousness in the Commentarii

The unadorned style of Caesar's *Commentarii,* the rejection of rhetorical embellishments characteristic of true *historia,* the notable reduction of evaluative language—all contribute greatly to the apparently objective, impassive tone of Caesar's narration. Beneath this impassivity, however, modern criticism has discovered, so it believes, tendentious interpretations and distortions of the events for the purpose of political propaganda. Some undoubtedly have pushed this too far, but the connection of the *commentarii* with the political struggle is equally beyond doubt. The connection is more immediate in the *De Bello Civili,* where the urgency of the burning themes of the day is alive and evident, than in the *De Bello Gallico.* The interpretation is unquestionably a forced one that regards the latter as written and published for the purpose of supporting Caesar's candidacy for his second consulship.

In any event, the presence of distortions in both works is undeniable. It is never a matter of large-scale falsifications, but of omissions of greater or lesser importance, a certain way of presenting the relations between events.

Caesar relies on very clever devices, almost perfectly concealed. He attenuates, insinuates, lightly anticipates or postpones, and arranges the topics in such a way as to justify his own failures.

The Gallic War as a defensive war

In a manner consistent with these tendencies of Caesar's narrative, the *De Bello Gallico* on the whole cannot be read as a glorification of the conquest. As we have seen, Caesar emphasizes instead the defensive needs that compelled him to undertake the war. It was, after all, the established custom of Roman imperialism to present wars of conquest as necessary for protecting the Roman state and its allies from dangers that arose abroad. In addition to the Romans, Caesar addresses the Gallic aristocracy, to assure them of his protection against the lawless men who behind their flaunted ideals of independence conceal their aspiration to tyranny. In the *De Bello Gallico* Caesar stresses how his actions have always remained within the laws; he presents himself as a political moderate from whom revolutionary outbursts certainly should not be expected.

Charisma and luck

In both works he makes evident his abilities in military and political action, but he does not create a halo of charisma about himself. In this he may have behaved differently from the way he behaved in *unwritten* forms of propaganda, which were addressed to the less educated, less shrewd populace. Luck is an element that plays a large part in his narrative, but it is not presented as a protecting divinity. It is, rather, a concept that serves to explain sudden changes in a situation, an imponderable factor that sometimes aids Caesar's enemies too; it is, above all, what lies beyond man's abilities of foresight and rational control. Caesar attempts to explain events through human and natural causes, to grasp clearly their inner logic, and he practically never has recourse to divine intervention.

5. THE CONTINUATORS OF CAESAR

Hirtius, Bellum Alexandrinum, Bellum Africum, Bellum Hispaniense

Caesar's lieutenant Aulus Hirtius wrote book 8 of the *De Bello Gallico* in order to link up its narrative with that of the *De Bello Civili* by recounting the events of 51 and 50. The *Bellum Alexandrinum* is probably also owed to Hirtius. We may presume that these works, with their sober, unadorned manner, respect the stylistic tradition of the commentary more consistently than the authentic works of Caesar. The Caesarian style, as we have seen, sometimes pushed the commentary towards *historia.* It did not reject the demand for sobriety, and yet it attained levels of lapidary elegance and of suggestiveness that remain unknown to Hirtius and the other continuators. Still, as far as we can tell, the genre of the *commentarius* was not very stable, and in those continuators of Caesar it opens itself to various influences. The *Bellum Africum* is often covered with an archaizing patina, whereas the *Bellum Hispaniense,* with its lack of balance and its discrepancies of tone, shows sporadic affectations of style against a background of popular, colloquial language, not without decidedly vulgar features. Its anonymous author is rightly identified as a *homo militaris* with a rudimentary rhetorical training that encouraged his vain literary ambitions.

6. LINGUISTIC THEORIES

Caesar as orator

The loss of Caesar's speeches is one of the gravest losses suffered by Latin literature, to judge by the enthusiastic opinions of those ancients who could read him, such as Quintilian, Tacitus, and others. In the passage of the *Brutus* already mentioned Cicero appears, to some extent, to contrast Caesar's style in the *Commentarii* with that in his speeches, in which rhetorical ornaments would not have been a defect. The judgment is not completely reliable, because Cicero's purpose (see p. 188), given that he could not deny the force of Caesar's oratory, was probably to trace this style back to non-Atticist models, emphasizing the rhetorical ornaments and minimizing elegance as a source of the speeches' success with the audience. Caesar's oratorical style probably avoided "swellings" *(tumores)* and excessively gaudy colors, but the adroit use of the ornaments saved him from the excesses of a spare, jejune style such as was dear to the extreme Atticists.

Caesar the analogist

It is Cicero again in any event who recognizes that Caesar acted as a purifier of the Latin language, "correcting a faulty, corrupt usage by a pure and irreproachable one." Caesar expounded his linguistic theories in the three books *De Analogia* (on the notion see pp. 124 f.), written in 54 and dedicated to Cicero, who certainly did not share those theories. As far as one can tell, the treatise expressed the desire for a rational and ascetic handling of Latin. The few fragments preserved show how Caesar laid down as the basis for eloquence the sensible choice of words, for which the fundamental criterion is analogy, rational and systematic selection, as opposed to anomaly, the accepting of that which gradually becomes customary in the *sermo cotidianus.* The choice should be limited to the *verba usitata,* the words already in use; Caesar advised the writer to avoid odd and unusual words as the steersman avoids a reef. The congruence is evident between these prescriptions and the spare, precise style of the *Commentarii.* Caesar's analogism is concern for simplicity, order, and especially clarity, to which he sometimes is willing to sacrifice even gracefulness. We have seen that Cicero recognized the greatness of the *Commentarii.* But Caesar's linguistic theories could not have won his agreement, and the fact that Caesar dedicated his essay to him is no more an indication of shared literary views than is Cicero's dedication of works such as the *Brutus* or the *Orator* to the Atticist Brutus (see p. 188).

7. LITERARY SUCCESS

Antiquity

For the most part, Caesar's *Nachleben* has been, not literary, but political. "Kaiser" and "czar" designate forms of power, not styles of writing, and if Napoleon studied Caesar's *Commentaries* in his last years on the island of Saint Helena, it was surely not only with a view to their grammar and diction. But this was not always the case: Caesar's contemporaries took him seriously not only as a general and statesman but also as a writer. Although Asinius Pollio cast doubt upon his veracity, both proponents such as A.

Hirtius (*De Bello Gallico* 8 *praef.*) and opponents such as Cicero (*Brutus* 262) could praise the style of his memoirs for its perfect lucidity and freedom from rhetorical artifice. Later, Quintilian refers to his speeches but not to the *Commentaries,* perhaps for the very same reason. Through most of the rest of antiquity, however, Caesar's works did not have an easy time. The peculiar character of the *Corpus Caesarianum*—their author's unexpected death had left his writings unfinished, incomplete, and unrevised, and they were subsequently supplemented by Hirtius and other loyal followers— posed considerable philological problems, with which ancient scholarship wrestled, not always with success. His lucid style made him uninteresting for the grammarians, who almost never cite him. The contents of his work had the same effect upon the church fathers. It was only the historians, for example, Livy, Nicolaus of Damascus, Plutarch, Tacitus, Appian, Dio Cassius, and Ammianus Marcellinus, who appreciated his qualities and sometimes exploited his materials (though they often diverged from his own account of events). But Livy also came to overshadow and supplant him as a historical source for the events of this period; it is not even certain that Lucan, who felt such keenly fascinated horror for Caesar, ever read him. Curiously, Orosius attributes the *Bellum Gallicum* to Suetonius, and the same attribution is found in some manuscripts.

Middle Ages

In the Middle Ages, Caesar was not a school author and was not widely known. Until the twelfth century he is relatively rare in medieval catalogues except in France. And those few medieval authors who had read him—mostly French and German—seem to know only his memoir of the Gallic War (which also became known in the East after Maximus Planudes translated it into Greek around 1300).

Renaissance

The Renaissance rediscovered Caesar not only as a military strategist and a canny, ambitious politician but also as a writer. Petrarch wrote a biography of him, and in the fifteenth century Andrea Brenzio forged a speech of Caesar's to his soldiers. In the following century, in England Arthur Golding translated him, in Germany Nicodemus Frischlin based a school drama, *Helvetiogermani,* upon book 1 of the *Bellum Gallicum,* and in France Montaigne, praising him in terms similar to Cicero's, adopted him as a

Modern period

model for prose style, thereby paving the way for the new rational style of French classicism, which was to culminate in such writers as Descartes. Since then, and especially starting in the nineteenth century, the *De Bello Gallico* has become one of the standard school texts for beginning students of Latin prose, not only because of its deceptively easy style, perhaps, but also because it treats matters of national interest to French, German, and English readers and provides models of dedication to the state and obedience to authority. We cannot know how many potential readers Caesar has thereby lost.

BIBLIOGRAPHY

The standard modern text of Caesar is that of A. Klotz (Leipzig 1927–50), supplemented for the *Bellum Gallicum* by the texts of O. Seel (Leipzig 1970) and W. Hering

(Leipzig 1987). There is an Oxford text by R. du Pontet (2 vols., Oxford 1900–1901), and there are three Loeb volumes (London) with translation: *Gallic War,* by H. J. Edwards (1917), *Civil War,* A. G. Peskett (1914), and other works, by A. G. Way (1955). The best commentary on the *De Bello Gallico* is in German, by F. Kramer and W. Dittenberger, rev. H. Meusel and H. Oppermann (3 vols., Zurich 1962–67); there are older historical commentaries by St. George Stock (Oxford 1898) and T. Rice Holmes (Oxford 1914). On the *Civil War* see again the German commentary by F. Kramer and F. Hofmann, rev. H. Meusel and H. Oppermann; there are brief English commentaries on books 1 and 2 by J. Carter (Warminster 1990) and on book 3, chaps. 102–11, together with the *Bellum Alexandrinum,* in G. B. Townend, *Caesar's War in Alexandria* (Bristol 1988). The *Bellum Alexandrinum* and *Bellum Africanum* are edited with German commentaries by R. Schneider (Berlin 1888, 1905), and the *Bellum Hispaniense* by A. Klotz (Leipzig 1927). See also the Italian commentaries on the *Bellum Alexandrinum* by R. Giomini (Rome 1956) and on the *Bellum Hispaniense* by G. Pascucci (Florence 1965, very full).

Among English studies note F. E. Adcock, *Caesar as Man of Letters* (Cambridge 1956), J. M. Collins, "Caesar as Political Propagandist," *ANRW* 1.1 (Berlin 1972) 922–66, L. Raditsa, "Julius Caesar and His Writings," ibid. 1.3 (Berlin 1973) 417–456 (the volume contains other studies), T. A. Dorey, "Caesar: the *Gallic War,*" in *Latin Historians* (London 1966) 65–84, C. E. Stevens, "The *Bellum Gallicum* as a Work of Propaganda," *Latomus* 11 (1952) 3–18, 165–79, and M. F. Williams, "Caesar's Bibracte Narrative and the Aims of Ceasarian Style," *ICS* 10 (1985) 215–26. Among foreign works, note esp. D. Rasmussen, *Caesars Commentarii: Stil und Stilwandel am Beispiel der direkten Rede* (Göttingen 1963), M. Rambaud, *L'Art de la déformation historique dans les Commentaires de César* (ed. 2 Paris 1966), F. Bömer, "Der Commentarius: Zur Vorgeschichte und literarischen Form der Schriften Caesars," *Hermes* 81 (1953) 210–50, and A. La Penna, "Tendenze ed arte del 'Bellum Civile' di Cesare," *Maia* 5 (1952) 191–233. There are many political biographies; see, e.g., Z. Yavetz, *Julius Caesar and His Public Image* (London 1983), and in German, C. Meier, *Caesar* (ed. 2 Berlin 1982). S. Weinstock, *Divus Iulius* (Oxford 1971), is an indispensable guide to Caesarian propaganda.

Sallust

LIFE

Gaius Sallustius Crispus was born at Amiternum, in the Sabine territory (today near L'Aquila), on 1 October 86 B.C., of a wealthy family, which, however, had never given magistrates to the state; thus Sallust is a *homo novus,* as is his fellow Sabine Cato the Censor, who was an important ideological and literary model for him. He probably completed his studies at Rome, where his interests soon began to gravitate towards politics. An unreliable notice has him as quaestor in 55 or 54. At first he was allied with the *populares;* as tribune of the plebs in 52 he led a fierce campaign against Clodius's killer, Milo, and against Cicero, who supported him. Shortly afterwards he must have suffered the revenge of the aristocrats, for in 50 he was expelled from the Senate for moral turpitude. After the outbreak of the civil war he fought on Caesar's side, and he was readmitted to the Senate after his victory. His career started again rapidly, so much so that in 46 he had already reached the praetorship. Once the Pompeians were defeated in Spain, Caesar named Sallust governor of the province of Africa Nova, made up of the larger part of the kingdom of Numidia, which had been taken from its king, Juba, who had supported the Pompeians. Sallust showed himself a bad administrator and rapacious, and upon returning from the province he was accused of embezzlement. To avoid his condemnation and a second expulsion from the Senate, Caesar probably advised him to withdraw once and for all from public life. From this moment on Sallust devoted himself to historical writing. Death came to him in 35 or 34, in his luxurious residence, with its large park, located between the Quirinal and the Pincian (the so-called Horti Sallustiani), leaving his major work, the *Histories,* unfinished.

WORKS

Two historical monographs: the *Bellum Catilinae* (or *De Catilinae Coniuratione,* as Sallust himself calls it in section 43) and the *Bellum Iugurthae,* written and published probably between 43 and 40. A work on a larger scale, the *Histories,* begun around 39 and left incomplete in the middle of book 5, covered the period between 78 and 67, from the death of Sulla to the end of Pompey's war against the pirates; many fragments remain, among them several large ones—a good part of the proem, four complete speeches, and two letters.

Spurious works: two *Epistulae ad Caesarem Senem de Republica* and the *Invectiva in Ciceronem.*

The poem *Empedoclea,* mentioned by Cicero, in which Empedoclean and Pythagorean doctrines were united, is probably not by Sallustius, but by an author of the same name, in all likelihood Cicero's friend Gnaeus Sallustius.

SOURCES

Jerome's *Chronicle* is the basis for the date of birth. For the other events of his life and political career we are dependent on references scattered through various historiographic and learned sources, especially Cassius Dio 40.63 and 43.9. For his retirement from political life the testimony of Sallust himself in the *Bellum Catilinae* 3.3–4.2 is important.

I. THE HISTORICAL MONOGRAPH AS A LITERARY GENRE

Sallust's proems: historiography and political science

To both his monographs Sallust prefixes proems of some length, in which he strives to justify the fact of having retired from political life and devoted himself to writing historical works. Even though filled with the commonplaces of popular philosophy, the proems meet his profound need to give an account of his own intellectual activity before a public such as that of Rome, which abided by the tradition according to which making history was a more important task than writing it. Cicero had several times had to give similar justifications, also in proems, for his philosophical works. But in Cicero the revaluation of intellectual activity is carried out with a pride greater than Sallust's, who attributes to historiography a far lesser value than he attributes to politics and who in any event does not grant it an independent significance. For Sallust historiography remains closely tied to political practice, and its greatest function is identified as a contribution to the training of the politician.

The monograph as investigation into the crisis

The few biographical references in Sallust's proems aim at explaining his abandonment of political life by means of the crisis that has irremediably corrupted institutions and society. Sallust denounces greed for wealth and power as evils that are poisoning Roman political life; the contrast is obvious here between the written word and what we know of his life. But what is most important is that Sallust's historical writing itself tends to take on the form of an investigation into the crisis. This accounts for the monographic form of his first two historical works, which was almost a complete novelty in Roman historiography; the only precedent of any importance is that of Coelius Antipater (see p. 121). The monograph form was excellently suited to delimiting and focusing upon a single historical problem against the background of an organic view of Rome's history. Thus the *Bellum Catilinae* illuminates the most acute point of the crisis, depicting a danger more threatening than any yet experienced by the Roman state. The *Bellum Iugurthae* directly confronts, through a paradigmatic episode, the problem of the incapacity of a corrupt nobility to defend the state and emphasizes the first successful resistance on the part of the *populares.* At the same time, the monograph form was affected by the demand for short works in a refined style that had grown as a result of the neoteric experiment. The choice of the monograph led Sallust to develop a new historiographic style (see below).

2. CATILINE'S CONSPIRACY AND THE FEAR OF THE LOWER CLASSES

Catiline's plan

Catiline, whose conspiracy Cicero had suppressed as consul in 63 (see p. 181), had perceived the possibility of creating a kind of social bloc opposed to the senatorial government and made up of the urban proletariat, the poorer classes from certain regions of Italy, the debt-laden members of the aristocracy, and perhaps more or less large masses of slaves.

Summary of the
Bellum Catilinae

After the proem (chaps. 1–4), Sallust begins with the portrait of Catiline. The personality of this corrupt aristocrat is made the focus of attention against the general background of the decline of Roman morals, which is due to the very growth of the Empire's power and to the spread of luxury and wealth. Taking advantage of this moral degeneration, Catiline surrounds himself with persons who, in order to escape poverty or judgment, for the most varied reasons, are hoping for a change of government (5–18). The nobility, who thanks to several leaks begin to get wind of the plot, affected by the fears this arouses, decide to entrust the consulship to Antonius and a *homo novus,* Cicero. Catiline continues his preparations, extending them to all Italy. With the help of an aide, Manlius, he gathers at Fiesole an army composed to a large extent of desperate men and people sunk in misery (18–25). Defeated in the consular elections, Catiline makes several attempts on Cicero's life, which come to naught. Cicero obtains from the Senate full power to crush the rebellion, and on 8 November 63 he openly accuses Catiline in the Senate (the first *Catilinarian*). Catiline flees Rome and goes to join Manlius and his army; the Senate declares both of them public enemies (26–36). At this point Sallust introduces a digression on Catiline's motives (37–39). The narrative begins again with the various events as a result of which Cicero comes to have in his hands tangible proofs of the plot. Cicero has those accomplices of Catiline who have remained in the city imprisoned, and the Senate meets to deliberate on their fate. After Decimus Junius Silanus declares his support for condemning them to death, opposing speeches are delivered by Caesar and Cato the Younger: the former demands a milder punishment, while the latter vigorously supports the necessity of putting them to death (40–52). After reporting the speeches, Sallust compares Caesar and Cato, two men of opposite and complementary virtues, the only great men of the time (53–54). His accomplices executed, Catiline, at the head of his army, tries to flee to Gallia Cisalpina but is intercepted by the regular army and forced to give battle near Pistoia (January of 62). The rebel army is annihilated, and Catiline himself, after fighting valiantly, dies in battle (55–61).

The fear on the part
of the landholding
classes

The phenomenon of Catiline aroused in the ruling classes fears that may seem excessive; but without such fear towards the lower classes the importance attributed to the conspiracy cannot be explained satisfactorily. Like many of his contemporaries, moreover, Sallust saw the Catilinarian danger as one of the symptoms of the very serious disease suffered by Roman society. The historian, interrupting the narrative, devotes a large excursus to this nearly at the beginning of the *Bellum Catilinae.* This is the so-called "archaeology," which, inspired by Thucydides, sketches a rapid account of Rome's rise and fall. The turning point is located at the destruction of Carthage. Sallust has the deterioration in Roman morality begin with the cessation of *metus hostilis,* the fear of the enemy that previously had kept the community of citizens firmly united. In this degeneration the democratic Sallust gives an important role to the aristocratic dictator Cornelius Sulla, whose example inspires individuals such as Catiline. The historian emphasizes the horror of the Sullan proscriptions, in which Catiline had distinguished himself at the beginning of his career.

A second excursus, placed at the center of the work, denounces the degeneration in Roman political life during the period from Sulla's domination to the civil war between Caesar and Pompey. The condemnation involves equally the two parties to the struggle, the *populares* and the supporters of the Senate: on the one hand are demagogues who by large donations and promises to the plebs arouse their emotions in order to make them the basis for their own ambitions; on the other hand are aristocrats who cloak themselves in the dignity of the Senate but in fact fight only to consolidate and extend their own privileges. Sallust sees an organic link between the factiousness of the opposing parties and the danger of social upheaval; to root out the deep-seated tendency towards conflict it is necessary to shield the landholding classes from that danger. The condemnation of government by party is thus consistent with the expectations that Sallust had of Caesar. From Caesar the historian probably hoped for the creation of a policy not unlike the one Cicero expected from his princeps: an authoritarian regime that would be able to end the crisis of the state by reestablishing order in the Republic, strengthening concord among the wealthy classes, and restoring prestige and dignity to a Senate that had been enlarged with new men from the elite of all Italy. The principal difference between Sallust's ideal and the policy actually pursued by Caesar was probably the function assigned to the army. Sallust—in this also not very different from Cicero—would have been disgusted by Caesar's "befouling" the Senate through the admission of people from the ranks of the military.

This general scheme explains Sallust's partial distortion of Caesar in the *Bellum Catilinae,* in which he cleanses him, so to speak, of any contact or link with the Catilinarians and avoids the explicit condemnation of his policy as leader of the *populares.* Sallust separates the Catilinarian phenomenon from the sound policy of opposition to the aristocracy and identifies the corruption of the young as the prime cause of the conspiracy. In reporting the session of the Senate at which the decision is made to condemn Catiline's accomplices to death, Sallust has Caesar deliver a speech that, in order to dissuade the senators from this course, appeals heavily to considerations of legality. The speech "recreated" by Sallust is not, it seems, a substantial falsification; but the emphasis on themes of legality, even if it had some justification in the speech actually given by Caesar on that occasion, is particularly consistent with the Caesarian propaganda of the last years, as seen in the *Commentarii* (see p. 228), and with Sallust's political ideal. The preoccupation with order and legality possessed a perennial value in the eyes of the historian. By showing it as operative in Caesar's thought as early as 63, Sallust implicitly suggested the consistency and continuity of his political line.

The comparison between Caesar and Cato

Immediately after narrating the session of the Senate, Sallust paints the portraits of Cato and Caesar, who on this occasion had given opposite opinions. The idea of the comparison between two persons is not unrelated to the controversy over Cato that had developed after his suicide at Utica and in which Caesar himself had taken part with his *Anticato* (see p. 226). Sallust seems to have been the first to attempt a calm consideration, which is nearly an ideal reconciliation between the two persons. The portrait of Caesar dwells not only upon his liberality, *munificentia,* and *misericordia* but also upon the unflagging energy that supports his desire for glory. The characteristic virtues of Cato, by contrast, are the virtues rooted in tradition, *integritas, severitas, innocentia,* and so on. In differentiating the characters of the two persons Sallust wanted to establish that both were positive for the Roman state, and in the two men he identified complementary virtues. In particular, moving beyond disagreements over the role of the nobility to which Cato gave voice, Sallust recognized in the ethical-political principles espoused by Cato an essential foundation of the Republic.

The devaluation of Cicero

By pointing to Caesar and Cato as the greatest Romans of the day, Sallust certainly did not aim at denigrating Cicero, but it is a fact that in the narrative of the *Bellum Catilinae* the consul who suppressed the conspiracy appears somewhat diminished if one recalls the boasts Cicero had lavished on himself. Sallust's Cicero is not the politician who dominates events by virtue of his own intelligence but a magistrate who does his duty, not a hero but a man overcoming doubts and weakness.

The moralistic portrait of Catiline

Catiline, however, does reach a kind of greatness, albeit an evil one. Sallust paints his portrait in strong, contrasting colors, emphasizing both his indomitable energy and his ready familiarity with every form of depravity. The portrait is dominated by the drive towards moralization: while treating his character, Sallust judges it. Sallust's moralism is consistent with his political moderation. By locating the causes of the Catiline phenomenon in a moral degeneration that involves many members of the ruling class, the historian can avoid pushing his inquiry deeper, to the point of seeing in that phenomenon a logical and necessary consequence of the crisis. This would have been nearly equivalent to a justification of the subversive movement rather than a condemnation of it. But more than once, probably more than the historian intended, the deep reasons for the crisis that had been afflicting the Roman state for some time emerge from the speeches Catiline delivers in Sallust's monograph: on the one hand, a few powerful men who hold a monopoly on political careers and riches, taking advantage of the people they dominate; on the other, a powerless mass, sunk in debt and without real prospects for the future.

3. THE *BELLUM IUGURTHAE*: SALLUST AND THE OPPOSITION TO THE NOBILITY

At the beginning of his second monograph Sallust explains that the war against Jugurtha, which took place from 111 to 105, was the first occasion on which "men dared to oppose the insolence of the nobility." The *Bellum Iugurthae* is largely intended to make clear the responsibilities of the aristocratic governing class in the crisis of the Roman state.

Summary of the Bellum Iugurthae

Jugurtha, after making himself master of the kingdom of Numidia through crime, had corrupted with money the representatives of the Roman aristocracy who were sent to fight him in Africa and had thus succeeded in concluding an advantageous peace. Metellus, sent to Africa, has successes that are notable but not decisive. Marius, Metellus's lieutenant, after long demanding it, secures Metellus's permission to go to Rome in order to stand as a candidate for the consulship. Elected consul in 107, he is given the task of bringing the war in Africa to an end. Marius alters the composition of the army by enrolling the *capite censi,* that is, proletarians not subject to taxation, because they lacked property, and thus "rated by head," registered in the censor's lists not by their property but merely by their physical person. The war in Africa starts over with various events; it is concluded only when Boccus, the king of Mauretania, betrays Jugurtha, his former ally, and hands him over to the Romans.

The polemic against the nobility

In Sallust's narration the war against the Numidian usurper acquires importance against the background of the degeneration of political life. The opposition to the nobility, to which Sallust attaches himself, stood for an expansionist policy and for the defense of Roman prestige. As in the previous monograph, Sallust introduces in the center of the work an excursus that points to government by parties *(mos partium et factionum)* as the chief cause of the Republic's being torn apart and destroyed, but the condemnation is probably more toned down than in the *Bellum Catilinae.* In the second monograph Sallust's principal target is the nobility, and the excursus clearly shows, for instance, the author's concern not to condemn the policy of the Gracchi altogether, but only its excesses.

In certain respects the picture that emerges from the *Bellum Iugurthae* is distorted. In order to represent the mob as a single bloc headed by a corrupt group, Sallust neglects to speak of that wing of the aristocracy that favored an active commitment to the war, the wing more closely linked to the business world and more inclined towards the policy of expansionist imperialism.

The policy of the populares: the speeches of Memmius and Marius

The main lines of the policy of the *populares* are exemplified in the speeches that Sallust puts into the mouths of the tribune Memmius, who protests against the inconclusive policy of the Senate, and later of Marius, when he persuades the plebs to enroll en masse. For Sallust both speeches represent the best ethical-political values expressed by Roman democracy in its struggle against the nobility. Memmius urges the people to rebel against the arrogance of the *pauci,* the controlling oligarchy; he enumerates the evils of aristocratic government: the betrayal of the interests of the *res publica,* the squandering of public funds, the monopolizing of wealth and offices. In Marius's speech, however, the central theme is the establishment of a new aristocracy, the aristocracy of *virtus,* which is based not on birth but on the native abilities of each man and his determination to develop them to the full. Marius appeals to the ancient values that made Rome great, those values that in a long-ago age made possible the emergence of the very founders of the aristocratic families that were now degenerate and distinguished only by incompetence.

The judgment on Marius

Marius's speech expresses above all the aspirations of the Italian elite to a greater share in power; still, Sallust's overall judgment on Marius is marked by ambivalences and nuances whose real bearing it is difficult to evaluate. Admiration for the man who opposed the arrogance of the nobility is tempered somewhat by the awareness of the responsibility Marius was to bear for the civil wars. The enrollment of the *capite censi* throws a disturbing light on him. Sallust seems not to approve of this measure, in which, as was commonly believed, lay the origin of those personal professional armies that would destroy the Republic; rather, he appears to view the establishment of the military proletariat as soiling that aristocracy of *virtus* that Marius, conscious of being a *homo novus,* glorifies in his speech. His fundamental moderation prevents Sallust from laying aside his important reservations about the man who had not hesitated to stir up the dregs of the populace in the struggle against the nobility and to place the fate of the state in the hands of the military proletariat.

The portrait of Jugurtha

We cannot leave the *Bellum Iugurthae* without mentioning the portrait of Jugurtha. As he had already done with Catiline, Sallust makes clear his perplexed admiration for the man's indomitable energy, which is the sure sign of *virtus,* even if of a corrupt *virtus.* An important difference from the portrait of Catiline is that the personality of the barbarian king is represented as evolving, so to speak: his nature is not corrupt from the very beginning, but becomes so gradually. The seed of corruption is planted in Jugurtha by Roman nobles and *homines novi* during the siege of Numantia. Sallust does not, however, offer justifications or extenuations for his character, nor does he even try to illuminate the situation from Jugurtha's point of view. Once his character is corrupted, Jugurtha is only a petty, treacherous tyrant, ambitious and unscrupulous. He is certainly not the hero of Numidian independence that some interpreters have imagined. In Sallust's eyes the national basis of imperialism was so obvious as to seem beyond discussion.

4. THE *HISTORIES* AND THE CRISIS OF THE REPUBLIC

The Histories *and the return to annalistic writing*

Sallust's greatest historical work was left unfinished on account of his death. The *Histories* began in 78 B.C., attaching themselves to Sisenna's narrative (see p. 122), but we do not know how far down Sallust intended to bring his account; the fragments we have do not go beyond 67 B.C. After the experiments with monographs Sallust now ventured upon a project of vast size. It was almost obligatory to return to the annalistic form, which afterwards would continue its stubborn existence in Latin historiography. The work, which is lost for us but was known at least until the fifth century, had much influence upon the culture of the Augustan age.

Speeches and letters in the Histories

Some of the remaining fragments from the *Histories* are particularly large. There are four speeches (of the tribune Licinius Macer, e.g., for the restoration of the tribunician powers, in 73; of Lepidus, against the Sullan system of government; of Marcius Philippus, a violent reaction to those elements in Lepidus's speech that most obviously aimed at demagogic incitement) and a couple of letters (one by Pompey, one by Mithridates). Among these letters the one Sallust represents as written by Mithridates is particularly important. From the words of the Oriental ruler who had long fought the Romans the reasons why the peoples subjugated and dominated by Rome complained emerge clearly. The only reason the Romans have for waging war upon all the other nations, writes Mithridates, is their unquenchable thirst for wealth and power. We also have several fragments of a geographic and ethnographic character, confirming an interest already present in the larger of the monographs.

The pessimism of the late Sallust

The *Histories* paint a picture in which dark colors predominate: the corruption of morals spreads inexorably, and with a few noble exceptions, among whom Sallust particularly admires Sertorius, the champion of *libertas* who, in rebellion against Sulla and the powerful *optimates,* had established a new republic in Spain, the political stage is occupied by adventurers, demagogues, and corrupt noblemen. In general, Sallust's pessimism seems to grow deeper in his last work. After the murder of Caesar and the frustration of the hopes that reposed in the dictator, the historian no longer has a party to side with, nor does he expect any savior.

5. STYLE

Historiography according to Cicero

The era that had witnessed both the revival of oratory and artistic prose by Cicero and the concern of the neoterics to achieve the most perfect form no doubt also looked forward to the creation of a new historical style. Cicero, who was expected by some to leave his mark on historiography too, desired a harmonious, fluid style, in accordance with his tastes; more precisely, he desired a historiographic writing that would be a suitable adaptation of the oratorical model, which he had perfected, and so he conceived of history as *opus oratorium maxime,* "a supremely oratorical work." This notion is essentially Hellenistic, based on the rhetorical principles of Isocrates, and yet it also makes sense if one considers that at Rome oratory had reached its maturity at least a generation before historiography.

Sallust as founder of the Latin historiographic style:
a) inconcinnitas

It was Sallust, however, who to a large extent, though not exclusively, determined the future stylistic evolution of Latin historical writing. Nourished on Thucydides and Cato the Censor, he developed a style based on *inconcinnitas* (the opposite of the Ciceronian pursuit of symmetry, the rejection of an ample, regular, balanced discourse) and on the frequent use of antithesis, asymmetry, and variations in construction. The difficult balance between this restless dynamism and a vigorous movement to restrain it produces an effect of austere, majestic *gravitas,* an image of deliberate thought. "Thoughts cut short and brusque interruptions and a concision that is nearly obscurity" *(amputatae sententiae et verba ante exspectatum cadentia et obscura brevitas)*—thus did Seneca define Sallust's style *(Epistulae ad Lucilium* 114.17), while ridiculing the clumsy excesses of his would-be imitators. "In Sallust," continues Seneca, "these stylistic traits are used with parsimony, whereas in his imitator Arruntius they multiply and turn up incessantly: Sallust simply found these forms of expression, the other went in pursuit of them."

b) *"Innovative archaism"*

The archaizing patina of this style contributes to its austere *gravitas.* Archaism, however, consists not only in the choice of obsolete words, marked by the dignity of the antique, but also in the tendency towards strings of paratactic phrases. Thus, like the independent blocks of a building, the thoughts are juxtaposed one next to the other. The creation of periods through syntactic subordination, in which one thought depends on the other, as in a hierarchically ordered expansion, is avoided; the balanced structures and rhythmic clausulae that developed oratorical discourse is fond of are also avoided. The economy of expression—asyndeta and a more general omission of syntactic links, ellipses of auxiliary verbs—is extreme, but in reaction to the condensing of the discourse, which is the inevitable consequence, there is operative the taste for the asyndetic accumulation of almost redundant words, which has an intensifying effect. The frequent alliteration lends an archaic color, but it also strengthens the meaning of the words. In short, we have an archaizing style, but an innovative one, in that its broken movement is completely contrary to convention and its vocabulary and syntax run against that process of standardization that was establishing itself in the literary language.

Tragic sobriety

As far as narrative technique goes, the need for sobriety and austerity demanded the rejection of a whole series of dramatic effects typical of tragic historical writing (see p. 121) that aimed at arousing emotions and so drew inspiration from a lively and, so to speak, realistic style of narrative. But the limitation is responsible for a more intense dramatic quality precisely because it is more controlled and less effusive. The protagonists of the two monographs, Catiline and Jugurtha, are tragic persons, and the subjects of the two works are chosen not only for their interest as revealing symptoms of the crisis but also because of the varied and dramatic nature of the events that the historian can present. The developed style of the two monographs must have become more fully mature, artistically, in the *Histories,* to such an extent that it constituted one of the standard models for later Latin historiography.

6. THE *EPISTULAE* AND THE *INVECTIVAE*

Immediate success of Sallust

The works of Sallust won an immediate, notable success. The Roman people had the delightful sensation of now possessing a historian who could satisfy their expectations for a literary genre that was arousing lively cultural interest. The very style of writing, personal and powerful, provoked admiration. The rhetorical schools could not remain untouched by the desire to emulate his manner of writing. They must have imagined, for instance, the great author of historical-political works in interesting situations: in a contrast with Cicero and his very different political-cultural ideals or in exhortations and advice addressed to the victorious Caesar (involved in this too was the familiar academic taste for filling out the empty periods in an author's life and works with skillful, plausible inventions). The manuscripts of Sallust preserve for us an *Invectiva in Ciceronem,* which Quintilian too considered authentic (4.1.68, 9.3.89), but it is likely that the author is a rhetorician of the Augustan age, since the work aims at seeming to be written in 54 B.C. (though this also presents problems). Its obvious pendant would be the *Invectiva in Sallustium* that was attributed to Cicero; this is certainly a forgery created in the rhetorical schools, since Sallust is there accused of having shamelessly exploited for his private enrichment the new province of Numidia, of which Caesar had put him in charge. The *Epistulae ad Caesarem Senem de Republica* are to be regarded as equally spurious. They are transmitted anonymously in a manuscript that contains letters and speeches drawn from Sallust's historical works. The style is almost more Sallustian than Sallust's; this is the ineradicable weakness of every forger, who is the prisoner of the model he must faithfully counterfeit and much less free than any authentic author. Yet the writing not only is excessively archaizing but also appears ill-suited to the literary forms of the oratorical discourse and the letter. The content is predictable: violent derision of Cicero, his political line and ambitions, and advice to Caesar to choose the path of *clementia* and, by combating the corruption of the nobility, to reconcile the factions and restore peace and liberty. The question of authenticity is still very controversial among philologists and historians, but it seems reasonable to regard these works as products of the rhetorical schools from the first half of the first century A.D.; let us recall the spreading use of *suasoriae,* those deliberative declamations that are mocked by Persius (3.45, where Cato delivers a speech explaining the reasons for his decision to die by suicide) and Juvenal too (1.16, where the theme to be developed is advice to Sulla to lay down his power and retire to private life) and of which the elder Seneca preserves examples.

The Invectiva in Ciceronem

The Epistulae ad Caesarem

7. LITERARY SUCCESS

Antiquity

Sallust's popularity in antiquity is attested by the five papyrus fragments of his transmitted writings and the further papyrus fragments of his lost *Historiae* that have been discovered up to now. Among Latin authors, only Virgil and Cicero seem to have been read more often. In general, with such exceptions as Pompeius Trogus and Livy, he was highly regarded as a historian and prose stylist (Quintilian could even, absurdly, say that he rivaled Thucydides [*Institutio Oratoria* 10.1.101]), and he was considered a model both for historians (thus Velleius Paterculus and Martial) and for writers of speeches and letters; hence the speeches and letters that he put into his historical works were eventually excerpted and collected, and this collection was transmitted together with his own (spurious) letters to Caesar. His linguistic peculiarities made him a favorite topic of study for such Roman literary and grammatical scholars as Valerius Probus and Aemilius Asper, but it is above all in later historians that we can trace his influence. In the Flavian period, Vibius Maximus composed a history of the world by epitomizing Sallust and Livy, while Silius Italicus drew upon his geographical excursus about Sardinia. Tacitus, his greatest admirer in antiquity (he called Sallust *rerum Romanarum florentissimus auctor* [*Ann.* 3.29]) and a writer of far greater genius, nevertheless adopted his austere moralism and imitated his style. A little later Florus used his works, and Zenobius translated them into Greek. In the Antonine Age, Sallust's archaisms—which had already been criticized in the first century B.C., when Asinius Pollio had complained that he used too many of them and an anonymous epigram had accused him of plagiarism because of his imitation of Cato the Elder—made him a favorite author; Fronto and Aulus Gellius refer to him frequently. In the fourth century A.D. he appealed to such pagan writers as Avienius and Ammianus Marcellinus and to such Christian ones as Sulpicius Severus and Ambrose. Augustine seems to have been the last person to have studied the *Historiae* at first hand (later quotations are derived from Priscian and Isidore): a fifth-century manuscript of this work apparently survived, at least in part, until the late seventh or early eighth century, when it was cut to pieces, partly to serve as bindings, partly to copy Jerome's commentary on Isaiah.

Middle Ages and Renaissance

Sallust was a school author and one of the most popular writers of the Middle Ages and the Renaissance. He appears frequently in catalogues of libraries starting in the eleventh century, and more than 500 manuscripts have survived, including 2 from the ninth century, 4 from the tenth century, and 330 from the fifteenth century. The medieval manuscripts fall into two families, an earlier Carolingian and French one, a later German one. In the early Renaissance he exercised an enormous influence upon humanist historiography, especially upon Leonardo Bruni's historical writings and political thought and upon Politian's account of the Pazzi conspiracy. But gradually he came to be overshadowed by Tacitus as a psychologist, a dramatist, a theoretician of the absolute state, and a stylist. As late as the eighteenth century, Alfieri admired and translated him, but he did not permit him to influence his own prose style. Nowadays he is scarcely read except by students of Latin.

BIBLIOGRAPHY

The standard modern text of the major works is that of L. D. Reynolds (Oxford 1991): see also the Teubner of A. Kurfess (Leipzig 1957) and the Loeb by J. C. Rolfe (London 1921, with English translation). The *Epistulae* and the *Invectiva* are edited by

Kurfess (Leipzig 1962); for the fragments, the edition by B. Maurenbrecher (Leipzig 1891–93) has not been superseded. There are English commentaries on the *Jugurtha* by L. Watkiss (London 1971, introductory) and G. M. Paul (Liverpool 1984, historical) and on the *Catiline* by P. McGushin (Leiden 1977; note also his commentary on the Penguin translation, Bristol 1980); see also the German commentaries by E. Koestermann (Heidelberg 1971, the *Jugurtha*) and K. Vretska (Heidelberg 1976, the *Catiline*). Vretska has also done a German commentary on the *Epistulae* and the *Invectiva* (Heidelberg 1961).

The most important English study is R. Syme, *Sallust* (California 1964); see also D. C. Earl, *The Political Thought of Sallust* (Cambridge 1961), U. Paananen, *Sallust's Politico-social Terminology* (Helsinki 1972), T. F. Scanlon, *The Influence of Thucydides on Sallust* (Heidelberg 1980) and *Spes frustrata: A Reading of Sallust* (Heidelberg 1987), E. Rawson, "Sallust in the 80s," in her *Roman Culture and Society* (Oxford 1991), and on the *appendix Sallustiana*, R.G.M. Nisbet in *JRS* 48 (1958) 30–32. Among foreign works might be cited K. Büchner, *Der Aufbau von Sallusts Bellum Jugurthinum* (Heidelberg 1953) and *Sallust* (Heidelberg 1960), and A. La Penna, *Sallustio e la rivoluzione romana* (ed. 3 Milan 1973), but there has been much work in German and Italian. In French note esp. P. Perrochat, *Les Modèles grecs de Salluste* (Paris 1949). There is a comprehensive bibliography by A. D. Leeman (ed. 2 Leiden 1965).

THREE — The Age of Augustus

43 B.C.–A.D. 17: Characteristics of a Period

1. INTRODUCTION

Under the title "Augustan age" historians of literature generally include the literary writings from the death of Caesar to the death of Augustus, or if we want two more specific chronological limits, from 43 B.C., the death of Cicero, to A.D. 17, the death of Ovid. Throughout this period, from Caesar's funeral to the last day of his life, Gaius Julius Caesar Octavianus stands on the stage of Roman politics and rightfully gives his cognomen, Augustus, to the entire period of culture at Rome.

There are, to be sure, several problems of imprecision. The appellation Augustus, which gives the period its name, was taken by Octavian only in 27 B.C. Less formally and nominally, in the whole first decade of the period in question, at least down to 36 and the defeat of Sextus Pompey at Naulochus, the power and charisma of the young Octavian are certainly not absolute. No Roman in that uncertain atmosphere could have said with assurance that Octavian was destined to triumph over the great Antony and concentrate unprecedented power in his own hands. Moreover, as we will see shortly, the literature of this first period has markedly distinct characteristics. And yet this sort of periodization does have very appealing advantages for literary chronology. In 44 and 43 Caesar and Cicero die, the two leading figures in the politics and culture of the late Republic. Cicero's voice was extinguished in December of 43; and beginning in 42, according to the ancient notices, the young Virgil is at work on the *Bucolics.* From this moment on, all the dominant figures of the new poetry have clear, documented relations with Augustus and his circle. The poetic career of Virgil and Horace, like a highway of literature, leads us right to the years of the principate and then, with the late Horace, to the threshold of the Christian era. In the meantime, without there being clear breaks, Ovid makes a name for himself and holds the stage uninterruptedly until his exile and then his death, which comes about only three years after Augustus's. In the same year as Ovid, Livy, the leading historian of the Augustan period, dies.

To define a period running from the beginning of Virgil to the end of Ovid is obviously useful for organizing our study of Roman poetry; thus it seems to us that the definition of Augustan poetry can and should be valid.

Of course, one should not employ it mechanically; outside the field of poetry its usefulness is less. In fact, the literary genres develop at very different times. A large part of Sallust's work falls after the death of Caesar and thus, according to the terms we have allowed ourselves, in the Augustan age. But Sallust's historical work is retrospective, directed entirely towards the events of the late Republic and the rise of Caesar. In Sallust's thought the new problems of the Augustan age do not play any role, and so it is customary to treat the historian, who died shortly after the battle of Naulochus and before Actium, in the context of the literature of the Caesarian period. Other serious confusions would arise if one stopped to consider minutely authors who were very important, far more important than the young Virgil and the young Horace, in the forties and thirties but of whom we have only fragments and indirect testimony, for example, Cornelius Gallus, Varius Rufus, or Asinius Pollio. Some of these authors show greater continuity with the past, whereas others are transitional figures; Gallus (see pp. 324 f.) seems at the same time both a late neoteric poet and a forerunner of Augustan elegy.

Virgil and Horace

Virgil and Horace, as we have seen, offer us a more secure ground. The development of their work accompanies the political fortunes of Octavian Augustus so conspicuously as to make our periodization acceptable. In 39 and 38 Horace and Virgil, through their friendship with Maecenas, are admitted into Octavian's political circle. Both are already poets of great inspiration. The *Bucolics* of Virgil and the *Epodes* of Horace show Octavian's influence only in occasional flashes. Instead, both these texts are profoundly influenced by the general crisis into which Italian society was plunged, that crisis that is the fertile field for the growth of Octavian's party.

The period of "the great fear"

The predominant theme of the works composed between the death of Caesar and the battle of Actium could be called "the great fear." Uncontrollable anxiety no longer pervades only Rome, which for some time has been unstable and convulsed by political vendettas, but also the once tranquil world of the provinces. Even the hopes for renewal sound confused and irrational. The armies of Caesar's murderers and of Antony and Octavian have strewn bloodshed and desolation all about the country. The civil war has reached inhuman excesses, striking, almost incidentally, harmless populations of farmers who had long lived beyond the reach of any political change. The wounds of the great fear experienced in the years 43–40 long remain painful in Augustan literature, a literature that is frequently praised above all for calm, clear balance and the lessening of contrasts. Contrasts and lacerations, however, remain wherever the memory of the civil war is still felt. In the *Georgics,* published after 30 in a climate of general peacefulness, Virgil composes a powerful reminder of the civil wars: the end of the first book describes the cataclysm that followed upon Caesar's death. It is evident that Virgil believes in Octavian's mission, but he does not intend that the past be forgotten. In the same years of peace the Umbrian poet Sextus Propertius publishes the first book of a collection of poems on love; at the end of the book, two brief poems, unexpectedly after so many elegies of courtship and amorous struggle, rudely recall the Roman blood shed by the civil wars and the human sacrifices that have devastated the peaceful cities of Umbria. Dark shadows still fall upon the first collection of Horace's *Odes,* published in 23, and even upon the *Aeneid,* in which the war between Trojans and Latins is represented in the painful and even incongruous tones of a genuine civil war.

The effects of the civil wars

The recollection of the civil wars, present as direct experience in the *Bucolics* and *Epodes* and influential then in all Augustan literature down to Ovid's generation, has a complex function, not easily summarized. Poets such as Virgil and Horace are to be reckoned among the many victims of the crisis. Sons of small Italian landholders, they had serious problems at the crucial point of the troubles. Virgil lost and then, in exceptional circumstances, won back his land. Horace when very young fought on the "wrong" side at Philippi in 42 and in the following years is a demobilized veteran without a definite position. Into these lives politics brought only disappointment and bitterness. These poets find protection and support in their contemporary Octavian. Octavian not only allows them a tranquil poetic career but presents himself as the promise of national reconstruction and order, which would need to pass through the new civil war with Antony and would be crowned with success after the great victory at Actium in 31.

Writers in the period after Actium

After 31 Octavian is no longer what he had been, a political agitator, the head of a struggling faction. His new powers declare a new political epoch, one that on the one hand aims at restoring certain republican traditions and on the other hand, far more concretely, lays the basis of the principate, the stable control of the *res publica* by a single man. What is the role of the writers in this process? The position of Virgil and Horace is quite clear. They did not jump onto the victor's bandwagon at the last moment; their hope in Octavian is identical with the hope in someone who would bring peace and end the civil wars, a sentiment that fills the *Georgics.*

Augustan ideology

After Actium, then, a period of concord and reconstruction begins. Augustus and Maecenas do not seem to have exercised a genuine control over literature. The greatest Roman poets were already tied to Maecenas and the party of Octavian, and since they were small Italian landholders, their personal interests coincided naturally with those of the party of the princeps. These people had no regrets over Cicero's aristocratic *res publica;* they felt in their own flesh the bloodbath provoked by Caesar's "republican" murderers. What we call Augustan ideology is certainly not the mechanical product of a ministry of propaganda that directly controls writers' pens; it is a political-cultural cooperation in which the poets often play an active, individual role. The new ideology produces works of extraordinary classical balance, such as Horace's *Odes* and Virgil's masterpieces, yet it is not a stable formation without contradictions. The new power derives its legitimacy from the need to end the civil wars, yet Octavian, before being a man of peace and the founder of the new equilibrium, was a destroyer, a protagonist in the apocalyptic encounter. The new epic hero, Aeneas, would conceal grave contradictions in his tormented soul: he is called to found the city of the future, but in order to do so he must become a bringer of war and deal with feelings of guilt. Aeneas, Virgil emphasizes, does not provoke the war, but neither can he avoid becoming an avenger; he must—and this will be his hardest test—even kill in fury an enemy who seems to ask for mercy.

Augustan poets and the Res Gestae *of Augustus*

The memory of the civil war would in the end be done away with by Augustan propaganda. According to the *Res Gestae,* the political testament in which Augustus gives the official, authorized version of the facts, what happened receives different, more honorable names: a young man took revenge for the assassination of his adoptive father (at Philippi in 42, where Caesar's murderers, Brutus and Cassius, were defeated); and the leader of a united Italy fought a just war against the queen of Egypt, Cleopatra (in the great naval battle at Actium in 31, in which Antony was defeated). In the distance between the *Res Gestae* and the Augustan poets we can measure the gap between propaganda and ideology.

The epoch of masterpieces

In the purely literary field the most salient characteristic of Augustan writing is its exceptional, inimitable density of masterpieces. In poetry the space of twenty years witnesses the activity of Virgil, Horace, Propertius, Tibullus, and Ovid. These authors create texts that remain, each in its own genre, the classics of Roman culture. We can add Livy in historiography; it would be wonderful were Asinius Pollio also preserved. Oratory is an exception, and it is easy to understand why: it is the only art that could not be fostered by the severe peace that Augustus imposed.

The re-creation of Greek masterpieces

Still more curious is the fact that these masterpieces are intended and expected, in a certain sense even planned for. Here, too, however, one must reject the idea of an omnipresent ministry of propaganda headed by Maecenas. The relations between literature and ideology are much less totalitarian. The most evident feature of this blossoming of masterpieces may be the desire to compete with classical Greece. Every poetic text of this period chooses illustrious models for itself; the declared models, however, are not always directly imitated. Virgil looks to Homer, Horace to Alcaeus, Propertius to Callimachus, but not exactly in the sense in which Accius offers up anew Sophocles' *Antigone* or Terence declares his Menandrian originals. The relationship of imitation that characterizes Augustan literature is freer and more complex. These poets announce their intention to "re-do" Homer, Alcaeus, and Callimachus, to produce here and now, under altered conditions of history, language, thought, and culture, something that stands on the same level as the model, a Roman equivalent that can present itself at the same time as both transformation and continuation of the model, but one that above all can take on the function of reference point and guide. Virgil toils with great perseverance on the form of his work in order to re-create a new epic style nourished on Homer, but something beyond a rivalry over form is at stake: his intention is to create an epic text that has the same cultural importance at Rome that Homer had had for the Greeks. This is the paradox of Augustan poetry: by comparison with Ennius and Plautus, Virgil and Horace are both more faithful to the Greek model and more independent of it. For the Augustans the great Greek literature is alive in its entirety and present all at once—the grandeur and pathos of Homer, the keenness of Euripides, the force of Archilochus, as well as the formal perfection of the Alexandrians.

A Mature Literary Consciousness: The System of the Genres

Already in Lucretius conscious artistic intention had wanted to show itself in the construction of an architecturally complex poem. The organization of the material according to the logic of rigorous argumentation was accompanied by the "Alexandrian" requirement that the book be an artistic unity, marked by correspondences and alternations. Augustan poetry would bring this process to full maturity. Attention to structure would become one of its characteristic traits, serving as an added instrument of meaning with which the modern poets show that they have taken full responsibility for the literary form they have adopted.

The Hellenistic poets and the contamination of literary forms

The Greek poets of the Hellenistic age (e.g., Callimachus and Theocritus) had before them an amply articulated and clearly defined literary system that was ordered by internal differences. For these *poetae docti* the literary genres were precise points of reference, possible modelings of meaning and form. Thus, by working with contamination and crossing the boundaries between the various genres and the different literary codes, the Alexandrians secured for themselves new possibilities of expression.

The neoteric poets, though reinstating the Alexandrian principle of *poikilia* and thus freely contaminating forms, had devoted themselves to the continued practice of single modes of composition rather than to a variety of different experiments. There was, however, an important difference for them: they worked as the Alexandrians did, but they did not possess those constant points of reference (from which to try new crossings) that were represented for the Alexandrians by the corpus of the different ancient genres, the heroic epic of Homer, the didactic poetry of Hesiod, and the various melic and lyric forms. They still needed to construct a complete canonic literary system like the one that had established a plurality of individual literary codes in Greek culture, each one distinct from the other. The genres, as diversified forms of literary discourse, were an objective still to be achieved.

The Augustans and the construction of a system of literary genres

In the wake of the neoterics, but with a greater ambition and a greater consciousness, the poets of the generation of Cornelius Gallus and Virgil embarked on a vaster project. It would fall to them to define within the possibilities of literature the marked traits belonging to a given genre, from the point of view of both expression (metrical and compositional structure, linguistic levels and registers, style) and content (selection and combination of themes and images, construction of individual details, representation of values and choices of life). In a certain sense, then, the Latin poets of the Augustan age work basically in an opposite direction from their Alexandrian models, from whom their poetics takes its rise. In all departments of poetry that are of Alexandrian derivation or inspiration, starting from a mixed-form literary reality and without denying the expressive richness that comes from *poikilia,* they devote their energies to selection, restricting the field of subjects and delimiting their languages, as they seek dominant principles around which to construct organic forms of literary discourse, that is to say, as they construct genres. Thus, Virgil worked with an edition of Theocritus that included *Idylls* of varying nature: bucolic, mimic, encomiastic, or generally narrative (whether they were authentic or spurious did not concern Virgil). There is no doubt, however, that the *Eclogues* create a consistent pastoral world and restrict the possibilities of the Syracusan Muse, which is understood as hexameter poetry of low or middle level; each exception (e.g., the fourth eclogue) is presented as such: *paulo maiora canamus,* "let us sing something on a slightly higher level." Bucolic poetry, in other words, is constructed as a genre provided with independent meaning and form, in which each element organically reflects the pastoral world and its imagery: from the characters to the countryside, from the actions of the protagonists to their desires, everything enters the text of the *Eclogues* only if it permits itself to be spoken of in the language of the shepherds.

Similarly, by comparison with the multiform variety of Hellenistic elegiac poetry, Roman elegy, thanks to Gallus, Propertius, and Tibullus, certainly receives its identity from a unitary project that selects and retains only those features that, once brought into systematic relation, make it possible to give consistent representation to a tortured and unequal love relation. The Augustan elegiac poets attempt to establish certain dominant principles as the basis on which they select the rich materials of the Hellenistic tradition, subordinating them to an organic project. Thus the *elegi* become chiefly love poetry, and then the poet can make his passion the exclusive reason for his existence and his poetry. Strong features of the literary code would include the *servitium amoris*—the poet's submission to the whims of a *domina* who is refined and frivolous, a shrewd dispenser of favors and infidelities—and the choice of a degrading life with which the poet-lover rejects any recognition or social success (an honorable career or the acquisition of wealth). Hence we have a poetry that alternates between suffering and joy, exulting and complaining, a totalizing, absolute universe that proposes an independent ideology of its own that contrasts with the official values of the *civitas.* In short, the construction of the elegiac code is the result of a process of selection. The literary tradition is decanted as if through a filter, and from its rich treasure of myths, symbols, and marked words only those elements that can be turned to new functions and new meaning are allowed to pass through.

In the space of around forty years, various writers succeeded in their extraordinary undertaking of producing a body of works comparable to those of Greek literature. They were moved by a common commitment to cultural planning, but each had his own personal literary preferences; hence the frequent need they felt to deliver declarations of poetics, to set their own choices into words, to make polemical *recusationes.* From the beginning they were held together by pride in the task they had undertaken, a pride that increased as new poetic realizations were achieved (Propertius did not restrain his enthusiasm for the great epic poem that Virgil was writing, and in a famous verse he declared of the *Aeneid* that "something greater than the *Iliad* is being born"). Literature now consciously aimed at organizing itself into an articulated system of genres, it possessed an ample variety of differentiated languages, and it was mature enough to meet all the various needs of representation and expression. The possession of mature formal categories was accompanied by the necessary ambition to make use of them. For the poets, with their new and stronger consciousness of the tasks entrusted to literature, perhaps even a new cultural state is born: they are no longer merely skillful makers of verses, no longer merely artists, but *vates,* inspired singers destined to find an excited and widespread hearing. Lucretius had already anticipated the ideal of an engaged poet, "master of the truth," holder of great secrets that are to be solemnly communicated; and certainly his poetry must have been an important precedent for the Augustan ideal of the useful poet, that model of the poet upon whom the title *vates* is traditionally bestowed. Both Virgil and Horace would represent a moment of valorization of the vatic poet, a sign of the new function that Augustan culture wanted to assign to poetic activity and engagement (even the late Propertius would rejoin this tendency, ambiguously). The idea that *vates* was an ancient word, a more ancient word for designating the poet in the sense of the inspirer and voice of his community, must have been rooted in late republican antiquarian interests. The two etymologies proposed for this word both seem Varronian: *a versibus viendis* ("from weaving words") and *a vi mentis* ("from mental vigor"). This second interpretation was probably the one that was more fruitful for Lucretius's imagery, if it is true that it can be found in his ardent declaration of poetics (*amorem / Musarum, quo nunc instinctus* mente vigenti / *avia Pieridum peragro loca* [*De Rerum Natura* 1.924–26]). But to valorize the connotation of poetic primitivism, which is implicit in the reverential label of *vates,* means, additionally and especially, to modify the Alexandrian image of poetry making and replace it with an ideal of the poet who is inspired by events and strongly committed to his society. In this, Augustan poetry exactly reverses the neoteric conception, not rejecting the refinements of style they had achieved, but rather bringing them to perfection.

Augustan Ideology and the Sincerity of the Poets

Thus several texts come into existence that were profoundly related to the tendencies of Augustan ideology. The effort to compete with the great Greek classics included also an effort to broaden subjects and experiences; it was no longer, as it had been for the *poetae novi,* an effort chiefly involving form and expression. Virgil gives form to the myth of the Italian countryside, and Horace in the "Roman odes" speaks to the community of citizens about great civic and moral subjects. The critical debate over the sincerity of these attitudes is still unresolved. We know that Augustus shared in these efforts. Augustan ideology proposes to rediscover the path of further growth; the traditions of the "republic of the peasants," with their twin pillars, the family and the property in land, are called back to life; Eastern influences, the consumption of luxury goods, and licentiousness are combated. A large part of this ideology remained mere sloganeering, without practical effects. The return to the "republic of the peasants," if that had ever existed, was impossible under a political system no longer based on direct participation. Horace's reenacting in his verses the bond between an archaic Greek poet and his *polis* has a somewhat unreal effect. The truer message of Horace's poetry was something else altogether: Maecenas was an exemplary figure of the new era. He wielded a power without name and definition, while remaining a knight, a well-to-do private citizen, and he showed that one could be active and engaged in public affairs without sacrificing *otium,* culture, pleasure, or luxury. And Horace is at his best when exploring the themes of the private man: the pursuit of wisdom, the passage of time, pleasures, private recollections, the sense of death, man's relation to nature.

Elegy and the Augustan regime

The development of the private dimension is undoubtedly the outstanding feature of Roman society during the transition from Republic to principate. And this development explains the explosion of the elegiac genre, poetry that presupposes a life completely withdrawn into a private sphere to which political duties and participation are alien. That withdrawal, of course, is the other side of the new political model. There is no necessary, immediate conflict between the official ideology and the elegiac ideology; rather, there is a certain division of roles. The poet can address Augustus gratefully as the one who assures the peace and rules the state securely. Thanks to the person who is concerned about the "serious" things, love at last can be the only serious thing. The new paradigm of the life of love, however, is not officially favored by the government. Propertius has a more modest place within Maecenas's circle, and Tibullus gravitates towards an independent circle gathered about Messalla. (In other cases, one may think of almost schizophrenic forms of life: Cornelius Gallus, before he ruined his life by falling into disgrace, seems to have succeeded in being an excellent official and an original poet of love, thus splitting himself between contrasting experiences.) These poets reject any epic exaltation of the national value or the civilizing mission of Rome: "Love is a god of peace." Still, they do show respect towards the princeps in a curiously hesitant, contradictory poetic form, the *recusatio.* They excuse themselves for not being able to sing of epic subjects, sometimes offering a brief attempt, almost for fun, but without ever recanting their own exclusive calling.

These poets, active in the central phase of Augustus's reign, have an ambiguous, unresolved relation with Augustan ideology. Propertius, for instance, shows traces of conflict. But the only poet actually to collide with power will be, paradoxically, the most unpolitical, the most unengaged of all: Ovid.

The second phase of Augustus's principate

The final phase of Augustus's reign was stormy, though in a hidden and sometimes deceptive way. Even the literary climate was different. After Virgil, poetry seems to bifurcate sharply: either it is celebratory, as in certain infelicitous passages in the fourth book of Horace's *Odes,* or it is apolitical and disengaged. Even the attempts to revive the social function of literature seem to falter. The efforts to restore a Roman national drama are crowned by no worthwhile result. An art form that had been so important during the Republic, as a reflection of the community and a mark of cultural identity, no longer succeeds in holding its own in the new climate. Horace in the second book of the *Epistles* analyzes in exemplary fashion the difficulties of the theater. After Horace's death—he had been preceded by Maecenas—there is no longer any connection between the circle of the princeps, which is increasingly remote and busy with obscure palace politicking, and the world of literary pursuits.

Ovid, the smiling destroyer

Ovid, the light of poetry in this last phase, is a kind of smiling destroyer. The literary genres practiced by him, the various types of elegy and epic, in the end transform unimaginably their traditional identity. Love elegy is no longer based on love as a choice of life, but with brilliant virtuosity it adapts itself to the life of a gallant society. Ovid has the greatest success ever achieved at Rome in attempting to give literary dignity to a modernist culture. For the first time, it is free from moralisms and from returns to its origins. Ovid sings of pleasures, spectacles, luxuries, free love, and at the same time, of course, he glorifies the princeps that has made possible this era of felicity in the metropolis. Without intending to, Ovid by his grave injury in the end touched upon an unresolved contradiction in the Augustan world: the split between certain current tendencies—real tendencies, which involved even sexual behavior in the house of Augustus!—and the continual proclamation of ideological values that appeared fundamental for the construction of the new society—civic zeal, moral purity, suppression of luxuriousness, and religious restoration. Perhaps for this reason he ended his career upon the shores of the Black Sea, anticipating a century of difficult relations between literature and absolute power.

2. LITERATURE, THE POLITICAL BACKGROUND, AND THE POETIC CIRCLES

The connective tissue of Augustan culture

The study of the masterpieces produced in the Augustan age may easily overshadow a more minute consideration of this period's connective tissue: the minor writers—some of them minor only for us, because their writings have been lost—and especially the intellectual life of the capital, with its talented dilettantes, Maecenas, Messalla, and Asinius Pollio. The importance of this should in no way be underestimated.

We will return in greater detail to the lost literature of this period after pausing over the principal figures of the Augustan age (on the minor poetry of Ovid's generation, see pp. 426 f.). We must, however, make an exception for two authors who already had direct influence upon the young Virgil and who therefore can in no way be classified as followers of the Augustan classics.

Cornelius Gallus

To judge from indirect testimony, Cornelius Gallus is undoubtedly an eminent poetic voice in the period of history between the death of Caesar and the battle of Actium. At the time of Virgil's *Bucolics* Gallus is already an established author, and his writing seems to be the most important link between neoteric poetry and the love poetry of the Augustan age. Although he was Virgil's contemporary, Gallus ended his literary activity in a hasty and untimely manner: a suicide in 26, he left the scene just when the Augustan elegiac poets were flourishing. We will deal with him more extensively in connection with elegiac poetry, for which his *Amores* provided a powerful stimulus (see pp. 324 f.).

Varius Rufus

Varius Rufus was slightly older than Virgil but longer-lived. We have few fragments of his, but every time he enters the scene he leaves his distinct mark. He is praised by Virgil already in the *Bucolics* (9.35); he was the one to introduce Horace to Maecenas (Horace, *Satires* 1.6.55); he is one of the friends Horace refers to most readily throughout the first book of the *Satires;* he is the man whom Augustus chose for the delicate task of publishing the *Aeneid* after Virgil's death. Varius is clearly a principal figure in the literary circles of Octavian Augustus, and what we know of his work stimulates our curiosity. He was concerned in some way with epic and composed a tragedy, a *Thyestes,* performed in 29 B.C. Culturally he seems to

The Epicureanism of Varius

have had Epicurean tastes, which comes as no surprise. Strong Epicurean coloring marks Virgil's first writings and, to an extent, all of Horace's work, and an Epicurean atmosphere surrounds Maecenas's private life too. Varius's Epicureanism would certainly be clearer if we had his mysterious poem *De Morte,* of which a few fragments remain, brief but of notable inspiration, preserved for the most part because they provided starting points for Virgil (they are quoted in ancient commentaries on Virgil's work). To judge from the title, the *De Morte* would seem to be a text of didactic poetry, and we know, from Lucretius and Philodemus among others, how important the problem of death was in the Epicurean philosophy. But it seems that Varius did not limit himself to philosophical speculation: one of the fragments contains a clear political attack on Octavian's great political enemy, Mark Antony. It looks as if Varius reproached Antony with greed for wealth and immoderate passion for luxury. Perhaps this polemic also had Epicurean undertones, since the connection between political ambition and uncontrolled desire is a typical target of Lucretius and Philodemus. Varius, in any event, appears to be a consistent partisan of Octavian. Later he also composed a *Panegyric* of the princeps. He is certainly one of the most intimate among the writers who surround Maecenas.

Maecenas and his circle

As already indicated by several references, Maecenas is the true center of attraction for the entire generation of Augustan poets, a generation of which he was more or less exactly a contemporary, since he was born around 70 and died in 8 B.C. A native of Arezzo, in Etruria, he was at the same time aristocratic and bourgeois: he came from a noble Etruscan family but as a Roman citizen he never rose above equestrian status, by his own choice, and he never held real public offices. All this in the end encouraged a personal myth that we find reflected several times in the poetry of Horace, Virgil, and Propertius. During the burning years of the civil wars Maecenas had been a very important diplomatic and political adviser to Octavian. After the triumph of Octavian's party and the establishment of the new regime, Maecenas ostentatiously continued to refrain from entering the traditional Roman political system, a system whose continuation was assured by Augustus in several respects. Aristocratic by birth, ordinary citizen by choice, and a great power in the political reality of the day (i.e., in the unwritten constitution that underlay all the official forms), Maecenas was a kind of living symbol of the new times. The most constant trait in his work is precisely the breaking with the traditions of the Republic. In him the rejection of official posts is joined to an intense behind-the-scenes activity and an ironic detachment from the "public virtues" of the traditional Roman politician. He displayed a taste for luxury and private pleasures, estheticism and the cult of private friendship, and he was not concerned to mask the personal character of his devotion to the princeps. At the same time, Maecenas with extraordinary intelligence promoted a national literature, not a mass literature, of course, since the masses did not read books, but a literature of powerful intellectual engagement: the *Georgics,* the *Aeneid,* the *Odes* and *Epistles* of Horace. His circle, however, though based on close private ties, aimed at a very widespread literature, one no longer withdrawn into private subjects and difficult avant-garde works as the world of the *poetae novi* had been. Personally, by contrast—and this is another paradox—Maecenas cultivated an ephemeral, playful, intimate, ironic poetry. As a writer he was not successful, and this was certainly not the main area of his ambitions.

Augustus as writer   Still more modest were the literary ambitions of the princeps. Augustus was too clear-headed a political leader, too free from illusion, to be deceived about his own literary talents. He spoke with irony of his poetic experiment, the *Ajax:* he used to say that his Ajax had died, not by the sword as Sophocles' hero had, but by the sponge, that is, the sponge used for erasing. Thus he did not seek publicity for his private literary diversions. His autobiography, however, had a certain circulation; though incomplete, it was probably used by the historians of the imperial age. One gets the impression that Augustus had a moderate degree of culture and could write with propriety but without particular literary satisfaction. But like his friend Maecenas, he had a strong sense of propaganda. His true self-portrait is found in the *Res Gestae,* finished shortly before his death, which came about in A.D. 14.

The Res Gestae *of*   The work is of extraordinary historical and ideological interest and in
Augustus   no way aims at competing with the more diffuse narrative technique of Caesar's *Commentarii.* It is a text that was intended to be reproduced in public inscriptions and that has in fact come down to us epigraphically. The most important testimony comes from the *Monumentum Ancyranum,* found at the site of modern Ankara, in Anatolia. We know that in the copies intended for Greek countries the text was accompanied by a Greek version. In a laconic, forceful style, apparently simple but carefully calculated in its tones, Augustus declares that he has freed the Roman Republic

from the threats posed by Caesar's assassins and the Egyptian queen. The civil wars are schematically summarized as a "liberation" of Italy from tyrants and external threats. The princeps is particularly concerned—this is the most delicate point in the mechanism of his power—to explain that the source of his offices is the desire of the Senate and the people; and he enumerates at great length all the benefits and gifts conferred on Rome and its citizens. The *Res Gestae Divi Augusti* is a text of ideological and political propaganda exemplary for its density and its ability to persuade.

Pollio as organizer of culture

The cultural richness of the Augustan age is not confined to the circle of Augustus and Maecenas. A person such as Asinius Pollio testifies to the vitality of a culture that is not integrated into the new regime. In creativity and intelligence Pollio has little to envy a Maecenas: he had merely chosen the wrong side in politics. After fighting for the cause of Antony, Pollio ended his promising political career before the disaster. Retired to private life, he led a sort of cultural opposition to the new regime, distinguishing himself by critical sentiment and by enthusiasm for literature. He founded the first public library at Rome in the atrium of the Temple of Liberty and encouraged the practice of *recitationes,* public gatherings that served to preview new writings. Concern over the decline of the oratorical tradition, a natural consequence of the new political arrangement, was surely operative in him.

Pollio as literary historian and critic

Pollio is praised by Horace and by Virgil in the *Bucolics*—it is not accidental that he is absent from all Virgil's later work—as the author of tragedies. His most significant work, however, was the *Historiae,* one of the most grievous losses in Latin historical literature. Pollio had the courage to deal with the period of history from the first triumvirate to the battle of Philippi (42 B.C.), in effect, the whole decline of the Roman Republic, a burning theme still in the years of the Augustan regime. It was distinguished, it seems, by a critical manner and by nonconformity, opposing the growing spread of tendentious memorials, that is, writings from the side of the victors (for more detailed notices of his historical work, see pp. 377 f.). Judgments of Pollio on Caesar and Cicero, on Sallust and Livy, are recorded. Whether they are malicious or clear-sighted is hard to say. We do not know whether his own work, which was in the tradition of republican Atticism, was on the same level as his skills as literary critic and polemicist.

Valerius Messalla and his circle

The position of Marcus Valerius Messalla (64 B.C.–A.D. 8), who is known to literary history chiefly on account of his connection with the poet Tibullus, is somewhat hazier. Messalla had a complicated political past—he fought at first along with the republican murderers of Caesar and later with Antony—but at the right moment he chose to join Octavian. We find him as a public figure throughout the Augustan age, even though he does not appear to be linked to the princeps's most intimate circle. His patronage of literature was an independent one, and it is not accidental that the inspiration of his most well-known protégé, Tibullus, is rather remote from the dominant tendencies of Augustan literature. Messalla's influence is not altogether comparable to Maecenas's; yet he devoted himself to his own literary work more than Maecenas did. Messalla seems to have been above all a notable orator, but we have evidence, too, of many scholarly, grammatical, and rhetorical writings. He also seems to have composed bucolic poems in Greek, which is significant both for his relations with Tibullus and for the degree of his literary sophistication. We may suppose that all the texts collected in the *Corpus Tibullianum,* whether Tibullan or not (see p. 330), had to do with Messalla's circle. The *Panegyric* transmitted in the collection, an occasional work of medium quality and certainly by one of his protégés, was written in his honor.

Virgil

LIFE

Publius Vergilius Maro was born near Mantua—the precise location is controversial—on 15 October 70 B.C., to small landholders. The places of his education must have been Rome and Naples, though the whole chronology of his youth is debated. An especially interesting notice is found in a short poem attributed to Virgil, the fifth of the collection *Catalepton* (see p. 431): allusion is made to a school that the young Virgil had attended in Naples, conducted by the Epicurean philosopher Siro. The value of the notice is debated, since the poem, as far as its quality goes, could be the work of a young Virgil, but by the same token the autobiographical content could also derive from a forger eager to fill a vacuum in the career of the young poet. Still, the first work Virgil certainly wrote, the *Bucolics,* clearly shows familiarity with Epicureanism.

The dating of the *Bucolics* is fairly secure, on the whole, but it is tied to an episode that is not altogether clear. Several times in the work Virgil alludes to the perilous events of 41, when the country around Mantua suffered great land confiscations, which were intended to recompense the veterans of the battle of Philippi. The period is marked by serious disorders, and Virgil reflects the tragedy of the dispossessed peasants. A notice originating in the classical period and greatly elaborated by the ancient commentators on Virgil has it that Virgil himself had lost his family farm in the confiscations and had then gotten it back. Through whose intervention? The ancient notices are not clear on this point. Octavian has been suggested, as have other people directly mentioned in the *Bucolics,* all somehow involved in the administration of the Transpadane territory: Asinius Pollio, Cornelius Gallus, and Alfenus Varus, the first two known as men of culture, among other things. Around the original nucleus of the notice a biographical fiction was later formed, involving the allegorical interpretation of many passages of the *Bucolics;* today it is very difficult to disentangle any underlying truth.

It is certain, however, that the *Bucolics* show no trace of Maecenas, who would be Virgil's great friend and patron. At the same time, the protecting figure of Pollio, who would later disappear altogether from Virgil's work, is of considerable importance. Immediately after the publication of the

Bucolics Virgil joins the circle of Maecenas's intimates, and thus Octavian's too. Shortly after, Horace also joins. During the long years of uncertainty and political strife before the battle of Actium (31 B.C.), Virgil is at work on the refined composition of his agricultural poem, in full harmony with the circle of Maecenas. He seems, however, not to have liked Rome: the end of the *Georgics* speaks of Naples as a beloved place of retirement and literary activity.

All of Virgil's life, as far as we know it, is extraordinarily lacking in external events and is centered instead on unremitting toil over poetry. In 29 Octavian, returning victorious from the East, stops at Atella, in Campania, and has Virgil read to him the *Georgics,* which he had scarcely finished. There are, however, somewhat controversial indications that place the actual publication of the poem a little earlier (see p. 269). From here onwards the poet was entirely absorbed in the composition of the *Aeneid.* It seems that Augustus followed the development of the work with great personal interest, as we learn from a fragment of a letter. Virgil lived long enough to read some parts of the poem to the princeps but not long enough to regard the work as finished; it seems that scruples, second thoughts, and revisions were typical of his character and his method of composing. The *Aeneid* was published at Augustus's behest by Varius Rufus: the poet had died on 21 September 19 B.C. at Brundisium, on returning from a voyage to Greece. Virgil was buried at Naples. The literary success of the work, which had already been awaited and heralded in literary circles before 19, was immediate and such as to establish it forever.

WORKS

Bucolics, ten brief poems in hexameters (going from a minimum of 63 verses to a maximum of 111, for a total of 829 hexameters), also called *Eclogues,* written between 42 and 39 (the chronology of the individual poems is much debated); *Georgics,* a didactic poem in four books of hexameters (each book containing slightly more than 500 verses, a total of 2188), completed in 29; the *Aeneid,* an epic poem in twelve books, in the meter appropriate to the genre, the hexameter (the books containing between 700 and 950 verses apiece, for a total of a just under 10,000). The last work was published by the executors of his will. Some instances of incongruence and narrative repetition remain, signs that the final touches are missing; the most obvious signs of incompleteness are the 58 unfinished verses, which Virgil himself called *tibicines,* "props" to support a building under construction. The poetic texts known collectively as the *Appendix Vergiliana* are mostly spurious (see pp. 430 ff.); only a couple of the poems from the collection *Catalepton* have a fair probability of being authentic, and, if they are, they belong to his youthful writings.

SOURCES

Apart from the evidence to be gotten from the genuine texts, we have a series of late ancient and medieval *Vitae* in which a nucleus goes back to Suetonius's biographical activity (see pp. 547 f.) and therefore deserves the greatest consideration. The most famous of these *Vitae* is owed to Aelius

Donatus, the great grammarian of the fourth century (see pp. 627 f.). All the genuine works are amply commented on beginning in the first century A.D.; among the preserved texts the commentary of Servius (fourth–fifth century) is particularly important, since it contains historical information, of varying value.

1. THE *BUCOLICS*

Theocritus and Virgil

The poetic world of Theocritus

Until the publication of Virgil's *Bucolics,* Theocritus was the least popular and least successful among the great Hellenistic authors read by the Romans. His world, at the same time simple, delicate, and artificial, was not perhaps the one most apt to seize the imagination of the *poetae novi.* His poetics did not lend themselves to manifestoes of innovation and experimentation. The new Roman culture, so strongly urban, preferred to turn to other models. Curiously, Theocritus had been, in his way, a poet of the city, indeed of the metropolis. The poetry of the *Idylls* looks to the nostalgic and learned reconstruction of a traditional pastoral world, a sight intended for the taste of an urbanized, cosmopolitan public and a court society. Settings such as Sicily and the distant island of Cos serve Theocritus as backdrops for his drama of shade and shadow. A strong Doric veneer helps to distance the poetic language. Shepherds were the protagonists of the action, and along with them a rich but static countryside, with everything suspended in an everyday existence that is rarefied, yet brightened by poetry. The material offered by the new genre is less monotonous than it seems: it can also treat large themes, but it does so, of necessity, in a simple and remote way. The sophisticated public of the city can admire in every detail the delicate balance between poetic learning and a taste for description of the particular.

Virgil appropriates Theocritus

The coming together of Virgil and this genre, which is also a world of imagination, was extremely fortunate. The young poet possessed a great store of feelings, and in Theocritus he read the rural world in which he had grown up. Touches of realism and of nostalgia were part of the poetic formula of this genre. Yet he was moved in the direction of Theocritus by a strong sense of literature, a tendency towards self-reflection. The shepherd-poets of the *Idylls* readily presented themselves to him as possibilities for investigating, obliquely, an entire literary vocation. Imitating Theocritus signifies, ultimately, a kind of symbiosis that is without precedent in Roman literature, and even perhaps, as far as intensity goes, one that is without real followers. Virgil did not limit himself to knowing thoroughly the Theocritean corpus and, probably, the minor bucolic poets of the second and first centuries and the commentators on Theocritus. He transported himself to within this literary genre and learned to observe its principles in a foreign language. The result cannot be reduced to a simple process of imitation. No single Virgilian eclogue stands in a one-to-one relation with a single Theocritean idyll. The presence of Theocritus has been resolved into a tissue of relations so complex that the new work is on a par with its model. In this sense the *Bucolics,* which are so neoteric for their learning, stylization, and devotion to poetry, are truly the first text of Augustan literature. They already interpret its basic drive, to rework the Greek texts while treating them as classics.

The Book of the *Eclogues*

The title of the collection, *Bucolics,* "cowherds' songs," contains the basic feature of this genre, which evokes a pastoral setting in which the herdsmen themselves are brought on as actors and even creators of poetry. By a tradition that goes back to the Latin grammarians, the term "eclogue," meaning "short selected poem," is preferred in the singular. One should not imagine, of course, that pastoral imagery or themes were completely absent from previous Latin poetry; but the originality of Virgil (cf. 6.1–2: "My Muse was the first not to disdain the Syracusan verse, and she accepted living in the woods") is guaranteed by the choice he made to devote to this genre an entire book, one held together by a carefully thought-out architectural composition. No other ancient poetry book that we know of before Virgil shows the same level of architectural complexity and unity. The plan of the work is as follows:

Summary of the Bucolics

Poem 1. Dialogue between two shepherds, Tityrus and Meliboeus. Contrast of destinies: the former, helped by a divine young man at Rome, will enjoy his tranquil life; the latter, dispossessed, will wander far and wide.

Poem 2. Love complaint of the shepherd Corydon, who is consumed with love for the young man Alexis.

Poem 3. Poetic contest between two shepherds, conducted in alternating songs (the "amoebean" form, in which remark is followed by reply).

Poem 4. Prophetic song for the birth of a child who will witness the coming of a new and happy cosmic age.

Poem 5. Lament for the death of Daphnis, a deified pastoral hero. It is divided between two shepherds, Menalcas and Mopsus.

Poem 6. The aged Silenus, captured by two young men, sings a catalogue of mythical and naturalistic scenes, the climax of which is the poetic consecration of the great elegiac writer Cornelius Gallus. The eclogue is prefaced by a declaration of poetics, which clearly, in Alexandrian fashion, serves to introduce the second half of the book.

Poem 7. Meliboeus recounts in the first person a duel between two poets, the Arcadian shepherds Thyrsis and Corydon.

Poem 8. A singing contest, dedicated to Asinius Pollio and divided into two lengthy stories of unhappy love: the lament of Damon, who will choose death, and the magical practices of a woman in love.

Poem 9. Dialogue between two shepherd-poets, with references to the reality of the Mantuan countryside and to the expropriations that followed the civil wars.

The originality of the Bucolics

Poem 10. Consolation by the bucolic poet Virgil for the love pangs of the elegiac poet Cornelius Gallus.

Architecture of the Bucolics

The principles of arrangement for the book's poems have been much discussed by critics. The number ten might go back to a collection of ten idylls of Theocritus (not all genuine) that Virgil used. The existence of many parallelisms between individual poems is beyond question. In the first place stands the poem that contains an homage to Octavian; in the last is the eclogue dedicated to Gallus; the two central places (eclogues 5 and 6) are occupied by a poem that alludes to the death of Julius Caesar (if the common allegorical interpretation is right) and by one that deals with questions of poetics and is supplied with a kind of proem.

Some eclogues are conceived in pairs and placed apart because of love for variety: 1 and 9 (references to the civil war in Italy); 2 and 8 (monologues of love); 3 and 7 (poetic contests); 4 and 6, which are not closely connected to one another but are the two least pastoral poems of the book. One could go on at length. Some of the symmetries proposed by the critics are surely too subtle and abstract, since they are sometimes based on mathematical relations and on assumptions of allegory.

The Limits of the Bucolic Genre

Variety of themes in Theocritus

The miscellaneous character of Theocritus's collection had sanctioned a certain variety of subjects. The new Theocritus, to be truly bucolic, needed therefore to abandon the limits of the pastoral world now and then. Theocritus's collection as we read it today includes forays into the world of the city and also poems of celebration, connected to historical occasions and dedicated to royal patrons (idylls 16 and 17). Furthermore, a certain variety of setting, with scattered references to Sicilian and Greek locales, or locales in Magna Graecia, was achieved even in the most strictly pastoral scenes.

Italian countryside and ideal countryside

Virgil exploits these possibilities to the maximum. On the one hand, some suggestions allow him to set the eclogues in the Italian countryside familiar to the poet; on the other hand, and this is a great contribution by Virgil to the tradition of the European pastoral, there are references, especially in eclogue 10, to a particular ideal landscape, Arcadia. In earlier Greek culture there are already allusions to this happy world of the shepherds, isolated among the mountains and still visited by divine presences, but the myth of Arcadia as a land of poetry owes a great deal to Virgil. Virgil's other, and more substantial, contribution to the bucolic tradition consists in the free use made of autobiographical material.

Autobiography in the Bucolics

The drama of the exiled shepherds in eclogues 1 and 9 certainly contains a core of personal experience. In the years 42–41 the confiscations of lands for the veterans struck the farmers around Cremona and then Mantua. According to the ancient biographical tradition, Virgil himself at first had been dispossessed, but then his property was restored to him through influential people: Asinius Pollio, Alfenus Varus, Cornelius Gallus, all of them in some way present in the bucolic collection. About this core, which may well be true, there later developed a historical reconstruction, a sort of allegorical fiction. Starting from the identification of Tityrus with Virgil—already a debatable premise—ancient and modern interpreters have seen behind all the figures of the pastoral world a confused mass of historical allusions. This way of explaining the eclogues is unsatisfactory, and it is clear that Virgil, when he really wants to allude to a historical background, does not have recourse to allegories. Thus, the implicit presence of Octavian in the first eclogue is certain (according to some, precisely because of the role that Octavian plays there, the eclogue can not have been written in the period of the confiscations, but must be later). Also clear, apart from the precise interpretation of the context, is the existence of a concrete historical reference in the fourth eclogue. Nearly all the rest is unconvincing conjecture.

Interpretations of eclogue 4   It is important to grasp the originality of inspiration with which Virgil reads the period of the civil wars in bucolic language. This happens, as was seen, in the "Theocritean" eclogues 1 and 9 and in the famous eclogue 4. As the beginning announces (*paulo maiora canamus,* "let us sing something on a slightly higher level"), the poet raises himself out of the pastoral sphere, which is still noticeable in the style and in the choice of several images, in order to sing of a great event. By a historical irony, this poem, so clear in itself, has given rise to a puzzle. Who is the *puer* who by his arrival brings the Golden Age back to a world in crisis? The late antique identification of the *puer* with Jesus Christ is merely the boldest of the many conjectures proposed. The eclogue belongs among the expectations of renewal that were characteristic of the age of crisis between Philippi and Actium, and it has a clear parallel in Horace's epode 16. We can distinguish the cultural threads that lead to this visionary poetry. Poems in honor of marriages and births had a rhetorical tradition of their own; moreover, Virgil has drawn on nonpoetic sources, in which philosophical influences are mixed with messianic teachings, expectations of a savior. According to the majority of interpreters, however, the figure of this young savior of the world must still have a concrete, proximate reference: the eclogue is securely dated to the consulship of Asinius Pollio, in 40 B.C. The best hypothesis, since among other things it explains the obscurity of the reference, which was clear for the readers of the time and already mysterious a few years later, is that the child of the eclogue was expected in that year but in fact was never born. In that year many hopes attended a power-sharing agreement between Octavian and Antony (which proved to be short-lived). Antony, who for long had been the most powerful man around, married Octavian's sister. The marriage lasted but a short time, and there were no male offspring. But the eclogue, precisely because of its delicate, oracular language, did not lose its value: it was retained and had great success as attesting a certain expectation and a moral climate. Without knowing it, Virgil thus opened the way to the Christian interpretation of his poetry, which was so important in the Middle Ages.

*The eclogues for
Gallus and the
definition of the
bucolic genre*

Two other eclogues, the sixth and ninth, allow Virgil to broaden the horizons of the bucolic song. The sixth is perhaps Virgil's most Alexandrian work. Silenus's revelations range from mythological to cosmological images; at its center the poem has an homage to the poet Cornelius Gallus in which the bucolic world strives to welcome the symbols of Alexandrian poetics, symbols probably introduced in his friend's poetry. Gallus returns as a poet of love in eclogue 10, a bucolic poem; it could hardly be otherwise, given its function as the leave-taking from the book. The Arcadian setting is typically bucolic, as is the idea that poetry can heal the sufferings of love by bringing man close to nature. But here, too, Virgil does not refuse to broaden the horizon. Gallus is represented as the incarnation of another poetry, elegiac poetry, which is also life choice, as it will be for Propertius and Tibullus. The elegiac poet Gallus, wearied by the unhappy love that is his chosen life, seeks refuge in his friend's bucolic poetry. The meeting of these two worlds allows Virgil to pay homage to a great friend. It also allows him to make completely clear the personal poetic dimension by exploring the boundaries, the similarities and differences, of the bucolic genre and the elegiac genre.

*Poetry and auto-
biography in the
Bucolics*

The *Bucolics,* taken all together, reveal not only the poetic maturity reached by Virgil but also the maturity of his life choices. Poetry is experienced as a refuge from the dramas of existence; the withdrawn life of the shepherds is hospitable to watered-down Epicurean tones. The passions are present with an intensity that can be fierce, but poetry is also a means of overcoming them through harmony. Beside the poet can be glimpsed the figures of great patrons who make possible his life of poetic *otium:* Pollio, to whom eclogue 7 is dedicated, and then, but only by implication, Octavian, who for Virgil will be the decisive choice. In the *Bucolics* there is no trace of another figure, Maecenas, who will be the direct inspirer of the *Georgics.*

In elegiac poetry the poet experiences the pains of love to the utmost, but in the bucolic genre the song of love is a consolation and reconciliation with nature. The bucolic setting absorbs and mediates in itself the contrast of models. As the great humanist Julius Caesar Scaliger wrote, "The bucolic genre summons to itself and reabsorbs every element of reality."

2. FROM THE *BUCOLICS* TO THE *GEORGICS* (38–26 B.C.)

In 38 B.C. the *Bucolics* had probably been completed, and Virgil already has a new and influential patron, Maecenas. In this year the young Horace joins the circle of *amici* and finds Virgil already installed there. Maecenas does not ask the talented young writers to participate directly in the vicissitudes of Octavian's party, but his influence is evident in a new generation of poetic works, Horace's *Epodes* and Virgil's *Georgics.*

The composition cost Virgil nearly ten years of work; an important impetus may have been the publication of Varro's work on agriculture in

37 B.C. In 29 B.C., as far as we know, the poem had reached a definitive stage and was recited to the princeps while he was returning victorious from his campaigns against Antony and Cleopatra. Such a long wait is not surprising; according to his biographers, Virgil worked assiduously on every detail and made many corrections. At the same time, the *Georgics* presupposes an extraordinarily rich reading, great Greek poetry (Homer, the tragedians, the Alexandrians) and Roman (Lucretius, Catullus, etc.), of course, but also technical material in prose and philosophical treatises of every sort. A lengthy process of composition is indicated also by the series of historical allusions scattered throughout the work. The end of the first book evokes an Italy in the grip of the civil wars, in which the rise of Octavian is merely a hope threatened by many dangers, a setting that makes sense only if conceived in the years around 36 B.C., when Octavian's power is not well established even in Italy and the devastations of the civil war are still fresh. In many other places the poem already shows the princeps as the triumphant bringer of peace to the world. This does not represent a discrepancy passively acquiesced in: Virgil has aimed at including within his poem, along with the victory of the new order, the wounds that led up to it.

The problem of the double ending

The date of the poem's publication thus coincided with that of Octavian's splendid triple triumph; but this raises a delicate problem. According to another ancient notice, preserved by the commentator Servius, Virgil altered the text of the poem, suppressing one part and substituting for it the story of Aristaeus (or, according to a variant, only the episode of Orpheus and Eurydice). The cause of this was the unexpected suicide of his friend Cornelius Gallus. Gallus's falling into disgrace with Augustus and his death are events of 26 (or, less probably, of the following year). What precisely was suppressed? Our source speaks of "praises" of Gallus. Praises of Pollio, Augustus, and Maecenas are frequent in Virgil, and it is clear what we ought to picture to ourselves. There are two large objections, however. If the work began to circulate in 29, as seems necessary, it is odd that these verses have disappeared without leaving any trace. Also, the epyllion of Aristaeus is more than two hundred verses long. If the suppressed passage was of comparable length, and it is practically necessary to suppose it was, since the books of the *Georgics* are all delicately balanced in length, what else will the fourth book of the "first edition" have contained? And to what was the praise of Gallus attached? One of the more attractive hypotheses is based on 4.290–93, a passage that deals with Egypt in relation to the *bugonia,* the spontaneous birth of the bees from the carcass of an ox. The text is rather incoherent and poorly transmitted; Egypt was Cornelius Gallus's province. All this would lead one to imagine a brief reference to Gallus. It will have been easier for Virgil to eliminate it without recourse to hurried rewriting. But in that case will the epyllion of Aristaeus and Orpheus really be a subsequent addition?

The notice of the reworking evidently poses grave problems. Still, no one has shown who could have invented it out of nothing, or why. What is certain, because it goes back to the common, legitimate experience of Virgil's readers, is that the narrative "digression" on Aristaeus, whenever it was written, has nothing false or improvised about it, not only because it is itself an example of great poetry but especially because strong ties link it to the fabric of the work and to the didactic structure of the context.

3. THE *GEORGICS*

The *Georgics* as a Didactic Poem

Hellenistic development of the didactic genre

The title *Georgics* promised the educated Roman reader something far more limited than the work's true ambitions. As earlier with the *Bucolics,* but to a much smaller extent, Virgil starts out from an immediate connection to Greek Hellenistic poetry: Aratus, Eratosthenes, and Nicander, authors of the third and second centuries who had brought about a change of taste and poetics within the tradition of the didactic genre. The *Phaenomena* and *Prognostika* of Aratus and the *Georgika* and *Alexipharmaka* of Nicander are works that contain, as the titles promise, instruction, or at least information, of the sort expected from didactic poetry. But this content is extremely specialized and restricted in the scope of its ambitions; compare what the didactic genre had been for Hesiod, Empedocles, or Parmenides. Not by accident do these Hellenistic poets often use scientific treatises in prose as their models: anyone deeply interested in the contents alone, whether theoretical or practical, could consult these technical sources directly (prose is the regular medium of information and textbook instruction). These poets do not claim to instruct a more or less ideal addressee by putting their own literary art at the service of great content. In their poems the addressee is more than anything else a formal survival, a mere given of the genre. The eagerness to argue and to persuade that is felt in early Greek poetry is replaced now by the passion to describe.

Predominance of form over content in the Alexandrian didactic genre

This passion, too, is relative. The refinement in the pursuit of form and the virtuosity of the versification unbalance these works on the side of form. They are formal devices that are designed almost to counteract the very subjects of instruction, to counteract the aridity or the humbleness of the subjects. Preference is given to apparently frigid subjects (poems on astronomical geography or the phases of the moon) or narrow, technical ones (the poisons of serpents, certain types of hunting). Aratus, the singer of celestial phenomena, has only a shallow knowledge of astronomy, but he uses the conventions of poetic language with great subtlety. His style is drenched in affected echoes of Homer. The unity of the work is assured by the uniformity of style and by the monographic specialization of the subject rather than by the genuineness of a didactic approach. For Virgil, the formal rigor of this poetry is a lesson to ponder. The alternation of catalogues, descriptions, and narrative digressions derives from a conscious pursuit of variety. But the *Georgics* would prove to be something quite different from the rendering into epic verse of technical treatises.

The tradition of didactic poetry had been lost at Rome and then, under the strong influence of Lucretius, revolutionized again. Pursuit of form and literary taste are, of course, an inheritance from Lucretius too. In his own day the Aratean didactic tradition had found practitioners such as the young Cicero or, later, Varro of Atax. But Lucretius had decisively distanced himself from this tradition. Guided by the trend of his own thought, he rediscovered by another path the line of the great didactic verse: the poetry of Hesiod, of Parmenides, of Empedocles. Each of these was the vehicle for an individual message addressed to a large community and directed towards well-defined goals of life transformation, liberation, and the re-foundation of wisdom—messages of salvation by means of knowledge. With this missionary impulse, the poetry of Lucretius surmounts the demands of the poetic game. Descriptions, digressions, and similes are meant to be strictly functional in relation to the structure of the work and its ideology. The beauty of the form is honey, an accessory to the severity of the philosophical medicine. The poet's commitment to the content of his own message of salvation becomes responsibility for form; it is the demand that controls the entire construction of his poetic discourse.

Virgil's reconciliation
of Lucretius and the
Alexandrians

Although more Alexandrian (and more neoteric) than Lucretius, Virgil feels closer to Lucretius than to the Alexandrians. Certainly, the taste for delicate things is not foreign to him, the drive to turn into poetry the physical details and minute realities that seem refractory to poetic diction. This may be the aspect in which Lucretius and the Alexandrians most lend themselves to reconciliation. The *Georgics,* not by accident, owe part of their fascination to such images as the crust on oil in a lamp (1.391), the behavior of the bees when ill (4.252), the consistency of earth crumbled between the fingers (2.248). It is Virgil's contribution to widening the horizons of literature that he sharpened perception and reworked as poetry realities that appeared negligible. *In tenui labor,* he says (4.6), "the subject of my labor is slender," a phrase that suggests a program: *labor* (like Greek *ponos*) alludes to the notion of poetry as formal toil; *tenue* (like Greek *lepton*) is the world of the bees, but the term has literary-critical connotations, of a subtle kind of poetry that eschews elevated subjects and pursues the greatest possible perfection of form. The phrase thus announces a poetic program that owes much to the Alexandrian pursuit of form and to Callimachus's poetics. Many passages of the poem in fact reveal direct emulation of such poets as Aratus, Eratosthenes, Nicander, and Varro of Atax. Technical sources in prose (Varro of Reate, but not he alone) are ransacked for material where the discourse becomes practical and the treatment systematic.

Nonetheless, the basic impulse for the *Georgics* came from a dialogue with Lucretius:

Fortunate the man who has been able to investigate the causes of
things and to set beneath his feet all fears, inexorable fate, the roar
of greedy Acheron. Fortunate, too, the man who knows the gods of

the countryside, Pan and aged Silvanus and the sister nymphs. That man cannot be affected by the fasces of the people, nor by the purple of a king, nor by the discord that troubles disloyal brothers, not by the Dacians who sweep down from the Danube, not by the happenings at Rome and the kingdoms condemned to destruction; and he never suffers with pity for the poor man or envy for the rich. He gathers the fruits that the branches and the fields have produced willingly and spontaneously: he knows nothing of the iron laws, of the madness of the Forum, of the public records. (2.490–502)

This is a new message of salvation and wisdom. It does not coincide with Lucretius's doctrine, nor is it directly opposed to it, but it measures itself by it, occupying a more withdrawn, more modest place. There are clear similarities. The wisdom of the peasant, who stands between the toil of work and the spontaneous generosity of the land, leads to a kind of material and spiritual self-sufficiency. This self-sufficiency is a response to the threat of the Roman Republic's social and cultural crisis; in the same way, the Lucretian sage freed himself at the same time from superstitious fears and from the pressure of history. There are also clear differences. Virgil's georgic space accepts traditional religion more openly; or rather, it is intimately linked with it. And the intellectual investigation of the mechanisms of the cosmos, undertaken in order to free men from the anxiety of living, gives way to a weaker understanding, one anchored in the rhythm of ordinary life. One has the impression that Lucretius looks to natural causes as the hidden manipulators of human culture. Virgil, however, seems to hold on patiently to all that civilizes and humanizes nature, and from this, to a great extent, is born the poetry of the *Georgics*.

The Augustan Background

Octavian in the Georgics

The georgic space of the poem has a protective enclosure about it. The young Octavian is portrayed as the only one who can save the civilized world from decline and civil war (1.500 ff.). We are in the period of crisis before Actium, in the uncertainty arising from the death of Caesar and from Philippi. Elsewhere, he appears already as a triumphator and bringer of peace: the triumph of Octavian in 29 (3.22 ff.); Caesar Augustus driving back the peoples of the East (2.170 ff.; 4.560 ff., the seal of the work), the divine figure who watches over the world and protects the life of the fields (1.40 ff.).

The Georgics and the era of the principate

The new princeps assures the conditions of security and prosperity within which the world of the farmers can find once again the continuity of its life. By virtue of this ideological frame, the *Georgics* can be considered the first true document of Latin literature in the age of the principate. The first proem is a clear instance. There, in a clear break with the Roman political tradition, the figure of the princeps appears as a deified sovereign, the unmistakable development of a Hellenistic tradition that had established itself at Rome only with difficulty. The princeps Augustus and, with him, his adviser Maecenas are introduced into the work not only as illustrious dedicatees (in the manner of Lucretius's Memmius) but also as genuine inspirers. Even if it is only through brief references (Augustus [1.40 ff.]; *tua, Maecenas, haud mollia iussa* [3.41]), these persons play the part of Epicurus and not of Memmius, inspirers of the teaching rather than interlocutors or, still less, pupils. The role of the addressees of the instruction is assigned instead to the collective figure of the farmer. Behind this addressee, present in the text as the point of orientation for the instruction, is portrayed the real addressee of the work: a public that knows the life of the cities and their crises. Formally dealing with the life of the country, the poem in the end also deals obliquely with the problems of city life and the more general problems of living.

Virgil and the national myth

It is difficult to believe that the *Georgics* were directly inspired by an Augustan program of agrarian reconstruction. If any such program was conceived in those years, it has not left any record in economic history. Furthermore, the image of the rural economy that emerges from the poem is an idealized retrospective construction and does not correspond to the reality of the period. The hero of the poem, if one can speak so, is the small landholder, the direct cultivator. Virgil has at best pale reflections of the great transformations then taking place—the extension of the latifundium, the depopulation of the countryside, the assignment of lands to the veterans, the transferral of certain forms of farm production from Italy to the provinces. Still more notable is the lack of any reference to slave labor, the real foundation of the farm economy. The idealization of the *colonus* evidently has a purely moral significance. At this level it is easier to accept the idea of close correspondences between Virgil and Augustan ideological propaganda. For example, the glorification of the traditions of the Italy of peasants and warriors, a world felt as unified, has for its background the climate of the war against Antony. Octavian's party presented it as a conflict between West and East, supported by the spontaneous harmony of an Italy that recognized in Octavian its charismatic leader. Nonetheless, the independence with which Virgil works out this legacy of ideas should not be neglected. Virgil's personal contribution to the national myth of Italian unity must have been very perceptible. The so-called Augustan ideology is not only a preexisting ideological device that the poet merely shows respect for; it is also, to an extent, the product of individual intellectual contributions. The complexity of this ideological world will become more evident if we examine the structure of the poem.

Structure and Composition

Subjects of the individual books

The themes of the four books are, respectively, the working of the fields, arboriculture, the raising of livestock, and beekeeping. These are four fundamental activities of the farmer, but not the only ones; comparison with Varro's *De Re Rustica,* for instance, shows that Virgil has been deliberately selective. The order in which these tasks are mentioned in the text describes a curve in which the contribution of human toil becomes less marked and nature becomes more the active agent. But nature is viewed in relation to man. The unceasing toil of the plowman, in the first book, corresponds in the fourth book to the terrible industry of the bees, animals that by their very nature become stands-ins for human diligence. The structure of the poem seems to move from the large to the small, from the cosmic laws of farm work to the microcosm of the beehives, but it is precisely the small world of the bees that comes closest to the nature of human culture.

Architecture of the Georgics

The work, therefore, is based upon a series of books possessing a clear, independent subject and linked together by an overall plan. Each book is introduced by a proem and contains digressive sections. Here, too, the lesson of Lucretius is evident, with two important differences: Virgil tends to weaken the logical constraints of the thought, the strong links of argumentation, the connections between one subject and another; yet the formal architecture of the poem becomes more controlled, more symmetrical. In this way a new poetic structure is born. The discourse flows naturally, sometimes willfully, concealing the logical transitions and moving along by associations of ideas or antitheses. At the same time, its dynamism ends by achieving balance in a carefully wrought architecture of the whole. This

Proems and concluding digressions

architecture is most evident in the symmetries between one book and another. Each book of the *Georgics* has a concluding "digression" of fairly uniform length: the civil wars (1.463–514), the praise of the rural life (2.458–540), the plague among the animals of Noricum (3.474–566), the story of Aristaeus and his bees (4.315–558). The proems clearly serve as hinges: those in books 1 and 3 are long and almost excessive, by comparison with the georgic themes of the individual books; those in books 2 and 4 are brief and strictly introductory. These formal resemblances also have a deeper function. Books 1 and 3 are thus paired, as they are also by the grand final digressions: the civil wars and the plague of the animals echo one another, and the horrors of history correspond to the disasters of nature. In relation to these dark endings, the effect of the other digressions is calming: the praise of the rural life is opposed to the threat of war, and the rebirth of the bees replies to the devastation of the plague (even though, with typically Virgilian allusiveness, the collective rebirth of the bees is not detached from the individual tragedy of the poet Orpheus). These great polarities between themes of death and themes of life give a meaning to the formal architecture. They make it into a chiaroscuro of ideas that provoke the reader's thoughts.

The contrasts in the Georgics

The *Georgics,* an object of devotion in periods of classicism, is in fact also a work of contrasts and uncertainties. The splendid balance of the style and the symmetry of the structure do not conceal the breaking out of apprehensions and conflicts. Man's toil is sent by divine providence as a kind of cosmic necessity (1.121 ff.), but the farmer's ideal recalls the myth of the Golden Age, when toil was not necessary, because Nature herself satisfied his needs. The simple, toil-filled life of the Italian farmer has led to the greatness of Rome, but Rome is also the City, seen as a place of degeneration and conflict, the opposite pole to the georgic ideal. Aristaeus, the patient farmer-hero, by following divine guidance, is able to regenerate his swarm; yet from this act of his, scarcely perceived, is born the irremediable unhappiness of the disobedient poet Orpheus.

The Story of Aristaeus and Orpheus

The concluding digression of book 4, unlike the others, is narrative in nature. In the Alexandrian manner, it is introduced as an *aition,* the "origin" and explanation of an astonishing fact, the bugonia. The ancient sources for natural history often speak of this property of the bees, that they can be born from the rotting of an ox's carcass. Virgil now recounts a story about the discovery of this miracle.

Summary of the story of Aristaeus and Orpheus

Aristaeus, a mythical figure, a great civilizer and discoverer of techniques, has lost his bees in an epidemic. Aided by his mother, the nymph Cyrene, the farmer-hero discovers the origin of the disease: unintentionally he had caused the death of Eurydice, the wife of the singer Orpheus. A seer now tells Aristaeus the poet's sad story: Having descended to Hades, he was able to bring his wife back to life by the power of his song. Then, by a fatal error, he had lost her again and forever. Then follows the forlorn death of the poet Orpheus. But Aristaeus derives a valuable lesson from this account. The curse is removed by a sacrifice of oxen, and miraculously the life of the new bees develops from the sacrificial victims.

Technique of embedded stories

Virgil has joined together two myths quite different from one another, rethinking both of them, as the analysis of the mythological sources proves, and arranging them in a framing structure. In this he was very much influenced by a tradition of Alexandrian and neoteric poetry, the tradition of interlocked stories. The most conspicuous example, and the one most present to Virgil, was certainly Catullus's poem 64. It was important that the two stories not be joined merely mechanically, as by a description or by a story within a story. The two stories in some way ought to recall one another. In achieving this, Virgil deploys great virtuosity: he joins the two stories by subtle narrative parallels. The farmer Aristaeus and the poet Orpheus both meet a series of difficulties: the former descends into a river as far as the fabled source of all waters; the latter descends into the abyss of the Underworld. The farmer-hero and the poet, by different paths, both in the end struggle against death. The two stories, parallel in their line of development (the search for a means to overcome a certain deprivation), are opposed in their conclusions: Orpheus's undertaking fails, since he does not respect a divine prohibition; Aristaeus's mission, by contrast, succeeds, since he is distinguished by scrupulous obedience.

The story of Orpheus and Aristaeus within the didactic genre

Yet the entire narrative is enclosed, in its turn, in the structure of the didactic poem. Virgil invites the reader to retrace a continuity. Several basic themes of the poem are found in disguise, that is, in a guise that is no longer didactic, but narrative. The figure of Orpheus fuses together the great possibilities of man, in that by means of his song he can even dominate nature, and the ultimate setback for man, the impossibility of defeating the natural law of death. The other civilizing hero points to a different path. Aristaeus, who in the mythic tradition "invents" hunting, the curdling of milk, the collection of honey, and so on, shows that the patient struggle against nature is maintained by a stubborn obedience to divine guidance and leads to the regeneration of the bees. In this way the narrative digression, allusively and by alteration of the myth, illuminates the substance of the didactic message and in turn is illuminated by it. Without prescribing a solution, Virgil allows his account to be pervaded by the contrast between different models of life.

4. FROM THE *GEORGICS* to the *AENEID*

The Georgics *as a lesson in form and subjective style*

The experience of the *Georgics* permits Virgil to think large without abandoning the requirements of the new poetics. The poem orchestrates a large diversity of themes, organizing them into a continuous whole, without neglecting thereby the refinement of the form. At the same time, Virgil enhances the subjective nature of his style. When describing, or when narrating, as in the miniature epic of Aristaeus, the poet immerses objects and persons in his subjective participation, or rather he immerses himself, for a moment, in the perspective of other subjects. He describes and narrates without rejecting emotion.

The expectation of an epic in Augustan culture

The expectation of a new epic was strong in Augustan culture. The poet who in the *Bucolics* refused to sing of *reges et proelia* (6.3) now is willing to accept this burden, but he brings a new sensibility with him. In the proem at the middle of the *Georgics* he gives us to understand that he is even willing to sing the deeds of Augustus (3.46–48). The Ennian tradition, which was opposed by the *poetae novi,* had never been altogether extinguished, but epic served for the most part to celebrate contemporary achievements. The people of Virgil's day thus must have been inclined to expect a kind of new *Caesareid.* The actual result could not have failed to astonish them.

5. THE *AENEID*

Homer and Augustus (I)

The confrontation with Homer: correspondences and differences

The new epic in fact did not propose to continue Ennius, but to replace him; thus a direct confrontation with Homer was inevitable. According to the ancient grammarians, the purpose of the *Aeneid* was twofold: to imitate Homer and to praise Augustus, "beginning with his ancestors." A first glance at the work shows that this is a reasonable simplification. The twelve books are conceived primarily as a response to the forty-eight books of the two Homeric poems.

The first six books of the *Aeneid* recount Aeneas's difficult voyage from Carthage to the shores of Latium, with a retrospective review of the events that had brought him from Troy to Carthage. With the beginning of book 7 the Trojans have arrived at the mouth of the Tiber, the place indicated by destiny, and there begins the narrative of a war (*dicam acies,* "I shall sing of battles" [7.42]) that will end only with the death of Turnus in the last verse of book 12. For this reason it is common to talk of an "Odyssean" half of the *Aeneid* (1–6) and an "Iliadic" half (7–12). This refers to a great structural partition, undoubtedly intended by the poet. This does not mean that there will not be instances of the *Odyssey's* influencing the latter part of the poem or of the *Iliad's* influencing the earlier part, but if we look at the great lines of Virgil's project, the basic choice is evident. The *Iliad* tells of the events that lead to the destruction of a city; the *Odyssey* narrates, as a sequel to this war, the return home of one of the destroyers. These two epic stories, these *fabulae,* are represented by Virgil in reverse sequence: first the voyages, then the war. But this arrangement involves an inversion of the contents as well. Aeneas's voyage is not a returning home like Odysseus's; it is basically a voyage towards the unknown. The war waged by Aeneas does not serve to destroy a city, but to construct a new city, which will be the ancestor of Rome. This complex transformation of the Homeric models has no precedent in ancient poetry. Apollonius of Rhodes had to some extent "contaminated" narrative sequences drawn from both Homeric poems, and Naevius's *Bellum Poenicum* appears to have been indebted to the *Odyssey* for Aeneas's voyage and to the *Iliad* for the narratives of war, but in each case we are dealing only with a remote impetus (on Naevius see p. 46).

Contamination and continuation of Homer

For convenience, one might distinguish different levels of transformation. First, the *Aeneid,* as we have seen, is a particular contamination of the two Homeric poems. Second, there is also a continuation of Homer. Aeneas's deeds follow upon the *Iliad* (Virgil's book 2 recounts the last night of Troy, which in the *Iliad* was glimpsed only in prophecy) and link up with the *Odyssey* (in book 3 Aeneas partly follows the track of Odysseus's adventures, meeting perils that the Greek hero had already come across). In this way Virgil repeats the experience of the epic cycle, the chain of epic narratives that combined Homer's poetry into a sort of continuum.

Repeating and surpassing the Homeric war

Third, the *Aeneid* includes within itself a sort of Homeric repetition. For instance, the war in Latium is often viewed as a repetition of the war at Troy, but it is certainly not a merely passive echoing. At the start the Trojans find themselves besieged and near defeat, as if they were condemned to repeat their destiny. In the end, however, the Trojans are victorious, and Aeneas slays his chief opponent, Turnus, as Achilles slays Hector: in the new *Iliad* the Trojans are victorious. But it is easy to see that the repeating is also a surpassing of Homer. The war, through struggles and sufferings, will lead, not to destruction, but to the construction of a new unity. In the end, Aeneas contains in himself the victorious Achilles and especially Odysseus, who after so many attempts retakes his country and restores peace.

The prehistory of Augustus

This brings us to Virgil's other intention: "to praise Augustus, beginning with his ancestors." Virgil's poem is separated from the Augustan present by an almost astronomical distance. The ancients placed an interval of about four centuries between the destruction of Troy and the foundation of Rome. The events of the *Aeneid* are treated as historical, although, technically speaking, they do not belong to *Roman* history. Virgil's Roman readers find themselves in the midst of a Homeric world, removed from the familiar present by a legendary space of more than a thousand years.

This displacement permits Virgil to regard the world of Augustus from a distance, just as in the *Georgics* the displacement towards the historyless world of the countryside allowed the poet a broader and more detached perspective. The *Aeneid* is full of prophetic passages that give an Augustan orientation to the story, but it does not thereby cease to be Homeric.

Homeric narrative techniques and Augustan Rome

The narrative techniques that allow Virgil to regard Augustan Rome from a distance are in fact Homeric. In the *Iliad* Zeus prophesies the destiny of the heroes and the destruction of Troy. In the *Aeneid* (1.257–96 and elsewhere) Jupiter safeguards not only Aeneas's destiny but also the future greatness of Augustus, who in the end will bring back the Golden Age. In the *Odyssey* Odysseus descends to Hades and obtains a vision of his own destiny. In the *Aeneid* Aeneas learns from the kingdom of the dead not only of his personal future but also of the great moments in Rome's history (6.756–886). In the *Iliad,* the poem of warrior might, the description of Achilles' shield introduces a sort of cosmic vision (scenes of nature, city images). In the *Aeneid* the description of Aeneas's shield is crowned by the image of the city of Rome, caught in the critical moments of its historical development (8.626–728). Thus a difficult balance is attempted between the tradition of the heroic epic and the need for a historical-celebratory epic.

The Legend of Aeneas

Italian legends and the story of Aeneas

The point of intersection between the Homeric dimension and the Augustan dimension was given to Virgil by an old legend. Ancient Italy knew a series of foundation legends tied to the Trojan War. Heroes of the Greek side and the Trojan, disbanded or in exile, are said to be the founders, or the colonizers, of Italian places. Among these stories the legend of Aeneas acquired particular significance in a long process that extended from the fourth to the second century B.C. In Homer he was an important, but not a principal, Trojan hero, his house seeming destined to rule over Troy after the extinction of Priam's line (*Iliad* 20.307 ff.). Later, however, Aeneas's flight from burning Troy with his father Anchises on his back became popular in figurative art as well as in literature. A link was soon established with ancient Latium: on one side, a Greek literary tradition worked in this direction; on another, as recent archaeological discoveries have shown, the cult of Aeneas as founder-hero is attested at Lavinium, south of Rome, from the fourth century onwards.

Roman power and the success of the myth of Aeneas

It does not appear that Aeneas was ever regarded as the founder of Rome or that he had a particular cult in archaic Rome. From the second to the first century, however, the figure of Aeneas acquired growing fame among the Romans. The reasons are political and not easy to disentangle. Chiefly, the myth of the Trojan origin of the Romans drew support from Aeneas; the most noble Trojan hero to have escaped from the catastrophe would thus be connected by genealogy with Romulus, the founder of the city. This permitted Roman culture to claim a kind of independent equality with the Greeks precisely at the time when Rome was securing hegemony over the Greek Mediterranean. The Trojans were confirmed as great antagonists of the Greeks by the Homeric myth. Their revenge would be carried out by Rome. (The third great power of the Mediterranean, Carthage, was also opportunely linked to the legend of Aeneas through its queen Dido.) Rome thus legitimized its new power by means of a deep historical background. Another factor in Aeneas's popularity depends on a circumstance of internal politics. Through the figure of Aeneas's son Ascanius/Iulus, the *gens Iulia,* a noble Roman family, claimed very noble origins for itself. A member of this clan, Julius Caesar, and later his adoptive son Octavian Augustus found themselves masters of Rome's worldwide empire. Here, then, the circle is formed that joins together Virgil, Augustus, and the epic hero.

Aeneas as ancestor of Augustus

Summary of the Aeneid

The *Aeneid* traces the legend of Aeneas from the last day of Troy up to Aeneas's victory and the fusion of Trojans and Latins into a single people. The plan of the work is as follows:

Book 1. Juno cannot forget her hatred towards what remains of the Trojan people. A storm, provoked by the goddess, shatters Aeneas's ships and compels him to put ashore in Africa, near Carthage. Aided by his mother Venus, the hero finds a warm welcome with the queen of the Phoenician city, the widow Dido. The queen, also an exile, asks her guest to recount the end of Troy.

Book 2. Aeneas's account: during the destruction of the city the hero, with divine protection, succeeds in fleeing along with his aged father, his little son, and the penates, the symbol of a race's continuity; his wife Creusa, however, is lost to him.

Book 3. Aeneas's account: leaving the Troad, the Trojans realize, after various uncertainties and puzzlements, that a new country awaits them in the west. After describing several miraculous happenings, the retrospective account concludes with the death of the aged Anchises.

Book 4. The tragic story of Dido's love. The Carthaginian queen, abandoned by Aeneas, who must follow the course intended by fate, kills herself, cursing Aeneas and prophesying eternal hatred between Carthage and the descendants of the Trojans.

Book 5. The Trojans make a stop in Sicily. Nearly the whole book is taken up with the funeral games in honor of Anchises.

Book 6. Arriving at Cumae, in Campania, Aeneas is obliged to consult the Sibyl and to gain access to the world of the dead. There he meets persons from his past: Deiphobus, fallen at Troy, Dido, dead on his account, the unfortunate pilot Palinurus, and especially his father Anchises. Anchises reveals to him the distant future. The world of the dead contains the heroes of the future too, the leaders who will make Roman history.

Book 7. Strengthened by this vision and by his father's advice, Aeneas disembarks at the mouth of the Tiber and, on the basis of signs foretold, recognizes the promised land. He now makes a pact with king Latinus. Juno launches Allecto, the demon of discord, against the pact; assailed by Allecto, Latinus's wife Amata and the Rutulian prince Turnus, the man betrothed to Latinus's daughter, stir up the war. With the first incident the pact with Aeneas is broken, and the dynastic marriage between Aeneas and Latinus's daughter Lavinia is off. A powerful coalition of Italian peoples marches on the Trojan camp. Lavinia, a new Helen, stands at the center of the discord.

Book 8. In great difficulty, Aeneas, upon divine advice, sails up the Tiber with a small detachment. Here, in the place where Rome will rise, he finds the support of Evander, the king of a small nation of Arcadians. Along with Evander's son Pallas, Aeneas next secures a powerful ally: the Etruscan coalition that has risen up against Mezentius, the cruel tyrant of Caere, now expelled, and an ally of Turnus. The divine aid for Aeneas culminates in the gift of a set of armor made by Vulcan; the shield is adorned with scenes from future Roman history.

Book 9. In Aeneas's absence, the Trojan camp finds itself in a critical situation. Turnus and his allies obtain partial successes. The courageous sacrifice of the young Trojans Nisus and Euryalus during a nocturnal expedition leads to no results.

Book 10. Aeneas, together with his allies, bursts upon the scene and tips the balance of the war. But Turnus in single combat kills the young Pallas, Aeneas's ally and protégé, and strips him of his sword belt; he puts on the sword belt as a reminder of his proud victory. Aeneas in exchange kills Mezentius, Turnus's strongest ally.

Book 11. After his first victory, Aeneas mourns the dead Pallas. His peace offerings lead to no result. Turnus again tries the luck of battle. In a great cavalry engagement another hero from the Latin side perishes, the virgin warrior Camilla.

Book 12. Wearied by his failures, Turnus must accept a decisive duel with Aeneas. The nymph Juturna, at Juno's urging, causes this truce also to fail. The battle starts again. When the victory of the Trojans is certain, Juno is reconciled with Jupiter and obtains his agreement that there will remain no trace of the Trojan name in the new people. Aeneas defeats Turnus in a duel; he hesitates over whether to spare his life, but when he catches sight of the young Pallas's sword belt, which Turnus is wearing, he kills him in a burst of indignation.

Reworking of the historical-antiquarian sources

From what we know of the historical-antiquarian sources used by Virgil, it is evident that the poet has thoroughly restructured the traditional data about Aeneas's arrival in Latium. The varying notices about a war with the Latins, or with a part of them, followed by the formation of an alliance, have been fused into a new, single war sequence, concluded by a historic conciliation. The war has been represented by Virgil as an encounter between Trojans and Latins. The latter form a coalition with numerous Italian peoples, many of whom, significantly, boast Greek ancestry; the former form a coalition with the Etruscans and with a small Greek population settled on the soil of the future Rome. In the effort to create a true Roman national epic, Virgil sets in motion, already in the period of the origins, all the great forces from which "modern" Italy will be born. No people is completely excluded from making a *positive* contribution to the genesis of Rome. The Latins themselves, after many sacrifices, will be reconciled and will thus form the core of the new people. The vast Etruscan power, extending from Virgil's Mantua all the way to the Tiber, is seen as playing a positive role. Even the Greeks, the traditional adversaries of the Trojans, supply a decisive ally, the Arcadian Pallas, and are presented as the noblest element in Rome's prehistory.

The Aeneid *is not a historical poem*

The *Aeneid* is thus a work of dense historical and political significance; it is not, however, a historical poem. The contents are dictated by a selection of the material according to a dramatic principle that recalls Homer more than Ennius. Despite the expectations aroused by the title, the work does not even draw a complete picture of Aeneas's life. We take leave of the protagonist before he can savor his triumph; it is not even quite clear whether he will live for much longer, and his future as a deified hero is glanced at only obliquely.

The New Epic Style

The newest and greatest quality of Virgilian epic style lies in the reconciliation of the maximum of freedom with the maximum of order (as the German scholar Friedrich Klingner was wont to say).

Rigidity of the neoteric hexameter

Virgil labored over the epic meter, the hexameter, bringing it to a culmination of both regularity and flexibility. The neoterics had established tight restrictions on the use of the caesuras, the alternation of dactyls and spondees, and the relation between syntax and meter. Catullus's poem 64 represents an extreme case of this, an extreme reaction to the rhythmic-verbal "anarchy" of the archaic poetry, a reaction naturally influenced by the formal discipline of the Alexandrians. This discipline involved an effect of monotony, which becomes more pronounced as the narrative text becomes longer. The placement of the words is not merely artificial but also rigidly fixed (hexameters formed by two adjective-noun pairs symmetrically placed are typical) and the rhythmic unity of the verse rejects clear sense-pauses within the line, with a resulting effect of almost unbending rigidity.

Order and freedom in the Virgilian hexameter

Virgil shapes his hexameter to be the vehicle of a long, continuous narration, articulated and varied. The rhythmic structure of the verse is based on a limited number of principal caesuras in certain preferred configurations. Thus a fundamental regularity is established that is indispensable to the epic style. At the same time, the combination of principal caesuras and secondary caesuras permits a notable variety of sequences. And the phrase is thereby set free from any slavish fixity in relation to the meter. The periods may be large or small; they may cross the boundaries of the metrical units or coincide with them. The hexameter thus adapts itself to a variety of expressive situations: broad, calm descriptions, or aroused and pathetic exchanges. The rhythm of the narration finds a formal reflex in the varying proportion of dactyls and spondees. Alliteration, a formal device characteristic of archaic Latin poetry, in Virgil becomes a controlled, motivated device that emphasizes pathetic moments, links key words with one another, creates phonetic symbolism, and produces echoes between different points in the narrative.

The traditions of the epic genre required an elevated language, removed from everyday usage. Thus it is natural that the *Aeneid* is the Virgilian work richest in archaisms and poeticisms, two categories that often coincide, but not always. Some of the archaisms pay homage to Ennius's style or to the strong expressiveness of early tragedy. Others simply form part of the established literary language. Poeticisms that are not archaic are, for instance, the calques from Greek or the neologisms. On the whole, however, this is not the most significant feature of the Virgilian style. A contemporary, cited in the Donatan life of Virgil (sec. 44), said that Virgil had invented a new *cacozelia,* a new "mannerism": "a mannerism that was elusive, neither swollen, nor thin, but made up of ordinary words." Ordinary words—a large percentage of the Virgilian vocabulary consists of terms not conspicuously poetic, "neutral" words, so to speak, employed in prose and the language of everyday usage (i.e., the Latin spoken at Rome by the educated classes). Virgil tends to avoid Grecisms, archaisms, and novel literary formations, which, though differing in their origins, are functionally alike in being opposed to this medium level of the language. Instead, the novelty

consists in new junctures among words. *Recentem caede locum,* "a place fresh with slaughter"; *tela exit,* "he leaves the missiles (dodges them)"; *frontem rugis arat,* "plows the forehead with wrinkles"; *caeso sanguine,* "blood slain" (i.e., "of the slain"); *flumen,* "stream (of tears that flow)"; *ventis dare vela,* "to give the sails to the wind"; *lux aena,* "light of bronze." Some of these junctures are familiar to us, in part because of Virgil's strong influence upon the Western literary tradition, but they must have struck the Roman reader as the revelation of new possibilities for the language. Others are more difficult to translate because they do violence to sense and syntax: *rumpit vocem,* not "breaks the voice" but "breaks the silence"; *eripe fugam,* "snatch away flight," based on the normal *se eripere,* "escape." This type of development of the everyday language has no precedents in Latin poetry; one thinks rather of Sophocles or Euripides. The experimentation with syntax operates with a vocabulary that remains simple and direct. In its effects, however, it proves to be a renewal; the words undergo a process of distancing that gives importance and a new perceptibility to the meaning in context.

The new epic style can also adapt itself to a series of traditional requirements. From Homer onwards, narrative is supposed to be gradual and without intervening gaps, "full," so to speak. Recurring, repeated actions lend themselves to verbal repetitions. Fixed, natural epithets accompany objects and persons, almost as if to fix their place in the world. The numbers of warriors and of ships, the names of the characters, the origins of objects are all elements to be catalogued with precision. Virgil accepts this tradition: the *Aeneid,* unlike his other writings, gives much space to formulaic procedures.

Virgil tends to preserve these forms and at the same time to charge them with new sensibility. The epithets, for example, tend to involve the reader in the situation, often even in the psychology of the persons of the action.

The narrative suggests more than what it says explicitly. For instance, in 1.469–71 Aeneas is looking at the pictures recording the tragic war at Troy. Among other scenes is Diomedes carrying out a nocturnal massacre:

> niveis tentoria velis
> adgnoscit lacrimans, primo quae prodita somno
> Tydides multa vastabat caede cruentus.

("Aeneas, weeping, recognizes the snowy-white canvas of the tents, betrayed by the first sleep, and Diomedes laying waste to them, bloodied with slaughter"). The reader perceives the intense white of the tents only to see them stained with blood; the red of the bloodshed is not openly stated by the text but is contained entirely in the epithet *cruentus*. And the perception of these details intensifies his participation in the state of Aeneas's soul, the more intensely as the reader must collaborate, make the hints explicit, fill in the empty blanks.

The subjective style and the intervention of the poet

The fundamental characteristic of Virgil's epic style is thus the increase of subjectivity. Greater initiative is given to the reader, who should respond to the stimuli, to the characters, whose point of view colors the narrated action at times, and to the narrator, who is present at several levels of the story. This increase of subjectivity would run the risk of breaking down the structure were it not checked in a number of ways. Objectivity is secured by the presence of the poet, who allows the individual subjective points of view to emerge in the text but is always responsible for recomposing them into a unitary project. To recognize and study the complexity of the style means to touch the very complexity of the ideological discourse that takes shape in the *Aeneid*.

Homer and Augustus (II): The Motives of the Defeated

The ideological subjectivity of the Aeneid

The development of subjectivity, which in a very schematic way one could contrast with Homeric objectivity, concerns not only the epic style and the technique of narrative but also the ideology of Virgil's poem. The *Aeneid* is the story of a mission willed by fate that would make possible the foundation of Rome and its salvation by Augustus. The poet is the guarantor and spokesman of this project, and he focuses his account on Aeneas, the bearer of this fated mission. (It is obvious therefore why Aeneas is not a character like the others.) Thus Virgil fully assumes the legacy of the Roman historical epic: his poem is a national epic, in which a collectivity needs to reflect itself and feel itself united.

And yet there is more to the *Aeneid* than this undertaking. Below the objective line willed by fate, characters move about in conflict with one another; the narrative adapts itself to contemplating the conflicting motives. The feelings of the characters (not only the "positive" characters such as Aeneas) are constantly in the foreground.

a) The motives of Dido

Take Dido, for example. Roman culture in the period of the conquests represented the Punic Wars as an encounter between different parties. Roman identity was based on the great opposition to Carthage. The enemy is treacherous, cruel, fond of luxury, devoted to perverse rites. For Virgil, however, the war with Carthage does not arise from difference: back at the time of its origins, the war arises from an excessive and tragic love between parties who are similar. Dido is defeated by destiny, as Carthage will be, but the text makes a place for her motives and transmits them.

b) Turnus the suppliant and Aeneas the avenger

This is also the case with Turnus. The war that Aeneas wages in Latium is not viewed as a necessary sacrifice. The peoples divided by the war are from the very beginning substantially similar and kindred to one another. To emphasize this point, Virgil even maintains that the Trojans, through their ancestor Dardanus, have Italian origins; in this sense Aeneas, too, like Odysseus, is one who returns. The war is a tragic error willed by demoniacal powers. It is in effect a fratricidal war (this is an incessant theme in the *Aeneid* even before it is in Neronian and Flavian poetry). The slaying of Turnus, prepared for by the death of Pallas, appears necessary. Turnus, disarmed and wounded, asks for pity. Aeneas has learned from his father to beat down the proud and to spare the one who submits. Turnus is a proud hero, but now he is also *subiectus.* The choice is difficult. Aeneas kills him only because at that crucial moment the sight of Pallas's sword belt overwhelms him in a fit of deadly anger. Thus, in the final scene of the story the pious Aeneas resembles the terrifying Achilles who takes his revenge upon Hector. The *Iliad,* however, ends with a pitying Achilles who finds himself no different from Priam.

c) The involvement of the reader

It is clear that Virgil demands a great deal of his readers. They must simultaneously appreciate the fated necessity of the victory and remember the motives of the defeated; look at the world from a high perspective (Jupiter, fate, the omniscient narrator) and share in the sufferings of the individuals; accept both epic objectivity, which from on high contemplates the great providential cycle of history, and tragic subjectivity, the quarrel of individual motives and relative truths. At this level, too, and not only at the level of style, Virgil shows he has profoundly pondered the lesson of the Greek tragedians, from whose influence his poem derives a very marked openness to the problematic elements in life, which renders it different from a typical national epic. In this light it is easy to understand why the reception of the work has remained vital and problematic long after the passing away of its Augustan message.

6. LITERARY SUCCESS

Virgil and Western literature

Virgil's *Nachleben* is Western literature. Virgil disliked publicity and cultivated a difficult Muse, but in vain. Anecdotal evidence suggests that already during his lifetime he was regarded not only by professional colleagues but also by many lay readers as Rome's greatest living poet; and the grammarian Caecilius Epirota had made him a school author by about 25 B.C., even before his crowning work, the *Aeneid,* had been published. At the time of his death Virgil left instructions that that epic, unfinished and (perhaps only for this reason) unsatisfactory, be burned—again in vain:

Augustus entrusted its publication to Varius, and it went on to become one of the central literary works of Western culture. Perhaps it is only with regard to Virgil that T. S. Eliot could begin a lecture entitled "What is a Classic?" by asserting as something obvious that "whatever the definition we arrive at, it cannot be one that excludes [him]—we may say confidently that it must be one which will expressly reckon with him." For Virgil, almost despite himself, became a European classic. Like his hero Aeneas, he rescued his idols from historical oblivion by betraying them, by transporting them, with considerable reluctance and many a backward glance, to a new domain, where he laid the foundation for a new cultural and political empire that he would not live to experience and that in many regards would have profoundly troubled him.

Antiquity   For the Romans, with a speed and completeness that has few parallels in world literature, Virgil had already become a classic. His works are quoted so often in antiquity that even if they had been lost, they could still be reconstructed in large measure. During his own lifetime, fellow poets such as Horace and Propertius admired him, from a distance, and parodies of his works flourished (Numitorius already composed *Antibucolica* in protest against his earliest poems), but apparently no poet earlier than Ovid dared to try to rival him. Very early he became a model author for grammarians (Caecilius Epirota; C. Julius Hyginus, the head of the Palatine Library) and for rhetors (thus already during the reigns of Augustus and Tiberius, on the testimony of Seneca the Elder), and throughout antiquity he remained one of the fundamental school texts (replacing republican epic poets such as Ennius and thereby condemning their works to full or partial destruction); one surviving papyrus transmits *Georg.* 4.1–2 written six times, another *Aeneid* 2.601 written seven times. But such scholarly attentions could be directed not only to admiring the beauties of his art. Such *obtrectatores Vergili* as Herennius, Carbilius Pictor, Q. Octavius, and Perellius Faustus wrote polemical tractates with titles such as *Aeneidomastix* (modeled on the Greek *Homeromastix*) and *Homoiotetes* in which, misunderstanding the character of Virgil's profound traditionality, they attempted to demonstrate his lack of originality by collecting what they called his *furta*, thefts from earlier authors, and thereby, in spite of their polemical intentions, helping to make a fundamental positive contribution to the development of Latin philology and elaborating lists of Virgil's "sources" (transmitted by Macrobius and Servius) that, properly used, can still be of great help for modern scholars.

In the first century A.D., Virgil remains the supreme Latin author (even if, during the reign of Nero, Seneca and his circle sought originality by ostentatiously preferring Ovid). It is to this period that most of the minor imitations of his poetry, later gathered into the *Appendix Vergiliana,* are likely to belong (these will be discussed in part 4, when we come to the age in which these pseudo-Virgilian works were composed); his verses are found scratched on the walls of Pompeii, and Petronius delighted in creating variations, sometimes obscene, on verses of the *Aeneid.* Towards the end of the century, Virgil's popularity seems to have reached a high point (coinciding, perhaps not accidentally, with Quintilian's conspicuous anti-Senecan polemics): Statius asked his *Thebaid* to follow the *Aeneid* "at a distance" and to revere its footsteps (*Theb.* 12.816–17), and Silius Italicus not only imitated Virgil's poetry with almost religious scrupulosity but even collected mementos of the poet, bought the land on which his tomb was located, and celebrated his birthday every year as his own.

Ancient exegesis   The foundations of the scholarly tradition of exegesis of Virgil's poems were laid in the first and second centuries A.D. by Valerius Probus and thereafter especially by C. Julius Hyginus, L. Annaeus Cornutus, and Aemilius Asper. Although the running commentaries for students that have survived (above all Servius, but also the smaller collections of scholia and the rhetorical commentary of Tiberius Donatus) all date from the fourth century, they preserve a considerable amount of earlier material, much of it deriving from this period, while the essays on Virgil in Macrobius's *Saturnalia* give us an idea of what earlier scholarly *hypomnemata* might have looked like. The rhetoricians, too, took their examples from Virgil's poems and debated whether he was more an orator or a poet; one declamation survives, composed by Ennodius and purporting to be a speech by Dido upon the departure of Aeneas. The ancient allegorical tradition of Virgil exegesis, already established by the time of Donatus and Servius, culminated in the sixth century in the work of Fulgentius, who interpreted the twelve books of the *Aeneid* as the twelve stages of man's life from infancy to old age, while the widespread conviction that Virgil knew everything, including the future, led to the use of his verses as oracles and prophecies *(sortes Vergilianae)*. And through late antiquity Virgil continued to be a favorite object for scholastic poetry; exercises on Virgilian themes and in Virgil's style flourished (in the fourth century, for example, Avienus rewrote Virgil's poems in iambic trimeters), as did so-called centos, in which every single verse was derived unchanged from Virgil but, because it was put into a different order and context, its meaning was completely changed (thus, e.g., the *Medea* "written" around 200 by Hosidius Geta and Ausonius's *cento nuptialis*). When such poetic exercises are transmitted in fragmentary form on papyri, we sometimes cannot be sure whether they are to be attributed to advanced students or to professional poetasters.

Manuscript tradition   No other Latin author survives so massively, so anciently, and so excellently as Virgil. We have three ancient manuscripts, almost complete, written in the fifth or sixth century in rustic capital scripts (known in the early Middle Ages as *litterae Virgilianae,* precisely because so few codices in this script survived for any other author), and four others, in more fragmentary condition, dating from the fourth or fifth century (of these ancient manuscripts, two have important illustrations and one, decorated initials); and of the surviving Latin papyri whose authors can be identified, Virgil appears on more than half (one papyrus, which dates perhaps from the first or second century, may have been written only a century later than his death).

For Christian late antiquity, Virgil is by far the most popular Latin poet: Jerome was intimately familiar with his works; Augustine cannot retell the story of his life without seeing crucial episodes through the lens of the *Aeneid;* the Christian poetess Proba even composed a Virgilian cento about Jesus. This continued unchanged throughout the Middle Ages, when Virgil (despite occasional protests by such figures as Alcuin and Ermenrich) was a central school author and the fourth eclogue and the *Aeneid* were the most widely read Latin poems; in Chaucer's *House of Fame* Virgil stands alone on a column of gleaming tinned iron. Inevitably, however, the pagan poet had to be Christianized if he was to remain a supreme authority for a changed world. According to medieval legend, St. Paul visited Virgil's tomb in Naples and wept because Virgil had died too soon to be converted by him; yet in mystery plays, Virgil appeared together with the Sibyl and the Prophets as a witness to the Incarnation. For those with eyes to see, the fourth eclogue was evidently an announcement of the birth of the Redeemer—thus already Lactantius and Eusebius, and somewhat later Augustine and Prudentius, among countless others—and Vincent of Beauvais could still report that three pagans had been converted to Christianity by reading this eclogue (and who can be sure that he was wrong?).

But it was above all the *Aeneid* that not only furnished, particularly in book 6, ample material for the many medieval legends of Virgil as a sage, a magician, a prophet, and a saint (confusion with *virga,* the term for a magician's wand, may even have contributed to the transformation of the Latin *Vergilius* into the vernacular *Virgil*) but also provided the greatest challenges and the greatest rewards to allegorical interpretation. The epic was seen as an image of human life in which wisdom and virtue (represented by Aeneas) triumphed with the help of the gods over folly and passion (represented by Dido and Turnus). Fulgentius's twelve-book allegory was drawn upon seven centuries later by Bernardus Silvestris, who explained books 1–6 as the six stages of life (the shipwreck onto the shores of Carthage in book 1, birth; the fires of Troy in book 2, the passions of youth; the visit to the Underworld in book 6, the passage to the next life). Similar readings are expressed or implied by such authors as John of Salisbury and Dante. Indeed, Dante's reverence for Virgil represents one of the high points of the Latin poet's *Nachleben* and one of the deepest sources for the Italian poet's creativity ("tu se' solo colui," he tells him in *Inferno* 1.86–87, "da cu'io tolsi / lo bello stile che m'ha fatto onore"). He respects "l'altissimo poeta" as the symbol of the highest limits attainable by unaided human wisdom and chooses him as his guide through *Inferno* and most of *Purgatorio* (where he must turn over his charge to Statius, who was born later and hence could be saved).

But the *Divine Comedy* was not the only poetic form assumed by Virgil's medieval reception. From the ninth to the twelfth century Virgil spawned new medieval epic genres, of myth, of chivalry, and of philosophy, such as Ekkehard's *Waltharius* and Walter of Châtillon's *Alexandreis.* In the second half of the twelfth century the *Roman d'Énéas* (adapted in Heinrich von

Veldeke's *Eneide*) provided an Ovidian continuation to the *Roman de Troie,* elaborating in detail upon Aeneas's love affair with Lavinia. And in the fourteenth century Petrarch (who admired Virgil and Cicero above all other Latin authors and whose carefully annotated manuscript of Virgil is preserved in Milan) wrote twelve Latin eclogues and an epic, the *Africa,* closely modeled on the *Aeneid,* and Boccaccio composed a *Theseid,* which contained not only the same number of books as the *Aeneid* (which is not remarkable) but even the same number of lines (which is).

Renaissance

Virgil remained one of the most important school authors long after the Middle Ages (though, unsurprisingly, in the sixteenth century Jesuit schools banned certain eclogues and the fourth book of the *Aeneid*). Imitations of his poems continued to dominate literature in the Renaissance and for another couple of centuries. The *Eclogues* found in Mantuanus a writer of Latin bucolic poems whose very name betrayed his literary affiliation and in Sannazaro an imitator so influential that his sentimental nostalgia for a lost Arcadia distorted readings of Virgil's tougher bucolic poetry for centuries, while in English poetry Spenser's *Shepherd's Calendar* created a tradition that was deconstructed in Milton's *Lycidas* and resynthesized in Pope's four *Pastorals.*

The Aeneid *and Renaissance epic*

But it was neither the *Eclogues* nor, of course, the *Georgics* that above all captured readers in this period, but rather the *Aeneid.* The epic was studied closely by humanist scholars, many of whom still accepted allegorical interpretations of it (thus in Latin Alberti and Coluccio Salutati, who cited Bernardus Silvestris, and in the vernacular Landino); it was "completed" by the addition of a thirteenth book that brought its plot to a natural close; it was set above Homer as the most perfect ancient epic (thus Vida, *De Arte Poetica* 1527, and generally until such eighteenth-century critics as Lessing); and it founded the Renaissance genre of historical epic, which went on from Petrarch to flourish in such poets as Camões, Tasso, and Milton, to subside in Ronsard's *Franciade* (unfinished, in four books), and finally to die out in Pope's unfinished *Brutus* and in Voltaire's unread *Henriade.* Parallel and complementary to these serious epics flourished a tradition of travesties and burlesques, in which the historical distance between Virgil and modern times was transposed into a stylistic tension between lofty characters and vulgar or obscene language and incidents (G. Lalli, *Aeneida travestita,* 1633; P. Scarron, *Le Virgile travesti,* 1648–53).

Translations

Virgil continued to be read in Latin for centuries. Shakespeare probably knew at least the earlier books of the *Aeneid* in Latin, while Milton's *Paradise Lost* attempts to provide an English equivalent not only for Virgil's epic themes but even for his syntax, diction, and, as far as possible, meter. But in Britain he was also particularly well served by translations. In the sixteenth century the epic was translated into Scottish verse by Gavin Douglas (the *Aeneid*) and into English by Henry Howard, earl of Surrey (*Aeneid,* books 2 and 4); in the seventeenth century it was translated by Dryden (the *Aeneid*). It was translated in the eighteenth century by Christopher Pitt (the *Aeneid*) and Joseph Warton (the *Eclogues* and the *Georgics*), and in the same century Eugenios Bulgaris translated the *Georgics* and the *Aeneid* "back" into Homeric Greek hexameters (already in antiquity Arrian had translated the *Georgics* into Greek, and a Greek translation of the fourth eclogue seems to lie behind a speech of Constantine's reported by Eusebius). Even those who could read Virgil in no language at all were not spared contact with his themes: although he was never as popular in music and the visual arts as Ovid, he did provide material for Purcell's *Dido and Aeneas* (Nahum Tate composed the words) and later for Gluck's *Orfeo ed Euridice* and Berlioz's *Les Troyens,* as well as for paintings by Tiepolo, Claude Lorrain, Turner, and others (thereby reviving a tradition found in ancient mosaics and wall paintings).

Modern period   Schiller still admired and translated Virgil, but with the advent of Romanticism, his fortunes suffered a decline; for certain tastes (thus Goethe) he could no doubt seem too literary, too reflective, too elitist. And although he has continued to remain one of the most popular school authors wherever Latin is taught, over the past two centuries he has gradually been displaced to the margins of modern culture. During the same period, however, he has continued to fascinate lyric poets in France (Hugo, Baudelaire, Valéry), Italy (Pascoli), and England (Tennyson, T. S. Eliot), and at least one novelist, Hermann Broch, has used the story of the poet's dying wish to burn the *Aeneid* as the basis for a profound meditation on life, death, art, and history (*Der Tod des Vergil,* 1945). If the nineteenth century could sometimes read Virgil as an apologist for imperialism and the various Fascist movements of the twentieth century could canonize him as a propagandist of ruthless service to the state, since the Second World War he has tended more to be prized as a poet of peace who loved bucolic tranquillity and abhorred the horrors of war. And over the last several decades, with the rise of environmentalism, first the *Eclogues* and then even the *Georgics* have enjoyed modest waves of renewed popularity.

Virgil the model of a poetic career   Beyond the influence exercised by his individual works, Virgil has also provided the Western literary tradition with its most compelling and durable model of a poetic career, one beginning with small, unambitious, personal works (the *Eclogues*), moving on to more difficult tasks of greater intellectual complexity and social significance (the *Georgics*), and culminating in a single massive work that subsumes all the earlier ones and provides an epic mirror for the destiny of a nation (the *Aeneid*). The influence exercised by this model can already be traced in the first century A.D. in some of the poems of the *Appendix Vergiliana* and in Lucan. And for many centuries it continued to provide poets with a guideline for their own development and with suggestions for what kind of poem to write next, through the Middle Ages (when the three genres involved were known as the "rota Virgilii") and the early modern period (when it fascinated such poets as Spenser, Milton, and Pope), and even into Romanticism (it stands behind the English Romantic poets' dream of concluding their career with a single great philosophical epic) and the twentieth century (Proust, Joyce, and Musil all begin with smaller and more personal works before moving on to their larger epics). If even today we sometimes tend to regard with suspicion a young author who presumes to begin his career with a large-scale epic or an aging one who has still not moved on from smaller and more precious literary modes, this is due not only to widespread general assumptions about what is appropriate to the different stages of human life but also, more specifically, to Virgil.

BIBLIOGRAPHY

The standard modern critical texts are those of R.A.B. Mynors (Oxford 1972) and M. Geymonat (Turin 1973, with fuller apparatus); the Loeb is by H. R. Fairclough (2 vols., London 1934–35), but there is a better bilingual edition of the *Eclogues* by Guy Lee (Liverpool 1980, with brief notes). There are numerous modern translations; note esp. those of C. Day Lewis with introductions by R.O.A.M. Lyne (*Eclogues* and *Georgics,* Oxford 1983) and J. Griffin (*Aeneid,* Oxford 1986), as well as D. West's prose version of the *Aeneid* (Harmondsworth 1990).

The last complete scholarly commentary in English was that of J. Conington and H. Nettleship (ed. 3 London 1881–83), which remains invaluable. There is an introductory Macmillan commentary on the complete works by T. E. Page (3 vols., London 1894–1900), which is complemented rather than replaced by the similar set by R. D. Williams (London 1979, 1972–73). For the *Eclogues,* see the editions of R. Coleman (Cambridge 1977) and, mainly for its bibliography, E. Coleiro (Amsterdam 1979); on the *Georgics,* those of R. F. Thomas (2 vols., Cambridge 1988) and R.A.B. Mynors (Oxford 1990). There is a commentary with brief notes on the whole *Aeneid* by J. W. Mackail (Oxford 1930, occasionally useful), and James Henry's *Aeneidea* (Edinburgh 1873–89) offers acute if sometimes eccentric discussion of selected passages. Modern work has concentrated on editions of individual books. The commentaries of R. G. Austin on books 1, 2, 4, and 6 (Oxford 1971, 1966, 1955, 1977) are particularly suggestive; note also the massive commentary on book 4 by A. S. Pease (Cambridge, Mass. 1935) and the less detailed commentaries on books 7 and 8 by C. J. Fordyce (Oxford 1977), on book 8 by P. T. Eden (Leiden 1975) and K. W. Gransden (Cambridge 1976), and on book 11 by K. W. Gransden (Cambridge 1991). There is a major edition of book 10 by S. J. Harrison (Oxford 1992). Among those in other languages might be mentioned the complete commentaries by C. G. Heyne and G.P.E. Wagner (ed. 4 Leipzig 1830–41, Latin) and T. Ladewig (Berlin 1876–86, German) and esp. the great commentary on book 6 by E. Norden (ed. 3 Stuttgart 1926, German). The plain text of the *Eclogues* by C. Hosius (Bonn 1915) has much useful information on sources and analogues in the brief Latin notes.

The critical literature is vast, but few works attempt to deal with the whole *oeuvre.* Note, however, J. Griffin's brief *Virgil* (Oxford 1986) and the more substantial books of W. F. Jackson Knight, *Roman Vergil* (ed. 2 Harmondsworth 1966) and B. Otis, *Virgil: A Study in Civilized Language* (Oxford 1964), as well as in German, F. Klingner's *Virgil* (Zurich 1967). There are a number of collections of essays, by S. Commager (Englewood Cliffs 1966), T. A. Dorey (London 1969), F. Robertson (*Meminisse iuvabit: Selections from the Proceedings of the Virgil Society,* Bristol 1988), and I. McAuslan and P. Walcot (Oxford 1990). For the views expressed above, see esp. G. B. Conte, *The Rhetoric of Imitation* (Ithaca 1986). On the *Eclogues,* H. J. Rose, *The Eclogues of Vergil* (Berkeley 1942), still makes a convenient starting point; among more recent work may be mentioned M.C.J. Putnam, *Virgil's Pastoral Art* (Princeton 1970), E. W. Leach, *Vergil's Eclogues: Landscapes of Experience* (Ithaca 1974), J. Van Sickle, *The Design of Virgil's Bucolics* (Rome 1978), and P. J. Alpers, *The Singer of the Eclogues* (Berkeley 1979). There is an English survey of work to 1977 by W. W. Briggs, *ANRW* 31.2 (Berlin 1981) 1265–1357. On the *Georgics,* L. P. Wilkinson, *The Georgics of Virgil* (Cambridge 1969), is again a convenient starting point; more recent works include M.C.J. Putnam, *Virgil's Poem of the Earth* (Princeton 1979), G. B. Miles, *Virgil's Georgics: A New Interpretation* (Berkeley 1980), P. A. Johnston, *Vergil's Agricultural Golden Age* (Leiden 1980), D. O. Ross, *Virgil's Elements* (Princeton 1987), C. Perkell, *The Poet's Truth* (Berkeley 1989), and J. Farrell, *Vergil's Georgics and the Traditions of Ancient Epic* (New York 1991). On the *Aeneid*, there is a collection of articles edited by S. J. Harrison, *Oxford Readings in Vergil's Aeneid* (Oxford 1990), with an introduction offering one view of twentieth-century Virgilian scholarship; see also W. R. Johnson, *Darkness Visible* (Berkeley 1976) 1–22, W. Suerbaum, *Vergils Aeneis: Beiträge zu ihrer Rezeption in Gegenwart und Geschichte* (Bamberg 1981), and the introduction to the Italian collection by F. Serpa, *Il Punto su Virgilio* (Rome 1987). The two most important books are both in German, R. Heinze, *Virgils epische Technik* (ed. 3 Leipzig 1915), and V. Pöschl, *Die Dichtkunst Virgils: Bild und Symbol in der Aeneis* (ed. 3 Berlin 1977); however, an earlier edition of the latter was translated into English by G. Seligson as *The Art of Vergil* (Ann Arbor 1962), and the essence of Heinze's views, especially on the source material, is summarized in H. W. Prescott, *The Development of Virgil's Art* (Chicago 1927). There is a brief and jejune *Introduction to Virgil's Aeneid* by W. A. Camps (Oxford 1969); brief, too, but better are R. D. Williams, *The Aeneid* (London 1987), and K. W. Gransden, *Virgil: The Aeneid* (Cambridge 1990). The "pessimistic" view of the epic was developed especially by scholars associated with Harvard; see, e.g., A. Parry, "The Two Voices of Virgil's Aeneid," *Arion* 2 (1963) 66–80, W. V. Clausen, "An Interpretation of the Aeneid," *HSCP* 68 (1964) 139–47, both frequently reprinted, and M.C.J. Putnam, *The Poetry of the Aeneid* (Cambridge, Mass. 1965). Recent work within this tradition includes two works by R.O.A.M. Lyne, *Further Voices in Vergil's Aeneid* (Oxford 1987) and *Words and the Poet* (Oxford 1989). On the other side, there have been two notable attempts to reestablish an "Augustan" reading: P. R. Hardie, *Virgil's Aeneid: Cosmos and Imperium* (Oxford 1986), and F. Cairns, *Virgil's Augustan Epic* (Cambridge 1989). But in general there are fewer book-length studies in English of the *Aeneid* than might be expected; in addition to those already mentioned, however, note K. Quinn, *Vergil's Aeneid: A Critical Introduction* (London 1968), and G. Williams, *Techniques and Ideas in the Aeneid* (New Haven 1983). In German might be mentioned also F. J. Worstbrock, *Elemente einer Poetik der Aeneis* (Münster 1963), V. Buchheit, *Virgil über die Sendung Roms* (Heidelberg 1963), and A. Wlosok, *Die Göttin Venus in Vergils Aeneis* (Heidelberg 1967).

On the relation of the *Aeneid* to earlier texts, see G. N. Knauer, "Virgil and Homer," *ANRW* 31.2 (Berlin 1980) 870–918 (with Kopff on Cyclic epic and Briggs on Hellenistic epic in the same volume; Knauer's massive *Die Aeneis und Homer* [Göttingen 1964] contains indexes that can be used without knowledge of German), R. R. Schlunk, *The Homeric Scholia and the Aeneid* (Ann Arbor 1974), K. W. Gransden, *Virgil's Iliad* (Cambridge 1984), W. Clausen, *Virgil's Aeneid and the Tradition of Hellenistic Poetry* (Berkeley 1987), M. Wigodsky, *Virgil and Early Latin Poetry* (Wiesbaden 1972), and in Italian, A. Barchiesi, *La Traccia del modello* (Pisa 1985). On Virgil's later reception, note esp. D. Comparetti, *Virgil in the Middle Ages,* trans. E.F.M. Benecke (London 1895), and the collection of essays edited by C. Martindale, *Virgil and His Influence* (Bristol 1984).

The famous ancient commentary of Servius was edited by G. Thilo and H. Hagen (Leipzig 1878–1902); this is gradually being replaced by the "Harvard Servius" (vol. 2 Lancaster 1946, vol. 3 Oxford 1965). For an introduction, see A. F. Stocker, "Servius servus magistrorum," *Vergilius* 9 (1963) 9–15.

On all aspects of the *Aeneid,* the monumental Italian *Enciclopedia Virgiliana* (Rome 1984–) is invaluable. The bibliographies by W. Suerbaum in *ANRW* 31.1 (Berlin 1980) are excellent; see also M. T. Morano Rando, *Bibliografia virgiliana* (Genoa 1987).

Horace

Quintus Horatius Flaccus was born on 8 December 65 B.C. at Venosa, a Roman military colony on the border between Apulia and Lucania, to a modest family. His father was a freedman, probably a former public slave, and owned a small farm at Venosa; later, after moving to Rome, he was a collector in auction sales. Despite his modest social position, Horace was given the best education. When his first studies were completed at the local school, his father brought him to Rome so that he could attend the school of the grammarian Orbilius. An admirer of the archaic poets, Orbilius was accustomed to use lashes to persuade his pupils to study the *Odusia* of Livius Andronicus; Horace would later coin the epithet *plagosus,* "lavish with blows," for him. At about the age of twenty, Horace, as was the custom for young men of means, went to Greece to complete his studies. At Athens he deepened his knowledge of philosophy by listening to the lectures of teachers such as Cratippus of Pergamum, a Peripatetic philosopher, and Theomnestos, an Academic. His student career was violently interrupted, however. Greece at the time was the scene of historic events. Caesar's murderers had made it their principal base of operations, and it was natural that the young Horace, fresh from his philosophical studies, was attracted by the ideals of *libertas* (as well as enticed by the outstanding career prospects offered). He enrolled in Brutus's republican army and was given the command of a legion with the title of military tribune, which was a great thing for the son of a freedman. The defeat at Philippi (42 B.C.) interrupted his military career; with bitter self-irony he would later say that like Archilochus, Alcaeus, and Anacreon, he had thrown away his shield. He was able to return to Rome in 41 B.C., thanks to an amnesty, but the farm at Venosa had been confiscated by the triumvirs, and he needed to take employment as a *scriba quaestorius* in order to earn a living. He also began to write poetry and came into contact with poets and other writers. Probably around the middle of 38 B.C. Virgil and Varius present him to Maecenas, Octavian's minister, a man of letters and a patron of writers. Nine months later Maecenas admits him to the circle of his friends. Probably in 33 B.C. Maecenas presents him with a farm in the Sabine country, which would give him financial peace of mind and assure him a much-valued refuge from the business and inconveniences of Roman life. From that point on, his life goes by without significant events, articulated only by the publication of his works under the patronage of Maecenas and later, with Maecenas's progressive withdrawal from the scene, of the princeps himself. Horace's relation to Augustus was quite close, one of devoted friendliness, but without servility: when the princeps asks him to become his personal secretary, Horace is able to decline the offer with grace and firmness. In 8 B.C. Maecenas died, fondly recommending the poet to the kindliness of Augustus. But Horace followed him to the grave only two months later, on 27 November.

WORKS

Epodes: Seventeen short poems, written between 41 and 30 and published together with the second book of the *Satires.* The name refers to the metrical form: an epode is, properly speaking, the shorter verse that follows a longer verse, forming a couplet with it. Horace calls them *iambi,* which refers to the rhythm that predominates in the *Epodes* and at the same time alludes to that aggressive tone that had been traditionally associated with Greek iambic poetry from its beginnings. The collection is arranged by the editorial criterion of meter that had been established in the Alexandrian period: poems 1–10 are in alternating iambic trimeters and dimeters, 11 in alternating iambic and elegiambic trimeters; in poems 12–16 the hexameter alternates with another verse, mostly the trimeter; the last poem, 17, in iambic trimeters, is not epodic. The collection is characterized by a variety of subjects. The prefatory poem is addressed to Maecenas: Horace declares himself ready to share with his friend any danger whatever—perhaps those connected with the expedition to Actium? Among the remainder various groups can be distinguished: poems of invective (8 and 12 against an old, lustful woman, 5 and 17 against the witch Canidia, 4 against a parvenu, 6 against an unknown slanderer, 10 against a poetaster; 3 is a playful invective against garlic and against Maecenas, who prepared it for him); erotic epodes (11, 14, 15); civil epodes (7 and 16, deprecations of the fratricidal war; 9, celebration of the battle of Actium); isolated, the "gnomic" epode 13 (an invitation to drink on a winter's day) and the ambiguous epode 2 (a praise of the rustic life put into the mouth of a hypocritical moneylender).

Satires: A first book of ten poems (from a minimum of 35 hexameters to a maximum of 143), dedicated to Maecenas, was published perhaps in 35, and in any event before 33. In 30 there appears, along with the *Epodes,* the second book (only eight satires, but the third, considerably longer than the rest, has 326 verses). In total the *Satires* amount to more than two thousand verses. The internal chronology is difficult: 1.7 and 1.2 are regarded as among the oldest; 1.2 is referred to in 1.4, which is certainly earlier than 1.10. The subjects vary: some satires have a literary-programmatic subject (in addition to 1.4, one satire that serves as an envoi, and another that serves as a preface: 1.10 and 2.1); 1.1 deals with human inability to be satisfied and with greed; 1.2 is against adultery, 1.3 about indulgence in dealing with defects; 1.5, modeled on Lucilius's *Iter Siculum,* is a diary of a voyage (Horace along with other friends of his circle had accompanied Maecenas on a diplomatic mission to Brundisium); 1.6 is a meditation on his own social condition and relations with Maecenas; 1.7 recounts a squabble between a Greek merchant and a proscribed man from Praeneste; in 1.8 a statue of Priapus recounts a night of spells; 1.9 is a kind of very lively mime, in which the poet brings himself on stage struggling with a bore through the streets of Rome; 2.2 sets forth the arguments of a farmer from Venosa, Ofellus, against table luxury; 2.3 is a dialogue between the poet and Damasippus, a Stoic neophyte, who recounts a long sermon of the philosopher Stertinius against the four capital vices in order to demonstrate the Stoic paradox that all men, except the philosopher, are mad; in 2.4 Catius expounds his gastronomic theory; 2.5 has a mythological-fantastic setting of the Menippean type and presents Tiresias instructing Ulysses in how to build up his estate by hunting for legacies; in 2.6, as in the corresponding satire of the first book, Horace reflects upon himself and his relations with his patron Maecenas; 2.7 is another dialogue, between the poet and his slave Davus, who, referring at second hand to the teachings of the philosopher Crispinus, demonstrates another Stoic paradox, that all men, except the sage, are slaves; in 2.8 Fundanius recounts to Horace a dinner in the house of the rich man Nasidienus, who has pretenses to gastronomy (something similar was in Lucilius, and Petronius would take his cue from this satire for the *Cena Trimalchionis*).

Odes (in Latin, *Carmina*): A collection of three books (88 poems in total) was published in 23 B.C. Horace had worked on it for about seven years: among the poems that can be dated, the earliest is 1.37, a song of joy for the death of Cleopatra, which occurred in 30 B.C. He returned to lyric poetry six years later, to compose, at Augustus's behest, the hymn that a chorus of twenty-seven girls and as many boys was to perform during the celebration of the Ludi Saeculares: the *Carmen Saeculare,* in Sapphic meter, an invocation to the gods, Apollo and Diana especially, asking that they assure prosperity for Rome and the government of Augustus. Horace devoted himself to lyric poetry again later and added to the previous books a fourth book of the *Odes,* with fifteen poems. The last one that can be dated (4.5) refers to Augustus's return from the north, in July of 13 B.C. Horace's lyric poetry experiments with various meters: predominant are the Alcaic strophe (37 poems out of 103), the minor Sapphic strophe (25 poems), and the Asclepiadic strophe in its various forms (34 poems). The other meters are represented for the most part in isolated examples. All told, the four books of the *Odes* contain 3,034 verses, to which are added the 76 verses of the *Carmen Saeculare.* Some odes are very brief (the famous 1.11 and also 1.38 are only eight verses apiece, for instance); some are longer, up to a maximum of 80 verses (ode 3.4).

The arrangement of the poems within the collection deserves attention. The impetus had come from Alexandrian editions of the Greek lyric poets. In Alexandrian poetry and then, by imitation, in Roman poetry, poetry books were organized artistically, in a significant architectural structure. The opening and closing odes are addressed to persons of note (1.1 to Maecenas, 2.1 to Pollio, 4.1 to Paulus Fabius Maximus, and 4.15 to Augustus), and often, in accordance with an established tradition, they deal with questions of poetics (1.1, 2.20, and 3.30 are the most famous). The second, the penultimate, and the central positions are also privileged. The poet often juxtaposes poems of similar content (e.g., 4.8 and 4.9 on the immortality conferred by poetry), and in one case he creates a genuine cycle (3.1–6), signaled by a proem (3.1) and by an intermediate proem (3.4) and dedicated to themes of national identity (the so-called Roman odes). But the preferred principle for the organization of the book seems to be *variatio*, both from the point of view of metrical form (the first nine poems of book 1 are in nine different meters, and 1.11 is in still another meter) and from that of tone and content (alternations of political subjects and private subjects, high style and light style). Unlike modern lyric poetry, the odes of Horace rarely express free meditation or introspection; they almost always have a dialogic structure and are addressed to a "you" who may be a real person (this is relatively more common, even though less common than in neoteric poetry), or an imaginary one (the women and the men with Greek names are usually considered such), or a god or the Muse, a collectivity, even an inanimate object.

Epistles: The first book of the *Epistles* was published in 20 B.C. Horace had worked on it for three years, after the publication of *Odes*, books 1–3. The collection comprises twenty poems in hexameters, from the 16 verses of the fourth epistle to the 112 of 1.18; in total the verses number slightly more than 1,000.

The prefatory epistle is dedicated to Maecenas and is a sort of combined presentation and justification of the new literary form; 1.2, to Lollius, is a meditation upon the moral lessons to be gotten from reading Homer; 1.3, to Florus, asks for information on the literary activity of Tiberius's friends; 1.4, to Albius (Tibullus), contains Epicurean precepts to his friend, the poet; 1.5, to Torquatus, is an invitation to dinner; 1.6, to Numicius, deals with the philosophical theme of impassiveness; 1.7, to Maecenas, is a graceful request for independence, and especially for the right to live at a distance from Rome; 1.8, to Albinovanus Celsus, is about the disturbing torpor that afflicts the poet; 1.9, to Tiberius, is a letter of recommendation; 1.10, to Fuscus, is on city life and country life; 1.11, to Bullatius, concerns the mania for travel and the *strenua inertia,* "frenzied torpor"; 1.12 is addressed to Iccius, administrator of Agrippa's estates, who is interested in philosophy; 1.13 contains instructions for Vinnius, who is charged with delivering to Augustus the first three books of the *Odes;* 1.14, to the bailiff of the Sabine farm, is about country life in contrast with life at Rome; 1.15, to Numonius Vala, requests information for a stay at Salerno and Velia; 1.16, to Quinctius, is on the ideal of the *vir bonus;* 1.17, to Scaeva, and 1.18, to Lollius, contain pieces of advice on how to deal with the powerful men of the world; in 1.19, addressed to Maecenas and on a literary subject,

Horace polemicizes against servile imitators and defends his own lyric poetry; 1.20, addressed to the book itself, is a farewell to the *Epistles* and a foretelling of the reception that awaits them.

The second book, which may have been published posthumously, was composed in the years 19–13. It contains two long epistles on literary subjects: the first, to Augustus, criticizes admiration for the archaic poets and examines the development of Roman literature; the second, to Julius Florus and more personal, is a sort of farewell to poetry, with a memorable picture of the Roman writer's daily life and a lengthy consideration of the pursuit of philosophical wisdom.

The epistle to the Pisos, the so-called *Ars Poetica,* is placed by many in the second book. Its date is debated: it is probably later than 13, the date of the epistle to Augustus, but many locate it between the first book of the *Epistles* and the *Carmen Saeculare.* The *Ars Poetica* is a treatise in 476 hexameters that sets forth basically Peripatetic theories on poetry, especially dramatic poetry. According to Porphyrio, Horace's source was Neoptolemus of Parium, a poet-grammarian of the third century B.C. With some difficulty a structure has been discerned within the work: verses 1–294 speak about the *ars,* 295–476 about the *artifex;* the first part, in its turn, seems divided into halves dealing with *poesis* (the content of the work, 1–44) and *poema* (the style, 42–294).

SOURCES

The principal source is Horace himself, whose works are strewn with autobiographical notices and allusions to contemporary reality; in the case of the latter it is often useful to consult the explanations of the ancient commentators. Several important Horatian manuscripts contain a *Vita Horati,* taken from Suetonius's *De Viris Illustribus;* in modern critical editions of the poet it is generally prefixed to the text.

1. THE *EPODES* AS POETRY OF EXCESS

The Epodes *and the youthful phase of Horace's poetry*

Horace's iambic writing seems linked, as the poet himself would declare, to the youthful phase of his poetic activity and to the particular conditions of life that marked the period immediately following the experience of Philippi:

decisis humilem pennis inopemque paterni
et laris et fundi, paupertas impulit audax
ut versus facerem

("I was on the ground, my wings clipped, deprived of the house and the farm of my father: insolent poverty drove me to compose verses" [*Epistles* 2.2.50–52]).

It is natural to link with this situation of hardship Horace's harsh polemics, loaded tones, and violent poetic language. This makes the *Epodes* in many regards an isolated case in Horace's literary writings and gives us an image of the poet far different from the stereotyped one with which Horace has always been associated in European culture (good taste, affability, warm humanity, detachment from passion, sense of proportion).

The Epodes *and their models*
Some interpreters of Horace, however, are rightly hesitant to link the *Epodes* so directly (and so mechanically) with this personal experience. What is required is the ability to judge how many of the distinctive features of this poetry go back to the rules of the genre, to the imitation of the models—that literariness that is not merely implicit but conscious and professed and is found as a characteristic throughout Horace's poetry:

> Parios ego primus iambos
> ostendi Latio, numerosque animosque secutus
> Archilochi, non res et agentia verba Lycamben.

("I was the first to transplant to Latium the iambs of the poet from Paros, following the rhythms and the spirit of Archilochus, not the subjects and the words that persecuted Lycambes" [*Epistles* 1.19.23–25]).

Of imitation in Horace and the Augustan poets generally we will speak later, in connection with the *Odes.* For the moment it is important to observe how this declaration, respectful and proud at the same time, is a claim to versifying ability, the merit of having transferred into Latin poetry the meters of Archilochus (and in fact the greater part of Horace's epodic

Horace and Archilochus: dependence and originality
schemes do have counterparts in the fragments of the poet from Paros). Yet Horace explicitly claims originality as well. He states that he has borrowed the meters *(numeri)* and the aggressive inspiration *(animi)* from Archilochus, but not the contents *(res)* and "the words that persecuted Lycambes" (Lycambes was the father of Neobule, Archilochus's fiancée; according to the tradition, the poet's invectives led to the suicides of father and daughter). Horace does not mean merely that the *Epodes* are not translations and that he draws on a Roman and personal reality; he probably also means to indicate several particular features of his Archilochean inspiration. If a sensibility that was irritated by hardship and bitterness could make him feel an affinity with the inflamed passion and fierce polemical spirit of Archilochus, the differences between him and Archilochus ought not to have escaped him. Archilochus expressed the hatreds and rancors, the civic passions and disappointments, of a Greek aristocrat of the seventh century B.C. Horace was writing in a Rome dominated by the triumvirs and would soon be joining Octavian's entourage. He was the son of a freedman and had barely escaped from a difficult and dangerous political experience. Horace's aggression can be directed only at smaller targets: unimportant, anonymous, or even fictitious people, such as a usurer, a parvenu, a sorceress, an aged woman. All this has contributed to create an impression of literary artificiality, and it has even been said that sometimes the *res* do come from Archilochus, without Horace's being able to recreate the *animi.*

Epode 10
A famous example is the tenth epode. In a kind of reversed *propempticon* (a poem wishing someone a good voyage) Horace wishes for Maevius to be shipwrecked. The model for this is a poem of Archilochus (or possibly Hipponax), a significant fragment from which, the "Strasburg epode," has

fortunately come down to us. But Horace proves to be quite distant from the model, not so much because he cannot reproduce the seriousness and drastic ferocity of the Archilochean invective as because unlike Archilochus, whose enemy is an ex-friend who has injured and betrayed him, Horace mutes the personal character of the invective (we are not told who Maevius is or why Horace has it in for him). In this case, as in others, the violence of the threats and the curses seems rather empty, sometimes even playful (as it is in the epode on garlic, the third).

Yet undoubtedly the Archilochean spirit, apart from the question of the real or fictitious character of the individual targets, must have seemed suitable to Horace for expressing the anxieties and passions, the fears and indignation, of an entire generation: consider, for example, epode 4, which is a reaction to the sudden social upheavals connected with the Roman revolution, or the apprehensions expressed in the epodes relating to the civil wars.

The Iambs *of Callimachus and the pursuit of variety*

Influenced also by the *Iambs* of Callimachus, another of the Greek models important for the *Epodes,* Horace must have felt that variety was essential for an iambic collection. Working simultaneously on the *Satires* and the *Epodes,* he seems to reserve for the latter that multiplicity of themes, tones, and stylistic levels that Roman tradition assigned to satire. A very distinct group, for example, is composed of the erotic epodes, poems of love that develop motifs and situations of Hellenistic erotic lyric and reproduce even their language and pathetic tone. The tradition of the rustic idyll, together with ideological themes that are more specifically Roman, can be sensed behind the ambiguous praise of the country in epode 2. And from the point of view of expression as well, despite the fact that the typical language of the *Epodes* is taut and charged and dwells on the cruder and sometimes more repugnant aspects of reality, Horace's iambic poetry can also accommodate a more careful diction: alongside the poet of excess, we glimpse the poet of moderation.

2. THE *SATIRES*

An Entirely Roman Genre: Horace and Lucilius

Lucilius as Horace's model

In Quintilian's judgment, *satura tota nostra est;* that is to say, he did not know Greek authors who could have served as reference points for the authors of this literary genre. And Horace, too, in the programmatic poems that give the coordinates of his satiric poetry, points to Lucilius as the inventor of the genre. This attribution must have been something of a surprise. Leaving aside the early dramatic *satura,* about which we are poorly informed (it must have consisted in rudimentary stage action, accompanied by the flute, with mime, dance, and clownish fights), Ennius had written satire, to be sure. Here, too, we lack sufficient information. It is generally believed that his *Satires* were characterized by variety, of meter, style, and content, and included autobiographical references, gnomic thoughts, anecdotes, fables, and dialogues—many elements that would reappear in later satiric poets. But Horace does not name Ennius, and Quintilian, too, would exclude him from the line that goes from Lucilius to Horace, Persius, and Juvenal.

The aggressiveness of satire

Lucilius therefore was identified as the one who had established the constituent features of satiric poetry. A fundamental element, particularly in the literary culture of the ancients, originated with him: the choice of the hexameter as the metrical form of satire. Lucilius had practiced this literary genre principally as a tool of personal aggression, of mordant criticism. The aggressiveness appeared to Horace as so characteristic an element that he was moved to link Lucilius, not with Ennius, but with the poets of Greek Old Comedy, Eupolis, Cratinus, and Aristophanes:

> siquis erat dignus describi, quod malus ac fur,
> quod moechus foret aut sicarius aut alioqui
> famosus, multa cum libertate notabant.
> hinc omnis pendet Lucilius

("If there was someone who deserved to be held up to ridicule, because he was a scoundrel or a thief or an adulterer or a killer or otherwise notorious, they branded him as such directly. Lucilius depends on this entirely" [*Satires* 1.4.3–6]).

Lucilius thus organized his representation of contemporary society, and of the ruling class in particular, along these same lines. In his poetry, though, he had included a great variety of themes and concerns: literary polemics, philosophical discussions, linguistic or grammatical questions, conversations. The autobiographical element was the most important of all. Lucilian satire accommodated facts, persons, and observations connected to the personal life of the poet. Horace would be conscious of this inheritance, too, from his master:

The autobiographical element

> ille velut fidis arcana sodalibus olim
> credebat libris, neque si male cesserat, usquam
> decurrens alio, neque si bene: quo fit ut omnis
> votiva pateat veluti descripta tabella
> vita senis.

("He used to entrust his secrets to books as if to faithful companions, and he had no recourse to anything else, not if things went badly for him, nor if they went well: thus it happens that the whole life of this old man stands before one's eyes, as if it were painted on a votive tablet . . . " [*Satires* 2.1.30–34]).

Satire and Diatribe: Horatian Morality

Aggressiveness and moral inquiry

To Horace's literary conscience his satire was "Lucilian" because he inherited from Lucilius the two distinctive traits of aggressiveness and autobiography. Yet Horace himself did not underestimate the differences that separated him from the *inventor* of the genre; he emphasized, however, chiefly those related to style, criticizing Lucilius's careless facility, especially in satires 1.4 and 1.10. But there were also important differences in the form of the contents. In Lucilius, though he devoted attention to themes of moral thought and reformulated motifs of the diatribe tradition, the relation between diatribe and aggressiveness was not clear. But a stable, organic connection between these two components is characteristic of Horace's satire. In him the personal attack is always tied to a purpose of moral inquiry. For the gratuitous pleasure of aggression, an Aristophanic trait still alive in Lucilius, Horace substitutes the need to analyze the vices (excess, stupidity, ambition, greed, fickleness) by means of critical observation and the comic representation of the characters. This empirical moral inquiry does not set out to proselytize, and it seeks neither to convert others to a preformed model of virtue nor to reform the world, but only to identify a path for a few, for himself and an enlightened group of friends, cutting across the mistakes of a society in crisis. In this sense Horatian satire is intimately linked, even more than his lyric poetry, to the circle of poets, writers, and politicians gathered around Maecenas, their intelligent guide. Lucilius's aggressiveness is conspicuously transformed precisely at the moment when its inheritance is being claimed. Lucilius virulently attacked eminent citizens, adversaries whose status he shared. This would not have been possible for the son of a freedman; what is more important, in order to derive instruction from the conduct of one's peers through criticizing their mistakes, it was not necessary to choose targets of high social level. Instead, Horace considers a small world of irregular types: courtesans, parasites, artists, swindlers, street philosophers, profiteers, small fry. As his father had taught him, he learns from those near him, those he meets in the street:

> insuevit pater optimus hoc me,
> ut fugerem exemplis vitiorum quaeque notando.

("that good man, my father, taught me to shun vices by having me learn them one by one from examples" [*Satires* 1.4.105–6]).

Horace's morality thus has its roots in education, in traditional good sense—and Horace proudly points out the Italian, rustic ingredient in his wisdom—but it is constructed with materials developed by the Hellenistic philosophies, which also reached Horace through the filter of the diatribe, that is, the tradition of popular philosophical literature, illustrated by dialogues and anecdotes.

The basic objectives of Horace's inquiry were *autarkeia* (inner self-sufficiency) and *metriotes* (moderation, the just mean). Neither of these concepts belongs to a specific philosophical sect, and in any event distinctions of doctrine were weak in the tradition of the diatribe. *Autarkeia* is the property of nearly all the schools, which were committed to protecting the individual from the blows of fortune and from slavery to external goods. If the extreme formulations of it are Stoic-Cynic, the demand for *autarkeia* also could not be alien to Epicureanism, which limited the rights of *voluptas* to the satisfaction of a few natural needs. The morality of the just mean had

Horatian satire and the circle of Maecenas

Horace's targets

Horace and the diatribe: autarkeia *and* metriotes

received its most coherent formulation with the Peripatetic school, but the concept belonged to the oldest Greek wisdom, and the pursuit of pleasure could not be confused by rigorous Epicureans with a practice of excess. We emphasize Epicureanism because this is the philosophical tradition that has greatest weight in Horace's satire. The empiricism and the realism of Horatian morality, features that have stamped the *Satires* with that warm, good-natured reasonableness that has been valued in every period, could not but come into conflict with the rigor and the abstractness of the Stoics; satire 1.3, for instance, is devoted to this controversy.

The satires and Epicureanism

Connected directly to Epicureanism is satire 1.2, against adultery and its pointless follies (natural satisfaction of the need for sex is recommended), and particularly the prominence given in the *Satires* to problems of friendship and the representation of Horace's group of friends. Intellectual affinity, indulgence, dedication, sharing of life, solidarity before external pressures—all this is influenced by Epicurean theories and reflects the value that *philia* had in the thought of Epicurus and his followers.

Philosophical satires and descriptive satires

Moral inquiry characterizes not only the satires that could be called "diatribal," that is, the ones, such as 1.1, 1.2, and 1.3, in which a discussion in the manner of diatribe, with arguments, objections, examples, and anecdotes, is developed about a specific moral problem, but also those satires in which the poet, following the model of the autobiographical Lucilius, represents a scene, recounts an episode, or describes a situation. In these cases the moral interest is inseparable from the representation itself; it is like the lens through which the poet observes actions and people. The best examples of this are the satire of the journey and the satire of the bore. And there are also several instances in which diatribe and representation are joined in a single poem. Satire 1.6, for example, moves from autobiography (the poet's origin, his presentation to Maecenas) to argument over the value of birth and ambition, only to return to autobiographical representation (recollection of his childhood and his father, diary of a day at Rome).

The Second Book and the New Stance of Horatian Satire

Gap between poet and satiric voice

The fundamental mechanism of the satiric genre in Horace's first collection was the comparison between a positive model, the objective of the moral inquiry of the poet and his friends, and a plethora of negative models, the types found in Roman society who are the targets of comic aggression. This stance is revealed as extremely precarious in that the second collection of the *Satires* shows substantial changes. Let us note first of all that the representative-autobiographical element recedes dramatically; despite a proem that promises this, in fact there is only satire 2.6 to justify that promise. Then, in the argumentative satires the dialogue form becomes dominant (six out of eight), and as for the distribution of parts, the leading role is given, not to the poet, but to the interlocutor to whom he himself yields the stage. Even in 2.2, which is not in dialogue form, the speaking role does not belong to the poet: the thoughts on temperance and simplicity of life are delivered by a certain Ofellus of Venosa. The coincidence of the poet and the satiric voice that argues and refutes had guaranteed a point of reference for the moral inquiry of the first book. Now that the poet withdraws to a second level, it is no longer possible to extract a unitary sense from the contradictions of reality. All the interlocutors are repositories of a truth of their own, even if not all the truths are equivalent and several discourses refute themselves on their own in an unintended irony. But the poet no longer seems to believe that satire can be the locus of a moral inquiry that could empirically identify a satisfactory code of behavior. The balance between *autarkeia* and *metriotes,* which ensured a good observation post on reality, appears lost. The poet no longer represents his own ability to live among people without losing his own moral identity, but he allows his interlocutors to denounce, even unjustly, the weaknesses and inconsistencies of their choices. The only refuge is the Sabine villa (satire 2.6), where *autarkeia* takes advantage of the isolation and is not obliged continually to take into account the contradictions in life at Rome.

The Style of the Horatian *Sermo*

Satire, Horace says, is not true poetry: to be called a poet one needs inspiration and a voice capable of sublime sounds:

> neque enim concludere versum
> dixeris esse satis, neque si qui scribat, uti nos,
> sermoni propiora, putes hunc esse poetam.

("neither would you say that to conclude a verse is sufficient, nor would you regard as a poet one who, like me, writes closer to prose" [*Satires* 1.4.40–42]).

Satire, then, is literature closer to prose, distinguished from it only by the obligation of the meter. But Horace should not be taken too literally, and in particular one should not infer that the style of the *Satires* is the

result of facile improvisation. The language of educated conversation that he proposes to reproduce intentionally is the one that is adequate to express the confidential thoughts of an elegant, educated man of the world. But in fact the *Musa pedestris* requires refined and patient attention, no less toilsome than for more valued levels of literature. This need is observed by Horace with programmatic clarity and is the only point in which he resolutely wishes to distinguish himself from Lucilius. Horace aims at a disciplined, simple language. By contrast with the exuberant and "muddy" (*lutulentus*) style of Lucilius, who included the loftiest literary parody along with the roughness of the *sermo vulgaris,* Horace tries to obtain vigorous effect with a great economy of means of expression. The poet of the *Satires* shows that he has assimilated well the essence of Callimachus's lessons. He demands for satire a standard of expression that is anything but accessible and looks for concentration and suppleness:

> est brevitate opus, ut currat sententia neu se
> inpediat verbis lassas onerantibus aures,
> et sermone opus est modo tristi, saepe iocoso,

defendente vicem modo rhetoris atque poetae,
interdum urbani, parcentis viribus atque
extenuantis eas consulto.

("brevity is necessary, so that the thought hurries along and is not hindered
by words that weigh down and weary the ears; and a tone is necessary that
is now austere, often playful, now taking the part of the orator, now of the
poet, now the man of the world who spares his strength and deliberately
weakens it" [*Satires* 1.10.9–14]).

Flexibility and variety of style

And indeed flexibility and variety are the first characteristics of the style
of the *Satires,* which from time to time shape themselves to suit their subjects, now familiar, now serious and oratorical, now solemn and poetic,
sometimes ironically solemn. To this we must add an affectation of negligence characteristic of prose: repetitions, free constructions, juxtapositions
of short clauses. As for the general course of the argument, Horace has
taken lessons from the popular, effective eloquence of the diatribe. The
lecture continually yields to dialogue, involves the interlocutors, anticipates objections, and introduces dramatic scenes, examples from myth or
history, parodies, anecdotes, and plays on words.

3. THE *ODES*

The Cultural and Literary Premises of Horatian Lyric

Horace and Alcaeus: imitatio *in Latin poetry*

Horatian lyric cannot be understood apart from its organic relation with
the Greek tradition. This is in fact true for a large part of Latin poetry,
and for Augustan poetry in particular. In these poets the consciousness of
dependence on the Greeks is so alive that it is revealed in explicit declarations of poetics. If in the *Epodes* Horace proclaimed himself an heir of
Archilochus, in regard to his lyric writings he proudly claims the title of
the Roman Alcaeus (*Carmina* 1.1.34, 1.26.11, 1.32.5). But such declarations can easily be misunderstood by the modern reader. They actually refer
to a relation of *imitatio* that signifies chiefly obedience to the *lex operis* (the
rules governing the literary genre in which the poet wants to work) and
thus respect for literary decorum, as well as the creation in the recipient of
a consistent set of expectations. Imitation, as understood by a Latin poet,
implies, in short, bringing into play the vast expressive possibilities offered
by the different forms of poetic memory; it is an element of the poetic
language, not an obstacle to originality of creation.

The theme of primus ego

For understanding these features of Latin poetry the *Odes* offer a special
observation post. Not by chance has the literary success of Horace as a lyric
poet always been closely linked to the more general question of the originality of Latin literature in comparison with Greek. Just as the Roman
poets themselves, and Horace more than the others, were conscious of their
literary ancestry, they were also jealous of their own original, creative contribution and did not fail to boast of it:

libera per vacuum posui vestigia princeps,
non aliena meo pressi pede

("I was the first to set my free feet upon free soil, and I did not tread with my foot upon the tracks of others" [*Epistles* 1.19.21–22]).

This is true especially of his relation with Alcaeus. Horace, *Latinus fidicen,* "the Latin lyric singer," is proud to have been the first to employ his measures; for this reason he deserves the appreciation that belongs to the one who opens unknown paths (*Epistles* 1.19.32 ff.). These proud claims, which become a commonplace of Augustan poetry, known as the *primus ego* motif, refer principally to the technical difficulties of transferring metrical and expressive structures from one language to another. The poet in fact behaved a good deal more freely towards his models: despite themes, occasions, and situations that were often traditional, a Roman setting and sensibility are always present, as is a specifically Horatian poetic language.

The multiple suggestions of the model

In recalling Alcaeus, Horace in any event was not merely meeting a requirement of Augustan classicism; he was availing himself of the *auctoritas* of his model to legitimize the conjunction of separate (and not always readily reconcilable) elements of his lyric world: attention to the happenings of his community and a song more linked to the private sphere (love, friendship, the banquet). Invoking the Aeolian cithara, the symbol of lyric in the style of Alcaeus, Horace himself indicates the multiplicity of suggestions that might come to him from the model:

> age dic Latinum,
> barbite, carmen,
>
> Lesbio primum modulate civi,
> qui ferox bello tamen inter arma,
> sive iactatam religarat udo
>   litore navem,
>
> Liberum et Musas Veneremque et illi
> semper haerentem puerum canebat
> et Lycum nigris oculis nigroque
>   crine decorum.

("Come, sing a Latin song, o lyre first tuned by the citizen of Lesbos, who, a valiant warrior, between one battle and another, or if he had tied his beaten ship to the damp shore, still sang of Liber and the Muses and Venus and the boy who is always by her side and Lycus, handsome with his dark eyes and dark hair" [*Carmina* 1.32.3–12]). Alcaeus in addition, as we now know from papyrus discoveries, had also been a gnomic poet. It is reasonable, then, to link to him the strong moralizing element in Horace's lyric, even though it is certainly more the result of more recent cultural traditions.

The "motto"

A feature typical of the way in which Horace understands his relation with early Greek lyric, and with Alcaeus in particular, is his borrowing of a poem's beginning. Several odes of Horace start with an obvious borrowing, sometimes nearly a quotation that serves as a "motto." Then, however, the poet proceeds in his own way, and the model is nearly forgotten (the most well-known instances are 1.9, 1.10, 1.14, 1.18, 1.37, 3.12). The famous ode to Thaliarchus (1.9), for example, opens with a winter landscape that recalls a fragment of Alcaeus. As in Alcaeus, an invitation to drink is connected with it; then, however, the poem develops into a series of gnomic thoughts and ends with a picture of love in the city, a scene close in taste to Alexandrian realism.

Alcaeus and Horace: militant poetry and the poetry of otium

If the traits that Horace shares with Alcaeus are important, the differences are certainly no less so. The verses of Alcaeus were the expression of the loves and the hates of an aristocrat of Lesbos, directly engaged in the harsh political struggles of his city. Tied, as it is, to genuine social occasions, such as a symposium or a religious celebration, Alcaeus's lyric expects to be performed, which implies a simplicity of subjects and language. In Horace, however, the interest in the *res publica* is lively, but it is that of an intellectual who, after a passing involvement in the civil upheavals, lives under the protection of the powerful masters of Rome. For Horace, then, poetry as a relief from toil or as a pause in the midst of battles is little more than a literary image, all the more so because the private aspect of his poetry could not be separated from that pursuit of inner happiness, composed of *autarkeia* and *tranquillitas animi,* that had been the principal lesson of the Hellenistic philosophies. Horace's lyric poetry, moreover, is written for reading, it frequently describes imaginary or at least highly stylized situations, and it aspires to a quite elevated level of literary refinement and sophistication.

Other models of the Odes: a) *Sappho*

The other great representative of Aeolic lyric, Sappho, has left a smaller trace in Horace's poetry. In a famous ode he imagines Sappho and Alcaeus bewitching an astonished Underworld with their song. The shades seem to prefer Alcaeus as singer of the civil disturbances over Sappho and her passionate laments (2.13.24 ff.); Horace certainly seems to have shared this judgment. The poetess who had sung of beauty and the upheavals of passion only occasionally seems to have provided the starting point for Horace's erotic verse. The ode on jealousy, already translated by Catullus, influenced 1.13, and Sapphic accents, as often happens, characterize the evocation of the poetess in 4.9.10 ff. (see also 1.22.23 f.). By contrast, Roman elegiac poetry is more indebted to Sappho for its own representation of love.

b) *Anacreon*

Horace's debt to another lyric monodist, Anacreon, is more significant (1.27 and 1.23 are the most evident cases). The delicate, elegant grace of the poet from Teos and his melancholy over lost youth appear to have more than a few affinities with the corresponding motifs in Horace's lyric.

c) *Pindar's choral lyric*

Choral lyric also played a notable role. Although Horace himself names him admiringly, Stesichorus does not seem to exert a conspicuous influence, and the same can be said of Simonides (*Carmina* 2.1.39, 4.9.8). More important was Bacchylides, from whom the mythological ode 1.15, with Nereus's prophecy to Paris, abductor of Helen, took its cue. Horace, especially in the first phase of his writing, must have contemplated a lyric poetry that, on a higher stylistic level, would accommodate material similar to that of the Alexandrian, neoteric epyllion; imitation of Bacchylides may have led in this direction. But there is no doubt that Pindar occupies the most important post among the choral lyric *auctores* of Horace. In recognizing his greatness, Horace notes all the perils to which the *aemulatio* of so bold and difficult a poet exposes one ("He who wants to imitate Pindar exposes himself to a flight as risky as Icarus'" [*Carmina* 4.2.1 ff.; see also *Epistles* 1.3.10]). Horace attempts a Pindaric lyric especially in the fourth book, where he is responding to Augustan cultural stimuli. But in the previous books as well (see, e.g., the motto of 1.12 or the fourth Roman ode) Horace's pursuit of the sublime, especially in the poems on civic subjects, seems to be fostered by suggestions originating in Pindar: ample periods, of impetuous movement, the solemn gravity of the *gnome* (the brief saying, packed with thought and having a moral bearing), improvised admonitions, bold transitions. Important ideas also come to Horace from Pindar, such as the consciousness of the high function of poetry, the poet's ability to confer immortality, and the appreciation of ethical-political understanding.

The experience of Alexandrian poetry

Horace's echoing of early Greek lyric undoubtedly had the characteristics of a precise programmatic choice and expressed his conscious desire to distinguish himself from the Alexandrianism of the *neoteroi.* Of course this does not mean that Horace is not a modern poet and that his lyric poetry neglects the Hellenistic experience. From this quarter comes a vast repertory of subjects, images, and situations, relating especially to love and courtship but also to public festivals and ceremonies, the banquet, and the countryside. And not this alone: Horace draws upon the Hellenistic world for central elements of his culture, his ideology, and his sensibility as a poet. The importance and richness of his relation with this poetry is today accepted as a given (and Italian philology has made important contributions to this), yet it is still uncertain whether the Hellenistic elements abundantly present in Horace go back to direct contact with Alexandrian lyric poetry, now mostly lost to us, or rather to contacts with different but kindred literary traditions, such as epigram and elegy.

But just as the example of Alcaeus as a civic poet met a contemporary need in Horace for passionate attention to the affairs of the *res publica,* so Alexandrian poetry does not have a purely literary attraction. It is the form of daily life at Rome, the Hellenized metropolis, a worldliness composed of loves, festivals, banquets, dance, and poetry.

Even though it is often neglected, the part played by prose literature in the culture of Horace the lyric poet is important, not only, of course, the tradition of the philosophical diatribe, but also Hellenistic treatises on good government, panegyrics, and rhetorical treatises.

Themes and Characteristics of Horace's Lyric Poetry

Meditation and philosophical culture in the Odes

Horace as the poet of serene balance, of detachment from passion, of moderation: this image is deeply rooted. And the traditional image, in this case as in others, is quite close to the truth. It leads us to sense, first of all, the central role that thought and philosophical culture plays in Horatian lyric. Here it is natural to think of the poet of the *Satires* and the assimilation, through the diatribe tradition, of concepts and problems of the Hellenistic schools of philosophy; this feature renders Horace's pronouncements substantially different from those of early Greek lyric. Nonetheless, it is no more than a genuine moral inquiry based on the critical observation of others. In a certain sense one may say that the *Odes* begin where the *Satires* leave off, with a thoughtful meditation upon a few fundamental achievements of philosophy, Epicurean philosophy in particular. These basic notions, which, to be sure, also owe something to common sense, receive from Horace a formulation that is so clear and incisive that they have become part of the European cultural heritage, which has often drawn upon Horace's poetry as a storehouse of maxims.

The brevity of life   The cardinal point is the awareness of the brevity of life, which implies the need to take the joys of the moment, without getting lost in the fruitless concern over hopes, ambitions, or fears. The exhortation to Leuconoe is the most famous of all:

> sapias, vina liques, et spatio brevi
> spem longam reseces. dum loquimur, fugerit invida
> aetas: carpe diem, quam minimum credula postero.

("Be wise, strain the wine; and since time is brief, reduce lengthy hope. While we are speaking, envious life will have fled: pluck the day, and do not trust to tomorrow" [1.11.6 ff.]).

Epicurus had said: "One is born only once, to be born twice is not granted to us, we will not be forever. Though not master of your morrow, you put off pleasure; thus life goes by in this delaying, and each of us dies without having enjoyed tranquillity" (*Gnomologium Vaticanum* 14). The wise man will deal with events as they are and will be able to accept them. He relies on the present alone, which he seeks to capture in its flight, and he acts as if each day of life were the last. The *carpe diem* therefore should not be misunderstood as a banal invitation to pleasure; in Horace, as also in Epicurus, the invitation to pleasure is not separate from the keen awareness that that pleasure itself is fleeting, as human life is fleeting. The only possibility is to erect, against the imminence of death or misfortune, the solid protection of possessions already enjoyed, happiness already experienced:

> ille potens sui
> laetusque deget, cui licet in diem
> dixisse "vixi: cras vel atra
> nube polum Pater occupato
>
> vel sole puro; non tamen irritum,
> quodcumque retro est, efficiet neque
> diffinget infectumque reddet,
> quod fugiens semel hora vexit."

("He will live as master of himself, in happiness, who from day to day will be able to say, 'I have lived: tomorrow let father Jupiter cover the sky with dark cloud or shining sun; still, he will not make naught of all that is behind, nor will he cancel or undo what the fleeting hour has already brought'" [3.29.41–48]).

The laborious achievement of wisdom

This reflection can sometimes be translated into a song of serenity—the happiness of *autarkeia*, the condition of the poet-sage, freed from the torments of human folly and blessed with the protection of the gods. Divine favor manifests itself by transforming circumstances of daily life, such as dangers survived, into miracles, and it is always intimately connected with his vocation as poet: the gods and the Muses save Horace to preserve him for that destiny. And yet wisdom, tranquillity, balance, mastery of oneself, the *aurea mediocritas* of the man who can avoid all excess and adapt himself to every fortune—none of these is a secure possession, acquired once for all time. The poet of the *Odes* is not unaware of the insidious, attractive force of the passions. He is familiar with the soul's weaknesses, and he knows that what he hopes for and recommends to his friends must be won and defended at every moment. Wisdom thus runs into the unchangeable givens of man's condition in the world: the fleeting nature of time, old age, and death, subjects that animate some of the loveliest odes (1.4, 2.3, 2.14, 4.7). No wisdom can counterbalance completely so heavy a negative weight. Against the anguish and the grief of life one can only wage a brave warfare, demanding energy and a certain heroism, in order to transform apprehension and bitterness into acceptance of destiny:

> immortalia ne speres, monet annus et almum
> quae rapit hora diem
>
> . . . .
>
> damna tamen celeres reparant caelestia lunae:
> nos ubi decidimus
> quo pater Aeneas, quo Tullus dives et Ancus,
> pulvis et umbra sumus.

("Not to nourish immortal hopes the year admonishes you, and the hour that carries away the life-giving day . . . still, in the sky the swift moons make good what they have lost: we, however, once we have fallen where father Aeneas has, and powerful Tullus and Ancus, we are dust and shadow" [4.7.7–8, 13–16]).

The civic poetry

The other pole of Horace's lyric, the poetry engaged with civic and national subjects, with the celebration of people, events, and myths of the Augustan regime, for long stretches is removed from the private subjects. Nonetheless, and this is an important difference from neoteric lyric, the private sphere in Horace always aspires to a general validity, aspires to express the comprehensive condition of man. The civic lyric, much discussed for its results, certainly does not lack originality. The celebratory poetry linked to the Hellenistic monarchs furnishes nothing more than some external features; onto this trunk (and of course onto that of early

Greek lyric) Horace has been able to graft national themes, suggestions originating in epic and historical writing. The procedure was ambitious and met profound personal needs that were deeply rooted in a generation that, after the devastations of the civil wars, with a combination of hope, enthusiasm, and some anxieties not yet laid to rest, looked upon the princeps as the victor and guarantor of the peace. It is not necessary therefore to think only of the energizing pressures of Augustan cultural politics. The image of Horace as a singer of Rome's greatness and of the eternal values of the Empire may be evaluated today, at last, without arousing the suspicions that the rhetoric of *Romanitas* has projected onto it in the twentieth century. Horace's civic lyric includes celebration and encomium and sometimes has a kind of official character, but it cannot be dismissed as propaganda in verse. The first reason is that even where he reflects, with a fidelity much valued by the sociologist and the historian, the themes and the successive stages of the ideology of the principate, he is able to take advantage of the amplitude and the flexibility of that very ideology in order to avoid dogmatic conclusions and to glorify the sublime quality of magnanimity, for instance, loyalty towards the republican cause and *its* unfortunate heroes (2.7, 1.12, 2.1) and admiration for *virtus* even in the most hated enemy (as in the famous picture of Cleopatra fearlessly facing death in 1.37). Another reason is that Horace as poet of the community can frequently become the interpreter of uncertainties and fears, of discouragement and then unexpected, liberating joy, of the deep sentiments and aspirations of contemporary society. Even the praise of the princeps generally avoids the courtly gestures of Hellenistic encomium to give utterance to the sincere, anxious gratitude toward the man who brought peace to the Empire. Horace's civic lyric shares in the moral structure of Augustan ideology; the crisis was produced by the decline of morals, the abandonment of that coherent system of ancient ethical-political and religious values that had brought about the greatness of Rome. This moralistic poetry may in places overlap with Horace's moral inquiry—in the criticism of luxury, extravagance, and folly, in the admiration for the self-sufficiency of *virtus,* in the appreciation of rationality against the forces of chaos (although generally a less vital note is heard in the civic poetry, one stiffened by the firmness of the Stoic sage). The conciliation, or rather the coexistence, of public sphere and private sphere was easier when some Hellenistic features of the civic poetry became dominant. A public festivity (a holiday, a ceremony, a joyous event) can also be an occasion of private joy: the poet celebrates with a banquet or an amorous encounter. Horace thus inaugurates a fashion that would be important for other poets of the Augustan age, for Propertius and especially for Ovid.

The polarity to which we referred is of course a simplification that ultimately obscures the thematic variety and vitality of Horace's lyric poetry, a variety that often corresponds to the different categories into which early Greek lyric was divided. These categories, functional for different occasions, would be classified normatively as true "genres" by later rhetorical

The ideology of the principate and the authenticity of Horace

Augustan ideology and Horatian morality

Variety of themes in the Odes

treatises. Thus we have convivial poems, which allude to the *sympotika,* the convivial poems, of Alcaeus but also owe much to Hellenistic epigram; and also invitations, with descriptions of the preparations traditional for the Hellenistic-Roman symposium (wine, flowers, music). Almost a quarter of the *Odes* can be classified as erotic. Horace's love poetry, unlike that of Catullus and the elegiac poets, seems to be fostered by ironic detachment from passion. With some exceptions, love is analyzed as a ritual the action of which is conventionalized and predictable: serenades, meetings, oaths, fallings-out, a sporting, gentlemanly life, banquets. The poet often observes with a smile the credulity of the young lover and the seriousness with which each person performs his part, swearing exclusive love and the undying nature of his own feeling. But Horace's irony is not ignorant of passion: he is familiar with its cruelty, he evokes its melancholy, he feels its unexpected arousal:

The love poetry

> iam nec spes animi credula mutui
> 　　nec certare iuvat mero
> nec vincire novis tempora floribus.
> 　　Sed cur heu, Ligurine, cur
> manat rara meas lacrima per genas?
> 　　cur facunda parum decoro
> inter verba cadit lingua silentio?
> 　　nocturnis ego somniis
> iam captum teneo, iam volucrem sequor
> 　　te per gramina Martii
> campi, te per aquas, dure, volubilis.

("Now I like neither the trusting hope of love requited, nor to vie with the wine, nor to bind the temples with fresh flowers. But why, Ligurinus, why does the occasional tear fall across my cheeks? Why does my eloquent tongue cease in the very midst of words and fall into an undignified silence? In my dreams at night I have seized you, I hold you, I pursue you as you flit across the grass of the Campus Martius or—you hard one—across the flowing waters" [4.1.30–40]).

The hymn

The hymn, too, is well represented in Horace's lyric poetry. Here, naturally, the differences from early Greek lyric are conspicuous, since Horace's religious lyric, apart from the *Carmen Saeculare,* lacks any link to a ritual occasion or performance. He frequently retains the formulaic language and movement of the hymn—the invocation in the second person, the *epiclesis,* or "summoning," of the god, the setting forth of the privileges and sites of the cult, the invitations to be present, the stipulations and requests—but it is interwoven with references and developments of a literary nature.

The contamination of the lyric categories

It is not always easy, however, to place a Horatian ode within a well-defined type, since the poet is often fond of combining in the same poem different categories of lyric, in accord with the Alexandrian procedure of "crossing of genres," for example, a *propempticon* (a bon-voyage poem) and a mythological poem (3.27); a hymn and a mythological poem (3.11); an epigram on spring and a banquet poem (1.4).

Recurrent themes in the Odes:
a) *The landscape*

Certain themes recur often in poems of varying nature. The country is usually stylized to become the *locus amoenus,* a pleasant Italian landscape that accommodates banquets, repose, and the simple rustic life. Yet Horace also knows the attraction of the "Dionysian" countryside, a nature that is mountainous, wild and harsh, composed of cliffs, woods, and springs, a nature not tamed by man.

b) *The* angulus *as the locus of poetry*

Yet the most distinctively Horatian places are those defined by the limited, closed space of the small individual farm, a space that is dear because known and certain, unassailable because separate and deliberately modest (*hic in reducta valle* [1.17.17; see also *Satires* 2.6.1: *modus agri*]; but to find oneself sometimes all that is needed is just a bit of quiet country or a lonely beach by the shore). This privileged space functions in the text as a symbol of the poet's existence (it is the form of his affections), but it is also a symbol of his poetic experience (it is the aesthetic form of it, in that it is space meant to represent an order and a meaning). This place of refuge becomes a literary topos in the theme of the *angulus* (*terrarum mihi praeter omnes / angulus ridet,* "that corner of land smiles at me more than any other" [2.6.13]), the designated place for song, wine, and wisdom. And however conventional the theme may appear, it finds new functions in Horace and becomes the nucleus from which much poetry is produced, in that it is associated with two other great themes: the theme of death (even the thought of death approaching with time becomes less bitter in this privileged space and is reduced to melancholy) and particularly the theme of

c) *Friendship*

friendship. Friendship in the *Odes,* as in all the poet's other works, has a fundamental role and provides the individual poems with a wide range of dedicatees, each with his specific qualities as friend, and to each one affectionate attention is shown. Important also is the motif of the vocation of

d) *The vocation of poetry*

poetry. The *vates* feels that he is related to the Muses and the other inspiring divinities (Mercury, Bacchus, Apollo). Through the Hellenistic topos he expresses enthusiasm for his mission and pride in his work.

The style of the Odes:
a) *The utter simplicity*

One of the hallmarks of Horace's lyric is the perfection of the style, a refinement that owes much to the lesson of Callimachus and Callimacheanism. Horace employs a very simple diction that permits even words regarded as prosaic in other poetic traditions. The simple, essential nature also guides the choice of adjectives, the moderate use of sound figures, the cautious employment of metaphors and similes. The syntax, less predictable yet still always quite simple, is prone to ellipsis, Greek constructions, hyperbaton, enjambment. The dignified elevation of the style is secured by carefully reducing the means of expression, with a diction free from all redundance, concise and polished. Expressiveness is guaranteed, too, by Horace's metrical virtuosity and by his skill in the collocation of words, a skill already to be seen in Alcaeus.

b) *The art of the* iunctura

Shrewd placement of the words within the verse means pursuing a strategy that, while binding together the words in the texture of the phrase, places some close together and separates others, letting them recall one another at a distance. Thus ordinary words, receiving a distinction of their own, are perceived as if new, as if they were now spoken for the first time;

their meanings, with the opaque veneer of custom stripped off, find a new luminosity in the text. The strategic configuration that the elements of the discourse take on revitalizes the exhausted meaning of words and images that ran the risk of being nearly insignificant. For instance, an adjective separated from the noun that it is to complement or modify and displaced to a position in the metrical-rhythmic sequence that somehow draws attention to it—placed early, say, or held back to the verse following, in enjambment—appears isolated in the phrase and thus recovers its original resonance. At other times the adjective (or the participle or adverb) can be added to a word that is not its proper referent, creating new effects or unusual associations, allowing implicit meanings to emerge, causing latent images to blossom, or suggesting forgotten senses. Horace himself, when theorizing, mentioned among the most powerful procedures the simple artifice of the *callida iunctura* (*dixeris egregie, notum si callida verbum / reddiderit iunctura novum*, "you will express yourself in a distinctive way if a clever combination will make a familiar word new" [*Ars* 47–48]). For instance, a very simple juxtaposition of words can create an effect of emphasis: *credulus aurea* in *qui nunc te fruitur credulus aurea*, "he who now credulous enjoys your gleaming beauty" (*Carmina* 1.5.9); *simplex munditiis*, "simple in affectation" (1.5.5); *palluit audax*, "he grew pale at his own boldness" (3.27.28). Quintilian expresses thus his admiration for a sober but very powerful style of writing: *insurgit aliquando et plenus est iucunditatis et gratiae et varius figuris et verbis felicissime audax*, "he rises to grandeur at times and is also full of liveliness and charm; he shows variety in his figures and a remarkably successful boldness in his choice of words" (10.1.96).

c) *Sobriety and neatness*

Horace deploys the maximum economy of linguistic inventiveness in order to have the maximum of expressiveness. That is, he is parsimonious in his use of novel formations. His style of composition relies rather on new analogies and prefers neat contextual correspondences—members arranged in parallel, elements disposed simply by contrast or antithesis—well-planned structures in which the individual words, the individual things, by reciprocal action reacquire their proper communicative energy in its entirety. In short, the style produces an effect of sobriety and classical neatness, to which not a small contribution is made by the structure of the individual poem, carefully planned in a unified, compact manner. This does not always mean symmetry; *variatio* is a no less important stylistic principle.

4. THE *EPISTLES*: CULTURAL PROJECT AND PHILOSOPHICAL WITHDRAWAL

The return to sermo

After the great experience of the lyric poetry, Horace returns to the conversational hexameter. It must have been difficult for the ancient Horatian commentators (grammarian-readers, guardians of rules, literary genres, and definitions) to devise a critical formula that could distinguish the *Epistles* from the two collections of *Satires*. May it not have been the poet who applied the term *sermones*, "conversations," to both works, which in this way were associated with one another by the same stylistic register "closer to prose"? In the final analysis the best definition was the one that emphasized two different pragmatic situations, or to put it another way, the different intensity of two voices: *hoc solum distare videntur, quod hic quasi ad absentes loqui videtur, ibi autem quasi ad praesentes loquitur,* "the only difference is that in the *Epistles* he appears to be addressing people who are absent, whereas in the *Satires* he addresses people who are present" (*Pseudoacronis scholia in Horatium vetustiora,* preface to epistle 1.1). In this way the ancient judgment, while it shrewdly recognizes the mimic-dramatic bent of the *Satires,* well emphasizes the specific epistolary configuration of the later work. As a collection of letters (such are the messages to the "absent" of pseudo-Acron), the *Epistles* acquire their first, important identity: all the poems have an addressee, and occasionally the typical signs of a letter, such as the formulas of salutation and farewell, are seen. The "real" character of these letters is debated. Of course, no one believes that they have a true private function, yet the possibility cannot be excluded that individual letters, though conceived as literary works and intended for the reading public, may occasionally have been sent to their addressees as a literary homage. In any event, the epistolary element guarantees for the Horatian *sermo* a more personal tone as well as the variety of styles and attitudes called for by regard for the addressee.

The verse epistle: a new literary genre

From the point of view of form the *Epistles* were almost certainly a novelty. In what remains to us, or what we have precise notice of, from Greek and Latin literature, we find nothing really similar. We know of epistles in verse (in the satires of Lucilius, for example, or certain poems of Catullus that proclaim themselves letters, such as 68), and there were well-known philosophical treatises in the form of prose epistles (Plato's letters and the letters of Epicurus to his pupils). But a systematic collection of verse letters such as Horace's is probably an original experiment; nor does the poet in this case refer, as he does in others, to an *inventor* of the genre he is practicing.

The loss of balance

But the factor that contributes the most to differentiating the *Epistles* from the collections of satires, in a novel way, gives it a physical distance, a different stage upon which the persona assumed by the author stands up to speak. The satire had belonged essentially to an urban setting, which corresponded to the social needs of the genre in that it opened room for movement among the cultivated classes—the *equites*—and provided easy

The poet's remote angulus *and the exhortation to wisdom*

material for the poet's comic imagination. All of Horace's letters, however, presuppose displacement towards a rustic periphery (the *angulus* of the *Odes,* as we will soon explain) that resonates with philosophical memories. Thus, exhortation is the truest aim of every single poem and of the whole of the first book of the *Epistles* as a collection. The addressees are invited to repeat the choice of wisdom that Horace visualizes as a journey towards the *angulus,* a road that signifies, metaphorically and metonymically, an entire mental *iter.* The poetic persona of the *Epistles* is portrayed against the background of a remote landscape that, if it sometimes refers to the Sabine refuge of individual lyric poems, proposes anew the Epicurean goal of

Lucretius's *De Rerum Natura.* The *angulus* translates into Horatian terms the experience of the *sapientum templa serena* that Lucretius proposes to his readers.

The Lucretian premise

Even so, the collection develops a didactic discourse that revives the Lucretian poem by altering its significant features, to such an extent, indeed, that the very conventions of the letter assure a Lucretian situation, that is, the situation (and it is a marked innovation in the genre) that continually involved the reader in the choices made by the text. The relation between author and reader, which was lively and dramatic in the *De Rerum Natura,* here is imposed by a communicative structure entirely directed towards injunction and exhortation. Thus the author-reader relation becomes itself the subject of the discourse, to the point of assuming the forms of meta-literary consciousness. The project of the *Epistles* now develops within itself (i.e., in the individual episodes that realize it) the model of a Lucretian teacher who teaches his pupils the love of a withdrawn life. But where the work shows most evidently the typical traits of moderate Augustan classicism (which are common to Virgil and Horace) is in the melancholy perplexity that it discovers precisely in regard to a real didactic power of its message: the addressees will not always prove to be receptive to the suggestion of a new philosophical world, which in some respects is akin to that of the *Bucolics,* though that is more literary and imaginative.

The revision of the Lucretian model

Yet, still from the point of view of the form of the content, there are other conspicuous differences from the *Satires.* The *Epistles,* for instance, lack that comic aggression that for Horace is still the obvious mark of the satiric genre. The moral thought now does not proceed by means of observing contemporary society critically. Horatian morality seems to become more clearly conscious of its own weaknesses and contradictions; the balance between *autarkeia* and *metriotes,* on which the very possibility of satire rested, now appears irrecoverable, and one does not glimpse any other balance. Whether directed at itself, in a lucid and sometimes pitiless introspection, or realized in dialogue with the interlocutor and his point of view, the moral inquiry is vivaciously animated in the *Epistles* by the need for wisdom. The Horatian sensibility for the inexorable passage of time, sharpened by the impression of a premature old age, makes the achievement of wisdom seem an urgent task that cannot be postponed. But at the same time Horace no longer seems prepared to construct, either for himself or for others, a satisfying model of life. The rejection of social life and of ethical optimism is symbolized by his flight from Rome towards the concentration of the Sabine country, a restless withdrawal but at least one removed from the engagements, harassments, and passions of the city, before which the poet now feels himself defenseless. The need for *autarkeia,* that "self-sufficiency" in which more than one philosophical school located the secret of human happiness, is now livelier than ever, but not even *autarkeia* appears to guarantee the poet a consistent and constant attitude. He seems to waver, without ever really identifying a point of reasonable balance, between a moral rigor that attracts but frightens him and a hedonism

Moral inquiry and the need for wisdom

whose concreteness and yet fragility he perceives. In the epistle that serves as proem Horace declares himself independent of any philosophical orthodoxy:

nullius addictus iurare in verba magistri,
quo me cumque rapit tempestas, deferor hospes.
Nunc agilis fio et mersor civilibus undis,
virtutis verae custos rigidusque satelles,
nunc in Aristippi furtim praecepta relabor
et mihi res, non me rebus subiungere conor.

("I am not obliged to swear according to the formula of any master; wherever the wind drags me, I let myself be carried as a guest. Now I become a man of action and immerse myself in the civic storms, guardian and unyielding defender of true virtue. Now I slip into the precepts of Aristippus and attempt to subject things to myself, not myself to things" [*Epistles* 1.1.14–19]).

The uncertainties in Horace's morality

It is not a question here of claiming an original mediation between concepts and positions drawn from different philosophical traditions, or even from the syncretistic tradition of diatribe preaching. Horace is speaking programmatically of the wavering that characterizes the morality of the *Epistles,* in which, for example, epistle 16, of a clearly Stoic nature, focusing on the theme of inner freedom and the true ideal of the *vir bonus,* is juxtaposed with the pair of epistles 17 and 18, which present in a didactic manner a series of pieces of advice and reflections on the way to live near the powerful and assure oneself of their favor.

Dissatisfaction with oneself: the strenua inertia

With the *aporiai* of Horace's moral inquiry one ought, it seems, to link the notable space now granted to the diatribist's theme, already wonderfully developed by Lucretius and come to fruition in the second book of the *Satires,* of dissatisfaction with oneself, of inconstancy, of anxious, impatient boredom. The restlessness is presented as a kind of *mal de siècle:*

caelum, non animum mutant qui trans mare currunt.
Strenua nos exercet inertia: navibus atque
quadrigis petimus bene vivere. Quod petis, hic est,
est Ulubris, animus si te non deficit aequus.

("He changes the sky overhead, not his soul, who runs across the sea. A restless lethargy wears us down, us who seek the happy life with ships and chariots: what you seek is here, is at Ulubri, if your soul does not lack balance" [*Epistles* 1.11.27–30]).

Yet the poet does not feel at all protected, nor do the promptings of wisdom seem able to assure his recovery from the tenacious, insidious disease afflicting him:

si quaeret quid agam, dic multa et pulchra minantem
vivere nec recte nec suaviter: haud quia grando
contuderit vitis oleamve momorderit aestus,
nec quia longinquis armentum aegrotet in agris;

sed quia mente minus validus quam corpore toto
nil audire velim, nil discere, quod levet aegrum;
fidis offendar medicis, irascar amicis,
cur me funesto properent arcere veterno,
quae nocuere sequar, fugiam quae profore credam,
Romae Tibur amem ventosus, Tibure Romam.

("If he will ask you what I am doing, tell him as follows: I, who threatened
many lovely things, do not live in accord with either virtue or pleasure.
This is not because the hail has pounded the vines or the heat has bitten
the olives, nor because the herd is ill in distant pastures, but because, sick
at heart rather than in my whole body, I do not want to hear, I do not want
to learn what could relieve my ills, I grow irritated with my trusted doctors, I become angry at my friends, because they strive to free me from
mortal torpor; I pursue that which I know does me harm; I shun that from
which I expect pleasure; I am like the wind: at Rome I like Tivoli, at Tivoli
Rome" [Epistles 1.8.3–12]).

The didactic structure

The weakness Horace demonstrates in his own ethical-philosophical
position is accompanied, rather paradoxically, by an increasingly didactic
structure to his discourse. The epistolary form itself corresponds in some
ways to the position of an eminent and respected intellectual, who is the
interlocutor and also a point of reference for the Augustan social elite. In
the relation of two parties that inheres in a letter there is room to confess
but also to warn and instruct, especially if the *persona* of an inexperienced
addressee—many of the letters are addressed to young friends—seems
somehow to call for it:

disce docendus adhuc quae censet amiculus, ut si
caecus iter monstrare velit, tamen aspice siquid
et nos quod cures proprium fecisse loquamur.

("Learn the view of your friend who himself needs instruction; it is as if a
blind man should want to show the way. But take thought whether I am
not also saying something that you might care to make yours" [Epistles
1.17.3–5]).

Horace as literary critic

This didactic aspect is accentuated in the letters of the second book and
especially in the *Ars Poetica.* Augustan society is a society of writers and
lovers of literature; the problems of literary criticism, poetics, and cultural
politics are among the liveliest questions of the day. Horace participates in
the discussion with the authority granted to him by a secure prestige and
his personal relation with the princeps. Thus it is Augustus who comes to
be the primary interlocutor, explicitly or implicitly, in these discourses on
art and literature. In order to secure a wider ideological and cultural basis
for the difficult social arrangement of the principate, Augustus looked with
favor upon national, popular literature. The *Aeneid* had been a response,
even if only a partial one, to the request for an epic-historic poem that
would give voice to the stern ideology of the *maiores* and sing of Rome's
imperial destiny. The question of Latin drama remained open (and in the

The question of Latin drama

eyes of the princeps, urgent). The generous reception accorded to Varius's *Thyestes* shows how much importance was attached to a form of art that was credited with the greatest possibilities for ideological penetration, in that it was the one most able to represent cultural values and models.

The question of drama is central in Horace's literary epistles. In the *Epistle to Augustus* (2.1) the poet polemicizes against the indiscriminate favoring of the poets of the archaic Roman theater. In a kind of "debate of the ancients and the moderns" Horace decisively takes the side of the latter, in the name of the Callimachean principle of cultivated, refined art. On this important point he resists Augustus's own preferences and recommends to the master of Rome a kindly attention to poetry that is intended for reading, the only poetry, according to him, that could achieve the levels of formal excellence that the culture and the very prestige of Augustan Rome necessarily demand. There is another reason why Horace does not show confidence in a true rebirth of the theater: an audience that is less select and refined than the one to which written literature is directed does not seem likely to appreciate a dramatic production of quality and prefers instead the pomp of spectacle and the commonplace jests of mimes and acrobats.

The Ars Poetica:
a) *Poetic theories of drama*

The *Ars Poetica,* nonetheless, orients its analysis of art and poetry by questions of dramatic literature, and not only tragedy and comedy, but even the satyr play, of whose vitality at Rome there is no trace. This orientation ought to be connected with the privileged position drama had in Peripatetic treatises, beginning with Aristotle's *Poetics,* with which Horace is linked in an indisputable, if problematic, manner. We must not imagine, however, a passive reception of a Greek source. After the perplexity and resistance expressed in the letter to Augustus, Horace agrees to offer in the *Ars Poetica*—the chronology is debated, but the later date of the letter to the Pisos is quite probable—his own contribution as theorist, if not as militant poet, to the question of the theater. In any event, in the *Ars* he remains faithful to his principles, preaching an art that is refined (it is recommended that one perfect one's writing with *labor limae* [v. 291]), patient (it is better to keep one's writings in the drawer for nine years before publishing them [v. 389]), cultivated (it is necessary to read and reread the great Greek models [v. 268]), and attentive (the fundamental principles are those of consistency and suitability, or decorum).

b) *A literary and cultural history*

In the framework of these thoughts Horace has occasion, among other things, to give a valuable sketch of the history of culture and literature, both Greek and Roman, as well as to open interesting perspectives on the daily life of the Roman writer and of the literary circles of the capital. In the latter regard the letter to Florus, with its more personal tone, is important.

5. LITERARY SUCCESS

Antiquity

Horace himself ironically foretold that he would become a school author (*Epistles* 1.20.17–18), and despite some initial coolness, at least on the part of the broader public (especially towards the first three books of the *Odes*), he quickly became canonized as a proto–poet laureate *(Carmen Saeculare),* and he has continued to be read in schools, virtually without interruption, almost until the present day. Although all his works seem to have become widely used school texts in antiquity, his influence as a satirist upon later Latin authors such as Persius and Juvenal was far greater than his impact as a lyric poet (only Statius's *Silvae* survive). His works were edited by the Neronian scholar M. Valerius Probus and were explained in at least two and perhaps three surviving ancient commentaries: by Pomponius Porphyrio (third century), the oldest and most important; by the "pseudo-Acron," an anonymous collection, in the Renaissance attributed arbitrarily to Helenius Acron (second century) but certainly postdating Porphyrio and Servius; and perhaps by the *commentator Cruquianus* (though much uncertainty and suspicion surround these notes, purportedly transcribed by the Dutch scholar J. van Cruyck from manuscripts now lost). As late as the sixth century, according to a subscription found in a number of manuscripts, Vettius Agorius Basilius Mavortius, the *consul ordinarius* for the year 527, aided by his assistant Felix, revised the text of the poet, but thereafter there are virtually no traces of familiarity with his writings for about three centuries.

Middle Ages   But Horace's poems had survived the Dark Ages in two, perhaps even three, codices, from which the medieval manuscripts are derived. Knowledge of the poet and manuscripts of his works reappear already in the eighth century: Alcuin took on the pen name of Flaccus and certainly knew the *Ars Poetica* and perhaps the *Sermones,* and a Carolingian commentary to the *Ars Poetica* survives that has sometimes been attributed to Alcuin himself. Thereafter he became one of the most important and best-known school authors after Virgil, excerpted frequently for philosophical maxims by anthologies and transmitted in around three hundred medieval manuscripts (these seem to have been more widely disseminated in Germany and especially in France than in Italy). For the Middle Ages, as for antiquity, Horace was above all a writer of epistles and satires (especially the *Ars Poetica*) rather than a lyric poet, perhaps not only for obvious reasons of content but also because the language and meter of his hexametric poems posed fewer difficulties. Over 1,000 medieval quotations from his *Satires* and *Epistles* have been traced, only about 250 from his *Carmina,* and for Dante he is still "Orazio satiro" (*Inferno* 4.89), second after Homer. In the tenth-century animal epic *Ecbasis captivi* a fifth of the verses are taken from Horace; a century later Horace inspired the satirist Amarcius. But as early as the tenth century Horace's lyric production gained in popularity as well. The ode to Phyllis (4.11) is set to music in a tenth-century Montpellier manuscript, and in the first half of the twelfth century Metellus of Tegernsee imitated a number of the odes and epodes in his polymetric praise of St. Quirinus.

Renaissance and   Petrarch admired Horace and was perhaps the first writer to quote from
after   his lyric and hexametric poems in equal measure, but it was above all because of Landino and Politian that in the Renaissance Horace's fame as a

lyric poet came to overshadow his *Satires* and the *Epistles* (with the exception of the *Ars Poetica*). For the vernacular literature from the sixteenth through the eighteenth century, Horace provides the dominant model both for private lyrics celebrating wine and love and for public lyrics celebrating affairs of state: in Italy, Spain, and France, especially in such sixteenth- and seventeenth-century poets as Bernardo Bembo and Fulvio Testi, Garcilaso de la Vega and Luis de León, Ronsard and the other poets of the Pléiade, Martin Opitz and his followers; and in England, for a longer and richer period, lasting from Ben Jonson through Herrick, Marvell ("Upon Cromwell's Return from Ireland"), Milton (who translated *carmen* 1.5), and Pope ("Ode on Solitude") to later poets such as Collins ("To Evening," "To Simplicity") and Keats (the beginning of whose "Ode to a Nightingale" was inspired by *Epodes* 14.1–4). Imitations of Horace in Horatian meters were also composed in Latin, especially in the seventeenth century (M. K. Sarbiewski, J. Balde, S. Rettenbacher) but even down to our own day. Even at its most inspired, lyric in the Horatian mode does not cease to aim at moderation and control, in language, meter, and length; those who preferred a wilder alternative could always turn to Pindar (misunderstood, to be sure, through the filter of Horace's own *carmen* 4.2). Although the *Ars Poetica* had already become extremely influential through its paraphrase by Robortelli (published in 1548 together with Aristotle's *Poetics*), it was the seventeenth century in general that saw the high point of Horace's satires and epistles: in the France of Louis XIV, Boileau composed Horatian *Satires, Epistles,* and an *Art Poètique,* which became manifestoes of classicism; in England, Dryden and Pope, as well as hosts of lesser poets, composed in the same genres. Horace's elegant rationalism and moral wisdom made his poems, especially the *Satires* and the *Epistles,* favorite reading for the Enlightenment. In England, Bentley published in 1711 a celebrated edition in which he altered over seven hundred passages, often against the consensus of the manuscripts, by appeal to *ratio.* In Germany, Wieland translated him and Kant quoted him. And in France, Diderot translated the beginning of satire 1.1 and published two Horatian satires of his own, each with a Horatian motto: a first one on characters and a second one, better known as *Le Neveu de Rameau,* in which the parasite Rameau is a near cousin of the slave Davus in satire 2.7.

With the advent of Romanticism, Horace, like other Latin poets, suffered a decline, except among classically trained and oriented writers such as Leopardi, Carducci, and Nietzsche. His place in the classroom, however, was never seriously called into question; carefully expurgated editions, especially in the nineteenth century, ensured that even there he would not be able to do much harm.

BIBLIOGRAPHY

There are modern critical editions by S. Borzsak (Leipzig 1984, esp. for the manuscript readings) and D. R. Shackleton Bailey (Stuttgart 1985, a bold text with many conjectures, and misprints). The older Teubner of F. Klingner (ed. 3, Leipzig 1959) remains usable and is better than the Oxford text of E. C. Wickham and H. W. Garrod (Oxford 1912). The Loeb edition and translation of the *Odes and Epodes* is by C. E. Bennett (Cambridge, Mass. 1927), with the hexameter works edited by H. R. Fairclough (Cambridge, Mass. 1929). The only complete English commentary of substance is that of E. C. Wickham (Oxford 1891–96). For the *Odes,* the editions of T. E. Page (London 1895) and P. Shorey and G. J. Laing (Chicago 1919) remain useful (see also those of K. Quinn [London 1980] and D. H. Garrison [Norman 1991]), but they are superseded for the first two books by the monumental commentaries of R.G.M. Nisbet and M. Hubbard (Oxford 1970, 1978). Book 3 has been edited with facing translation and running commentary by G. Williams (Oxford 1969). There is a small edition of *Epistles* 1 by O.A.W. Dilke (London 1966) and major commentaries on the *Ars Poetica* and *Epistles* 2 by C. O. Brink (Cambridge 1971 and 1982); see also *Horace on Poetry: Prolegomena to the Literary Epistles* (Cambridge 1963), and the smaller edition of N. Rudd (Cambridge 1989). The small text and translation of *Epistles* 1 by C. W. Macleod (Rome 1986) contains much of value. There is no substantial commentary on the *Satires* in English, but there is a good French edition by P. Lejay (Paris 1911) with a substantial introduction to each piece. In German the complete commentary by A. Kiessling and R. Heinze (ed. 10 Berlin 1961, with bibliography by E. Burck) is fundamental, and the running commentary on the *Odes* by H.-P. Syndikus (Darmstadt 1972–73) is often acute. There is a good Italian edition of the *Epodes,* with commentary, by A. Cavarzere (Venice 1992).

There is a collection of introductory essays, now dated, by C.D.N. Costa (London 1973). Other general works in English include E. Fraenkel, *Horace* (Oxford 1957, dated in approach but the starting point for much later work), D. R. Shackleton Bailey, *Profile of Horace* (London 1982, brief), and D. Armstrong, *Horace* (New Haven 1989); there is a Greece and Rome survey by G. Williams (Oxford 1972). There is much on Horace in J. K. Newman, *Augustus and the New Poetry* (Brussels 1967). On the *Odes,* see also L. P. Wilkinson, *Horace and His Lyric Poetry* (ed. 2 Cambridge 1951), S. Commager, *The Odes of Horace* (London 1962), D. A. West, *Reading Horace* (Edinburgh 1967), G. Davis, *Polyhymnia: The Rhetoric of Horatian Lyric Discourse* (Berkeley and Los Angeles 1991), and the chapter on Horace in R.O.A.M. Lyne, *The Latin Love Poets* (Oxford 1980). In Italian, G. Pasquali's *Orazio lirico* (Florence 1920) is fundamental; see also A. La Penna, *Orazio e l'ideologia del principato* (Turin 1963). In German, R. Heinze's short essay "Die horazische Ode," reprinted in *Vom Geist des Römertums* (Darmstadt 1960) 172–89, has been extremely influential. There is no satisfactory English treatment of the *Epodes* (an edition by L. Watson is in preparation), and the only monograph of value is V. Grassman, *Die erotischen Epoden des Horaz* (Munich 1966). On the *Satires,* see N. Rudd, *The Satires of Horace* (Cambridge 1966) and the various general books on satire (E. Knoche, *Roman Satire,* trans. E. S. Ramage [Bloomington 1975] 17–30, and M. Coffey, *Roman Satire* [ed. 2 Bristol 1989] 24–32, with bibliography 282), as well as the pieces in W. S. Anderson, *Essays on Roman Satire* (Princeton 1982); there is a good German survey by M. von Albrecht in *Die römische Satire,* ed. J. Adamietz (Darmstadt 1986) 123–78. G. C. Fiske's *Lucilius and Horace* (Madison 1920) contains much of interest among unreliable reconstruction of Lucilian satire. On the *Epistles,* see M. J. McGann, *Studies in Horace's First Book of Epistles* (Brussels 1969), and two volumes by R. S. Kilpatrick, *The Poetry of Friendship: Horace Epistles I* (Edmonton 1986), and *The Poetry of Criticism: Horace Epistles II and Ars Poetica* (Edmonton 1990). Note in French E. Courbaud, *Horace: La vie et sa pensée à l'époque des Épîtres* (Paris 1914), and in German, another influential essay by R. Heinze, "Horazens Buch der Briefe," *Vom Geist des Römertums* 295–307.

On the *fortuna* of Horace, there is a collection of essays edited by D. Hopkins and C. Martindale, *Horace Made New* (Cambridge 1993).

Elegy: Tibullus and Propertius

Judgment of the ancients on Latin elegy

A celebrated statement by Quintilian, *elegia quoque Graecos provocamus* (10.1.93) attests Roman literary culture's proud consciousness of the high level achieved in the elegiac genre at Rome. The same passage also provides us with the canon of its most representative authors: Gallus, Tibullus, Propertius, and Ovid. Ovid in *Tristia* 4.10.53 f. already designates himself as the youngest in the sequence. (The taste for drawing up canons was widespread in antiquity.) The greatest flourishing of elegy, which at Rome means chiefly love poetry with markedly subjective features, therefore takes place in the second half of the first century B.C. The origin and formation of this literary genre, however, is complex and difficult to pin down, although during the period mentioned it presents, despite the rifts within it, clear characteristics of homogeneity and unity.

Versatility of the Greek elegiac genre

In ancient Greek literature, "elegy" meant a poem the meter of which was the *elegos,* that is, the elegiac couplet, composed of a dactylic hexameter and pentameter. The precise etymology of the word is unknown; according to some, it is the Phrygian name, or the name in another Eastern language, of the flute, the sound of which accompanied the recitation of the poems. Originally from Ionia, elegy spread from the seventh century onwards and was used on various occasions of both public and private life. We find poems that are not only warlike, exhortatory, and polemical (Callinus, Tyrtaeus, Archilochus) but also political, moralizing (Solon, Theognis, Phocylides, Xenophanes), and, more conspicuously, erotic (Mimnermus). Elegy must also have been used as an expression of grief, in funereal lamentations (the association of elegy with weeping would later become fundamental; see, e.g., Horace, *Ars Poetica* 75 ff., and Ovid, *Amores* 3.9.1 ff.). We do not have an ancient example of this use, but clear traces of it are not lacking, in the *Andromache* of Euripides, for instance; and Antimachus of Colophon (fifth–fourth centuries B.C.), in his *Lyde* (the name of his dead beloved), also seems to depend on such a tradition. The work of Antimachus is probably an important junction in the development of this literary genre. A personal event, the death of the woman he loved, was the occasion for him to recall and narrate various myths of tragic love; thus he established the connection, however slight and external it may have been, between autobiography

Antimachus of Colophon: the connection between autobiography and myth

and myth and at the same time introduced into elegy myth, which would become one of its steady and typical features later on. Following the example of Antimachus, and also of Mimnermus earlier, who, it seems, had called his elegiac collection *Nanno*, from the name of his beloved, several Hellenistic poets collected elegiac poems under the title of a woman's name, as did Philitas with his *Bittis*, and Hermesianax, who in his *Leontion* gave a catalogue of poets in love, probably establishing a connection with his personal life.

The origin of Latin elegy:
a) From Hellenistic elegy

All this is important for its bearing on the origins of Latin elegy, one of the most disputed questions in the history of classical philology, and one that we will deal with only in a summary manner. One theory was propounded chiefly by the German scholar F. Leo: noting certain affinities between New Comedy and Latin elegy, he traced them back to a hypothetical model now lost, the presumed Hellenistic subjective-erotic elegy. This theory, that Latin elegy was derived directly from Hellenistic elegy, is generally rejected today. The distinctive trait of Latin elegy, the strongly subjective, autobiographical style, has no precedent in any of the Hellenistic elegiac poets, neither in Callimachus, who excludes all autobiographical elements from the elegies of the *Aitia,* reserving them instead for the epigrams, nor in what we can read of Phanocles or Hermesianax. An opposing

b) From Greek epigram

theory is that of F. Jacoby, who regarded Latin elegy as an enlargement and development of Greek epigram, from which it will have derived its subjective character, its situations and motifs. The influence of epigram is quite evident, it is true, but it seems to be noticeable in several individual elegies rather than in the genre as such, and in particular it does not succeed in explaining the presence and function of myth in Latin elegy, where it serves to illuminate and at the same time dignify the personal situation.

The autobiographical element

While it is indisputable that the subjective nature of Latin elegy contrasts with the objective, nonautobiographical tone of Greek elegy, the contrast should not be exaggerated to the point of excluding shared traits. The subjectivity of Latin elegy would indeed have been new as a characteristic feature, as a distinctive mark, but it must not have been altogether absent from Greek elegy, neither early elegy nor Alexandrian. The mythological elegy of Antimachus, Philitas, and Hermesianax must in all likelihood have contained *in nuce,* as suggested above, an autobiographical element, a connection, perhaps hardly explicit, between the adventures of the mythic heroes and the personal experiences of the poet. Latin elegy would develop this aspect strongly, preserving, however, certain objective, gnomic qualities that generalize the personal story into a wider vision and accommodate elements absorbed from other literary genres, such as comedy, epigram, tragedy, lyric, and bucolic.

The elegiac world

Explicitly, often polemically, autobiographical poetry that insists on proclaiming its roots in the concrete, subjective experience of the poet, elegy tends to frame the individual experiences in typical forms and situations, in recurring ways; this should alert us to the dangers of biographical criticism. One may speak of an elegiac world, with conventional roles and behaviors, and of an ethical principal belonging to it, an ideology associated with its founding values. Its most characteristic form is represented in Propertius's first book.

Servitium amoris

Above all it is a poetry of love, since for the elegiac poet love is the sole and absolute experience, completely filling existence and giving it meaning. It is his *aristos bios,* the "perfect form of life" chosen by him, which proudly contrasts itself with the other ethical models available, proclaiming its own superiority and its achievement of *autarkeia,* the satisfying self-sufficiency sought by the philosophies of the day. The poet's life, entirely devoted to love, is figured as *servitium,* as enslavement to the *domina,* who is capricious and unfaithful. His relation to her is made up, naturally, of occasional joys and much suffering. Apart from betraying the lover and making him jealous, she gives herself to him only with difficulty. This is the typical situation of the *paraklausithyron,* in which the rejected lover bewails her cruelty in front of her closed door. And yet the poet, irremediably ill with his passion, abandons himself to a sort of pleased acquiescence in the pain, in the enjoyment of suffering; only occasionally can he make the feeble gesture of rebellion. This is the situation of the

Projection into myth

renuntiatio amoris. The bitter feelings and continual disappointments lead him to project his own experience into the pure realm of myth or into the happy innocence of a golden age, to exalt his experience by assimilating it to the heroic loves of literature, to transfer it, in other words, to a wholly satisfying, ideal world. Imprisoned in an irregular love, in a passion that alienates and humiliates him, even socially, he leads a life of *nequitia,* a life of degradation and dissipation, since in everyone's eyes his life lacks positive qualities. He repudiates his duties as *civis,* the glorious values of the citizen-soldier, contrasting the softness of love with the harshness of war and with the other forms of degradation associated with it, such as greed and ambition. And he transfers to this sphere all his moral energy, to the point of absolute devotion: he becomes, not a hero of war, but—an oxymoron—a hero of love.

Elegy and the mos maiorum

It is interesting to observe how elegy, which avowedly rebels against the established values of the tradition, against the *mos maiorum,* in fact reclaims them by transferring them into its own world, and it does this while remaining their prisoner still (this is a contradiction, and one of the most conspicuous reasons for the instability of the elegiac system, as is evident, for instance, in the work of Propertius). And when we come to Propertius, we will see (as we have already, in a way, with Catullus) that the love relation, although institutionally irregular, in that it involves only courtesans or "free" women, never women of respectable society, tends to be figured as a conjugal relation and therefore to be bound by *fides,* safeguarded by *pudicitia,* and suspicious of *luxuria* and urban sophistication.

Poetry as a means of courtship

In this sort of bohemian life led by the elegiac poet, the motives for love and for poetry writing naturally become identical and delimit the same world. The poetry that is produced by the poet-lover's direct experience and resembles his life should at the same time perform a practical function and serve as a means of courtship (*ite procul, Musae, si non prodestis amanti,* says Tibullus [2.4.14]); it should cooperate in seducing the beloved with the mirage of fame and immortal glory. One natural consequence, of course, is a certain choice of poetics, the rejection of elevated poetry in favor of the light muse, with tones and content inspired by the immediacy of passion. This takes the traditional form of the *recusatio,* in which the poet justified such a rejection as a necessary choice determined by his own inability.

Neoteroi and elegy

Here one sees clearly the enormous debt that elegiac poetry owes to Catullus and neoteric poetry. It shares with it, first of all, the revolution in literary taste. Callimachean poetics, the pursuit of formal refinement and concise elegance, several times affirmed by the elegiac poets, Propertius in particular, is now a definite acquisition for Latin literature. At the same time, elegy inherits, from Catullus chiefly, the sense of moral rebellion, the taste for *otium,* for a life remote from civic and political engagement and disposed instead to cultivate private sentiments and to make them the object of poetic activity. Thus it is precisely the connection of its two characteristic traits, elegance of form and intensive affective participation, that elegy derives from neoterism and especially from Catullus, in whom it could also find the outline for the new form of composition. Catullus's poem 68, in particular, in which the mythological element has an important function, is often pointed to as the embryo of the future literary genre. Elegiac poetry itself several times shows that it is fully conscious of this continuity with the neoteric-Catullan tradition, by paying due homage to its predecessors (Propertius 2.34.85; Ovid, *Amores* 3.9.61 ff.).

1. CORNELIUS GALLUS

Life of Gallus

C. Cornelius Gallus, about whose life our chief source is Suetonius, was born of a humble family perhaps in 69 B.C., in Narbonese Gaul, at Forum Iulii (today Fréjus). At Rome he was a fellow student of Virgil, whom later, once his political career had begun, he may have assisted in preserving his lands near Mantua at the time of the distribution to the veterans. He sided with Octavian against Antony, fighting in Egypt in 30. Immediately after the victory he was appointed *praefectus Aegypti,* a post that he must have held with excessive independence and pride, since he ventured to speak with scant regard for Augustus himself. He thus fell into disgrace and was condemned to exile and the confiscation of his property; he had no choice but to kill himself (26 B.C.).

The friends of Gallus: Virgil and Parthenius

The friendship that joined Gallus to Virgil is well known. Virgil dedicated the tenth eclogue to Gallus, drawing accents and motifs from his friend's verses, and also, it seems, may have concluded the fourth book of the *Georgics* with his praises, which later, when Gallus fell into disgrace, Virgil replaced, at Augustus's behest, with the fable of Aristaeus that we now read there (but see p. 269). Also important is Gallus's friendship with the Greek poet, Parthenius of Nicaea, who, after coming to Rome around

73, played a significant role as mediator between Hellenistic culture and neoteric poetry (see p. 141). Parthenius dedicated to Gallus a prose collection of myths about love, *Erotika pathemata,* from which to draw inspiration for his poetry.

*Gallus and
Euphorion*

We know that Gallus was the author of four books of elegies, published under the title *Amores,* in which he sang of his passion for Lycoris (the customary poetic pseudonym of the beloved woman, which, it seems, concealed the mime actress Volumnia, whose stage name was Cytheris; Antony may also have been her lover). Thus the erotic element was central in Gallus's poetry, but mythological learning must also have played an important part. In this connection it should be recalled that, as Virgil's tenth eclogue itself attests (v. 50), Gallus was an admirer of Euphorion of Chalcis, the Greek poet of the third century whose inauspicious influence upon the poetic taste of the time was deplored by Cicero (see p. 136); Gallus too will have been one of the *cantores Euphorionis.* And the idea that Euphorion's precious mythological and geographical learning—he had the reputation of being a hermetic poet—exercised an important influence upon Gallus's poetry seems to be confirmed by a verse of his (*uno tellures dividit amne duas,* said of a Scythian river, the Hypanis, which separates Asia and Europe), that pentameter that until a short time ago was all that remained to us of his work.

*The new Gallus:
progenitor of elegy*

In 1979 a lucky papyrus discovery in the sands of Egypt restored to us a set of ten verses (on whose authenticity and attribution, however, doubt has been cast). Despite their fragmentary form, they seem to provide interesting confirmation of a number of hypotheses that scholars, lacking concrete textual references, had previously formulated. Already to be found in Gallus, it was suspected, was the kernel of several basic themes of elegy: the beloved as a source of inspiration and the addressee of the poetry; the identification of poetry with life; the *servitium amoris,* that is, the poet's enslavement to the capricious and tyrannical *domina;* the poet's bad conscience over his life of *nequitia,* which betrays an inner conflict with the system of traditional values. All this emerges from the few verses that were rediscovered, as does also that poetics of courtship through poetry that later would have an important function in the other elegiac poets. Gallus, the heir—through Euphorion and Parthenius—of Alexandrian poetry, thus confirms his great significance as a mediator between neoterism and Augustan elegy. He was probably the one who gave this genre its own form, bestowing upon it a range and a compositional movement that was ampler than that of the brief epigram and fusing in it the mythological learning of Alexandrian elegy and his own personal experience. In short, the new Latin elegy acquires its formal independence and its distinctive character as love poetry from him, whom the ancients regarded as its creator. Unfortunately, only a dim echo has come down to us of Gallus's own voice, of that work of his that was so greatly valued in his day (although later Quintilian would judge it to be *durior* than that of Tibullus and Propertius).

2. TIBULLUS

LIFE AND
EVIDENCE

About Tibullus's life we do not have abundant and precise information. What we do know comes to us from a *vita* transmitted, without author's name, in the oldest Tibullan manuscripts (according to some, it goes back to Suetonius's *De Poetis*) and from references in his elegies or in other poets, especially a funeral epigram by Domitius Marsus, Horace's epistle 1.4, and Ovid's epicedion, *Amores* 3.9.

His death, shortly after Virgil's (September of 19 B.C.), we may with a fair approximation date to the last months of the same year or the first months of 18. On the basis of unreliable notices, his birth is placed between 55 and 50 B.C., in rural Latium, perhaps at Gabii or Pedum. His well-to-do family belonged to the equestrian class; this is true despite his complaints of economic reverses and poverty, which is a motif he has in common with the other elegiac poets.

The central reference point of his biography is the relation of friendship and patronage between him and Messalla Corvinus, a republican nobleman and politician who maintained a position of prestige even under the Augustan regime (see pp. 260 f.). Tibullus followed his patron on several military expeditions entrusted to him by Augustus; he took part, for example, in the expedition to Aquitania, the victorious outcome of which secured for Messalla the honor of a triumph (September of 27); this was celebrated by the poet in elegy 1.7. Another elegy (1.3) informs us that Tibullus took part as a member of Messalla's general staff in another mission to the East, of uncertain date, but that illness kept him at Corcyra (Corfu) until his forced return to Italy. The last years of his life he may have lived in the countryside of Latium, where Horace depicts him as withdrawn and melancholy.

WORKS

Antiquity has transmitted to us under the name of Tibullus a heterogeneous collection of elegies, the so-called *Corpus Tibullianum,* in three books (which became four with the division of the third book into two parts during the Renaissance). Today only the first two books are attributed to our poet with certainty. In addition, the last two poems of the present fourth book and the five poems about the love of Messalla's niece, Sulpicia, for a certain Cerinthus (numbers 2–6 of the same book) should also belong to him. For the other poems, see below.

The first book, begun after 32 and published in 26 or 25 B.C., is dominated by the figure of Delia, a name that, according to Apuleius, derives from the translation into Greek of the woman's real name, Plania *(planus = delos);* five of the ten elegies that make up the book are devoted to her (1, 2, 3, 5, 6). These poems, in conformity with the topos of the elegiac genre, describe a woman who is inconstant, capricious, and fond of luxury and mundane pleasures; their relation is a tormented one, always threatened by the risk of betrayal. Alternating with the elegies on Delia are the elegies on a young man, Marathus (8, 9, and 4, which illustrate the art of conquering the *pueri*), written in a less suffering tone and full of playful irony; yet the contours of this relation, which may intersect momentarily or overlap with the relation to Delia, remain very hazy. The first book is completed by an elegy (7) for Messalla's birthday and by the concluding elegy (10), which celebrates peace and the country life.

Three of the six elegies in the second book (3, 4, 6), which perhaps remains unfinished, are devoted to Nemesis, the woman who is its new protagonist. Nemesis, whose name means "revenge" (she is the one who has ousted Delia from the poet's heart), is a figure with harsher features, a greedy and unscrupulous courtesan. Of the remaining elegies, one sings of the birthday of Tibullus's friend Cornutus (2), the first describes the celebration of a farm festival, the Ambarvalia, and another (5) celebrates the appointment of Messalla's oldest son, Messalinus, to the priestly college of the *quindecemviri sacris faciundis*. In the works of Tibullus that have come down to us there is no trace of Glycera, Tibullus's unhappy love for whom is mentioned by Horace (*Carmina* 1.33).

The Myth of Rural Peace

Rural peace and city life

Tibullus is known commonly as a poet of the fields, of the serene rural life. And yet even in him we find the regular setting of elegiac poetry, the life of the city, which serves as background for the loves and intrigues, the secret meetings and the betrayals, in short, for the moments and occasions about which the wheel of amorous society turns. It is not in this sense, therefore, but in another, more exact sense that one can uphold the centrality of the rural world in his poetic universe.

The rural world as the substitute for myth

We have already referred to a tendency, a typical drive of elegiac poetry, to construct an ideal world, a place of evasion, a refuge from the bitterness of a tortured existence and the disappointments of a relation that is never wholly satisfactory. This agonizing tension finds its outlet in the world of myth, where the elegiac poet projects his experience ideally, assimilating it to the great heroic paradigms. In Tibullus, however, the world of myth is absent—this trait distinguishes him sharply from the other elegiac poets—and its function is performed instead by the rural world. The Tibullan countryside is a place of idyllic happiness, of a simple and serene life harmoniously responding to the rhythms of nature and pervaded by a sense of ancestral rustic religiosity. Tibullus makes this ideal space the place of regret and desire; he yearns for it as the lost setting of a distant, happy golden age and, at the same time, as the hoped-for harbor in which to anchor a precarious, suffering existence. In a space that is conventional and stylized several undoubtedly autobiographical references stand out; such references are not unimportant in regard to a poet over whose biography there has been debate concerning whether it is real or invented. Among these references the lovely image of the boy Tibullus running through his house is noteworthy: *aluistis et idem, / cursarem vestros cum tener ante pedes,* "Lares of my ancestors, protect me: you nourished me when as a child I ran by your feet" (1.10.15–16).

Longing for peace

In Tibullus there is a strong need for refuge, for an intimate, quiet space in which to protect and cultivate his feelings in the face of the treacheries and storms of life; the picture sketched in 1.1.45–48 is a splendid emblem of this. And such a need is met by the other dominating theme of Tibullus's poetry, peace. His opposition to militarism and his execration of war and its horrors, which corresponds to a call for peace widespread in the culture of the day, following the long tragedy of the civil wars, harmonizes with his longing for this ideal counterworld, which is populated by simple people and warmed by the love of a faithful woman. Behind the features of bucolic idyll, in which Virgilian influence is notable, the countryside of Tibullus reveals its Italian character, with its wealth of ancient rural values celebrated by the archaizing ideology of the principate. In this, in his close adherence to the traditional values, in his anti-modern attitude, Tibullus is perhaps the most obvious instance of the contradiction that elegiac poetry, so avowedly nonconformist and rebellious, harbors within itself. It is no coincidence that Ovid, who will address and in his own way resolve that contradiction (see pp. 341 f. and 345 f.), when thanking the good fortune that caused him to be born in the opulent Rome of his day, would reverse Tibullus's regret for the mythical happy age of Saturn (1.3.35 ff.).

Tibullus as *Poeta Doctus*

Tibullus and Hellenistic poetry

Whereas Propertius looks upon Callimachus and Philitas as masters of elegy and, in his eagerness to rival the models of Greek love poetry, proclaims that he feels he is the Roman Callimachus, Tibullus is not inclined to similar declarations of poetics. But this does not mean that the work of the great Alexandrian poets was not as familiar to him as to Propertius. Our knowledge of Alexandrian poetry today allows us to find in Tibullus's work many of the distinctive traits of Hellenistic poetry; and although there are no traces in him of that subtle learning displayed by the Alexandrians and scarcely any evocation of precious myths to adorn his composi-

The style of Tibullus

tion, Tibullus, too, undoubtedly deserves the title *poeta doctus*. His style reveals at every point, and with extraordinary regularity, the effort made towards a writing of extreme care, in which simplicity itself is the laborious result of an artistic choice, or rather the visible sign of a trust in words and their expressive force, without the need for distortions or pathetic intensifications of the discourse. The limpid expression seems to be the product of immediacy; the effort of composition remains hidden beneath the smooth surface of an apparently spontaneous writing. This limpidity of expression is matched by a restrained, unexcitable voice—intensity without shouting, the discretion of a low voice. The rhythm has a certain light, singable quality, a regular cadence, which often approaches the resonance of rhyme when, with the words distributed in a balanced way between the first and the second part of the pentameter, the sound that ends the second half of the verse echoes the end of the first. This form of expression exerts a conspicuous influence on the technique of the Ovidian couplet (even though Tibullus's terse simplicity lacks the sharpness of mannerist writing that belongs to Ovid's style).

"Terse and elegant": thus described by Quintilian (10.1.93), who sees in him the classic of Roman elegiac poetry, Tibullus is already admired by the ancients for his style, which is simple and luminous, free and refined. The lexical purity, the fluid movement of the thoughts, harmoniously linked together and without the abrupt swerves of Propertius, the fine, delicate tones, often gently dreaming, the very economy of mythological learning, the lightly ironic smile—all these qualities give to his poetry the charm of stylistic maturity and expressive naturalness.

Literary Success

To judge at least from Horace, Domitius Marsus, Ovid, and the *Corpus Tibullianum,* Tibullus seems to have been quite popular among his contemporaries, and he remained so at least until the first century A.D. Quintilian prefers him to Propertius, though he acknowledges that others do not share his view. Ancient readers may have found Tibullus's elegant balance and his dampened emotions, his *elegantia* and *suavitas,* more consoling, and less irritating, than the rough, frenetic Propertius. But Tibullus's fortunes started to be overshadowed in late antiquity by Ovid's, and outside of a few French cultural centers, he was not widely known in the Middle Ages. A single manuscript of his poems seems to have existed at the Carolingian court in the late eighth century, and from there knowledge of his works radiated to Fleury on the Loire and thence in the twelfth century to Orléans. But the main vehicle for Tibullus's survival in the Middle Ages was anthologies. The *Florilegium Gallicum,* composed at Orléans in the mid-twelfth century, contained extensive extracts; many others contained brief ones, chosen sometimes for their moral sentiments, sometimes apparently simply as an aid in teaching metrical composition.

It may have been Petrarch who brought Tibullus to Italy from France. At first he seems not to have been very popular, but then in the 1420s two manuscripts of his poems were copied, and by the middle of the century he had become a favorite author; there are well over a hundred manuscripts (often accompanying Catullus, Propertius, and Ovid) and three *editiones principes* (all dating from about 1472). His popularity as a sentimental, melancholy poet of love and the countryside lasted into the nineteenth century and inspired generations of poets. Luigi Alamanni's fifteenth-century *Felicità dell'amore* translated the opening lines of poem 1.1; Pietro Bembo praised Lucrezia Borgia in elegies inspired by Tibullus; Goethe's *Roman Elegies* reveal intense study of his poems (for example, the eighteenth elegy is obviously based in part upon Tibullus 1.1). Among nineteenth-century authors, Mörike and Carducci were particularly influenced by him, while Chateaubriand's *Mémoires* (bk. 2, chap. 3) provides a memorable account of how, as an adolescent in love, he rediscovered his own sorrows in the text of Tibullus.

So far the twentieth century, which seems to prefer sterner stuff, has tended to neglect Tibullus in favor of Propertius. It may be doubted whether Tibullus's sentimental nostalgia for the beauties of nature will win him very many new readers in the coming years.

3. THE *CORPUS TIBULLIANUM*

The two most important manuscripts of Tibullus, the *Ambrosianus* and the *Vaticanus* (of the fourteenth century), have transmitted to us, as was already said, a collection of poems only a part of which is to be attributed to the poet under whose name it has come down to us and to whom in fact they were attributed until the end of the eighteenth century. This collection is known as the *Corpus Tibullianum.* In the manuscripts it was divided into three books, but the humanists divided the third in two, and so today we speak of four books.

Lygdamus

Difference between Lygdamus and Tibullus

The first six poems of book 3 of the *Corpus,* addressed to a woman named Neaera, are the work of a poet who calls himself Lygdamus. Since this is a pseudonym—Lygdamus is a Greek name and as such could have belonged only to a slave; but the poet is a free man and from an old Roman family, as he himself says—it was thought to conceal Tibullus himself. The German scholar J. H. Voss, however, was the first to realize that Lygdamus sets his birth in the year 43 B.C.; he indicates this with the verse *cum cecidit fato consul uterque pari* (3.5.18, used by Ovid for the same purpose in *Tristia* 4.10.6), when both consuls, Hirtius and Pansa, died in the battle of Modena. Now, 43 B.C., the year of Ovid's birth, cannot also be the year of Tibullus's, who in that case would have been only thirteen or fourteen at the time of Messalla's expedition to the East (around 30 B.C.). Thus Lygdamus cannot be identified with Tibullus, as had been thought up to that time. But then who is this poet?

The identification of Lygdamus

The hypotheses about Lygdamus's identity have been numerous, ranging from poets such as Cassius Parmensis or Valgius Rufus to Ovid's brother and Messalinus, Messalla's son, but they are all unsatisfactory, in different ways. The most obvious, which identifies the young Lygdamus as Ovid, who later in the *Tristia* would have repeated a verse previously used, may also be the most plausible, but it runs into contrary indications, mostly of a linguistic-stylistic nature. Moreover, the many parallelisms between Lygdamus and the other works of Ovid suggest instead an influence exerted by Ovid upon this mysterious poet.

The problem of Lygdamus's identification thus remains open; he was probably a poet of Messalla's circle. His poems center on his painful separation from the woman he loves, and they elaborate recurring motifs of elegiac poetry. Despite recourse to conventional clichés and a certain stylistic immaturity, the reader appreciates a vein of fresh sentimentality shadowed by the obsessive thought of death.

The *Panegyric of Messalla* and the Other Poems

The Panegyricus Messallae

Following Lygdamus's six elegies in the manuscripts of the *Corpus Tibullianum* comes a long poem of 211 hexameters, the *Panegyricus Messallae,* and a group of thirteen other poems, which make up the present book 4. The mediocre *Panegyric of Messalla,* probably written not long after 31, the year of his consulship, is, as the name says, a praise of this important politician (see pp. 260 f.), whose virtues it celebrates and whose brilliant career it passes in review. The unknown author would have been a poet of the circle.

Sulpicia
Of the other thirteen poems of book 4, the first five (2–6) are generally attributed to Tibullus and concern the love of Sulpicia, niece of the jurist Servius Sulpicius and of Messalla himself, for Cerinthus, whose name some have seen as the Hellenized name of Cornutus, Tibullus's friend from elegy 2.2; the last pair (13–14, the latter an epigram) are also attributed to Tibullus. Although these are shorter than the poems that are certainly by Tibullus, the greater stylistic consciousness and the typical fluid movements suggest the hand of the poet. Elegies 7–12, by contrast, form a cycle of brief love notes by Sulpicia to Cerinthus and are attributed to Sulpicia herself.

4. PROPERTIUS

LIFE
Sextus Propertius was born in Umbria, very probably at Assisi, between 49 and 47 B.C. His family was well-to-do and of equestrian rank, but as a result of the Perusine War (the revolt of the Italian landowners, which was put down by Augustus, in 41–40) it suffered losses and the confiscation of lands. Now in straitened circumstances, the young Propertius moved to Rome to try a legal and political career. But already in 29 we see him, not busy with rhetorical training, but belonging to the fashionable literary circles of the capital and connected to an elegant, unscrupulous woman, Cynthia; her true name, according to Apuleius, was Hostia, and she would have been a descendant of a poet named Hostius, who wrote an epic-historical poem, the *Bellum Histricum* (see p. 110) during the second half of the second century B.C. Besides his relation with Cynthia, the other important event in the life of Propertius is his contact with Maecenas and his famous circle. The approach to this circle probably took place in 28, after the publication of his first book of poems, and his familiarity with the other poets who belonged to it, especially Virgil, is repeatedly documented from this point on; yet he also had particularly close ties to Ovid, who from his youth belonged to Messalla's circle.

Like Catullus and Tibullus, Propertius had a short life. In his verses we have no chronological references later than 16 B.C., and so his death should be put in that year or shortly after.

WORKS
We possess four books of Propertius's elegies. The first book, published in 28 B.C., is known also by the Greek name, transmitted by several manuscripts, of *Monobiblos,* "single book." As for books 2 and 3, it is not certain whether they were published together or separately; separate publication of the two books, in around 25 and 22 B.C., respectively, is regarded as more likely. It is certain, however, that the order in which these books appear repeats the order in which they were written. This is different from

what happens during the same period with the first three books of Horace's *Odes,* the architecture of which is the final outcome of a planned, unified arrangement that ignores the real chronology of composition. All the elegies of Propertius's second book, by contrast, were written before those of the third book. Book 4, which differs from the previous ones in content too, is later and does not refer to events after 16 B.C., a date taken as that of publication. Some analytic information on the four books follows:

Book 1: twenty-two elegies, varying in length from ten to fifty-two verses, for a total of about seven hundred, or 350 elegiac couplets. The book opens with the name of Cynthia (*Cynthia prima suis miserum me cepit ocellis* [1.1]), and the fascination exerted by the cultivated, refined woman upon the young man in love animates, more or less directly, all the elegies of this first book. An autobiographical poem, or rather a testimonial of a generation and a milieu, of this sort does not go along with an interest in civil society and in the new political arrangement that Octavian was creating at Rome in the wake of his victory at Actium (31 B.C.). The sole reference to politics is the mention of the *bellum Perusinum* and the death of a relative of the poet in that tragic episode; the mention, which was certainly not welcome to the new regime, occurs in the leave-taking (elegy 22) that forms a kind of *sphragis,* or "signature," to the *Monobiblos.*

Book 2: thirty-four elegies, some divided in two by the critics, of from six to ninety-four verses, for a total of about fourteen hundred verses, or slightly fewer than seven hundred elegiac couplets. Published probably in 25, book 2 in its very first elegy shows a clear sign of Propertius's contact with the official milieu of Maecenas: the rejection *(recusatio)* of epic poetry, which amounts to a rejection of celebratory poetry. Cynthia, with her moods and loves, her desertions and rejections, is still at the center of the book. But already, with the tenth elegy, poetic homage to the princeps and his triumphs slips in.

Book 3: twenty-five elegies, of from eighteen to seventy-two verses, a total of about a thousand. The book is still dominated by the figure of Cynthia, but it is shadowed now by the imminent *discidium,* the definitive break. And yet alongside the theme of elegiac love there appear in this book, published probably in 22, other motifs relating to the fortunes and the ideology of the Augustan regime: good wishes for the expedition against the Parthians, planned in 22 (elegy 4); in an elegy dedicated to Maecenas (9), the promise of the engaged poetry that will be the material for the "Roman elegies" of book 4; the praise of Rome and Italy (22); the epicedion, "funeral song," for the young Marcellus, son by adoption and son-in-law of Augustus, who died in 23 (Virgil too had memorialized him, in the sixth book of the *Aeneid*). We find, moreover, in this book a new attention on Propertius's part to the established morality, a greater openness to the themes that were pleasing to official circles—a clear indication of the journey the poet was completing towards his integration with the regime.

Book 4: eleven elegies, more engaged and longer than those of the preceding books, varying in length from the 48 verses of the tenth elegy to the 150 of the first, for a total of almost 1,000 verses. Only two elegies are still devoted to Cynthia: the eighth, which represents the fascinating violence of Cynthia when jealous and victorious, and the ninth, in which Cynthia, a shade in the realm of the dead but still bitter and aggressive, appears to the poet in a dream. The other elegies are for the most part a concession, though a limited and controlled one, to the directives of the official culture. Nonetheless, it is not celebratory poetry. Propertius does not betray the principles of Alexandrian poetics and the *Musa tenuis* of elegy; rather, following the path marked out by the *Aitia* ("The Causes," "The Origins") of Callimachus (the third-century poet from Cyrene), he sets out to illustrate myths and rituals of the Roman and Italian tradition: the god Vertumnus, the treachery of the virgin Tarpeia, the dedication of the Temple of Palatine Apollo, the legend of Hercules and Cacus, the worship of Jupiter Feretrius. (Ovid in his *Fasti* would follow him in turn, only more systematically, as usual.)

SOURCES

Many autobiographical references are found in Propertius's elegies themselves; on his homeland and youth, see in particular 1.22 and 4.1.121 ff. Various other references are in Ovid, for instance, *Tristia* 4.10.45 f. and 4.10.51 ff. We do not have ancient biographies of him. About the real person Cynthia, as about the other women sung of by the love poets, we are informed by Apuleius, *Apologia* 10.

In the Name of Cynthia: The First Book

The name of Cynthia

It was already a custom of the Alexandrian poets, which then came to Rome with the *neoteroi,* to give to a collection of poems the name of the woman celebrated therein. The young Propertius followed this usage when in 28 B.C. he published under the name *Cynthia* his first book of elegies, known also by the Greek name *Monobiblos.* This extraordinary woman stands out from the very beginning, from the first word of the prefatory poem, which describes the poet's condition:

Cynthia prima suis miserum me cepit ocellis,
    contactum nullis ante cupidinibus.

("Cynthia was the first to capture me, unfortunate, with her eyes: no passion had touched me before" [1.1–2]).

Social degradation

He presents himself as being for a year the prisoner of his passion for her, his first passion, and as being inexorably destined for a life of dissipation *(nullo . . . consilio)* on her account. Cynthia, as was already said, is an elegant, refined woman, of great literary and musical culture—the very pseudonym the poet created for her is emblematic: it is derived from Cynthus, a mountain of Delos that was sacred to Apollo—who lives as a courtesan in the fashionable circles frequented by politicians and writers. Joining oneself to such a woman, a "free" woman of the demimonde, signifies for

Propertius compromising his social status, contravening the code of respectability by which a man of his position was bound.

The pleasure in degradation

But the degradation to which the elegiac poet condemns himself by rejecting career and social decorum is not merely justified by him: he glories in it. The relation with the beloved woman, who is haughty and capricious, tyrannical and unfaithful, is imaged as *servitium,* as slavery, but the poet-lover proudly justifies his difference from others and takes pleasure in his suffering; the attitude has been called that of the "cursed poet." He makes love the center and the absolute value of life, and Cynthia becomes the only reason for his existence, to which she gives meaning and satisfying fullness:

> Tu mihi sola domus, tu, Cynthia, sola parentes,
> omnia tu nostrae tempora laetitiae.

("You alone, Cynthia, are my house and my parents, you are all the hours of my happiness" [1.11.23–24]).

Propertius's ethical revolt

Propertius carries to an extreme and produces a rationale for that revolt already raised by Catullus, the rejection of the *mos maiorum,* of the primacy of the values of the *civitas,* in favor of an existence totally dedicated to love (1.6.27–30). This decided acceptance of his own different destiny, when contrasted with the leading ethical models of the day, in particular the moral degradation and corruption that stained public life, sometimes takes on the character of an almost philosophical life choice, one that can provide inner self-sufficiency, the *autarkeia* promised by the Greek philosophies.

Unity of life and poetry

An existence devoted to *otium,* to *servitium* towards the beloved, becomes completely one with the poet-lover's literary activity, since he makes his life the material of poetry and in turn uses that as a device for courting the woman, as the only tool of seduction that the poor elegiac poet has at his disposal in the contest with the other, wealthy suitors. It is evident that the motivations of life, of practical convenience, here accord perfectly with the basic choices of elegiac poetry. The Callimachean choice of "slender" poetry, as opposed to the overblown qualities of epic, is favored because of its greater effectiveness in achieving the goals of courtship (*plus in amore valet Mimnermi versus Homero,* "in love the verse of Mimnermus [i.e., the elegiac couplet] is worth more than the poetry of Homer" [1.9.11]).

Cynthia and the traditional values

And yet Propertius's love, the type of relation that he pursues as an ideal, is not libertine love, the casual comedy of amorous adventures that will constitute the art of Ovid's Don Juan. For himself and Cynthia, Propertius dreams of the great loves of myth, exclusive and eternal passions that last beyond death (*traicit et fati litora magnus amor* [1.9.12]). For Cynthia, the brilliant and unscrupulous courtesan, he desires the traditional models and values, and like Catullus with Lesbia, he would like to imagine his love for her as a *foedus,* a strong inner bond assured by the gods and fostered by

Neoteroi *and elegy*

castitas, pudor, and *fides,* the cornerstones of female morality. The reality, of course, is quite different, and the elegiac poet is tormented by the contradiction in which he is imprisoned: he is attracted by the charm and fashionable elegance of the beloved woman, and yet at the same time he looks for simplicity, loyalty, and absolute devotion in her. From this dissatisfaction, this unresolved tension, is born the need for flight, for escape into the pure world of myth: transfigured into mythic characters, the poet-lover and his woman would be an exemplary love, an unblemished dream.

A Larger Corpus and the Break with Cynthia

The new collection: the recusatio

The large and immediate success of the first *libellus* cast Propertius into the literary limelight and attracted Maecenas's interest. Augustus's refined and shrewd "minister of culture" attempted to guide Propertius towards new poetic forms, to win him over as a collaborator in the cultural policy promoted by the regime. We find evident traces of these pressures and of the poet's resistance in the new, larger collection, books 2 and 3, probably published in 22 B.C. The second book opens with a *recusatio,* an elegant but firm refusal, in the Callimachean tradition, on the part of the poet, who declares himself unequal to the task of facing the sublime Muse of the epic-historic poem, of playing the part of seer, and affirms the unity of poetics

Propertius's discomfort

and style of life. And yet Propertius's attitude in book 2, as compared with that in book 1, is more complex, less straightforward. On the one hand, his sense of discomfort with the life of *nequitia* is sharpened, a sense that sometimes results from a consciousness of incompleteness, of an unresolved existence; on the other hand, his relation with Cynthia becomes more painful, his need for idealizing her greater, since she is evidently not able to stand comparison with the great mythic paradigms.

Book 3 and Propertius's detachment

Such a process, which is accompanied by experimentation with more complex forms of composition, reaches a more advanced stage in the third book, where a more varied material, embracing themes less closely connected to love for Cynthia, is especially notable. The love elegies are less frequent, and Propertius's attitude in particular is less impassioned. The self-irony already present in book 1 becomes more conspicuous, and the poet regards himself with greater detachment, often with witty levity. This detachment shows itself also in a broadening of perspective and in the emphasis on the gnomic-didactic stance, which is sometimes inspired by the themes of diatribe. The choice of the slender Muse and the rejection of epic are reconfirmed, but as the prefatory elegy significantly demonstrates, they are no longer closely connected to a style of life, no longer seen in relation to love, but are motivated only by esthetic-literary concerns. The book concludes, emblematically, with the definitive *discidium,* the farewell to Cynthia, bringing to a close the cycle that had begun with her name.

Civic Elegy

Elegy uncoupled from eros: the "Roman Callimachus"

The apparently irremediable crisis of Propertius's relation with Cynthia and his abandonment of love elegy take place at a moment in which the poetry of political engagement, meeting the ideological and cultural needs of the Augustan regime, is producing its ripest and finest fruit, the *Aeneid.* Propertius himself had solemnly announced as much a few years earlier (*nescio quid maius nascitur Iliade* [2.34.66]). External events, the pressure exerted by Maecenas and perhaps by Augustus himself, together with the crisis that had destroyed from within the precarious coherence of erotic elegy drive Propertius, after several years of silence, towards a different kind of poetry. He does not reject Callimacheanism, and he does not turn to epic-historic poetry; rather, carrying to its limit a process already under way in the third book, he uncouples elegy from eros and makes it an independent genre. Propertius will be the "Roman Callimachus" (4.1.64); he will be, like the master of his style, the careful investigator of causes: in the manner of the *Aitia* he will study and sing of the origins of the names, myths, and cults of Rome (4.1.69).

Civic poetry and ironic grace

His fourth book of elegies, probably published in 16 B.C., thus is produced under the impetus of a new and ambitious commitment (from which the Ovid of the *Fasti* will take his cue [see pp. 355 f.]), but Propertius's civic poetry will not in general have the weightiness, the *gravitas,* the seriousness of so much national poetry. Early Rome and the world of myth are interpreted for the most part in accordance with Callimachean taste, which allows for gracefulness, irony, and occasionally a light, comic pleasantry (as in elegy 9, on Hercules). And along with engaged, solemn poems (e.g., elegies 6 and 10) there are also elegies in which pathos is noticeable, the lyricism of the love poetry. In the fourth elegy, for instance, on the myth of Tarpeia, the poet adapts the myth as it was preserved in the tradition (for which see Livy 1.11.6) and reshapes it on the model of the dramatic story of Scylla's love for Minos, thus making amorous passion for Titus Tatius, king of the enemy Sabines, the reason for which the heroine betrays

Love in book 4

her own people. Love in fact is not absent from Propertius's last collection—the lack of homogeneity in the book is attested in the prefatory elegy, where the astrologer Horus draws attention to the contrast between Propertius's ambitions and his natural vocation for erotic poetry—nor is Cynthia absent; she reappears here in the dark (yet seductive) light of vice and corruption, or returns like a shade after death, to recall the love of a former time and to confirm its eternal existence, which had been so often proclaimed by the poet. But in the fourth book, especially in elegies 3, Arethusa's letter to her distant husband Lycotas, and 11, the famous epicedion of Cornelia, an important feature is the revaluation of conjugal love, the celebration of family feelings and domestic virtues, of chastity and tenderness. Moves in this direction were already found among the neoterics, in Catullus and Calvus; in Propertius it is one of the most evident signs of that movement towards integration that accompanies his poetic career.

Density of Style

Concentration and obscurity

Propertius has the reputation of being a difficult, sometimes obscure poet. In contrast to the crystalline naturalness of Tibullus, his style is characterized by concentration, density of metaphor, and constant experimentation with new expressive possibilities. The Callimachean inheritance, which is evident in his mythological learning and sophisticated literary consciousness, also manifests itself in the careful pursuit of unusual, often audacious *iuncturae* and of a complex syntactic structure, which is strained and often forced to the point of obscurity. These features of the style and composition of the Propertian elegy have contributed to the great damage that has complicated and often irremediably distorted the manuscript tradition of the poet, especially in book 2. Not only are there corruptions, lacunae, and transpositions, but it is often difficult even to establish with

The harsh elegance of
Propertius

certainty the divisions between one elegy and the next. This is the most typical feature of Propertius's style: abrupt beginning (*Tune igitur demens . . . ?* [1.8]; *Et merito . . .* [1.17]), proceeding by unpredictable movements, by leaps, through images and concepts, not making connections explicit but following a hidden, inner logic. In this form of expression, which mingles irony and pathos (note, for instance, the large number of questions, exclamations, and interjections), in its harsh elegance, and also in the complexity of the psychological attitudes it portrays, lie the principal reasons for the fascination that Propertius's poetry has exercised upon the taste of modern readers.

Literary Success

Antiquity and
Middle Ages

Propertius, like Tibullus, enjoyed an immediate success that lasted for at least a century. His verses are found inscribed on the walls of Pompeii, and even in Martial's time the *Monobiblos* was a favorite gift. Poets have always been particularly attracted to him. In antiquity, Ovid seems to have been especially adept at taking up and further developing generic hints he found adumbrated in Propertius: the *Heroides* work out in detail poetic possibilities apparently first explored in Propertius's elegy 4.3; the same applies to the relation between the *Fasti* and the aetiological poems in Propertius's fourth book. But from the end of antiquity (Ausonius, Claudian, Paulus Silentiarius) until about the middle of the twelfth century Propertius seems to have been little known; the few traces of apparent familiarity with his poetry during this period are likely to be indirect. During the twelfth century he began to circulate in northern France, perhaps in the Loire valley. The earliest references to him and imitations of his poetry are found in the works of John of Salisbury. The earliest surviving manuscripts were copied in Orléans on the Loire at the end of the twelfth century or the beginning of the thirteenth century, and all other surviving manuscripts derive from them.

Renaissance and
after

Once again, Petrarch seems to have played a decisive role in the return of Latin literature from France to Italy: he found a manuscript of Propertius in the Sorbonne, copied it, and brought the copy back to Italy. From then on, Propertius's increasing popularity was assured. Two *editiones principes* were published in Venice in 1472, and his combination of *doctrina* and *verborum novitas* inspired such Renaissance vernacular poets as Ariosto, Tasso, and Ronsard and such neo-Latin ones as Aeneas Silvius Piccolomini (the later Pope Pius II, whose *libellus* of nineteen erotic elegies entitled

"Cinthia" was suppressed during his lifetime and rediscovered only in the nineteenth century). If Tibullus was compared to a languid, pleasant brook, Propertius reminded his admirers of a rushing, uncontrollable torrent. Goethe's *Roman Elegies* represented one high point in the poet's modern fortunes, Ezra Pound's *Homage to Sextus Propertius* another. His peculiar combination of technical refinement, imagistic complexity, unpredictable sequences of thought, erudition, and suffering tends to make readers nervous, which is one reason why contemporary audiences find him, like Catullus, one of the most congenial of all Latin poets.

BIBLIOGRAPHY

General works on elegy are numerous; see esp. G. Luck, *The Latin Love Elegy* (ed. 2 London 1969), D. O. Ross, *Backgrounds to Augustan Poetry: Gallus, Elegy, and Rome* (Cambridge 1975), R.O.A.M. Lyne, *The Latin Love Poets* (Oxford 1980), P. Veyne, *Roman Erotic Elegy,* (badly) translated by D. Pellauer (Chicago 1988), and the essays collected in *Elegy and Lyric,* ed. J. P. Sullivan (London 1962). On the origins, see A. A. Day, *The Origins of Latin Love Elegy* (Oxford 1938) and compare the appendix to F. Cairns's *Tibullus: A Hellenistic Poet at Rome* (Cambridge 1979); the seminal German article by F. Jacoby, "Zur Entstehung der römischen Elegie," *Kleine philologische Schriften* 2 (Berlin 1961) 65–121, is still worth consulting. P. Oxy. 3725 offers new evidence; see P. J. Parsons in *MH* 45 (1988) 65–74 (German). Among works on particular topics note F. O. Copley, *Exclusus Amator: A Study in Latin Love Poetry* (Madison 1956), S. Lilja, *The Roman Elegists' Attitude to Women* (Helsinki 1965), and R. Whitaker, *Myth and Personal Experience in Roman Love-Elegy* (Göttingen 1983). In German see esp. W. Stroh, *Die römische Liebeselegie als werbende Dichtung* (Amsterdam 1971); for the viewpoint adopted above, see G. B. Conte, "Love without Elegy," in *Genres and Readers,* trans. Glenn W. Most (Baltimore 1994) 35–65.

The new fragment of Gallus was first published by R. D. Anderson, P. J. Parsons, and R.G.M. Nisbet in *JRS* 69 (1979) 125–55, with detailed commentary; the text has often been reproduced, e.g., in Büchner's *Fragmenta poetarum latinorum* (Leipzig 1982) and Courtney's *Fragmentary Latin Poets* (Oxford 1993). There have been many studies, including a monograph by L. Nicastri, *Cornelio Gallo e l'elegia ellenistica-romana* (Naples 1984). Doubts over the authenticity are resolved by J. Blänsdorf in *ZPE* 67 (1984) 43–50.

There are critical editions of Tibullus by F. W. Lenz and G. K. Galinsky (ed. 3 Leiden 1971) and by G. Luck (Stuttgart 1988); the Oxford text of J. P. Postgate (Oxford 1915) is still usable. The Loeb edition with translation by the same editor (in the same volume as Catullus) has been revised by G. P. Goold (Cambridge, Mass. 1988). The text by Guy Lee, with translation and notes, is excellent (ed. 3 with Robert Maltby, Leeds 1990). The detailed commentary by K. F. Smith (New York 1913, reprint Darmstadt 1964) is better than that of M.C.J. Putnam (Norman 1973); see also for book 1 that of P. Murgatroyd (Pietermaritzburg 1980). Among general studies note Cairns, *Tibullus,* and R. J. Ball, *Tibullus: A Critical Survey* (Göttingen 1983). For the *appendix Tibulliana,* see the commentary by H. Tränkle (Berlin 1990).

The best modern critical text of Propertius is that of P. Fedeli (Stuttgart 1984); see also the rival Teubner of R. Hanslik (Leipzig 1979) and the Oxford Classical Text of E. A. Barber (ed. 2 Oxford 1960, new text in preparation by S. J. Heyworth). G. P. Goold's Loeb of 1990 contains a completely new text and translation. There are helpful brief commentaries on all four books by W. A. Camps (Cambridge 1961–67);

also helpful is the older, single-volume commentary of H. E. Butler and E. A. Barber (Oxford 1933). See also the edition by L. Richardson, Jr. (Norman 1977), and the commentary on book 1 by R.I.V. Hodge and R. A. Buttimore (Cambridge 1977). D. R. Shackleton Bailey, *Propertiana* (Cambridge 1956), is a discussion of textual problems but also contains many parallels. In other languages, the German commentary by M. Rothstein (Berlin 1920–24) remains useful, but the fullest commentaries are those of P. J. Enk on books 1 and 2 (Leiden 1946, 1962, Latin) and P. Fedeli on books 1 and 3 (Florence 1980, Bari 1985, Italian). Fedeli's edition of book 4 (Bari 1965) is on a smaller scale.

English discussions include M. E. Hubbard, *Propertius* (London 1974), J. P. Sullivan, *Propertius: A Critical Introduction* (Cambridge 1976), T. D. Papanghelis, *Propertius: A Hellenistic Poet on Love and Death* (Cambridge 1987), H.-P. Stahl, *Propertius: "Love" and "War"* (Berkeley 1985), and the chapter in Lyne, *The Latin Love Poets*. The most important foreign works are J.-P. Boucher, *Études sur Properce* (Paris 1965), E. Lefèvre, *Propertius ludibundus* (Heidelberg 1966), and A. La Penna, *L'integrazione difficile: Un profilo di Properzio* (Turin 1977). There is a bibliography for 1946–83 by P. Fedeli and P. Pinotti (Assisi 1985).

On Ezra Pound's *Homage to Sextus Propertius,* see esp. J. P. Sullivan, *Pound and Propertius: A Study in Creative Translation* (London 1965).

Ovid

Publius Ovidius Naso, who himself gives us much information on his life, especially in elegy 4.10 of the *Tristia,* was born at Sulmona, a city of the Paelignians, in what is today the Abruzzo, of a prosperous equestrian family, on 20 March 43 B.C. At Rome he attended the best schools of rhetoric, those of Arellius Fuscus and Porcius Latro, aiming at a career in law and politics. He completed his studies with the required visit to Greece, but on returning to Rome, after holding several minor offices, he abandoned his political career. He joined the literary circle of Messalla Corvinus and established relations with Rome's greatest poets. After his precocious and brilliant literary efforts his life headed towards calm and complete success; at about the age of forty he also found conjugal felicity with his third wife. Just at the apex of success, in A.D. 8, an unexpected punishment from Augustus befell him, and he was relegated to the Black Sea, at Tomi (today Costanza). The causes of his relegation, which, unlike exile, did not include the loss of citizenship and possessions, have never been made fully clear (Ovid refers to them in a veiled manner at *Tristia* 2.107); the suspicion is that behind the official accusations of the immorality of his poetry, especially the *Ars Amatoria,* the real intention was to punish his involvement in the scandalous adultery of Julia Minor, Augustus's granddaughter, with Decimus Junius Silanus. Ovid died at Tomi in A.D. 17 or 18. Jerome's *Chronicle* attests the date of 17, but in book 1 of the *Fasti* reference is made to Roman events from the end of 17, knowledge of which could hardly have reached all the way to Tomi in a short time; and for this reason some regard it as prudent to put the date back a year.

The dating of Ovid's youthful works is problematic. Ovid published an edition of his first work, the *Amores,* in five books several years after 20 B.C.; a second edition in three books, the one that has come down to us, must have been published many years later, perhaps in A.D. 1. The *Amores* comprises forty-nine elegies, ranging in length from about 20 to 100 verses, for a total of 2,460 verses. The meter is the usual one of the genre, the elegiac couplet. To the same period as the *Amores* is traditionally assigned the composition of the first series (letters 1–15) of the *Heroides* (literally

"The Heroines"), which would have been published around 15, though some place them between 10 and 3; the second series (letters 16–21) is dated quite a bit later, to the years immediately before exile, A.D. 4–8. The twenty-one letters, the shortest being 115 verses, the longest 378, amount in total to about 4,000 verses. The meter is the elegiac couplet.

The (lost) tragedy *Medea,* which had great success, may have been written in the period between 12 and 8 B.C.

The publication of the first two books of the *Ars Amatoria* falls between 1 B.C. and A.D. 1 and is soon followed by the publication of the third book and of the *Remedia Amoris.* The *Ars* comprises three books, more than 2,300 verses, the first two dedicated to men, the third to women. The meter is the elegiac couplet, as it is for the 814 verses of the *Remedia Amoris.* In the same period are also placed the *Medicamina Faciei Femineae* ("The Cosmetics of Women"), also in elegiac couplets, of which only a hundred verses remain; the work is already mentioned in the third book of the *Ars.*

The years from A.D. 2 to 8 see the composition of the *Metamorphoses*—the Latin title is *Metamorphoseon Libri*—an epic poem in fifteen books (the shortest is of 628 verses, the longest of 968, for a total of nearly twelve thousand hexameters; exile prevented the final revision), and of the *Fasti,* a poetic calendar in elegiac couplets that was broken off when but half-finished: it comprises only six books, each one devoted to a month, from January to June, with a total of about 5,000 verses altogether.

Of the works from exile, all in elegiac couplets, the *Tristia* comprise five books, of about 3,500 verses all told: book 1 was composed during the voyage to Tomi; book 2, a single long elegy of self-defense, in 578 verses, was composed in 9; and the others were written from 9 to 12 and published separately. Of the four books of *Epistulae ex Ponto* (forty-six elegies, numbering around 3,200 verses), the first three are published in 13 and the fourth probably appears posthumously. The short invective poem *Ibis,* of 322 verses, should belong to the years 11–12.

Poems of doubtful authenticity have also come down to us under Ovid's name, such as the fragment (135 verses) of a didactic hexameter poem on fishing *(Halieutica)* and poems that are certainly spurious, such as the *Consolatio ad Liviam* or the elegy *Nux.* In addition to the *Medea,* various pieces of light or occasional poetry have been lost and two brief poems on the death or apotheosis of Augustus, one of them in the Getic language that was spoken at Tomi.

1. A MODERN POETRY

Relative adherence to elegy

After Propertius and Tibullus the reader who comes to Ovid is struck by the enormity of his production and the variety of poetic genres handled. This might seem to be an external fact, a pure problem of classification, but in reality it indicates a different attitude towards literary choices, which in turn involve or reflect life choices. Adherence to a genre such as love elegy does not mean for Ovid, as it did for his predecessors, an absolute life choice, centered on love. In particular it does not delimit a horizon or exclude other poetic experiences, as was the case for the love poets, who were bound to a practice of poetry that was suitable for their modes of life; we recall the motif of the *recusatio,* the protested inability to attain poetic subjects and tones of greater dignity. That experimentation that would lead him to attempt the most varied poetic genres without identifying himself with any one of them is the most conspicuous indication of Ovid's attitude, which makes the practice of poetry as such (i.e., not limited to one sphere or another, nor subordinated to other values) the center of his own experience.

The practice of poetry as the new center of life

This powerful literary self-consciousness also accords with Ovid's tendency to analyze reality in its most various aspects, excluding nothing and maintaining an attitude of extreme relativism. Opposed to absolute choices, he can follow the various aspects of reality, privileging those that seem more in accord with his taste, or he can follow the ethical-esthetic tendencies of his age as well as his own. This explains the most significant feature of his poetry, particularly the youthful poetry, namely, Ovid's acceptance, which proceeds from conviction and is often enthusiastic, of the new forms of life in the Rome of his day; this does not exclude, especially in the more advanced works of his maturity, a more conciliatory attitude and an openness to the values of tradition.

Relativism and openness to the new

Ovid, the last of the great Augustan poets, is outside the bloody period of the civil wars. When he enters the literary scene, that specter is far removed, peace is established, and people in general, intolerant of the archaic models of life proposed by the regime, are full of growing aspirations—to more relaxed manners of life, to a less severe morality, and to the ease and refinement that were introduced at Rome by its conquests in the East and that shape the fashionable society of the capital. Ovid becomes the interpreter of these aspirations, yet without rigidly opposing the regime and its guiding ideology; the recurrent attempts to attribute to the poet the role of political opponent, an anti-Augustan attitude, are not persuasive. He develops a type of poetry that palpably corresponds to this taste, to the style of life dominated by *cultus* and its refinements.

Ovid, poet in an era of peace

This is equally true in regard to content and to form. As for his poetics, the conception of poetry that Ovid repeatedly manifests is essentially anti-mimetic and anti-naturalistic and strongly innovative in comparison with the classical tradition, the line represented by Aristotle and Horace. Ovid's poetry claims to be independent of reality and instead declares, or rather exhibits, its literary nature and alludes to its models. This literary modernity is also revealed in Ovid's poetic language, which is to a very large extent the language of Latin poetry from Catullus onwards. It is revealed, too, in the terse and elegant style, in the musical flow of the verse (he brings the elegiac couplet to perfection, creating the standard towards which so many imitators in later centuries would strive), and in the richness and boldness of expression, this last a characteristic brilliantly cultivated and refined during the years he attended the rhetorical schools. The pleasing

A modern poet

Skeptical elegance

esttheticism and skeptical elegance of this poetry are also the expression of a taste that turns literature into an ornament of life.

2. THE *AMORES*

Ovid and the elegiac tradition

Ovid made his debut as a poet with a series of sparkling poems written when he was not yet twenty, a collection of elegies on the subject of love, the *Amores*. These still show visible traces of the great models and masters of erotic elegy, Tibullus and especially Propertius. Ovid, too, expresses, in the first person, the traditional themes of the elegiac genre: along with occasional poetry (e.g., the epicedion on the death of Tibullus) or poetry of obviously Alexandrian character (e.g., the elegy on the death of his mistress's parrot), there are love adventures, fleeting rendezvous, nocturnal serenades, quarrels with the beloved, scenes of jealousy, protests against her venality or her caprices, her harshness and her betrayals, and so on. But together with the manner and the themes and tones of the tradition, new features are already clearly observable, the elements proper to and characteristic of the Ovidian elegy.

The lack of a unifying figure

Above all, and this may be the most conspicuous innovation, the poetry lacks a female figure around whom the various amorous experiences gather, who constitutes the unifying center of the poet's work and life. The earlier love poets, Catullus, Gallus (as far as we know), and Propertius, had built their poetic activity around a single woman, a single great love that would be the goal and the meaning of that activity. With Ovid it is otherwise: Corinna, the woman evoked now and then under a Greek pseudonym, is a tenuous figure, present intermittently and in limited ways, who, one suspects, did not really exist; moreover, the poet himself declares on several occasions that he cannot be satisfied with a single love, that he prefers two women (2.10), or even that he can be charmed by any beautiful woman (2.4).

Love and irony

Just like the figure of the inspiring woman, who lacks the clear outlines of a protagonist and tends to appear as a vestige, a mere conventional function of the elegiac genre, so the pathos typical of the great Latin love poetry also dissolves into banality in Ovid. The drama of Catullus or Propertius, the intense adventure of their existence, becomes in Ovid little more than a *lusus,* and the experience of eros is examined by the poet with irony and intellectual detachment. Equally significant is the virtual absence from the *Amores* of a motif that was absolutely central in earlier elegiac poetry: the *servitium amoris,* the profession of total dedication on the part of the lover towards the beloved, her desires, and her caprices; in Ovid the motif has a very limited function. It is noteworthy, however, that an entire elegy, and one prominently placed (1.2), is devoted to the profession of *servitium* towards Amor: it is no longer the individual woman that is central, but the experience of love itself. Moreover, the poet's literary consciousness becomes more important than it had been in earlier elegiac poetry (see especially 1.15 and 3.12), as can be seen from the emphasis on poetry as an

The literary consciousness of the poet

instrument of immortality and as the independent creation of the poet, set free from the obligation to reflect reality. The Ovidian elegy no longer presents itself as subordinate to life, as its faithful reflection, but it asserts its own primacy, its own centrality in the poet's existence.

3. THE DIDACTIC LOVE POETRY

Precepts on love

The facts that there are in the *Amores* several didactic elegies (1.4 and, still more, 1.8) that develop hints from previous elegiac poetry (Propertius 1.10 and 4.5, Tibullus 1.4) and that the experience of love is ironically emptied of content, as can already be perceived in Ovid's first works, conveniently explain the link between the *Amores* and the group of erotic works constituted by the *Ars Amatoria,* the *Remedia Amoris,* and the *Medicamina Faciei Femineae,* which form a veritable cycle of didactic poetry; they are also close in time. The same conception, the same project of writing a work such as the *Ars* and its sequels in which one could impart instruction in love, seems to be the natural (and also the extreme) outcome of the conception of love already delineated in the *Amores,* after which elegy, exhausted, could only extinguish itself.

The poet as director and the playing of roles

An important link between the two works is, as was said, elegy 1.8 of the *Amores,* in which the poet elaborates a motif already traditional in elegiac poetry, that of the old *lena,* the cunning, experienced procuress who advises a young woman on the best way to capitalize on her qualities with the various suitors. Leaving aside the conventional features, however, Ovid's attitude is quite different. To him, the *lena* so deprecated by the elegiac tradition (Propertius 4.5) appears in a fundamentally positive light; her shrewd realism and cynical views do not sound different from the advice that the poet himself imparts to the lover in his didactic work. The *lena* is the parent of the didactic poet, of the teacher of love, since the conception of love presupposed by the two works is analogous. The only difference is that in the *Amores* the poet, bound by the elegiac convention, is also the lover, the protagonist in the love adventures, a part he would put aside in the *Ars* in order to take on fully the part of the director of the love relation, the knowledgeable supervisor over the playing of roles.

Erotic code and amorous diversion

Playing of roles is precisely what we have. For Ovid, once it has lost its character of a devastating passion, the love relation is an intellectual game, an amorous diversion, subject to a set of its own rules, to an ethical-esthetic code that can be extracted from Latin erotic elegy. Roles, situations, behavior are all already foreseen and codified; they are written in the literary texts that the chief figures of amorous society are supposed to regard as exemplary models. The only part Ovid can play is to draw up an inventory of the elegiac universe, to write the textbook giving the rules of behavior that one conforms to.

The Ars Amatoria: *the strategy of seduction*

The *Ars Amatoria* is a work in three books, written in elegiac meter, that gives advice on ways to conquer women (book 1) and to retain their love (2); the third book, added later in order to compensate the women for the harm done to them in the first two—such is the jesting premise—provides instruction in how to seduce men. Ovid describes the meeting places and the fashionable haunts of the capital (dinner parties, theaters, shows in the circus, promenades), the moments of relaxation and pastimes, the very varied occasions of urban life (the work is an important document of the everyday habits and customs of Rome) in which the lover is to carry out the campaign of seduction. The outer form is that of the didactic poem (the great Roman models were Lucretius and the *Georgics* of Virgil), from which Ovid wittily borrows formulas, stances, and compositional schemes. The course of instruction is interrupted here and there by inserted mythological and historical narratives (a kind of tryout for the future *Metamorphoses*), which are intended to illustrate, in the manner of *exempla,* the validity of the advice given.

Irony towards the traditional morality

The perfect lover described by Ovid is characterized, of course, by his (or her) shameless lack of scruple, by impatience and combativeness towards traditional morality, ancient Roman usage—and this sphere of sexual and matrimonial morality is a very delicate one, to which Augustus in his reforming zeal attached particular importance (and so the scandal created by the *Ars* could be made the official charge against the poet at the time of his expulsion from Rome). In fact, the libertine, unscrupulous character of the *Ars,* which has brought down upon the poet the disapproval of moralists in every age, is no more than the glittering, provocatively seductive outer covering of the work; precisely in becoming a *lusus,* an amusing intellectual exercise, the Ovidian eros loses all ethical purpose, all inclination to rebel against the prevailing morality. The absoluteness of love as a life choice upon which to base new values and a new morality, which had been the most revolutionary feature in elegiac poetry and earlier in Catullus, is lost in Ovid, and his work's apparent libertinism can actually be brought within the bounds of the traditional ethic and its conventions. Ovidian eros demands, not an open rejection of every inclination towards conflict, but only a certain tolerance, a free zone, a sector of the social scene in which to suspend the severe moral code that is now inadequate for the usage of the Hellenized metropolis (the poet several times is concerned to delineate a restricted space, that of libertine love, from which respectable society is excluded).

The reconciliation of elegy with contemporary society

In addition to fomenting the tendency to rebellion, Ovidian elegy entertains ambitions in the opposite direction (this is the aspect that criticism has focused on most recently). In denying the total commitment that was characteristic of earlier love poetry, in neutralizing its more aggressive drives, Ovid attempts a sort of reconciliation between elegiac poetry and the society in which it has its roots; in the harmonious complementariness of the private sphere and the civic, he indicates the best path towards a contented adherence to the present. He clearly identifies, and in his own way tries to resolve, a conspicuous contradiction in elegiac poetry, namely, that in its proud opposition to the traditional system of social and cultural values it had not been able to develop alternative ethical models, but had in fact borrowed from the tradition some of its most characteristic standards (see p. 323). To this contradictory, and potentially archaizing, tendency of elegiac poetry Ovid opposes the values of modernity, an enthusiastic acceptance of the lifestyle of the brilliant Rome of Augustus, the capital of consumption and high living and urban splendor (*aurea sunt vere nunc saecula*—thus does he wittily reverse the theme of the Golden Age, which was honored in every nostalgic evocation of the past).

The Medicamina: *cosmetic art legitimated*

Also corresponding to the celebration of *cultus,* of comforts and refinements, is the poem on cosmetics for women, *Medicamina Faciei Femineae,* of which only a hundred verses are left, in elegiac meter. The work opposes the traditional rejection of cosmetics and explains the technique for several beauty preparations.

The Remedia Amoris *and the end of elegy*

The didactic cycle is concluded by the *Remedia Amoris,* the work that, reversing certain precepts of the *Ars,* teaches how to free oneself from love. It was a commonplace of erotic poetry that there is no remedy for the sickness of love, and the elegiac poet seemed almost to take delight in his being condemned to heartsickness, since he could not free himself from it, and yet inwardly was also proud of his complete devotion, of his choice of *nequitia.* Ovid reverses this position, asserting that it is not only possible but even obligatory to free oneself from love if it brings suffering. (He thus sets himself a goal of Stoic and Epicurean philosophy, which condemned love as a sickness of the soul, a goal that had earlier inspired Lucretius's fourth book.) A work such as the *Remedia,* teaching how to heal oneself of love, represents the extreme development of elegiac poetry and brings to a symbolic close the brief period of its intense existence.

4. THE *HEROIDES*

The theme of myth

If love is the unifying theme for Ovid's youthful works, the other great source of his poetry is myth. Before the *Metamorphoses* the work that draws from it the most is the *Heroides.* This title (the original one was probably *Epistulae Heroidum*) designates a collection of verse letters. The first series, letters 1 to 15, comprises letters written by famous women, heroines of Greek myth (though Virgil's Dido is also present, along with a historical figure, Sappho), to their distant lovers or husbands: in order, Penelope to Ulysses, Phyllis to Demophoon, Briseis to Achilles, Phaedra to Hippolytus, Oenone to Paris, Dido to Aeneas, Hypsipyle to Jason, Hermione to Orestes, Deianira to Hercules, Ariadne to Theseus, Canace to Macareus, Medea to Jason, Laodamia to Protesilaus, Hypermestra to Lynceus, and Sappho to Phaon. The second series, 16 to 21, is made up of the letters from three lovers and the replies from their respective women: Paris and Helen, Hero and Leander, and Acontius and Cydippe. The two groups are distinct, though they are always found together in the tradition (letter 15, Sappho's, has its own tradition, however, and its authenticity has always been suspect, though now suspicion has been almost completely banished), and in their distinctness they represent two different phases of composition: the first is very difficult to date (the tendency is to make it coincide with the composition of the *Amores,* before 15 B.C., but some place it between 10 and 3), whereas the second is probably to be put shortly before Ovid's exile (i.e., between A.D. 4 and 8).

The problem of authenticity

The doubts about the authenticity of the letter of Sappho have already been mentioned. In fact, the fifteenth is not the only letter whose Ovidian authorship has been questioned. Occasionally some scholar, on the basis of alleged metrical and stylistic irregularities, or more generally (and more questionably) on the basis of alleged weaknesses and narrative defects, goes back to approving, in whole or (most often) in part, the judgment of Lachmann, who considered not only the double epistles spurious but also all those that Ovid does not explicitly name in *Amores* 2.18. This elegy guarantees the authenticity of nine letters, namely, those of Penelope, Phyllis, Oenone, Canace, Hypsipyle and/or Medea (it names the recipient, Jason, who is the same for both epistles), Ariadne, Phaedra, Dido, and Sappho (to be sure, the passages *Amores* 2.18.26 and 2.18.34, which refer to the epistle of Sappho, are sometimes considered invalid by those who maintain the inauthenticity of the letter itself). Nonetheless, given the substantial inconsistency of the greater part of the attacks made on the authenticity of several of these *Heroides,* one must wonder whether such attacks would ever have been launched, and whether they would ever have been launched precisely at those and not other letters, if the passage of the *Amores* had not been there from the first to arouse suspicion. Yet it is obvious, as everyone recognizes, that nothing compelled Ovid in *Amores* 2.18 to name *all* the epistles in his collection.

A new genre: myth and elegy

Ovid proclaims his pride in the originality of this work, with which he creates a new literary genre (*Ars Amatoria* 3.345); and indeed before him we have no evidence of similar works, that is, collections of verse letters on the subject of love. The idea of the letter in verse probably came to him from an elegy of his friend Propertius (4.3, written by Arethusa to her faraway husband Lycotas), which is echoed several times in the *Heroides.* The literary material is drawn, in various ways, chiefly from the Greek epic-tragic tradition, but along with the more remote models Callimachus too is present, and Hellenistic poetry as well as Latin, in particular Catullus and Virgil. Although the characters and situations belong to the large inheritance of myth, many elements are borrowed from the Latin elegiac tradition, in which certain motifs are common, such as suffering on account of the remoteness of the beloved, recriminations, laments, entreaties, suspicions of unfaithfulness, accusations of betrayal, and so on. For example, among the letters that clearly have the feel of the elegiac model (themes, situations, attitudes) is the letter of Phaedra to Hippolytus, in which the Euripidean heroine sheds her noble, tragic dignity and comes to resemble an unscrupulous woman of amorous society, ready to seduce her stepson with the enticements of a casual *furtivus amor,* boldly asserting a new sexual morality, scoffing at old-fashioned conventions.

Elegiac modeling of material from epic and tragedy

In the *Heroides* Ovid makes the elegiac model into a filter through which he passes the narrative material of epic, tragedy, and myth. But the elegiac modeling does not consist solely in narrative materials and techniques nor even in the unifying theme of love. Instead, it acts as a perspective that selects and reduces to its own language every other possible theme. It is a restricted and conventional perspective that leads Ovid's heroines to impose an elegiac shape on the narrative material of epic, tragedy, and myth. It is a process of distortion, systematic reinterpretation, consistent rewriting.

Thus, in the seventh letter Dido selects from the Virgilian original the elements useful for her persuasive purpose (to convince Aeneas not to leave). This may explain, for instance, her insistence on a notion such as pregnancy (7.133 ff.), which destroys the formulation of the motif in the *Aeneid*, where it was a matter of a painfully disappointed hope. In the ninth letter the arrival of Hercules' concubine Iole (9.121 ff.) is described by Ovid's Deïanira in terms that systematically contradict all the features found in the corresponding scene of Sophocles' *Trachiniae*. The same events are often interpreted and evaluated in a different and even opposite way, according to the different points of view and different persuasive forces of the various heroines. A particularly clear case can be observed in the letters of Hypsipyle and Medea, the two rivals for Jason's love, and another good example is the way an event such as the Trojan War or a person such as Helen is regarded from different points of view.

Recodifying in elegiac terms stories of heroines from epic and drama, who were not born "inside" and "for" the elegiac code, Ovid introduces the reader into a new literary universe, neither ancient nor modern, neither epic nor tragic nor mythic nor elegiac, but based on the coexistence of codes and values and on their interaction. Obviously the rewriting often significantly distorts the models; the differences become the most evident signs of the new literary code.

Limits imposed on the genre: the monotony of the Heroides

The choice of the epistolary form naturally imposed limitations on the poet, particularly in regard to the letters of the first series. The letters are presented as monologues (they are "closed" texts, expecting no reply) and are based for the most part on a standard situation, the "lament of the abandoned woman" (an example Ovid certainly had in mind was Ariadne in Catullus's well-known epyllion, poem 64). The structure of the letter did not allow much variation. Given that the educated reader was familiar with the basic situation, the course of the monologue (movement between the heroine's desperation and her calling for the return of the beloved and urging him to abide by his promises—the influence of the rhetorical exercise of the *suasoria* is evident) is interrupted only occasionally by a flashback of memory, which evokes distant events in narrative fashion but lacks dynamic development.

Each letter is meant to be set at a well-determined point in time, a fruitful moment fixed in a narrative continuum. The continuum is guaranteed by the echo of well-known models and of literary or, more generally, mythological texts.

For obvious reasons of dramatic economy, the epistles are far more interesting if they are sufficiently open not only to the past but also to a future that is not yet decided. Verisimilitude demands that the person writing be able to refer to past events but that she be ignorant of her future. Only the author, therefore, who is omniscient but outside the text, can be responsible for forecasting future events. Because he cannot participate in his own person, he employs irony to insert himself into the voice of the person herself. Thus, tragic irony becomes the means Ovid uses most often in the *Heroides* to prevent the contraction of the narrative space. By dividing the person's voice in two, without violating the rules of the epistolary form, he can secretly introduce his own voice and thus broaden the heroine's confined perspective into a synoptic view of the myth, into a narrative of her own that is synthetic yet complete. Then the reader's collaboration and literary competence are required in order to recompose into a unity the various segments of the narrative line, filling in the gaps that separate them. Play with chronology thus often comes to have an important role: Ovid succeeds in deriving remarkable effects from the relation between the time of the model (the durative time of the story) and the time of the letter (the point in time at which the reader imagines the heroine writing).

The double epistles provide Ovid with new possibilities. First of all, the new formula allows a clash of different points of view on the same reality, a clash that can sometimes prove of great interest (as in the cases of Paris and Helen and, especially, Acontius and Cydippe; the latter pair of letters looks like a genuine legal controversy). Above all, it makes possible a greater freedom of movement, an ampler narrative field. Moreover, because of the dramatic context, the three pairs that close the collection provide a full justification of the epistolary form (one could not say that this was certainly true of all the single letters; we need think merely of an extreme case such as that of Ariadne, who writes from the deserted shore of Naxos). The exchange of letters is no longer a gratuitous narrative form, condemned to betray its artificial nature, as is often the case with the letters of the first series, but it becomes an integral part of the story's dramatic development. (In this juxtaposition of two points of view a certain affinity with the rhetorical *controversiae* may also be recognized.)

The Heroides *as poetry of lament*

Another aspect should also be emphasized. The *Heroides* are, properly speaking, a poetry of lament, the expression of the unhappy situation of the woman who has been left alone or abandoned by her far-off husband or lover. But if for the most part this abandonment by her beloved, or her own disaffection, the cooling of her love, is the cause of her suffering, there are other causes of unhappiness as well for the female figures of the *Heroides,* for example, Laodamia's suffering over her sudden separation from Protesilaus on account of the war, or the special suffering of Phaedra, or of Canace and Hypermestra, both victims of the pitiless cruelty of their fathers. The heroines suffer, in short, not only as people whose love is betrayed or not returned but also, and especially, as women. This is the condition they share (a condition sufficient in itself) that condemns them to an existence marked by abandonment, humiliation, weakness, and the inferiority of the one who must endure and not be able to assert herself. In the *Heroides* the elegiac genre seems to return to its origins as a poetry of grief and lament; consider the frequency in the elegiac vocabulary of key terms such as *queri* and *querimonia* ("complain," "complaint"). Sappho's words well express the almost necessary relation between the elegiac verse form and the condition of the heroines whose love is unhappy: *flendus amor meus est: elegi quoque flebile carmen.*

The space for pathos   A feature that distinguishes this work from Ovid's other early writings is the considerably greater space given over to pathos rather than play and that ironically detached attitude that is particularly characteristic of the poet of the *Ars Amatoria.* There are, to be sure, letters that strongly echo the themes, situations, and attitudes of elegy. Perhaps the best instance of this is the letter of Phaedra to Hippolytus, already mentioned: Phaedra, the heroine in a well-known play of Euripides, leaves behind the elevated world of tragedy; Ovid's treatment turns her into a contemporary, the unprincipled would-be seductress of her stepson, a socially prominent woman who aims at replacing traditional morality with a revolutionary one. The impulse towards modernizing the ancient literary material and reducing it to the elegiac register is occasionally evident, but this is not the most typical aspect of the *Heroides,* in which the tendency to pathetic-tragic tones remains strong.

Psychological penetration   Instead, Ovid's rewriting is of a different sort. On the one hand, he takes up again the great subjects of the literary tradition, emphasizing situations and aspects that suit the new context; on the other, he reworks those texts, displacing the perspective and giving a voice to the women and their motives, which until then had remained unexpressed for the most part or had been sacrificed. The exploration of female psychology, in which the influence of Euripides is strong, is one of the most notable features of the *Heroides.*

5. THE *METAMORPHOSES*

Alexandrian poem and epic poem   With the *Aeneid* Virgil had realized the grandiose project of a Homeric-style poem, a national epic for Roman culture. Ovid in realizing his ambitions for a work of great scope (after the love poetry that had brought him success) takes another direction. The outer form was to be epic (the hexameter is its distinctive mark), as was the ample scale (fifteen books), but the model, which is based on Hesiod *(Theogony, Catalogue),* is that of a "collective poem," one that gathers a series of independent stories linked by a single theme. This type of poetry had been popular in Hellenistic literature; such was the basis of, for example, the *Aitia* of Callimachus (a series of aetiological tales in elegiac meter) and a (lost) hexameter poem by Nicander of Colophon (second century B.C.) that actually collected stories of metamorphosis. Yet while he followed this preference of Alexandrian poetry (in both content and the form that organized it), Ovid at the same time also reveals his intention to compose an epic poem, a genre that, notoriously, Callimachean poetics had banished. The proem (1.1–4), which is brief and thus all the more charged with meaning, seems to say just that:

Ovid utters a ritual prayer to the gods to inspire him to write a poem of metamorphosis *(mutatas . . . formas)* but in the style of epic *(perpetuum deducite . . . carmen,* all terms from the vocabulary of Callimachean literary polemic). Ovid's ambition therefore is grand: to realize a universal work, one that goes beyond the limits of the various poetic creeds.

The very chronology of the poem confirms this. It is boundless, going from the origins of the world down to Ovid's day, and thus realizes a project long desired and hitherto only sketched out in Latin culture (the inspiration of Virgil's sixth eclogue). It also corresponded, in a way, to a tendency widespread at the time, the synthesis of universal history (now that Rome dominated the world scene), which was particularly noticeable in Hellenistic historiography.

The rapprochement to the principate

This also allowed Ovid to be active in fields less remote from the interests of the principate and even to meet, in his own way, the needs of the nation and of Augustus, by making the new regime the crowning culmination of world history. In this regard his "little Aeneid" in the poem's last section is noteworthy, conceived as it is on the margin of the Virgilian text: it fills several narrative ellipses of the *Aeneid* by developing episodes suitable to the context.

Composition and Structure

Principles of association among the stories

Between the two chronological extremes the structure in which the content is disposed is necessarily flexible. About 250 mythical-historic episodes are recounted in the course of the poem. They are arranged on a chronological principle that soon after the opening grows weaker to the point of almost disappearing (it will become more perceptible again, obviously, when in the final books the poem passes from the vaguely timeless world of myth into the historical period); this in turn leaves room for other principles of association. The various stories can be linked, for example, by geographical contiguity (as with the Theban tales, from the third book onwards), by thematic parallels (e.g., the loves of the gods, their jealousies, their revenges), by contrast (episodes of piety counterposed with others of impiety), by simple genealogical relation among the characters, or even by similarity of metamorphosis.

Summary of the *Metamorphoses*

After the very brief proem, the narrative begins with the birth of the world from the original formless chaos and with the creation of man. The universal flood and the regeneration of the human race at the hands of Deucalion and Pyrrha mark the passage from primordial time to mythic time, with its divinities and semidivinities, their passions and their whims: Apollo and Daphne, the latter metamorphosed into the laurel; Jupiter and Io, guarded by Argo with his hundred eyes (book 1); Phaethon, who falls to earth with the chariot of the sun and sets the world on fire (2); Actaeon transformed by Diana into a stag and torn to pieces by his own dogs; Narcissus, who spurns Echo's love and is consumed by love for himself; the impious Pentheus punished by Bacchus (3). Next follows the tragic love of Pyramus and Thisbe and that of Salmacis for Hermaphroditus; Perseus's rescue of Andromeda from the sea monster (4); the rape of Proserpina and the metamorphoses of Cyane and Arethusa (5); the jealousy of the gods, with Minerva's revenge on Arachne, who is changed into a spider; the slaying of Niobe's children; the grim story of Tereus, Procne, and Philomela (6); the incantations of Medea; the tragic error of Cephalus and Procris (7); the fatal flight of Daedalus and Icarus; Meleager and the Calydonian boar hunt; the piety of Philemon and Baucis rewarded and the impiety of Erysicthon punished (8); the labors of Hercules and Byblis's incestuous passion (9); the story of Orpheus and Eurydice, which includes within it other stories of love: Cyparissus, Hyacinthus, Pygmalion, Myrrha, Venus and Adonis, and others (10). With the marriage of Peleus and Thetis, which is followed by the touching story of the conjugal love of Ceyx and Alcyone (11), we are at the border of the fluid chronology of myth: the characters of the Trojan War usher us into history, which concludes with the age of Augustus.

Thus we have the labors of Achilles and the battle between the Lapiths and the Centaurs (12), then the contest for the arms of Achilles between Ajax and Ulysses, the series of Trojan losses, and Polyphemus's love for Galatea (13). Following the trail of the *Odyssey* and then the episodes with Aeneas (Ovid is also keen to write a little Aeneid, without overlapping with Virgil), the scene shifts to ancient Latium, with its tales and its rural gods (Pomona and Vertumnus). Now we are at Rome with its kings (14). By way of Numa is introduced Pythagoras, who gives a lengthy speech on metamorphosis as the law of the universe (which should constitute the philosophical basis of the poem); the apotheosis of Caesar, the last of Aeneas's descendants, and the celebration of Augustus conclude this "history of the world" (15), whereupon the last verses proclaim the poet's proud certainty that he has achieved immortal fame.

Variety of the content and narrative skill

The variety of the content corresponds to the fluidity of the structure. The dimensions of the stories told vary widely, from a simple allusive reference, extremely elliptic, to several hundred verses, which makes many stories genuine epyllia. Especially diverse are the manner and the pacing of the narrative, which lingers upon the outstanding moments and pauses over dramatic scenes and events, such as the act of metamorphosis generally is: metamorphosis is minutely described in the course of taking place. Ovid's narrative skill is also shown in the care with which stories of different character and content are juxtaposed or alternated—cosmic catastrophes and delicate tales of love, violent battle scenes and pathetic stories of unhappy love, dark, incestuous passions and touching conjugal love, and so on. The mutability of themes and tones goes along with the mutability of style, which is now solemnly epic, now lyrically elegiac, now echoing passages of dramatic poetry or bucolic attitudes. The *Metamorphoses* is, among other things, a sort of art gallery of the various literary genres.

Continuous narration

Ovid does not strive for unity and homogeneity in content and form so much as for a calculated variety. He strives particularly for continuity of narrative, for its fluid, harmonious unfolding. A proof of this lies in the technique of division between the several books of the poem: unlike in the *Aeneid* of Virgil, where each individual book is given its own relative completeness and independence, the breaks between the various books of the *Metamorphoses* for the most part fall at the liveliest points, in the very middle of an episode, in order to awaken the reader's curiosity and keep it aroused in the pauses within the text, in order not to slacken the narrative tension.

The embedded tale: narrative that reproduces itself

In this regard the very technique of narrating the various stories is important. Not only is the chronological ordering rather vague in general, as we have said, but it is continually disturbed by the recurrent insertion of prior narratives. Ovid, the principal narrator, has frequent recourse to the Alexandrian technique of the embedded tale, which allows him to avoid the unvarying, cataloguelike succession of the various tales by embedding one or more inside another, which is used as a frame. But most often it is the characters themselves who seize control of the narrative in order to recount other stories, within which the same mechanism may be repeated again, in an unbroken proliferation of stories; entire books are constructed by this technique, among which the complex structures of book 10 and especially 5 are noteworthy. In addition to varying the form of exposition, this complication of the narrative syntax, by multiplying the narrative levels and voices, produces an effect of giddiness, of a labyrinthine fugue: the account seems to be sprouting continually from itself and moving away in an infinitely receding perspective, in a dimension out of time. But the technique of the story within the story has still another function: it sometimes allows the poet to adapt the tones, style, and color of the story to the character who tells it; this is the case, for instance, in the solemnly epic account of the rape of Proserpina, narrated by Calliope, the muse of epic.

Metamorphosis and the World of Myth

Metamorphosis and aetiology

Metamorphosis, the transformation of a human being into an animal, a plant, a statue, or some other form, was a theme already present in Homer, but it was especially favored, as has already been suggested, in Hellenistic literature (in addition to Nicander, Parthenius of Nicaea had dealt with it, and others too), for which it satisfied the characteristic taste for aetiology, the learned investigation of causes (in that metamorphosis describes the origin of present-day things and beings from some earlier form of theirs; and Ovid insists on continuity, on the traits common to the old and the new form). In Ovid's poem, as we have already said, metamorphosis is the theme that unifies the numerous stories told. In the final book the poet also attempts retrospectively to give philosophical dignity to his work (and also to emphasize its unity) by means of Pythagoras's lengthy speech, which points to change (*omnia mutantur, nil interit* {15.165}) as the law of the universe, to which man must conform (hence, as a consequence of the theory of metempsychosis, the exhortation to vegetarianism). But Ovid does not seem deeply committed to this eclectic philosophy of history (which is basically Pythagorean, with an admixture of Stoic and Platonic elements), and his attempt to provide the poem with a philosophical interpretation does not bear the stamp of true conviction.

Love in the Metamorphoses

Metamorphosis, as we have remarked, is the poem's unifying theme (although in some stories it does not appear at all or has a quite marginal role). Nonetheless, the central subject of the work is love, which had been the source and inspiration of all Ovid's earlier poetry. Love, to be sure, is no longer set in daily life, in the Rome of fashionable society (which, however, Ovid often does sketch into the background through clever anachronisms); rather, just as in the earlier *Heroides,* it is set in the world of myth, among gods, semi-divinities, and great heroes.

Myth as decorative element

The mythic dimension, however, is not matched by an idealizing ethos, a grandness or solemnity of values. For Ovid myth does not have the religious value or the profundity that it has for Virgil; in this respect, he accentuates a tendency already present in Hellenistic culture and turns myth, along with the figures that populate it, into an ornament of daily life, a decorative backdrop. Thus the divinities of the Greco-Roman religious tradition are brought down to earth and operate under the force of completely human sentiments and passions, and often not the noblest of them. Love, jealousy, rancor, and revenge are the impulses that drive them and that overwhelm the human beings, victims of their capricious power.

Intertextuality of the Metamorphoses

For the highly literary Ovid, the world of myth is above all the world of poetic fictions, and the *Metamorphoses,* the work of his that more than any other is nourished by myth, that would come to be a kind of grand encyclopedia of myth for millennia to come, is also a concise summary of a vast literary inheritance, extending from Homer to the Greek and Latin tragic poets, to the vast, many-faceted literature of the Hellenistic period, and on to the poets of Ovid's Rome. Ovid's poem is both conscious and proud of its complex, intertextual nature, and it is fond of frequent displays of its own ancestry, the sources of its own poetic memory. Such delighted consciousness of its own literariness naturally translates itself into a detached smile at the fictitious character of the content, into graceful irony at the improbability of the legends narrated. The poet who so often joked at the *fecunda licentia vatum* (*Amores* 3.12.41) occasionally smiles at the credibility of what he is recounting, at the poets' innate lack of fidelity to the truth. In the skeptical distance from its own content, from the world of the venerable mythological tradition by which it is inspired, lies the narcissistic triumph of this poetry that aims to entertain and astonish.

Self-contentment and self-irony

Poetry as Spectacle

Ambiguity and illusion in the world of the Metamorphoses

The fundamental characteristic of the world described by the *Metamorphoses* is its ambiguous and deceptive nature, the uncertainty of the boundaries between reality and appearance, between the concreteness of things and the inconstancy of their appearances. The characters of the poem behave as if lost in this insidious universe, which is governed by change and error; disguises, shadows, reflections, echoes, and fugitive semblances are the snares in the midst of which the humans move about, victims of the play of fate or the whim of the gods. Their uncertain action and the natural human disposition to err are the object of the poet's regard, now touched, now amused; they are the spectacle that the poem represents. (The very language and the style are apt for demonstrating the ambiguous nature of things. By displaying its innate duplicity, even language reveals the danger it itself offers, the gap between the illusory nature of appearance and the concreteness of reality.)

The intervention of the narrator

The characters act each according to his own point of view, each certain that he has grasped reality. The poet, sole possessor of the "true point of view," analyzes this multiplicity of perspectives and follows the characters along the path that progressively distances them from reality, showing the reader the fatal outcome that awaits them. Rejecting the impersonal objectivity of the epic poet, the narrator of the *Metamorphoses* often intervenes to comment upon the course of events, to involve the reader by interrupting the narrative fiction, to share the reader's ironic detachment and amused smile.

The "photographic" narrative technique

The way in which the world is seen as a spectacle, as marked by extraordinary, marvelous events, is matched by a narrative technique that, as already suggested, emphasizes the salient moments of those events and isolates the individual scenes in them by diminishing their dramatic movement and fixing them in their visual clarity. Noteworthy in this regard is the special emphasis on the visual perception of reality, which is particularly conspicuous in the description of the event that recurs most often in the poem, metamorphosis. This is generally characterized by traits of the marvelous and is presented "before the eyes" of a viewer; in describing it Ovid dwells on the intermediate phases of the process, on the uncertain boundaries between the old and the new form, on the paradox of the split between the new appearance and the old psychology of the beings subjected to the change.

Towards mannerism

With its predominantly visual nature and its immediate plastic clarity (a quality that helps explain its immense success as a model for the figurative arts), with its interest in the paradoxes that lurk in reality and its fondness for spectacle, often under the most hideous forms, this poetry anticipates important characteristics of the literary taste of the coming century, the "mannerism" of the Empire.

6. THE *FASTI*

Ovid as civic poet

It is the *Fasti* rather than the *Metamorphoses* that is the work of Ovid's least remote from the cultural, moral, and religious tendencies of the Augustan regime. Following in the footsteps of the late Propertius and his "Roman elegies," Ovid, too, devotes himself to composing civic poetry. His project is to illustrate the ancient myths and customs of Latium, following the course of the Roman calendar. Thus twelve books (in elegiac meter) were projected, one for each month of the year, but the poet's unexpected exile interrupted the work in the middle, at the sixth month, June; the work was partially revised during the years of exile.

The Callimachean model and the anti-quarian sources

In addition to Ovid's direct predecessor, Propertius, the work owes much to the model that is common to the two poets, Callimachus's *Aitia,* both in its technique of composition and in its aetiological character, that is, its investigation into the "causes," the origins of present-day reality in the world of myth. Even more than the poet who was his friend, Ovid himself desires to become the Roman Callimachus (Propertius 4.1.64), producing a finished work, a new poetic genre, in place of what in Propertius had been experimental attempts alternating with the usual erotic subject matter. In this new guise as bard celebrating the idea of Rome, Ovid undertakes careful, learned researches in a variety of antiquarian sources. From Verrius Flaccus (the grammarian who was the author of a commentary on the Roman calendar [see p. 386]), Varro, Livy, and others he reaps a huge harvest of antiquarian, religious, legal, and astronomical lore, which he employs to illustrate beliefs, rites, usages, and place names—all this part of the rediscovery of ancient origins that was a fundamental tendency of Augustan ideology.

Civic poetry and elegiac pathos

But Ovid's allegiance to the regime's cultural program, despite his insistence upon the value of his own civic poetry (*Fasti* 2.9–10), naturally remains superficial. Into the antiquarian background, which makes the *Fasti* an exceptionally important document for early Roman culture, he inserts mythical material of Greek origin (e.g., the legends of Proserpina and Callisto, both also treated in the *Metamorphoses*) or material of an anecdotal character, with frequent references to contemporary reality and events. This allows him to overcome the limits imposed by the nature of the poem, to escape the difficulties of a dry "calendar in verse," and instead, at certain idyllic moments, to satisfy his taste for delicate pathos or, at other times, to make room for an erotic element (not without a few touches of juicy realism) and for his usual playful, ironic tones and his smiling skepticism about myth.

An alternative interpretation

This interpretation of the *Fasti* tends to free the poem from any responsibility to Augustan ideology; Ovid, as one recent critic has written, speaking for many, would pay "his debt listlessly performing his duty as a *civis Romanus.*" It is an interpretation that goes well with the modern interest in the *Fasti* as a source of valuable anthropological information; the Ovid that Frazer used is basically only a transmitter of traditional stories, and the poet's stance towards the tradition does not have much importance for him. But more recent studies suggest that some caution is in order. The use Ovid makes of the aetiological scheme proves to be considerably more playful than had been thought: the poet plays with his duty as antiquarian (precisely as Callimachus had, with regard not only to the form but also to the form of the content and the crisis of knowledge). This is not to say that the poet's play stops at the edge of Augustan ideology, just short of it; no one can forget the important part that the reconstruction of the past has in Augustus's ideological program. Thus, when Ovid deconstructs and puts in doubt the relation between past and present, the game threatens to turn serious. It is the *Romanitas* conveyed by the calendar that is attacked and decentralized. The real gap in the poem, obviously from the point of view of the emperor, is not that Ovid does not take Augustus seriously but, as has been noted, that he does not take Romulus seriously. The *Fasti* is a poem in which there is still much to investigate from an ideological-literary perspective, and one wonders whether criticism has been somewhat hasty in separating the poem's form from its content, and the poem from all the rest of Ovid's works.

7. THE WORKS OF EXILE

The shock of exile

The unexpected banishment from Rome naturally signals an abrupt break in Ovid's poetic career. He more than others surely bewailed the separation from the capital, from the society to which his poetry was addressed and by which it had been nourished, from its fashionable circles and literary haunts (for some time now he had been the greatest living poet). He finds himself banished from the limelight to the very borders of the Empire, in the midst of a primitive people who do not even speak Latin. Accustomed to success, to the fervent admiration of a public captivated by his virtuosity, Ovid all at once finds himself alone, composing poetry for himself; and his condition as an artist without a public, lacking contact with an audience, suggests to him the gloomy image of a man dancing in the darkness (*Epistulae ex Ponto* 4.2.33 f.).

The Tristia

Ovid's first work composed at a distance from Rome—and sent not without some hesitation, as the prefatory elegies of the first and third books show—is the collection of the *Tristia,* five books whose common feature, explicitly emphasized (*flebilis ut noster status est, ita flebile carmen* [5.1.5]), is lament over the exiled poet's unfortunate condition. Equally insistent is the recurring appeal to his friends and wife to obtain, if not a complete remission of his punishment, then at least a change of location. The repeated expressions of regret for his faraway homeland and the frequent descriptions of the inhospitable and squalid landscape around him, of the dangers from the continual raids of the barbarians, of the desolation of an existence deprived of its lifeblood—all these seek to bring about a change of mind that may grant the exiled poet the minimum conditions to be himself. The elegies of the first book carry the reader through the departure from Rome, the long voyage towards Tomi, and the winter crossing of the Adriatic and the Aegean, with storms making the sailing more difficult and anxious. The second book, consisting of a single long plea addressed to Augustus, is supposed to exonerate Ovid's love elegy from the charge of immorality; notable as well for the literary-critical matters that it takes up, this stoutly argued self-defense reviews *sub specie amoris* the chief Greek and Latin literary genres. In the following books there are more elegies addressed to precise recipients, who are not explicitly named but are sometimes identified through indirect indications—another aspect of that uncertainty that the poet, now fallen into disgrace and far from his public, harbors about the possible reactions provoked by his verses.

The Epistulae ex
Ponto

The epistolary form characterizes all the elegies gathered in the four books of the other collection from his exile, called for that reason *Epistulae ex Ponto.* This accentuation of the epistolary character is manifested in various ways: in the regular use of the formulas appropriate to the genre (as at the beginning and the close of a letter), in the reference to letters sent in reply by the addressees (who are now all mentioned expressly, the caution of the *Tristia* no longer seeming necessary), and particularly in the density of certain topoi that recur in epistolary literature, such as the emphasis on the letter as a conversation between distant friends, the illusion of presence despite the distance, the comfort furnished by this instrument of communication that mitigates the solitude of the exile, and so on.

Elegy as poetry of lament

The *Epistulae* in this regard offer interesting analogies to Ovid's other epistolary work, the *Heroides,* for instance, in the parallelism between the remoteness experienced by the abandoned woman and that experienced by the exiled poet. Yet it is important to notice in the two major works of exile the conscious rediscovery of elegy as a poetry of lament, of weeping, virtually a return to the supposed classical Greek origins of this genre, of which Ovid was so fond and which, in its most authentic form, his experience of grief now rendered tragically present to him. The brilliant singer of Roman worldliness, making a pact of winking complicity with his reader, had previously amused himself by treating the entire world of literary fictions with a detached smile. Now, forced to become the subject of his own poetry (*sumque argumenti conditor ipse mei* [*Tristia* 5.1.10]), he declares the absolute authenticity of his poetic material and summons the most famous mythological paradigms to affirm the unusual significance of his own tragedy. Ovid puts all remaining hope for the future into his poetry, which has become more than ever the totality of his existence, the only thing capable of providing a motive, and a comfort, for living (to such an extent that it sometimes inspired in him the moving tones of a hymn). Although so far removed from Rome, without the experience and the direct participation in events, he does not refuse to celebrate the successful military campaigns of those years with his verses (*Tristia* 4.2, *Epistulae ex Ponto* 2.1). Yet this anticipation of his possible role as a poet who would interpret the great collective emotions did not avail in rescuing him from the desolate loneliness of Tomi.

The Ibis

Fallen into disgrace, Ovid during his exile must still defend himself from the attacks of his enemies. This purpose is met by a poem in elegiac couplets entitled *Ibis* (from the name of a coprophilic bird) and modeled on a lost poem of the same name by Callimachus that was supposedly directed at Apollonius of Rhodes. The poem consists of a long series of invectives against a detractor of Ovid's. The compositional scheme is borrowed from Callimachus, as is the enigmatically learned nature of the poem.

8. LITERARY SUCCESS

Even Ovid, who was obsessed with the fame and survival of his literary works (*Amores* 3.15, *Metamorphoses* 15.871–79, *Tristia* 4.10), might have been satisfied by his extraordinary *Nachleben,* which was second only to Virgil's and lasted in literature and the fine arts well into the Romantic period —and even seems to be enjoying a modest contemporary revival.

But already in antiquity his reception was bifurcated into the two branches that continued to characterize it in the following centuries. On the one hand, there can be no doubt that Ovid was extremely popular with many readers and decisively influenced later poets. His love poetry and his lost tragedy *Medea* seem to have been especially popular among his contemporaries, and he himself attests to imitations of his work by other poets during his own lifetime (e.g., the letters of response to his *Heroides* written by his friend Sabinus, *Amores* 2.18.27–34) and to frequent stagings of his poems in the theaters of Rome (*Tristia* 2.519–20, 5.7.25–28). The apparent facility of Ovid's style not only made it easy to imitate him deliberately—Sabinus inaugurated a tradition followed by the numerous medieval and humanist poets who composed apocryphal Ovid texts, and nineteenth-century English schoolboys knew how much easier it was to compose Ovidian couplets than Virgilian hexameters—but also made his unconscious influence upon later poets both more massive and easier to trace. In general, after his death for the rest of antiquity, Ovid was above all the poet of the *Metamorphoses*. His profound influence upon such immediate successors as Lygdamus, Manilius, and the authors of the *Ciris* and of some of the *Carmina Priapea* is unmistakable; in the Neronian period his poetic influence offers a welcome alternative to Virgil's for Seneca's tragedies and for Lucan's epic; in the Flavian period his influence upon Statius and Valerius Flaccus (which they seem hesitant to admit) rivals Virgil's (which they proudly acknowledge); and in late antiquity poets such as Ausonius and Claudian attest to his continuing fascination. Nor was his popularity limited to elite cultural spheres: the subliterary graffiti on the walls of Pompeii and ancient verse inscriptions on stone are filled with quotations and reminiscences from his works.

On the other hand, already in antiquity he was the object of suspicion and polemic. Augustus banished Ovid from Rome and ordered all the works of the *doctor adulterii* (*Tristia* 2.212) removed from the three public libraries, and although this did not prevent his poems from finding numerous readers, it was a first signal of an official hostility that never ceased to accompany him (and no doubt contributed to his popularity). If Augustus may be thought to have attached more importance to moral considerations than to stylistic ones, Quintilian's acerbic criticisms of the man and his poetry—he accused him of being *lascivus . . . et nimium amator ingenii sui* (10.1.88, cf. 10.1.93 and 10.1.98)—not only attest involuntarily to Ovid's contemporary fashionableness (even Quintilian must acknowledge that he is *laudandus tamen partibus* [10.1.88]) but also indicate the difficulty of any clean separation between the two registers in dealing with Ovid. Ovid never became a canonical poet in antiquity, and he seems to have been studied neither in ancient grammar schools (except for late scholia on the *Ibis* and perhaps on the *Metamorphoses,* his works do not seem to have received any commentaries at all in antiquity) nor, after Augustan times, by teachers of rhetoric (no ancient author who lived later than the Augustan orator Cestius ever complains, as he did [Seneca the Elder, *Contr.* 3.7], that his contemporaries were all full of Ovidian *sententiae*). Christian authors regarded him with understandable (but not always deeply felt) suspicion: Isidore calls him the one pagan poet who must most be avoided (but quotes him twenty times).

Middle Ages

For the Middle Ages, Ovid was not only a philosopher (readers recalled the beginning and end of the *Metamorphoses*) and encyclopedist (again the *Metamorphoses:* Vincent of Beauvais quotes Ovid more than any other Latin poet) but also a moral guide and a teacher of the rules of proper conduct (once more the *Metamorphoses,* this time suitably allegorized, and, astonishingly, the *Amores* and *Ars Amatoria*). Although his star ascended slowly, it came to outshine almost all others. In the Carolingian period, Ovid's poetry, especially the *Metamorphoses,* the exile poems (popular among poets suffering the same fate), and the *Heroides* (a useful model of poetic epistles for poets often absent from court), was certainly known (the oldest surviving manuscripts date from this period), but he was less popular not only than Virgil and Terence but even than Horace, Lucan, and Juvenal. Although one poet of the Carolingian court assumed the pen name Naso, another, Theodulf, had to resort to allegorical explanation to defend Ovid's poetry as a repository of profound truths.

Aetas Ovidiana

But this changed by the late eleventh century, and the twelfth and thirteenth centuries were called by Ludwig Traube the *aetas Ovidiana* (nowadays the term is often extended to include the fourteenth century as well). This is above all the age when Ovid's love poetry attained a cultural preeminence unmatched before or since. But it is also the period in which the minor works (*Ibis, Nux, Medicamina Faciei Femineae*) reappear and in which, next to the traditional manuscripts that transmitted his individual works, for the first time omnibus codices, containing some or all of his elegiac works (sometimes together with the *Metamorphoses,* often together with medieval pseudo-Ovidiana), become popular. Although there is some evidence for an Ovidian renaissance in the early twelfth century in southern Germany, especially at the Benedictine monastery of Tegernsee, it was almost certainly in the Loire valley that Ovid first became a canonical author. Excerpts from his works were included in the *Florilegium Gallicum* (Orléans, mid-twelfth century); Arnulf of Orléans, the leading literary scholar of his age, lectured and commented on the *Metamorphoses,* the *Fasti,* and other works; and the *Remedia Amoris* and other love poems were used in the schools to teach the elements of Latin grammar.

Love poetry in the Middle Ages

If in the tenth and eleventh centuries Ovid was still read less in the schools than the standard pagan authors (Virgil, Terence, Cicero, Plautus, Horace, Sallust, Lucan, and Juvenal), this changed after the eleventh century. Surprisingly, it was above all his love poetry that came to be used widely, to teach medieval pupils not only language but also manners. The *Amores* could be read (though not without some difficulty) as the serious ethical discourses of a *praeceptor morum* and became perhaps the most popular of Ovid's poems in the schools; the didactic genre of the *Ars Amatoria* made the text appropriate for teaching purposes in spite of its scandalous contents; and the *Remedia Amoris* was redeemed (despite its many scabrous details) by its purported intention of providing a cure for the illness of love. As a guide to proper conduct, Ovid was sometimes brought up to date and down to earth in ways that can amuse the modern reader: if Ovid recommended that the lover feign tears by moistening his hand, the Middle Ages recommended the use of an onion.

Perhaps for obvious reasons of content, perhaps also because they were what most students first read (and hence all that some students ever read), Ovid's erotic poetry seems to have exerted the most influence in this period. Alain of Lille calls him "amorigraphus." Chaucer terms him "Venus clerk, Ovyde, / That hath y-sowen wonder wyde / The grete god of Loves name"; this is how he is viewed by such writers as Héloise, John of Salisbury, William of Saint-Thierry, and many others. He is frequently cited by the troubadours and Minnesänger and seems to have made a fundamental contribution to medieval notions of "courtly love." His erotic works were much used by Marie de France, Chrétien de Troyes (whose translation of the *Ars Amatoria* is lost), Gottfried of Strassburg, and Brunetto Latini; the monks who take part in the twelfth-century "Love Council of Remiremont" declaim his writings on love "quasi evangelium."

The Metamorphoses   But most of Ovid's nonerotic poetry, too, was widely known and highly influential in the high Middle Ages. The *Medea* had unfortunately been lost forever by the end of antiquity, and the *Ibis* and the *Halieuticon* were not rediscovered until the fourteenth century by Boccaccio and the early sixteenth century by Sannazaro, respectively. Among his surviving writings, the least popular were, as always, his exile poems, which had been neglected in late antiquity but attained a brief popularity during the uncertain times following the death of Charlemagne, when exiled poets such as Ermoldus Nigellus could use Ovid's example to console themselves. There are relatively few traces of the exile poetry thereafter (except in the Loire circle, e.g., Baudri of Bourgueil), though the separation from friends is a common theme and the separation from Rome could be allegorized as separation from Paradise. The *Metamorphoses* and, to a lesser extent, the *Heroides* (read in the Middle Ages without the letter of Sappho) remained popular throughout this period. Albrecht von Halberstadt translated the *Metamorphoses* into German in 1210, and Maximus Planudes translated both poems into Greek around 1300; Conrad of Würzburg made liberal use of both poems when writing on the Trojan War; and there are frequent traces of Chaucer's intense study of these two poems and of the *Fasti* throughout his career, from the story of Ceyx and Alcyone in his earliest poem, *The Book of the Duchess,* through the *Legend of Good Women* and up to the metamorphosis of the crow in the Manciple's tale. Chaucer, who quotes Ovid more than any other Latin poet and who was compared to Ovid in his own lifetime by Eustache Dechamps, is particularly interesting as an example of a medieval reader who gladly took over Ovid's literal narratives without seeming to bother much with the prevailing allegorical interpretations.

Allegorical interpretations

But the dominant tendency was in the opposite direction: the racy stories were always enjoyed, but they had to be legitimated by earnest exegesis. The fashion of *Ovide moralisé*, loose translations of the *Metamorphoses* with lengthy, explicit, and often banal, sometimes bizarre ethical allegorical explanations, began in the early fourteenth century in France, with Philip de Vitri's 570,000 lines of octosyllabic couplets dedicated to Jeanne de Bourgogne, the wife of Philip V, and Pierre Bersuire's *Ovidius Moralizatus,* and spread from there to Italy (Bonsogni, Bonsignore, Dolce), Germany (Boner, Lorch, Spreng), Spain (Bustamente, Perez Sigler, Sánchez de Viena), and other countries. Indeed, the many allegorical interpretations of Ovid's works are among the best indexes of his problematic popularity. In the twelfth century, allegorizing could even render the *Ars Amatoria* suitable for nuns. The *Heroides* were interpreted ethically; at least Penelope could be a positive paradigm for chaste conjugal love, but most of the other heroines had to be explained as counterexamples, showing what not to do. But of course it was the *Metamorphoses* that most attracted the allegorists. Dante, who proposed this poem as a model of style in his *De Vulgari Eloquentia*, declared in his *Convivio* that it required allegorical interpretation, and his younger contemporaries were only too happy to oblige. Giovanni del Virgilio provides one example of fourteenth-century allegorizing, explaining the story of Daedalus and Icarus rationally (the father escaped in a ship as fast as birds, but his son fell overboard). Pierre Bersuire provides four at once—historical (Ovid was criticizing certain people who had built labyrinths), moral (the devil Minos shuts up the sinner Daedalus within the labyrinth of the cares of this world), familial (warning sons not to be rash and disobedient), and religious (Daedalus is God the architect; Icarus represents any Christian in danger of falling). As late as the sixteenth century, Arthur Golding was still explaining Daedalus as a symbol for men's love of liberty and for necessity as the mother of invention, and Icarus as proof of the necessity for moderation and obedience.

Allegorizing is usually a symptom of discomfort with an authoritative writer deemed indispensable but dangerous; and the fundamental tension in the medieval view of Ovid as a poet both wise and immoral, and in any case fundamentally un-Christian, is well illustrated by the medieval legend of two students who visited his tomb. Upon pondering his best line, *virtus est licitis abstinuisse bonis* (Her. 17.98), and his worst line, *omne iuvans statuit Juppiter esse bonum* (cf. Her. 4.133), they decided to pray for Ovid's soul, whereupon a voice sent them brusquely away, declaring *nolo Pater Noster; carpe, viator, iter.*

Renaissance

During the Renaissance the discomfort largely vanishes, and Ovid becomes the most popular Latin author after Cicero. Petrarch still criticizes Ovid, in terms borrowed from Quintilian, as *magni vir ingenii . . . sed lascivi et lubrici et prorsus mulierosi animi* and the *Ars Amatoria* as *insanum opus et meritam . . . exilii sui causam* (*De Vita Solitaria* 2.7.2), but he mentions him frequently in his *Res Familiares* and does not omit the *Metamorphoses* from his reading list (Ovid's story of Apollo and Daphne is cited in *Canzone* 23). But a new spirit can be heard in Boccaccio's admiration for the *Ars Amatoria* as "il santo libro d'Ovidio, nel quale il sommo poeta mostra come i santi fuochi di Venere si debbano ne' freddi cuori con sollecitudine accendere" (*Il Filocolo*). To be sure, allegorizers continued for a long time to cloak Ovid's poetry in veils of higher meaning. In his *Ovid's Banquet of Sense* (1595), George Chapman depicted the poet watching Augustus's daughter Julia bathe naked and play the lute, but as a neo-Platonist admirer of beauty, not as a voyeur, while the Elizabethan poet Thomas Howell spoke of "Ovid's meaning strange / That wisdom hideth with some pleasant change." But most Renaissance readers seem to have preferred to gaze upon Ovid bare.

The Renaissance's Ovid is primarily the author of the *Metamorphoses* and the erotic elegies, the poet of flippant wit, elegant language, bizarre passion, and inventive narrative. Translations made him accessible to wider groups of readers and decisively influenced Renaissance poetic language. The *Heroides* were translated by Turberville in 1567, the *Amores* by Marlowe around 1597; one English version of the *Metamorphoses* in fourteen-syllable lines was published by Arthur Golding in 1565–67, another by George Sandys in 1621–26. Ovid was the favorite classical author of Shakespeare, whose intense study of Golding's translation and, to a lesser extent, of Ovid's other works can be documented throughout his career, not only in the sonnets and *Lucrece,* but in the plays as well, as late as *The Tempest,* in which Prospero's celebrated and affecting farewell to his art begins with an evident reminiscence of the invocation Ovid wrote for his Medea (*Metamorphoses* 7.197 ff.). Indeed, in 1598 Francis Meres could write, "The sweet witty soul of Ovid lives in mellifluous and honey-tongued Shakespeare"; but Ovid was so much the presiding genius of Elizabethan poetry that contemporaries also termed Chapman, Daniel, and Drayton modern Ovids. From Ovid, Spenser learned how to use the technique of the aetiological flashback to moralize a whole landscape, while Marlowe (*Hero and Leander*), Shakespeare (*Venus and Adonis*), and a host of minor poets learned how to write the erotic epyllion, the most Ovidian of all genres of Renaissance poetry; perhaps it was for this very reason that Milton turned so often to Ovid when he sought a seductive rhetoric of pagan passion as a foil for the Christian austerities of *Paradise Lost.* But Ovid's wit and passion inspired not only writers: the first opera, Peri's *Dafne* (about 1597), was based upon the *Metamorphoses,* as was, for example, Handel's cantata *Apollo e Dafne;* while the painters and sculptors who depicted Ovidian themes included Titian, Brueghel, Rubens, Bernini, Poussin, Luca Giordano, Boucher, and Benjamin West.

Modern period

By the end of the seventeenth century the *Metamorphoses* had become so thoroughly absorbed within European culture that poets who sought the wellsprings of Ovidian influence had to study poems that had once been marginal (though even then they were reluctant to turn to his exile poems).

Dryden translated the first book of the *Ars Amatoria,* and he declared of the *Heroides* that they were "generally granted to be the most perfect piece of Ovid." Pope, following his advice, translated the letter of Sappho and with his own letter of Eloisa to Abelard created one of the most popular poems of the eighteenth century. But aside from such exceptions as Rousseau's *Pygmalion,* that was the first century to witness the beginning of a decline in Ovid's fortunes. It is exemplary that in 1770 the young Goethe tried to convince Herder that the *Metamorphoses* had any poetic merit whatsoever—and failed. Keats remembered Glaucus when writing "Endymion," and Wordsworth, who liked Ovid as a boy, returned to him in *The Excursion* and *Laodamia.* On the Continent, Sappho's letter inspired a number of Romantic authors to use the figure of the doomed poetess in love to elaborate the oppositions between man and woman, life and art, poetry and love (Verri, Leopardi, Grillparzer). But in general, Romanticism marked the low point in Ovid's popularity: he was decried as superficial and insincere, immoral and degenerate, witty and soulless; as is often the case, a revolution in taste did not judge by new criteria, but simply changed the values attached to traditional criteria. There are occasional traces of Ovid's inescapable influence through the course of the nineteenth century (Thackeray, Browning, Matthew Arnold, Meredith), but it is only towards the end of the century, in such Decadents as d'Annunzio and Swinburne, that precisely these qualities begin to be appreciated again.

Ovid in the twentieth century

The twentieth century's fascination with myth, its rediscovery of cultivated, reflective poetry, and its experience of exile have made Ovid one of its favorite ancient poets. Over and over again, poets, especially English ones, have chosen figures from Ovid as projections of their personal aesthetic dilemmas: Joyce put an Ovidian Stephen Daedalus at the center of his *Portrait of the Artist as a Young Man* and balanced him with a Homeric Leopold Bloom in *Ulysses;* Shaw used *Pygmalion* to ask whether art could change life if the artist was not only opposed to society but also in complicity with it; while T. S. Eliot, in a note to *The Waste Land,* put Ovid's Teiresias into the very heart of the poem's meaning. Even in more recent times, Ovid has continued to prove useful in examining the limits of the imagination's capacities—in Anglo-American literature, more often in lyric (Geoffrey Hill, "Ovid in the Third Reich," 1968; C. H. Sisson, "Metamorphosis," 1968); in continental European, more often in the novel (Christoph Ransmayr, *Die letzte Welt,* 1988; Cees Nooteboom, *Het volgende verhaal,* 1991).

BIBLIOGRAPHY

The best plain text of the amatory works (*Amores, Ars Amatoria, Remedia Amoris,* and *Medicamina Faciei*) is that of E. J. Kenney (Oxford 1961). For the *Heroides,* see the old edition of H. Sedlmayer (Vienna 1886) or the edition with Italian translation by G. Rosati (Milan 1989); the large edition by H. Dörrie (Berlin 1971) is extremely inaccurate. For the *Metamorphoses,* see the edition by W. S. Anderson (ed. 2 Leipzig 1982; an

Oxford text by R. J. Tarrant is in preparation); for the *Fasti,* that of E. H. Alton, D.E.W. Wormell, and E. Courtney (Leipzig 1978). The exile poetry is edited by S. G. Owen (Oxford 1915); see also the Teubner edition of the *Ex Ponto* by J. A. Richmond (Leipzig 1990). Five of the volumes in the Loeb series have been revised by G. P. Goold and now offer good texts and translations: *Heroides* and *Amores* (Cambridge, Mass. 1977), *Ars Amatoria* and other poems (1979), *Metamorphoses* (2 vols., 1977–84), *Tristia* and *Ex Ponto* (1988). The Loeb edition of the *Fasti* was by the distinguished anthropologist J. G. Frazer (1931). The Budé series with French translations should also be consulted (Les Belles Lettres, 1924–77).

Among English commentaries note esp. those on the *Amores* by J. C. McKeown (Leeds 1989–; see also the editions of book 1 by J. Barsby [Oxford 1973] and book 2 by J. Booth [Warminster 1991]), on *Ars Amatoria* 1 by A. S. Hollis (Oxford 1977), on *Heroides* by A. Palmer and L. C. Purser (Oxford 1898), on *Remedia Amoris* by A.A.R. Henderson (Edinburgh 1979), on the *Fasti* by J. G. Frazer (5 vols., London 1929), on *Metamorphoses* 1 by A. G. Lee (Cambridge 1953) and 8 by A. S. Hollis (Oxford 1970), and on *Tristia* 2 by S. G. Owen (Oxford 1924). There are large-scale German commentaries on the *Fasti* and the *Metamorphoses* by F. Bömer (Heidelberg 1957–58, 1969–86); the older commentary on the latter by M. Haupt, O. Korn, and R. Ehwald, revised by M. von Albrecht (ed. 10 Zurich 1966), is not entirely superseded. There is an edition of the *Tristia* on a similar scale by G. Luck (Heidelberg 1967–77). For the *Ars Amatoria,* see the German edition of P. Brandt (Leipzig 1911) and the Italian one of E. Pianezzola with G. Baldo and L. Cristante (Milan 1991); for the *Epistula Sapphous,* that of H. Dörrie (Munich 1975), for the *Remedia,* that of P. Pinotti (Bologna 1988; see also the editions of 1–396 by H. J. Geisler [Berlin 1969] and of 397–814 by C. Lucke [Bonn 1982]), for the *Medicamina,* that of G. Rosati (Venice 1985), for the *Ibis,* that of A. La Penna (Florence 1957), and for the *Halieutica,* that of F. Capponi (2 vols., Leiden 1972).

There is a good Greece and Rome survey by J. Barsby (Oxford 1978), as well as a collection of essays by J. W. Binns (London 1973); see also H. Fränkel, *Ovid: A Poet between Two Worlds* (Berkeley 1945), L. P. Wilkinson, *Ovid Recalled* (Cambridge 1955), and S. Mack, *Ovid* (New Haven 1988). Among recent work on the amatory poetry, note J. T. Davies, *Fictus Adulter: Poet as Actor in the Amores* (Amsterdam 1989), and M. Myerowitz, *Ovid's Games of Love* (Detroit 1985, on the *Ars Amatoria*). On the *Heroides,* see H. Jacobson, *Ovid's Heroides* (Princeton 1974), and F. Verducci, *Ovid's Toyshop of the Heart* (Princeton 1983). On the *Metamorphoses,* the best general works are K. Galinsky, *Ovid's Metamorphoses: An Introduction to the Basic Aspects* (Berkeley 1975), and J. B. Solodow, *The World of Ovid's Metamorphoses* (Chapel Hill 1988); see also B. Otis, *Ovid as an Epic Poet* (ed. 2 Cambridge 1970), O. S. Due, *Changing Forms* (Copenhagen 1974), F. Ahl, *Metaformations* (Ithaca 1985), P. E. Knox, *Ovid's Metamorphoses and the Traditions of Augustan Poetry* (Cambridge 1986), and S. Hinds, *The Metamorphosis of Persephone* (Cambridge 1987). On the *Fasti,* see J. F. Miller, *Ovid's Elegiac Festivals* (Frankfurt 1991), and the essays in *Arethusa* 25.1 (1992). On the exile poetry, see H. B. Evans, *Publica Carmina* (Lincoln 1983), and B. R. Nagle, *The Poetics of Exile* (Brussels 1980); there is much of interest in R. Syme, *History in Ovid* (Oxford 1978).

There is a recent German introduction to Ovid by H. Wissmüller (Neustadt/Aisch 1987); see also on the *Metamorphoses* W. Ludwig, *Struktur und Einheit der Metamorphosen Ovids* (Berlin 1965), and among very recent work U. Schmitzer, *Zeitgeschichte in Ovids Metamorphosen* (Stuttgart 1990). Again an article by R. Heinze has been influential: "Ovids elegische Erzählung," reprinted in *Vom Geist des Römertums* (Stuttgart 1960) 308–403 (English summary in the introduction to Otis *Ovid as an Epic Poet*). Among recent Italian works note M. Labate, *L'arte di farsi amare* (Pisa 1984), and G. Rosati, *Narciso e Pigmalione* (Florence 1983). In French, G. Lafaye, *Les Métamorphoses d'Ovide et leurs modèles grecs* (Paris 1904) is still useful; see also S. Viarre, *L'Image et la pensée dans les Métamorphoses d'Ovide* (Paris 1964), M. Boillat, *Les Métamorphoses d'Ovide: Thèmes majeurs et problèmes de composition* (Bern 1976), and H. Le Bonniec, *Études Ovidiennes: Introduction aux Fastes d'Ovid* (Frankfurt 1989).

Livy

LIFE

Titus Livy—his cognomen is unknown—was born at Padua in 59 B.C. He went to Rome, where, even though he did not take part in public life, he became known to Augustus. His interest at first lay in philosophy, but soon, at about the age of thirty, Livy devoted himself entirely to his grand historical work. He was greatly admired and conspicuously honored; among other things, he undertook to guide the historiographic interests of the future emperor Claudius. He alternated living at Rome with long sojourns in his native Padua, where he died in A.D. 17.

WORKS

Ab Urbe Condita Libri, the history of Rome from its foundation down to the contemporary period. The work comprised 142 books, of which 1–10 and 21–45 are preserved (book 45 is damaged at the end), along with a handful of fragments from the other books; among these are the famous fragments containing the death of Cicero and Livy's judgment upon him, transmitted to us by Seneca the Elder. The books we have are of differing lengths, ranging from the twenty-three chapters that make up book 43 to the seventy-two chapters of the third book; the average book contains fifty chapters.

We also hear of historical-philosophical dialogues and other philosophical works, all composed in his youth.

SOURCES

Information about Livy's life and activity is provided by Jerome's *Chronicle;* Pliny, *Epistulae* 2.3.8; and several passages from Quintilian, Tacitus, and others.

1. THE PLAN OF LIVY'S WORK AND HIS HISTORIOGRAPHIC METHOD

The return of annalistic writing

In the books *Ab Urbe Condita* Livy returned to the annalistic structure that had characterized Roman historical writing from the very beginning (see pp. 68 f.), implicitly rejecting thereby the monograph format of Sallust's early works. Thus, the narration of an activity such as a military campaign is carried through its course during one year, and upon the completion of the year it is left suspended while Livy begins the narration of other events belonging to that year. Then the same narrative method is employed for the events of the next year: Livy picks up the narrative of the campaign where he left off at the end of the previous year, and so forth.

The plan of the work and the preserved books

Livy's narrative began with the mythic origins of Rome, that is, with Aeneas's flight from Troy, and in book 142 it came down to the death of Drusus, Augustus's stepson, which took place in Germany in 9 B.C., or perhaps even down to the defeat of Varro in the Teutoburg Forest in A.D. 9. It is possible that Livy's plan, interrupted by his death, was to have the work comprise 150 books and reach the death of Augustus in A.D. 14. Books 1–10, called the "first decade," are preserved, reaching the Third Samnite War, which ended in 289 B.C. Also preserved are books 21–45, the third and fourth decades and the first half of the fifth, which cover the events from the Second Punic War (218 B.C.) to the end of the war against Macedonia (167 B.C.). Of the lost books, except for numbers 136 and 137, we possess *periochae,* brief summaries probably written in the third or fourth century A.D., perhaps themselves based in turn on earlier epitomes, or abridgments, of Livy's work.

The division into decades

The loss of vast parts of Livy's history is probably to be explained by its subdivision into distinct groups of books, which suffered separate fates. The division into decades is first referred to near the end of the fifth century A.D. but in all likelihood goes back to an earlier date. According to some scholars, it might even go back to Livy himself, who brought out his own work in groups of books that treated distinct periods and who prefaced some of the books opening a new section with introductory remarks. One of the most famous is the preface that opens the third decade, which contains the narrative of the Second Punic War. The use of a preface to open a decade suggests that such a subdivision marks the stages in the publication of the work by Livy himself.

Interest in the most recent period

Like a good number of previous Latin historians, beginning with Cato (see pp. 86 f.), Livy enlarged the scale of his narrative as he approached his own day; for the period from the age of the Gracchi onwards, which amounts to less than a century and a half, 85 books of the 142 are required. This enlargement satisfied the expectations of his readers, who were more interested in more recent events, especially the story of the enormous political and social crisis out of which the Augustan principate had emerged. Livy himself in the general preface to his work refers to this impatience on the part of the public.

Livy's sources

Livy obviously used many sources. For the first decade, containing Rome's most ancient history, he had at his disposal almost exclusively the annalists, among whom he prefers the most recent; he seems to have used Valerius Antias, Licinius Macer (an annalist writing after the civil wars of the eighties B.C. who tended to favor Marius), and Claudius Quadrigarius much more than he used Fabius Pictor. In the following decades, in which the expansion of Rome in the East was narrated, the Roman annalists were joined by the great Greek historian Polybius, from whom more than anyone else Livy derived his unified vision of the Mediterranean world and of the relations between Rome and the Hellenistic kingdoms. His use of Cato's *Origines,* by contrast, seems to have been sporadic.

Lack of criticism in using sources

It has often been emphasized that Livy does not appear to carry out his historical work on the basis of a careful critical evaluation of his sources. In some cases ease of access and location seems to have determined his choice. Furthermore, he conspicuously fails to fill the gaps in the historiographic tradition by having recourse to other kinds of documentation, which may have been readily accessible; thus Livy makes very scant use of the documentation to be found in manuscripts and ancient inscriptions or of the results obtained by the scrupulous research of antiquarians from the previous generation, such as Atticus and Varro. Consequently, he has frequently been seen as a mere *exornator rerum,* whose chief concern is to amplify and embellish what he found in his source by dramatizing it, by giving it variety and movement. By taking this line, scholars have tended to leave Livy outside the development of major Latin historical writing between Sallust and Tacitus, that is, outside the great senatorial historiography. According to this view, Livy is not a historian who had been a senator and statesman, whose bitter, disillusioning experience in contemporary political life has led him to form a considered personal judgment on the events of the past as well, and whose position facilitates his access to guarded sources of documentation, such as the *acta senatus,* and so on; rather, he is the literary historian who works principally at second hand, using the narrative of previous historians.

Livy as an honest historian

The notion contains some elements of truth, but it should not be pushed so far that it establishes a diametrical opposition between senatorial historiography, written by one who knows how history is made and intended for the guidance of the politician, and a historiography that is the literary exercise of men incapable of making history and that therefore is vitiated by vapid moralization. Livy may well be less aggressive than Tacitus in using sources and documents, nor does he have the rationalism and skepticism of Sallust or Tacitus, their indifference to the slogans of propaganda. Yet this does not mean that he is not a fundamentally honest historian or that he writes in a spirit that exalts the Augustan regime joyfully and without a touch of doubt.

2. THE NEW REGIME AND THE TENDENCIES OF LIVY'S HISTORIOGRAPHY

Patavinitas

The Augustan regime, it seems, did not attempt to dominate historical writing as it did poetry. Livy certainly was not part of the opposition, but neither was he an uncritical supporter. We know from Quintilian that Asinius Pollio detected in him traces of *Patavinitas,* "Paduan provincialism." Pollio referred chiefly to certain elements of Livy's style, which we have trouble identifying today, as perhaps Quintilian himself already did.

It is more difficult to say whether *Patavinitas* also referred to a certain political-cultural stance, an especially close attachment to the traditions of the Republic, which were keenly felt—so Cicero attests in the *Philippics*—in a provincial city where the *mos maiorum* was still vigorous and the recent corruptions of luxury and vice still were not widespread. A passage from Tacitus (*Annals* 4.34) is more explicit about Livy's allegiances: Augustus is said to have jokingly called the historian a "Pompeian" because of the nostalgic sympathy towards republican ideals that was probably reflected in his work. The loss of the section dealing with the recent civil wars makes it impossible to form an adequate idea of how Livy recounted the crisis of the Republic, and in particular of the tone in which it was recounted. But we do know, again from Tacitus, that Livy praised Pompey and was respectful towards Caesar's other opponents, including his very murderers, Brutus and Cassius.

In the age of Augustus such an attitude did not arouse special hatred. Augustus himself, especially after the constitutional reform of 27, was more eager to present himself as the restorer of the Republic than as Caesar's heir and thus not only tolerated but even, to some extent, himself utilized the devotion paid to the martyrs of the Republic. The regime could thus find the historian in substantial agreement with it on certain subjects, without exercising the least pressure. The chief of these subjects was probably the condemnation of the social and political disorder during the last decades of the Republic, the party strife, and the greed of the rich, but even more the furious revenges of the poorer classes. The new regime claimed to have reestablished harmony in the body of society by eliminating the political parties. These were conditions suitable to a historian who, as we often find, was eager to abominate the evils of demagoguery. Given the loss of the sections dealing with recent history, in pursuing this subject we need to go to Livy's narrative of the internal conflicts during the first centuries of the Republic, onto which the historian often seems to project problems and interpretations related to much more recent conflicts. Another important element joining Livy to the princeps was the Augustan policy of restoring ancient moral and religious values, which naturally was dear to the historian from Padua.

Nonetheless, as has already been said, Livy's agreement with the regime did not translate itself into an unconditional celebration. This would be completely clear to us if we possessed his narrative of the civil wars and the principate of Augustus. Still, some basic tendencies can be grasped in the general preface to the history. In the preface there is evident an acute consciousness of the crisis Rome has recently passed through, which the historian seems not to regard as resolved in a completely satisfactory way. "We can tolerate," he says, "neither our vices nor their remedies." Indeed Livy does not accept the whole part of Augustan ideology that insists on the charismatic value of the principate and that views it as the realization of a new golden age. Virgil, despite many reservations, in the end justified a providential design that sanctioned the notion that history could reach its

Livy as a "Pompeian"

Worship of the res publica *and condemnation of demagoguery*

Detachment from the principate

destined climax only by means of the vast bloodshed of the civil war. Livy, by contrast, probably failed to discern in Augustus's victory the miraculous remedy that had destroyed forever the seeds of corruption that had caused the Roman state to decline.

The flight from the crisis

Several times, both in the preface and elsewhere, Livy refers to the fact that for him the narrating of Rome's glorious past is a refuge from the distress he feels when he comes to narrating more recent and contemporary events, an attitude that implicitly polemicizes against the historiography of Sallust, who had placed Rome's crisis at the center of his research. Livy's pessimism, while it exists, is not so clear as Sallust's. Although he recognizes that the crisis was epochal rather than episodic, Livy refuses to focus on that alone; rather, he strives to view it within the general context of Roman history. He recognizes that corruption and moral decadence have made their way even to Rome, but later than in any other state: on the whole, no other people can offer more outstanding instances of moral greatness and upright behavior.

Justification of Rome's empire

Justification of Rome's empire emerges forcefully from the preserved parts of Livy's work; its creation is due to a strong cooperation between *fortuna* (in substance, the same as divine providence) and the *virtus* of the Roman people. No other people, no general can successfully stand up to this, since none can deploy a moral force comparable to that on which the Roman state is founded. At one point Livy poses the question of how matters would have turned out if Alexander the Great, the greatest conqueror in antiquity, had attacked Rome rather than the East, and he does not hesitate to claim that not even Alexander would have succeeded in overcoming the Romans. Such thoughts probably helped console Livy for the bitterness he felt towards his own time. The pessimism that shows itself in the preface must have been far more pervasive, as has been said, in the narration of the more recent periods. Perhaps what appears in Livy as unbroken nationalistic pride, as continuous, unswerving exaltation and embellishment of all the deeds of the Romans—for example, in the narrative of the Second Punic War—may only be due to his general tendency to idealize the past. He probably darkened appropriately the picture of the latest century of Rome's history.

The images of the past as paradigms of behavior

When Livy turns his gaze to the more than seven centuries that have brought a small city of Latium to mastery of the world, he shows reverence, almost dismay, before such vast time and such vast achievements. In evoking that immense journey, he feels the pressure of history, the weight of the influence that the images of the past exercise upon the consciousness of the present time. These images act as models of social and individual behavior, positive and negative; they are invitations to virtue or warnings against wickedness. Rome's grandiose past indicates the path of salvation to those who ought to reenact its valuable example in the present. The mythology of the past, in short, not only *has* meaning for contemporary men but also *gives* meaning to their actions, in that it can illustrate through examples their own ideological needs.

3. NARRATIVE STYLE

Lactea ubertas

In his stylistic preference Livy is sharply opposed to the tendency of Sallust (see pp. 241 f.); instead, he comes close to the style Cicero had hoped for in Roman historical writing. Quintilian, who recognized the superiority of Sallust as a historian, contrasts with his austere and epigrammatic *brevitas* the *lactea ubertas* of Livy (*Institutio Oratoria* 10.1.32), a style that is ample, flowing, and luminous, without artifice and without hindrance, one that avoids all harshness and in which the periods run along smoothly. Throughout, Quintilian stresses the *candor*, the limpid clarity, of Livy's style. Yet Livy can also make his style admirably flexible and varied.

Flexibility and variety of Livy's style

In the first decade his concessions to the archaizing taste are more evident, in accordance with the distant solemnity of the events recounted, whereas in the later parts the principles of the new classicism come to the fore.

The dramatization of the account

Poetic coloring is conspicuous and frequent. Inheriting a tendency that had long been present in Latin historiography (see p. 122) but had been greatly reduced by Sallust, Livy gives much more space to the dramatic presentation of the story, yet without allowing this to overwhelm the factual framework. The drama of Lucretia, a legendary heroine of early Rome, with its succession of scenes filled with pathos, is justly famous, as is that of Sophonisba, the Carthaginian noblewoman, daughter of Hasdrubal and wife of Massinissa, who courageously preferred to take poison rather than fall into the hands of the Romans. But dramatization is a tendency present nearly everywhere in Livy's narrative. We find it in the description of battles (which are frequently represented with a *peripeteia*, that is, the sudden turning of an initially unfavorable situation into a victory for the Romans), in the description of popular uprisings, and in the reports of debates in the Senate.

"Tragic" historiography

Livy conceives of history not as a political study that explains attitudes and events and takes into account strategies of parties and factions, ideologies and material interests, but rather as a narrative that is conducted in terms of human personalities and representative individuals. The moral passion that marks such a conception derives in part from the Hellenistic historiographic tradition. This was probably the manner of historical interpretation that characterized the works, now lost, of historians such as Ephorus and, later, Duris and Phylarchus, the style of historical writing that is called "tragic" (and also "Peripatetic," on account of the influence exerted by Aristotle's theoretical model). In this way *historia,* instead of being "investigation" of the truth, could become a rhetorical activity and so once again return to being a literary genre (for some theoreticians it was close to oratory, for others close to poetry). Livy explicitly admits that he ranks dramatic conception and narration of the story above investigation of the truth for its own sake. His purpose is to show that moral and intellectual qualities have a decisive impact on events. The atmosphere of a city in distress, the feelings of a people or of a mob, the thoughts and desires of a person, his psychological uncertainties and his calculations—none of these

The dramatic description of the characters

is "objectivity," the impersonal detachment that all theoreticians, ancient and modern, expect from a trustworthy historian. Livy immerses himself in the affairs he describes; with a number of suggestive strokes of the brush, which could hardly be called exact, he aims at giving the impression of a witness who has experienced the story he recounts from within. For Livy, writing history is above all bringing to life the men who make it: if the author judges his characters, they also judge one another. And in this his literary gifts, which are certainly of a high order, secure impressive results. His sense of gradation and composition is marvelous, as are the artistry of his phrases and above all the impressionistic qualities through which words are able to convey great mass scenes. The frequent passages of indirect discourse become a means of expression for evoking the hidden states of mind of crowds and groups of persons. Skillful speeches directly reported are often composed, with effective oratorical art, for the purpose of delineating the thoughts of individuals, and their impetuous ardor is often reflected later in the comments and reflections of the spectators or listeners, almost as if they wanted to represent the effects of the speeches upon themselves. Frequently, too, the extreme and most pathetic point of an episode is rendered in a direct or an indirect speech that characterizes the soul of the protagonist.

The speeches in Livy

But the pathetic quality of Livy is in no way comparable to the heightened pathos of Sallust or to the marked passion of a style of writing that had punctuated the narrative with sharp judgments and had clothed it in a thought that was always alert, dense, severe. Livy's style is rather an airy manner of representing and narrating, what we might call a "sentimental" manner, with more ethos than pathos, one that can combine a certain grandeur of imagination with the pleasure created by the account. And not rarely this lends a kind of epic majesty to the text: the figures often take on a monumental character, which nonetheless never becomes academically mannered or excessively emphatic. The model of historical style produced by Livy rapidly became a classic and for a long time rivaled the other model, that of Sallust, even if it was that rival model that exerted a predominant influence in antiquity.

Pathos and epic majesty

If, in conclusion, we wished to define the tendency of Livy's historiography, it would be easy to say that as the declared opponent of Sallust, he was a follower of Cicero. Seneca the Elder, in *Controversiae* 9.1.13 f., informs us that what Livy criticized in the Sallustian style was its taste for excessively concise expression, that pursuit of *brevitas* with which Sallust wanted to rival Thucydides, almost to the point (so runs the charge) of falling into obscurity. In fact, the precepts that Cicero had given for historical style must have been regarded by Livy as good in themselves, and he readily conformed to them: the style of the historian should "have variety of tones" but especially should be distinguished by the "gentle and regular movement of the expression" (*De Oratore* 2.54). Still more clearly, Cicero had wished for "a style smooth and ample, which flows gently, following an even and regular course" (*genus orationis fusum atque tractum et cum lenitate*

Livy as a follower of Cicero

quadam aequabiliter profluens [ibid. 2.64; cf. *Orator* 66]), a great river, majestic, broad, and calm, rather than a tumultuous, headlong torrent.

Yet it is also true that Livy's periods, compared with those of Cicero, are often loaded, crowded, nearly encumbered on account of the desire to accumulate too many important details in a single long movement. If Cicero's are created to be heard, Livy's expect to be read. Madvig, in a happy analysis, passed this judgment: "Not only does Livy represent the true written language, but in addition his language, with its methodical, calculated movement, tends towards heaviness and in places becomes, because of excessive art, incorrect and unnatural in the relation it establishes between the construction of the period and the thought."

4. LITERARY SUCCESS

Despite the prevalence of the Sallustian model in Roman historiography, Livy already became a widely popular figure during his lifetime—Pliny reports (*Epistulae* 2.3.8) that one fan traveled all the way from Cadiz to Rome, simply to see Livy, and returned home once he had accomplished his goal—and went on to influence and inform historians such as Tacitus and Florus (and even such Greek ones as Plutarch and Cassius Dio), specialist authors such as Valerius Maximus and Frontinus, and poets such as Lucan and Silius Italicus. His literary qualities are praised by both Senecas, Quintilian, Tacitus, and other writers; when Caligula decided to banish the works and the portraits of two authors from all public libraries, he chose Livy and Virgil. As late as the fourth century, Avienus transposed Livy's history into iambic verse; and two centuries later he was still being read and quoted by Priscian.

Nevertheless, the enormous mass of his work posed difficulties for its survival. At least three different strategies were designed to preserve parts—and thereby helped to condemn the whole. Epitomes, called *Periochae* ("Summaries") from the titles found in the manuscripts, were prepared, probably for didactic purposes; these are attested already in a witty epigram by Martial, *pellibus exiguis artatur Livius ingens, / quem mea non totum bibliotheca capit* (14.190). Excerpts were assembled: during the reign of Domitian, Mettius Pompusianus collected the speeches of Livy's kings and generals. And the *Ab Urbe Condita* was divided up into pentads and decades, groups of five and ten books, which were transmitted separately.

In 401, Q. Aurelius Symmachus corrected a set of manuscripts containing the whole of Livy's work, as we know from a subscription; this was a large-scale cooperative venture of the Nicomachi and Symmachi families and is the ultimate source for all surviving manuscripts of the first decade. Livy was not a school author in the Middle Ages, but although he suffered a decline in popularity during this period, he continued to be read—already Einhard studied his works and imitated his style—and in the eleventh century starts to appear more frequently both in library catalogues and in such authors as Lambert of Hersfeld and John of Salisbury. Dante praises him as "Livio che non erra" (*Inferno* 28.12), uses him as a source in book 2 of his *De Monarchia*, and lists him among the great prose authors in his *De Vulgari Eloquentia*. And in the fourteenth century Pierre Bersuire translated him into French for King John III.

Rediscovery

Livy's fragmentation into pentads and decades was the indispensable premise for his survival through the Dark and Middle Ages (for no work of that length could have been transmitted as a whole), but the story of his transmission in the Renaissance is that of the gradual joining up of these fragments in the vain attempt to reconstitute the whole. Petrarch found manuscripts containing the first, third, and fourth decades at Chartres, emended the text, and—for the first time since antiquity—put them together; his collection was later used by Lorenzo Valla. But it was not until 1527 that Simon Grynaeus discovered a manuscript of the first half of the fifth decade in Lorsch; and the first part of book 33 did not turn up until 1615, when the Jesuit Horrio found it in Bamberg. The *editio princeps* (Rome 1469) contained only books 1–10, 21–32, 34–39, and part of 40; an edition published in Mainz in 1518 added the rest of book 40 and the second part of book 33; another printed in Basel in 1531 added the five books of the fifth decade; the first part of book 33 was not published until 1616 in Rome. Rumors of the survival of complete manuscripts of Livy haunted the Renaissance, sending humanists scurrying to a Benedictine abbey near Lübeck, to the archives of the cathedral of Chartres, to the Cistercian monastery of Soröe near Röskilde in Denmark—but all in vain. Nor was the energy of scholars directed solely to discovery: it could also aim at a perhaps easier target, invention. In the seventeenth century Johannes Caspar Freinsheim "restored" sixty of the lost books.

Renaissance and
after

But while the hunt for actual new texts of Livy brought everdiminishing returns, the influence exercised by the contents of what did survive continued to increase. Petrarch (who was inspired by Livy for some of the episodes of his epic *Africa*) and Boccaccio (who may have prepared an extant Italian translation of the third and fourth decades) bequeathed Livy to the Italian Renaissance as one of the most important sources for Roman history, as an important model for humanist historiography, and even as an instrument of international diplomacy—Cosimo de Medici sent a manuscript of Livy to Alfonso of Aragon, who dared to take it into his hands despite his court's fears that it might have been poisoned. He was a favorite humanist author: Cola di Rienzi and Lorenzo Valla studied him, and the poet Beccadelli is even said to have sold a piece of property in order to buy a manuscript of Livy copied by Poggio Bracciolini. In Latin, the same Poggio and Leonardo Bruni wrote Livian histories of the Florentine republic. In Italian, Macchiavelli wrote *Discourses on the First Decade of Livy*, the first modern reflection on Roman history, which sought both to recover the truth of the events Livy reported and to draw from them permanently valid moral and political lessons. Livy's anecdotal style furnished excellent material for tragedies in Italy and France and (together, to a lesser extent, with Ovid) for Shakespeare's *Lucrece*, as well as for countless historical paintings. The death of Lucretia appealed particularly to painters and patrons who felt the need of a historically erudite and morally edifying pretext for the display of a highly erotic naked woman stabbed to death, while heroic themes from Livy's stories of early republican history dominated French historical painting at the end of the eighteenth and the beginning of the nineteenth centuries.

Through the fifteenth century (with occasional exceptions, e.g., Alciato and Justus Lipsius) Livy was usually preferred to Tacitus; by 1530 there were more than thirty editions and translations of Livy but only about six of Tacitus. But in the sixteenth century his fortunes began to decline as the republican hopes of the Renaissance gave way to the realities of absolutism; and they never fully recovered from the shock of the sack of Rome. Even nowadays some of Livy's stories still form part of the intellectual baggage of the moderately cultured, but he is little read, except by classicists, especially anthropologically minded ones, who have long since learned to distrust his version of early Roman history but who hope to find in his stories material for the reconstruction of the customs of primitive Rome.

BIBLIOGRAPHY

The best complete edition of Livy is the Teubner set by W. Weissenborn, M. Müller, and W. Heraeus (Leipzig 1887–1908); there are revised editions of books 21–22 and 23–25 by T. A. Dorey (Leipzig 1971, 1976), of 26–27 by P. G. Walsh (Leipzig 1982) and of 41–45 by J. Briscoe (Stuttgart 1986). There are Oxford texts of books 1–35; those of 1–5 by R. M. Ogilvie (1974) and of 31–35 by A. H. McDonald (1965) are better than the older volumes by R. S. Conway, C. F. Walters, and, for 26–30, S. K. Johnson. The Budé set is still incomplete but is making rapid progress (Paris 1947–). The Loeb set in fifteen volumes concludes with a useful index by R. M. Greer (Cambridge, Mass. 1919–67, various editors). There are good English commentaries by R. M. Ogilvie on 1–5 (ed. 2 Oxford 1969) and by J. Briscoe on 31–33 (Oxford 1973) and 34–37 (Oxford 1989); the only complete commentary, however, is that of W. Weissenborn and H. J. Müller (ed. 4 Berlin 1910, German).

Among general works in English note esp. P. G. Walsh, *Livy: His Historical Aims and Methods* (Cambridge 1961; Walsh also produced a useful Greece and Rome survey, Oxford 1974), T. J. Luce, *Livy: The Composition of His History* (Princeton 1977), and J. Lipovsky, *A Historiographical Study of Livy, Books VI–X* (New York 1981). There is a set of essays edited by T. A. Dorey (London 1971); on the style, see also A. D. Leeman, *Orationis Ratio: The Stylistic Theories and Practice of the Roman Orators, Historians, and Philosophers* (Amsterdam 1963) 190–97. In German see esp. E. Burck, *Die Erzählungskunst des T. Livius* (Berlin 1934), A. Klotz, *Livius und seine Vorgänger* (Amsterdam 1964), H. Tränkle, *Livius und Polybius* (Basel 1977), and the collection *Wege zu Livius*, ed. E. Burck (Darmstadt 1967).

Directions in Historiography

I. ASINIUS POLLIO AND THE HISTORY OF THE CIVIL WARS

The tradition of senatorial historiography continues in the Augustan age with Asinius Pollio, whose cultural importance in his time we have already described (see p. 260).

Life of Pollio

Gaius Asinius Pollio (76 B.C.–A.D. 4), from Teate (Chieti) in the country of the Marrucini, was a follower first of Caesar and then of Antony; in the party of the latter indeed he was the person second in importance. Consul in 40 and proconsul in 39, in which year he celebrated a triumph over Dalmatian peoples, he subsequently withdrew from political life, maintaining a position of notable independence under Augustus. His diverse talents found expression in the fields of politics, oratory, historiography, poetry, the patronage of poets, and literary criticism. In his youth he had been a friend of Catullus and Helvius Cinna; in the year of his consulship Virgil dedicated the fourth eclogue to him (see p. 267). Asinius wrote tragedies, but was particularly known as an orator: an Atticist, he always remained hostile, even personally hostile, towards Cicero, and even after Cicero's death he did not cease to blacken his memory. Asinius carried his Atticist tendencies over into his literary criticism; we know from Seneca the Elder (*Controversiae* 4 *praef.* 3) that few writers of the day escaped the censure of his *strictum et asperum et nimis iratum iudicium.*

Pollio's Histories

The *Histories* of Asinius Pollio, begun in the year of Sallust's death, 35 B.C., seem to have covered the period from the first triumvirate (60 B.C.) onwards, the most tumultuous period of recent Roman history, including the civil war between Caesar and Pompey, the dominance of Caesar, and the new conflicts that arose after his death, perhaps going down to the battle of Philippi. In the first ode of the second book Horace could rightly claim that Asinius did not hesitate to advance across a fiery terrain and concern himself with the conflicts that were still lurking beneath the ashes. Unfortunately, only a few fragments are left of the *Histories,* which makes it very difficult to reconstruct the tendencies of Pollio's historiography; the independence he displayed towards the new princeps probably did not take the form of open opposition.

Pollio's critical
judgments

From the stylistic point of view, Pollio was, as has already been said, the exponent of a trenchant Atticism, of a "primitive," Thucydidean manner. Pollio's tastes were also expressed in poisonous judgments on other writers: Caesar, in his view, lacked *diligentia* and regard for the historical truth; Sallust went too far in his archaisms, obscurity, and use of metaphors; Cicero lacked a sense of correct and pure *Latinitas*, heaped up too many metaphors, and was guilty of *neglegentia*; and the criticism of Livy for *Patavinitas*, "Paduan provincialism" (see pp. 369 f.), goes back to Pollio. The loss of Pollio's work makes it impossible to judge to what extent he himself as a writer reached the high level he expected of others. But such notion as we can form is of an affected spareness, of an odd verbal mosaic composed with meticulous care. Seneca in one place refers to Asinius Pollio's *compositio salebrosa* ("rough composition"). The fragment on Cicero's death, preserved by Seneca the Elder, who stresses that it is not a typical example of Pollio's style, is striking for the oddness of its word order and for the large number of *traiectiones* ("transpositions"), which in the end make the fragment scarcely clear. The fragment also brings to mind the criticism Cicero levels in the *Orator* against the Latin orators of Thucydidean tendency who speak in broken, disconnected phrases.

A style spare to the
point of obscurity

2. AUTOBIOGRAPHY AND PROPAGANDA: AUGUSTUS

The Commentarii of
Agrippa and
Augustus

Reference has previously been made (see p. 123) to the moderate flourishing of autobiographical *commentarii* beginning in the age of Sulla. The tradition continued in the age of Augustus, when Agrippa, Augustus's close collaborator and son-in-law, wrote an autobiography. We know, moreover, of the *Commentarii de Vita Sua* composed by Augustus himself. From the few pieces of evidence on it that we have, it seems that the princeps promoted the creation of a charismatic halo about himself, as Sulla had done; he recorded prodigies and prophecies that referred to him. The funeral inscription Augustus composed for his own tomb is very different, in that its official character caused the charismatic elements to be made thoroughly marginal. The inscription has been preserved for us in a double version, Greek and Latin, on a temple dedicated to Augustus and the goddess Rome at Ankara in Asia Minor *(Monumentum Ancyranum)*; its usefulness as a work of propaganda has already been discussed (pp. 259 f.).

3. POMPEIUS TROGUS AND REFLECTIONS OF ANTI-ROMAN OPPOSITION

The Historiae
Philippicae

Pompeius Trogus, an approximate contemporary of Livy, originally from Gallia Narbonensis, came from a family that had loyally cooperated with their Roman masters. His grandfather had fought under Pompey's command in the war against Sertorius, and his father had served under Caesar. Trogus apparently wrote some works of natural history, but his fame is owed principally to the *Historiae Philippicae,* in forty-four books. These are lost, but an abridgment survives, compiled by a certain Justin in the second or third century A.D. This is sufficient to give us a notion of some historiographic tendencies in Pompeius Trogus, but it does not allow us to appreciate the qualities of his style.

The change in perspective

The title of Pompeius Trogus's work echoes that of the *Philippic Histories* of the Greek historian Theopompus (fourth century B.C.), which celebrated the deeds of Philip of Macedon. The structure of the two works was different, since Theopompus limited himself to affairs of Greece and Macedon, whereas Pompeius Trogus wrote a genuine universal history that extended from the earliest events of Babylon to the author's own day. The echo of the title was justified, nonetheless, in that the greater part of the narrative (books 7–40) was reserved for the history of Macedon and only the last two books were concerned with the history of Rome and the western regions.

One notices here a conception profoundly different from that of Livy, for whom Rome was the pivot upon which the episodes of universal history turned and the other peoples were taken into consideration to the extent that they came into contact with Rome and fell inexorably under her control. The same choice of title probably shows that Pompeius Trogus regarded the Macedonian empire as the greatest that had ever appeared in the world. It is clear, in any event, that the place of Rome in world history is redefined: for Pompeius Trogus, the Roman hegemony is only one among the many that have succeeded one another through the ages.

The independent approach

Pompeius Trogus relied heavily on the contemporary Greek historian Timagenes, who was notoriously hostile to Rome and the principate, as a source. Some have wanted to draw the conclusion that the *Historiae Philippicae* was dominated by a decidedly anti-Roman approach. To be sure, indications of anti-Roman polemic surface here and there in Justin's abridgment: we find some of the gravest setbacks that the Romans suffered recorded almost with satisfaction; we see people such as Hannibal, Pyrrhus, or Mithridates praised; and considerable importance is attached to the affairs of a people traditionally hostile to Rome, the Parthians, who had again become special objects of fear at the time Trogus was writing. But as far as we can judge from Justin's abridgment, it is not likely that anti-Roman polemic was the fundamental inspiration of Pompeius Trogus's work or that it was conducted as systematically as some interpreters have supposed.

Trogus's models: Sallust and Caesar

As we have said, it is very difficult to get an idea of Pompeius Trogus's style. As far as we can tell, he was an imitator of Sallust who tended to develop Sallust's taste for concise antitheses into a taste for pathetic amplification, which in the end weakens the original stylistic force of the model. We know, too, that when he had to let his characters speak, he preferred indirect discourse to direct. Trogus probably inherited this tendency, which stands in contrast to the general tendency in Roman historical writing, from Caesar, who in turn had derived it from the tradition of military and governmental reports. Yet Trogus, as far as we can see, was inclined to swell the size of the indirect discourses; a lengthy *oratio obliqua* of Mithridates has been preserved by Justin precisely so that the reader can get an idea of the style of the *Historiae Philippicae.*

4. THE HISTORIOGRAPHY OF CONSENSUS: VELLEIUS PATERCULUS AND VALERIUS MAXIMUS

Life of Velleius Paterculus

The principate's relation with the intellectuals had already deteriorated in the last phase of Augustus's rule (see p. 256 f.). Unlike him, the second emperor, Tiberius, for the most part lacked ability as an organizer of consensus about the regime. He found an impassioned celebrator, nonetheless, in Velleius Paterculus, from Aeclanum in Irpinia. Velleius himself gives us notices about his own life. He reveals that he came from a prosperous family and had served under Tiberius as a cavalry commander in Germany and Pannonia; in A.D. 14 Tiberius designated him praetor for the following year. Velleius's autobiographical information stops in the year 14; but he certainly lived until after 30, since the *Historiae* was dedicated to Marcus Vinicius on the occasion of his consulship, which fell in that year. The *Historiae,* in two books, which are preserved with some considerable lacunae, covered Rome's history from the remote past to the contemporary period. Contemporary events were given a far more conspicuous importance than had been usual in earlier Latin historical writing, whereas the earliest eras were treated summarily, almost as in an abridgment. Velleius is not outstanding either for his gifts of historical penetration or for his literary merits, but he does often succeed in giving to his narrative a lively movement that makes it pleasant to read.

The Historiae: *general characteristics*

The interpretation of recent history centers on the celebration of the social improvement, the internal pacification, and the suppression of civil conflicts that had been begun by Caesar and consolidated by Augustus, whose policy Tiberius is regarded as continuing and bringing to completion. When it comes to deal with Tiberius, Velleius's history is virtually transformed into a panegyric: Tiberius is depicted as a general of immense experience and a wise and clement politician, in short, the best leader that the Empire could desire. In senatorial historiography, the hostility shown towards the principate by the aristocracy, which had been excluded from power, was always smoldering to one degree or another (recall Tacitus's grim picture of Tiberius [see p. 540]). Velleius, by contrast, is the spokesman for loyalty to the principate on the part of the military class, from which he himself and his ancestors came. The attentiveness with which he follows the rise of the *homines novi* is understandable: among these stands out especially Tiberius's close collaborator the notorious Sejanus, of whom Velleius sketches a highly laudatory portrait.

The panegyric of Tiberius

The paradoxical portrait

Velleius shows a particular sensitivity towards the emergence of new values and of personalities of a new type. In his narrative he succeeds in bringing to life paradoxical characters, that is, characters who contain within themselves an indivisible mixture of virtues and vices; an instance is the portrait of Maecenas, both an energetic politician and a debauched pleasure-seeker. The relative subtlety with which Velleius manages to capture the changes in custom corresponds, in a way, to the interest with which he follows the unfolding of cultural history, a subject earlier historiography had never dealt with systematically. Velleius reports on the penetration of Greek culture into Rome, on the evolution of the public's tastes, and on events having to do with the literary genres (this last according to the naive scheme by which every genre declines rapidly after it has reached maturity, an "organicist" evolutionary model that had already been applied to the life of nations and empires); he even goes into digressions on the architectural aspects of the city.

The work of Valerius
Maximus

Warm support for the regime of Tiberius is also expressed in the nine books of *Factorum et Dictorum Memorabilium,* which Valerius Maximus probably published around A.D. 31–32, shortly after the fall and slaughter of Sejanus. To the praises Velleius had already heaped upon Tiberius, Valerius adds praise for having saved the Empire from the ruin Sejanus was preparing for it.

The Exempla

We know almost nothing about the life of Valerius apart from the very little that he tells us: he was not rich and was a client of a Sextus Pompeius, consul in A.D. 14, in whose train he had visited Asia Minor in 27. Valerius Maximus's work—which we have placed in a section dedicated to historiography only for convenience and on account of a degree of thematic affinity—is, properly speaking, a collection of *Exempla,* a handbook of models of vices and virtues intended for the use of the rhetorical schools. The *Exempla* is divided into chapters by subject (*De religione, De patientia, De humanitate et clementia, De severitate, De mutatione morum ac fortunae,* etc.), and each chapter in its turn is usually subdivided into sections devoted to the Roman and the foreign examples, respectively. In general Valerius gives the impression of looking on the other peoples with an unshakeable cer-

The celebration of the
traditional values

tainty that Roman morality is superior. From the collection, which despite rhetorical ambitions is composed in a slack and rather colorless style, there emerges with great clarity the system of values that Valerius Maximus holds to: as with the "Catonian" inspiration of the Augustan regime and, still more, with the drab morality of the Tiberian, the traditional, archaizing values of the *mos maiorum* are the dominant ones, even though some chapters are devoted to more modern ethical values, such as *liberalitas* and *humanitas.*

Literary success of
Valerius Maximus

Valerius Maximus's enormous popularity seems inversely proportional to his modest literary qualities. In antiquity his convenient and easy anthology of useful and entertaining stories was much quarried by later writers, including Pliny, Aulus Gellius, Lactantius, and Priscian; even Plutarch cites him twice. In the fourth century it was twice reduced to the form of compendia, one by Julius Paris, which has survived intact, and another by Januarius Nepotianus, which stops at book 3.2.7.

Both complete and compressed, Valerius Maximus survived to become one of the most famous Latin authorities for the Middle Ages and to inspire the numerous collections of *exempla* that proliferate starting in the eleventh century. In the ninth century, he was excerpted at least twice, by Eric of Auxerre and Sedulius of Liège; in the eleventh century, Rodolfus Tortarius, a monk at Fleury, wrote the *De Memorabilibus,* a poem in nine books based on his work; and Petrarch took him as his model for the structure and content of his *Libri Rerum Memorandarum.* At least excerpts were available in southern Germany by the end of the eleventh century, and a manuscript of the whole work returned to Italy by the thirteenth century. From that time on, his popularity increased explosively for several centuries. While no tenth-century manuscript survives, only one eleventh-century one, and five twelfth-century ones (including excerpts), there are fourteen manuscripts from the thirteenth century and about five hundred from the fourteenth to sixteenth centuries. In the fourteenth century his work was explained in at least three Italian commentaries (by Dionigi da Borgo San Sepolcro, Luca de Penna, and Benvenuto da Imola), two French ones (by Simon de Hesdin and Nicolas de Gonesse, the latter with a translation), and one German one (by Heinrich von Mügeln), and by the end of the Middle Ages he had been translated into Catalan, Castilian, Italian, and Sicilian.

In the first century of the Renaissance, his popularity increased even further, extending beyond literature to include cycles of paintings by Beccafumi and Pordenone. But thereafter his fortune began to wane, in part because of the fading away of the public orations for which he had gathered his materials, in part because of a gradual loss of faith in the exemplary power of ancient models in general, in part because most of the stories he reported could be found in other surviving and more interesting texts. Inexplicably, despite his reductive moralism and his soothing intelligibility, he never became a school author in the modern period; nowadays almost no one reads him.

5. THE HISTORIOGRAPHY OF THE SENATORIAL OPPOSITION

The opposition to Tiberius: Labienus and Cremutius Cordus

Under the regime of Tiberius the strongest and most vital historiographic current was the one dominated by an approach hostile to the principate. The opposition was varied and expressed itself as much in the worship of the republican martyrs, Cato of Utica in particular, as in the literature that was favorable to Germanicus and his family, upon whom the illusory hopes for a conciliation between the principate and liberty were concentrated. The regime, once it had lost control over historical writing, went in for gestures of repressive intolerance, the first signs of which had already appeared towards the end of Augustus's principate. It was decreed that the historical work of Titus Labienus, which evidently dealt with recent events, be publicly burnt. Labienus, nicknamed "Rabienus" on account of his polemical animosity, who was also a well-known orator, could not bear to survive his work and in A.D. 12 killed himself in the tomb of his ancestors. Under the reign of Tiberius, while Sejanus was still in power, a similar fate was decreed for the *Annales* of Cremutius Cordus, who, as we learn from Tacitus, had glorified Brutus and termed Cassius the last of the Romans. Fortunately, Cremutius Cordus's historical work was saved from the fire and subsequently published; Cremutius himself by his suicide forestalled the outcome of the trial that had been set in motion against him by Sejanus.

Other historians of the Tiberian period

Nostalgia for the republican past was probably also expressed in the historical work of Seneca the Elder (see pp. 404 f.). It is more difficult to discern the approach taken by the *Annales* of Fenestella, who was chiefly a scholar and antiquarian from the time of Augustus or Tiberius. Also to be placed in the Tiberian period are Servilius Nonianus, an opposition historian and an important source for Tacitus, who shows great respect for him, and probably Aufidius Bassus, the author of a work on the war against the Germans and of another in which the history of Rome was narrated, perhaps beginning with the period of Caesar. The historical work of Pliny the Elder would follow upon the latter, just as Sallust in his *Histories* had followed upon the work of Sisenna.

6. HISTORIOGRAPHY AS LITERARY ENTERTAINMENT: CURTIUS RUFUS

Dating the work of Curtius Rufus

Quintus Curtius Rufus, a person otherwise unknown (an identification has been proposed with a rhetorician mentioned by Suetonius), is the author of the *Historiae Alexandri Magni,* in ten books, of which the first two have been lost, while the remaining eight have come down to us with lacunae. Dating the work of Curtius Rufus continues to be one of the most difficult problems for classical philology, with hypotheses ranging from the age of Augustus to the age of Theodosius. For lack of any notice of him whatsoever in other authors, scholars have been forced to rely exclusively on what they regard as allusions to more or less contemporary events contained within the work. The hypothesis that has prevailed for a long time, however, is that Curtius Rufus writes during the reign of Claudius, shortly after the death of Caligula; among other things, a possible play of words on the name of Caligula has been detected in the work.

The figure of Alexander the Great

The "myth" of Alexander the Great was always alive in the Rome of the Empire, helping, among other things, to inspire the poses and attitudes struck by some emperors. Moreover, the Macedonian ruler was an "example" well known in the schools of rhetoric, as we know from Seneca the Elder and can see in Valerius Maximus's collection, where he occupies a place of honor and appears under the most varied rubrics: *amicitia, patientia,*

Alexander as a hero of romance

iracundia, clementia, superbia, and, of course, *cupiditas gloriae.* And yet the figure of Alexander was not merely an element in political iconography or a subject of rhetorical exercises; it had acquired an important place in the tradition of entertainment literature as well. Hellenistic culture had already made the Macedonian ruler a kind of romance hero and took pleasure in the account of his adventure-filled conquests in remote Oriental lands, which often were conducted in an atmosphere of the fabulous and marvelous. Curtius Rufus's work derives from the combination of all these aspects of the tradition about Alexander, and in its turn it would greatly influence the various versions of the so-called *Romance of Alexander*, which was destined to have immense popularity in the culture of the late Empire and the Middle Ages (see p. 653). Curtius Rufus, who writes in a style that is intensely rhythmic and full of color, with the easy flow that is characteristic of the Livian tradition, exerted himself as a narrator more than as a true historian, as is shown by his quite casual employment of Hellenistic sources that are occasionally divergent, some favorable to Alexander, some unfavorable. Curtius Rufus echoes Clitarchus and Timagenes, but his use of other authors is also evident. Given the loss of the vast quantity of Hellenistic historical writings about Alexander, the work of Curtius Rufus, quite apart from the author's intentions, proves on occasion to be a valuable source of information. As is consistent with Curtius Rufus's purpose, which is chiefly to interest the reader and excite his imagination, the character of Alexander emerges from his work as a mixture of cruelty and generosity, of virtue and corruption. The events of his life were more than anything a pretext for a narrative taste that was comfortable with romancelike episodes, exotic landscapes, and scenes heavy with pathos. The result is a work of multifaceted pleasure.

The narrator's taste

BIBLIOGRAPHY

The fragments of Asinius Pollio and the other historians mentioned above can be found in volume 2 of H. Peter, *Historicorum Romanorum Fragmenta* (Leipzig 1906). The *Monumentum Ancyranum (Res Gestae Divi Augusti)* is conveniently edited by P. A. Brunt and J. M. Moore (Oxford 1967); see also the editions of J. Gagé (ed. 3 Paris 1977) and H. Malcovati in *Imperatoris Caesaris Augusti Operum Fragmenta* (ed. 5 Turin 1969). For Justin-Trogus see the editions by O. Seel of the fragments of Trogus (Leipzig 1956) and of Justin's epitome (Leipzig 1972); for Velleius Paterculus the editions of W. S. Watt (Leipzig 1988) and J. Hellegouarc'h (2 vols., Paris 1982, with French translation and commentary), as well as the important commentaries on 2.94–131 and 2.41–93 by A. J. Woodman (Cambridge 1977, 1983). The Loeb edition of Velleius by F. W. Shipley (London 1920) includes a text and translation of the *Res Gestae*. For Valerius Maximus, see the editions of C. Kempf (Leipzig 1883) and R. Faranda (Turin 1971, with Italian translation), and for Curtius Rufus, that of K. Müller (Munich 1954, with German translation). There is a two-volume Loeb edition of Curtius by J. C. Rolfe (Cambridge, Mass. 1946).

For English studies, see A. D. Leeman's *Orationis Ratio: The Stylistic Theories and Practice of the Roman Orators, Historians, and Philosophers* (Amsterdam 1963), E. Badian, "The Early Historians," in *Latin Historians*, ed. T. A. Dorey (London 1966) 1–38, esp. 2–7, B. W. Frier, *Libri annales pontificum maximorum: The Origins of the Annalistic Tradition* (Rome 1979) with R. M. Ogilvie's review in *JRS* 71 (1981) 199–201, C. W. Fornara, *The Nature of History in Ancient Greece and Rome* (Berkeley 1983) 23–28, and E. Rawson, "The First Latin Annalists," in *Roman Culture and Society* (Oxford 1991) 245–71. On Pollio, there is a French monograph by J. André, *La Vie et l'oeuvre de Asinius Pollio* (Paris 1949), and an Italian survey by G. Lecchini in *ANRW* 30.2 (Berlin 1982) 1265–96;

the best English account is the brief introduction by R.G.M. Nisbet and M. Hubbard to their commentary on Horace *Odes* 2.1 (Oxford 1978). On Justin-Trogus see Leeman, *Orationis Ratio* 244–47, O. Seel, *Eine römische Weltgeschichte* (Nuremberg 1972), and H.-D. Richter, *Untersuchungen zur hellenistischen Historiographie* (Frankfurt 1987). On Velleius, see the introductions to Woodman's volumes mentioned above and his article in *Empire and Aftermath,* ed. T. A. Dorey (London 1975) 1–25; there is a survey by J. Hellegouarc'h in *ANRW* 32.1 (Berlin 1984) 404–36. The same volume contains a survey on Valerius Maximus by G. Maslakov (437–96); see also C. J. Carter in the Dorey collection (30–34). There is a good recent bibliography to Curtius Rufus in the Penguin translation by J. Yardley and W. Heckel (London 1984) 259–64; see esp. W. W. Tarn, *Alexander the Great,* vol. 2 (Cambridge 1948) 91–122, and E. I. McQueen in T. A. Dorey, ed., *Latin Biography* (London 1967) 17–43.

Scholarship and Technical Disciplines

1. SCHOLARSHIP AND GRAMMATICAL STUDIES IN THE AUGUSTAN AGE

Hyginus and the Palatine library

The establishment of three public libraries at Rome undoubtedly signifies an increased demand for reading. A freedman of Augustus, Gaius Julius Hyginus, who was either a Spaniard (according to Suetonius) or from Alexandria (according to others), was placed in charge of one of these libraries, the Palatine (this Hyginus should not be confused with the somewhat later mythographer, author of a collection of *Fabulae*). Subsequently, it seems, Hyginus fell into disgrace and died in poverty; still, his appointment as prefect of the Palatine library indicates that men of servile origin could rise in society through cultural activities as well as economic ones. Hyginus wrote a commentary on the works of Virgil, a treatise on agriculture, another on the origin of bees, and various works, all lost, of antiquarianism and scholarship, somewhat in the manner of Varro.

Verrius Flaccus

The Fasti *of Verrius Flaccus*

The greatest grammarian of the time was Verrius Flaccus, from Praeneste, whom Augustus chose as tutor for his grandsons Lucius and Gaius. He wrote various works, of grammar and scholarship, all lost, among them the *Fasti* that Ovid used extensively in his work of the same name. Verrius himself had these *Fasti* carved in marble in the forum at Praeneste, where a statue had also been erected to him. A part of them has been recovered from excavations, and we know that they reached A.D. 22 and therefore that the death of Verrius must be placed after this date.

The De Verborum Significatu: *grammar and antiquarianism*

Among Verrius Flaccus's scholarly works one may mention the *Rerum Etruscarum Libri*. But his name is principally linked with the *De Verborum Significatu,* an alphabetical glossary of difficult or obsolete terms. As in Varro's works, the grammatical interest was closely connected to antiquarian research; the individual lemmata continually offered the author opportunities for *excursus* on ancient Rome and its Italic peoples, which were filled with quotations from early and often relatively unknown authors. Varro himself was quoted a number of times and is one of the principal sources of the *De Verborum Significatu.*

The epitome of Festus

Verrius Flaccus's original text has been lost, but we do have, though only in part, the abridgment made of it by a grammarian of the second and third centuries, Sextus Pompeius Festus. Festus, however, did not confine himself to a simple summary but often used notices drawn from other sources to argue against Verrius.

The epitome of Paulus Diaconus: the success of Verrius Flaccus

Festus in his turn was abridged, in the Lombard-Carolingian age, by Paulus Diaconus. This abridgment is preserved entire; yet in bulk and critical competence it amounts to little in relation to Festus's work, let alone that of Verrius. These remains, nonetheless, do allow us to glimpse what a treasure of antiquarian, historical, and grammatical learning there was in Verrius Flaccus; and this in turn explains the success he enjoyed among the scholars of the Empire (Pliny the Elder, for instance, used him extensively). Moreover, the work of Verrius, Festus, and Paulus even now provides valuable information for scholars of the language, institutions, and civilization of Rome.

2. THE TECHNICAL DISCIPLINES IN THE AGE OF AUGUSTUS AND THE JULIO-CLAUDIANS

The problem of a scientific prose at Rome

Latin culture in general is poor in scientific prose. The prestige attaching to rhetoric hindered the creation of a prose that, on the model of Aristotle's philosophical prose, would reject ornamentation and strive towards precise terminology and rigorous argumentation. At the same time, the strong tradition of didactic poetry, upon which Lucretius and Manilius, for instance, had drawn, also helped to prevent the formation of a true scientific prose. Nonetheless, the early Empire, in the period after Varro and before Pliny the Elder, witnesses a modest flourishing of scientific literature.

Architecture: Vitruvius

Vitruvius's De Architectura: *date of composition and contents*

Vitruvius Pollio, an officer in Caesar's engineering corps who had been entrusted with constructing war machines (but he had also been an architect in peacetime: he himself mentions having designed and constructed the basilica of Fano), between 27 and 23 B.C. published a treatise on architecture, *De Architectura,* in ten books. It is dedicated to Augustus, who had secured a pension for him and so permitted him to make use of his education and his technical experience in composing a work by means of which he sought to win fame among posterity. It is probably not a coincidence that the work appeared during the years in which the princeps was proposing a vast program for improving the public buildings of Rome and the Empire. The first book deals with the places suitable for construction, the second with materials, the third and fourth with sacred buildings, the fifth with public buildings, the sixth and seventh with private buildings, the eighth with hydraulics, the ninth with sundials, the tenth with mechanics, that is, the construction of cranes, hydraulic devices, and machines of war. In the course of the work's transmission the diagrams Vitruvius tells us accompanied it were lost.

Architecture as imitation of nature

In Vitruvius's conception, architecture is seen, in almost Aristotelian terms, as an imitation of the providential order of nature. Thus he requires in his architect a rich and varied education, almost of the sort that Cicero required in the orator (the comparison is not out of place, since the model of Cicero's *De Oratore* is certainly present to Vitruvius's mind). Particularly in the proems, which are of great interest for understanding the status of the technical disciplines at Rome, Vitruvius insists that the architect not only must be a specialist but must possess a wide culture: knowledge of acoustics is required for the construction of theaters, knowledge of optics for the lighting of buildings, knowledge of medicine for the hygiene of the areas to be built on. But the encyclopedic education that Vitruvius expects his ideal architect to have hinges principally upon philosophy. In Vitruvius's proems it is easy to perceive the need he felt to bestow upon the architect the social and cultural prestige that ancient society customarily denied to the technical disciplines. He seeks to justify architecture before the public through a connection with philosophy, which is ultimately a subordination to philosophy. The deference to philosophy, which Vitruvius announces in the proems, has little to do with the treatment proper, in which the architect's actual experience naturally dominates. The difference between the sections of proem and of instruction in Vitruvius's work is reflected also in the style: the former make quite abundant use of rhetorical ornaments, whereas in the latter the sentences are spare and unadorned, and the language does not hesitate to allow vulgarisms and technical expressions of Greek origin.

The architect as philosopher

Medicine: Celsus

Celsus's encyclopedia: the section on medicine

A different way of bestowing dignity upon the technical disciplines was to set them within a comprehensive encyclopedia of the *artes,* as Varro had done in the *Disciplinarum Libri IX* (see p. 211). This was the path chosen by Aulus Cornelius Celsus, who lived in the age of Tiberius and was the author of a vast encyclopedic handbook that treated six *artes:* agriculture, medicine, military art, oratory, philosophy, and jurisprudence. Only the eight books on medicine (books 6–13 of the entire work) are left to us. Celsus's treatment is so extremely clear and effective that it has led respectable scholars of ancient medicine to suppose that he was a doctor by profession. The question, much discussed, has not yet found a solution: Celsus certainly uses Greek sources, but his treatment has many typically Roman features, which lead one to believe that he was not simply a compiler.

Balance shown by Celsus as doctor

Celsus, displaying remarkable gifts of balance and critical spirit, eschews entering into the dogmatic controversies of the Greek medical schools and tries to maintain a position midway between empiricism and rationalism. (These were the two opposing directions that medicine took in his day: the latter investigated the "hidden causes" of disease and so was inclined towards anatomy and vivisection; the former confined itself to considering the evident causes, with experience as its guide, and was more concerned with cures than with comprehension.) These qualities of sobriety and balance, joined to the excellence of the style—Quintilian regarded Celsus as an elegant writer, and the humanistic tradition placed him among the best

Latin prose writers—contributed to make the work successful over the centuries.

Shortly after Celsus falls the life of another writer, Scribonius Largus, who, unlike Celsus, was concerned exclusively with medicine. He lived, we know, in the time of Claudius. From him we have a book of prescriptions (in Latin, *Compositiones*), written without literary pretensions and intended only for practical use.

Under the name of Antonius Musa, Augustus's doctor and Horace's, a writing entitled *De Herba Vettonica* has come down to us; it is, however, a work from a later period.

Agriculture: Columella

Among the technical disciplines agriculture occupied a special position. Given the landowning tradition of the Roman aristocracy, distinguished members of the ruling class such as Cato and Varro did not disdain to write on this subject. A more exacting treatise, *De Re Rustica,* was published by Lucius Junius Moderatus Columella, who was a contemporary of Seneca and hailed from Gades (Cadiz) in Spain. We know little about his social origins. An inscription from Taranto mentions him as tribune of the *legio VI Ferrata,* stationed in Syria. For the provincial aristocracy the post of legionary tribune was often the means of beginning their career outside their native city. Residing at Rome or in the vicinity, Columella devoted himself chiefly to the practice and the study of agriculture.

Columella's treatise had two editions. From the first we have only the book *De Arboribus,* whereas the far larger second edition, in twelve books, we possess in its entirety. Columella deals successively with the cultivation of fields, trees, and vines, the raising of large animals and barnyard animals, the raising of bees, vegetable and flower gardens, and the duties of the bailiff and his wife. The tenth book, *De Cultu Hortorum,* in hexameters, is Columella's homage to the tradition of Virgil's *Georgics* and also an attempt to fill a gap deliberately left by Virgil, who in the fourth book of his didactic poem, in which he referred to gardens only briefly and complained of the lack of space, had left to others the task of treating them more thoroughly.

Columella writes in a smooth, limpid prose, and his verses, too, are finely constructed. The sources are the usual ones, the Greek and Latin writers on agriculture, from Xenophon to Cato and Varro, and echoes of Virgil, even in the prose parts, are far from rare. But the author's personal experience dominates. Columella's work begins by acknowledging an immense crisis in Italian agriculture, the causes of which are to be sought in the lack of

interest on the part of the proprietors, in the inadequate use made of the vast latifundia, and in the lack of serious scientific preparation in the discipline. This has brought about a structural weakness in Italian agriculture and has led to the dominance of some provinces in exporting products such as wine and oil.

In his introductory pages Columella criticizes the fact that there are no schools and teachers for farmers (in contrast to the situation in the other arts and professions) even though agriculture is the most beautiful and most noble of activities. Yet the training of the perfect farmer seems an impossible task, so vast and varied are the required areas of competence. As a solution to the problem, Columella seems to embrace the idea of an encyclopedic education such as the one Cicero had envisioned for the orator (not by chance are Cicero's treatises frequently referred to by Columella) or the one Vitruvius required for his architect. The spread of this encyclopedic ideal among the various disciplines demonstrates the enduring need for them to be subordinated to philosophy, which appears to be the obligatory path for them to follow in order to acquire dignity and, paradoxically, independent status.

Small properties and latifundia

The frequent reference in Columella's pages to the idealized figures of the old Roman landowners, who divided their time between care for their fields and political activity, may lead one to think that the author's preference is for the small farm, of the sort that the owner can run directly; and confirmation might seem to be found in the frequent criticism of the absentee landlords of the latifundia. In fact, even though Columella gives no explicit dimensions for his ideal farm, it is apparent from the work that his advice is directed for the most part to owners of very large estates. This emerges clearly, for instance, from the section (1.6) devoted to the size of the villa and its parts, which describes the places intended for the slaves and for the processing and storage of the products and the utterly separate places intended for the residence of the owner. It enumerates a whole series of comforts that would have scandalized the Romans of ancient type, whom

A modern view of agriculture

Columella nonetheless praises. The reference to old-time morality in all likelihood is not a mere reflex. A contradiction similar to the one in Columella appeared, perhaps with greater consciousness on the part of the author, in Vitruvius, who, while he continued to value the ancient model of the frugal citizen, also gave directions for constructing the luxurious abodes of wealthy Romans. Columella realizes that in order to bring the urbanized owners back to the country—the best way to increase production, according to him, is to place it under the direct supervision of the *dominus,* who ought to make frequent visits to his farms—moral exhortation is not enough: it is necessary to provide the farming villas with all the amenities offered by a mansion in the city.

Columella and Pliny the Elder

Columella supports a trend towards the maximum intensification and rationalization of agricultural activity, regardless of the size of the estate. Thus he seems sincere in his hostility to the latifundium, which is abandoned and neglected by its owners and increasingly unproductive, and acute in his plans for organizing the work of the slaves, who are subject to the iron control that the *vilicus,* or "bailiff," himself a slave, ought to exercise. Nonetheless, the remedy proposed by Columella was largely utopian. Pliny the Elder would prove to be more realistic in understanding that as long as slave labor prevailed, it would be impossible to rationalize agricultural production effectively: slaves, lacking incentive and indifferent to the work, would never toil to their utmost.

Geography: Agrippa and Pomponius Mela

The domination of Rome and the development of geography

Varro and Nepos

It is understandable how, at a time when Rome's domination was being extended to include a large part of the known world and even lands hitherto unknown, geography acquired importance, both for practical purposes and for celebratory reasons. Varro had already concerned himself with geography, having perhaps dedicated specific works to this science, as is suggested by the titles *De Ora Maritima,* cited by Servius, *Ephemeris Navalis,* and others. From the few fragments we have we may assume that in his geographical books Varro worked in his usual way, paying attention to the more practical aspects, such as the distances between various places. Notices of a geographical character from Nepos have also come down to us, but, as mentioned (see p. 221), we know very little about his work in this field.

Agrippa's map

An interest in geography was also shown by one of the most important political figures of the Augustan age, Marcus Vipsanius Agrippa, commander of Augustus's army and the emperor's son-in-law (of precisely the same age as Augustus, being born also in 63 B.C., Agrippa married Augustus's daughter Julia). He has been referred to in the previous chapter (see p. 378) as the author of an autobiography. Agrippa, certainly motivated by patriotic purposes, drew up a gigantic map of the known world. This map was accompanied by *commentarii,* either published separately or placed at the bottom of the map, which gave information on the extent of the various territories, on the distances between places, and so on. When Agrippa died, in 12 B.C., Augustus personally saw to it that his map was completed and set up in a portico constructed for the purpose in the Campus Martius. Pliny the Elder, in the section of the *Naturalis Historia* devoted to geography (further evidence of how important this science was), cites Varro and Agrippa with the greatest respect.

Pomponius Mela, the first "pure" geographer

A generation earlier than Pliny, under the reign of Caligula or Claudius, we find the first Latin author whom, to the best of our knowledge, we can call a "pure" geographer and whose work has come down to us complete. This is Pomponius Mela, a Spaniard from Tingentera, near Gibraltar, whose *Chorographia,* "Description of Places," in three books, is preserved.

Technical prose and stylistic ambition

In the foreword to the *Chorographia* Pomponius Mela complains that the subjects he is preparing to treat leave no room for an elevated style, a deployment of eloquence. This "inferiority complex" seems shared by a great part of Latin technical prose, which regularly aims at a style that is elevated and often full of archaisms, in contrast to the prosaic quality of the contents. Mela's style, for example, is chiefly based on the style of Sallust and abounds in archaisms and linguistic affectations.

Mela's Chorographia

As for its content, the *Chorographia* describes the world, taking the Mediterranean as its basic point of reference. It proceeds counterclockwise from the Strait of Gibraltar, whither it returns at the end of the description. Mela does not seem interested in the more specifically technical aspects of the subject; he lacks numbers and precise data, though he shows an outstanding knowledge of the Greek and Latin sources. Mela is moved rather by ethnographic interests, and his *facundia* is employed particularly when he comes to speak of distant or scarcely known regions; in that case he often lets himself be carried away by his fondness for fabulous and marvelous details.

Culinary Instruction: Apicius

The corpus *of Apicius*

Marcus Gavius Apicius was a contemporary of Tiberius. His true name seems to have been simply Marcus Gavius; the cognomen was probably derived from the fact that a famous gourmet of the end of the second century B.C. was named Apicius. To this man the manuscripts assign a *corpus* of cooking recipes divided into ten books, with the title *De Re Coquinaria*. In fact the *corpus* is made up of various strata, the latest of them from the fourth century A.D. The Apician nucleus of this collection, itself probably derived in turn from two separate works (one on sauces, one on the complete preparation of certain dishes), is not easily recoverable from the composite mass of recipes that has reached us. This is the fault of an inept late antique compiler, who shows that he understands little of the technical terminology and the culinary material.

Sources of Apicius

The basis of the *De Re Coquinaria* is formed by works of a medical character (the recipes are often given for their dietetic qualities or as medicines for disorders of the digestive system) and treatises of Greek cuisine. The style of exposition lacks any rhetorical or formal elegance, and the ingredients are indicated in minimal fashion in a language that is often pedestrian. Behind this utter simplicity, however, one still discerns the attention to creativity and to the dramatic preparation of the dishes, the extreme of which can be summarized in Apicius's own paradoxical conclusion that "at table no one will recognize what he is eating."

BIBLIOGRAPHY

Paul the Deacon's epitome of Festus's *De Verborum Significatu,* based on the work of Verrius Flaccus, is edited by W. M. Lindsay with the fragments of Festus's original work (Leipzig 1913; see also the edition in *Glossaria Latina,* vol. 4, Paris 1930). There are respectable Loeb editions (Cambridge, Mass.) of Vitruvius by F. Granger (1931), of Celsus by W. G. Spencer (1935), and of Columella by W. B. Ash, E. S. Forester, and E. H. Heffner (1941–45). The principal critical editions of Vitruvius are those of V. Rose and H. Müller-Stübing (Leipzig 1867) and G. Fensterbusch (Darmstadt 1964, with German translation and commentary); a Budé edition is in progress, with books 8 by L. Callebat, 9 by J. Soubiran, and 10 by L. Callebat and P. Fleury published thus far (Paris 1973, 1969, and 1986, respectively). Note also the Italian edition of S. Ferri (Rome 1960). The best edition of Celsus is that of F. Marx in the *Corpus Medicorum Graecorum* (Leipzig 1915), of Columella, the Uppsala edition of V. Lundström, A. Josephson, and S. Hedburg (Uppsala 1897–1968). There is a German translation of Columella with brief notes by K. Ahrens (Berlin 1972) and a similar Italian volume by R. Calzecchi Onestri and C. Carena (Turin 1977). For Pomponius Mela, see the editions of G. Randstrand (Gothenburg 1971) and P. Parroni (Rome 1984, with extensive Italian commentary); for Apicius, those of M. E. Milham (Stuttgart 1969) and J. André (Paris 1974, with French translation and notes). There are several popular translations of Apicius; see esp. that of B. Flower and E. Rosenbaum (London 1958, with Latin text and practical advice).

On all aspects of the technical writers, E. Rawson, *Intellectual Life in the Late Roman Republic* (London 1985) is again invaluable. There is an Italian monograph on Verrius Flaccus by F. Bona, *Contributo allo studio del "De verborum significatu" di Verrio Flacco* (Milan 1964); on Vitruvius, note H. Plommer, *Vitruvius and Later Roman Building Manuals* (Cambridge 1973), and E. Romano, *La capanna e il tempio: Vitruvio dell'architettura* (Palermo 1987). Celsus is discussed in most books of Roman medicine (e.g., J. Scarborough, *Roman Medicine* [Ithaca 1969]), and Columella, in books on farming (see esp. K. White, *Roman Farming* [London 1970]). For Pomponius Mela, see J. O. Thomson, *A History of Ancient Geography* (Cambridge 1948) 225–26. There is an *ANRW* survey (32.3) in French of Columella by R. Martin (Berlin 1985), 1959–79. T. Janson, *Latin Prose Prefaces* (Stockholm 1964), is worth consulting, especially on Columella and Mela, and there is much of relevance in W. H. Stahl, *Roman Science* (Madison 1962).

Legal Literature: From Its Beginnings to the Early Empire

The Laws of the Twelve Tables and the rigid formalism of early Roman law

The historical evolution of Roman law is marked at its beginning and end by two legislative enactments that are utterly unique in the history of law, and not only of Roman law: the Twelve Tables and the complete Justinianic codification in the sixth century. The Twelve Tables were never abolished, and formally they remained in effect until the time of Justinian. In all likelihood they represented the publication of the most important principles of the customary law obtaining at the time. All the early law and all the judicial procedure in that period was characterized by a rigid formalism, according to which in every legal transaction and every judicial suit it was necessary to employ solemn oral formulas. These formulas were framed in unvarying forms of words, marked by artificial language, with figures of sound and parallelisms similar to those of religious and liturgical language. In the second half of the third century B.C. Roman commerce and domination expand; it is significant that in 242 the office of *praetor peregrinus* was created, with jurisdiction over controversies involving a non-Roman. At about this time new legal institutions appear, which naturally produced a first flowering of legal thought and literature. Models and stimuli from Greek culture certainly must have played a part, but from the beginning, despite the paucity of direct evidence, the character of this jurisprudence seems substantially Roman, at least in its practical flexibility; it was meeting the requirements of an empire that was growing and continually running into new, real needs. Thus, that knowledge of law and legal procedure that down to the third century had been the exclusive prerogative of the patrician *pontifices* was placed in the hands of lay jurists. Jurisconsults such as Gnaeus Flavius and Tiberius Coruncanius informed the people about civil law and the procedural forms of the *pontifices*. Coruncanius, though he was pontifex maximus, the first one of plebeian extraction (except for the consul of 280, who had triumphed over the Etruscans), admitted the public, or at least pupils, to his legal consultations. Flavius, the freedman and secretary of Appius Claudius Caecus, published a manuscript of his patron's *legis actiones*. Still, it remains true during the entire period of the Republic that the most important jurists came from senatorial families and as a rule combined their juridical activity with the various

Creation of new legal institutions

Gnaeus Flavius and Coruncanius

Function of the jurisconsults

duties of a public career. Since judge and magistrate were not necessarily expert at law, the function of the jurisconsult was quite important in the Roman legal system. In addition to advising private individuals in legal controversies, he assisted the state magistrates with his consultations; in particular he saw to the correct formulation of the edicts of praetors, aediles, censors, and provincial governors. The principal forms of this legal literature, apart from the collection of *responsa* and *quaestiones,* were commentaries on the praetorian edicts.

The Tripertita *of Aelius Paetus*

Giving a commentary on the laws was perhaps the most typical activity of the jurisconsult in his capacity as teacher. The *Tripertita* of Aelius Paetus (called *Catus,* "the Cunning," consul in 198 B.C.) must have been a culminating monument of this activity. The work contained first the Laws of the Twelve Tables, then an explanation of their development by means of legal interpretation (in effect a commentary), and finally the *legis actiones.* Valued even several centuries afterwards as "the cradle of the law," it must have been the basis upon which a judicial literature grew up in the following period and became increasingly refined. A leap forward in the quality of these studies was certainly taken in the work of a number of famous orators who devoted their abilities to the construction of a systematic legal thought. In particular one must mention Quintus Mucius Scaevola the Augur (son-in-law of the Laelius who was linked to the so-called Scipionic circle), who had Cicero as his pupil and figures as a venerable character in several of his dialogues; and, on the same level with him, though perhaps more productive, Quintus Mucius Scaevola the Pontiff, slightly younger than the other, author of a systematic treatment of civil law that was the basis of many later legal commentaries. The next generation finds in Servius Sulpicius Rufus a deliberate continuator of these studies. Famous as a jurisconsult, he enjoyed the esteem and admiration of Cicero, who, despite having ridiculed him in the *Pro Murena* (see pp. 181 f.), praised him enthusiastically in the ninth *Philippic,* recalling his eagerness for peace and his exemplary morality. He wrote numerous legal works (around 180 books); he also commented on the Twelve Tables and added notes to Scaevola's systematic work. But he distinguished himself principally for having devoted various monographs to individual parts of the law. Equipped, as far as we can judge, with excellent theoretical abilities, he also had subtle skills in dialectic, not to mention an elegant style of writing, which is evidenced in two beautiful letters he wrote to Cicero, one a consolation for the death of Tullia, the other giving a fine description of the murder of Marcus Marcellus (*Epistulae ad Familiares* 4.5 and 4.12, respectively).

The two Scaevolas

Sulpicius Rufus

Law in the Augustan age: the schools of Labeo and Capito

The great flourishing of studies continued in the Augustan age. Indeed, it reached the point of allowing two different tendencies of thought to spring up. The two different schools (we forbear to describe their opposing principles) were headed by the eminent figures Antistius Labeo and Ateius Capito. In origin not very different from one another (both plebeians, the latter perhaps more humble), they must have had contrasting characters, ambitions, and styles of life. Capito pursued a political career up to the consulship (A.D. 5), whereas Labeo refused the consulship Augustus offered him. A convinced republican (hence probably his refusal to accept the post of consul under Augustus's regime), Labeo was fond of living a withdrawn life and writing and teaching, whereas Capito, a supporter of the new order, had a more public life and in the end wrote less than his opponent.

Antistius Labeo

Labeo, a man of enormous culture, an expert in dialectic, in the history of the Latin language and grammar, and in philosophy, wrote around four hundred books (he was accustomed to spending six months in Rome teaching and six months in the country writing). From the references of other jurists we know some titles of his immense production: the *Pithana* ("Plausible Cases," a survey of decisions relating to individual cases), the *Responsa,* the *Epistulae,* a large treatise *De Iure Pontificio* (in fifteen books), as well as commentaries on the laws and legal works. In his writings he showed an unusual independence of judgment and was a marked innovator in a subject that had been deeply influenced by the weight of tradition *(plurima innovare instituit).*

Ateius Capito

Sabinians and Proculians

His opponent Gaius Ateius Capito, by contrast, while in politics he had accepted the new Augustan regime, was conservative in his activity as jurisconsult. He seems to have been chiefly concerned with constitutional law and sacred law: among the titles of his books are recorded *De Iure Pontificio, De Iure Sacrificiorum,* and *Coniectanea.* In the two opposing schools (innovative and conservative—but the contrasts between the two founders were personal and political) later jurisprudence saw the origin of the opposition between the juridical schools that would come to be called the "Sabinians" and the "Proculians." The *secta* that followed the path of Labeo was called Proculian, from the name of Proculus, a jurist of the first half of the first century A.D., who published the *Notae* to the posthumous works of his predecessor Labeo. The other, going back to Capito, took the name Sabinian from the jurist Masurius Sabinus (they were also called "Cassians" from the name of Cassius Longinus, a scholar and successor to Sabinus as head of the school). The differences between the two schools must have been manifested in individual legal points rather than in a consistent basis of doctrine (and the matter can be easily understood if one considers the lack of interest on the part of these jurists in vast constructions of theoretical thought and, correspondingly, the eminently practical character of this literature). It can be argued with a high degree of probability that the organization of jurisprudence had taken the form of corporations of jurisconsults; much of what we are told is unintelligible unless the divergences were embodied in corporations. What is certain is that the authority of Masurius Sabinus, and in particular of his three books of civil law, was very great and, as a model, shaped all subsequent legal literature.

BIBLIOGRAPHY

For the fragments of early legal writers, see F. P. Bremer, *Iurisprudentia Antehadriana* (Leipzig 1896–1901), E. Seckel and K. Kübler, *Iurisprudentiae Anteiustinianae Reliquiae*

(Leipzig 1907–27), and S. Riccobono, *Fontes Iuris Romani Antejustiniani* (Florence 1941). There is an edition of Ateius Capito by W. Strzelecki (Leipzig 1967). Introductory works in English include H. F. Jolowicz and B. Nicholas, *Historical Introduction to the Study of Roman Law* (ed. 3 Cambridge 1972) 374–94, W. Kunkel, *An Introduction to Roman Legal and Constitutional History,* trans. J. M. Kelly (Oxford 1973; the original German work is in its eighth edition, Vienna 1978), and more generally J. A. Crook, *Law and Life of Rome* (London 1967); see also the trilogy by R. A. Bauman, *Lawyers in Roman Republican Politics, Lawyers in Roman Transitional Politics,* and *Lawyers and Politics in the Early Roman Empire* (Munich 1983, 1985, 1989). Three important works in Italian deserve mention: G. Nocera, *Iurisprudentia: per una storia del pensiero giuridico romano* (Rome 1973), A. Schiavone, *Nascita della giuridico nella Roma tardo-repubblicana* (Bari 1987), and the same author's *Giuristi e nobili nella Roma repubblicana* (Rome 1987).

FOUR — The Early Empire

Culture and Spectacle: The Literature of the Early Empire

1. THE END OF PATRONAGE

The second Augustan generation

The second Augustan generation had scarcely been touched by the bloody period of the civil wars and thus, in comparison with the generation that had been assailed by it, it felt less gratitude towards the princeps who had restored harmony and social peace. It had already given signs of disaffection, if not open intolerance, towards the literature that had lent its agreement and support, more or less indirectly, to that program of moral and political restoration. Ovid is a symbol of this changed attitude towards politically committed high poetry (represented by Virgil primarily) and of the corresponding preference given to light literature in a Hellenistic style.

Writers and the principate of Tiberius

The death of Maecenas and the loss of his shrewd mediation between the political powers and the intellectual elite created a rift that would be healed only occasionally and then only temporarily. The crisis in patronage is already manifest with Tiberius, who does not even appear to address the problem of organizing a program of cultural hegemony (his own taste for light Alexandrian poetry is indicative of this indifference), and this despite the fact that he faced a reinvigorated historiography so deeply opposed to the principate that it had its own "martyrs of freedom," such as the historian Cremutius Cordus, dead by suicide in A.D. 25. This historiographic trend, rooted in the republican tradition of the senatorial elite, produces that attitude of hostility towards the Julio-Claudian dynasty that would extend its influence to Suetonius and Tacitus and originate the image of the Julio-Claudians that would be transmitted to posterity.

The principate of Claudius

The situation does not seem to improve with Claudius, although personally he had an excellent reputation as a man of learning and wrote many works in both Greek and Latin. In Latin, under the guidance of Livy, he had even written history. He began with the death of Caesar, passed rapidly over the period of the civil wars, which he treated in only two books, and dwelt instead on the period of Augustus's principate, to which he devoted forty-one books. In Latin too, Claudius had composed a work in defense of Cicero, a reply to a work written by Asinius Gallus, the son of Pollio, who maintained that his father's style was superior to Cicero's. Claudius also wrote a grammatical work, in which he proposed to introduce three new letters into the Latin alphabet.

*Nero's first years
and the revival of
patronage*

Nero alone, in the first years of his principate, which were guided by Seneca, attempted to recover the good will of the Senate and to reestablish patronage. This project made possible that brief period of classicism that aimed at a new flourishing of literature as in the extraordinary age of Augustus and from which only several modest products are left to us, such as the so-called *Ilias Latina* (see p. 437) or the bucolic poetry of Calpurnius Siculus and others (see pp. 435 f.). In these trends one notices clearly the predominant influence of Virgil, who was taken as the highest paradigm of Augustan literature, both as embodying formal perfection and as representing the values of that age and of the role that literature played in relation to political power.

Nero was a poet himself, with a predilection for epic on Trojan themes that itself exemplifies the trend just referred to, and he promoted artistic activities in various ways. Among other things, he instituted a public poetic competition in 60, the Neronia, a quinquennial contest of song, music, poetry, and oratory. The enterprise is interesting, since it provides evidence not only of Nero's ambition to create a new system of patronage but also of the particular direction he wanted to head these new cultural manifestations: they were to be public and in the nature of spectacles. The traditional image of Nero—the histrionic emperor, lover of theatrical spectacles and the circus, an actor himself and driven by a notion of all life as performance (even his immense *Domus Aurea* aims at representing the world that turns about its sovereign)—reflects not only the character and obsessions of this singular figure, as has long been believed, but also the precise aims of a cultural policy. His histrionic spirit and drive towards Hellenization explain the widespread demand for a cultural renewal and for the recognition and legitimization of tastes and tendencies now widespread among the masses of the people. These tendencies, which, as threats to the social system, are strongly resisted by the senatorial aristocracy, who see in Nero an enemy of the Roman tradition, are the tool that he brazenly uses to win favor and consent, as well as to legitimize the Hellenistic and absolutist elements in his regime.

*The principate of the
Flavians and moral
and civic restoration*

The fashion of public poetic contests, held on the occasion of certain festivals, persists and even becomes more popular under the principate of the Flavians, but the advent of the new imperial dynasty signals a clear break with Nero's cultural policy. In opposition to its openness to Greek influences they set forth a program of moral and civic restoration. They come to power with the abundant good will they have won by bringing back peace and harmony after the grave crisis and bloodbath that accompa-

nied the end of the hated Julio-Claudian dynasty. In literature two phenomena stand out in this return to the celebration of the traditional values: the renewal of epic poetry, with Virgil as its paradigm, and in prose the rise of Cicero as a model of a style and also of an education based on rhetoric. (The establishment of the first state-supported chairs of rhetoric under Vespasian is the most visible sign of the program that entrusts to this discipline the training of the ruling class, that is, of the imperial officials.)

*Persistence of the
new taste in the era
of the Flavians*

Beside the classicist tendencies of the regime, we also find in the literature of the Flavian era, especially in poetry, the traces of the taste that had
slowly grown up in the first part of the first century A.D., and this even
without the organic renewal of patronage that the poets of the time had
hoped for. The life of Martial, who was forced to earn his *sportula* as a client
in trying fashion, is instructive about the conditions in which even a very
successful poet lived. Equally instructive is the notice that Statius, despite the immense renown he achieved through the public readings of the
Thebaid, was compelled to earn his livelihood by writing a libretto for a
pantomime (an *Agave,* as we know from Juvenal 7.87).

2. LITERATURE AND THEATER

That the same man should be active both as a librettist (Lucan too was
a librettist) and as the greatest court poet of the day not only demonstrates
the necessity that existed, even for an author such as Statius, to turn to the
theater in order to reap more substantial rewards from his literary activity
but also indicates the success that was enjoyed by a genre such as pantomime. This was a theatrical representation (introduced at Rome under
Augustus, it seems), often of an intensely dramatic character, in which an
actor sang the libretto *(fabula saltica)* to musical accompaniment while a
second, masked actor mimed the event with body movements and hand
gestures. This genre of spectacle at Rome was immensely successful during
the Empire. Despite the lack of direct evidence (i.e., despite the loss not
only of the music but of the libretti as well), the indirect evidence offered
by writers such as Seneca or Juvenal gives us significant information on the
unbridled enthusiasm aroused by pantomime and the immense popularity
enjoyed by the actors (e.g., the Paris referred to in the passage quoted from
Juvenal, who also had great influence at court, before falling afoul of Domitian). Alongside other, minor theatrical forms, such as the mime and the
Atellan, the pantomime was the genre with the greatest popular success
during the entire first century of the Empire and beyond. The favor it found
was matched only by the circus games, which under the Empire became
more and more spectacular, on account both of the ingenuity of the stage
machinery, which often could represent such myths as those of Pasiphae,
Prometheus, or Orpheus, and of the brutality of contests such as those
between gladiators. (We should not leave the subjects of mime and spectacle without mentioning the very famous mime writer Catullus, who lived
under Caligula, and from whom are recorded a *Phasma* and especially a
Laureolus, the stage effects of which particularly amazed the public: an actor
vomited blood on the stage, a crucifixion was represented, etc.)

We find here, then, a phenomenon of great importance, touching many
aspects of the social and cultural life of a metropolis that is populated by
large masses of Italians and urbanized provincials, to whose simple taste,
sensitive to violent emotions, these spectacles can make their appeal. It is
a phenomenon that can hardly be rivaled by the senatorial elite's attempt to

restore the great tragic drama, intended for a cultivated and ideologically restricted audience. In the face of this it is not surprising that contemporary literature, poetry especially, tends, within certain limits and in certain respects, to become a form of spectacle and to take on theatrical traits.

3. SENECA THE ELDER AND DECLAMATION

The declamatio

Before proceeding with the characterization of the literature of the first century, it will be useful to pause and consider another important cultural phenomenon of the period: the spread of public declamation. The *declamatio* was a kind of exercise that had been used for some time in the schools of rhetoric. We have valuable evidence about this in Seneca the Elder, who also gives us a picture of oratorical activity and the chief rhetoricians in his day. His work is called *Oratorum et Rhetorum Sententiae Divisiones Colores.* *Sententiae* are epigrammatic phrases intended to impress the listener or reader, phrases that are often sententious, such as aphorisms; *divisiones* are the ways in which the declaimer articulates the legal aspects of the matter; *colores* are the stylistic colorations with which the declaimers present characters and situations. Since the work is the product of Seneca's school recollections, it is inappropriate to apply to him, as is commonly done, the epithet "Rhetor": he was the pupil of rhetoricians, not a rhetorician himself.

Seneca the Elder and the decline of rhetoric

Born in Cordoba, Spain, around 50 B.C., of equestrian ancestry, Seneca divided his long life between Rome and Spain, probably living long enough to see the reign of Caligula (though his death precedes the exile of his son, Seneca the philosopher, in A.D. 41). Although he moved in the highest social circles at Rome, we know nothing certain about his public activity. The work through which he is known to us, written in the last years of his life (perhaps towards the end of Tiberius's principate), testifies to the change that the advent of the principate and the progressive loss of political liberty had produced in rhetorical activity at Rome. When scope for political and judicial oratory is lost, the civic function of rhetoric is lost. Rhetoric, which had once been the instrument par excellence for training future citizens, now serves chiefly to train brilliant lecturers. Rhetoric sinks into pointless exercises, the *declamationes,* in fact, which center on themes and subjects that are fictitious, novelistic (mocked, for instance, by Petronius in the first surviving chapters of the *Satyricon*), and chosen precisely for their unusual or odd character, which was supposed to act as a stimulus to the audience, the students of the schools and also the general public. The declamation has now become, in fact, a public spectacle in which even persons eminent in political life do not disdain to participate.

Controversiae *and* suasoriae

Seneca the Elder illustrates the two types of exercise most in vogue: the *controversia,* which belonged to the judicial genre and consisted in the trial, by opposing sides, of a fictitious case, which was based upon Roman or Greek law or upon imaginary legislation; and the *suasoria,* belonging to the deliberative, or political, genre and consisting in the orator's attempt to guide the action of a famous historical or mythical person facing an uncertain or difficult situation. From his work one book remains containing seven *suasoriae* (but the plan was for more), and five of the ten books of *controversiae* (1, 2, 7, 9, and 10; extracts are extant from the other, lost books). Along with the various subjects of exercise, Seneca also provides an interpretation of the history of oratory at Rome, down to the decline in his own days, which he attributes to the moral corruption of the whole society.

The pursuit of effect and the colores

Given the fictitious character of the situations and many of the premises, the orator's aim is not so much to persuade as to astonish his audience, and he therefore resorts to the most ingenious contrivances of language and imagination. The mannerism of the forms makes exaggerated use of the *colores,* the technical term indicating the clever manipulation of a situation or a concept and capable of presenting the matter in hand under the most surprising aspect. In the pursuit of effect, and of the audience's applause, the orator also makes use of a brilliant, precious style, one that has recourse to all the artifices of Asianism (see p. 120), from the accumulation of the rhetorical figures to densely epigrammatic expression to care over the rhythm of the period.

4. RECITATION, OR LITERATURE AS SPECTACLE

The recitationes *and the transformation of literature*

Besides the declamation, another form of cultural public entertainment is *recitatio,* the reading of passages of literature by the author to an invited audience. The use of these public readings was introduced by Asinius Pollio (see p. 260), whose many merits as a man of culture have already been mentioned. It is obvious that the new custom of public readings of literary texts and the now established genre of school declamations bring with them important transformations in oratory and all forms of literary production. This phenomenon did not escape the notice of contemporaries, as is evident from the trenchant remarks in Persius, Petronius, and Juvenal directed against the widespread mania for *recitatio* and from the lengthy analysis in Tacitus's *Dialogus de Oratoribus,* which gives us an account of the debate over the causes of the corruption of eloquence. As often happens,

Change in addressee and change in the formal characteristics of the work

the change in a literary work's intended audience brings about a transformation in the formal characteristics of the work itself. Now an article of consumption in public halls or theaters, literature tends to acquire theatrical, "spectacular" features. The measure of worth becomes the audience's applause, and this audience is no longer the restricted aristocracy of taste that the Augustan poets addressed, but a much larger public, of a social and cultural level that is not always high, which necessarily implies a vulgarization of the literary product. In view of this, it would hardly be surprising if the author in the end behaves as a sort of magician of the word, always hunting for the effect that can arouse the admiration and astonishment of the listeners.

The independence of the individual parts of the work

In the light of this notion of literature as performance, as exhibition of talent, one can understand the typical tendency of so many first-century works to consist of a series of virtuoso pieces intended to wring applause from the audience. This is a hallmark of the new taste, as in Seneca's tragedies or Statius's *Thebaid.* This tendency moves towards the independence of the parts, at the expense of the organic quality and overall economy of the work. The abuse of rhetorical artifices—the age has been called "the age of rhetoric"—signs of which can already be seen in Ovid, the brilliant pupil of the best rhetoricians of his day, is one of the characteristic features of the literature of the first century A.D.; it also illustrates the functioning of this discipline as a unifying agent in taste and as the medium of cultural popularization. Silver Age literature is generally so called in order to indicate, from a classicizing point of view, a decline from the Golden Age of Augustus but also a fundamental change in taste and tendencies. Apart from the invasion of rhetoric, the period is characterized by a strong element of anti-classical reaction, which is manifested both in content (in a preference for themes and subjects that are unusual, exotic, or in some way reducible to the marvelous) and in form (in an accentuation of expressionistic colors and gloomy, pathetic tones, in a frantic pursuit of expressive tension that, precisely because of its deliberate opposition to Augustan classicism, has led some to speak of stylistic mannerism). The new distrust of what had been the sober self-composure of classical expression shows indirectly how the clear, measured style that characterized the age of Caesar and still more the age of Augustus must be regarded as an extraordinary tour de force, an achievement of art and culture that is a parenthesis in the history of Latin literary taste. In the expressive tension animating it, the literature of the early Empire also reveals the inner discomfort of a society and culture that witnesses changes in its own horizons and values and that no longer can find satisfactory expression in the objective forms of a classical art.

The anti-classical reaction

BIBLIOGRAPHY

On Julio-Claudian literary culture, see G. Williams, *Change and Decline* (Berkeley and Los Angeles 1978), and J. P. Sullivan, *Literature and Politics in the Age of Nero* (Ithaca 1985), but the best treatment is that in M. Griffin, *Nero: The End of a Dynasty* (London 1984); see also F. M. Ahl, "The Rider and the Horse: Politics and Power in Roman Poetry from Horace to Statius," *ANRW* 32.1 (Berlin 1984) 40–110, and H. Bardon, *Les Empereurs et les lettres latines d'Auguste à Hadrien* (ed. 2 Paris 1968). More generally, note G. Boissier, *L'Opposition sous les Césars* (ed. 10 Paris 1932), and C. Wirszubski, *Libertas as a Political Ideal at Rome* (Cambridge 1950).

On spectacle in Roman culture, see esp. P. Veyne, *Bread and Circuses,* trans. B. Pearce, intro. O. Murray (London 1990; this is an abridgment of the original French edition). On the theater, see W. Beare, *The Roman Stage* (ed. 3 London 1964) 233–40, and there is much of interest in R. J. Tarrant, "Senecan Drama and Its Antecedents," *HSCP* 82 (1978) 213–63.

There is a good Loeb edition of Seneca the Elder by M. Winterbottom (2 vols., Cambridge, Mass. 1974), and monographs by L. A. Sussman, *The Elder Seneca* (Leiden 1978), and J. A. Fairweather, *Seneca the Elder* (Cambridge 1981). On declamation, see S. F. Bonner, *Roman Declamation* (Liverpool 1949) and M. Winterbottom's collection of texts with brief notes with the same title (Bristol 1980), as well as H. Bornecque, *Les*

Déclamations et les déclamateurs d'apres Sénèque le père (Lille 1902). There is much of relevance in D. A. Russell, *Greek Declamation* (Cambridge 1983). On recitation, see A. Dalzell, "C. Asinius Pollio and the Early History of Public Recitation in Rome," *Hermathena* 86 (1955) 20–28, J. C. McKeown, ed., *Ovid: Amores 1* (Liverpool 1987) 68–73, and A. Hardie, *Statius and the Silvae* (Liverpool 1983) passim.

Seneca

Lucius Annaeus Seneca was born in Spain, at Cordoba (a city with republican traditions: it had sided with Pompey at the time of the civil wars), of a wealthy equestrian family (his father is Seneca the Elder), in the last years before the common era, perhaps in 4 B.C. He soon came to Rome, where he was educated in the schools of rhetoric, with a view to a political career, and of philosophy. Among his teachers were the Stoic Attalus and Papirius Fabianus, a former rhetorician who was close to the Stoic-Pythagorean school of the Sestii, which was characterized by ascetic tendencies as well as an interest in natural science. Around A.D. 26 he went to Egypt, in the entourage of an uncle who was a prefect. Upon returning to Rome, in 31, he began his forensic activity and political career. He must have achieved a considerable success if it is true that Caligula (37–41), jealous of his oratorical fame, decreed his condemnation to death, from which a lover of the emperor is said to have saved him. He was not saved, however, from the relegation that the new emperor Claudius inflicted upon him in 41, accusing him of involvement in the adultery of Julia Livilla, Germanicus's younger daughter and Caligula's sister; Claudius's actual intention was to strike at the political opposition gathered around the family of Germanicus. Seneca remained in wild, inhospitable Corsica until 49, when Agrippina succeeded in securing from Claudius his return from exile and chose him as tutor for her son by her first marriage, the future emperor Nero. In this role as educator, which he performed jointly with Afranius Burrus, the praetorian prefect, Seneca shared in the young Nero's accession to the throne (A.D. 54) and from then on guided his governance of the state. This is the celebrated period of Nero's good government, based on principles of balance and conciliation between the powers of the princeps and the Senate. Subsequently it deteriorated (Nero killed his mother in 59), and the philosopher was forced into serious compromises. Around 62, after the death of Burrus, with Nero now in the hands of Poppaea and beginning the notorious concluding period of his reign, Seneca saw the loss of his influence as a political adviser and gradually withdrew into private life, devoting himself to his studies. Disliked now and suspect in the eyes of Nero and Tigellinus, the new praetorian prefect, Seneca was implicated in the famous Pisonian conspiracy (April of 65), which he may merely have known about but not participated in, and was caught up in the repression that followed it. Condemned to death by Nero, he committed suicide in the same year, 65 (Tacitus gives a famous account of the death of Seneca in *Annals* 15.62–64).

WORKS
Among the works that survive from Seneca's huge literary output, those of a philosophical character occupy the larger part. Some of these works were collected, after Seneca's death, in twelve books of *Dialogi* (a title already known to Quintilian, one that does not generally imply dialogue form, but seems due rather to the great tradition of philosophical dialogue extending back to Plato). They are treatises, brief for the most part, on ethical and psychological questions: 1, *Ad Lucilium de Providentia*; 2, *Ad Serenum de Constantia Sapientis*; 3–5, *Ad Novatum de Ira Libri III*; 6, *Ad Marciam de Consolatione*; 7, *Ad Gallionem de Vita Beata*; 8, *Ad Serenum de Otio*; 9, *Ad Serenum de Tranquillitate Animi*; 10, *Ad Paulinum de Brevitate Vitae*; 11, *Ad Polybium de Consolatione*; and 12, *Ad Helviam Matrem de Consolatione*. The other philosophical works, transmitted to us independently, are the seven books *De Beneficiis*, the *De Clementia*, addressed to Nero (of the original three books, the first and the beginning of the second survive), and the twenty books containing the 124 *Epistulae Morales ad Lucilium* (we know that there were originally more, since we have notice of a twenty-second book). More properly scientific are the *Naturales Quaestiones*, in seven books, originally perhaps eight. We have, in addition, nine *cothurnatae* tragedies of Seneca, that is, ones with Greek subjects (*Hercules Furens, Troades, Phoenissae, Medea, Phaedra, Oedipus, Agamemnon, Thyestes, Hercules Oetaeus*, arranged in that order in the most authoritative manuscript, the Etruscus); as well as the *Ludus de Morte Claudii* (or *Apocolocyntosis*), a Menippean satire on the strange apotheosis of the emperor, a work that today is generally regarded as authentic. By contrast, many doubts persist about the Senecan authorship of the *Epigrams* (see below).

The lost works are of various sorts: a biography of his father, numerous speeches, various physical, geographic, and ethnographic treatises, and many other philosophical works, among them the *Moralis Philosophiae Libri*, to which Seneca himself refers a number of times. There are also several works of doubtful attribution or certainly spurious; among the latter, the most famous example is the correspondence between Seneca and St. Paul, the product of a legend that contributed to enhancing Seneca's reputation in the Middle Ages.

SOURCES
Seneca himself supplies many autobiographical notices, especially in the *Epistulae* and the *Consolatio ad Helviam Matrem*. Among the other sources, the most important are books 12–15 of Tacitus's *Annals*, a section of the *Roman History* by the Greek historian Dio Cassius, and the Suetonian biographies of the emperors Caligula, Claudius, and Nero.

1. THE *DIALOGI* AND STOIC WISDOM

The genre of the consolatio

Very few of the Senecan works left to us can be dated with certainty or close approximation, and so it is difficult to trace a possible development of his thought or to connect it to events in his life. Among those that can be dated is the *Consolatio ad Marciam,* written under the principate of Caligula, perhaps around 40, and addressed to the daughter of the historian Cremutius Cordus, whom it seeks to console for the loss of a son. The genre of the consolation, already practiced in the Greek philosophical tradition, centers upon a stock of moral themes—the fleetingness of time, the precariousness of life, death as man's inevitable destiny, etc.—that form the basis for a large part of Seneca's philosophical thought. He refers to this stock again in the other two consolations that are preserved, both from the years of exile. The *Ad Helviam Matrem,* perhaps from 42, aims at reassuring his mother about the condition of her exiled son and emphasizes the positive aspects of his isolation and his contemplative *otium.* The other (43?), *Ad Polybium,* addressed to a powerful freedman of Claudius in order to console him for the loss of a brother, reveals itself in fact as an indirect attempt to flatter the emperor in order to secure his return to Rome (and it is the work that more than any other has brought down on Seneca the charge of opportunism).

The books De Ira

The individual works of the *Dialogi* are independent treatises on particular aspects or problems of Stoic ethics, which is the general framework for all of Seneca's philosophical writings. His is a Stoicism that has moderated the earlier strictness of doctrine, following the so-called "middle school," and eschews dogmatic conclusions. The three books of the *De Ira,* for instance, written in the first part of his exile but not published until after Caligula's death, are a kind of phenomenology of the human passions: they analyze the mechanisms of their origin and the ways of checking and mastering them (the third book is devoted to anger in particular). The work is dedicated to Seneca's brother Novatus; some years later, when Novatus was called Gallio, from the name of his adoptive father, the rhetorician Junius Gallio, he would also dedicate to him the *De Vita Beata* (perhaps from 58),

The De Vita Beata *and the problem of wealth*

which addresses the problem of happiness and the role that comfort and wealth can play in achieving it. It appears that in reality, behind the general problem, Seneca wants to meet the accusations that we know were made against him (Tacitus, *Annals* 13.42) to the effect that there was an inconsistency between his professed principles and the actual conduct of his life. Thanks to the position of power he occupied at court, he had come to possess an immense estate (through moneylending, among other things). Even though the essence of happiness lies in virtue, not wealth and pleasure (the polemic is directed principally at Epicureanism, or at least its inferior versions), Seneca nonetheless justifies the use of wealth if it proves helpful in the pursuit of virtue. Wisdom and wealth are not necessarily antithetic (*nemo sapientiam paupertate damnavit,* "no one has condemned wisdom to poverty" [23]). Seneca for the most part is not attracted to the Cynic model, which he regards as dangerously asocial. The man who aspires to *sapientia* (an ideal that can never be fully realized) must be able to endure the comfort and well-being that the circumstances of life have brought, without allowing himself to become ensnared in them. The principle, in other words, is that the important thing is, not to forgo possessing riches, but not to let oneself be possessed by them.

The dialogues to Serenus and the detachment of the Stoic sage from earthly contingencies

The superior detachment of the sage from earthly contingencies is also the unifying theme of the three dialogues dedicated to his friend Serenus, who abandons his Epicurean principles to adhere to Stoic ethics: *De Constantia Sapientis, De Otio, De Tranquillitate Animi.* The first of these three so-called dialogues, published after 41, glorifies the imperturbability of the Stoic sage, who in the face of injury and adversity is strengthened by inner firmness. The *De Tranquillitate Animi,* the only work partially in dialogue form, addresses a fundamental problem in Seneca's philosophical thought, the sage's participation in political life. Seneca seeks a middle term between the extremes of contemplative leisure and the engagement proper to the Roman citizen; he proposes a flexible approach, related to the political conditions. The objective to be attained, by withdrawing both from the tedium of a solitary life and from the obligations of the harried life of the city, is always the serenity of a soul that can assist others, if not by public engagement then at least by example and precept. If the tension between commitment and renunciation remains unresolved here (and this is one of the reasons for placing the dialogue shortly before 62), the choice of a withdrawn life, by contrast, is evident in the *De Otio.* There it is an obligatory choice, made necessary by a political situation so gravely compromised that to the sage, who has been rendered incapable of helping others, it offers no alternative but flight into contemplative solitude, the merits of which are celebrated (the work is to be dated perhaps to 62, the period of Seneca's withdrawal from political life).

The De Brevitate Vitae *and the* De Providentia

The *De Brevitate Vitae* seems to go back to an earlier moment, perhaps to the years 49–52. Dedicated to Paulinus, the prefect in charge of the food supply and possibly a relative of Seneca's second wife, it deals with the problem of time, with its fleetingness and the apparent brevity of a life, which seems brief because we do not know how to grasp its essence but which we fritter away in so many useless pursuits without fully realizing it. The dialogue that opens the collection, the *De Providentia,* dedicated to the Lucilius of the *Epistulae,* ought to belong to Seneca's last years. It deals with the problem of the contradiction between the providential scheme that, according to Stoic doctrine, governs human affairs (a polemic against the Epicurean notion of divine indifference) and the disconcerting recognition of a fate that often seems to reward the wicked and punish the good. Seneca's answer is that the adversities that befall the undeserving do not contradict such a providential scheme, but rather give evidence of the divine will to put the good to the test and exercise their virtues. The Stoic *sapiens* realizes his rational nature in recognizing the post that is assigned to him in the cosmic order ruled by the *logos* and in adapting himself to it completely.

2. PHILOSOPHY AND POWER

The Naturales
Quaestiones

The *Naturalium Quaestionum Libri VII,* the only scientific work of Seneca's
extant, is also dedicated to Lucilius and written after the author's withdrawal from public life. It deals with various atmospheric and celestial phenomena, from storms to earthquakes to comets. It is the result of an
immense labor of compilation, probably extending over many years, from
varied, principally Stoic sources (such as Posidonius). It appears to represent the physical underpinnings of Seneca's philosophical system, but in
fact there is neither integration nor organic connection between the physical investigation and the moral inquiry.

The De Beneficiis
*and reflection upon
individual morality*

Another philosophical work transmitted independently of the *Dialogi,*
the seven books *De Beneficiis,* which is dedicated to Seneca's friend Aebutius
Liberalis, is from more or less the same period (it is finished by 64, as Seneca
himself attests in *Epistulae ad Lucilium* 81.3). It treats the nature and the
various modes of acts of beneficence, the link they establish between the
benefactor and the benefited, the obligations of gratitude that bind them,
and the moral consequences that befall the ungrateful (a veiled allusion has
been suspected here to Nero's behavior towards him). The work, which
analyzes beneficence principally as a cohesive element in social relations,
seems to transfer to individual morality the project for a balanced, harmonious society that Seneca had based upon the ideal of an enlightened monarchy. The appeal to the duties of philanthropy and liberality, addressed
mainly to the privileged classes, because it aims at establishing more
humane and more cordial social relations, presents itself thereby as an alternative to that failed project; it has a kind of reversed perspective but the
same paternalistic approach.

The De Clementia
*and the problem of
the good sovereign*

Seneca expounded his notion of power most fully in the *De Clementia,*
opportunely dedicated to the young emperor Nero (in the years 55–56) as
the sketch for an ideal political program based on fairness and moderation.
Seneca does not discuss the constitutional legitimacy of the principate or
the openly monarchic forms that it had now assumed; the only power was
the power that conformed to the Stoic conception of a cosmic order governed by *logos* ("universal reason"), the power most suitable for representing
the ideal of a cosmopolitan universe and for serving as a link and unifying
symbol of the many peoples making up the Empire. Seneca's notion did
not take into account that this power had now been imposed upon reality,
and it did not seem realistic to place any confidence in that mirage of a
restored republican *libertas* that was animating the Stoically inclined circles
of the aristocratic opposition. The problem, rather, is to have a good sovereign. And in a regime of absolute power, without any external check, the
only restraint upon the emperor is his own conscience, which ought to
prevent him from ruling tyrannically. Clemency (which is not the same as
pity or unmotivated generosity, but expresses a general attitude of philan-
thropic benevolence) is the virtue that ought to shape his relations with his
subjects. By exercising clemency and not striking fear into his subjects, he

can win their consent and their devotion, which are the securest guarantee of a state's stability.

In this notion of an enlightened, paternalistic principate, which entrusts good government to the sovereign's conscience, to his moral perfection, the importance of the education of the princeps is evident, as is, more generally, the role of philosophy as guarantor and inspirer of the political direction of the state. Seneca long employed his energies in this noble illusion, which seemed to revive Plato's old project of government by philosophers and which dramatically affected the very course of his life. Moved by the impulse towards the duties of social life, and equally far removed from the extreme positions of intransigently rejecting collaboration with the princeps and of servilely acquiescing in his despotism, he cherished an ambitious project of a balanced, harmonious distribution of power between a restrained sovereign and a Senate secure in its right to liberty and aristocratic dignity. Within this project, as was said, a prominent role is assigned to philosophy, that of promoting the moral training of the sovereign and the political elite, but the rapid degeneration of Nero's government, after the parenthesis of the "happy quinquennium," lays bare the limits of that plan and brings it to naught. Seneca's philosophy then needs to redefine its tasks, loosening its ties to the *civitas* and emphasizing more its eagerness to work upon the conscience of individuals. Deprived of his political role, the Stoic sage places himself at the service of humanity.

3. THE DAY-TO-DAY PRACTICE OF PHILOSOPHY: THE *EPISTULAE AD LUCILIUM*

In Seneca's philosophical development one cannot distinguish clearly between two drives, towards civic engagement and towards meditative *otium.* The hope of performing a social function, in the forms allowed by circumstances, remains strong even in the late works. Nonetheless, it cannot be denied that in the writings composed after his withdrawal from the political scene Seneca is mainly concerned with the individual conscience. The principal work among his late writings, and the one that is unquestionably the most famous, is the *Epistulae ad Lucilium,* a collection of letters, varying considerably in length (some are as long as an essay) and in subject, addressed to his friend Lucilius. Lucilius is a person of modest origins, slightly younger than Seneca and originally from Campania, who had risen to equestrian status and various political-administrative offices, a man of good culture, and a poet and writer himself. Whether the correspondence is real or fictitious is a question that continues to be discussed. There are no insurmountable difficulties in believing the exchange genuine (various letters reply to letters from Lucilius); and yet this view is not irreconcilable with the possibility that other letters, in particular the longer and more systematic ones, were in fact not sent and instead were added to the collection at the moment of publication. The work has come down to us incomplete, as was said, and may date from the period of political withdrawal (62 to the beginning of 63). In any event, it is unique in ancient literature and philosophy.

The philosophical letter as a literary genre

The impetus to compose philosophical letters addressed to friends probably came to Seneca from Plato and especially from Epicurus. However that may be, he is fully conscious, and not a little proud, of introducing a new genre into Latin literature. Polemically, he wants to distinguish it from ordinary epistolary practice, even the illustrious practice of a Cicero. The model he strives to match is Epicurus, who in his letters to friends was able to realize perfectly the relation of spiritual training and education that Seneca establishes with Lucilius. His letters aim at being an instrument of moral growth, a diary of spiritual victories along the road towards *sapientia*. Taking up a topos that is very common in ancient epistolography, Seneca emphasizes that epistolary exchange makes it possible to hold a *colloquium* with the friend, to create with him an intimacy that, by being a direct example of life, shows itself to be pedagogically more effective than doctrinal instruction. More than the other genres of philosophical literature,

The daily practice of philosophy

the letter is close to the reality of ordinary life, from which it picks up various elements, using them as points of departure for moral considerations and so lending itself perfectly to the daily practice of philosophy. By proposing each time a new theme, one that is simple and easily understood, for the reflection of the pupil-friend (on the model of the philosophical schools), the letter accompanies and articulates the stages of his successful progress towards inner improvement. The same purpose is served by the custom of closing each letter in the first three books with a *sententia*, an aphorism offering a bit of wisdom to contemplate. Returning to a procedure used in the school of Epicurus, who graduated the various stages along the road towards *sapientia*, Seneca employs the letter as an ideal instrument particularly for the first phase of spiritual guidance, which is based on the acquisition of certain key principles; with the growth in the pupil's analytical ability and the enlargement of his knowledge, the teacher will next resort to more demanding and more complex devices of learning. That the literary form conforms successively to the different stages in the process of education is proved by the tendency of the individual letters to resemble a philosophical essay increasingly as the correspondence proceeds. No less important than the theoretical element—Seneca in fact several times polemicizes against the excessive logical subtleties of the philosophers, especially the Stoics—is the paraenetic element: the letter tends not so much to demonstrate a truth as to exhort and invite the reader to the good.

Seneca's philosophy and the tradition of diatribe

Besides being useful for a specific phase in the process of spiritual guidance, the epistolary genre also proves suitable for accommodating a philosophy such as Seneca's, which is not systematic but is inclined rather to deal with particular aspects or individual themes in ethics. The subjects of the letters, suggested for the most part by everyday experience, are quite varied but generally derive ultimately from the themes of the diatribe tradition. In their variety and occasional nature and in the link between real life and moral thought, they show their affinities with satire, especially Horatian satire. They center upon the principles by which the sage shapes his life, his independence and self-reliance, his indifference to mundane attractions, and his scorn for ordinary opinions. In the calm, cordial tone of one who is not striking the pose of a stern teacher but is himself pursuing the path towards wisdom, a goal that can never be fully achieved, Seneca proposes the ideal of a life that is directed towards concentration, meditation, and inner improvement and is achieved through an attentive reflection upon the weaknesses and vices of oneself and others. Consideration of the human condition that is common to all living beings leads him to condemn the treatment regularly employed towards slaves, and his tones of intense piety have reminded some of the sentiment of Christian charity. In fact the Senecan ethic remains profoundly aristocratic, and the Stoic *sapiens* who expresses his sympathy for ill-treated slaves also manifests openly his inalterable disdain for the masses of people who have been rendered brutish by the spectacles in the circus.

The aim of the Stoic sage

In the *Epistulae,* detachment from the world and from the passions that stir it runs parallel with the attraction to a withdrawn life and with the elevation of *otium* to a supreme value, an *otium* that is not inactivity but the active pursuit of the good, carried out in the conviction that spiritual conquests can aid not only the friends committed to the pursuit of *sapientia* but also others and that the *Epistulae* can exercise a beneficial influence upon posterity. Once it is necessary for him to give up all expectations in the field of politics, the Stoic sage sets the achievement of inner freedom as his ultimate objective, and along with it the daily meditation upon death, which he can look upon with serenity as the symbol of his own independence from the world.

4. "DRAMATIC" STYLE

Seneca's style in theory and practice

If the chief aim of philosophy is to assist inner improvement, the philosopher will need to be concerned with *res,* not with studied and elaborate language: *non delectent verba nostra sed prosint* (*Epistulae ad Lucilium* 75.5). Such language will be justified only if by virtue of its expressive power, in the form, for example, of *sententiae* or poetic quotations, it performs a psychagogic function, that is, if it contributes to fixing a precept or moral principle in the memory and the soul. In fact, despite a program of a style *inlaboratus et facilis* (*Epistulae ad Lucilium* 75.1), Seneca's philosophical prose becomes virtually the emblem of an elaborate style, both taut and complex, characterized by the pursuit of effects and concise, epigrammatic expression. Seneca rejects the compact classical architecture of the Ciceronian period, which by means of hypotactic arrangement organizes the hierarchy of its inner logic. Instead, he creates a highly paratactic style, which, because among other things it aims at reproducing the spoken language, breaks up the structure of the thought into a series of pointed and sententious phrases, the linking among which is effected primarily by antithesis and repetition; this produces the impression of "sand without lime" with

Seneca's style and Asianic rhetoric

which the malevolent Caligula reproached him. This prose, which is opposed to harmonious Ciceronian periods and, as Quintilian observed with concern, is revolutionary in taste (and destined to exercise great influence on the artistic prose of Europe), has its roots in Asianic rhetoric—which celebrated its triumph in the schools of declamation with which Seneca was so familiar—and in the preaching of the Cynic philosophers. This style proceeds by a studied play of parallelisms, antitheses, and repetitions, in a rapid series of nervous, staccato phrases (the *minutissimae sententiae* deplored by Quintilian), with a kind of pointillist effect. It gives the impression of considering an idea from all possible angles by providing ever more pregnant and more concise formulations, to the point where it crystallizes the idea in an epigrammatic expression. This pointed and penetrating style, which with its continuous tension does not escape a certain theatricality, is employed by Seneca as a probe with which to explore the secrets of the human soul and the contradictions that torment it and also as a device through which to speak to the heart of men and exhort them to the good. It is a style that is inwardly antithetic and confrontational ("dramatic" is a helpful definition), alternating the quiet tones of inner meditation with the resonant tones of preaching, a style that emblematically reflects the drives animating Seneca's philosophy, which is torn between pursuing freedom for the ego and liberating mankind.

Style and thought in Seneca

5. THE TRAGEDIES

The impossibility of dating Seneca's tragedies

The tragedies occupy an important place in Seneca's writings. Nine are generally regarded as authentic (doubts remain only about the *Hercules Oetaeus*), all on subjects from Greek mythology. And yet we know very little about them, about the circumstances of their actual performance or the date of their composition. In regard to the latter it is impossible to draw inferences even on the basis of stylistic criteria or, still less, of references to contemporary events. Given the impossibility of sketching a plausible chronology, they are listed here in the order in which the most authoritative tradition transmits them.

Summary of Seneca's Tragedies

The *Hercules Furens*, based on Euripides' *Heracles*, deals with the madness of Hercules, which, provoked by Juno, leads the hero to slay his wife and sons. When, upon recovering his sanity, he is resolved to kill himself, he allows himself to be dissuaded from his plan and goes to Athens to be purified. The *Troades*, the result of conflating the subjects of two Euripidean plays, the *Trojan Women* and the *Hecuba*, represents the fate of the captive Trojan women when they find themselves helpless before the sacrifice of Polyxena, daughter of Priam, and of the little Astyanax, son of Hector and Andromache. Based on Euripides' *Phoenician Women* and Sophocles' *Oedipus at Colonus*, Seneca's *Phoenician Women*, his only incomplete tragedy, turns on the tragic destiny of Oedipus and the hatred that divides his sons Eteocles and Polyneices. The *Medea*, of course, also goes back to Euripides, but perhaps also to a tragedy by Ovid of the same name, which was successful but is now lost. It is the grim story of the princess from Colchis, who, because she has been abandoned by Jason, takes vengeance upon him by murdering their sons. The *Phaedra,* too, presupposes a famous Euripidean original (the surviving *Hippolytus* and also an earlier, lost one), as well as, in all likelihood, a lost tragedy by Sophocles and the fourth of Ovid's *Heroides.* It deals with Phaedra's incestuous love for her stepson Hippolytus and the dramatic fate that befalls the young man, who has rejected the advances of his stepmother: she takes revenge by denouncing him to her husband Theseus, Hippolytus's father, and causing his death. The *Oedipus Rex* of Sophocles is the basis of the *Oedipus,* which recounts the well-known Theban myth of Oedipus, unwitting murderer of his father Laius and husband of his mother Jocasta, who, upon discovering the awful truth, reacts by blinding himself. Seneca's *Agamemnon,* loosely based on the play of the same name by Aeschylus, represents the assassination of the king, upon his return from Troy, at the hands of his wife Clytemnestra and her lover Aegisthus. The *Thyestes* takes up the grim tale of the Pelopidae, which had previously been dealt with in lost works by Sophocles and Euripides as well as in early Latin drama and, more recently, in a play of the same name by Varius, the friend of Horace and Virgil. Moved by mortal hatred of his brother Thyestes, Atreus gets his revenge with a feigned banquet of reconciliation at which he serves to his unwitting brother the flesh of his sons. In the *Hercules Oetaeus* (i.e., upon Oeta, the mountain on which the culminating event of the hero's drama is enacted), modeled on the *Trachinian Women* of Sophocles, Seneca treats the myth of Deianira's jealousy. In order to recover the love of Hercules, who is now enamored of Iole, she sends him a tunic soaked in the blood of the centaur Nessus, which she thinks is a love philter but which is really endowed with murderous power. In hideous pain, Hercules has a pyre erected and hurls himself upon it to end his life, which is followed by his assumption among the gods.

Tragedies in the Julio-Claudian period and anti-tyrannical inspiration

Seneca's are the only Latin tragedies to have come down to us complete. Apart from this, which makes them valuable witnesses to an entire literary genre, they are also important as documents of the revival of Latin tragic drama, which took place after the scarcely successful attempts of Augustan cultural policy to promote a rebirth of theatrical activity (one event in this program was the production in 29 B.C. of Varius's *Thyestes,* in which the anti-tyrannical polemic embodied in the subject may have had Antony for its target). In the Julio-Claudian period and in the beginning of the Flavian period, until the Flavians reformed the Senate socially and thereby altered its political attitude as well, the intellectual senatorial elite seems actually to have turned to tragic drama—Persius, Lucan, and others had written tragedies—as the literary form most suitable for expressing its opposition to the regime (Latin tragedy, taking up and glorifying an aspect already basic to classical Greek tragedy, had always been strongly influenced by republicanism and the hatred of tyranny).

Tragedians of the Julio-Claudian and Flavian periods

The tragedians of the Julio-Claudian and Flavian periods whom we know of are all people of some importance in Roman public life. We know from Tacitus's *Annals* that under the reign of Tiberius, Mamercus Scaurus, who was famous as an orator too, was compelled to take his own life because allusions to the emperor had been noted in a tragedy of his, the *Atreus.* In the time of Claudius, Pomponius Secundus, who had been consul, was well known; his friend Pliny the Elder would write a biography of him. Pomponius wrote not only tragedies with Greek subjects but also a *praetexta* entitled *Aeneas*. One may mention, finally, Curiatius Maternus, from the time of Vespasian, who was an orator and figured as an interlocutor in Tacitus's *Dialogus de Oratoribus*. We know various titles of his tragedies, among them those of two *praetextae*, the *Cato* and the *Domitius*.

Seneca's tragedies were intended chiefly for reading

The lack of external notices about Seneca's tragedies does not make it impossible for us to know anything certain about the manner of their performance. What we do know about the realization of tragic literature in the period before Seneca—tragedy did continue to be performed upon the stage normally, but it could also be limited to reading in recital halls—has led scholars to believe, on the basis of their stylistic peculiarities among other things, that Seneca's tragedies were intended chiefly for reading; this does not exclude, at some times or for some of them, performance upon the stage. This view still prevails, rightly, even if not all the arguments supporting it are equally forceful. The use of machines or the cruel spectacles called for in certain scenes, which were certainly incompatible with the principles of performance in the classical Greek theater, might seem to presuppose rather than give the lie to stage performance in situations where a mere reading would limit, if not destroy altogether, the effects required by the dramatic text.

Philosophy and tragedy in Seneca

The various tragic stories are figured as conflicts of contrasting forces (especially within the human soul), such as the opposition between *mens bona* and *furor,* between reason and passion. The use of important themes and motifs from the philosophical works (e.g., in the story of Hercules, the theme of the strong man who overcomes the trials of life to rise to a higher freedom) makes clear the fundamental consonance between the two areas of Seneca's writing. It has also encouraged the notion that Senecan drama is only an illustration of Stoic doctrine presented in the form of mythic *exempla.* The analogy should not be pressed too far, however. For one thing, the specifically literary matrix remains strong in the tragedies; this may have offered, as in the case of Euripides, the most popular model, paradigmatic representations of conflicts within the human psyche. In the

The logos *defeated*

tragic universe, moreover, the *logos,* the rational principle to which Stoic doctrine entrusts the governance of the world, is shown to be incapable of restraining the passions and checking the spread of evil. The background to the various tragic tales is in fact a reality of dark, hideous colors, and against this backdrop of horrors is played out the struggle of the malign forces, a struggle that involves not only the human psyche, which is explored even to its most secret corners, often in lengthy, elaborate monologues, but the entire world, which is conceived of, in Stoic fashion, as a physical and moral unit; this gives to the conflict between good and evil a cosmic dimension and a universal bearing. Among the forms in which this emergence of evil into the world is manifested most expressly, the figure of the tyrant is especially prominent. Bloodthirsty, greedy for power, closed to moderation and clemency, tormented by fear and anxiety, he provides frequent occasions for an ethical debate on the theme of power, which, as we have seen, occupies an important place in the thought, as well as the life, of Seneca.

The relation to the Greek models

In the case of nearly all of Seneca's tragedies, as was said, we have the corresponding Greek originals; through comparison we can assess his stance towards them. Compared with the stance taken by the early Latin tragedians, Seneca's shows greater independence (after the great age of Augustus, Latin literature no longer limits itself to "translating," but regards itself as equal to Greek, in free rivalry with it), and yet at the same time it presupposes a continuous relation with the original, which Seneca contaminates, restructures, and rationalizes in its dramatic approach. The relation with the Greek originals, even though direct, is mediated nonetheless through the filter of Latin taste and the Latin tradition. The poetic language of the tragedies has its roots in Augustan poetry (Ovid's presence is conspicuous and pervasive), from which Seneca also borrows the refined metrical forms, such as the Horatian lyric meters that he uses for the choral interludes; he also employs the particular type of senarius adopted by Augustan tragic drama, which in its rigid scheme resembles the Greek and Horatian iambic trimeter rather than the freer senarius of early Latin drama. The traces of early Latin tragedy are noted principally in the taste for heightened pathos and in the tendencies towards expressive accumulation (carried out, however, in the manner of Augustan style) and towards the sententious phrase, which is isolated and stands out, although it is the rhetorical taste of the time that chiefly fosters this. The same tendency is manifested also in the fragmentation of the dialogues into closed, stichic responsions (one verse for each character), in a constant pursuit of Asianic *brevitas*. Senecan drama in fact bears everywhere the mark of Asianic rhetoric. It can be perceived in the continuous tension, the declamatory emphasis, the display of weighty learning (e.g., in the geographic or mythological catalogues), and those dark, macabre colors that have contributed to Seneca's success as a tragedian in modern times. The dramatic tension is often enhanced through the introduction of long digressions *(ekphraseis),* which are excessive in comparison with epic and, particularly, with tragic usage. These affect the pace of the dramatic development and belong to the general tendency of Seneca's plays to have isolated individual scenes, virtually independent pictures, outside of the dramatic dynamic (this supports the notion that such bravura pieces were supposed to be read in recital halls). It is, in short, a style that despite its most unusual features easily fits within the canons of contemporary literary taste, of which it is one of the most representative documents.

In addition to the nine tragedies discussed, the secondary branch of the tradition transmits another, entitled *Octavia.* It recounts the fate of Octavia, Nero's first wife, whom he rejects once he has fallen in love with Poppaea and whom he causes to be killed. It is thus a tragedy on a Roman subject, a *praetexta,* the only one extant. Its authenticity, however, is generally denied today. The principal reasons for regarding it as inauthentic, apart from the very suspicious appearance of Seneca himself as a character in the play, are,

The preponderant influence of Augustan poetry

Early Latin tragedy and Asianic rhetoric

The digressions

The Octavia

first, the description of the death of Nero, which took place in 68, three years after Seneca's death, and which is announced ahead of time by the ghost of Agrippina (the description corresponds so closely to the historical reality that it is hard not to believe that the prophecy was written *ex eventu* by someone who knew precisely how things had turned out); and second, the fact that the author, who shows great familiarity with all Seneca's work, seems to transfer to the tragedy versified passages from his philosophical works. Therefore, the *Octavia,* which has notable stylistic affinities with the genuine tragedies, must be placed in a milieu close to Seneca and at a time not long after his death, perhaps the decade A.D. 70–80.

6. THE *APOCOLOCYNTOSIS*

The oddity of the title

A truly unusual work within the vast range of Seneca's writings is the *Ludus de Morte Claudii* (as it is called in the two chief manuscripts that transmit it) or *Divi Claudii Apotheosis per Saturam* (according to a kind of gloss in the third), most commonly known under the Greek title *Apocolocyntosis,* provided by the historian Dio Cassius (60.35). This word would imply a reference to *kolokynta,* that is, the pumpkin, perhaps as a symbol of stupidity, and according to Dio it would be a parody of the deification of Claudius decreed by the Senate upon his death. Since no reference is made to a pumpkin in the text, and since the apotheosis does not in fact take place, doubts have arisen over the identification of the work mentioned by Dio with the *Ludus;* today, however, these doubts are almost completely dispelled. The curious term should be understood not as "transformation into a pumpkin" but rather as "deification of a pumpkin, a pumpkin head," referring to the not exactly flattering reputation that Claudius enjoyed. Other doubts and confusions have been created by the fact that, as we learn from Tacitus (*Annals* 13.3), the same Seneca had written the *laudatio funebris* for the dead emperor, which was delivered by Nero, and so radical a contrast in behavior has appeared untenable to many. Given the difficulty of assuming that immediately after the official elogia Seneca could sarcastically give vent to his resentment against the emperor who had condemned him to exile, some scholars have been led, mistakenly, to push forward the date of composition of the lampoon to around 60. But a lampoon makes sense only if published (even anonymously) hard on the heels of an event, such as the deification of Claudius, which behind the thin veil of official response must have aroused the irony of the same court circles and of public opinion; thus the composition of the work should be placed in 54.

The Apocolocyntosis *as parallel to the funeral elogium of Claudius*

Contents and literary genre of the work

The work narrates Claudius's death and his ascent to Olympus in the vain hope of being admitted among the gods, who instead condemn him, as they do all mortals, to descend to the Underworld, where he becomes the slave of his nephew Caligula and in the end is assigned to the freedman Menander, an appropriate fate for a man who in life had the reputation of having been under the thumb of his own powerful freedmen. Seneca offsets scorn for the dead emperor with words of praise for his successor; at the beginning of the work he foretells an age of splendor and renewal for the new principate.

The work belongs to the genre of the Menippean satire (so called from Menippus of Gadara, the originator of this literary form [see pp. 215 f.]). Certain similarities between Seneca's work and several dialogues of Lucian point to this genre as the common direct model. It alternates prose and varying kinds of verse in a remarkable linguistic and stylistic mixture that juxtaposes the even tones of the prosaic parts with the often parodically solemn tones of the metrical parts, adding to them vivid, colorful colloquialisms and mocking vulgarisms. The style shows occasional correspondences with Seneca's philosophical prose and enhances the picture of his inventiveness and versatility as an artist. The many quotations of verses, including Greek verses, produce a farcical counterpoint; sometimes they are famous passages, already exploited by a long Greek comic tradition. But literary parody reappears, as we were saying, in the constituent elements of the Menippean genre, which to a considerable extent is represented for us by the *Apocolocyntosis*. Thus Ennius, Catullus, Virgil, and Ovid give opportunity for amusing additions, short literal quotations inserted into an incongruous context or employed for a different meaning. Other, longer passages are elaborate literary pastiches, cento-like compositions that mock the fashionable genres, such as epic and tragedy. In a high-toned passage in iambic senarii one may even recognize a delightful self-parody of Seneca as tragedian, with allusions to the *Hercules Furens*.

7. THE EPIGRAMS

The epigrams

Several dozen epigrams in elegiac couplets, transmitted in a manuscript of the ninth century, also go under Seneca's name. They are anonymous, but since three of them are attributed to Seneca in another manuscript, it has been proposed to attribute the others to him as well, even though in many cases the Senecan origin is scarcely tenable. The level is generally respectable but not particularly outstanding. Some of the epigrams refer to the philosopher's experience in exile on Corsica.

8. LITERARY SUCCESS

Seneca the philosopher and stylist

Throughout antiquity, it was Seneca's prose philosophical works that were most popular, despite periodic polemic and controversy (already Caligula rejected his style as sand without lime). His tragedies, on the other hand, seem to have been almost completely neglected (except by Quintilian and the grammarians, who occasionally cite them, and Sidonius Apollinaris, who distinguishes their author from the philosopher Seneca). Contemporary Latin prose was profoundly influenced by his pointed, nervous style, but at the end of the first century Quintilian, in the name of a new Ciceronianism, sharply criticized him and his fashionable imitators, while in the next century Fronto and Aulus Gellius attacked him from the point of view of the proponents of the archaizing style. In late antiquity, however, Christian writers refer to him frequently and admiringly and even occasionally mention the tragedies; they considered him, though a pagan, to be nevertheless a morally serious philosopher, and they were strengthened in this conviction by his notorious correspondence with St. Paul, forged in the fourth century, first mentioned by Jerome and thereafter celebrated throughout the Middle Ages (and perhaps in part responsible for the fact that Seneca's works have reached us). So popular was Seneca that he sometimes even survived in disguise. In the late sixth century, Martin of Braga wrote a *De Ira* based upon Seneca's treatise of this name and a *Formula Honestae Vitae,* which seems to have been largely plagiarized from a lost work of Seneca's, probably his *De Officiis,* and which enjoyed considerable popularity in the Middle Ages. Indeed, a number of his philosophical works that were most popular in antiquity have not survived: Lactantius quotes from *Exhortationes, De Immatura Morte,* and *Moralis Philosophiae Libri,* Jerome from *De Matrimonio,* Augustine from *De Superstitione,* and Cassiodorus from *De Forma Mundi,* all now lost. And the lone ancient manuscript of his prose works, written in the third or fourth century and surviving in incomplete form, contains fragments of two other lost works, *Quomodo Amicitia Continenda Sit* and *De Vita Patris.* The *Letters to Lucilius* survived but were split into two groups (1–88 and 89–124), which were transmitted separately for centuries (the former group was the more popular) and not recombined until much later, especially starting in the twelfth century. Even where Seneca's prose works were not themselves known directly, his epigrammatic and jumpy style made him an ideal author for excerpting, and many *florilegia* contained extracts from these texts, especially from *Letters* 1–88, *De Beneficiis,* and *De Clementia.* One such anthology, called the *Liber Senecae* or *Liber Senecae de Moribus,* was already cited as an authority in 567 by the Council of Tours and remained particularly successful through the Middle Ages.

Medieval rediscovery of the philosophical works

The prose works (except for the *Dialogues*) reemerged in the ninth century but then faded away again until their popularity increased explosively in the twelfth and thirteenth centuries; at this time, too, Seneca's separately transmitted works started to be put together again (the process had been completed by the fourteenth century). The earliest works to reappear were the *De Beneficiis* and the *De Clementia,* and these two remained particularly popular through the Middle Ages; including epitomes and excerpts, they are transmitted in three hundred manuscripts of the twelfth century and later. It was such moralistic prose works that were read in medieval schools and that, together with his scientific writings, which were rediscovered in northern France by the early twelfth century, determined his reputation for erudition, wisdom, and rectitude among medieval readers. For Dante he is still "Seneca morale"; and Roger Bacon and other medieval philosophers quote him as an authority more often even than they do Cicero. The *Dialogues* did not reappear until the end of the eleventh century, at Montecassino, and only became generally available in northern Europe in the second half of the thirteenth century. Roger Bacon discovered a manuscript containing them in Paris in 1266, but already earlier there are traces of acquaintance with them in northern Europe. Later they, too, went on to become very popular: over a hundred late manuscripts transmit them.

Literary works in the late Middle Ages

But Seneca's poetic works had a more difficult time. The *Apocolocyntosis* was rare until the thirteenth century and remained one of his least popular writings through the Middle Ages. Of his tragedies, which were not widely known in late antiquity or in the early Middle Ages, some excerpts were disseminated in the *Florilegium Thuaneum* (second half of the ninth century, central or northern France, perhaps Fleury), and one Italian manuscript from the end of the eleventh century has been preserved, but most of the oldest surviving manuscripts derive from northern France in the second half of the twelfth century, and it was not until the early fourteenth century that these works, too, started to be read more widely. But once they did, they too participated in Seneca's extraordinary late medieval popularity: they are transmitted in almost four hundred manuscripts. Particularly important centers for their study and diffusion in this period were Padua (the scholars Lovato Lovati and Albertino Mussato) and the papal court at Avignon (a commentary by Nicholas Trevet); there are marginal notes by Petrarch on one manuscript, which perhaps he discovered in the latter city.

Renaissance

Seneca's prose writings remained popular in the Renaissance, and most of them had already been printed by 1475 (though the *Naturales Quaestiones* were not published until 1490). Erasmus devoted two editions to his works (1515, 1529), arguing in the second and much improved one on the authority of Jerome that Seneca was a saint; Calvin wrote a commentary on the *De Clementia;* Montaigne's conception of philosophical writing was deeply influenced by Seneca; and Seneca's moral treatises have left unmistakable traces on Corneille and Diderot. The *Apocolocyntosis,* which was not published for the first time until 1513 (in a poor edition, based upon an inferior manuscript which omitted the Greek), rose somewhat in fortune during this period: it inspired Lipsius's satirical *Somnium: Lusus in nostri aevi criticos* (1581), which started a fashion for Menippean satires in the six-

Tragedies in the Renaissance

teenth and seventeenth centuries. But in the Renaissance it was above all Seneca's tragedies (first published in Ferrara in 1484) that, for the first time, dominated within the reception of his works. Renaissance tragedy is inconceivable without Seneca. He not only supplied the genre with its only Latin exemplars but filled it out with plots, style, and details that were to become the stock in trade of European tragic drama for several centuries: exaggerated, heroic characters, among them sanguinary kings and treacherous courtiers, lubricious women and virtuous youths; conflicts of power and politics; violent passions, merciless revenge, and terrific carnage; drastically heightened language and wittily pointed epigrams. His influence upon Italian tragedy was massive in the Renaissance and continued to the time of Metastasio (who at the age of fourteen wrote an original tragedy modeled on Seneca) and Alfieri (whose violent polemics against tyranny are influenced in equal measure by Seneca and by Lucan). The same applies to the French classical tragedy of Corneille (whose *Médée* was the only French baroque tragedy whose plot as a whole was directly taken from Seneca), Racine, and later Voltaire, and to German tragedy, from the baroque *Trauerspiel* through Lessing (who wrote an essay on Seneca's tragedies) to the Romantics. So, too, in England, where Seneca inspired many of the most familiar figures and themes of Marlowe, Shakespeare, and the Jacobean tragedians: tyrants *(Richard II)*, ghosts invoking revenge *(Macbeth, Julius Caesar, Hamlet)*, witchcraft *(Macbeth)*, madness *(The Spanish Tragedy, The Duchess of Malfi, King Lear)*, torture and mutilation, corpses littering the stage and murder performed before the audience's eyes; in *Richard III* Shakespeare even seems to have experimented with an English version of Senecan stichomythia.

Modern period   But with the growth of a taste for literary realism and for Greek tragedy and with the decline in courtly culture, especially starting in the eighteenth century, Seneca suffered a sharp decrease in popularity; traces of familiarity with his works during the Romantic period and later are few and far between (an exception is Schopenhauer). But contemporary audiences, especially those of cinema and the novel, seem once again to have become keenly interested in themes and tastes such as those typical of Seneca's tragedies; and some recent films, for example Peter Greenaway's *The Cook, the Thief, His Wife, and Her Lover* (1989), are certainly reminiscent of Seneca, whether or not they were directly inspired by him. Nevertheless, modern philosophy has taken little interest in his moral writings; his scientific works have at most an antiquarian and historical appeal; and his plays themselves, though still occasionally produced, are too remote from modern stage conventions to be able to affect most audiences nowadays as viscerally as they affected readers for centuries.

BIBLIOGRAPHY

There are good Oxford texts by L. D. Reynolds of the *Dialogi* (Oxford 1977) and the *Epistulae Morales* (Oxford 1965) and by O. Zwierlein of the *Tragedies* (Oxford 1986, reprint with corrections 1992, complemented by his *Kritische Kommentar* [Mainz 1986]). For the *De Beneficiis* and *Naturales Quaestiones,* reference must still be made to the editions of C. Hosius (Leipzig 1914) and A. Gercke (Leipzig 1907, reprint Stuttgart 1970, with bibliography by W. Schaub; see also the edition of P. Oltramare [Paris 1929]). For the *Apocolocyntosis,* see the edition with commentary by P. T. Eden (Cambridge 1984), and for the epigrams, that of C. Prato (Rome 1964, with Italian commentary). There are few English commentaries on the philosophical works, but the older selection of letters by W. C. Summers (London 1910) is still useful and is now complemented by C.D.N. Costa, *Seventeen Letters of Seneca* (Warminster 1988), while there is a commentary on the *De Brevitate Vitae, Ad Polybium,* and *Ad Helviam Matrem* by J. D. Duff (Cambridge 1915). H. M. Hine's edition of *Natural Questions,* book 2 (New York 1981), offers both a new text and a rich commentary. In other languages, note the Italian editions with commentary of *De Brevitate Vitae* by A. Traina (Turin

1970), *De Tranquillitate Animi* by M. G. Cavalca Schiroli (Bologna 1981), and *De Otio* by I. Dionigi (Brescia 1983), as well as those of *Epistulae* 1–12 and 65 by M. Scarpat (Brescia 1975, 1965) and of 94–95 by M. Bellincioni (Brescia 1979). See also the German edition of letter 88 by A. Stückelberger (Heidelberg 1965). The tragedies are better served, with English commentaries on *Agamemnon* by R. J. Tarrant (Cambridge 1976), *Hercules Furens* by J. G. Fitch (Ithaca 1987), *Medea* by C.D.N. Costa (Oxford 1973), *Phaedra* by A. J. Boyle (Liverpool 1987) and M. Coffey and R. Mayer (Cambridge 1990), *Thyestes* by R. J. Tarrant (Atlanta 1985), and *Troades* by E. Fantham (Princeton 1982).

The major English study is M. Griffin, *Seneca: A Philosopher in Politics* (Oxford 1976); see also V. Sorenson, trans. W. Glyn Jones, *Seneca: The Humanist at the Court of Nero* (Edinburgh 1985), and P. Grimal, *Sénèque ou la conscience de l'empire* (Paris 1978). There is a collection of essays edited by C.D.N. Costa (London 1974); volume 32.2 of *ANRW* is devoted to Seneca and includes a detailed bibliography (Berlin 1985). There have been few English monographs on the philosophical works; however, A. L. Motto, *Seneca Sourcebook* (Amsterdam 1970), is extremely useful. On the tragedies, see N. T. Pratt, *Senecan Drama* (Chapel Hill 1983), D. and E. Henry, *The Mask of Power* (Warminster 1985), and C. Segal, *Language and Desire in Seneca's Phaedra* (Princeton 1986). The essay "Senecan Tragedy" by C. J. Herington has been influential; it appeared first in *Arion* 5 (1966) 422–71 and was reprinted in *Essays on Classical Literature*, ed. N. Rudd (Cambridge 1972). On the question of performance, the seminal work from a skeptical point of view is O. Zwierlein, *Die Rezitationsdramen Senecas* (Meissenheim 1966); see also the introduction to E. Fantham's edition of *Troades*. On the other side, see D. F. Sutton, *Seneca on the Stage* (Leiden 1986) and esp. the important article of R. J. Tarrant, "Senecan Drama and Its Antecedents," *HSCP* 82 (1978) 213–63 (though note also the introduction to his edition of *Thyestes*).

On Senecan drama in the Renaissance, see T. S. Eliot, "Seneca in Elizabethan Translation," in *Selected Essays* (London 1951), and G. Braden, *Renaissance Tragedy and the Senecan Tradition* (New Haven 1985).

The Poetic Genres in the Julio-Claudian Period

The taste for the so-called minor genres

In the history of Latin poetry the period from the beginning of Tiberius's principate to the accession of Nero is one of the most difficult to describe succinctly. On the one hand, the influence of figures such as Virgil, Horace, and Ovid is overwhelming; on the other, we lack impressive new writers who might serve as points of reference and attraction. The most conspicuous fact about the literature of this period, its rage for minor poetic genres, is precisely what hinders the identification of constants and well-defined literary schools. It is interesting to compare these characteristics of the poetry with the artistic tastes of the various emperors. Tiberius, for instance, is an enthusiast for certain minor trends within Alexandrian poetry, for learned, mythological poems, epyllia such as those rehandled by Ovid in the *Metamorphoses*. This preference is all the more significant if one recalls the effort made under Augustus by the circle of Maecenas to attach greater value to a literature that was more creative and more committed to large themes—the didactic and epic poetry of Virgil, the civic poetry, the ethical poetry, and the literary criticism of Horace, as well as the intended rebirth of Latin drama (the lost tragedies of Varius Rufus, Asinius Pollio, and Ovid, for instance, had responded to this dictate of cultural policy). It is easy to believe that the fragmentation of works and literary genres under Tiberius, Caligula, and Claudius also corresponds to a decline in these expectations.

1. THE MINOR POETRY OF OVID'S GENERATION

Valgius Rufus and Domitius Marsus

Among the contemporaries of Horace and Ovid stand out several elegiac poets of whom we have only indirect evidence and a few fragments. Valgius Rufus, consul in 12 B.C., wrote epigrams, elegies, and hexameters on bucolic subjects; he was also important as a scholar. Domitius Marsus is slightly more significant, the author of elegant epigrams, among them a famous one on the death of Tibullus. It is likely that these poets published mixed collections containing epigrammatic or elegiac poetry or both.

Aemilius Macer

Aemilius Macer, who died in 16 B.C., was more closely connected to Ovid. He practiced principally that genre of Hellenistic didactic poetry that we mentioned in connection with Virgil's *Georgics* (see pp. 270 ff.). He wrote brief hexameter poems on birds *(Ornithogonia)*, serpents *(Theriaca)*, and herbs *(De Herbis)*, developing naturalistic and scientific themes in verse. This kind of interest increases in the Roman culture of the Empire and culminates in Pliny the Elder's great *summa.* In general, Macer was probably linked to that neo-Alexandrian trend that left a trace in Ovid but comes to dominate the minor poetry of the Julio-Claudian period.

Grattius

Macer can be likened to Grattius, to whose name it is customary to add the epithet "Faliscus" because, when speaking of the Faliscans in his work, he uses the adjective *nostri.* Grattius is the author of a short didactic poem on hunting *(Cynegetica),* which has come down to us incomplete (around five hundred hexameters). In this modest work Virgilian influences coexist with an affected fondness for mythological digression. The work antedates the exile of Ovid, who names Grattius in the *Epistulae ex Ponto.*

2. ASTRONOMICAL POETRY: GERMANICUS AND MANILIUS

Aratus in Latin literature

To this neo-Alexandrian tendency one can also link Manilius and Germanicus, who, though they give new emphases and accents and differ from one another in various ways, both choose as the model for their own work the didactic poetry of Aratus. The learned poet of the fourth–third century B.C. exerted enormous influence on Roman poetry; he was translated by Cicero (see pp. 200 ff.) and would be translated again, in late antiquity, by Avienus (see p. 661 f.).

Spread of astrology at Rome

The interest in astrology and astronomy is a notable element in Roman culture beginning at least in the time of Caesar. It is not merely a scientific or scholarly interest: faith in the stars becomes tinged with philosophy and also, under the ever-pervasive influence of the Oriental civilizations, with religion. The Stoics, for example, lay great stress on man's relation with the cosmos and on the link between human destiny and natural laws. In popular religion, too, the notion of astral predestination, controlled by celestial "attractions," becomes more common. But it is not solely a matter of cosmology or folklore. The emperors also, beginning with Augustus, who attributes great importance to his horoscope, make political and propagandistic use of belief in the stars. And Virgil himself, in one of the most propagandistic and fawning passages in all his work, the proem to the first book of the *Georgics,* foretells the catasterism (the transformation into an immortal star after death) of Octavian.

Germanicus

It is not surprising, then, that Germanicus (15 B.C.–A.D. 19) is a politically powerful figure. Adoptive son of the emperor Tiberius, and his designated successor, Germanicus (he inherited the appellation from his father Drusus, who died fighting in Germany [see p. 368]) distinguished himself at an early age as a general fighting against the Germans; his unexpected death was attributed to a political plot. As a writer he has left us nearly a thousand hexameters: an incomplete poem (we have about 725 verses from it) entitled *Aratea* and fragmentary excerpts that go by the name of *Prognostica*. These are, respectively, a version of Aratus's *Phaenomena* (on celestial bodies) and a rather free reworking of the same author's *Prognostica* (on weather signs). To judge by what remains, the *Prognostica* was handled much more freely in the reworking; we do not know whether Germanicus conceived of the pair as a unified work. The proem of the *Aratea* contains a dedication to a *genitor* who is certainly Tiberius (note that in the corresponding proem Aratus addressed Zeus). The text gives the impression that it dates from shortly after the death of Augustus, that is, between 14 and 19, under the reign of Tiberius. Given the intense military and diplomatic activity of Germanicus during this period, one can only admire the work's smoothness and the care bestowed on its form. The philosophical elements, however, receive little emphasis (especially in comparison with Manilius). The ensemble represents the learned activity of a curious young man of great culture who does not feel called to a literary mission.

Manilius and Latin astrology in prose

Unlike Germanicus, Manilius for us is an enigmatic figure; few Latin authors have as obscure a life. All that we know of him comes from a text completely lacking in autobiographical clues: the five hexameter books (slightly more than forty-two hundred verses) of the didactic poem *Astronomica*.

The Astronomica

The first book is devoted to astronomy, with a description of the cosmos that includes theories about its origin, the stars, the planets, the celestial circles, and the comets. The second book analyzes the characteristics of the signs of the zodiac and the possibilities of their conjunctions; the third describes the twelve athla, the *locus Fortunae,* and the way to determine a horoscope; the fourth analyzes the decans of the zodiacal signs (each sign consists of three units, or decans, each of ten degrees, for a total of thirty-six decans) and their influence on human characteristics; the fifth examines the extra-zodiacal signs that accompany the movement of the zodiac and the magnitudes of the stars.

In the course of the first century A.D., as was remarked, star lore had been accepted at the most varied levels within the official culture of Rome, even if suspicion and distrust persisted, especially towards some astrologer-magicians. Serious representatives of the official culture such as Varro and Nigidius Figulus had concerned themselves with these problems systemat-

Manilius's Stoicism

ically, in prose. Manilius's poem is the most persuasive attempt to confer poetic dignity on this line of thought. The structure of the poem, which breaks off rather abruptly in the fifth book and for that reason in all likelihood remained unfinished, is entirely shaped by the search for a universal order, a cosmic *ratio* that moves the great machine of the universe. Manilius is clearly a Stoic. In a very interesting passage he compares the delicate order of nature to the hierarchical structure of Roman society: even in the immensity of the cosmos, he says, there is a *res publica* (5.734 ff.). For Manilius, revealing this order is identical with adhering and submitting to it.

Manilius and Lucretius

Manilius's poetry thus has a much greater element of instruction to it than the neo-Alexandrian didactic poetry (e.g., of his contemporary Grattius), which limits itself to descriptive concerns. His eagerness to instruct carries Manilius towards the great model of Lucretius's poetry. Completely alien to the atomistic materialism of the *De Rerum Natura,* even opposed to it, the Stoic Manilius nevertheless sees in Lucretius the only possible model of a "high" didactic genre, one that is not merely a learned curiosity or pointless description. The *Astronomica* thus emulates Lucretius, especially in the structure of its exposition and the disposition of its material among the books.

The influence of Ovid   Lucretian in his didactic enthusiasm, Manilius is in other respects perhaps the first real exponent of what we usually call the "Silver Age" of Latin poetry. His hexameter, with its fluid, regular structure, shows the dominant influence of Ovid. This is the expressive principle which would become dominant in the great masters of the Silver Age hexameter, Lucan and Statius. Ovid's presence is also felt in the sentimental and rococo taste of certain mythological digressions, which stand out from the astronomical context; a conspicuous example is the narrative about Andromeda (5.549 ff.).

Date of the
Astronomica   The work must have been composed towards the end of Augustus's reign. Among other things, it clearly presupposes the influence of Ovid's *Metamorphoses.* Some critics, however, while acknowledging that various passages presume that Augustus is still alive, believe that the poem contains at least one allusion (4.764) to the succession of Tiberius. The most likely date is one that spans the two principates. Manilius's relation to Germanicus, who is close in time and literary interests, is not clear.

The refinement of Manilius's verses, with a certain tendency to *brevitas,* the difficulty of the subjects treated, and the numerous instances of obscurity and imprecision make him one of the most difficult poets of Latin literature.

3. DEVELOPMENTS IN HISTORICAL EPIC

Loss of a great part of
Latin epic   As we have already seen (see pp. 101 f.), epic poetry on historical subjects has an unbroken success at Rome, and it seems lacunose only to us, who from the long period between Ennius and Lucan, between the ages of Scipio and Nero, possess but isolated fragments, often merely titles and authors' names.

Varius and
Albinovanus Pedo   The failure of these works to be preserved might be an indication of their quality, but perhaps it is more sensible to ascribe it to changes in taste. Catullus, Horace, and Propertius attacked a certain kind of historical, panegyrical epic; thus it is difficult to form an objective judgment on the quality of these historical poems. The new era of historical epic opens with Virgil and Ovid. We should particularly regret the loss of the *forte epos* (so Horace terms it in the *Satires*) of Lucius Varius Rufus, a prominent poet in the circle of Maecenas and the highly valued author of a tragedy, *Thyestes,* of a possibly didactic poem, *De Morte,* and of a *Panegyric of Augustus.* The most significant historical poet of the later Augustan age, Albinovanus

Pedo, is an elegant rival of Virgil and Ovid. His poem dealt with Germanicus's adventurous expedition to the northern seas (A.D. 16). We have a considerable fragment of it (around thirty hexameters), which in a forceful, image-filled style develops a theme dear to the rhetoricians and the schools of declamation, namely, whether it is right for man to push himself ever farther, beyond the natural limits of his world. The theme arose from celebrations of the deeds of Alexander the Great. Albinovanus rehandles it with an abundance of poetic colors, mostly from Virgil's palette, and with considerable pathos. Pathos and rhetorical tension already look forward to the style of Lucan; the poem's ideology, however, seems based on the imperialism that runs through Roman culture in the early Empire. This rhetoric of conquest would find new scope, after the Neronian parenthesis, in the culture of the Flavian period (see pp. 488 ff. on Valerius Flaccus and his *Argonautica*).

Rabirius

Rabirius and Cornelius Severus appear to be historical poets of less force; we have very brief fragments of them. Although they are contemporaries of Ovid, some anticipations of Lucan are evident. Rabirius chose the civil war between Octavian and Antony as his subject. From the little that is left, it seems that Rabirius also had naturalistic interests; this would be another feature typical of Lucan's epic and in any event an interest felt more and more in the Neronian-Flavian period. One can set beside Rabirius a wretched anonymous fragment on the battle of Actium, found among the papyri from Herculaneum. Sextilius Ena, one of the authors of epic-historical poetry on the civil wars, and so comparable to these others, is practically a mere name to us.

Cornelius Severus

Cornelius Severus must have been somewhat less modern and more archaizing: the title of his historical poem (or were they several separate works?) is controversial, but the generic *Res Romanae* is probable. Cicero's death was certainly among the subjects treated (a fragment we have is an emphatic tirade upon it), as was the war in Sicily between Octavian and Sextus Pompey. One has the impression that Severus represents the extreme point of a convergence of epic poetry, oratory, and historiography. Not surprisingly, Lucan would later be accused of being more a prose writer than a poet. With just this meaning Quintilian terms Severus (10.1.89) better as a *versificator* than as a *poeta*. Taken all together, then, the Ovidian generation of historical poets made interesting attempts at modernizing the epic genre. Lucan would follow this trend, at least partly, and the classicist revival of the Flavian era would combat it.

4. THE *APPENDIX VERGILIANA*

The Appendix *a work of the first century* A.D.

The rather heterogeneous collection of poetic texts that goes by the name *Appendix Vergiliana* has created among critics and historians of literature an interest that is out of proportion to its intrinsic value. The stimulus to this interest was the question of Virgilian authorship, which today is almost completely closed, that is, answered in the negative. Consequently, the poems of the *Appendix* find their correct place, not beside Virgil's work, but in the framework of the minor poetry of the first century A.D. There alone, in fact, could one locate poetic texts that not only presuppose Virgil but also are steeped, the vast majority of them, in Ovid's style—just as the poetry of Statius or some of the poetic sections of Petronius's *Satyricon* are.

History of the attribution to Virgil

The term *appendix* is modern (used for the first time by J. C. Scaliger in 1572) and refers to the custom of printing these texts all together after the genuine works of Virgil. It is not likely that any of the works included in the *Appendix* is by Virgil, except perhaps for a pair of short poems in the *Catalepton*. The attribution of the various individual works to Virgil—and, we repeat, the collection was formed in the Renaissance—rests on pieces of evidence that vary in number, authority, and antiquity. The *Culex,* for example, was regarded as a youthful work of Virgil's already in the time of Lucan (see the *Vita Lucani* and the preface to the first book of Statius's *Silvae*), but the *Moretum* is identified as Virgilian solely upon evidence from the Middle Ages.

Origin of the Appendix

The scarcity or abundance of these pieces of evidence does not, of course, by itself constitute conclusive proof that Virgil was not their author. Stylistic investigation of the individual works is conclusive, however: vocabulary, metrics, prosody, and allusions are indications that accumulate to prove a date that is often much later than the age of Augustus. The poems are not all to be dated to the same period, and they are undoubtedly by different hands; moreover, one cannot say for certain whether they were *intentionally* conceived of as Virgilian falsifications. The large number of imitations of Virgil does not in itself prove that there was such an intention, since all the poetry of the Empire is more or less marked by this classical model. Some of these poems are probably the works of undistinguished poets that someone later attempted to attribute to Virgil, in order to satisfy the curiosity of the educated public, which must have been aroused by the absence of genuine minor and youthful writings by the greatest Roman poet.

All that remains is to consider one by one the various poems of the (pseudo-)Virgilian *Appendix.*

The Dirae *or* Lydia

The *Dirae,* or "maledictions," is a poem of invective, like Ovid's *Ibis* and, earlier still, Callimachus's *Arai.* This slight hexameter work seems to be a variation on the theme of the land confiscations, which is well known— and was a popular literary subject at Rome—on account of Virgil's *Bucolics.* The manuscripts follow the *Dirae,* no separation being indicated, with about eighty hexameters on a completely different subject: a pastoral love lament devoted to a woman named Lydia. Since this Lydia is also named in the *Dirae,* it is likely that someone joined together these two poems, which otherwise are similar in their bucolic background. Stylistically, the two poems appear to have been composed within the Augustan age. They are to be seen as a first instance of that post-Virgilian bucolic development that would flower again in the time of Nero.

The Catalepton

The *Catalepton*—with Greek accentuation, *Katà leptón,* or with Latin, *Catalépton*—is, as the name says ("a few at a time" or "small collection"), a "container" of small texts, various in subject and meter. The title is already attested in Greek poetry of the Hellenistic age. The fifteen poems of the collection must be different in origin as well as in subject and meter; some are linked only by the fact that they present themselves explicitly as works by Virgil. A couple of these poems might even be considered authentic, namely, the fifth and the eighth, which are occasional poems attributable to the young Virgil. Nonetheless, the activity of a forger cannot be excluded, since Virgil's fame, from the late Augustan period onwards, was such as to encourage the search for unpublished poems and juvenilia. They are, in any event, texts of modest poetic value in which a certain Catullan inspiration (the Catullus of the *nugae*) is evident. Other poems of the *Cata-lepton,* such as the ninth, a panegyric for Messalla, the patron of Tibullus who held a triumph in 27 B.C., are simply too bad to be by Virgil.

The Culex

The *Culex* is a miniature epic, an epyllion, that recounts in hexameters an episode in which the protagonist is a shepherd. The shepherd was about to be killed by a snake while he slept; the mosquito (the *culex* of the title) saved him by stinging it, but the shepherd in his ignorance kills the kindly insect. Then, after the shepherd has fallen asleep again, the mosquito appears to him in a dream, complaining of the wrong done to him; the shepherd, to set matters right, upon awakening gives the mosquito burial. In the dream the mosquito tells the shepherd about the Underworld. The notion of a mosquito who, like Odysseus, Orpheus, or Aeneas, descends to Hades and tells of his experience shows that the *Culex* is conceived as a parody of serious epic, or rather, a reduction of it to a small scale. The attribution of the poem to the young Virgil is, as we saw, quite ancient and widespread. It is obvious that its style and content caused the ancient critics to see this clever work as a plausible preliminary exercise for a poet who was destined for poetic genres far more solemn, and for hugely successful results in them.

The Ciris

The *Ciris* (the term indicates a kind of heron) is also an epyllion, this time mythological. In over five hundred hexameters it tells the pathetic story of Scylla, who betrays her father, the king of Megara, out of love for his enemy Minos; it ends with Scylla's metamorphosis into a heron. This type of poetry had been introduced at Rome by the *neoteroi,* but it also had some success under Tiberius and then under Nero. The *Ciris* is clearly influenced not only by Virgil but also by minor neoteric poetry and by Ovid's *Metamorphoses.* The author is chiefly inspired by neoteric poetry and does not seem particularly close to Virgil in his literary taste. The date of the poem is controversial.

The Copa

The *Copa* is a sketch in elegiac couplets (thirty-eight verses). It describes a scene set among the common people: a lady innkeeper (the *copa,* feminine of *copo/caupo,* "innkeeper") who draws customers to her place of business by her dancing.

The Moretum

Taste for minute realism is also evident in the *Moretum* ("The Loaf"), a short hexameter poem that describes minutely the morning rising of a peasant and the preparation of his meal. It takes pleasure in the description of the simple life of the peasants, a popular subject in the poetry of the Empire as a result of the public's taste for cameo scenes and rustic moralizing.

The Priapea

Three *Priapea* are also transmitted under the name of Virgil, though they should be regarded as spurious. The genre had been practiced by Catullus and has a mild literary success in the Julio-Claudian period (see below).

The Elegiae in Maecenatem

The *Elegiae in Maecenatem* form a text of considerable historical-cultural interest, since they recall the death and the personality of Augustus's most influential political-literary adviser. These two small elegiac works are undoubtedly composed in a period not long after the death of the illustrious man, in 8 B.C. Virgil, whom some manuscripts name as the author, had died eleven years earlier!

The Aetna

Finally, the scientific poem *Aetna,* 645 hexameters treating causes and phenomena of volcanoes, has no connection to Virgil. It is an original experiment in didactic poetry, though in form it leaves much to be desired. The work can be dated between the time of Manilius, whom the author of the *Aetna* imitates, and A.D. 79, the year of the eruption of Vesuvius, which the author could not have failed to mention if he had written afterwards. Strong similarities in content remind one of Seneca's *Naturales Quaestiones,* and the rejection of mythology recalls to a degree the attitude of Persius. Thus, a date in the Neronian era seem plausible, on the whole.

5. PHAEDRUS: THE FABLE TRADITION

A marginal poet

Up to this point the minor poetry of the Julio-Claudian period ha· shown us the learned activities of high circles, mostly close to the imperial court. Phaedrus, by contrast, represents a completely isolated voice. In many respects, he is a marginal author. As a person, he has a quite modest social position, and as a poet, he cannot be called a virtuoso; and he practices a minor literary genre, which is itself marginal to the great literary currents of the early Empire.

The founder of a new poetic genre

Nonetheless, in certain respects Phaedrus is one of the greatest glories of Latin literature. That may seem astonishing, but to this humble artisan belongs an important historical first: he is the first author in Greco-Roman culture to give us a collection of fables conceived as an independent poetic work and intended for reading. This is no small matter: only in satire and the novel does Roman culture display an equally marked independence.

The fable is the most universal and most profoundly popular genre. The "authors" of fables are almost always the heirs of a popular, oral narrative tradition that has already been consolidated. Phaedrus, too, as narrator, invents very little, and it is not in that area that his merits should be appreciated. His fables, taken one by one, are scarcely original, indebted as they are to the Aesopic tradition. And in literary elaboration no tale of Phaedrus's can rival the fables that the great poets or narrators—from Hesiod to Callimachus, from Ennius to Horace, and Petronius too—are fond of including in their works as occasional experiments. Instead, Phaedrus's merit lies in his constant, systematic commitment to giving the fable a standard, a rule, a well-defined, recognizable voice.

Aesop's fables and Phaedrus's codification

The Aesopic tradition—anecdotes, usually with animals for characters, that presented humorous ideas and bits of moral wisdom—had been fixed in Greece around the fourth century B.C. in literary collections that were, as far as we know, written in prose. The custom had developed of there being a foreword *(promythion)* or an afterword *(epimythion)* or both, in which the subject was established or the moral of the fable was made clear. Working with these Greek prose models, which were probably his only source, Phaedrus made this custom a rule and created a regular poetic form for the fable. A characteristic of this genre is the use of animals as masks, creatures humanized and given a stable, recurring psychology (the clever fox, the wicked wolf, etc.), and a virtual constant is the presence of a moral, a universal truth that is extracted from the tale, sometimes forcedly. In this field Phaedrus does not achieve the refinement and taste that characterize a fable such as Horace's about the country mouse and the city mouse (*Satires* 2.6).

The morals of Phaedrus and the world of the marginal

The morals of Phaedrus, however, are an original feature, at least insofar as they express a social mentality. The embittered tone in which the poet often comments on the "law of the stronger" that prevails in animal society seems to express the point of view of the subservient classes of Roman society. Phaedrus is one of the very few Roman writers to let the marginal people of Roman society speak; in this sense, his work contains the urgency of a social reality. Although descriptive and linguistic realism is almost completely absent—the world of the fables tends to be abstract, the scenery generic, the language terse and scarcely serving to characterize—it is precisely in these moralizing notes that we seem to catch a genuine fidelity to the mind of the humblest classes and to the common sense of the people.

Phaedrus's realism and offenses against the powerful

And yet the work does not lack touches of fidelity to contemporary reality, sometimes in tones that come close to satire. Phaedrus does not always limit himself to the tradition of animal fables, and sometimes he appears to strike out on his own, as in the amusing tale that has Tiberius as its chief character (2.5). In the prologues to the individual books he shows a notable literary consciousness; he defends his own type of poetry, celebrates its virtues (brevity, variety, instructive content), and also emphasizes increasingly his independence from the Aesopic model. Indeed, Phaedrus seems to have found himself in trouble on account of his views, through their relation to contemporary reality. From the prologue to the third book one gathers that the poet was persecuted by Sejanus, Tiberius's powerful righthand man. In the fables that we have it is not clear what can have injured the powerful or aroused their suspicions; but Phaedrus does not lack polemical references to society, and indeed he even claims for his work a certain satiric character, which aims its blows, if not at individuals (this would have been truly dangerous, especially for an obscure freedman), then at least at certain human types and patterns of behavior. His fables are intended to be entertaining as well as instructive. For us, they often do not succeed, but they do have the great merit of preserving a genre of the people, reinterpreted in the light of real life and of a mentality that for the most part is excluded from high literary expression.

Life of Phaedrus

Phaedrus must have been born at a fairly early date in the principate of Augustus (around 20 B.C.?). He was active under Tiberius, Caligula, and Claudius, and a date of death around A.D. 50 is likely. In book 3, written after A.D. 31, Phaedrus says he is close to old age. In the literature of the early Empire he is one of the very few authors not of free birth (it is clear that the social origins of writers have been inverted from the times of Andronicus and Plautus). As far as we know, he was a slave of Thracian origin. In the manuscripts of his works he is referred to as *libertus Augusti* and therefore seems to have been set free by the emperor.

The fables of Phaedrus and the Appendix Perottina

The manuscripts transmit to us slightly more than ninety fables, divided into five books, all in iambic senarii (the usual verse form of the *palliata* of the republican era). It is certain that the original *corpus* was far larger. Among other things, some books appear exceptionally brief: the second contains only eight fables; the fifth, ten; and both have fewer than two hundred verses. The approximately thirty fables that are gathered in the so-called *Appendix Perottina,* named for its editor, the humanist Niccolò Perotti, are also certainly genuine. Other fables can be reconstructed from prose paraphrases that were popular in late antiquity (among which the *Romulus* is important).

Changes in the literary success of Phaedrus

The humble fabulist does not appear to have been very popular, at least with the educated public. Seneca says (*Ad Polybium de Consolatione* 8.3) that no Latin author has ever devoted himself to the Aesopic genre, and Quintilian, even if he knows Phaedrus, finds no reason to name him. But in compensation, as it were, Phaedrus's writings, rediscovered in the fifteenth century, have been notably successful in the modern period. A French classic such as La Fontaine owes much to him, and the fables, because of their simple style and moral content, were heavily used for teaching Latin in the schools.

6. THE POETIC GENRES IN THE NERONIAN AGE

The Return of Pastoral

The flourishing of literature under Nero

Among all the emperors of the Julio-Claudian dynasty, the last, Nero, is the one who leaves the deepest mark on literary history. His era witnesses a conspicuous flourishing of literary talents (in addition to Seneca, we have Lucan, Petronius, and Persius), joined by a host of lesser figures. We know that the emperor, especially in the tranquil first years of his reign, gave a strong stimulus to the arts. Greek poets as well, such as the epigrammatist Lucillius, who is preserved in the *Anthologia Palatina,* were connected to the poetic circles of the Neronian period.

The eclogues of Calpurnius Siculus and the taste for allegory

The bucolic genre in particular flourished: Virgil's influence is now dominant in Roman poetry. A certain Calpurnius Siculus, whose life is completely unknown, has left us seven eclogues, pastoral poems in the manner of Virgil, who has now replaced Theocritus as the model of the bucolic genre. The allusions to Nero allow the work to be dated securely. Calpurnius is important not so much for his metrical technique (though he does take pains over that) as because he provides the first instance of an allegorical conception of pastoral poetry. It is evident that some of Calpurnius's shepherds are simple allegories of historical figures. The tendency to employ Arcadia as a disguise for contemporary realities would reappear in the Italian Renaissance and then in the European pastoral tradition down to the eighteenth century.

It is equally evident that Calpurnius reinforces certain allegorical tendencies already present in Virgil's *Eclogues.* Now, of course, everything is clearer and more explicit. The mysterious prophecy of the Golden Age found in Virgil's fourth eclogue becomes, in Calpurnius's courtly vision, the golden age embodied in the good government of the princeps Nero. Virgil's subtle, ambiguous references to real circumstances become here a true poetry *à clef,* intended for a restricted audience, yet not without touches of propaganda.

The Carmina Einsidlensia

Along with Calpurnius's eclogues, there are transmitted four eclogues by Nemesianus, a poet of the third century (see pp. 613 f.), who continues the pastoral genre. By contrast, the so-called *Carmina Einsidlensia,* two bucolic fragments discovered in 1869 in a manuscript from the monastery of Einsiedeln, in Switzerland, can be dated to the Neronian period and placed somewhere near Calpurnius. The poetic technique, which recalls Calpurnius, and the references to Nero make the date certain.

Mythological Poetry and Minor Genres

Laus Pisonis

Some attribute to Calpurnius as well the *Laus Pisonis,* a long panegyric (260 verses) in hexameters. If this Piso is Calpurnius Piso, the member of the court who in 65 led a conspiracy against Nero, which was later destroyed in a bloodbath, one might also believe that the mysterious Calpurnius Siculus is connected to this milieu (perhaps a freedman of Piso?). The panegyric genre must have flourished especially throughout the early Empire, since it won immediate support for the poets.

The poetry of Nero

The gravest loss in this literary underbrush is perhaps the poetry of Nero himself. He wrote much, to judge from the titles we have (but it was an age of feverish activity: Nero died at the age of 30, Persius at 27, Lucan at 25). From the titles it is evident that Nero favored a return to mythological poetry, clearly based on neo-Alexandrian models. We have notices of an odd poem on the war at Troy, the *Troica,* the hero of which is Paris rather than Hector (handsome, luxurious, and elegant, was Paris perhaps a figure in whom Nero wished to see his own reflection?). Nero must have particularly sought to display mythological and geographic learning, precisely the type of decadent poetry that Persius attacks harshly in his *Satires.* A slanderous rumor has Nero reciting his lines on the burning of Troy while Rome was itself burning, in 64, and the fire, some opponents said, was set by Nero himself! However that may be, it is extremely likely that the literary taste favored by the emperor is reflected in some of the poetic parts of

Petronius's *Satyricon,* in which, among other things, there occurs a poem in iambic senarii called the *Capture of Troy (Troiae Halosis).*

Nero as patron and baroque taste

Nero encouraged many writers and sponsored regular poetic contests, with rewards offered to the best poets. The practice of recitation is increasingly widespread in this period, and a luxurious, baroque style becomes popular, one that astonishes the public with its unusual images, bold metaphors, and sonorous preciosities. The parodies by Persius and Martial give us a window upon the contemporary atmosphere and the culture of these poets.

The Greek fashion and the Ilias Latina

The display of Greek culture becomes increasingly vital to the prestige of the poets. Lucan himself, who for us is the standard-bearer of the historical epic, also distinguished himself at a very early age by his mythological poetry. A modest poetic abridgment of the *Iliad,* the so-called *Ilias Latina,* may belong to this period. Slightly more than a thousand hexameters narrate the Homeric events in a mannered style that smacks of the rhetorical schools. The historical importance of the *Ilias Latina* lies more than anything in its literary success during the Middle Ages. In a period that did not have direct access to Homer, this modest composition, along with other prose abridgments, performed the invaluable function of being a popularization, a temporary surrogate serving until Western culture once again had direct knowledge of classical Greek poetry.

Caesius Bassus

It is natural that in this period there were also outstanding philologists (on whom see pp. 577 f.). One of them, Caesius Bassus, the author of an important metrical treatise dedicated to Nero, of which only fragments remain, was also a lyric poet praised by Persius (who was a great friend of his and whose *Satires* he published posthumously) as well as by Quintilian.

Sulpicia

Finally, among the lyric poets of this period a woman must also be mentioned, Sulpicia, whom Martial praises, comparing her even to Sappho. She was famous for the crude erotic realism of her lyric poems, dedicated to her husband Calenus, of which we have but two verses.

BIBLIOGRAPHY

For all the poets mentioned above of whom only fragments are preserved, see W. Morel, ed., *Fragmenta poetarum latinorum epicorum et lyricorum praeter Ennium et Lucilium* (Leipzig 1927, reprint 1963), and the much-criticized revision by K. Büchner, Leipzig 1982, with bibliography), as well as A. Traina and M. Bini, *Supplementum Morellianum* (Bologna 1986) and E. Courtney, *The Fragmentary Latin Poets* (Oxford 1993). The standard work on them and on all the other "lost" poets is H. Bardon, *La Littérature latine inconnue* (2 vols., Paris 1952; the second volume deals with the imperial period, esp. 123–75); see also Bardon's *Les Empereurs et les lettres latines d'Auguste à Hadrien* (ed. 2 Paris 1968). In English see G. Williams, *Change and Decline* (Berkeley and Los Angeles 1978), and J. P. Sullivan, *Literature and Politics in the Age of Nero* (Ithaca 1985), as well as E. Cizek, *L'Époque de Néron et ses controverses idéologiques* (Leiden 1972). *ANRW* 32.1 (Berlin 1984) contains many relevant articles; on Valgius Rufus and Varius Rufus see also H. Dahlmann, *Zu Fragmenten römischen Dichtern* (Mainz 1983).

There is an edition of the remains of Domitius Marsus by D. Fogazza (Rome 1981);

see also E. S. Ramage in *CPh* 54 (1959) 250–55 (speculative). For Aemilius Macer, see esp. A. S. Hollis in *CR* 23 (1973) 11; there is an *ANRW* survey in French by J. P. Néradeau (30.3, Berlin 1983). There are major editions with commentary of Grattius, *Cynegetica*, by P. J. Enk (Zutphen 1918, Latin), R. Verdière (Wetteren 1964, French), and C. Formicola (Bologna 1988, Italian); the work is included in the Loeb *Minor Latin Poets* of J. W. Duff and A. M. Duff (Cambridge, Mass. 1934, later split into two volumes).

Germanicus's translation of Aratus was edited with English translation and commentary by D. B. Gain (London 1976); see also the Budé edition of A. le Boeuffle (Paris 1975). The five-volume text of Manilius with Latin commentary by A. E. Housman (ed. 2 London 1937) is one of the most celebrated works of twentieth-century scholarship; there is now also a Teubner by G. P. Goold (Leipzig 1985), who produced an excellent Loeb text and translation (Cambridge, Mass. 1977). There is an Italian introduction to Manilius by C. Salemme (Naples 1983); in English note esp. A. M. Wilson, "The Prologue to Manilius 1," in *Papers of the Liverpool Latin Seminar* 5 (Liverpool 1985) 283–98.

On Varius Rufus, see esp. A. S. Hollis in *CQ* 27 (1977) 187–90 and H. Jocelyn in *CQ* 30 (1980) 387–400. There are German monographs by W. Wimmel, *Der tragische Dichter L. Varius Rufus* (Mainz 1981), and E. Lefèvre, *Der Thyestes des Lucius Varius Rufus* (Mainz 1976), and an *ANRW* survey by Wimmel (30.3, Berlin 1983), 1562–1621.

On Albinovanus Pedo and the other writers of historical epic, see esp. V. Tandoi, "Albinovano Pedone e la retorica giulio-claudiana delle conquiste," in *SIFC* 36 (1964) 129–68 and 39 (1967) 5–66. There is a German monograph on Cornelius Severus by H. Dahlmann (Mainz 1975), which also discusses Albinovanus Pedo.

The standard edition of the *Appendix Vergiliana* is that of W. V. Clausen, F.R.D. Goodyear, E. J. Kenney, and J. A. Richmond (Oxford 1966). The texts are included in the second volume of the Loeb *Vergil* by H. R. Fairclough (Cambridge, Mass. 1935). Among editions of individual texts may be mentioned those of the *Dirae* and *Lydia* by C. van den Graf (Leiden 1945), of the *Catalepton* by R.E.H. Westendorp Boerma (2 vols., Assen 1949–63, Latin), of the *Ciris* by R.O.A.M. Lyne (Cambridge 1978), of the *Copa* by F.R.D. Goodyear (*BICS* 24 [1977] 117–31) and A. Franzoi (Padua 1988, Italian), of the *Moretum* by E. J. Kenney (Bristol 1984) and A. Perutelli (Pisa 1983, Italian), of the *Elegiae in Maecenatem* by H. Schoonhoven (Groningen 1980, English), of the *Epigrammata* and *Priapea* by E. Galletier (Paris 1920, French) and A. Salvatore (Naples 1963, Italian), and of the *Aetna* by F.R.D. Goodyear (Cambridge 1965; the German edition of S. Sudhaus [Leipzig 1898] remains useful on the subject matter). There is an *ANRW* survey by J. Richmond (31.2, Berlin 1981), 1112–57; see also *Enciclopedia Italiana* s.v. "Appendix" (Italian) and the entries under the individual poems. Among English articles may be mentioned D. O. Ross, "The *Culex* and *Moretum* and Post-Augustan Parody," *HSCP* 79 (1975) 235–63.

There is a good Loeb text of Phaedrus with translation and important introduction by B. E. Perry (New York 1965, along with an edition of the Greek writer Babrius); see also his *Aesopica* 1 (Urbana 1952). There is an *ANRW* survey by H. M. Currie (32.1, Berlin 1984), 497–513.

There is a useful text of Calpurnius Siculus and the *Carmina Einsidlensia* with German translation and notes by D. Korzeniewski, *Hirtengedichte aus neronischen Zeit* (Darmstadt 1971); see also the edition in Duff and Duff, *Minor Latin Poets,* the older English commentary on Calpurnius by C. H. Keene (London 1887), and the French edition by R. Verdière (Brussels 1954). Verdière also wrote the survey in *ANRW* 32.3 (Berlin 1985), 1845–1924.

On the *Ilias Latina,* see the text and detailed Italian commentary by M. Scaffai (Bologna 1984), as well as A. Grillo, *Critica del testo, imitazione, e narratologia: Ricerche sull'Ilias Latina e la tradizione epica classica* (Florence 1982).

All we know of Sulpicia comes from Martial 10.35 and 38; there is a single two-line fragment (p. 134 in Morel, *Fragmenta Poetarum Latinorum*); p. 361 in Courtney, *Fragmentary Latin Poets*).

Lucan

Marcus Annaeus Lucan was born at Cordoba, in Spain, on 3 November A.D. 39, the son of Annaeus Mela, Seneca's brother, and thus the nephew of the philosopher. In 40 he moved with his family to Rome, where he was educated. His teacher was the Stoic Annaeus Cornutus, in whose school he met Persius, who became his friend. Intellectually brilliant, he entered the court of Nero, who for some while numbered him among his intimate friends. By special grant of the princeps, Lucan held the quaestorship before the minimum age specified by law, and he joined the college of augurs. At the Neronia of 60 he recited *laudes* of the princeps, specially written for the occasion. According to some ancient sources, he published the first three books of the *Pharsalia,* the poem to which he had been devoting his efforts. For reasons that are unclear, there was an abrupt break with the emperor. The ancient sources refer to literary jealousy on the part of Nero, but it is also possible that Nero did not look with favor upon those ideas expressed in Lucan's poem that were too clearly marked by a nostalgic republicanism. Fallen into disgrace with the emperor and removed from the court, Lucan joined the conspiracy of Piso. When the plot was discovered, he, like many another, received the order to take his life. He died by his own hand on 30 April 65, not yet twenty-six years old.

WORKS

His chief work has been preserved, the epic poem *Bellum Civile* or *Pharsalia* (*Bellum Civile* is the title gotten from the ancient biographies and the manuscripts; Lucan himself at 9.985 calls the work *Pharsalia,* from Pharsalus, the site of the decisive battle in the civil war between Caesar and Pompey). The poem, in ten books, with a total of 8,060 hexameters, was left unfinished because of the author's death; book 10, which is far shorter than the others, breaks off abruptly. Lucan probably began work on the poem in 60.

Lost works: We have the titles (and in some cases a very few fragments) of works that are nearly all certainly earlier than the *Pharsalia:* an *Iliacon* (a poem on the Trojan War); a *Catachthonion* (a poem on the descent to the Underworld, identified by some with an epyllion on Orpheus, another work of which we hear); a *De Incendio Urbis;* an unfinished tragedy, *Medea;*

the *Saturnalia;* ten books of *Silvae,* a collection of poems of varying sorts; the *Laudes Neronis* already mentioned; and also epigrams, libretti for pantomimes, and declamations.

SOURCES Three ancient biographies of Lucan, one composed by Suetonius (in the *De Poetis*), another attributed to Vacca, and a shorter, anonymous one in the *Codex Vossianus II;* the ancient *Life* of Persius; book 15 of Tacitus's *Annals* (on the conspiracy of Piso); Statius, *Silvae* 2.7, a lengthy encomium of the poet. There are abundant and important collections of exegetical notes from the Middle Ages, some of which in all likelihood go back to late antiquity.

1. VERSIFIED HISTORY?

The early Lucan, poet of the regime

Lucan's intellectual training is almost wholly unknown to us, and the loss of his writings before the *Pharsalia* only aggravates the situation. The number and the variety of the compositions we know of indicate an unusual artistic precocity, as well as a remarkable versatility. To judge from the titles of the lost works, he seems to have conformed to Nero's tastes and commands: the *Iliacon* satisfied the princeps's passion for Trojan antiquities, and the *Silvae* and the libretti for pantomimes fall readily into the category of that entertaining poetry, refined in form and strongly inspired by specific occasions, that the emperor appeared to be fond of. The *Pharsalia* represents a completely different genre. Even if it did not right from the start stand in marked contrast to Nero's cultural tendencies—he himself was planning an epic poem on Roman history—the manner in which Lucan chose to deal with his subject, the civil war between Caesar and Pompey, turned the poem into a glorification of ancient republican liberty and an explicit condemnation of the imperial regime.

Summary of the Pharsalia

Book 1. After setting forth the subject of the poem and delivering a long praise of Nero, Lucan tells the causes of the war. Next he narrates Caesar's crossing of the Rubicon and the terror that fills Rome at word of his approach. A series of omens announce the imminent catastrophe.

Book 2. The Romans lament as they recall the earlier civil conflict between Marius and Sulla and realize that the one between Caesar and Pompey will be far more terrible. Brutus and Cato hold a discussion at night: is it right, they ask, to keep aloof from a conflict that in any event will result in the absolute domination of the victor, or is it advisable to join Pompey's side in the hope of influencing him? Cato persuades Brutus to choose the second alternative. Under pressure from Caesar's legions, Pompey flees from Italy.

Book 3. In a dream Pompey sees the ghost of Julia, Caesar's daughter and Pompey's first wife, who threatens him with terrible disasters. Caesar enters Rome and takes possession of the public treasury. Pompey assembles the allies, in large part Oriental, of whom Lucan gives a lengthy list, in the manner of the catalogue of ships in the *Iliad.* Then the theater of war shifts to Marseilles, which is besieged by Caesar. A naval battle takes place between the people of Marseilles and Caesar's army.

Book 4. This book describes Caesar's actions in Spain; the heroism of a Pompeian, Vulteius, who at the head of a small band holds off the attack of many enemies; and the death in Africa of Curio, a young partisan of Caesar's defeated by Numidian troops.

Book 5. The Senate, in exile from Rome, meets in Epirus. A Pompeian, Appius, goes to consult the oracle at Delphi, but the reply is ambiguous. After putting down an attempted rebellion, Caesar transports his troops to Epirus. Annoyed by delay on the part of Antony, who is slow to follow him with the rest of the army, he tries to rejoin it by recrossing the sea, incognito, in a small boat, but a furious storm drives him back to land. Pompey conveys his wife Cornelia to safety on the island of Lesbos, and both grieve over their enforced separation.

Book 6. Pompey is shut in and besieged at Dyrrhachium with his army. The Caesarian Scaeva performs heroic deeds. The armies of Pompey and Caesar reach Thessaly, which would be the site of the definitive meeting. Sextus, one of Pompey's sons, goes to consult the sorceress Ericthon, which introduces a scene of necromancy: by her magical arts Ericthon summons back to life a soldier fallen in battle, who reveals to Sextus Pompey the ruin that awaits him, his family, and the entire Roman political order.

Book 7. In a dream Pompey reviews the triumphs of his past. In a council of war Pompey tries to recommend avoiding battle, but he is overcome by the eagerness of his partisans, including Cicero. As part of the preparations for the battle of Pharsalus, Caesar and Pompey harangue their troops. The battle takes place, and Caesar is victorious; the Pompeian Domitius Ahenobarbus, an ancestor of Nero, meets a heroic death. Pompey flees. Caesar refuses to grant funeral honors to the dead. During the night distressing visions disturb his sleep.

Book 8. Joined once again by Cornelia, Pompey suggests to his men that they continue the fight with the help of the Parthians, but the proposal is rejected after a vigorous speech by Lentulus. He then heads for Egypt, where he hopes to find refuge. King Ptolemy, however, on the advice of his courtiers, has Pompey killed upon his arrival. Pompey's headless body is abandoned on the seashore; a certain Cordus gives it humble burial.

Book 9. After Pompey's death, Cato assumes command over the remains of the republican army and crosses the Libyan desert, meeting dangers of every sort, including sandstorms and snakes. He refuses to consult the oracle of Ammon: knowledge of the future cannot alter the wise man's decisions. Caesar, after seeing the ruins of the Troad, arrives in Egypt, where Pompey's head is presented to him; he feigns a chivalrous disdain for the treacherous murder of his rival.

Book 10. At Alexandria Caesar visits the tomb of Alexander the Great, virtually his teacher in tyranny. He holds a splendid banquet at which Cleopatra is present; there is a long discussion of the sources of the Nile with the Egyptian priest Achoreus. The Alexandrians attempt a rebellion against Caesar. At this point the poem breaks off abruptly.

Criticisms of the ancients

Ancient criticism, as evidenced by the scholiastic tradition and the judgments of grammarians (Servius) and rhetoricians (Quintilian, Fronto), repeatedly expressed set complaints about Lucan's poems: the use and abuse of elaborate *sententiae* (which made the style of the *Pharsalia* resemble that of oratory), the rejection of divine intervention, and an almost annalistic manner of narrative (which was more typical of historical works than poetic). All this amounted to a series of innovations in the epic genre that left room for disagreement.

We shall see later how the motives urging Lucan along this path involve more generally his attitude towards Roman epic tradition and its models. For now, let us confine ourselves to pointing out the difficulties in a precise evaluation of the objections raised by the ancient critics. The loss of the historiographic material upon which Lucan most probably relied—Livy's books on the civil wars and the *Histories* of Seneca the Elder—prevents us from testing whether he followed his sources slavishly or not. Scrupulous fidelity to his historical source was certainly sacrificed to distortions of the truth for ideological purposes, especially in regard to Pompey, Caesar, and their supporters. In such cases the alteration has to do with the manner of presenting or coloring some of the events recorded by the sources, but at other times Lucan inserts episodes that lie outside the true facts, such as the scene of necromancy in book 6 or Cicero's presence at Pharsalus in book 7. Lucan's innovative work received not only criticism but also great and immediate success, as we can see from the statements of Martial and Statius, not to mention the many echoes found in later epic poetry.

Lucan's distortions

2. LUCAN AND VIRGIL: THE DESTRUCTION OF THE AUGUSTAN MYTHS

The Pharsalia *as an anti-*Aeneid

The criticisms of Lucan mentioned presuppose, in the ancients as well as in the moderns, a more or less explicit comparison with Virgil's *Aeneid* that can also be misleading. It is not out of the question, for instance, that the annalistic manner that came in for criticism was a "defect" traditional in all historical epic of the late Republic and early Empire, and it is probable that the authority of Ennius's *Annals* also contributed to preserving such a narrative structure. Moreover, we know that already in the age of Augustus various poets had chosen the civil wars as a subject for epic (Cornelius Severus, Rabirius, the author of the *Bellum Actiacum*), though the few fragments preserved do not allow us to establish precise links with the *Pharsalia*. It is the case, in any event, that the *Pharsalia* itself urges the comparison with Virgil: the poem has rightly been described as a sort of anti-*Aeneid,* the author as an anti-Virgil.

The overthrow of the epic genre

In Lucan's hands the epic poem completely alters the features that had characterized it in the Roman literary tradition ever since the times of Naevius and Ennius. From a monument erected to the glories of the state and its armies the epic is transformed into an indignant denunciation of fratricidal war, of the subversion of all moral values, and of the arrival of the kingdom of injustice. This extremely problematic attempt to open the literary genre to radically new content is carried out through polemical confrontation with its own past. Essentially reflective, Lucan's poetry aims not so much at drawing the tradition into itself in order to reshape it as at projecting itself, as if by contrast, onto that background, a background in which the largest space is certainly occupied by Virgil's *Aeneid*. Lucan seems to propose a systematic refutation of the model by virtually over-turning its assertions, a polemical (or "antiphrastic," as it has been called) rehandling of Virgilian expressions and situations. This new type of allu-siveness is sustained by a tone of resentful *indignatio* towards the model. It is as if Virgil had perpetrated a deception in the *Aeneid,* covering in a veil of mystification the end of Roman liberty and the transformation of the old Republic into a tyranny. Lucan seems to set himself the task of unmasking the deception, of writing a poem that does not justify the power of the princeps by resorting to old religious fables but, on the contrary, shows how the imperial regime was born out of the ashes of the *libera res publica.*

The path Lucan chooses for disavowing Virgil is, first of all, to change the subject: he does not rework mythic tales, but sets forth, with substantial fidelity, a recent, well-documented, universally known story. This pro-grammatic choice of fidelity to the historical truth explains in large part the rejection of divine intervention that so scandalized ancient critics.

Nonetheless, it would be one-sided to see in Lucan only the heated oppo-nent of Virgil. His relation with his model is far more complex, probably because Virgil himself presented ambiguous and contradictory aspects. The Virgil who may have appeared to the young poet as the convinced and compromised singer of the optimism of Augustan ideology was the same one who in certain passages of the *Georgics* had lamented the horror of the civil wars; in the *Aeneid* itself, moreover, the credit given to the providen-tial nature of history goes along with commiseration felt for the innocent victims of fate (see pp. 283 f.). At the moments when he was deeply engaged in the cases of certain unfortunate persons, doubts about the good-ness of destiny surfaced in Virgil's verses too. But the bitterness of doubt was not enough for Lucan: from the first verses of the *Pharsalia* every illu-sion appears utterly shattered.

3. THE PRAISE OF NERO AND THE EVOLUTION OF LUCAN'S POETICS

It is quite likely that Lucan's pessimism ripened during the course of the poem's composition; in an initial phase, Lucan may have shared the hopes for political and social revival aroused by Nero's accession. The polemic against Virgil begins to appear in the verses immediately following the proem, where the allusions to Virgil seem to strike a pose of opposition. In Virgil's epic the historical theme of the civil wars shows itself here and there in the text, but it was projected into a mythic past, merely adum-brated in the distant conflict between Trojans and Latins (who were des-tined to fuse later into a single people). Lucan, by contrast, aims at bring-ing civil war before us in all its inescapable historical reality, presenting its awful consequences for later history. Furthermore, it seems possible to interpret Nero's appearance in the proem as a kind of compensation for the disasters provoked by the civil conflict. The praise of Nero picks up from

Virgil a whole series of motives relating to the glorification of the princeps. It obviously echoes the words with which Jupiter, in the first book of the *Aeneid* (291 ff.), Jupiter had prophesied to Venus the arrival of a new golden age after Augustus has ended the civil strife. The attribution of Augustan features to Nero is widespread in the literature of the day, in Calpurnius Siculus, for instance, and in the *Carmina Einsidlensia* (see p. 436). For Lucan, in any event, the new Augustus is far better than the first, and singing his praises implies entering into a veiled controversy with Virgil. Nero, not Augustus, the poet seems to be saying, is the true realization of the promises made by Virgil's Jupiter.

Lucan and Nero: Lucan's fundamental consistency

This interpretation presupposes that the praise of Nero is sincere, a view that is not shared by all modern scholars. Some ancient scholia had already seen in the exuberant *tumores* of the praise a sign of a kind of concealed irony towards the emperor. This interpretation has been repeatedly revived, by moderns too, but in our opinion it cannot be accepted. Greater plausibility is to be found in a second line of interpretation, which presupposes in Lucan an evolution that in certain regards is similar to Seneca's. The approach taken in the first three books of the poem (the only ones, according to Vacca's biography, that were published by the author) would present analogies with the approaches of Seneca's *De Clementia* and *Apocolocyntosis,* in which the conciliation of the principate and liberty is still considered possible with a return to Augustus's pro-senatorial policy. This does not mean that one should mark too sharp a break between a "first" and a "second" Lucan. Along the same lines, there are some who assert that in the course of composition the poet changed his judgment on Caesar and Pompey. According to this theory, Lucan starts from a position of neutrality but after book 3 begins openly to take the side of the latter and express his poisonous hatred towards Caesar. In fact, a relative change in his judgment on Pompey was implicit in the very structure of the *Pharsalia,* in which Pompey gradually moves towards the acquisition of wisdom, whereas the aversion towards Caesar is constant from the beginning of the poem to the end.

The praise of Nero and the progress of pessimism in Lucan

It remains true that within the *Pharsalia* the praise of Nero sounds a strident note. The contradiction between the radically pessimistic vision Lucan had been developing of the previous century of Roman history and the expectations aroused by the new emperor was embedded in the very plan of the poem. The split that was present from the start could only grow deeper—and actual events must have urged things in the same direction—with the result that Lucan was freed from the last traces of an already enfeebled notion of providence. Nero is not named again in the work.

4. LUCAN AND THE ANTI-MYTH OF ROME

The anti-myth of Rome: the inversion of Virgil's words

In the remainder of the poem Lucan's pessimism grows far more radical and comes closer to a consistent darkness of conception, a genuine anti-myth of Rome, the myth of its collapse, its inexorable decline, opposed to Virgil's myth of the rise of the City from humble beginnings. A paradigmatic example (which is also a paradigm of Lucan's "antiphrastic" technique of allusion) is found in *Pharsalia* 7.391–93:

> tunc omne Latinum
> fabula nomen erit: Gabios Veiosque Coramque
> pulvere vix tectae poterunt monstrare ruinae.

("Then the Latin name will be known only by hearsay: ruins covered in dust will scarcely be able to indicate Gabii, Veii, and Cora"). Lucan, contemplating the terrible blow Pharsalus inflicted on Rome, inverts the words in which Anchises had revealed to Aeneas the names of the first lands destined to fall to Roman domination:

> hi tibi Nomentum et Gabios urbemque Fidenam,
> hi Collatinas imponent montibus arces,
> Pometios, Castrumque Inui, Bolamque Coramque.
> haec tum nomina erunt, nunc sunt sine nomine terrae.

("These men will establish for you Nomentum and Gabii and the city of Fidenae, these will set upon the mountains the citadels of Collatia, Pometia, Castrum Inui, Bola, and Cora. These then will be illustrious names, now they are lands without name" [*Aeneid* 6.773–76]).

The prophecies of disasters

Like the *Aeneid,* the *Pharsalia* is structured around a series of prophecies that reveal, not the future glories of Rome, but the ruin that awaits it. The most important undoubtedly is the *nekyomanteia,* "necromancy," in book 6. In introducing the Underworld, Lucan reveals his obvious desire to create a kind of counterpart to the *katabasis,* "descent to the dead," of Aeneas. The placement of the episode in book 6, just as in Virgil's poem, is a likely indication of the central position Lucan intended to give it within the architecture of the poem and therefore an indication, too, of the projected size of the *Pharsalia:* twelve books, the same number as in Virgil's poem.

Lucan inverts his Virgilian model even in the smallest particulars. The soldier restored to life by the Thessalian sorceress tells of having seen the dead greatly agitated: the souls of Rome's heroes were in tears, lamenting the unhappy fate that awaits the city, while the spirits of the *populares* (among them Catiline), Caesar's political predecessors and the eternal enemies of the Roman state, were exulting. The choice of Sextus Pompey as recipient of the revelation is explained by, among other things, the fact that Lucan intended to link Pompey's family to the myth of Rome's ruin, as Virgil had linked the *gens Iulia* to the myth of its glorious rise. Moreover, Sextus Pompey, a degenerate and impious son, represents in many ways a reversal of pious Aeneas.

5. THE CHARACTERS OF THE POEM

Caesar, the dark hero

Unlike the *Aeneid,* the *Pharsalia* does not have a principal character, a true hero. The action of the poem, except for various minor figures, turns upon the personalities of Caesar, Pompey, and (especially in the last part)

Cato. Caesar for a long while dominates the scene with his malign greatness; often guided by an inspired idea of the moment, or even by his own temerity, he becomes the incarnation of the *furor* that a hostile Fortune unleashes against Rome's ancient power. In the ceaseless activity displayed by Caesar, the poem's dark hero, some have seen virtually a sign of Lucan's admiration. It is unquestionable that the poet here and there seems to succumb to the sinister charm of his character, who represents the triumph of those irrational forces that in the *Aeneid* had been curbed and defeated; *furor, ira, impatientia,* and a culpable desire to put oneself above the state are the passions that principally stir his soul. These features are typical of the representation of tyranny, which is found already in early Roman tragedy and then again in Seneca's drama. Ferocity and cruelty also join this set: violating historical truth, Lucan in the *Pharsalia* deprives Caesar of his principal attribute, clemency towards the defeated, as when he decides to leave the dead at Pharsalus unburied.

Pompey, the passive hero

From the start of the poem Caesar's frenetic energy is contrasted with the relative passivity of Pompey, a person in decline, affected by a kind of military and political senility. Such a characterization also serves, paradoxically, to limit Pompey's responsibility: Caesar's mad desire for power is chiefly responsible for the catastrophe that brings Rome to its ruin. Lucan aims at making Pompey a sort of Aeneas whom destiny opposes instead of favoring; he thus becomes a tragic figure, the only one who evolves psychologically during the course of the poem. The *Pharsalia* represents Pompey's fall from the greatest heights, as Fortune, once so favorable, turns against him with implacable hostility. In proportion as he loses political authority, Pompey withdraws into the private sphere of family affection (in contrast to Caesar's self-centered attitude); Lucan emphasizes Pompey's attachment to his children and especially to his wife. In the end, abandoned by Fortune, Pompey moves towards a kind of purification. He becomes aware of the wickedness of fate and understands that death in a just cause is the only path to moral redemption.

Cato, the new Stoic sage

This awareness, which for Pompey is the result of a long and painful process, is for Cato, by contrast, a firm possession from his first appearance in the poem. A justly famous lapidary verse defines the ideology of this character, which to a large extent reflects Lucan's own ideology: *victrix causa deis placuit, sed victa Catoni,* "the victorious cause had the support of the gods, but the vanquished had the support of Cato" (1.128). The philosophical background to the *Pharsalia* is unquestionably Stoic; but the traditional Stoicism, which assured the dominance of reason in the cosmos and of divine providence in history, comes to its end in the character of Cato. Once he is aware of the wickedness of a fate that is bent upon the destruction of Rome, it becomes impossible for Cato to give his voluntary allegiance to the will of destiny (or of the gods) in the way Stoicism expected. Thus there arises the idea that the criterion of justice is now to be sought somewhere other than in the heavenly will, that henceforth it resides exclusively in the conscience of the sage. In his Titan-like rebellion Cato makes himself equal to the gods. He no longer needs their advice to distinguish the just from the unjust. Since he no longer submits himself to the will of destiny, neither does the sage any longer maintain his traditional imperturbability before the realization of that will. Cato commits himself to the civil war in full consciousness of the defeat that awaits him and of the consequent necessity to take his own life, the only path left to him for continuing to affirm law and liberty.

The other characters   Around the three protagonists move a number of minor figures, whose characterization is shaped by their belonging to one or the other of the parties in the conflict. Thus many of the Pompeians and Catonians are presented as courageous, though unlucky, fighters. Among the others stands out Domitius Ahenobarbus, whom Lucan characterizes as a hero, which conflicts with the historical reality as we know it (it is still debated whether this distortion is intended to flatter Nero, who was a descendant of Ahenobarbus). Caesar's army, by contrast, is composed mostly of bloodthirsty monsters, who are tied to their leader by a psychological dependence and by eagerness for booty. Even when presenting individual acts of heroism, as in the case of Scaeva, the poet does not fail to emphasize the injustice of the cause for which they are fighting. Among the female characters Pompey's wife Cornelia stands out, the very portrait of absolute faithfulness and devotion to her husband, with whom she shares to the very last the blows of fate.

6. STYLE

Excess as stylistic principle   *Ardens et concitatus:* thus did Quintilian (10.1.90) describe Lucan, and he probably meant to refer, among other things, to the urgent narrative rhythm of the periods, which follow one another in unbridled haste and leave parts of the phrase overflowing the boundaries of the hexameter; the impassioned urgency of the thoughts is reflected in the continual enjambment, and the syntax of the words aims at escaping from the bonds of the hexameter while giving an unusual expressive tension to the verse. Because of its continuous drive towards pathos and sublimity, Lucan's style has many points of contact with the style of Seneca's tragedies. Some have called it "baroque" or "mannerist," the latter especially in connection with the taste for paradoxes and conceits, which is no less important in Lucan's style than the *tumores.* The poet's concern to avoid elision is also significant in this connection, as he sacrifices the fluidity of the verse to the sententiousness of the content. The poet's persona is nearly omnipresent, judging and often condemning in an indignant tone. Hence the extraordinary frequency of apostrophe in the *Pharsalia* and, in general, of the poet's personal interventions by way of comment upon the events he is narrating.

Crisis of values and crisis of the epic genre   The style is certainly one that hardly knows control and measure, and for this reason it can quickly sate the reader. But it is just as certainly a style that does not merely reflect the literary fashions of the day; nor does it aim solely at satisfying the taste of the declamation halls. The expressive tension of Lucan's epic is created by the enthusiasm and the passion with which the young poet experienced the crisis of his culture. Now that the entire world could no longer be what it had been before, could the representation of a catastrophe such as the civil war (Roman against Roman) still be based on a traditional form such as the epic genre offered? The epic tradition had constructed an entire complex language, capable of giving an attractive narrative form to the great cultural models on which Roman society was based. Tenacity, fairness, spiritual strength, resistance, willingness to sacrifice oneself, respect for divinity and justice, worship of the state and loyalty to its laws—these were some of the basic values that, when interpreted by the great structures of the epic-heroic language, were transformed into resonant poetic accounts in which the heroes who embodied those values in their deeds became true models of virtue. The grand, solemn style of these poems, which, significantly, used a language with archaic coloring, was the style that, in the hierarchy of literary genres, made epic the highest form of poetic expression. In the fiction of heroic epic the conscience and the pride of a people had found forms capable of transfiguring the events of their own past. The deeds preserved in the collective memory, or those experienced more recently, had become the strong points in an edifying account that could harmonize myth with history and join together the evocation of ancient magical beliefs with the "truth" of a state ideology put to the test in its actions, an account that proposed not only the contemplation of the religious and the superhuman but also the admiration of the achievements of exceptional men. But now that the course of events had betrayed that ideal world and discredited the literary forms that narrated it, epic could no longer deal with this task of celebrating the great heroic

The crisis within the epic genre

models. At the same time, it created new expectations in the public. Lucan does not have the strength to free himself from a literary form that he regards as inadequate for his needs. Rather than attempting to create epic language anew, he seeks a compensating remedy in the ideological ardor with which he denounces the crisis. Thus the presence of a political-moral ideology in him becomes obsessive. It invades his language; indeed, it becomes nothing more than language, since it is shouted, displayed. Championed in language (in *sententiae* constructed for effect or in coldly intellectual antitheses), it is reduced to rhetoric. But the rhetoric animating this language is not a sign of empty ornamental artifice but the gesture of a style that, paradoxically, in order to recover its authenticity, in order to be certain of not betraying with words the message of an ideology without hope, can no longer entrust itself to simple, direct expression, but of necessity speaks by having recourse to the emphatic schemata of rhetorical discourse. Thus it looks to rhetoric, to its laborious and calculated constructions, to compensate for the loss of credibility into which the simple forms of epic language have fallen.

7. LITERARY SUCCESS

Antiquity

When Lucan died, his epic was unfinished and only partially revised, but it went on to become one of the great successes of world literature. Two sets of ancient commentaries (though it is only starting with Servius that Lucan is cited by grammarians) and over four hundred manuscripts, distributed throughout Europe and including fragments of three ancient codices and five complete (and one fragmentary) ninth-century ones, testify to its enormous popularity in antiquity and the Middle Ages. Martial attests that the poem sold well during his time (14.194); Tacitus in his *Dialogus* associates Lucan with Horace and Virgil (20); Statius and Florus admired the *Bellum Civile* and exploited it. The stature of Lucan's epic is further suggested by the frequent literary polemics directed against it: Petronius's *Bellum Civile* has often been interpreted as a critical demonstration of how Lucan's material should have been handled by an epic poet; Quintilian tempered his praise for Lucan's heat, rapidity, and aphorisms with the personal advice that he be imitated less by poets than by orators; Fronto attacked Lucan's style, justly, as being repetitive and full of superfluities; and Servius, in his commentary on the *Aeneid*, dismissed Lucan as a writer not of poetry but of history.

Middle Ages   He was read through late antiquity, especially in the schools, and went on to become a central medieval school author. The Middle Ages revered him not only as an important source of Roman history, geography, and natural science and the master of rhetorical pathos and pointed epigrams but also as a repository of the secrets of witchcraft (as demonstrated by the episode of Erictho in book 6). Dante's admiration led him to place Lucan fourth and last among the "spiriti magni" after Homer, Horace, and Ovid (*Inferno* 4.90), to model his Cato upon Lucan's (*Purgatorio* 1.28–108), to cite Lucan in one passage in an explicit attempt to outdo him (*Inferno* 25.94–96), and to borrow his tragic style and horrific expressionism in many others. Chaucer placed him on top of an iron column in his *House of Fame,* a location of honor otherwise reserved only for Homer, Virgil, Ovid, and Statius. He was quoted by Geoffrey of Monmouth and John of Salisbury, among many others. He was a principal model of Gunther's *Ligurinus* (1187) and a main source of such medieval romances as the *Roman de Jules César* (which, however, gave special prominence to the love affair of Caesar and Cleopatra); as early as 1310 he had been translated into Italian. But sometimes his effect upon medieval readers could be devastating: Otloh of St. Emmeran reports that he became so fascinated by Lucan that he stole away from his monastery so as to read him outside the gates, whereupon a hot wind blasted his skin, he was terrified by a vision of a monster, and finally a giant in a dream beat him.

Renaissance   Lucan remained, together with Seneca, the teacher of the pathetic style until the seventeenth century. His constant effort to surpass expectation provoked poets not merely to imitate him but to try to surpass him in turn: *Lucano ipso lucanior* became a seventeenth-century cliché, sometimes in disparagement but sometimes in praise. In the fifteenth century, the humanist Pomponio Leto wrote a manuscript commentary on his poem, extending to verse 8.733. Such Renaissance epics as Petrarch's *Africa* and Tasso's *Gerusalemme liberata* are heavily indebted to him both for details of language and style and for larger aspects of tone and conception—though Tasso, too, in the theoretical context of his essay on the heroic poem, placed Lucan far below Virgil and termed him a historian rather than a poet. For Renaissance tragedy as well, his influence was the most important after Seneca's. His tragic epic provided material for plays on such themes as the death of Pompey (Corneille, *La Mort de Pompée*), the suffering of Cornelia (Robert Garnier, *Cornélie*), the martyrdom of Cato (Addison, *Cato*), and Caesar's affair with Cleopatra and his other exploits (Shakespeare, *Julius Caesar*). In the first half of the seventeenth century, his fame reached its peak, especially in England, where Christopher Marlowe translated book 1 (1600) and Thomas May translated the whole (1627) and wrote one continuation of the poem in English (1630) and another one in Latin in an imitation of Lucan's style (1640); curiously, this last was reprinted as late as 1728 in Oudendorp's scholarly edition of the *Bellum Civile*. At the same time, even Kepler worked intensively upon the chronological aspects of verses 1.639 ff. During this period, French and English commentaries and translations (by Thomas Farnaby in 1618, Thomas May in 1626, G. de Bréboeuf in 1655) often emphasized a political reading of the work of the writer whom Hugo Grotius called *poeta phileleutheros:* the epic was intended as a manual of political education; its readers would become better citizens. But such arguments could backfire. Louis XIV banned Lucan from the editions *ad usum Delphini* for fear that the Dauphin's mind might become poisoned by Lucan's love for freedom and hatred for kings. In general, Lucan's popularity declined during the course of the seventeenth century. Not only did his thirst for freedom become suspect in the age of political absolutism but his violent excessiveness provoked aversion among the proponents of the rational aesthetics of classicism. Julius Caesar Scaliger, in his *Poetics* (1561), was the first of many to reject Lucan as unnatural and irrational, and at the end of the sixteenth century he was banished from Jesuit schools.

Rediscovery by the Romantics

After a period of obscurity, however, he was rediscovered by the Romantics of the late eighteenth and early nineteenth centuries, and he was briefly fashionable as a prototypical poet of irrational genius. In England, Lucan was Shelley's favorite Latin poet. In Italy, he influenced Alfieri's libertarian and anti-tyrannical politics, left evident traces in Foscolo's *Sepolcri,* and helped shape Leopardi's sublime tones and anti-religious themes (especially *Bruto Minore*). And in Germany, Lucan's Erictho contributed mood and details to the *Walpurgisnacht* in Goethe's *Faust*. During the French Revolution, the sabers of the national guard of the First Republic bore an inscription from Lucan (4.579). But neither the politics nor the literary style of the nineteenth century was very congenial to him, and by the second quarter of the century, with rare exceptions (e.g., Macaulay), he had largely ceased to be a vital presence in world literature.

BIBLIOGRAPHY

Lucan was edited by A. E. Housman (ed. 2 Oxford 1927), and his text was the basis of the Loeb by J. D. Duff (Cambridge, Mass. 1928); there are more recent texts by G. Luck (Berlin 1988) and D. R. Shackleton Bailey (Stuttgart 1988). Useful English editions of individual books include those of R. J. Getty on book 1 (Cambridge 1955), V. Hunnink on book 3 (Amsterdam 1992), J. P. Postgate and O.A.W. Dilke on book 7 (Cambridge 1960), and R. Mayer on book 8 (Warminster 1981). In other languages note esp. the Dutch edition of book 2 by F.H.M. Van Campen (Amsterdam 1991), G. B. Conte, *Saggio di Commento a Lucano* (Pisa 1974, reprint Urbino 1988) on 6.118–260, and M. F. Schmidt, *Caesar und Cleopatra: Philologischer und historischer Kommentar zu Lucan. 10, 1–171* (Frankfurt am Main 1986). Detailed commentaries on the rest of the work remain desiderata.

A good general work in English is F. Ahl, *Lucan: An Introduction* (New York 1976); see also the briefer but stimulating works of M.P.O. Morford, *The Poet Lucan* (Oxford 1967), and esp. W. R. Johnson, *Momentary Monsters: Lucan and His Heroes* (Ithaca 1987), and J. Masters, *Poetry and Civil War in Lucan's Bellum Civile* (Cambridge 1992). M. Griffin, *Nero: The End of a Dynasty* (London 1984), is good on the historical context. Among works in other languages may be mentioned R. Pichon, *Les Sources de Lucain* (Paris 1912), H.-P. Syndikus, *Lucans Gedicht vom Bürgerkrieg* (Diss., Munich 1958), W. D. Lebek, *Lucans Pharsalia: Dichtungsstruktur und Zeitbezug* (Göttingen 1976), and E. Narducci, *La provvidenza crudele: Lucano e la distruzione dei miti augustei* (Pisa 1979). Fondation Hardt's *Entretiens* 15 (Geneva 1968) was devoted to Lucan (see esp. the piece by O. S. Due, "Lucain et la philosophie"); see also the bibliography and studies in *ANRW* 32.3 (Berlin 1985), the collection of essays by W. Rutz (Wege der Forschung 235, Darmstadt 1970), and the surveys by R. Haüssler in *Das historische Epos von Lucan bis Silius und seine Theorie* (Heidelberg 1978) and E. Burck and W. Rutz in *Das römische Epos,* ed. E. Burck (Darmstadt 1979).

From among the mass of articles in English, note esp. L. Thompson and R. T. Bruère, "Lucan's Use of Vergilian Reminiscence," *CPh* 63 (1968) 1–21, B. M. Marti, "Lucan's Narrative Techniques," *Latomus* 30 (1975) 74–90, C. Martindale, "Paradox, Hyperbole, and Literary Novelty in Lucan's De bello civili," *BICS* 23 (1976) 45–54, M. Lapidge, "Lucan's Imagery of Cosmic Dissolution," *Hermes* 107 (1979) 344–70, and J. Henderson, "Lucan / The Word at War," in *The Imperial Muse: To Juvenal through Ovid,* ed. A. J. Boyle (Bendigo 1988) 122–64. The chapter in D. C. Feeney, *The Gods in Epic* (Oxford 1991), again offers a good introduction to current criticism.

Petronius

If the author of the *Satyricon* is the person described by Tacitus in *Annals* 16.17 f. (as today seems highly probable, but see below), he is Titus Petronius Niger (the praenomen is disputed), consul around 62 and a suicide by command of Nero in A.D. 66. The cognomen Arbiter attested in the manuscript tradition of the *Satyricon* and in several indirect pieces of evidence should be linked to the description of him reported by Tacitus, *elegantiae arbiter,* even if the connection is disputed.

As a writer Petronius is named rarely, and by no one earlier than the third century. The identification with the courtier of Nero, however, has in its favor an unforgettable Tacitean portrait in book 16 of the *Annals* and several other mentions, especially Pliny, *Naturalis Historia* 37.20.

A long narrative fragment in prose, with parts in verse, the remains of a far longer narrative, probably titled *Satyrica* (according to others, *Satirica* or even *Saturae*). The title seems to combine two Grecisms: *satyri* ("the satyrs," figures from Greek myth and folklore) and the Greek derivative suffix *-icus (-ikos),* which also serves to form such titles as *Georgica* or *Aithiopica* (neuter plurals: "The Georgics," "The Ethiopics," i.e., something like "Poem of the Peasants" and "Stories of the Ethiopians"). According to others, the title derives from the Latin word *satura.* It should be noted, in any case, that the usual title *Satyricon* is inexact; it is a genitive plural neuter, dependent on *libri,* just as *Georgicon libri = Georgica =* "The Georgics." We will continue to use the form *Satyricon* solely for convenience.

The part we have covers (with some gaps, no doubt) parts of books 14 and 16 and all of book 15; it is likely that book 15 coincided in large part with the Feast of Trimalchio. We do not know how many books the novel comprised.

It is not certain that Petronius wrote other literary works. The *Anthologia Latina* (the large collection of poems by various authors or anonymous, made in the fifth or sixth century) preserves some poems and poetic fragments transmitted under Petronius's name; others have been attributed to Petronius by moderns on stylistic grounds. It is quite possible that some of this poetic material was originally included in the *Satyricon,* which, to judge from the parts we have, must have contained very many and varied poetic inserts.

The text had a complex and capricious fate. It was mutilated and anthologized in late antiquity and came to include real interpolations too. Of this version of the *Satyricon* a section—the famous episode known as the *Cena Trimalchionis,* the part of the novel that is most popular today—reappeared only in the seventeenth century, in a manuscript that was rediscovered in the Dalmatian town of Trogir (the *Codex Traguriensis*); other parts were already known to the Italian humanists from 1423.

Moralistic prejudices for a long time inhibited the spread of Petronius's work and in any case prevented it from being read in the schools. But the development of the European novel (especially during the fifteenth and sixteenth centuries, when the text that was known corresponded to the one we have today) was deeply influenced by this narrative of comic, satiric, and paradoxical adventures. Great modern artists such as Flaubert and James Joyce have clearly acknowledged their debt to this singular and impressive experiment of ancient narrative.

1. THE *SATYRICON*

Problems posed by the Satyricon

Few masterpieces of world literature are so shadowy as this: the author of the *Satyricon* is uncertain, as are the date of composition, the title and the meaning of the title, the original extent of the work, and its plot, not to mention less concrete but important matters such as the literary genre to which it belongs and the reasons why this work, which is unusual in so many regards, was conceived and published. The artistic greatness of the work—the sole feature that does not appear controversial—only heightens our curiosity. Still, not all aspects of the work are equally uncertain. For the problems of attribution and dating, as we will see in a moment, a fully satisfactory solution exists. In regard to other matters, we would do well to keep constantly in mind the extent to which our knowledge and the hypotheses we base upon it are limited and partial.

The Author and Dating

The portrait of Petronius in Tacitus

No ancient author tells us who was the mysterious Petronius Arbiter who, according to the manuscript tradition, was the author of the *Satyricon.* To judge from the indirect tradition of the *Satyricon,* which is slight, to be sure, the work must have been written before the end of the second century A.D., but we have nothing more precise.

Tacitus, however, who does not mention the *Satyricon,* does present us in book 16 of the *Annals* with a remarkable portrait of a courtier of Nero's by the name of Petronius, who was regarded by Nero as the judge par excellence of chic and refinement, his *elegantiae arbiter.* The identification of this Petronius of Tacitus with Petronius Arbiter the author of the *Satyricon* is accepted today by the great majority of critics, even though in actual fact it does not rest on any explicit identification.

The resonances between Tacitus's portrait and the *Satyricon* are unquestionably intriguing. Describing the circumstances of Petronius's death—the procedure is typical of the historian's brilliant narrative technique—Tacitus depicts a paradoxical, inimitable character. This Petronius had been a strong and effective wielder of power, but the quality that made him valuable to Nero was his refinement, his esthetic taste. Among the suggestions that come to mind—inevitably arbitrary, but always appealing—are certain figures of the European seventeenth century or of Decadentism: the courtesan, the dandy, the devotee of estheticism, the intellectual pleasure seeker. However that may be, this Petronius, driven to suicide by palace intrigues in 66, had one more surprise up his sleeve, a suicide that was as paradoxical as his life. This was no display of Stoic severity; on the contrary, his suicide seems to have been conceived as a parody of the theatrical suicide typical of certain opponents of the regime. Opening his veins and then deliberately delaying the moment of his end, Petronius passed his last hours at a banquet; he was busy with poetry, it seems, and did not hurl forth philosophical proclamations or political testaments. And yet, along with these indications of provocative mockery, he also wanted to show his own seriousness and responsibility: he was concerned for his slaves, and chose to denounce openly the emperor's crimes (in his testamentary letter the princeps' wicked and indecent deeds were listed and revealed). He then destroyed his signet ring, lest it be used in some act of counterfeiting or political intrigue.

Identification of the Tacitean character with the author of the Satyricon

It is clear that the portrait owes much to Tacitus's art, yet to many readers of the *Satyricon* the resemblances to the atmosphere of the novel have seemed too close to be coincidence. Open-mindedness, a sharp critical eye, disillusion, a sense of mystery, not to mention, of course, an aristocratic literary culture, are all qualities that the author of the *Satyricon* must have possessed to a high degree, just as Tacitus's Petronius did. This master of literary parody might very well have carried out his own death in the manner of a parody.

Fate of Tacitus's character

It is understandable that Tacitus's Petronius, Petronius the person, has enjoyed his own success, independent of that of the *Satyricon.* This model of the esthete appealed greatly to the leaders of European Decadentism, and the figure of Petronius in Sienkiewicz's *Quo Vadis?*—taken in a historically arbitrary way as the symbol of the moral crisis of the pagan aristocracy—has contributed greatly to the spread of this myth among the wider public.

Inferences from Tacitus's text

It is necessary to act with greater prudence when dealing with the inferences to be drawn for the interpretation of the *Satyricon.* We do not know whether Tacitus knew the novel directly; if he did know it, he may have taken it into account when painting his portrait of Petronius, and he was surely not obliged, in his austere historical work, to refer to so odd and outrageous a text. It has even been supposed that the testament in which Petronius attacked the shameful conduct of the court is meant as a reference to the *Satyricon,* but the hypothesis seems silly. A novel that, for all we know, might have been as long as *I Promessi Sposi* or even *War and Peace,* a text that in form and style has little to envy the great modern narratives, surely cannot be produced just like that, out of the desire to denounce others before killing oneself.

Petronius and the Neronian milieu

At the same time, it is legitimate to inquire about some of the aspects of the text we have, looking for points of contact with Nero's court. It has been thought that Petronius's taste for the life of the lowest social classes has some subtle relation to the emperor's tastes; the anti-Neronian historians attribute to Nero an intense, secret nocturnal life in which he frequents low drinking places and brothels and gets mixed up in brawls. Nero's poetic tastes have also been brought into the discussion and compared with some of the poetic insertions in the novel. It is possible, for instance, that the *Capture of Troy* sung by the poet Eumolpus is not unrelated to Nero's poem on the Trojan War. Certainly, if the author is Tacitus's Petronius, we could expect subtle references to the milieu of Nero's court. But the intent of this insert (satiric or polemic? or perhaps entertainment for the court?) continues to elude us, and in any case nothing authorizes us to see in this complex, imaginative work a *roman à clef,* whose characters are masks for historical personages.

The Satyricon *as a work of the Neronian age*

The linguistic vulgarisms

All internal indications of date, that is, ones derived from the very text of the novel, fit with a date no later than Nero's principate. The references to historical figures, the names of all the characters in the novel, the social background of the plot (economy, law, institutions, and general setting) are all compatible with this period of composition, and no indication implies a later date. The novel's style has given greater trouble to the critics. The language spoken by some minor figures of the novel—the freedman at the party in Trimalchio's house—is profoundly different from the literary Latin that is familiar to us. We have in this a valuable source of information on the popular, spoken language, which can be combined with instances of subliterary Latin, such as the graffiti of Pompeii and glosses (rare words, which, precisely because they are not literary, are mentioned by the grammarians and lexicographers of late antiquity), and also with those traces of the spoken language that can be recovered, often with difficulty, from poets such as Plautus and Catullus and from the less stylized prose writers. The language of the freedmen fits perfectly with the general picture of such evidence and is distinguished from the Latin that Petronius, through his narrator Encolpius, uses in the narrative portions of the novel. The contrast is deliberate and implies conscious artistry. It is evident that the vulgarisms are not the sign of a late date for the work, not even when certain terms and constructions seem to us unique and unparalleled. Putting it schematically, one may say that the vulgarisms indicate, not a historically late stratum of the language, but a low stratum, which lasts during a long historical period and is normally excluded by the selective literary language. To bring this low stratum into the spotlight is an artistic aim of Petronius, one guided by a precise literary program.

In summary, one can say that the novel must have been written in the Neronian period and may even be set in an earlier period. This much at least is certain, regardless of the identification of Petronius. The dating of the composition is still more exact if we accept that the *Bellum Civile,* Eumolpus's historical poem (see below), contains precise references to Lucan's *Pharsalia.* There are, however, delicate problems of chronology here: Lucan died only a year before Tacitus's Petronius, leaving his work unfinished, yet it is likely that at least the first part of the poem had already been in circulation for a while. The question cannot be called settled today, but it is clear in any event that the debate over historical poetry fits particularly well the literary climate of the Neronian age.

The Plot of the Novel

Fragmentary nature of the novel

As we briefly review the plot of the *Satyricon* we should keep in mind that the way the text we have took shape is quite problematic. We are certainly dealing with a fragment of narrative that is continuous in its broad outlines but must have been cut here and there, perhaps interpolated too, and transposed in sections. The most nearly integral passage is the famous episode of the Feast of Trimalchio; evidently it had a particular attraction for whoever handled the text of Petronius. The text we have was certainly preceded by a long section (narrated in fourteen books, if we rely on the indications in the manuscripts) and followed by a part the length of which we cannot fix with precision.

Summary of the Satyricon

The story is narrated in the first person by the protagonist Encolpius, the only character, apart from Giton, who appears in all the episodes of the novel. Encolpius experiences an awful series of mishaps. The rhythm of the story varies, too, sometimes terse and summary, sometimes (as in the banquet at Trimalchio's house) slow and full of realistic details.

At the beginning Encolpius, a young man of good education, comes into contact with a teacher of rhetoric, Agamemnon, and discusses with him the problem of the decline of oratory. The problem is similar to the one discussed in Tacitus's *Dialogus de Oratoribus,* but Agamemnon gives the impression of being a third-rate professor.

Encolpius, we learn, is traveling with another adventurer with a checkered past, Ascyltos, and with a handsome young man, Giton; among these characters a romantic triangle exists. A woman named Quartilla enters the story, involving the three in a rite honoring the god Priapus. This comic god, who symbolizes the masculine sex, seems to have an important role in all the stories told by Encolpius. The rites of Priapus furnish, more than anything else, a pretext for subjecting the three young men to Quartilla's lustful desires.

Barely escaped from Quartilla, the three are invited to a banquet in the house of Trimalchio, an extremely wealthy freedman of annoying crudeness. The course of the banquet is described in abundant detail; it is a theatrical display of riches and bad taste. The scene is dominated by Trimalchio's freedmen friends and their conversation. Encolpius here again is forced into a passive and subordinate role; only an accident puts an end to the dinner and sets our heroes free again. The homosexual rivalry between Encolpius and Ascyltos comes to a head; the two men, jealous of Giton's love, have a violent quarrel, and Ascyltos takes the boy away. Encolpius, upset, casually enters a picture gallery and meets a new character, who will have a central part in all his subsequent adventures. This is Eumolpus, an elderly, wandering poet who is insatiable both as a writer and as an adventurer. Eumolpus begins by showing off his poetic abilities, reciting a poem of his on the *Capture of Troy,* which is badly received by those present; in this Eumolpus recalls the failures of the ambitious rhetorician Agamemnon. After a swift series of mishaps Encolpius succeeds in recovering his Giton and in getting away from Ascyltos (who apparently disappears from the story); he does not succeed in getting away from Eumolpus, who shows a growing interest in Giton's charms. Thus a new romantic triangle is formed.

Up to this point the action has unfolded in a *Graeca urbs,* a coastal city of Campania. Its precise identification is controversial, and Petronius may not have had an exact place in mind. Encolpius, Eumolpus, and Giton hastily leave the city and embark incognito on a merchant ship. En route the master of the ship turns out to be Encolpius's worst enemy, a merchant named Lichas, who has some reason for wanting to avenge an earlier happening (which obviously was narrated in the earlier portion now lost to us). With Lichas is traveling a woman of dubious morality, Tryphaena, who is also known to Encolpius. An inept attempt to disguise themselves leads to catastrophic results; discovered, Encolpius is now liable to Lichas's revenge. Eumolpus attempts a reconciliation and, among other things, tries to divert the travelers by recounting the racy tale of the Matron of Ephesus. The situation, nonetheless, is not looking good, when a providential storm intervenes. The threatening Lichas is swept overboard, Tryphaena escapes on a boat, the ship sinks, and the three find themselves alone on the shore.

Thus begins a new adventure. Eumolpus discovers that they are near the city of Croton. This city, which had a glorious past, is now completely engaged in a deplorable pursuit: legacy hunting. The entire city is in the hands of the heirless rich and the legacy hunters, who load the rich with honors and favors in order to secure their inheritances. Eumolpus has an inspired plan: he will play the part of a wealthy, childless old man, assisted by Encolpius and Giton, who will play his slaves. On the road to Croton Eumolpus gives his companions a lecture on epic poetry and declaims a long poem on the war between Caesar and Pompey, the so-called *Bellum Civile.*

The last stage of the story is harder to follow because of the lacunose state of Petronius's text. At first Eumolpus's play-acting works, and the three live comfortably at the expense of the legacy hunters. Encolpius has an adventure with a woman named Circe, but he unexpectedly loses his sexual ability. Persecuted, as Encolpius himself claims, by the god Priapus, the protagonist submits to humiliating magical practices, without any success whatever; then, all of a sudden, he recovers his virility. At this point, however, Eumolpus's play-acting begins to fall apart; the people of Croton are on the verge of discovering the fraud.

In the last scene we have, Eumolpus tries a peculiar ploy. An absurd will, according to which whoever wants to enjoy Eumolpus's estate must eat his corpse (Eumolpus is ill or dead, or pretends to be; this detail is not clear), is read. The claimants, blinded with desire, are ready to become cannibals . . .

When our text resumes, we once again find the protagonist in a difficult situation, one created by his attempt to get free from an impending threat. We do not know how the adventure at Croton finished nor how much longer the novel went on; to imagine the work's ending is utterly impossible. None of the episodes we have gives a hint of what is to come, nor do we even know how Encolpius's picaresque life began. Furthermore, one may even ask to what extent the *Satyricon* was a novel according to our modern concept of this literary genre.

The Literary Genre: Menippean and Novel

The ancient novel, a nearly invisible genre

None of the modern terms that we use to designate a fictional narrative (short story, novel, etc.) has a classical tradition, nor does the ancient world have anything that corresponds to these terms. The ancients apply to these narrative works either very general terms, such as *historia* or *fabula,* or particular designations used without any strictness, such as *Milesia* (see below). We do not possess theoretical discussions of such texts; rhetoricians, philosophers, and literary critics are not concerned with them; and the titles, too, are generic and do not distinguish these from other types of narrative. We suspect that there was much reading of narratives, but few ancient writers are directly interested in them; some presumably are ashamed to admit to such frivolous reading.

The term "novel" as applied to the ancient world

Modern critics generally use the term "novel" for a restricted group of works, which fall into two very different categories: (*a*) two Latin texts, independent of one another and not very similar, the *Satyricon* of Petronius and the *Metamorphoses* of Apuleius; and (*b*) a series of Greek texts, written from the first century A.D. (Chariton) to the fourth (Heliodorus), the *Chaereas and Callirhoe* of Chariton, the *Leucippe and Clitophon* of Achilles Tatius, the *Ephesiaca* of Xenophon of Ephesus, the *Daphnis and Chloe* of Longus the Sophist, and the *Ethiopica* of Heliodorus. We have papyrus fragments of other, similar works or notices of them (summaries, quotations). The debate over the origins of this literary stream is still inconclusive.

Plot type of the Greek novel

Unlike the Roman novels, this series of Greek works is unified by a notable homogeneity and the persistence of distinctive traits. The plot is almost invariable, dealing with the difficulties encountered by a pair of lovers, a young man and a girl who are separated by troubles and endure a thousand adventures and perils before reuniting and achieving their love. The plots consist entirely of incidents that retard the happy outcome—confusions of identity, shipwrecks, the intrigues of rivals, feigned deaths, voyages to distant countries, and so forth. The tone is almost always serious, or at least the protagonists and their love are taken seriously and viewed as sufferers who arouse sympathy. The setting, however, is variable and may be anywhere in the Greek-speaking lands of the Mediterranean; the interest in contemporary reality is small, the historical setting slight. Love is treated with modesty, as a serious and exclusive passion. Much of the story's suspense lies in the heroic ways the heroine preserves her chastity for the young man she loves and how she escapes various traps set for her. This Greek novel could be called a narrative version of plots that are typical of Athenian New Comedy, that is, stories of love that meets with opposition. An important difference is that the setting is now enormously expanded, no longer a quiet middle-class corner of the city, but the open spaces of the sea and of exotic lands, the wide horizons of the Hellenistic world.

Love in the Satyricon: *the Greek anti-novel*

In Petronius's novel love is viewed quite differently. There is no room for chastity, and no character is a serious and believable vehicle of moral values. The protagonist is tossed around amid sexual mishaps of every sort, and his preferred partner is male; sex is treated explicitly and is viewed as a continual source of comic situations. It has even been thought that the *Satyricon* in its broad outlines is structured as a parody of the idealized Greek love romance. Thus, the homosexual relation between Encolpius and Giton, for instance, would be a parody, an ironic degradation, of the romantic love between the lovers in the Greek novel. This notion includes elements of truth—parody is fundamental to Petronius's poetics—and explains well many comic effects in the *Satyricon,* but it becomes rather forced if it is understood as exclusive. Among other things, though it is true that in the part we have Encolpius is always in Giton's company, this pair is not the sole focus of the story; moreover, the two are almost never separated, as would be the case in the typical narrative of the Greek novel.

The ancient short story: the nonidealized tradition

And yet serious narration is not the only narrative genre in which Petronius may have been working. Beginning no later than the first century B.C., great success is enjoyed by a literature of short stories, characterized by comic situations that are often racy and amoral. An important tradition is the one that the ancients frequently labeled as *fabula Milesia,* since it goes back to a Greek work of considerable popularity, the *Milesiaka* of Aristides (the title refers to the city of Miletus, in Asia Minor). Aristides' short stories were taken up at Rome by Sisenna (first century B.C., perhaps to be identified with the historian Sisenna [see p. 123]). More or less the same material had been brought on to the stage at the same time by the mime of the Romans.

We are certain that Petronius made ample use of this tradition of nonidealized narrative. A typical Milesian tale is the one recounted by Eumolpus (*Satyricon* 111–12): a matron of Ephesus, an inconsolable widow, yields to the desires of a soldier and, through a series of circumstances, ends up exposing her husband's corpse on the cross in order to save her lover. The typical themes of such short stories, which in style are rather like Boccaccio's, are antithetical to any idealization of reality: men are fools, women are disposed to yield. We must suppose that a large amount of this popular narrative writing, which embraced a certain variety of literary forms and subgenres, has been lost, both on account of its literary level, which made it unworthy of the attention of medieval scholars, Western and Byzantine, and, perhaps even more, on account of its immoral contents. Papyri from Egypt have restored to us some examples of comic narrative, and it is possible that not only short stories but also genuine novels belonged to this tradition. The *Satyricon* and Apuleius's *Metamorphoses* must have been far less isolated than they seem to us.

Literary complexity of the Satyricon

No classical narrative that we know of even remotely approaches the literary complexity of Petronius. The novel's plot, to begin with, is complex. The part we have is a loose succession of scenes, in varying tones, but these scenes are linked by a complex of narrative echoes. There are characters who appear and then reappear much later, such as Lichas and Tryphaena. There are typical situations that are repeated: settings and minor characters change, but Encolpius continues to be entrapped, humiliated, and forced into attempts at flight that, by the perversity of an implacable fate, land him in still worse situations.

The form of the novel: the alternation of prose and poetry

The form of the novel is still more complex. The prose narrative is quite often interrupted by inserts of poetry. Some of these verse passages are spoken by the characters, especially Eumolpus, who at inappropriate moments spews forth a torrent of poetry; this is the case with the *Capture of Troy* and the *Civil War,* to name the longest inserts. These inserts are motivated by and are addressed to an audience made up of the novel's characters. But

Poetic inserts and the intervention of the narrator

many other poetic passages represent interventions by the narrator, who in the middle of his story gives up relating events in order to comment upon them. These comments often have an ironic function, not because they are bad poetry (indeed, in them Petronius shows his extraordinary technical versatility as a poet), but rather because the poetic comment fails to correspond, either in style and literary level or in content and orientation, to the situation into which it is supposed to fit. The result of this is contrasts, sudden shifts between expectation and reality, between illusions fabricated out of fantasy (fantasy that is nourished in turn on culture and literature) and abrupt awakenings of a brutal vulgarity. When Encolpius compares a drunken, sinister sorceress to a character from Callimachus, or when, in Catullan verses, he sings of his joys as a lover just before he is betrayed by Giton, the reader finds an ironic counterpoint, at the expense of the narrator's naiveté.

The passive narrator

The passive, naive narrator, subjected to continual changes of fortune, is as characteristic of Petronius as of Apuleius's novel or the modern picaresque novel. It is a mode of constructing the account. But the continual free use of poetic inserts separates the *Satyricon* from the tradition of the novel and puts it closer, from a formal point of view, to other literary genres.

The Satyricon *and Menippean satire*

The free alternation of prose and verse is not a markedly common feature in the ancient narrative texts we know, such as, for example, Apuleius's novel. The closest point of reference is a Menippean satire, Seneca's *Apocolocyntosis.* The history of the genre is complicated. With reference to the Cynic philosopher Menippus of Gadara (second century B.C.), Varro had called his satiric writings "Menippean satires." From the fragments we have, this type of satire seems to have been an open vessel, varying greatly in the themes it accommodated and especially in its form. It must have included prose parts also, and Varro seems to have given much room to realism. To this tradition, in any event, clearly belongs the *Apocolocyntosis,* a prose text that admits varied poetic inserts, not only quotations from classical authors, which in the narrative context have the value of distorting or parodying the original, but also poetic parts specially composed, often pastiches themselves, reworkings of traditional poetic formulas. An interesting feature of this Menippean is the continual juxtaposition of serious and playful tones, of literary echoes and crude vulgarities. The whole is done with a sophisticated technique of composition that resembles that of Petronius.

Differences from Menippean satire

Some clear differences remain, however. The Senecan satire is a narrative of very brief compass and cannot be compared to the extended development of the *Satyricon.* It is, moreover, a libel, a personal attack conceived in a precise situation and directed against an explicit target, the deceased emperor Claudius. In Petronius, no such intent can be perceived, and beyond the individual parodies or distorted portraits (which involve Seneca, Virgil, Homer, rhetoric, occasional poetry, the *nouveaux riches,* parasites, and a thousand other figures of contemporary society, etc.), a unifying polemic purpose does not appear. Petronius may have looked to the Menippean tradition for many features of his work, for example, the mixture of styles, the prosimetron (i.e., the mixture of prose and verse), and perhaps even the narrative structured in blocks. But this literary tradition does not seem to have provided him with a ready-made formula for the *Satyricon.* Furthermore, that alternation of prose and verse that in the Menippean was only a formal resource becomes in Petronius a novel way of constructing the account: the poetic inserts often reveal to the reader the perspective from which the narrator Encolpius sees things.

The new use of the prosimetron

Realism and Parody

Models and originality: realism in the Satyricon

To summarize, the *Satyricon* is very indebted to narrative, both serious and comic, for the plot and structure of the story and somewhat indebted to the Menippean tradition for the formal texture (the prosimetron), yet in its complexity and richness of effects it transcends both traditions.

The most original feature of Petronius's poetics may be its strong charge of realism, which is evident especially in the Feast of Trimalchio, where it becomes even a linguistic phenomenon, but is also present elsewhere. The novel has its story to relate, the adventurous life of Encolpius, but in relating the story it pauses to describe places that are not viewed in the abstract and outside of time, as in much of the Greek novel. They are characteristic, central places of the Roman world—the rhetorical school, the mystery rites, the picture gallery, the banquet, the marketplace, the brothel, the temple. The author has a lively interest in the mentality of the various social classes and, at least in the section describing Trimalchio's feast, in their everyday language. Clearly, realism is found in many other types of Roman literature, in satire, mime, epigram, and sometimes comedy. Satire (Lucilius, Horace, Persius, and Juvenal) in fact provides us with a helpful contrast. The realism in satire generally attaches to quite precise social types—the parasite, the rich fool, the poetaster, the woman who makes a show of virtue—and these types are all seen through a moralizing lens. The satiric poet looks at them from the point of view of his ideal. There is continual moral commentary, even if it is often implicit, and the reader is

The Satyricon *and Latin satire*

always in a position to form his own judgment upon these realities. It makes little difference whether the tone is one of aggressive indignation (as in Juvenal) or pursuit of inner balance (as in Horace).

Petronius's amorality

Petronius, however, gives his readers no tool with which to judge. It could not be otherwise in a narrative carried on in the first person by a character who is completely immersed in that dissolute world. Even where Encolpius distances himself from the events and himself criticizes or ironizes, a positive ideology is never offered to the reader. The characters that announce the moral, moreover, are in no way superior to the others. The originality of Petronius's realism consists not so much in giving us fragments of daily life as in giving us a vision of reality that is critical in that it is without illusion; when it follows the path of satire it stops short of adopting the stance of protest, invective, and preaching.

Parody in Petronius

The novel thus is something less than full satire, but it is completely dominated by a drive to parody. We have already seen the large role played by the verse parts in creating ironic contrasts. The result of the contrasts is often twofold: the irony seems directed at times towards literature and the models it proposes (of convention, of rhetoric, even of nonsense), at times towards life and its delusions. Petronian parody is a way of seeing things that is charged with ambiguity; in some cases its ultimate meaning is elusive. Eumolpus presents his criticism of the historical poem and then exemplifies it by composing verses on the *Bellum Civile;* he explains, among other things, that epic poetry cannot dispense with divine apparatus. He seems to be criticizing Lucan's *Pharsalia,* which does violate the principles of the tradition by eliminating the Olympian deities. The *Bellum Civile* includes both imitations of Virgil, which fit Eumolpus's poetic approach, and allusions to Lucan. Yet it is difficult to translate all this into anything constructive. The *Bellum Civile* is overwhelmingly conventional poetry, and it is difficult to believe that Petronius intended it as a positive model; the poet Eumolpus, moreover, is a dreamily ambitious and frustrated outcast. The situation produces laughter, but no clear message emerges. It seems too simple to hold that his intention is to ridicule Lucan, or to exalt him.

Ironic use of the models: Odysseus and Encolpius

Subtle ironic effects are continually arising from the use of elevated literary models, which are not directly imitated in the poetic parts but form a kind of trail through the narrative parts. A clever maid quotes Virgil in order to convince her mistress to yield to a suitor. Encolpius, persecuted by Priapus, compares himself to Odysseus persecuted by Poseidon.

Echoes of grand epic are especially common, the allusions to the *Odyssey* being particularly numerous. The structure of the novel as a journey makes this preference quite natural, but some have also thought that the whole story of Encolpius is, in a way, conceived as a parody of the *Odyssey,* a down-at-heels *Odyssey.* The notion is appealing, and parody of Homer has an immense literary tradition (comedy, epigram, and even the *Priapea* go in for it heavily); it has even been thought that the whole genre of the novel goes back, more or less directly, to Homeric epic. And yet it seems risky to turn these allusions into a general key to interpretation. It is true that

Encolpius on several occasions seems to take into consideration the angered god Priapus; this makes him resemble the wandering hero Odysseus, who is persecuted by Poseidon and by Helios, the sun god. One suspects that Encolpius's misfortunes go back to an earlier incident, told in the part that preceded, a sacrilege, for instance, or a divine curse. But it is necessary to observe that Priapus's role in the fragment we have is sporadic, and the place of divine persecution is quite small in the plot of the *Odyssey.*

The game of parody

The most natural explanation is that the parody of Homer is part of the overall game of parody, an element in the variegated texture of Petronius's novel. If Priapus had a prominent role, it is easy to understand why: this comical god of rustic sex gives the right tone to the story, just as the noble Olympian divinities are the distinguishing sign of epic and mark its lofty level. We may recognize as a unifying feature of the work, then, the fact that Petronius has collected, reinterpreted, and parodied all the literary genres and cultural myths of his day (Homer and Virgil, tragedy, elegy, history, and philosophy), as well as popular literature (sentimental novels, short stories, mimes, declamations, and sensational tales of witches, magic, and werewolves). Petronius may be studied as a shrewd depicter of customs and also as the author of a kind of literary encyclopedia of imperial Rome. Nor is this encyclopedia surprising in a period that opens with Ovid's *Metamorphoses* and was to have, on the constructive, institutional side, its Pliny the Elder and its Quintilian.

Literary Success

Antiquity

The *Satyricon* left very few traces indeed in antiquity (Jerome, Sidonius Apollinaris, Macrobius, Joannes Lydus), and in late antiquity the text seems to have been willfully mutilated, excerpted, and interpolated. In the ninth century, the novel was known at Auxerre and Fleury, but for obvious reasons Petronius never became a medieval school author, and there are few signs, if any, of acquaintance with his work in the Middle Ages. It would not have required much bad luck for the *Satyricon* to have vanished forever.

Renaissance

The story of Petronius's partial rescue during the Renaissance is full of twists and ironies; Petronius himself would have enjoyed it. He was saved from oblivion by Poggio Bracciolini's discovery, in 1420 in Cologne, of a manuscript containing Carolingian excerpts written continuously. This version, which favored verse and dialogue over description and narration and attempted to suppress the novel's exuberant homosexuality, formed the basis of the *editio princeps,* published in Milan in 1482. It was not until the sixteenth century that scholars doubled the amount of text available, by discovering another family of manuscripts, likewise excerpts, but this time representing a different editorial decision, one in favor of narrative, no matter how sordid it might be. The first expanded edition, the *editio Tornaesiana,* was published in Lyon in 1575. The *Cena Trimalchionis* had been copied for Poggio in 1423 in Florence, but then vanished; it was not rediscovered until almost a century later, by Marino Statileo in Trogir in Dalmatia, and was not published until 1664. The first edition to contain all the fragments of the novel we currently possess was published in 1669. A few decades later, François Nodot tried to give fate a helping hand by forging a *Satyricon cum fragmentis Albae Graecae recuperatis* (Cologne 1691).

Modern period

By this time, however, the genuine remains of the original text had already become popular and influential. Novelists from the seventeenth century through Flaubert and Joyce learned techniques of characterization and humor from studying it. Even in translation (as in that of the eighteenth-century German novelist Wilhelm Heinse), Petronius's vitality, humor, erudition, and cynicism, not to mention his fascination with erotic matters, have long made him one of the most popular of all ancient authors (though his sexual license has made certain periods quite uncomfortable). And contemporary readers used to twentieth-century novels are likely to have fewer difficulties with the fragmentary and discontinuous character of his text than they should. Nor has his impact been limited to those who have read him. Leibniz reports in a letter about a theatrical performance of the *Cena Trimalchionis* at the court of Hanover in 1702. And in 1969 Federico Fellini made a colorful film based upon the novel, which outraged some classicists but certainly won Petronius many new admirers, who, having seen the movie, may have been surprised by what they then found when they read the book.

2. THE *PRIAPEA*

Priapus in Roman culture

The *Satyricon,* because of its theme, lends itself to comparison with the poems in the book of *Priapea.* This is a collection that has come down to us anonymously, about eighty poems of varying length and meter. The date is uncertain, but the second half of the first century A.D. is quite likely.

The poems are closely linked to one another, united by the figure of the god Priapus, who protects orchards and gardens with his unrestrained sexuality. He is a god connected to fertility, but in Roman culture he is no longer treated with serious respect; in folklore as well as literature he is associated with salacious jokes and obscene witticisms. The Priapean genre is thus a particular type of epigram, joking in tone and for the most part explicitly sexual in subject. The genre was practiced sporadically by famous writers—by Martial, by an author of the *Appendix Vergiliana* (see p. 433), and apparently also by Catullus, a poet very much in touch with folklore. Here instead we have a unified work, very probably owed to a single specialized author.

The pursuit of variety in the Priapea

Given the relative monotony of the subject, the author's virtuosity (the *Priapea* are notable for their technique) consists in producing a variety of effects by alternating his meters and turning the Priapean material to a variety of purposes. Thus we have dedication poems, satiric portraits, curses, and riddles, all written from the limited perspective of this rustic divinity. An outstanding piece in the collection is a Goliardic, very amusing recasting of the *Odyssey* in a pornographic mold (poem 68), which reminds one (though with a considerable difference in quality and extent) of certain parodic sallies in the *Satyricon.*

BIBLIOGRAPHY

The main critical edition of Petronius is that of K. Müller (ed. 3 Munich 1983, with German translation by W. Ehlers); the Loeb edition by M. Heseltine revised by E. H. Warmington (Cambridge, Mass. 1969) is usable but suffers from a number of misprints. For a commentary on the whole work, recourse must still be had to the Latin edition of P. Burmann (2 vols., Amsterdam 1743); on the *Cena* there is an English commentary by M. S. Smith (Oxford 1975), to be supplemented by the older editions of L. Friedländer (ed. 2 Leipzig 1906, German) and A. Maiuri (Naples 1945, Italian). There is a separate English commentary on the *Bellum Civile* by F. T. Baldwin (New York 1911); most of the other verse passages are treated (with the fragments) in E. Courtney, *The Poems of Petronius* (Atlanta 1991).

Most works on the ancient novel include discussion of Petronius; see esp. B. E. Perry, *The Ancient Romances* (Berkeley 1967) 186–210, P. G. Walsh, *The Roman Novel* (Cambridge 1970) 67–140, and T. Hägg, *The Novel in Antiquity* (Oxford 1983) 168–75. He also figures in some works on satire; see esp. M. Coffey, *Roman Satire* (ed. 2 Bristol 1989) 178–203. The two principal monographs in English on the *Satyricon* are J. P. Sullivan, *The Satyricon of Petronius* (London 1968), and N. W. Slater, *Reading Petronius* (Baltimore 1990); see also H. D. Rankin, *Petronius the Artist* (The Hague 1971), and B. Boyce, *The Language of the Freedmen in Petronius' Cena Trimalchionis* (Leiden 1991). On the questions of date and authenticity, see K.F.C. Rose, *The Date and Author of the Satyricon* (Leiden 1971); on the Greek background, P. J. Parsons, "A Greek *Satyricon?*" *BICS* 18 (1971) 53–68, R. Heinze, "Petron und der griechische Roman," in *Vom Geist des Römertums* (Darmstadt 1967) 417–39, and A. Barchiesi, in *Semiotica della novella latina* (Rome 1986) 219–36. Among other works may be mentioned E. Auerbach, *Mimesis* (Princeton 1953) 24–49, E. Courtney, "Parody and Literary Allusion in Menippean Satire," *Philologus* 106 (1962) 86–100, P. Veyne, "Le 'Je' dans le *Satyricon,*" *REL* 42 (1964) 301–24 (cf. R. Beck, "The Satyricon: Satire, Narration, and Antecedents," *MH* 39 [1982] 206–14, and F. Jones, "The Narrator and the Narrative of the *Satyricon,*" *Latomus* 46 [1987] 810–19), A. Cameron, "Myth and Meaning in Petronius: Some Modern Comparisons," *Latomus* 29 (1970) 397–425, J.H.D'Arms, *Commerce and Social Standing in Ancient Rome* (Cambridge, Mass. 1981) 97–120, J. P. Sullivan, *Literature and Politics in the Age of Nero* (Ithaca 1985) 153–79, and J. Adamietz, "Zum literarischen Charakter von Petrons Satyricon," *RhM* 130 (1987) 329–46. There is a bibliography by G. Schmeling and J. H. Stuckey (Leiden 1977); see also that by M. S. Smith in *ANRW* 32.3 (Berlin 1986) 1624–65, along with the articles in the same volume, and the survey of recent scholarship by S. J. Harrison in *JRS* for 1993. There is an annual *Petronian Society Newsletter.*

The most convenient edition of the *Priapea* is that of I. Cazzaniga in *Carmina Ludicra Romana* (Turin 1959). There is a text with English translation and notes (not always reliable) by W. H. Parker, *Poems for a Phallic God* (London 1988), which draws heavily on the major German study by V. Buchheit, *Studien zum Corpus Priapeorum* (Munich 1962).

Satire under the Principate: Persius and Juvenal

The satire of Persius and Juvenal: the change in audience

Even though their poetry is separated by about half a century (one writes under Nero, the other in the span of time from Nerva to Hadrian), Persius and Juvenal have important characteristics in common. Both declare their connection to the satiric poetry of Lucilius and Horace and therefore place themselves in that tradition; but programmatic purposes aside, this literary genre undergoes a marked transformation in their hands. The innovations are considerable in regard both to the form that satire now takes and to the audience for the work in society. The satires of Lucilius and Horace assumed as a likely audience the circle of their friends, whereas those of Persius and Juvenal, even though formally addressed to an individual, are actually directed to a general public of reader-listeners, before whom the poet plays the part of a censor of vice and morals. The form of the discourse is no longer the constructive conversation that, while examining human weaknesses, aimed at arousing laughter. From this there arose, especially in Horace's satire, a kind of complicity between author and listener that was the sign of a shared language, a successful communication. The author himself could figure in the text as implied audience for his own discourse, and the listener, now the poet's companion and partner in the satiric discourse, came close to becoming his active collaborator in developing a model of life. But now that the listener is denied any closeness to the poet and any possible identification with him, the satiric poet's discourse places itself on a different plane of communication, one that is detached and loftier. The courteous, confidential manner, the smile of self-irony, the indulgent understanding towards mankind's common foibles that characterized Horatian satire are replaced by invective, the unsparing denunciation that humbles and destroys its victim. The poet, while engaged in correcting men, appropriates those forms of stern moralism (the strictness of Cynic-Stoic philosophy) that Horatian satire had rejected, or rather mocked, as being one of the excesses to be guarded against. Along with this change in the role and position of the satiric poet, one notes in the poetry of Persius and Juvenal the clear signs of a new literary taste, of that anti-classical mannerism that arises in reaction to the classicism of the Augustan age and flourishes in the first century A.D. and later. But above all, the transforma-

The detachment of the poet from the listener

Invective

Satire and recitation

467

tion in the formal characteristics of post-Horatian satire is owed to the changed manner of its creation and reception. The satire of Persius and Juvenal is intended not for private reading but for oral performance, recitation in public, and it naturally aims at having a striking effect upon the audience. This purpose is directly served by the use of the showiest techniques of rhetoric.

I. PERSIUS

LIFE AND
EVIDENCE

Aules Persius Flaccus, about whose life we are informed by a *vita* thought to go back to Valerius Probus, the grammarian of the first century A.D. and the first commentator upon the poet, was born of a wealthy equestrian family in A.D. 34 at Volterra, in Etruria (a trace of his Etruscan origin remains in his praenomen, *Aules,* a compromise between Etruscan *Aule* and Latin *Aulus*). When he was six years old he lost his father. At the age of twelve or thirteen he was sent to Rome to be educated in the best grammatical and rhetorical schools, but the teacher who left a decisive mark on his life was a philosopher, the Stoic Annaeus Cornutus, who brought him into touch with the circles of the senatorial opposition to the regime. Persius met, among others, not only Caesius Bassus and Lucan, whose friend he became, but also Seneca and Thrasea Paetus, to whom he was tied by bonds of admiration and also kinship. (Thrasea Paetus, who fell victim to Nero in 66, wrote a life of Cato of Utica that was famous in antiquity and would serve as a model for Plutarch's life of Cato.) Persius's conversion to philosophy caused him to lead an austere, withdrawn life devoted to study and family affection. His life was also quite short, for he died in 62, not yet twenty-eight years old.

WORKS

Persius did not write much—*scriptitavit et raro et tarde,* his biographer says—and he published nothing during his lifetime. His friend Caesius Bassus saw to the publication of his works after they had been revised by Cornutus (to whom Persius upon his deathbed had also left his extensive library). Cornutus advised against publishing Persius's first poetic attempts (a tragedy *praetexta* of uncertain title, a book of travels, an elogium of the heroic Arria Maior, daughter-in-law of Thrasea Paetus) but did authorize the publication, after he had lightly retouched the last part, of the book of *Satires,* which was greeted with immediate success.

**Summary of the
Satires**

A prefatory poem (which according to some is an epilogue, since several manuscripts transmit it at the end of the collection), consisting of fourteen choliambics (i.e., scazons, or "limping" iambic trimeters, the meter of invective), polemicizes harshly against the literary fashions of the day. It is followed by six satiric poems in dactylic hexameters (669 verses altogether), the meter now traditional for this literary genre. Satire 1 illustrates the deplorable mannerisms of contemporary poetry (which tended equally towards affected neoteric frivolity and hollow epic-tragic pomposity) and the moral degeneration that accompanies it (shameless exhibitionism, vanity, and craving for success); the poet contrasts this with the disdainful protest of his own verses, which are addressed to free men. Satire 2 attacks the merely formal, hypocritical religiosity of those who do not know what honest feeling is and who ask the gods only to satisfy their own cupidity for money. The third is addressed to a young gentleman who is leading a slothful, dissipated life and urges him to follow the path of moral liberation by obeying the precepts of Stoic philosophy. Satire 4 shows the necessity of practicing the principle of *nosce te ipsum* for one who has ambitions for a political career and wants therefore to give moral commandments to others. The fifth, addressed to his teacher Cornutus, develops the theme of freedom according to Stoic doctrine, contrasting the commonest human vices with the freedom of the sage who frees himself from the passions and lets himself be guided by his own conscience. The sixth satire, finally, in form a letter addressed to his friend Caesius Bassus, deplores the vice of avarice and holds up as an alternative model the Stoic sage who uses his possessions with moderation.

Satire and Stoicism

Stoic moral tension and the satiric genre

For the young poet, animated by the strong moral tension that was fostered by Stoicism, the satiric genre was a virtually obligatory choice (the first verse of the first satire, which is believed to be derived from Lucilius, may be a sign of this). His polemical spirit and enthusiastic desire for truth found in satire their most suitable instrument for expressing sarcasm and invective, as well as moral exhortation. Persius several times, especially in the more evidently programmatic poems, returns to the reasons for his literary choices: in conformity with the moral-pedagogical conception of literature that was held by the Stoics, his poetry is inspired more than anything by an ethical need, the need to expose and combat corruption and vice, and for that reason it is polemically opposed to the literary fashions of the day. For the moralist Persius, contemporary poetry is ruined by a degeneration in taste that is also a sign of moral worthlessness. He does not hesitate therefore to polemically claim for himself the quality of *rusticitas* (this would appear to be the meaning of the controversial term *semipaganus,* with which Persius describes himself in the opening choliambics). This means opposing the fatuous affectation and the inane mythological subjects of the fashionable poetry and taking upon himself with pride the task of violently assaulting people's consciences in order to try and redeem them. A real need therefore lies at the base of both his literary and his philosophical activity, which is represented as a drastic operation of moral surgery. *Radere, defigere, revellere,* terms recurring in his poetry, which denote the individual actions of this severe therapy, point to the process of demystifying reality, the removal of the scab of deceptive appearances that is necessary for a radical renewal of the conscience.

Morality and literary polemic

The vocabulary of the body

In describing the multiple forms in which vice and corruption manifest themselves, Persius often has recourse to a particular lexical field, that of the body and sex, where he has at his disposal a wealth of metaphors. The obsessive image of the belly becomes the center about which man's existence turns and the very symbol of his degradation (the likeness between moral fault and bodily illness was a common assumption of Stoic philosophy and its therapy of the passions). In just this area Persius gives us some of his most famous pictures, in which he shows to best effect that taste for the macabre distortion of reality that is typical of the moralists's hallucinatory vision—the bald poet with the upset stomach in the first satire (56 f.), for instance, or the wealthy young man of the third satire, brutalized by sleep and revelry (3–4, 32–34, 58–59), or the depraved pleasure-seeker stretched out in the sun (4.33–41), or, most notable, the intensely expressionistic picture of the glutton dying in his bath amid the stench emanating from his own body (3.98 ff.).

The phenomenology of vice

In denouncing vice and harshly describing its manifestations, Persius links himself to the tradition of satire and diatribe (this explains his tendency to portray unchanging types and the impression thereby created of an almost academic quality). But he heightens its tones, moving them towards a macabre baroqueness that would reach its culmination in Juvenal. The phenomenology of vice becomes the most prominent aspect in Persius's satire, relegating to the margins the positive stage in the process of moral liberation; in comparison with the description of the negative aspects of reality, there are few directions on how to *recte vivere,* on the principles by which to shape one's existence. The precepts set forth—every satire is focused on a specific ethical theme—originate in Stoic doctrine and its theory of virtue. The sage sees the conduct of his life within the framework of a cosmic order that is assured by God, and he finds in it the ultimate end to which natural law has destined him. Persius's Stoicism does not openly take on the characteristics of political engagement; rather, it tends towards an inner concentration that is the condition required for worshiping virtue and is similar to the withdrawn existence and the tranquil freedom from disturbance of the Epicureans.

The private dimension of Persius's Stoicism

From Satire to Examination of Conscience

The interrogation of Augustan models

But more than anything, Persius's book of *Satires* offers the historian of literature the rare opportunity for an important examination. It is necessary, however, to abandon the esthetic prejudice that would diminish the literary intentions of the work, reducing them almost solely to an exuberant exercise in philosophical morality, and to recognize behind the clear intertextual echoes that animate the work the real presence of exemplary models and authors, voices that are different and far removed from the Roman literary tradition and that are summoned to dialogue and contrast with one another. In this view the *Satires* may appear like a rich pool into which many sources have flowed, or like a body of harmonic resonances in which one can still recognize notes that had been dominant in the Augustan poetic programs. The first presence, constant and uniform, is the Horatian *sermo,* a form of discourse that had been able to adapt itself to satiric purpose as well as to epistolary thought.

But questions of more general bearing prove to be involved in the thorough understanding of the work. In part because of Lucretius, Augustan literature had attached importance to educational ambitions, to pragmatic applications (if we do not wish to say "didactic," a term that defines a precise tradition); that is to say, beyond the forms that belong to the didactic genre, the poet sought an intense contact with the recipient, whom he provoked and involved, and for whom he proposed choices and values. Persius takes up this Lucretian model and develops it into its opposite; he practically turns Lucretius into an anti-model. And thus the traces of the Epicurean concept of a didactic relation on which to base literature find in the *Satires* of Persius their point-by-point liquidation.

Lucretius, Horace, and the model of the poet-teacher

It was Horace who, especially in his *Epistles,* had been the medium of introducing Lucretian attitudes and applications into Augustan classicism (see p. 313). Literary writing had then acquired the substance of a protreptic discourse, of a continually repeated exhortation to wisdom. Those texts had chosen to seek and to invoke, insistently, the cooperation of the reader-pupil. The poet had assigned to the imagined recipient the part of a friend whom the poet-teacher was striving to accompany along the path towards his own truth, towards the lofty and serene garden of the sages (the *angulus* of the *Epistles,* the *templa edita sapientium* of Lucretius's poem), from which he might contemplate without acrimony the surrounding desolation of the nonphilosophers. In this regard Horatian satire, to which Persius is indebted for many verses, proposed various alternatives. One of its characteristic features, in fact, is that it teaches but also travels with the friend it addresses along a common path towards the proposed objective. It is a gesture of association, a maieutic procedure, a gradual conquest, in which mutual understanding and indulgence are the basis of the relationship.

This is the model established in the tradition. Persius's poetic *liber* is like a meditation upon it and also an act of apostasy from it. Radically transforming what had been the cordial figure of the author-philosopher reaching out amicably towards the reader, Persius's *Satires* describe the journey of a perennially unheard teacher, a teacher destined never to find satisfaction and obedience. Although some of the scenic backdrops are changed from one text to another, the functional types remain opposed— the author-teacher, the mass of the *stulti* (who mock him, however), and the young recipient (who does not allow himself to become a pupil, however). Deprived a priori of any apostolic effectiveness, the didactic discourse in Persius does not permit itself any expectations of success, statutorily denies itself the possibility of a positive response from the recipient, and in the end sinks into that angry monotony that inevitably has an unfavorable effect on modern readers. The tranquil good humor of Horace's *sermo* is replaced by a consciously harsh and aggressive attitude, which is necessary in order to overcome the indifference of the *miseri* who are prey to vice, an attitude that does not scruple to display that rustic rudeness from which Horace's urbane cordiality had always fled.

An unsuccessful teacher

The monologue of the examination of conscience

Yet precisely from this, from the loss of a recipient who is receptive to teaching, an advantage accrues to the work, or rather to the work's form of discourse. Once contact is weakened with the other pole of the communication (the one who should receive the message), space is won for a literature of interiority, for the confessional monologue; and this, too, is in part derived from Horace. In the "useless" teaching that is developed by the

Satires, then, one glimpses the scheme of a personal itinerary towards philosophy. The code of the examination of conscience is the cultural code (pre-Senecan) that seals the entire book. Thus the one who uses the voice and the function of a teacher in the text will reveal, if observed attentively, the features of a young person not yet free from difficulty, who perceives in his various pupils his own disease, which needs to be treated. In the end he comes all alone to the Elysian Fields of his philosophy and the Stoics who were his inspiration, a metaphorical destination that, in a significant coincidence, repeats the connotations of the *angulus* of which Horace had spoken in the *Epistles:*

> Hic ego securus volgi, et quid praeparet Auster
> infelix pecori, securus et angulus ille
> vicini nostri quia pinguior.

("Here I live, not worried about the mob or what the unfortunate south wind has in store for my flock, not worried because the field of my neighbor is more fertile" [*Satires* 6.12–14]).

The Harshness of the Style

The means of preaching: obscurity and harsh language

This aim of salutarily assaulting the reader, of shaking him up and showing him the crude reality of things, is chiefly responsible for the main characteristic of Persius's style, his well-known obscurity. This obscurity is in line with a tendency to conceal the train of thought behind a series of pictures that apparently are juxtaposed without there being inner connection between them, a technique originating in diatribe that some have compared to surrealism. The real need that, as was said, animates his verses (and that is innate in the satiric genre) leads him to choose ordinary, common language (*verba togae* [5.14]) and to reject rhetorical embellishments (*tectae pictoria linguae* [5.25]) that are the instrument of general mystification. A harsh language, polemically avoiding the refinements of smoothly exotic or fashionably archaic language and open instead to the brusque forcefulness of vulgarism, would prove to be the best means for expressing

The iunctura acris

authentic feelings and the natural reality of things. For this purpose, since style is the faithful mirror of reality and does not betray its unpleasant ugliness, where Horace had recommended the careful choice of the *callida iunctura,* Persius regularly has recourse to the technique of the *iunctura acris,* of the collocation that provokes by its harshness (*lapidosa cheragra; noctem . . . purgas; avias . . . revello; murmura . . . secum et rabiosa silentia rodunt*), a harshness that can be either of sound or, more often, of sense (as in the frequent oxymorons that convey a surprising, hidden truth: these have a distancing effect analogous to that secured by the *aprosdoketon,* "the unexpected element," which surprises the reader and frustrates his expectations).

The distortion of ordinary language

Thus the language is ordinary, but the style undertakes to distort it and compel it to express a truth that is not banal, to shed light on new aspects of reality, to establish unexpected relations between things (sometimes with truly cryptic results, e.g., *puteal . . . flagellas* [4.49], *salivam Mercurialem* [5.112]). Another typical technique of Persius's moves in the same direction: the very bold employment of metaphor, which is useful for exploring new relations between things and capable of effects of extraordinary density and expressive power (*pallentis radere mores; de gente hircosa centurionum*).

The esthetics of obscurity

It is evident that a gap tends to open up between the need for a natural language and the pursuit of bold, innovative expression and that the asserted desire for clarity is subverted in the end by the obscurity of the artificial style, that is, by the implicit Callimacheanism that Persius himself inherited from his *auctor* Horace and scrupulously professes (in this way he fatally restricted his audience to that public of literary refinement that can decipher its secrets). Nonetheless, the proverbial difficulty of Persius's style is not, as has long been believed, the gratuitous habit of a stilted, academic poet; nor is it the harsh, striking expression of the strict Stoicism on which his satires are based. Instead, it derives from his desire to serve the esthetic and, especially, the ethical drives of his poetry. The risk of obscurity is the price to be paid for an art that is capable of blinding flashes.

Literary Success

Antiquity

Persius's satires achieved immediate success both among poets (during a recitation Lucan is said to have become so excited that he exclaimed that Persius's works were true poetry, his own merely trivialities) and with a wider readership. The popularity and the difficulty of his poetry are indicated by the fact that shortly after their publication his satires had already received a learned commentary from Valerius Probus; many others followed in late antiquity, when his works were the object of intense philological activity. Quintilian (*Inst. orat.* 10.1.94) and Martial (4.29.7) attest to his continuing popularity, which, if anything, increased in late antiquity both among pagan poets and among church fathers such as Tertullian, Lactantius, Jerome, and Augustine, who appreciated his commitment to an austere morality.

Middle Ages and Renaissance

The many surviving medieval manuscripts and his frequent appearance in medieval library catalogues from the eighth through the twelfth century prove that he remained popular in the Middle Ages, when he became a school author and was venerated as an intransigent moralist. His works provided edifying quotations for such authors as Hrabanus Maurus, Bishop Rather of Verona (the all too eager rediscoverer of Catullus), Gunzo of Novara, and John of Salisbury. It was only during the later Renaissance that his occasionally arid and obscure style began to cost him readers; twenty-one editions of his works appeared before 1500. With the end of the Middle Ages Persius ceased to be read as a universally wise poet. And even when he was interpreted philosophically, as in Politian's lectures, he came to be seen increasingly within the limits of the genre of satiric poetry; but even here, among Roman satirists he came to be overshadowed by the more accessible Horace and Juvenal. Yet where these were read he was never entirely neglected, as, for example, in neo-classical England and during the Enlightenment. It is not surprising that he was one of Kant's favorite authors; but it is somewhat odder to find Goethe praising him for having concealed bitter discontent in Sibylline gnomes and expressed his despair in somber hexameters. Whether the obscurity and intellectualism of some contemporary poetic modes will win him many new readers may be doubted.

2. JUVENAL

LIFE AND
EVIDENCE

On Juvenal's life the information we have is scarce and unreliable, derived from the rare autobiographical references in his satires and from some epigrams addressed to him by his friend Martial. The many extant *vitae,* the most ancient of which goes back to the fourth century, are of little worth. Decimus Junius Juvenal was probably born at Aquinum, in southern Latium, between A.D. 50 and 60 (though some put his birth in 67). His family must have been prosperous, since he had a good rhetorical education, though he showed little interest in philosophy. He seems to have practiced law, but without earning the rewards he expected, and to have devoted himself to the declamations then in vogue. He probably came to write poetry at a mature age, after the death of Domitian (96), and he continued to compose into the reign of Hadrian. Like his oldest friend Martial, he lived in the shadow of the great, in the difficult position of a client, a man without economic independence. We know nothing of his death, which was certainly later than A.D. 127, the latest chronological reference in his verses. The ancient tradition that says he left Rome for Egypt, where he was sent at the age of eighty (so the story goes), under pretext of a military command, on account of certain verses that gave offense to a favorite of the emperor, is scarcely reliable.

WORKS

His poetic works consist of sixteen satires, in hexameters, subdivided into five books perhaps by the author himself (book 1: satires 1–5; book 2: 6; book 3: 7–9; book 4: 10–12; book 5: 13–16, a total of 3,869 verses); a fragment of 36 verses, regarded by most as authentic and belonging to the sixth satire, was discovered in 1899. The very few chronological indications there are lie between A.D. 100 and 127, and the publication of the satires, or at least their composition, must take place during this period.

**Summary of the
Satires**

In satire 1, which is prefatory and programmatic, Juvenal polemicizes against the fashionable declamations and their fatuousness and declares his disgust at the widespread moral corruption that compels him to become a satiric poet (*difficile est saturam non scribere* [v. 30]). But in order not to bring hatred and revenge upon himself, he will not attack the present generation, only past ones. Satire 2 attacks the hypocrisy of those who cloak the foulest vice beneath the appearance of virtue; the poet's principal target is homosexuality. The third describes the poet's old friend Umbricius's abandoning Rome, the chaotic metropolis where life has become dangerous for honest men. In the fourth satire he tells of the council called by Domitian to deliberate upon a grave question: how to cook the gigantic turbot presented to the emperor as a gift. Satire 5 describes the dinner given by the rich Virro and the humiliating situation of the clients invited. The sixth and longest satire is the famous tirade against the immorality and the vices of women. Satire 7 deplores the general decline in study and the wretched condition in which the writers of the day are forced to live; by contrast, it pines for the patronage that nourished Augustan literature. Satire 8 contrasts the false nobility of birth with the true nobility that derives from talent and feeling. The ninth recounts, in the form of a dialogue, the protests of Naevolus, a homosexual ill-rewarded for his difficult services. Satire 10 focuses on the folly of human desires. In satire 11 the poet contrasts the ostentatious luxury of rich men's banquets with the modest dinner offered him by a friend. In 12 he attacks legacy hunters; in 13, cheats and swindlers. In 14 Juvenal discusses the upbringing of children and the need to accompany precept with example. Satire 15 describes an episode of cannibalism that took place in Egypt (which the poet claims to know [v. 45]) and was provoked by religious fanaticism. The last satire, which is incomplete, lists the advantages offered by the military life.

Indignant Satire

The poetics of indignatio

The literature of the day, with its foolish delight in hackneyed mythological stories, is, according to Juvenal, absurdly far removed from the corrupt moral climate and the deep degradation of Roman society at the end of the first century and in the first decades of the second, the very years that to others seemed to herald a new glorious era following the grim period of Domitian. In the face of the unhalting spread of vice (*quando uberior vitiorum copia?* [1.87]), indignation will be the poet's muse (*si natura negat, facit indignatio versum* [1.79]), and satire will be the required genre, the kind of poetry most suitable for conveying the fury of his disgust. Juvenal thus, in the first satire, announces the reasons behind his poetics and the central place occupied by *indignatio,* marking thereby a perceptible departure from the Latin satiric tradition. Unlike Horace and even Persius, who, though fascinated by the representation of vice, did not refuse to propose a remedy (one based upon stern philosophical precepts), Juvenal does not believe that his poetry can influence the behavior of men, whom he regards as irremediably prey to corruption. His satire will limit itself to denouncing, to shouting out his rancorous protest, without cherishing any illusions of redemption.

The rejection of Roman moral thought

Juvenal refuses to conform, in other words, to the earlier rationalistic and reflective tradition of satire, but his rejection of that tradition is more general: it attacks the very forms of moral reasoning and judgment, the categories and structures of Roman moral thought. This last, as is well known, takes shape when a large number of topoi from Cynic-Stoic diatribe are adapted to Roman society, and it shapes in turn, in the most varied ways, Roman thinking about problems of personal ethics and social morality, providing it with structures of thought and types of solution. Juvenal rejects precisely the answers that are given by moral diatribe, by that morality that teaches men to remain indifferent to the world of concrete, external things, to regard them with irony and detachment, and to cherish instead inner goods, to strive for the *apatheia* and *autarkeia* of the sage, which are the goals of a superior nobility of the spirit. Juvenal rejects and demystifies this consoling morality with the disdain of a man who is offended at seeing vice and wrongdoing rewarded and with the rancor of a social outcast, one who sees himself as excluded from the benefits that society confers on the corrupt and forced into the humiliating position of the client.

The invective of the outcast

Rancor towards society, hidden resentment at not belonging to it, is an important element in the indignant satire of Juvenal, who represents the Italian middle class that in the daily life of the Empire's cosmopolitan capital witnessed the constant subversion of the moral and political values of the national, republican tradition. Lacking an ethical-political awareness that could explain this turbulent development, the variety and mutability of the social picture, Juvenal looks upon this confused spectacle (which relegates him to the edges of the scene) as a tragedy performed in grotesque masks, and he does not have even the bitter satisfaction of invective. In the moralist's distorted view, Roman society appears irremediably perverted, and the roles of the several classes overturned, beginning with the nobility, which has unworthily abdicated its rightful functions (e.g.,protecting and promoting culture, as under the great patronage of the Augustan age) and

Aggressive fury against all

which brutalizes itself in carousal and lust. His aggressive fury spares no one, and it grows especially heated against the figures who best symbolize the society and the manners of the swarming metropolis—the vulgar arrogance of the nouveaux riches, the excessive power of the freedmen, the cunning boldness of the Orientals, the moral degradation of the starveling

Misogyny

writers. Women, both free and emancipated, are a special target. By their easy movement in society they personify for the poet the destruction of modesty; they inspire him to write the sixth satire, one of the most ferocious misogynistic documents of all time, in which the dark grandeur of Messalina, the imperial prostitute, stands out especially.

Apparent democratism

This radical aversion to his own day and the rabid protests he registers against injustice and against the oppression and misery in which the humble and the outcast live have led some to speak of a democratic attitude on the part of Juvenal. This is a mistaken view, however; apart from some occasional expressions of solidarity with the poor and the helpless, his attitude towards the crowd, towards the uncouth and unlettered, towards whoever engages in commerce or manual labor, is one of deep and inalterable scorn. His intellectual pride and nationalistic resentment of flattering, intriguing Greeks and Orientals (whose competition harms Roman *clientes*) permit him to claim for himself, at most, affluence and social recognition but leave him far from harboring any aspirations to social solidarity.

Sterile idealization of the past

Instead, injured and rejected by a society that destroys and scorns his values, Juvenal tends to idealize nostalgically the past, the good old days dominated by a sound farmer morality and polemically contrasted with the corrupt citizenry of the present, a society not debased by Orientals, ex-slaves, and businessmen. This flight from the present, this archaizing utopia (a topical motif in Roman moral thought), seems the only possible outcome of Juvenal's *indignatio* and amounts to an implicit admission of his frustrated powerlessness.

The later Juvenal and the return to diatribe

A marked change of tone is observable in the second part of Juvenal's work, that is, in the last two books, in which the poet expressly renounces violent *indignatio* and assumes a more detached attitude, which aims at the *apatheia* of the Stoics. In this he is returning to that diatribe tradition of satire from which he has drastically departed. His view thus widens into a more general observation and allows itself the time to take a more tranquil view, one that is resigned in the face of the world's incurable corruption. And yet upon this facade of impassability cracks open here and there, showing the old fury, and the undying rage sometimes breaks out again. Not even the remedy of philosophic indifference succeeds in calming his wounded and frustrated mind.

The Sublime Satiric Style

Indignatio *and loftiness of tone*

Whereas in the earlier tradition the fact that satire had ordinary reality as its subject led it to adopt a humble stylistic level, a familiar and unpretentious tone (*sermo,* in fact), now, when this reality has become unusual and vice has peopled it with *monstra,* satire must match it with grandiosity. It therefore no longer adopts a lowly style, but one like that of the genres traditionally contrasted with satire, epic and especially tragedy. Satire would lack an essential feature of these genres, their fictionality (which Juvenal several times polemically rejects), because it would remain realistic, but it would have their loftiness of tone, that grandeur of style that would correspond to the violence of his *indignatio.*

"Tragic" satire

Juvenal thus transforms profoundly the formal principles of the satiric genre, breaking the traditional link with comedy (i.e., dispensing with the *ridiculum*) and bringing satire near to tragedy, on the level of content (the *monstra*) and style, which is similarly "sublime." A familiar technique in Juvenal is the employment of epic-tragic language precisely in connection with the coarsest, most vulgar content; his purpose is to bring out the lowness of the material by contrasting it with the loftiness of the form of expression. His realism, which richly documents for us the habits and usages of daily life at the time, strongly tends to distortion, of course, because he is dealing with figures and scenes of such coarseness that the indignant moralist's biliousness vents itself on them.

Rhetorical training and ideological authenticity in Juvenal

His expression, which is always prone to explode in hyperbole and in which courtly and plebeian tones and lofty and obscene words clash, with intentionally striking effect, is visual and pregnant, dense and sententious (many of Juvenal's verses have become proverbial). In his declamatory emphasis, in this tone which is always ready for denunciation and invective (and which rarely relaxes into reflection or laughter), in the fixity of the targets he attacks and in the repetition of the moralizing topoi, some have perceived the influences of the rhetorical schools and of the declamations that Juvenal had long practiced, and his poetry has always been burdened with this accusation of academicism. But the studies of the last decades have examined Juvenal's poetics more deeply and shown how his means of expression serve the ideological purposes of "the most tragic and greatest poet of human vices."

Literary Success

Antiquity

Juvenal seems to have been relatively neglected in the second and third centuries; neither Donatus nor Jerome ever refers to him. He is first mentioned by Lactantius, and Ammianus Marcellinus attests his rise to popularity in the last quarter of the fourth century, especially among poets and grammarians—Servius cites him more than seventy times in the course of his commentary on Virgil, and Servius's student Nicaeus published an edition of the *Satires*. One evident result of this brief spurt of interest in Juvenal, which seems to have reached its climax by the end of the century, is the two sets of scholia on his poems, which go back in part to this period but continued to grow through the Middle Ages (when one was attributed to Valerius, the other to Persius's friend Cornutus). He was read by such poets of late antiquity as Ausonius, Rutilius Namatianus, and Claudian, while his presence in bilingual glossaries suggests that he was used in the eastern part of the Empire to teach Latin to speakers of Greek.

Middle Ages

Juvenal returned to prominence during the Carolingian revival and figured in Charlemagne's court library. Throughout the Middle Ages his popularity as a moralist secured him both a wide circulation (besides fragments of three ancient manuscripts, well over five hundred medieval ones have been found) and a firm place in the medieval school curriculum. Heiric of Auxerre studied him and is mentioned in the scholia; students practiced the rules of meter on his verses; he provided examples for the teaching of rhetoric; and in 1086 the grammarian Aimericus gave him the first place in his canon of authors. For the genre of medieval Latin satire, which flourished in the twelfth century, Juvenal provides the most important model. Both medieval prose authors and poets refer to him often. Dante and Petrarch knew his works; Geoffrey of Monmouth, John of Salisbury, Vincent of Beauvais, and other medieval authors quoted him frequently; and in his *Troilus and Creseide* Chaucer provides explicit confirmation for a judgment expressed in the tenth satire by "Juvenal lord." Indeed, according to one of the ribald university songs of the twelfth and thirteenth centuries, "they believe more in Juvenal than in the doctrine of the prophets" (*magis credunt Juvenali, quam doctrinae prophetali*).

Renaissance and later

In the Renaissance Juvenal's popularity, like Persius's, decreased somewhat. In particular he ceased to be regarded as a universal sage and was understood instead within the more limited confines of the moralizing satirical tradition; but within this genre he remained a dominant influence. It was Juvenal, for example, rather than the other Roman satirists, who contributed most to Luigi Alamanni's thirteen satires on the vices of Italy, to Ariosto's seven on social corruption (including not only women and priests but also patrons and humanists), to the satires of Parini and Alfieri, of Hugo and Carducci and Joseph Régnier. English translations by Stapylton (1660), Holyday (1673), and Dryden (1693) suggest his importance to neo-classical satire, and in the next century Samuel Johnson modernized, sanitized, and humanized his third satire ("London") and his tenth ("Vanity of Human Affairs").

The strange taste for neo-Latin satires in the Juvenalian mode lasted longer than anyone might have expected. In the eighteenth century they were written on English matters by Pope's contemporary William King and on Polish ones by Antonius Loz Poninski, in the nineteenth century on Swiss matters by Petrus Esseiva and on Croatian ones by Junius Resti, and as recently as the 1960s on American matters by Harry C. Schnur, who also published a supplement to Juvenal's last satire, perhaps inspired by the miraculous feat of a young Oxford undergraduate, E. O. Winstedt, who in 1899 discovered thirty-six previously unknown verses in a manuscript of the sixth satire.

BIBLIOGRAPHY

There is an Oxford text of Persius and Juvenal by W. V. Clausen (ed. 3 Oxford 1992); the Loeb is by G. G. Ramsay (London 1918). Persius is now well served by English commentaries; see those of J. Conington and H. Nettleship (ed. 3 Oxford 1893, with text and translation), J. R. Jenkinson (Warminster 1980, with text and eccentric translation), R. H. Harvey (Leiden 1981, the fullest), and G. Lee and W. Barr (Liverpool 1987, with text and translation), to be supplemented by the clear and helpful Latin commentary of D. Bo (Turin 1969), the older editions of O. Jahn (Leipzig 1843) and F. Villeneuve (Paris 1918), H. Beikircher, *Kommentar zur VI Satire des A. Persius Flaccus* (Vienna 1969), and the vast German commentary with text and translation by W. Kissel (Heidelberg 1990). There is a very full English commentary on Juvenal by E.Courtney (London 1980, text published separately, Rome 1984); see also the texts of A.E. Housman (Cambridge 1931), U. Knoche (Munich 1950), and J.R.C. Martyn (Amsterdam 1987) and the commentaries of J.E.B. Mayor (ed. 4, 2 vols., London 1888–89, still entertaining and useful), J. D. Duff (Cambridge 1898, reprint with intro. by M. Coffey, Cambridge 1970), J. Ferguson (New York 1979), and L. Friedländer (2 vols., Leipzig 1895, German).

Both Persius and Juvenal receive full treatment in books on satire; again the treatment in M. Coffey *Roman Satire* (ed. 2 Bristol 1989) is among the most useful. The most important English monograph on Persius is J. C. Bramble, *Persius and the Programmatic Satire* (Cambridge 1974); see also R.G.M. Nisbet in *Satire*, ed. J. P. Sullivan (London 1963), C. S. Dessen, *Iunctura callidus acri: A Study of Persius' Satires* (Urbana 1968), J. P. Sullivan, "In Defence of Persius," *Ramus* 1 (1972) 48–62, E. Paratore, *Biografia e poetica di Persio* (Florence 1968), and A. La Penna, "Persio e le vie nuove della satira latina," introduction to *Persio, Satire* (Milan 1979). There is a bibliography of recent work by M. Squillante Saccone in *ANRW* 32.3 (Berlin 1985).

On Juvenal, see G. Highet, *Juvenal the Satirist* (Oxford 1954), R. Jenkyns, *Three Classical Poets* (London 1982) 151–221, M. M. Winkler, *The Persona in Three Satires of Juvenal* (Hildesheim 1983), J. Ferguson, *A Prosopography to the Poems of Juvenal* (Brussels 1987), S. Braund, *Beyond Anger: A Study of Juvenal's Third Book of Satires* (Cambridge

1988), J. De Decker, *Iuvenalis Declamans* (Liège 1913), J. Gérard, *Juvénal et la réalité contemporaine* (Paris 1976), F. Bellandi, *Etica diatribica e protesta sociale nelle satire di Giovenale* (Bologna 1980), and J. Adamietz, *Untersuchungen zu Juvenal* (Wiesbaden 1972, on satires 3, 5, and 11). Among articles, note esp. those by W. S. Anderson collected in his *Essays on Roman Satire* (Princeton 1982) and, e.g., E. J. Kenney, "Juvenal, Satirist or Rhetorician?" *Latomus* 22 (1963) 704–20, G. B. Townend, "The Literary Substrata to Juvenal's Satires," *JRS* 63 (1973) 148–60, and L. I. Lindo, "The Evolution of Juvenal's Later Satires," *CPh* 69 (1974) 17–27. In recent criticism feminist approaches have become important, not only in relation to satire 6; see, e.g., A. Richlin, "Invective against Women in Roman Satire," *Arethusa* 17 (1984) 67–80, eadem, *The Garden of Priapus* (New Haven 1983), and J. Henderson, "Satire Writes 'Woman': Gendersong," *PCPhS* n.s. 25 (1989) 50–80. On Juvenal's *fortuna,* see Highet, *Juvenal the Satirist,* and C. J. Classen, "Satire—The Elusive Genre," *SO* 63 (1988) 95–121.

Epic in the Flavian Period

Virgil's three epigones   Although relations among the three contemporary poets Statius, Valerius Flaccus, and Silius Italicus are quite obscure and their relative chronology is complex, they tend to be studied as a group, since they share considerable similarities in taste and cultural climate, similarities that may be less marked in Statius, who is the liveliest and most original of the three. The poetry of the three authors supposes as its reference Virgil's now-classic *Aeneid.* The *Aeneid,* which for Lucan had been a model yet also a stimulus to innovation, now becomes a kind of shelter, a closed field. Equally important for the Flavian writers is the influence of Ovid, who above all determines the basic features of their narrative style.

I. STATIUS

LIFE   Publius Papinius Statius was born at Naples sometime between A.D. 40 and 50, the son of a learned schoolmaster. The young poet had notable successes at Rome in public recitations and poetic contests. A protégé of Domitian, he suffered some failures in his last years. After returning to Naples he died shortly before the emperor, perhaps in 96.

WORKS   The *Silvae,* five books of verses in various meters, published gradually from 92 onwards. Two epic poems, in hexameters: the *Thebaid,* in twelve books (over ten thousand verses), published in 92; and the *Achilleid,* an unfinished epic poem, of which only the first book and the beginning of the second are left (altogether slightly more than eleven hundred hexameters). A historical poem on the deeds of Domitian *(De Bello Germanico)* and a successful pantomime *(Agave)* are lost.

SOURCES   The *Silvae* provide many valuable observations on Statius's milieu, life, and personal relations. Juvenal's evidence is also helpful on the public recitations of the *Thebaid* and on the commercial composition of a script for pantomime (Juvenal 7.82 ff.). Late antique scholia on the *Thebaid* are preserved, bearing the name of Lactantius Placidus.

The *Silvae*

The Silvae *as an occasional work*

In comparison with all three epic poems of the Flavian period, Statius's *Silvae* stands out, a nonepic work that is both original and closely tied to contemporary taste. Unlike Silius and the mysterious Valerius, Statius is a professional writer who lives from his work. Because the character of the *Silvae* is occasional and thus varied and miscellaneous—the title probably indicates a collection of "sketches" (Quintilian 10.3.17), as if to give an air of improvisation to the whole—these poems are an extremely valuable document on the society of the day. The people who commissioned the several poems are reflected in many of them, revealing to us the mind and attitude of a cultivated, prosperous class engaged in an active social life and often employed in government and the imperial bureaucracy. The values shaping this social system emerge clearly: on the one hand, withdrawal into private life (passion for the arts, conspicuous consumption, estheticism, family affection), and on the other, the ideology of a public service carried on within the structures of the imperial power.

The people who commissioned the Silvae: *a cross section of Flavian society*

Of equal historical importance are the courtly poems addressed directly to Domitian, which illustrate for us the development of imperial worship, the ceremonies and public displays connected with it. A series of descriptive poems attest to the tastes of the time. The artifices of the poetry are well adapted to imitating the artificial architecture of the patrons' villas and gardens, where nature is cleverly transformed into spectacle. The poems, thirty-two in all, are organized book by book in carefully constructed sequences, with complex effects of balance and variation; the meters range from hexameters to lyric verses. The structure of the individual poems is shaped by traditional schemes that are closely adhered to (e.g., poems for weddings and birthdays, poetic epistles); these are certainly influenced by rhetorical training. These schemes do not preclude an abundance of original variations, since the poet's virtuosity consists precisely in adapting them to the occasions. The poet shows himself perfectly at home in a hierarchical society, within a network of powerful patrons, having the deified image of the princeps as its fixed center.

An artificial poetry for an artificial society

In a hieratic imperial setting, the poet sometimes claims for himself a solemn calling as a conciliator, almost as if he were in charge of systematically supervising public sentiments. A spectator of earthly and celestial scenes, the poet of the *Silvae* strikes the pose of an Orphic singer who is a part of his community. This is the model of the poet that he likes the most and that he recalls on numberless occasions, with varying periphrases. He feels like a psychagogue who arouses pathetic emotions, but only for the purpose of calming them immediately in the sweetness of a composed and melancholy contemplation. Juvenal forcefully expressed an excellent judgment: *tanta dulcedine captos / adficit ille animos.* Poetry now serves as ornamentation; it creates a padding on which the things and gestures of the everyday are laid like precious objects. Thus, in this extreme decadence, poetry becomes the other face of luxury, since intellectual futility has been turned into precious wit.

A sentimental and precious poetry

This mild futility, however, is the heir of a great and vigorous poetry (Virgil, Horace, Propertius, Catullus). From this tradition the poetry of the *Silvae* inherits expressive modes and phrases, values and moral structures, but it sets out to exploit this residual splendor in order to highlight everyday kitsch (which includes the emperor and his worship). It also exploits skillfully some vices originating in that great literature (e.g., its ambiguous relation to power), and it even succeeds, without doubts or problems, merely by carefree superficiality, in bringing the Augustan poets into the imperial cult. This poetry's new function is estheticizing, in the sense that it needs to render objects, men, and deeds beautiful and agreeable, but it

Ornamental function of the digressions

can do this only by distancing itself from them. Statius's ecphrases are not so much descriptions as encomia, and they do not so much show something to the reader as aim at leaving him content and satisfied. The ornamental curlicues cover and hide the essential line of things so that the text can produce a forceful "rhetoric of sweetness," a sweetness that, starting with the style, ends up permeating the things themselves. (Herein lies the secret of Statius's extraordinary success among the mannerist courtiers of late antiquity, such as Claudian and Sidonius Apollinaris, or of the Middle Ages, such as Venantius Fortunatus at the Merovingian court, who transmitted the pompous-epideictic style to the courtly world of the Middle Ages.)

Statius and verbal virtuosity

Nonetheless, the *Silvae* contain some of the greatest moments in all the lyric poetry of the Empire. Since they are a refined, traditional, and reflective poetry, they have not often found their due admirers. They have failed to win appreciation even more because of a certain repugnance created by the courtly and conformist nature of the whole. But it is precisely when dealing with arid subjects or situations of base flattery that Statius proves to be a remarkably gifted artisan of the word. His ability at "improvising," his *celeritas* in composing, which is flaunted more than factual, is the rhetorical gesture of the poetics of the minor, or minimal, work, which captures the original impulse that comes from the epigrammatic tradition. The proclaimed rapidity of composition pretends to be directly in touch with real life (the preface to the first book is instructive in this regard), and it aims at programmatically contrasting the *Silvae* with the highly polished *Thebaid* (which was worked on for more than a decade); at the same time, it announces the playful self-contentment of the professional writer who takes a break in this way from his demanding epic *labor*.

Statius's tender, sentimental poetry, orthodox and conciliatory, aspires to present itself as the faithful, authorized portrait of good imperial society. But the taste and the poetics of feeling that characterize the *Silvae* are a response—within the scheme of an organic culture that the Flavians pro-

The control of culture: poetic certamina *and imperial patronage*

mote—to a broad policy of directing and controlling public emotions. The Neronian age had begun the fashion of public contests of poetry, celebratory *certamina* connected to holidays and festivals. Now the fashion had become established, but it serves instead a program of civil and moral restoration, the exaltation of the traditional values and literary forms (the most famous were the Ludi Capitolini and the Ludi Albani, with contests in prose and poetry, in both Greek and Latin). This leads to a substantial theatricalization of literature, transforming poetry into spectacle; the public and social occasions instituted by imperial patronage create and at the same satisfy the need for shared sentiment.

The feeling for spectacle that inspires these poetic contests, which are intended to please the heterogeneous masses of a now immense metropolis, is fully congruent with the extraordinary success forms of spectacle such as the mime now find with the Roman public (see pp. 402 f.). Between the celebratory *certamina* and the mime theater there is probably a difference in level but not in cultural attitudes. Not only is the official culture willingly recognized in the rhetoric of ornamentation and sweetness but it also legitimizes and fosters the taste for the alluring elementary emotions. The satire of Juvenal, who is a frustrated educator and, as such, the lone teacher of opposition, observes with outrage the new "patronage for all" that the imperial authority promotes. The spectacle of the mime, which arouses easy and sensual emotions (voluptuously satisfied [see Juvenal, *Satires* 6.63 ff.]), meets with the ordinary theatricalization of the imperial myth. Thus the central figure in the mythological imagery and the undertakings inspired by the *certamina* is frequently, and significantly, Jupiter, whom an allegory identifies with the ruling emperor. A fine example is the speech that Jupiter as absolute master of the universe delivers in the Greek verses of a certain Quintus Sulpicius Maximus, who in 94 at the age of twelve was the winner of the Ludi Capitolini.

The *Thebaid*

If Lucan had sung "wars more than civil" (1.1), Statius's theme is "battles between brothers," *fraternae acies* (1.1). In opposition to Lucan, Statius chooses a mythological subject, complete with an elaborate divine apparatus; yet the substance of the material inevitably recalls the *Bellum Civile*.

Summary of the Thebaid

Book 1. The aged Oedipus summons the Furies of the Underworld to persecute the royal house of Thebes. Oedipus's two sons, Eteocles and Polyneices, are ready to break the agreement by which they take turns at governing, each year one reigning and the other leaving Thebes. Polyneices, who is at Argos, is recognized by the aged king Adrastus as the stranger destined to marry one of the two Argive princesses.

Book 2. The Underworld is opened, and Laius, the father whom Oedipus killed, returns to the earth. His ghost inspires Eteocles to break the pact with his brother and to keep all power for himself. The hero Tydeus, Adrastus's son-in-law, goes to Thebes in order to claim the throne that belongs to his brother-in-law Polyneices. An ambush set by the tyrant Eteocles fails.

Book 3. Argos decides to wage war against Thebes and makes military preparations. The pious soothsayer Amphiaraus is contrasted with the blasphemer Capaneus.

Book 4. While at Thebes Laius's ghost predicts death and suffering, seven great heroes (Adrastus, Polyneices, Tydeus, Capaneus, Parthenopaeus, Hippomedon, and Amphiaraus) march on the city with their bands. Weakened by thirst during their journey, they receive the aid of Hypsipyle, who tells them her sad story.

Book 5. A monstrous serpent kills Opheltes, the infant entrusted to Hypsipyle's care. In expiation of the occurrence the Seven establish the Nemean Games.

Book 6. The games are celebrated. Obscure presages declare that only one of the Seven will return from Thebes alive.

Book 7. Hostilities begin before the walls of Thebes. The soothsayer Amphiaraus is swallowed up into Hades.

Book 8. The battle heats up, urged on by the Fury Tisiphon. Tydeus, mortally wounded, gnaws the cranium of his opponent Melanippus.

Book 9. The Thebans have some successes. A battle is fought in the river, during which Hippomedon falls. The young Parthenopaeus dies a pitiable death.

Book 10. The Argives make an expedition by night and massacre the Thebans. The young Theban Menoeceus, Creon's son, willingly sacrifices his life for the good of the city. The impious Capaneus, while breaching the city's walls, is struck by the thunderbolt of Jupiter.

Book 11. The two rival brothers, Eteocles and Polyneices, kill one another in single combat. Jocasta kills herself. Oedipus is driven out of Thebes. The Argive army withdraws, Adrastus being the only survivor of the Seven. Creon becomes the new king of Thebes.

Book 12. Creon forbids that the corpses of the enemy receive burial. Theseus, king of Athens, intervenes and restores justice and piety. Together upon the funeral pyre, Eteocles and Polyneices remain in conflict, two flames divided from one another in hatred (12.429 ff.).

The many models of the Thebaid

In an unusual programmatic epilogue Statius states that he has a lofty model, the *Aeneid,* which the *Thebaid* should "follow at a distance," with humble reverence (12.816 f.). The poem's ambitions are very clear. It is composed of twelve books, divided into two hexads. The second hexad, like the Iliadic half of the *Aeneid,* is all a story of war; the first, which is more varied, serves as a long preparation and also contains Odyssean features (the vicissitudes of travel), like the first half of the *Aeneid.*

The poetic models are legion. The grim exploits of the Seven had been sung in epic poetry, particularly in the popular work of Antimachus of Colophon (fourth century B.C.), and had been treated in Greek tragedy too. The Theban Cycle had especially inspired Seneca (*Oedipus* and *Phoenissae*). The choice of heroic epic brings with it many direct echoes of the *Iliad,* some through the mediation of Virgil, some independent (especially standard episodes—funeral games, catalogues, river battles, supplications, etc.). In certain short digressions unexpected models also appear—Euripides, Apollonius of Rhodes, even Callimachus (reminding us of the rich literary culture of Statius's father). Statius's narrative style and metrics are inconceivable without the technical lessons learned from Ovid. Moreover, his view of the world cannot be divorced from the influence of Seneca. And precisely here, in the contrast between loyalty to the Virgilian tradition and modern anxieties, is located the true center of Statius's epic inspiration.

Recurrence of themes and moods: iron necessity

Although it is indebted to this constellation of influences, the work does not lack unity. The most characteristic weakness of the *Thebaid,* indeed, is the obsessive recurrence of themes and moods. The entire story is governed by an iron necessity: "Who can deny that presages come from hidden causes? Destiny is unfolded before man, but he does not want to read it, and anticipation of the future is lost. Thus we turn presages into accidents, and Fortune has the power to smite us" (6.935–36). The house of Oedipus is crushed not so much by a curse of family revenges (the notion found in Greek tragedy, which would look out-of-date here) as by a universal iron necessity. Statius's ideological choice is obviously Virgilian: to keep epic's divine apparatus but to render it more modern by enlarging the role of Fate. But the choice of so profoundly negative a theme brings Statius very close to Lucan's position. The result is a compromise that was to be very influential on the history of Western epic. The traditional epic divinities appear empty and flat; the most vital divine forces are personifications of abstract ideas, sometimes having even an allegorical coloring. The Fury who sets in motion a large part of the action is an Evil Genius, pure and simple. Overwhelmed by the laws of the cosmos and predestination, the human figures in their turn are also flat. Statius makes few concessions to psychological nuance; from one end of the poem to the other, Eteocles remains the very type of the tyrant, Tydeus the incarnation of anger, Capaneus a blasphemer, Hippomedon a kind of war machine. The few attractive characters are equally schematic. To complete this Manichean view of reality, the eleven books on the war of the Seven close with something that compensates for them, the triumph of clemency and humanity brought about by Theseus the civilizer.

Divinities and abstract forces: the compromise between Virgil and Lucan

Schematism of the characters

Overcoming the dangers of dissipation

The large number of heroes entailed both a very complex plot, almost as in a novel, and the absence of a true protagonist (here again one is reminded of Lucan). The dangers of dissipation, however, are vigorously resisted. Even in the longer episodes that retard the beginning of the war one often notes the desire to establish recurring thematic links. The lengthy funeral games in the sixth book, for instance, serve in many ways (perhaps even more than in Virgil) to advance the development of the plot. The similes are often conceived of in similar sequences, with an effect that at times is almost obsessive: the images of nature reflect the course of the human events. This is the Stoic conception of *sympatheia* that Seneca had been able to transform into a literary theme.

Statius and his times

The absence of direct references to contemporary Roman life does not mean that Statius necessarily avoided the nightmares of his times (cf. the attempted evasion in the *Achilleid* or in Silius). A civil war seen as a conflict between equals who are mirror images of one another, the decline of a ruling family into fanatical despotism, the ethical problem of living under tyrants while still having regard for moral law—the emphasis upon these problems, set in a hallucinatory scene of dark, ancestral mythology, makes the *Thebaid* valuable reading for historians of Roman culture.

The *Achilleid*

The poem scarcely begun: a more relaxed and idyllic tone

Unlike the poem about Thebes, which would be popular for a long time, especially in medieval epic, the poem on Achilles has had a hard life. Any judgment upon it is difficult, since the text we have (interrupted by the author's death) deals only with episodes of the young Achilles on Scyros. Perhaps because of the subject, or because of a deliberate choice of poetics, the tone is more relaxed and idyllic than that of the *Thebaid;* for this reason the work does not displease those critics who find the *Thebaid* excessively baroque. The plan of narrating all of Achilles' life (1.4 ff.) suggests large literary ambitions. Statius, had he been able to continue, would have found himself facing Homer. And beginning with its title the work seems, even more than the *Thebaid,* to be heading towards a perilous confrontation with the ghost of its father Virgil.

Literary Success

Antiquity

Statius's *Thebaid* won instant popularity, both among the wider public and in imperial circles, and his fame continued throughout antiquity. In the third century the emperor Gordian I based his *Antoninias* upon the *Achilleid* and the *Aeneid*. Servius and Priscian cite one commentary on Statius, and we possess another on the *Thebaid,* written by Lactantius Placidus in the second half of the fifth or in the sixth century. Even his *Silvae* left traces upon such ancient poets as Ausonius, Claudian, and Sidonius Apollinaris.

Middle Ages

But it was above all in the Middle Ages that Statius achieved greatest popularity, at least as an epic poet, rivaling even Ovid; and in the early Middle Ages even the *Silvae* became relatively popular. Although there was some doubt about his person—one medieval legend had Statius, a loyal follower of Virgil, converting to Christianity upon reading the fourth eclogue, and he is often supplied with the surname Sursulus or Surculus and called a native of Toulouse, by confusion with a Gallic rhetor, Statius Ursulus, mentioned by Jerome—nothing could stand in the way of his poems: there are over 160 medieval manuscripts of the *Thebaid,* an epic that was probably copied more often in the Middle Ages than it has been read in modern times. Yet even this poem was not well known in the eighth and ninth centuries, except at the court of Charlemagne (Alcuin also refers to the *Silvae* and Paulus Diaconus imitates them once). Only in the tenth century, radiating outwards from the north of France, did it start to become as popular as Lucan's *Bellum Civile,* and it then remained so throughout the Middle Ages. The *Thebaid* was appreciated by medieval readers for its allegorical personifications and for its stark moral conflict between the forces of good on Olympus and those of evil in the Underworld; it became a widely used school text that influenced Chaucer's *Troilus and Creseide,* among other works. In his *House of Fame,* Chaucer placed Statius on top of a column of iron painted with tiger's blood; the only other poets he honors by such elevation are Homer, Virgil, Ovid, and Lucan. But the most spectacular episode in Statius's *Nachleben* was the central role Dante, inspired by the legend of his conversion, assigned him as Virgil's successor in guiding him through Purgatory. In other episodes, too, Dante makes use of Statius's epic poetry, but he entirely ignores his lyric production. As for Statius's unfinished *Achilleid,* this poem, too, became a set text in schools, once it had been added in the thirteenth century to the *Liber Catonis* because of its mythology and moral content (it already appears in similar company in one eleventh-century manuscript). Thereafter manuscripts containing it proliferated (there are about two hundred), and it influenced such authors as Joseph of Exeter and Conrad of Würzburg.

Renaissance

In 1418, during the Council of Constance, Poggio Bracciolini sent to Italy a manuscript containing the *Silvae* together with Manilius and Silius Italicus and transcribed for him by a local German scribe he called *ignorantissimus omnium viventium,* but this text does not seem to have circulated before Poggio's final return to Florence in 1453. The *editio princeps* of the *Silvae* was published in Venice in 1472; that of the *Thebaid* and *Achilleid* had appeared about two years earlier in Rome. The generic diversity and Silver Latinity of the *Silvae* made them of some interest to a number of humanists—thus Politian used his inaugural lecture to discuss Quintilian and Statius's *Silvae* (though he had to justify himself for not having chosen Cicero or Virgil). Thereafter Statius continued to influence Renaissance occasional lyric and, to a far lesser extent, epic, but his fortunes began an inexorable decline that has continued to our own days.

2. VALERIUS FLACCUS

LIFE

Since he gives no autobiographical references, the life of Valerius Flaccus is practically unknown. His name is transmitted to us as Gaius Valerius Flaccus Balbus Setinus. The work is dedicated to Vespasian but also contains references to Titus. From Quintilian 10.1.90 (*multum in Valerio Flacco nuper amisimus,* "recently we have sustained a great loss in the death of Valerius Flaccus") we infer that he died shortly before A.D. 92.

WORKS

Argonautica, in eight books of hexameters (for a total of about fifty-six hundred verses), an epic poem left unfinished probably because of the author's decision or his death.

The *Argonautica*

An unfinished poem

The poem, which either was not finished or, as is less likely, suffered damage in the manuscript transmission, is preserved only for seven books and a part of the eighth; these comprise a series of episodes corresponding to about three quarters of the story as told by Apollonius of Rhodes in the four books of the *Argonautica.* Valerius recounts Jason's expedition in search of the Golden Fleece (book 1); the journey, full of adventures and obstacles right up to the arrival in Colchis (books 2–4); the intrigues and struggles at the court of King Aeëtes and the love between Jason and Aeëtes' daughter Medea; and the winning of the Golden Fleece and the beginning of the difficult return (books 5–8).

Although he takes up nearly all the principal episodes from Apollonius's poem, which had established itself as the canonical version of the myth, Valerius aims at a reworking of the Argonaut theme that is mostly independent, and he does not limit himself to simply Romanizing it, as had Varro of Atax in his version, which was still famous (see p. 141). He abridges and adds material and makes important changes in the psychology of the characters, the manner of conceiving the divine intervention, and the rhythm of the story. Variations and innovations, however, are worked upon a text that in its narrative structures as well as its expression remains indebted to Apollonius in varying degrees. The Alexandrian poem is always present in the background, not merely a source of mythic tradition but a true poetic model.

The model of Apollonius of Rhodes and the pursuit of effects

Where Valerius follows the Greek text closely (even to the point of sometimes testing himself in small attempts at artistic translation), his reworking seems guided by the pursuit of effect. Accentuation of the pathos, dramatization, visualization, and concentration of the model, the consequent taste for brevity of expression (which becomes bold and allusive almost to the point of obscurity), and rhetoricization are the techniques most often used to secure a greater emotional involvement on the part of the reader.

Multiplicity of models and dispersal

Apollonius's text, imitating Homer and imitated in turn by Virgil, is at the center of a network of relations that tie together a vast epic tradition. Thus the Flavian poet, in his self-conscious, "mannerist" role as an epigone, is led to do things in a way that is different but consistently marked by literary imitation. He can recover for his text the necessary Homeric antecedents, yet he must integrate the same text with materials derived from Virgil. In his lively awareness that literature is, among other things, all the language that has been gradually deposited like sediment to constitute an organic poetic tradition, he cannot even avoid deriving suitable suggestions from other writers of Augustan literature, Ovid in particular, and from "moderns" such as Seneca the Younger and Lucan. And so this reflected and elaborated poetry, which is characterized by a mannerist virtuosity in the development of the various models, runs the risk of sometimes being dissipated under the not always harmonious influences exerted by an excessively vast multiplicity of models.

Attention to detail and lack of narrative cohesion

Although elegant and refined in particulars, in descriptive details, in psychological depiction, and in the individual scene, Valerius is often unsuccessful in creating articulated narrative structures. The lack of clarity and of linear movement and, still more, the inadequate specification of temporal and spatial coordinates for the action suggest that he composed in separate blocks and thus gave more attention to the clarity and effect of the individual scene than to the perspicuity and consistency of the whole.

Reactionary poetics

The fundamental influence of Virgil pushes Valerius towards a reactionary poetics. The subject is mythological, the divine apparatus omnipresent, the moral approach unquestionably edifying. Whereas Apollonius had made Jason a problematic and ambiguous hero, nearly an anti-hero, Valerius once again places his protagonist on a high epic level. Virgil's providential Fate, with its spokesman Jupiter, controls the entire course of events.

Subjective style and psychologizing of the story

Valerius Flaccus's narrative exaggerates the Virgilian tendency to the subjective style, that is, the tendency to render events and situations from the point of view and through the feelings of the various characters. This obviously entails a continuous psychologizing of the story. If in Virgil the feelings of the various characters sometimes acquired greater importance than the events themselves, in Valerius the importance they take on is so great as even to eliminate the description of particulars or the narration of events, often including those that are vital for understanding the text. It is natural that the expansion of Apollonius's original is directed especially towards the enhancement of pathos, which is sought on all possible occasions and applied to every type of character, without much regard for the incongruities it may produce. The result is a narrative text that is difficult,

A text addressed to learned readers

often obscure, and extremely learned even in relation to its audience (the public that is envisioned as the ideal reader). The reader sometimes does not find in Valerius's text all the necessary information, but must already be familiar with the events in order to understand them; most of the time one needs to have Apollonius at hand for ready consultation. This is, in short, a work that, in order to realize an arduous and sophisticated poetics, presupposes a broad literary competence in its audience.

Touches of contemporary reality in Valerius Flaccus

Evidences of the poem's roots in contemporary culture are, on the whole, scarce. In several additions that Valerius makes to the Greek original, however, one does find moments of a more contemporary sensibility. In the first book (vv. 747 ff.), for instance, there is the episode of the suicide of Aeson, who has been persecuted by the tyrant Pelias: the inspiration is obviously the Stoic suicide typical of the anti-tyrannical opposition. The political happenings in the kingdom of Colchis are also more developed than in Apollonius and represent the theme of civil war between brothers, which is characteristic of Flavian imagination and culture. This situation allows Valerius to give in book 6 a large-scale (and not very successful) description of combat. Apollonius has no comparable battle scenes, and the Latin poet introduces them to round out the heroic idealization of the Argonauts as well as to create a more exact correspondence to the two-part structure (voyage + war) of Virgil's epic. It is also an opportunity to show (where Apollonius no longer interposes) a more modern interest in barbaric peoples. The growing ethnographic interest in the peoples bordering the Empire is characteristic of the Flavian period.

Emphasis on domination of the sea and Vespasianic ideology

Contemporary reference can be lightly sensed also in the work's overall structure. For Valerius the exploit of the Argonauts is crucial in the plans of divine providence: the Argo, the first ship, must open up the seas so that civilizations can develop; thus world power will pass from Asia to Greece, and from there to still another civilization that is to arise (Jupiter at 1.531 ff.). Valerius's subject is truly prehistoric: the exploits of his pioneers are performed before the events narrated by Virgil and even by Homer. This frontier spirit and the emphasis on domination were probably welcome to the ideology of the house of Vespasian. Yet in the course of the Argonauts' adventurous journey the ideological suggestions get lost. This moderate classicist keeps his distance both from Lucan's grand historical visions and from Statius's mannerist outbursts.

Literary Success

Valerius Flaccus's subtle and elegant epic deserves more readers than it has ever found. He is not mentioned by any writer before Chaucer, who cites him in his *Legend of Good Women* for the list of the crew members who landed on Lemnos, yet it is unlikely that Chaucer knew his works directly. The first part of the epic (through line 4.317) was rediscovered by Poggio Bracciolini in St. Gall in 1416; by 1429 Niccolò Niccoli had found a manuscript containing the whole poem. The *editio princeps* appeared in Bologna in 1474.

3. SILIUS ITALICUS

LIFE

Tiberius Catius Asconius Silius Italicus was born around A.D. 26. A lawyer, he was politically connected to Nero (he was consul in 68). Later, under Vespasian, he was proconsul of Asia. Retiring to private life, he devoted his last years to his large historical poem. In 101, suffering from an incurable disease, he let himself die by starvation.

WORKS

The *Punica*, in seventeen books of hexameters (over twelve thousand verses). Some critics think the text is incomplete; it is suggested that the original plan called for eighteen books, parallel to the size of Ennius's *Annals*.

SOURCES

Mostly notices by contemporaries, including Tacitus, *Histories* 3.65 (political activity), and Pliny the Younger, *Epistulae* 3.7 (obituary).

The *Punica*

A museumlike conception of literature

Pliny the Younger's letter not only registers the chief moments of Silius Italicus's public and official life but also shows a conspicuous taste for anecdote, Pliny's usual mode for illuminating, with forceful rapidity and brilliant lightness of touch, the more curious aspects of others' private lives. Pliny records how Silius's familiarity with the emperor Vitellius and the status he acquired with his proconsulate in Asia under Vespasian contributed to keeping his obscure past concealed (he had been an informer for Nero). Still, the attention of the reader of the letter is drawn especially to the account of the day spent at the Campanian villa, which is devoted to a learned and literary *otium* that for Pliny may have constituted the chief grounds for excusing Silius's earlier notoriety (*maculam veteris industriae laudabili otio abluerat* [par. 3]).

For this reason he gives much space to the description of an almost maniacal *philokalia,* a museumlike worship of Virgil. Silius Italicus liked to collect the relics of the Augustan poet and had even purchased his tomb. In this attitude of a private museum there is much of the spirit with which the elderly ex-consul prepares to write literature in the first person. His work is a frigid gallery of historical busts and antiquarian curiosities, collected with sincere but undiscriminating passion. Not by chance did a sophisticated critic such as G. C. Scaliger dutifully give a qualitative evaluation of Silius's *Punica* in just a few lines: *quem equidem postremum bonorum poetarum existimo: quin ne poetam quidem* (*De Arte Poetica,* p. 324). As can be seen, with the passage of time Pliny's famous judgment, *scribebat carmina maiore cura quam ingenio* (par. 5) is regarded virtually as a euphemism.

Livy, the most evident model

The *Punica* is the longest Latin historical epic to come down to us (and the worst, as is usually, and cruelly, added). Its seventeen books recount the Second Punic War from Hannibal's expedition to Spain to Scipio's triumph after Zama (201 B.C.). The very subject of the poem immediately poses the question of its historical sources. The annalistic line shows the poet's desire to link himself to the most imposing treatment in Latin of the events from 218 to 201, Livy's third decade.

A first significant indication is the use of the architectonic framework of the original. Silius, too, places his portrait of Hannibal (1.56 ff.) shortly after the preface, and like Livy, he ends with the reassuring image of Scipio's triumph (17.618 ff.). When developing the narrative, he always makes ample use of the Augustan historian, though he responds to different needs. The description of the first years of the war down to Cannae (216 B.C.) follows Livy very faithfully. The first ten or eleven books of the *Punica* cover in effect the events of Livy's books 21–22 and the beginning of 23. Silius shows that he can divide his energies equitably among the employment of the historical material, the reworking of epic models, and the *excursus* of varying nature. The rapidity and lessened accuracy in detail of the second part of the poem affect mostly the economy of the historical account; a large number of minor clashes are concentrated and summarized on the basis of rigorous principles of selection. From book 11 on, the author seems to be more drawn to bestowing epic dignity on some events that are particularly endowed with potential symbolic value. This is the case with the battle beside the walls of Rome, in the twelfth book, in which the Olympian divinities participate by driving back the attack that the Titan Hannibal launches against the Capitoline.

Attention deserves to be paid to the attempt, which was already made in the nineteenth century, to attribute scenes and episodes not found in Livy to the influence of the minor ancient annalists (Valerius Antias, Coelius Antipater). In view of the mass of historical, mythological, antiquarian, and naturalistic sources a poem such as Silius Italicus's presupposes, the hypothesis is plausible. Nonetheless, it has rightly been suggested that for lack of a compelling necessity, it is unmethodical to postulate alternative historical sources every time Silius detaches himself a little from his principal model or, worse, where he shows that he has chosen a variant discarded, but mentioned, by Livy himself.

The Annals *of Ennius*

The most obvious parallel to the *Punica* is Ennius's *Annals,* which provided a textbook example for the composition of an annalistic epic. (Since there were eighteen books to the *Annals,* and since the end of the *Punica* is unusually abrupt, it is possible that an additional book was foreseen in the original plan.) The fragmentary state of Ennius's work and the nature of Silius's style (which avoids archaisms) make it very difficult to identify precise imitations. But it cannot be doubted that the consciousness of his derivation from the great model must have been firmly rooted in the Flavian poet. This is indicated by a sketch (12.390 ff.) celebrating the heroic poet from Rudiae, who fought with the Roman army in Sardinia. An Orpheus *redivivus,* Ennius liked to relax from the toil of battle by playing the cithara; when attacked by an enemy, he sees intervening in his behalf no less a figure than Apollo, who sings his coming glories as a poet, his marvelous fusion of the abilities of Homer and Hesiod.

Another archaic predecessor, still more distant and certainly less direct, was Naevius, the author of the *Bellum Poenicum,* which narrated the events of the First Punic War. He too, presumably, receives an homage to his memory, if that is how we ought to understand the flashback devoted to Atilius Regulus's *constantia* (6.118 ff.), a passage that is important as a sign of intertextual connection but is also fully integrated into the ideological system of the *Punica.*

Virgil, Ennius, and the improbability of the divine interventions

The basic impulse came from the *Aeneid.* The war with Hannibal is presented as a direct continuation of Virgil. It derives from Dido's curse against Aeneas and his descendants. After the rupture represented by Lucan's *Pharsalia,* Silius Italicus restores the structural function of the mythological apparatus, even to historical epic. By a mechanical extension of the *Aeneid*'s structure, Juno continues to oppose the descendants of the Trojans while acting at the same time as the protector of Carthage. Until the victory at Cannae the goddess seconds Hannibal's initiatives. Then, in the face of Jupiter's inalterable decision, Juno must cease to harbor plans of defeating the Romans. Before the walls of Rome it is she herself who attempts to halt the Carthaginian leader by showing him (the echo of *Aeneid* 2.604 is clear) that the gods themselves are his opponents. Ennius's *Annals* also certainly contained scenes set on Olympus, in which Juno's hostility played a role; but it does not seem possible that in Ennius things were done in the same way.

In the *Punica* Jupiter desires to put the Romans to a hard test. Urged by Venus, the traditional protector of the descendants of Troy, he explains the inner reasons for the imminent conflict (3.571 ff.): The Roman race does not run the risk of being extinguished, but by proving its valor it must demonstrate that it is worthy of aspiring to dominion over other peoples. In view of this, even the terrible defeats that are to follow will find a higher justification.

Silius's intention of developing a theory does not remove the annoyance provoked in the reader by the improbability of the divine intrusions upon the course of the historical action. Silius's readers are asked to accept without difficulty not only the conventions of Virgilian epic but those of Homeric epic as well. At Zama, for instance, Scipio is about to slay Hannibal with his own hands when Juno intervenes to rescue Hannibal, making use of a kind of specter (17.522 ff.)

This restoration of the mythological apparatus, with its paradoxical results, should not be separated from a notable sensibility for some stylistic *colores* that were common in the poetry of the Neronian age (Seneca the tragedian and Lucan) and that exaggerate a particular taste already present in some passages of the "classic" *Aeneid,* a taste for dark and macabre tones. The antiphrastic overturning of Virgil's providence, which is celebrated by Lucan, is replaced by an epic with a reassuring *lysis,* but the lesson, which has been enhanced by valorizing Virgil's expressionistic ideas (Ovid's mediation in this is fundamental), seems definitively absorbed in the Flavian era.

Awkwardness in the annalistic method and the lack of a protagonist

There is no absolute protagonist, but it is emphasized several times that Hannibal, the only character continuously present from beginning to end, best deserves this title. The characterization of the negative hero—the titanic adversary of the Romans, the gods, and Fate—shows the influence now of Virgil's Turnus, now, in his more demoniacal fits, of Lucan's Caesar. Against the impious protagonist there rise up a sizable group of Roman heroes, who are worthy representatives of the fundamental ideological values of Rome, *fides, pietas, constantia,* and *fortitudo.* Among these Scipio and Fabius Maximus stand out. The distinctive glories of the former are significantly anticipated by a favorable *auspicium* before the battle of the Ticino, in which he takes part even though he is very young (4.115 ff.). Scipio will actually begin to affect the course of the conflict only later. In book 13, where he makes a remarkable descent to the Underworld, following in Aeneas's footsteps, he receives a symbolic investiture that maintains his semi-official status. In book 15 his elevation to the role of leader of the Roman troops is formalized by a new series of presages and, especially, by the traditional motif of Hercules at the crossroads: between the two paths indicated by the personifications of *Virtus* and *Voluptas* the young hero cannot but choose the former. The ostentatious addition of Scipio to the list of the semi-divine heroes, the *megalourgoi* (Hercules first, also Bacchus, Romulus-Quirinus, etc.), culminates in the concluding image of his triumph.

Fabius Maximus represents the Roman senatorial tradition, which is more tied to the ancient (we might almost say anti-imperialistic) prerogatives. His *virtus,* though realized in an action of containment, of endurance, has an exceptional significance, which is already to a large extent celebrated by Livy. His example of resistance (to which nearly the entire seventh book is devoted) is an indispensable basis for the future successes.

The splendid representation of such heroes is the principal vehicle of the poem's ideological motifs, but several essential scenes must not be forgotten, even if from an artistic point of view they are not always successful.

The work joins the rich tradition of Roman patriotic literature, without adding much that is new. The mythological and aetiological digressions (often of an Ovidian taste, such as the *aition* of the cult of Bacchus and Falernian wine, 7.162 ff.) and the antiquarian exactness directed towards the world of archaic Italy (see, e.g., the catalogue of the Roman troops and the *socii* in book 8) declare Silius's attention and sensitivity to the charm of Alexandrian *poikilia,* or "variety." The *excursus,* which often arouse greater interest than the plot proper, reflect the oscillation of epic in this period between the Homeric path and the Hesiodic-Hellenistic taste for variety. This is a phenomenon that seems to produce strong centrifugal thrusts within a structure whose unity shows itself to be ever more formal and less substantial.

Literary Success

Of Silius Italicus it cannot be said that his *Nachleben* greatly exceeded his merits. Readers interested in epic poetry have always preferred Virgil, Ovid, and Statius, while those who wanted to know more about the Punic Wars have turned to the historians. Silius's contemporaries Pliny and Martial refer to him, but for five hundred years thereafter no one except Sidonius Apollinaris names him. In the Middle Ages he never became a school author, and there are only three traces of the *Punica* after the sixth century, all localized near the Lake of Constance. It was in the same area, perhaps at St. Gall, that Poggio Bracciolini rediscovered him in 1417 during the Council of Constance; there are thirty-two Renaissance manuscripts, all derived from the one Poggio found. The *editio princeps* was published in Rome in 1471. In 1508 J. Constantius published eighty-two newly discovered lines. Petrarch, a far greater poet than Silius, seems to have been entirely ignorant of the *Punica* when he composed his own Latin epic on the Punic Wars, the *Africa.*

BIBLIOGRAPHY

Statius

There are Teubner texts of the *Thebaid* by A. Klotz and T. C. Klinnert (Leipzig 1973) and of the *Silvae* and *Achilleid* by A. Marastoni (Leipzig 1970, 1974). There is a new Oxford text of the *Silvae* by E. Courtney (Oxford 1990), and an older edition of the epics by H. W. Garrod (Oxford 1949); the Loeb is by J. H. Mosley (London 1928). Note also D. E. Hill's major edition of the *Thebaid* (Leiden 1983) and the edition of the *Achilleid* with commentary by O. A.W. Dilke (Cambridge 1954). There is a good modern commentary on *Thebaid,* book 9, by M. Dewar (Oxford 1991); other commentaries of varying quality include those on book 1 by H. Heuvel (Zutphen 1932, Latin) and F. Caviglia (Rome 1973, Italian), on book 2 by M. M. Mulder (Groningen 1954, Latin), on book 3 by H. Snijder (Amsterdam 1968, English), on book 10 by R. D. Williams (Leiden 1972), and on book 11 by P. Venini (Florence 1970, Italian). On the *Silvae* the only complete commentary is that of F. Vollmer (Leipzig 1898, German), but there are good English commentaries on book 2 by H. J. Van Dam (Leiden 1984) and on book 4 by K. M. Coleman (Oxford 1988). The scholia (Lactantius Placidus) are edited by R. Jahnke (Leipzig 1898).

On the *Thebaid* see esp. D.W.T. Vessey, *Statius and the Thebaid* (Cambridge 1973), and on the *Silvae,* A. Hardie, *Statius and the Silvae* (Liverpool 1983), as well as L. Legras, *Étude sur la Thébaide de Stace* (Paris 1905), W. Schetter, *Untersuchungen zur epischen Kunst des Statius* (Wiesbaden 1960), S. J. Newmyer, *The Silvae of Statius: Structure and Theme* (Leiden 1979), D. Bright, *Elaborate Disarray: The Nature of Statius' Silvae* (Meisenheim 1979), and H. Cancik, *Untersuchungen zur lyrischen Kunst des P. Papinius Statius* (Hildesheim 1965). *ANRW* 32.5 (Berlin 1985) includes a general survey of work on Statius by H. Cancik and H. J. Van Dam (German) and important articles in English by H. J. Van Dam, D.W.T. Vessey, and F. Ahl; see also C. S. Lewis, *The Allegory of Love* (Oxford 1936), the final chapter in D. C. Feeney, *The Gods in Epic* (Oxford 1991), and E. Burck in *Das römische Epos* (Darmstadt 1979) 300–308. Among other articles J. Henderson, "Statius' *Thebaid* / Form Premade," *PCPhS* n.s. 37 (1991) 30–80 is outstanding.

Valerius Flaccus

There are Teubner texts of Valerius by E. Courtney (Leipzig 1970) and W. W. Ehlers (Stuttgart 1980) and a Loeb by J. H. Mozley (ed. 2 Cambridge, Mass. 1936). There is a commentary by P. Langen (Berlin 1896–97), but detailed modern discussion remains a desideratum (note the German commentary on 4.1–343 by M. Korn [Hildesheim 1989]). There is no comprehensive English monograph, but the chapter in D. C. Feeney, *The Gods in Epic* (Oxford 1991), again serves as an excellent introduction. In other languages note F. Mehmel, *Valerius Flaccus* (Diss., Munich 1934), J. Adamietz, *Zur Komposition der Argonautica des Valerius Flaccus* (Munich 1976), E. Burck, *Das römische Epos* (Darmstadt 1979) 208–53, A. Perutelli, "Pluralità dei modelli e discontinuità narrativa: l'episodio della morte di Esone in Valerio Flacco (1,747 sgg.)," *MD* 7 (1982) 123–40, and the articles by M. Scaffai and A. J. Kleywegt in *ANRW* 32.4 (Berlin 1986) 2359–2447 and 2448–90.

Silius Italicus

The standard critical text of Silius is that of J. Delz (Stuttgart 1987); there is a Loeb by J. D. Duff (2 vols., London 1934), and a Budé edition is in progress (books 1–4 ed. P. Miniconi and G. Devallet, Paris 1979; 5–8 ed. J. Volpilhac, P. Miniconi, and G. Devallet, 1981; 9–12 ed. J. Volpilhac-Lenthéric, M. Malin, P. Miniconi, and G. Devallet, 1984). There are French commentaries by F. Spaltenstein on books 1–8 and 9–17 (Lausanne 1986, 1990). There is again no English monograph of substance, but the *ANRW* survey by F. Ahl, M. A. Davis, and A. Pomeroy is extensive (32.4 [Berlin 1986] 2492–61); the discussion in D. C. Feeney, *The Gods in Epic* (Oxford 1991), is less successful than in the case of the other epicists. In German, note esp. M. von Albrecht, *Silius Italicus: Freiheit und Gebundenheit römischer Epik* (Amsterdam 1964), R. Häussler, *Das historische Epos der Griechen und der Römer* (vol. 2, Heidelberg 1976), E. Burck, *Das römische Epos* (Darmstadt 1979) 254–99 and *Historische und epische Tradition bei Silius Italicus* (Munich 1984), and J. Küppers, *Tantarum Causas Irarum: Untersuchungen zu einleitende Bücherdyade der Punica des Silius Italicus* (Berlin 1986).

H. Juhnke, *Homerisches in römischer Epik flavischen Zeit* (Munich 1972), is of importance especially for Statius and Silius.

Pliny the Elder and Specialist Knowledge

Pliny's career is the exemplary one of an effective equestrian toiling in the service of the imperial court. Gaius Plinius Secundus was born at Como in A.D. 23 or the following year. As a young man he began his career with military service, which he did in Germany during two long stretches, both falling within the period A.D. 46–58. He took part in military campaigns on the frontier and met important people, such as the great general Gnaeus Domitius Corbulo, the general (and writer) Pomponius Secundus, and the very young Titus, who many years later would be emperor. Pliny's interest in military questions is attested by a small treatise, lost to us, called *De Iaculatione Equestri* (i.e., on the techniques of fighting from horseback). He also wrote a (lost) biography of his influential friend, the *De Vita Pomponii Secundi,* which was presumably similar in genre and approach to Tacitus's *De Vita Iulii Agricolae.*

The German campaigns gave Pliny the idea for a historical work, the *Bella Germaniae,* which must have had a notable success: Tacitus would make considerable use of it as a source. After Claudius's death Pliny must have led a withdrawn life. From several allusions in the *Naturalis Historia* we know that he was fiercely hostile to Nero. His withdrawal from public offices and political activity was a salutary move, however, for it is likely that in this period he devoted himself instead to oratory and law; if so, we can place in this stage of his life the composition of an essay in six books called (so it seems) *Studiosus.* From the few fragments we have, the subject appears to be comparable in some ways to that of Quintilian's *Institutio Oratoria;* it was probably a handbook for the student of rhetoric. In one fragment Pliny, with characteristic conscientiousness, explains how the orator should arrange his hair. In this same period when his career was at a standstill, Pliny must have developed interests in grammar. A handbook of his, entitled *Dubius Sermo* because it was concerned with problems and variations of linguistic usage, had considerable success. We have a good number of fragments from it, since it was used and cited a great deal by the grammarians of the late Empire.

With the accession of Vespasian, Pliny, rather surprisingly, entered upon an intense career as imperial procurator, holding many important posts.

Despite these tasks, Pliny during the seventies devoted himself to the two works that brought him most fame as a writer. The first of these, the Roman history *A Fine Aufidi Bassi,* has not been preserved, but it seems to have been by far his most important and ambitious work. It is a history of Rome that, attaching itself to the end of a text by the great historian Aufidius Bassus (on whom see p. 383), covered approximately the years from 50 to 71, from the end of Claudius's reign to the accession of Vespasian. It was a very delicate task to write about a period so inflammatory and so close to the present day. The work could not fail to have a marked pro-Flavian tendency, but Pliny, with wonderful insight, did not wish it to be published during his lifetime; as he tells us (*Naturalis Historia praef.* 20), he wanted to avoid charges of servility towards the princeps Vespasian. In any event, the success of Pliny's histories was rapidly outstripped by competition from Tacitus.

Around 77–78 Pliny also completed the monumental effort of the *Naturalis Historia* and presented it to the new emperor Titus. In the meantime he held an apparently tranquil post, as prefect of the imperial fleet stationed in Campania. It was in this capacity, and in the service of the state, that he met his death on 24 August A.D. 79, overcome by the eruption of Vesuvius.

WORKS

All the works just mentioned have been lost, except for the *Naturalis Historia.* An atmosphere of excess surrounds the work. We know that Pliny claims never to have read a book so bad as not to have any value at all; and Pliny was constantly reading, taking notes, and indexing. The final result was a work in thirty-seven books, intended to inventory the total knowledge possessed by man. The indefatigable Pliny worked his way through impressive numbers: 34,000 notices, 2,000 volumes read, from 100 different authors, and 170 dossiers of notes and preparatory files ("I have not knowingly omitted any piece of information, if I have found it anywhere" [17.137]).

The plan of the work is as follows: book 1, general table of contents of the work and bibliography for each book; 2, cosmology and physical geography; 3–6, geography; 7, anthropology; 8–11, zoology; 12–19, botany; 20–32, medicine; 33–37, metallurgy and mineralogy (with large excursus on the history of art).

The text of the *Naturalis Historia* ("Natural History" in English, but the exact meaning would be rather "The Knowledge of Nature") is preceded by a dedicatory letter addressed to the future emperor Titus, in which Pliny explains the motivations and limits of his work. The letter allows us to date the completion of the work to A.D. 77–78.

SOURCES

Various passages of the *Naturalis Historia* contain autobiographical notices or hints, places he saw, for instance, and relations with famous people; moreover, as a famous historian of Rome, Pliny merited a biography in Suetonius's *De Viris Illustribus* (frag. 80 Reifferscheid). But by far the most interesting information comes from three letters of his nephew Pliny (called the Younger, to distinguish him from his uncle). Pliny gives a fascinating account of his uncle's literary activity and a catalogue of his writings (*Epistulae* 3.5), and separately, in two letters to the historian Tacitus (6.16, 6.20), a narrative of the unusual circumstances in which he died.

The account of his death has contributed greatly to Pliny's renown as an exemplary figure, a "proto-martyr of experimental science" (I. Calvino), who braved a cataclysm in order to satisfy his scientific curiosity. It should be said, however, that Pliny's conception of science has little of the experimental or empiric and that, according to the account of the Younger, Pliny exposed himself to danger in order to bring aid to some citizens threatened by the eruption. The virtue that emerges from this noble death is thus philanthropy and the spirit of service rather than thirst for knowledge, just the virtue that drove Pliny to the immense undertaking of the *Naturalis Historia*, a work intended in its entirety to be of service to mankind.

1. PLINY THE ELDER AND ENCYCLOPEDISM

Theoretical thrust and systematization of acquired knowledge

An attempt to systematize knowledge is evident in all Roman culture of the early Empire, and it finds expression particularly in works of a handbook nature, that is, in texts that aim at gathering the best information in a certain area of knowledge or practical activity and providing the reader with an accessible and comprehensive guide to it. The practical aim of these syntheses tends invariably to weaken their theoretical thrust and the scope for individual experimentation. At the same time, the goal of complete information does not foster the development of critical abilities. The times become readier for the development of genuine encyclopedias, in the sense of inventories of acquired information.

Imperial Rome and the demand for technical knowledge

Given the level of scientific achievement in Greece and the Hellenistic world, it is evident that works of this sort are for the most part popularizations of Greek originals, a significant exception being, under the Republic, the Latin translation of agricultural treatises written by the Carthaginian Mago. Imperial Rome witnesses a great expansion of the classes that we would call technical and professional—doctors, architects, experts in aqueducts and sewer systems, agronomists, and administrators partly coinciding with the nascent imperial bureaucracy. Moreover, greater technical abilities are required of politicians, too. Those who administer the provinces, for example, are less often military leaders and more often technicians; they are concerned with economy and finance, with the land's resources and means of transportation, and with the exploitation of nature. Among all these classes the demand for information, for accessible knowledge, is on the rise.

Scientific curiosity and cultural consumerism: the paradoxographers

At the same time, scientific curiosity is established as a form of entertainment, of cultural consumption. We can document this phenomenon at least as early as the age of Seneca. The popular writings on nature are not, of course, Aristotle's stern works nor Seneca's *Naturales Quaestiones*, which are too rigorous. The authors who promote a genuinely new literary genre are the so-called paradoxographers (from the Greek *paradoxon,* "oddity, unexpected thing"). Their works are extremely uneven and miscellaneous collections of anecdotes, small scientific curiosities, anthropological notices of varying worth, and extracts from more serious scientific works. The authors often present themselves as travelers who gather their material firsthand. In some cases it can be shown that the writers of *paradoxa* and *mirabilia* did have access to fresh information and thus did not merely reproduce traditional notices and hearsay. The most famous author of *mirabilia,* Licinius Mucianus, is also the chief military leader and politician in the early days of Vespasian's reign. Mucianus, a decisive supporter of Vespasian in the crisis of A.D. 69, spent much time in the eastern provinces, and from his experiences he wrote a work in which curiosities of the natural world, passion for sensationalism, and taste for the exotic must all have been combined. These journalistic reports from the frontier provinces were very successful; in the fragments that we have he speaks of shells, immense fountains, tame elephants, and the effects of the moon on monkeys.

Licinius Mucianus

It is evident that these naturalist-travelers, even when not simply inventing details or copying them from older compilations, are still dilettantes. The interest in concrete detail and exploration is not supported by any method and lacks that systematic spirit that the Romans maintained towards other aspects of the culture. One should not be too severe: the paradoxographic tradition had already been started by Greek writers in the train of Alexander the Great, more than three centuries earlier. Nor is it always easy, moreover, to draw a sharp line between direct experience and the conditioning created by reading. Even the European travelers of the sixteenth century, although they "see" the apes in the jungle, call them satyrs. The man who claims to have met Amazons and unicorns is simply "reading" the New World with the eyes he has at his disposal, the eyes of the classical tradition and of academic culture.

Dilettantism of the paradoxographers

The paradoxographic literature conveys very well the limit of Roman scientific culture; it contains genuine curiosity and lively practical interests but no systematic principle. Still more important is the lack of connection between practical experience and tradition. The enlargement of experience does not lead directly to an alteration of the prior models, that is, the classic models, the great models of the Greek tradition, not only in mathematics and astronomy but in geography, botany, and zoology as well. At the very most, new experiences and new data may be accepted and catalogued alongside the traditional.

Lack of connection between practical experience and tradition

Pliny the Elder's gigantic work of erudition is the fullest realization of these tendencies in Roman culture. Roman culture had already known large and small works of synthesis, such as the various treatises by Varro and Celsus, Vitruvius's handbook on architecture, Mela's summary of geography, or Columella's treatise on agriculture, and a few years after Pliny, Quintilian was to produce a work of great importance for rhetoric and education. Yet none of these authors conceived a project of preserving all

Pliny the Elder and the other Roman encyclopedists

knowledge, nor did Greek works exist that were at all comparable; indeed it is difficult to point to another writer as prolific as Pliny, apart from Varro.

Eclecticism and the Encyclopedic Project

Pliny's encyclopedia was thus an undertaking original in size and scope. It was a helpful circumstance, and not necessarily accidental, that the author was close to certain positions of the Stoics (during the time of Pliny's education, traces of Stoic physics and ethics are found in Persius and Lucan as well as in Seneca). Certainly the idea of the universe as a complex whole governed by divine foresight, as a cosmic machine that man must be familiar with in order to reflect its virtues within himself, was a very suitable idea for guiding the project of an encyclopedia that began with the movements of the stars but also included man's artistic creations, as well as the life of the smallest animals. Indeed, a certain adherence to Stoicism is evident in the cosmology (book 2), which is the most enthusiastic section of Pliny's treatise. But one should not make too much of this. The encyclopedic mentality in Pliny's case is an accommodating eclecticism; an overprecise philosophical choice would end up by reducing too much the quantity of materials to be registered and classified in the *Naturalis Historia.* In the same book of cosmology Pliny comfortably juxtaposes Stoic professions with weird magical-astrological notions, which are utterly foreign to Stoic thought and derive instead from some Eastern source.

Pliny's accommo-dating eclecticism

From Stoicism Pliny retains, more than anything else, a general sense of the sage's mission. Yet this is the moderate Stoicism, colorless and banal, which is found in the Roman governing class of that period; it is not a deep ideological inspiration. Another aspect of Pliny's personality, that commitment of his that we might call "the spirit of service," is far more evident in the *Naturalis Historia.* Within the immense mass of notions and theories belonging to others, this contribution can be regarded as personal and original. To his encyclopedia of nature Pliny brings a spirit of service all his own, as well as a practical sense and moral seriousness, qualities typical of a hardworking imperial functionary.

Moderate Stoicism and the spirit of service

Stylistically, Pliny is regarded by many critics as the worst Latin writer. The judgment needs some qualification. First of all, the enormity of the work was not compatible with regular stylistic elaboration; furthermore, the Roman encyclopedic tradition did not include a particular effort to write well. The greatest Roman encyclopedist, Varro, is far superior to Pliny in competence and clarity, but as far as we can tell, his style is careless and inelegant, almost casual. Pliny in fact does not always write in the same way. The scattered, muddled style that dominates entire books contrasts with true rhetorical tirades; his praises of science, nature, and Italy and his moral condemnations of luxury and the exploitation of nature are demonstrative passages in which one detects a certain literary ambition. (It is likely, moreover, that Pliny's historical work had a different style: historical works in Latin literature observe a principle of greater attention to form than do technical and natural works.) Like all prose writers of the Neronian

Encyclopedic tradition and careless style

and Flavian periods, Pliny tends to undo the large, balanced structure of Ciceronian periods. This new freedom in writing, which in the case of Seneca and Tacitus produces a revolution in literary art, in Pliny's case dissolves into an impersonal confusion.

A work destined for consultation

The work was too long to be read straight through—not many are likely to have had the courage to attempt it in any period—and too long also, of course, to be used in school. Moreover, the whole is separable into homogeneous blocks (e.g., the geography of the earth, botany, pharmacological remedies, etc.), and the table of contents and index of authors used make consultation easier. It is necessary to recognize that until our modern encyclopedias brought alphabetic order and other practical aids into general use, the *Naturalis Historia* was one of the best-organized and most easily consultable ancient texts.

Literary Success of the *Naturalis Historia*

Antiquity

Because of the richness of the information Pliny supplied in his *Naturalis Historia,* he was used by grateful readers throughout antiquity (fragments of five ancient manuscripts have survived); but the enormous scope of his work made it particularly liable to be excerpted and epitomized. One medical breviary compiled around the beginning of the fourth century from his work, the *Medicina Plinii,* went on to become very popular in the Middle Ages. So did the *Breviarium Rerum Memorabilium,* composed probably in the third century by C. Iulius Solinus. This collection of wondrous and abnormal "facts," three quarters of which were drawn from Pliny, is transmitted completely in 153 manuscripts and was itself frequently epitomized and excerpted in turn. Such manipulations proved fatal to the transmission of Livy's monumental work in its entirety, but they did not prevent Pliny's from being transmitted in parallel as a whole: even in the Dark Ages the *Naturalis Historia* was still being copied as the sole surviving link to the vast resources of ancient knowledge.

Middle Ages

In the Middle Ages Pliny was not a school author, but despite his own disclaimers to originality, or rather because of them, he was surrounded by an aura of authority and prestige. Parts of his text were available in Northumbria in the eighth century; they were known to the Venerable Bede and were listed by Alcuin as being available at York. Alcuin, in answering questions on astronomy posed him by Charlemagne, cited Pliny as a standard authority; so, too, did the Irish scholar Dungal. In the ninth century, astronomical excerpts were prepared, especially in Aachen (where Charlemagne's palace school was located) and in Constance. And in the twelfth century Robert of Cricklade prepared nine books of excerpts, entitled *Defloratio* and dedicated to Henry II.

Renaissance

Pliny remained popular in the Renaissance. He was one of the most frequently consulted authorities on many subjects for Valla and many other humanists; there were at least forty-six editions of his work by 1550; and he was translated into Italian by Landino (published in 1501) and into English by Philemon Holland (1601). But gradually the intense philological work of humanist scholars on the one hand and the new discoveries of the scientific revolution on the other began to throw doubt upon Pliny's reputation as an infallible authority, and in the end his reputation could not even be rescued by blaming the manuscripts. Yet as Pliny has lost his practical value as a reference handbook in the modern period, he has gained in historical importance for the information he transmits concerning ancient art, science, folklore, religion, and material culture. It is precisely Pliny's intellectual defects—his bland indifference to theoretical rigor, his refusal to engage in systematic analysis and selection—that make him so precious for modern scholars interested in the ancient world. Unlike scholars who had greater intelligence, more self-confidence, or simply more time at their disposal, he preserves everything and passes it on to us.

2. A TECHNICAL WRITER: FRONTINUS

Life and works of Frontinus

Comparable to Pliny in period, life, and to some extent interests as well is Sextus Julius Frontinus, consul in 74, legate of Britain, and then in 96–97, under Nerva, *curator aquarum,* that is, director of the aqueducts. He died under Trajan, after having been consul a second time.

Like Pliny, Frontinus is distinguished for vigor both in his career and in the range of his technical works. The two texts of his that are preserved, *De Aquis* (or *De Aquae Ductu*) *Urbis Romae* and *Strategemata,* show but limited literary ambition. They are works of the *commentarii* type ("notes and observations," "recollections," "studies," a kind of writing with flexible boundaries that includes a masterpiece of memoir writing, such as Caesar's, along with the humblest collection of personal notes [see p. 226]).

Analysis of Frontinus's works

The *De Aquis Urbis Romae* is a good, concrete treatment of the problems of Rome's water supply; it reflects Frontinus's technical skill as the man responsible for the aqueducts, an area in which the Romans had achieved excellent results. The four books of the *Strategemata* (the authenticity of book 4, however, is somewhat problematic) are not so distinguished for competence and precision. The work is in effect a collection of military anecdotes, a more restricted derivative of the seam opened by Valerius Maximus with his *Facta et Dicta Memorabilia.* Although Frontinus really intended to be of practical use to warriors (he himself had fought successfully, in Britain), the result is questionable: the information is generic and the result of an occasionally imprecise compilation.

Frontinus and the land surveyors

Apart from military art and waterworks, Frontinus had also dealt with land surveying, that discipline whose object is to survey, to represent upon a map, and to delimit the surface of a piece of land. This science, which employs an instrument that resembles the modern theodolite and is called *groma* (whence the name *gromatici* for surveyors), had many practitioners at Rome. Only extracts of Frontinus's treatise remain, but we have several others by his contemporaries and by authors of later date, which testify to the importance of land surveying among the Romans.

BIBLIOGRAPHY

The standard critical edition is that of C. Mayhoff (5 vols., Leipzig 1892–1909); there is a complete Loeb edition by H. Rackham, W.H.-S. Jones, and D. E. Eicholz (10 vols., Cambridge, Mass. 1938–63), and an almost complete Budé edition with French translation and notes by A. Ernout and others, esp. J. André (Paris 1947–). The edition with Italian translation and brief notes by G. B. Conte and others (Turin 1982–) includes a detailed introduction and bibliography. There is no complete commentary, and there are few discussions of individual books; the notes in the Budé edition are the most useful aid.

There is a collection of English essays edited by R. French and F. Greenaway, *Science in the Early Roman Empire: Pliny the Elder, His Sources and Influence* (London 1986). Several similar volumes were issued to commemorate the nineteen-hundredth anniversary of Pliny's death; see esp. *Helmantica* 37 (1986) and 38 (1987) and the proceedings of the congresses *Plinio il Vecchio sotto il profilo storico e letterario* (Como 1982) and *Plinio il Vecchio* (Rome 1983). The *ANRW* survey (French) is by G. Serpat (32.4, Berlin 1986) 2069–2200; see also J. Miller, *Der Stil des älteren Plinius* (Innsbruck 1883), F. Münzer, *Beiträge zur Quellenkritik der Naturgeschichte des Plinius* (Berlin 1897), P. C. Cova et al., *Studi sulla lingua di Plinio il Vecchio* (Milan 1980), R. König and G. Winkler, *Plinius der Ältere* (Munich 1979), and S. Citroni Marchetti, *Plinio il Vecchio e la tradizione del moralismo romano* (Pisa 1991).

The standard edition of Frontinus's *De Aquis* is that of C. Kunderewicz (Leipzig 1973), of the *Stratagemata* that of R. J. Ireland (Leipzig 1990). There is a Loeb of both by C. E. Bennett, C. Herschel, and M. B. McElwain (London 1925). C. Herschel's *The Two Books of the Water Supply of the City of Rome of Sextus Julius Frontinus* (ed. 2 London 1913) is a text, translation, and commentary by a practicing engineer; see also T. Ashby, *The Aqueducts of Ancient Rome* (Rome 1935), and the publications of the Frontinus-Gesellschaft in the series *Geschichte der Wasserversorgung* (Munich 1983–).

The standard text of the *Corpus Agrimensorum* is still that of C. Lachmann et al. (2 vols., Berlin 1848–52, with German notes); see also the partial edition of the *Opuscula Agrimensorum Veterum* by C. Thulin (Leipzig 1913). There is an excellent English introduction by O.A.W. Dilke, *The Roman Landsurveyors* (Newton Abbot 1971); see also Å. Josephson, *Casae Litterarum* (Uppsala 1950).

Martial and the Epigram

LIFE AND
EVIDENCE

Marcus Valerius Martial was born at Bilbilis, in Hispania Tarraconensis, on 1 March in some year between A.D. 38 and 41 (this and other biographical notices come to us from his own verses and from a letter of Pliny the Younger). In 64 he went to Rome, where he found the generous support of the most conspicuous Spanish family in the capital, the family of Seneca, which introduced him into good society. He became acquainted with Calpurnius Piso and the circles of the senatorial opposition to Nero, whom the emperor in 65, as a result of the Pisonian conspiracy, would bloodily suppress. For some years thereafter he probably led a modest life, pursuing his poetic activity as a client. He must have won a certain notoriety, since in 80 he composed (probably on commission from people at court) and published a collection of epigrams celebrating the inauguration of the Flavian Amphitheater. The work won for him the appreciation (including monetary appreciation) of the new emperor Titus. From 84–85 he began to publish his poems regularly. Success smiled upon him, and he also held honorific posts: he was military tribune, and thus achieved equestrian status. He came into contact with eminent people—the future emperor Nerva, for instance, and writers such as Silius Italicus, Pliny the Younger, Quintilian, and Juvenal—but this did not bring him a steady income (in antiquity, copyright did not exist, so only the bookseller profited from the sale of books). He complains repeatedly of the hardships he suffered and the difficulties he experienced in finding patrons and sponsors who were ready to offer him recognition and support.

In 87–88, annoyed by city life, he left Rome to stay at Forum Corneli (today Imola) and other cities in Emilia, but after a short time he returned to the capital. He left it again, definitively, in 98, when he decided to return to his native Bilbilis (Pliny the Younger helped him by paying for his voyage). There he found the tranquillity he was seeking but also the pettiness of a provincial atmosphere, and he missed the turbulent life of Rome. Disappointed and still unhappy, he died at Bilbilis around 104.

WORKS

We possess a collection of Martial's epigrams divided into twelve books that were written and gradually published from A.D. 86 to 101–102. The body of the collection is preceded by another book with about thirty epigrams *(Epigrammaton Liber),* composed independently (as was said) in 80 and known today as the *Liber de Spectaculis* or *Liber Spectaculorum.* Two other books (usually referred to as books 13 and 14), which are also independent, follow. These are, respectively, the *Xenia* and the *Apophoreta,* published in 84 and 85. They consist of very short inscriptions, each one a single couplet, which, like labels on an object, accompany presents of varying sorts given on the occasion of the Saturnalia (the *Xenia,* or "gifts for guests") and gifts presented to guests at banquets (the *Apophoreta,* or "carry-outs"). The present arrangement of Martial's complete works probably is that of an ancient edition made after the author's death.

The meters vary: along with the elegiac couplet, which is the most common, the Phalacaean and scazon are frequent, but other meters are found as well. The epigrams also vary in length, ranging from a single couplet (or even a single verse) to ten or more verses and even to twenty, thirty, or forty. In arranging the epigrams in books, Martial distributed them in a balanced and varied way, paying attention to their meter and length and being alert especially to avoid repetition and dullness. There are in total over fifteen hundred epigrams, with about ten thousand verses altogether.

1. THE EPIGRAM AS REALISTIC POETRY

Coexistence of epic and epigram in the Flavian period

An important aspect of the literary culture of the Flavian period, which is characterized by a climate of moral restoration, is the movement back towards the highest poetic genre, the epic (Statius, Silius Italicus, Valerius Flaccus). Yet the period also witnesses the popularity and notable success of a genre such as the epigram, which, as Martial himself attests (12.94.9), is regarded as the humblest of all.

Epigram as commemorative and as occasional poetry

The epigram originates in the archaic period of Greece, where its function (the name itself means "inscription") was essentially commemorative. Epigrams were engraved, for instance, on tombstones or on votive offerings, in order to record a person, a monument, a famous place or event (e.g., Simonides' famous epigram over those who fell at Thermopylae). In the Hellenistic era, however, the epigram, though preserving its characteristic brevity, frees itself from its epigraphic form and practical purpose. Now it is a type of poem suitable for occasional poetry, suitable for fixing, within the compass of a few verses, the impression of a moment or of a small, everyday happening (this is the function performed by the sonnet or the lyric in modern poetry). The subjects are often light (erotic, sympotic, satiric-parodic), but more traditional subjects are also found, such as funereal poetry, sometimes in the gently parodic form of an *epicedion* for small animals. The *Garland of Meleager,* which later passed into the *Anthologia Palatina,* is the document that best illustrates the nature and popularity of epigram in the Hellenistic period. In Latin poetry the epigram did not have a great tradition, and little of what there was has come down to us. Except for Catullus, we know virtually nothing of the poets whom Martial points to as his *auctores* (Domitius Marsus, Albinovanus Pedo, Lentulus Gaetulicus). It is true, moreover, that apart from professional poets, many politicians wrote *versiculi* (as Pliny the Younger attests); for them, epigrammatic poetry was little more than a refined way of enjoying their *otium,* almost a pastime without great ambitions to literary dignity. Only with Martial's work, in fact, does the epigram find artistic recognition. Thus a minor poetic form, once courtiers and patrons allow it a legitimate space in which to fulfill its destiny, readily becomes an element of social etiquette and in the end acquires independent value and artistic dignity also.

But it should not be forgotten that in the Rome of the early Empire the Greek epigram also flourished notably; it should be enough to recall the publication of the *Garland of Philip* in the time of Caligula and the success of Lucillius's witty epigrams in Nero's time. A few decades before Martial began his activity the epigrammatic genre had become very popular, the courtly function (the epigram could lend itself to an act of homage or to accompanying a gift, as happens in the *Garland of Philip*) alternating with the possibility of jesting and playful entertainment (the case of the witty epigrams).

Catullus's epigrams

At Rome Catullus valued the brief form, already given a special place by Callimachean poetics, as the one most suitable for expressing feelings, tastes, and passions (i.e., the subjects of private life), as well as for being a device of lively polemical attack (the epigram was exploited for this pur-

Martial's epigrams and closeness to everyday life

pose by other neoteric poets also). Martial makes the epigram his exclusive genre, the sole form of his poetry, because he values highly its flexibility, the ease with which it suits the many aspects of reality. The variety and the mobility of a lively genre such as epigram are the qualities Martial polemically contrasts with the qualities of the noble genres, epic and tragedy, with their serious tones and much abused contents, those trite mythological stories that were so far removed from the reality of everyday life.

It is precisely its realism, its closeness to actual life, that Martial claims as the distinctive mark of his poetry (*hominem pagina nostra sapit* [10.4.10]), and he proudly regards this as confirmed by the enormous acclaim with

Success and the subjects of Martial's epigrams

which the public received it. In his epigrams the public could find the concise evocation of a spectacular event (as in the *De Spectaculis*), or the idea for a *bon mot,* a clever poetic tag, to accompany a gift for a friend or a guest (as in the collections of *Xenia* and *Apophoreta*), or the commemoration of actual events, of important moments in the life of the various recipients, such as births, weddings, holidays, celebrations, and so on. In other words, the public found in the epigram their own experiences filtered and ennobled by an artistic form possessing flexibility and potent expressiveness. It is, in short, a poetry that combines practical usefulness and literary amusement, painting an incisive and variegated picture of everyday reality with all its contradictions and paradoxes.

Martial and the diverting spectacle of the world

Martial observes the spectacle of reality and of the various people who occupy its stage with a distorting glance. He accentuates their grotesque features and reduces them to recurring types (parasites, vain people, plagia-

rists, misers, swindlers, legacy hunters, petulant poetasters, dangerous doctors, etc.). Deformation and grotesqueness are the result of a representation
from close up, an optical effect that, like the witty epigram, focuses upon
individual persons and features in isolation, denying them background and
contours—as if, in order to show them better, they were wrenched out of
context, as if they were suspended in a vacuum, "de-realized," so to speak.
The poet's attitude, however, is that of an alert but mostly detached
observer who rarely engages in moral judgment or condemnation. His is a
social satire without harshness (*parcere personis, dicere de vitiis* [10.33.10]),
and he prefers laughter to indignation at the absurd spectacle of the world
in which he finds himself. For that reason, all the more does he occasionally
like to contemplate, by contrast, a life of simple, natural pleasures, of tranquil recreations and sincere affections (see, e.g., 1.55 and 10.47), a dream
that sometimes takes on the idyllic features of his Spanish homeland
(1.49, 10.96).

2. THE MECHANISM OF WIT

Prevalence of the comic-satiric element

The subjects of Martial's epigrams are varied and embrace the whole of
human experience. Some are rooted in tradition (such as the funerary epigram, of which Martial presents us with examples of great delicacy), while
others deal more closely with the poet's personal experiences (many epigrams are literary polemic, in which Martial explains his poetic preferences
or laments the decline of literature and patronage) or with the social usage
of the day (e.g., the celebratory epigrams or those that flatter the emperor
Domitian).

Martial's epigram in general develops the comic-satiric aspect more than
the tradition had. In this he follows a tendency already begun by an earlier
writer of epigrams, Lucillius, a Greek poet of the Neronian period, who
had given much space to persons with conspicuous physical defects and to
social types whom he represented comically, and he thereby joined the
Roman satiric tradition, which was attentive to the analysis of social usage

The technique of the closing quip

and quick to sketch its most characteristic representatives. But Martial also
changes several formal techniques of Lucillius, for instance, the technique
of the closing quip, the witty remark that brings the brief course of the
thought to a brilliant close. The tendency to localize the wit in the ending
was already perceptible in the Hellenistic epigram, but Lucillius had developed it and Martial perfected it. In his hands the epigram acquires a typical
physiognomy and form; it becomes a comic mechanism constructed around
the *fulmen in clausula,* the parting thrust. This trait goes along with that
taste for the *pointe* that was so dear to the rhetoric of the day (Seneca the

Typical scheme of the epigram

Elder had already collected a number of significant examples). The compositional forms are varied but can generally be reduced to a recurring mode,
which has led critics from Lessing on to establish a typical scheme for the
epigram: a first part describes the situation, the object, or the person, creating in the reader the tension of expectation, and the last part, with an effect

of surprise *(aprosdoketon)*, releases that tension in a paradox, a brilliant flare that it sends up.

A preference for realistic poetry such as Martial practices and repeatedly affirms is naturally accompanied by a language and a style that are similarly open to the liveliness of colloquial manner and to the richness of everyday vocabulary. In addition to words for humble, ordinary realities, Martial often enjoys introducing extremely obscene words (obscene realism is an important aspect of his poetry, which he feels called upon to justify through the motif, already found in Catullus and Ovid, of the distinction between art and life: *lasciva est nobis pagina, vita proba* {1.4.8}); the expressive force of these words is sometimes enhanced by his skill at collocation. But a

flexible poet such as Martial can alternate the most varied forms of expression, passing from tones of sober clarity to others that are more elegant and even precious (particularly noteworthy is his parodic use of the solemn phrases of famous poetry). In this context, his celebratory and flattering epigrams are an important document of the mannered language employed at court and in the realm of the official culture. What we find, then, is a richness in modes of expression that corresponds to the multiplicity of subjects and reproduces the flexibility and the variety of the real world that the epigram sets out to interpret.

3. LITERARY SUCCESS

Martial's popularity was immediate and long-lasting. Hadrian's adoptive son, Aelius Verus, called Martial his Virgil. In late antiquity Martial exercised an enormous influence upon such poets as Ausonius, Claudian, Sidonius Apollinaris, and Luxorius; it is Martial who mediates Catullus to late antiquity and the Middle Ages. From the fourth to the sixth centuries he is quoted often in grammarians, from Victorinus, Charisius, and Servius up through Priscian and Isidore of Seville. There are traces of at least three ancient editions of his epigrams, from one of which, prepared in 401 by Torquatus Gennadius, descends one family of medieval manuscripts.

In the Middle Ages, Martial was not a school author but still circulated, less, however, in his own right (there are only about fifteen medieval manuscripts) than in anthologies, which emphasized his *sententiae* and transmitted (often uncharacteristic) moralistic fragments. Starting in the twelfth century, he became an important model for the popular genre of medieval epigram. But the medieval Martial was not always one we would easily recognize. The archetype had provided some of the epigrams with titles that were misleading or on occasion absurdly mistaken. One family of manuscripts tried to expurgate all traces of heterosexual obscenity (remaining, however, generously hospitable to homosexual ones). And a legend followed by such authors as John of Salisbury, Walter Map, Conrad of Mure, and Vincent of Beauvais attributed the authorship of the transmitted poems to an apocryphal Martial the Cook.

Boccaccio, who discovered a manuscript of Martial, helped contribute to his popularity in the Renaissance, which increased dramatically starting in the second quarter of the fifteenth century; there are about 130 Renaissance manuscripts. It was Martial, more than Catullus or even the *Greek Anthology,* who provided poets such as Pontano and Sannazaro a model for new ways to write epigrams. The numerous ribald and obscene epigrammatists of the fifteenth and sixteenth centuries look back to him as their chief model. And it was with the apogee of the genre of epigram in the sixteenth to eighteenth centuries that Martial's own fortunes reached their highest point. English poets from Ben Jonson to Pope imitated him and sought ways to reproduce in English language and meter the effects of concision and point he had perfected in Latin. In German literature, Martial's polemical and demystifying wit was much admired and imitated by the epigrammatic poets of the seventeenth century and later by Lessing. But not everyone admired Martial: Andreas Navagero objected so strongly to his immorality that once a year, on a day dedicated to the Muses, he solemnly burnt a copy of his epigrams.

The last major poets to be strongly influenced by Martial were Goethe and Schiller, who in 1796 published the *Xenia,* three hundred satirical epigrams on contemporary literature, philosophy, and politics. Thereafter, with the collapse of aristocratic society and the unprecedented expansion of the reading public, the genre of epigram, together with the conditions upon which it had depended, declined. And with it declined Martial's own popularity.

BIBLIOGRAPHY

There is an Oxford text of Martial by W. M. Lindsay (Oxford 1903) and Teubners by W. Heraeus, revised J. Borovskij (Leipzig 1976), and D. R. Shackleton Bailey (Stuttgart 1990). The Loeb is by W.C.A. Ker (2 vols., Cambridge, Mass. 1919–20, rev. ed. with complete English translation 1968). The only complete commentary is the German one of L. Friedländer (Leipzig 1886), but there are good editions of book 1 by M. Citroni (Florence 1975, Italian) and P. Howell (London 1980) and of book 11 by N. Kay (London 1985).

There is a recent comprehensive study in English by J. P. Sullivan, *Martial the Unexpected Classic* (Cambridge 1991). In German note esp. R. Reitzenstein, *Epigramm und Scholion* (Giessen 1893), O. Weinreich, *Studien zu Martial* (Stuttgart 1928), K. Barwick, *Martial und die zeitgenössische Rhetorik* (Berlin 1959), and E. Siedschlag, *Zur Form von Martials Epigrammen* (Berlin 1971); in French, P. Laurens, *L'Abeille dans l'ambre: Célébration de l'épigramme de l'époque alexandrine à la fin de la Renaissance* (Paris 1989; see also his article "Martiale et l'épigramme grecque du 1er siècle antique," *REL* 43 [1965] 315–41); and in Italian, C. Salemme, *Marziale e la poetica degli oggetti* (Naples 1976). Three articles in English by P. White have been influential: "The Presentation and Dedication of the *Silvae* and Epigrams," *JRS* 64 (1974) 40–61; "The Friends of Martial, Statius, and Pliny, and the Dispersal of Patronage," *HSCP* 79 (1975) 265–300, and "*Amicitia* and the Profession of Poetry in Early Imperial Rome," *JRS* 68 (1978) 74–92. See, however, for some corrections, M. Citroni, "Pubblicazione e dediche dei libri in Marziale," *Maia* 40 (1988) 3–39, and note R. P. Saller, "Martial on Patronage and Literature," *CQ*

33 (1983) 246–57. Several other articles by Citroni are important; see esp. "La teoria lessinghiana dell'epigramma e le interpretazioni moderne di Marziale," *Maia* 21 (1969) 215–43, and his article on Martial in the *Dizionario degli scrittori classici* (Milan 1988) 1297–1312.

On Martial's extensive *fortuna,* see Sullivan, *Martial the Unexpected Classic,* and Laurens, *L'Abeille dans l'ambre.* Howell's edition of book 1 is particularly useful; see also T. K. Whipple, *Martial and the English Epigram from Sir Thomas Wyatt to Ben Jonson* (Berkeley 1925).

Quintilian

Marcus Fabius Quintilian was born at Calagurris (modern Calahorra), in Spain, around A.D. 35; his father was a teacher of rhetoric. While still young he went to Rome, where he received instruction from the grammarian Remmius Palaemon and the rhetorician Domitius Afer. Later, returning to Spain, he probably practiced law. He was summoned to Rome by Galba in A.D. 68 and began his work as a teacher of rhetoric, without ceasing to be a lawyer. His teaching was very successful (among his pupils he had Pliny the Younger and probably Tacitus), so much so that in 78 Vespasian appointed him the first state professor, with an annual salary of a hundred thousand sesterces. Domitian put him in charge of educating two of his nephews, a circumstance that brought Quintilian the *ornamenta consularia*. In 88, after twenty years, he retired from teaching and forensic activity and devoted himself exclusively to his studies. He died after 95.

A treatise *De Causis Corruptae Eloquentiae* has been lost. Lost, too, are the two books *Artis Rhetoricae*, a set of notes that Quintilian's students derived from his lessons and published against their teacher's will. Quintilian's principal work, however, has been preserved, the twelve books of the *Institutio Oratoria,* which may have been begun in 93 and was probably published shortly before the death of Domitian, in 96. The manuscripts also transmit to us under Quintilian's name two collections of declamations (19 *declamationes maiores* and 145 *declamationes minores,* the latter the surviving part of a collection that originally numbered 388). Despite some opinions to the contrary, criticism now agrees in regarding these two books of *Declamationes* as spurious. The 19 *maiores* in particular it seems impossible to attribute to Quintilian, because they have a strong stylistic coloring that is foreign to the tastes and the judgments he expresses on a number of occasions (see, e.g., *Institutio Oratoria* 2.10.4); already in the fourth century they were circulating under Quintilian's name, and they appear to be derived from a collection made in this period or slightly earlier. The *minores,* however, go back to an earlier period, the first or second century;

some of them may even be authentic (though this is impossible to demonstrate) or at least belong to his school.

SOURCES

Quintilian gives some notices about himself and his activity in several passages of the *Institutio Oratoria*. Others are provided by Jerome's *Chronicle* and references scattered in various other authors (e.g., Martial 2.90 and Juvenal 7.186 ff.).

I. REMEDIES FOR THE CORRUPTION OF ELOQUENCE

The corruption of eloquence: the moral and the literary aspects

The problem of the corruption of eloquence involved questions both of morality and of literary taste. The first aspect was particularly evident in the widespread practice of informing, which often made eloquence serve the purposes of material and moral blackmail. Moreover, the schools, as it seems, often harbored corrupt teachers, who in their turn corrupted the morals of their pupils (Remmius Palaemon, who was one of Quintilian's teachers, was a notorious example). The other aspect of the problem had to do with literary choices, since some saw the expression of virtues and vices of character in the virtues and vices of style. The debate among the various schools of thought about oratory (archaizing, modernizing, Ciceronian) was particularly heated in the Flavian period. From the point of view of literary tastes, Quintilian was the standard-bearer of a classicist reaction to the "corrupt" or "degenerate" style whose chief exponent and principal source was, in Quintilian's eyes, Seneca.

The remedies: moral reconstruction and academic reform

Like other ancient authors, Quintilian sees the problem of the degeneration of eloquence in moral terms, and he locates its cause in the general decline of manners. Yet he is first and foremost a man of large experience in teaching, deeply convinced of the efficacy of education, and so for him the corruption of oratory also has technical causes, which he perceives in the decline of the schools and the absurd inanity of the rhetorical declamations. Thus he trusts in a renewed seriousness in instruction to carry out the task of eliminating the problem to the extent that is possible. The *Institutio Oratoria* sketches out accordingly a comprehensive program of cultural and moral training, which the future orator ought to follow scrupulously from his infancy to his entrance into public life.

Summary of the Institutio Oratoria

The *Institutio Oratoria* is dedicated to Victorius Marcellus, an orator who was also admired by Statius and was a friend of Valerius Probus, and is preceded by a letter to Tryphon, the "publisher" who was to see to its circulation; it is composed of twelve books, as was said. The first two books are properly didactic and pedagogic. They treat elementary instruction and the basis of rhetorical instruction and discuss, among other things, the instructors' duties. Books 3–9 provide a thorough, more technical treatment. They examine analytically the various parts of rhetoric, from its subdivisions to *elocutio* and the figures of speech and of thought. Book 10 teaches the ways of acquiring *facilitas,* that is, ease of expression. In reviewing the authors who ought to be read and to be imitated, Quintilian adds here a famous literary-historical digression on the Greek and Latin writers. This is invaluable evidence for the canons of ancient criticism, but the critical judgments expressed are exclusively rhetorical, and in some ways this produces odd evaluations and unexpected omissions: Quintilian is disposed to show that Latin literature can bear comparison with Greek. (Many of his judgments have become classical formulations of criticism; on Menander, for instance, Thucydides, Sallust, Livy, and Lucan.) Book 11 is concerned with the techniques of memorization and the art of delivery. Finally, book 12 deals in quite desultory manner with various questions of the cultural and moral requirements for the orator, and it also touches upon the problem of relations between the orator and the princeps.

The return to Cicero

Quintilian's stated goal was to take up and adapt to his own times the legacy of Cicero, a task that he was able to carry out with subtlety and a sense of proportion. Quintilian's return to Cicero expresses the need to recover a soundness of expression that at the same time would be a sign of moral strength. Such a need ought perhaps also to be explained by the larger social changes to which Tacitus refers at one point (*Annals* 3.55): he observes that with Vespasian's accession the excesses of the Neronian period had to give way to more sober standards, in part because the *novi homines* of Italian or provincial origin, who were now attaining positions of eminence, tended to reintroduce codes of behavior that were closer to the old Roman tradition.

The establishment of the new classicism

When, presumably around A.D. 90, Quintilian published his (lost) *De Causis Corruptae Eloquentiae,* the New Style, of which Seneca, several decades before, had been the most illustrious exponent, still had its followers and admirers. Yet only a few years later, at the time of the *Institutio,* the situation already seems somewhat altered: the new classicism is establishing itself, and Quintilian, its cultural leader, has practically won the day. Nonetheless, it is still necessary to condemn several intolerable features of modernist excess, intolerable, that is, for Quintilian, who is not an intransigent classicist, to be sure, and who is capable of acknowledging good qualities in Seneca's style. Book 8 of the *Institutio* preserves a lively polemic against the *sententiae* of the Senecan manner. Originally, Quintilian argues, *sententia* had the simple general meaning of "judgment" or "opinion." Now, however, it refers to "the bright passages of the speech, especially those placed at the end of the period" (*lumina praecipueque in clausulis posita* [8.5.2]). The *sententiae* have become a device for making the speech lively. It is easy to recognize the object of the polemic: the continual glittering of short sentences that break up the speech and make it discontinuous and unpredictable, like starts and fits of thought that aim at striking the reader. Seneca's disconnected and fragmented style, his writing "for effect," is created by these devices; and his epigones and imitators must have been attracted to him especially by these devices. "Today," Quintilian continues, shortly after, "people want every passage and every thought that ends a period to strike the ear. And it is regarded as a shame, almost as a crime, to catch one's breath without having provoked applause every time. This is the origin of all those petty thoughts [*sensiculi*], broken into pieces, spoiled, far-fetched, and irrelevant to the matter in hand. Obviously, there cannot be

The polemic against the sententiae

Docere *and* movere:
the importance of the
audience

as many good *sententiae* as there are occasions when the phrase needs to be concluded." Quintilian, in the final analysis, held that elocution should be developed chiefly in relation to the "substance of things" (*rerum pondera* [10.1.130]), whereas Seneca aimed at the listener and the need to capture his interest and shape his reactions. Thus Quintilian's polemic against Seneca and the New Style (as we might say with some simplification) actually represented the clash between two different impulses of discourse. One was the need to *docere,* which bases discourse on the objectivity of the things said and regards the author (i.e., the one speaking or writing) as the sole "performer" of the text. The other, which is characteristic of the New Style, was the need to *movere,* which places the burden of the discourse's meaning upon the audience, the listeners, and makes them (or rather, makes their perception and the emotions with which they react) the real "chief performer" of the text.

2. QUINTILIAN'S EDUCATIONAL PROGRAM

Rhetoric and literary
culture

The type of the ideal orator that Quintilian describes is close to the Ciceronian ideal (see p. 187) by virtue of the extent of the cultural training it demands. But in this general training philosophy seems to have lost ground to rhetoric and literary culture, whose primacy is defended by Quintilian. Thus the program of readings sketched in book 10 gives first place to the choice of Greek and Latin writers. Although sometimes he merely echoes conventional schemes, Quintilian demonstrates notable balance, especially when he takes a position in the ongoing dispute (ongoing since the times of Cicero and Horace) over the superiority of the old or the modern writers. He sees, for instance, considerable deficiencies in the early writers, but he can distinguish between what should be attributed (by way of praise or blame) to the poet specifically and what should be attributed to the age in which he lived.

Style: the reinter-
pretation of the
Ciceronian model

In Quintilian's program, the chief purpose of reading the greatest variety of authors is to shape the orator's style. For this purpose Quintilian recommends the Ciceronian model above all, yet he does so without slavishness. The Ciceronian model is reinterpreted for the purpose of achieving an ideal balance between terseness and bombast. Quintilian was just as opposed to the archaism that would shortly find its leader in Fronto (see pp. 580 f.) as to the excessive modernity of Seneca's Asianism, the *corrupta oratio,* with its sometimes turgid, more often stilted and affected periods. Nonetheless, the style of Quintilian himself is not harmoniously ample and symmetrical as Cicero's is; in some ways, it appears to have been influenced by Seneca's prose. Still, it must be admitted in general that Quintilian's style represents the best example of the virtues he himself recommends. It strives for the utmost clarity and avoids the excesses of ostentatious expression; flexible and undogmatic, rather than pursuing originality it shows balance in the choice of models by which to shape the discourse. This same taste, because it is moderate and its judgments are supported by experience (and it is thus free from preconceived extremism), made Quintilian an author especially dear to the Middle Ages and to the culture of the Renaissance.

3. THE ORATOR AND THE PRINCEPS

The last book of the Institutio: *the defense of professionalism*

A particular problem is posed by the twelfth and last book of the *Institutio,* where Quintilian touches upon the question of the relations between the orator and the princeps. Some interpreters have attributed to Quintilian the ideal of the orator as a "bureaucrat of the word," a subordinate functionary who employs the oratorical technique he possesses in order to transmit the emperor's directives to his audience, the Senate chiefly. This view obviously attaches great importance to the fact that Quintilian became at a certain point the first holder of an official chair of rhetoric. Quintilian is more likely to have been one of those intellectuals who, like Tacitus (see below), accepted the principate as a necessity. Within the limits of this given situation, he strove to secure for the orator the maximum professional recognition and a high degree of dignity. Quintilian's orator does not, to be sure, question the regime, but the moral gifts that he should have—on which Quintilian strongly insisted, as we saw—are useful not so much to the princeps as to society in general (such moral qualities keep the orator away from, for instance, the temptations to become an informer, which was an important tool of the emperor's power and of his control over the aristocracy). Quintilian attempted to win back for the orator a role in civil life that was as far removed from pointless rebellion as from humiliating servility.

Quintilian's illusions and Tacitus's realism

The ideal championed by Quintilian of an orator who is still, as formerly for Cato, *vir bonus dicendi peritus* and who guides the Roman Senate and people remains nonetheless a completely baseless illusion, virtually a negation of the historical reality of the Empire. A very different view of the orator's position, a bitterly realistic one, has been preserved for us in the more or less contemporary *Dialogus de Oratoribus* of Tacitus, which is strongly marked by an awareness of the orator's reduced role and by a disillusioned declaration of an irreversible political impotence.

4. LITERARY SUCCESS

Antiquity

Quintilian long remained a symbol for the program and practice of rhetoric he had tried to establish (and precisely for this reason tended to be neglected by the archaizers of the second century). His ideal of universal knowledge inspired such pedagogues as Augustine, Martianus Capella, and Cassiodorus and, codified as the seven liberal arts, went on to determine the fundamental shape of Western education for many centuries; and the authority of his name attracted to him the *Declamationes* composed by many other rhetors. The *Institutio Oratoria* itself served as a model for Hilary of Poitiers in the fourth century and was studied by Rufinus in the fifth century and Cassiodorus in the sixth, but in general it was little used in late antiquity (Jerome's seventieth letter provides a rare exception). Instead, as with many other handbooks, its text had to be manipulated and abbreviated if it was to become fully effective. It was epitomized by Consultus Fortunatianus and Julius Victor for their own rhetorical handbooks, was used in a rhetorical collection prepared in the eighth century in Montecassino, and some excerpts are found in Cassiodorus's *Institutiones*. The intact text of the whole continued to be copied, but only two ancient manuscripts of it survived the Dark Ages.

Transmission during the Middle Ages

The mostly lacunose medieval tradition of Quintilian is largely French and is centered in Fleury, though one complete manuscript of the *Institutio Oratoria* may have been extant in Germany starting in the tenth or eleventh century. Although he never became a school author, he was known to John of Salisbury, Vincent of Beauvais, and a number of other medieval writers, more perhaps from excerpts in anthologies than from direct contact. Indeed, Quintilian became a crucial reference point for medieval forerunners of the humanists (see especially John of Salisbury's *Metalogicon,* 1159) and helped shape the twelfth-century ideal of education founded upon eloquence. In the Middle Ages, as in antiquity, his text was abbreviated; thus in the twelfth century the poet Étienne de Rouen prepared an abstract, one third the length of the original.

By the end of the Middle Ages, then, incomplete manuscripts of Quintilian were not rare, at least in France, but complete ones were. It was from France that Quintilian returned to Italy, by the fourteenth century, but for generations Italian humanists sought in vain a complete manuscript of the *Institutio Oratoria.* Petrarch complained that he had to make do with an imperfect manuscript; Coluccio Salutati tried in vain to obtain a complete manuscript from France; Gasparino de Barzizza even supplied the missing parts by inventing them himself. It was not until 1416 that Poggio Bracciolini discovered a complete text at St. Gall. Thereafter Quintilian went on to become, next to Cicero, the most important influence upon such Renaissance teachers of rhetoric as Valla, Politian, and Gabriel Harvey, not only inspiring the humanist ideal of the perfect orator but also providing an important stimulus for the Renaissance reform of medieval dialectic. His influence remained strong during the Reformation. He was one of Luther's favorite authors, and Erasmus devoted intense study to his work.

Renaissance

Modern period

Gradually the very bulk of Quintilian's treatise began once again to obstruct its usefulness. He vanished from the Jesuit schools and had to compete with excerpts and summaries (e.g., those of Rollins, published in 1715 in Paris, and of Andres, published in 1782 in Würzburg) as well as with independent handbooks of rhetoric. Nevertheless, as late as the eighteenth century Quintilian still provided an important pedagogical model. In 1779 Frederick the Great tried to have Quintilian read in the schools of Prussia (he ended up having to permit the use not only of the full text but also of a summary). And as a young man in Strasbourg, Goethe filled notebook after notebook with extracts from Quintilian—whom he later came to abhor. But with the decline of public oratory and with Romanticism's new ideas of the nature of children and the proper way to educate them, Quintilian's ideal came to seem increasingly abstract and his goal increasingly unrealistic. Even the modern proponents of the study of the great books with the goal of verbal proficiency in the service of the public good would be surprised to learn that one of their ultimate sources is Quintilian.

BIBLIOGRAPHY

The standard modern text of Quintilian is that of M. Winterbottom (2 vols., Oxford 1970); see also the Budé edition with French translation and notes by J. Cousin (7 vols., Paris 1975–80). The Loeb is by H. E. Butler (4 vols., Cambridge, Mass. 1920–22). There are English commentaries on book 1 by F. H. Colson (Cambridge 1924), on book 10 by W. Petersen (Oxford 1891), and on book 12 by R. G. Austin (Oxford 1928), and a German one on book 3 by J. Adamietz (Munich 1966).

There is a brief introduction to Quintilian by G. Kennedy, *Quintilian* (New York 1969); see also his *Art of Rhetoric in the Roman World* (Princeton 1972) 487–514 and "An Estimate of Quintilian," *AJP* 83 (1962) 130–46, M. L. Clarke, *Rhetoric at Rome* (London 1953) 109–29, H.-I. Marrou, *A History of Education in Antiquity*, translated badly by G. Lamb (London 1956), A. D. Leeman, *Orationis Ratio: The Stylistic Theories and Practice of the Roman Orators, Historians, and Philosophers* (Amsterdam 1963) 287–310, M. Winterbottom, "Quintilian and Rhetoric," in *Empire and Aftermath: Silver Latin II,* ed. T. A. Dorey (London 1975) 79–97, M. L. Clarke, "Quintilian and Education," ibid. 98–118, and S. F. Bonner, *Education in Ancient Rome* (London 1977). In other languages, note esp. J. Cousin, *Études sur Quintilien* (2 vols., Paris 1935–36); his *Recherches sur Quintilien* (Paris 1975) is principally on the textual tradition. There is an *ANRW* survey in German by J. Adamietz (32.4, Berlin 1986, 2226–71).

The *declamationes maiores* have been edited by L. Håkanson (Stuttgart 1982), and the *minores* by M. Winterbottom (Berlin 1984, with detailed English commentary). There is a useful English translation of the *maiores* by L. A. Sussman (Frankfurt 1987); note also M. Winterbottom's brief selection *Roman Declamation* (Bristol 1980). For discussion, see S. F. Bonner, *Roman Declamation* (Liverpool 1949), and J. Dingel, *Scholastica Materia: Untersuchungen zu der Declamationes Minores und der Institutio Oratoria Quintilians* (Berlin 1988).

The Age of the Adoptive Emperors

I. A PERIOD OF PEACE AND STABILITY

The period that begins with the principate of Nerva and ends with the death of Commodus (A.D. 96–192) constitutes, if we except the last twelve years, those of Commodus's principate, an entire century of tranquillity that has no equal, in length and benefits, in any earlier period of Roman history. If the first century of the Empire had been characterized by relative political instability, by tensions and conflicts in government, the second century, though varying somewhat with the emperors who ruled, is characterized by a substantial uniformity in the handling of power. The Senate, though now deprived of its authority, recovers a small amount of its power in relation to the emperor and in the end adapts itself to a role that is limited (or rather, subordinate) but no longer exposed to those violent and insulting attacks that had so stained the government of the Caesars under the first Empire. The problem of the imperial succession had found a satisfactory solution (at least as long as it lasted) in the system of adoption; this assured, at least down to Marcus Aurelius, a series of emperors endowed with high personal qualities. The stability achieved by governmental organization reduced what had been the continual nuisance of conspiracies and rebellions set in motion by the powerful generals of the army, who had been inclined to use their military might to realize their personal ambitions for power. It also allowed the emperors to undertake institutional and social reforms that had previously been unthinkable.

The pursuit of grace and courtesy

Although the Empire's boundaries now reached their greatest extension, this period could certainly not be called heroic. Instead, due especially to the absence of serious political and social tensions, the prevailing climate was generally one of harmony and active cooperation. This picture of widespread serenity should not lead us to forget the vigor of strong moral spirits, which we find, for example, in the deep convictions and unyielding commitment of writers like Tacitus and Juvenal; nor was the spirit of adventure lacking, as we are reminded when we look at the Pantheon or the Column of Trajan or when we recall the wars of Trajan himself and the opening of trade with the Far East. Yet it is true that the whole period is dominated by a new pursuit of grace and courtesy, by an elegant sense of culture as the art of social forms that were capable of censuring and concealing the less pleasant aspects of life. In this sense Pliny the Younger may be regarded as the person who symbolizes the age of Trajan, an age that was pleased to believe in the recovered felicity of the Empire and found it almost astonishing that everything had not always been so calm and tranquil as it seemed to be at that time. In Pliny's *Panegyric* of Trajan not only courtliness and mannered rhetoric are present; present as well is the genuine enthusiasm (transposed into declamatory form) of a man who believes, and wants others to believe, that to the extent that Roman authority is now stronger, *pietas* is more widespread. Even Tacitus's lucid bitterness is directed only at the past and thus implicitly acknowledges that now, unlike in the past, things were truly just as Pliny's self-satisfied superficiality was fond of portraying them.

2. CULTURAL REFINEMENT AND ERUDITE PHILOLOGY

Accommodating itself to the ease of social life and to the felicity of the times—the Empire never enjoyed such economic prosperity, political stability, and security on its borders—culture now tends towards a showy refinement. The dominant cultivated class chooses a life made esthetic by sophisticated literature and ornamental arts; thus a precious mannerism of style is produced that corresponds to a widespread erudite philology. There may never have been another period of Roman history in which literature and culture in general enjoy wider public patronage than in this one—this despite the many complaints that poets and writers in general utter against the lack of disinterested patronage. A number of public libraries were created by the political powers; Trajan indeed created in the Basilica Ulpia, which was located in the Forum of Trajan, the largest library Rome had ever had. Instruction in Greek and Latin rhetoric was instituted not only at Rome but in the provinces too; Gaul alone in this period came to have eleven such schools. The number of illiterates was never as low as at this time. The many inscriptions incised or scratched on marble that belong to this period indirectly attest (many times the inscriptions are crudely scribbled) the widespread knowledge of reading and writing even among the humbler classes.

Along with this flourishing of the academic institutions of intermediate and upper level, Roman culture in this period witnesses an extraordinary renaissance' of literature in Greek. There is reason to believe that the emperor Hadrian's predilection for Greek culture (some nicknamed him *Graeculus*) had much to do with favoring this movement, but the most important cause is surely to be sought in the exceptional situation of peace, security, and relative prosperity in which the entire eastern Mediterranean now found itself. The most conspicuous result of this Greek renaissance was undoubtedly the formation of the school called the Second Sophistic, an ambitious restoration of the one that had flourished in the time of Gorgias and Socrates. These new sophists, however, were not philosophers but rhetoricians such as Aelius Aristides, Herodes Atticus, or Fronto, the teacher and friend of the emperor Marcus Aurelius. Greek in origin, often remarkably talented, frequently traveling about as representatives and ambassadors of their native cities or provinces, they could compose or deliver speeches on topical subjects or on religious, ethical, political, or consolatory themes. They were readily accepted in the Roman upper classes, and they were received with such warm welcome by the imperial government that they were admitted to the equestrian order and the Senate. Some were also important in the political and administrative life of the Empire; often, as in the case of the historians Appian and Arrian, they joined the imperial bureaucracy. In much the same way, Greek intellectuals such as Plutarch or Lucian or Galen, the great medical encyclopedist, were drawn into the orbit of Roman power, where they were welcomed and appreciated in every way.

The emperor Hadrian

Although Hellenism and the sophistic movement seem to reach their culmination in the memoirs "To Himself," which the emperor Marcus Aurelius composed in Greek, nonetheless it is the *Graeculus* emperor Hadrian who best represents his era's taste for this late renaissance of Greek culture. A poet himself, slight but refined, he wrote short poems in the neoteric style of the Catullans (some fragments are preserved, full of soft tones and gentle verbal caprices). A knowledgeable admirer of the antique, interested in philology and literary controversies, he was largely responsible for the establishment of the new literary ideal. His philology led him to side with the archaicists then in fashion (and to prefer Ennius over Virgil, Cato over Cicero, the annalists over Sallust). Yet he exercised his most decisive influence less as a highly literary poet than as a promoter of culture. He established at Rome a kind of academy known as the Athenaeum, in which noted rhetoricians and intellectuals held lessons and gave lectures. The classicism that inspired him was shown even more fully in the figurative arts, especially in sculpture and in magnificent works of architecture. In his splendid villa at Tivoli, which he had made a true museum, he collected many works of the ancient masters (many of the pieces are today in the Vatican Museums). He also had an immense number of copies made of the classic works of Greek sculpture; and it is from these that the modern period derived its first notion of what great Greek art was.

3. THE SIGNS OF THE FUTURE: RELIGIOUS SYNCRETISM AND THE REVIVAL OF BELIEFS IN AN AFTERLIFE

Cultural contacts with the East

We have referred several times to a certain serenity that the second century as a whole shows to the eye of the historian. But we ought to note that this widespread social-political tranquillity, projected into an ideal of restored classicism, concealed within itself, and also fostered, new developments that would be decisive for later culture. The Roman world was about to be transformed—even if those transformations would not emerge clearly before the age of the Severans and only the first inklings could be perceived now—into a social reality that because of wider cultural contacts with the East was to become more markedly cosmopolitan. This is the only way to understand how several decades later, when interest in politics had declined almost completely and new spiritual concerns had come to the fore, a climate of religious syncretism arose in which divinities and beliefs from the most diverse forms of faith came to be mixed. (Severus Alexander is said to have constructed two chapels in his palace, one dedicated to Orpheus, Abraham, Christ, and Apollonius of Tyana, the ascetic, wandering holy man who spread the neo-Pythagorean creed, and the other dedicated to Cicero, Virgil, and those of his ancestors who had been benefactors of mankind.) The chief reason one can point to is the convergence of two basic tendencies. First, the pagan religions practiced in the first two centuries undergo a sort of general leveling, in that many of the religions and cults belonging to the different provinces of the Empire are assimilated through analogy, and so absorbed, by the official cults of Rome. Second, even among educated people, or rather especially among them (one thinks of people important in such different ways as Suetonius and Plutarch), we find the revival of beliefs and practices tied to a belief in the hereafter: oracles, presages, dream interpretation, magical practices, faith in supernatural powers and in the thaumaturgic qualities of the (deified) emperors all return to favor, the signs of a widely felt spiritual need.

The return of beliefs in the hereafter

The exhaustion of Stoicism

Once the attraction of philosophical sects and doctrines such as Stoicism was exhausted (Stoicism would soon be absorbed in some ways by Christianity), it was inevitable that new religious faiths would be established, ones that could offer, not the exemplary model of imperturbable wise men shut in their own egoism, but the fascinating and complex instruction of those religious reformers who preached altruism as the decisive test of a truly moral human behavior. The Stoic (and especially Cynic) injunction to "live according to nature" could no longer satisfy the more demanding spirits; Stoicism would have its last triumphs in the lay strictness of the emperor Marcus Aurelius.

The cults of Isis and Mithras

New beliefs and new cultural practices not only imposed more demanding duties but also offered the hope of higher rewards. The joint cult of Isis and Serapis reached the outmost regions of Germany and Britain in the first and second centuries, but it soon gave way before another Eastern cult, that of the Persian Mithras. Originally a divinity of light and truth, the agent of Ahura-Mazda (who was the power of good opposed to Athriman, the power of evil), Mithras was transformed, just at the end of the pre-Christian era, into the central divinity of a Roman mystery cult. Following in the paths of merchants and soldiers, he spread from Asia Minor throughout the Romanized world. The cult, which derived in part from Persian Zoroastrianism (Mithras was identified with the Sun), had many features in common with the cult of the Phrygian goddess Cybele. Because of the syncretism that blurred the distinctive features of each mystery cult, it soon supplanted the cult of Isis, in whose path it followed and not a few of whose external features it adopted. It was more attractive than the Isiac cult in that it not only promised future immortality but also could impose a living, practical code of morality. In certain respects, it was not very different from Christianity, which inculcated the obligation to do good and made altruism and brotherhood the center of its virtues. Under the veil of the mysteries, the initiates began on the path towards knowledge of the truth and freedom from impurity (the journey of the immortal soul); the initiation also included a kind of baptism (with bull's blood, derived from the cult of the goddess Cybele).

Mithraism and Christianity

In Mithraism very great importance was attached to a symbolism connected to the zodiacal signs and the planetary divinities (and Mithraic art appears strongly marked by such representations). Initiation and worship were limited to men, however; it seems to have been addressed especially to wealthy businessmen and army officials. It does not seem to have been widespread among the lower classes, which may have been put off by the complex and sophisticated esoteric symbolism. In this it is completely different from Christianity, whose first followers were people of humble situation. Men and women, free and slave, took part in the Christian gatherings, drawn by the simplicity of the rituals. Even though it remains rather obscure to some scholars how and why Christianity easily defeated the Mithraic religion with which it was competing (and which, among other things, could count on the connivance or the explicit support of the second-century emperors), one may readily believe that Christianity succeeded in establishing itself against any other religion practiced in the Empire by virtue of the solid, articulated organization with which the faithful soon provided it. Already at the beginning of the second century (after a period of initial experimentation in which dominant figures such as apostles, prophets, and teachers of doctrine were active), a hierarchical structure existed, a clergy, with its own bishops, under whom were placed many elders and deacons; this clergy had wide powers over the lay faithful. Along with this sturdy hierarchical structure, moreover, a unique system of communication among the various Christian communities soon began to function.

Creation of a Christian religious literature

The early creation of a vast religious literature must have contributed greatly to the consolidation of Christianity. This literature aimed not simply at establishing norms but also at preserving Christian doctrine from contamination by other religions and other systems of thought, by Stoicism, for example, and Platonism. Already by about 130 the doctrinal corpus of the four Gospels and the thirteen epistles of Paul was commonly accepted as the New Testament, a collection of books analogous to the Hebrew collection of the Old Testament. The Christian communities also had written records of their own histories and thus produced a literature of testimonies that has come down to us under the name *Acts of the Martyrs* (see pp. 598 f.), accounts of trials and scenes of martyrdom, of persecutions and moving acts of courage and faith, in which the numerous miraculous and legendary traits are intended to offer pictures of exemplary spiritual edification. The same combativeness with which the church had had to defend itself led, in the second century, to a large, zealous literature written by apologists (see pp. 600 f.), learned defenders of the Christian creed who wanted to show to a vast public of readers how ethically superior the new religion was (and also how unjustly defamed). In addition to the need to defend Christianity from the violent attacks made on it (no other religion in antiquity was ever opposed so strongly), the need to protect its doctrine from the numerous heresies that immediately sprang up around it explains why so intense and abundant a literary activity developed. At the beginning, in the climate of syncretism of religion and mystery that characterizes this whole period, it was easy for the Christian beliefs to lose their simple essential quality and to become infected with complex notions, in which there were mixed together magical, philosophical, mythological, and cosmological elements, the property of other religions or the residue of old beliefs. Hence the need for writing, in order to reason, to explain, and to rebut, through argument and confutation.

Pliny the Younger

Gaius Caecilius Secundus was born at Como in A.D. 61 or 62. Upon the death of his father he was adopted by Pliny, his maternal uncle, whose name he took. He studied rhetoric at Rome under the tutelage of Quintilian and Nicetes Sacerdos, a Greek rhetorician of the Asianic school. He soon began his legal career, in which he obtained notable successes, and also the *cursus honorum;* he was successively quaestor, tribune of the plebs, and praetor, and in 98 he was appointed *praefectus aerarii Saturni* (roughly, "minister of the treasury"). In 100 Pliny, along with the historian Tacitus, who was his friend, brought an accusation against Marius Priscus, the proconsul of Asia. Towards the end of that same year he was appointed *consul suffectus.* Evidently, the passage from Domitian's principate to those of Nerva and Trajan caused no harm to Pliny's career in law and politics. In 111 Trajan appointed him his legate in Bithynia. He died not long afterwards, probably in 113.

Panegyricus, an enlarged version of the speech of thanks that he delivered to Trajan in the Senate on the occasion of his appointment as consul, in A.D. 100. A collection of *Epistulae* in ten books, the first nine containing letters composed from 97 to 108 and published by Pliny himself, the tenth containing private and official letters from Pliny to Trajan, as well as the emperor's replies. The letters collected in the tenth book belong for the most part to the period in which Pliny was governor of Bithynia; it is likely that they were published after his death and added to his own collection as a tenth book. Nothing remains of his many poetic works and speeches, which are often mentioned in the *Epistulae.*

Details of Pliny's life and activities come for the most part from his own correspondence.

I. PLINY AND TRAJAN

The *Panegyricus* has come down to us as the first in a collection of later panegyrics of various emperors (on which see pp. 632 ff.), the virtual beginning of a literary genre. (The title may not be original: the term originally indicated the speeches delivered at the pan-Hellenic ceremonies; in the first century A.D. it came to indicate the encomium of the monarch.) The *gratiarum actio* before the Senate becomes an encomium of the emperor, who had the power to recommend to the Senate the appointment of the magistrates. Pliny enumerates and celebrates the virtues of the *optimus princeps* Trajan, who has restored freedom of speech and thought. After Domitian's grim tyranny, which he defames bitterly (although, as was said, even under Domitian Pliny had had a peaceful life and had gone through the entire *cursus honorum* except for the consulship), Pliny expresses his hopes for a renewed collaboration between the emperor and the Senate and attempts to describe a model of behavior for the future emperors, a model obviously based on continued concord between emperor and aristocracy and on close political understanding and cultural integration between the latter and the equestrian class, which is the chief source of manpower for the bureaucracy and the administration. Despite the fundamentally hopeful tone, here and there in the *Panegyricus* the concern emerges that wicked emperors could come to power again and that the Senate could once again suffer as much as it had under Domitian.

The attempt to educate the princeps

Pliny, not without a certain ingenuousness, seems to take a pedagogic stance towards the princeps. In the midst of the many praises and the formulas of courteousness, he is clearly attempting to exercise a mild form of control over the wielder of absolute power. It is not an accident that scholars have noticed a certain affinity, even from the stylistic point of view, between the *Panegyricus* and Cicero's *Pro Marcello* (see p. 184).

The real relations between Pliny and Trajan

Despite the pedagogic stance taken by Pliny, the real relations between him and Trajan emerge clearly from the correspondence they conducted during the former's governorship in Bithynia, which is preserved, as was said, in the tenth book of the *Epistulae*. Pliny behaves like a scrupulous and loyal yet somewhat indecisive official, informing Trajan about all the problems he faces—public works, problems of finance and public order, among them the trials of the Christians—and waiting for advice and orders from him. In Trajan's replies one occasionally catches a light hint of annoyance at the continual queries Pliny puts to him, even on matters of secondary importance. The emperor is famous for his attitude of calm tolerance towards the Christians. There being no relevant laws on the books, he instructs Pliny not to try them except in the case of declarations that are not made anonymously and in any event to suspend the trial if the accused, by sacrificing to the pagan gods, gives evidence that he is not a Christian or is no longer one. He is obviously concerned not to punish offenses against religion, thus freeing himself from responsibility in regard both to informers and to public opinion.

Trajan and Christianity

2. PLINY AND THE SOCIETY OF HIS DAY

Careful arrangement of a correspondence intended for publication

The first nine books of the *Epistulae* were published, as was said, by Pliny himself, possibly in groups. In the prefatory letter to Septicius Clarus, Pliny claims that in grouping his letters he has not followed any exact criterion, in particular that he has not paid attention to chronology; the letters are supposed to follow one another in a completely casual sequence. Pliny's claim is to be regarded as disingenuous. It is likely that the arrangement is based on a principle of alternation in subjects and motifs, in such a way as to avoid monotony for the reader. Pliny's letters are in fact usually devoted each to a single theme, which is always handled with careful attention to literary elegance. That is one of the most important differences between this correspondence, which from the outset is intended for publication, and the correspondence of Cicero (see pp. 202 f.), in which the eagerness to communicate often compelled the author to jumble together the most varied subjects, and to do so occasionally with references that are extremely brief and far from clear to a reader other than the original recipient. The style of Pliny's correspondence aims at grace and elegance, which

Ciceronian model and hints of mannerism

it secures chiefly by a firm self-discipline; it is fond of antithesis, for instance, but does not use it excessively. The preferred model is Cicero, from whom Pliny takes over the taste for clear phraseology, the harmonious architecture of the period, and the recurring rhythmical schemes, even though the periods are shorter (but Pliny, as lay in his nature, does not like excess, and he openly declares to his friend Tacitus that he does not approve of his *brevitas*). And yet one does glimpse some touch of mannerism in his fondness for asyndeton and anaphora, in the care he devotes to avoiding repetitions, and especially in the affectation of a spontaneous correspondence, not intended for publication.

Content of Pliny's letters

Pliny's letters are really a series of brief essays chronicling the fashionable, intellectual, and civil life of his day. The author always addresses his interlocutors with extreme ceremoniousness (phrases of more or less affected courtesy abound in his correspondence, even to the point of becoming cloying). He informs them about his activities and recreations and his concerns as a large landowner. He depicts the country in mannerist tones, describing it principally as a panorama enjoyed through the windows of his villas, although some descriptions, such as of the sources of the Clitumnus or of the eruption of Vesuvius, in which his uncle, Pliny the Elder,

Pliny's addressees and enthusiastic ceremoniousness

died, are very powerful and have enjoyed great success with posterity. He praises various people, especially writers and poets who are alive or but recently dead, such as Silius Italicus and Martial. It is rare for him not to find for each person mentioned in his letters some courteous phrase that calls attention to his good qualities. Pliny shows himself to be a frequenter of the halls where *recitationes* and *declamationes* were held, cultural events that he himself to a large extent helped organize. He is an enthusiast who is not stingy with words of praise for nearly all the versifiers and lecturers he hears. But Pliny praises above all his own poetic activity, for which he is distressed at not being able to find sufficiently suitable and educated appreciators.

Pliny's formalism and his literary tastes

Unlike his teacher Quintilian or his friend Tacitus, Pliny is not concerned with the cultural crisis. He discerns, at most, a certain decline in the taste of the listeners, who are less keen on attending literary events than formerly. The literature he likes is essentially frivolous, intended for entertainment and for an ephemeral consumption during the dinners of aristocrats or in the public halls—passages of oratory declaimed, and especially *versiculi*, poetic *nugae* often somewhat insipid, the origin and product of a relaxation without worries and without enthusiasms. Moreover, the social relations that emerge from Pliny's correspondence also often appear marked by an empty and ceremonious formalism, the symptom of the advanced impoverishment and banalization of what had been the great cultural tradition of the Roman ruling class.

Pliny and the culture of his time

It is easy to understand how Pliny's worldliness and his being simultaneously a very wealthy man, an important political figure, and a valued author placed him in a privileged position as an observer of his time. The greatest figures of the day appear in Pliny's letters, from the emperor Trajan (of whom we have already spoken) to Tacitus (to whom the letter on the eruption of Vesuvius was addressed; Tacitus is frequently addressed by Pliny, who is delighted at having been mistaken for his friend the historian in the Circus, evidently by someone who, as Pliny must have thought, confused the two greatest writers of the day), and on to Suetonius (whom Pliny urges to publish once and for all the *De Viris Illustribus* that he has had in the drawer for some while). The occurrences of the day also appear, from the most important and tragic, such as the eruption of Vesuvius (but Pliny, who already at the age of seventeen must have had the character he would have as a man, is not fond of strong sensations: while everything is in commotion and his uncle sets out to meet his death, he remains behind to summarize Livy), to the petty rumors circulating in high, cultivated circles. It is Pliny's correspondence alone that preserves for us the names of many authors and gives us an overall picture of literature in the period of the Flavians and Trajan.

3. LITERARY SUCCESS

Antiquity

The calm and balanced civility of Pliny's letters and the superficiality of his interests may make him less appealing for modern readers but help explain his success among ancient ones. The very accessibility of the model he provided may have contributed to the formative influence he exercised upon later epistolary authors in antiquity. In particular he was revived in the late fourth century when Silver Latin literature became newly fashionable. It was at this time that Symmachus published a collection of nine books of his own private letters and one of public ones and that Ambrose put together nine books of his speciously private letters and one of documents. But the fact that a century later Sidonius Apollinaris published his letters in nine books suggests that two collections of Pliny's letters may have circulated in antiquity, a nine-book edition and a ten-book one (with indexes); our manuscripts all go back to a French archetype derived from the latter source. The *Panegyricus* served as a model in late antiquity, when such public eulogies became a favorite literary genre in Gaul.

Middle Ages and Renaissance

In the Middle Ages, when the epistle ceased to be an important literary mode, the younger Pliny was not as widely known as his maternal uncle.

He did not become a school author, and references to him are rare. Bishop Rather of Verona quoted his letters once, John of Salisbury his *Panegyric*. It was in the Renaissance that Pliny's fortunes reached their high point (though his correspondence never became as popular as Cicero's): he provided a model of the tactful, shrewd, but not thoroughly dishonest courtier for a society that desperately needed one. In 1338 in Avignon Simon of Arezzo bequeathed to Dominicus of Arezzo a manuscript containing Apuleius's *Golden Ass* and ten of Pliny's letters. In 1419 in Venice Guarino discovered a manuscript containing 124 new letters besides the 100 that had become known in the meantime. But it was not until after 1494 that Fra Giovanni Giocondo discovered a manuscript containing all ten books of the letters. Pliny's *Panegyric* to Trajan had been discovered in Mainz by Aurispa in 1433. For generations Pliny's letters, together with Cicero's, taught European men what tone to adopt in their own correspondence, and his *Panegyric* taught them how to address supreme political authority in public oratory. Nowadays the former remain of interest primarily for ancient historians studying Roman administration and social life of the late first century, and the latter, if at all, only for experts on ancient rhetoric.

BIBLIOGRAPHY

The standard modern texts are those of R.A.B. Mynors, *Epistulae* (Oxford 1963) and *Panegyricus* in *XII Panegyrici Latini* (Oxford 1964), which are those used in the Loeb edition with translation by B. Radice (2 vols., Cambridge, Mass. 1969); see also the Teubner text of M. Schuster, revised by R. Hanslik (Leipzig 1958). There is a commentary on the *Epistulae* by A. N. Sherwin-White (Oxford 1966); for the *Panegyricus* see the edition of M. Durry (Paris 1938).

There are good English introductions to the *Epistulae* by A. N. Sherwin-White in *G&R* 16 (1979) 76–90 and to the *Panegyricus* by B. Radice in *G&R* 15 (1968) 166–72; on the latter see also S. MacCormack, "Latin Prose Panegyrics," in *Empire and Aftermath: Silver Latin II*, ed. T. A. Dorey (London 1975) 143–205. See also F. Gamberini, *Stylistic Theory and Practice in the Younger Pliny* (Hildesheim 1983). In other languages, see E. Allain, *Pline le Jeune et ses héritiers* (4 vols., Paris 1901–2), M. Guillemin, *Pline et la vie littéraire de son temps* (Paris 1929), P. V. Cova, *La critica letteraria di Plinio il Giovane* (Brescia 1966), H.-P. Bütler, *Die geistige Welt des jüngeren Plinius* (Heidelberg 1970), and F. Trisoglio, *La personalità di Plinio il Giovane nei suoi rapporti con la politica, la società, la letteratura* (Turin 1972). *ANRW* 33.1 (Berlin 1989) deals with Pliny and includes surveys of research on the *Epistulae* by E. Aubrion (French) and on the *Panegyricus* by P. Fedeli (Italian).

Tacitus

LIFE

Publius (or Gaius?) Cornelius Tacitus was born around A.D. 55, in Terni according to some sources but more probably in Narbonese Gaul, of a family that may have had equestrian status. He studied at Rome, and in 78 he married the daughter of Gnaeus Julius Agricola, an influential statesman and military commander. Thanks in part to the help of Agricola, Tacitus began his political career under Vespasian and continued it under Titus and Domitian. After having been praetor in 88 (in the same year he is attested as one of the *quindecemviri sacris faciundis,* one of the greater priestly colleges), Tacitus was away from Rome for several years, probably on a posting in Gaul or Germany. In 97, under Nerva, he was *consul suffectus.* Already a famous orator, he delivered the funeral elogium over Virginius Rufus, the consul who had died during his year of office and whom Tacitus had replaced. One or two years later, under the principate of Trajan, together with Pliny the Younger, who was his close friend, he conducted the prosecution for the provincials of Africa against their ex-governor Marius Priscus, who was accused of corruption; after some delays the trial ended in 100 with the condemnation of Priscus to exile. Subsequently Tacitus was proconsul of Asia in 112 or 113. He probably died around 117.

WORKS

De Vita Iulii Agricolae, published in 98; *De Origine et Situ Germanorum,* more commonly known as the *Germania,* probably from the same year; *Dialogus de Oratoribus,* from shortly after 100 (it is dedicated to Fabius Justus, consul in 102); *Histories,* in twelve or fourteen books, written between 100 and 110; *Annals,* or *Ab Excessu Divi Augusti,* in sixteen or eighteen books, written after the *Histories* and possibly left incomplete by the author's death. Of the *Histories* only books 1–4 have come down to us, along with part of book 5 and some fragments. Of the *Annals,* we have books 1–4, a small portion of 5, book 6, part of 11, books 12–15, and part of 16. There is much controversy concerning the number of books that made up the *Histories* and the *Annals:* some hold that they comprised twelve and eighteen books, respectively; others, fourteen and sixteen. The latter hypothesis is supported by the numbering in the Second Medicean manuscript, but the problem is complicated by the fact that the two works, though published separately, very soon began to circulate in a combined edition of thirty books, in which, reversing the sequence of composition, the *Annals* preceded the *Histories,* thus forming a continuous narrative of Roman history from the death of Augustus to the death of Domitian.

SOURCES

General information about Tacitus's life and career is derived chiefly from some passages of the *Agricola,* the *Dialogus,* and the *Histories* and from various letters of Pliny the Younger.

I. THE CAUSES OF THE DECLINE OF ORATORY

Authenticity of the
Dialogus

The *Dialogus de Oratoribus* is not, in all likelihood, Tacitus's first work. The prevailing notion today is that it was composed after the *Agricola* and the *Germania.* Yet on account of various features that tend to separate it from his work as a whole, it is a well-established tradition to begin any treatment of Tacitus with it. This separation is such as to have brought into question the authenticity of the *Dialogus,* which is transmitted in the manuscript tradition along with the *Agricola* and the *Germania.* Its authenticity has been contested ever since the sixteenth century, chiefly on stylistic grounds, by philologists of the highest abilities, and among modern scholars as well there are some grave doubts about Tacitean authorship. The sentence construction in the *Dialogus* resembles far more closely the neo-Ciceronian style, polished but not prolix, which was the basis of instruction in Quintilian's school, than it does the severe and asymmetric *inconcinnitas* that was typical of Tacitus's larger historical works. Even among those who defend its authenticity, therefore, the hypothesis has won credence that regards the *Dialogus* as a youthful work composed between 75 and 80 by a Tacitus who is still tied to the classicizing preferences of the Quintilianic school. On this hypothesis, the *Dialogus,* even if written under the reign of Titus, would have been published only much later, after Domitian's death, and the dedication to Fabius Justus would refer, obviously, to the time of publication. But it is more likely that the unusual classicism of the style is to be explained by the fact that the *Dialogus* belongs to the rhetorical genre, for which the structure, vocabulary, and style of Cicero's rhetorical works still constituted a canonic model.

Summary of the
Dialogus

The *Dialogus de Oratoribus,* set in 75 or 77 (one gets partially contradictory indications from the text on this point), is connected with the tradition of the Ciceronian dialogues on philosophical and rhetorical subjects. It reports a discussion that is imagined as taking place in the house of Curiatius Maternus, rhetorician and tragedian, among Curiatius himself, Marius Aper, Vipstanus Messalla, and Julius Secundus (Tacitus claims to have been present at this discussion in his youth). Since Aper at the beginning of the conversation has reproached Maternus with neglecting eloquence in favor of dramatic poetry, we have at first antithetic speeches by Aper and Maternus, defending, respectively, eloquence and poetry. The course of the debate takes a sudden turn with the arrival of Messalla, whereupon it shifts to the theme of the decline of oratory. Messalla locates the causes for it in the deterioration of the future orator's training, both at home and at school, which is not looked after as in early days: the teachers are unprepared, and a vacuous rhetoric often takes the place of general culture. After a section that contains several lacunae, the dialogue ends with a speech by Maternus, evidently the spokesman for Tacitus, who argues that a great oratory may have been possible only with the freedom, or rather with the anarchy, that prevailed in the days of the Republic, in the heat of civil turmoil and conflict. It becomes anachronistic and impracticable in a tranquil, orderly society such as the one that came into being after the establishment of the Empire. The peace that this assures must be accepted without undue regrets for a past that, to be sure, did offer a more favorable soil for the blossoming of literature and the flourishing of great personalities.

The inevitability of the principate

The view attributed to Maternus represents a constant in Tacitus's thought. At the base of all his thought is the unarguable acceptance of the Empire as the sole force that can save the state from the chaos of civil war. The principate hinders and limits the orator and the politician, but there are no alternatives to the principate. This does not mean that Tacitus welcomes the imperial regime, nor that within this limited space he does not point out the opportunity left for making choices that are more or less honorable, more or less useful to the state. This indeed was the theme he had already dealt with in his biography of Agricola.

2. AGRICOLA AND THE FUTILITY OF OPPOSITION

The Agricola *as* laudatio funebris

Near the beginning of Trajan's reign Tacitus took advantage of the revival of freedom after Domitian's tyranny to publish his first historical work, which records for posterity the memory of his father-in-law Julius Agricola, who was a loyal imperial official and the man chiefly responsible for conquering a large part of Britain under Domitian's reign. Because of its occasionally encomiastic tone the *Agricola* recalls in part the style of the funeral *laudationes.* After a brief summary of the protagonist's career before his post in Britain, the work focuses chiefly on his conquest of the island, allowing a certain amount of space for geographic and ethnographic digressions; these last derive from Agricola's notes and recollections but in part also from the notices about Britain found in Caesar's *Commentarii.* Because of these digressions, the subject of the *Agricola* has appeared to exceed sometimes the limits of a simple biography. In fact, the author never loses sight of his principal character: Britain is the principal field in which Agricola's *virtus* is unfolded, the scene of his remarkable deeds.

Agricola and the glorification of the "middle path"

In praising the character of his father-in-law, Tacitus emphasizes how, as governor of Britain and head of an army at war, he had been able to serve the state faithfully, honorably, and well even under a terrible princeps such as Domitian (Tacitus explicitly criticizes the latter and his cruel system of espionage and repression more than once). In the end Agricola, who did not favor opposition for its own sake and yet was not inclined to dishonor himself by servility, also fell into disgrace with Domitian, but not without having demonstrated to what extent a man could work usefully on behalf of the community until such time as the clash could no longer be avoided. Encountering the corruption of others without being corrupted himself, Agricola can die in silence—and Tacitus draws a veil over the real causes of his death, whether natural or intended by Domitian—and die without seeking the death of an ostentatious martyr, that *ambitiosa mors* (such as the suicide of the Stoics) that Tacitus condemns as being of no use to the *res publica*. Agricola's shining example indicates how under a tyranny a man can, without necessarily running grave risks, stick to the path that lies in the middle between those alternatives that Tacitus would describe, in a famous passage of the *Annals* (4.20.7), as *deforme obsequium* and *abrupta contumacia*. The praise of an emblematic figure such as Agricola becomes a defense of the "sound" part of the governing class, that is, men who, without any desire to be martyrs, had collaborated with the emperors of the Flavian house in developing the laws, governing the provinces, extending the boundaries, and defending the frontiers of the Empire, men who, once freedom was recovered, would have regarded as unjustified an indiscriminate condemnation of the service they had rendered the state.

The composite character of the Agricola

The *Agricola*, as we have indicated, is situated at the intersection of several different literary genres. It is a panegyric developed into a biography, a *laudatio funebris* interspersed, enlarged, and integrated with historical and ethnographical materials. Thus the work shows traces of different styles, which also contribute to its composite character. In the preface, in the speeches, and especially in the moving peroration at the end the influence of Cicero is paramount (these sections may also give us an idea of what Tacitus's oratory must have been like). In the narrative and ethnographic parts, by contrast, one notes the presence of the two different models of historical style, the Sallustian and the Livian.

3. BARBARIAN VIRTUE AND ROMAN CORRUPTION

Ethnographic literature at Rome

Ethnographic interests, already amply present in the *Agricola*, are at the center of the *Germania*. The latter furnishes practically our sole instance (apart from the more or less large *excursus* found in historical works) of a specifically ethnographic literature that must have enjoyed a certain popularity at Rome; we know, for instance, of monographs by Seneca on India and Egypt. But ethnographic interests had already been strong in Hellenistic culture (e.g., in Posidonius). At Rome they may have gone back to Caesar's *De Bello Gallico,* which had also dealt with the life of the Germans. Later historians such as Sallust and Livy probably had recourse, in lost sections of their works, to large ethnographic digressions, which introduced an element of variety into the lengthy accounts of events and at the same time allowed learning and versatility to be displayed. An *excursus* on Germany must have been found in book 3 of Sallust's *Histories,* and Livy may have dealt with the subject near the end of his work, when he was concerned with Drusus's campaigns beyond the Rhine (see p. 368).

It has been emphasized how the ethnographic notices found in the *Germania* do not derive from direct observation, but almost exclusively from written sources. Although Tacitus shows that he has consulted various sources, it has been suggested that he may have drawn the larger part of the documentation from the *Bella Germaniae* of Pliny the Elder, who had served in the Rhine armies and taken part in expeditions that crossed the river and invaded the territory of those Germans who had not yet been subjected to Roman rule. Tacitus appears to have followed his source faithfully, being content to improve and embellish the style (Sallustian coloring is frequent in the *Germania,* and epigrammatic sayings are quite common too) and to add a few details in order to bring the work up to date (Pliny's notices went back about forty years). Nonetheless, some discrepancies remain, since quite often the *Germania* appears to describe the situation as it was before the Flavian emperors advanced across the Rhine and the Danube.

Tacitus's intentions in the *Germania* have been the object of a longstanding debate among scholars. A long-held hypothesis, which seems well-founded to us, though in need of some clarification, sees in the work the glorification of a primitive, naive civilization, one not yet corrupted by the refined vices of a decadent civilization. The *Germania* is pervaded by an implicit opposition between the barbarians, full of energies that are still strong and fresh, and the Romans. Still, one should not insist too much on the idealization of the savage peoples, a theme that is customary in ethnographic literature and is influenced by dissatisfaction with the decadence and corruption of city life. In insisting on the untamed strength and valor in war of the Germans, Tacitus probably intends not so much to praise them as to stress the threat they pose to the Empire. The weakness and frivolity of Roman society must have alarmed the budding senatorial historian; the Germans, with their bravery, their freedom, and their numbers, may have represented a serious threat to a political system that was based on servitude and corruption. Still, it is not surprising that Tacitus also draws up a long list of the weaknesses of a people who seemed essentially barbaric to him: indolence, a passion for games, a tendency towards drunkenness and quarreling, and innate cruelty. Whether the *Germania* is basi-

cally a short ethnographic-geographic treatise or a work with a political bearing, it is appropriate to connect it with an event nearly contemporary with its composition, namely, the presence of Trajan on the Rhine with a strong army, bent, it seems, upon warfare and conquest. In the course of his historical work Tacitus would continue to regard the German frontier (more than the Parthian frontier, say) with particular interest, showing admiration, for instance, in the *Annals* for the aggressive policy of Germanicus. In this interest of his, a conviction of the danger presented by the northern peoples crosses with the complementary conviction that the greatest possibilities for expanding the Empire lie in that direction. The persistence of this interest confirms the coherence of the thoughts and concerns of the man from whom the ethnographic treatise originates.

4. THE PARALLELISMS OF HISTORY

Plan of the Histories

The project for a vast historical work was already present in the *Agricola,* where, in one of the early chapters, Tacitus expresses his intention to narrate the years of Domitian's tyranny and then the freedom recovered under the regimes of Nerva and Trajan. In the *Histories* the project appears modified. Although the extant part narrates the events of the years 69–70, from the reign of Galba to the Jewish rebellion, the work in its entirety was to be extended to 96, the year of Domitian's death. In the preface, Tacitus expressly says he is saving for his old age the treatment of the principates of Nerva and Trajan, "richer and less risky material." The *Histories* thus dealt with a gloomy period, one disturbed by civil wars and finished by a long tyranny.

Summary of the *Histories*

The first book (which follows the annalistic tradition and is concerned with events beginning on 1 January 69) opens with the narration of Galba's brief reign. Next we read of his murder and the elevation of Otho. In Germany, however, the legions acclaim Vitellius as emperor. The struggle between Otho and Vitellius, which ends with the defeat and suicide of the former, and the ensuing struggle between Vitellius and Vespasian form the subjects of books 2 and 3. Vespasian, acclaimed as emperor by the legions of various countries, leaves his son Titus in the East to deal with the Jews and, going to Egypt, leads his troops against Rome, where Vitellius has taken refuge; Vitellius is captured and slain. Book 4 deals with the sack of Rome by the Flavian soldiers and the mutinies against Vespasian that break out in Gaul and Germany. Book 5 (which has come down to us in damaged condition and breaks off in chapter 26), after an *excursus* on Judaea, where Titus is, moves on to the events in Germany and the first signs of weariness shown by the rebels.

Galba and Nerva: a) *The problem of adoption*

The year in which the *Histories* opens, 69, had seen four emperors succeed one another (Galba, Otho, Vitellius, and Vespasian). A secret of the Empire had also been revealed, as Tacitus emphasizes: the princeps could be chosen elsewhere than at Rome, since his strength was based chiefly on the support of the legions stationed in more or less remote lands. Vitellius had been raised to power by the legions of Germany, Vespasian by those of the East. Otho, made princeps at Rome, based himself on the support of the praetorians, the imperial guards stationed in the capital. Tacitus was writing the *Histories* more than thirty years after 69, but the year of the four emperors was, in all likelihood, a lively issue in the political debate that had accompanied Trajan's accession to power. A certain parallelism has been noted between this accession and the events of 69. Trajan's predecessor Nerva, like Galba, had found himself dealing with a revolt of the praetorians that was undermining the basis of his power, and like Galba, he had designated a successor by means of adoption. At this point the analogy breaks down, however. Galba, whom Tacitus describes as a lethargic old man, ruined by wicked advisers, and anachronistically and uselessly adopting a pose of republican *gravitas,* had chosen as his successor Piso, a noble of the old school, a man of stern morals who, because of his archaic strictness, was hardly suitable for winning the good will of the troops; he was basically a puppet, the victim of his illustrious ancestors, the ineptitude of Galba, and the criminal ambitions of Otho. Nerva, by contrast, had consolidated his own power by associating in his rule Trajan, an influential military leader, the commander of the army in Upper Germany. It is impossible therefore to share the view that has Tacitus see in Galba an unlucky precursor of the reconciliation between the principate and freedom that was later realized by Nerva and Trajan. Tacitus had probably taken part in the imperial council that decided to adopt Trajan. At this meeting anachronistic views not very different from Galba's probably emerged from among the traditionalist members of the senatorial aristocracy, but the council evidently was able to reject them. In the speech that Galba is made to deliver in the first book of the *Histories* on the occasion of Piso's adoption, the historian aimed at making clear, virtually by contrast, through the very words of the emperor, significant aspects of his own ideological-political position. Tacitus wanted to show the split in Galba between the model of behavior strictly based on the *mos maiorum,* a model now reduced to empty respect for the forms and out of touch with any political reality, and the real ability to dominate and control events. Basing himself on that model, Galba could not choose a course that would assure the security of the state, and a period of bloody civil conflict followed. By contrast, the adoption of Trajan, an old-fashioned commander who knew how to be liked by his soldiers without surrendering the sternness and decorum of his position, calmed the turmoil among the legions and put an end to any rivalry. Trajan showed that he was able to maintain the unity of the armies, control them, and prevent them from becoming the arbiters of the Empire. Tacitus, with the pessimistic realism that is characteristic of him, may not have totally shared the enthusiasm that Pliny the Younger showed in the *Panegyric* for the solution to the crisis that was represented by the choice of Trajan, but he certainly saw that it was impossible to put off any longer the need to heal the fracture, dramatically revealed in 69, between the *virtutes* of the old republican ethical model and the ability to establish a genuine rapport with the military masses.

b) *Impracticability of the* mos maiorum

The only solution: the moderate principate

As we have said, Tacitus is convinced that only the principate can assure peace, the loyalty of the armies, and the cohesion of the Empire. Already in the proem to the *Histories,* when referring to the accession of Augustus, he emphasizes how after the battle of Actium the concentration of power in the hands of a single person was proven to be indispensable for maintaining peace. Naturally the princeps must not be a criminal tyrant like Domitian, nor inept as Galba was (Tacitus's sarcastic epigram summing up the latter is famous: "In the judgment of all worthy to rule, if only he had not ruled" [*Histories* 1.49]). Instead he must have the qualities necessary to rule the whole Empire, and at the same time he must guarantee the remnants of prestige and dignity that the governing senatorial class possessed. In the moderate principate of the adoptive emperors Tacitus sees the only practicable solution.

The narrative style of the *Histories,* as is consistent with the rapid succession of the events, has a varying, swift rhythm that never slackens or stands still. This implies that Tacitus had worked to condense the material given by his sources. Occasionally something is omitted, but most often Tacitus is able to give dramatic force to his narrative by breaking the account up into individual scenes; thus, for example, the march of Fabius Valens (first a supporter of Galba, then of Vitellius) from the Rhine to the Alps is narrated through a series of lively vignettes depicting the behavior of the soldiers during the civil war. Vitellius's three attempts at abdication, known to us through Suetonius, are condensed into a single, dramatic, picturesque episode in which Tacitus has employed to the utmost all his powers of color and suggestion. Tacitus is a master at the description of masses, which is

often haunting and frightening. He can be equally powerful when he depicts the crowd as calm, or threatening, or dispersing when gripped by panic. In his description of the crowd one notes the senator's fear mixed with disdain at the turbulence of the soldiers or the dregs of the capital. Yet the aristocratic historian manifests an almost equal disdain for his peers, the members of the Senate, whose behavior is described with a subtle malice that emphasizes the contrast between the facade and the reality of their feelings: their flattery of the emperor masks the hatred they secretly feel towards him, and their concern for the public welfare conceals intrigue and ambition.

The *Histories* recounts for the most part acts of violence, dishonesty, and injustice. As a result human nature is painted in tones that are always dark. This does not prevent Tacitus from treating the characters he introduces skillfully and variously, alternating brief, incisive remarks and full-length portraits. Take, for example, Mucianus, the governor of Syria, who played an important role in the accession of Vespasian. Mucianus is described as the type of the paradoxical character, as a mixture of sensuality and industry, of cordiality and arrogance, excellent in his public activities but unsavory in his private life. Tacitus seems to have taken special pains over the character of Otho. Tacitus emphasizes the consciousness with which he adopts a subservient position towards the lower strata of the city and the soldiery, which he condenses into an epigrammatic phrase: *omnia serviliter pro dominatione* ("In every matter he behaved like a slave in order to acquire power" [*Histories* 1.36.3]). And yet Tacitus shows how it is precisely this conscious servility of Otho towards the crowd that is a condition of his demagogic energy and his perverse ability to affect affairs, qualities that place him on a different (though not morally superior) level from a Galba or a Piso. Like certain Sallustian characters (one thinks above all of Catiline), Otho is dominated by a restless *virtus,* which leads him to contemplate, in a monologue like that of a tragic hero, an ascent to power that will not stop at crime or infamy. But Otho is also, in some regards, a person who evolves: his character seems to undergo a change when, once he is certain that he will be defeated by the Vitellians, he decides to die a glorious death in order to spare the state further bloodshed.

Tacitus's technique of portraiture shows many affinities with Sallust. Tacitus relies on *inconcinnitas,* dislocated syntax, and disjointed stylistic structures to penetrate to the depths of the characters. But whereas Sallust's abrupt style exerts its influence over all of Tacitus's narrative, Tacitus develops it to such a point that it marks a genuine leap in quality. It accentuates the tension between archaic *gravitas* and dramatic pathos, enhances the poetic coloring, and multiplies the unexpected *iuncturae.* Tacitus is fond of ellipses of verbs and conjunctions; to lend variety and movement to the narrative he has recourse to irregular constructions and frequent shifts of subject. When a phrase appears to be over, he often extends it with a surprising finish, which adds an epigrammatic comment or modifies, preferably by allusion or indirection, what has just been stated.

5. THE ROOTS OF THE PRINCIPATE

The link with Livy

Not even in the last phase of his activity did Tacitus keep his promise of narrating the story of the principates of Nerva and Trajan. Once he finished the *Histories,* he turned to investigating the still more remote past and in the *Annals* undertook to recount the earliest days of the principate, from the death of Augustus to the death of Nero. The date chosen by Tacitus for the beginning of the *Annals* has suggested that he intended his work as a continuation of Livy's (we saw that Livy's original plan, interrupted by his death, probably included 150 books, which would have treated Augustus's entire principate [see p. 368]; nothing prevents the supposition that in the preface to some book lost to us but known to Tacitus, Livy stated explicitly some such intention on his part). The title found in the manuscripts of Tacitus *(Ab Excessu Divi Augusti)* seems to echo Livy's title, *Ab Urbe Condita.*

Summary of the Annals

From the *Annals,* books 1–4 have been preserved, a fragment of 5, and part of 6, embracing the events from the death of Augustus (A.D. 14) to that of Tiberius (A.D. 37), with a gap of a couple of years from 29 to 31; as well as books 11–16, with the account of the reigns of Claudius (beginning in 47) and Nero (book 11 has lacunae, and 16 is damaged, ending for us with the events of 66). Books 1–5 trace in parallel Rome's internal and external affairs: in the capital, the progressive revelation of Tiberius's closed, suspicious, and touchy character, the growth of trials for *lèse majesté,* the rise and then the fall of the sinister Sejanus (but we lack the part in which his death is told), and the regime's degeneration into cruelty and dissolution, down to the death of Tiberius; abroad, Germanicus's successes in Germany, the quarrels between him and Piso, his death in the East, as a result of which Piso is suspected of poisoning him, and also minor events, such as the victorious war in Africa against the Numidian Tacfarinas and the suppression of the revolt of the Frisians, a Germanic people.

Books 11 and 12 recount the events of the years 47–54, the second half of the principate of Claudius. He is represented as a weak man who after the death of his first wife, Messalina, is controlled by the powerful freedman Narcissus and his second wife, Agrippina, who in the end has her husband poisoned and places Nero, her son by a previous marriage, upon the throne.

In books 13–16 Tacitus narrates the reign of Nero. At first the princeps is affected in alternation by the diverse influences of his mother, of the philosopher Seneca, and of Burrus, the praetorian prefect; the latter two work together, having in mind the (improbable) reconciliation of the principate with freedom. Subsequently, the emperor becomes independent but falls prey increasingly to his own depraved instincts. While the Roman commanders (chiefly Corbulo) report notable successes upon the frontiers, Nero begins to rule in the manner of a Hellenistic monarch, devoting himself primarily to games and spectacles, and persists in his plan to get rid of all those who could restrain his perverse and extravagant behavior. After a first attempt that fails, he succeeds in having his mother Agrippina killed. Three years later, in 62, Tigellinus, a detestable person, succeeds Burrus as praetorian prefect, in the wake of the latter's mysterious death. At the same time Seneca withdraws to private life. From this moment onwards Nero abandons himself to excesses of every sort; discontent grows, and around Gaius Piso there forms a band of conspirators who plan to murder the princeps. The famous fire of Rome breaks out. Tacitus seems to credit the rumors according to which Nero himself had it started, but the Christians are persecuted as the ones responsible for the fire. Piso's conspiracy is discovered and suppressed, and many of the most distinguished people are ordered to take their lives. In this way perish Seneca, Lucan, Petronius, and finally Thrasea Paetus, in the middle of the account of whose death the preserved part of the *Annals* comes to an end.

The progress of Tacitus's pessimism: a servile Senate and useless heroes

In the *Annals,* Tacitus retains his idea of the necessity of the principate, but his view seems to be still darker than before. In a famous passage (3.28), at the same time that he affirms that Augustus assured peace for the Empire after long years of civil war, the historian also emphasizes how ever since then the yoke has become heavier. Tacitus gives a uniformly gloomy coloring to his picture of life under the Caesars. The history of the principate is also the history of the decline of political freedom for the senatorial aristocracy, which is itself experiencing moral decline and corruption; these in turn make it eager for a servile assent (Tacitus calls this *libido adsentandi*) to the wishes of the princeps. The historian also shows little sympathy (as we have already seen in regard to the *Agricola*) for those who choose the opposite path, of martyrdom, which is virtually useless to the state, and who continue to enact philosophical suicides. A literature of *exitus illustrium virorum* flourished beginning in the Neronian age. It is hardly coincidence that when describing Petronius's suicide Tacitus emphasizes his ironic inversion of this philosophical model.

The good officials

In recounting Roman history Tacitus leads the reader across a human territory that is desolate, without light or hope. Nonetheless, the good part of the political elite—and here we find a certain continuity with the *Agricola*—continues to give its best efforts to governing the provinces and leading armies: Germanicus's achievements in war are great in comparison to Tiberius's wretched policy in Rome, and even Corbulo's military action is, in Tacitus's eyes, more useful and perhaps more important than the dark passions stirring Nero's Rome.

Tacitus's tragic historiography

It has been said that Tacitus is above all else a great dramatic artist, but this probably undervalues his specific skills as a historian. Yet it is true that tragic historiography (see p. 122) plays an essential role in the *Annals.*

Tacitus's tragedies, the dramas of the soul that he presents, are not so much provoked by the desire to stir the emotions as they are fostered by the pessimism that is deeply rooted in the Latin historiographic tradition, in Sallust especially. To the element of tragedy that is prominent in his historical writing Tacitus assigns the task of exploring the inner lives of his characters, in order to reveal not only the passions that move them but also the ambiguities, the chiaroscuro, that inhere in them. The passions that dominate in Tacitus's characters, with only the partial exception of Nero, who is in some ways pathological, are political passions: the lust for power unleashes the fiercest fights. The bitterest conflict develops inside the imperial palace, of course. But the historian also turns elsewhere in order to bring out the ambition and the tension involved in social climbing, which is often accompanied by envy, hypocrisy, or arrogance, defects from which no person or class is exempt. Compared with ambition, vanity, and the desire for power, the other passions (e.g., erotic desire or eagerness for wealth) play a quite secondary role, yet Tacitus still pays due attention to crimes and jealousies of sexual origin, and he shows a keen perception in matters of money.

The portrait of Tiberius

The art of portraiture, already shrewdly exploited in the *Histories,* is further improved in the *Annals.* For some, the culmination is reached in the portrait of Tiberius, which is of the indirect type; that is, the historian does not give a portrait once and for all, but lets it emerge in stages through observations and comments embedded in the narrative. The portrait of Tiberius is painted with the whole range of gradations. He liked to seem grim and was fond of austerity. Oppressed by *tristitia,* he made his own conduct cruel and harsh. Eternally suspicious, taciturn because accustomed to keep his own thoughts concealed, often frowning, sometimes wearing a false smile upon his face, he had made dissimulation the first among his virtues. Tacitus generally prefers a moral portrait over a physical one, but in a passage written in a quite affected style he lingers over a description of Tiberius's repulsive old age—tall, but bent and emaciated, his face marked by scars and covered with pimples, his head completely bald.

The paradoxical portrait of Petronius

As in the *Histories,* the paradoxical type of portrait is used to a certain extent, the most notable example being the portrait of Petronius (*Annals* 16.18), to whom reference has already been made. The fascination of the character lies precisely in its contradictory aspects. Petronius has won by *ignavia* the reputation that others win by unstinting toil, but the laxness of his character contrasts with the energy and ability shown when he held important public offices. An air of supreme nonchalance, a *neglegentia* that enhances its refinement, surrounds his whole existence. Petronius faces death almost as if it were a final pleasure and at the same time gives evidence of self-control, courage, and resoluteness. In a deliberate polemic against the Stoic tradition of theatrical suicide, he entertains himself through conversations with his friends on subjects quite different from those that served to create an aura of *constantia;* he has read aloud to him, not dissertations on the immortality of the soul or sayings of philosophers, but rather light poetry and casual verse (*Annals* 16.19). Without holding him up as a model—Tacitus's own tastes were more austere—the historian seems implicitly to emphasize that his *virtus* is ultimately stronger than the *virtus* often displayed by the Stoic martyrs in death.

The style of the Annals: the increase in variatio

The style of the *Annals* is different in certain respects from the style of the *Histories.* At least before book 13, the style evolves perceptibly towards greater distancing from conventional norms, a pursuit of the odd that is expressed in the preference for unusual forms and for an archaic, solemn diction that is full of power. The *Annals* are less eloquent and less smooth than the *Histories,* more concise and austere. The taste for *inconcinnitas* persists and even becomes more marked. It is secured especially by means of *variatio,* that is, by joining to one expression another that one would expect to be parallel to it but that in fact is different in structure (two examples taken from the burning of Rome are: *pars* **mora**, *pars* **festinans**, *cuncta impediebant,* and *{incendium} in edita* **adsurgens** *et rursus inferiora* **populando** *anteiit remedia* [*Annals* 15.38]). The verbal disharmonies reflect the disharmony of events and the ambiguity in human behavior. Violent metaphors are common (the images are of light and shadow, destruction and fire), as is the bold use of personification. Poetic coloring is frequent, especially from Virgil, but there are also notable traces of Lucan in Tacitus's prose.

The regression of style in the last part of the Annals

Nonetheless, one notes within the *Annals* a certain modification of the style, in which some scholars have seen a regression. Beginning with book 13, Tacitus seems to return to more traditional standards, ones less removed from the dictates of classicism. His style becomes richer and more elevated, less tight, sharp, and insinuating; in choosing synonyms the historian moves from choice, decorative expressions to those that are more sober and normal. The difference has been attributed to the different subject matter. The reign of Nero, quite close in time, needed to be treated with a less solemn distancing than the now far-off reign of Tiberius, which seemed still to be anchored in the ancient *res publica.* Some signs of negligence noted especially in books 15 and 16 have even suggested that the *Annals* did not receive final revision.

6. SOURCES

The acta, *the speeches, the multiplicity of sources*

The problem of the sources Tacitus used in the *Histories* and the *Annals* has long been debated, and a definitive answer cannot be said to have been reached. The issue involves relations with the rest of the historiographic tradition that has transmitted to us the events of the same period (Suetonius, Cassius Dio, Plutarch). Some points, nonetheless, are firmly established. First of all, Tacitus could have consulted official documents, the *acta senatus* (the minutes of the sessions, more or less) and the *acta diurna populi Romani* (which contained the acts of the government and notices about whatever happened at the court and in the capital). He had at his disposal, moreover, collections of speeches by some emperors, such as Tiberius and Claudius. The care shown by ancient historians in handling documents was not, on the whole, the same as that shown by modern historians, but Tacitus was unquestionably among the most scrupulous (his uncommon *diligentia* in this regard is praised in a letter of Pliny the Younger). The historical and literary sources are many. Once the notion had been laid to rest that in each of his major works Tacitus had constantly followed, at least for each section, a single source (a common proceeding in the rest of the historiographic tradition), to which he merely gave a new artistic covering, the idea emerged that he freely used a multiplicity of sources, alternating (e.g., in regard to Tiberius's principate) between sources of opposite tendency. Tacitus himself, moreover, mentions some of his sources: Pliny the Elder, who had written *Bella Germaniae* in twenty books and a history in thirty-one books, the continuation of Aufidius Bassus's (see p. 383); and Vipstanus Messalla—one of the interlocutors in the *Dialogus*—the author of memoirs on the civil war, in which he had fought on Vespasian's side. Particular importance seems to be attached to Cluvius Rufus and Fabius Rusticus. The first was a consul under Caligula and probably died under Vespasian. He was on friendly terms with Nero, but he refused to become an informer. He seems to have written about contemporary events, and he was one of the sources of the *Histories*. Fabius Rusticus, of whom we know very little, was favorable to Seneca and had a hostile attitude towards Nero. He was important as a source for the last phase of Nero's principate.

The exitus
illustrium virorum

Tacitus could also have made use of correspondence and memoirs (e.g., Corbulo's memoirs on the war against the Parthians), and he certainly drew upon that vast literary genre that is called *exitus illustrium virorum,* pamphlets originating with the opposition that recounted the sacrifice of the martyrs of freedom, particularly of those who had committed suicide on the basis of Stoic doctrines. Tacitus availed himself of this literature in telling, for instance, of the death of Seneca or Thrasea (the latter, on whom see p. 468, had himself written a life of Cato of Utica, the archetype of the martyrs of freedom). He used it chiefly to add dramatic coloring to his own account, and not because he was one of those who admired this kind of suicide, which, as we have stressed several times, appeared to him vitiated by a kind of ambitious and politically unproductive ostentation.

7. LITERARY SUCCESS

Antiquity

Tacitus seems to have been surprisingly unpopular in antiquity. Although the younger Pliny foretold the immortal fame of the *Historiae* (*Epist.* 7.33), thereafter traces of familiarity with Tacitus's works are rare indeed: among pagan authors, only in the fourth-century historian Ammianus Marcellinus, who probably intended his own history to continue Tacitus's, as Xenophon's had continued Thucydides'; and among Christian writers, only in Sulpicius Severus, Orosius, Sidonius Apollinaris, and Cassiodorus (who seems to have known the *Agricola* and the *Germania*). Otherwise there seems to be no sure evidence for his ancient *Nachleben*.

Middle Ages

In the Middle Ages, too, Tacitus was hardly known and could easily have failed to survive to our times. Books 1–6 of the *Annales* are transmitted in a single medieval manuscript, as are books 11–16 and the *Historiae,* and most quotations are taken from Orosius. The minor works left few traces in medieval authors outside the Carolingian period (e.g., Einhard and Rudolf of Fulda) and no certain ones at all in medieval catalogues. He was entirely unknown to Dante (this may be why Dante eulogizes Tiberius in his *Paradiso*) and even to Petrarch.

Rediscovery in the Renaissance

Not until the Renaissance did Tacitus's fortunes begin slowly to rise. Zenobi da Strada discovered the lone medieval manuscript of *Annales* 11–16 and the *Historiae* in Montecassino; it may have been removed from there by Boccaccio and then acquired by Niccolò Niccoli from the latter's private library. Poggio Bracciolini rediscovered the three minor works in 1425 in the German monastery of Hersfeld (in 1455 Enoch of Ascoli brought this manuscript back to Pope Nicholas V in Rome), but it was not until 1508 that *Annales* 1–6 were rediscovered at Corvey and brought to Rome and not until 1515 that they were first published. Boccaccio, the first humanist to demonstrate knowledge of Tacitus's works, used Tacitus's account of the death of Seneca for his commentary on Dante, and he used other passages for his *On Famous Women.* Otherwise, although Niccoli's manuscript was transcribed several times, Tacitus remained largely unknown until the publication around 1470 of the *editio princeps* (containing only *Annales* 11–16, the *Historiae,* the *Germania,* and the *Dialogus*) and Puteolanus's publication in 1476 of the *Agricola* (together with the collection of miscellaneous panegyrics). The number of quotations from his works in the fifteenth century is remarkably low.

The first, republican generations of the Renaissance tended to prefer Livy to Tacitus. After all, Livy told of heroes and the rise of a city, Tacitus of villains and its decline. But at the end of the fifteenth century the *Dialogus* became an important document in discussions of the relationship between eloquence and politics, and already Guicciardini foreshadowed not only the Counter Reformation fashion of "Tacitism," which found in the historian's works instructions for how to become a tyrant, permanently valid rules for the conduct of politics, and a legitimation for absolute power and *raison d'état,* but also the complementary and contemporary reading of Tacitus as providing instructions for how to survive under a tyrant without either becoming servile or wasting one's energy (and life) in sterile opposition. After about 1530, as the political atmosphere in Europe changed, Tacitus came to surpass Livy in popularity. The *Historiae* were translated for the first time in 1544, the *Annales* in 1563, both into Italian, and Sir Henry Saville's English translation of four books of the *Historiae* and the *Agricola* in 1591 achieved great success. His influence extends in the next century to the French classical drama of Corneille (*Othon,* 1665) and Racine (*Britannicus,* 1669), and a century later to the historical dramas of the Italian Alfieri (*Ottavia,* 1780) and the French writer Joseph Marie Chénier (*Tibère,* 1807). In the age of Enlightenment, Tacitus's works were usually celebrated as handbooks of opposition to tyranny—the ideologues of the

French Revolution preferred him to Livy and Plutarch—but Diderot, in his *Essai sur les règnes de Claude et de Néron,* could derive from Tacitus's account of the relations between Seneca and Nero arguments to justify the philosopher's willingness to collaborate with his ruler.

While Livy's historical work nowadays is of interest mostly only to classical anthropologists and Sallust's is largely neglected, Tacitus's psychological acuity and his sensitivity to the constraints imposed upon a cultured elite forced to live in a totalitarian state ensure that he continues to find readers, even outside the philological profession.

BIBLIOGRAPHY

The standard modern editions of Tacitus are, for the minor works, that of R. M. Ogilvie and M. Winterbottom (Oxford 1975), for the *Histories,* that of K. Wellesley (Leipzig 1989), and for the *Annals,* that of H. Heubner (Stuttgart 1983), to be supplemented for books 1 and 2 by the editions with commentary by F.R.D. Goodyear (Cambridge 1972, 1981). The Loeb edition of the minor works by W. Peterson and M. Hutton, revised by M. Winterbottom, R. M. Ogilvie, and E. H. Warmington (Cambridge, Mass. 1970), is excellent, those of the *Histories* and *Annals* by C. H. Moore and J. Jackson (4 vols., Cambridge, Mass. 1925–37) tolerable.

English commentaries include, on the *Agricola,* that by R. M. Ogilvie and I. Richmond (Oxford 1967), on the *Dialogus,* that by W. Peterson (Oxford 1893), and on the *Germania,* that by J.G.C. Anderson (Oxford 1938); on the *Histories,* books 1–2 and 4–5, those by G.E.F. Chilver (Oxford 1979, 1985 [with G. B. Townend], "historical"), and on book 3, that of K. Wellesley (Sydney 1972); and on the *Annals,* the complete commentary by H. Furneaux, H. F. Pelham, and C. D. Fisher (Oxford 1896–1907), with individual commentaries on books 1 and 2 by F.R.D. Goodyear (noted above; see also the useful edition by N. P. Miller, London 1959), on book 4 by R. H. Martin and A. J. Woodman (Cambridge 1989; see also that of D.C.A. Shotter, Warminster 1989, with translation), on books 11 and 12 by H. W. Benario (London 1983), and on book 15 by N. P. Miller (London 1973). Important commentaries in German include those on the *Dialogus* by A. Gudeman (ed. 2 Leipzig 1914; see also the small Italian edition by D. Bo, Turin 1974), on the *Germania* by R. Much, H. Jankuhn, and W. Lange (ed. 3 Heidelberg 1967), on the *Agricola* by R. Till (Berlin 1961) and H. Heubner (Göttingen 1984); on the *Histories* by H. Heubner (4 vols., Heidelberg 1963–82); and on the *Annals* by K. Nipperdey and G. Andresen (ed. 11 Berlin 1915) and E. Koestermann (Heidelberg 1963–68).

The most important modern work on Tacitus is R. Syme's monumental *Tacitus* (2 vols., Oxford 1958; see also his *Ten Studies in Tacitus,* Oxford 1970). There are shorter general introductions by D. R. Dudley, *The World of Tacitus* (London 1968), and R. H. Martin, *Tacitus* (London 1981), and a Greece and Rome survey by F.R.D. Goodyear (Oxford 1970). See also R. Scott, *Religion and Philosophy in the Histories of Tacitus* (Rome 1968), B. Walker, *The Annals of Tacitus* (Manchester 1952), J. Ginsburg, *Tradition and Theme in the Annals of Tacitus* (New York 1981), H. Y. McCulloch, *Narrative Cause in the Annals of Tacitus* (Königstein 1984), and A. J. Woodman, *Rhetoric in Classical Historiography* (London 1988) 160–96 (cf. D. West and A. J. Woodman, *Creative Imitation in Latin Literature* [Cambridge 1979] 143–55). There is a collection of essays edited by T. A. Dorey (London 1969); cf. the German collection by V. Pöschl, Wege der Forschung 97 (Darmstadt 1969). Volumes 33.2–33.5 of *ANRW* contain a wide range of surveys and articles on Tacitus, many in English.

General works in other languages include R. Haüssler, *Tacitus und das historische Bewusstsein* (Heidelberg 1965), A. Michel, *Tacite et le destin de l'empire* (Paris 1966), G. Wille, *Der Aufbau der Werke des Tacitus* (Amsterdam 1983), and E. Aubrion, *Rhétorique et histoire chez Tacite* (Metz 1985), with a large number of monographs; see esp., on the style, B.-R. Voss, *Der pointierte Stil des Tacitus* (Münster 1963; cf. E. Löfstedt, "On the Style of Tacitus," *JRS* 38 [1948] 1–8, and the survey by J. Hellegouarc'h in *ANRW* 33.4:2385–2453), and on the sources, C. Questa, *Studi sulle fonti degli Annali di Tacito* (ed. 2 Rome 1967; note R. Syme, *Roman Papers* 3 [Oxford 1984] 1014–42, 4 [Oxford 1988] 199–222). On Tacitus's *fortuna,* note esp. K. C. Schellhase, *Tacitus in Renaissance Political Thought* (Chicago 1976).

Suetonius and the Minor Historians

We do not know the exact year of Gaius Suetonius Tranquillus's birth or of his death. On the basis of the meager autobiographical indications that he provides us with (we get other details from Pliny the Younger's correspondence, the *Historia Augusta,* and an inscription discovered several decades ago), we can only suppose that he was born shortly after A.D. 70 to an equestrian family of modest condition (nothing certain is known about the place of his birth). For a while he must have engaged in legal work. Later—when he had already begun to devote himself to learned studies— thanks to the patronage of influential people, at first Pliny the Younger, then Septicius Clarus, he entered the court as an official. At first he was put in charge of the public libraries by Trajan (which would confer upon him the *ius trium liberorum*); later, under Hadrian (117–38), he was employed on the imperial archives and the correspondence of the princeps himself, an office that would have determined the direction of his researches.

His brilliant bureaucratic career was rudely interrupted in 122, when, along with Septicius Clarus, the praetorian prefect and his patron, he fell into disgrace. After his dismissal from court, all traces of Suetonius are lost; we do not know how much later he died.

WORKS

Our knowledge of his many learned works, in Greek and Latin, is derived not so much from the scanty fragments that are preserved as from the so-called lexicon of the Suda (tenth century), which lists their various titles. Their subjects are diverse, ranging from Roman customs to the calendar, from the diacritical marks used by philologists to famous courtesans, from Cicero's physical defects to his political writings. *Pratum,* or *Prata,* is probably an encyclopedic work, subdivided into different sections on the basis of the subjects treated; according to others, the title designates rather the entire corpus of antiquarian-erudite writings that we have mentioned.

De Viris Illustribus is the title of a collection of biographies of writers subdivided by genres—poets, orators, historians, philosophers, grammarians. We possess only one section, *De Grammaticis et Rhetoribus,* which is damaged at the end. The first twenty-four chapters are devoted to grammarians (i.e., philologists, scholars who work on literary texts) and extend from Crates of Mallus, the Greek who introduced grammar at Rome, to Valerius Probus; the remaining chapters are the six that alone survive from those devoted to the rhetoricians. Of the other sections we have only scattered material that has come down to us through the indirect tradition. From the *De Poetis,* in particular, are derived the extant lives of several poets, such as Terence, Virgil, Horace, and Lucan; we do not know whether and to what extent these lives were reworked by the compiling authors, such as Donatus and Jerome.

By contrast, the *De Vita Caesarum,* a collection of twelve biographies (of the emperors from Julius Caesar to Domitian) in eight books, is preserved intact, except for the introductory chapters of the first biography and the dedication of the work to Septicius Clarus.

I. BIOGRAPHY IN SUETONIUS

Suetonius's predecessors

Biography was a literary genre of Greek tradition that had been practiced and approved at Rome especially by Varro and Cornelius Nepos. More or less during the same years, both Varro (who was also the author of biographies of poets, now lost) in his *Imagines* and Nepos in his *De Viris Illustribus* had sketched the lives of famous people (distinguished by category—statesmen, military commanders, artists, writers, etc.), using as a basis the same format that Suetonius would follow in his *De Viris Illustribus.* Brief information on origins and place of birth, instruction received, principal interests and works composed, features of character (the last often illustrated through interesting anecdotes or details of private life)—this, approximately, is the model structure for the succinct portraits of grammarians and rhetoricians that Suetonius paints. For the *Lives of the Caesars,*

Format of Suetonius's biographies

Suetonius's other biographical work, the basis seems to be a similar format. The differences lie only in the activities engaged in (instead of the instruction received, we are told of the various ways the subject exercised power) and in the much larger scale of the imperial biographies. The latter begin with notices relating to the family and the place, date, and circumstances of birth of the princeps. Next a chronological account traces his youthful growth and development up to his accession to power. At this point the chronological arrangement is abandoned for a synchronic description of the various aspects of the emperor's personality, presented under separate headings, which themselves in turn are further subdivided. Then the biography, returning to chronological order, concludes with the death of the princeps and the funerary honors paid to him.

The rejection of chronological arrangement: the extension of the format of the viri illustres *to the Caesars*

The most significant feature in the organization of the biographical material is thus the rejection of a chronological arrangement that follows the development of the person under discussion. Suetonius himself, in a passage of the *Life of Augustus* (9.1), explains how his exposition proceeds, not *per tempora* but *per species,* that is, by a series of categories, or headings, that deal separately with the various aspects of the princeps' personality. Thus, rather than following a single, linear course and illuminating the events in the full complexity of the elements that may explain them, the biographer prefers to compose in episodic fragments and to give an analysis that is centered on the person and his private life and character. He places his *virtutes* and his *vitia* under appropriate headings, which has the obvious consequence of orienting judgment along decidedly moral lines. On the basis of these analogies between Suetonius's two biographical works, scholars have come to accept the theory, propounded chiefly by the great philologist F. Leo at the beginning of the century, that Suetonius unwarrantedly extended to the *Caesars* the biographical model he had already used in the *De Viris Illustribus.* This model, according to the theory, had been developed in Alexandria to describe men of culture (poets, philosophers, historians, etc.) and was a type of biography intended for the learned and lacking any artistic pretensions, one in which chronological narrative, since private lives were the subject, naturally did not have the same importance as in a work that treated the personality of a statesman or a military leader. For this second type of biography Greek culture (more exactly, the Aristotelian school) had developed another model, the Plutarchan type (so called because Plutarch, contemporaneously with Suetonius, had given the most outstanding instance of it in his *Parallel Lives*). This type, by virtue of its chronological arrangement of the events, was suited for shedding light on complex, public figures such as great politicians and statesmen; it was the type of biography, that is, that Suetonius ought to have adopted for the *Lives of the Caesars.*

Alexandrian biographies and Plutarchan biographies

Today, however, this theory, which is based on a reconstructed history of the biographical genre in antiquity that cannot be defended and which attributed the ahistorical, fragmentary character of Suetonius's imperial biographies to his familiarity with the Alexandrian biographical format, has come to be replaced by a different evaluation, one that pays more attention to the intrinsic reasons for Suetonius's choices. First of all, Suetonius's adoption of the biographical genre shows his awareness that this is the form of historical writing best suited to explain the new form that power has assumed, the individual, personal form of the principate, and also that the biography of individual emperors is best adapted to periodizing the history of the Empire. In the rejection of the annalistic scheme (i.e., the narrative of events year by year), which senatorial culture had tied to the regular succession of the republican magistrates, one perceives the realistic awareness that those magistracies, though still existing formally, are now a mere fiction and that only the duration of each emperor's reign can articulate the succession of periods. Whereas an earlier age saw the influence of Alexandria as being strongest, the trend today is to note specifically Roman features. The tradition of the *elogia* and of the *laudationes funebres,* which enumerated the civil and military achievements, the services, and the honors of the dead man, seems to show its influence on the way Suetonius selects and arranges the material. The *Res Gestae* of Augustus, which summarizes the offices bestowed on the princeps, the grants to the state, his gifts to the people, the monuments he erected, in short, the various services he

Evolution of the principate and evolution of the format for biography

Suetonius's Roman models: elogia *and* laudationes funebres

performed, constitutes an important example of the impetus that so eminently Roman a tradition could give to the exposition *per species* that we find in Suetonius's *Lives*. Suetonius has a notable tendency to emphasize the private lives of the emperors, which is often deplored as a low taste for gossip. He is fond of describing their excesses and intemperance and dwelling on petty or scandalous details, a tendency that has enhanced the success of the work, since it was read as a handbook of royal perversions. In this tendency one is also inclined to see the manifestation of a desire for objectivity and demystification and of an intention to provide a comprehensive portrait of the person, illuminating all the aspects of both his public and his private life, without falling into encomium and without rejecting the concrete notices the imperial archives made available to him.

Gossip and demystification

A fine example of minor historiography

The result is a kind of minor historiography (minor in comparison with Tacitus's, for instance, according to the canons of aristocratic historiography) that draws on the most varied sources, from archival documents to oral tradition, from satiric pamphlets to earlier historiography, especially of the anti-Caesarean tradition. It also depicts, in some ways, the features of its intended audience, which is to be identified as the equestrian order, to which Suetonius himself belongs and which constitutes the point of view from which the individual episodes are observed and evaluated. An audience of officials and bureaucrats would have appreciated the feeling of concreteness in Suetonius's pages, the curious detail he registers (in the scrupulous spirit of the chancellery), the unpublished document he makes known, and his exposition of the material in a manner that is clear and organized by distinct headings. Such an audience would also have enjoyed Suetonius's sober, laconic language, which is untouched by archaizing affectations and modern preciosities and is open to colloquial turns without failing to be decorous. His is a smooth and nimble style of writing, whose narrative liveliness is the chief recompense for the work's most conspicuous limitations, the greatest of which is the superficiality of the historical and psychological analysis. Although it does not rise to the level of truly great historiography, the *Lives of the Caesars* is nonetheless exceptionally rich in notices and information for the historical reconstruction of the early Empire.

2. LITERARY SUCCESS

Antiquity

It was Suetonius who determined the form of the genre for biographers until at least the eighteenth century. Later biography in antiquity, both pagan *(Historia Augusta)* and Christian (Jerome), depends heavily upon the model of his lives of the Caesars and the *De Viris Illustribus*. His scholarly works apparently also remained popular until the fifth and sixth centuries, when the erudite compilers of late antiquity, such as Censorinus, Servius, Macrobius, Johannes Lydus, and Isidore of Seville, seem to have preferred his writings, which were short, snappy, and above all easy to consult, to Varro's for the history of Roman antiquities.

Although over two hundred manuscripts of Suetonius are extant, only one seems to have survived the Dark Ages. But he seems to have become a central author during the Carolingian Renaissance (though he did not become a medieval school author); Einhard based his *Vita Karoli Magni* upon Suetonius's life of Julius Caesar and others of his imperial biographies. The ninth century also witnessed the first medieval excerpts from Suetonius, compiled by Heiric of Auxerre and extremely popular in the later Middle Ages. Further excerpts were disseminated as part of the *Florilegium Gallicum* (Orléans, mid-twelfth century). Indeed, most of the traces of his reception during the Middle Ages can be localized in France, in the eleventh century in the Loire Valley, for example, and in a French translation in 1381.

Suetonius was one of Petrarch's favorite authors, which is not surprising in view of Petrarch's intensely personal relation to the individual great men of antiquity. Of the ten surviving fourteenth-century manuscripts, two belonged to him, and he also owned a twelfth-century manuscript. Petrarch also took over Suetonius's model and title for his own *De Viris Illustribus*. Boccaccio also made extensive use of Suetonius as a historical source; a manuscript of excerpts written in his own hand is preserved in

Florence. Suetonius's popularity increased through the Renaissance, and although no commentaries were written on him before the late fifteenth century (Domitius Calderinus, Philippus Beroaldus), two *editiones principes* of his works were published in Rome in 1470, and thirteen other editions were printed before 1500. And through the centuries that followed, despite gradual refinement of the methodology of biography and a shift in the interest of professional historians away from the lives of great men, nevertheless, wherever readers have retained an interest in the bizarre excesses of absolute power and in the mixture of the significant, the banal, and the salacious, Suetonius has continued to be read—up to the present day.

3. FLORUS AND THE "BIOGRAPHY OF ROME"

The need to reform the traditional historiographic models, or to alter their characteristics, seems to be documented not only by Suetonius but also by the work that is transmitted to us under the title of *Epitoma de Tito Livio Bellorum Omnium Annorum DCC* (in two or four books, according to the manuscripts) and is attributed to Lucius Annaeus (or Julius) Florus. We know very little of the author. The tendency today is to identify him with the Publius Annius Florus who wrote the dialogue *Vergilius Orator an Poeta* (which represents a fashion popular in the rhetorical schools) and with the Annius Florus who, as a friend of Hadrian's, exchanged with that emperor jesting poems of the type dear to the *poetae novelli* (see pp. 588 ff.). We have, then, a single person of African origin (the proem of the above-mentioned dialogue, the only part extant, furnishes us with these meager biographical data), who left Rome in the time of Domitian, was a schoolteacher in Spain, and later returned to the capital, where he moved in circles close to the court.

Sources other than Livy

Here we are concerned only with his historical work, which is interesting in various regards. The title, which was probably added by someone else, is inappropriate, since Florus's summary is not made from Livy. He is the principal source, it is true, but certainly not the only one. The influence of historians such as Sallust and Caesar is perceptible, as is that of poets, too, such as Virgil and Lucan. Furthermore, Florus's work, which deals with the history of Rome at war from the origins to the principate of Augustus, also includes events subsequent to Livy's treatment.

Biological scheme for the growth of Rome

Epitoma denotes the concise, pithy character of this work, which consists essentially of a reconstruction of Roman military history, detailing the various stages of the inexorable expansion of a small city that was destined to become an empire. The progressive growth of Roman power is modeled on the scheme of biological growth. Florus personifies the Roman people, making it a kind of collective protagonist of the narrative, and he describes its various ages, from infancy (monarchy) on to youth (early Republic) and maturity, which is reached in the *pax Augusta* and destined to be followed by the old age of the first century of the Empire, which Florus avoids dealing with (it would have been very difficult to continue to make the *populus* the protagonist of Roman history). With obviously apologetic and panegyric purpose, he dodges the necessarily pessimistic conclusions about the Empire's destiny and instead claims to see a new flourishing under Trajan, a second youth that heralds a new felicity. The adoption of the biological scheme, which has early Stoic precedent and is already found in Varro and Seneca the Elder, betrays the influence of Suetonian biography (in the sense that it figures the history of a political organism as the life of a person) and also the search for new forms of historiography, forms that are more adapted to the taste of the public; the quick, concise narrative and the rhetorically colored style seem aimed at satisfying such a taste.

Influence of Suetonius and the search for new forms of historiography

Granius Licinianus

Among historical abridgments of predominantly Livian character we must mention one from the second century, carried out by Granius Licinianus, who lived in the time of Hadrian and was the author not only of an encyclopedic work, *Cenae Suae,* in the manner of Gellius, but also of a large historical work. The few surviving fragments, discovered in the last century, presuppose at least thirty-six books. The concise, schematic narrative is keen on anecdotes and curious details.

Lucius Ampelius and Justin

The date of Lucius Ampelius is more uncertain. He may have been from the time of Hadrian or Antoninus Pius, but some, chiefly on linguistic grounds, place him much later, even as late as the fourth century. He was the author of a *Liber Memorialis,* which is mostly geographical and mythological in nature but also contains many selected historical notices (the primary source is Livy again). The notices are arranged in a summary (and rather confused) manner, for the purpose of making the Romans' historical inheritance easily accessible, and they show a marked taste for *mirabilia.* Let us recall, finally, that Justin, the epitomator of Pompeius Trogus's *Historiae*

Philippicae (see pp. 378 f.), must almost certainly be placed in this century.

BIBLIOGRAPHY

The standard edition of the *Caesares* is that of M. Ihm (editio maior Leipzig 1907, ed. minor 1908); for the *De Grammaticis et Rhetoribus,* see the editions of L. Brugnoli (Leipzig 1963) and A. Rostagni, *Suetonio de poetis e biografi minori* (Turin 1944), and for the fragments, that of A. Reifferscheid (Leipzig 1860), as well as J. Taillardat, ed., *Peri blasphemon, Peri paidion (extraits byzantins), Des termes injurieux, Des jeux grecs* (Paris 1967). The Loeb is by J. C. Rolfe (2 vols., Cambridge, Mass. 1914–28). There are English commentaries on *Julius* by H. E. Butler and M. Cary (ed. 2 Bristol 1982, with additions by G. B. Townend), on *Augustus* by E. S. Shuckburgh (Cambridge 1896) and J. M. Carter (Bristol 1982), on *Tiberius* by M. J. du Four and J. R. Rietra (Philadelphia 1941 and Amsterdam 1928, reprinted together 1979), on *Claudius* by J. Mottershead (Bristol 1986), on *Nero* by B. H. Warmington (Bristol 1977) and K. R. Bradley (Brussels 1978), on *Galba* to *Domitian* by G. W. Mooney (London 1930), and on *Vespasian* by A. W. Braithwaite (Oxford 1927).

There are two comprehensive studies in English, by A. Wallace-Hadrill (London 1983) and B. Baldwin (Amsterdam 1983); see A. R. Birley in *JRS* 74 (1984) 247–51. See also R. C. Lounsbury, *The Arts of Suetonius* (New York 1987). Foreign monographs include W. Steidle, *Sueton und die antike Biographie* (ed. 2 Munich 1963), F. Della Corte, *Suetonio: Eques Romanus* (ed. 2 Florence 1967), B. Mouchova, *Studie zu Kaiserbiographien Suetons* (Prague 1968), P. Venini, *Sulla tecnica compositiva suetoniana* (Pavia 1975), E. Cizek, *Structures et idéologie dans les Vies des Douze Césars de Suétone* (Paris 1977), and F. Gascou, *Suétone historien* (Rome 1984). There is an introductory article by G. B. Townend in *Latin Biography,* ed. T. A. Dorey (London 1967), 79–111; see also R. Syme, *Roman Papers* 4 (Oxford 1984) 1251–75, and the discussions in works on ancient biography, esp. F. Leo, *Die griechisch-römische Biographie* (Leipzig 1901), D. R. Stuart, *Epochs of Greek and Roman Biography* (Berkeley 1925), and A. Momigliano, *The Development of Greek Biography* (Cambridge, Mass. 1971). The *ANRW* surveys are in volume 33.5 (3576–3851) and include a comprehensive bibliography by P. Galland-Hallyn (French).

There are editions of Florus by P. Jal (2 vols., Paris 1967, with French translation) and E. Malcovati (ed. 2 Rome 1972); the Loeb edition is by E. S. Forster (Cambridge, Mass. 1929). See esp. W. den Boer, *Some Minor Roman Historians* (Leiden 1972) 1–18. For Granius Licinianus, see the edition by N. Criniti (Leipzig 1981), as well as the Italian translation and commentary by B. Scardigli (Florence 1983), for Ampelius those of E. Assmann (Leipzig 1934) and N. Terzaghi (Turin 1947).

Apuleius

Given the complete silence of his contemporaries, we obtain all that we know about Apuleius's chronology and biography from the works of the author himself. His praenomen is unknown; some manuscripts give it as Lucius, but in all probability they have merely taken this over from the name of the novel's protagonist-narrator. An African from Madaura (the present-day Mdaourouch), which lies in a borderland between Gaetulia and Numidia (today it is approximately Algeria), he was born around A.D. 125. He came from a prosperous family (his father was a *duovir iuri dicundo*), which made it possible for him to complete his studies at Carthage, the hub of the province's cultural life, and then at Athens, where he could pursue better his philosophical interests. Afterwards he was at Rome for a while—it is uncertain when—and traveled to the East on several occasions, giving lectures of great renown and success in various places. Back in Africa, while on a journey to Alexandria he stopped at Oea (Tripoli today), around 155–56. His meeting there with Pontianus, a schoolmate from Athens, led to an event of great consequence for Apuleius's life and literary career, his marriage to his friend's wealthy, widowed mother, Pudentilla. As a result of this marriage, Apueleius in 158 found himself accused of magical practices and at Sabrata had to defend himself in a suit brought by his wife's parents. Evidence of the trial survives in Apuleius's *Apology* (which, along with the *Florida,* is our chief source for the writer's life), a subsequently reworked version of the speech that Apuleius delivered in his own defense and that probably secured his acquittal. The last years of his life, spent at Carthage, saw him at the center of public life, a famous and valued orator. Our information on him does not go beyond 170.

WORKS

Surviving works include the *Metamorphoseon Libri,* a novel in eleven books, known since antiquity under the title *Asinus Aureus* ("The Golden Ass"); the *Apology,* already mentioned (in the manuscripts that transmit it the title is *De Magia*); *Florida* (= *Anthera,* "Selection of Flowers"), a collection of twenty-three oratorical passages; the philosophical treatises *De Platone et eius Dogmate* (in two books), *De Deo Socratis,* and *De Mundo.* Works traditionally attributed to Apuleius include a *Peri Hermeneias,* a Latin treatise of Aristotelian logic, and a dialogue, *Asclepius,* about whose authenticity there are grave doubts. Other probable works, which are entirely lost or of which we have only a few fragments, include another novel, the *Hermagoras;* some translations from Plato *(Phaedo, Republic)* and a translation from the neo-Pythagorean Nicomachus of Gerasa (the *Arithmetic Art);* some *ludicra;* and also texts of an encyclopedic nature *(De Proverbiis, De Medicinalibus, De Re Rustica, De Arboribus, De Musica).* We also have a brief fragment that may plausibly be attributed to Apuleius from a Latin translation of Menander's comedy *Anechomenos* (a work of which we have no further notices).

I. A COMPLEX FIGURE: ORATOR, SCIENTIST, PHILOSOPHER

The Platonic philosopher

"To the Platonic philosopher, the citizens of Madaura"—thus the dedication engraved on the base of a statue erected to Apuleius by his fellow citizens summarizes the personality of the writer, and he is called *Platonicus* in some manuscripts of his works. "Platonic philosopher" (of middle Platonism, from the first century B.C. to Plotinus) must have been in some way the official description and probably the one favored by Apuleius, who in his trial had based his defense against the charge of magic precisely on his claim to be regarded as a philosopher. Such a label appears to us rather as the expression of the cultural field in which Apuleius's many-sided studies are located. He is a representative of the cultural climate that we call the Second Sophistic, in which performances by famous rhetoricians increased enormously and the various religious observances were massively penetrated by the irrational (in the form of ascetic mysticism or simple superstition). As such, Apuleius shares the various aspects of this phenomenon—curiosity about the world of nature, anxiety and tension over the occult (a region presupposed by the cracks in reality, whose exploration was now felt necessary for a satisfactory understanding of the world), initiation into the mystery cults, and the career of a brilliant itinerant lecturer, who is master of both the Greek and Latin languages to the point of virtuosity. Apuleius

Elements of popular culture

is so imbued with popular culture (in addition to academic learning) that in him one can easily recognize the echoes not only of Platonic, Peripatetic, and generally philosophical thought but also of Isiac and even gnostic and Jewish religious conceptions (though towards the latter two he takes a polemical stance). There are significant traces of doctrines accepted at a lower cultural level, such as physiognomy (which despite its popular diffusion had distant origins in the Aristotelian schools) or the art of dream interpretation (which flourished in the second century, as is suggested to us by the *Oneirocritica,* a work in five books written by Artemidorus of Daldis at the end of the second century). Platonism itself, moreover, to which Apuleius himself appealed, had now grown very far from the original orthodoxy of the Athenian philosopher. Regardless of whether there did or did not exist a well-defined school headed by the middle Platonist Gaius (a controversial question), it is certain that middle Platonism showed strong Peripatetic and Stoic influences and embraced a plurality of interests, as seems evidenced by the numerous works attributed to Apuleius, not only those still extant but also the many we know to be lost.

The treatises on natural science

Tradition associates the name of Apuleius with many philosophical works. Some of these that for us are certainly spurious owe their attribution solely to the fame that surrounded this remarkable figure, a scholar, a naturalist, and a doctor of extraordinary thaumaturgic powers. We have, however, only the titles of some treatises on natural science (see above), which are the expression of an interest in nature that corresponded to the taste of the period.

The extant writings are the three treatises *De Deo Socratis, De Platone et eius Dogmate,* and *De Mundo,* about whose authenticity there are no longer serious doubts; they are generally considered to be the products of Apuleius's studious youth. There is a strong, though not uniform, skepticism about the authenticity of the *Peri Hermeneias,* the reworking of a homonymous Greek treatise of the Peripatetic school, a kind of short handbook that summarizes the Aristotelian doctrine of the syllogism (in particular, of the assertive syllogism) and that had a fundamental importance in the Middle Ages as a school text. The dialogue *Asclepius,* however, is generally regarded as spurious. The attribution to Apuleius is not surprising if one keeps in mind that the physician-god who was venerated by Aelius Aristides (as his *Sacred Discourses* show) was certainly not unknown to the philosopher of Madaura.

The De Mundo

The *De Mundo,* a reworking of the pseudo-Aristotelian *Peri Kosmou,* goes along with Apuleius's speculative interest in the forces governing the universe. The choice of subject is explained by the tendency of middle Platonism to accept Aristotelian ideas that might conciliate natural investigation and metaphysical-theological interests; however, the spirit that is its basis—a spirit that is close to the determinism of Stoicism, which denied the individual's free will, subordinating it to the designs of Providence—seems to be even more removed from Platonic orthodoxy. But if all this does not belong exclusively to Apuleius (it was already found in the pseudo-Aristotelian treatise that served as model), certainly the coloring that characterizes the work in its Latin version is Apuleian. The effort to introduce into Latin the technical-specialist language of the natural sciences, an effort that is shared by the other philosophical works, is particularly in evidence here. The fact that chapters 13 and 14 seem to draw heavily on Gellius's *Noctes Atticae* (2.22) has affected the dating of the *De Mundo,* which should be later than the publication of Gellius's work (the second half of the second century). Some who maintain the general thesis that the philosophical works we have are from Apuleius's youth have gone so far as to deny the Apuleian origin of the work. To avoid this difficulty, some have preferred to date the publication of Gellius's work earlier (there are no serious obstacles to this).

The two books *De Platone et eius Dogmate,* a synthesis of Plato's physics
and ethics (Apuleius, as he announces in the proem, was going to treat
logic in a third part—which some scholars identify as the *Peri Hermeneias*),
are a useful witness to the extensive exegetical labors that were devoted to
the master's doctrine, since they probably derive from elaborations going
back to commentators.

The most important of these writings is certainly the *De Deo Socratis,* the
most systematic treatment of the doctrine of demons that has come down
to us from antiquity. The structure has three parts: the first section examines the separate worlds of gods and of men; the second is devoted to the
position of demons in the hierarchy of rational beings and their function
as intermediaries between the two worlds (this makes them the guarantors
that a providential plan will be fulfilled in the history of the world); the
conclusion concentrates on Socrates's demon, the inner voice that, regarded
as the vehicle of a divine order, compelled the philosopher to continue his
pursuit of truth. An exuberant, effective style, suitable to the tone of a
lecture, enlivens the many-sided, dynamic picture of a universe inhabited
by mysterious forces that lie outside sense perception and whose work can
be grasped only by the wise man.

Apuleius has left us ample documentation of the most striking feature
of the Second Sophistic, the activity of itinerant orators. Fortunately, the
same manuscript that has preserved for us the novel and the *Apology* also
contains a collection of twenty-three oratorical passages, of various lengths
and on various themes, extracted from the text of lectures and public readings that Apuleius gave in Africa, after his return to Carthage. The identity
of the compiler is unknown to us, but the nature of the passages in the
brief anthology, which are all marked by a rhetorical preciosity that is often
close to tightrope-walking, allows us to perceive the criteria of his choice.
Probably following the taste of the time, he anthologized the pieces of
greatest rhetorical virtuosity, without regard for the content. From these
extracts emerges an image of a lecturer who is ready to deal with any matter: he is the orator of official political speeches, the religious panegyrist,
the scholar, the writer, the moralist, the teller of interesting tales, and the
philosopher convinced that the art of living and the art of speaking can be
approached with the same intellectual grace and the same elegance. These
are exceptional examples of rhetorical virtuosity. Among other things, they
evidence the extraordinary success that the art of the word could secure for
a talented rhetorician able to charm a sophisticated public: in the *Florida*
Apuleius thanks the Carthaginian citizenry that out of admiration dedicated a statue to him. We can only admire the flexibility of his lively and
brilliant prose, which can adapt itself to the most varied subjects at the
most varied levels, from philosophy to myth to the unusual anecdote. (An
excellent example is the fragment devoted to the parrot, *Florida* 12, which,
going beyond the purely naturalistic interest, competes with the genre of
the *epainos,* adapting itself to that particular form of humorous praise given
to animals or inanimate things that the Second Sophistic so enjoyed.) Here
already one can recognize some of those features that will especially delight

the reader of the *Metamorphoses*—adroitly constructed discourse, forceful rhetoric of the period, marked by parallelism and figures, and a varied vocabulary enriched with new coinages.

The Apology

By contrast, the long speech that makes up the text of the *Apology* (or *Apulei Platonici pro Se de Magia Liber,* according to the manuscripts, which altogether arbitrarily divide the work into two books) is a judicial speech, the only one we have from the imperial period. Since the speech, if delivered in its present form, would certainly have lasted for many hours, and since it does not have the actual feel of a trial (it does not have, for instance, a point-by-point discussion of the proofs), the reader is led to suspect that this work, too, though apparently produced by a real historical circumstance, actually has a strongly literary nature and purpose. The pleasing digressions, which are very close to the taste of a Fronto (see, e.g., the praise of toothpaste), are so numerous and so varied in nature—philosophical, scientific, and literary by turns—that one may call the *Apology* a lecture rather than a speech of defense, and doubt has even been cast on its historicity. It seems obvious, in short, that the work, before being used as a direct document of Apuleius's life, asks to be interpreted as a sophisticated literary product. The famous rhetorician is here utterly committed to the attempt to leave posterity a carefully modeled portrait of himself as a talented and brilliant Platonic philosopher.

Summary of the
Apology

The origins of the trial seem to lie in economic interests. Pontianus's father-in-law (see p. 533), Herennius Rufinus, perhaps soon after Apuleius's marriage to Pudentilla, sought the support of Pontianus himself and, after his death, the support of his still underage brother, Pudens, in attacking Apuleius. The purpose was to prevent him from having access to the inheritance of his wife, who was considerably older than he, and the pretext was protecting Pudens's interests. When a first, obviously trumped-up charge—that Apuleius was responsible for the death of Pontianus—failed almost immediately, the charge of magic was brought against Apuleius (for which the *lex Cornelia,* as we are told by Paulus, a jurist of the third century, prescribed even capital punishment); only by recourse to magical practices, evidently, could he have been able to induce a wealthy, no longer young widow to marry him. Despite obvious reworking, the text we have of the *Apology* must be faithful to the order of the arguments developed in court. First (chaps. 1–25) the orator attempts to meet one by one the arguments the prosecution had drawn from his private life, multiplying learned disquisitions on disparate subjects, so as to gain the upper hand completely over his opponents in the realm of culture. Next he rebuts the specific accusation that he is a magician by proudly declaring his activity as a philosopher (25–65). The third and last section (66–103) is then devoted to the reconstruction of the events following his arrival in Oea, for the purpose of showing how the marriage was entirely due to Pontianus. The decisive proof, which must have secured acquittal (no source mentions condemnation, and the cocky, resolute tone itself of the written version accords well with a favorable outcome to the trial), was the reading of Pudentilla's will, which named as principal heir, not Apuleius, but her son Pudens himself.

Apuleius and Cicero

The skill as advocate that Apuleius shows in the *Apology* has led to frequent comparisons with Cicero, in particular with the Cicero of the *Pro Caelio,* a speech full of plays on words, invective, irony, and sarcasm. From

Cicero, who was considered, though often reluctantly, the leader of Roman oratory, Apuleius not only borrowed his sentence construction but also more than once employed entire passages, in a subtle and amusing play. Yet he never crossed the boundary into open irony (as happens at several famous points in the novel: see *Metamorphoses* 7.20 and especially 3.27: *quo usque tandem — inquit — cantherium patiemur istum?* "just how long will we endure that nag?" where one notes the parody of the most famous of all Ciceronian openings); the genre did not allow ridicule of its most important (and standard) representative. The color of the speech, however, is certainly not Ciceronian. It is far removed from republican taste, being inclined instead to a mixture of vulgarisms, neologisms, archaisms, poeticisms, and everything else that gives Apuleius's style its peculiar quality. As for content, one cannot but admire the coolness with which the orator ridicules the grounds of the accusation. Apuleius in fact always speaks in lofty tones of his encyclopedic culture, which he constantly displays. There are allusions and winking references, from which his accusers are excluded (this is another way of making fun of their ignorance) and which, by contrast, are shared with Maximus, the presiding judge, who thus is promoted to the position of sole auditor, an ideal recipient because he is cultivated and sensitive. The free and lively stance of the speech, which consists wholly of allusions and digressions, makes possible graceful exercises in learning that are comprehensible only to an audience able to recognize the literary *exempla* quoted in the author's arguments for the defense. Thus a text is produced that sometimes preserves unusual notices and observations, such as the one in the tenth chapter, where Apuleius, defending himself against charges of licentiousness for having sung of his love for two handsome boys, who are mentioned under false names, records the real names of the women whom the Latin elegiac poets had sung of under appropriate pseudonyms (these have the same metrical shape and number of syllables as the real names: Clodia for Lesbia, Hostia for Cynthia, and Plania for Delia).

Apuleius the magician

But what is most fascinating to moderns is the disturbing shadow that Apuleius does not succeed in banishing (or does not care to banish) cast by his own undeniable vast knowledge about magic. The sharp distinction that he pretends to draw between magic and philosophy, or in more exact terms, between black magic and theurgic magic, is based on a distinction between powers. But the ability to dominate natural forces that belongs to the scientist (or therapist or soothsayer), of which he several times boasts, nonetheless retains a certain ambiguity throughout the speech. And if, as is often thought, the judges and accusers, while acquitting the accused with a *non liquet,* were not fully satisfied and convinced, with all the more reason does the modern reader ask questions to which the text of the *Apology* does not reply: was Apuleius not already at a disadvantage because Gaetulia (along with Numidia, his native country) was a land famous for magicians? when defending himself against the charge of having used fish for wicked ends, why does Apuleius claim that sea animals have nothing to do with black magic, when we know that exactly the opposite is the case? is Apuleius sincere? Even the picture of the philosopher that he draws, far from having the clear, unequivocal features of a Platonist (which Apuleius claims to be), denotes an eclecticism that is not easily distinguished from the neo-Pythagoreans, who are very close to a magic that is not solely theurgic (he can, for instance, call upon the intervention of demons to assure his salvation from hostile forces). It cannot be doubted, in any case, that regardless of the outcome of the trial, which must have been favorable to the accused, as the self-confident and haughty tone seems to indicate, Apuleius's fame as a magician lasted for centuries and was associated with that of other great magicians, among them Apollonius of Tyana (this would be attested by, among others, Lactantius in *Divinae Institutiones* 5.3.7 and especially Augustine, who in books 8 and 9 of the *City of God* rebuts point by point Apuleius's teachings, in particular his demonology, and in his correspondence, especially letters 102 and 138, directs harsh criticisms at Apuleius as magician, who is acclaimed by the pagans of Africa and contrasted with Christ).

Apuleius certainly did not forget his misadventure at Sabrata, if it is true, as has been observed, that echoes and recollections of it would become those many episodes of the novel in which a trial, with all its suffocating mechanisms, constitutes the center of the scene.

2. APULEIUS AND THE NOVEL

The only completely preserved Latin novel

To the neo-Platonist Macrobius, two centuries later, it seemed almost incredible that a Platonic philosopher had sunk to composing a novel of erotic, licentious adventures such as the *Metamorphoses.* This sort of moralistic reservation, however, had no influence on the work's fate in medieval times. Along with Petronius's *Satyricon,* Apuleius's work represents for us the only example of an ancient novel in Latin, and it is the only one that has survived intact.

Date and title of the work

The *Apology* provides the *terminus post quem.* Given the tone of the accusation, alert to every detail of Apuleius's private life, one presumes that the existence of a novel such as the *Metamorphoses,* the episodes of which are connected to magic in various ways, would not have been passed over in silence. We should conclude therefore that at the time of the trial the novel had not yet become known to the public, even if some part of it was written.

The title preserved by the manuscripts, *Metamorphoses,* soon competed with the title under which the work was referred to by Augustine (*De Civitate Dei* 18.18): *Asinus Aureus,* in which it is uncertain whether the adjective should be taken as referring to an appreciation of the text's quality or to the animal's tawny color. Recently, on the basis of arguments made by historians of religion (the most important argument, which takes into consideration the fact that the eleventh book is a profession of faith in Isis, recalling that the ass in the cult of Isis is identified with Tiphon-Seth, the god of evil), the title testified to by Augustine has been defended; it probably coexisted with the other.

<table>
<tr><td>

Summary of the
Metamorphoses

</td><td>

Of the eleven books, the first three are concerned with the adventures of the young protagonist Lucius before and after his arrival at Hypata in Thessaly, which was traditionally a land of magic. Involved already during his journey in the mysterious atmosphere surrounding the place, through the dark tale of his traveling companion, Aristomenes, the young man shows at once the basic feature of his character, *curiositas*. This leads him deeper and deeper into the witchcraft that lies at the heart of the life of the city, in which he at once finds himself experiencing an outrage disguised as a kindness by his friend Pythias. The guest of Milo, a rich local man, and of his wife Pamphila, who is connected to magic, Lucius succeeds in winning the favors of their servant Fotis and persuades her to let him be present secretly at one of the transformations that her mistress undergoes. Upon seeing Pamphila change herself into an owl by the aid of an unguent, Lucius cannot resist and insistently begs Fotis to help him try such a metamorphosis on himself. Fotis agrees but makes a mistake with the unguent, and Lucius becomes an ass, though he retains his human faculties of thought. This is the crucial episode in the novel, the one that sets the rest of the plot in motion. Lucian learns from Fotis that in order to recover his human appearance, he must eat roses. This escape from his predicament, though he pursues it at once, is put off until the end of the novel and is achieved only after a long series of mishaps has befallen the ass. A second section of the novel includes the ass's experiences with a group of brigands who have carried him off: his removal to the mountain cavern in which they live, a failed attempt at flight along with a girl, Charite, who is their prisoner, and the final deliverance of the two by the girl's fiancé, who, pretending to be a brigand, succeeds in tricking the gang (4–7.14). The principal narrative becomes the frame for a second narrative, in the form of a story told to Charite by the old woman watching over her, the beautiful and famous tale of Cupid and Psyche, which occupies parts of three books (4.28–6.24). The following books, except for the last, cover the tragicomic calamities of the ass, who passes from self-styled priests of the Syrian goddess, who devote themselves to lascivious practices, to a miller, who is killed by his wife, on to a very poor vegetable gardener, a Roman soldier, and then to two brothers, one a cook, the other a pastry chef. Lucius, who always remains unobserved under the ass's skin, is able to witness the unhappy stories of adultery and death that fill out the last books, varying and enlarging the basic form that Apuleius seems almost to announce at 8.22. Everywhere the ass observes and records actions and plans with his human mind, impelled equally by his curiosity about the surrounding world and by the desire to find the roses that can free him from the magic spell. The cook and the pastry chef are the first to recognize his two-sided nature, a discovery that leads to the final event. Told of its unusual character and amused, the master of the two artisans buys the ass to show it off to his friends. In the course of the exhibitions made of him, Lucius succeeds in getting away from the arena at Corinth, in which he was to copulate with a woman condemned to death, and in his flight he reaches a deserted beach, where he falls asleep. Lucius's abrupt awakening in the middle of the night opens the last book. The ritual purification that follows and the prayer to the Moon prepare the way for the decidedly mystical atmosphere that dominates the concluding part. Lucius recovers his human form on the next day by eating the roses of a crown taken from a priest in the sacred procession of Isis, just as the goddess herself had prescribed

</td></tr>
</table>

when she appeared to him on the beach. In the procession there also reappear, as masqueraders, many of the characters of the novel, including the symbol of the baseness Lucius has endured, a kind of asinine Pegasus, who is the mockery of all. In gratitude, he becomes initiated into Isis's cult at Corinth. Then at Rome, at the behest of Osiris, he becomes a pleader of cases in the Forum.

The Metamorphoses *and the genre of the novel*

Reading the *Metamorphoses* raises some preliminary questions. The first has to do with the genre to which the text, which is usually called a novel, belongs. Within the system of genres transmitted to us by antiquity, the novel seems to lack a definite physiognomy (see p. 459); it appears to be the result of the intersection of various genres (epic, biography, Menippean satire, mythological story, etc.). Moreover, it is difficult to form a true picture of the novel genre on account of the lack of evidence, at least in Latin literature. Roman society lacked a large class of readers of middling culture of the sort that seems to be the minimum necessary for creating and maintaining a genre that by definition is popular.

The fabulae Milesiae

In the case of the *Metamorphoses,* furthermore, it is necessary to consider another element that is vital for characterizing the work's genre, though no less problematic, namely, its relation to the *fabulae Milesiae,* with which the author himself connects the substance of his work (*sermone isto Milesio varias fabulas conseram* {1.1}). But the nearly total loss of the translation that Cornelius Sisenna made (see p. 123) of the original *fabulae Milesiae* by Aristides of Miletus (second century B.C.) leaves the origins of this narrative genre obscure beyond recovery. The only thing that is certain is the erotic character of these short stories, which they share with the novel (as one infers from the Greek writings of the imperial period, which are preserved in far greater number than the Latin). The *Metamorphoses* preserves this feature, too, and develops it through a series of mishaps, in the form of the *insertae fabulae.*

The story of the ass-man, in its basic erotic-licentious form, also seems to have been a *fabula Milesia.* But the addition of the magical element is probably due to Apuleius. This feature must have already been present in the Greek text that (as we will soon argue) served as a model, but certainly not with so important a role. And Apuleius shows that he is quite conscious of the innovation when he adds to the first books of the novel a series of notably magical tales. From the very start the work marks its departure from the Milesian tradition. The characters in these tales—Socrates, Aristomenes, and Thelyphron, who, hardly by accident, is a native of Miletus—represent typical figures of traveling merchants or idle students, characters who must have been very common in the Milesian tale, for we find them again, with their regular repertory of acts and attitudes, in Petronius's *Satyricon.* Here, in Apuleius's novel, the logic of their lives appears frustrated, not to say overthrown, by their encounter with the pitiless world of magic. Thus, if Socrates, for instance, lives under wretched conditions, the true cause is not, as Aristomenes thinks, that he lost his head chasing prostitutes but that he has been subjugated by the spell of the witch Meroe. The case of Thelyphron is similar: Upon hearing that in that city people are paid to guard the dead, he wonders, with a skeptical smile, *Hicine mortui solent aufugere?* That smile is destined to fade quickly from the unlucky man's lips when he meets realities that are stronger and more mysterious. The ordinary logic of cleverness—which is characteristic of the narrative structure of the Milesian tale—is frustrated by the assault of magic, defeated by the strange logic of the magical tale. The opening tales, in short, are not solely, as has often been noted, narrative prefigurations whose purpose is to give exemplary warnings to Lucius (who later will experience a similar, though not so tragic, fate, suffering not only injury but also mockery, once in the episode of Pythias and then in the episode of the festival of the god Laughter). The opening tales also seem to correspond to the author's desire to define, in terms of novelty, his own work in relation to the genre to which it belongs.

The sources of the **Metamorphoses**

Another important question has to do with a difficult problem of sources. It is known that a novel preserved for us among the works of Lucian of Samosata, but certainly spurious, has the same plot as the Latin novel and bears the title *Lucius, or the Ass;* it is written in Greek and is a good deal shorter than Apuleius's. Then we have the testimony of the Byzantine patriarch Photius (ninth century), who claims (on folio 129 of his *Bibliotheca*) to have read stories of transformations in the work of an otherwise unknown Lucius of Patrae, in several books. The first two of these, it is supposed, were copied from Lucian's work, or—Photius judges this hypothesis more likely—Lucian took them from Lucius. The interpretation of this notice has given rise to a debate that still continues among scholars over the relations and the priority of the two surviving works (the very identity of Lucius of Patrae has been disputed, with great probability, because of the ease with which his name could be reconstructed from the name of the protagonist in the *Lucius*). Whatever solution be adopted (a common source for Apuleius and pseudo-Lucian, or, less likely, that the *Lucius* is the original version), the question remains open about the parts that are found only in Apuleius, that is, how many of them are to be attributed with certainty to Apuleius and were not found in the original. In this case, too, scholars are divided. Some grant Apuleius little more than the central story of Cupid and Psyche (about which, for various reasons, no one entertains any doubts). Others, who are more numerous today, considering the intention that the author expresses at the beginning of the *Metamorphoses* (the *varias fabulas conseram* already quoted), attribute to him all the episodes that are lacking in the *Lucius* (such as the major part of the initial episodes). It appears certain, in any event, that the end, with the appearance of Isis and the successive initiations into her mysteries and those of Osiris, belongs to Apuleius (in the *Lucius* the story ends when the ass succeeds in escaping from the disgraceful copulation by eating rose petals carried by a spectator in the amphitheater), all the more so if one considers that the protagonist, a young man who is presented as Greek throughout the novel, suddenly becomes *Madaurensis* in this book, with an obvious superposition of the writing "I" on the narrating "I."

More interesting than the complicated question of how individual passages originated is the difference in general significance and narrative tone between Apuleius's text and the one by pseudo-Lucian, that is, to what extent each reflects the general shape of the original. A reading of the *Lucius* reveals that the narrative was intended to be pure entertainment and that the plot has absolutely nothing to do with any moral purpose; instead, there are ludic, erotic, humorous, and scabrous elements, combined in an amusing mixture. The case of the *Metamorphoses* is different. The story pretends to offer reading of pure diversion (*lector, intende: laetaberis* [1.1]), with lots of humorous and licentious episodes, but in fact it takes on the qualities of an exemplary tale. For this reason Apuleius never overdoes the coarseness in his novel, which would certainly have been easy for him, and he uses only sparingly and at intervals those obscene elements that the *Lucius* joins together in crude vignettes.

It is not surprising, therefore, that practically all editors, despite recent attempts to defend it, expunge as not belonging to Apuleius the so-called *spurcum additamentum* at 10.21, a short, very racy addition to the already coarse episode of Lucius-the-ass's lovemaking with a noble matron. Various views have been taken of this. Some have recognized in it a relic of a more vulgar edition of the novel that was redone by others and circulated in parallel (a relic going back to what is for us a shadowy translation of the *Milesiaka* done by Sisenna). Others, with greater likelihood, have seen in it a skillful forgery of the Middle Ages. Still others have believed it could be Apuleian. The discussion has been and continues to be one of the liveliest and most heated of modern philology, because, among other reasons, it is obviously connected with the more general problem of the transmission of Apuleius's text. One sign of the work's moral earnestness is the use of Lucius's *curiositas* as a structural element. Right from the beginning it leads the character to the calamitous transformation from which he will be delivered only after a long expiation, culminating in a drastic change of life. As if to confirm that this is an interpretive key provided by the author, some minor episodes of the plot have exact correspondences with episodes in the story of Lucius, either anticipating or reflecting its features, the episode with Byrrhena, for instance, in which Lucius sees the statues representing the myth of Actaeon, who was punished for his curiosity. The tale of Cupid and Psyche is also clearly symbolic. Because of the importance it has by virtue of its central position and great extent, it becomes a prefiguration of Lucius's destiny, and the interpretation of the entire novel depends on the interpretation of this.

Summary of the
tale of Cupid and
Psyche (4.28–6.24)

The plot reflects traditional tales familiar from all periods. The youngest daughter of a king arouses Venus's envy by her extraordinary beauty; because the goddess wills it, she is given into the power of a monster. (Not by chance is the oracle that seems to order Psyche's marriage to a horrible monster composed in the elegiac meter, contrary to the convention by which oracles are composed in hexameters.) The figure of the terrible husband adumbrates Cupid, the god of love, who has fallen in love with the girl. Psyche, who was expecting to die on top of a cliff, is thus transported to a very beautiful palace. Here she meets her husband, whose identity she does not know and the sight of whom is forbidden to her: if she looks upon her husband—this is the condition—she will be immediately separated from him. Goaded by her two envious sisters, however, Psyche disobeys the order and looks upon Cupid as he sleeps. Of course she is immediately separated from him, and this is ended only by the painful expiation she undergoes through various tests, among them a descent to the Underworld. The story concludes with marriage and the honors paid to Psyche, who is taken up to heaven as a goddess.

In the *bella fabella* (so Lucius terms the tale of Cupid and Psyche at 6.25) a strong allegorical purpose is immediately evident. It apparently influenced and redefined for contemporaries and for immediately succeeding readers the very nature of the Milesian genre, which it explicitly recalls (*propter Milesiae conditorem,* Apuleius says in reference to himself at 4.33). If in fact, as the *Historia Augusta* tells us (*Clodius Albinus* 12.12), Septimius Severus reproached Clodius Albinus with growing dull-witted because of reading the *Milesiae Punicae* of his Apuleius and throwing himself away on *neniae aniles* (in the term, which is generic, there may also be an ironic reference to the tale of Cupid and Psyche, which is told by an *anicula* who wants to console a girl who has awakened with a start), the polemical tone of the passage does not warrant us to believe in the existence of a definite genre of *Milesiae Punicae* of which Apuleius was the founder. But according to Tertullian (*Adversus Valentinianos* 23), whose testimony is itself not free from polemic, the gnostics wrote *Milesiae,* giving them the coloring as well as the substance of their own allegories, which seems to indicate that the example of Apuleius had caused the term *fabula Milesia* to lose its specific original value.

The differing interpretations of the tale of Cupid and Psyche

The *fabella* became the immediate object of numerous interpretations. The oldest one that has come down to us, a polemic directed against the many pagan or gnostic interpretations of the *fabella,* is by Fulgentius (*Mythologiae* 3.68), who interpreted the tale in a Christian way, as a myth of the meeting between the Soul and Desire. It is obvious that Apuleius, even though he breathed the same atmosphere as the gnostic thinkers, could certainly not have written a Christian myth, being as he was a harsh critic of Judaism (see *Metamorphoses* 9.14, where he violently criticizes monotheistic worship). The Christianizing interpretation, which descends to Boccaccio, in whom it already seems tinged with Platonism (see his allegorical exegesis of the *fabella* at *Genealogiae Deorum Gentilium* 5.22, which is probably also influenced by the demonological writings of Martianus Capella, an author who knew Apuleius), may be a useful document for the historians of religion, but it is altogether foreign to the author from Madaura. The interpreter who believes he should look for some coherence of thought between the narrator-allegorist and the speculative philosopher would thus regard as historically better founded the interpretation of the tale as a philosophical myth, with a rigorously and exclusively Platonic basis. Not very different from this is the more recent interpretation that makes the fable a tale of initiation into the cult of Isis; this view sets a high value on the eleventh book, which is in effect a great aretalogy of the Egyptian divinities Isis and Osiris.

Yet, besides radical doubts about the seriousness of Apuleius's Platonism and religiosity, the context of the tale does not seem to authorize excessively definite interpretations, because in it Platonic and Isiac elements appear not only indissolubly linked, so that they cannot be easily distinguished, but also confused with one another. The philosophical interpretation cannot forget that the Plato of the *Republic* would have condemned a myth in which the Olympian divinities are so openly ridiculed. Venus, for instance, is reduced to a matron who is as lecherous as she is capricious; Zeus appears little more than a miserable and hypocritical bourgeois. The religious interpretation, which sees in Psyche's story a doublet of Lucius's difficult journey towards Isiac salvation, meets similar difficulties. Psyche does not seem to evolve towards a true chaste morality, as happens with the protagonist of the novel, but at the end she is rejoined to a Cupid who is even more lascivious than in the rest of the story, and she is taken up to an Olympus that is certainly not heavenly but, with its banquets and dances, as earthly as can be. *Curiositas* too, which in the rest of the work is the burning, profaning desire to know, seems to be reduced in the tale to something quite weak. Psyche's *curiositas* is neutralized by that childish *simplicitas* of hers that typifies her and protects her from negative connotations. Thus, her extreme act of *curiositas* is motivated by her silly desire to please her husband (see 6.20).

Moreover, if one reads the tale in the context of the novel, it is difficult to attribute to it a simplistically positive value—which is what a tale conveying an explicit revelation, Isiac or Platonic, would convey. That would be contradicted by the reaction of Lucius the ass, the ironic listener to the story: *sed astans ego non procul dolebam mehercules, quod pugillares et stilum non habebam, qui tam bellam fabulam praenotarem* (7.25), where the adjectival addition to *fabellam* is significant, since it is a nexus that appears constantly charged with ironic connotations in Apuleius. Then, too, Charite, the girl to whom the tale is told to console her for her sufferings, is going to die a terrible, melodramatic death, as the eighth book reveals to us. Contradictions of varying weight, in short, discourage an unambiguous interpretation of the tale of Cupid and Psyche, and they invite one to attach value rather to the delicate and complex literary functions that the story acquires within the structure of the novel.

The tale of Cupid and Psyche as a prefiguration of the entire novel

The tale of Cupid and Psyche reproduces the whole story on a smaller scale and provides the key for reading it. How indeed, we may ask, would we read the novel if we did not have the tale of Cupid and Psyche (contained, as was said, in books 4, 5, and 6)? We would certainly read it as at first we read books 1, 2, and 3, that is to say, as a kind of novel of adventure in which the marvelous and the scabrous play a large part; we certainly would not read it as a mystagogic novel, that is, as the account of an initiation into the mystery rites. It is the task of the secondary tale to complicate the first reading by starting a second theme (religion), which not only prefigures the epiphany of the goddess Isis, which will conclude the whole narrative in book 11, but also overlaps with the first theme (adventure) in order to give it the meaning of an initiation. As soon as they are brought into contact with Psyche's parallel experience, Lucius's metamorphoses can no longer be read except as tests imposed upon a being who, after a period of alienation and misadventure along the way, from the very beginning has been promised salvation by the goddess who is the mistress of transformation. But in the context in which it is set (i.e., before the explicit revelation of the divinity that takes place in the eleventh book) the tale of Cupid and Psyche appears isolated from the narrative context, and in a certain sense it is destined to fail for the moment. Its structure as a story of salvation with a happy ending will be reactivated and brought to completion only with the close of the narrative.

The literary format of the tale of Cupid and Psyche

The obvious allegorical meaning in no way destroys the lightness of the tale. A basic plot that is probably influenced by popular fable (whether Iranian or Egyptian or western African has been a matter of discussion) is joined both to Alexandrian and Milesian elements and to specifically Latin elements; the suggestions of Virgil for the descent to the Underworld and of elegy for the love of Cupid and Psyche are important. Everything is fused together and executed with that superiority and levity that Apuleius seems to share with Ovid, another nonchalant recounter of myths.

The Metamorphoses, *popular story and mystical-symbolic account*

The other digressions inserted into the principal plot are events of various sorts, in which the magical (in the first three books) alternates with the epic (in the stories of the brigands) and with the tragic and the comic, an experiment with various genres that is paralleled by the work's experimentation with language. But the numerous literary motifs of varying origin are arranged in a design that seems dense with meaning. To give a single example, this is the case with the short stories of adultery that make up the last books, the darkest stories of the entire novel, in which the power of a blind, merciless fortune makes itself felt most strongly, in marked contrast to the pure light of the last book, which is dominated by Isis-Tyche, the *Fortuna videns.* The whole novel is structured as a journey through a world of literary signs and symbols towards a liberation into light and morality. The continual mutual penetration of the mystical-religious element (which opens itself to symbolism) and the original texture of the Milesian tale constitutes the most original quality of the novel (and also explains its success even in periods of mystical fervor). The criticisms that have been brought against the imperfect fusion of the two levels of reading, the popular-story level and the mystical-symbolic, are not sufficient to affect the overall success of the experiment that is constituted by the text. With the sole exception of book 11, in which the mystical element prevails and Lucius's animal form has lost its importance almost completely, it should not be forgotten that in the course of the novel it is precisely the constant presence of the ass's thoughts that creates a continuity uniting the two levels and articulates the overall meaning of the story as a progressive *iter* towards wisdom.

Thus the final outcome, which on the one hand identifies the narrator Lucius with the author Apuleius, calling him *Madaurensis,* and on the other provides the key that is needed for interpreting the novel as a story of religious salvation, does not arrive completely unexpected and is firmly tied to the rest of the novel; indeed, it appears to be the necessary culmination of it. Nor is it accidental that the author's direct interventions, which seem to be peculiar to the *Metamorphoses* (cf. the *Satyricon*), become more frequent in the last books, to the point that they produce effects of an ironic rupture. The very conventions of the ancient novel are called into question: *sed nequis indignationis meae reprehendat impetum secum sic reputans: — ecce nunc patiemur philosophantem nobis asinum! — unde decessi revertar ad fabulam* ("But let no one find fault with the fury of my indignation, thinking 'Now we will have to endure an ass prattling philosophy!'—I return to my story at the point where I left off" [10.33]). It is as if the author were warning us of the imminent reversal and resolution of the expectations aroused by the story, a change of course to which the reader cannot remain indifferent. Whereas the *lector* of the stories that form the first ten books had been called *scrupulosus* (9.30) and his ideal behavior ought to have been that exemplified by Lucius himself (see 1.20: *sed ego huic et credo hercules et gratas gratias memini, quod lepidae fabulae festivitate nos avocavit,* "but I have faith in the man and am deeply grateful that he has diverted us with a charming and delightful story"), now in the eleventh book, after the revelation of Isis, the same *lector* is called *studiosus* (11.23). Thus the *lector* is involved in the *gaudere* that closes the last phrase of the novel, *gaudens obibam* (11.30), replacing, or rather amplifying, the *laetari* that was promised to the reader in the prologue. All the coincidences of an ironic play? or genuine mystical passion? One cannot give a final answer to the doubts. The only thing certain is that the novel concludes with the positiveness of a salvation, a manner of ending behind which, after all, everyone may suspect (beyond the possibility of a positive verification) a light gesture of superior irony.

3. LANGUAGE AND STYLE

For some time now, scholars, following Norden, who insisted on seeing in Greek Asianism the basis of the culture and taste of the African rhetoricians, among them Apuleius, have given up the notion of *Africitas* as a common denominator in the language of the Latin writers from Africa. The notion, in any case, would not help in defining Apuleius's language, which is the result of a remarkable and highly original mixture of different features. Living in a period of enthusiasm for the archaic, Apuleius naturally shares the fondness of his contemporaries for obsolete words (to give but a single example, he makes ample use of the adverbs ending in *-im,* which are quite common in Sisenna's language) and for archaic authors (as far as we can tell from his works, he was very fond of Plautus, whom he often echoed), but he makes it part of a more general pursuit of literariness. This feature, associated with the practice of oratory, gets translated into a

*The literary
language: the
prominence of the
form of expression*

complete mastery of different registers, which are combined in the texture of the language in various ways. Hence the absolute freedom in juxtaposing archaisms and neologisms, vulgarisms and poeticisms, and the technical vocabulary of science and the crafts. If, then, one recognizes that the primary purpose of literary language is to valorize itself by distancing itself from the purely communicative use of language, Apuleius's language seems the perfect expression of that purpose. The words become evocative; they appear surrounded by a penumbra of marginal meanings and call up suggestive implicit connotations.

Still more interesting is the way Apuleius occasionally puts into practice his own choices. Because of his great knowledge of literature, he seems to have at his disposal a kind of specialized literary lexicon, gathered and organized around a set of typical situations based on the classics (Ennius, Virgil, etc.). It is as if he knew formulas, repertories of established *iuncturae,* for describing scenes of grief, pictures of heroism, the effusion of passions and states of mind. He has ready recourse to these, with his rhetorical ability to compose set pieces on a given theme by recombining in a new and personal way the material drawn from tradition and by renewing it from within through frequent neologisms. This procedure, which especially in the novel enlivens various genre scenes, is obviously based on the multiplication and superabundance of passages, in order to make the register he wants immediately perceptible. This more than anything creates the impression of stylization that Apuleius's language ultimately produces in the reader.

The highly rhetorical quality of the vocabulary corresponds to the character of the construction of phrase and sentence, in which isocolon, homoeoteleuton, assonance, accumulation of synonyms, and deliberately repeated rhythms give the discourse a very particular movement, which tends to show as many facets as possible to every notion. Apuleius's prose, though it respects in general the standards of classical rhetoric, in the end carries the Latin rhetorical system to its ultimate limits of expression. And yet, in opening itself to new rhythms and new constructions, at the same time it allows us a presage of the age of medieval Latin prose that was now not so very far away.

4. LITERARY SUCCESS

Apuleius was celebrated in late antiquity—but as a sorcerer and philosopher, not as a novelist. His *Apology, Metamorphoses,* and *Florida* are preserved in a single manuscript, copied in the second half of the eleventh century, which in turn goes back to a manuscript revised by a certain Sallustius in Rome in 395 and in Constantinople in 397. His philosophical writings, on the other hand, emerged and circulated in northern Europe in the Middle Ages. It was not until the fourteenth century that the two separate strands were combined to form the corpus of his writings. Unsurprisingly, he never became a medieval school author.

It was Boccaccio who rediscovered and transcribed the lone manuscript containing the *Metamorphoses* and the other two opuscules. In the Renaissance the text was often printed in Latin (the *editio princeps* already appeared in 1469 in Rome) and often translated into the vernacular, into Italian (by Boiardo and by Firenzuola), into French (by Guillaume Michel), into German (by Johannes Sieder), into English (Thomas Adlington), and into other languages. It exercised a considerable influence upon the growth of the modern novel, above all upon the genre of the picaresque novel in Spain. In more modern times, one of its fervent admirers was Flaubert, who in a letter praised its treatment of nature, simultaneously ancient, Christian, and modern: "One smells there the odor of incense and of urine, bestiality is linked with mysticism." The inset story of Cupid and Psyche enjoyed enormous popularity independently of its context; its first separate translation into English was published by Shakerley Marmion in 1637.

Apuleius remains one of the Latin authors most likely to fascinate modern readers. His exploration of abnormal and supernatural realms of experience and his fascination with sex, violence, and redemption exert an appeal even upon the many readers who are spared the bizarrely sensuous pleasures of his Latin style.

BIBLIOGRAPHY

The best editions of Apuleius's works are in the Budé series: the *Metamorphoses*, ed. D. S. Robertson (4 vols., Paris 1936–45), the *Apologia* and *Florida*, ed. P. Vallette (1924), and the philosophical works, ed. P. Beaujeu (1973; see also the Teubner of C. Moreschini, Stuttgart 1988). There is also a Teubner edition by R. Helm and P. Thomas (latest editions Leipzig 1955–69) and a good new Loeb of the *Metamorphoses* by A. Hanson (2 vols., Cambridge, Mass. 1989). There is an English commentary on the *Apologia* by H. E. Butler and A. S. Owen (Oxford 1914), and there are a number of commentaries on single books of the *Metamorphoses*: on book 1 by A. Scobie (Meissenheim am Glan 1975), on book 3 by R. T. van der Paardt (Groningen 1971), on book 4 by B. L. Hijmans et al. (Groningen 1977), on the *Cupid and Psyche* episode by E. J. Kenney (Cambridge 1991), on books 6–7 and 8 by B. L. Hijmans et al. (Groningen 1981, 1985), and on book 11 by J. G. Griffiths (Leiden 1975). See also B. J. de Jonge's Latin commentary on book 2 (Groningen 1941).

The general works on the novel mentioned above on Petronius (B. E. Perry, *The Ancient Romances* [Berkeley 1967], P. G. Walsh, *The Roman Novel* [Cambridge 1970], and T. Hägg, *The Novel in Antiquity* [Oxford 1983]) also deal with Apuleius's *Metamorphoses*. See also B. L. Hijmans and R. T. van der Paardt, eds., *Aspects of Apuleius' Golden Ass* (Groningen 1978), J. Tatum, *Apuleius and the Golden Ass* (Ithaca 1979), A. Scobie, *Apuleius and Folktale* (Leiden 1983; see also *Aspects of the Ancient Romance* [Meissenheim am Glan 1969]), J. J. Winkler, *Auctor et Actor: A Narratological Reading of Apuleius' The Golden Ass* (Berkeley and Los Angeles 1985, the most influential modern study), P. James, *Unity in Diversity: A Study of Apuleius' Metamorphoses* (Hildesheim 1987), and C. C. Schlam, *The Metamorphoses of Apuleius: On Making an Ass of Oneself* (Chapel Hill 1992). For the Greek *Lucius*, see vol. 2 of the Oxford Classical Text Lucian by M. D. Macleod (1974); there is a translation in vol. 8 of the Loeb Lucian by the same editor (Cambridge, Mass. 1967) and in B. P. Reardon, *Collected Ancient Greek Novels* (London 1989). For Photius's paraphrase, see R. Henry, ed., *Photius, Bibliothèque*, vol. 2 (Paris

1960) cod. 129, pp. 103–4; on the relationship between the Greek *Lucius* and the *Metamorphoses*, see Perry, *Ancient Romances,* and G. Bianco, *La fonte greca delle Metamorfosi di Apuleio* (Brescia 1971).

Among foreign monographs on the *Metamorphoses* may be mentioned M. Bernhard, *Der Stil des Apuleius von Madaura* (Stuttgart 1927), P. Junghanns, *Die Erzählungstechnik von Apuleius' Metamorphosen und ihrer Vorlage* (Leipzig 1932), P. Callebat, *Sermo Cotidianus dans les Métamorphoses d'Apulée* (Caen 1968; see also his article in Hijmans and van der Paardt, *Aspects of Apuleius' Golden Ass*), and D. Fehling, *Amor und Psyche* (Wiesbaden 1977). More generally, see A. Pennacini, P. L. Donini, T. Alimonti, and A. Monteduro Roccavini, *Apuleio, letterato, filosofo, mago* (Rome 1979).

On the *Apology,* see esp. A. Abt, *Die Apologie des Apuleius von Madaura und die antike Zauberei* (Giessen 1908), and on the *Florida,* K. Mras, "Apuleius' *Florida* im Rahmen ähnlichen Literatur," *AAWW* 86 (1949) 205–23; there is a brief discussion of both in G. Kennedy, *The Art of Rhetoric in the Roman World* (Princeton 1972) 604–7. On the philosophical works, see J. Dillon, *The Middle Platonists* (London 1977) 306–37, and more broadly, C. Moreschini, *Apuleio e il platonismo* (Florence 1978); see also B. L. Hijmans in *ANRW* 36.1 (Berlin 1987) 395–475.

On the *Peri Hermeneias,* which may or may not be by Apuleius, see D. Londey and C. Johanson, *The Logic of Apuleius* (Leiden 1987).

Philology, Rhetoric and Literary Criticism, Law

I. LATIN PHILOLOGY: A SUMMARY OF ITS HISTORICAL DEVELOPMENT

A view of the history of Roman philology

The philological and critical study of Latin texts comes to its full maturity in the period from the Flavians to the Antonines. This may be the right moment to consider the lines of development of this scholarly production. It might be useful to give a summary that, starting from the beginning, presents an orderly historical picture of Roman philology and also shows the earlier progress and the causes that led to the great flourishing of these studies in the first and second centuries A.D.

Our information on the development of philology at Rome is based for a long period on indirect notices and later sources, that is, texts that we have in their entirety from later antiquity, the work of scholars, grammarians, and commentators from the second to the sixth century A.D.; especially valuable is the section *De Grammaticis* from Suetonius's *De Viris Illustribus.*

The Birth of Philology at Rome

The sophistication of early literature and the development of philology

The first flourishing of philological studies is closely connected to the development, in the archaic period, of a literature that was sophisticated, oriented towards Greek models, and alert to the technical problems of style and poetry. Authors such as Ennius, Terence, Accius, and Lucilius give direct evidence in their writings of familiarity with Greek studies in philology, rhetoric, and poetics. In this sense Ennius proclaims himself *dicti studiosus,* "lover of the word," that is, a philologist. We may recall Terence's penetrating discussions of poetics; from Accius and Lucilius we have fragments dealing in precise technical terminology with problems of literary criticism and linguistics.

The earliest philology practiced on Greek texts

It is obvious that an intimate familiarity with the Greek culture of the Alexandrian period comes to fruition in these writers. It is less obvious at what precise moment philological studies could first have been applied to texts. Around the middle of the second century B.C., in any event, the study and the cultivation of the word, that vast field in which rhetoric, philology, and linguistics operate, receives a powerful stimulus from the presence in Rome of eminent Greek specialists. Until at least the Augustan age, moreover, all forms of rhetorical, philological, and literary training are based primarily on Greek texts. Yet even within this tendency events occur that are important for the development of a Latin philology: the studies on Plautus by Stilo and Varro or the critical teaching of the grammarian-poet Valerius Cato, in the sophisticated circle of the *poetae novi.*

An accident seems to have played an important role in philology's first steps at Rome. The great scholar Crates of Mallus, having traveled to Rome on a political mission, broke a leg, and this had the effect of detaining at Rome for some considerable time a distinguished figure (he was not a mere schoolmaster) of Greek intellectual life. The year is 168 B.C., and Crates is at that time the chief representative of the Pergamene school, which shares the primacy in humanistic studies with Alexandria. The Alexandrian

school excelled especially in formal philology, the grammatical study of the literary language and the careful publication of critically revised editions. Crates, however, claimed to be more than a mere grammarian: he claimed also to be a *kritikos,* a "judge" of literary matters. We know that the Pergamenes had what is known as an anomalist point of view in their linguistic studies. They recognized a spontaneous creation, a natural development, in language, which was shaped by everyday usage. Thus they were very tolerant towards exceptions and neologisms. Being careful collectors of linguistic oddities, they rejected the excessively rigid rule of grammatical norms. The Alexandrians, by contrast, were more inclined to a rationalistic view, which is known as analogism. If one regards language less as a fact of nature than as the result of a convention among men (a position that had won the authoritative agreement of Epicurus), then it is necessary to go along with the rational logic of the norm, the intrinsic *ratio* of language. This linguistic *ratio* was rigorous in judging differences, exceptions, and impromptu innovations. The analogists are inclined to purism, at least by tendency.

From these opposite tendencies, anomaly and analogy, the two schools also derived different attitudes towards the study of literary facts. The analogist Alexandrians, for instance, as textual editors were much more disposed to look for a consistent logic in individual linguistic usages. The studies of the great Aristarchus, who claimed to "explain Homer by Homer," aimed precisely at extracting from an objective, deep knowledge of Homeric language a system of norms that would make it possible to evaluate the places in which the text indicated uncertainties, waverings, and obscurities.

Aelius Stilo and the Tendencies of Philology in the Second Century B.C.

From mid-century, then, the two schools began to exercise their influence over Rome. Roman culture would produce scholars of both anomalist and analogist tendencies, as well as attempts to mediate and conciliate the two directions.

A direct line joins the Pergamene Crates to the greatest grammarian and philologist of the second century, Lucius Aelius Stilo. Born around the middle of the century, Stilo continued his teaching into the time of Varro and Cicero, who were able to study with him. Deeply influenced by the Pergamenes, Stilo nevertheless also had contacts with the rival tendency: at Rhodes he studied with the great analogist grammarian, Dionysius Thrax.

We know little directly about Stilo's work, but it is likely that he began the tendency towards mediation that we see in the grammatical works of Varro of Reate (see pp. 211 ff.). Like Varro, Stilo was concerned with the authenticity of texts circulating under Plautus's name. Moreover, he worked on texts such as the extremely obscure *Carmen Saliare,* texts that on account of their prehistoric linguistic nature were in need of careful exegesis.

Philology applied to the law

It is important to recall that parallel to literary exegesis, and indeed prior to it, the interpretation of legal texts had developed extensively at Rome. The very characteristics of Roman law, which was so conservative that it was still based on extremely archaic texts that were sometimes difficult to understand, made it necessary for there to be a school of interpreters, specialists in law who also had competence in linguistics and exegesis. Lucius Acilius, for instance, commented on the Twelve Tables, and a large-scale commentary on the Twelve Tables made up a part of the *Tripertita* of Sextus Aelius Paetus, consul in 198 B.C. The school of jurists continued into the Gracchan era with such influential persons as Marcus Junius Brutus, Publius Mucius Scaevola the pontiff, and his son, Quintus Mucius Scaevola, consul in 95 B.C.

Chronological studies (Accius) and the canons of writers (Volcacius Sedigitus)

The philology of the second century reflects the influences of both Alexandria and Pergamum. An interest in questions of literary chronology—of the sort "Did Homer or Hesiod live first?"—or in the lives of the classical authors was typical of Pergamum. The researches of the poet Accius on the chronology of the earliest Latin poets, Livius Andronicus in particular, obviously belong to this trend. It was regarded as one of the principal tasks of the critic to establish canons of writers, that is, series of authors approved as classics and ranked according to preferences that were based on critical judgment, deciding, for example, who were the best epic poets, or the best iambographers, and in what order they were to be ranked. Thus, around 100 B.C. the critic Volcacius Sedigitus established a canon of the best Roman comic poets (the genre now offered a large number of texts on which to base it), in which the first three places were awarded to Caecilius, Plautus, and Naevius, respectively.

Division of classical texts into books: Octavius Lampadio

The creation of literary canons was a typical activity of the Alexandrian philologists. Still more typical of the Alexandrians was an interest in the structure of poetic books. These philologists saw to the formal arrangement of earlier texts, such as Homer, Sappho, and Pindar, and they were responsible for, among other important undertakings, the division of the Homeric poems into books. We ought to connect with this activity the work of the grammarian Gaius Octavius Lampadio, who divided into seven books the *Bellum Poenicum,* which, as far as is known, Naevius had published in a continuous form. Lampadio evidently aimed at bringing this ancient Roman poem up to the modern standards of form established by Alexandrian philology for the classics of Greek epic.

*Absence of editorial
activity in the second
century* B.C.

The work of the Latin philologists in the second century was thus quite rich and variegated, including researches into chronology, problems of authenticity, literary canons, formal interests, and, more generally, researches into linguistic and grammatical problems of Latin. Up to this point, however, little is heard of true editorial activities, of the sort then making Alexandrian philology famous: the preparation of texts that were provided with conventional signs indicating the critic's work on the text (the "diacritical signs") and were accompanied by volumes of critical annotations and textual analysis. Here attention should be drawn to some limitations that continued to hinder the development of an independent philological activity. The first limitation, and perhaps a decisive one, was the lack of real public libraries. The philological researches of Alexandria and Pergamum had flourished around public libraries. The acquisition of manuscripts and the work of the librarian-philologists were financed by the sovereigns. In the second and first centuries, to be sure, Rome must have seen a great increase in library resources. Large donations of Greek texts arrived as war booty, or, in any event, in the train of commanders and politicians returning from the East. Writing in Latin increased rapidly. Yet for a very long time the concentration of library resources remained a private phenomenon. The chief owners of books were wealthy private collectors, such as Licinius Lucullus, the great politician of the Ciceronian period. Of course, these private libraries may have been available to scholars, but there was no stable public structure to look after the transmission and improvement of library resources. The decisive step—the institution of the first state library at Rome—was taken by Asinius Pollio only in 39 B.C., after which the emperors, from Augustus onwards, bore responsibility for the institution.

*Lack of public
libraries at Rome
before Pollio*

A second, important limitation was set by the academic structures at Rome. At least down to the Augustan age, the Roman school mostly follows the Greek model. It not only imitates the organization of study found in the Greek world but is based, directly and principally, upon Greek texts of poetry, oratory, philosophy, and history. Both the social status of the teachers and the state's support of educational structures, however, for a very long time remained far below those of the Greek world. In other words, not until the Empire did education cease to be a private matter. Until the time of Augustus, teachers usually were not Roman citizens, and no chairs of literature were financed by the state before Vespasian.

*Limitations of the
academic structures
at Rome*

Thus, there is neither a homogeneous class of teachers, nor a steady connection between instruction and research. The great teachers of literature in the first century B.C. are isolated figures, at the center of private circles and coteries for the most part. The most eminent philologist in the age of Caesar, Valerius Cato, is not coincidentally a leader of the neoteric literary movement; his work is closely tied to an exclusive literary elite.

*Absence of connection
between instruction
and research*

Valerius Cato and Philology in the Age of Caesar

*Valerius Cato, a
critic-poet*

Among Roman literary scholars Valerius Cato best fits the Alexandrian model. He truly combined critic and poet in a single person. As a neoteric poet, he was known for his *epyllia*, short mythological poems that were prized by the *poetae novi* of his circle, the *Dictynna* and the mysterious *Lydia*. As a professor, he had a long career and a vast public following. He was born before 90 and had a long and active life. Suetonius tells us that *docuit multos et nobiles visusque est peridoneus praeceptor, maxime ad poeticam tendentibus* ("he had many important students and seemed a teacher of unusual ability, good especially for those who wanted to become poets"). This is an important point. The teaching of poetry was not normally separable from the teaching of rhetoric; or rather (and increasingly so as Roman culture developed), the study of the poets was intended for the preparation of the orator. We will see shortly what consequences followed from the close cooperation between rhetoric and literary studies, but it is evident that Cato, going against the current the day, gave his students an instruction that was completely oriented towards literary education. If, as is likely, his tastes tended towards the sophisticated avant-garde of the *neoteroi,* clearly he could not have had much liking for the more standardized aspects of forensic and political rhetoric.

Valerius Cato's philological activity

It would be interesting to have more information on Valerius Cato's actual philological activity. To his contemporaries he is "the only one who reads and makes poets," that is, the interpreter par excellence, the guide of young writers and also, in all likelihood, the man who creates the standards for what counts in literature. One of his admirers compares him to Zenodotus and Crates put together. This is a huge compliment, since they are not only two very great philologists but also the leaders of rival, opposing tendencies. We know that Valerius Cato had a deep interest in the text of Lucilius; we do not know whether we may speak of an edition in the Alexandrian sense, and our source about this (the beginning of Horace, *Satires* 1.10) is difficult to interpret.

Philology in the Age of Augustus

The age of Augustus and the spread of Greek culture at Rome

After Cato it is hard to find others who combine the roles of teacher, philologist, and avant-garde writer. Instead we observe a growing specialization. A typical phenomenon in the following period, the age of Augustus, is the increasing spread of Greek learning at Rome. Notable scholars of literature and esthetics are active in Rome, such as Dionysius of Halicarnassus, the historian and student of literary matters, and Caecilius of Caleacte, who wrote a treatise *On the Sublime,* used by the later author of the famous extant treatise of the same name.

Limited knowledge of Greek literature in Rome

Even though the Hellenization of Roman culture had begun more than two centuries earlier, there was still room for knowledge of it to increase, and one should not exaggerate the spread of Greek literature in Rome. Virgil undoubtedly knew Theocritus and Homer by heart, and a part of his educated public was in a position to judge competently the use he made of his Greek models. But Propertius, who so often cites Callimachus as his model, does not, at least as far as we can tell, really seem to have an extensive familiarity with the sacred Callimachean texts. Callimachus is a difficult poet. In the early Empire, Statius knows and imitates him more than the "Callimachean" Propertius, but Statius, as he himself tells us, was the son of a learned professor of Greek literature!

Growth of literary and esthetic taste: Maecenas and Pollio

Yet the growth of Greek learning is not the chief phenomenon of the Augustan period. Still more typical is the growth of literary and esthetic taste, of which the most enduring testimony is the *Ars Poetica* of Horace (who in important ways was preceded by Cicero as a literary critic). Persons such as Maecenas and Asinius Pollio are, to judge from anecdotes and indirect notices, the true arbiters of literary taste; their judgments are swift and sharp. The influence exerted by men of this sort, who, to be sure, were in no sense professional writers or educators, is sufficient testimony to the cultural level reached in this period, which for the first time in Roman history saw its own classics come to maturity, classics written in the Latin language.

The creation of Latin classics

The emergence of Cicero, Horace, and Virgil was truly a turning point in the development of philological and literary studies. The expectation of new classics was keen, virtually a hunger. Literary studies had in a sense anticipated their arrival, and, as we have seen, they continued to draw from the great Greek classics. Authors such as Ennius, Plautus, and Lucilius were widely read, of course, and were the starting point for learned research and analysis, but they had not taken on that unchallenged cultural centrality that is the hallmark of the classic. They were not classics but illustrious forebears. By a curious (and typically Roman) phenomenon of expectation, the new classics were recognized as such immediately, even while they were still being presented. Cicero's speeches were already being studied in the schools before their author died. While the *Aeneid* still lay on Virgil's desk, the world was already talking of a "new *Iliad*." The new classics had only to fill the space that had long been waiting for them. Roman culture now had its own center of thought and education. Around 25 B.C. a grammarian (i.e., a teacher), Caecilius Epirota, became famous because he gave lectures on Virgil and other modern poetry (according to Suetonius, *De Grammaticis* 16.2). The path was now marked out, and the high Augustan period soon witnessed a great flourishing of philological studies applied to the new literary texts, even the most sophisticated and elite—a certain Crassicius Pasicles wrote a commentary on Cinna. The first librarian, in the Alexandrian sense, also appears: Gaius Julius Hyginus, a freedman of Augustus, directed the new public library on the Palatine and was an important promoter of studies on Virgil. He wrote at least five books (we have indirect notices of them, mostly from Gellius) full of observations on Virgilian problems—questions of content, antiquarian researches, difficulties of interpretation. Starting with Hyginus, we can trace a continuous line of research on Virgil that leads us directly to the commentators of the fourth and fifth centuries, who, in the collections of scholia that have come down to us, avail themselves of the abundant fruits of this work.

Philology applied to the new classics: Caecilius Epirota, Hyginus

Poetic texts as tools for learning rhetoric

The centrality of the classics in instruction had important consequences, not always positive ones. Education remained entirely oriented towards the student's abilities at expression, the preliminaries to the training of the orator. The elementary teacher, the *litterator,* emphasized the alphabet, pronunciation, and recitation. Then the teacher of literature, the *grammaticus,* dealt with poetic texts, or rather, with their exposition, *enarratio.* This involved exercises that we find rather arid: the passages of poetry were reduced to prose paraphrases, without any critical appreciation. The poetry, that is to say, was the platform from which the studies of rhetorical forms and means of expression took off. Rhetorical education thus increased the interest in preserving the classics and promoted the moderate diffusion of literary culture (only to the extent that education was available at all, of course); yet this was not a setting particularly favorable to the development of philological or esthetic or literary-critical studies. In the early Empire we find authors such as Quintilian, who offer interesting perspectives on literary history yet have concerns that are fundamentally different, and wholly centered on the creation of the perfect orator; or learned men such as Gellius, not lacking in acuity, but unsystematic, sporadically curious, excellent yet erratic.

Remmius Palaemon and Asconius Pedianus

Portrait of Remmius Palaemon

The most eminent *grammaticus* of the early Empire was Remmius Palaemon, a freedman born at Vicenza who was self-made, having learned to read while he accompanied his master's son to school. Suetonius in the *De Grammaticis* gives an amusing portrait of him. We know from him that Palaemon was a teacher of indisputable learning but dubious morality, to the point that Tiberius and then Claudius regarded it as impossible to entrust boys to him. He was dissolute, a ladies' man, and he even washed several times a day!

A megalomaniac philologist

From a scholarly point of view, Palaemon had remarkable abilities, accompanied, however, by arrogance and, above all, by an unrestrained megalomania. He circulated stories about himself, such as the one of the brigands who, after capturing him, had at once released him when they realized whom they had in their hands. Moreover, he used to say that philology had been born with him and would die with him. He even maintained that his charisma had been almost prophetically recognized by Virgil himself, who had given the name Palaemon to one of the characters in his *Bucolics* (in the third eclogue Palaemon, the *grammaticus ante litteram,* takes the part of judge in a poetry contest between shepherds). Nor did he stop short of attacking an untouchable paragon such as Varro, upon whom he conferred the epithet "pig."

The introduction of modern authors into the schools

Unfortunately, the *Ars Grammatica* of this self-styled genius (who was, however, recognized as such by his own contemporaries, who also valued highly his poetry) has been lost to us. But on the basis of the fragments that do remain, Palaemon appears to be a continuator of Hyginus's work; or rather, with him the introduction of modern authors as a special object of study is established once and for all. Only with Palaemon, it seems, is Virgil definitively consecrated as a school author. Palaemon had as students Quintilian and Persius, among others.

Another notable philologist, Asconius Pedianus, who was born at Padua, is more or less a contemporary of Remmius Palaemon. Jerome tells us that he became blind at the age of 72 and lived for another twelve years, in an atmosphere of general respect. The year 75 mentioned by Jerome is for some the year he became blind and for others the year of his death. We have Asconius Pedianus's commentary on five speeches by Cicero: *In Pisonem, Pro Scauro, Pro Milone, Pro Cornelio,* and *In Toga Candida* (the last two speeches are lost, and so the commentary is valuable also for reconstructing them). It is understandable how this commentary, composed, it seems, in the period 54–57, made the author famous during the last years of his life, in the climate of that "return to Cicero" of which we spoke when dealing with Quintilian (see p. 514) and which Asconius had anticipated by several years. The approach of Asconius's commentary is more historical than linguistic. His notes, which aim at reconstructing the historical framework of the speeches, are based on excellent sources, which have often been consulted at firsthand and subjected to critical evaluation by the author, who thus sometimes acts exactly as a good modern philologist would. Little is known about Asconius's other works. He had written a *Contra Obtrectatores Vergilii* ("Against the Detractors of Virgil"), which thus follows in the path of Palaemon and the new philology. Of a *Vita Sallustii* only the title is left to us.

Valerius Probus and Later Developments in Philology

The most important philologist of the century, Marcus Valerius Probus, the great Virgil scholar, is from the age of the Flavians. Probus is, as far as we know, the Latin scholar who comes closest to the specialization practiced by a modern philologist, that is, the editing of the classics. He was concerned with Virgil and also Terence and Persius. From Suetonius, who annotated his own texts carefully, we know that his work included *emendare, distinguere,* and *adnotare.* Probus, in other words, obviously corrected the errors that had cropped up in the manuscript tradition, saw to the punctuation, put diacritical signs beside the text, and wrote his notes corresponding to the signs. We do not know whether these notes took the form of a genuine commentary, but it is significant in any case that there has come down to us a list of the signs that Probus had adopted, in the manner of the Alexandrians. It is likely, moreover, that Probus, who was concerned with the best possible reconstruction of the texts, sought out particularly old and authoritative manuscripts. Of course, he did not arrive at the modern techniques of collecting and comparatively evaluating the manuscript tradition; rather, from what we can see of his work on Virgil, Probus felt free to intervene in the text, incorporating his own conjectures or expelling verses that his taste or his reason found unacceptable. Probus's work as commentator and teacher left enduring traces among later scholars and commentators (Gellius, Macrobius, Aelius Donatus, Servius), and to us it appears to represent the summit of Latin philology. It is unlikely, however, that Probus directly shaped any manuscript tradition that has come down to us, for instance, that of Virgil. It should be kept in mind that before Gutenberg the influence of scholars on the circulation of manuscripts could be only sporadic and confined to small groups of experts.

Towards the crystallization of the school authors

A second, and even less positive, consequence of the meeting between rhetorical education and the study of the classics was the growing tendency to restrict the school authors by separating them from the others. At the end of this selection process, in late antiquity, Terence and Virgil form practically the sole basis of school study; considerations of stylistic purity, linguistic clarity, and exemplary moral nature had produced this shrinking of the horizons. But this outcome is still quite far off in the second century, in the period from Trajan to the Severans. Indeed, this is the period in which studies reach their greatest degree of openness: meter, grammar, linguistics, and rhetoric, early and classical writers, both Greek and Latin, are all widely studied. The repute and social position of academics rises continually. We will soon see the case of Fronto, and Juvenal remarks ironically: *si Fortuna volet, fies de rhetore consul* ("Fortune permitting, you can even go from being a teacher of rhetoric to being consul!" [7.197]).

Aemilius Asper, Caesellius Vindex, Sulpicius Apollinaris

Aemilius Asper wrote on Terence, Sallust, and Virgil. Caesellius Vindex was concerned with archaic Latin. Sulpicius Apollinaris's teaching was influential on questions of grammar and vocabulary. We have only very modest remains of his work, the summaries he prefixed to the books of the *Aeneid* and to Terence's comedies. It is evident that he was increasingly concerned to produce continuous and detailed notes as aids to accompany the reading of the most popular texts.

The collections of scholia

In this setting there appear, towards the end of the second century, the first real collections of scholia of which we have notice, the true predecessors of our modern commentaries. The scholia presented themselves as a continuous commentary on a text, divided verse by verse, and so problem by problem, and preceded by introductory remarks. This kind of erudite writing obviously lends itself in particular to gathering the fruits of earlier researches, of monographs on different aspects of the texts to be interpreted. In this way the Virgilian researches of a Hyginus, a Probus, an Asper, became a sedimentary deposit and left a trace in the scholiasts who have come down to us. The activity of Helenius Acron, a skilled interpreter of Horace, is placed at the end of the second century. We do not have his actual commentary on Horace; this kind of work (like today's school commentaries!) is very prone to being reworked and enlarged by later hands. Thus we have instead a pseudo-Acron, a text extensively redone by late and, especially, by medieval interpreters. Pomponius Porphyrio's commentary on Horace, however, has come down to us in its original form, a genuine school commentary of the third century A.D., and one of the earliest organic examples of scholiastic activity that we possess. We are thus in a position to evaluate which were the dominant interests of exegesis: on one side, the reconstruction of the historical background, with biographical, legal, and antiquarian notes; on the other, the formal analysis of the text, with attention to the rhetorical figures and the difficulties of interpretation.

Acron and Porphyrio

If we turn back to the world of scholarship in the second century, however, we have only indirect notices to go on. The nearest witness we have, Aulus Gellius (see below), dwells a good deal on the diffusion of learned and philological curiosity. From the traces we have, it appears that the chief characteristic of the period was the growth of interest in archaic Latin in all its principal forms of transmission—inscriptions and very early laws (Festus, the epitomator of Verrius Flaccus, should probably be located in this period [see p. 386 ff.]); historians and orators, especially Cato the Elder and the archaizing Sallust; and poets such as Ennius, Plautus, and Caecilius. This backward-looking taste did not threaten the fame of such classics as Cicero, Virgil, and Horace, which was now accepted by everyone, but the attention philologists paid to archaic Latin is a sign of the times, and it is clearly linked to the archaizing movement in contemporary artistic prose and rhetoric.

2. THE ARCHAIZING TENDENCY OF THE SECOND CENTURY

The recourse to archaic linguistic and literary models—separate from and discontinuous with the contemporary language and literature—is a recurring temptation in the history of Latin literature. Around the middle of the second century this attitude becomes a more marked and organic tendency; one can now speak of a new dominant taste, a tendency towards the archaic.

Certain historical circumstances prepared the ground suitably. In the learned coteries and literary circles at Rome, erudite research had become a genuine passion. We have a perfect testimonial to this in the *Attic Nights* of Aulus Gellius (on whom see below). What had by now become a professional class devoted itself to instruction in rhetoric, the philological study of the ancient texts, in particular those from the Republic, instruction in that literature, and, more generally, the study of vocabulary. These scholars naturally were led to revive the texts of an era now in mothballs, not only Cicero, Virgil, and Ovid, who were the inheritance of all, but also more remote and difficult authors. Moreover, already in the period of the Flavians, with Quintilian, a reaction had set in against the linguistic and stylistic modernism that Seneca had proclaimed so successfully. Quintilian reacted chiefly by harking back to the classical style of Cicero. The period following carried the reaction further back.

The Roman culture of the second century is increasingly a bilingual culture, starting with the emperors themselves. Hadrian carries the Hellenization of culture and art to its extreme, and Marcus Aurelius would deserve a place of honor in this book had he not written his meditations in Greek. The Greek culture of the second century is itself wholly pervaded by archaism. The writers and rhetoricians inaugurate a new form of purism: they reject the naturally evolved Greek of the Hellenistic era and rediscover the language and style of the great Attic prose writers of the fifth and fourth centuries. To write in the manner of Xenophon or Lysias signifies, of course, an artificial detachment from everyday reality and a striving (linked to a certain national pride) towards an idealized, unachievable world. This tendency is usually called Atticism, a purism of fine writing that has little to do with the traditional opposition between Atticists and Asianists.

Establishment of the archaizing movement and its limits

All these factors, in combination, contributed to the growth of the archaizing movement at Rome. The texts from republican Rome were now a world to be rediscovered. For some while now the orators had been looking to Cicero, and the poets to Catullus (and no one before him), as their models, while Plautus and Cato promised forgotten treasures of expression. Archaism brought renown to professors of rhetoric and literature. For the teachers of epideictic rhetoric (such as Apuleius), it served to make their stylistic virtuosity the more precious, even to the point of shocking the ordinary public. It strengthened the philologists in their worship of the past. And it offered a powerful response on the part of the Romans to the renewed nationalism of Greek intellectuals.

Despite all this, one should not exaggerate the purity and the theoretical orthodoxy of these tendencies. Archaic Latin was not a perfectly developed and self-sufficient artistic language, as the Greek of Isocrates and Demosthenes might have been. The masters of Roman archaism themselves do not get beyond salvaging a certain number of learned features, which they sprinkle over a style that is nonetheless substantially a new one. Fronto himself, with his mannered imitations of Sallust, does not quite suppress the lessons learned from the two centuries of prose writing that have gone by in the meantime. The despised Seneca, for instance, is not easily forgotten even by his worst enemies.

Fronto

Limits to our knowledge of Fronto

The limits and the variations of the archaizing tendency are neatly symbolized by its triumphant leader, Marcus Cornelius Fronto. It appears from indirect notices that he was valued as a kind of new Cicero. Intellectuals such as Gellius revered and imitated him. The imperial family entrusted the education of the princes Marcus Aurelius and Lucius Verus to him. Later ages, down to the end of the Empire, considered him a classic of the first rank. Our own judgment makes him a much smaller figure.

It is necessary, however, in Fronto's case to make allowance for a number of extenuating circumstances. His reputation in antiquity was based on his teaching of rhetoric and his public orations. We have only fragments and titles of these. In 1815 the future cardinal Angelo Mai discovered some writings by Fronto in a Milanese palimpsest. Even in the light of the reputation Fronto had acquired on the basis of indirect information, the enthusiasm was great. Several years later another fragment completed the discovery. The deciphering of the manuscript, however, brought disappointment. It proved to contain a miscellany of minor writings, and we do not even know whether the author actually intended to publish them. We have here a private correspondence, letters from and to members of the imperial family (Antoninus Pius, Marcus Aurelius, Lucius Verus), and some very modest occasional compositions—brief declamations, narrative sketches in Greek and Latin, and other odds and ends. Nothing remains of the more ambitious public speeches, such as the historic discourse against the Christians to which Minucius Felix's *Octavius* must have been an indirect response.

Calpurnius Flaccus

The only direct evidence we have about rhetoric during this period is the extracts from fifty-three declamations by an otherwise unknown Calpurnius Flaccus, a rhetorician who is thought to have flourished in the time of Hadrian or Antoninus Pius. In the extracts we read grim stories of kidnappings, rapes, murders of tyrants, and so on, more or less the same subjects found in the work of Seneca the Elder (see pp. 404 f.) and in the pseudo-Quintilianic *Declamations* (see p. 512 f.).

Life of Fronto

Our judgment on Fronto must therefore be limited. The prominent rhetorician was a provincial from Africa (as were Apuleius, Minucius Felix, and Tertullian), a native of Cirta. His date of birth is around 100. He had a distinguished public career under Hadrian and Antoninus Pius, and he was *consul suffectus* in 143. He had for a long time the prestigious duty of educating the two adoptive sons of the emperor Antoninus Pius. The one destined for greater fame, Marcus Aurelius, was personally inclined in a different direction: rather than the art of the word that Fronto preached, he cared for ethical and philosophical meditation. Fronto died quite old, perhaps around 170.

Fronto's stylistic theories

Fronto's stylistic theories have certain clear chief points. Fronto pursues a style that sounds new and original yet does not seem modern. It thus draws upon the rich resources of pre-Augustan literature, being on the lookout especially for *insperata atque inopinata verba*. Fronto likes linguistic creativity but not neologism; the creativity he likes is that of the archaic writers, upon whom lies the patina of the antique. In Cicero he values especially the liveliness of the epistolary style, not the regular periods of the speeches. He is very open to colloquial language (resembling Apuleius in this), and is not biased against Grecisms. His archaism, in fact, is not a purism that rejects outside influence and mixture with everyday language.

The empire of rhetoric

The aspect that most attracts Fronto to archaic literature is its taste for sonorous effects and plays on words. His own prose is a vindication of the claims of rhetoric to absolute power; it thrives on parallelism, rhyme, chains of imagery, and plays with sound and sense. Even in the modest passages of occasional writing that we have, it is evident that this worship of rhetoric exists at the expense of content. Fronto has little interest in philosophical, moral, social, and political subjects. We get a good picture of him from the *Principia Historiae*, which must have been the preface to his historical narrative of Lucius Verus's campaigns against the Parthians. Questions of historical method are disposed of superficially; history is seen only as the rhetorical embellishment of a preconstituted outline. The empire of rhetoric is undisputed. The correspondence with Marcus and Lucius, moreover, seems to show that Fronto understood his educational task as purely and simply a training in rhetoric. It is difficult to believe that he was involved in the discussion of affairs and problems of state. From what we can gather, Fronto embodies the total divorce of rhetoric from the social responsibility it had long borne in the Roman world, and he also represents the restriction of rhetoric to an artistic prose that makes no pretense of persuading or arousing, not even for show. It is difficult to say, however, what the formal results were of this exclusive worship of the beautiful word.

3. AULUS GELLIUS

The Noctes Atticae, *the unsystematic work of a dilettante*

In the period that is dominated by Fronto and Sulpicius Apollinaris, teachers who remain for us rather dim figures, there appears before us a dilettante man of letters (as Pliny the Elder had been a dilettante scientist) and eclectic writer, Aulus Gellius. About the author of the *Attic Nights* we have only information derived from the work itself. He is a man passionate about culture (not a rhetorician or a successful writer) who had made the grand tour to Greece. He must have been born around 130, a generation after Fronto and Sulpicius Apollinaris, who was his teacher at Rome. In fact the *Attic Nights,* probably written shortly before 170, presents itself as collections of notes taken on evenings *(noctes)* during a winter spent near Athens. The structure of the work aims at preserving a sense of spontaneous variety, without any attempt at systematization or homogeneity. Gellius clearly intends to go back to a popular tradition, the miscellanies, which had titles such as *silvae, pratum,* or (at most) *naturalis historia.* He utterly refuses, however, to set his kaleidoscopic material into any framework; it is not arranged by subject, for instance, nor structured as a dialogue with a narrative setting. The pleasure of variety and arbitrary sequence thus is carried to the extreme (the complete opposite of Pliny the Elder's carefully thought out "scale of nature"). *Usi sumus ordine rerum fortuito:* we are not amazed at going from a chapter on the names of the winds to a comparative analysis of the comic poets Menander and Caecilius Statius, and ambling about among linguistics, poetry, oratory, philosophy, history, and law. The work is divided into twenty books, subdivided into short chapters (a passage from the preface and all of book 8 are lost). As far as we know, Gellius never published anything else.

Gellius's literary sensibility

Gellius's greatest merit is his open literary sensibility. The influence of Frontonian archaism is conspicuous in him and formative, but it does not become dogmatism. Gellius, in fact, has a profound interest in all archaic Latin, especially the comic writers of Plautus's day, and he is a passionate investigator of antiquarian traditions and obsolete linguistic oddities. We owe to this archaizing taste of his the careful preservation of a number of fragments of archaic prose and poetry, accompanied by anecdotes, information, and unremarkable judgments, as well as a contribution of his personal sensibility. Among these treatments of archaic literature, the comparison of a passage of the comedian Caecilius Statius with the corresponding passage of its original, by Menander, has remained justly famous (2.23). It is a critical event of some importance: the method of comparing point by point the style of a Latin poet with that of his source has remained basic to modern philology.

Gellius's sources and originality: his literary tastes

It should not be forgotten, however, that Gellius was able to draw on a robust tradition of Greco-Latin philology of the sort sketched at the beginning of this chapter. Given, moreover, the arbitrary and unsystematic way in which Gellius names his learned sources, we cannot know precisely to what extent he drew on scholars and philologists such as Valerius Probus or Sulpicius Apollinaris. It is certain, in any event, that Gellius has a taste of his own and a deep understanding of the texts he reads. His archaizing passion does not lead him into hasty depreciation of the classics. He reads Cato's speeches with intelligence (6.3) but also has a balanced understanding of Cicero (10.3). Like Quintilian before him, of course, he has an antipathy for Seneca's stylistic anti-classicism and rejects it. He is quite close to Quintilian in his style, too. Gellius writes in a smooth and deliberate way, and he is also an agreeable narrator (see the story of Androcles and the lion, 5.14). His prose would later please Augustine, and his work, full of details and small antiquarian discoveries, was to have considerable success in the Middle Ages. Even now Gellius must be heeded by those who study Roman sensibility towards the problems and techniques of literature.

4. LEGAL LITERATURE: THE SYSTEMATIZATION OF DOCTRINE

The systematization of legal doctrine

The age of Hadrian witnesses the completion of that systematization of the individual *artes* that had begun in the early Empire and been carried out in all the various scholarly disciplines. As in the *ars grammatica,* in jurisprudence, too, the oppositions between the different schools become increasingly less important, and an effort is made to give an organic structure to the doctrines. It is as if reaching maturity required systematic elaboration rather than discussion and polemic.

The Constitutiones Principis *and the change in Roman law*

At the start of the principate the constitutional basis of the emperor's legislative power was not altogether clear. In practice the imperial *edicta* were treated as expressions of a magistrate's *imperium,* and the Senate still needed to approve the legislative wishes of the emperor, that is, at least in appearance to promulgate the laws. But later the resolution of the Senate became a mere formality, with the result that the *Constitutiones Principis* (imperial decrees and rescripts, decisions that the emperor as supreme magistrate rendered in particular legal matters) acquired the force of law. In this way all the legal doctrine that had been employed up to now in interpreting the *edicta praetoris* came to be employed directly on the decisions of the princeps, who now held the new *imperium* of supreme magistrate. This inevitably altered profoundly the practical aspect of law and jurisprudence; among other things, it brought a new centralizing order to this field.

The great unitary reorganization of Roman jurisprudence that was carried out in the time of Hadrian is indissolubly linked to the name of the great jurist Salvius Julianus, a pupil of Javolenus Priscus, who was the head of the Sabinian school in the Trajanic period. Lucius Octavius Cornelius Salvius Julianus was probably the most remarkable representative of Roman legal learning. Because of his highly original thought, legal science is regarded as reaching its apogee in him. Even though several jurists from the period of the Severans (Ulpian, for instance, and Papinian) were superior to him in the number of their works and their encyclopedic learning, they all experienced the powerful influence of his creative personality. He had an extraordinary career in public life (he was part of the *consilium principis* under Hadrian and Antoninus Pius), but the prestige he enjoyed as a jurist was undoubtedly exceptional. Before reaching the age of thirty he had been entrusted by the emperor Hadrian with completing the revision of the *edictum praetorium;* this was completed around A.D. 130. (The *edictum praetorium* functioned as a series of procedural remedies that had indirect but decisive force. Its aim was to bring the dispositions of civil law into relation with circumstances. Normally, it was entrusted to the individual praetors, who could occasionally intervene with modifications. This was the situation that obtained until the definitive codification ordered by Hadrian.) This revised edition was confirmed by a senatorial decree; thus the praetorian edict took on permanent form *(edictum perpetuum),* and the praetors lost the right to modify it. Vast commentaries on the *edictum perpetuum,* as it had been fixed by Salvius Julianus, were written by later classical jurists (and from them in turn the compilers of Justinian's *Digest* made large extracts, which have been the basis of attempts to reconstruct its outline). Following the new disposition that he had given to the *edictum perpetuum,* Salvius Julianus composed his monumental *Digesta* (in ninety books), a systematic, large-scale survey of civil and praetorian law. Much of its content is known to us from Justinian's *Digest,* which cites it. (The greatest part of Roman legal literature is known to us only through the Justinianic *Digest,* the section of the *Corpus Iuris* [see p. 713] that consists of a kind of anthology of classical jurisprudence over the entire course of its development.)

Sextus Pomponius was a contemporary of Julianus in whom, it seems, one must recognize unusual gifts as a compiler (he wrote more than three hundred books on law, more than any other Roman jurist). He did not hold any public office (unlike most of the jurists from the late principate, who are often high officials in the service of the emperor). Justinian's *Digest* preserves a large fragment of his *Liber Singularis Enchiridii,* a brief compendium of the history of the sources of Roman law, of the magistrates, and of legal science down to Salvius Julianus.

The celebrated jurist Gaius is to be placed, it seems, in an only slightly later period. We know virtually nothing about him, although the imaginative ingenuity of scholars has sought to derive an exact biography from a few uncertain details. We do not know his family name or his cognomen, nor even his origin (he may have come from a Greek province) or where he studied. He lived at Rome and wrote a great deal in the period from Hadrian to Marcus Aurelius. He probably did not hold any public office or have the *ius respondendi* (i.e., the recognized right to give opinions on legal matters), since his opinions *(responsa)* are not referred to. He was probably a teacher of law, and we are told that many of his works (commentaries and monographs) were devoted to different areas of legal science, but his reputation rests on the four commentaries of his *Institutiones,* the only classical legal work that has come down to us in substantially its original form (it was completed probably after 161). From its very beginning the *Institutiones* shows, in its division of the material, the systematic attempt at an articulated treatment: "The laws we use all refer either to persons *(ad personas)* or to things *(res)* or to actions *(actiones)*." This triple division of the legal material may not be due to Gaius's originality—there is reason to believe he had a predecessor—but he certainly exercised an enormous influence upon later legal thought. His qualities of orderliness, simplicity, and clarity made Gaius a touchstone of the legal discipline—a fate that often befalls intelligent works of compilation, which are valuable, if for no other reason, at least for the economy of the information they purvey, representing the conclusion and summary of long, laborious earlier discussions. Gaius's *Institutiones* seems to possess for legal literature the same significance that Quintilian's *Institutio* possessed for the art of rhetoric several decades earlier. And this too, as we remarked earlier, is the sign of a profound cultural maturity in a period that was inclined to produce, in the most diverse fields of knowledge, practical tools of learning such as these *summae* of doctrines.

BIBLIOGRAPHY

For the early period, Elizabeth Rawson's *Intellectual Life in the Late Roman Republic* (London 1985) is fundamental for all branches of Roman scholarship; see also *PBSR* 46 (1978) 12–34. On the ancient book, there is still no comprehensive replacement for T. Birt, *Das antike Buchwesen* (Berlin 1882); for subsequent work, see the bibliographies to the collection of studies edited by G. Cavallo, *Libri, editori e pubblico nel mondo antico* (ed. 2 Rome 1977), and his article "Alfabetismo e circolazione del libro" in M. Vegetti, ed., *Oralità scrittura spettacolo* (Turin 1983) 166 ff. In English, note F. G. Kenyon, *Books and Readers in Ancient Greece and Rome* (ed. 2 Oxford 1951), O.A.W. Dilke, *Roman Books and Their Impact* (Leeds 1977), C. H. Roberts and T. C. Skeat, *The Birth of the Codex* (ed. 2 London 1987), W. V. Harris, *Ancient Literacy* (Cambridge, Mass. 1989), and the special edition of *Arethusa* 13.1 (1980) devoted to Augustan poetry books. On libraries, see C. E. Boyd, *Public Libraries and Literary Culture in Ancient Rome* (Chicago 1915), and G. Cavallo, *Le biblioteche nel mondo antico e medievale* (ed. 2 Rome 1989).

On the history of education and the development of rhetoric, see the works of Marrou, Bonner, Clarke, and Kennedy cited above on Quintilian (H.-I. Marrou, *A History of Education in Antiquity,* trans. G. Lamb [London 1956], S. F. Bonner, *Education in Ancient Rome* [London 1977], M. L. Clarke, "Quintilian and Education," in *Empire and Aftermath: Silver Latin II,* ed. T. A. Dorey [London 1975], 98–118, G. Kennedy, *The Art of Rhetoric in the Roman World* [Princeton 1972]) and the fundamental work of A. D.

Leeman, *Orationis Ratio: The Stylistic Theories and Practice of the Roman Orators, Historians, and Philosophers* (Amsterdam 1963), which has been frequently mentioned. E. Norden, *Die antike Kunstprosa* (2 vols., Berlin 1898), is still of great value; the Italian translation by B. Heinemann, *La prosa d'arte antica* (Rome 1985), contains a useful supplementary study by G. Calboli. For literary criticism, see G.M.A. Grube, *The Greek and Roman Critics* (London 1965), D. A. Russell, *Criticism in Antiquity* (London 1981), esp. 52–68, and the relevant sections of the *Cambridge History of Literary Criticism*, vol. 1, ed. G. A. Kennedy (Cambridge 1989). J.E.G. Zetzel, *Latin Textual Criticism in Antiquity* (New York 1981), discusses the development of textual criticism.

Texts of the grammarians whose works are preserved only in fragments may be found in the collections of G. Funaioli, *Grammaticae Romanae Fragmenta* (Leipzig 1907), and A. Mazzarino, *Grammaticae Romanae Fragmenta Aetatis Caesareae* (Turin 1955). On Remmius Palaemon, see the important monograph by K. Barwick, *Remmius Palaemon und die römische Ars Grammatica* (Leipzig 1922). The standard text of Asconius's commentary on Cicero is that of A. C. Clark (Oxford 1907); see also the edition with translation by S. Squires (Bristol 1990) and the historical commentary by B. A. Marshall (Columbia, Mo. 1985). On Probus, see J. Aistermann, *De M. Valerio Probo Berytio* (Bonn 1910), Zetzel, *Latin Textual Criticism* 41–54, and M. L. Delvigo, *Testo virgiliano e tradizione indiretta* (Pisa 1987). For Pseudo-Acron and Porphyrion on Horace, see the editions by O. Keller (2 vols., Leipzig 1902–4) and A. Holder (Innsbruck 1894); there is a brief account of their works in the commentary of R.G.M. Nisbet and M. Hubbard (Oxford 1970) xlvii–li.

The standard text of Fronto is that of M.P.J. van den Hout (Leipzig 1988; see also his earlier edition, Leiden 1954); see also the older Teubner of S. A. Naber (Leipzig 1867) and the Loeb of C. R. Haines (London and Cambridge, Mass. 1919–20). There is a comprehensive study by E. Champlin, *Fronto and Antonine Rome* (Cambridge, Mass. 1980); see also R. Marache, *La Critique littéraire de la langue latine et le développement du goût archaïsant au IIe siècle de notre ère* (Rennes 1952) and *Mots nouveaux et mots archaïques chez Fronton et Aulu-Gelle* (Paris 1957), and P. V. Cova, *I "principia historiae" et le idee storiografiche di Frontone* (Naples 1970). There is much of interest in R. B. Rutherford's *Meditations of Marcus Aurelius: A Study* (Oxford 1989); see also L. Pepe, *Marco Aurelio Latino* (Naples 1957).

The standard edition of Aulus Gellius's *Noctes Atticae* is that of P. K. Marshall (2 vols., Oxford 1968–90); the *editio maior* of M. Hertz (Berlin 1883–85) remains important. There is a Loeb by J. C. Rolfe (3 vols., London and Cambridge, Mass. 1946–52), and a Budé edition with French translation and brief notes by R. Marache is in progress (Paris 1967–). The only modern commentary is that of H. M. Hornsby on book 1 (Dublin 1936). L. Holford-Strevens, *Aulus Gellius* (London 1988), deals with all aspects of the work; see also L. Gamberale, *La traduzione in Gellio* (Rome 1969).

For the legal writers, see F. P. Bremer, *Iurisprudentia Antehadriana* (Leipzig 1896–1901), E. Seckel and K. Kübler, *Iurisprudentiae Anteiustinianae Reliquiae* (Leipzig 1907–27), and S. Riccobono, *Fontes Iuris Romani Antejustiniani* (Florence 1941). There is a good English translation of Gaius's *Institutes* by W. M. Gordon and O. F. Robinson (London 1988), including the text of E. Seckel and B. Knebler (ed. 7 Leipzig 1935). A critical edition by M. David and H.L.W. Nelson is in progress (Leiden 1954–); see also F. de Zulueta, *The Institutes of Gaius* (2 vols., Oxford 1951–53). There is a study of Gaius himself by A. Honoré, *Gaius* (Oxford 1962), which also contains much information on the early imperial lawyers. Volumes 13–15 of *ANRW* 2 are devoted to law; volume 15 contains a number of studies of individual jurists, including Gaius. Although it is by now a little dated, A. Berger, *An Encyclopedic Dictionary of Roman Law* (Philadelphia 1953), which includes articles on the major jurists, remains useful.

Developments in Poetry: The *Poetae Novelli*

The second century, taken as a whole, presents a social, artistic, and cultural picture of unusual liveliness. Rome's great economic, moral, and cultural crisis will not occur until the next century, and it is this historic rupture that will lead to the late Roman Empire, which will prove to be new in so many ways. The different periods of poetry vary a good deal. The prosperous, vital years of Trajan, Hadrian, Antoninus Pius, and Marcus Aurelius do not witness a significant flourishing of poetic talents. In Pliny the Younger's correspondence poetry appears as a refined hobby of the upper classes rather than as a serious vocation. In the day of the great rhetoricians, with learning triumphant, poetry seems to have lost any cultural centrality it had. The dark years of the third century, in fact, have left us a greater number of important works in this field. The unbroken trail of the great traditional poetic genres starts to peter out already at the beginning of Hadrian's reign. We have no epics, either historical or mythological, after the Flavian period; satire ceases with Juvenal; elegy, at least the genre of personal poetry established by the Augustans, has only feeble successors; and after Seneca and the *Octavia* poetry for the stage does not show itself.

A minor genre of poetry, however, does continue to be practiced. It is realized in a variety of forms, which cannot be traced back to any earlier literary precedents; it is a poetry without definite genre (we have followed certain lines from the age of Tiberius to the age of Nero: see pp. 426 ff.). In this literary field, which can hardly be defined except by opposition to grand poetry, several minor figures appear, of whom we have a few fragments. Historians of literature, who because of the nature of their work have a horror of vacuums, tend to fill in the poetry of the second (and the third) century by reconstructing a genuine school, that of the so-called *poetae novelli*.

The poetae novelli:
*the archaizing
rehabilitation of
the* poetae novi

The label *poetae novelli* is ancient, and it contains many literary-historical presuppositions. The key to the reference is the neoteric school of the first century B.C., the group of the *poetae novi,* including Catullus, Cinna, Calvus, Valerius Cato, and even some of their predecessors, such as the original formalist Laevius. The *novelli* would thus be *poetae novi* in a minor key. Their novelty does not lie in being avant-garde and modernizing, as were the *poetae novi,* but they salvage for their own use what is archaic, obsolete, and out of fashion. They thus represent a clear parallel to that pursuit of novelty that, in artistic prose, is characteristic of Fronto's stylistic antiquarianism. In order to escape from the domination of the great classics, style renews itself by turning to earlier experiences that have been discarded. Moreover, the success of the neoterics is not a complete novelty. Already in the first century A.D. the texts of the so-called *Appendix Vergiliana* and the minor poetry of the Neronian age clearly showed the influence of the *poetae novi,* though without abandoning the principles of Augustan classicism. We suspect therefore that the *poetae novelli* represent not so much a sudden renaissance as the development of a secondary stream in Latin poetry.

Annianus and the other novelli

The term *poetae novelli* goes back to a reference made by the great metrician Terentianus Maurus (second to third century A.D.) to several poets of whom we have but very poor remains. Annianus, who is also mentioned by Gellius, wrote *Carmina Falisca,* composed in an anomalous meter (which would be called "Faliscan" in fact—three dactyls and an iamb), and also mysterious *Fescennini.* Alfius Avitus wrote poems about the celebrated men of Roman history. A certain Marianus composed *Lupercalia.* Septimius Serenus sang of rural and pastoral subjects.

Metrical experimentation

One can perhaps catch some affinity among these umbratile poets. The most obvious is their metrical experimentation. They invent new forms (the "Faliscan" of Annianus, for instance) or, breaking with the great classics, sing traditional subjects in unexpected and apparently inappropriate meters. Thus, Serenus treats pastoral themes, not in Virgilian hexameters, but in iambic dimeters. Then, forms of figured verse flourish—"reciprocal" couplets, in which the pentameter repeats the words of the hexameter backwards, or poems that, arranged on the page in verses of varying length, create the image of the object they mean to describe. The *Egg* of Simias, a Greek poet of the Alexandrian period, had been of this sort, for instance. From this point of view, the *poetae novelli* take up the formal experimentation that was typical both of certain neoteric poetry (Laevius rather than Catullus) and of the Greek versification of the last Alexandrians. The acrobatics of the *carmina figurata* are an obvious adoption of these experiments, which in themselves are already marginal and ludic.

The archaizing taste

Furthermore, a pursuit of the antique and archaic is evident, both in the picturesque subjects (titles such as *Falisca* or *Lupercalia*) and in the vocabulary used. Idyllic scenes, set in the old Italian countryside, obsolete, archaic, colloquial, and dialectal words, and certain aspects of the prose of Apuleius and Fronto all find close formal equivalents here.

The emperor Hadrian

Some scholars extend this "school" to include much of the poetry of the third century, texts such as the *Pervigilium Veneris,* Nemesianus, and Reposianus (which we will treat later). We are dealing, in any event, with a quite undefined and undefinable field. The most interesting person in this minor flourishing is, in the second century, a Roman emperor. We know from his biographers that Hadrian was a man of extremely refined and versatile culture. His policy of universal integration embraced Rome, the provinces,

Greece, and the East in an effort at fusion that was cultural no less than administrative. He had a profound acquaintance with Greek culture, literary and artistic, and encouraged every aspect of art and scholarship. He was also, we know, an excellent versifier; not by chance does he compose in both the languages of the Empire's culture. Only a few verses of his are left. The most remarkable is an occasional poem, an apostrophe to his soul that he probably composed shortly before dying. It is deservedly famous for its neoteric musical grace and apparent facility, which is in fact based on literary sensibility. It has appeared to many as virtually a harbinger of decadence:

> Animula vagula blandula
> hospes comesque corporis,
> quae nunc abibis in loca
> pallidula rigida nudula
> nec, ut soles, dabis iocos!

("Soul sweet and shifting, guest and companion of my body, now you will depart for places pale, harsh, and barren, and you will not make sport as before").

BIBLIOGRAPHY

For the fragments of various figures mentioned above, see W. Morel, ed., *Fragmenta poetarum latinorum epicorum et lyricorum praeter Ennium et Lucilium* (Leipzig 1927, reprint 1963), and E. Courtney, *The Fragmentary Latin Poets* (Oxford 1993), and the much-criticized revision by K. Büchner (Leipzig 1982, with bibliography), as well as E. Castorina, *I poeti novelli* (Florence 1949; cf. his *Questioni neoteriche* [Florence 1968]), and esp. S. Mattiacci, *I frammenti dei poetae novelli* (Rome 1982), but see the skeptical discussion by A. Cameron, "Poetae Novelli," *HSCP* 84 (1980) 127–75, and the recent survey by P. Steinmentz, "Lyrische Dichtung im 2. Jahrhundert n. Chr.," *ANRW* 33.1 (Berlin 1989) 259–302, esp. 300–302. Both Cameron and Steinmetz discuss the fragment ascribed to Hadrian in the *Historia Augusta;* see also I. Mariotti, "Animula vagula blandula," in *Studia Florentina A. Ronconi Oblata* (Rome 1970) 233–49. In general see H. Bardon, *Les Empereurs et les lettres latines d'Auguste à Hadrien* (ed. 2 Paris 1968) 393–424.

FIVE

The Late Empire

From the Severans to Diocletian (193–305)

I. THE GREAT SOCIAL CHANGES

The great crisis

The third century was a dramatic moment in the life of Rome, as the very survival of the Empire seemed in doubt. It faced recurring civil wars, which decimated the ruling classes, impoverished the economic system in the regions that were the battlegrounds, and weakened the frontier defenses with which the pressure of the barbarians was to be resisted. It also faced immense internal changes—social, institutional, and religious—which brought into question the very foundations of the state. Nonetheless, contrary to every expectation and in a way that still astonishes the modern historian, the Empire succeeded in getting over what is unquestionably its gravest crisis before the definitive disintegration at the end of the fifth century. It emerged from it profoundly changed but robust, substantially reorganized in the crucial points of its governmental apparatus, and able to face all external threats for two centuries more.

Centrifugal tendencies and a policy of centralization

One of the most evident manifestations of this crisis is the rise of centrifugal tendencies and separatist movements, which tend to replace the state's central structures with independent, decentralized administrations. These administrations themselves in turn sometimes claim the dignity of being states, as is the case with the kingdom of Palmyra in the East and with the *imperium Galliarum* in the West. The imperial courts reacted against this danger of disintegration in various ways, depending on the circumstances and the possible courses of action. In the earliest years of the century the dynasty of the Severans promoted a rigorous policy of centralization, which accompanied a sort of democratization of society, especially in the provinces. Particular attention was devoted to the needs of the poorest classes, and the representatives of the central power took upon themselves the task of seeing to it that the rich and powerful did not infringe the rights of the *humiliores* and paid their taxes regularly to the treasury. As a facet of this policy Caracalla in 212 issued the *Constitutio Antoniniana,* which granted Roman citizenship to all the free residents within the territory of the Empire; this was an attempt to heal the disparities that led, in law and in fact, to much unfairness in administration.

The years of military anarchy

With the end of the dynasty of the Severans, in 235, the most confusing period of this tormented century opens. It is characterized by the emperors who remained in power a few months or even only a few days, who opposed one another and created ephemeral administrations and even more ephemeral political projects. Amidst this disorder, particular interests naturally came to prevail, regional concerns and the economic or military needs of the Empire's different zones, which tried to resolve on their own the problems that the central power could no longer deal with through concrete, credible initiatives. Particularly noticeable was the political-administrative and cultural rift between the West and the East, in which from mid-century onwards *rectores* or *correctores* ruled over large areas of Asia that were menaced by Persian expansionism, creating the conditions for that division between *pars Orientis* and *pars Occidentis,* and thus between the two empires, that would create fundamental differences and decisive separations in European history.

Pressures at the Empire's frontiers

In the meantime the two chief frontiers, European and Asian, were subjected to constant pressure made worse by simultaneous attacks on the two fronts. On the border of the Rhine and the Danube the Germanic peoples were capable of incursions that reached deep within the territory of the Empire and were halted only at the cost of great military efforts and grave economic sacrifices. On the eastern border the new Persian kingdom of the Sassanids, which in 224 succeeded the kingdom of the Parthians, began a military expansionism that relied on modern, effective arms and was supported by a solid governmental organization, a flourishing economy, and an unshakeable confidence in the nation's imperial destinies. Other frontiers were also threatened at the same time: the English border (Hadrian's Wall) by the Scots, the African territories by the peoples coming from the south.

Power controlled by the army

The importance of the army in this situation assured the survival of the state but also had consequences for the entire organization of the Empire. It increasingly became the norm that the choice of the emperor was made by the troops rather than by the Senate. At the same time, career officers from the army's lower ranks were taking the place of young and not-so-young senators in commanding the troops, and even though this met the undeniable need that existed to secure commanders who were experienced and respected by their soldiers, it also broke the last links binding military power to constitutional organs of government and created in fact a new path of recruitment into the governing classes, one that was destined to be much followed throughout late antiquity. The composition of the army also underwent important changes. The need for ever larger military levies extended recruitment to the citizens of the entire Empire and even to the barbarians who were inclined to serve under Roman standards; hence a social mobility that saw Arab soldiers reach the imperial throne and, in general, saw military men, even those born outside the Empire, lead enviable careers and hold positions of fundamental importance.

The economic crisis

As for economic problems, they were in great part connected to the military problems. The countryside was becoming depopulated. The cities were a more secure refuge, because of the walls that surrounded them (even Rome, the capital, felt the need to surround itself with a new city wall under Aurelian), but they were exposed to siege and sack. The routes of communication were unsafe, and this contributed to a general reduction of commerce. The need to spend money in order to defend the Empire from enemy armies worsened the state's finances and brought many economic activities into crisis, especially in the urban centers, and the strong inflation led to price increases that, again, hit the cities hardest. To this very negative picture we need to add natural catastrophes such as earthquakes (which shook even Rome) and epidemics, which were more frequent and more deadly than in other periods. The result was a remarkable decrease in the size of the population, which at certain points was virtually half the average of earlier decades.

The Establishment of Christianity

This climate of insecurity, extending to all parts of the Empire (and not limited to the marginal areas, which by their nature were more exposed to external dangers), had direct influence on more specifically cultural aspects of life too. An accurate overview would require a joint treatment of Greek and Latin literatures, since in this period the cultural unity of the two parts of the Empire was still quite strong, despite the difference in language. Intellectuals often moved from the East to the West, and similar subjects and problems cropped up even more often, especially in Christian milieus. *Vitality of Eastern culture* One should not forget, however, the intense fervor over doctrine that agitated the eastern Mediterranean, and especially Egypt, in a period when texts in Latin, by contrast, except for a few Christian writers, seemed to be repeating themes from earlier times in a wearisome way. In speculative philosophy special importance attaches to developments in neo-Platonic doctrine, which would shape the last centuries of paganism and leave deep traces upon Christian thought as well. At the same time the need for religious certainties and an increased striving for transcendence were manifested in attachment to Oriental cults and mystery religions. The desire for individual salvation, neglected by ancient paganism, was satisfied by the cults of Mithras, Cybele, and Isis, the cult of the Sun, and Christianity. What all these new religions had in common was the promise of a future salvation, an expectation of redemption that would compensate men for their precarious and unhappy life on earth.

The Christian cult The most important among all these cults was undoubtedly Christianity, which in the course of a couple of centuries succeeded in prevailing over all the others, going from a minority cult to the religion of the majority within the Empire. Pagan culture at the time did not understand the special proselytizing force of this religion, which brought a message from which no one was excluded a priori and which was better able to answer the needs felt by the great masses. To the pagans it seemed a superstitious cult like so many others, and a peculiarly obstinate one; its faithful were prepared to face even harsh persecution for not performing the customary liturgical services to the gods of the Empire.

Spread of Christianity Christianity spread rapidly in all parts of the Empire, and during the third century it became a decisive element in the balance of forces. Arising chiefly as an urban religion of the lower classes (especially in the East, or still more in the capital), it now included faithful from all social classes, and at Rome especially it succeeded in winning over many women of rich and noble families, who provided substantial donations and also won it attention and prestige at the highest levels of society. Whereas Christianity in the East established itself increasingly as a current of thought and gave birth to philosophical developments that reached some of the highest levels attained in the history of third-century culture, in the West a certain backwardness in theoretical developments is accompanied by an organizational ability that creates a structure solid enough to resist the recurring persecutions at the hands of the political powers.

Christianity and the power of the state

Throughout the century the relations between the Christian communities and the institutions of the state were complex and ambiguous. Periods of toleration, in which trials of Christians were rare or altogether absent, were succeeded by periods in which martyrdoms were common. Furthermore, not all regions and not all classes were affected in the same way by these waves of violence. Thus, in Italy there were relatively few victims of persecution, and very few among the members of the upper classes, whereas the situation was a good deal more dramatic in Africa, where the leaders of the church were repeatedly struck. Hence the different attitudes that the Christians showed towards the Empire and its traditions. Sometimes more strict and intransigent, sometimes more inclined to a secularization that would be accentuated in the capital, the Christians held a wide range of positions between orthodoxy and heresy, with notable divergences that are nevertheless easily explained in the tumultuous expansion of those years.

Christianity: cultural subversion and new literature

The Christians also showed that they could produce an imposing literature, with works of the highest importance, and not only from a theological or religious point of view. To all effects, Christian literary writing is the principal cultural event in an era that otherwise, at least in the Latin West, does not have many significant writers or important literary movements. In the great cultural and social ferment of those years, with extensive internal migration and the rapid rise of some classes at the expense of others, and with the dimming of classical ideals and the emergence of eschatological concerns (heralding the imminent end of the world), Christian culture became the point of convergence for many traditions scattered across the Empire. It constituted a unifying force in the following decades, suitable for holding together a state that was troubled by so many events and yet remained sturdy enough to administer the entire Mediterranean area for more than a century.

2. TOWARDS THE ORIGINS OF A CHRISTIAN LITERATURE

The East: Christianity and Jewish culture

Over many decades Christianity grew as one among many Jewish sects within the Roman Empire. Despite the Hellenizing influences introduced by Paul or the evangelist Luke, the basic religious and cultural positions of

Christianity in its first stage remained tied to Judaism. The Jews, whether in Palestine or, especially, in Alexandria, where hundreds of thousands lived, had for a while maintained close relations with the thinking that was dominant in the eastern Mediterranean, but they had never lost their own original characteristics. The Jews (and thus the Christians) often, or even mainly, wrote in Greek and spoke of *logos* and *pneuma,* but their interpretations always derived from the national book, the Old Testament, which was an indisputable point of reference, however numerous and varied the interpretations they drew from it.

Within this variegated Jewish world the Christians are distinguished by a conspicuous activism. They composed texts of notable significance, both those that would later be joined in the New Testament (the four canonic Gospels, the *Acts of the Apostles,* the canonic *Letters,* and *Revelations*) and various others that later generations would not accept with the same devotion (various other Gospels known as apocryphal, other letters, a whole literature in which relations with Jesus's teaching are less evident). They also created an organization of solidarity, marked by a particular efficiency, which was of great utility to the faithful. These were advantages for the solidarity of the group and its possibilities of expansion, which were directed to the conversion not only of the other Jews but also of all those peoples among whom the new religion had good chances of catching on, first the lower classes (who constituted the most marginal segment in the Empire's great metropolises), then the Greeks and Romans themselves.

Christianity in the West

The development in the West is slower. Christianity certainly arrived in Italy around the middle of the first century, at Rome, Pozzuoli, Pompeii, and probably other commercial or maritime centers, but the possibilities for expansion were considerably reduced by the low esteem in which the eastern communities were held: they were scorned as different and feared as potential sources of disorder and catastrophe. Under Nero the murder of many Christians, carried out under the pretext that they were to blame for the fire that had broken out in Rome, shows how political power and public opinion saw in them only criminals, or potential subverters, to be extirpated without concern. The difficulties deriving from this almost total marginalization and the slow spread of the religion, which for more than a century was linked to groups that spoke Greek even in Rome and Italy, explain why for a long time Greek was the language of Christianity even in the West. Moreover, the writings that were coming to be recognized as texts of faith were in Greek. For such reasons the first Christian writings composed in the West are also in Greek, such as the letter of Clement of Rome (Clement was, according to tradition, the fourth bishop of Rome) or the *Shepherd* of Hermas, a work not without literary interest, which recounts five symbolic visions in a Greek that is full of Hebraisms and Latinisms. Writers would continue to write in Greek up to the start of the third century. By then, however, the need to communicate with much larger, Latin-speaking groups had already led to the birth of a parallel Christian literature in Latin.

The Greek language of the earliest Christianity

The Translation of the Sacred Texts

The Bible translated: the Vetus Latina

It has been customary to locate the origins of this literature in the translations of the sacred texts that were carried out in Africa and Italy. Beginning in the second century, Christian communities that did not speak Greek—they were more numerous at first in Africa, then increasingly present in Europe, as gradually in the course of the third century knowledge of that language diminished in the West—felt the need to have the Bible available in Latin. This early translation of the sacred book is commonly referred to as the *Vetus Latina,* that is, "the old Latin translation" ("old" by comparison with Jerome's translation, which would become the official one later). In fact, a single translation was not in use among all the Christians of the West. First of all, there were certainly differences between the African texts, the *Vetus Afra,* and the Italian, the *Vetus Itala.* Second, even within these two geographical areas there were several translations, which sometimes seriously disagreed with one another. These first Bibles in Latin have not come down to us directly, since Jerome's *Vulgata* replaced them all, but we do have numerous samples of them, because of the quotations from Christian writers who worked before the *Vulgata* became the sole official text.

The Vetus Afra *and the* Vetus Itala

To meet the needs of Latin-speaking Christians, other works in addition to the Bible were translated that do not now form part of the New Testament but were considered of great authority at the time. We have, for example, Latin translations of Clement's letter and of the *Shepherd* going back to the second century.

The *Acta Martyrum* and the *Passiones*

The first independent works written directly in Latin come from Africa and belong to the second half of the second century. There is some doubt over the exact chronology of several speeches that have been transmitted to us among the works of Cyprian, but they are certainly earlier than that writer. There exists no uncertainty, however, about the *Acta Martyrum Scillitanorum,* from the year 180, with which a genre already attested in Greek begins in the Latin language. The work is an account of the trials that ended with the martyrs' condemnation to death and their passion. Between the end of the second century and the first years of the fourth, periods of toleration (in which, to be sure, individual episodes of repression did take place) alternated with true, organized persecutions. There were some who out of fear repented of their choice and agreed to change religion, or at least to carry out the formal sacrifices demanded in exchange for acquittal. But the resistance of the majority of the Christians and their determination to endure torture and death were very useful to the cause, since they testified to the sincerity of their faith and the trustworthiness of their doctrine. Hence the name "martyrs," which in Greek means "witnesses," was given to the victims of these judicial episodes.

The Acts of the Scillitan Martyrs

In order to make the martyrs' courage better known and at the same time to preserve and venerate their memory, accounts were published of their trials and last hours. The narratives were sometimes written by the martyrs themselves, as long as they could write, and completed by others of the faithful for their last hours of life and the description of their death. These are nearly always powerful, vital works that owe their ability to strike and move the reader chiefly to the brevity of the exposition and the apparent detachment of the writing.

The *Acta Martyrum Scillitanorum* has to do with an isolated judicial episode in which several Christians of the African town of Scillum were tried and condemned to death by the proconsul Saturninus, who had tried in every way to convince the accused to declare that they were not Christians, in order to be able to acquit them, but in the end was obliged to condemn them because of the resoluteness with which they had affirmed their faith.

Other acts of martyrs

After the description of the episode at Scillum—as was said, the first in Latin—we have various other descriptions, increasingly complex and sometimes skillfully reworked in order to be more effective. The contrast emerges between the Christians, bringers of the new order, nonviolent, and certain of their life after death, and the Roman magistrates, defenders of the old order, compelled to rely on force and to be cruel even beyond their personal intentions, and lacking all hope for the future. The writing of these acts covers the entire third century (Acts of the Martyrdom of St. Cyprian, 258; Acts of Fructuosus; Acts of Marcellus; Acts of Maximilian, 295). Along with the acts written originally in Latin, we also find translations of Greek texts regarded as especially suitable for anti-pagan propaganda.

The Passiones

The *Passiones* are less closely linked to the official account. They are narrative works, developed out of larger or smaller autobiographical cores, that allow the authors to insert scenes that are touching and full of edifying details. Here, too, the earliest texts are in Greek, but the masterpiece of the genre is Latin, the *Passio Perpetuae et Felicitatis,* about the martyrdom of a prosperous young African woman of good family, Perpetua, and of her slave Felicitas and their catechist Saturus, which took place at Carthage in 202.

The Passio Perpetuae et Felicitatis

The text presents itself, in the first part, as the work of Perpetua herself, who tells of her father's attempts to make her deny Christianity in exchange for the freedom promised by the judges, of the difficulties imprisonment created for a young mother, who had her suckling infant with her, and of the signs pointing to her future martyrdom and joy in paradise. The following parts were probably written by Saturus, who recounts some of his visions. The work ends with the narrative of the martyrdom in the games at the amphitheater, a narrative written by an editor, to whom we also ought to attribute the coordination among the various parts that make up this passion.

Whether the role of the editor goes beyond the simple stitching together of Perpetua's and Saturus's texts and the adding of the final part is not of primary importance. Even if Perpetua and Saturus left nothing, as some have thought, and we owe everything to the pen and the imagination of this single author, who according to some might be Tertullian (but there is no valid ground for this attribution), the *Passio Perpetuae* loses nothing of its humanity and immediacy. The description of life in prison, which is unthinkable in that form for a classical writer, is an innovation introduced into literature by Christianity, and the character of Perpetua's brother, a boy who died at the age of seven from a cancer of the face, could acquire the importance it has here only in a literature that elevates scenes of daily life to literary dignity but in its form of expression never rejects that mine of invention that is represented by the schools of rhetoric, with their controversies and declamations.

Another important fact about the *Passio Perpetuae* is that the persons held up to the admiration of the faithful are not part of the ecclesiastical hierarchy of Carthage. This is evidence of a moment in which the designation of exemplary models was not yet in the hands of the ecclesiastical authority, which very soon would turn the propaganda of the martyrs to its own purposes.

A form of popular literature

The power of the *Passio Perpetuae,* which is evident to any modern reader, who cannot but be gripped by the simplicity and candor of the descriptions—and it makes little difference whether it is genuine or, as is more likely, derives from a sophisticated rhetorical exercise—is confirmed by its success among the Christians. It was the model for other, later African *passiones* written by heretical groups, and it was even translated into Greek. The latter is an extremely unusual occurrence in those days, in which Latin Christendom was considered a debtor to Greek in the development of thought and the creation of literary works. The *Passio Perpetuae* is certainly one of the very first (and one of the very few) Latin texts the Easterners thought worth knowing. In a later period the genre of the passions evolved towards a greater similarity to other narratives, especially the novel. Thus is born the epic passion, which is predominantly Greek, in which the martyr takes on the role of the victorious hero, who, though dying, in fact defeats his or her own executioner through a series of fantastic events, *coups de théâtre,* and genuine miracles. But the composition of these texts flourishes after Constantine, when martyrdom is no longer a reality or a looming threat, and for this reason the faithful take pleasure in exaggerated, improbable accounts of events that never occurred. Such narratives, steeped in a sense of triumph, met the needs of a public that until then had turned for entertaining literature to the Greek novel, which shared with the passions a taste for plot and attention to the element of imagination.

3. THE APOLOGISTS

Alongside these forms of literature that may be popular but are not on that account less interesting for their stylistic value, there begin to appear at the end of the second century the first Christian Latin writers about whom we have enough information to form a more complete picture. The writing that aims at spreading the Christian theories and defending them from the attacks of the pagans is called "apologetic," and these writers who are active from the last years of the second century to the first years of the fourth are commonly called "apologists." The development of these works, too, is more rapid in the East and relatively slower in the West. The first apologies written at Rome are the work of Justin, martyred in 165, but they are written in Greek. The various other, slightly later works written for the same purposes in different parts of the Empire are also in Greek. The first to write in Latin are Minucius Felix and Tertullian, and they are called the first Christian Latin authors. Which of the two is earlier is a nearly insoluble problem. We know many events of Tertullian's life and can make a reasonable reconstruction of their chronology. Everything is far more uncertain, however, for Minucius Felix, and the arguments that are the basis for regarding him as earlier or later than Tertullian are mostly subjective and reversible, or they can be interpreted in different ways, according to the theories of individual scholars. It is important to observe, in any event, that from the very beginning a feature manifests itself in the different positions taken by Minucius and Tertullian that will remain constant in Christian writing: on the side of Minucius, a conciliatory tendency, which seeks to avoid breaking with the classical past and to recover from it whatever is not in flagrant contrast with the Christian message; on the side of Tertullian, a rigid intransigence, which demands a decisive turning away from the pagan world and its values, even though such a turning is itself expressed in a literary language that is influenced by the rhetorical precepts of school training (which was common to pagans and Christians).

Tertullian

Quintus Septimius Florens Tertullianus was born at Carthage around the middle of the second century, to pagan parents. He studied rhetoric and law in the traditional schools, where he also learned Greek. He practiced as a lawyer in Africa and then for a while at Rome before he returned to his country and was converted, which took place only at a rather advanced age, probably around 195. He was also a priest, and his religious views were very strict, to such an extent that in 213 he became an adherent of one of the heretical sects most known for intransigence and fanaticism, the Montanists. During the last years of his life he abandoned even this group and founded a new one, called the Tertullianists. He died after 220, the year from which we have the latest notices of him.

We have more than thirty writings of Tertullian's, of a theological and polemical nature, polemics against pagans and against Christians who did not share his views. Among the most notable should be mentioned the *Ad Martyras,* an exhortation to a group of Christians imprisoned and awaiting martyrdom; the *Ad Nationes,* the *Apologeticum,* and the *De Testimonio Animae,* all three composed in 197 to defend Christianity from the attacks of the pagans; the *De Praescriptione Haereticorum,* of around 200, against Christians who contaminated their faith with pagan philosophical doctrines and proposed excessively free interpretations of the Bible; the *De Anima,* written around 211, perhaps the most notable work of Tertullian's maturity, in which he broadly reworks pagan sources; the *Ad Scapulam,* of 212, addressed to the governor of Africa Proconsularis, who was conducting a campaign against the Christians. Also worth mentioning are the works that deal with moral problems and the behavior of Christians in daily life, which therefore offer the reader interesting glimpses of African society in the second and third centuries: the *De Spectaculis,* against taking part in the spectacles of the theater, the amphitheater, and the circus; the *De Cultu Feminarum,* on the clothing of women, which should be particularly modest; the *De Virginibus Velandis,* on the appropriateness of a woman's leaving the house with her face uncovered; the *De Pudicitia,* against sexual relations outside marriage; the *De Corona,* against military service, which is declared to be incompatible with allegiance to the Christian faith; and the *De Idololatria,* against all economic activities connected in any way with the pagan cults. Other works have a liturgical and theological subject, and still others are devoted to violent polemics against religious adversaries (*Adversus Marcionem, Adversus Praxean,* etc.).

Aggressive language and anti-feminine ideology

The professional experience of the lawyer, the spirit that is combative and prone to convert every work originating in defensive needs into a fierce attack upon one's adversaries, the taste for abuse, for unpleasant and annoying description, and for a "baroque" style that is furnished with very powerful rhetorical tools—these are characteristics common to virtually all of Tertullian's writing, from whatever period they come. One can get the impression of an arrogant person, inclined to defend his own theories with any type of argumentation whatsoever, sometimes even with questionable reasoning and obviously false proofs. This picture, which on the whole is not positive, is made worse by certain views of Tertullian's that are wholly unacceptable out of context, such as his stubborn demonizing of all that is feminine and his notion that woman is Satan's most dangerous instrument. Such preliminary dislikes should be overcome, however, if one wants to understand the role and the position of a person who is certainly impetuous yet not without courage and often in the grip of intense strictness and moralism. Tertullian in the final analysis appears as a tragic figure who does not love humanity and who takes pleasure in imagining and describing all the misfortunes that sooner or later will befall his enemies, a man who cannot find a moment of peace and tranquillity, at least not in this life.

The greatness of the thinker

Yet the man who is subject to these limitations is also a great theoretician and an acute thinker. Leaving aside more strictly doctrinal matters, which are only of secondary importance here, one should keep in mind the importance that the *Apologeticum* attaches to defining the legal relation between state and religion, which is established with the clarity and professionalism of a Roman lawyer. Also from the *Apologeticum* comes the famous discussion of the *anima naturaliter Christiana,* which exerted so much influence in the following centuries: the soul itself, if not indoctrinated to the contrary, would demonstrate the primacy of monotheism with invocations to a single god in moments of difficulty. His inability to mediate and his intransigent devotion to consistency at all costs set Tertullian against the whole world. In this regard the *De Idololatria* is particularly important, in that it regards nearly all daily activities as full of paganism and thus unacceptable for the good Christian. It is the problem of the relation that the opponent of a regime—of a state, in fact—ought to have to the reality that surrounds him: how far can opposition and refusal be taken without becoming fanatical rejection and exasperated isolation, which remove even the possibility of intervening to alter a situation that one regards as unjust?

Tertullian deserves an important place in the (on the whole, rather poor) panorama of his period on account of his qualities as a writer too. His combination of technical terms from lawyer's jargon with words of indisputable literary dignity is entirely his own. He is the complete master of a deliberately irregular, broken sentence construction. Questions and exclamations often interrupt the flow of his discourse; he knows how to write concise, effective phrases; and he pushes to the utmost metaphors that belong to a visionary, almost hallucinatory imagination. His renown in African culture is confirmed by the survival of the Tertullianists as late as the time of Augustine and by the fact that many of his favorite subjects return insistently in the Christian literature of the first centuries. Nor is it a small merit of Tertullian's to have contributed greatly to creating a new Christian language, one able to express on a literary level the dogmas of faith and the problems of the believer's daily behavior.

Minucius Felix

LIFE AND
WORKS
Another lawyer and African (he was probably born at Cirta, the native city of Fronto), Marcus Minucius Felix was active at Rome, where he was comfortably off economically. A contemporary of Tertullian, he wrote, according to some scholars, several years before him, at the end of the second century; but according to others his work should be located in the first decades of the third century, between the writings of Tertullian and of Cyprian. In addition to the dialogue *Octavius,* which is extant, Minucius is said to have written a work *De Fato,* which is lost.

Summary of the Octavius

The dialogue *Octavius* takes place on the shore at Ostia, between three people: the pagan Caecilius, the Christian Octavius, and Minucius himself. Octavius reproaches Caecilius for an act of adoration to a statue of the god Serapis, and Caecilius proposes to expound his reasons in turn and to name Minucius as judge of the contest. But after the two speeches, Caecilius's against Christianity and Octavius's in favor of it, there is no need for judgment, since Caecilius admits he has been defeated.

The subjects discussed are the ones that also appear in the other apologists, including Tertullian: monotheism is preferable to polytheism, even rationally; not only are the Christians innocent of the misdeeds imputed to them but it is often their accusers who are stained with such guilt; if the

Intransigent consistency (margin note)

Expressiveness of a pungent style (margin note)

The persuasive language of reason

pagans understood Christianity's insistence on peace and love, they would not be opposed to it but would convert to it at once. And yet the difference between Minucius's treatment and Tertullian's, in the *Apologeticum,* for instance, could not be more evident. Minucius is a fine, delicate writer, and he shuns the crudity that Tertullian, by contrast, is fond of. Minucius bases his argument on logic and calm reasoning, whereas Tertullian tries to arouse emotions and stir feelings. Minucius addresses the cultivated pagans, in order to convert them, and therefore he abounds in quotations from the classical authors and refrains from references to the Bible; Tertullian lets fly at the pagans in order to strengthen the Christians in their faith and at the most may think of winning over to Christianity the future generations, not yet stained with the sin of idolatry. In short, if Tertullian stuns the reader by his taste for irritation, Minucius Felix, by contrast, appears a model of balance and good sense.

This difference has often brought upon Minucius accusations of weakness and incompetence, of uncertainty in his faith, and of the dominance of literary interests over religious. But whoever has sufficient sensitivity to catch his nuances and half-tones and sufficient good taste to appreciate a work that programmatically rejects any lowering of its level, any concession to the pathetic, is bound to appreciate the serenity and the dignity of the discussion. This does not mean, however, that Minucius does not pay much attention to the literary aspect: Cicero is always present as the model for sentence construction. Some scenes of the dialogue's frame are justly appreciated bravura pieces, such as the famous description of the boys on the beach making flat rocks skip across the water and of the protagonists walking along the extreme edge of the wave-soaked sand and halting on the reef, where they sit to talk in the fresh fall morning, and the ending in which the three friends take their leave of one another, content with the fine discussion and happy to have smoothed out their differences.

Balance and classical elegance

Continuity of the dialogue tradition and moderation

With its serene and yet melancholy tone and its composed rationality, the *Octavius* marks the end of the classical world and the transition to Christianity as a process of continuity and not, as Tertullian wished, of rupture. It is the Christianity of the ruling classes, who have no desire to see the change of religion accompanied by social upheavals and who are convinced that the refinement and balance created by centuries of Greco-Roman civilization must survive. In Minucius's program there is no place for the peculiarities of Judaism or the extremism of Christian radicals. It cannot be denied that his Christianity is authentic and sincere, but it certainly has none of the revolutionary drive that had helped it to spread among the lower classes and that for some intellectuals, including Tertullian, was even the principal attraction of the new religion.

Cyprian

LIFE

Thascius Caecilius Cyprianus was born around 200 at Carthage and was educated in the schools of that city. He was a renowned teacher of rhetoric until 246, when he converted and gave all his goods to the poor. Chosen bishop at the end of 248, he had to deal with the very harsh persecution decreed by the emperor Decius in 250, during which he showed great courage and was able to protect the Christian community from still graver sufferings. He did not escape, however, the persecution of Valerian in 257–58, when he was tried and condemned to exile and then recalled for a second trial, which ended with his condemnation to death and his martyrdom on 14 September 258.

WORKS

Various apologetic writings, such as the *Ad Donatum,* on his own conversion (where the autobiographical element makes this seem a precedent for Augustine's *Confessions*), and the *Ad Demetrianum,* on the attacks of the pagans and divine punishment, or the *Quod Idola Dii Non Sint,* about the authenticity of which there is some doubt. Other essays deal with matters connected with his role as bishop of Carthage, such as the *De Lapsis,* on the attitude to be adopted towards those Christians who had denied their faith during the persecutions but later repented and wanted to return to the ecclesiastical community; the *De Catholicae Ecclesiae Unitate,* a firm stand against all heresies and schisms, which Cyprian considered a major calamity of the persecutions against the Christians (the work was sent to Rome and used as the most complete theoretical justification of papal primacy, which was threatened at the time by the schism of Novatianus [see below]); and the *De Habitu Virginum,* on the rules of conduct that ought to be followed by the women who have vowed to consecrate themselves to God. Cyprian's correspondence, consisting of eighty-one letters, sixty-five written by him and sixteen addressed to him, is also very important. From it we can draw precise information on the conditions of life in Africa Proconsularis at the middle of the third century and on the problems that the persecutions created for the Christian communities.

Cyprian's balance

Cyprian thought very highly of Tertullian, whom he valued for the severity of his doctrines. In various works he took up subjects and even titles that had previously been employed by his older fellow countryman. But unlike Tertullian, he never allowed the taste for extremism to get out of hand. His position as bishop and the obligations it imposed towards all the faithful, along with his innate, admirable balance and a remarkable dose of common sense, always helped him to make the most reasonable choices. Thus, after the persecution of Decius, he decided to accept back into the church the renegades *(lapsi)* who were repentant, despite the opposition of those who had risked martyrdom by not abjuring their faith, but he imposed severe penitences on those who wanted to earn readmission to communion. This attitude should not be confused with laxity or permissiveness: a few years later Cyprian demonstrated with his own martyrdom that he was not disposed to surrender, and he showed a similar firmness on the occasion of a clash with Stephen, the bishop of Rome.

The collision with the pope

The matter had to do with the baptism performed by heretics. For the Africans, this baptism was not valid, and in their opinion all who had received the sacrament from priests outside of the church needed to be rebaptized. For the pope, however, this baptism was valid because it had been done in accordance with the forms prescribed by rite, and it could not be renewed. Although it arose from a problem of pastoral practice, the conflict involved the much larger question of the autonomy of the different episcopal sees in relation to the see of Rome; the latter appealed to the so-called primacy of Peter, on the basis of which the pope claimed an authority superior to that of all the other bishops. Cyprian was able to weave skillfully a dense web of alliances, which included many Eastern bishops, in order to check what was perceived at the time as an illegitimate invasion on the part of the pope, but the persecution of Valerian and his own death interrupted this initiative.

A classical style

Cyprian's characteristics as a writer are very different from those of his dear Tertullian. He has a firm grasp of the techniques of classical prose, into which he inserts biblical quotations without altering the elegant construction of the phrase and the grand solemnity of the period. Far removed from Tertullian's provocations and excesses, yet with less nuance and delicacy than Minucius, he provided the chief model for the great Christian prose writers of the following century. The deacon Pontius, who knew Cyprian personally, wrote a *Vita Cypriani,* the first Latin example of those biographies of bishops and saints that would become numerous in subsequent centuries.

Other Apologists

Tertullian, Minucius Felix, and Cyprian are the three principal writers of this century, but many other apologists, known to us to a greater or lesser extent, flourished along with them, and the polemic among Christianity's various sects gave rise to a vast literature on theology and doctrine, which cannot be treated here exhaustively or even mentioned with adequate coverage. It will be enough to recall Novatianus, a priest of Rome, who sided against Cyprian in the controversy over the *lapsi.* When, after the see had been vacant for more than a year, pope Cornelius, who shared Cyprian's position on the *lapsi,* was elected in 251, Novatianus, placing himself at the head of the strict party, had himself elected in turn as pope of his own followers, which gave rise to a heresy that would last for more than a century. His principal work is a *De Trinitate* (a title that would be used often in later literature), in addition to a *De Spectaculis* and a *De Bono Pudicitiae* that are obviously based on Tertullian.

Novatianus

Victorinus of Poetovium

Victorinus of Poetovium (today Ptuj in Slovenia), who died as a martyr in 304, a victim of the persecution unleashed by Diocletian, is another ecclesiastic who has left us works in Latin. He wrote many biblical commentaries, about which Jerome informs us. We possess from them only a commentary on *Revelations,* the earliest work of biblical exegesis in Latin that has come down to us.

4. COMMODIAN

LIFE

The notices about Commodian are so uncertain that some scholars place him even in the fifth century, but a date in the middle of the third century appears more likely, since some of his verses may refer to the persecutions of Decius and Valerian, which broke out at that time. From another passage one learns that he was a native of Gaza in Palestine. He must have left Palestine to go west, however, probably to Africa, as is indicated by the similarities of content between his works and those of the contemporary African apologists and by certain metrical peculiarities, which also appear in many African inscriptions of the third and fourth centuries. Yet scholars disagree even about these points, and some deny his Eastern origins, while others hold that his activity took place in southern Gaul, or even at Rome.

WORKS

Instructiones, in two books, eighty hexameter poems in all, of varying length, from six to forty-eight verses. The first book includes the poems against the pagans and against the Jews; the second, the poems for the Christians, who are reproached for their sins and exhorted to follow a more devout life. The poems are acrostics, the first letters of the individual verses of a poem, read in sequence, forming the title of the poem; for instance, in the *De Infantibus,* the first verse begins with *d,* the second with *e,* the third with *i,* the fourth with *n,* and so on.

Carmen Apologeticum, in 1,060 hexameters, the real title of which was probably *Carmen adversus Iudaeos et Graecos,* or *Carmen de Duobus Populis.* The work is transmitted without any indication of author, but the attribution to Commodian is now regarded as beyond question. The subject of the poem is the history of the world, that is, the history of the Old Testament and Rome, which is seen as a clash between God and the devil, coming down in time to the destruction of the Empire, the Apocalypse, and the Last Judgment.

Emotive and doctrinaire naiveté

Among the many prose writers that early Christianity produced, Commodian was the only poet, yet he was a significant one. He is an unusual poet in many regards, an anomalous voice in the history of Latin poetry: he is interested in the lower levels of society, and in his works he represents the beliefs and the aspirations of the underprivileged, their strong and direct passions, and he uses a Latin that is influenced by the developments of the spoken language and a metric that lacks continuity with the metric of the classics. In the field of Christian doctrine, too, his knowledge is rather approximate and crude, far removed from the rich elaborations of the Western apologists and from the refined lucubrations of the Eastern. He does not explain well the role of the Holy Spirit. He believes that the pagan gods are sons of the angels and mortal women. And he is convinced that the end of the world will be preceded by a happy age upon earth, that states founded on injustice and exploitation of the weak will be overturned, to be replaced by an earthly kingdom of God, in which the poor, the underprivileged, and the downtrodden will see their hopes fulfilled and their rights recognized. This millennial hope, which believed in a concrete change in the conditions of life on earth, a change that precedes and is greater than the celestial rewards of paradise, was quite widespread in the Christianity of the humbler classes and met precise social needs.

Expectation of the millennium

If Commodian as a theoretician is confused, to say the least, he also shows certain limitations as a polemicist. He has the vehemence and force of a Tertullian, and like him he can find popular, rough insults for the pagans and the Jews, but he lacks the imagination and rhetorical ability of the Carthaginian lawyer; the repetitions are rather frequent, the vulgarities predictable and lacking in force. His sharpest features are his strict moralism, his deep conviction of being in the right, and his clash with the dying institutions of classicism. Because of the ardor with which he presents his apocalyptic visions and the revolutionary hopes that he places in them, Commodian has come to be termed the last of the prophets, and the only one to express himself in Latin. It is very difficult to determine to what extent the author makes himself the convinced spokesman of popular demands and to what extent he gives way to a demagogic attitude; in this regard Commodian always leaves readers uncertain and disconcerted: we ask ourselves whether a writer who is certainly cultured could descend to these levels of crudity, or whether he has not rather appropriated to himself a standpoint for the purpose of literary, religious, and political provocation.

A raging prophet

Rhythmic-accentual metrics and syntactic-lexical vulgarisms

Commodian's verse is striking for its anomalous prosody, which is completely different from that of classical Latin. The hexameter is no longer a regular succession of short and long syllables, but a line composed of a certain number of syllables (not more than seventeen and not less than twelve); it is the sequence of the tonic accents of the words, not the alternation in quantity, that creates the rhythm of the whole. Commodian thus anticipates the evolution that will lead from quantitative metrics to the accentual poetry of the Romance languages.

This novelty is combined with an elementary and repetitious vocabulary, with a syntax simplified to the utmost, and with a logic that is summary and at times absurd in its partisanship. From it one forms the picture, as we said, of an unusual and stimulating figure—a writer who does not completely ignore classical models and their conventions, but reuses them in forms that are banally academic or utterly altered, rendered vulgar and popular; a poet who presents himself as spokesman of people on the margins of society, with all their irrational, violent drives, but also with a thirst for justice that is slaked by the divine promise; a polemicist who alternates the petty meanness of personal invective against his opponent with vast cosmic pictures of the return of Christ and the fire that will burn the wicked and spare the few honest persons that there are in this world.

5. THE LAST FRUITS OF THE POETICS OF THE NOVELLI

A society with little interest in poetry

The poetry of traditional inspiration, by contrast, gives an overall impression of weariness. It consists for the most part of poems that rework themes and subjects of classical poetry, with a marked tendency to pursue a rarefied atmosphere and technical feats in accord with the taste of the poets from the previous century, the *novelli* of the Antonine period. In quantity, too, the writings that have come down to us do not seem significant: there were few writers, few works, not a large number of verses, to such an extent that it is not difficult to deduce that the society of the day had a reduced interest in poetry. We must keep in mind, however, that the Christians (whose major innovations in literature had been in prose) do not devote themselves to poetry (Commodian, if in fact he lived in the third century, would be the sole exception); poetic form is not regarded as suitable for the necessity of confuting one's adversaries and spreading the divine message, a necessity that is primary in the entire period of the persecutions.

Literary Genres and Poets of the *Anthologia Latina*

Many of the poems customarily assigned to this period have been preserved by the *Anthologia Latina*. This title embraces a vast collection of poems assembled in Africa in the sixth century that contains chiefly writings of African poets of late antiquity but does not neglect texts from earlier periods, especially if they are attributed to authors of great renown (as with some of the epigrams that go under the name of Seneca and Petronius). The anthology originates in an educational milieu, where those verses may have survived even after the barbarian invasions, and it has the value of transmitting to us authors and works that otherwise would have been irretrievably lost. One copy, in an ancient codex now preserved at Paris, was in the possession of the French humanist Claude de Saumaise (or, in Latin, Salmasius, 1588–1653); hence the name *Codex Salmasianus,* for this fundamental witness of the *Anthologia Latina.*

A school anthology

It is not always easy to date the various poems gathered in the *Anthologia,* since we often lack any sort of comparable material, and the names of the authors are otherwise unknown. In some cases, however, sufficiently convincing chronological hypotheses have been advanced.

Pentadius

Pentadius, who probably belongs to the third century, was an elegant writer of "echoing couplets," the term used for those couplets in which the first part of the hexameter is the same as the last part of the pentameter, as in the following: *Sentio, fugit hiems, Zephyrisque moventibus orbem / iam tepet Eurus aquis; sentio, fugit hiems.* The technical difficulty does not seem to pose particular problems for the writer, who can paint his graceful, mannered vignettes, refined and pleasant, full of learning and classical Greek and Latin reminiscences, on the theme of spring and the rebirth of the world or on mythological subjects. According to some, he is to be identified with the *Pentadius frater* to whom, in 314, Lactantius dedicated the *Epitome,* which summarized and elaborated his *Divinae Institutiones* (see p. 640).

The *Pervigilium Veneris*

The theme of nature, so very present in Pentadius's verses, is a constant in many of the poems that make up the *Anthologia,* from the numerous poems on roses to the one that is perhaps the most famous among the pieces of the collection, the anonymous *Pervigilium Veneris*. Problems of dating surround this fresh poem (consisting of ninety-three trochaic tetrameters), which some assign to the age of the Antonines, because of certain coincidences of style with the taste of the *poetae novelli* (in this case, an attribution to Florus has been proposed), while others want to place it in a later period, in the third, fourth, fifth, or even sixth century.

Popular themes and literary learning in the Pervigilium Veneris

In this "Vigil of Venus" popular themes and literary learning combine in strophes of varying length, separated by the refrain *Cras amet qui numquam amavit, quique amavit cras amet*. It describes the festivities of Venus to celebrate the spring in accordance with the customs of Hybla, in Sicily. The goddess, who symbolizes love, is also the principal force of nature, invoked to render the fields fertile, in a context in which sensual descriptions combine with legends of Rome's origin, mythology with agriculture.

The only instance of its genre in Latin literature, the *Pervigilium Veneris* recalls by its meter the form of the acclamations that soldiers and people used to shout during the triumphs of their victorious generals. Although the vocabulary is largely classical, some traits of the popular language can be recognized in the syntax. But the simplicity of expression aimed at and the clearness of the descriptions give the poem an extraordinary freshness; the apparent spontaneity only adds elegance.

The Other Poets of the *Anthologia Latina*

Reposianus and descriptive mannerism

The *Anthologia Latina* has also preserved for us a brief hexameter poem of Reposianus, entitled *De Concubitu Martis et Veneris*. In this case too, while the work is usually attributed to the third century, the dating is far from certain, and others have attributed it to the fourth century or the fifth. The subject is drawn from the famous episode in the eighth book of Homer's *Odyssey;* the characters are Mars, Venus, and her husband Vulcan. Vulcan, learning of Venus's betrayal, prepares a remarkable chain, with which he binds the two lovers while they are asleep after making love and thus exposes them to the ridicule of the other gods. Elegant, mannered descriptions are fitted into this story, such as of the forest in which the meeting between Venus and Mars takes place and the meadow in which the two make love. Subjects and tones of which Pentadius and the author of the *Pervigilium Veneris* were fond reappear here, namely, the cosmic sense of love, the relation between love and the rebirth of nature, formal elegance, and subtle learning. The plastic representation of the couple has suggested the performances of the mime, which was often on erotic subjects and which is attested throughout the imperial period.

Vespa and the controversiae

The *Iudicium Coci et Pistoris Iudice Vulcano,* written by Vespa, is on a different subject. We have here an amusing example of satiric poetry, with a cook and a baker-confectioner arguing over the superiority of their callings. Each defends his thesis with subtle mythological and philosophical arguments as well as references to tasty dishes and exquisite desserts. The play shows Vespa's great ability in *controversiae* (rhetorical disputes on a given theme, with the speakers defending the two opposing positions [see also pp.

404 f.]). Vespa himself, moreover, tells us of his own activity as a lecturer, which took him to the various cities in search of paying spectators, of any class whatever. Agreeably mocking his own calling and his fate, the poet demonstrates in a hundred hexameters the futility of those very rhetorical spectacles that were probably his only source of support. After the two contenders have defended themselves and their arts at length, Vulcan, called upon to pass judgment, declares that they are equal and threatens to deny his fire to their furnaces if they do not make peace with one another.

Hosidius Geta and the cento

Another genre well represented in the *Anthologia Latina* is that of the cento. These were compositions made by using whole or half-verses taken from famous classical poems (in the Latin world, nearly always Virgil's works) and stitched together in such a way that the original meaning of the verses was completely changed. The Latin name *cento* derives from a kind of cloth made by joining together various pieces and is extended metaphorically to this type of verse, of which Tertullian already makes mention and which is found throughout late antiquity.

Among all the authors of centos registered in the *Anthologia,* the one we know best is Hosidius Geta, the author of a *Medea,* which was probably written in the last years of the second century and the first years of the third. A fellow countryman of Tertullian, who refers to him in the *De Praescriptione Haereticorum* as his contemporary, this African poet takes up the subject of Seneca's *Medea* using Virgilian hexameters for the spoken parts and half-hexameters for the choruses; the second half of the hexameter, after the penthemimeral caesura, may even suggest the anapestic movement that characterized the choruses in Sophocles' tragedies.

Other poems of the Anthologia Latina

Along with these and other poems preserved by the *Codex Salmasianus* and along with a few other poems that have come down to us in other manuscripts and have also been collected under the name *Anthologia Latina* by Riese, the most famous editor of these texts, a number of longer, perhaps more important poems deserve mention. These belong to the genre of didactic poetry and purport to offer instruction in the most diverse fields of knowledge, from metrics to medicine, from ethics to hunting. Other sources for the literary culture of this period are the various epigraphic compositions in verse, especially tomb inscriptions, which for the most part have been edited by Buecheler in another section of the *Anthologia.*

Terentius Maurus

Terentius Maurus's versified work on grammar and metrics is far from agreeable to read, on account of the extreme dryness of the subject, but it is of importance for an understanding of the poetic techniques of this period. He is regarded as having lived in the last years of the second century, but some locate him about a century later. He was an expert on grammar but also a capable theoretician of the poetics of the *novelli,* and he could play skillfully with the different metrical structures.

Three works of his are extant, transmitted in a single volume but in fact quite clearly distinct from one another: a brief *De Litteris,* a *De Syllabis,* and a longer *De Metris,* which has reached us incomplete. These treatises, according to the preface, were composed at an advanced age, perhaps after many years of teaching, in order to fix definitively a series of precepts. The *De Litteris* describes the sounds and the signs of the vowels and consonants and also includes a section on the numerical value of the letters and their mystical-magical powers in certain particular formulas. The *De Syllabis* examines vowels and diphthongs and then prosodical questions about the length of the various syllables in the versification of the hexameter. Terentius's metrical theory, which is expounded in the *De Metris,* belongs to the "derivationist" school that went back to Caesius Bassus and, still earlier, to Varro. According to this theory, all the Greek and Latin meters are nothing but modifications of two basic metrical structures, the hexameter and the iambic trimeter, which gave rise to the other verses through additions, subtractions, and modifications of syllables. In this system an important role is also assigned to the Phalacaean, Catullus's characteristic verse. Terentius's treatise does not confine itself to expounding theory, but always cites actual examples and for some meters is the only source that we have.

Wisdom and Medicine in Verse

The Disticha
Catonis

The so-called *Disticha Catonis* were famous during the Middle Ages as small summaries of wisdom, easy to remember and suitable for quotation. This collection of maxims, each one consisting of two hexameters, fills four books and was assembled between the end of the second century and the beginning of the fourth. The name of Cato the Elder, alleged author of the maxims, was chosen for various reasons: it associated the work with a man of great wisdom and integrity and a renowned moralist, and it recalled the existence of a genuine work by Cato, a *Carmen de Moribus.* In order to make the Catonian origin of the verses more credible, a dedication to his son was invented (some works of Cato were actually dedicated to his son Marcus), and a letter addressed to the son was added to the collection, along with a series of maxims in prose, each just a few words long. The couplets are based on the typical popular wisdom of Rome, yet they also include references to the literary tradition and to archaic models, of the sort that had been ideologically represented by the nostalgic writers of the good old days. It has been observed, and it deserves to be mentioned, that this invitation to keep in mind the virtues of the ancestors and the qualities that had made Rome and Latium great is made precisely during the years in which the Roman citizenship was extended to all the free inhabitants of the Empire (by the Edict of Caracalla) and in which that tendency to extend rights that had so outraged the moralists of the previous centuries, such as Juvenal, came to its fulfillment. As for the fields in which the *Disticha* offer their precepts, these are mostly minor matters of everyday life: behavior towards friends, neighbors, and women (and here the misogyny that the sources uniformly attribute to Cato allows the compiler to indulge in multiple variations on the theme of the nagging wife). Few couplets deal with more complex questions, such as the relation between man and divinity, or man and death. In particular there is no theoretical structure that could be consistently referred to a well-defined philosophy.

Serenus Sammonicus   By contrast, Quintus Serenus Sammonicus, an important figure at the court of the Severans and the Gordians, was interested in health, diseases, and remedies. His father had been a writer in the time of Septimius Severus (193–211), and a *Rerum Reconditarum Libri* by him is recorded. Quintus, however, had connections with Severus Alexander (222–35) and then with Gordian I, who wanted him to be tutor to his son, Gordian II (238). He had an immense library of sixty-two thousand volumes, and it was on his extensive reading rather than on his actual experience as a doctor that he based the cures listed in the approximately sixty prescriptions that make up his *Liber Medicinalis,* a work consisting of more than eleven hundred hexameters. The chief source is Pliny the Elder, but there are others, including Dioscorides. Serenus is fond of enhancing his prescriptions with literary quotations from Plautus, Lucretius, Horace, and other Greek and Latin writers, as if to prove that he is a learned reader, not an empiricist. The suggested cures have to do with various illnesses, which are listed in order from the head to the feet, and include remedies against white hair, warts, and hemorrhoids. Serenus proposes not only medicines derived from natural essences but also magical formulas and objects, such as slips of paper with the word *abracadabra* on them. He seems concerned to provide medication for all patients, not only the wealthy, since he emphasizes the difference between his prescriptions, of which even the poor can avail themselves, and those of certain doctors, who cause prosperous gullible persons to spend immense sums of money.

Nemesianus and Didactic Poetry

LIFE   Marcus Aurelius Olympius Nemesianus was an African, probably from Carthage. He lived in the second half of the third century, as is proved by the dedication of his principal work to the emperors Carinus and Numerianus (283–84).

WORKS   The most ambitious work is the *Cynegetica,* on the techniques of hunting. Only 325 of its hexameters have been preserved for us, since the rest of the work was lost through damage to the manuscript that transmitted it. It is dated to 283–84 by the dedication to the emperors reigning at that time, and it opens with a long proem that belongs to the genre of the *recusatio:* the poet declares that he does not want and does not know how to write other genres of poetry. We also have four eclogues by Nemesianus, based on Virgil's *Bucolics* and their imitators. Other works on fishing and navigation, however, have been lost, and we have only references to them.

The tradition of didactic poetry on the subject of hunting had a Roman precedent of some significance, the poem of Grattius Faliscus (see p. 427), who was also the author of a *Cynegetica;* in fact, in the manuscript that Sannazaro recovered (the one we possess today) the text of Nemesianus is joined with that of Grattius (and also the *Halieutica* attributed to Ovid). But the cynegetic genre had enjoyed and continued to enjoy in that period a great success in Greek as well, as is indicated by various works in prose and verse. As far as one can judge from the relatively few hexameters that have come down to us, the didactic purpose often serves as justification for elegant descriptions of landscapes, carried out for the most part in a Virgilian style. Hunting is viewed as an activity that brings man into constant contact with nature, frees him from the urban environment (which is regarded as unnatural and harmful), and allows him to roam about through the fields and forests. The hunter is a noble and rich gentleman in search of emotions and distractions who wants to taste adventure and to recapture a literary dimension of the setting. In truth, the real conditions of agriculture in many areas of the Empire had changed for the worse since the second century, and by choosing to present the landscapes in the Virgilian manner the poet can conceal this decline in the name of a poetic model of indisputable authority. This also allows him to draw a parallel, comforting even if unrealistic, between the present day and the Augustan age.

Estheticization of hunting

The eclogues of Nemesianus

The four eclogues are also closely tied to the Virgilian model, though they show influence from Calpurnius Siculus too. Indeed for a long time the eclogues formed a single corpus together with the poems by Calpurnius (who is usually dated under Nero [see pp. 435 f.], though some have suggested that he be dated to a period closer to Nemesianus).

Although the models are present, in the overall structure of the individual poems or in various episodes or in expressions and nexus that contain exact verbal repetitions, in reading Nemesianus's eclogues attentively one is bound to be aware of a new sensibility and new attitudes. The second eclogue, regarded by some as an unsuccessful reworking of Calpurnius Siculus's third eclogue, is instead an evident example of this originality on account of the situation it describes: Idas and Alcon, two fifteen-year-old boys, have both fallen in love with Donace after having raped her together in the fields, and now each one tries to win her for himself, and for himself alone, by means of his song.

6. LEARNED LITERATURE

A phenomenon of some importance that emerges in the third century and would reach its greatest height in the fourth is the growing importance and utility of the schools. The gradual transformation of the state administration from the exclusive privilege of members of the most important families to a genuine career reserved for professionals of varying social origin, who are specifically trained and prepared for such activity, entailed the creation of educational centers suitable for creating this class of bureaucrats. Thus the number of public schools increases on both state and municipal levels, and these, now a match for the private schools, show themselves active in various fields of knowledge, from the more traditional and always very important fields of grammar, rhetoric, and jurisprudence to "scien-

The public schools

Replacement of the
volumen *by the*
codex

tific" ones such as medicine, architecture, and music. This remarkable diffusion of culture, and therefore of the book as well, contributes to the replacement of the old, expensive *volumen,* the papyrus roll, by the new codex, which is made of parchment pages and is more economical and more suitable for taking notes and keeping course materials and collections of school lessons.

The Christian schools

The Christians are particularly active in the world of education, often devoting themselves to teaching in public and private institutions. The Christian school, however, was nondenominational. Their programs were identical to those of the non-Christian schools and aimed at training a corps of well-prepared officials that would be sufficiently homogeneous in outlook and culture. At the base of all instruction there always remained the classics, especially Cicero and Virgil, from whom the children learned to read and then, as they grew up, mastered the rules of grammar and the precepts of rhetoric. It was from the classics, moreover, that they got the erudite and antiquarian information that made up the cultural baggage common to all members of the upper-middle classes. Along with the classics, however, were employed many handbooks, greatly varying in size, dealing with the many disciplines that are the object of instruction. Thus beside grammatical works of the traditional type, commentaries on the classics, and rhetorical treatises, we find writings on law, medicine, and other technical subjects, and we see a rich flourishing of encyclopedic works in various formats.

The handbooks

Among the grammarians and authors of treatises are Julius Romanus and Marius Plotius Sacerdos, the latter of whom taught metrics at Rome and also composed a *De Metris.* One of the works that derives from grammatical interests is the previously mentioned epitome of the Augustan grammarian Verrius Flaccus's *De Verborum Significatu* that Sextus Pompeius Festus made in the second century or at the beginning of the third (see pp. 386 f.). Among the commentaries on the classics, those by Acron and Porphyrio on Horace, which have already been referred to, stand out in particular.

The Jurists: Papinian, Ulpian, and Others

Aemilius Papinian

Several of the most important jurists in the history of Roman law also belong to the third century. Aemilius Papinian was a friend of the emperor Septimius Severus and influenced his policy in the field of law. He held important magistracies, among them the praetorian prefecture, but then, after coming into conflict with the new emperor Caracalla, he was murdered in 212. His vast writings (thirty-seven books of *Quaestiones,* nineteen books of *Responsa*) had a profound influence upon later jurisprudence and legislation, even upon those of the Germans after their invasion of the Empire. We have various fragments from them, which have sometimes come down to us along with commentaries compiled by jurists of later periods.

Domitius Ulpian

Along with Papinian, Domitius Ulpian stands out, a Phoenician from

Tyre who enjoyed great favor at the court of Caracalla and Severus Alexander until his death in 228 at the hands of the praetorians. He wrote even more than Papinian: eighty-one books *Ad Edictum Praetoris,* which are fundamental for the theoretical definition of praetorian law; fifty-one books *Ad Masurium Sabinum,* on civil law; books of *Disputationes, Responsa,* and *Institutiones;* and a *Liber Singularis Regularum.* Only fragments and summaries remain of these and his other works.

Julius Paulus

The triad of Severan jurists is completed by Julius Paulus, who was also praetorian prefect after a career that in part followed that of Papinian. He was the author of 86 works in a total of 319 books; the longest fragments come from his *Sententiae ad Filium.*

Herennius Modestinus

From a slightly later period comes Herennius Modestinus, who wrote the *Differentiarum Libri IX,* on the subtle differences between cases that appear similar. The end of the century saw the compilation of the *Codex Gregorianus,* probably by a jurist by the name of Gregory, with the rescripts promulgated by the emperors of the second and third centuries. This work too, which anticipates later and more famous collections, such as the *Codex Hermogenianus* of the fourth century and especially the *Codex Theodosianus* and the *Corpus Iuris Iustiniani,* confirms the tendency to define a legal norm that is well articulated, consistent, and likely to assure the certainty of the law.

The Testamentum Porcelli

The importance of studies on the laws and law finds a curious confirmation in an amusing parody of testamentary law that goes by the name *Testamentum Porcelli,* or more exactly, *Testamentum Grunni Corocottae Porcelli.* A pig, having understood that the hour of his death is come (at the hands of the cook), draws up his last will and testament, in perfectly legal form, with notaries and witnesses; he leaves his goods to friends and relatives. The combination of the fable of the speaking animal with the parody that degrades a serious subject makes this brief text an interesting literary document. New methods of reading, applied recently and with good results, have emphasized the basic role of the pig in agrarian societies and the traditional customs that accompanied the killing of it.

Censorinus

Among the works of encyclopedic learning that deal with what might be regarded as "scientific" subjects, the *De Die Natali* of Censorinus may be mentioned. A grammarian and writer of grammatical texts (now lost), Censorinus in 238 dedicated the *De Die Natali* to the rich and noble Quintus Cerellius upon the occasion of his birthday. The work consists of two parts: the first examines the relation between man and his *dies natalis,* and the second talks more generally about the calendar and the divisions of time.

Astrology and the guardian angel

Astrological theory, though it is analyzed in detail in the first part, does not have the importance that we might expect and that it would acquire in later works. Censorinus still assigns a significant role to the *Genius,* the personal divine protector, for propitiating whom he sets forth the necessary practices. Much room is given, moreover, to philosophical and scientific theories about human reproduction and the different ages of man. The second part deals with the different temporal divisions (centuries, lustra, years, months, days) according to the differing customs of the various nations.

Censorinus shows a remarkable erudition throughout the short work. In addition to Varro and especially Suetonius, whom he cited frequently, Censorinus used other sources that were less easy to locate, which he may have known at second hand. The whole work is developed with considerable ability, even though the poor condition in which the text has been transmitted does not always allow us to catch and appreciate the qualities of elegant writing that some ancients attribute to the work.

The Fragmentum Censorini

Along with the text of Censorinus has come down to us an anonymous small-scale encyclopedic treatise, quite damaged, which is called the *Fragmentum Censorini,* even though the attribution is more than doubtful. It discusses the sky, the stars, the earth, geometry, music, and Latin metrics, a mixture of scientific and grammatical interests that might lead one to think of the author of the *De Die Natali* but that must not have been uncommon among the learned men of the period.

Gargilius Martial

We are put in mind of a similar combination of studies that for us are very different from one another by the works of Gargilius Martial, who died in 260 and was commemorated by his Mauretanian fellow citizens (he was born at Auzia, in Mauretania Caesariensis) in a long inscription that registers his military and political services. He had written works of history, such as a biography of Severus Alexander that is completely lost to us, and a *De Hortis.* As far as one can judge from the various extracts that have come down to us in medicinal collections, the chief concern of this work was the curative powers of the various plants. The *Curae Boum,* which is also partially preserved, shows an interest in veterinary medicine.

Solinus

Gaius Julius Solinus, who probably lived between the middle and the end of the third century (his dating varies from the beginning of the third to the end of the fourth century), was concerned with geography, though not in the modern sense of the term. His work is entitled *Collectanea Rerum Memorabilium,* but in the Middle Ages, when it was widely read, it was also known as *Polyhistor,* to emphasize the great number of curiosities that were collected there.

An encyclopedic compiler

The work is a careful compilation from many literary sources, chiefly Pliny the Elder but also Pomponius Mela and Suetonius, along with various other geographical treatises that are no longer extant. Solinus noted down all the unusual things he came across when reading these works, about peoples and their customs, animals, and plants; he sometimes also made large mistakes. The resulting book, written with a degree of elegance, well represents the qualities and the limitations of the intellectual class in this period, which was devoted chiefly to works of varied learning rather than of precise theoretical engagement.

The work opens with a full treatment of Rome and Roman history from the kings to the principate of Augustus. The area examined is then extended to Italy, and then to Greece and the Black Sea, Germany, Gaul, Britain, and Spain; this counterclockwise tour ends with Africa, Arabia, Asia Minor, India, and the kingdom of the Parthians, in accordance with a systematic geographical plan that is one of the most characteristic features of the work. Reference has already been made to the considerable success Solinus's work had in the Middle Ages, when it was also read and studied as a summary of the excessively vast *Naturalis Historia* of Pliny the Elder. It did not, however, altogether replace it, with the result that it enjoyed, so to speak, a success parallel to that of its more illustrious predecessor.

BIBLIOGRAPHY

Social Change

There are many works on history and society in the later Empire; see esp. A.H.M. Jones, *The Later Roman Empire* (3 vols., Oxford 1964), S. Mazzarino, *The End of the Ancient World* (London 1966), P.R.L. Brown, *The World of Late Antiquity* (London 1971), and R. Lane Fox, *Pagans and Christians* (London 1986). Note esp. work on sexuality in late antiquity in the wake of M. Foucault's *History of Sexuality,* vol. 3, *The Care of the Self,* and vol. 4, *The Uses of Pleasure,* trans. R. Hurley (New York 1985); see the review by A. Cameron, *JRS* 76 (1986) 266–71, P. Brown, *The Body and Society* (New York 1988), and A. Roussell, *Porneia,* trans. F. Pheasant (Oxford 1988).

The Origins of Christian Literature

There are texts of most Latin Christian authors in the Corpus Scriptorum Ecclesiasticorum Latinorum, or CSEL (Vienna 1866–), to be supplemented by the Corpus Christianorum (CC), Series Latina (Tunhout 1954–), and the volumes with French translation of the series Sources Chrétiennes (Paris 1941–). Where modern editions are not available (as is more often the case with later writers) recourse must still be had to the famous Patrologiae Cursus Completus, Series Latina, of J. P. Migne (229 vols., Paris 1844–). There are a number of guides to patristic literature; see esp. the *Patrologie* of B. Altaner and A. Stuiber (ed. 8 Fribourg 1978), the fifth edition of which has been translated into English by H. C. Graef (Fribourg 1960), and the four-volume *Patrology* of J. Quasten (Utrecht 1950–86; volume 4 is a collaborative work edited by A. di Bernardino, first published in Italian in 1978 and translated by P. Solari, Westminster, Md., 1986). Specifically on the Latin tradition, see S. D'Elia, *Letteratura latina cristiana* (Rome 1982), with bibliography. The *Oxford Dictionary of the Christian Church,* by F. L. Cross (ed. 2 Oxford 1974), is an invaluable reference work; of the many large-scale dictionary projects in the field of patristics and biblical studies, note esp. the German *Reallexikon für Antike und Christentum* (Stuttgart 1950–), the French *Dictionnaire de spiritualité* (Paris 1937–), and the short but comprehensive Italian *Dizionario patristico e di antichità cristiane* (Rome 1983–88).

The major edition of the Old Latin versions of the Bible by B. Fischer and others is still in progress (fasc. 1 Genesis, Fribourg 1951); see the introductory work *Kirchenschriftsteller Verzeichnis und Sigel,* by H. J. Frede (Fribourg 1981; cf. the "Aktualisierungsheft" of 1988), and the various studies *Aus der Geschichte der lateinischen Bibel* published as part of the same enterprise. See also the volumes of the series Collectanea Biblica Latina (Rome 1951–) and for the New Testament, A. Jülicher, *Itala* (Berlin 1938–63, Gospels only). The classic work comparing the older versions with Jerome's Vulgate is H. Rönsch, *Itala und Vulgata* (Marburg 1875). There is a lucid introduction to the texts by B. M. Metzger, *The Early Versions of the New Testament* (Oxford 1974).

There is an edition with English translation of several early martyr acts by H. Musurillo, *The Acts of the Christian Martyrs* (Oxford 1972).

There is a good general study of Tertullian by T. D. Barnes (ed. 2 Oxford 1985). For texts see the first two volumes of the CC; among the many other editions of his works might be singled out that of the *Adversus Marcionem* by E. Evans, with English translation (Oxford 1972), and the celebrated edition of the *De Anima* with English translation and commentary by J. H. Waszink (Amsterdam 1947). There is a convenient list of some other standard editions in the edition with English commentary of the *De Idolatria* by J. H. Waszink and J.C.M. van Wirken (Leiden 1987) 298–99. There is a Loeb edition of the *Apologia* and *De Spectaculis* by T. R. Glover (Cambridge, Mass. 1931).

The standard editions of Minucius Felix are the Teubner edition of B. Kytzler (Leipzig 1982) and the Budé of J. Beaujeu (Paris 1964), with French translation and notes; there is a Loeb edition by G. H. Rendall with Tertullian *Apologia* and *De Spectaculis* (Cambridge, Mass. 1931). See also the English translation with notes by G. W. Clarke (New York 1974).

Most of Cyprian's works are edited in CC 3 and 3A; for the letters, see the edition of le chanoine Bayard (2 vols., Paris 1945–61), as well as M. Bévenot, *The Tradition of Manuscripts* (Oxford 1961) and the English translation by G. W. Clarke (New York 1984–). There is a general study in English by M. M. Sage, *Cyprian* (Cambridge, Mass. 1975); see also C. Saumage, *St. Cyprien, évêque de Carthage, pope d'Afrique* (Paris 1975), and V. Saxer, *Vie liturgique et quotidienne à Carthage vers le milieu du IIIe siècle* (Rome 1969).

There is a text of Novatian in CC 4; for Victorinius of Pettou, see CSEL 49.

There is an edition of Commodian by A. Salvatore (Naples 1965–68); see also H. A. M. Hoppenbrouwers, *Commodien poète chrétien* (Nijmegen 1964), and A. Salvatore, *Interpretazioni commodianee* (Naples 1974).

The Final Poetry in the Style of the *Novelli*

For the *Anthologia Latina,* see the editions of A. Riese (Leipzig 1894–1906) and D. R. Shackleton Bailey (Stuttgart 1982; see the review of M. D. Reeve in *Phoenix* 39 (1985) 174–80; on the *Codex Salmasianus,* see M. Spallone in *Italia Medievale e Umanistica* 25 (1982) 1–71. A number of poets mentioned above may be found in the Loeb volume *Minor Latin Poets,* ed. J. N. and A. M. Duff (ed. 2 London and Cambridge, Mass. 1935). There is a separate edition of Pentadius by A. Guaglianone (Padua 1984, with bibliography).

There are useful editions of the *Pervigilium Veneris* by R. Schilling (Paris 1944) and E. Cazzaniga (Turin 1959, *Carmina Ludicra Romanorum*) and a full text with English translation and commentary by L. Catlow (Brussels 1980). The older edition by C. Clementi (Oxford 1936) is eccentric but includes much useful information in the notes. The edition in the Loeb Catullus by J. W. Mackail was revised by G. P. Goold (Cambridge, Mass. 1988). On the date and authorship, see most recently A. Cameron in *La poesia tardo-antica* (Messina 1984, conference proceedings) 209–34 (the volume contains a number of other articles of interest, though it is mainly on later figures) and D. Shanzer in *Rivista di Filologia* 118 (1990) 306–18.

On Reposianus, see J. Tolkiehn in *JKPh* 155 (1897) 615–23.

For Vespa's *Iudicium Coci et Pistoris,* see A. J. Baumgartner, *Untersuchungen zur Anthologie des Codex Salmasianus* (Baden 1981, with text, German translation, and commentary).

Hosidius Geta's *Medea* is edited by G. Salanitro (Rome 1981) with a survey of the cento and bibliography; see also the Teubner text of R. Lamacchia (Leipzig 1981). There are a number of articles on the text in *Studi in onore di A. Barigazzi* 1 = *Sileno* 10 (1984) 309–41. In English, see *Oxford Classical Dictionary,* s.v. "Cento."

The works of Terentius Maurus are edited by H. Keil in volume 6 of his *Grammatici Latini* (Leipzig 1864) 313–413; see also B. Effe, *Dichtung und Lehre* (Munich 1977) 231–32. There is a major edition of the *Disticha Catonis* with Latin commentary by M. Boas and H. J. Botschuyver (Amsterdam 1952); see also P. Roos, *Sentenza e proverbio nell'antichità e i "Distici di catone"* (Brescia 1984). Serenus Sammonicus's *Liber Medicinalis* has been edited by F. Vollmer (Leipzig and Berlin 1916) and R. Pépin (Paris 1951); see also Effe, *Dichtung und Lehre*, 199–204, which also has a section on Nemesianus (165–73). There are editions of the last by H. J. Williams (Leiden 1986), C. Giarratano (ed. 3 Turin 1943), and P. Vopilhac (Paris 1975, with French translation and brief notes); see also R. Verdière, *Prolégomènes à Nemesianus* (Leiden 1974), and H. Walter, *Studien zur Hirtendichtung Nemesians* (Stuttgart 1988).

On the schools of later antiquity, see H.-I. Marrou, *A History of Education in Antiquity,* trans. G. Lamb (London 1956), and S. F. Bonner, *Education in Ancient Rome* (London 1977). The grammarians are to be found in Keil's *Grammatici Latini* (7 vols., Leipzig 1857–80, with supplement by T. Hagen 1870): K. F. Halm, *Rhetores Latini Minores* (Leipzig 1863), is useful for the minor rhetorical treatises, some of which have separate editions.

For the legal writers, see F. P. Bremer, *Iurisprudentia Antehadriana* (Leipzig 1896–1901), E. Seckel and K. Kübler, *Iurisprudentiae Anteiustinianae Reliquiae* (Leipzig 1907–27), and S. Riccobono, *Fontes Iuris Romani Antejustiniani* (Florence 1941). The controversial work of A. Honoré (*Emperors and Lawyers* [Oxford 1981], *Ulpian* [Oxford 1982]) is discussed by F. Millar in *JRS* 76 (1986) 272–80, which offers further bibliography on the jurists between Gaius and the *Digest*. See also P. Lanfranco, *Il diritto nei retori romani* (Milan 1938), M. Villey, *Recherches sur la littérature didactique du droit roman* (Paris 1945), and G. G. Archi, ed., *Istituzioni guiridiche e realtà politiche nel tardo impero* (Milan 1976).

The standard edition of Censorinus is that of F. Hultsch (Leipzig 1867); this is not superseded by the edition of N. Sallmann (Leipzig 1983; see A. Grafton in *CR*, n.s. 35 [1985] 46–48), but the latter includes an up-to-date bibliography. There is a useful French translation with notes by G. Rocca-Serra (Paris 1980). There is an edition of Gargilius Martialis by S. Condorelli (Rome 1978; see also that of E. Lommatzsch in his edition of Vegetius, Leipzig 1903, and that of I. Mazzini, Bologna 1978, with Italian translation). For Solinus, the standard edition is still that of T. Mommsen (Berlin 1895).

From Constantine to the Sack of Rome (306–410)

1. THE GREAT CULTURAL RENAISSANCE

If the third century marked one of the most difficult periods for Latin culture, the fourth witnesses an impressive revival, which proceeds in step with the reestablishment of relative internal tranquillity. Diocletian's reforms and Constantine's economic and political policy, the long period during which his dynasty held the Empire unopposed, the military successes enjoyed on various fronts and the skillful external policies that made it possible to resolve the problems that could not be resolved by military means—all these were responsible for a surprising revival and for a literary flourishing that is one of the most impressive in the history of Rome.

Consolidation of the state

A state structure was consolidated that was strongly centered around the emperor and his court, with a high-level bureaucratic administration that, along with the army, constituted the principal support of the state. The economic reforms assured good revenues for the treasury, though at the cost of a grave worsening in the conditions of life, especially for the lower and lower-middle classes. The great latifundia, however, did well, especially the Gallic ones, with their *villae,* rural settlements where the proprietors now more and more often tended to settle, along with their field workers. The proprietors left the cities in order to manage their own interests better and to escape from the heavy administrative burdens that were laid upon the most prominent and prosperous persons of every urban center. Thus the gap in society widened between the wealthy large landowners and the

The flight from the cities

poor classes. The latter consisted of the urban proletariat, of peasants who were free at first but were then, in effect, enslaved to the owners of the latifundia through the institution of the *patrocinium potentiorum,* and of artisans impoverished by the cities' decline in importance. Various attempts to avoid the flight to the country were made by the central power through legislation that tended to bind each citizen to his *status* and his residence, but these were always ineffective, since mobility in this period was far greater than is generally recognized and far greater than the rulers would have liked. It must be said, however, that these phenomena were not found in equal measure across the territory of the Empire. Stronger in the West, the flight from the cities was far less noticeable in the East, where in some regions there were even phases of intense urbanization linked to an overall improvement in economic conditions.

In this centralized society with marked feudal traits, the senatorial classes, which had long since lost political and institutional power (which had passed into the hands of the military and the higher echelons of the bureaucracy), had come to wield economic power, which made them necessary participants in determining the political balance. The Empire was ruled through the consent of the few who were members of these privileged classes and the indifference of the great masses. The latter were concerned with problems of day-to-day survival and beyond this were interested, at best, only in religious matters, which, by a deliberate policy of the church, could not call into question the political and economic arrangements. By virtue of having become the representative of large segments of the population, however, the church, especially at the highest levels of the ecclesiastical hierarchy, was in a position to play a prominent role in the affairs of the Empire, and not solely in regard to religious problems. The figure of the bishop grew in prestige and authority, and, especially in the West, bishoprics increasingly came to be held by members of eminent Christianized senatorial families, who were tied to the groups that wielded economic power. The action of the bishops became more influential, while ultimately the church was profoundly transformed in its goals and its behavior.

Bishops from senatorial families; secularization of the church

The Great Heresies

The period from Constantine's recognition of Christianity to Theodosius's decision to make it the only state religion marks the passage for the new religion from the era of persecutions endured to the era of persecutions enforced, enforced against the pagans and all who did not declare their allegiance to Christianity, or professed it in forms regarded as heretical. Religion became an *instrumentum regni,* and in order to be able to take advantage of it the emperors were disposed to grant it favors and privileges. This undoubtedly contributed to the stability of the Empire, but it often obliged the court to intervene in disputes among the various Christian sects. The event of greatest moment, which risked compromising Christianity's function as a possible unifying element for the state, was the clash between Arianism and the doctrine that later proved victorious, the doctrine of the *homousia.* For Arius, a priest of Alexandria who lived in the first half of the century, Christ could not be considered equal to God the father without running the risk of introducing into Christianity elements of polytheism. The official church, however, maintained the substantial identity (*homousia*) between God the Father and Christ. From this arose a long controversy that saw the theologians taking up opposing positions: Arius won great approval in the East, though resolute opponents were not lacking, whereas in the West nearly all were against him, and they wrote numerous works to confute his theories. Between one council and another, one imperial intervention and another, the dispute dragged on for the entire century, and it had consequences in the following periods as well. The controversy

The heresy of Arius

began to introduce differences between the Eastern church and the Western, and it was exiled Arian bishops who converted the Germans, with the result that, after the invasions, relations between these peoples and Rome were rendered more difficult by this religious difference too.

The Manichean heresy

The Manichean heresy originated earlier (it goes back to the third century) but was still active in the fourth century. The Manicheans (so called from Mani, their leader, who was crucified perhaps in 276 in Persia) believed that there were two opposing principles, the good and the evil, that were engaged in constant struggle with one another. This dualism purported to explain the existence of evil in the world, which could not have been willed by God and therefore must go back to an independent origin; it ended up, however, by creating a double divinity and thus violating the principle of divine unity.

The Donatist heresy

The dispute over the Donatist heresy was violent, though it did not pose a serious threat to the unity of the church. The schism arose in Africa at the beginning of the fourth century and became widespread in that province after the end of the persecutions. Donatus and his sect maintained a severe and intransigent position, which set the church against the Empire and demanded of Christians a life of complete spiritual perfection. This strictness, which is typical of the African church (one thinks of Tertullian), had a notable success, and Donatism remained an enemy for the orthodox to combat at least to the end of the fourth century.

The heresy of Priscillian

The heresy of Priscillian lasted less long and was for the most part confined to Spain, with some influence on the Gallic church. We do not have precise details of its content—our chief source is the *Chronicorum Libri* of Sulpicius Severus, who devotes much space to Priscillian and his sect and shows a certain sympathy for it—but the theory of the Priscillianists appears to have contained Manichean elements, sometimes along with features of an exaggerated mysticism. What is certain is that the theological dispute was transformed into an internal division within the Spanish clergy, with mutual accusations of immorality and impiety, until the Empire intervened by decreeing that Priscillian be condemned to death, in 385. The sect survived for several more years, at least until the council of Toledo, in 400, which promoted the reabsorption of Priscillianism into the orthodox religion; but its decline was rapid, among other reasons because it was clearly condemned by many of the principal representatives of Christian culture.

The heresy of Pelagius

The story of Pelagianism is more complex. This heresy developed in the first half of the fifth century and thus should have been treated later, but it is appropriate to discuss it here in order to unify the treatment of the chief heretical movements and because Pelagius's greatest adversary was Augustine, who in his last years opposed the spread of his theories by every means he could (see pp. 685, 687).

Pelagius was a monk of British origin, active at Rome at the beginning of the fifth century and linked in friendship with many Christian writers of the day, such as Paulinus of Nola. We have an *Epistula ad Demetriadem seu Liber de Institutione Virginis* by Pelagius, a *Libellus Fidei ad Innocentium Papam,* and a commentary on Paul's *Epistles.* His fundamental work, however, the *De Libero Arbitrio,* in four books, is lost except for several fragments. The central point of Pelagius's heresy is the affirmation that good works, honest behavior, and a pure life can by themselves earn salvation and that man therefore, if he avoids sin and guilt, can win paradise for himself. The doctrine takes no account of the need for divine grace, by which God saves only those whom he has resolved to save in his plan of redemption; the role of human beings in salvation is thereby increased, and the role of Christ diminished. The fundamental place that Pelagius assigns to the individual, who strives with all his might for his own salvation, was not looked upon kindly by the official church, whose mediating role does not figure in his scheme. That explains not only the condemnation of Pelagius but also the success that he and his doctrine achieved in the high senatorial aristocracy of Rome, which was interested in choosing independently the ways in which to practice self-discipline. Pelagius's position, moreover, could not but arouse sympathy in the most zealous Christian circles, especially those that extensively practiced a life of privation and prayer, precisely because by valuing such behavior, Pelagianism provided grounds for monasticism and asceticism. For this reason, despite the fact that the Pelagian heresy was condemned officially and definitively in the second decade of the fifth century, forms of a more or less occult Pelagianism survived for a long time, particularly in the more prestigious religious houses of southern Gaul.

The Empire of the West and the Barbarians

The barbarian invasions

The other grave problem that the West found itself facing in the fourth century was, first, the pressure of the Germanic peoples and, then, their invasions into the territories of the Empire. Driven themselves by westward migrations of people living on the steppes, the Germans were forced to seek new lands beyond the Rhine. The emperors tried to resist this advance, alternating a policy of peaceful accords (conceding small slices of territory to be preserved and defended in the name of Rome) with military engagements (such as the one in which Julian was victorious in 357, assuring a decade of relative tranquillity). At the end of the century, however, the situation changed. The resistance by the Romans had been weakened by their need to reinforce the eastern border with the Persians, and the thrust of the Germans across the Rhine and the Danube became unstoppable. First the Visigoths, later the Ostrogoths, Vandals, Alanni, Suebi, and other peoples crossed the frontier. At first they were absorbed into the state and in some ways integrated into its administration, but then they were like enemy invaders. The front along the Rhine collapsed in 406, and bands of Germans crossed over, devastating all of Gaul and even reaching Spain. In the same years the Visigoths entered Italy from the east, led by their king Alaric, who in 410 succeeded in capturing and sacking Rome. This first wave of invasions did not, however, bring about the immediate collapse of the Empire: that did not occur for several decades.

The Germanic question was not confined to military aspects. Roman society in the fourth century saw members of those peoples placed in positions of great responsibility, first in the army, then in the state administration. Even though these Germans were always mindful of their obligations and defended the Empire courageously against the other Germans, nonetheless they were always regarded with great anxiety by the Romans, who were afraid that their institutions had been taken over, so to speak, by their own tenants. This danger seemed imminent especially in the time of Stilicho, but Roman civilization's ability to absorb and assimilate the barbarians who were to be found at the higher levels of the army and the political hierarchy always prevailed and carried the day.

The incursions of the Visigoths and the sack of Rome in 410 marked, for the Romans and particularly for the few pagans still tied to the traditional religion, the end of a world upon which the standards of value and the guiding principles of their existence had been based. The Christians, for their part, reacted to the invasions in a more complex but no less intense

manner. Many were deeply affected by them, to the point that they wondered whether the end of the world had come, with the destruction prophesied by *Revelations*. Others had moments of crisis: if the Roman Empire had been willed by God to make possible the spread of the true faith (a theory that retains a firm place in the theological and eschatological interpretations of history developed by Christian intellectuals down to Dante and beyond), and if the Roman peace was the necessary preliminary to the Christian peace, and ultimately was to be identified with it, how could God have permitted such destruction and the overthrow of everything that had been regarded as eternal and inalterable? But the more intelligent minds, and especially Augustine, drew from the unforeseen fall of the city that had been considered the "capital of the world" grounds for a substantial rethinking of the relation between religion and politics, in opposition to the tendency towards the secularization (and the Romanization) of Christianity. Refuting the charge that the last pagans had made against the Christians, namely, that the new religion had weakened the military and intellectual resistance of the state by putting its traditions into a state of crisis, this new apologetic proposes a different opposition, no longer between states and peoples, but between the two cities, the city of God and the city of man, coexisting spatially in all parts of the world, and engaged in a continuous struggle for salvation or damnation. It is a position that would become widespread in later periods and especially in the Middle Ages. Along with the seeds of the feudal economic system and the fusion between Latin and Germanic civilization, this religious innovation marks the passage from the ancient world to a different society.

The Grammarians: Charisius, Diomedes, Dositheus

The continuity with the past is quite strong, however, in the world of the school, which continues to follow the paths of quantitative and qualitative growth already noted in the previous century. The sons of senators and future bureaucrats passed through the schools, and in them were laid the foundations of the future ideological arrangements of the state; hence the great attention paid to them by the Christians, and also by the government, which passed much legislation about them. The legislation becomes especially precise under Julian, called the Apostate, emperor from 361 to 363, who attempted to restore the traditional religion: he prohibited Christian teachers from teaching in the schools and imposed the reading and study of pagan authors exclusively. As for the programs of teaching and the writing of textbooks, the tendency was towards creating large collections and encyclopedic repertories, which gathered together all classical culture in order to transmit it to posterity.

Among the works most important in this regard one can mention the grammar of Flavius Sosipater Charisius, who around the middle of the century taught at Rome and Constantinople and composed an *Ars Grammatica* in five books, dedicated to his son, with additional observations on stylistics and metrics; the *Ars Grammatica* of Diomedes, in three books, on morphology, stylistics, and metrics; and the *Ars Grammatica* of Dositheus, which is interesting because it is a Latin grammar intended for Greek-speaking students. All these works, but particularly Charisius's, preserve for us fragments of Latin works that would otherwise be lost.

Nonius Marcellus

By far the most important work in the field of grammar was the encyclopedic treatment by Nonius Marcellus, an African of perhaps the Constantinian period, who wrote a treatise entitled *De Compendiosa Doctrina,* in twenty books of greatly varying length (they run from the single page of the last book to the more than three hundred of the fourth book). The work, dedicated to his son, can easily be divided into two parts: the first, comprising books 1–12, which is incomparably more interesting for us, has a more properly linguistic and grammatical content, whereas the second, books 13–20, which is considerably shorter (it amounts to barely a twentieth of the *De Compendiosa Doctrina*), is devoted to individual subjects of a mostly antiquarian nature (ships, domestic utensils, clothing, food, etc.) and is concerned with describing Roman usages and customs.

Linguistic interests

Antiquarian interests

Quotations of early authors

In the history of Latin literature Nonius has a special importance, of what we might term a secondary character. The first part of the *De Compendiosa Doctrina* is organized as a series of lemmata, whose significance or use of particular meanings, and so on, Nonius explains, illustrating his explanation in each case by quoting from early authors, many of whom have not come down to us by direct tradition. The tragedies of Livius Andronicus, Naevius, Ennius, and especially those of Pacuvius and Accius; the *palliatae* comedies of Turpilius and the *togatae* of Titinius and Afranius; the Atellans of Pomponius and Novius; Laberius's mimes; the satires of Lucilius and those of Varro (the *Menippeans*); the historical works of Quadrigarius and Sisenna, Varro's *De Vita Populi Romani,* and Sallust's *Historiae*— all or at least a considerable part of these writings would be lost to us without Nonius's quotations.

It is therefore fortunate for us that Nonius is predominantly interested in the authors of the republican period, including the very earliest. This predilection, moreover, which has caused Nonius to be regarded as one of the last figures of the archaizing movement, is reinforced by his quotations of other authors, who have come down to us by direct tradition as well. Apart from the obvious names of Virgil and Cicero, those which recur most frequently in the *De Compendiosa Doctrina* are Plautus, Terence, and Lucretius.

Regardless of whether he is rightly accused of disorder, confusion, and quotations that are mistaken in form and substance, it is understandable why Nonius has always been the object of careful studies (which have intensified recently). Scholars seek to improve their understanding of the valuable library that Nonius must have had available and to reconstruct the criteria by which the grammarian arranged his lemmata. These are not arranged alphabetically, with the partial exception of books 2–4, in which, as was usual among the Romans, the alphabetization does not go beyond the first letter of the word, and even in those books it is believed that the alphabetical order is due, not to Nonius, but to later grammarians. Scholars

have even succeeded in discovering correspondences between the sequence in which the quotations from a given work appear in Nonius's text and the sequence in which the quoted passages were found within the original work (which is lost for us). If we did not have Nonius's quotations, a number of authors (e.g., Lucilius) would be little more than mere names for the modern reader, but thanks to the *De Compendiosa Doctrina* and the studies carried out on it, we now have many fragments and even, for some books, the possibility of a likely reconstruction of the whole. In short, every student of the fragments of early Latin must also be a student of Nonius Marcellus.

The Commentators: Donatus and Servius

The grammarians did not limit themselves to composing handbooks, but often wrote commentaries on the classics as well. These works are valuable for us because they not only document the complex grammatical teaching of some of the most distinguished schoolmasters but also allow us to understand how the great writers of earlier centuries were read and interpreted. Thus, Aelius Donatus, who was perhaps the greatest of the

fourth-century grammarians and who, around mid-century, had Jerome among his pupils at Rome, composed two treatises on grammar, an *Ars Minor* (more elementary, on the eight parts of speech) and an *Ars Maior* (for more advanced studies of stylistics and metrics). These were destined to become the textbooks through which for centuries, to the Middle Ages and beyond, the young would learn Latin. In addition to these very successful handbooks, he composed a commentary on Virgil, which, unfortunately, is almost completely lost, and also a commentary on Terence. Of the former,

all we have is a *Life of Virgil* (extremely helpful since it uses a reliable source such as Suetonius), an introduction to the *Bucolics,* and a dedication to Lucius Munatius. The latter has reached us virtually intact, lacking only the part on the *Heautontimoroumenos,* and includes stylistic and learned notes that are not confined to the text of Terence but touch upon various aspects of the ancient theater as well.

Tiberius Claudius Donatus

Tiberius Claudius Donatus, who until the past century was confused with Aelius Donatus, probably lived from the end of the fourth century to the beginning of the fifth. He was the author of *Interpretationes Vergilianae,* a commentary on Virgil, divided into twelve books, each of which discusses a book of the *Aeneid;* this work has come down to us intact.

Servius: the commentary on Virgil

The commentary on Virgil by Servius, who was probably a pupil of Aelius Donatus and then had a school at Rome, is exceptionally rich and complex. His fame is confirmed by Macrobius, who in his *Saturnalia* entrusts the discussion of difficult problems of Virgilian exegesis to Servius. The commentary belongs more or less to the first decades of the fifth century.

Servius Danieli

Today we possess two different versions: a shorter one, transmitted explicitly under Servius's name, and a longer one, which was discovered around 1600 by the French humanist Pierre Daniel and therefore called Servius Danielinus or Servius Auctus. It was long believed that the larger text was closer to the original commentary, which in the course of transmission through the centuries had undergone a series of reductions. Only at the end of the nineteenth century did intensified study of Servius make clear the unity of the short text (thus undermining the hypothesis that it is a drastically reduced version) and indicate, conversely, the often additive character of the Danieline notes. The tendency today is to regard Servius Auctus as the work of a compiler active sometime in the seventh or eighth century A.D. who combined Servius's commentary with other valuable ancient material, chiefly the commentary of Aelius Donatus, upon which Servius himself had drawn heavily.

Characteristics and importance of Servius's commentary

Both Servius proper and the expanded version of the commentary provide us with information about the composition of the works and interesting stylistic and grammatical observations on them. Much space is given to exegesis: different interpretations of the text are often given and are almost always discussed and judged. Much of this material is drawn more or less explicitly from older grammarians and Virgilian commentators. In addition, there are many scholia that preserve valuable antiquarian information, about religion and cult, or linguistic and prosodical observations, or allegorical interpretations of Virgil's works.

The entire commentary is interesting also for the purpose of reconstructing Virgil's text. In addition to the readings of the lemma, other readings found in different manuscripts are frequently cited. Servius, however (as well as Servius Danielinus, of course), is not important solely for the study of Virgil; he is also valuable evidence for the way the study of literary works was approached in antiquity. Nor should one undervalue the important role that this scholiastic material played in preserving, even if only fragmentarily, texts that would otherwise be lost. Thus the indirect tradition enriches our knowledge of authors whose work has not been transmitted to us intact but who owe their partial survival to grammarians and commentators.

The Rhetoricians

Arusianus Messius and the quadriga

Along with grammar, the study of rhetoric, which corresponded to secondary and higher education, flourished during this period. And for rhetoric, too, textbooks and treatises of great learning were produced, even if they were destined to be less popular than the grammatical works. Among the principal authors of this period one may mention Arusianus Messius, a political figure of some importance, who at the end of the century dedicated his *Exempla Elocutionis* to Olybrius and Probinus. This is an alphabetically arranged repertorium containing models of constructions drawn from four authors who from then on became exemplars and constituted the *quadriga,* the four fundamental writers whom every person of culture should know perfectly—Virgil, Sallust, Terence, and Cicero, listed in this order in the work's subtitle. Probably also belonging to the fourth century is the

Fortunatianus

Ars Rhetorica of Consultus Fortunatianus, who was long known, erroneously, as Chirius Fortunatianus. This is a manual in three books that became very popular in the schools, both for its organization of the material (subdivided into *inventio, dispositio,* and *elocutio*) and for its exposition, which is presented in the form of questions and answers.

Julius Victor

Finally, let us mention Gaius Julius Victor, chiefly to point out that his *Ars Rhetorica* reports examples drawn from a rhetorician whose name, Marcomannus, indicates a Germanic origin. Members of this nationality had become participants in Roman tradition and culture to such an extent that they took an interest in questions of rhetoric, one of the most refined products of classical civilization.

Macrobius

LIFE

There are few notices about Ambrosius Theodosius Macrobius, and scholars have proposed quite different reconstructions of his life. He was certainly not Roman, but neither is it certain that he was a native of Africa, as some think. He had a brilliant political career at Rome and had connections with the great families of the day, the Symmachi above all. According to the most accepted theory, his writings should be later than 384 and before the last decades of the fifth century. Many identify him with the Macrobius who was the prefect of Spain in 399 and the proconsul of Africa in 410. If this hypothesis is right, Macrobius was born shortly after the middle of the fourth century, perhaps around 360, and composed his principal work, the *Saturnalia,* between 384 and 395. Others, however, think that the writer should be identified with the Theodosius who was the praetorian prefect for Italy in 430. If this second hypothesis is right, Macrobius would not be born before 390, and the *Saturnalia* would be written between 430 and 440.

WORKS

Commentary on the *Somnium Scipionis* (a long passage from the last book of Cicero's *De Republica*), in two books, dedicated to his son Eustathius. The passage is not explicated word by word, as in the grammatical commentaries on Virgil or Terence that were common in this period, but it is more or less a pretext for expounding scientific and philosophic theories. *Saturnalia,* seven books of dialogues arranged over three days. *De Differentiis et Societatibus Graeci Latinique Verbi,* a treatise on Greek and Latin words dedicated to a Symmachus (we have only fragments of it). Macrobius's works belong in the line of that erudite literature, common in the fourth century, that ranges from linguistic, exegetical, and stylistic problems to scholarship and history, and from philosophy to religion.

Chronological problems with Macrobius

An evaluation of Macrobius's works is not easy, and it varies greatly according to the chronology one adopts. If we place these writings, which are deeply bound to the Roman and pagan tradition, in the last years of the fourth century, when conspicuous pagan circles continued to exist and writers and poets tied to the old religion were still at work, even in the milieu of the court, then the *Saturnalia* will be seen as one of the last cries of a paganism that is embattled in defense of its values. If, however, we place this work nearly at the middle of the fifth century, when Christianity had decisively defeated all pagan resistance and when the profession of Christianity had become a legal requirement for anyone who wanted to join the state administration, then the *Saturnalia* can be read as the idealized representation (in a world that is Christian by convention or convenience) of an epoch now closed, whose cultural message it wishes to preserve for posterity. In treating the *Saturnalia* as a work from the end of the fourth century, we follow the theory most commonly accepted, though we recognize that there are also valid arguments in favor of setting the author and his works in a period several decades later.

The Saturnalia: *characters of the dialogue*

After a preface dedicating the work to the author's son Eustathius, the *Saturnalia* is introduced by a prologue between two characters, Decius and Postumianus. The latter recounts to the former the learned conversations that took place in December of 384 at the houses of the leading members of the Roman aristocracy and were carried on by a group of important people in politics and culture who had gathered to celebrate the holiday of the Saturnalia (17–19 December). Figures of the first rank at Rome from the second half of the fourth century participate in the dialogue, including Vettius Agorius Praetextatus, who entertains the guests at his house on the first day, Virius Nicomachus Flavianus, the host of the second day, and Quintus Aurelius Symmachus, in whose house the third day's conversation is set. Among the other characters we find writers such as Avienus, grammarians such as Servius, philosophers such as Eustathius and Horus, doctors such as Disarius, orators such as Eusebius, politicians, and others. In order to enliven the setting, a character who is probably invented, Evangelus, distinguishes himself for ignorance and arrogance and provokes the corrections of the other characters. The first day, to which two books are given, is devoted to learned discussion of religious problems and to an account of the witticisms of the ancients. The second and third days, which fill the remaining books, concern Virgil, in whose works antiquarian information of every sort and valuable stylistic models are found. The work has several lacunae, including some large ones, which on occasion make it difficult to follow the thread of the discourse.

The typical setting

The setting chosen for the *Saturnalia* is based on principles followed in other, similar Greek and Latin works, which start with banquets and celebrations in order to recount the speeches made there. In this way they provide the doctrines treated with a literary framework that is supposed to lighten the reader's task and make the exposition more pleasant. Macrobius is very good at describing the pagan society of Rome, and his persons are felicitously characterized. The three hosts, Praetextatus, Flavianus, and Symmachus, stand out, especially the first of the three. From inscriptions and other works of the time, not to mention from the historical events of the second half of the fourth century, it is evident that these three senators are the principal representatives of the pagan party. Praetextatus was a high priest and an expert on Oriental cults but also a skillful politician who was able to tackle and resolve, among other things, the difficult problem of the clashes between Christian factions that plagued Rome after the election of pope Damasus. On the strength of his authority as prefect of Rome, he eliminated all strife by favoring the pope then in office, though he himself was a pagan. Flavianus was the praetorian prefect, and he played an important role in behalf of the usurper Eugenius, who was proclaimed emperor to support the claims of the pagans. Defeated by Theodosius, Flavianus chose suicide, in accordance with ancient Stoic tradition. In addition to his engagement in politics, he pursued literary activity and wrote historical works (see p. 645). Symmachus is the famous orator and epistolographer, about whom we will speak below; for us he is the most famous representative of these circles.

Macrobius assigns to these and the other persons remarks and speeches that accord well with their characters: the great expert on religion, Praetextatus, speaks about the calendar, pontifical law, and religious problems in general; the orator Symmachus speaks about Virgil's elegance; Servius comments on several difficult passages of Virgil's works; the philosopher Eustathius talks about philosophy in Virgil; and so on. On the whole, the exposition is carefully articulated, and monotony is avoided through various literary devices. The *Saturnalia* thus is readable in ways that other works of the same sort are not, and it becomes a work of a high order, quite apart from the usefulness of the information it contains. This derives from the most varied Greek and Latin sources, from Varro to Plutarch, from Suetonius to Gellius to many other minor men of learning who are more or less known to us. But Macrobius's ability lies in being able to combine his notes taken from this work or that into a unitary discourse, without noticeable differences between one section and the other.

Vitality of the classical tradition

In the peaceful circle of learned men that is presented to us, the questions under discussion are anything but trifling. The fundamental subject is the presence and the inheritance of classical culture, which is understood as a tradition both poetic and religious. Through persons such as Praetextatus and Flavianus the crucial questions of late paganism are taken up, with a theological and ethical systematization that moves towards defining a religious and philosophical system opposed to triumphant Christianity. Macrobius's interests in philosophy, especially neo-Platonism, are confirmed by the other work, the commentary on the *Somnium Scipionis,* which is full of astronomical observations as well as mystical and allegorical interpretations. This work was accompanied in the ancient manuscripts by the Ciceronian text that was the object of its commentary, and thus the *Somnium* was able to avoid the fate of the other books of the *De Republica.*

The Editing of the Classics

Other cultural activities that also flourished in this century derive from the passion for study. A lively textual criticism produces editions that are increasingly more correct and reliable; the transition from papyrus roll to parchment codex is now definitively completed, and the need is felt to finish this operation by preparing texts that are free from errors. Along with specialists in the field, the chief members of the most eminent families devote themselves to this task, emending the classics to the forms that subsequently will come down to us through the medieval manuscripts. Livy's history is edited by the families of the Symmachi and the Nicomachi, who are related to one another. Other learned men devote themselves to the works of Martial, Juvenal, Apuleius, and other ancient texts. Engagement in this first humanism was regarded as a fundamental duty of the intellectual and the politician, and its energy would not be spent in the course of a few decades but rather, at least in Italy, would last for a couple of centuries.

Chalcidius and Plato's Timaeus

Also stemming from this period is another work that was very popular in the Middle Ages, the translation of Plato's *Timaeus* and the partial commentary on it that were carried out by a Christian author, Chalcidius, at the suggestion of Hosius of Cordoba (on whom see p. 645). Until the humanists of the fifteenth century recover direct contact with the Greek language, Chalcidius's translation would be the West's only approach to the text of Plato.

The Panegyrists

Oratory, too, is linked to the world of education and to rhetorical culture, not only because declaiming speeches based on fictitious situations was still one of the most common and most important exercises in the rhetorical schools but also because the schoolteachers were often the ones to give the official speeches in which the emperors were thanked for what they had done on behalf of the state or a particular region. This is a well-defined literary genre, not a new one, but one recently sanctioned by Greek orators and especially by Menander of Laodicea (third century A.D.), the genre of the panegyric.

An important collection of such speeches has come down to us under the name *Panegyrici Latini,* comprising twelve speeches that cover the period from the end of the third century to the end of the fourth, with the exception of the first in the series, which is the panegyric of Trajan delivered by

Pliny the Younger (see p. 526). After this speech, which is placed at the beginning on account of the importance of the author and because it is by far the oldest, the other eleven follow in loose order. Two of these are dedicated to Maximian, Diocletian's colleague in the Empire, and a third is dedicated to Maximian and Constantine jointly; one is for Constantius, the father of Constantine; four speeches are addressed to Constantine (plus the one to him and Maximian jointly), one to Julian, and one to Theodosius; and one, finally, is intended, not for an imperial person, but for the governor of Gaul.

The collection, as it has come down to us, was assembled in Gaul sometime between the end of the fourth and the beginning of the fifth century. After Pliny's panegyric, which must have been a sort of undisputed model, three other speeches follow that give the authors' names: Latinius Pacatus Drepanius, author of the panegyric on Theodosius, the last in chronological sequence (389); Flavius Claudius Mamertinus, who thanks Julian for having appointed him consul for 362; and Nazarius, a Gallic rhetorician, the author of a panegyric on Constantine from the year 321. The other seven speeches, collected under the title *Panegyrici Diversorum,* all go back to the milieu of the Gallic schools, and most of them are anonymous.

This collection of speeches covers exactly a century of eulogistic oratory, and it allows us to analyze, on the basis of adequate data, a literary genre of great importance in late antiquity. Modern readers may be astonished and annoyed by the excessive praise and unjustified glorification lavished on the powerful addressees, but they must keep in mind that in the ancient world the written speech was the sole means of mass communication and the vehicle for spreading and advertising political programs. The professional orator delivering his panegyric thus performed the same function as the publicist organizing a campaign of persuasion, but perhaps with greater independence and creativity. In citing the qualities of the emperor he described a series of values, and if he tried to win his listeners over to the project of those who wielded power, yet he was also able to stress to the latter those elements he regarded as more important and play down aspects that seemed less persuasive to him. The panegyric, therefore, was not a one-way communication, proceeding from the throne to the subjects, since it also caught in some ways the needs and desires of the people and presented them to the ruler skillfully blended with his praises.

The panegyrics thus are interesting on several levels, which often cannot be separated. They inform us about the schools of rhetoric, the instruction offered in them, and therefore the cultural and ideological training not only of the rhetoricians but also of the entire important class of the bureaucrats and those who exercised economic power. They show us the literary tendencies of late ancient prose, its substantial continuity with the prose of the first and second centuries (it is not coincidental that the first piece in the collection is Pliny's panegyric of Trajan). They illustrate for us the political principles according to which different emperors acted, or wished people to believe they acted. They also document for us the conditions of

The panegyric as instrument of propaganda and participation

The panegyric as a vehicle of political and cultural thought

life or specific occurrences in the period. Of course, not all the speeches are equally valuable or equally successful. Sometimes the speaker, because of his concerns and his fear of compromising himself by adopting too precise a position, falls into generalities, avoids the hottest issues, or takes refuge in the most convenient commonplaces. And yet, if one looks carefully, one notes that this happens quite rarely, and often it is merely our own fault if we cannot catch the indications and the precise references that, though skillfully contained in subtle allusions, did not escape the notice of the ancient public, which was familiar with them.

One of the most famous panegyrics is Eumenius's, delivered in 298 at Autun before the governor of Gallia Lugdunensis and commonly entitled *Pro Instaurandis Scholis.* The devastations that had afflicted the Empire in the third century had struck that city also, depriving it of its schools, which at one time were renowned. Now, however, in the new climate of peace and hope created by Diocletian's tetrarchy, one could hope for their rapid reconstruction. Eumenius, named head of these schools and given a high salary, appears before the governor in order to hasten the reconstruction, and to this end he devotes a considerable part of his speech to the importance that the instruction and training of the new generation has for the well-being of the state.

Symmachus

Oratory, since it was chiefly practiced by the teachers of rhetoric, true professionals of the word, was closely connected with the world of education. And yet the most famous of the fourth-century orators, Symmachus, who is also a great writer, does not come from an academic setting, but rather from the Roman senatorial aristocracy.

Quintus Aurelius Symmachus, nicknamed Eusebius, was born into a noble family around 340–45. His father, Lucius Aurelius Avianius Symmachus, called Phosphorius, was an important senator. Symmachus had a rapid and successful political career. Among his more important posts one must mention the proconsulate of Africa and especially the prefecture of Rome, which he held from 383 to 385. As consul in 391, he was often sent to the court as the representative of the Roman Senate. He died around 402–3. By his wife Rusticiana he had two children, a girl who married a son of Nicomachus Flavianus and a boy, Quintus Fabius Memmius Symmachus, who continued his father's literary interests.

Of the many speeches he wrote, which made him famous, only eight have come down to us, mostly in quite lacunose form; three are addressed to the emperors Valentinian and Gratian and are true panegyrics, and five were delivered in the Senate. The *Letters* are better preserved, a correspondence in ten books containing more than nine hundred letters. The *Relationes,* finally, are about fifty official letters sent to the emperors during the time he was prefect of Rome.

In the judgment of the ancients Symmachus was the orator par excellence, and they paid little attention to his other works. Moderns, however, are obliged to value him above all for his letters, which have come down to us in great numbers and constitute one of our best sources on late antiquity. Only a few fragments of the speeches are extant; some speeches that the ancients extolled as masterpieces of oratorical art and political ability we do not have at all, and even those of which some part is preserved are seriously lacunose.

The latter are mostly youthful works: two panegyrics of Valentinian, which can be dated to 369 and 370, one of Gratian, from 369; a later speech *pro patre,* delivered in the Senate, offers thanks for the consulship granted to his father and takes the opportunity to praise the emperors. Only a few sentences remain to us from the other senatorial speeches, which dealt with the political career of persons more or less eminent in the senatorial milieu. If the speeches to the emperors show all the characteristics proper to panegyrics, what we can reconstruct of the senatorial speeches goes back to the structures typical of the schools of rhetoric, with their declamations, skillfully articulated and full of pathos.

Symmachus's correspondence belongs to a literary tradition made famous for the imperial period by Pliny the Younger. It presents us with a gallery of the most important persons of the day. Praetextatus, Nicomachus Flavianus, Ausonius, Ambrose, and other great men of culture find their place here alongside generals of barbarian origin, such as Richomeres, Stilicho, and Bauto; close relatives; and people whom Symmachus may never have seen in person and whom he addresses only because of the requirements of courtesy that were so operative in a complex society like that of late antiquity. So great a mass of letters is a valuable source of information, much still waiting to be exploited. Among the subjects most often dealt with is friendship, which is understood as the assurance of mutual favors exchanged by two friends. For this reason there are many letters of recommendation (even Augustine made use of a recommendation from Symmachus to obtain the chair of rhetoric at Milan). Yet the letters also contain information on building activity in Latium and Campania, references to several large administrative scandals and their judicial consequences, and
complaints about the exorbitance of the taxes. The style is agreeable throughout, tending to a brevity that Symmachus declares the principal virtue of a letter and not without the odd flash of wit.

The correspondence was not published by Symmachus, but by his son Memmius, between 402 and 408; thus we cannot with any certainty attribute to the author the criteria by which the letters were selected and collected. It is evident that all the letters addressed to the more awkward figures, such as usurpers or treacherous commanders, have been eliminated and that in general a discreet censorship has been exercised, the terms of which we do not know. The last book, which completes the collection and brings the total number of books to ten, the same number as in Pliny the Younger's correspondence, contains the personal letters to the emperors.

Most of this book has been lost, with only a letter to Theodosius and one to Gratian remaining.

The Relationes: *a vivid picture of bureaucratic and political reality*

The *Relationes,* by contrast, are official letters, sent to the emperors in regard to administrative matters about which the prefect of Rome needed to inform the court and to receive orders from it. If the correspondence is valuable for its notices about everyday life, the *Relationes* reveals the world of the bureaucracy and the complex web of legal questions and political interests that shaped the activity of a high state official. Full of information about law and procedure, they have been studied more by historians and jurists than by philologists, except for the famous third *relatio,* about the altar of Victory, which saw Symmachus and Ambrose adopt opposing positions and which has always been taken as a symbol of the final conflict between pagans and Christians, ending in the decisive supremacy of the latter.

The third relatio *and the problem of the Altar of Victory*

The Altar of Victory had been placed in the Senate house by Augustus and had remained there without problem until Constantine, who had had it removed because it was a symbol of the old religion. Put back in its place by Julian, it was removed again by Gratian in 382. The Senate, the majority of which was still pagan, sent Symmachus and other influential senators to court, but the delegation was not received, because Pope Damasus and Ambrose intervened with Gratian. In 383 Gratian was killed by the usurper Maximus, and the pagans made a strong recovery, Praetextatus being appointed praetorian prefect and Symmachus prefect of Rome. The senators then made an attempt, once again through Symmachus, to obtain from the emperor Valentinian II the restoration of the altar. The third *relatio* is the text in which he is asked, in the name of religious freedom, to grant the pagans the right to worship their divinities. Once again the response was given by Ambrose, who by means of two letters threatening the emperor with excommunication saw to it that the petition was rejected and Christianity confirmed as the only permitted religion (see p. 680).

Symmachus's essay is elegant and moving. Rome itself, personified, asks that Victory always remain by her side, making her plea in the name of a glorious past and of the mystery that surrounds faith: *uno itinere non potest perveniri ad tam grande secretum* ("by following only one path it is not possible to attain to so great a mystery"). But along with the devotion to Rome's ancient glory and the worship of its past we find more concrete economic motives as well: the emperor should restore its finances to the cult, because the pagans know well that if the sum necessary for maintaining the priests is not forthcoming, the maintenance of the ancient cults and the traditional priests will become increasingly problematic. Behind a dispute that in appearance is entirely ideological—in engaging in it, Symmachus distinguishes himself by his formal elegance and his ability to touch the most powerful emotional cords, and Ambrose by his firmness, which nearly becomes arrogance, and by his certainty of being on the winning side—there is thus more than an altar or a question of respect for traditions: the argument has to do with large amounts of money and thereby with immediate, pressing questions of prestige and power.

Matters of power in sublimated form

The Scientific Disciplines

Grammar and rhetoric held a dominant position in the late ancient schools, but they did not occupy the whole field of the disciplines; there was room also for scientific subjects, from medicine to veterinary science, from agriculture to geography. And in these subjects, too, handbooks for the use of students and treatises for practical use are produced, with particular attention to the technical aspects. Late antiquity, in fact, witnesses in this field a particular flourishing of specialist works, fostered by favorable legislation and motivated by practical economic or military needs. Even for the armies and the sciences of war, specially composed works deal with the chief theoretical problems and furnish us in addition with indications of how people acted in particular situations.

The so-called *Medicina Plinii* was probably composed in the first half of the century. In three books, it reworks material drawn from the *Naturalis Historia,* also adding new prescriptions devised by the author and including as well some suggestions for the preparation of cosmetic products. In the preface the author declares that he wants to furnish everyone with protection from the greed of doctors, who demand exorbitant fees for their services. At the beginning of the fifth century, Theodorus Priscianus wrote *Euporiston Libri,* which have come down to us virtually intact. From the end of the fourth century to the start of the fifth several other medical works were also composed, among them a *Herbarium,* which during the Middle Ages were attributed to Apuleius on account of his reputation as a scientist. For veterinary medicine, in addition to a treatise on diseases of

horses, the work of Pelagonius (second half of the fourth century), the anonymous *Mulomedicina Chironis,* a Latin reworking in ten books of a Greek original, and especially the *Mulomedicina* of Flavius Vegetius Renatus

deserve mention. Vegetius, a Christian, lived at the end of the fourth century, held important military and political offices, and composed four books of notes on veterinary medicine derived from earlier Greek and Latin handbooks. Almost as if to demonstrate the close connections between this science and the problems of military art (horses were vital for the armies of late antiquity), Vegetius also wrote a treatise entitled *Epitome Rei Militaris,* also divided into four books, which reuses earlier sources on recruiting, formations, the tactics of battle and siege, and naval engagements.

Another treatment of military art is the anonymous *De Rebus Bellicis,* written in the second half of the fourth century. It is one of the most intelligent works of late antiquity, both because of the many technological innovations it proposes in the field of military machines and because of the acute observations on economy and politics found here and there in the work.

The fourteen books of the *Opus Agriculturae,* or *De Re Rustica,* of Palladius Rutilius Taurus Aemilianus deal with agriculture. Palladius devotes books 2–13 to the tasks to be done in the individual months of the year, the first book functioning as a general introduction. At the end Palladius adds a section on grafting, in verse, as book 14 (Columella, we recall, had also written the tenth book of his treatise on agriculture in hexameters). Palladius's work, written between the end of the fourth century and the beginning of the fifth, presents the point of view of the landed proprietor in the West, facing rapid technological innovation and social change that would lead to a different organization of work.

Geography: Vibius Sequester

Vibius Sequester had an interest in geography. He is the author of *De Fluminibus Fontibus Lacubus Nemoribus Paludibus Montibus Gentibus per Litteras,* an alphabetical listing of information drawn from the poets, especially Virgil and Lucan, and from the various commentaries available. Several geographical handbooks, itineraries, and maps also belong to the same period, from the fourth to the fifth century, such as the so-called *Itinerarium Antonini,* composed after Diocletian, which describes the travels of the emperor Antoninus Pius, and the *Itinerarium Hierosolymitanum,* which tells of a trip made in 333 from Bordeaux to Jerusalem (hence the title), on to Rome, and finally to Milan. Among all these accounts of travel, the most

The Peregrinatio Aetheriae

famous is the *Itinerarium Egeriae,* also known as the *Peregrinatio Aetheriae* (the name of the woman author is not reported uniformly by the manuscripts). Written by a noblewoman, who was probably Spanish, and dedicated to her sisters in Christ, it narrates a pilgrimage to Sinai, Palestine, and Mesopotamia made around the end of the fourth century. The work is justly famous for the captivating simplicity of its exposition and especially for the very peculiar language that the author employs, which combines classical forms with words and syntactic structures that are characteristic of the spoken language. This is a Latin that in various aspects foreshadows the future developments of the Romance languages.

The De Ponderibus et Mensuris

A genuine treatise of metrology in verse is the *De Ponderibus et Mensuris,* 280 hexameters addressed by a certain Remius Favinus (thus the manuscripts, but some prefer to read Remmius Flavianus) to a Symmachus, who could be the son of the famous orator. It deals not only with the weights and measures of the Greeks and Romans and the mathematical formulas to be used for converting from one system to another but also with liquids and some interesting problems of physics.

2. THE TRIUMPH OF CHRISTIANITY

Constantine's empire marks a stage of profound changes for Christianity that go beyond the official recognition contained in the Edict of Milan (313), which sanctioned the legality of the new religion. The expansion of Christianity in the prosperous and powerful classes, the emperor's attention to theological disputes, and the rapid change in the Christians from a stance that was defensive (though lively and sometimes violent, like the stance of the earlier apologists) to a position of power and even ideological monopoly all necessarily entailed profound upheavals that left their mark on dogma as well as on organization, on the social composition of the clergy as well as on literature. One can get an idea of the rapidity with which these changes occurred by comparing the positions of three writers who lived only a few years apart from one another: Arnobius, Lactantius, and Firmicus Maternus.

Arnobius

Arnobius was born in Africa, at Sicca Veneria, around the middle of the third century. A schoolteacher in that city, he converted to Christianity rather late, in the last years of the century. He died at a fairly advanced age, around 327.

Adversus Nationes, in seven books, written after the persecutions of Diocletian, which are mentioned in the work, but before the Edict of Milan, and so probably between 305 and 310. The first two books expound Christian doctrine and dismiss charges that the Empire's recent misfortunes are due to it. Books 3–5 deal with the theological doctrines of polytheism, which are refuted in the last two books.

The anti-pagan polemic of a convert

Arnobius's defense shows strong traces of the violence that characterizes the first Christian writers from Africa. It is no accident that Arnobius chose for his work a title that closely echoes that of Tertullian's first work, the *Ad Nationes.* But Arnobius is also a newcomer, converted only in adulthood, if not on the very threshold of old age, and for this reason, too, he feels more keenly the need to polemicize against the things he had believed in since his youth. His recent conversion, however, also proves to be theologically questionable in certain regards; it shows itself in gross confusions that go well beyond any heresy and in an uninformedness that often borders on real ignorance. The entire work moves along these two tracks, anti-pagan aggressiveness and doctrinal inexactness, as Arnobius alternates pages of elegant rhetoric (he taught in the rhetorical schools, we recall) with bizarre, fantastic passages, which combine themes of Christianity with theories of the philosophical and religious sects that Arnobius wants to combat.

The polemic against neo-Platonism

His chief aim was to demonstrate the error of neo-Platonism. But Arnobius must himself have passed through these experiences, and the influence of the mystery cults remained with him. Because of his profession, he was more familiar with the pagan classics than with the Bible. He used the New Testament little and criticized the Old Testament as a Jewish fable. For Arnobius, the human soul had not been created by God, but by a kind of demiurge, who was inferior to God and thus capable only of an imperfect creation; thus the soul is mortal, and immortality is reserved exclusively for the good and depends on a special, subsequent divine intervention. On Christ, too, Arnobius's position is rather odd: certainly inferior to the Father, he had only the function of a teacher. But while Arnobius is unreliable on Christian theology, he is well informed on paganism, which he criticizes with irony and sometimes with relish, and always with literary

Satiric realism against paganism

success, with a realism of satire or comedy that recalls the best writers of the classical era.

With his tormented and unresolved movement from paganism to Christianity, Arnobius represents for us the journey of many men of culture from the third and fourth centuries, who found themselves beset by doubt and persecutions, emotional ties and fears of retaliation. If it is true, as it seems to be, that the *Adversus Nationes* was written by Arnobius to demonstrate the doctrinal solidity of his own faith to a bishop who questioned it, reading the seven books confirms that the bishop's concerns were not unfounded. But the occasional circumstance that led to the work's composition has provided us with a valuable picture of the complicated intersections between old faith and new, between philosophy, the mysteries, and theosophy.

Lactantius

LIFE

Lucius Caelius Firmianus Lactantius was born around the middle of the third century in Africa. He was a pupil of Arnobius, and like him, he became a teacher of rhetoric. He taught Latin rhetoric at Nicomedia, in Bithynia, where he was at the time when Diocletian's persecutions burst out and forced him to abandon teaching: at Nicomedia Lactantius had been converted to Christianity. In 317 he was chosen by Constantine as tutor for his son Crispus, and he went to Gaul to take up this task. He died after 324.

WORKS

The writings from his pagan period are completely lost: a *Symposium,* a *Hodoeporicum,* describing in verse his voyage from Africa to Bithynia, and a grammatical treatise. From the later period his *Letters,* in eight books, are also lost. Six works are extant: the *De Opificio Dei,* written between 303 and 305, on the perfect harmony of nature and the immortality of the soul, which Lactantius defends with conviction; the *Divinae Institutiones,* in seven books, dedicated to Constantine, which were begun in 304 and completed in 314, with additions in the years 322–24, of which the first two books are against paganism, the third is against philosophy, the fourth is about Christ, the fifth and sixth are about Christian theology, and the seventh is about the Last Judgment and the destiny of souls; from 314, an *Epitome* that summarizes and reworks the *Divinae Institutiones;* from the same year, the *De Ira Dei,* on the necessity for God to grow angry against the wicked in order to demonstrate his love for the good; the *De Mortibus Persecutorum,* of 315, with additions of 320, which records the dramatic deaths of all who persecuted Christians; and finally the poem *De Ave Phoenice,* an elegy upon the phoenix, the symbol of Christ, whose attribution to Lactantius is uncertain.

Systematic argumentation and classically balanced exposition

Although he was a pupil of Arnobius, Lactantius, especially in his earlier and larger works, is a systematic and balanced thinker, far removed from his teacher's excesses in both argumentation and style. Traditionally compared to Cicero, Lactantius employs large, well-articulated periods, does not like phrases used for effect, and puts his trust in a reasoning that is engaging and calm. Whereas the *De Opificio Dei* still shows the influence of a philosophical approach that had its origin in classical schools of thought, and especially in Stoicism, and only occasionally displays more definite traits of Christianity, the *Divinae Institutiones* sets out to be a fundamental book for the systematization of Christian doctrine, just like the many *institutiones* composed in late antiquity on various subjects, especially law. It is another question whether Lactantius succeeded in painting the organic picture he intended, and again whether the acuity of his thought is comparable to that of the great Greek Christian thinkers or, among the Latins, Augustine. There is no doubt that Lactantius is more a careful philologist and a scrupulous scholar than an original philosopher or creator of theories, but one should appreciate all the more the importance of his achievement in moving apologetic from the level of passionate argument to that of rational analysis. Lactantius studies polytheism, seeking its roots in the divinization of great men who have died and exploring a line of continuity from ancient wisdom to modern. He thus tends to reduce the differences by treating them as due to evolution, an evolution from error to truth, from philosophy to faith.

Lactantius thus breaks with the apologetic tradition of Tertullian, which was still clearly present in Arnobius, and, in accordance with Constantine's program, he tries to present a Christianity that is dominant because it is able to avail itself of the best of ancient culture. Christianity becomes virtually the natural result of classical *sapientia;* it ought not to inspire fear, therefore, and can become Rome's new religion without too many problems. The confirmation of ancient values, reaffirmed without excessive changes in the light of the new faith; a liberal inspiration deeply consistent with the calm classicism of his style; a view of salvation following upon an end of the world that is no longer catastrophic but is described with the colors of the Golden Age—all these are clear signs of how much the Western world has changed in the ten years from the persecutions of Diocletian to the Edict of Constantine.

Even the two works with the most severe and vindictive titles, the *De Ira Dei* and the *De Mortibus Persecutorum,* do not contradict this picture. The first text affirms the equilibrium of the world, which is maintained through the divine punishment of the wicked, and ends up being actually more consolatory than threatening. The second, which is apparently so far removed from Lactantius's other attitudes that doubts have often been cast on its authenticity, fits in well with the Constantinian program, but from another point of view and along the lines of another literary genre, the genre of historiography. The emperors are divided into two categories: those that have tolerated or helped Christianity and those that have persecuted it. The latter are the wicked emperors, who have harmed the state and have rightly suffered divine punishment, whereas the former are the good emperors, and among all the best is Constantine. The conditions are thus established for the emergence of a religious historiography in Latin, and at the same time a start is made towards creating the myth of Constantine, who is the symbol of the relation between political power and the church. It is interesting to observe that the two leading themes of the *De Mortibus,* the triumph of the church and the glorification of Constantine, are present on an ampler scale in the work of his Greek-speaking contemporary Eusebius of Caesarea. In those same years Eusebius, with his *Historia Ecclesiastica,* was opening up a new perspective for historical writing, one in which the church and its affairs became the center of interest for the narrative.

Firmicus Maternus

A rhetorician and lawyer from Sicily—he may have been born at Syracuse—Julius Firmicus Maternus was active about twenty years after Lactantius. Before his conversion, which occurred between 337 and 346, Firmicus wrote the *Matheseos Libri VIII,* the most complete Latin treatise of astrology that has come down to us. Its philosophical basis is neo-Platonism, onto which are grafted astrological and divinatory doctrines, presented as the only science that can put man in touch with divinity and his own fate. The work contains many moralistic digressions and references to persons and events of the day. After conversion Firmicus wrote the *De Errore Profanarum Religionum,* dedicated to the emperors Constantius and Constantine. The refutation of paganism is carried out with the violence that had characterized the early apologists, with heavy sarcasm and a forensic manner of oratory. It is accompanied by exhortations to the emperors to confiscate all the property of the pagan temples, to compel by force all who still believe in the old religion to renounce it, and, if necessary, to put to death those not prepared to convert. The work is the most evident testimony of how things have now changed in favor of Christianity. In some circles, which Firmicus represents well, a climate of intolerance has arisen, which would alternate with more reasonable, more humane positions until all pagan resistance is eliminated or absorbed.

Firmicus and the climate of intolerance against the pagans

The Anti-Arians

Among the Christian writers who lived under the reign of Constantine's descendants, some are distinguished for being particularly active in the polemic against the Arians. Lucifer, bishop of Cagliari, was even exiled, from 356 to 361, for his fierce anti-Arian position. During the years of exile he wrote five treatises attacking the emperor Constantius, who was an Arian. Another determined adversary of the Arians was Eusebius, bishop of Vercelli from 345 onwards, who was also exiled to the East for religious reasons. Some letters of his are extant. And Zeno, the bishop of Verona from 360 to 370, was clearly anti-Arian. We have several speeches of his, as well as summaries of unelaborated sermons. But the most important figure in the battle against the heresy of Arius is certainly Marius Victorinus.

Lucifer of Cagliari

Marius Victorinus

Gaius Marius Victorinus was of African origin. Born around 300, he went to Rome to practice the profession of rhetorician, which he did with great success. For his academic abilities and his qualities as a forceful orator, a statue was erected to him in the Forum in 353.

In this period his positions were far removed from Christianity, showing rather the influence of neo-Platonism. His conversion, which must be placed around 355, greatly astonished his contemporaries. When the

LIFE

emperor Julian forbade Christians to teach in the pagan schools a few years later, Victorinus retired from teaching (362) and devoted himself entirely to Christian writings on religious subjects. We have no information about the date of his death.

An *Ars Grammatica,* two books of commentary on Cicero's *De Inventione,* and a *De Definitionibus,* which takes up Aristotelian theories, all belong to the period of his activity as a teacher. To his Christian period belong the *Ad Candidum Arianum,* which includes among other things three books *Adversus Arium;* three sacred hymns; and a series of commentaries on Paul's *Epistles.*

Marius Victorinus, despite his great zeal in the struggle against Arianism, does not reach the level of importance of other distinguished persons, for example, Hilary of Poitiers, of whom we shall speak next. Even the church of the day passes rather varied judgments upon him. Jerome did not like him and considered him too obscure and comprehensible only to a restricted number of educated persons, whereas Augustine esteemed him highly, since he could better appreciate a Christianity that was born from neo-Platonism and was still full of philosophical elements deriving from that school of thought. The studies of logic to which Victorinus had

Logical studies and neo-Platonic training, the basis of Victorinus's anti-Arian thought

devoted himself before conversion, and to which he had made the significant contribution of a specific Latin vocabulary for formal logic, make him a rather isolated thinker and one not understood in the late ancient and medieval Christian world; only recently have we returned to positive judgments of him, following in the footsteps of Augustine. Today we appreciate the originality of his thought directed against Arianism, one that does not merely follow the official position but was personally drawn from his neo-Platonic training. In the exegesis of Paul's *Epistles,* too, Victorinus employs a system different from that of the Christian tradition and closer to that of the commentaries on the classics that were produced in the schools, with ample paraphrases explaining the text word by word.

His principal work, the *Ad Candidum Arianum,* has a structure that is interesting in literary terms as well. This Arian Candidus is certainly a fictitious figure, a heretic in good faith, and a friend of Victorinus, who tries to convince him to return to orthodoxy.

In the hymns, too, Victorinus is different from the other writers we know of by virtue of his free verse technique, which more nearly resembles rhythmic prose than any precise meter. Here again we find a large neo-Platonic element and strong anti-Arian tones, which are joined to a biblical lyricism that renders these three poems even more remote from the classical tradition.

Hilary of Poitiers

Hilary was born around 315 at Poitiers to a prosperous family. He converted at a mature age and in 350 became bishop of his city. Exiled in 356 because of his explicitly anti-Arian position by the emperor Constantius, who was a follower of Arianism, he remained for several years in Phrygia, where he composed his most famous works. Returning to Gaul in 360, he continued the struggle up to the time of his death, which came about in 367.

WORKS

Among his many writings, the most important are the twelve books *De Trinitate;* the *De Synodis,* which describes for Westerners the discussions held in several Eastern synods; a series of shorter works against Constantius; and the *Hymns,* which are the first written in the West.

The Christological problem

Important for the political role he played in the battle against Arianism, Hilary was certainly the most subtle and original of the Western Christian thinkers before Augustine. At the center of his speculation stands the problem of Christ, about which the controversy between Arians and Catholics raged most fiercely. Hilary treats the problem with the refinement typical of Greek theological developments, yet always with a lively attention to the relevant biblical passages and to several central questions of Western patristics, such as the question of time (in this respect as well Hilary may be considered a precursor of Augustine). His style is heavy and monotonous, though recently its monumentality and nobility have come in for renewed appreciation.

Hilary's Hymns

The *Hymns,* which are the first in Latin whose author is known, deserve separate treatment. Of all the hymns written by Hilary and collected in the *Liber Hymnorum,* only three are extant, and they are lacunose for the most part, though sufficiently preserved for us to note certain characteristics, such as the variety of meters (aeolic meters, iambs, trochees), the frequent liberties with prosody, the preference for alphabetic poems (where the first strophe begins with *a,* the second with *b,* and so forth), and the constant presence of the anti-Arian theme. In this regard as well Hilary is a precursor (of Ambrose, the greatest of the Latin hymnographers).

Poetry: Juvencus, Optatianus, Tiberianus

Until the age of Constantine, Christian authors had written in prose, both because the subjects addressed did not belong among those traditionally treated in poetry and also on account of prejudice towards a mode of writing that attached particular importance to formal elegance and mythological references. After the achievement of religious peace, the slackening of anti-pagan polemic made possible a less hostile stance towards poetry, which educated Christians were in any event accustomed to appreciate because of the instruction they received in school. Furthermore, the various Latin texts of the Bible that circulated in the *pars Occidentis* (see p. 598) were of questionable literary value, and so Christians felt a growing need for writings that would narrate the history of salvation in a more worthy and elevated manner. Against this background a new literary genre becomes popular: the reworking of the Bible in verse. Juvencus, a Spanish priest of Giliberri (today Elvira, near Granada), who may have come to court with his fellow countryman Hosius of Cordova, Constantine's ecclesiastical adviser, renders into hexameters the Gospel of Matthew, to which have been added episodes drawn from the other Gospels; the whole bears the title of *Evangeliorum Libri IV.* Among the traditional literary genres, the one to which Juvencus is closest is epic; a fact of fundamental importance for mankind such as the redemption cannot be sung of except in the highest style.

The work, produced in 329–30, derives from an ambitious project: to join together Christianity's principal text, the Gospels, from which the material is drawn, and the principal pagan Latin author, Virgil, whose hexameter verse is put to use and who is echoed in many phrases and collocations. To give the elegance of Virgilian poetry to the biblical narrative was an enterprise beyond Juvencus's powers, however; he was crushed beneath the weight of his two models. His personal presence in the poem is limited to a preface, depicting the new Christian poetics that assures the validity of the product by virtue of the sacred nature of the subject and the authenticity of the inspiration, which is due, not to the Muses, but to the Holy Spirit; several descriptions embellished according to the principles of classical rhetoric; and several mild liberties in the translation of the dialogues. Altogether, Juvencus is extremely faithful to the sacred text. His learned reworking found many imitators in antiquity.

The compositions of Publilius Optatianus Porfyrius share this tendency towards learned poetry and technical refinements that are virtuoso displays of patient labor. Optatianus was a pagan senator. After falling into disgrace with Constantine, he succeeded in winning his favor again by sending him a volume of figured poems, many of them on Christian subjects. Such poems are based on a difficult poetic game that somewhat resembles our crossword puzzles. If the verses of the poem are aligned letter by letter one above the other, other verses are formed vertically or diagonally, and these, moreover, make a geometric or allegoric design. The effect was emphasized by using a different ink for their letters.

Pagan poetry is poorly exampled in this first part of the century. To find instances one is obliged to look in the *Anthologia Latina,* of which we have spoken in connection with third-century poetry. Among the few authors whose names we know and some of whose poems we have, one may mention Tiberianus, the governor of Gaul in 355 and author of three moralizing poems and a description of the countryside that in its better parts may remind us of the *Pervigilium Veneris.*

3. THE LAST PAGAN HISTORIOGRAPHY AND THE NEW CHRISTIAN HISTORIOGRAPHY

The historical writing of the fourth century is particularly vast, and the leading figures of political life, such as Nicomachus Flavianus, author of *Annales* that are lost to us (and a character in Macrobius's *Saturnalia*), devoted themselves to this genre.

The numerous works that have come down to us are chiefly from the second half of the century, beginning with the so-called "Chronograph of the Year 354," a collection of texts assembled in that year and attributed by the manuscripts to a certain Philocalus, who might be the collaborator of Pope Damasus (see p. 663). The "Chronograph of the Year 354" includes, among other things, a splendid calendar with illustrations. Composed certainly in a Christian milieu, the work contains very useful information that is transmitted only here. The list of prefects of Rome, for instance, is fundamental for the reconstruction of political events in the third and fourth centuries.

Aurelius Victor and the *Historia Tripertita*

The Liber de
Caesaribus

From a slightly later date comes the work of Sextus Aurelius Victor, an African of humble origins who succeeded in pursuing a distinguished career up to the prefecture of Rome in 389. In 360 he composed a *Liber de Caesaribus,* which is also known under the title *Historiae Abbreviatae,* containing the biographies of the emperors from Augustus to Constantius. Its purpose is to combine the annalistic technique of Livy with the biographical technique of Suetonius. It interprets events in accord with the position of the Roman aristocracy, to which Aurelius Victor was very close in that he defended tradition, condemned Christianity, and was concerned over the excessive powers of the military.

The Historia
Tripertita

The *Liber de Caesaribus* is accompanied by three small historiographic works forming a corpus that is certainly to be attributed to authors other than Aurelius Victor, even though the manuscript tradition assigns it to him at least in part. The corpus includes an *Origo Gentis Romanae,* giving the history of Rome from the mythic god Saturn to Romulus; a *De Viris Illustribus,* virtually a continuation of the preceding work, from Proca, king of Alba Longa, to Antony and Cleopatra; and an *Epitome de Caesaribus,* from Augustus to the death of Theodosius (395).

The Origo Gentis
Romanae

Its intention is clearly to create a kind of treatise subdivided into three parts (a *Historia Tripertita,* according to the name usually given to this collection), from the most remote period to the end of the fourth century, when the collection was probably assembled. The *Origo* is remarkable for the incredible number of quotations supposedly derived from annalists (e.g., Fabius Pictor and Cincius Alimentus) and pontiffs of the early period. If these quotations were authentic, we would have a text of extraordinary documentary value, but the reliability of the quotations is still controversial.

Eutropius and the *Breviaries*

A handy manual of history for the use of educated people appears to have been a need very much felt in the second half of the fourth century. Various such works appear during this period, among which the most famous is Eutropius's *Breviary,* which was destined to be very popular in later centuries.

Eutropius was a rhetorician of Italian origin and took part in Julian's expedition against the Parthians. He held important posts under the emperor Valens (364–78), who appointed him his *magister memoriae.*

The *Breviarium ab Urbe Condita,* written at the request of Valens, in ten books, covering the period from Romulus to the death of Jovian in 364. The large number of books should not deceive anyone: Eutropius's *Breviary* is a short manual that in a modern edition might fill a hundred pages; the division into books serves basically to separate the subjects. Its principal sources are Livy for the first six books, Suetonius for book 7, and for the

remaining three books repertories barely known to us. The chief quality of this work is its clarity and elementary style, which for centuries have made it one of the earliest texts for students to read in learning Latin. Eutropius aimed at informing the emperor in a simple, unlaborious way about the principal events of Roman history. The didactic purpose is fully achieved, by virtue of both the form it employs and its ability to select from the mass of events those that are most important for a reconstruction of the past that is completely positive, with a glorification of Rome and its governing classes. The success of the *Breviary* was immediate and is confirmed by a recognition granted to few Latin works, translation into Greek by a contemporary, Paeanius.

Another *Breviary* was composed by Rufius Festus under Valens. The work, written after 371, includes an introduction on the chronology of the kings, consuls, and emperors, then a review of the different provinces, in order to narrate the conquest of them, and finally the history of relations between Rome and the Parthians, from the time of Lucullus (first century B.C.) to the author's own day, ending with an exhortation to Valens to resolve the Eastern question definitively. Unlike Eutropius's *Breviary,* which aimed at a global treatment of Rome's history, Festus's is obviously based on two principal themes, the conquests that led to the creation of the Empire, and the war against Persia.

The fourth century was probably also the time of composition for that breviary of history from 293 to 337 that goes under the name "First Anonymus Valesianus" (to distinguish it from a second, similar breviary covering the period 474–526), so named from the French humanist Henri Valois (Valesius), who published it in the first half of the seventeenth century. Let us mention finally the so-called *Periochae* of Livy. This consists of

brief summaries of the individual books, which in the end replaced the original text, on account of its enormous mass. The *Periochae* have the merit of informing modern scholars about the distribution of the material in the books of Livy that are not extant, allowing us to reconstruct the outline of Livy's work in its entirety (see p. 374).

Ammianus Marcellinus

Ammianus Marcellinus was born at Antioch in Syria around 330–35 to a prosperous family of Greek language and culture. He began his career under the emperor Constantius, as an officer. He took part in various campaigns against the Persians, only to retire later to private life in his native Antioch. At Rome subsequently, he improved his knowledge of Latin and began to write his historical work. He came into contact with the circle of the pagan senatorial aristocracy but never succeeded in joining it fully. In the last decade of the century he gave public readings of his *History,* with remarkable popular success. His death can be placed around 400.

WORKS The *Rerum Gestarum Libri XXXI.* The work started with the reign of Nerva (96) and went down to the death of the emperor Valens at Adrianople (378), but it is not preserved in its entirety. We have books 14–31, dealing with the years 353–78. The history of Julian (355–63) forms the chief section of the extant part, the rest of which is devoted to the events of the reign of Valentinian and his brother Valens.

Ammianus's history presents at first appearance two features that deserve further investigation: the obvious disproportion between the part devoted to Julian and the space to which the other events are confined, and the deliberate choice of the year 96 as starting point for the treatment, which evidently sets out to present itself as a continuation of Tacitus's historical work. In the first thirteen books, which are lost today, 250 years of history and more were narrated, whereas the eleven books on Julian cover a span of fewer than ten years, and only six books are devoted to the last fifteen years covered. Thus we find operative in Ammianus not only the natural tendency to narrate in greater detail the facts that are more recent, and therefore better known directly, but also the desire to give greater weight to a particular era, and one that, moreover, has a strong ideological character: Julian's brief reign marked the temporary revival of paganism and a momentary interruption of Christianity's triumphal march.

Continuator of Tacitus

Ammianus's critical spirit

One should not think, however, that Ammianus wants to present Julian, the apostate emperor, as a completely positive hero, utterly without defect, idealized for his utopian plan of a return to the past. Julian's defects are also presented objectively, and his stance towards the Christians does not go uncriticized, but is regarded as sometimes uselessly repressive and unjust. Towards the Roman aristocracy, which was his chief point of political reference, Ammianus is anything but tender. He denounces its faults and moral degeneration and reproaches its avarice and exclusiveness, which he must have experienced personally. In short, the historian gives evidence of an independence and a free judgment, which are a basic merit of his work. His evaluations are heavily influenced by his personal disappointments and his Greek upbringing, which positioned him to view the conventions and customs of Roman society from without.

Tacitus as model

Still more interesting for us is Ammianus's relation to Tacitus, whom he resembles in his ambition to be dispassionate, to consider his material *sine ira et studio.* To choose Tacitus as a model meant to oppose the established tendency towards biographical history in the manner of Suetonius, to suggest again the priority of events over their protagonists, to link oneself to a pro-senatorial historiography in order to propose its revival in a contemporary mode. Ammianus wants to present himself as an objective layman, concerned with all excesses and convinced that a strong senatorial group could balance the imperial power, which now was greater than ever because of the coincidence of interests between the emperor and the Christian church. His chief aspiration is a strict system of guarantees, a pacific tolerance that avoids repression and persecution, which are always reprehensible, from whichever side they come. He does not lack prejudices and idiosyncrasy of his own, of course: he is too cultivated, too refined to understand the motivations and the behavior of the urban plebs. Even so, showing an openness and an interest that are rare in an ancient writer, he gives space to events such as urban or military revolts, which the classical historians would have quickly passed over.

Erich Auerbach devotes a chapter of his famous book *Mimesis* to the arrest of Peter Valvomeres, the leader of a popular revolt, which is described by Ammianus in 15.7. Auerbach's aim is to demonstrate the attention that the author pays to the most grotesque and degrading aspects of the scene, with a taste for the macabre and the miraculous that, though of distant Tacitean origin, is the antithesis of Tacitus's realism. These descriptions in dark colors show the coexistence in Ammianus of a lively interest in the horrifying and the sensual; into a courtly style there thus bursts a pictorial realism that spares nothing. This tendency does not belong to Ammianus alone. It is shared by other learned men of the day, Jerome in particular, who not uncommonly alternates lofty language with crude realism.

Pessimism and distrust

The excursus

The profoundly pessimistic framework, the conviction that the state is now in decline, at the center no less than at the periphery, the slight hope, or absence of hope, in a Roman future that could renew the glories of the past—all these also make one think of Tacitus. Rome will remain eternal, since that is its destiny, but in an increasingly squalid existence. This is the picture gotten from several famous digressions in the work, which describe geographical or sociological oddities (the portrait of Eastern pleaders is famous), anecdotes, or philosophical meditations on justice. In these *excursus* particularly, yet in the rest of the work as well, Ammianus uses extensively, perhaps excessively, the artifices of rhetoric. It has been observed that his style is always pitched somewhat above the appropriate tone, and so it flattens the expression instead of heightening it. It is not easy to say to what extent this results from a limited knowledge of Latin, which Ammianus learned only in adulthood and therefore did not employ with the spontaneity that one has in one's native language, but it is evident that the tension, which is pleasant and stimulating when applied to brief episodes, is ultimately wearying when extended uniformly to the entire work. Moreover, lexical and syntactic Grecisms were long ago identified in Ammianus's language, hints of the author's double culture. It must not be forgotten either that the author is not a school man but a soldier, or rather a retired general, *miles quondam et Graecus,* as he himself says, and his skill at the fine points of rhetoric could not be particularly high.

Lexical and syntactic Grecisms

Another characteristic revealed by scholars is a certain contradiction between various parts of the *History,* and not solely in the evaluation of this or that person (which might change from one place to another, if different sources were used for the two passages). It has been noted that the methodological preface to book 15, which opens the section on Julian, is in sharp contrast to the one at the beginning of book 26, which introduces the section devoted to Valens and Valentinian. In the first the author stresses the need to say everything, even at the risk of becoming too lengthy, whereas in the second he declares his preference for a historiography that selects the matters to be recounted and limits itself only to the most significant. This difference and the very presence of separate prefaces confirm that the work was composed over a long period and so may have been subject to some changes in approach, depending on the period treated and the author's stance towards it.

Like ancient historiography in general and that of late antiquity in particular, Ammianus makes use of fictitious speeches and letters, but he prudently advises the reader that these are communications reconstructed by the imagination, composed with the freedom that the literary genre permitted to writers. From this scrupulousness in informing the reader one receives the impression again of a serious and serene writer, conscious of his limitations but intending to set forth whatever he regards as true together with his own points of view on individual events, and convinced of the value of supplying for the Empire's last centuries a record that would be comparable to that available for its first.

The *Historia Augusta*

The historical work closest to Ammianus Marcellinus's, because of its richness of information and amplitude of structure, is the so-called *Historia Augusta,* which presents the most complex philological and historiographic problems of any work from the fourth century. It is a collection of biographies that was probably supposed to include the lives of the emperors from Nerva to the immediate predecessors of Diocletian (Carus, Carinus, and Numerianus), and thus the entire period from 96 to 284. It is missing, however, the first two lives, of Nerva and Trajan, and several lives of emperors who reigned at the middle of the third century (Philip the Arab, Decius, Gallus, Aemilianus, and also the first part of the life of Valerian). The title given by the manuscripts is *Vita Diversorum Principum et Tyrannorum,* but by now it has become customary to refer to it as the *Historia Augusta.* The work is said to have been written by six different authors— Aelius Lampridius, Aelius Spartianus, Flavius Vopiscus, Julius Capitolinus, Trebellius Pollio, and Volcacius Gallicanus—who lived under Diocletian and Constantine. The distribution of the lives among the authors is very uneven, and the length of the biographies varies considerably, some being very long (the so-called "principal lives"), other quite short.

The question of the *Historia Augusta* concerns, in essence, the reliability of the attributions to the six names mentioned above, which are unknown to us from any other source. If this attribution is rejected, the question arises of the period and setting to which the work should be assigned. Doubts on the subject are well grounded: there are contradictions in the attribution of several lives to this author or that, and the dedications to the emperors stand in contradiction to other chronological data. Given the many problems, the theory has emerged that the six names are wholly fictitious and that the work was composed in a later era, probably by a single writer. Others have preferred an intermediate hypothesis, that someone in the second half of the fourth century took up and reworked lives originally written in the time of Diocletian or Constantine.

The discussion of this difficult problem is still open, but the contradictions and the absurdities entailed by acceptance of the attributions as they are indicated in the text are such that the idea of a forger seems preferable.

The problem of dating

The problem thus arises of determining the period in which this forger worked and the reasons for his inventing six different authors' names for biographies written by him. Because of several clearly pro-senatorial and pro-pagan features, scholars have for the most part thought of the years of Julian's reign, or the brief but intense pagan revival in the time of Symmachus, under the reign of Theodosius, or the first decades of the fifth century. Still others have preferred much later dates, at the beginning or even in the second half of the sixth century. On the whole, however, most agree upon the period from 390 to 420.

The motives for the forgery

Those who believe in a forgery maintain that the historian did not want to make himself vulnerable to the possible reactions of those holding opposing views and that he avoided the risk by antedating the work, so as to lend it greater authority and credibility. There are, however, those who have emphasized how the anachronisms, the inconsistencies, the confusions, the *post eventum* prophecies, the obvious invention of certain sources, and the gross exaggerations point to a parody of the more or less official historiography, whose defects it accentuates to the point of absurdity. But those who, by contrast, think the work serious, so serious that it could be dangerous for its author, locate the risk in the anti-Christian polemic present in the work and in the support it gives to the senatorial class against the new powers, especially those coming from the army.

Banal biographies or subtle display of ingenuity?

The *Historia Augusta* thus poses problems that can be solved only with great difficulty and permits the most widely divergent evaluations. The text can be seen as a banal collection of biographies constructed in an utterly unoriginal way on the basis of schemes by then widely diffused and mechanically applied, or as a clever mockery directed against this tendency towards narrative and historiographic flattening; as a work of popularization intended for the masses, with a general intention to inform, or as a subtle pamphlet *à clef,* written perhaps by high palace officials and intended for an audience of the educated few. It is certain, in any event, that the chief historiographic model is Suetonius.

The lives have a number of defects that were widely noted long ago.

They dwell on secondary details and lose sight of the major historical problems; they are full of tiresome gossip and notices that are certainly false; they are written in a flat and monotonous style, a journalistic style, as Arnaldo Momigliano calls it. And yet for us they are fundamental, because they constitute the principal source, and in many cases the sole source, of information for a good part of the second and all of the third century.

Taste for gossip and journalistic style

The Histories by Subject

The two principal tendencies of fourth-century historiography are towards the continuous exposition of events, in the form of a breviary or annals, and towards biography. And yet there are also instances of histories by subject, which deal in monographic form with a specific subject, looking for examples in all Roman or ancient history, or which select a historical or mythical episode and narrate it in the manner of a novel. Thus, Julius Obsequens, for instance, composed a *Liber Prodigiorum* that proposed to collect and list all the miracles performed by the pagan gods that were recorded in Livy's work. It aimed at fighting the attacks of Christian historians who denied the favorable intervention of the pagan divinities in the history of Rome and at proving the necessity of abiding by the ancient worship in order to assure oneself of their continued protection.

Julius Obsequens

"Hegesippus" (so-called) in his *De Bello Iudaico* was interested in Jewish history. His work is in effect a reworking, almost a translation, in Latin of the work by Flavius Josephus (the very name "Hegesippus" arises from a distortion of *Josephus,* which first became *Joseppus* and then was ennobled into *Egesippus* or *Hegesippus*). The work, from the second half of the fourth century, was erroneously attributed to Ambrose. Undoubtedly composed in a Christian setting, it is full of anti-Jewish feelings, made evident right from the prologue.

Hegesippus

Novelized Histories

Also very popular were novelized histories on Oriental subjects, with the Trojan Cycle and the adventures of Alexander the Great as preferred subjects. They were escape literature (stories of heroes, of unknown and marvelous places) intended for a public not particularly educated but prosperous. They were often reworkings or translations from Greek originals, which were sometimes from several centuries earlier. The line of popular medieval romances begins with these works and is destined to have a huge success.

Escape literature

The most famous fourth-century work in this genre is the *Ephemeris Belli Troiani.* The author, a Latin writer who claims to be named Lucius Septimius, takes up and abridges a Greek text of the first century A.D. about the war at Troy. We cannot be certain that the author of the Latin text was really named Septimius, since the imagination of these novelists was exercised on names and attributions too, but the existence of the Greek model is secure, since two papyri have preserved several short pieces of it. The prologue recounts that Dictys Cretensis, a Greek who had taken part in the

Lucius Septimius and "Dictys Cretensis"

Trojan War, had kept a diary, in which he noted the events he witnessed. This diary, it is alleged, was found in the Neronian period and given to the emperor. The work claims to be a translation of it.

The first five books contain the episodes of the siege and destruction of Troy, narrated from the point of view of one of the besiegers, who is an eyewitness. The remaining books contain the stories of the heroes' home-comings, thus completing the theme of the *Iliad* with that of the *Odyssey*. Septimius shows many traces of the Latin of Sallust, who is his chief linguistic and stylistic source, but there are echoes of the other classics commonly read in schools, especially Cicero and Virgil.

Two other works that belong to the saga of Alexander are the *Historia Alexandri Magni* and an *Itinerarium Alexandri,* in which, unlike in the other itineraries of which we have spoken (see p. 638), the historical interest predominates over the geographical.

(see p. 638)

Poetry to celebrate the powerful

It has been thought that the author of the two works, which are found together in the manuscripts, may be Julius Valerius Polemio. The basis of each of the Latin works is a Greek original, which for the *Historia* is the *Romance of Alexander,* a text so popular in the East that we have Armenian and Syriac versions of it. The fantastic inventions, the confusions, and the absurdities of the Greek text remain, and Julius Valerius has clothed them in a popular Latin, full of terms from everyday usage and suitable to the public the author addresses.

The Historia Apollonii Regis Tyrii

From the same cycle derives also an *Epitome Rerum Gestarum Alexandri Magni,* which can be dated between the late fourth and the early fifth century and has come down to us incomplete. The *Historia Apollonii Regis Tyrii* is far more difficult to date (the dates proposed range between the end of the third century and the first half of the sixth), among other reasons because a basic plot may have been repeatedly reworked and elaborated as it grew and was improved. A Greek original may be presumed for this tale as well. Among all the novelized histories of this period, this text presents the most obvious characteristics of invention, with persons and fantastic events mingling in a very complicated plot. Amidst stories of love and incest, flight and rape, pirate ships and brothels, unfolds the story of Apollonius, who, though first an exile from Antioch, later becomes king. The novel has all the requisites for fascinating the public, from an exotic and suggestive setting to the most disparate elements of fable; taken up in the ancient fable tradition, these have been preserved down to modern times (for instance, marriage with the king's daughter is promised to whoever solves a riddle, but anyone who tries to solve it and fails pays with his life).

In the version that we have, the *Historia Apollonii* is the most "medieval" of the narratives of Latin antiquity, yet it is also the one most similar to the tradition of the Greek novel.

The Lives of Saints

The lives of saints, monks, and bishops, which the Christians produce in ever greater numbers, also belong to the historiography of lives of famous persons. They take up various elements from different literary forms. The structure is drawn fundamentally from late ancient biography on the Suetonian model; the influence of the *Passions* and the *Acts of the Martyrs,* which go back to the period of the persecutions, is also undeniable; and there are also ideas derived from the literature of prodigies and the fantastic. These writings had a double purpose: to reinforce the unity of the believers through the worship of exemplary persons who had distinguished themselves in ecclesiastical administration or religious ascesis, and to strengthen the role of the ecclesiastical hierarchy, whose functions grew in importance as Christianity established itself as an element of cohesion among the several realities of the Empire. This explains a difference from the traditional lives of emperors or illustrious persons, in which information and a taste for the learned or spicy detail undoubtedly prevailed over any educational purposes. In this regard, the works were more similar to other pagan lives that tended to present non-Christian "saints" as a possible alternative (e.g., the itinerant "saint" Apollonius of Tyana).

Hegesippus

The *Life of Anthony,* the desert hermit, was one of the most popular among Christian biographies. Written in Greek by Athanasius, bishop of Alexandria, shortly after the monk's death, which occurred in 356, it had a great and immediate success and was translated throughout the Mediterranean world. At Rome it achieved such great popularity that in slightly more than fifteen years two versions of it were published. The reasons for such success are multiple. Curiosity about the exotic setting (Anthony was a Copt) and the novel-like liveliness of the biography may have played a part, and Christian circles undoubtedly had a strong interest in the mode of life described in the work, the rejection of earthly things that seemed to go in the direction opposite to that of the official church, which was increasingly eager to augment its institutional power.

The Life of Anthony

Following a brief summary of Anthony's youth, the center of the work is his summons to the hermit's life. First he leads an ascetic life at home; then he installs himself in an isolated place at the edge of the village; next, persisting in the path of perfection, he goes to an abandoned cemetery; and finally he retreats to the desert and attracts other monks who, like him, reject civilization. To this theme of flight from society and aspiration to solitude are joined accounts of miracles and meetings with pilgrims, moral meditations and maxims, with sufficient variety to avoid, almost always, any feeling of tediousness.

Summary of the
Life of Anthony

Apart from the account of Cyprian (see p. 606), which stands midway between passion and biography, the earliest Latin lives are those of three bishops—Ambrose, Martin of Tours (see p. 695), and Augustine. Compared with the Eastern biographies, these have scarcely anything of the miraculous, and the three protagonists, though endowed with monastic virtues, nonetheless form part of the ecclesiastic hierarchy. These writings, therefore, composed in the West, where functions proper to the political sphere continue to be delegated to the bishop, agree in proposing a model of active sainthood that is seen as operating within society

The earliest Latin lives

and that lacks the subversive force that marked the rise of Eastern monasticism.

4. POETRY AND DRAMA

Poetry to celebrate the powerful

The imperial courts in the second half of the fourth century are important centers of poetry. The phenomenon is explained by the presence of a relatively large educated public, by the opportunities for a brilliant career offered by a well-composed poem, and by the rulers' interest in being surrounded by writers and in particular by poets, who could, if necessary, spread the dominant ideologies among the classes of greatest economic and political significance.

Different kinds of writers surrounded the emperors: wealthy gentlemen who loved literature and composed in the time that was not taken up by political activity and care for their estates; respectable school men who had distinguished themselves by their culture and for this reason had been summoned to court; and finally, true wandering poets, ballad singers almost, who were obliged to secure the necessities of life from their skill in poetry and who thus were accustomed to composing verses to exalt the powerful. Although these differences brought about notable variations in subject and stance, it is possible to point to at least one feature common to this poetry, namely, the return to the classics of the Augustan era, both because they were regarded as the authors of absolute excellence and thus deserved to be imitated and because Augustus's principate was always the ideal model on which the late ancient emperors claimed to base themselves.

Ausonius

LIFE

Decimus Magnus Ausonius was born at Burdigala (Bordeaux) around 310 and studied at Tolosa from 320 to 328, and then at Bordeaux, where he became a professor, first of grammar, then of rhetoric. Summoned to court in 364 to teach the future emperor Gratian, he subsequently held important public offices. He retired to private life after Gratian's death, in 383, and died around 393–94.

WORKS

Very many works (nearly all poetry, but there are some in prose) have come down to us with the comprehensive title *Opuscula;* we shall mention only the chief ones below. They are preceded by three *Praefatiunculae* in elegiac couplets, probably written after 383.

Ausonius is the most famous of the learned poets active in the second half of the fourth century. His poetry is strongly marked by his work as a schoolteacher. The subjects of many of his poems, which are mostly short, are typical of the academic world, and even his scrupulous attention to choice of words and his taste for metrical play show the experience of the rhetorician who is accustomed to working with words. It would be an error, however, to believe that contemporaries considered such poetry abstruse, completely unworldly, concerned with ridiculous, abstract problems of grammar; this is proved to us by the personal experience of Ausonius himself, for whom political activity opened the way to court and assured success and power. School, grammar, and the word were rather different realities for the late ancient world than for our culture. In those days the tools of persuasion and the very definition of values and ideals were entrusted in large part precisely to those circles and those disciplines, and to write poetry about them, even if one made good-natured fun of their limitations and parodied the more questionable aspects of instruction, meant to respond to the cultural interests of what was one of the most important sectors for the social organization of the state. The subject was intrinsically important and of great contemporary interest.

Only if one regards them from this point of view can one understand works such as the *Commemoratio Professorum Burdigalensium,* in which the people are honored in their daily occupations, the gossip typical of academic milieus not being neglected: "Even though you have unjustly usurped a professorial chair, as is said, . . . " (10.1). From these epitaphs, these fictitious tomb inscriptions, which recount the stories of so many persons, telling of an incredible variety of events that nonetheless are rather similar to one another, we get a clear and substantially believable picture of an educated provincial society. The *Commemoratio* (an illustrious poetic precedent, one might say, of Edgar Lee Masters's *Spoon River Anthology*) is thus an exceptional document for the customs of social life in a lively fourth-century city.

An educated provincial society

Two other groups of poems also refer to the academic world: the *Eclogarum Liber,* about some of the most typical subjects of instruction (how mankind became honest, the parts of the year, the labors of Hercules, etc.), and the *Protrepticus ad Nepotem,* a genuine plan of study to be followed for cultural education. The same may be said for the many works made up of short pieces devoted to describing famous persons (e.g., the *Caesares*), or the seven wise men *(Ludus Septem Sapientium),* or the most important cities of the Empire *(Ordo Urbium Nobilium).*

Technical-formal virtuosity

Virtuosity in versification and a complete mastery of language and vocabulary reign supreme in works such as the *Oratio,* a prayer written entirely in rhopalic verses (i.e., verses in which the first word has only one syllable, the second two, the third three, etc.); the *Griphus Ternarii Numeri,* a lengthy riddle on the number three, full of Pythagorean doctrine; the *Cento Nuptialis,* employing verses of Virgil that are cut and put together so as to alter their original significance completely and instead made to describe, in ample detail, the celebration and the consummation of a marriage; the *Grammaticomastix* ("Grammarian-whipper"), a kind of list of the most difficult linguistic questions with which the poor grammar teacher was forced to contend.

The most successful works: the Parentalia, *the* Bissula, *and the* Mosella

To the category of funerary poetry belong both the *Epitaphia,* fictitious inscriptions for the tombs of the great figures of literature (Agamemnon, Achilles, Ulysses, etc.), and the *Parentalia,* poems the author dedicates to his own dead. In the latter work one finds expressions of tenderness and affection (but always discreet ones), as in other works that are traditionally held to be his most successful: the *Bissula,* for a German slave woman who was set free and instructed in Roman culture, and the *Mosella,* an epyllion devoted to that river, with ample descriptions of landscapes. The latter presents itself, even externally, because of its length (483 hexameters), as Ausonius's most ambitious work, and it is full of reminiscences of Virgil, Horace, Ovid, and others.

Among the other works that are left to us, the 114 epigrams and 25 metrical epistles to friends ought to be mentioned, for among the friends are some of the most important persons of the day, such as the orator Symmachus, Paulinus of Nola, and the rhetorician Axius Paulus, to whom Ausonius sends, among other things, a curious bilingual Greco-Latin letter, the first instance we have of macaronic poetry, in which Greek endings are added to Latin words, and vice versa. Of the prose writings one should recall not only several prefaces in the form of a letter but also the *Gratiarum Actio,* delivered in 379 in honor of Gratian.

Homage to the high bureaucracy

The *Ephemeris,* finally, describes the typical day of a high imperial bureaucrat. Here, too, preciosities of form are not lacking, such as the use of different meters for the various activities of the day—awakening and checking up on the servants to be sure they are not sleeping too much, the morning prayer, leaving the house to meet one's friends, giving instructions to the slaves for preparing dinner and delivering invitations, and giving orders to the cook.

The eyes closed to the present

In works such as the *Parentalia,* the *Professores,* and the *Ephemeris,* Ausonius gives a certain amount of space to the affairs of his own life and the lives of those around him, all with a simple, everyday realism. By contrast, he shows a total indifference to the real problems—social, economic, and political—that threaten the soundness of the Empire. The contrast with the consciousness of Ambrose, who gradually would supplant him as adviser to the young Gratian, could not be greater. In Ausonius's ideal vision there is no room for unsecured frontiers, the depopulation and impoverishment of the country, or religious disputes between one sect and another. For him, the state is still the same as in the first century A.D., the barbarians are always inferiors who provide Rome with slaves and military defeats, and the border areas (the Moselle, for instance, subject of an epyllion), where battles are now fought continually, are still regarded as pleasant sites of tourism and recreation.

Homage to the classical literary tradition

In conformity with this view, the great literary tradition of the happiest of past eras is taken over in its entirety, though in different forms. Thus we find the employment of various types of verse (polymetry) and poetic experimentation resembling that of the neoteric poets of the Republic (filtered through the poetics of the *novelli,* and thus rendered less provocative, less revolutionary, and so more adapted for the court); the elegance in composition and formal equilibrium of the Augustans, reduced to the smaller scale called for by the new taste; and the passion for witty remarks in the epigrams, which sometimes recall those of Martial.

The great erudition that characterizes Ausonius's work is not (or is not merely) a narcissistic display of learning. The interest in the uncommon observation, in the obscure detail of a story or myth, tends towards the recovery of a tradition that is felt to be the worthy subject for a poetry that draws part of its significance from its ability, by means of a novel reworking, to deal with subjects that have been hallowed by centuries of literature. This tendency to prevent even a small part of Rome's culture from being lost is important for understanding Ausonius's attitude towards Christianity. Let us recall, first of all, that the division between pagans and Christians in the fourth century was less sharp than is commonly believed. The two religions coexisted peacefully at all social levels, and sometimes even within the same family. Moreover, the presence within each of the two religions of a great range of positions brought it about that a Christian and a pagan might not be hindered by sectarianism and might agree on various problems more readily than two Christians or two pagans. Ausonius thus belongs to the Christian sector but is far removed from extreme strictness, and he is determined to defend everything in paganism that could be used to glorify Rome and the Empire.

An estheticizing ideal of cultural conciliation

Partly for his ability, partly for his concrete political power, partly for his conciliatory attitude, Ausonius was highly esteemed by his contemporaries. The emperor Theodosius, addressing him with great respect, asks him for a copy of all his writings, and Symmachus, one of the leaders of the pagan senatorial group, engages in an extensive and friendly correspondence with him, on literary topics as well as others. Yet his success diminished in time, a process continued down to the excessively negative evaluations of some recent criticism, which is not inclined to forgive those superficial and joking, if not downright fatuous, attitudes of good-natured play with language and meter that are the most personal aspect of Ausonius's poetry, and perhaps his principal merit.

Claudian

LIFE

Claudius Claudianus was born at Alexandria in Egypt around 370. He was at Rome in 395 and then went to the court of Honorius at Milan, where he was connected to the general Stilicho especially. In 400 the Senate of Rome decreed a statue in the Forum for him. He died around 404.

WORKS

Many poetic compositions in Latin, nearly always in hexameters or elegiac couplets, dating from the period 395–404 (we will review them below). Three chief groups can be identified: poems for the emperor Honorius, poems for Stilicho, and epic poems on mythological subjects. Among his juvenile works there was a *Gigantomachy,* of which two fragments remain.

A courtly poet

Claudius Claudian, who was active at the Western court a few years after Ausonius, belongs to another category, that of the professional poets who lived from their own verses. Despite the formal affinity, there is an extraordinary difference between the two. Ausonius, who is an important and powerful political figure, seems to live in a happy, unreal world, whereas Claudian, who is only indirectly in touch with the news and the directives from the state's decision-making centers, appears nonetheless far better informed and conscious of the problems.

A Greek-speaking Easterner who had begun his career by writing his first poems in Greek, Claudian arrived in Italy and in a short time became the most acclaimed Latin poet and also a confidante of the barbarian Stilicho, the supreme general, of Vandal origin, who occupied the highest post in the hierarchy of power. This mixture of East and West, of Greek, Latin, and Germanic, of the Empire's constitutional organs and the strength of the armies, may give an idea of the conditions at Rome in the fourth and fifth centuries, when the presence of the Germans had profoundly changed the general picture. They exerted pressure on the frontiers, to be sure, but they also occupied the most important posts within the Empire's institutions; and the image of Germany is no longer Bissula, Ausonius's sweet slave, but Stilicho, the harsh general on whom it was necessary to rely for defending the peace and the survival both of individuals and of the Empire as a whole.

The ideal of Rome persists, along with the aspiration to a classical perfection, but all the paths are more twisted and more complex. Although he was accused by the historian Orosius (see pp. 702 f.) of being a *paganus pervicacissimus,* Claudian did not assimilate himself culturally to the pagan party represented by Symmachus, and he developed all his activity as a Latin poet at a Christian court. He is attracted to an Eastern paganism strongly pervaded by the presence of elements of Orphism and the mysteries; hence a taste for images of the other world and a certain mystical tone that is remote both from the serenity of the official poetry of the classical era and from the balanced good sense of an Ausonius.

A pagan tinged with mysticism

From Claudian's earliest writings, in Greek, we have several fragments of a *Gigantomachy,* on the mythical war of the Giants against the gods of Olympus, and some epigrams.

The poems for Honorius

In 395, at a public *recitatio* in Rome, Claudius delivered the panegyric for the consulate of Anicius Olybrius and Anicius Probinus, which brought him to the attention of the court; he was subsequently charged with celebrating Honorius's third consulship (396), and then the fourth (398) and the sixth (404) as well. The three panegyrics combined praises of the emperor with praises of Rome and her empire. Also for Honorius is the *De Nuptiis Honorii et Mariae,* an epithalamium for his marriage to the daughter of Stilicho, which is one of the moments of greatest power for the Vandal general and so for his entourage. The text is full of mythological references and praises worthy of a panegyric, whereas the *Fescennina* are very different, licentious verses in varying meter, in accordance with the classical tradition of the nuptial rite.

The poems in honor of Stilicho

A number of poems belong to a kind of Stilicho cycle: the *De Bello Gildonico,* the *Laus Stilichonis* (in three books), and the *De Bello Gothico.* Stilicho is compared to Scipio Africanus, and, though a barbarian, he is placed without difficulty in the company of the great Romans who have fought foreign enemies; just as these had their poets, beginning with Ennius, so it is right that the Muses sing their songs for Stilicho too. Claudian also wrote two invectives against two powerful persons who were enemies of Stilicho, *In Rufinum* and *In Eutropium*. The *Laus Serenae* also honors Stilicho, indirectly. Serena was Stilicho's wife, and Claudian regards her as one of his benefactors; and he attributes to her, among other things, the merit of her fortunate marriage. Naturally, the praise of the great woman permits large digressions on her powerful husband.

Mythology

Two of Claudian's poems are based on mythology: a *Gigantomachy,* which takes up in Latin the subject of his youthful Greek poem (but of the Latin text, too, we have scarcely more than a hundred verses), and the *De Raptu Proserpinae.* The subject of the latter is the myth of Proserpina carried off by the god of the Underworld, Hades. The descriptive passages are particularly extensive: Claudian enjoys representing the settings of the story in detail and with all the colors of rhetoric (particularly appealing are the descriptions of the realm of the dead), and the characters are also subjected to minute analysis—all to a degree at the expense of the action, which is rendered sluggish and fragmented in juxtaposed scenes.

Other poems

Worth mentioning, finally, are some occasional poems, written for influential persons, some verse letters, some idylls, mostly on scientific subjects, and various epigrams. The idylls are of interest for the subjects they take up, which aroused much curiosity in the educated public (for example, the phoenix, the mythical bird that was reborn from its own ashes and had a great symbolic value for both Christians and pagans, on account of the idea of renewal and rebirth connected with its resurrection).

A professional poet

Claudian wrote a great deal, and the quantity of his works is all the more surprising if one keeps in mind that they all fall within the decade 395–404. The high technical quality of his verses is also surprising; his hexameter, prosodically impeccable, shows affinities with that of the poets of the first century of the Empire and is constructed in accordance with the best Latin tradition. Claudian also belongs to the same expressive Latin tradition by virtue of his return to myth and the treatment of themes of Greek origin.

Stilicho must have been a demanding patron, who expected from his "propaganda attaché" a constant production of literary novelties. In these poems of his that are engaged but at the same time occasional, Claudian calls into question the literary genres as they had been defined by the classical age, and the mixture of epic and panegyric, although it has had precedents, is nonetheless codified here in its clearest form.

A new celebratory epic

By reclaiming the epic on a contemporary historical subject, a poetry but little practiced under the Empire, and fusing it with the typical characteristics of encomiastic poetry, Claudian could look for success among the educated senatorial public, to whom the poems were addressed and whom Stilicho wished to reach. For this purpose he made certain changes in the genre: he reduced the scale and made the message explicit, since too long a poem could weary the reader, and the public might not be quick to decode ambiguous allegories.

The poems on mythological subjects depart from this tendency somewhat, since the poet has other aims: to consolidate his own fame and thus enhance the value of his services and to defend his philosophical and religious conceptions in a society that was seeing Christianity establish itself increasingly as a state religion.

The English poet Coleridge, who considered Claudian "the first of the moderns," admired the tension in him between the ancient expectation of an objective poetry and the modern tendency towards subjectivity and the necessity of obtaining an effect. Another who esteemed Claudian greatly, Huysmans, who dedicates a passage of his famous *Rebours* to him, appreciated above all his artistic abilities in constructing the hexameter and his linguistic taste. More recent evaluations of Claudian have often been less favorable, because of the prejudices against a poetry for hire, or even because of classicist reservations. Only very recently, as part of a comprehensive revaluation of late antiquity, have we succeeded in appreciating once again this poetry of a refined artificiality that has grand ideals and can interpret a difficult moment of cultural and political transition.

Other Court Poets: Avienus, Naucellius, Avianus

Avienus

Claudian's official debut as a Latin poet had taken place at Rome with his panegyric for Probinus and Olybrius, who belonged to the illustrious family of the Anicii. Thus, alongside the imperial court, there existed another milieu eager to foster the writing of poetry—the senatorial circles, with their educated audience and their passion for literature. Rufius Festus Avienus, a friend of Symmachus, belonged to these circles. His passion was geography, both celestial and terrestrial, as is evidenced by his short didactic poems: *Aratus,* a translation in hexameters of Aratus's *Phaenomena,* the astronomical treatise already translated by Cicero and Germanicus; the *Descriptio Orbis Terrae,* in hexameters; and the *Ora Maritima,* with a description of the coasts of the Empire, in iambic trimeters and incomplete.

Naucellius

To the same circles also belonged Junius (or Julius) Naucellius, to whom are to be attributed some of the *Epigrammata Bobiensia,* a collection of seventy poems, including the famous satire *Sulpiciae Conquestio,* whose author pretends to be the poetess Sulpicia (who lived at the end of the first century A.D. [see p. 437]) in order to complain about the situation in which intellectuals find themselves.

Avianus

The fabulist Avianus, whose membership in these Roman circles is less certain but likely, redid forty-two Aesopic fables in elegiac couplets. The work, which is of slight literary value, had a notable success in the Middle Ages.

Christian Poetry of Religious Inspiration

Along with court poetry, which is predominantly occasional poetry or official poetry, and therefore celebratory, the other great poetic current in the second half of the fourth century is the Christian poetry of religious inspiration. Under this heading one can place works that are very different from one another in literary genre, in verse technique, and in their intended audience but are united by their shared purpose of publicizing the new faith and combating the remains of paganism, which was still strong in both the higher and the poorer classes. A Christian Latin poetry, though not widespread, had already existed in the previous decades, even before Constantine, but it grew greater, obviously, with the new turn that events took after the Edict of Milan. The greater security assured by the emperors' religious choice in favor of Christianity, the rapid spread of the new faith through the classes that were educated and so able to compose literary texts, and the general return of the taste for poetry during the period from the reign of Constantine's descendants to the reign of Theodosius's are the principal reasons for this increase in poetic production and for its progressive differentiation in the second half of the century.

Hymns continue to be written, a genre that had to be present even in the earliest church but that now enjoys its period of greatest flourishing, with authors such as Hilary of Poitiers and especially Ambrose; the traditional funereal inscriptions in verse take on a new literary dignity thanks to the epitaphs of Pope Damasus; bravura pieces such as centos are produced by Christians for the purpose of edification and are even more popular than among the pagans; above all, Christian poets emerge who recover the tradition of classical poetry, in order to write ancient verses about new concepts. Thus the Christian poetry of the fourth and fifth centuries helps to heal the rupture between strict Christianity and the classical tradition, an opposition that would continue to cause distress for many centuries. Is it legitimate, men wondered, to study and to love classical literature, which is the work of pagan authors and thus recounts myths and events culturally bound to that pagan religion that the Christians must combat? When Damasus, Proba, Prudentius, and Paulinus of Nola choose Virgil and Horace as their chief sources, they in effect assist the victory of the most conciliatory, least exclusionary policy on the part of Christianity, providing these poets and the other classical writers a patent of legitimacy, to which they owe, at least in part, their preservation during the Middle Ages. This choice was certainly not always clear and conscious, and often it conformed to a tendency already under way. Nonetheless, the role of Christian Latin poetry was invaluable, not only because it aided that mediation between classicism and Christianity that is at the heart of all modern civilization but also because it laid the basis for much of the later medieval writing in verse.

Damasus

Damasus's literary fame is tied to the epigrams that he had inscribed on the tombs of the martyrs venerated at Rome, even though we also have some letters of his. As part of a project of restoring Christian architectural monuments, this enterprising pope, who governed the church from 366 to

Poetry celebrating the establishment of Christianity

Hymns, epitaphs, centos

The acceptance of the great pagan literature

The epigrams inscribed on the tombs of the martyrs

384, charged a distinguished calligrapher, Furius Dionysius Filocalus, with inscribing the verses composed by him upon slabs of marble in elegant letters. The homage thus paid to the martyrs did not serve solely devotional purposes. In a period when the primacy of Rome had not yet been definitively established, Damasus was concerned to emphasize, by the testimony of the martyrs and in an easily accessible literary form, the centrality of Rome in bearing witness to the faith. The novelty of a pope who was a poet, the devotion to the martyrs, and the beauty of Filocalus's lettering impressed visitors, and the epigrams of Damasus were soon recopied into manuscripts and so escaped the destructions and the sacks of Rome, which caused the originals to be lost. The genuine compositions, about sixty in number, were later joined by others that cannot be attributed to Damasus. The texts, like many others of the period, show some prosodic irregularities and often repeat expressions used by the classical poets. The influence of Virgil is evident, a characteristic that Damasus's inscriptions have in common with contemporary epigraphic poetry. This use of the classics finds an echo in the policy Damasus followed during his pontificate, when he always strove to assure good relations with the pagans. In more strictly literary terms, we find in him, as was said, an attitude that is open to the profane literary inheritance, especially Virgil, a poet particularly dear to the Christians, who studied him in school and had begun to read the fourth eclogue as referring to Christ's coming. The great prestige enjoyed by Virgil among the Christians in the second half of the fourth century is also indicated by Proba's activity as a writer of centos.

Proba

A poetess, author of a cento

If Damasus represents the rare case of a pope who was a poet, Proba, too, is a rarity in Latin literature, a poetess, and what is more, the author of an unusual poem, a long Virgilian cento on subjects of the Old and the New Testaments. Active at Rome around the middle of the fourth century, Proba belonged to one of the most illustrious families of the aristocracy and was the wife of an important magistrate. She had great success in this particular literary genre, which consisted in taking verses and parts of verses from Virgil and recomposing them so as to create a new poetry, with completely different content and meaning. The success of Proba's cento was such that it was regarded as almost a doctrinal text. Not long after its composition, a decree attributed to Pope Gelasius is careful to list it among the texts that have no authority in the field of faith, a sign that for some, at least, Proba's work had acquired the same value as the works of the church fathers.

Endelechius

At the end of the century Endelechius, a friend of Paulinus of Nola, writes a *De Mortibus Boum.* Full of Virgilian echoes, it speaks of a plague upon animals, in order to reach the conclusion that only in Christianity can one find salvation.

Prudentius

Aurelius Prudentius Clemens was born at Calagurris (Calahorra, in Spain) in 348. He was a lawyer and then entered government administration. From 401 to 403 he was at Rome. The latest notices of him are from 405.

Praefatio, from 405, in forty-five lyric verses, serving as introduction to the entire collection of works. *Cathemerinon,* twelve hymns in various meters. *Apotheosis,* in hexameters, dealing with the mysteries of the Trinity and of Christ's Passion. *Hamartigenia,* in hexameters, on the origin of sin and mankind's responsibility. *Psychomachia,* in hexameters, on the struggle between the virtues and the vices in the human soul. *Contra Symmachum,* from 402–3, in two books of hexameters, on the Altar of Victory, which the Christians had had removed from the Senate and the pagans wanted to reconstruct (see p. 636). *Peristephanon,* fourteen hymns in various meters, composed in honor of Christian martyrs. *Dittochaeon,* forty-eight strophes of four verses apiece, on episodes of the Old and New Testaments. *Epilogus,* thirty-four lyric verses concluding the collection.

Prudentius is, along with Paulinus of Nola, the most important figure in Christian poetry. Apart from the *Praefatio* and the *Epilogus,* Prudentius's works can be put into three groups: hymns, didactic poetry (but with strong epic coloring), and a single poem of apologetic character. The two most famous collections are those containing the twenty-six hymns, namely, the *Cathemerinon Liber* and the *Peristephanon.*

The *Cathemerinon* includes six songs to be sung daily at certain moments of the day; six others are for particular Christian holidays or festivals. Thus the life of the believer is articulated rhythmically, from dawn to night and in accordance with the principal occasions of the year.

The first hymn is devoted to the rising of the sun and the cock's crow, a symbolic event especially dear to the hymn writers of the day because of the multiple allegories that could be constructed between awakening and resurrection, and between the cock and Christ as savior, and also because of the obvious echo of the episode of Peter that was familiar from the gospel: three times on the night of Christ's arrest, before the cock crowed, Peter denied that he knew his master. The second hymn is also a morning song, but the return of the light is seen particularly in relation to the Christian's daily activities and his struggle not to fall into sin. The second pair of hymns is related to the hour of eating: the third was sung before eating, to thank God for giving man the possibility to feed himself; the fourth, *post cibum,* praises moderation and recalls how God does not allow believers to die of hunger. The third pair includes the evening hymns: the fifth, for the lighting of the lamp, declares that the light of fire, like the light of day, is a gift of God, and the sixth, to be sung before going to sleep, mentions the possibility of having revelatory dreams and recommends the sign of the cross. The other six hymns, for annual festivals or special functions, are also arranged in three pairs. The seventh and eighth have to do with periods of fasting, which one should practice, but not to excess, since the will of Christ is always that of the good shepherd. The ninth is the *Hymnus Omnis Horae,* which can be sung at any moment of the day, recounting the story of Christ, with special reference to his descent to the Underworld and ascension; the tenth is a hymn for the dead that recalls how Christianity assures the immortality of the soul and the resurrection of the body. The last two hymns, finally, are for two solemn festivals, Christmas (11) and Easter (12).

The Peristephanon

The *Peristephanon* includes fourteen hymns in honor of saints who because of their faith had received the crown of martyrdom. The title derives from the crowns (*peri stephanon* means "about the crowns" in Greek) that were the symbol of the martyrs' victory over sin and over the forces of evil represented by those who persecuted Christianity. The protagonists of the poems are often Spanish, such as Emeterius and Chelidonius of Cala-horra (first hymn), or Eulalia, celebrated in the third, which is one of the most famous and successful hymns, or the eighteen martyrs of Saragossa (4), Vincent (5), and others. There are also other saints, such as the Apostles Peter and Paul (12) or the Romans Lawrence (2), Hippolytus (11), and Agnes (14). The tenth hymn, honoring St. Romanus, stands out because of its unusual length, 1,140 verses; but Romanus is the protector of the mute, since his tongue was cut off in his martyrdom, and it therefore seemed just that he was compensated with a longer song (in which much space is given to the saint's prolix speeches).

The *Cathemerinon* is more pleasurable to the modern reader than the *Peristephanon.* The latter is weighed down by macabre descriptions, which precisely because of the excess of revolting details risk becoming unintentionally ridiculous, and it is also full of narratives that are improbable even for miracles. Yet at the end of the fourth century, when the persecutions began to be reasonably distant, an interest developed in reconstructing the past of martyrdom, the heroic aspects of which were increasingly idealized. The combination of the horrible and the miraculous was attractive to the public, as is evidenced by the great success that a narrative genre such as the *passiones* would experience during the fifth century.

The competition with
the classics

Both the *Cathemerinon* and the *Peristephanon* contain valuable information on the customs of the Christians, their aspirations, and the new poetics that compares itself with that ancient poetics without the shyness produced by reverence, since the excellence of the subjects compensates amply for the personal limitations of the poets. Hence comes the intention to compete with the classics, in the certainty of proving superior to them by the help of God. Prudentius chooses as model and rival Horace, from whose odes he takes many of the meters adopted in the hymns, as well as many images and phrases. He no longer has the mythology, but in its stead he uses biblical tales or the sometimes fantastic narratives of the martyrs.

Literary success of
Prudentius's hymns

Even though the exposition is often difficult, obscure, and pointlessly prolix and the transitions from one theme to another do not always follow an impeccable logic, Prudentius's hymns enjoyed great popularity and success, and they were used for centuries in the liturgy of the church. From the literary point of view as well, these are works of primary importance.

The extent of the learning, in both the classical tradition and biblical culture, the full mastery of meter, and the rhetorical and oratorical ability employed even to excess (we should not forget that Prudentius was active for a considerable time as a lawyer) all make the reading of the hymns, if not agreeable, at least interesting.

The **Apotheosis** and the **Hamartigenia**

Three shorter poems, the *Apotheosis,* the *Hamartigenia,* and the *Psychomachia,* are didactic, as is the *Dittochaeon.*

The *Apotheosis,* consisting of slightly more than a thousand hexameters, is preceded by a hymn on the Trinity, also in hexameters, and by a preface in iambs. The subject is strictly theological and has to do with the mysteries of the Trinity and the Passion of Christ. The doctrines maintained by several heretics are confuted by being contrasted with the orthodoxy of the church of Rome. Among the questions treated at greater length are the divinity of the Son and the relation between the human soul and God. The Jewish religion and the Jews are referred to in tones of violent opposition. Among the historical personages mentioned in the *Apotheosis* is Julian the Apostate, the emperor who had abandoned Christianity to embrace ancient philosophy and the pagan faith. Prudentius recalls him with great respect for his abilities as commander, legislator, and writer, even though he condemns, naturally, his choice of religion: *perfidus ille Deo, quamvis non perfidus orbi,* "he was lacking in faith towards God, but not towards the world." So favorable a mention of a person towards whom Christian propaganda was hostile deserves to be remembered; it attests to attitudes considerably less rigid than those that, in the *De Mortibus Persecutorum* (see p. 641), attributed abilities of ruling to the emperors who were not hostile to God but judged the persecutors as bad rulers. Prudentius's experience as an official may have promoted the positive judgment on Julian's administration.

The *Hamartigenia* ("Origin of Sin") discusses the human soul and man's responsibilities, for the purpose of confuting heresies. After a doctrinal opening passage, the poem dwells on the examination of sin and various manifestations of evil in the world (harmful plants and animals, storms, floods). It includes elegant descriptions and attractive vignettes, moral condemnations of luxury and aggrieved attacks against women, who are the instruments the devil employs to corrupt men. The poem concludes with a representation of hell and paradise, the former full of flames, pitch, molten lead, and worms, the latter full of flowers, perfumes, and brooks. At the end is the poet's prayer asking God to watch over him with special indulgence.

The **Psychomachia**

Of the three poems, the most complex and most successful is the *Psychomachia,* the combat between the vices and the virtues in the human soul, with the epic description of duels between Faith and Idolatry, Chastity and Lust, Patience and Anger, Humility and Arrogance. The work consists of 915 hexameters.

The encounters are described with all the devices of epic technique, and the personifications of the virtues and the vices behave like Homeric or Virgilian heroes, or perhaps even more cruelly. Faith, for example, strangles

Idolatry, causing her eyes to pop out of their sockets, Chastity butchers Lust, Humility cuts off Arrogance's head, and so on. Patience alone can avoid cruel acts, since Anger kills herself, enraged at not having succeeded in defeating her enemy. The taste for the macabre that characterizes the descriptions of the martyrs in the *Peristephanon* returns here, with its emphasis on the details of the slayings, even though this time the roles are reversed, and it is the good that puts the evil to death.

Duels alternate with speeches, to which most of the moral instruction is entrusted; thus the combination of epic and didactic poetry becomes even closer and is found throughout the poem. The description, which is lively and detailed, continually tends towards allegory and in some cases becomes almost a picture, an iconographic representation of a peculiar virtue or vice. Such representations would have great success during the Middle Ages, and then again in the Renaissance, not only in literature but also in figurative art. The allegorical types created by Prudentius would move outside the regions of Latin and Romance culture, and they would become widespread in those of German culture as well.

The *Dittochaeon* may also be considered didactic. In about fifty strophes equal numbers of scenes from the Old and the New Testament are illustrated; the "two nourishments" to which the title refers are the two testaments. The brief poems were composed to serve as captions for painted or mosaic representations in a church. This confirms Prudentius's interest in the relation between text and image, between poetry and painting, which is already heralded in the marked representational character of many scenes in the *Psychomachia*.

The *Contra Symmachum,* finally, is an apologetic poem in two books. The subject is the dispute, already twenty years old (it went back to 382–84), between Ambrose and Symmachus over the suitability of replacing the altar of the goddess Victory in the Senate (see p. 636). Prudentius naturally takes the part of Ambrose against pagan idolatry, affirming the absurdity of classical polytheism and the value of eliminating it and confuting Symmachus's arguments: the tradition to which the senator appeals must not prevail over the truth of the new faith, and the greatness of Rome was not willed by the pagan gods, but by God, who in this way was preparing the diffusion of Christianity throughout the world that had been politically unified by the Empire. Once again, and more clearly than elsewhere, Prudentius insists on the necessity of not creating an opposition between Christianity and Roman civilization (and so he represents his opponent Symmachus as a learned man worthy of great respect who has unfortunately fallen into error). From this perspective, to attribute the successes of Rome to the divine will is a way of recovering the tradition, limiting the changes exclusively to the religious sphere, without renouncing classical culture.

Paulinus of Nola

LIFE

Meropius Pontius Paulinus was born in 353 at Burdigala (Bordeaux). He was a pupil of Ausonius and began a brilliant political career. Consul in 378, he was the governor of Campania. He married a wealthy Spanish woman, Therasia, and because of her influence, among other reasons, he gave up politics. He retired first to Spain, where he became a priest in 394, and then to Nola in Campania, where he oversaw the construction of a monumental architectural complex, imposing remains of which are extant near the Campanian village of Cimitile. Bishop of Nola from 409 on, he died in 431.

WORKS
Epistulae, numbering about fifty, written mostly from 394 to 413. *Carmina,* slightly more than thirty, in various meters, but mostly hexameters. A panegyric of Theodosius and some other writings have been lost. It is virtually certain that the *De Obitu Baebiani* and the four poems of the *Appendix* attributed to him by the manuscripts are not by Paulinus.

Paulinus's letters: aspirations to peace and tranquillity

The recipients of the letters are often persons of the highest rank, from Jerome to Augustine, from Ausonius to Rufinus to Sulpicius Severus. The letters often speak of concrete matters or give simple though interesting notices of daily life, and they are occasionally accompanied by the addressees' replies. Themes of greater theological importance are also found, especially in the correspondence with Augustine, but Paulinus was far from having the intelligence of the philosopher or the combativeness of the defender of orthodoxy. His ideal was a pacific, tranquil world in which everything was to one's liking, thanks (if need be) to the providential intervention of some saint who would resolve the most difficult problems at the right moment. On this view, even faith ought not to demand an excessive effort, since it runs the risk of becoming arrogance; the instinctive devotion of the humble is better. In the controversies over the heresies, too, Paulinus tried to keep aloof, sometimes even risking reprimand for what was considered lukewarmness towards the true faith but was rather a profound aspiration to peace and brotherhood, joined to a clear consciousness of his own limitations as a thinker and theologian.

Among the subjects investigated in one letter is the relation between Christianity and pagan culture. The latter, according to Paulinus, is dangerous if it is cultivated for its own sake (this is Jerome's position), but it may be preserved if it is used for publicizing the new faith. His prose style seems to adopt the same position: it uses all the artifices of rhetoric but is also full of words and whole phrases taken bodily from the Bible, in an odd collage that sometimes reminds one of the centos.

The Carmina Natalicia

The best part of Paulinus's writing is his poetry. Nearly half of his poems are devoted to St. Felix, the patron of Nola, who is celebrated with a poem every year, on the occasion of his *natalicium* (the day of martyrdom; such a poem is called a *natalicium* because on that day the saints are born into the true life, the one in heaven). Fourteen *Natalicia* of varying length have come down to us, from the first, written in 395, to the one of 408, which is partially lost. Sometimes they are simple, brief prayers, at other times accounts of the martyr's life, at still other times a narration of some of his miracles. In some cases Paulinus dwells on events of the moment, as in poem 26, which is chiefly devoted to concerns over the presence of Alaric and his Goths in Italy.

The style of Paulinus The style of Paulinus as poet is reserved, his language epic on the whole. He reaches out to his flock more by his choice of subjects (often drawn from the rural reality of Nola) than by his form of expression. The most successful scenes are the ones that describe, with lively freshness, the popular festivals held on St. Felix's day; in these cases Paulinus can find notes of enchanting candor and disarming sincerity.

Good examples are the precautions taken so that pilgrims do not become drunk; or the miracle of the cow that runs away, to the desperation of the peasants, and then reappears just in time to be slaughtered for the festival; or the episode of the peasant who protests to the saint that he did not perform a miracle for him and by these reproaches succeeds in obtaining it; or the story of the troubles that Paulinus met in trying to have two old houses destroyed that were ruining the view of the new church (in this case a "miraculous" fire resolved the problem).

Paulinus's other poetry Among the poems not devoted to the *natalicia* should be mentioned the verse epistles to Ausonius, which reply to those in which his old teacher tried to dissuade his pupil from his decision to abandon the things of the world and devote himself to the church: Paulinus reaffirms his choice and extols the superiority of the spiritual life and the devotion to faith.

Several other poems deserve mention: an epithalamium of 403, for the marriage of Julian of Eclanum (on whom see p. 704); a *propempticon,* or poem wishing a friend a good voyage; and a *consolatio* for a couple that have lost a young son. Epithalamium, *propempticon,* and *consolatio* were three typical literary genres of classical poetry. Paulinus returns to them, bringing important innovations, especially in the case of the epithalamium, which is transformed into an exhortation to the couple to practice chastity.

Prudentius and Paulinus Prudentius and Paulinus represent two different levels and aspects of Christian poetry in these years. Prudentius uses the viewpoint of the middle level of state officials, who constituted the backbone of the late Empire; Paulinus belongs to the rich senatorial nobility. Prudentius owes everything to his studies, to his professional abilities, while Paulinus can make the gesture of renouncing his goods and can be closer to the poor, feel as they do, and participate in their joys and sorrows over small matters. Hence the different roles the two writers assign to their poetry: Prudentius, who has lived at court and learned the publicity value of his poetry, proposes to realize his own Christian faith through literature, to give the new faith a poetic voice that can help to spread it. Paulinus aims rather to give his faith material expression, which he is able to do since he is (or would be) a bishop as well. At the center of a network of epistolary relations with the most important men of his day (some engaged in polemic with one another), and concerned over the social problems of his diocese, Paulinus also sees in poetry a means of edification and participation, but he does not regard it—as Prudentius, who is far more distant from the circles that count, seems to do—as the principal means of exercising his influence.

The construction of a church can engage him more than poetry. The noble Paulinus has lesser ambitions in this direction than Prudentius the official; indeed, all his effort seems directed at the attenuation of tones and passions that are too intense, of expressions that are too strong. The life of the peasants and the stories of animals are his preferred subjects, and this passion for the fields also helps make him comparable to the great model that he had proposed for himself, the Virgil of the *Bucolics* and the *Georgics*.

The *Querolus*

The only extant comedy from imperial times

The second half of the fourth century marks not only the revival of poetic activity but also a return to drama. The comedy entitled *Querolus sive Aulularia* is the work of an anonymous author from a Gallic milieu. The *Querolus* ("Complainer") is to be placed in the last years of the fourth century or the first of the fifth, and it is important because it is the only instance of Latin comedy under the Empire that has reached us. It shows us how the structure of a theatrical script has changed from the texts of Plautus and Terence and how its enjoyment by the public is different now. The author says he has written his work *fabellis atque mensis,* that is, to be read or performed during banquets, at private recitals, in other words, and no longer on the stage. Another important innovation is that the text is written, not in verses, as had been the custom of the Greek and Roman theater, but in prose, though the prose is peculiar, full of suggestions of meter. It is significant that the late ancient dramatic texts, intended for an audience that was different and more select than the one that had attended performances in the theater, adopt a different form of expression, one that anticipates by many centuries modern prose drama.

A text in prose, intended for reading

Summary of the Querolus

Leaving aside these formal differences, the *Querolus* is different from the ancient comedies in its plot and characters. The reference in the title to Plautus's *Aulularia* does not mean that we have here a reworking of a classic. The *Querolus* is, if anything, the sequel to the *Aulularia,* a continuation of the story, in which the theme of avarice, which is central in Plautus's comedy, is much less important.

The story goes as follows: The elderly Euclio, the miser of the *Aulularia,* dying in a foreign land, confides to Mandrogerus that he has hidden a treasure in his house, and he asks him to tell his son Querolus about it; in return, Mandrogerus will be co-heir. Mandrogerus, along with two swindlers, enters Querolus's house, after convincing him that he alone can free him from bad luck by means of magic, and steals the treasure. When the strongbox is opened, the three thieves find a funerary urn; convinced that they have been deceived by Euclio, they throw it out of the window. The urn breaks, and out comes the gold for all to see. Mandrogerus now asks Querolus for the promised share in the inheritance, and Querolus reproaches him with the attempted theft. In the end they resort to an arbitrator, who assigns all the gold to Querolus but compels him to maintain Mandrogerus as a parasite.

The character of Querolus

The protagonist Querolus is well portrayed. He is unlucky, but he seems to bring about the unluckiness by his continual complaining about everything and everybody. He is a misanthrope convinced that the defects and the faults lie always in others, but he is obliged to have a long conversation, or rather interrogation, with the *Lar familiaris.* The *Lar,* the tutelary genius, also appears in the *Aulularia,* where he performs the function of prologue, but in the *Querolus* he becomes much more important. In a certain sense, he is Querolus's double, his more intelligent half, and the scene of the dialogue between them is like an examination of one's conscience, of the sort that the late ancient Stoics recommended to the *vir bonus* every day. We are not, to be sure, at the level of Augustine's *Confessions,* but the emphasis on the fact that no one has the right to consider himself just in the abstract is the result of the same moral conception, which was common among the prosperous classes of late antiquity.

A morality meeting the ideals of gentlemen

The comedy responds not only to the ideals of these cultivated gentlemen but also to their customs, with the description, which is quite plausible, of a villa in Gaul and the people who inhabit it, from the master to the slaves. A long monologue describing the life of the slaves is given to a slave. It is not, certainly, a description of the real situation, or of how the slaves themselves saw it. The point of view, even though spoken by a slave, is always that of the masters, and it is so consoling that one concludes that slaves have nothing to envy in the life of their masters; on the contrary, the latter cannot allow themselves liberties and pleasures that are permitted to those from the lower strata of society.

The moral purpose, which is pervasive, but not in so oppressive a manner as to destroy the pleasure of the tale, has assured the *Querolus* popularity even during the Middle Ages. It was read and quoted, and there were those who went back to it in order to write a new *Aulularia,* continuing thus the success of the Plautine title.

BIBLIOGRAPHY

The Great Cultural Renaissance

In addition to A.H.M. Jones, *The Later Roman Empire* (3 vols., Oxford 1964), S. Mazzarino, *The End of the Ancient World* (London 1966), P.R.L. Brown, *The World of Late Antiquity* (London 1971), and R. Lane Fox, *Pagans and Christians* (London 1986), see F. Lot, *The End of the Ancient World and the Beginning of the Middle Ages* (New York 1932), A. Momigliano, *The Conflict between Paganism and Christianity* (Oxford 1963), E. R. Dodds, *Pagan and Christian in an Age of Anxiety* (Cambridge 1965), and J. Geffcken, *The Last Days of Greco-Roman Paganism* (Amsterdam 1978). On the literary side, see T. R. Glover, *Life and Letters in the Fourth Century* (Cambridge 1901), P. Courcelle, *Late Latin Writers and Their Greek Sources* (Cambridge, Mass. 1969), J. W. Binns, ed., *Latin Literature of the Fourth Century* (London 1974), and Fondation Hardt Entretiens 23, *Christianisme et formes littéraires de l'antiquité tardive en l'occident* (Geneva 1977). S. G. MacCormack's *Art and Ceremony in Late Antiquity* (Berkeley and Los Angeles 1981) is a rich and wide-ranging study. There are good treatments of many of the writers mentioned in the new *Handbuch der lateinischen Literatur der Antike,* vol. 5, ed. R. Herzog et al. (Munich 1989); the long introduction (1–51) is especially useful.

The *Oxford Dictionary of the Christian Church,* by F. L. Cross (ed. 2 Oxford 1974), offers useful introductions to the principal "heresies"; see also D. Christie-Murray, *A History of Heresy* (Oxford 1976). On Arianism, see most recently R.P.C. Hanson, *The Search for the Christian Doctrine of God: The Arian Controversy, 318–381* (Edinburgh

1988). Much interest has been excited in the study of Manichaeism by the discovery of the Greek "Cologne Mani Codex" (see L. Koenen and C. Roemer, *Der Kölner Mani Kodex: Abbildungen und diplomatischer Text* [Bonn 1985, *Kritische Edition* Opladen 1988], as well as the English translation of R. Cameron and A. J. Dewey, Missoula 1979); for a comprehensive survey, see S.N.C. Lieu, *Manicheanism in the Later Roman Empire and Medieval China* (Manchester 1985), as well as the papers of the symposium, *Codex Manichaeus Coloniensis,* ed. L. Cirillo (Cosenza 1990). On the Donatists, see J. L. Maier, *Le Dossier du Donatisme* (2 vols., Berlin 1987–89); on Priscillian, H. Chadwick, *Priscillian of Avila* (Oxford 1976); and on Pelagianism, B. R. Rees, *Pelagius: A Reluctant Heretic* (Woodbridge 1988).

For Charisius, Diomedes, and Dositheus, see H. Keil, *Grammatici Latini* (7 vols., Leipzig 1857–80), vols. 1 and 7. Note also A. C. Dionisotti, in *JRS* 72 (1982) 83–125, on the *Hermeneumata pseudo-Dositheana* (which are not in any way connected with Dositheus). There is a useful bibliographical survey of work on the *Grammatici Latini* by A. Della Casa in *BStudLat* 15 (1985) 85–113.

Nonius Marcellus's *De Compendiosa Doctrina* is edited by W. M. Lindsay (Leipzig 1903); see also his monograph on Nonius's methods of citation, *Nonius Marcellus' Dictionary of Republican Latin* (Oxford 1901). The Italian series of *Studi Noniani* (Genoa 1967–) contains many important articles.

Aelius Donatus's commentary on Terence was edited by P. Wessner in three volumes (Leipzig 1902–8): see G. B. Waldrop, "Donatus, the Interpreter of Virgil and Terence," *HSCP* 35 (1927) 75–142, and L. Holtz, *Donat et la tradition de l'enseignement grammatical* (Paris 1981) 15–36. See also *Scholia Terentiana,* ed. F. Schlee (Leipzig 1893), and *The Scholia Bembina in Terentium,* ed. J. F. Mountford (Liverpool 1934), as well as N. Marinone, *Elio Donato, Macrobio, e Servio commentatori di Virgilio* (Vercelli 1946). The *Interpretationes Vergilianae* of Tiberius Claudius Donatus were edited by H. Georgii (2 vols. Leipzig 1905–6); see M. Squillante Saccone, *Le Interpretationes Vergilianae di Tiberio Claudio Donato* (Naples 1985), and *BStudLat* 13 (1983) 3–28. The commentary of Servius was edited by G. Thilo and H. Hagen (Leipzig 1878–1902); this is gradually being replaced by the "Harvard Servius" (vol. 2 Lancaster 1946, vol. 3 Oxford 1965). For an introduction, see A. F. Stocker, "Servius servus magistrorum," *Vergilius* 9 (1963) 9–15.

For the minor rhetoricians, see again C. Halm, *Rhetores Latini Minores* (Leipzig 1863). There is an edition of Arusianus Messius's *Exempla Elocutionum* by A. Della Casa (Milan 1977). Fortunatianus has been edited by L. Calboli Montefusco (Bologna 1979), and Julius Victor by R. Giomini and M. Silvana Celentano (Leipzig 1980).

The standard edition of Macrobius's *Commentary* and *Saturnalia* is that of J. Willis (2 vols. Leipzig 1970); the older edition of L. Jahn is still useful. On the *Saturnalia,* see esp. the annotated translation by P. V. Davies (New York 1969); on the *Commentary,* the major Italian edition with text, translation, and notes by L. Scarpa (Padua 1981) and the annotated English translation by W. H. Stahl (New York 1952). See also T. Whittaker, *Macrobius or Philosophy, Science, and Letters in the Year 400* (Cambridge 1923), A. Cameron, "The Date and Identity of Macrobius," *JRS* 56 (1966) 25–38, and J. Flamant, *Macrobe et le Néo-Platonisme latin à la fin du IVe siècle* (Leiden 1977). The bibliographical survey by L. Fiocchi in *BStudLat* 12 (1982) 34–85 includes extensive discussion.

On the *subscriptiones* that attest "editorial" activity in this period, see J.E.G. Zetzel, *Latin Textual Criticism in Antiquity* (New York 1981) 211–31. For Chalcidius's *Timaeus,* see the major edition by J. H. Waszink (London 1962), as well as J. Dillon, *The Middle Platonists* (Leiden 1977) 401–8.

There are editions of the *Panegyrici Latini* by E. Galletier (3 vols., Paris 1949–55), R.A.B. Mynors (Oxford 1964), and P. Fedeli and V. Paladini (Rome 1976). For other panegyrical texts, see conveniently the introduction to T. Janson, *Latin Prose Prefaces* (Hildesheim 1979), as well as S. D'Elia, *Ricerche sui Panegirici da Mamertino a Massimiano* (Naples 1961), S. MacCormack in *Révue des Études Augustiniennes* 22 (1976) 29–77, and U. Asche, *Roms Weltherrschaftsidee und Aussenpolitik in der Spätantike in der Spiegel der Panegyrici Latini* (Bonn 1983). There is a good Italian survey by G. Barabino in the *Dizionario degli scrittori greci e latini* (Milan 1987). On Eumenius, see W. S. McGuiness in *G&R* 21 (1952) 97–103.

There is a complete edition of the works of Symmachus by O. Seeck (Berlin 1883); for the *Letters*, see the edition of J. P. Callu (2 vols., Paris 1972–82), and for the *Relationes*, that of R. H. Barron, *Prefect and Emperor* (Oxford 1973, with translation, introduction, and notes). There is a series of Italian historical commentaries on the *Letters* published in the Biblioteca di Studi Antichi (Pisa 1981–). See A. Cameron in Fondation Hardt Entretiens 23, *Christianisme et formes littéraires,* and J. M. Matthews in Binns, *Latin Literature of the Fourth Century,* as well as the papers of the *Colloque genevois sur Symmaque,* ed. F. Paschoud (Paris 1986), and G. Haverling, *Studies in Symmachus' Language and Style* (Gothenburg 1988).

The *Medicina Plini* is edited by A. Önnefors (Berlin 1964); see his *In Medicinam Plini Studia Philologica* (Lund 1963). For the *Euporiston Libri* of Theodorus Priscianus, see the edition by V. Rose (Leipzig 1894), as well as T. Meyer, *Theodorus Priscianus und die römische Medizin* (Jena 1909). The pseudo-Apuleian *Herbarius* is edited by E. Howald and E. Sigerist (Leipzig 1927). The *Mulomedicina Chironis* is edited by E. Oder (Leipzig 1901); for the Latin veterinary tradition, see K. D. Fischer in *Papers of the Liverpool Latin Seminar* 5 (Liverpool 1981) 285–303.

Vegetius's *Mulomedicina* is edited by E. Lommatzsch (Leipzig 1903); for the *Epitome Rei Militaris* see the edition of C. Lang (ed. 2 Leipzig 1885), as well as B. Campbell in *JRS* 77 (1987) 12–29. For the *De Rebus Bellicis,* see the edition by R. I. Ireland (Leipzig 1984), and E. A. Thompson, *A Roman Reformer and Inventor* (Oxford 1952, with translation); see also H. Brandt, *Zeitkritik in der Spätantike* (Munich 1988).

For Palladius, see the editions of J. Svennung (Gothenburg 1926) and R. H. Rodgers (Leipzig 1975); a Budé edition of the *Opus Agriculturae* by R. Martin is in progress (Paris 1976–). See R. H. Rodgers, *An Introduction to Palladius* (London 1975, mainly on the text), and the massive linguistic study by J. Svennung, *Untersuchungen zu Palladius* (Uppsala 1935).

Vibius Sequester has been edited by P. Parroni (Milan 1960) and R. Gelsomino (Leipzig 1967); see also J. O. Thomson, *A History of Ancient Geography* (Cambridge 1948).

The best edition of the *Peregrinatio Aetheriae* is that of A. Franceschini and R. Weber, Corpus Christianorum, or CC, 175 (Turnholt 1965). E. Löfstedt's *Philologische Kommentar zur Peregrinatio Aetheriae* (Uppsala 1936) is a famous study of later Latin. See also the annotated translation of J. Wilkinson (ed. 2 Jerusalem 1981) and P. W. L. Walker, *Holy City, Holy Places?* (Oxford 1984).

The *De Ponderibus et Mensuris* may be found in A. Riese's edition of the *Anthologia Latina* (Leipzig 1906); see also B. Effe, *Dichtung und Lehre* (Munich 1977) 227–30.

The Triumph of Christianity

On the age of Constantine in general, see A. Alföldi, *The Conversion of Constantine and Pagan Rome,* trans. H. Mattingly (ed. 2 Oxford 1969), D. Bounder, *The Age of Constantine and Julian* (London 1978), T. D. Barnes, *Constantine and Eusebius* (Cambridge 1981), *The New Empire of Diocletian and Constantine* (Cambridge, Mass. 1982), R. Macmullen, *Constantine* (ed. 2 London 1987), and M. Grünewald, *Constantinus Maximus Augustus: Herrschaftspropaganda in der zeitgenössischen Überlieferung* (Stuttgart 1990).

There is an edition of Arnobius's *Adversus Nationes* by C. Marchesi (ed. 2 Turin 1934), and there is a good annotated translation by G. E. McCracken (2 vols., Westminster

1949). A Budé edition with notes by H. Le Bonniec is in progress (Paris 1982); see also G. Gierlich's commentary on the first two books (Diss., Mainz 1985). See also F. Gabarrou, *Arnobe* (Paris 1921), and E. Rapisarda, *Arnobio* (Catania 1945).

There are texts of Lactantius's works in Corpus Scriptorum Ecclesiasticorum Latinorum, or CSEL, 19 and 27; there are also important later French editions of the *De Opificio Dei* by M. Pervin (2 vols., Paris 1974), of books 1, 2, and 5 of the *Institutiones* by P. Monat (Paris 1986, 1987, 1973), and of the *De Ira Dei* by C. Ingremeau (Paris 1982; see also the German edition of H. Kraft and A. Wlosok, ed. 2 Darmstadt 1971) and an English edition of the *De Mortibus Persecutorum* by J. L. Creed (Oxford 1984). See R. M. Ogilvie, *The Library of Lactantius* (Oxford 1978), T. D. Barnes in *JRS* 63 (1973) 29–46, R. Pichon, *Lactance* (Paris 1901), V. Loi, *Lattanzio nella storia del linguaggio e del pensiero teologico preniceno* (Zurich 1970), and F. Amarelli, *Vetustas-Innovatio* (Naples 1978).

The *Mathesis* of Firmicus Maternus is edited by W. Kroll, F. Skutzsch, and K. Ziegler (2 vols., Leipzig 1897–1913), the *De Errore Profanarum Religionum* by K. Ziegler (Leipzig 1907, ed. 2 Munich 1953); there is also a Budé edition with French translation and commentary by R. Turcan (Paris 1982), and there is an Italian commentary by A. Pastorino (Florence 1956). There is an English translation with notes by C. A. Forbes (New York 1970). See also F. H. Cramer, *Astrology in Roman Law and Politics* (Philadelphia 1954), A. J. Festugière, *Trois dévots païens* (Paris 1944), A. Bouché-Leclercq, *L'Astrologie grecque* (Paris 1899), F. Boll, *Sphaera* (Leipzig 1903), and W. Gundel and H. G. Gundel, *Astrologoumena* (Wiesbaden 1966).

For Lucifer of Cagliari, see the edition by G. F. Diercks (Turnholt 1978); for Eusebius of Vercelli, that of V. Bulhart (Turnholt 1957), as well as E. Crovella, *S. Eusebio di Vercelli: Saggio di biografia critica* (Vercelli 1961), and L. A. Speller in *JThS* 36 (1985) 157–65.

An edition of the works of Marius Victorinus is in progress in the CSEL; the first part, edited by P. Henry and P. Hadt, is of the *Opera Theologica* (Vienna 1971). There is also a Teubner text by A. Locher (Leipzig 1976), who also edited the commentaries on the letters of St. Paul (Leipzig 1972). For the *Ars Grammatica*, there is an excellent edition with Italian commentary by I. Mariotti (Florence 1967); for the other rhetorical and grammatical works, including the commentary on Cicero's *De Inventione*, see Keil, *Grammatici Latini*, vol. 6, and Halm, *Rhetores Latini Minores*. The major study is P. Hadot, *Marius Victorinus, recherches sur sa vie et ses oeuvres* (Paris 1967); see also his edition of the *Traités théologiques sur la Trinité* (2 vols., Paris 1960) and *Porphyre et Victorinus* (2 vols., Paris 1968, on the connection with the neo-Platonist Porphyry).

The main editions of the works of Hilary of Poitiers are in CSEL 22 and 65. For the *De Trinitate*, see the edition by P. Smulders (CC 62 and 62A, Turnholt 1979–80). There are a number of separate editions with French translation and commentary in the Sources Chrétiennes series; see esp. that of *In Matthaeum* by J. Doigner (2 vols., Paris 1978–9). See G. M. Newlands, *Hilary of Poitiers: A Study in Theological Method* (New York 1978), M. F. Butrell, *The Rhetoric of Saint Hilary of Poitiers* (Washington, D.C., 1933), C.F.A. Borchhardt, *Hilary of Poitiers' Role in the Arian Struggle* (The Hague 1960), P. Galtier, *Saint Hilare de Poitiers, le premier docteur de l'Église latine* (Paris 1960), H. C. Brennecke, *Hilaris von Poitiers und die Bischoffsopposition gegen Konstantinus II* (Berlin 1984), and the papers collected in *Hilare de Poitiers, évêque et docteur* (Paris 1968) and *Hilare et son temps* (Paris 1969).

On Juvencus and biblical epic, see esp. M. J. Roberts, *The Hexameter Paraphrase in Late Antiquity* (Liverpool 1985), and R. Herzog, *Die Bibelepik der lateinischen Spätantike* (Munich 1975). There are texts by J. Huemer (CSEL 24, Vienna 1891) and K. Marold (Leipzig 1886).

For Optatian, see the edition of G. Polara (2 vols., Turin 1973), as well as T. D.

Barnes in *AJP* 96 (1975) 173–86 and W. Levitan in *TAPA* 115 (1985) 245–69. For Tiberian, see the edition of U. Zuccarelli (Naples 1987) and A. Cameron's discussion of Tiberian and the *Pervigilium Veneris* in *La poesia tardo-antica* (Messina 1984) 209–34.

The Last Pagan Historiography and the New Christian Historiography

For the "Chronographer of 354," see the edition by T. Mommsen, *Chronica Minora* 1 (Monumenta Germanica Historica, Auctores Antiquissimi, 9, Leipzig 1892), as well as M. R. Salzman, *On Roman Time* (Berkeley and Los Angeles 1990), and H. Stern, *Le Calendrier de 354* (Paris 1953). There is a recent Budé edition of Sextus Aurelius Victor by P. Dufraigne (Paris 1975), but this is unreliable (see R. J. Tarrant in *Gnomon* 50 [1978] 355–62). For a general historical study, see F. den Boer, *Some Minor Roman Historians* (London 1972) 19–113, and H. W. Bird, *Sextus Aurelius Victor* (Liverpool 1984). The *Origo Gentis Romanae* is edited by J. C. Richard (Paris 1983); see esp. A. Momigliano in *Secondo contributo alla storia degli studi classici* (Rome 1960) 145–76. For the *De Viris Illustribus,* the best edition is still that of F. Pichlmayr and R. Gruendel (Leipzig 1966); see also that of W. K. Sherwin (Norman 1973), as well as M. M. Sage in *TAPA* 108 (1978) 217–48 and *Hermes* 108 (1980) 83–100 and L. Braccesi, *Introduzione al De viris illustribus* (Bologna 1973).

The standard edition of Eutropius is that of C. Santini (Leipzig 1970); see also den Boer, *Some Minor Roman Historians,* 114–72, and M. Capozza, *Roma fra monarchia e decemvirato nell'interpretazione di Eutropio* (Rome 1973). For the *Breviarium* of Festus, see the English edition with commentary by J. W. Eadie (London 1967), as well as den Boer, *Some Minor Roman Historians,* 173–223, and B. Baldwin, "Festus the Historian," in *Studies in Late Roman and Byzantine History, Literature, and Language* (Amsterdam 1984) 79–99. For the *Excerptum Valesianum,* see the edition of V. Velkovad and J. Moreau (ed. 2 Leipzig 1968) and the full text and commentary of I. König (Trier 1987), as well as T. D. Barnes in *Phoenix* 43 (1989) 158–61. The *Periochae* of Livy were edited by O. Rossbach in the Teubner series (Leipzig 1910); see also L. Bessone in *Atene e Roma* 29 (1984) 42–55.

There is a convenient modern edition of Ammianus Marcellinus by W. Seyfarth (2 vols., Leipzig 1978; see his earlier edition with German translation and notes, Berlin 1970–71); a Budé edition with French translation and notes by E. Galletier et al. is in progress (Paris 1968–), and there is a Loeb by J. C. Rolfe (3 vols., Cambridge, Mass. 1935–40). There is a commentary on books 14–19 by P. de Jonge (Groningen 1935–82, book 14 in German, 15–19 in English), which is being continued by J. den Boeft, D. den Hengst, and H. C. Teitler (book 20 Groningen 1987); see also J. Szidat, *Historische Kommentar zu Ammianus Marcellinus, Buch XX–XXI* (2 vols., Wiesbaden 1977–81). There is a comprehensive English study by J. Matthews, *The Roman Empire of Ammianus Marcellinus* (London 1989, with full bibliography).

The standard edition of the *Historia Augusta* is that of E. Hohl, W. Seyfarth, and C. Samberger (Leipzig 1965); there is a Loeb edition by D. Magie (Cambridge, Mass. 1922–32). For the skeptical position, see esp. the work of R. Syme: *Ammianus and the Historia Augusta* (Oxford 1968), *Emperors and Biography* (Oxford 1971), *The Historia Augusta: A Call for Clarity* (Bonn 1971), and *Historia Augusta Papers* (Oxford 1983), as well as T. D. Barnes, *The Sources of the Historia Augusta* (Brussels 1978), P. White in *JRS* 57 (1967) 115–33, and I. Marriot in *JRS* 69 (1979) 65–74. The most important scholar to accept multiple authorship was A. Momigliano; see *Secondo contributo alla storia degli studi classici,* 104–43 (and note *Ottavo Contributo* [Rome 1982] 392–98). The volumes of the series Beiträge zur Historia-Augusta-Forschung (Bonn 1963–, mostly proceedings of the annual Historia-Augusta-Kolloquium) contain many important treatments of detail.

For Julius Obsequens, see the edition of O. Rossbach in *T. Livii Periochae* (Leipzig 1910), as well as P. L. Schmidt, *Iulius Obsequens und das Problem der Livius-epitome* (Mainz

1968); for Hegesippus, see the edition by V. Ussani (CSEL 66, 2 vols., Vienna 1932–60) and L. H. Feldman, *Josephus and Modern Scholarship* (Berlin 1984) 40–43.

Dictys Cretensis has been edited by W. Eisenhut (ed. 2 Leipzig 1973, with a text of the papyrus fragment of the Greek original); there is an English translation by R. M. Frazer (Bloomington 1966). See also S. Merkle, *Die Ephemeris belli Troiani des Diktys von Kreta* (Frankfurt 1989).

For the *Res Gestae Alexandri Macedonis,* see the edition by B. Kübler (Leipzig 1888), as well as D. Romano, *Giulio Valerio* (Palermo 1976); for the *Itinerarium Alexandri,* that of H.-J. Haussmann (Diss., Cologne 1968); and for the *Epitome,* that of P. H. Thomas (ed. 2 Leipzig 1966). On the Latin Alexander Romances in general, see R. Merkelbach, *Die Quellen des griechischen Alexander-Romans* (Munich 1977).

The Latin version of the *Vita Antonii* is edited with Italian translation and commentary by G. J. M. Bartelink (Milan 1981, with an important introduction by C. Mohrmann).

Poetry and Drama

Ausonius is edited with English commentary by R.P.H. Green (Oxford 1991); see also the older editions of R. Peiper (Leipzig 1886) and S. Prete (Leipzig 1978, but see M. D. Reeve in *Gnomon* 52 [1980] 444–51). There is a Loeb by H. G. Evelyn White (London and Cambridge, Mass. 1919–21). Much has been written on the *Mosella;* see the editions by C. Hosius (Marburg 1909) and C. M. Ternes (Paris 1972), as well as, most recently, E. J. Kenney in *G&R* 31 (1984) 190–202, M. Roberts in *TAPA* 114 (1984) 343–53, and C. Newlands in *TAPA* 118 (1988) 405–19. For a plea for the revaluation of the other works, see S. Georgia Nugent, in *The Imperial Muse,* ed. A. J. Boyle (Bendigo 1990) 236–60. In French, note the collection of articles by C. M. Ternes, *Études ausoniennes* (2 vols., Luxembourg 1983, 1980), as well as his bibliography in the *Bulletin des antiquités luxembourgeoises* 14 (1983) and Wege der Forschung 652, ed. M. J. Lossau (Darmstadt 1991); there is also a very full bibliography in Green's edition.

The standard text of Claudian is that of J. B. Hall (Leipzig 1985); there is a Loeb by M. Platnauer (2 vols., Cambridge, Mass. 1922). Among commentaries may be mentioned those in English by H. L. Levy on *In Rufinum* (Cleveland 1971), J. B. Hall on *De Raptu Proserpinae* (Cambridge, 1969; see also the German commentary on book 1 by E. Potz, Grax 1984), and W. Barr, *De IV consulatu Honorii* (Liverpool 1981; see also J. Lehre, *Poesie und Politik in Claudians Panegyrikus auf das vierte Konsulat des Kaisers Honorius* [Königsberg 1984]); for others, see the list in Hall's edition, p. xxi. The major English study is A. Cameron, *Claudian: Poetry and Propaganda at the Court of Honorius* (Oxford 1970); see also his brief survey in Binns, *Latin Literature of the Fourth Century,* as well as S. Döpp, *Zeitgeschichte in Dichtungen Claudians* (Wiesbaden 1980), and A. Fo, *Studi sulla tecnica poetica di Claudiano* (Catania 1982).

There is a complete edition of Avienus's works by A. Holder (Innsbruck 1887); for the *Descriptio Orbis Terrae,* see the edition by P. van de Woestijne (ed. 6 Bruges 1961), for the *De Ora Maritima,* those of A. Schulten (Barcelona 1922) and D. Stichtenoth (Darmstadt 1968), and for the translation of Aratus, that of J. Soubiran (Paris 1981). See esp. A. Cameron in *CQ* 17 (1967) 385–99 and J. Matthews in *Historia* 16 (1967) 484–509. For Naucellius, see the editions of the *Epigrammata Bobbiensia* by F. Munari (Rome 1955) and W. Speyer (Leipzig 1963), as well as the latter's *Naucellius und sein Kreis* (Munich 1959). Avianus has been edited by A. Guaglione (Turin 1958) and F. Gaide (Paris 1980, with French translation and notes). The older English commentary of R. Ellis (Oxford 1887) is still useful; see also the article of Cameron mentioned above, Gaide's introduction, W. R. Jones in *Classical Studies Presented to B. E. Perry* (Urbana 1969) 203–9, and J. Küppers, *Die Fabeln Avians* (Bonn 1977).

For the Christian Latin poets, the first chapter of F.J.E. Raby, *A History of Christian-Latin Poetry* (Oxford 1953), remains fundamental; note also the works of J. Fontaine,

La letteratura latina cristiana (Bologna 1973), *Études sur la poésie latine tardive* (Paris 1980), and *Naissance de la poésie dans l'occident chrétien* (Paris 1981).

On Damasus, see A. Ferrua, *Epigrammata Damasiana* (Rome 1942), A. Ferrua and C. Carletti, *Damaso e i martiri di Roma* (Rome 1985), A. Salvatore, *L'epigramma damasiano In laudem Davids* (Naples 1960), and the proceedings of the conference *Saecula Damasiana* (Rome 1986).

For Proba's *Cento Vergiliana,* see esp. the edition with English translation and commentary by E. A. Clark and D. F. Hatch (Ann Arbor 1981), as well as D. F. Bright in *ICS* 9 (1984) 79–90 and D. Shanzer in *REAug* 32 (1986) 232–46. The *De Mortibus Boum* of Endelechius is included in C. Bücheler and A. Riese, eds., *Anthologia Latina* (Leipzig 1894) vol. 1.2, pp. 334–39; see W. Schmid in *RhM* 96 (1953) 101–65, as well as his article in *RAC* 5 (Stuttgart 1962).

The standard editions of Prudentius are those of J. Bergman (CSEL 51, Vienna 1926) and M. P. Cunningham (CC 126, Turnholt 1966); there is a Budé edition by M. Lavarenne (Paris 1943–51) and a Loeb by H. J. Thomson (2 vols., Cambridge, Mass. 1949–53). There is a commentary on the morning and evening hymns by M. van Assendelft (Groningen 1976). See also M. Smith, *Prudentius' Psychomachia: A Reexamination* (Princeton 1976), A.-M. Palmer, *Prudentius on the Martyrs* (Oxford 1985), S. Georgia Nugent, *Allegory and Poetics: The Structure and Imagery of Prudentius' Pscyhomachia* (Frankfurt am Main 1985), M. A. Malamud, *A Poetics of Transformation* (Ithaca 1989), C. Witke, *Numen Litterarum: The Old and the New in Latin Poetry from Constantine to Gregory the Great* (Leiden 1971), R. Herzog, *Die allegorische Dichtung des Prudentius* (Munich 1966), K. Thraede, *Studien zur Sprache und Stil des Prudentius* (Göttingen 1965), and I. Lana, *Due capitoli prudenziani* (Rome 1962). The older work by M. Lavarenne, *Études sur la langue du poète Prudence* (Paris 1953), has a good bibliography.

The standard edition of Paulinus of Nola is that of W. Hartel (CSEL 29–30, Vienna 1894). There is an introduction by W.H.C. Frend in Binns, *Latin Literature of the Fourth Century;* see also *JRS* 60 (1969) 1–11, R.P.H. Green, *The Poetry of Paulinus of Nola: A Study of His Latinity* (Brussels 1971), Witke, *Numen Litterarum,* 75–101, P. de Labriolle, *La Correspondence d'Ausone et de Pauline de Nole* (Paris 1910), W. Erdt, *Christentum und heidnisch-antike Bildung bei Paulinus von Nola* (Meissenheim am Glam 1976), and K. Kohlwes, *Christliche Dichtung und stilistische Form bei Paulinus von Nola* (Bonn 1979). In Italian, S. Prete has published a number of studies (see esp. *Paulino di Nola e l'umanesimo cristiano* [Rome 1964]), and the *Biblioteca Diocesana S. Paolino* of Nola publishes a series of essays under the title *Disce Paulinum* (Nola 1985–). See also A. Fo in *Metodologie della ricerca sulla tarda antichità* (Naples 1990) 361–82.

The standard edition of the *Querolus* is that of R. Peiper (Leipzig 1875); see also that of F. Corsaro (Bologna 1964) and his large-scale study *Querolus: Studio introduttivo e commentario* (Bologna 1965), as well as J. Küppers in *Philologus* 133 (1989) 82–103 and in English, D. P. Lockwood in *TAPA* 44 (1913) 215–32.

The Apogee of Christian Culture

1. THE FATHERS OF THE CHURCH

The "golden century" of Christian thought

The years from the second half of the fourth century to the sack of Rome are one of the most fertile eras in Latin literature, on account of the quantity of the works, their cultural richness, and the elegance of their form; yet there is above all one field of truly prodigious fertility, and that is patristics. "Fathers of the church" is the term used for the Christian writers of this period, both Greek and Latin, who successfully mediated between classical and Christian culture and carried the analysis of ethical and religious problems to depths and degrees of subtlety never before achieved. One may say, and it has been said, that in antiquity there were two epochs that were fundamental for the definition of man, of his social and cultural characteristics: the fifth and fourth centuries B.C. in Greece and the fourth and fifth centuries A.D. for Christian thought.

Emergence of great thinkers in the Latin world

The Latin world continues to be indebted to the Greek world, at least in theological thought and biblical exegesis, as is shown by the many translations made, but it also succeeds in producing its own figures of the very highest rank, in the fields of ecclesiastical policy, catechesis, and doctrinal analysis. It is rendered especially lively by a large group of what we might call intermediate intellectuals, who successfully undertake the task of transmitting the notions of the great thinkers to the faithful, orienting the latter in the difficult controversies between official doctrine and heresy, and making the church's organizational network more comprehensive and serviceable. Standing out, however, are the names of three great fathers who in different ways have shaped the entire history of Western Christianity: Ambrose, Jerome, and Augustine.

2. AMBROSE

LIFE

Ambrose was born around 339–40 at Treviri, one of the chief cities of Germany, where his father resided as praetorian prefect for Gaul. From an important senatorial family, already Christianized (and related to the powerful *gens Aurelia,* to which the pagan Symmachi belonged), Ambrose pursued the typical studies of young men of good family, who were expected to follow a career in public administration, and he attended the best schools of Rome. Around 370, when he was slightly more than thirty years old, he was sent to Milan as *consularis Liguriae et Aemiliae,* in effect, governor of all northern Italy, in which post he won the esteem and affection of the citizens and resolved a number of difficult situations. After the death in 374 of the bishop of Milan, Auxentius, who was an Arian, Ambrose had such success in calming the conflicts and the violence between Arians and orthodox Christians that the only way out of an otherwise insoluble predicament was to appoint Ambrose himself as bishop, despite the fact that he was a catechumen and so had never received baptism. He died in 397, after playing for more than twenty years a role of the greatest importance in the principal affairs of the Empire and the church, in which Ambrose always took part with the ability of a great politician but also with vehement combativeness. He had a fundamental role in the council of Aquileia in 381, which marked the defeat of Arianism in the West. He opposed Symmachus in the dispute over the Altar of Victory in the Senate. He intervened in problems of the Eastern church. He pressured Theodosius to adopt a rigidly anti-Jewish policy. And he threatened the emperor with excommunication and imposed public penitence on him after a police action against the city of Thessalonica. Ambrose was, in fact, one of the principal authorities of the state, and his part was considerably more influential than that of many popes, who were pushed into the background by his vigorous personality.

WORKS

Despite his political and ecclesiastical commitments, Ambrose composed a large number of works, even though not everything that has come down to us under his name should be certainly attributed to him. His works include ninety-one letters, some famous hymns (though the ones that are securely his are only four), sermons, and funeral and polemical speeches. His sermons were sometimes reworked and joined together to form new works. This is the case with the *Hexameron* (six books containing nine speeches on the Creation), with the *De Sacramentis,* and with many of his works on virginity (the *De Virginibus,* the *De Virginitate,* the *Exhortatio Virginitatis,* the *De Institutione Virginis,* etc.). Trinitarian theology is dealt with in the treatise *De Fide,* in three books, and in various other writings; on sin and grace we have the *De Paenitentia.* One of his most famous works is the *De Officiis Ministrorum,* in three books, which lists the duties of priests and provides them, and all Christians, with precepts for living. Also interesting is the *De Nabuthae,* about the problem of property and the relation between the rich and the poor. He wrote many commentaries on books and passages of the Old and the New Testament, including some Psalms and the Gospel of Luke.

Ambrose and the secularization of the church

The figure of Ambrose is exceptionally rich and complex. One can trace back to him, at least in part, that secularization of the church that brought it to intervene increasingly in the affairs of the world and gradually to take the place of the political institutions that were in decline. In particular, Ambrose witnesses a limiting of the independent decision-making power of the emperor, who, as a Christian, is subject to the church in all political initiatives of a moral bearing. The two funeral speeches delivered by the bishop of Milan for Valentinian II and Theodosius are interesting in this connection. In them Ambrose paints the picture of the *pius princeps* and at the same time establishes a kind of link between the emperor's Christian piety and his right to govern. Ambrose's preaching did not have reverberations solely in the political field. To his homilies, whose beautiful style was especially valued by the professor of rhetoric Augustine, is also due the conversion of the latter and the acquisition for Christianity thereby of a spirit that was one of the most subtle and most skillful in dealing with questions of theology and philosophy at the highest level.

The hymns

Although Ambrose's greatness as a historical figure is certainly beyond question, the evaluation of him as a writer is more controversial. The judgment on his hymns, however, is unanimously positive, and the authenticity of *Aeterne rerum conditor* (the most famous), *Iam surgit hora tertia, Deus creator omnium,* and *Veni redemptor gentium* is assured by the testimony of Augustine.

These lively poems (in iambic dimeters catalectic), which have shaped Christian song and music, have an interesting story, which is recounted by Ambrose himself in his *Sermo contra Auxentium,* an anti-Arian speech. In 386 the bishop had succeeded in wresting all the churches of Milan from the heretics, and when the empress Justina decided that at least one, the Portian, should be reserved for the worship of the Arians, who until a few years earlier had been half of the Christian population, Ambrose went to occupy it along with a mass of the faithful, in order to prevent the entry of the forces of public order who were to restore it to the Arians. To entertain those occupying the church during the long days when it was under siege by the army and to raise their spirits, Ambrose thought of having them sing these texts, whose rhythm was easy and whose content was edifying. The success that they had among the faithful and the successful outcome of the battle for the Portian church led to the hymns' being made a regular part of the Milanese liturgy and then of all Christian liturgy.

The correspondence

Ambrose's correspondence is also forceful, alternating familiar letters and official letters, expressions of affection and tender concern for the flock entrusted to him and grim threats of divine punishment. When he deals with fundamental events in the history of the Roman West and with the duties of Christians, Ambrose shows a refined elegance in narrative and a brilliant ability always to present all matters in the light that is most favorable to him. One theme that naturally recurs is the fight with the Arians, which Ambrose waged not only before the highest tribunals of the church, as at the council of Aquileia of 381, but also in the midst of the people; he operated with a multiplicity of edifying initiatives, such as the great fuss made over the rediscovery of the bodies of St. Gervase and St. Protase, who at the time were very famous in Milan. We also hear in Ambrose's letters the echo of the last battle against paganism, the dispute (already mentioned several times) over the Altar of Victory, which the senators wanted to put back in the Senate house. Symmachus, as we have seen, prepared a very elegant and persuasive speech to this effect, but two stern letters from Ambrose dissuaded the emperor from heeding the requests of the pagans. Frequently using biblical quotations, yet also a clear and even elegant

Latin, the correspondence depicts the role of the bishop, or at least of a great bishop, in late antiquity, his spiritual and temporal commitments and his duties towards the diocese and the entire church.

The De Officiis Ministrorum

Ambrose was particularly concerned with the duties of the clergy, to the point that he devoted an entire work to them, the *De Officiis Ministrorum,* which already in its title and in the number of its books, three, refers to Cicero's *De Officiis.* All the values and standards of behavior of the ancient world that are compatible with the new Christian ethic are retained—the cardinal virtues, the concept of natural law, and the priority of the rights of the collectivity over the rights of individuals. But the thesis of the book is that these principles achieve their full realization only within a system based on the Christian faith. Ambrose, in his constant comparison of classical and modern ideas, is more or less conscious of the adjustments and distortions of concepts and positions that he is producing, and we have more than merely a Christianization of ancient thought. The classicization of Christianity is equally evident and is fully consistent with the program of integrating church and Empire, of which Ambrose was the chief proponent.

The Hexameron

Like other writings, the *De Officiis Ministrorum* was created from several speeches delivered to the priests of the diocese. Ambrose's most famous exegetical work, the *Hexameron,* originated in a series of homilies for Holy Week. As the title indicates, it is a commentary on the six days of Creation, and therefore on the Old Testament book of Genesis. The *Hexameron* is in six books, and it shows the influence of similar writings by Greek Christian authors. Here perhaps more than in his numerous other exegetical works, Ambrose succeeds in giving literary charm to his writing: he can stand before the created world with the naive astonishment of the man seeing nature for the first time, but he can also describe it with a refined exposition that uses the traditional figures of rhetoric to the greatest advantage.

The theme of wealth

A theme taken up in various works is wealth and private property, which Ambrose condemns when it brings with it inadmissible differences between rich and poor. Especially in the *De Nabuthae* (the story of the poor Naboth, who has been deprived of his small vineyard and murdered by King Ahab) but also in the *De Tobia,* strong charges are leveled against avarice, which is closely connected to the passion for possession. Even in the *De Officiis Ministrorum* there are observations on the necessity of regarding the earth and its goods as the inheritance of all.

Ambrosiaster

Over the centuries many works that certainly do not belong to Ambrose have been attributed to him. For some of these (e.g., a commentary on Paul's *Epistles*) the author is usually identified by the name *Ambrosiaster* ("false Ambrose"), which was given to him by the humanists.

3. JEROME

LIFE

Sophronius Eusebius Hieronymus was born at Stridon in Dalmatia around 347. He went to Rome in 354 and studied in the city's best schools; his teachers included Marius Victorinus and Donatus, and his future enemy

Rufinus was a fellow student. He traveled a great deal, especially in the East, where he learned Greek and was ordained a priest. He spent three years leading a monastic life in the desert of Chalcis (where he did not get a favorable impression of the monks, who were too devoted to theological controversies). In 382 he returned to Rome, where he had great success. Pope Damasus chose him as his secretary, and many noblewomen selected him for their spiritual adviser, forming a circle that was based on his instruction. Upon the death of Damasus, in 384, Jerome's authority and prestige declined rapidly, and the excesses of his asceticism came in for heavy criticism. In 385 he therefore left the city for the East, followed by some of the matrons who had put themselves in his hands. Monasteries and convents were established on his initiative, one of them in 389 at Bethlehem, where Jerome passed the last part of his life and where he died, in 419 or 420.

WORKS

Jerome's principal work, which has shaped all Western culture, is the Latin translation of the Bible, the so-called *Vulgata.* We also have from him a large correspondence; three lives of hermit monks; commentaries on books of the Old and the New Testament; texts of religious polemic, such as the *Apologia adversus Libros Rufini,* in three books, and the *Contra Iohannem Hierosolymitanum Episcopum,* on the Origenian controversy; the *Adversus Iovinianum,* on asceticism and virginity; the *Adversus Vigilantium,* on the cult of the martyrs; the *Dialogus adversus Pelagianos,* in three books, against the heresy of Pelagius; and translations of Greek Christian authors. Two works are especially important for literary studies: the *Chronicon,* which translates, expands, and updates the work of the same title by the Greek writer Eusebius, including many important notices on ancient Latin authors, and the *De Viris Illustribus,* with 135 biographies of Christian writers, from St. Peter to Jerome himself.

Jerome's difficult character and the polemic with Rufinus

Jerome on a number of occasions shows a decidedly difficult character, if not as a writer, at least as a man of the church, and this may account for the many enmities that he created for himself during his own lifetime and for the often very severe judgments passed on him by many modern scholars. His harsh polemic with Rufinus (on whom see below) is typical from this point of view. Jerome had long shared Rufinus's enthusiasm for Origen and his method of interpreting the Bible, which was based on allegorical reading. According to this method, the various passages were not to be understood in a literal sense; rather, a hidden deeper meaning needed to be looked for. Jerome had promoted a wider familiarity with Origen and his theories in the West by translating some of the Greek thinker's works into Latin. Consequently, Jerome's about-face in 395 was very disturbing. Concerned by certain unorthodox aspects of Origen's thought, he wrote a harsh attack against John, the bishop of Jerusalem, who did not share his own new position and was a sincere supporter of Origen. Rufinus replied to the attack on John, but in relaxed and tranquil tones, declaring that he did not share Jerome's second thoughts and wanted instead to continue his work, going ahead with the translations of Origen's writings. Jerome then penned a violent reply to Rufinus, in 402–3, in which he avoids any discussion of the religious ideas and problems that ought to have been at the center of the debate and instead chooses the path of personal invective and abuse.

Jerome and Tertullian

In this Jerome recalls the violence of a Tertullian, but his aggressiveness is much less justified, since the times have changed profoundly and Christianity is no longer threatened by the persecutions. Moreover, one notes right from the beginning personal motives that are not always disinterested and ambiguities large and small, the excesses of one who wants to make up for positions he has previously taken by later presenting himself as the stoutest defender of their contraries.

Jerome's correspondence

Jerome's correspondence also testifies to his harsh character. Leaving aside the many letters that deal directly with the Origenian controversy, we see emerge from the correspondence the clear figure of a man who is brilliant, fascinating, and full of intelligence but also violently emotional, controlled by his desire to excel, and not disposed to accept objections calmly or to tolerate opinions different from his own. Already with Cicero and Pliny epistolography had shown itself to be an open literary genre, into which subjects of every sort fitted, problems of politics, literature, and daily life. With Jerome this tendency reaches its culmination. We find not only a greater richness of themes and subjects but a structural change as well; in its occasional developments the letter is transformed to the point of resembling different, specific literary forms. Thus we have in Jerome's correspondence a long biography (*epistula* 108, the so-called *epitaphium Sanctae Paulae*), a short treatise on the techniques of translation (*epistula* 57, *de optimo genere interpretandi*), exhortations to virginity, *consolationes,* and finally, long exegetical disquisitions on problematic passages of the Bible.

Some letters have become famous, especially those in which Jerome deals with the relation between Christianity and classical tradition. In one Jerome records the very famous dream he had during his first stay in the Holy Land. He had brought some classical works with him into the desert and continued to read them, alternating them with texts of faith, until one night the divine judge appeared to him in his sleep and reproached him and asked who he was. To Jerome's answer, "I am a Christian," God replied, *Ciceronianus es, non Christianus,* and this persuaded Jerome to solemnly abjure classicism and promise not to take a Latin author in his hand again. But the promise was not kept, and Jerome's relations with Rome and its culture were more intense than perhaps the writer himself would have wished. In another letter, after the sack of Rome in 410, he expresses his dismay at the fall of the world's capital and his sense that now everything is changing, and he says that the decline of the Empire's solid political and cultural structures must have consequences for religion as well.

The Vulgata

Jerome's masterpiece is, as was said, the *Vulgata.* Various Latin translations of the Bible were already in circulation. Precisely because of their number and the many differences among them, various problems arose; hence the need for a revision that would establish a definitive, standard text.

During his Roman period, at the behest of pope Damasus, Jerome prepared the translation of the New Testament and a translation of the Psalms, the latter made from the most common Greek text, the Septuagint, which in its turn was a translation of the Hebrew original. After his departure from Rome, during his long years in Bethlehem Jerome started on the work once again, using for his translation the edition of the Bible prepared by Origen (the so-called Hexapla), which gave under six columns the Hebrew text, its transliteration, and four different Greek translations. Jerome became convinced very quickly that it was necessary to translate into Latin directly from the Hebrew original, the *Hebraica veritas,* without going through the intermediary of a Greek text, and for this purpose he took up again his studies of Hebrew and completed them. In fifteen years of constant and fervid toil, from 391 to 406, the work was finished. With Jerome's translation, the Western church finally had a unitary and reliable text, which virtually down to our own day was destined to remain the only authorized version circulating in all the lands first of Latin speech and then of the Romance and the Germanic languages.

The later history of the Vulgata

The success of the *Vulgata* was not immediate, however. There were practical problems that slowed the spread of the new text, such as the necessity of having a sufficiently large number of copies in circulation. Then there was the natural resistance of Christians who were accustomed to read and quote the sacred books in another version, and in particular there was some resistance from within the church, from Augustine, for instance. The latter expressed his concern over the danger that a Latin text completely independent of the Greek text of the Septuagint, because translated directly from the Hebrew, could provoke a separation of the Western church from the Eastern, which used the Septuagint as its official text. Indeed, relations between the Latin church and the Greek church did become increasingly difficult with the passage of time; moreover, the distance between the two parts of the Empire was destined to grow larger for reasons more concrete and ineluctable. Nonetheless, the *Vulgata* represented a fundamental moment of cohesiveness for a West that had been devastated and divided by the invasions of the various Germanic peoples, with the result that its unifying function was far greater than the rupture that it may have helped to provoke.

The Chronicon

It remains to speak of the *Chronicon* and the *De Viris Illustribus.* The *Chronicle* of Eusebius was a brief synthesis of notices down to 325, a preparation for the Greek writer's more ambitious historical works, and as a repertory of information it was valuable. During his stay in Constantinople, in 381, Jerome translated it into Latin, and he supplemented it with more recent notices, from 325 to 378, and with information on the Latin world that Eusebius had not been able or had not wanted to include. Jerome is especially attentive to events of literary history, for which he may have used excellent sources, such as Suetonius's *De Viris Illustribus.* Despite instances of inexactness, which were due among other things to the speed with which Jerome usually worked, the *Chronicon* is valuable to us because, having lost all Jerome's sources, we have in him our only witness to much important information, especially on literary-historical subjects.

The De Viris Illustribus

Jerome's other historical work, the *De Viris Illustribus,* which belongs to the genre of biography, takes its title from Suetonius, and in part it reworks material drawn from Eusebius's *Historia Ecclesiastica,* to which it adds many interesting lives of Christian Latin writers. The evaluations are very personal and show the writer's likes and dislikes; it is clear that Jerome prefers rigid, ascetic figures such as Tertullian, in whom perhaps he recognizes something of his own quality as a fierce polemicist, whereas he treats badly those who support the secularization of the church, Ambrose above all.

4. AUGUSTINE

LIFE

Aurelius Augustinus was born at Thagaste, a city of Numidia, in northern Africa, in 354; his mother, Monica, was a fervent Christian. He studied first at Madaura and then at Carthage, where, while very young himself, he had an illegitimate son. When he was 19, reading Cicero's *Hortensius* brought on a profound spiritual crisis, which led him to subscribe to the doctrine of Manichaeism, which attempted to reconcile the transcendent character that belongs to every religion with aspects of rationalism that were stimulating to an intellectual. Augustine taught at Thagaste, then at Carthage, and finally (384) at Rome. Thanks to the recommendation of Symmachus, the leader of the pagan senatorial group, he obtained the chair of rhetoric at Milan, and he taught there from the fall of 384 onwards. At Milan his close relations with the city's neo-Platonic circles, his hearing Ambrose's sermons, and the presence of his mother, who had come to him along with his son, led to Augustine's definitive conversion. After giving up teaching and receiving baptism (387), he returned to Africa (on the return voyage his mother died), and there he devoted himself to the monastic life. In 391 he was ordained a priest at Hippo (today Bône, in Algeria), of which he became the bishop in 395 or the following year. As head of the diocese, he fought against various sects and heresies, especially the Manicheans, the Donatists, and the Pelagians, but he was also concerned with the concrete problems of his flock, which became graver and more urgent as the structures of the Empire gave way before the invasions. He died in 430, while Hippo was besieged by the Vandals, who, led by Genseric, were on the way to conquering northern Africa.

WORKS

According to a calculation made by his friend and disciple Possidius, Augustine was the author of 1,030 writings. Not all of them have come down to us, and some may be joined in collections, such as the *Sermons* or the *Letters;* in any event, they are so numerous that one cannot reasonably think of indicating all of them. They cover a span of fifty years, from the first works written at Carthage around 380 to the treatises that can be dated to the last years of his life. A traditional division groups them into: autobiographical works, philosophical works, apologetic works, dogmatic works, polemical works, moral works, exegetical works, letters, sermons, and poetic works.

The *Confessiones,* his most well-known and popular work, in thirteen books, belongs to the autobiographical works. The title does not refer to a confession of one's sins, but means rather "praise, exaltation of God." It was written in the first years of his episcopate, from 397 to 400. Books 1–9 narrate Augustine's life from his birth to the death of his mother. With book 10, autobiography gives way to philosophical reflections (especially the problem of memory) that are developed in the last books in the form of commentary on the biblical text about the Creation; in particular, book 11 is concerned almost entirely with examining the concept of time. One can assign to the same group the *Retractationes,* two books written in 426–27, in which Augustine reexamines and corrects all his earlier works, except for the *Sermons* and the *Letters,* which he did not have time to review.

Among the philosophical works, some of which are lost, one must mention at least the *Dialogues* of Cassiciacum (386–87), three works in dialogue form (three books *Contra Academicos,* a *De Beata Vita,* two books *De Ordine*), which report the discussions of the group of intellectuals who had retreated with him to a villa at Cassiciacum, near Milan, after the spiritual crisis that preceded his conversion; and also the *Soliloquia,* in two books, containing the dialogue between Augustine and Reason on God's knowledge and the soul. To this group one can also assign the *De Musica,* in six books, in which it is maintained that musical harmony is based on precise mathematical norms and reflects the divine harmony of the creation; and the *De Magistro,* a dialogue with his son on the methods and limitations of academic instruction.

The *De Civitate Dei,* in twenty-two books, written and published in groups from 423 to 427, is an apologetic work. It is, along with the *Confessions,* one of the most important of his writings, destined to have wide popularity among contemporaries and great success with posterity. After the sack of Rome in 410 the pagans accused the Christians of having provoked the disintegration and decline of the Empire. Augustine replies by emphasizing the errors of paganism and then predicating the existence of two cities, the earthly city, belonging to the devil, and the heavenly city, belonging to God. The boundaries of the two cities do not coincide with political boundaries; rather, they coexist within each individual. States, the expression of the earthly city, are destined to die, but the city of God is eternal.

The principal dogmatic work is the *De Trinitate,* fifteen books that occupied Augustine for twenty years, from 399 to 419. It deals with the problem of the Trinity on the basis of biblical quotations and philosophical-theological speculations.

The polemical works oppose the doctrines of the Manicheans, for example, the three books *De Libero Arbitrio,* completed at Hippo, in defense of that freedom of choice that the Manicheans denied or especially the thirty-three books *Contra Faustum Manichaeum,* of 397–400, which define the relation between faith and reason. Directed against the Donatists are the seven books *De Baptismo,* of 400–401, and the *Post Conlationem contra Donatistas,* of 412; the latter defends the validity of the sacraments, independent of the priest's state of grace, and opposes forms of violent protest that mixed religious strictness and claims of social justice and gave rise to bands of fanatics such as the *circumcelliones,* who went about devastating the large estates. To the dispute with the Pelagians belong the *De Spiritu et Littera,* of 412, and the *De Praedestinatione Sanctorum,* of 428–29, which aims at clarifying the role of divine grace in salvation and the impossibility of man's saving himself by his unaided actions. Other writings are concerned with Arianism and other heresies.

The moral works include writings against lying, on virginity, on marriage, and generally on the behavior to be observed in various situations of life. Also belonging to this group are the *De Opere Monachorum,* of 400, on the activities to which monks should devote themselves, and the *De Doctrina Christiana,* in four books, another of his more important writings, begun in 397 and finished only in 426. In it Augustine is concerned with how sermons should be delivered and especially with how biblical texts should be interpreted; the fourth book is particularly important, in that it analyzes the relations between classical rhetoric and Christian rhetoric, and thus between the Greco-Roman cultural tradition and the new requirements of a faith that does not want to make distinctions of class or education.

Very many works dealing with the first three books of the Old Testament, and especially Genesis, are among the exegetical works. On the New Testament one needs to mention, among others, the four books *De Consensu Evangelistarum,* written around 400, which examine and attempt to resolve the contradictions among the four Gospel narratives and also the various writings on the text of John.

There are more than two hundred letters, varying in length and subject, and, along with Augustine's own letters, some from his correspondents have also been preserved. They range from simple notes to actual treatises or stenographic reports of sessions of the clergy of Hippo. Among the most famous recipients are Jerome, to whom Augustine writes about problems of biblical exegesis, and Paulinus of Nola.

To the letters of Augustine that were already known another twenty-three previously unknown have now been added; these have been transmitted to us by two manuscripts preserved in France. They constitute a significant discovery on account of both the enlargement of our material and the subjects that are treated in them, which go back to Augustine's last years. Letter 1*A is particularly interesting; it had earlier been wrongly regarded as the prologue to the *De Civitate Dei,* and published as such.

The sermons number more than five hundred, even if not all those attributed to Augustine are really his. Some examine biblical passages, others have as their subject the lives of the saints and martyrs, others take their start from problems of morality and behavior or from particular occasions. They are always marked by clarity of exposition and by the forcefulness of their rhetoric, that new Christian rhetoric discussed theoretically in the *De Doctrina Christiana.*

Augustine's compositions in verse are very few. Only the poem *Psalmus Abecedarius contra Partem Donati,* of 394, deserves to be mentioned. It is an innovative poem, composed of couplets beginning with the letters of the alphabet in sequence; and its rhythm is no longer based on classical prosody, but on word accents. Such features made the poem easy to memorize even for uneducated people. This is a further proof of the flexibility of Augustine, who can adapt his style and expressive techniques to the audience he is addressing.

Augustine and the *Confessions*

Originality and profundity of thought

Augustine is the richest and most original of the Latin thinkers and at the same time a writer of great elegance who can give to his profound thoughts both an admirable clarity and an emotional force that lets the reader know he is in the presence of powerful ideas. His theories dominated a large part of the Middle Ages, or rather, one may say that they were the origin of them. And yet, when Western society faced the new epochal change, from the Middle Ages to the modern era, it was in him that the Protestant Reformation found the theoretical bases of its doctrines. His philosophical arguments are subtle and extraordinarily modern. One needs merely to think of his discovery of the relativity of time, which is not an absolute category but exists only in relation to the individual subjects who make use of it. The past, as such, no longer exists; the future does not yet exist; and the present is the fleeting moment of transition between these two nonentities, so that it is more appropriate to speak of a present memory of the past, of a present expectation of the future, and of a present consciousness of the present. No less subtle and fertile in development are his reflections on the relation between destiny, divine grace, original sin, and free will, which led him to a complex doctrine that at the same time rejects both the Manichean position, more strictly deterministic, which deprives man of any possibility of influence upon his own destiny, and the more attractive position of Pelagianism, which emphasizes man's independent space and assures salvation solely on the basis of personal merit.

Introspection and psychological analysis

To give even an approximate idea of the vast literary writings produced by a man who could illuminate the most obscure and disturbing aspects of his own soul and could write about them using all the formal artifices of rhetoric in magisterial fashion is a disheartening enterprise. Augustine always has some surprise, makes some unexpected leap, making all systematizations precarious and questionable. His introspection is at its greatest in the *Confessions,* where he reaches levels of psychological analysis never reached before and difficult to find again in later periods—distress over sin, which is oppressively present in the descriptions of his infancy and childhood; the dramatic sufferings of his various crises; the famous scene of his conversion, with the child's voice repeating in singsong fashion, *tolle, lege,* "take and read"; Augustine opening the Bible at random and finding in Paul's letter to the Romans the words that signal his transition from worldly life to the discipline of Christianity. All these vignettes are highly effective because of their ability to emphasize the feeling involved and to mix pathos with a lyrical language full of poetic coloring, in which the frequent reminiscences of the Bible create an atmosphere of inspired sacredness. The diary of an anxious pursuit of truth that culminates in conversion, the *Confessions* is far removed from the ordinary journeys of salvation known to the pagan world (a classic example being the happiness that Lucius, the protagonist of Apuleius's *Metamorphoses,* secures by his initiation), because there remains in Augustine, even when he is converted, a sense of anxious precariousness, which makes him feel like an eternal convalescent, always threatened by possible relapses into sin. This consciousness that no victory is definitive makes the *Confessions* unique in patristic literature, which in general sees in conversion the happy creation of an achieved certainty.

The Confessions: *a revolution in literary genre*

The work is exemplary, too, for the innovations that Christianity brings to the canons of the ancient literary genres. The protagonist is not an exceptional person because of the role he plays or the events he participates in; he is a common sinner who, like so many others before him, by the will of God has found the path of salvation. The events are not exceptional or marvelous in themselves; they become so only by the author's presentation of them, by his ability to blow up the tiniest detail out of proportion and to give dignity to facts that traditional literature passed over in silence or reduced to the merely comic. It is sufficient to recall the famous episode of stealing the pears, a prank that takes on a density of meaning because it allows the author to discover, at the base of this transgression, a taste for the gratuitous act. In company with a group of reckless age-mates he had stolen from a neighbor's tree several pears, most of which were later thrown to the pigs. The recollection of that youthful act of bravado, apparently without importance, gives Augustine the starting point for a series of exceptionally profound thoughts on the nature and the motives of sin:

> So you love nothing but the theft itself. . . . Who understands sins? Laughter quickened our hearts, so to speak, at the thought of deceiving all the people who did not suspect such an action from us and would have been greatly annoyed. Then why did I enjoy not acting alone? Perhaps because it is not easy to laugh by oneself? . . . So here it is before you, my God, the living record of my soul. Alone I would not have carried out that theft, to which I was drawn, not by what we stole, but by the very act of stealing; to do it alone did not really appeal to me, and I would not have done it. O hateful

friendship, inexplicable seduction of the spirit, eagerness to do harm that arises from play and games, thirst for someone else's loss unaccompanied by desire for one's own gain or eagerness for revenge. One says, Come on, let's do it, and the others are ashamed not to be shameless. (2.16 ff.)

Problems posed by the Confessions

A modern reader would have no doubt about the literary genre to which the *Confessions* belongs: it is an autobiography. But the matter cannot have been equally obvious for an ancient reader, who did not find in Augustine's writing much of the information obligatory in a biography—notices about his parents, the city where he was born, the course of his studies, and so on. The notices that Augustine does give about himself, however, are but marginally connected to such data, which receive attention only insofar as they reverberate in the protagonist's soul. In addition to being one of the very few ancient autobiographies, Augustine's work, precisely because of its nonconformist features, is the first autobiography in the modern sense of the term.

Furthermore, so avowedly autobiographical a work—even though an inner biography, the history of a soul—concludes with four books that the modern reader finds difficult to connect with the first nine. Even the idea that the transition from the personal biography to the allegorical commentary on Genesis serves to underline the relation between man and nature, the role of God as creator, and the appropriateness of singing his praises, still appears to be an unsatisfactory connection for a project that in the author's mind must have been more complex and significant. It is certain, however, that for a late ancient public the very variety within the *Confessions* could have had a positive value: if the first nine books showed all sinners that one should never despair of salvation, the last three books deployed a learning that could be appreciated by educated Christians interested in the exegesis of Scripture. Even the title itself is far from clear. It does not refer to a confession in the sense that we moderns give to the term, even though Augustine declares so many of his sins publicly and accuses himself of them in order to ask pardon of God; rather, it is witness rendered to God, the expression of gratitude for having shown him the road through sin and also praise for the marvelous architecture of the Creation. The *Confessions* is, from beginning to end, a single, immense prayer to God, the omniscient interlocutor to whom Augustine addresses his discourse in a language that, not by chance, is strongly influenced by the style of the Psalms.

Literary success of the Confessions

Over the centuries, every time the *Confessions* has met with the passion for interior dialogue, the form of inner investigation, or the taste for the literature of recollection, it would find admirers quick to succumb to its lure. The model would be actively operative (or at least presupposed, sometimes in polemic) in a humanist prone to confession, such as Petrarch, in the religious ardor of Luther and Calvin, in the contemplative fervor of the Spanish mystics, in the tranquil thought of Montaigne, in the Jansenists, and especially in Pascal, until the "poetry of memory" would make the young Augustine a romantic hero.

The *City of God*

Problems of background posed by the De Civitate Dei

Something similar is true for Augustine's other masterpiece, the *City of God*. Here, in order to evaluate properly the grandeur of the basic idea— that history must no longer be the history of nations, but the history of humanity—and the fundamental contribution that it makes to the construction of an ideological system of Christianity, we must take into account problems of background that are still unresolved for us and rendered more complex by the publication of the books in groups as the writing proceeded. This may explain the repetitions and some contradictions, but it does not adequately clarify the difficulties Augustine has in settling the relation between church and city of God and the relation between earthly city and pagan-temporal state, which sometimes seem to be identified with one another but at other times seem to have quite distinct roles.

The most consciously designed of Augustine's works

In Augustine's vast production, the *City of God* is not only the most imposing work on account of its length and the effort that went into it (the author himself called it "a great and arduous work," *magnum opus et arduum*) but also the work with the most conscious and ambitious project. It attempted to oppose definitively the force of the great pagan intellectual tradition and to dismiss the threat that lay in the literary and philosophical neo-Platonism that was still attempting to impose its own cultural primacy. It was not so much a question of opposing intransigent but individually isolated conservatives as it was a question of preventing the intellectual aristocracy, which was consciously and consistently organized, from forming a coherent ideology out of the prestigious pagan tradition and using it to inhibit the spread of Christianity. Seen in this light, the *City of God* is the final act in a long drama. Written by a former protégé of Symmachus (the powerful champion of the pagan party), it must have sanctioned the definitive repudiation of paganism by an aristocracy that claimed to dominate the intellectual life of its time.

Resistance of the last pagan culture

To recognize clearly the tastes of this conservative circle, it will be enough to recall Macrobius's *Saturnalia,* a book of imaginary conversations portraying the great Roman traditionalists at the time of their apogee (around 380). In these conversations we can glimpse something more than the aristocratic enjoyment of a great past; it is an entire culture struggling to survive. The old tradition, the *vetustas,* now must be "venerated always." We find ourselves before a curious phenomenon, the preservation in the present of an entire system of life that is trying to save itself by transfusing into itself the inviolable certainty of a venerated past. But that was not all. These men were also profoundly religious; they could rival the Christians in their firm belief in rewards and punishments after death. We may recall that Macrobius had also written a commentary on the *Somnium Scipionis* in which he showed how "the souls of those who have deserved well from human society leave their body to return to Heaven, to enjoy there an eternal blessedness." To these men Christianity appeared like a religion severed from the natural assumptions of an entire culture. The great Platonists of the time, Plotinus and Porphyry, could offer to these men a profoundly religious view of the world that, with utter naturalness, derived from an ancient and deeply rooted tradition. The assertions of the Christians, by contrast, lacked intellectual foundations and did not contain rationally acquired knowledge.

The demythologizing of Roman history

This, then, is the educated pagan aristocracy to whom, or rather against whom, Augustine speaks in the *City of God*. And while he aims at constructing an intellectual foundation for Christianity, he also demythologizes the great past of the Romans, that idealized refuge in which pagan culture sought shelter against the bitter reality of the present. With passionate irony Augustine shows that Roman history is not in fact full of moral *exempla;* that grave disasters of every sort were as common in the past as in the present; that these were nothing but the signs of human sinfulness; that the virtues or vices of the Romans counted for nothing; that the Romans were neither better nor worse than other peoples; that the Roman Empire, far from being the privileged object of Divine Providence, was completely unessential for the salvation of humanity and that it was, if anything, a historically determined phenomenon that was destined to disappear in time. Each point in his argument required historical examples and discussions. The public Augustine was addressing was accustomed to think in terms of Roman history. Thus, the *De Civitate Dei,* and especially its first books, is one long detailed polemic against the facts, persons, beliefs, and cultural and religious practices of Roman history (especially of the republican period); Augustine shows an extraordinary knowledge both of the historical classics and of more recent epitomators. His philosophy of

A philosophy of history: the action of Providence and the destiny of the two cities

history reaches unusual heights by virtue of its amplitude in time and space. Through the whole universe and for all time the Divine Providence miraculously guides and directs all things and all events, preparing the salvation of mankind. Augustine declares that men are not forever existent and are not destined to exist forever and that social justice in this world (the *civitas mundi*) has never been completely achieved. The two cities (the earthly and the heavenly) have had their beginning and will have their progression and their end. The two cities have opposite characters even though in fact they coexist mixed and bound up in every man. The future of mankind is that this inseparable mixture of the two realities will eventually undergo a separation. With the eye of his hope Augustine separated what he still saw joined and mixed in the reality of the world. Beyond the appearances he saw two peoples, the faithful and the unfaithful.

The contradictions of the peregrinus *in the city of the world*

The need to preserve one's identity as citizen of Heaven is, accordingly, the center of gravity in Augustine's conception, in his concrete way of understanding the relations between the city of God and the city of the world. Ordinary human society must make room for a group of men conscious of being different, for a *civitas peregrina,* a community of citizens who are "strangers in their own country." The *peregrinus,* the pilgrim-stranger, will need to complete his journey in order to leave the world in which he finds himself existing and come to the city of God. He is *peregrinus* insofar as he is a "stranger" who temporarily resides in the world because he cannot reject a close dependence on the life that surrounds him. This may be Augustine's most remarkable lesson: the consciousness that man, even the Christian, is truly bound to this world, bound by chains that, solely because they are human, are in some way necessary and can never be completely refused; they impose common duties that must be accepted. Thus, in the final analysis, the *City of God* does not propose flight from the world: it is a fervent invitation to live both within the world and detached from it.

Thought and Style

A cultural world of extraordinary immediacy

Augustine's complicated personal journey has enriched his thought with a large number of themes and starting points, which may not have found a definitive systematic placement but precisely for this reason exercise all the greater a fascination upon those periods that, like the present, shun naively integral constructions. A schoolteacher, he was brought up on texts of the classical period, and from these he got to know the best products of Greek and Latin culture. A Manichean, he came into contact with the thought of a sect that was one of the liveliest and most stimulating of the period, a sect whose importance in ancient thought is an object of careful analysis and revaluation today. A neo-Platonist, he learned deeply the lesson of the one who is for him the greatest philosopher of antiquity, Plato, and at the same time he took part in the philosophical developments of the latest current of pagan thought. In the *De Civitate Dei* he reappraises the role of Rome and her empire, yet he does not hesitate to request, in letters of impressive harshness, the aid of the state in repressing the Donatist schism. Profoundly tied to classical culture, he does not hesitate to question it in the *De Doctrina Christiana*. A sophisticated intellectual, he chose to wrestle with the most complex problems, which for some time had agitated the toughest thinkers, and he also focused on new questions, ones no less anxious and difficult than the earlier ones. A man of the church, he considered it his duty to reach the weakest and least educated of his flock, and he strove to write for all, not only for an elite of scholars.

A personal style

Augustine's style, which varies considerably from one work to another, also meets the need to reach every sort of audience. Reserved in the writings intended for learned readers and men of the church, it is considerably more colloquial in the *Sermons,* in which he attempts, through the repetition of individual words and phrases, to fix fundamental concepts in the memory of the faithful. The style of the letters similarly varies a good deal, including tones of deferential courtliness towards correspondents who hold important posts in the administration of the Empire or belong to the ranks of the *nobilitas.* His writing is articulated in phrases composed of short elements, musically arranged within the period according to precise correspondences in length, rhyme, and assonance. It is a style that presupposes reading aloud (as the ancients usually did) and loses much of its force in our silent reading. In any event, we cannot fail to notice the elegance of his composition, which tends at times even to an excess of artifice, as he incorporates the numerous biblical quotations in a continuous discourse without making the reader aware of any disagreeable sudden changes in tone.

Augustine lends himself to the most varied readings. One may take pleasure in identifying his techniques of construction and his reassuring system of perfect balances, which guarantee the stability of the whole. One may follow the difficult course of his thought, striving to keep up with an intelligence that rises towards God along steep roads traced by a subtle, relentless logic. One can sometimes cast a glance into the deep abysses that lie beside these roads or towards the heights that can on occasion be glimpsed, even though one realizes that one cannot remain standing long amidst these tensions. The greatest intelligences of all times have struggled with Augustine, but it is not easy to find one who has been able to interpret and to comprehend his vital difficulty without somehow diminishing it.

5. OTHER FATHERS OF THE CHURCH

Rufinus

Along with these three—Ambrose, Jerome, and Augustine—who had the most significant role in Latin patristics, many other authors were active, some of greater importance for theological and doctrinal questions, others more interested in literary aspects. One needs to mention first Tyrannius Rufinus of Aquileia (circa 345–411), who was initially a companion and friend of Jerome and then the object of his fiercest attacks.

Rufinus and Origen

Rufinus's original work is almost all tied to the controversy over Origen, whom he defends by hypothesizing—in the *De Adulteratione Librorum Origenis*—that the various unorthodox passages found in the writings of the Greek author are the work of forgers; and other writings, especially the two books of the *Apologia contra Hieronymum,* serve to justify his own position of warm appreciation for the great Greek thinker. At the invitation of Paulinus of Nola, he wrote the *De Benedictionibus Patriarcharum,* a work of Old Testament exegesis. But as with Jerome, Rufinus's work as translator is more important than his work as writer. He made many translations from Origen and also from the great Eastern fathers of the fourth century. The most interesting perhaps are those that deal with the monks of Egypt, which aided the spread of monasticism in the Latin West, and the reworking of Eusebius's *Historia Ecclesiastica,* which Rufinus translated, supplemented, and completed by adding to it the part dealing with the years 324–95.

Sulpicius Severus

Life of Sulpicius Severus

The Gaul Sulpicius Severus is a brilliant and attractive writer. Born in Gallia Aquitanica in 360, he studied at Bordeaux, became famous as a lawyer, and contracted an excellent marriage with a wealthy young woman of consular family. The untimely death of his wife and the suggestions of his friend Paulinus of Nola urged him towards the ascetic life when he was about thirty years old. After several years passed in various localities of

Gaul, in 396 he went to Tours. There he met the famous bishop Martin, who had a great influence upon his future activity as a writer. In 399 he gave up all his possessions, and with the financial aid of his mother-in-law, he built a monastery in southern Gaul, at Primulacium. He remained there until his death, in about 420.

The Vita Sancti Martini

Much of Sulpicius Severus's writing turns about the figure of Martin, to whom he devoted various works, among them the *Vita Sancti Martini,* one of the very earliest examples of a saint's life written in the West (see p. 654). All the available sources are used, though they are not subjected to a critical evaluation, and much room is left for miracles and fantastic descriptions; the historical reliability of the reconstructions suffers in part, but the result is forceful enough as propaganda, and, like the lives of the Eastern saints, the work is attractive to read. Martin is presented as an ideal of asceticism and devotion to God. He is engaged in a continuous struggle with the devil and carries out edifying feats that often have obvious supernatural features. Although this may astonish the modern reader, all the more since these scarcely credible deeds are told to us by a rather snobbish intellectual, it is necessary to keep in mind, first, that in late antiquity even persons of culture shared in those superstitious beliefs that today tend to be regarded as belonging to popular religion and, second, that Sulpicius appears to be extraordinarily chary of demoniacal visions and miraculous feats if his account is compared with the Eastern lives. In any case, the remarkable ability Sulpicius shows for striking the imagination of his readers has undoubtedly had a primary role in creating the legend of St. Martin, which is widespread in all the West and especially in France.

Other works of Sulpicius Severus

From the cycle for Martin come also two *Dialogi,* of slightly later date than the *Vita,* which recount the saint's miracles and deeds in still more popular tones. The work is in the form of a two-day dialogue conducted by Sulpicius himself, a Western monk, and a traveler returned from the East. It is structured upon the contrast between the miraculous acts of the Egyptian monks and the miracles performed by Martin, who, of course, proves to be not a whit inferior to the Easterners. We also have some letters that relate to the episodes of Martin's life and death and to his cult, and a historical work, in two books, entitled *Chronica.* This last aims at providing a short, easy manual of ecclesiastical history from the origins of the world to the year A.D. 400. The treatment of the heresy of Priscillian (see p. 623) is particularly full; and Sulpicius is not altogether unsympathetic towards some heresies.

Sulpicius Severus and Paulinus of Nola

The affinities between Sulpicius Severus and Paulinus of Nola are not confined to biographical events. As a writer, too, Sulpicius has much in common with his friend and fellow countryman. Although both men came from the upper classes and had an excellent education, they can capture whatever marvelous or fascinating material is circulating in the lower classes and become the singers—Paulinus in verse, Sulpicius in prose—of a fabulous world inhabited by saints and devils. Thus, through Christianity, with its subversion of values and hierarchies, milieus and realities that until then had remained at the margins of classical culture emerge and are destined to become among the most vital elements in the new medieval reality.

BIBLIOGRAPHY

For general introductions to the fathers of the church, see the *Patrologie* of B. Altaner and A. Stuiber (ed. 8 Fribourg 1978), the fifth edition of which has been translated into English by H. C. Graef (Fribourg 1960), and the four-volume *Patrology* of J. Quasten (Utrecht 1950–86; volume 4 is a collaborative work edited by A. di Bernardino, first published in Italian in 1978 and translated by P. Solari, Westminster, Md., 1986). Specifically on the Latin tradition, see S. D'Elia, *Letteratura latina cristiana* (Rome 1982), with bibligraphy. Note also the article by M. Simonetti, "Padri della Chiesa," in the *Dizionario degli scrittori greci e latini*.

For the works of Ambrose, see Corpus Scriptorum Ecclesiasticorum Latinorum, or CSEL, 32, 62, 64, 73, 79, and 82 and Corpus Christianorum, or CC, 14. There are more recent editions of some works, notably in the Sources Chrétiennes series, and a complete Italian bilingual edition by the Biblioteca Ambrosiana in Milan is in progress (1977–). Note also the Budé edition of *De Officiis*, book 1 (Paris 1984), and the text with English translation and commentary of the *De Consolatione Valentiani* by T. A. Kells (Washington, D.C., 1940). There is no comprehensive English treatment of Ambrose after F. Homes-Dudden, *The Life and Times of St. Ambrose* (2 vols., Oxford 1935); in other languages, note H. von Campenhausen, *Ambrosius von Mailand als Kir-chenpolitiker* (Berlin 1929), P. Courcelle, *Récherches sur Saint Ambroise* (Paris 1973), G. Lazzati, *Il valore letterario dell'esegesi ambrosiana* (Milan 1960), G. Madec, *St. Ambroise et la philosophie* (Paris 1973), J. R. Palanque, *St. Ambroise et l'empire romain* (Paris 1933), S. Mazzarino, *Storia sociale del vescovo Ambrogio* (Rome 1989), and the papers collected in the volume *Ambrosius Episcopus* (Milan 1976). A bibliography is *Cento anni di bibliografia ambrosiana (1874–1974)* by P. F. Beatrice et al. (Milan 1981).

On "Ambrosiaster," see A. Souter, *A Study of Ambrosiaster* (Cambridge 1905), P. C. Martini, *Ambrosiaster* (Rome 1944, Latin), and the introduction to the first volume of H. J. Vogel's edition of the *Commentary on the Pauline Epistles* (CSEL 81–83, Vienna 1966–69). There is an Italian edition of the *Commentary on Romans* by A. Pollastri (Rome 1984).

A complete edition of Jerome's works is in progress in the CC (72–80 published to date, Turnholt 1959–82); there is a full bibliography to 1958 in the first volume in the series. There is an edition of the *Contra Rufinum* in the Sources Chrétiennes series by P. Lardet (Paris 1983). For the letters, see the edition of I. Hilberg (CSEL 54–56), as well as the Budé of J. Labourt (8 vols., Paris 1949–63); there is an edition of letter 57 with German commentary by G.J.M. Bartelink (Leiden 1980) and of letter 60, with English commentary, by J.H.D. Scourfield (Oxford 1993). The translation of Eusebius's *Chronicle* is edited by R. Helm (ed. 2 Berlin 1956, in vol. 7 of the edition of Eusebius's works; see his monograph *Hieronymus' Zusätze in Eusebius' Chronik und ihre Wert für die Literaturgeschichte* [Berlin 1929]), the *De Viris Illustribus* by G. Herding (ed. 2 Leipzig 1924; see also the edition by A. Ceresa-Gastaldo, Florence 1988). The major edition of the *Vulgate* is the *Biblia Sacra* (Rome 1926–), the best small edition that of F. Weber (2 vols., Stuttgart 1975). For the New Testament, see the edition of J. Wordsworth and H. J. White (3 vols., Oxford 1889–1954). There is a comprehensive English survey by J.N.D. Kelly, *Jerome* (London 1975); among many works in other languages, note J. Steinmann, *St. Jerôme* (Paris 1958), Y. Bodin, *St. Jerôme et l'église* (Paris 1966), P. Artin, *Receuil sur St. Jerôme* (Brussels 1968), I. Opelt, *Hieronymus' Streitschriften*

(Heidelberg 1973), H. Hagendahl in *VCHr* 28 (1982) 372–82, and the papers in *Gerolamo e la biografia letteraria* (Genoa 1989) and *Jérôme entre l'occident et l'orient* (Paris 1988).

In addition to the editions of the works of St. Augustine in the CSEL and CC series, there are French volumes in the series Bibliothèque Augustinienne and Italian in the series Nuova Biblioteca Agostiniana. There are Teubner editions of the *De Civitate Dei* by B. Dombart and A. Kalb (ed. 5, with new letters ed. J. Divjak, Stuttgart 1981) and of the *Confessions* by M. Skutella, H. Juergens, and W. Schand (Stuttgart 1981); see also the Loeb volumes of G. E. McCracken et al. (7 vols., Cambridge, Mass. 1957–72) and W. Watts (2 vols., Cambridge, Mass. 1950). There are general studies by P. Brown, *Augustine of Hippo* (London 1967) and *Religion and Society in the Age of St. Augustine* (London 1972); see also R. H. Barrow, *Introduction to St. Augustine "City of God"* (London 1950), H. Hagendahl, *Augustine and the Latin Classics* (Gottenburg 1967), G.J.P. O'Daly, *Augustine's Philosophy of Mind* (Berkeley and Los Angeles 1987), R. A. Markus, *Saeculum: History and Society in the Theology of St. Augustine* (Cambridge 1988), C. Kirwan, *Augustine* (London 1989), P. Courcelle, *Recherches sur les Confessions de St. Augustin* (Paris 1950) and *Les Confessions de St. Augustin dans la tradition littéraire* (Paris 1963), H. I. Marrou, *St. Augustin et la fin de la culture antique* (ed. 4 Paris 1958), and P. Ranson, *Saint Augustin* (Paris 1988). There have been numerous conferences; see esp. *Internationales Symposion über den Stand der Augustinus-Forschung*, ed. C. P. Mayer and K. H. Chelius (Würzburg 1989). The *Bulletin Augustinien* published with the *Révue des Études Augustiniennes* gives a full annual bibliography; see also C. Andriesen, *Bibliographia Agostiniana* (Darmstadt 1973), and T. L. Mirle, *Augustine Bibliography, 1970–1980* (Westport, Conn. 1982). An *Augustinus-Lexikon* of major topics is in progress, ed. C. Mayer (Stuttgart 1986–).

On Rufinus, see F. X. Murphy, *Rufinus of Aquileia* (Washington, D.C., 1945). The works apart from the translations are edited by M. Simonetti (CC 20, Turnholt 1961, with good bibliography); the *Historia Monachorum* is edited by E. Schulz-Flügel (Berlin 1990, also with full bibliography). On the translations, see M. Wagner, *Rufinus the Translator* (Washington, D.C., 1945, concentrating on Gregory of Nazianzus's *De Fuga*).

Sulpicius Severus's works are edited by C. Halm in CSEL 1 (Vienna 1866). There are editions with commentary of the *Life of St Martin* by J. Fontaine (3 vols., Paris 1967–69, French) and A.A.R. Bastiaensen and J. W. Smit (Verona 1975, with the *Life of St. Hilarius* and the *Epitaphium Sanctae Paulae,* Italian). See G. K. van Andel, *The Christian Concept of History in the Chronicle of Sulpicius Severus* (Amsterdam 1976), C. Stancliffe, *St. Martin and His Hagiographer* (Oxford 1983), P. Hylten, *Studien zu Sulpicius Severus* (London 1940), S. Prete, *I cronica di Sulpicio Severo, saggio storico-critico* (Rome 1955), and F. Ghizzoni, *Sulpicio Severo* (Rome 1983). The older work of J. Bernays, *Über die Chronik des Sulpicius Severus* (Berlin 1861), is still useful.

From Honorius to Odoacer (410–476)

1. THE END OF THE WESTERN EMPIRE: NEW POLITICAL INSTITUTIONS

The divisions between the Eastern Empire and the Western Empire

Disintegration of the Empire

The last decades of the Western Empire are marked by a succession of invasions and increasingly unsuccessful efforts to resist them. The division between the two parts of the Empire, the East and the West, was now definitive, and cultural relations between the two *partes* had also become more precarious. Within the West, moreover, the individual regions underwent different experiences, which led to a progressive differentiation among the various zones, in regard to language and literature as well as other things. The more peripheral areas had, in fact, been abandoned even before the Germanic invasions, because it was impossible to assure their connection with the center. This is what happened to Britain, which in the course of the century became separated from Roman tradition and culture. At the same time it witnessed a recovery on the part of the Celtic substratum, which became dominant and remained so until the arrival of the Angles and the Saxons. The other provinces underwent a series of dramatic episodes that did great harm to their productive capacities, weakening their economies and gravely worsening the conditions of life. Africa, along with Sardinia, Corsica, the Balearic Islands, and later Sicily, was conquered by the Vandals. From 429 on, these barbarians constituted an independent national state, the first Germanic state on the Empire's territory, which deprived Italy of the valuable foodstuffs that came from that province. Spain was crossed by successive waves of Vandals, Alans, Suebians, and finally Visigoths, who settled there, at first as Roman allies and later, from 466, as an independent state. Gaul was divided among the same Visigoths to the south, the Burgundians in the center, the Franks in the northeast, and the Bretons in the northwest. The territory that was left between these last two settlements continued to be recognized as Roman, even though, having lost all contact with Italy, it was an independent kingdom for a while. Italy, after the invasion of Alaric and the Visigoths, managed to avoid nearly all the waves of invasion and was attacked only marginally by the strongest wave, that of the Huns.

The Huns and the establishment of the Germanic states

The problem of the establishment of the Germanic peoples on the former territories of the Empire was aggravated by the raids of this nomadic people from the steppes, who devastated all Europe at mid-century. It was only the death of their king, Attila, rather than defeats inflicted by the Roman army or political action by the church under pope Leo I, that put an end to the power of the Huns and to the great empire that they put together in the space of a few years, an empire bounded by the Rhine, the Urals, and the Danube. With the end of this threat, the various Germanic states began to establish themselves. They still experienced many changes, to be sure, in the extent of their territory and in the settlement of different peoples, but a process was begun of defining their relations with the Roman *nobilitas*—the great landowners—and with the church, which was governed by members of this same *nobilitas*. This would lead to accords that in their turn would make possible, in most cases, a relatively peaceful integration.

General economic crisis

This institutional change, with the breakup of the Empire and the rise of various kingdoms that tended to become like national states, was accompanied by a severe economic recession. At the beginning of the fifth century the imperial treasury could still meet its expenses, even if only by very onerous taxation; farmland, especially in Gaul and Africa, produced immense wealth, and the owners of the latifundia possessed vast liquid capital in valuable gold coin; merchants were active in the larger cities, where money still circulated satisfactorily. By the middle of the century, however, the crisis was grave and involved not only the state's finances, which were completely exhausted, but also private wealth. The destruction of the cities, the reduction of the land under cultivation, and the very large increase in taxation in the territories still subject to the Empire had disastrous consequences for the economy, especially for the lower and middle classes. Peasants and slaves, reduced to desperation, banded together in armed groups to fight against both the barbarians and the representatives of imperial power. In Spain and France especially, popular revolts were frequent, and in order to put them down armies of Romans were often mobilized along with armies of German *foederati,* that is, Germans settled in the territories of the Empire and joined by a pact of alliance. Some members of the senatorial classes used their wealth to provide themselves with private militias, others formed agreements with the invaders, and many simply fled, taking all their treasures with them.

From the Crisis to a New Cultural Synthesis

In so altered a reality, one nonetheless finds some of the most typical characteristics of the imperial system preserved, though at a lower level. The Germans, for example, did not have bureaucratic and administrative traditions of their own that could compete with those of the Romans, and so they had to make use of the structures already in existence. This made it necessary to continue training capable personnel and thus assured the survival of the schools. In most cases the Germans had already been in close contact with Roman culture, and this rendered the impact of the occupation less grievous. Despite many difficulties, it made possible an integration that took place in different times and forms but did eventually take place throughout the territory of the former Empire. This complex combination of factors, which gave very different aspects to the various regions, produces a far from uniform picture of the cultural and literary life of the West. Some zones go through a period of serious decline, while others continue to produce writers and works comparable to those of earlier ages. The ideals of the classical tradition, which remained very strong, were now enhanced, in some cases, by the need to identify values with which to unify the Roman group and to oppose the values of the Germans. At the same time, some writers, acting with greater or lesser self-interest, were inclined to come to terms with the world of the victors, to transpose their culture into Latin standards, and to present themselves as mediators between past and present.

Martianus Capella

The genres common in the previous century that were still widely practiced included grammar. We have new handbooks, such as Agroecius's *Orthographia,* Consentius's *Ars,* and Pompeius's commentary on Donatus. And along with the grammatical works, one needs to mention, as in the fourth century, commentaries and encyclopedias of greater scope, such as that of Martianus Capella.

A Carthaginian, a lawyer who became a writer at an advanced age, and a pagan (or at least not a Christian), Martianus Capella was active in Roman Africa during the period between two disastrous events of Roman history: the sack of Rome in 410 and the sack of Carthage, which was carried out by the Vandals in 439. He compiled an encyclopedia of classical learning, the *De Nuptiis Mercurii et Philologiae,* in nine books. But this title, though it has now become current, is not uniformly attested by the *superscriptiones* of the manuscripts and is correctly applied only to the narrative-allegorical section of the work (books 1 and 2). It is likely that the title of the entire encyclopedia was *Philologia,* as seems to be indicated by several references in a metrical *institutio* that has recently been attributed to Martianus Capella with complete certainty (previously it was customary to attribute it to the grammarian Servius or to a lesser known Sergius). In this metrical work, the author, referring to a work of his own, says explicitly, *in tertio* Philologiae *libro,* and elsewhere, *ut est in* Philologia *meus versus.* The work is in prose, though it has many parts in verse, which almost constitute an anthology of the ancient meters and bring the work's literary genre close to that of the *satura Menippea* (see pp. 215 f.). The work, which would be popular in the Christian Middle Ages, shows a strong taste *The allegorical taste* for allegory. It takes up themes and images from Apuleius—an African himself—and presents personifications that closely resemble those in certain of Prudentius's works and anticipate Philosophy in Boethius's *Consolatio.*

In this allegorical *fabula* of a wedding, the first two books contain the preliminaries, which take place in Jupiter's galactic palace. Then in the remaining books (3–9), seven of the nine liberal arts from Varro's *Disciplinarum Libri* (see p. 211) are presented as Mercury's wedding gift to his bride

Philology. They are the encyclopedic *Artes* or *Disciplinae* (all summed up in the symbolic figure of the learned Philology), who, addressing the heavenly Senate gathered for the wedding ceremony, expound in the first person the *ars* of which each is an eponym: Grammar, Dialectic, Rhetoric, Geometry, Arithmetic, Astronomy, and Music (expounded by the *virgo Harmonia*); Medicine and Architecture are excluded here and thus would not form part of the medieval organization of study, the trivium and the quadrivium, which undoubtedly takes Martianus's encyclopedia as a model. The *De Nuptiis* had immense success, as is evidenced by the enormous number of medieval manuscripts.

The work, the literary, cultural, and historical importance of which is beginning to be recognized today, is a *summa* of ancient culture and science, laboriously reclaimed by a late pagan neo-Platonist. Its greatness and historical importance lie precisely in this, and even though the *fabula* has other significances as well, it clearly belongs to the same religious-mystical world of late ancient syncretism.

The style of the prose and poetry is extremely artificial and complicated, difficult to read and to understand. It is composed in a highly rhetorical tone, is deliberately (though not always successfully) structured, and is filled with echoes of classical authors, though these too are varied so as to form new images. The style represents a linguistic mixture that one needs to analyze patiently and resolve into its component elements before branding it ugly and illegible, as is still done today. The exposition of the doctrine of the several arts, by contrast, is carried out in a prose that, though technical and packed with ideas, is certainly simpler.

Scientific Handbooks

Medicine:
a) Marcellus
Empiricus

Interest in the various sciences was also lively; medicine in particular was much cultivated. Among the writers in this field we find Marcellus, known as Marcellus Empiricus, a high official of the Eastern Empire and native of Bordeaux, who dedicates a *De Medicamentis* to his sons, to enable them to avoid excessive recourse to doctors. Among the sources explicitly referred to are Pliny the Elder, pseudo-Apuleius, and Celsus. More than twenty-five hundred prescriptions are suggested, listed by order of the illnesses, going from the head to the feet. They are written in a Latin full of technical terms, Grecisms, words of popular usage, Gallicisms, and even words showing some Germanic influence. There are also several magic formulas. Another manual covering the same material is Cassius Felix's *De Medicina,* written in 447. The author, an African Christian, reports various terms from the local languages.

b) Cassius Felix

A geographical
compendium

Among works of geography Julius Honorius's *Cosmography* should be mentioned. It is a series of lessons transcribed by a pupil of the author and published against his will. Commenting on a map composed in the fourth century, Honorius, who probably lived in the fifth century, illustrates the various regions of the earth, with particular attention to physical geography and especially to rivers.

Law and Bureaucracy

The greatest continuity with the works of previous decades may be found in legal and bureaucratic writing. Two works stand out in particular, both composed under Theodosius II, emperor of the East (408–450): the *Codex Theodosianus* and the so-called *Notitia Dignitatum*. The *Codex Theodosianus* collects the laws promulgated from the age of Constantine onwards, divided by subjects (civil law, administrative, penal, financial, constitutional, ecclesiastical).

The Codex
Theodosianus

The work is fundamental for our knowledge of not only law but also the history of late antiquity. It is a valuable source on the political stances of the different emperors and provides information of great worth on the magistrates to whom the laws were entrusted for concrete application.

The *Notitia Dignitatum Omnium tam Civilium quam Militarium* is a genuine organic plan of the Empire, both West and East, which gives a list of all its administrative posts, with the tasks belonging to each and the competences of the hierarchic relations. It also provides a picture of the dioceses and the provinces of the Empire and thus adds geographical interest to the historical and legal interest.

The Notitia
Dignitatum

2. CHRISTIAN CHRONICLE AND HISTORIOGRAPHY

Historiography in the fourth century had been practiced predominantly by pagan authors (one need only recall its principal representatives, Ammianus Marcellinus and the *Historia Augusta*). During the fifth century the leadership in this field also passed to Christian writers, who with Augustine developed a new historiographic methodology. After him, two names are to be recorded: Orosius and Salvianus.

Orosius

LIFE

Paulus Orosius was born around 390, a Spaniard, perhaps from Tarragona. A priest, he was forced by the invasion of the Vandals to flee from the Iberian Peninsula. In Africa in 414 he came into contact with Augustine, and in Palestine in 415 with Jerome. He finished his *Historiae* in 417, after which we no longer have notice of him.

WORKS

The *Commonitorium de Errore Priscillianistarum et Origenistarum,* his first work, dedicated to Augustine, on the heresies most widespread in Spain. The *Liber Apologeticus,* against the Pelagian heresy. The *Historiae adversus Paganos,* in seven books, his principal work, which was requested by Augustine as a collection of material to be used later for his own *De Civitate Dei.* The first six books are devoted to the history of mankind, from its origins to the advent of Christ and the empire of Augustus, and the seventh treats the imperial period down to 417.

*Orosius's small value
as a historian*

Orosius does not have Augustine's originality; he follows traditional schemes and relies for the most part on the most familiar sources, not without serious misunderstandings. The most useful information concerns the period closest to him, the last years of the fourth century and the first two decades of the fifth. For this period Orosius provides us with details not preserved by other writers. But Orosius is important for his overall interpretive approach, which is substantially different from Augustine's, even though this comes about neither consciously nor willingly. For Orosius, divine providence willed the Roman Empire, and the coincidence of the birth of Christ with the empire of Augustus is not casual. The Empire's mission is to aid the spread of Christianity, and after the many dramatic events of the period before Christ's coming, the condition of mankind is now, by the will of God, growing better. As a result of this view, Orosius obviously undervalues the problem of the Germanic invasions (which in his view would soon be resolved by the absorption of the barbarians into Roman-Christian culture), but his development of a system based on the sacredness of the state and its providential function would be very influential in the Middle Ages. Orosius's text had a wide diffusion, and the chief works of Christian historiography in future centuries, down to Dante's *Commedia,* were based on it.

The providential vision of the Empire

Salvianus

Slightly later than Orosius is the Gallic Salvianus (circa 400–470), who wrote an *Ad Ecclesiam,* in four books, in which he invited all Christians to donate their private wealth to the church in order to strengthen the resistance that was needed against the barbarian invasions.

The revaluation of the invaders

The distressing threat posed by the invasions and by the resulting mishaps that involved the Empire is also present in the eight books of the *De Gubernatione Dei,* written around 450. Salvianus's response to the historical and moral problems raised by the conquest of the Germans is different from both Augustine's (in the *De Civitate Dei*) and Orosius's. For Augustine, the opposition Romans/barbarians ought to be eliminated as a historiographic category in favor of the new antithesis earthly city/heavenly city; for Orosius, there was no reason to worry, since everything was part of a providential design, and in any event the barbarians would be reabsorbed in Roman-Christian culture.

Salvianus does not deny the dramatic nature of contemporary events, but he attributes it to a divine design to punish Christians for their faults. For Orosius, the Roman Empire was the instrument that God used for spreading the faith. For Salvianus, however, it is the barbarians who are the divine instrument. This view leads to a revaluation of the barbarians' character that is almost excessively favorable: they are considered more honest, more moral, less degenerate and cruel than the Romans, and yet less culpable, since they have not yet been touched by the true faith.

Minor Historians

Prosper of Aquitaine

Prosper of Aquitaine, who was born around 390 and died in 463, is less important as a historian but nonetheless is a figure of some importance as a writer and man of the church. He wrote a *Chronicon,* which takes up Jerome's work where it left off and continues it down to 455, with firsthand information for the last years, from 425 on. Active in the battle against the Pelagian heresy, he wrote among other things a poem in hexameters entitled *De Ingratis,* on those who are ungrateful towards God and on all those who deny the fundamental importance of divine grace in human salvation, as the Pelagians did. Another writer who continued Jerome's *Chronicon* is Hydatius, a Spanish bishop, who extended the work to 468, being especially interested in the barbarian invasions and the dramatic struggles provoked by them. The many lives of bishops and saints from this period also belong to the field of historiography. Among others, one ought to mention the life of Ambrose, composed by Paulinus of Milan, and the life of Augustine, by Possidius, written before 439. Gennadius of Marseilles, during the last years of the century, wrote a series of biographies that are helpful for our knowledge of the Latin Christian writers; to Jerome's *De Viris Illlustribus* he added about ninety other lives.

Gennadius

The Sermons

One of the genres most cultivated in this period is the sermon. As an official duty, many bishops and men of the church delivered homilies, often of a notable stylistic level, which were transcribed and preserved. Among the authors of sermons most well known to us, we should single out Maximus of Turin, who died probably around 423; Quodvultdeus, a pupil of Augustine, who in 437 became bishop of Carthage, the author of a *De Promissionibus et Praedicationibus Dei,* traditionally assigned to Prosper of Aquitaine; Petrus Chrysologus, bishop of Ravenna, who died around 450; and Leo the Great, pope from 440 to 461, from whom we have sermons, letters, and the *Tomus ad Flavianum,* a theological work directed against the heresy called "monophysitism," which denied Christ's double nature, divine and human, and held that he had a single, divine nature.

Julian of Eclanum, Cassian

Julian of Eclanum

Among the authors of exegetical works, Julian of Eclanum needs to be mentioned first and foremost. An Apulian, born between 380 and 390, bishop of Eclanum, he supported the Pelagian theories and therefore broke relations with Augustine, who earlier regarded him almost as a pupil. The attention Augustine devotes to confuting his theories shows that he feared him and considered him the most intelligent and dangerous among the Pelagians, and the few works of Julian's that have come down to us (commentaries on the texts of the Prophets, plus long quotations from some other writings preserved for us in the works of Augustine) prove that Augustine's evaluation was fully justified. Despite the censorship exercised by later ages, we can discover in Julian a logical rigor and a modern aspiration to a "lay morality" that intrigue us and make him an interesting and unique figure in the last decades of the Empire.

Cassian

Other important names of fifth-century Christianity were also involved in the Pelagian controversy and took anti-Augustinian positions; they too made fundamental contributions to the church's development in other regards. The first was John Cassian, one of the fathers of Western monasticism. His *De Institutis Coenobiorum,* from 420, explains the rules of the monks in Palestine and Egypt and contains a list of the principal sins and ways of combating them. Cassian's principal work is the twenty-four *Conlationes,* lectures that appeared from 420 to 429, in some of which he quite explicitly condemns Augustine's theories on grace.

Novelized Histories

"Dares the Phrygian"

Novelized histories and fabulous stories, which had been popular in the previous century, continue to have a certain success. The *De Excidio Troiae Historia* is probably to be placed in the last years of the fifth century (but according to others, well into the sixth). The author, who pretends to be Cornelius Nepos and to dedicate his work to Sallust, presents the story of Troy from the point of view of the Phrygians. It is supposedly a Latin translation from the original by a Trojan priest mentioned in the *Iliad,* Dares the Phrygian. The work is, so to speak, the mirror image of Dictys of Crete and wins great popularity in the Middle Ages, especially since to the same Dares there was attributed a *Historia de Origine Francorum,* which maintained the Trojan origin of the Franks and thus claimed for them a nobility equal to that of the Romans.

3. THE NEW POETRY

Rutilius Namatianus

LIFE

Rutilius Claudius Namatianus, of Gallic origin, moved to Rome at a relatively young age. His father held important posts in the administration, and Namatianus's career was even more brilliant than his father's: he was prefect of Rome in 414. In 417 he returned to his native country because the grave news coming from Gaul urged him to supervise his properties personally.

WORKS

The *De Reditu Suo,* in two books of elegiac couplets, which has come down to us incomplete. The part we have (the entire first book and a few verses of the second) recounts his sea voyage from Ostia to the northern part of Tuscany; there are some references to Liguria in a fragment of the second book that has only recently been recovered.

A pagan who takes refuge in the past

A pagan poet, linked to the last circles of neo-Platonic intellectuals and in contact with some of the persons of pagan senatorial Rome described by Macrobius, Namatianus fills his travel journal with melancholy regrets for a world that is ending. Christians faced the problem of the barbarians in different ways, but always with attention to the future and to what was to be done in order to overcome present difficulties under a new political and social system that could do without the Empire but not without religion.

Rutilius does not share this hope. For him the only refuge is the past, which is to be glorified uncritically and to be contrasted with the present, invariably to the disadvantage of the latter.

Namatianus, to be sure, explicitly maintains that Rome is eternal, saved from the destiny of the other empires, since she can find in herself the strength to be reborn after disaster. In one of his most famous passages, the praise of Rome in the first book, he writes verses that would become commonplaces in celebrations of the Empire's historical role, such as *fecisti patriam diversis gentibus unam* ("for the various nations you made a single homeland") or *urbem fecisti quod prius orbis erat* ("you made a city of what had previously been a world"). And yet the descriptions of places seen during his journey present a nearly unbroken series of ruins and devastations: ravaged cities, abandoned countryside, desolation and poverty ruling everywhere. This completely negative picture makes still more painful his return to Gaul, which is really a flight.

Anti-Christian polemic

Namatianus knows whom to blame for all that has happened: he has harsh words for the Christians, in particular for the monks, and for the Germans who have become part of the Empire's structures, especially Stilicho. The monks, refusing social life and military and political engagement, deprive the state of forces that would be useful in a moment of crisis, and they show a disdain for humanity that makes them enemies of the world. Stilicho has betrayed Rome, forming an agreement with his fellow Germans to harm the Empire (this was the claim made by the emperor Honorius and the literature favorable to him when it was decided to eliminate the excessively powerful general), and he has shown how imprudent it is to trust barbarians and assign them important military and political positions. Other objects of Namatianus's attacks are the Jews, who are dishonest and greedy, and corrupt administrators, a category the poet must have gotten to know well during his career as a high official.

Namatianus and Claudian

Often compared to Claudian as the last poet of the Empire and the pagan world, Namatianus is actually very different from him. Nor are they divided only by their opposite evaluations of Stilicho, who is praised by Claudian and condemned by Namatianus, a difference that could be explained by the fact that Claudian wrote at the moment of the barbarian general's greatest success, while Namatianus wrote after his downfall. It is rather that Claudian and Namatianus express quite different interests and experiences. The former is a professional who lives from his poetry and needs to win patrons and backers and put his abilities as a writer at the service of their ideas; the latter is a wealthy landowner and an important state official who writes in order to defend his own ideas and positions, and not those of a patron. A historical vision that tended to separate clearly the pagan part from the Christian had made Rutilius the energetic and uncompromising champion of dying paganism; many references in the first book, and especially the attack on the monks, confirm this view. Nonetheless, the fragment of the second book recently found leads to the discovery of a less rigid attitude. In the new verses, in fact, we find praise of the

Christian Flavius Constantius, the future emperor Constantius III. It will be necessary therefore to make our judgment more nuanced and conclude that Rutilius, though not fond of Christianity, condemned it without possibility of appeal only when it assumed destructive forms, such as withdrawal from the world, and thus caused the loss of any protection it might have rendered to a state whose crisis it recognizes.

Merobaudes

Life of Merobaudes

More similar to Claudian is another court poet, often unjustly undervalued: Flavius Merobaudes. Of Spanish origin, he combined writing poetry with military service. He lived in Ravenna, at the court of Valentinian III, and had as his patron the powerful general Aetius. For his literary services he, too, like Claudian, was recognized with a statue at Rome, which was erected to him in the Forum of Trajan in 435. His chief work, the *De Christo,* in hexameters, was for a long time mistakenly attributed to Claudian. He also wrote panegyrics and poems for Aetius and his relations as well as for the emperor. These compositions have not always come down to us in their entirety.

Merobaudes and Claudian

The close connection with Claudian is not based solely on similarity between the two poets' personal histories, but grows also from an evident imitation on the part of Merobaudes. Titles and subjects, images and phrases of Claudian are taken up, in an *aemulatio* that is not ordinary dependence on a model but elegant reelaboration, learned recuperation, the modernizing of ideas and episodes.

Other models of Merobaudes

Along with Claudian, many other writers of earlier ages are evoked, among them Seneca, Virgil, Statius, and Prudentius. Unfortunately, the larger part of his poetry has come down to us in terrible condition, transmitted as the lower writing of a palimpsest, that is, a manuscript that has been erased and then used again for a new text (by "lower writing" we mean the earlier one, which has been erased and has nearly disappeared). We cannot therefore give a fully documented evaluation of Merobaudes's literary qualities. There are no doubts, however, about his usefulness as a historical source for the first half of the fifth century, not to mention his ability as a versifier and his knowledge. Leopardi was interested in Merobaudes's text and proposed several supplements for lacunose passages.

Sidonius Apollinaris

An official at the end of the Empire

Namatianus witnesses the fall of the Empire with profound melancholy, incapable of initiative or resistance. Merobaudes, twenty years later, at the apex of that ephemeral revival that followed Aetius's victories, presents us with the optimistic view of the court. A few years later another official and poet, Sidonius Apollinaris, saw the last moments of the Empire and could demonstrate an honorable commitment and an admirable organizational ability.

LIFE

Gaius Sollius Modestus Apollinaris Sidonius was born at Lyon around 431 to an important family, and he married a daughter of the emperor

Avitus (455–56). He was consul in 468 and later prefect of Rome, but he unexpectedly abandoned politics in order to devote himself to an ecclesiastical career. As bishop of Auvergne (Clermont-Ferrand) from perhaps 470 on, he organized the resistance against the invasion of the Visigoths under Euric; they settled in the region, however, and took possession of it. After a period in prison, he was freed by the same Euric and returned to his position as bishop, which made him the representative of the Roman community to the new German masters. He died around 486.

WORKS

Twenty-four *carmina,* divided into panegyrics (in hexameters) to the emperors Avitus, Majorian, and Anthemius, and occasional poems (epithalamia, descriptions of buildings, verse epistles, etc.); these poetic compositions precede his appointment as bishop. The nine books of the *Letters,* published from 469 to 482, are more important. Sidonius often inserts verse compositions into them, which shows that he continued his poetic activity even during his episcopate. Noteworthy among these is a praise of Euric, which certainly served to soften the heart of the German king and probably had a certain influence on his decision to release the bishop from prison.

The fusion of classical tradition and Christianity

Sidonius represents the wealthiest class of the Gallic nobility, their position within the state and the church, and their attitude towards the barbarians. In him classical tradition and Christianity coexist without difficulty, in regard to both form and content. Or rather, we may say, with him there begins the definition of a cultural inheritance that overcame those earlier oppositions by which people such as Jerome had been tormented and replaced them with a new distinction that views Greeks and Latins, pagans and Christians all on one side against the new world of the Germans.

An attempt to recover the past in order to change the present

This is not an antithesis between the happy past—of the great classics and the Bible, invoked as an ideal tranquil refuge—and the dramatic present. Sidonius's engagement in the affairs of the world is genuine, and so his work as a writer also needs to be seen as a way of taking part in reality, an attempt to lay the basis for the return of tranquil times so that the inheritance from previous eras can flourish again, eliminating whatever is uncivil and unpleasant in the Germans and their conquest.

Hence he pays learned attention to minute details, to the more technical aspects of language and meter; hence he aspires to assemble in his works again all the formal refinements accumulated during centuries of rhetorical tradition. Even in his choice of words Sidonius sets out to recover whatever he finds to be more elaborate in his predecessors. At the same time, he does not refuse to propose new words, in order to show that the Latin language is still alive and vital and able to deal with the new needs and new problems. His work, especially the letters, is also a valuable historical source, documenting for us the situation in Gaul at the waning of the Empire. Naturally, as was already said about Symmachus, it would be a mistake to look for precise references and specific events in Sidonius's letters. The allusions are often subtle, but they are sufficient to document for us a reality that is culturally far more lively than is usually believed for these last years of the Roman state.

The Minor Poets

Around these more important persons many other poets are also active. We will indicate here only some of the more notable. Cyprianus Gallus, a poet working in the first decades of the fifth century, wrote a *Heptateuch* (seven books of hexameters), a paraphrase of the first seven books of the Old Testament. Claudius Marius Victorius (or Victor), from Marseilles, who died sometime between 425 and 450, wrote in hexameters an *Alethia* ("The Truth"), a paraphrase of Genesis, the first book of the Old Testament.

Sedulius

Sedulius (perhaps Caelius Sedulius), who was trained in classical studies in Italy and then went on to religious poetry, wrote between 425 and 450 a *Carmen Paschale* (five books of hexameters) on several episodes of the Old Testament and the life of Christ, based on the account in the Gospels. Of this poem the author himself published a second version in prose, the *Opus Paschale*.

Orientius

Orientius, bishop of Auch in Gascony during the first half of the century, wrote a *Commonitorium* (two books of elegiac couplets) exhorting the faithful to devote themselves completely to God and to avoid sin. He frequently refers to the devastations in Gaul caused by the invasion of the barbarians, and he makes interesting use of the sixth book of the *Aeneid* as a model for his description of the Underworld.

Paulinus of Pella

Paulinus of Pella, a nephew of Ausonius, wrote in 459, when he was more than eighty years old, a *Eucharisticos*. In this poem he thanked God for all the misfortunes he had sent him, from the many family struggles endured to the poverty that overtook him after the invasions, when the barbarians took possession of his vast estate, saying that it was these sufferings that had made it possible for him to turn towards a more devout life. Paulinus of Périgueux around 470 composed a Life of Martin (six books of hexameters), a reworking in verse of the life written by Sulpicius Severus.

The Aegritudo Perdicae

Let us mention, finally, the *Aegritudo Perdicae,* an anonymous composition that is usually placed in the fifth century. Slightly fewer than three hundred hexameters narrate the story of Perdicas, the son of Alexander I of Macedon, who falls in love with his mother and wastes away because of this. Summoned to court, the great doctor Hippocrates understands what the problem is that is afflicting the young man, and he informs the parents of his diagnosis. To no avail they have him meet the most appealing women of the country, but for Perdicas no one can match his mother. Given the impossibility of solving his predicament, in the end the protagonist kills himself. The story, which is well documented in other Greek and Latin works, both prose and verse, is interesting in the *Aegritudo* version on account of the large role given to Hippocrates and medicine.

The End of the Empire in the West

On the "barbarian" invasions, see E. A. Thompson, *Romans and Barbarians* (Madison 1982), and W. Goffart, *Barbarians and Romans, A.D. 418–584* (Princeton 1980, with bibliography) and *The Narratives of Barbarian History* (Princeton 1988).

There are Teubner editions of Martianus Capella by A. Dick (Stuttgart 1925) and J. Willis (Leipzig 1983). There is an English commentary on book 1 by D. Shanzer (Berkeley and Los Angeles 1986; see also her review of Willis's edition in *CPh* 81 [1986] 62–81), and there are Italian commentaries by L. Lenaz on book 2 (Padua 1975) and by L. Cristante on book 9 (Padua 1987). See W. H. Stahl, R. Johnson, and E. L. Burge, *Martianus Capella and the Seven Liberal Arts* (New York 1971; vol. 2 is a translation, New York 1977), and F. le Moine, *Martianus Capella: A Literary Revaluation* (Munich 1972).

Marcellus Empiricus, *De Medicamentis,* is edited by M. Niedermann and E. Leichtenhan (Berlin 1968, with German translation); there is an old Teubner by C. Helmreich (Leipzig 1889). See also E. Leichtenhan, *Sprachliche Bemerkungen zu Marcellus Empiricus* (Basel 1917).

Cassius Felix, *De Medicina,* is edited by V. Rose (Leipzig 1879); see esp. H. Orth, "Der Afrikaner Cassius Felix, ein methodischer Arzt Sudhaus Archiv" 44 (1960) 193–217. The *Cosmografia* of Julius Honorius is included in A. Riese's *Geographi Latini Minores* (Heilbrunn 1878); see also J. O. Thomson, *History of Ancient Geography* (Cambridge 1948) 381–82.

The *Codex Theodosianus* was edited by T. Mommsen and P. Meyer (2 vols., Berlin 1905), and the works that make up Justinian's *Corpus Iuris Civilis,* by P. Krüger et al. (3 vols., Berlin 1954). For the fragments of early legal writers, see F. P. Bremer, *Iurisprudentia Antehadriana* (Leipzig 1896–1901), E. Seckel and K. Kübler, *Iurisprudentiae Anteiustinianae Reliquiae* (Leipzig 1907–27), and S. Riccobono, *Fontes Iuris Romani Antejustiniani* (Florence 1941). There is an edition of Ateius Capito by W. Strzelecki (Leipzig 1967). Introductory works in English include H. F. Jolowicz and B. Nicholas, *Historical Introduction to the Study of Roman Law* (ed. 3 Cambridge 1972) 374–94, W. Kunkel, *An Introduction to Roman Legal and Constitutional History,* trans. J. M. Kelly (Oxford 1973; the original German work is in its eighth edition, Vienna 1978), and more generally J. A. Crook, *Law and Life of Rome* (London 1967); see also the trilogy by R. A. Bauman, *Lawyers in Roman Republican Politics, Lawyers in Roman Transitional Politics,* and *Lawyers and Politics in the Early Roman Empire* (Munich 1983, 1985, 1989). Three important works in Italian deserve mention: G. Nocera, *Iurisprudentia: per una storia del pensiero giuridico romano* (Rome 1973), A. Schiavone, *Nascita della giuridico nella Roma tardo-repubblicana* (Bari 1987), and the same author's *Giuristi e nobili nella Roma repubblicana* (Rome 1987). Although it is by now a little dated, A. Berger, *An Encyclopedic Dictionary of Roman Law* (Philadelphia 1953), which includes articles on the major jurists, remains useful. There is a particularly clear account in B. Nicholas, *An Introduction to Roman Law* (Oxford 1962) 38–42.

The *Notitia Dignitatum* is edited by O. Seeck (Berlin 1886); see esp. R. Goodburn and P. Bartholomew, eds., *Aspects of the Notitia Dignitatum* (Oxford 1976), as well as R. Grigg in *JRS* 69 (1979) 107–24 and 73 (1983) 132–42.

Christian Chronicles and Historiography

Orosius's history is edited by K. Zangemeister (CSEL 5, Vienna 1882); see also the Portuguese edition of J. Cardoso (Minho 1986). See J. Svennung, *Orosiana* (Uppsala 1922, German), B. Lacroix, *Orose et ses idées* (Paris 1965), E. Corsini, *Introduzione alle storie di Orosio* (Turin 1968), F. Fabbrini, *Paolo Orosio: uno storico* (Rome 1979), D. Koch-Peters, *Ansichten des Orosius zur Geschichte seiner Zeit* (Frankfurt 1984), and A. Marchetta, *Orosio e Ataulfo nell'ideologia dei rapporti romano-barbarici* (Rome 1987).

The works of Salvian of Marseilles are edited by G. Lagarrique (2 vols., Paris 1971); see also the German translation of A. Mayer (Munich 1983). See M. Pellegrino, *Salviano di Marsiglia* (Rome 1940), H. Fischer, *Die Schrift des Salvian von Marseille an der Kirche* (Bern 1976), and J. Badewien, *Geschichtstheologie und Sozialpolitik im Werk Salvians von Marseille* (Göttingen 1980).

An edition of the work of Prosper of Aquitaine is in progress in the CC series; so far only volume 68A, *Expositio Psalmorum and Liber Sententiarum,* has appeared (Turnholt 1972). Other works are in Patrologia Latina 51; for the *De Providentia Dei,* see the edition with commentary by M. Marcovich (Leiden 1989, English), for the *Epitoma Chronicon,* T. Mommsen, *Chronica Minora* 1 (Leipzig 1892), as well as S. Muhlberger in *CPh* 81 (1981) 240–44. See also S. Muhlberger, *The Fifth-Century Chroniclers* (Leeds 1990).

Gennadius's *Liber De Viris Illustribus* is edited by E. C. Richardson (Leipzig 1896); see also S. Pricoco, *Storia letteraria e storia ecclesiastica dal De viris illustribus di Girolamo a Gennadio* (Catania 1979).

For the sermons of Maximus of Turin, see the edition of A. Mutzenbecher, Corpus Christianorum, or CC, 23 (Turnholt 1972), as well as the annotated translation of B. Ramsey (New York 1989); see also P. Bongiovanni, *S. Massimo vescovo di Torino e il suo pensiero teologico* (Turin 1952), and M. C. Conroy, *Imagery in the Sermones of Maximus* (Washington, D.C., 1965). For Quodvultdeus, see the editions of R. Braun (CC 60 Turnholt 1976, Sources Chrétiennes 101–2 Paris 1964), as well as his introductions; for Petrus Chrysologus, the edition of A. Olivar (3 vols., Turnholt 1975–81) and *Los Sermones de San Pedro Crisologo* (Montserrat 1962); and for the *Sermones* of Leo the Great, the edition of A. Chavasse (CC 138, Turnholt 1973), as well as that in the Sources Chrétiennes series by R. Dolle (4 vols., Paris 1964–73), P. Brezzi, *S. Leone Magno* (Rome 1947), and W. Halliwell, *The Style of Pope St. Leo the Great* (Washington, D.C., 1939).

For Julian of Eclanum, see the edition by L. de Coninck (CC 88, Turnholt 1977), as well as the editor's introduction; for John Cassian, see the edition by M. Petschenig (2 vols., Corpus Scriptorum Ecclesiasticorum Latinorum, or CSEL, 13 and 17, Vienna 1886–88), as well as H. Chadwick, *John Cassian* (Cambridge 1968).

There is an edition of Dares Phrygius by F. Meisler (Leipzig 1873); see also N. E. Griffin, *Dares and Dictys: An Introduction to the Study of the Medieval Versions of the Story of Troy* (Baltimore 1907), O. Schüssel von Fleschenburg, *Dares-Studien* (Halle 1908), and W. Schetter in *Hermes* 116 (1988) 94–109.

The New Poetry
    The most convenient edition of Rutilius Namatianus's *De Reditu Suo* is that of J. Vessereau and F. Préchac (ed. 2 Paris 1961). There is an English commentary by C. H. Keene and G. F. Savage (London 1907), Italian commentaries by E. Merone (Naples 1955) and E. Castorina (Florence 1967), and a German commentary by E. Doblhofer (2 vols., Heidelberg 1972–77). For the fragment discovered in 1973, see *Maia* 27 (1975) 3–26. See also J. Vessereau, *Cl. Rutilius Namatianus* (Paris 1904), I. Lana, *Rutilio Namaziano* (Turin 1961), E. Merone, *Aspetti dell' ellenismo in Rutilio Namaziano* (Naples 1967), F. Corsaro, *Studi Rutiliani* (Bologna 1981), and A. Fo in *MD* 22 (1989) 49–74, with bibliography.

The standard edition of the poetry of Flavius Merobaudes is that of F. Vollmer (Berlin 1905); see the reprint of that text with English translation and commentary by F. M. Clover (Philadelphia 1971), S. Gennaro, *Da Claudiano a Merobaude: Aspetti della poesia cristiana di Merobaude* (Catania 1958), and A. Fo in *Romanobarbarica* 6 (1981–82) 101–28.

There is a Teubner edition of Sidonius Apollinaris by P. Mohr (Leipzig 1895), a good Loeb by W. B. Anderson (Cambridge, Mass. 1936–65), and a good Budé by A. Loyen (3 vols., Paris 1960–70). See C. E. Stevens, *Sidonius Apollinaris and His Age* (Oxford

1933), A. Loyen, *Recherches historiques sur les panégyriques de Sidoine Apollinaire* (Paris 1942) and *Sidoine Apollinaire et l'ésprit précieux en Gaule aux derniers jours de l'empire* (Paris 1943), and I. Gualandri, *Furtiva lectio: Studi su Sidonio Apollinare* (Milan 1979).

The *Heptateuch* of Ciprianus Gallus (?) is edited by R. Peiper (CSEL 23, Vienna 1891); see esp. J.E.B. Mayor, *The Latin Heptateuch* (Cambridge 1899), S. Gamber, *Le Livre de la Genèse dans la poésie latine au Ve siècle* (Paris 1899), and M. Roberts, *Biblical Epic and Rhetorical Paraphrase* (Liverpool 1985) 93–95.

For the *Alethia* of Claudius Marius Victor, see the edition by P. F. Hovingh (CC 128, Turnholt 1960).

Sedulius's *Carmen Paschale* and *Opus Paschale* are edited by J. Huemer (CSEL 10, Vienna 1885); see also C.P.E. Springer, *The Gospel Epic in Late Antiquity: The Paschale Carmen of Sedulius* (Leiden 1988, with full bibliography).

The *Commonitorium* of Orientius has been most recently edited by C. A. Rapisarda (ed. 2 Catania 1970, with Italian translation; see also *Nuovo Didaskaleion* 8 [1958] 1–78); there is a critical edition by L. Bellanger (Paris 1903), as well as a text with English translation by M. D. Tobin (Washington, D.C., 1945).

Both Paulinus of Pella and Paulinus of Périgueux are edited by C. Schenkel in CSEL 16 (Vienna 1888); for the former, see also the edition by C. Moussy (Paris 1974), and for the latter, A. H. Chase in *HSCP* 43 (1932) 51–76.

There is an edition of the *Aegritudo Perdiccae* by L. Zurli (Leipzig 1987); see also the edition published in Rome in 1966 under the direction of S. Mariotti, based on that of F. Vollmer in *Poetae Latini Minores* 5.2 (Leipzig 1914). On the authorship, see E. Wolf in *Révue de Philologie* 62 (1958) 79–89.

The Dawn of the Middle Ages

1. CONTINUITY AND INNOVATION IN MEDIEVAL LITERATURE

Differences in liter-ary development in the various regions

After the fall of the Empire, writing in Latin continued, but the breakup of the political unit had various consequences for literature. In a first stage, down to the empire of Charlemagne, the gradual establishment of the various kingdoms and the different times at which Romans and Germans were integrated in the different regions led to dissimilarity in literary activity. Italy was still quite active in the sixth century, with figures such as Boethius and Cassiodorus, who among other things produce an encyclopedic body of philosophical, religious, and scientific thought to transmit to future generations. Spain and England, however, play a prominent role only some decades later, at the beginning of the seventh and of the eighth century, respectively, when with Isidore of Seville and Bede they express the most important aspects of European culture.

Priscian

These great men of learning are, in a certain sense, the bridge between the classical world and the medieval world, collecting and summarizing as much as possible of the ancient tradition. From this point of view a figure of no less significance, though his interests are more restricted, is the great grammarian Priscian, who was active at Constantinople during the first half of the sixth century and was the author of that *Institutio de Arte Grammatica* that would be the principal textbook of all the Middle Ages (and would earn Priscian a place in Dante's *Commedia*).

The Corpus Iuris

In the preservation of ancient tradition, the *Corpus Iuris Civilis,* or more simply *Corpus Iuris,* played a fundamental role. This is the name that was used, from the early Middle Ages on, for the monumental synthesis of Roman law compiled from 528 on at the behest of the emperor Justinian.

The first fruit of this activity was a collection of laws, which was published in 529 under the name *Codex Iustinianus* and is lost today. After three years of work (530–33) a collection of passages from the classical jurists was published, with the title *Digesta* (or *Pandectae*), to which we owe the greater part of our knowledge of ancient Roman law. Justinian gave it a normative as well as a historical role, and the passages, where necessary, were modified to adapt them to practical needs. Immediately after the *Digesta,* in the same year, 533, the *Institutiones* were published, in four books (compared with the fifty of the *Digesta*), a kind of summary of the larger work made for teaching purposes.

The intense legal-legislative activity of the last years made necessary the publication of a new codex, which would replace that of 529. After a year of work, at the end of 534, the *Codex Repetitae Praelectionis* was promulgated, in twelve books, which are extant.

Finally, the laws that came into effect during the following thirty-year period, to the death of Justinian (565), have come down to us, though not organically collected, under the name *Novellae* (with *Constitutiones* understood); many of these are written in Greek, or in both Greek and Latin.

Changes in the Latin language: the birth of the Romance languages

In the meantime, however, the ethnic and social upheavals profoundly altered the European and Mediterranean West. The profoundest changes touched the Latin language, in which the split between written language and spoken language grew to the point that the latter can no longer be recognized as a popular form of the language in which books continued to be written. Thus were born the Romance languages, and Latin becomes a learned language, destined to be used for cultural exchange at a high level and to be an effective source of continuity as the liturgical language of the church in the West. Already in the time of Charlemagne it is almost an artificial language, a system of communication for a few educated persons. This fact would decisively mark all literature from the ninth century onwards.

The renaissance under Charlemagne

A court gathered around Charlemagne, the ruler's ambitions encouraged literary men, and thus a circle of poets was created, whose literary works—which in many aspects take up myths and subjects of Augustan poetry—are far from contemptible in quantity and quality. And yet the relation between the Latin language and society was now deeply altered and compromised. There were to be renaissances, recoveries, noble instances of philology and learning, but the connection, the thread of continuity, was now irremediably broken. The writing of Latin had become a secondary and symbolic act.

2. CULTURE IN SIXTH-CENTURY ITALY: BOETHIUS AND CASSIODORUS

Boethius: man of culture and intransigent politician

The three centuries that lead to this new situation no longer have the characteristics of classical antiquity but do not yet have those of the Middle Ages; they are a complex border region calling into question our periodizations and classifications, valuable as they are as a framework for knowledge. In Italy, before the Lombards, the late ancient literary period seems to be prolonged and to continue to live, incredibly. Boethius is a man of most remarkable learning (and not remarkable merely because of the time in which he lived), a politician engaged in a difficult struggle to eliminate at least the most obvious and unpleasant effects of the defeat of the Roman Empire and a thinker who represents one of the highest points of contact between the world-views of pagan philosophy and Christianity.

The influence Boethius had on the Western Middle Ages, his ability to appreciate the significance of the classical tradition and to draw a balance that was mindful of its great intellectual problems, his farsightedness, which paradoxically contradicted his basically conservative program—these have made Boethius the figure of greatest distinction in this period and have in some ways obscured the existence of another area of Roman intellectual activity, one that was more realistic, more disposed to compromise with the Goths in order to rescue something of the classical tradition for the moment and not for an uncertain future. This other line is in a sense more subtle and more difficult, in that it is liable to unjust accusations of self-interested collaboration. The most important representative of this line is, of course, Cassiodorus, who in his difficult life, full of complex mediations, did not experience the head-on clashes that cost Boethius his life, but certainly needed to accept many bitter defeats and who lived long enough to see all his efforts to fuse Goths and Romans into an Italian nation completely annulled.

Cassiodorus: realism and mediation

Boethius

LIFE

Anicius Manlius Severinus Boethius, born at Rome around 480, studied philosophy in the Greek East and was one of the chief members of the Roman nobility. Prefect of Rome, praetorian prefect for Italy, consul in 510, *magister officiorum* in 522, he obtained from political activity the greatest satisfactions that a Roman of those days could hope for. Then, unexpectedly, his fortunes fell: accused of conspiring against Theodoric (the king of the Goths, who was then the master of Italy), he was imprisoned and later put to death in 524.

WORKS

Boethius conceived of an encyclopedic corpus that was to treat systematically all the problems of knowledge; to this belong the *Institutio Arithmetica* and the *De Institutione Musica.* His philosophical works on logic and dialectic are fundamental: translations and commentaries on the works of Aristotle, the neo-Platonist Porphyry, and Cicero; and two writings on the syllogism, a treatise in four books *De Differentiis Topicis* and a *De Divisione.* Among his theological works an essay on the Trinity and a polemical text directed against several heresies may be mentioned. His most famous work is the dialogue *De Consolatione Philosophiae,* which in form is a Menippean satire, that is, composed of prose and verse (see p. 216). The dialogue takes place between the author while a prisoner and Philosophy, who has visited him in jail in order to console him and to discuss the great themes of philosophy—unhappiness, good and evil, free will, and so on.

The De Consolatione Philosophiae

The importance of the *De Consolatione* does not lie solely in the immense success it had throughout the Middle Ages, but also in the role that the work plays in the history of an intellectual who, starting with the ambitious program of sketching the *summa* of ancient thought in order to demonstrate Greco-Roman superiority over the Germans, is forced to the bitter conclusion that success does not always attend good deeds and virtue and who therefore seeks to explain this injustice in a wider perspective. Philosophy and great literature, Greek and Latin culture, and dramatic personal experiences are fused in a mixture that is made more appealing by the circumstances in which the work was written. A rigorous theoretical structure based on Aristotle, the Stoics, the neo-Platonists, and also on Cicero, Seneca, and Augustine is joined with a moral perspective that makes the work an exhortation to the good. Boethius's fine rhetorical ability and his vast literary learning do not preclude attempts at bold experimentation, such as the alternation within each book of passages in prose with passages in verse and the employment of anomalous and unusual metrical forms.

Cassiodorus

LIFE

Flavius Magnus Aurelius Cassiodorus Senator, born at Squillace in Calabria before 490, was quaestor and then consul and in the end replaced Boethius as *magister officiorum*. When the Byzantines conquered Ravenna in 540, taking it from the Goths, he went to Constantinople, where he remained until the Eastern Empire won its decisive victory, in 554. He then returned to Calabria and founded the monastery of Vivarium. He died there after 580 at an age of more than 90.

WORKS

Cassiodorus's many writings can be divided neatly into two groups: one includes the works down to 540, which are more engaged in political life; the other includes the works after that date, which are mostly on religious or erudite subjects. To the first phase belongs the *Variae,* published in 538, which collects in twelve books 468 official letters written by him in his capacity as a high official of the state. From the same period comes the *Chronica,* which, on the model of Jerome, surveys events from Adam to the year 519. A historical work in twelve books has been lost, the *De Origine Actibusque Getarum,* composed between 526 and 533, which would have been valuable evidence about the Goths and the complex, tortured relations that Cassiodorus had with them. All we have is a summary of it and a continuation to 551, the work of Jordanes (or Jordanis), a Goth who was bishop of Crotona.

To the second phase of Cassiodorus's writing belongs the *Institutiones,* in two books, an encyclopedic handbook devoted to sacred and profane literature, with a good bibliography on its various subjects. In extreme old age, at 92, Cassiodorus composed a *De Orthographia* for the use of the monks of Vivarium.

Cassiodorus is the figure who can best illuminate the typical characteristics of Boethius's works and be illuminated by them in turn, so great are the similarities and differences between their personal histories and their cultural programs.

A political project destined to fail

Cassiodorus was a Roman who tried to understand the world of the German victors and looked forward to a fusion of the two peoples. In the Italy of that time he was one of the few to see clearly that the Empire was now finished and that it was necessary to build the new state and the new civilization in peace and without unproductive opposition. His political project was destined to fail, and after the war with the Goths it was transformed into a cultural enterprise of an encyclopedic type, comparable to Boethius's, though very different from it. Boethius had in mind an elitist ideal of culture and emphasized the theoretical aspects of the disciplines, their more abstract features. Cassiodorus, however, was concerned with the practical (today we would say technological) content of the various arts, in a line of encyclopedic thought that would have greater success as it more nearly approached natural history: not much literature, but many texts teaching how to carry out a variety of activities, from agriculture to medicine, from letter writing to the copying of manuscripts. In the monastery of Vivarium, a valuable library was collected under his guidance and work was begun on the classical texts (collation and emendation of manuscripts, translations, summaries, popularizations, etc.); this anticipates the scriptoria of the great abbeys during the following centuries.

A practical knowledge

The Poets

Ennodius

In poetry, too, authors of great formal elegance are to be found, men of originality who composed well-made poems, such as Ennodius, who was born at Arles in 473 or 474 but lived chiefly at Pavia, of which he was bishop until 521, the year of his death. He was the author not only of prose works but of poems and epigrams, in which the presence of the classical, pagan world is quite marked and is referred to with a regret that is surprising in a bishop. One of his pupils, Arator, was a successful poet. In 544, before pope Vigilius and an enthusiastic crowd gathered in the church of San Pietro in Vincoli, he read his poem entitled *De Actibus Apostolorum,* in two books of hexameters.

Arator

Maximian

Even more interesting than Ennodius, who is sometimes burdened by his academic erudition and taste for belles-lettres, is another poet, Maximian. A native of Tuscany who probably lived at the middle of the sixth century, he is the author of six elegies, in which the imminence of death and the sadness of growing old are seen as representing the end of pagan culture and its joy in living.

Benedict of Nursia and Gregory the Great

Alongside these authors in whom continuity with the Roman past is prominent, we also find authors who express the new medieval reality, such as Benedict of Nursia (ca. 480–ca. 547), the founder of the abbey of Montecassino, whose Rule, the reworking of the earlier *Regula Magistri,* was destined to govern monastic communities for centuries, and especially Pope Gregory the Great (540–604), a figure of great political significance and hardly less important in literature.

Convinced of the need to consolidate the primacy of the bishop of Rome, Gregory was not above using money and alliances to achieve this goal.

Worried by the ambitions of the Eastern emperor, who aimed at being the guardian of the papacy, he took advantage of the clashes and conflicts between the barbarian kingdoms and the Empire. Conscious of the advantages deriving from landholdings and a strong economic situation, he laid the basis of the Pontifical State and theorized about the suitability of its having at its disposal profane means to be employed in the service of the church. This is the source of the love and the hatred that the Guelfs and Ghibellines of all ages have harbored for him, creating a series of ideological superimpositions that make it practically impossible to evaluate his historical personality calmly and that often affect our judgment of his literary writings as well. We are informed about these activities of Gregory by the fourteen books of his *Epistles,* which are an extremely valuable source for reconstructing the political and religious life of the time.

Of noble family, Gregory already as praetorian prefect of Rome rejected the profane cultural inheritance, as is shown by his letter to Desiderius, bishop of Vienne. The bishop had opened a school for his clergy in which the course of instruction was the usual one, which included the classics, and Gregory forbade it. The author of ponderous exegetical works, Gregory also essayed a literary form that in subject and style was more immediately relevant to a not particularly educated public: the four *Dialogorum Libri,* the second of which is a biography of Benedict of Nursia. In this work— on which we owe to Auerbach, in *Literary Language and Its Public in Late Antiquity,* a number of felicitous observations—the pope uses a colloquial language and portrays a rural reality far removed from the world of the scholars and theologians to whom his other works are addressed.

The Carolingian renaissance in Italy

During the last decades of the century conditions in Italy changed profoundly. With the arrival of the Lombards, everything became more difficult, and for two centuries literature was not an activity to which it was easy or practical to devote oneself. It would be necessary to wait for the last years of Lombard domination and the new Carolingian atmosphere to find a historian such as Paul the Deacon, the author of the *Historia Langobardorum,* or a grammarian such as Peter of Pisa, and, more generally, a significant revival of studies.

3. LITERATURE IN AFRICA

Dracontius

The mixing of Christian and pagan subjects

In Africa, too, the last years of the fifth century and the first half of the sixth are a period of notable literary flowering, despite the harshness of the Vandal occupation. A poet such as Dracontius, who lived in the last years of the fifth century and died around 500, deserves to be remembered for his mixing of pagan and Christian subjects. A tragedy, *Orestis Tragoedia,* or more simply *Orestes* (actually a hexameter poem), and two epyllia, the *De Raptu Helenae* and the *Medea* (joined together with other poems of very varying character to form a collection entitled *Romulea),* already with their titles alone carry us back to classical mythology, which is relived through the experience of school and rhetorical studies, as well as through the tradition of dramatic performances (mimes in particular), which continued to be popular in fifth-century Africa. The Christian character is more evident in the *Satisfactio,* a poem in elegiac couplets, addressed to Gunthamund, king of the Vandals, in order to ask his pardon for a fault Dracontius had committed (having celebrated, instead of Gunthamund, another person, probably the emperor of the East, Zeno), and in the *De Laudibus Dei,* three books of hexameters, which proposes to sing God's benevolence towards man and his *pietas,* in order thus to move the king's piety and obtain his pardon.

Culture as a commodity of exchange

This attempt to use culture, the technical ability to write verses, as a commodity of exchange with the king is interesting. There was a tradition of poets who, after falling into disgrace, had regained, or attempted to regain, their fortunes by means of their own works, and Dracontius shows by his quotations from Ovid and Optatianus that he knows them well, but the novelty lies in the interlocutor: to address a poem to Augustus or Constantine was quite different from writing for the barbarian Gunthamund. Nevertheless, the poet's confidence in his art is striking, as is his willingness to believe that relations between power and culture can still exist as they did during the first four centuries of the Empire.

Fulgentius

The interpretation of the classics during the transition to the Middle Ages

Also active in the Vandal period is Fabius Planciades Fulgentius (though some regard him as being a century earlier), an odd and erudite author of four works: the *Mythologiarum Libri,* which seeks the "scientific" grounds behind the stories of pagan religion in order to extract from these symbolic tales the truths hidden within and to make them accessible to the Christian; the *Expositio Vergilianae Continentiae,* a dialogue in which Virgil explains to the author the allegories beneath the verses of the *Aeneid* and proposes a possible moral reading of the epic; the *De Aetatibus Mundi et Hominis,* a summary of history from the Fall to the second half of the fourth century (the text is certainly incomplete), the principal feature of which is that it was written in the technique of the *lipogramma,* by which in the first chapter the letter *a* never appears, in the second *b,* in the third *c,* and so forth; and the *Expositio Sermonum Antiquorum,* which explains the meaning of seventy-six words by a series of quotations from various authors (these occasionally give the impression of being wholesale fabrications or at least considerably altered).

The ensemble of these four works marks a stage in the transition from antiquity to the Middle Ages. The new attempts at interpreting and using the classics, the new place of mythology that these presuppose, and the new evaluation of history as salvation are combined with a language that is select and forceful but far removed from the norms that had been followed until a few decades earlier.

Victor of Vita

Also belonging to the last years of the fifth century is Victor, bishop of Vita, a city of northern Africa, who wrote a *Historia Persecutionis Africanae*

Provinciae, which recounts the cruelties of the Vandals from the invasion of 429 to the end of Hunerich's kingdom in 484. With its macabre descriptions it emphasizes the religious persecutions of the Christians.

Corippus

In comparison with this considerable flourishing of writers in the period from 480 to the reconquest of the province by Justinian's troops in 534, literary production oddly diminishes when the region returns to being a part of the Empire. The only poet of importance to deserve mention is Corippus, who in the middle of the sixth century sang the glory of the imperial armies under the leadership of the general John in an epic poem, the *Iohannis,* which follows the *Aeneid* closely not only in the form of its title but also in its characters. The poem, eight books of hexameters, recounts the war against the Moors of 546–48. Of slightly later date is an *In Laudem Iustini Augusti Minoris,* in four books, devoted to the installation of the emperor (565) and the first period of his rule. Corippus is a poet of great culture who combines Christianity and classical tradition as we have seen other writers of the period doing; one also notes in him certain particular characteristics, more evident perhaps in the *In Laudem Iustini,* such as a taste for describing ceremonies and displays and a notable slowness in the pace of the action, which is often replaced by the description of settings and by speeches made by the characters.

The Iohannis

In Laudem Iustini

4. LITERATURE IN SPAIN

A society of learned men and a Visigothic poet-king

In Spain the development of positive relations between Romans and Visigoths produced, at the end of the sixth century, a society of learned men, including bishops and men of the church, and even a Visigothic king, Sisebut, who cultivated poetry and the sciences. The interest in scientific studies is one of the most remarkable elements of this Visigothic renaissance, which created a summary of knowledge on which the learned men of all Western Europe would rely for centuries to come. The undoubted protagonist of this renaissance, even though there are many minor writers along with him, is Isidore, the *doctor egregius* of the Middle Ages.

Martin of Braga

A notable figure in this context is Martin, bishop of Braga (in what is today Portugal). Originally from Pannonia, he moved (for reasons we do not know) to the other extreme of Europe and became, after the middle of the sixth century, the bishop of Braga; he died in 580. His moral writings (the *De Ira* and the *Formula Vitae Honestae*) draw on Seneca as their chief source. His major work, the *De Correctione Rusticorum,* gives us evidence of how pagan practices still survived in the sixth century among the lower classes of the population in the Galician countryside.

Isidore of Seville

LIFE

Born in Seville, which in ancient times was called Hispalis (whence his Latin name, *Isidorus Hispalensis*), in around 570 to a family of Roman origin, Isidore was educated by his older brother Leander, the bishop of Seville, who was an important figure of literature in his own right. Upon his brother's death, in 600, Isidore succeeded him as bishop, devoting himself to the reorganization of the Spanish church, carefully tending relations with the Visigothic kings, and enhancing the temporal power of the bishops. He died in 636.

His literary works are impressively ample. They are in large part of a strictly religious or ecclesiastical nature, but there are also many historical writings (the *De Viris Illustribus;* the *Chronica,* from the creation to 615; the *Historia Gothorum, Vandalorum, Sueborum*). His encyclopedic works are fundamental, especially the *Origines sive Etymologiae,* in twenty books. Starting with the words used to define the various arts and sciences and with the terms relating to their concepts and instruments, Isidore attempts by means of etymology to return to the roots, to the original truth, and at the same time to preserve and spread knowledge and technology that would otherwise be lost. The twenty books are divided by subject: at the beginning are the arts of the trivium and the quadrivium, next follow other activities such as medicine and law, then matters of religious life, the different languages, nations, states, armies, citizens, and relatives. The tenth book is a genuine dictionary, explaining a series of difficult words. The second ten books deal with subjects that we might call more "scientific": men and monsters, animals, the universe and its parts, the earth and its parts, houses and country, rocks and metals, agriculture and gardening. The last books are curious because of the odd pairings of their contents: book 18 is on war and games, 19 on ships, buildings, and clothing, and 20 on food types and utensils for the household and the farm.

A cultural recovery with a view to progress

Isidore was not nostalgic for the Empire and did not want to oppose the Germans. A true follower of Cassiodorus, he sees the Goths as the founders of the new nation-state. The Romans of the Eastern Empire are the enemy, against whom it is right to fight. The recovery of classical culture is not carried out, therefore, with a sense of nostalgia, but in order to equip the new people for its future history and to furnish it with all the essentials of ancient knowledge in the forms that are simplest and easiest to understand, making no distinction between Christian and pagan texts, since the ideological threat posed by the latter is now greatly reduced. His scrupulous faithfulness to the ancient texts has often caused medievalists to accuse Isidore of being barely original and inferior in intelligence to a Boethius, a Cassiodorus, or a Bede. But the novelty of the project and the fact that it is accompanied by a concrete political engagement suggest that the ensemble of his works should be considered, not as an aseptic product of the study, but as an organic proposal (and a functional proposal, as his fortune throughout the Middle Ages would demonstrate) to systematize culture for the purpose of training new generations and new ruling classes.

Later, at the beginning of the eighth century, Spain becomes part of the

Islamic sphere of influence, and Latin literature there enters a period of crisis.

5. LITERATURE IN FRANCE

A constantly high level of culture

The literary history of France is considerably more complex, because the establishment of a Germanic kingdom in this region was more laborious. The Franks first had to drive the Visigoths from the southern regions and then absorb the Burgundians, and for a long time they had grave internal problems on account of the divisions between the various branches of the Merovingian ruling families. The last years of the fifth century and the first years of the sixth century are characterized by the same high cultural level that had characterized Gaul for more than a hundred years. One may recall Avitus, bishop of Vienne, author of, among other things, an epic poem on a religious subject (the *Libelli de Spiritalis Historiae Gestis,* in five books of hexameters, written in the first years of the sixth century), and Caesarius, archbishop of Arles from 502 to 542, the author of 238 *Sermones,* in which, perhaps for the first time, sacred eloquence takes on popularizing features, adapting itself thus, in both language and content, to the now modest cultural level of the audience. But the persons of greatest importance are active in the second half of the sixth century: Venantius Fortunatus, with his fresh poetic compositions, is perhaps the most significant author, but Gregory of Tours also holds special interest.

Venantius Fortunatus

LIFE

Venantius Honorius Clementianus Fortunatus was born at Valdobbiadene (then called Duplavilis) near Treviso around 530. He studied at Ravenna and then left Italy around 565 on a long pilgrimage across France and Germany. He traveled from Tours to Mainz, from Cologne to Triers, from Metz to Verdun, from Reims to Soissons to Paris, writing panegyrics of bishops and local lords and earning his living by his writing. At Poitiers, finally, in 567 he met Radegunda, the widow of King Clotaire, who had retired to a convent of that city. He became her secretary and a priest, remaining in the tranquil refuge of his monastery even after the death of Radegunda, which occurred in 587. Bishop of Poitiers from 597 on, he died around 600 at the age of seventy.

WORKS

In prose he wrote several saints' lives and a biography of Radegunda, composed after her death. In verse are the *Vita Martini,* in four books of hexameters, various hymns destined to survive in the Western liturgy (among them the famous *Vexilla Regis Prodeunt* and *Pange Lingua*), and many short poems collected in the eleven books of the *Miscellanea.*

A "different" poetic voice

Leaving aside moral evaluations of the doubtful aspects of his person, first an occasional writer and then a priest for convenience, Venantius is on many grounds a voice different from that of most contemporaries, especially on account of the facility and freshness of his poetry. His linguistic and metrical competence may give rise not only to criticism because of their distance from the classical models but also to enthusiasm for the new authenticity that makes Venantius the initiator of a medieval poetry that recovers the elegiac experience and turns it to singing new subjects, spiritual love not the least among them. In this regard Venantius is regarded by some as a precursor of troubadour poetry.

His facility as a poet allows him to find the right words and images, even if his cultural inheritance is not comparable to that of other Italian and African writers. Venantius can pass from the rarefied level of the small everyday events in the life of the convent to the grand constructions of the hymns, which in the harshness of their descriptions of Christ's Passion inaugurate the new esthetic of the medieval audience.

Gregory of Tours

Life and works of Gregory

Born in 538 at Clermont-Ferrand to one of the most distinguished Roman families of the city, in 563 he made a pilgrimage to Tours for reasons of health and remained there as deacon with his relative, the bishop Euphronius. Upon Euphronius's death, in 573, he succeeded him and for twenty years held the most prestigious episcopal see in France with great ability and courage.

The author of verse works that are totally lost and of a number of religious works, Gregory is known above all for his masterpiece, the *Historiae,* more commonly known as the *Historia Francorum,* in ten books, a fundamental text of medieval historiography. Written between 575 and 594 (the year of Gregory's death), the *Historia Francorum* begins with Adam and narrates events down to the year 591, devoting particular space to the more recent events, of which he had direct knowledge.

The historian's impassiveness

The history of the Franks is predominantly the history of crimes and cruelty, of usurpations, assassinations, and tortures, which arouse our indignation but which the author narrates with a detached imperturbability that has even brought down upon him accusations of insensitivity. It is likely that in order to live in those times, one needed to become accustomed to certain behavior and to regard it as practically usual. It is possible, too, that Gregory saw the futility in filling his history with moral tirades, which would have been so frequent as to lose all value and to become merely annoying to the reader. It is important, however, to recall that history for him is a constant conflict between the good, which is present on earth in the organization of the church, and the evil that lies in the vices of many of the powerful, in their lust for blood and riches. On this view, every misdeed is a modest, marginal episode in the greater cosmic war between good and evil, which will end with the certain victory of the former and thus with compensation for all the acts of injustice.

History of deeds and minor characters

Gregory's history includes the great but does not neglect more modest characters nor the kinds of deeds that an ancient historian would have excluded from his work; this is especially the case of those that took place in his own diocese. In these cases Gregory cannot help telling the story, even if it is merely the murder of a slave or an enmity between private citizens, scenes full of complications and surprises but of small importance in the context of great events. This sensitivity to the conditions of life of all the social classes brings the *Historia Francorum* close to modern historical writing, but its motives are not the same. Gregory's historical and political horizon is more restricted than that of other writers of the time, and for him almost only France exists, and in particular the territory of Tours. Moreover, his use of sources is different, because he attaches great value to viewing things directly. This leads to a new hierarchy of events that favors those that Gregory is sure he has seen with his own eyes, which is one of the most significant aspects of his work. It remains to mention the enjoyment that the reader derives from his pages, which are marked by exceptional narrative skill, animated by his descriptive power and moved by the dramatic quality of a varied and turbulent style, which is not without its novelty but which also shows a patient assimilation of the great traditional models of historiography.

A restricted horizon

Narrative skill

6. THE VENERABLE BEDE

In France, even more than in Italy, the seventh century is the "age of iron," in which there is little or nothing of importance to record, and literature seems to fall silent. In Britain, however, the revival of cultural activity came later, after cultural contact with the Latin world had been completely interrupted, in the fifth century: it may be said to date only from around the middle of the sixth century, when the Briton Gildas writes the *De Excidio et Conquestu Britanniae,* a work that depicts the historical happenings of his people but also provides a dramatic picture of the moral situation in which he finds himself. But although the revival came late, it lasted longer. The dominant figure in this process is the Venerable Bede.

LIFE

Bede was born in 672–73 on the eastern coast of northern England (Northumbria) near Hadrian's Wall. At the age of seven he was entrusted to the monastery at Wearmouth to be educated, and he spent his whole life in the twin monasteries of Wearmouth and Jarrow. A deacon and later a priest, he never went far from his monasteries and certainly never left his region. He died in 735.

WORKS

His works in verse are nearly all lost (only three are extant, among them a poem *De Die Iudicii* about the Final Judgment). The prose writings include letters, sermons, and religious, scientific, grammatical, and historical works. Among the scientific works the *De Natura Rerum,* based on Pliny and Isidore, is notable, as is the *De Temporibus,* about the year and its divisions, which uses Isidore, Pliny, and Macrobius. Grammatical works include the *De Orthographia,* the *De Metrica Arte,* and the *De Schematibus et Tropis,* on the rhetorical figures, with examples drawn from the Bible. The historical writings are the most important: the *De Ratione Temporum,* on the divergent chronologies in existence and the value of dating years from the birth of Christ; the *Historia Ecclesiastica Gentis Anglorum,* in five books, with a description of the island and the narrative of events from Caesar to his own days; and the *Historia Abbatum,* about the abbots of Wearmouth and Jarrow.

Bede's rigor and acuity

The rigor of Bede's historical method, the acuteness of his judgments, and the fullness of his documentation are all surprising. He understands the importance of a document and of comparing different notices. He reports the text of inscriptions and cites literary sources. He is punctilious in chronological tables and geographical notices, and he even tries to provide statistics on the population and the number of families. In his reconstructions he does not confine himself to simple occurrences, but shows an appreciable interest in the history of culture, in local traditions, and in material culture. The religious element naturally holds first place in the narrative, but not because of a deviation due to the author's personal vision. The fact is that religion and its problems really did play a leading part in the life of the period. Miracles, anecdotes, virtues, and weaknesses are mixed into a credible and enjoyable narrative that aims at a comprehensive reconstruction of historical events, and among the writer's many merits is certainly the elegance of his writing, which is clear and straightforward.

One of the fathers of the Middle Ages

Bede is one of the most remarkable figures in the literary history of the early Middle Ages. Dante places him in an ideal series that starts with Boethius and continues with Isidore; he thus identifies the three great mainstays, who, along with Cassiodorus, provided the whole Middle Ages with the wealth of information and ideas that constituted the cultural baggage of every intellectual. In this company Bede distinguishes himself by the attention he devotes to historical studies and also by the particular characteristics of his life. The others are all persons of great importance in politics, administrators of the state or ecclesiastical wielders of concrete temporal power, whereas Bede is an ordinary monk, who did not belong to powerful families and did not reach any grade in the ecclesiastical hierarchy, not even of his own monastery.

7. TOWARDS THE CREATION OF NATIONAL LITERATURES: A DIFFUSION RATHER THAN A TERMINATION

Creation of national literatures

After Bede an interesting phenomenon is to be observed: Anglo-Saxon scholars and Irish monks reimport into France and Italy the Latin culture that has been developed in the British islands. When this is carried out by individuals who do not speak Latin as their native language and do not have it as part of their national tradition, a cycle of literary history is brought to a close. Now the national literatures are created in Romance or Germanic languages, which previously coexisted with a Latin literature that was increasingly reserved for the narrow circles of the learned but later came to replace it completely at the birth of the modern world.

A great effort of synthesis

In the centuries between the fall of the Roman Empire in the West and the imperial restoration of Charlemagne, Latin literature carries out an important task in the history of culture, the transmission of knowledge from the old state system to the new Europe. In performing this function, the originality of the reconstructions, the strength (sometimes even excessive and oppressive) of the intellectual systems, and the difficult synthesis between paganism and Christianity, between Roman world and Germanic world, in short, everything produced by these intellectuals, presupposes an effort such as may never have been made in other stages of mankind's history.

Intellectuals and society in the Middle Ages

Whether this effort occurred apart from the social conditions that were troubling the medieval masses or whether, rather, the writers and men of letters took part in these events and played leading roles in them is a complex question that remains open. Certainly a view that sees in them a completely conventional culture, closed to relations with a world that no longer speaks Latin and looking upon the classical tradition as distant, not to say foreign, is too extremist. The personal histories of many writers serve to prove this, and it is indirectly confirmed by the role their work played in creating new literatures, for which they provided both content and formal structures.

This Latin that long survived its own death, this literature written in a language that no one used as a natural instrument of communication but that continued to be the official language of the church and met, and met quite well, the need for information felt by scholars and scientists are among the most curious and contradictory features of a period that was rich in incongruities and torn between aspirations towards the universal and centrifugal tendencies towards the particular. They are a language and a literature that, though closely tied to the past, have their own characteristics and their own independence, in that complex alternation of continuity and rupture that is perhaps the greatest fascination of the Middle Ages.

BIBLIOGRAPHY

There are a number of general surveys in English of medieval Latin literature. See esp. M.R.P. McGuire and H. Dressler, *Introduction to Medieval Latin Studies* (ed. 2 Washington, D.C., 1977), K. Stecker, *Introduction to Medieval Latin,* trans. R. B. Palmer (Berlin 1957), E. R. Curtius, *European Literature and the Latin Middle Ages,* trans. W. R. Trask, (London 1953), M.L.W. Laistner, *Thought and Letters in Western Europe* (ed. 2 London 1957), F.J.E. Raby, *A History of Christian Latin Poetry* (Oxford 1953) and *A History of Secular Latin Poetry* (ed. 2 Oxford 1957), E. Auerbach, *Literary Language and Its Public in Late Antiquity and the Middle Ages,* trans. R. Manheim (London 1965), P. Dronke, *Medieval Latin and the Rise of the European Love Lyric* (ed. 2 Oxford 1968) and *The Medieval Lyric* (London 1978), and P. Godman, *Poetry of the Carolingian Renaissance* (London 1985). In French note J. de Ghellink, *Littérature latine au moyen age* (Paris 1939), and D. Norbers, *Manual pratique de latin médiéval* (Paris 1968).

Priscian's *Institutio De Arte Grammatica* is edited in the second and third volumes of H. Keil's *Grammatici Latini* (Leipzig 1855) by M. J. Hertz; around four hundred manuscripts are known (cf. *BollStudLat* 15 [1985] 107).

The most recent critical edition of Boethius's *Consolatio* is that by L. Bieler in the Corpus Christianorum, or CC (ed. 2 Turnholt 1984); there is a Loeb by H. F. Stewart and E. K. Rand (Cambridge, Mass. 1918), and there is an excellent German commentary by J. Gruber (Berlin and New York 1978). There is a general study by H. Chadwick, *Boethius: The Consolations of Music, Logic, Theology, and Philosophy* (Oxford 1981), and a volume of essays edited by M. Gibson (Oxford 1981) that includes discussion and bibliography for the other writings. See also S. Lever, *Boethius and Dialogue: Literary Method in the Consolation of Philosophy* (Princeton 1985), P. Courcelle, *La Consolation de philosophie dans la tradition littéraire* (Paris 1967), M. Fuhrmann and J. Gruber, *Boethius* (Wege der Forschung 482, Darmstadt 1984), and for the poetic sections of the *Consolatio*, G.J.P. O'Daly, *The Poetry of Boethius* (London 1991).

The *Variarum Libri XII* of Cassiodorus are edited by A. J. Fridh (CC 96, Turnholt 1973), the *Institutiones* by R.A.B. Mynors (Oxford 1937, 1963); for the other works, see the bibliography in Mynors, pp. xviii–xx. In general see J. J. O'Donnell, *Cassiodorus* (Berkeley and Los Angeles 1979), A. Momigliano in *Secondo contributo alla storia degli studi classici* (Rome 1960) 191–229, R. McPherson, *Rome in Revolution: Cassiodorus' Variae in Their Literary and Historical Setting* (Poznan 1989), and the papers in the *Atti della settimana di studi su Flavio Magno Aurelio Cassiodoro* (Rubbettino 1986).

For Ennodius, see the edition by G. Hartel, Corpus Scriptorum Ecclesiasticorum Latinorum, or CSEL, 6 (Vienna 1882), as well as the detailed *RAC* article (in German) by J. Fontaine (vol. 5, Stuttgart 1962), and for Arator, the edition by A. P. McKinlay (CSEL 72, Vienna 1951), as well as R. J. Schrader in *Classical Folia* 31 (1977) 64–77. Maximianus is edited by M. Petschenig (Berlin 1890); there is a French commentary by F. Spaltenstein (Rome 1983). See esp. W. Schetter, *Studien zur Überlieferung und Kritik des Elegikers Maximians* (Wiesbaden 1970), C. Ratkowitsch, *Maximianus amat, zu Datierung und Interpretation des Elegikers Maximian* (Vienna 1986; but see D. Shanzer in *Gnomon* 60 [1988] 259–61), and A. Fo in *Hermes* 115 (1987) 348–71.

There is a major edition of the *Rule of St. Benedict* by A. de Vogüé and J. Neufville (7 vols., Paris 1972–77); note B. Jaspert, *Die Regula Benedicti — Regula Magistri Kontroverse* (Hildesheim 1975) and his *Bibliographie der Regula Benedicti 1930–1980: Ausgaben und Übersetzungen* (Hildesheim 1983).

An edition of the works of Pope Gregory the Great is in progress in the CC series, 140–44 (7 vols. to date, 1963–); see also the editions in the Sources Chrétiennes series of the *Dialogues* by A. de Vogüé (3 vols., Paris 1975–80) and the *Moralia in Job* by R. Gillet and A. de Gaudemans (3 vols., Paris 1974–89). See F. H. Duden, *Gregory the Great* (London 1905), C. Straw, *Gregory the Great* (Berkeley 1988), and C. Dageud, *Saint Grégoire le Grand* (Paris 1977), as well as the collection *Grégoire le Grand*, ed. J. Fontaine, R. Gillet, and S. Pellistrandi (Paris 1986), and the *Bibliografia di Gregorio Magno (1890–1989)*, by R. Godding (Rome 1990).

For Paul the Deacon, Peter of Pisa, and the beginnings of Carolingian poetry, see esp. Godman, *Poetry of the Carolingian Renaissance,* with bibliography.

There is an edition of Dracontius's *De Laudibus Dei* by C. Moussy and C. Camus (2 vols., Paris 1985–88, with French translation, commentary, and detailed introduction). For the other works, see F. Vollmer, *Poetae Latini Minores* 5 (Leipzig 1914). See D. F. Bright, *The Miniature Epic in Vandal Africa* (Norman 1987), F. Stella and W. Speyer in *Philologus* 132 (1988) 259–85 (with further bibliography).

The standard edition of the works of Fulgentius is that of R. Helm (Leipzig 1898, reprint with addenda by J. Préaux 1970). There is a useful English translation with notes and bibliography by L. G. Whitbread (Columbus 1971); see also J. C. Relihan in *AJP* 105 (1984) 87–90.

For the *History* of Victor of Vita, see the edition of M. Petschenig (CSEL 7, Vienna 1881), along with most recently S. Costanza in *VetChr* 7 (1980) 229–68 and R. Pitkäranta, *Studien zum Latein des Victor Vitensis* (Helsinki 1978).

There are good English editions of Corippus's *Iohannis* by J. Diggle and F.R.D. Goodyear (Cambridge 1970) and *In Laudem Iustini* by A. Cameron (London 1976); there is also an edition of the latter by S. Antès (Paris 1981).

There is an Oxford text of Isidore's *Origines sive Etymologiae* by W. M. Lindsay (Oxford 1911); a major new French edition is in progress in the series Auteurs Latins du Moyen Age (Paris 1986–). Note also the editions of the *De Rerum Natura* by J. Fontaine (Bordeaux 1960), the *De Ecclesiasticis Officiis* by C. M. Lawson (CC 113, Turnholt 1989), the *De Differentiis* by C. Codoner (Paris 1992), and the *Historia Gothorum* by T. Mommsen (Berlin 1894). For the many other works, see Patrologia Latina 81–84 and suppl. vol. 4.4 (Paris 1970) 1801–41; there are a number of modern Spanish editions. See H. J. Diesner, *Isidor von Sevilla und das westgotische Spanien* (Berlin 1971), E. Jones, ed., *Visigothic Spain: New Approaches* (Oxford 1980), and J. Fontaine, *Isidore de Séville et la culture classique dans l'Éspagne wisigothique* (3 vols., Paris 1959–84), as well as the articles collected in *Tradition et actualité chez Isidore de Séville* (London 1988). There is a bibliographical survey by J. N. Hilligarth in *Studi Medievali* 2 (1983) 845–53.

The standard edition of the poems of Venantius Fortunatus is that of F. Leo (Monumenta Germaniae Historica 4.1, Berlin 1881); see also R. Koebner, *Venantius Fortunatus* (Leipzig 1915), D. Tardi, *Fortunat* (Paris 1927), and W. Meyer in *Abh. der Göttingen Gesellschaft der Wissenschaften, phil.-hist. Kl.*, n.s. 4.5 (1901).

For the *History* of Gregory of Tours, see the edition by W. Arndt in *MGH Script. Merov.* 1 (Berlin 1884), as well as B. Versere, *Strutture e modelli culturali nella società merovingia* (Galatina 1979), and the papers in *Gregorio di Tours* (Todi 1977). See also F. Thürlemann, *Der historische Diskurs bei Gregor von Tours: Topoi und Wirklichkeit* (Berlin 1974), and W. Goffart, *The Narrators of Barbarian History (A.D. 550–800): Jordanes, Gregory of Tours, Bede, and Paul the Deacon* (Princeton 1988).

There is an edition of Bede's *Ecclesiastical History of the English People* by B. Colgrave and R.A.B. Mynors (Oxford 1969, with English translation); see also the *Historical Commentary* by J. M. Wallace-Hadrill (Oxford 1988), which contains on pp. 244–45 a useful list of editions of the other writings. There are short introductions by J. Campbell in *Latin Historians*, ed. T. A. Dorey (London 1966) and by G. H. Brown (Boston 1987). See esp. the papers in *Famulus Christi: Essays in Commemoration of the Thirteenth Centenary of the Birth of the Venerable Bede*, ed. G. Bonner (London 1976), and *Bede and Anglo-Saxon England*, ed. R. T. Farrell (Oxford 1978), as well as P. Hunter Blair, *The World of Bede* (London 1970). There is a short Italian life with bibliography by I. Cecchetti in the *Biblioteca Sanctorum* 2 (Rome 1962) 1006–74.

Appendix 1 Chronological Tables

EIGHTH–FOURTH CENTURIES B.C.

Roman History and Culture		Greek History and Culture
Date of the contemporary founding of Rome and Carthage according to Timaeus.	814	
	776	Traditional date of the first Olympiad.
		The written versions of the two poems attributed to **Homer**, the *Iliad* and the *Odyssey,* are commonly dated to this century.
		About mid-century, Greeks begin to colonize the West. According to tradition, the earliest colony founded was Cumae. It is followed in this century by Metapontum, Rhegium, Naxos, Syracuse, Zancle (Messina), Catania, Leontini, Megara Hyblaea, Sybaris, Crotona, and Tarentum.
Date of the founding of Rome according to Varro (21 April).	754	
Date from which the years *ab urbe condita* are reckoned (753 = year 1 A.U.C.).	753	
Date of the founding of Rome according to Cato.	751	
Date of the founding of Rome according to Polybius and Diodorus.	750	
Date of the founding of Rome according to Fabius Pictor.	747	
Date of the founding of Rome according to Cincius Alimentus.	728	
Death of **Romulus,** according to tradition.	716	

Roman History and Culture		Greek History and Culture
Beginning of the reign of **Numa Pompilius,** the legendary founder of Rome's religious institutions.	715	
	ca. 700	Floruit of Hesiod, the author of the *Works and Days* and the *Theogony.*
		The foundings of the colonies of Gela, Parthenope, Selinunte, Himera, and Posidonia belong to the seventh century.
	676–673	In this period the lyric poet **Terpander of Lesbos** wins the victory at a festival in honor of Apollo Carneios at Sparta.
		The elegiac poet **Callinus of Ephesus** is active during the first half of the century.
Legendary death of **Numa Pompilius,** who is succeeded by **Tullus Hostilius** (673–642). Under his reign, Alba Longa is destroyed after the duel between the Horatii and the Curiatii.	673	
	648	Total eclipse of the sun mentioned by the iambic poet **Archilochus of Paros** (6 April)—the first certain date in Greek literature.
		In the second half of the century is placed the poetic activity of the elegiac poet **Tyrtaeus of Sparta** and of **Alcman,** the founder of choral lyric.
		Greek sculpture begins to represent the nude male body *(kouroi)* and the draped female body *(korai).* From this derive the two themes, the nude and drapery, that will be the basis of European art.
Traditional date of the death of **Tullus Hostilius.** He is succeeded by **Ancus Marcius** (642–617), the founder of Ostia.	642	
Death of **Ancus Marcius.** He is succeeded by an Etruscan ruler, **Tarquinius Priscus** (616–579). The Etruscans evidently occupy Rome in this period, though they do not completely subdue it.	617	
	ca. 590	In this period the two greatest lyric poets of Lesbos, **Sappho** and **Alcaeus,** flourish.
	581	Founding of the Greek colony of Agrigentum, which quickly rises to great power.
Traditional date of the death of **Tarquinius Priscus.** He is succeeded by **Servius Tullius**	579	

(578–535), who institutes the centuriate organization, the base of Rome's social organization, and concludes a first treaty with the Latins.		
	ca. 550	These decades witness the activity of the two earliest Greek philosophers, both from Miletus in Ionia: **Thales** and **Anaximander.** The same decades also see the flourishing of the elegiac poet **Mimnermus,** of **Solon,** and of **Stesichorus of Himera,** the first Greek poet of Italy about whom we have knowledge.
	546	The Persians, led by King Cyrus, conquer Lydia.
	ca. 540	Battle of Alalia, in Corsica: the Carthaginians and Etruscans, joined in alliance, defeat the Greek fleet of the Phocaeans. The elegiac poet **Theognis** is active, also **Hipponax,** the author of iambs, the philosopher **Anaximenes of Miletus,** and **Ibycus,** the lyric poet from Rhegium, in Magna Graecia.
Servius Tullius dies. He is succeeded by the last king of Rome, **Tarquin the Proud** (534–510). The most ancient Latin documents we have (inscriptions of various sorts) go back at least to this century.	535	
	531	The philosopher **Pythagoras** emigrates from Samos to Crotona, in Magna Graecia.
	527	Pisistratus dies, after holding power at Athens on and off for forty years.
	525	**Aeschylus** is born at Eleusis.
	522	The poet **Anacreon** comes to Athens. In this year (or 518) **Pindar,** the greatest lyric poet, is born.
	514	The tyrant Hipparchus is slain at Athens by those who will become known as the "tyrannicides"—Harmodius and Aristogeiton.
Tarquin the Proud is expelled. The Etruscan king Porsenna wages war on Rome. This is the period of the legendary heroes Mucius Scaevola, Horatius Cocles, and Cloelia.	510	The west pediment of the Temple of Athena Aphaia at Aegina. End of tyranny in Athens.

Roman History and Culture		Greek History and Culture
		The tragedian **Phrynichus** is active, as are the philosopher **Heraclitus of Ephesus** and **Hecataeus of Miletus,** the first Greek historian of whom we have sure knowledge.
The first two consuls of the Republic, **Brutus** and **Collatinus,** are elected. Polybius records in this year the first commercial treaty between Rome and Carthage.	509	
	497	The tragedian **Sophocles** is born.
Struggle in Rome between patricians and plebeians; tradition places **Menenius Agrippa** in this context.	494	
Treaty with the Latins *(foedus Cassianum).*	493	
	492	**Phrynichus** writes *The Capture of Miletus,* a tragedy the subject of which is a contemporary event.
According to tradition, the expedition of **Coriolanus** and the Volsci against Rome.	491	
	490	Landing in Greece of the Persians, led by Darius; the battle of Marathon and Athenian victory. The east pediment of the Temple of Athena Aphaia at Aegina is contemporary.
	ca. 485	The tragedian **Euripides** is born.
	484	The historian **Herodotus** is born.
	480	Second landing in Greece of the Persians, led by Xerxes; battle of Salamis, and victory of the Greeks, led by Themistocles. The Syracusans, in coalition with many of the Greek cities of Sicily, defeat the Carthaginians in the battle of Himera. The original theater at Syracuse is built during these years.
	472	**Aeschylus:** *The Persians,* the earliest Greek tragedy that we possess.
		These years witness the activity at Elea, in Campania, of the philosophical school founded by **Xenophanes,** the greatest representatives of which are **Parmenides** and **Zeno.**
	ca. 470	**Socrates** is born. The Temple of Zeus at Olympia is built.
	467	**Aeschylus:** *The Seven against Thebes.*

Roman History and Culture		Greek History and Culture
	ca. 460	The great historian **Thucydides** is born. The pediments of the Temple of Zeus at Olympia date to this time.
	458	**Aeschylus** stages the trilogy of *Agamemnon, Choephoroe,* and *Eumenides,* which is called the *Oresteia,* one of the masterworks of all time.
	456	**Aeschylus** dies.
The consuls are replaced by decemvirs, who begin drawing up the Laws of the Twelve Tables.	451	
The decemvirs finish drawing up the Laws of the Twelve Tables.	450	The philosopher **Empedocles of Agrigentum** is active during these years.
Expulsion of the decemvirs; the consulate is restored.	449	
Creation of the quaestorship.	447	Construction of the Parthenon begins at Athens. **Pindar** dies sometime after this year.
Lex Canuleia: marriages are now possible between patricians and plebeians.	445	**Aristophanes,** the greatest Athenian comic playwright, is born.
Abolition of the consulate and creation of the *tribuni militum consulari potestate.*	444	
Creation of the censorship.	443	
	442	**Sophocles:** *Antigone,* his earliest datable tragedy extant.
	438	Construction of the Parthenon completed. The sculptor **Phidias** creates the Athena Parthenos, one of the most famous statues of antiquity. In the same year **Euripides** presents the *Alcestis,* his first extant tragedy.
	436	**Phidias** sculpts another famous statue, the Zeus of Olympia.
	433	Construction of the Propylaea is completed on the Acropolis of Athens.
	432	**Phidias** completes the frieze and the pediments of the Parthenon.
Victory of the Romans over the Aequi at Mt. Algidus.	431	**Euripides:** *Medea.* The Peloponnesian War between Athens and Sparta breaks out.
	429	Death of Pericles, who for more than thirty years has guided the policy of Athens. First performance of a comedy by **Eupolis.**

	428	**Euripides:** *Hippolytus.* Plato is born this year or the next.
	425	**Aristophanes:** *Acharnians,* his earliest comedy to have come down to us. The comic playwright **Cratinus** is active at Athens.
	424	**Herodotus** dies. In this and the following years **Aristophanes** presents some of his masterpieces.
	420–417	The sculptor **Polycleitus,** artist of the Doriphorus, flourishes during these years.
	415	**Euripides:** *The Trojan Women.*
	411	**Aristophanes:** *Lysistrata.*
	406	**Euripides** dies; his last tragedies, from this year, are *Iphigenia at Aulis* and the *Bacchae.* The Erechtheum on the Acropolis of Athens is finished.
	405	**Sophocles** dies. The *Oedipus at Colonus* will be performed posthumously.
	403	The orator **Lysias** delivers *Against Eratosthenes,* one of his most famous speeches. During these years **Thucydides,** the author of a historical work on the Peloponnesian War (which ended the previous year with the victory of Sparta over Athens), dies.
	399	Execution of **Socrates. Plato** begins to write his dialogues. During the first years of this century is to be located the activity of **Antimachus,** author of a *Lyde* and a *Thebaid.*
	388	**Aristophanes:** *Plutus,* the last securely dated play of his. **Plato** founds the Academy in Athens.
	388–366	From this period come **Plato's** most famous dialogues—*Symposium, Phaedo, The Republic, Phaedrus,* etc.
The Gauls burn Rome (in 390 according to other sources).	387	Dionysius of Syracuse has de facto hegemony over all the Greeks of Sicily.
	385	**Aristophanes** dies.
	384	**Aristotle** and **Demosthenes** are born.
	380	The Athenian orator **Isocrates** (436–338) delivers the *Panegyricus.*

Roman History and Culture		Greek History and Culture
Construction of the so-called Servian Walls in Rome.	378	
	371	Battle of Leuctra: the Thebans defeat the Spartans. Thebes is the most important city in Greece.
	368	**Aristotle** comes to Athens.
	367	Dionysius of Syracuse dies, after holding for nearly forty years a power that brought him hegemony over Greek Sicily.
Reintroduction of the consulate, now open also to the plebeians. Creation of the praetorship.	366	
Livy tells us of a performance of Fescennine verses at Rome.	364	
	364–361	The activity of the sculptor **Praxiteles,** creator of the Aphrodite of Cnidos, culminates in these years.
	362	**Xenophon** narrates events down to this year in his historical work *Hellenica.*
	359	Philip II becomes king of Macedon.
	355	**Isocrates** delivers his speech *On the Peace.*
	351	**Demosthenes** delivers the *First Philippic.*
		During these years **Archestratus of Gela** composes a poem on the art of eating well.
Commercial treaty between Rome and Carthage.	348	
	347	**Plato** dies. These years see the activity of **Alexis,** Middle Comedy author who will be a model for Plautus and Turpilius.
First Samnite War.	343	**Demosthenes** delivers the *Second Philippic.*
	341	The comic writer **Menander** and the philosopher **Epicurus** are born. **Demosthenes:** *Third Philippic.*
The Campanians and the Latins form an alliance against Rome.	340	
Rome defeats the Latin League; among the Roman generals are **Manlius Torquatus** and **Decius Mus.**	338	At the battle of Chaeronea Philip II secures domination of Greece
	336	Philip II is murdered; the twenty-year-old Alexander becomes king of Macedon.
		From this period, more or less, come the historical works of **Ephorus** *(Histories)* and **Theopompus** *(Philippic History).*

Roman History and Culture		Greek History and Culture
	333	Alexander the Great defeats the Persians in the battle of Issus.
	331	Alexander the Great routs the Persians in the battle of Gaugamela. Founding of Alexandria, in Egypt.
	330	The orator **Aeschines** delivers the speech *Against Ctesiphon.* **Demosthenes:** *On the Crown.*
	328–325	The activity of the sculptor **Lysippus** culminates in these years.
Siege of Naples and beginning of the Second Samnite War.	327	
	326	Alexander the Great reaches the boundaries of the known world.
	323	Alexander the Great dies. In Egypt the ruler is Ptolemy I Soter (323–283). **Hyperides:** *Against Demosthenes.*
	322	**Aristotle** and **Demosthenes** die.
The Romans, defeated by the Samnites, endure the humiliation of the Caudine Forks.	321	
	320	**Menander** presents his first comedy. In these (or the following) years the poets **Callimachus, Theocritus,** and **Aratus** are born, and **Philitas** may be beginning his activity.
	319	Aristotle's two principal students are active: **Dicaearchus** and **Theophrastus,** who in this year writes *The Characters.*
	317	**Menander:** *Dyskolos.*
Renewal of the fight against the Samnites.	316	
Appius Claudius constructs the *Via Appia.* **Appius Claudius** is censor.	312	The philosopher **Zeno,** founder of the Stoic school, comes to Athens. Historical writing about **Alexander the Great** and his deeds flourishes during these years. The author who will have the most influence on Latin literature is **Clitarchus.**
Appius Claudius is consul.	307	
New treaty between Rome and Carthage.	306	**Epicurus** founds his school at Athens.
Peace between Rome and the Samnites.	304	
	301	**Zeno** founds his school at Athens, in the Stoa, whence the name Stoic for his philosophical tendency.

Roman History and Culture	Greek History and Culture
	The rhetorician **Hegesias,** regarded as the founder of Asianism, is active in this period.

THIRD CENTURY B.C.

Roman History and Culture		Greek History and Culture
		In the first decade of this century, approximately, the comic writer **Diphilus** dies, **Euhemerus** composes the *Sacred Writing,* and the great epic poet **Apollonius of Rhodes** is born.
The Third Samnite War begins.	298	
Second consulate of **Appius Claudius.**	296	
Battle of Sentinum, a great Roman victory over the Samnites.	295	
Peace between Rome and the Samnites.	290	**Menander** dies.
		During these years **Asclepiades** flourishes, along with the elegiac poet **Hermesianax** and the comic writer **Apollodorus of Carystus,** who is one of Terence's principal models.
	287	**Theophrastus** dies.
	283	The king of Egypt, Ptolemy I Soter, dies. He is succeeded by Ptolemy II Philadelphus (283–247).
		More or less in this period **Duris of Samos** writes his *Macedonian History.* The philologist **Zenodotus** is the head of the Library of Alexandria.
		Two Cynic philosophers are active in this period, **Menippus of Gadara,** author of works in which prose alternated with verse, and **Bion of Borysthenes,** considered to be the developer of the diatribe. More or less during the same years, at the court of Ptolemy Philadelphus, **Sotades of Maronea** writes licentious poems.
		In approximately this period **Theocritus** writes the *Idylls.*

Speech against Pyrrhus by **Appius Claudius,** old and now blind (whence the appellative *Caecus,* "blind," added to his name). The jurist **Coruncanius** is consul.	280	
Pyrrhus, king of Epirus, landing in Italy at the invitation of Tarentum, defeats the Romans at Heraclea.		
Battle of Ascoli and peace between **Pyrrhus** and the Romans.	279	
Pyrrhus lands in Sicily. Rome and Carthage form an alliance against him.	278	
Pyrrhus is decisively defeated at Beneventum.	275	
Livius Andronicus, perhaps a child, is brought to Rome from Tarentum as a slave.	272	
Tarentum surrenders to the Romans.		
Rome conquers Rhegium and becomes mistress of all of peninsular Italy.	270	**Epicurus** dies.
		A youthful **Apollonius of Rhodes** writes the *Argonautica* at about this time.
Naevius is born in Campania.	ca. 270	
	ca. 265	**Apollonius of Rhodes** succeeds **Zenodotus** as director of the Library at Alexandria.
The First Punic War begins. The first gladiatorial exhibition takes place at Rome.	264	The comic writer **Philemon** dies at a very advanced age. The *History of Sicily* by **Timaeus of Tauromenium,** a work in which Roman historical events are also treated, narrates events down to this year.
	262	**Zeno,** the founder of the Stoic school, dies; he is succeeded by **Cleanthes.**
The Romans' first naval battle results in victory at Mylae.	260	**Theocritus** dies shortly after this date.
The jurist **Coruncanius** is the first plebeian pontifex maximus.	254	
Before this year **Plautus** is born at Sarsina.	251	
During years that are uncertain (probably the last ones of the conflict) **Naevius** takes part in the Punic War.		
	247	The ruler of Egypt, Ptolemy II Philadelphus, dies. He is succeeded by his son, Ptolemy III Euergetes.
	ca. 247	The great scientist and polymath **Eratosthenes** succeeds **Apollonius of Rhodes** as director of the Library of Alexandria.

Roman History and Culture		Greek History and Culture
		Apollonius retires to Rhodes (hence the appellation) and teaches grammar until his death.
	246	Ptolemy Euergetes marries Berenice. **Callimachus** writes the *Lock of Berenice,* adding it perhaps to a new edition of the *Aitia,* his most famous work, which may have been published in the preceding years.
Battle of the Aegates: the Carthaginian fleet is decisively defeated. End of the First Punic War.	241	Attalus I becomes king of Pergamum. Under his dynasty the city will achieve a great economic, cultural, and artistic splendor, taking up to an extent the heritage of Alexandria, which begins to decline.
At the Ludi Romani, a festival in honor of Jupiter Optimus Maximus, **Livius Andronicus** stages a tragedy on a Greek subject; it is the first regular dramatic text written in Latin.	240	
	ca. 240	**Callimachus** dies.
Ennius is born at Rudiae.	239	
Naevius makes his debut as a dramatic author.	235	
Cato is born at Tusculum.	234	
In a period hard to specify, but not too distant from these years, **Livius Andronicus** writes the *Odusia.*		
	232	**Chrysippus** becomes head of the Stoic school; he will continue as head until 207.
In the decade that opens with this year is placed the birth of **Caecilius Statius,** perhaps at Milan.	230	
Sicily and Sardinia become Roman provinces.	227	
The historian **Fabius Pictor** takes part in the war against the Insubrian Gauls.	222	
Claudius Marcellus defeats the Insubrian Gauls at Clastidium and attacks Milan. **Naevius**'s *Clastidium* is subsequent to this date.		
	221	Ptolemy III Euergetes dies. He is succeeded on the throne of Egypt by Ptolemy IV Philopator. During these years the poet **Euphorion of Chalcis,** later a model for Latin neoteric poetry, flourishes.

Roman History and Culture		Greek History and Culture
Pacuvius is born at Brundisium.	220	
Construction of the *Via Flaminia*.		
Naevius writes the *Bellum Poenicum* after this year.	218	
The Second Punic War begins; **Hannibal** crosses the Alps and defeats the Romans at Ticino and on the Trebia.		
Roman defeat at Trasimene.	217	
Fabius Pictor is sent to consult the oracle at Delphi.	216	
Battle of Cannae (2 August) and nearly total destruction of the Roman army.		
Plautus's *Asinaria* may be from this year. In the same year the Ludi Apollinares are established.	212	In the capture of Syracuse, the scientist **Archimedes** is slain.
The Romans retake Syracuse. Many works of art are transported to Rome.		
The historian **Cincius Alimentus** is praetor.	210	
Livius Andronicus writes a sacred hymn in honor of Juno. Establishment of the *collegium scribarum histrionumque*.	207	
Battle of the Metaurus; the Carthaginian general, Hasdrubal, is defeated and slain.		
The Metelli have **Naevius** imprisoned.	206	
Scipio, elected consul, carries the war to Africa.	205	
Scholars place **Plautus**'s *Miles Gloriosus* here.	ca. 205	
Cato meets **Ennius** in Sardinia and brings him to Rome. **Cethegus**, the first great Roman orator, is consul. The cult of Cybele is introduced from Asia Minor; in her honor the Ludi Megalenses are established.	204	
Battle of Zama and decisive defeat of the Carthaginians.	202	
Naevius dies in this year, or slightly earlier.	201	
Peace treaty between Rome and Carthage; end of the Second Punic War.		

SECOND CENTURY B.C.

Roman History and Culture		Greek History and Culture
Plautus: *Stichus*.	200	
	ca. 200	The historian **Polybius** is born.
The jurist **Aelius Paetus** is consul.	198	

Roman History and Culture		Greek History and Culture
Quinctius Flamininus, a young general with cultural interests, defeats the Macedonians at Cynoscephalae.	197	The great ruler Eumenes II accedes to the throne of Pergamum. His city, which will rise to a position of great prestige, will be Rome's faithful ally.
Flamininus solemnly proclaims the freedom of Greece, at Corinth.	196	
Cato is consul. In this year or the next (rather than in 185 or 184, as the tradition asserts) scholars commonly fix the birth of **Terence,** at Carthage.	195	The philologist **Aristophanes** is in charge of the Library of Alexandria.
Theatrical works begin to be presented at the Ludi Megalenses.	194	
Plautus: *Pseudolus.*	191	
Ennius is already an established dramatic writer. In the following years **Cato** will undertake a series of cases against the Scipios.	190	
Scipio Asiaticus defeats at Magnesia the king of Syria, Antiochus III, an ally of Hannibal.		
Ennius takes part in the expedition of **Fulvius Nobilior** against Ambracia; as a result he will write the *Ambracia.* Around this year **Plautus** writes the *Bacchides.*	189	
	188	Peace of Apamea: the territory of Syria is divided between Rhodes and Pergamum, which become the most important cities of Asia.
		The Nike of Samothrace, at Rhodes, comes from this period.
Plautus: *Casina.*	185	The Stoic philosopher **Panaetius** is born.
Plautus dies. In the same year (or the previous one) ancient tradition located the birth of **Terence. Ennius** obtains Roman citizenship. **Cato** is censor.	184	
Scipio Africanus dies, having been tried several times at Rome. **Hannibal** kills himself so as not to fall into the hands of the Romans.	183	
Cato speaks in defense of the *lex Orchia,* against excessive luxury.	181	The construction of the Altar of Pergamum begins.
According to some scholars, **Lucilius** is born in this year, at Suessa Aurunca (the traditional date, 148, is certainly wrong). It seems that the activity of **Titinius,** the author of *togatae* comedies, is to be set in this period.	180	
Caecilius Status flourishes.	179	

Institution of the Floralia, during which mimes are performed. The expulsion of the two Epicurean philosophers from Rome may belong to this year.	173
Ennius has already written books 1–12 of the *Annals*.	172
The activity of the comic writer **Luscius of Lanuvium** is placed in these years.	
Accius is born at Pesaro.	170
Ennius: *Thyestes*. He dies during the Ludi Apollinares of the same year. **Cato** supports the *lex Voconia*, which limits women's rights of inheritance.	169
Aemilius Paullus defeats Perseus, the king of Macedonia, at the battle of Pydna.	168
Caecilius Statius dies. After this year falls the *Paulus* of **Pacuvius**. According to some scholars, **Lucilius** is born in this year (and not 180); this seems the more likely date. After Pydna, Aemilius Paullus transfers the library of Perseus to Rome. The grammarian **Crates of Mallus,** chief defender of the anomalist theory, arrives in Rome.	
Among the prisoners of the Macedonian War the historian **Polybius** comes to Rome. **Cato**: *Oratio pro Rhodiensibus*. He is probably already working on the *Origines*.	167
Terence: *Andria*.	166
Terence: *Hecyra* (first performance).	165
Terence: *Heautontimoroumenos*.	163
Terence: *Eunuchus, Phormio*. An edict bans rhetoricians and philosophers from Rome.	161
Terence: *Adelphoe, Hecyra* (second and third performances).	160
Terence dies.	159

159 — The Altar of Pergamum is finished. Eumenes II dies; with his successor, Attalus II (159–138), the golden age of Pergamum comes to an end.

During these years **Panaetius** takes up Stoic philosophy.

The philosophers Carneades, Diogenes, and Critolaus come to Rome as an embassy; they have great success, and the annalist **Gaius Acilius** perhaps acts as their interpreter. They are expelled from Rome at the urging of **Cato**.	155

Roman History and Culture		Greek History and Culture
Cato visits Carthage. The great philologist **Aelius Stilo,** from Lanuvium, is born in these years.	153	
The last year treated in **Cato's** *Origines*.	152	
The annalist **Postumius Albinus,** who writes in Greek, is consul. The orator **Sulpicius Galba** is praetor. Around this year **Lutatius Catulus** is born.	151	
Cato dies.	149	
The Third Punic War begins (149–146).		
The *Annales* of **Cassius Hemina** is subsequent to this date.	146	**Polybius's** *Histories* narrate events down to this year.
Scipio Aemilianus destroys Carthage, ending the Third Punic War. **Lucius Mummius** sacks and destroys Corinth.		
	145	The king of Egypt, Ptolemy Physcon, removes Greek scholars from Alexandria. The grammarian **Dionysius Thrax** withdraws to Rhodes, which, along with Pergamum, is the liveliest city of the East.
		During these years **Panaetius** moves to Rome, where he is welcomed into the "Scipionic Circle."
The orator **Sulpicius Galba** is consul.	144	
Acilius writes Roman history in Greek.	142	
	141	**Panaetius** accompanies Scipio Aemilianus on his voyage to Asia. His essay *On Duty,* which will influence Cicero, is from this period.
Accius makes his debut as a tragedian, while the aged **Pacuvius** is still on the scene. **Laelius,** the friend of Scipio Aemilianus, and an esteemed orator, is consul.	140	
	138	The king of Pergamum, Attalus II, dies; Attalus III succeeds him.
Accius: *Brutus*.	ca. 136	
Accius makes an educational voyage to Pergamum.	135	
	ca. 135	**Posidonius** is born, Stoic philosopher, historian, and scholar.
Lucilius takes part in the war of Numantia, where the historian **Sempronius Asellio** fights as a military tribune. **Tiberius Gracchus,** an	133	

orator as well as a politician, is tribune of the plebs; he is slain in the same year. The annalist **Calpurnius Piso Frugi** and the jurist **P. Mucius Scaevola** are consuls.

Scipio Aemilianus conquers Numantia and puts down the revolt of Spain. In the same year the last king of Pergamum makes the Romans heirs to his kingdom. Disorders at Rome and murder of **Tiberius Gracchus** over the agrarian question.

Publication of the first books of **Lucilius**'s *Satires,* the death of **Pacuvius,** and perhaps also the flourishing of **Afranius,** the author of *togatae.*	ca. 130	
The *Bellum Histricum,* of the epic poet **Hostius,** refers to events of this year.	129	**Panaetius** takes over the direction of the Stoic school; he is less frequently at Rome.
Scipio Aemilianus dies suddenly.		
In this period the historian **Sisenna** is born.	124–114	
Gaius Gracchus, celebrated orator, is tribune of the plebs.	123	
The annalist **Gaius Fannius** is consul.	122	
Murder of **Gaius Gracchus.**	121	
	120	**Polybius** dies around this year.
Accius is the preeminent figure in the *collegium poetarum,* which will erect a statue to him.	ca. 120	
Debut of the orator **Licinius Crassus.**	119	
Marius is tribune of the plebs.		
Varro is born at Reate.	116	
Aemilius Scaurus, author of autobiographical *Commentarii,* is consul.	115	
The war against Jugurtha begins, after various years of skirmishing.	111	
Coelius Antipater composes his historical work.	ca. 110	
In this year (or the preceding one) **Atticus** is born.	109	**Panaetius** dies.
Caecilius Metellus and his lieutenant **Marius** assume command of operations in the war against Jugurtha.		During these year **Aristides of Miletus** writes the *Milesian Stories,* which Sisenna will translate into Latin.
Lucilius: *Satires* (the latest internal references allude to events of this year).	107	
Marius is consul. Jugurtha is repeatedly defeated.		

Roman History and Culture		Greek History and Culture
Cicero is born at Arpinum. The mime-writer **Laberius** is born. The orator **Licinius Crassus,** already a "democrat," leaves the party of the aristocracy.	106	
Sulla, Marius's quaestor, starts peace talks with Boccus, Jugurtha's ally.		
Rutilius Rufus, author of autobiographical *Commentarii,* is consul.	105	
In this decade is probably to be set the activity of the poets who were friends of **Lutatius Catulus**—**Valerius Aedituus, Porcius Licinus,** and **Volcacius Sedigitus.**		
Jugurtha is brought to Rome, where he will be executed. The war is over.		
Marius, consul for the second time, is the most prominent man at Rome.	104	
Turpilius, the author of *palliatae,* dies in advanced old age.	103	
Lutatius Catulus is consul, along with Marius. **Lucilius** dies.	102	
Marius defeats the Teutons at Aquae Sextiae.		
Marius, together with Lutatius Catulus, defeats the Cimbri at Campi Raudii.	101	

FIRST CENTURY B.C. — FIRST CENTURY A.D.

Roman Culture		Roman History	Greek History and Culture
Caesar is born at Rome. In about the same period **Cornelius Nepos** is born in the Po Valley. In the wake of the suppression of Saturninus's rebellion, **Aelius Stilo** follows his friend Metellus Numidicus, the conqueror of Jugurtha, into exile.	100	The tribune of the plebs **Saturninus** proposes radical reforms but is slain.	
The orator **Marcus Antonius** is consul.	99		
Lucretius is perhaps born in this year.	98		
The pre-neoteric poet **Laevius,** author of *Erotopaegnia,* flourishes.	97		

Roman Culture		Roman History	Greek History and Culture

The orator **Licinius Crassus** and the jurist **Q. Mucius Scaevola** are consuls. — 95

During these years the poet and philologist **Valerius Cato** is born.

The orator **Licinius Crassus** is censor. The school of **Plotius Gallus** at Rome is closed. — 92

The orator **Licinius Crassus** dies. The historical work of **Sempronius Asellio** is written after this year. — 91 — **Drusus** proposes and succeeds in passing a body of laws and reforms of democratic tendency.

In these years the death of **Aelius Stilo** is to be located.

90 — **Drusus** is murdered. The Social War breaks out; for Rome a sixty-year period of warfare begins.

Pomponius, from Bologna, the author of Atellans, flourishes. A near contemporary is **Novius,** another author of Atellans. The orator and tragedian **Julius Caesar Strabo** is consul. — 89

The Asianic orator **Sulpicius Rufus,** tribune of the plebs, is killed. The eclectic philosopher **Antiochus of Ascalon** comes to Rome from Athens. — 88 — **Sulla,** elected consul, ends the Social War. He then marches on Rome, forcing **Marius** to flee.

Repression by Sulla; **Julius Caesar Strabo** and the orator **Marcus Antonius** are slain, and **Lutatius Catulus** takes his own life. In this year or in the years immediately following, **Catullus** is born at Verona. — 87 — **Sulla** is sent to the East, against Mithridates, king of Pontus. **Marius's** follower **Cinna** is elected consul and is the master of Rome.

Latest evidence that **Accius** is alive is from this year; his death should be placed in this year or in the years immediately following. **Sallust** is born at Amiternum. The Greek **Posidonius** is at Rome. — 86 — **Marius** is consul for the seventh time; he dies in the same year. His followers control Rome: there are anti-Sullan reprisals.

Rhetorica ad Herennium. — ca. 85

Cicero: *De Inventione.* Before this date **Varro's** *De Antiquitate Lit-* — ca. 84

Roman Culture		Roman History	Greek History and Culture

terarum, dedicated to Accius, is written. Sulla brings to Rome a collection of Aristotle's works.

| | 85 | | The historical work of **Posidonius** narrates events from 145 to this year. |

| | 84 | **Cinna** is slain, while **Sulla** has successes in the East. | |

| | 83 | **Sulla** returns to Italy and begins war against Marius's followers. | |

Varro of Atax is born at Atax, and **Licinius Calvus** is born at Rome. **Furius Bibaculus** of Cremona appears to be of about the same age as they. Among the political prisoners brought to Rome by Sulla are **Tyrannio the Elder,** the analogist grammarian, and the theoretician of anomaly **Alexander Polyhistor.** — **82** — Battle of the Colline Gate (1 November): **Sulla** defeats the Marians and becomes the master of Rome.

Cicero: *Pro Quinctio,* the first of his speeches.

In these years the annalist **Valerius Antias** flourishes. — **81** — **Sulla** becomes dictator and unleashes the notorious proscriptions. Among his collaborators are the young Pompey, Crassus, and Lucullus.

Cicero: *Pro Roscio Amerino.*

Varro may begin to compose his *Menippean Satires* around this period. — **80**

Cicero makes a long trip to Greece and Asia. — **79** — **Sulla** rearranges the structure of the Roman Republic with a body of laws and then retires to private life.

Sisenna is praetor: his *Historiae* come after this year. **Sulla** writes autobiographical *Commentarii.* — **78** — **Sulla** dies.

Varro: *Ephemeris Navalis.* **Atta,** the author of *togatae,* dies. — **77** — Sertorius has conquered all Spain; **Pompey** is sent against him.

Asinius Pollio is born at Chieti. — **76**

The Epicurean philosopher **Philodemus** comes to Rome from Greece in about this year; he will — **75** — **Pompey** battles with Sertorius, who has formed an alliance with Mithridates.

Roman Culture		Roman History	Greek History and Culture
give lessons at Herculaneum. **Cicero** is quaestor in Sicily.			
	74	Lucullus as consul is sent against Mithridates.	
The annalist **Licinius Macer** is tribune of the plebs. **Varius**, slightly older than his friend Virgil, is born around this year. **Parthenius of Nicaea** comes to Rome as a slave; he will become a friend of Gallus's and dedicate his *Erotika Pathemata* to him.	73	Sertorius defends himself, committing atrocities. The slaves, headed by Spartacus, rise up in rebellion.	
	72	Sertorius is slain by his lieutenant Perperna. Crassus is sent against the rebellious slaves.	
Cicero: *Pro Tullio*.	71	**Pompey**, after defeating Perperna, suppresses the slave revolt.	
Virgil is born near Mantua (15 October). **Cicero** writes the *Verrines*.	70	Consulship of **Pompey** and **Crassus**.	
Cicero: *Pro Fonteio, Pro Caecina*. The orator **Hortensius** is consul. Around this year **Gallus** is born.	69		
Beginning of the correspondence between **Cicero** and Atticus. **Caesar** is quaestor.	68		
Sisenna dies.	67	**Pompey** routs the pirates and, by the *lex Manilia,* is sent against Mithridates.	
Cicero is praetor and delivers the speech *Pro Lege Manilia.* The annalist **Licinius Macer** kills himself.	66		
Horace is born at Venosa (8 December). **Caesar** is aedile. After more than twenty years in Athens, **Atticus** returns to Rome.	65		
	64	**Pompey** wins great victories over Mithridates, who kills himself.	
Cicero is consul. He delivers four speeches—*De Lege Agraria, Pro Rabirio, Pro Murena,* and the *Catilinarians.* **Octavian** is born, as is his future general **Agrippa**.	63	Discovery and suppression of the conspiracy of Catiline.	

Roman Culture		Roman History	Greek History and Culture
Cicero: *Pro Sulla, Pro Archia Poeta.* **Caesar** is praetor.	62	Catiline is defeated and slain. **Pompey** returns triumphant from the East.	
Catullus's love for Lesbia begins.	61		
	60	First triumvirate: **Pompey, Caesar,** and **Crassus.**	
Livy is born at Padua. **Cicero:** *Pro Flacco.*	59	**Caesar** is consul. He obtains a command in Gaul for the next year.	
Cicero in exile. **Catullus**'s love for Lesbia is finished. The philosopher and polymath **Nigidius Figulus** is praetor. **Varro of Atax**'s *Bellum Sequanicum* is subsequent to this year. Gaius Memmius, the friend of Lucretius, Catullus, and Cinna, is praetor.	58	**Caesar** begins his campaign in Gaul.	
Cicero returns from exile: *De Domo Sua.* **Catullus** and **Cinna** take part in an expedition to Bithynia.	57		
Cicero: *De Haruspicum Responso, Pro Sestio, In Vatinium, Pro Caelio, De Provinciis Consularibus, Pro Balbo.* **Cinna** writes a *Propemptikon* for Pollio.	56	The congress of Lucca extends Caesar's command in Gaul for five more years.	
Around this year **Lucretius** dies; perhaps in the same period **Tibullus** is born. **Cicero:** *In Pisonem* and *De Oratore.* The Greek historian **Timagenes** is brought to Rome as a prisoner. Construction of the first stone theater at Rome, the Theater of Pompey.	55	**Pompey** and **Crassus** are consuls.	
Perhaps in this year **Catullus** publishes his *Liber* and dies. It is alleged that in this same year Cicero (?) publishes posthumously **Lucretius**'s *De Rerum Natura.* **Cicero:** *Pro Plancio, Pro Scauro, Pro Rabirio Postumo.* **Caesar:** *De Analogia.*	54	**Crassus** is sent to the East against the Parthians.	
	53	Battle of Carrhae: **Crassus** is slain.	
Cicero: *Pro Milone.* **Sallust** is tribune of the plebs.	52	Anarchy in Rome, where rival bands confront one another (Milo kills Clodius). **Pompey** is consul	

Roman Culture		Roman History	Greek History and Culture
		without colleague. **Caesar** attacks Alesia and conquers Gaul.	
Cicero: *De Re Publica.* **Caesar:** *De Bello Gallico.*	51		**Posidonius** dies.
Hortensius dies. **Sallust** is expelled from the Senate for moral turpitude.	50		
Seneca the Elder is born during these years. Around this time begins the construction of the Theater of Marcellus.			
	49	**Caesar** crosses the Rubicon; this means civil war. **Pompey** flees to Greece.	
	48	Battle of Pharsalus (9 August): **Caesar** defeats **Pompey,** who, withdrawing to Egypt, is killed by King Ptolemy.	
Licinius Calvus dies. **Propertius** may be born in this year, perhaps at Assisi. **Varro:** *Antiquitates Rerum Divinarum.* **Atticus:** *Liber Annalis.*	47	**Caesar** defeats Pharnaces in the East, then lands at Tarentum.	
Caesar: *De Bello Civili.* **Cicero** delivers the speeches *Pro Marcello* and *Pro Ligario* but chiefly devotes himself to rhetoric *(Brutus, Orator)* and philosophy *(Paradoxa Stoicorum).* **Sallust,** rehabilitated by Caesar, is praetor; in the same year he will become governor of the province of New Africa. Mime contest between **Laberius** and **Publilius Syrus** in Caesar's presence. Suicide of Cato at Utica.	46	Solemn honors for **Caesar,** who at the battle of Thapsus, in Africa, defeats Pompeian resistance.	
Cicero delivers *Pro Rege Deiotaro,* then plunges into philosophical works *(Academica, De Finibus Bonorum et Malorum, Tusculanae Disputationes, De Natura Deorum).* **Varro:** *De Lingua Latina.* **Nigidius Figulus** dies in exile.	45	At Munda, in Spain, **Caesar** overcomes the last Pompeian resistance. He returns to Rome as its master, has himself honored in the manner of an Oriental ruler, and passes a large number of constitutional reforms.	
Caesar is murdered. **Cicero** writes a rhetorical work *(Topica)* and many	44	**Caesar** is murdered (15 March). The murderers, **Brutus** and **Cas-**	

Roman Culture		Roman History	Greek History and Culture
philosophical works *(De Divinatione, De Fato, Cato Maior, Laelius, De Officiis)*.		sius, flee from Italy; **Antony** appears as Caesar's moral heir. The young **Octavian**, whom Caesar has adopted in his will, appears on the scene.	
Cicero: *Philippics.* He is slain on 7 December. **Varro,** also proscribed, succeeds in saving himself; he writes the *De Gente Populi Romani.* **Laberius** dies. **Sallust's** *Bellum Catilinae* may be from this year. **Ovid** is born at Sulmo. **Lygdamus** is born.	43	War between **Octavian** (allied with the two consuls for the year, Hirtius and Pansa) and **Antony.** Battle of Mutina: **Antony** is defeated and the two consuls perish. Accord is reached between the two enemies, and the second triumvirate formed: **Antony, Octavian,** and **Lepidus.** Consequent proscriptions and murders of their enemies, especially those of **Antony.**	
Virgil begins the *Bucolics.* **Horace** fights at Philippi on the side of Caesar's murderers.	42	Battle of Philippi: the army of **Antony** defeats Brutus and Cassius.	
Horace begins the *Epodes.* **Virgil** succeeds in retaining his farm near Mantua.	41	Distribution of lands to veterans and consequent expropriations.	
Sallust: *Bellum Iugurthinum.* **Asinius Pollio** is consul and to an extent the arbiter of Roman politics.	40	Lucius Antony, brother of the triumvir, is defeated in the battle of Perugia. **Antony** marries Octavia, sister of **Octavian.** Peace appears to return to Rome.	
Cornelius Nepos flourishes.			
Virgil: *Bucolics.* In this year he probably joins Maecenas's circle. **Sallust** begins the *Histories.* **Varro:** *Imagines.* **Asinius Pollio** establishes the first public library at Rome.	39		
Virgil and **Varius** introduce **Horace** to Maecenas, who will admit him to his circle.	38		
Varro: *Rerum Rusticarum Libri.* **Virgil** begins the *Georgics.* **Virgil** and **Horace** accompany Maecenas on a journey to Brundisium.	37		
	36	**Octavian** defeats Sextus Pompey at Naulochus. **Lepidus** is eliminated from the triumvirate.	The *Library* of **Diodorus Siculus** is subsequent to this date.

Roman Culture		Roman History	Greek History and Culture

Horace: *Satires,* book 1 (according to others, it dates from 33). In this year (or the next) **Sallust** dies. **Pollio** begins the *Historiae.* — 35

Cornelius Nepos publishes the *De Viris Illustribus.* He survives **Atticus,** who dies in 32. — 35–30

Varro: *Disciplinarum Libri.* **Horace** receives a Sabine farm from Maecenas. — 33

32 — **Antony,** who has already married Cleopatra, officially repudiates Octavia, which leads to open war between him and **Octavian.**

Valerius Messalla is consul. — 31 — Battle of Actium (2 September): **Octavian** routs the fleet of **Antony,** who kills himself.

Horace: *Satires,* book 2, and the *Epodes.* **Gallus** is governor of Egypt. **Horace** begins the *Odes* not later than this year. — 30 — Cleopatra kills herself. Egypt becomes a Roman province.

Virgil reads the *Georgics* to Octavian as he returns from the East; he begins the *Aeneid.* **Propertius** falls in love with Cynthia. **Varius:** *Thyestes.* — 29 — Triumph of **Octavian,** whose legal position is not yet clear.

Propertius: *Monobiblos.* He enters the circle of Maecenas. — 28

Varro dies. Messalla triumphs over the Aquitani; **Tibullus** takes part in the expedition. — 27 — **Octavian** regularizes his position by a constitutional reform. He takes on the appellative **Augustus.**

Suicide of **Gallus.** From this year (or the following) comes the first book of **Tibullus's** *Elegies.* **Caecilius Epirota** opens a school at Rome in which Virgil is commented upon. — 26

Propertius finishes the second book of the *Elegies;* perhaps he does not publish it separately but joins it later with the third. **Livy** is already at work on his history. — 25

Roman Culture		Roman History	Greek History and Culture
Horace: *Odes,* books 1–3. **Vitruvius:** *De Architectura.*	23	New and definitive constitutional reform. Marcellus, not yet twenty years old, the son of Augustus's sister (and married to Augustus's daughter Julia) and his designated heir, dies.	
Propertius: *Elegies,* books 2–3.	22		
Agrippa marries Augustus's daughter Julia, the widow of Marcellus.	21		
Horace: *Epistles,* book 1. Slightly later is the first edition of **Ovid's** *Amores.*	20		
Virgil: *Aeneid* (left incomplete at his death, on 21 September, and published by **Varius**). In the same year (or the beginning of the following) **Tibullus** dies.	19		
Augustus celebrates the Ludi Saeculares. **Horace:** *Carmen Saeculare.*	17		
Propertius: *Elegies,* book 4. The didactic poet **Aemilius Macer** dies.	16		
Ovid: *Heroides* (first collection). **Germanicus** is born.	15		
Propertius dies in this year (or at any rate after 16).	14		
Horace: *Odes,* book 4, and *Epistles,* book 2.	ca. 13		
Agrippa dies. The elegiac poet **Valgius Rufus** is consul.	12		
The scholar **Hyginus** flourishes. Inauguration of the *Ara Pacis Augustae.*	9	Drusus, Tiberius's brother and Augustus's stepson, dies.	
Horace dies, on 27 November, a few months after his friend Maecenas.	8		
Gaius Melissus, the inventor of the *fabula trabeata,* flourishes. Around this year **Seneca** is born at Cordova in Spain.	4		
Ovid: *Amores* (second edition), *Ars Amatoria, Remedia Amoris.*	ca. 1		

Roman Culture		Roman History	Greek History and Culture
Ovid begins the *Metamorphoses* and the *Fasti*.	2	Gaius, Agrippa's son and the designated heir to the Empire, dies.	
Asinius Pollio dies.	4	Lucius, Agrippa's other son, dies. Augustus is obliged to adopt his stepson Tiberius, on condition that he in turn adopt, not his son Drusus, but Germanicus, the son of his brother.	
The jurist Ateius Capito is consul.	5		
Ovid is relegated to Tomi, on the Black Sea. During the voyage he composes the *Tristia,* book 1. The scholar Verrius Flaccus flourishes. Before this year Grattius composes the *Cynegetica.* Valerius Messalla, a writer and patron of poets, dies.	8	A Roman army led by Varus is defeated by the Germans at Teutoborg. The Roman advance into Germany is halted; the boundaries will remain the Rhine and the Danube.	
Ovid: *Tristia,* book 2. Around this year Pompeius Trogus publishes the *Historiae Philippicae.*	9		
Ovid: *Ibis.* Labienus commits suicide after his historical work is burnt.	12		
Ovid: *Ex Ponto,* books 1–3.	13		
Augustus dies, leaving the *Res Gestae* as his literary and historical testament.	14	Augustus dies (9 August). After a month's interregnum Tiberius succeeds him.	
The *Astronomica* of Manilius may come from these years. Germanicus's *Aratea* and *Prognostica* are of this year or those immediately following.			
Velleius Paterculus holds the praetorship, which is conferred on him by Tiberius.	15	Germanicus wins notable successes against the Germans.	
Livy dies. In the same year or the following Ovid dies in exile.	17	Germanicus is sent to the East, against the Parthians.	
Germanicus dies. The historian Fenestella dies perhaps in the same year.	19	Mysterious death of Germanicus.	
After this year Verrius Flaccus dies.	22		

Roman Culture		Roman History	Greek History and Culture
In this year or the following one **Pliny the Elder** is born at Como.	23	**Tiberius**'s son Drusus dies.	
Suicide of the anti-Tiberian historian **Cremutius Cordus**.	25		
Seneca leaves for Egypt. **Silius Italicus** is born.	26		
Around this year **Celsus** writes the *De Medicina*. **Valerius Maximus** accompanies his friend Sextus Pompeius to Asia.	27	**Tiberius** withdraws to Capri. The praetorian prefect Sejanus is at the height of his power.	
Velleius Paterculus: *Historiae*. During these years the gastronome **Apicius** is the friend of Sejanus.	30		
Seneca returns to Rome and begins his forensic activity. **Phaedrus** has already composed the first book of the *Fables*. **Valerius Maximus**'s *Factorum et Dictorum Memorabilium Libri* is subsequent to this year.	31	Sejanus is killed; Caligula, son of Germanicus, is chosen as Tiberius's successor.	
	33		**Paul of Tarsus** begins preaching.
The tragedian **Mamercus Scaurus**, incriminated by his *Atreus*, commits suicide. **Persius** is born at Volterra.	34		
The historian **Servilius Nonianus** is consul. During these years **Quintilian** is born at Calagurris in Spain.	35		
	37	**Tiberius** dies on Capri; **Caligula** succeeds him.	
Seneca the Elder publishes the *Controversiae* and the *Suasoriae*. He dies shortly afterwards (before 41).	ca. 37		
Lucan is born at Cordova in Spain.	39		
Statius is born in Naples.	40–50		
Seneca is exiled: he has recently written the *Consolatio ad Marciam*. In some year between 38 and 41 **Martial** is born in Spain.	41	**Caligula** is killed. His uncle **Claudius**, Germanicus's brother, succeeds him. Claudius grants much power to his freedmen, among	

Roman Culture		Roman History	Greek History and Culture
		whom the most powerful is Polybius.	
Curtius Rufus in the *Historia Alexandri Magni* may refer to events of 41 as recent. **Seneca:** *Consolatio ad Helviam Matrem* (he is in exile on Corsica).	42		
Seneca: *Consolatio ad Polybium.*	43		
	44	**Claudius** conquers Britain.	
Chorographia of **Pomponius Mela**.	ca. 44		
Scribonius Largus: *Compositiones.* The grammarian **Remmius Palaemon** flourishes.	48		
	ca. 48		**Plutarch** is born. During these years the Stoic philosopher **Epictetus** is born.
Seneca is recalled from exile. In these years **Phaedrus** dies.	49	**Germanicus,** after his wife Messalina is killed, marries Agrippina, the daughter of Caligula. Her son by a previous marriage, Nero, will be adopted by the emperor in the following year. Expulsion of the Jews from Rome.	
The tragedian **Pomponius Secundus** triumphs in Germany; his friend **Pliny the Elder** takes part in the expedition. In the decade that starts with this year is usually set the birth of **Juvenal,** at Aquinum.	51		
Seneca: *De Brevitate Vitae.*	ca. 52		
	53	Nero marries Octavia, the daughter of **Claudius.**	
Seneca: *Apocolocyntosis.*	54	**Claudius** dies; **Nero** succeeds him.	
	55	**Nero** has Britannicus, the son of Claudius and Messalina, killed.	
Tacitus is born at Terni or, more probably, in Gaul.	ca. 55		

Roman Culture		Roman History	Greek History and Culture
Seneca: *De Clementia*. This is the year of his consulate.	56	Seneca (the consul) and Burrus (the praetorian prefect) have great influence over **Nero**.	
The grammarian **Valerius Probus** begins his activity. Another grammarian, **Asconius Pedianus**, publishes his commentary on Cicero's speeches.	57		
Seneca: *De Vita Beata*.	ca. 58		
The historian **Servilius Nonianus** dies.	59	**Nero** kills his mother; Seneca's part in the crime is not clear.	
The historian **Aufidius Bassus,** one of the most famous authors of his day, is very old. **Lucan** recites praises of Nero at the Neronia: he may already be working on the *Bellum Civile (Pharsalia)*.	60	Institution of the Neronia, poetic games.	
In this or the following year **Pliny the Younger** is born at Como. The grammarian and poet **Caesius Bassus** has already written his lyrics.	61		
Perhaps from this year comes the *De Otio* of **Seneca,** who gradually withdraws from public life. **Persius** dies. The bucolic poet **Calpurnius Siculus** is active. **Petronius** is consul around this year.	62	Burrus dies, perhaps poisoned. Tigellinus is the new praetorian prefect.	
In this year, or perhaps the preceding one, **Seneca** begins the *Epistulae ad Lucilium*.	63		
Seneca: *De Beneficiis*. **Martial** arrives at Rome. Construction begun on the Domus Aurea.	64	Nero's persecution of the Christians.	
As a result of the Pisonian conspiracy **Seneca** and **Lucan** are obliged to take their own lives; the philosopher **Cornutus** is exiled.	65	The Pisonian conspiracy is thwarted.	
The *De Re Rustica* of **Columella** dates to about this time.			
Suicide of **Petronius** and **Thrasea Paetus**.	66		

Roman Culture		Roman History	Greek History and Culture

A possible date of birth (in addition to 51) for **Juvenal**.

67 Unsuccessful conspiracy of the general Corbulo, who kills himself. **Nero** travels to Greece and proclaims its freedom.

Silius Italicus is consul. **Quintilian** begins activity as a teacher of rhetoric at Rome.

68 Insurrection by Julius Vindex is put down. It is followed by another insurrection—this time successful—by **Galba,** who proclaims himself emperor. **Nero** kills himself. Nymphidius Sabinus also rises up; his revolt is suppressed.

69 On 15 January the praetorians kill **Galba** and proclaim **Otho** emperor; the legions acclaim **Vitellius**. Three months later **Otho** is defeated and kills himself. On 1 July the legions of the East acclaim **Vespasian,** who sends Licinius Mucianus to Rome. Battle of Cremona: **Vitellius** is defeated, and **Vespasian** is left as sole emperor.

Shortly after this date **Suetonius** is probably born. Construction begins on the Colosseum. The activity of the philologist **Valerius Probus** culminates in this decade.

70 Titus, the son of the emperor, puts down a Jewish revolt and occupies Jerusalem.

Frontinus is consul. Between this year and 77 the polymath **Licinius Mucianus** dies.

74

In this year, or the following, **Pliny the Elder** publishes the *Naturalis Historia*.

77

Quintilian is summoned by Vespasian to hold the first state chair of rhetoric. **Tacitus** marries Agricola's daughter and begins his political career.

78

Pliny the Elder dies in the eruption of Vesuvius; his historical work *A Fine Aufidii Bassi* is published posthumously.

79 **Vespasian** dies; his son **Titus** succeeds him.

The *Argonautica* of **Valerius Flaccus** is placed after this year.

Roman Culture		Roman History	Greek History and Culture
Martial: *Liber de Spectaculis.* Inauguration of the Colosseum; the Arch of Titus is begun (it will be finished under Domitian).	80		
	81	**Titus** dies; his brother **Domitian** succeeds him.	
Between the previous year and this year **Martial** publishes the *Xenia* and the *Apophoreta.*	85		
Martial: *Epigrams,* books 1 and 2. The other books will be published one at a time during the following years.	86		
Tacitus is praetor. **Quintilian** retires from teaching.	88		
Statius: *Thebaid.* From this year on he devotes himself to writing the *Silvae.* **Valerius Flaccus** has died recently.	92		
In this year or the next, **Quintilian** publishes the *Institutio Oratoria.* His death is slightly later.	95	Persecution of the Christians.	
Forum of Nerva. Around this year **Statius** dies.	96	**Domitian** is killed; a senator, **Nerva,** succeeds him.	
Tacitus is consul. **Frontinus:** *De Aquis Urbis Romae.*	97		
Tacitus: *Agricola, Germania.* **Martial** returns to Spain for good.			
	98	**Nerva** dies after having adopted **Trajan,** who succeeds him.	

SECOND—THIRD CENTURIES A.D.

Roman Culture		Roman History	Greek History and Culture
Pliny the Younger is consul and writes the *Panegyricus.* Around this year **Silius Italicus** publishes the *Punica.*	100		

Roman Culture		Roman History	Greek History and Culture

In this period **Juvenal** begins to write the *Satires*.

Silius Italicus dies. — 101

Martial: *Epigrams,* book 12 (the last). Around this year **Tacitus** writes the *Dialogus de Oratoribus*. — 102

Martial dies. — ca. 104

106 — **Trajan** conquers Dacia, which becomes a Roman province.

Tacitus: *Histories*. Perhaps in this year **Pliny the Younger** finishes publishing the first nine books of the *Epistulae*. — 110

In this year, approximately, **Pliny the Younger** dies. In this year too (or in the previous one) **Tacitus** is proconsul of Asia. Column of Trajan erected. — 113

114 — Armenia becomes a Roman province.

From after this date comes **Florus**'s *Epitoma de Tito Livio*. Reconstruction of the Pantheon begins. — 115 — Conquest of Mesopotamia and Arabia. The Roman Empire reaches its greatest extent.

117 — **Trajan** dies. **Hadrian,** who was adopted by him, succeeds him; he gives up the recently acquired provinces.

The *Annals* of **Tacitus,** who shortly afterwards dies. **Suetonius** is assigned to the emperor's correspondence and the imperial archive. — ca. 117

Suetonius: *De Vita Caesarum*. — ca. 120 — — Death of **Plutarch** and birth of **Lucian**.

121 — **Hadrian** travels in the western provinces of the Empire.

Suetonius falls into disgrace, along with his patron Septicius Clarus, and we hear no more of him. — 122

124 — **Hadrian** travels in Greece.

Apuleius is born at Madaura in Africa. Construction of Hadrian's Villa begins. — ca. 125

Roman Culture		Roman History	Greek History and Culture
Latest chronological reference in the *Satires* of **Juvenal**. Completion of the Pantheon.	127		
During this period the grammarian **Caesellius Vindex** flourishes; the great jurist **Salvius Julianus** revises the *edictum perpetuum;* and another jurist, **Pomponius**, writes the *Enchiridion*. The scholar **Gellius** is born.	130		
Construction begins of the Mausoleum of Hadrian.	132	A Jewish revolt breaks out. **Hadrian** assumes the title "Pan-Hellene."	
Fronto flourishes, considered the greatest orator of his day.	135	**Hadrian** suppresses the Jewish revolt, with heavy losses.	
The historical work of **Granius Licinianus** belongs to this period. Construction of Hadrian's Villa and the Temple of Venus and Rome.			
The emperor **Hadrian** dies, author of poems akin to the movement of the *poetae novelli*.	138	**Hadrian** dies; his adopted successor **Antoninus Pius** succeeds him.	
Mausoleum of Hadrian.	139		
Fronto is consul. His correspondence with the future emperor Marcus Aurelius begins; letters down to 147 are extant.	143		
The jurist **Salvius Julianus** is consul.	148		
Around this year (or slightly later) **Tertullian** is born at Carthage.	150		
Apuleius: *Apologia (De Magia)*. The *Metamorphoses* must be from after this year.	158		
The great scholar **Sulpicius Apollinaris,** the teacher of Fronto and Gellius, dies.	ca. 160		
After this year falls the publication of the *Institutiones* of the jurist **Gaius.**	161	**Antoninus Pius** dies; his adopted successor **Marcus Aurelius** co-opts his brother **Lucius Verus.**	
From this year, or slightly before, comes **Gellius's** *Attic Nights*. The	169	**Lucius Verus** dies. The Germanic peoples of the Quadi and Marco-	

Roman Culture		Roman History	Greek History and Culture
most famous of the *poetae novelli*, **Annianus,** flourishes during this decade.		manni advance almost as far as Italy.	
Apuleius: *Florida* (the latest references in the work belong to this year). After this year there are no further notices of him.	170		
After this year (but according to others, a year earlier) **Fronto** dies. Perhaps from this period come **Justin's** epitome of Pompeius Trogus and **Festus's** epitome of Verrius Flaccus.	175		
	177	**Marcus Aurelius** co-opts his son **Commodus** to the Empire.	
Acta Martyrum Scillitanorum.	180	**Marcus Aurelius** dies; **Commodus** succeeds him.	**Lucian** dies after this year.
	192	**Commodus** is murdered; **Pertinax** is acclaimed as emperor.	
Column of Marcus Aurelius erected.	193	**Pertinax** is murdered; his successor **Didius Julianus** is murdered in his turn by **Septimius Severus,** who becomes the sole emperor and does away with various other pretenders.	
The conversion of **Tertullian** takes place around this year. In the view of the majority of scholars, the writings of **Terentianus Maurus** belong to the last decade of this century.	195		
Tertullian: *Ad Nationes, Apologeticum, De Testimonio Animae.*	197		
Before this year the jurist **Papinian** composes the *Quaestiones;* his *Responsa* are from the following years.	198		
Cyprian is born at Carthage.	ca. 200		
Passio Perpetuae et Felicitatis. **Minucius Felix's** *Octavius* belongs to this decade, according to many scholars.	202	Edict against Christians and Jews.	
Arch of Septimius Severus.	203		
	ca. 205		**Plotinus** is born.

Roman Culture		Roman History	Greek History and Culture
Tertullian draws near to the Montanist heresy.	207		
	211	**Septimius Severus** dies; his sons **Caracalla** and **Geta** succeed him.	
Tertullian: *De Anima*.	ca. 211		
Papinian is slain. **Tertullian**: *Ad Scapulam*. Much of the work of the jurist **Ulpian** is placed in these years.	212	**Caracalla** kills his brother and promulgates the *Constitutio Antoniniana*, which gives Roman citizenship to all free inhabitants of the Empire.	
	212–ca. 215		**Origen**: *De Principiis*.
Tertullian officially adopts Montanism.	213		
Baths of Caracalla.	216	**Caracalla** makes an expedition against the Parthians.	
	217	**Caracalla** is killed; the praetorian prefect **Macrinus** is named emperor.	
Solinus: *Collectanea Rerum Memorabilium* (but the dating is very controversial).	218	**Macrinus** is killed; **Elagabalus** is acclaimed emperor (but in fact his grandmother, Julia Maesa, and his mother, Soaemias, are in command). The worship of the Sun is introduced, and freedmen return to power. Some fundamental aspects of Roman culture are rejected.	
Tertullian dies after this date.	220		
Ulpian is praetorian prefect.	222	**Elagabalus** and his mother are killed; **Severus Alexander** becomes emperor and once again values Roman military traditions, also giving ample political room to the jurists.	
	224	In the East the kingdom of the Parthians is succeeded by that of the Sassanids, who are even more anti-Roman.	
Ulpian is murdered. The *Liber Medicinalis* of **Serenus Sammonicus** dates from this period.	228		

Roman Culture		Roman History	Greek History and Culture
	229	Second consulate of **Cassius Dio,** Greek author of a history of Rome.	
	235	Murder of **Severus Alexander** and end of the dynasty of the Severans. The soldiers begin to be arbiters of the Empire; they name **Maximinus the Thracian** (235–38), who does not even come to Rome.	
Censorinus: *De Die Natali*.	238	The Senate's last attempts to be effective in naming the emperor: the two **Gordians** (father and son), then **Pupienus** and **Balbinus**. But the period of military anarchy has begun. **Gordian III** (238–44) is chosen.	
	244–49	**Philip the Arab** is emperor.	
Conversion of **Cyprian**; composition of his *Ad Donatum*.	246		
Cyprian becomes bishop of Carthage.	248		
	249–51	The emperor is **Decius,** who in 250 unleashes a great persecution of the Christians.	
Cyprian: *De Lapsis, De Catholicae Ecclesiae Unitate*. Schism of **Novatianus**.	251		
	251–52	**Trebonianus Gallus** is emperor.	
	252		In this year (or the following one) **Origen** dies as a result of the persecution of Decius.
	252–59	**Valerian** is emperor together with his son **Gallienus**.	
	257	Persecution of Christians.	
Martyrdom of **Cyprian**. The majority of scholars place **Commodian**'s poetry in these decades.	258		
	259–68	**Gallienus**, alone, is emperor.	
Gargilius Martial, the writer on botany and medicine, dies.	260		

Roman Culture		Roman History	Greek History and Culture
	268–70	Claudius the Goth is emperor.	
	270		Plotinus dies.
	270–75	Aurelian is emperor.	
The Aurelian Walls are built (construction will go on for about a decade).	271		
	275–76	Claudius Tacitus. Crucifixion of Mani.	
	276–82	Probus is emperor; he returns to a pro-senatorial policy.	
	282–85	Carus is emperor, then his sons Carinus (in the West) and Numerianus (in the East).	
Nemesianus: *Cynegetica*.	284		
	285	Diocletian is sole emperor.	
	286	Diocletian associates with himself Maximian as emperor of the West.	
	293	Diocletian establishes a complex mechanism for the imperial succession.	
Eumenius: *Panegyric* for the governor of Gaul. Construction begins on the Baths of Diocletian.	298		

FOURTH–EIGHTH CENTURIES A.D.

Roman Culture		Roman History
	301	Measures in defense of the currency.
Lactantius, who has received a professorship of rhetoric at Nicomedia from Diocletian, converts to Christianity.	303	Diocletian unleashes the fiercest of the Christian persecutions.
Martyrdom of Victorinus of Poetovium.	304	
Lactantius: *De Opificio Dei*.	305	Diocletian and Maximian abdicate; they are replaced by Galerius (East) and Constantius Chlorus (West).
	306	Constantius Chlorus dies. Four pretenders contend for the succession: the main ones are Constantine (the son of Constantius Chlorus) and Maxentius (the son of Maximian).

Arnobius writes the *Adversus Nationes*. In the same period **Ausonius** is born at Bordeaux.	ca. 310	
	312	After complex military events, **Constantine** defeats **Maxentius** at the Milvian Bridge and is sole emperor of the West.
	313	**Constantine** and **Licinius** (emperor of the East) proclaim the edict of tolerance towards the Christian religion (Edict of Milan).
Lactantius: *Divinae Institutiones* (first edition), *Epitome, De Ira Dei*.	314	
Lactantius: *De Mortibus Persecutorum*. The Arch of Constantine.	ca. 315	
Lactantius, in Trier, is named tutor of Crispus, the son of Constantine; it is the last certain notice of him.	317	
Nazarius: *Panegyric of Constantine*.	321	
An African inscription mentions a **Nonius Marcellus,** perhaps to be identified with the grammarian who was the author of the *De Compendiosa Doctrina*. **Lactantius** dies after this year.	324	**Constantine** defeats **Licinius** twice and is left the sole emperor.
Optatianus: *Carmina*.	325	Council of Nicaea.
Arnobius dies.	ca. 327	
Juvencus: *Evangeliorum Libri IV*. In this period **Ammianus Marcellinus** is born at Antioch.	330	Constantinople becomes the capital of the Empire.
Firmicus Maternus: *Matheseos Libri*.	337	**Constantine** dies. He is succeeded by his three sons—**Constantine II, Constans,** and **Constantius.**
Ambrose is born at Trier.	ca. 339	
	340	**Constantine II** is killed. **Constans** is the emperor of the West, **Constantius** the emperor of the East.
Eusebius becomes bishop of Vercelli. Around this year **Symmachus** is born.	345	
Jerome is born at Stridon, in Dalmatia.	ca. 347	
Prudentius is born at Calagurris, in Spain.	348	
Firmicus Maternus: *De Errore Profanarum Religionum*. **Hilary** becomes bishop of Poitiers.	350	**Constans** is killed by Magnentius, who proclaims himself emperor.
	351	In a bloody battle Magnentius is defeated by **Constantius,** who is left as sole

		emperor in Rome. He has embraced the Arian heresy.
The rhetorician **Marius Victorinus** is granted a statue in the Forum. **Paulinus of Nola** is born at Bordeaux.	353	
Augustine is born at Thagaste, in Africa. The grammarian **Aelius Donatus** flourishes. The "Chronographer of the Year 354" writes his work.	354	
	355	**Constantius** names as Caesar in Gaul Julian, who will be nicknamed "the Apostate."
Hilary of Poitiers and **Lucifer of Cagliari** are exiled by the emperor Constantius, a follower of Arianism.	356	
The conversion of **Marius Victorinus** may date to this year.	357	Solemn visit to Rome by **Constantius,** while Julian defeats the Alamanni.
The grammarian **Charisius** obtains a professorship at Constantinople.	358	
Hilary of Poitiers: *De Trinitate*. From these years come the *Cento* of **Proba**.	ca. 359	
Zeno becomes bishop of Verona.	360	**Julian** is acclaimed as emperor by his army.
	361	**Constantius** dies; **Julian** is left as sole emperor.
Marius Victorinus is compelled to give up teaching. **Mamertinus**: *Panegyric of Julian*.	362	**Julian** attempts to restore paganism; he excludes Christians from teaching. He establishes his capital at Antioch.
	363	**Julian,** while attacking the Persians, is wounded and dies; **Jovian** succeeds him.
Ausonius is at Trier, tutor of the future emperor Gratian.	364	**Jovian** dies; he is succeeded by **Valentinian,** who co-opts **Valens** as emperor of the East. Both emperors are fervent Christians.
Marius Victorinus: *Adversus Arium*.	365	
Damasus is elected pope. In the following years his epigrams will be carved on the tombs of the martyrs.	366	
Hilary of Poitiers dies.	367	**Valentinian** associates his son **Gratian** in the Western Empire.
Ausonius: *Bissula*.	369	
Ambrose goes to Milan as *consularis Liguriae et Aemiliae*. **Claudian** is born at Alexandria, in	370	

Egypt. Around this year **Eutropius** writes the *Breviarium ab Urbe Condita.*

Ausonius: *Mosella.* The *Breviarium* of **Rufius Festus** comes after this year.	371	
Augustine's first spiritual crisis, at Carthage. **Jerome** leaves for the East.	373	
Ambrose is elected bishop of Milan (7 December).	374	
	375	**Valentinian** dies. **Gratian** associates **Valentinian II** in the Western Empire.
Paulinus of Nola is consul, **Ausonius** praetorian prefect.	378	In the battle of Adrianople **Valens** is defeated and killed by the Goths.
Ausonius is consul: *Gratiarum Actio* to the emperor Gratian.	379	**Gratian** names **Theodosius** emperor of the East.
	380	Edict of Thessalonica: **Theodosius** proclaims as the sole state religion the Christianity that results from the dictates of the council of Nicaea.
Jerome is at Constantinople, where he writes the *De Viris Illustribus* and meets Gregory of Nazianzus and Gregory of Nyssa.	381	**Theodosius** makes a pact with the Goths. The council of Aquileia sanctions the defeat of Arianism in the the West.
Jerome, returning to Rome, is charged by pope **Damasus** (who chooses him as his secretary) with translating the Bible into Latin.	382	**Gratian** has the Altar of Victory removed from the Senate.
Praetextatus is praetorian prefect. **Ausonius** retires to private life. **Symmachus** is prefect of Rome (and will remain so until 385).	383	**Maximus** rebels in Spain and defeats and kills **Gratian**.
Jerome: *Vulgata* (New Testament). **Symmachus:** *Relatio III.* Pope **Damasus** dies.	384	**Theodosius** recognizes **Maximus** as emperor of the West.
Jerome leaves again for the East. At Trier **Priscillian** is condemned to death as a heretic.	385	
Ambrose: *De Officiis Ministrorum, Hymns.* **Augustine** converts; composition of *De Ordine, Contra Academicos, De Beata Vita, Soliloquia.*	386	
Augustine is baptized. His mother dies.	387	**Maximus** invades Italy: **Valentinian II** flees and is protected by **Theodosius.**
	388	Decisive defeat of **Maximus.** **Valentinian II** remains sole emperor of the West.
Ausonius: *Parentalia, Commemoratio Professorum Burdigalensium.* **Drepanius:** *Panegyric of Theodosius.* **Jerome** founds a convent at Bethlehem. **Aurelius Victor** is prefect of Rome.	389	

Roman Culture		Roman History
Augustine: *De Magistro.* **Ambrose's** *Hexameron* may be from this year.	390	**Theodosius** slays seven thousand inhabitants of Thessalonica. Ambrose compels him to admit his guilt publicly.
Augustine is ordained a priest. **Symmachus** is consul.	391	
	392	**Valentinian II** dies. **Eugenius,** though not recognized by **Theodosius,** proclaims himself emperor; he animates the last revival of paganism in Rome.
In this or the following year **Ausonius** dies. During these years, under the rule of Eugenius, the *Rerum Gestarum Libri* of **Ammianus Marcellinus** is published; a few years later he dies.	393	
Paulinus of Nola is ordained a priest; beginning with this year we have his *Epistulae.* **Nicomachus Flavianus** is consul; he commits suicide after the defeat of Eugenius. **Augustine:** *Psalmus contra Partem Donati.*	394	In the battle of the Frigidus (6 September), **Theodosius** defeats **Eugenius,** and for the last time the Roman Empire has a single emperor.
Augustine becomes bishop of Hippo. **Jerome:** *Contra Iohannem Hierosolymitanum Episcopum.* **Claudian** is at Rome, which he leaves for Milan and the court of Honorius. The *Saturnalia* of **Macrobius,** according to the early dating, is written before this year. Around this year **Ammianus Marcellinus** dies. **Paulinus of Nola** begins to write, year by year, fourteen *Carmina Natalicia.*	395	**Theodosius** dies, entrusting his sons to the barbarian general Stilicho; **Arcadius** will have the Eastern Empire, **Honorius** the Western. Alaric the Goth invades Illyria.
Ambrose dies. **Augustine** perhaps begins the *Confessions* this year.	397	
Claudian: *De Bello Gildonico* and other court poetry. **Rufinus** translates the *De Principiis* of Origen.	398	**Honorius** marries Maria, daughter of Stilicho.
Augustine begins the *De Trinitate.* **Sulpicius Severus** renounces his possessions and founds a monastery; his *Vita Sancti Martini* is from these years.	399	
Augustine perhaps finishes the *Confessions* in this year; from the same year is the *Contra Faustum Manichaeum* and the *De Opere Monachorum.* **Claudian** is given a statue in the Forum.	400	
Augustine: *De Baptismo.* **Prudentius** comes to Rome and begins his poetic activity.	401	
Claudian: *De Bello Gothico.* **Symmachus** dies; his son Memmius publishes posthumously the *Epistulae.*	402	Stilicho defeats the Goths of Alaric at Pollentia and Verona.

Roman Culture		Roman History
Jerome: *In Rufinum*. **Prudentius**: *Contra Symmachum*. **Paulinus of Nola**: *Epithalamium* (for the marriage of Julian of Eclanum).	403	
Claudian: *De VI Consulatu Honorii*. He dies shortly thereafter. The *Cathemerinon Liber* and *Peristephanon* of **Prudentius** may date from this year.	404	
Prudentius: *Praefatio*.	405	
Jerome: *Vulgata* (Old Testament). The *Commonitorium* of **Orientius** is from after this year.	406	New victory of Stilicho over the Goths, but the Rhine frontier has already been broken.
Paulinus of Nola writes the last of the fourteen *Carmina Natalicia*.	408	Stilicho comes to terms with Alaric but soon afterwards is killed at **Honorius's** order. In the East **Arcadius** dies; **Theodosius II** (408–50) succeeds him.
Paulinus is elected bishop of Nola.	409	
Pelagius goes to Carthage. Around this year perhaps are to be dated the *Commentary on Virgil* by **Servius** (but the dating is quite uncertain) and the *Querolus sive Aulularia*. Later than this date (but before 439) is the *De Nuptiis Mercurii et Philologiae* of **Martianus Capella**.	410	**Alaric** sacks Italy and Rome itself; afterwards he dies at the river Busentus, near Cosenza.
Rufinus dies.	411	
Augustine: *Post Conlationem contra Donatistas*, *De Spiritu et Littera*.	412	
Augustine begins to write the *De Civitate Dei*. **Paulinus of Nola**: *Epistulae*.	413	
Rutilius Namatianus is prefect of Rome. The *De Medicamentis* of **Marcellus** may date from this year. **Orosius** meets **Augustine** and, in the next year, **Jerome**.	414	The new king of the Goths, **Athaulf**, marries Gallia Placidia, the sister of Honorius and Arcadius. The Goths settle in Spain.
From this year, or the previous one, comes the *De Reditu Suo* by **Rutilius Namatianus**. The narrative of **Orosius's** *Historiae adversus Paganos* reaches this year.	417	
	418	Settlement of the Goths in Gaul, in the region of Toulouse.
Augustine: *De Trinitate*.	419	
Jerome dies in this or the previous year. **Pelagius** dies; around this year **Sulpicius Severus** also dies. **Cassian**: *De Institutis Coenobiorum*.	420	
	421	Gallia Placidia marries the Roman general Flavius Constantius.

Macrobius dies after this year, according to the most accepted theory.	422	
	423	**Honorius** dies; the functionary **John** takes control of the Western Empire.
	425	With **John** slain, Gallia Placidia's young son **Valentinian III** is proclaimed emperor under the tutelage of his mother.
Augustine: *De Civitate Dei, Retractationes.*	427	
Augustine: *De Praedestinatione Sanctorum.* **Cassian:** *Conlationes.*	429	The Vandals, led by Gaiseric, conquer Africa and form an independent national state.
Augustine dies. **Sedulius:** *Carmen Paschale* (before 450, in any event). **Macrobius:** *Saturnalia* (according to the later dating, the work is to be placed in the decade that opens with this year).	430	
Paulinus of Nola dies.	431	
Merobaudes composes a *Panegyric* for Aetius's first consulate.	432	The general Aetius is the actual arbiter of the Western Empire.
	433	The Huns settle in Pannonia.
Merobaudes is awarded a statue at Rome, in the Forum of Trajan.	435	Rome recognizes the sovereignty of Gaiseric over Mauretania and Numidia.
Quodvultdeus becomes bishop of Carthage.	437	**Valentinian III** marries the daughter of **Theodosius II.**
Codex Theodosianus.	438	
Before this year **Possidius** writes the biography of Augustine.	439	The Vandals conquer and sack Carthage.
Julian of Eclanum dies. **Leo the Great** is elected pope. Around this year is placed the *Ad Ecclesiam* of **Salvianus.**	440	
	444	Attila becomes the sole king of the Huns.
Merobaudes writes a *Panegyric* for Aetius's third consulship; for fifteen years he is the official court poet.	446	
Cassius Felix: *De Medicina.*	447	
	450	**Marcian** is the emperor of the East (450–57).
Salvianus: *De Gubernatione Dei.*	ca. 450	
	451	Aetius defeats Attila in Gaul.
	452	Attila marches on Italy; pope Leo the Great stops him.

Roman Culture		Roman History
Quodvultdeus, the likely author of the *De Promissionibus et Praedicationibus Dei,* dies.	453	Attila dies.
	454	Aetius is assassinated.
The *Chronicon* of **Prosper of Aquitaine** comes down to this year.	455	**Valentinian III** is murdered. He is succeeded by **Petronius Maximus,** who marries his widow. But Gaiseric, king of the Vandals, occupies Rome and puts the senator **Avitus** on the throne.
Sidonius Apollinaris writes a *Panegyric* for the emperor Avitus, whose daughter he has married.	456	**Avitus** is deposed. Now the barbarian general Ricimer is the arbiter of power at Rome.
	457	Ricimer puts **Majorian** on the western throne. In the East there is **Leo** (457–74). The new emperor of the West is pro-senatorial and a traditionalist.
Sidonius Apollinaris writes a *Panegyric* for the emperor Majorian.	458	
Paulinus of Pella: *Eucharisticos.*	459	
Pope **Leo the Great,** the author of *Sermons* and *Letters,* dies.	461	Ricimer gets rid of **Majorian** and names **Libius Severus.**
	465	For two years there is an interregnum in the Western Empire.
	466	Founding of the Visigothic state in Spain.
	467	The neo-Platonist **Procopius Anthemius** is named emperor of the West.
Sidonius Apollinaris is consul: *Panegyric* for the emperor Procopius Anthemius. The *Chronicon* of **Hydatius** reaches this year.	468	
Sidonius Apollinaris: *Letters.*	469–82	
Sidonius Apollinaris becomes bishop of Auvergne. Around this year **Paulinus of Périgueux** composes the *Vita Martini.*	470	
	472	Conflict between Ricimer and **Procopius Anthemius,** who both die. **Olybrius** is the emperor.
	473	The Burgundian Gundobad names **Glycerius** emperor.
	474	Orestes, previously Attila's secretary, names **Julius Nepos** emperor. In the East the emperor is **Zeno** (474–91).
	475	**Julius Nepos** flees. Orestes names his son **Romulus Augustulus** emperor.

Roman Culture		Roman History
	476	Odoacer kills Orestes and deposes **Romulus Augustulus** (23 August) without naming a successor; he assumes the title *patricius,* which **Zeno** recognizes. It is the end of the Roman Empire in the West.
Boethius and **Benedict of Nursia** are born.	480	
Victor of Vita's *Historia Persecutionis Africanae Provinciae* comes down to this point in its narrative.	484	
	484–96	**Gunthamund** is king of the Vandals, succeeding Huneric.
Sidonius Apollinaris dies.	ca. 486	
The African poet **Dracontius** flourishes in the last decade of the century; his *Satisfactio,* dedicated to Gunthamund, is from before 496.	490	
At the end of the century **Gennadius** adds an appendix to Jerome's *De Viris Illustribus.*		
	491–518	**Anastasius** is emperor of the East.
	493	Theodoric, king of the Goths, has Odoacer assassinated and becomes master of Italy.
Boethius is consul.	510	
Cassiodorus is consul.	514	
Avitus of Vienne dies.	518	
	518–27	**Justin** is emperor of the East.
Priscian's *Institutio de Arte Grammatica* belongs to this period (and in any event is later than 510).	520	
Ennodius, poet and bishop of Pavia, dies.	521	
Boethius is *magister officiorum.*	522	
Boethius: *De Consolatione Philosophiae.* He is executed in the same year.	524	
	526	Theodoric dies.
	527–65	**Justinian** is emperor of the East.
The *Corpus Iuris* begins to be compiled in this year.	528	
Benedict of Nursia founds the monastery at Monte Cassino.	529	
Venantius Fortunatus is born at Valdobbiadene.	ca. 530	
Corpus Iuris: Digesta, Institutiones.	533	

Roman Culture		Roman History
Corpus Iuris: Codex Repetitae Praelectionis.	534	**Justinian** defeats the Vandals and reconquers Africa.
	535–53	Greek-Gothic war, waged by the generals Belisarius and Narses (who were sent by **Justinian**) against the Goths under the successive leadership of Theodatus, Witigis, Totila, and Teias. Italy is completely devastated.
Gregory of Tours is born. In this year or the previous one **Cassiodorus's** *Variae* is published.	538	
	540	**Justinian** reconquers Ravenna, taking it from the Goths.
Gregory the Great is born. **Cassiodorus** founds the community of Vivarium.	ca. 540	
Caesarius of Arles, the author of *Sermones,* dies.	542	
Arator gives a public reading in Rome of the *De Actibus Apostolorum.*	544	
Benedict of Nursia dies.	ca. 547	
Corippus composes the *Johannis.* From the same decades come the *Elegies* of **Maximian** and the *De Excidio et Conquestu Britanniae* of **Gildas.**	ca. 550	
Venantius Fortunatus leaves Italy and begins his pilgrimage through Europe.	565	**Justinian** dies. **Justin II** is the emperor of the East.
Corippus: *In Laudem Iustini.* His death follows soon after.	567	
	568	The Lombards, led by Alboin, descend into Italy.
Isidore of Seville is born.	570	
Gregory becomes bishop of Tours.	573	
Gregory of Tours begins to write the *Historia Francorum.*	575	
Venantius Fortunatus: *Vita Martini.*	576	
	580	The Senate of Rome is mentioned for the last time.
Cassiodorus and **Martin of Braga** die.	ca. 580	
Venantius Fortunatus: *Vita Radegundis.*	587	
Gregory the Great is elected pope.	590	
The *Historia Francorum* of **Gregory of Tours** stops with the events of this year.	591	
Gregory the Great: *De Vita et Miraculis Patrum Italorum.*	593	
Gregory of Tours dies.	594	

Roman Culture		Roman History
Venantius Fortunatus is elected bishop of Poitiers.	597	
At the death of his brother **Leander, Isidore** becomes bishop of Seville. After this year falls the death of **Venantius Fortunatus.**	600	
	603	Peace between the Byzantines and the Lombards, under the auspices of pope Gregory the Great. The Lombards convert to Catholicism.
Gregory the Great dies.	604	
	612–20	Sisebut, a literary author of Latin poetry, is king of the Visigoths in Spain.
Isidore of Seville: *Chronica* (dedicated to Sisebut, king of the Visigoths).	615	
Isidore of Seville: *De Viris Illustribus*.	ca. 618	
	632	Mohammed dies.
	634	The Arab expansion begins.
Isidore of Seville dies. The *Etymologiae sive Origines* will be published posthumously.	636	
	643	Edict of Rothari.
The **Venerable Bede** is born.	672	
	697	The Arabs conquer all Africa.
Bede: *De Temporibus*.	703	
	711	The Arabs overthrow the kingdom of the Visigoths in Spain.
	728	Donation of Sutri: beginning of the Pontifical State.
Bede: *Historia Ecclesiastica Gentis Anglorum*.	731	
Bede dies.	735	
	776	Charlemagne establishes his dominion over Italy by defeating the Lombards.
Paulus Diaconus: *Historia Langobardorum.* The date of the *Epitome a Festo* is uncertain.	ca. 787	
	800	Coronation of Charlemagne in Rome: the Holy Roman Empire is born.

Appendix 2 Greek Authors and Texts

Achilles Tatius, 2d c. A.D., author of the *Leucippe and Clitophon,* one of the best examples of the Greek erotic novel to come down to us. The rhetorical-sophistic element is strong, reminding one of Apuleius.

Aelian Claudius, a native of Praeneste, rhetorician at Rome in the 2d–3d c. A.D., known for his miscellanies and collections of curiosities on animals and human history.

Aelius Aristides, 2d c. A.D., very popular orator and traveling lecturer, author of, among other things, a *Panegyric* of Rome and a number of idealizing evocations of Athenian civilization.

Aeschines of Athens, 4th c. B.C., famous Attic orator, an opponent of Demosthenes and linked with him in the Greco-Roman oratorical tradition.

Aeschylus, 525–456 B.C., one of the three great Greek tragedians, the one most remote from Roman taste but the one whose use in individual cases is likely, as, for instance, in Ennius's *Eumenides.*

Aesop, semi-legendary Thracian slave, said to have lived in the 6th c. B.C., to whom belongs the origin of the fable tradition, which is exampled for us principally in Phaedrus and Babrius. The abundant notices of his biography make up a kind of popular novel.

Alcaeus of Mytilene, lyric poet of the 7th–6th c. B.C. His poetic work was rearranged by the Alexandrians in ten books, divided according to genre and subject. Always valued by the greatest Greek poets, and the object of scholarly study, he makes his influence felt especially on Horace's lyric poetry.

Alciphron, rhetorician and sophist of the 2d c. A.D., important chiefly in the history of the epistolary genre. The subjects of his epistles are set in the remote world of Attic New Comedy.

Alcman, lyric poet of the 7th c. B.C., given first place in the Alexandrian canon of the lyric poets. He was distinguished also as the founder of choral melic poetry (he wrote famous *Partheneia,* choruses performed by young girls). His difficult language, a mixture of various literary dialects, did not help his success at Rome.

Alexander, Romance of, a complex series of narrative texts in various languages, several times reworked and transformed (we have versions in Greek, Latin, Armenian, Coptic, and Syriac), which go back to earlier compilations of historical-novelistic sources (*see also* **Pseudo-Callisthenes**). The Latin representative of this tradition is Julius Valerius (3d–4th c. A.D.).

Alexander Polyhistor, a scholar and polygraph of the 1st c. B.C. Brought to Rome as a slave in the wake of Sulla's campaigns in the East, he was set free by him and gave lessons in Rome. In the linguistic field he sided with the anomalists; his learned works had great success in Latin literature.

Alexis of Thurii, 4th c. B.C., poet of Attic "Middle Comedy," so called because it is the transition between the Old Comedy of Aristophanes and the New of Menander. Known to us only in fragments, he had some influence on the Roman *palliata*—the model of Plautus's *Poenulus* is Alexis's play *The Carthaginian*—although in general Middle Comedy was overshadowed by New Comedy.

Anacreon of Teos, 6th c. B.C., author of lyrics, elegies, and iambs; an authoritative edition in five books was issued by the Alexandrian philologist Aristarchus. He enjoyed enormous literary success in the Hellenistic-Roman period, especially as the representative of a frivolous love poetry; indeed his genuine work was gradually supplanted by a wave of counterfeit Anacreontics. At Rome he was important chiefly as a model for Horace's poetry.

Anaxagoras, philosopher of the 5th c. B.C. who worked at Athens and was Pericles' teacher. To him is due the theory of the *homoeomereiae,* the infinitely small original particles that, arranged by a divine intelligence, were said to have given rise to the various forms of reality.

Anthologia Palatina, huge collection of Greek epigrams in fifteen books, assembled in the Byzantine period and based on three collections of very different times: those of Meleager, 70 B.C.; Philip, 40 B.C.; and Agathias, 6th c. A.D. It is an invaluable source for our knowledge of the models of the Latin epigram.

Antigonus of Carystus, writer and probably sculptor of the 3d c. B.C., popular biographer and important source for the history of Greek art.

Antimachus of Colophon, epic and elegiac poet of the first half of the 4th c. B.C. A rich and problematic figure, he was criticized by Callimachus, yet he seems also to have anticipated in certain regards the erotic-mythological poetry of the Alexandrians. The Roman elegiac poets repeat rather passively Callimachus's strictures on him. As an epic poet, he may have influenced early Roman epic, and his *Thebaid* may have influenced Statius's poem of the same name.

Antiochus of Ascalon, philosopher of the beginning of the 1st c. B.C. He taught at Athens, where he had among his pupils the young Varro and Cicero, upon whom he exerted considerable influence by virtue of his position as an eclectic skeptic.

Antipater of Sidon, esteemed poet of epigrams at the end of the 2d c. B.C., preserved for us in the *Anthologia Palatina.*

Antipater of Thessalonica, poet of epigrams from the 1st c. B.C., also active at Rome and connected to L. Calpurnius Piso. His poems are preserved in the *Anthologia Palatina.*

Antisthenes of Athens, philosopher of the 5th–4th c. B.C., considered a precursor of the Cynics, author of dialogues and epideictic orations (e.g., a debate between Ajax and Odysseus, which was known to Ovid).

Antoninus Liberalis, mythographer of the 2d c. A.D. A collection of myths called *Metamorphoses,* put together by him, is important since it uses lost Hellenistic poets (Nicander, Boio) whom Ovid had before him when writing his *Metamorphoses.*

Antonius Diogenes, active towards the end of the 1st c. A.D., author of a huge novel of fantastic adventures, *The Wonderful Things beyond Thule,* of which we have a Byzantine summary. Its interest in travels and sensational adventures distinguishes it from the main tradition of the erotic novel.

Apollodorus of Carystus, minor poet of Attic New Comedy, used by Terence in the *Hecyra* (together with a text by Menander) and the *Phormio;* the corresponding titles from Apollodorus are *Hekyra* and *Epidikazomenos.*

Apollodorus of Pergamum, famous rhetorician of Atticist tendency, also the teacher of Octavian. A theoretical work of his was translated into Latin by Valgius Rufus.

Apollonius of Rhodes, epic poet of the 3d c. B.C., a native of Alexandria who later retired to Rhodes. He was also important as a scholar; among other things, he succeeded Zenodotus as head of the Library of Alexandria. His literary success rests more than anything upon his poem the *Argonautica,* in four books, a monumental compromise between the Homeric tradition and the new Alexandrian taste, and the only Greek epic poem extant in its entirety that was composed between Homer's time and the period of the Roman Empire. It was one of Virgil's favorite models; Varro of Atax's *Argonauts* was a Latin version of it; under the Empire it was imitated by many epic poets and was the chief source of Valerius Flaccus.

Apollonius of Tyana, Pythagorean holy man of the 1st–2d c. A.D. He was the object of a personal cult around a century later at the court of the Severans, when **Philostratus** (q.v.) devoted a novelized *Life* to him.

Appian of Alexandria, imperial official of the 2d c. A.D. His *Roman History,* in twenty-four books, from the city's origins to the time of Trajan, is preserved only in part.

Aratus of Soli, outstanding poet and scholar of the 3d c. B.C., famous at Rome above all for his astronomical poem, the *Phaenomena.* The object of intense commentary in the 2d–1st c. B.C., it had a large number of Latin translators (Cicero, Varro of Atax, Germanicus, even the laté Avienus), and it influenced the whole tradition of didactic poetry (in particular the Virgil of the *Georgics,* Ovid, and Manilius).

Archestratus of Gela, active in the 4th c. B.C. His gastronomic poem *Hedypatheia,* written in epic-style hexameters and devoted to the pleasures of the table, is preserved only in part; it was the direct source of Ennius's *Hedyphagetica.*

Archias of Antioch, 2d–1st c. B.C., a modest poet specializing in laudatory epics on the deeds of Roman commanders (Marius, Lucullus). He was defended by Cicero in a famous speech.

Archilochus of Paros, iambic and elegiac poet of the 7th c. B.C., regarded by the Alexandrians as the greatest representative of iambic poetry. His influence at Rome is attested from Ennius and Lucilius onwards and culminates in Horace's epodic poetry.

Archimedes of Syracuse, mathematician and scientist who died in 212 B.C., during the Roman capture of Syracuse. He was universally honored as a mathematician, astronomer, and inventor.

Arctinus of Miletus, epic poet of the 7th c. B.C.? A dim figure, in the classical period he was already known as the author of epic poems of the Trojan Cycle, among them an *Aethiopis,* which may have been one of the minor sources of Virgil's *Aeneid.*

Aristaenetus, 5th c. A.D., composer of letters on amorous themes, which presuppose Alexandrian poetic models. He documents the development of epistolary narrative (see Ovid's *Heroides*).

Aristarchus of Samothrace, philologist of the 3d–2d c. B.C., the most well-known representative of the philological school of Alexandria. The author of editions and fundamental studies of classics such as Homer, Pindar, and so on, he influenced the whole Hellenistic-Roman tradition of literary studies. A famous controversy over philological method pitted his analogist position, according to which language was based on regularity and respect for the recognized models and therefore did not allow neologisms or deviations from the norm, against the anomalist position of the Pergamene scholars, led by **Crates of Mallus** (q.v.), who considered language a free creation of usage and admitted deviations from the norm as a necessary phenomenon.

Aristarchus of Tegea, tragic poet contemporary with Euripides, known indirectly as a source used by Ennius in his tragedies.

Aristides of Miletus, perhaps at the end of the 2d c. B.C., author of a collection of *Milesiaka* ("Milesian Tales"), translated into Latin in the 1st c. B.C. by Sisenna. Both works are lost, but Aristides is considered the founder of the comic novel, a genre of great commercial success that clearly influences the novels of Petronius and Apuleius.

Aristophanes of Athens, 5th–4th c. B.C., unanimously considered the greatest poet of Attic Old Comedy and as such celebrated also at Rome. His direct influence was small on the Roman comic theater, which generally follows New Comedy (Menander, Diphilus, Philemon).

Aristophanes of Byzantium, great philologist of the 3d–2d c. B.C., librarian of Alexandria, editor of epic, lyric, and tragic texts, grammarian, and metrician. He was the teacher of Aristarchus.

Aristotle of Stagira, 384–322 B.C. His immense philosophical and scholarly work is one of the principal points of reference for Roman culture. In 84 B.C. a vast collection of his works was brought to Rome by Sulla, and important editions were made at Rome. This period witnesses an increase in the fame of the works that derive from Aristotelian teaching but were not published by Aristotle himself; conversely, some works published by Aristotle but lost to us had a fundamental influence on Roman culture during the Republic (e.g., the *Protrepticus,* an important model for Cicero).

Arius Didymus of Alexandria, eclectic philosopher who was one of Augustus's teachers. He is also known as the author of a *Consolatio* to Livia for the death of Drusus.

Arrian Flavius of Nicomedia, a prose writer of the 2d c. A.D. He preserved for us the teaching of **Epictetus of Hierapolis** (q.v.), and he is the author of a historical work in six books about Alexander the Great *(Anabasis).*

Asclepiades of Samos, 3d c. B.C., an Alexandrian poet connected to Theocritus. Asclepiades was the author of refined epigrams.

Athenaeus of Naucratis, a scholar of the 2d–3d c. A.D. He wrote in fifteen books the *Deipnosophistae* (which has reached us partly in the original form, partly in abridgment), a priceless collection of anecdotes and information about classical Greece.

Athenodorus of Tarsus, Stoic philosopher of the 1st c. B.C., one of the models for Seneca's ethical works.

Babrius, 2d c. A.D., perhaps a Hellenized Roman, author of (originally in ten books, it seems) a collection of Aesopic fables in choliambic meter (an abridged collection has come down to us). In the fourth century he influenced the Latin fabulist Avianus, and in the Middle Ages his work, with its elements of fable and romance, had great popularity.

Bacchylides, choral lyric poet of the 5th c. B.C. whose writings were collected in nine books by the Alexandrians. A difficult poet somewhat overshadowed by Pindar, he nonetheless left some traces in Latin poetry (Virgil, Horace's *Odes*).

Bion of Borysthenes, 3d c. B.C., considered one of the primary founders of the diatribe genre. Eclectically open to various philosophical influences, he influenced in turn Horace's ethical poetry and Seneca's philosophical prose.

Bion of Smyrna, poet of the late Alexandrian period (end of the 2d c. B.C.) who imitated Theocritus's pastoral manner. His *Epitaph of Adonis,* which may also have been known to the Roman poets of the 1st c. B.C., is preserved.

Boio, mysterious Alexandrian (?) author of an *Ornithogonia,* a likely source for Ovid and Aemilius Macer.

Caecilius of Calacte, rhetorician and literary critic active also at Rome (end of 1st c. B.C.), known particularly for having influenced "**Longinus**" (q.v.).

Callimachus of Cyrene, ca. 320–240 B.C., the Hellenistic poet who had the profoundest influence on Roman culture. His poetics can already be perceived in Ennius, who in the proem to the *Annals* is influenced by the proem to the *Aitia,* and in Lucilius, who is influenced by the *Iambs* principally. The poetry of Callimachus then becomes the programmatic model of the *poetae novi;* Catullus imitates him, and he translates him in poem 66. The elegiac poets and Virgil found in Callimachus the model of a refined poet; typically Callimachean is the Augustan *recusatio* (the contrast between the genres of fine-spun and elevated epic, found in Virgil, Horace, Propertius, Ovid). Now assimilated to Latin literary culture, Callimachus was still read firsthand in the 1st c. A.D. (Petronius, Statius). Among the elegiac poets of the previous century, Propertius presents himself as the "purest" Callimachean (though it is more a literary gesture than a real closeness), but the more cautious Tibullus is also in fact deeply touched by Callimachean influence.

Callinus of Ephesus, 7th c. B.C., the earliest elegiac poet of whom we have notice. His elegies (of which we have only fragments) seem to be of a predominantly warlike nature, exhortations to fight the invaders.

Callisthenes. *See* **Pseudo-Callisthenes**.

Carneades of Cyrene, distinguished philosopher of the 2d c. B.C., founder of the Third Academy. He was important in Roman culture for having headed, along with a Peripatetic and a Stoic, a historic embassy of Greek philosophers to Rome in 155 B.C.

Cassius Dio of Nicaea, an influential Roman politician in the age of the Severans. He left a *History of Rome* in eighty books, partially preserved, partially reconstructable on the basis of Byzantine reworkings. The *History* is an important source for the period from the late Republic to the early Empire, an era for which we possess few historical treatments in either Greek or Latin.

Castor of Rhodes, 1st c. B.C., compiler of valuable synoptic tables of Oriental, Greek, and Roman chronology, which were used by Varro and other later scholars of chronology.

Celsus, author of the 2d c. A.D., an anti-Christian polemicist known from Origen's vehement reply to him *(Contra Celsum)*.

Cercidas of Megalopolis, 3d c. B.C., author of *Meliambi* in a Cynic-diatribic vein. Along with Bion of Borysthenes and Menippus, he shapes the diatribe tradition, which can still be perceived in Roman culture (satire, philosophical dialogues).

Chariton, novelist of the 1st c. A.D., representative of a genre of idealized love stories that was to be very successful and may have been parodied in Petronius's novel.

Choerilus of Iasus, 4th c. B.C., an epic poet who is a typical (and therefore ill-famed) representative of courtly historical epic poetry. He sang the deeds of Alexander the Great.

Choerilus of Samos, 5th c. B.C., author of a historical epic on the Persian Wars that included ethnographic interests.

Chrysippus of Soli, Stoic philosopher of the 3d c. B.C., a prolific thinker and second founder of the Stoa.

Claudian, Greek epic poet, very probably identical with the celebrated homonymous Latin poet (who was well known for being bilingual).

Cleanthes, philosopher of the 4th–3d c. B.C., successor to Zeno as head of the Stoic school. He also wrote a *Hymn to Zeus*.

Clement of Alexandria, 2d–3d c. A.D., distinguished theologian converted to Christianity and persecuted by Septimius Severus. During his last years he was the bishop of Jerusalem. His work is important for its theoretical originality and rich pagan classical culture.

Clitarchus, historian of 4th–3d c. B.C. He was the author of a historical work on Alexander that had unusual success and remained for centuries the most-read work on the subject. Curtius Rufus cites it, but other Roman historians, from Sisenna to Livy, also were influenced by his "tragic" historiography.

Cornutus (Lucius Annaeus Cornutus), 1st c. A.D., the teacher of Lucan and Persius at Rome. He wrote in both Latin and Greek. We possess a compendium of mythology (in Greek) from him that is shaped by Stoic doctrine. Together with Caesius Bassus, he published posthumously Lucan's poem on the civil war.

Crates of Mallus, philosophical historian and grammarian, head of the school of Pergamum, one of the most influential intellectuals of the 2d c. B.C. In 168 he remained for some time at Rome, where his lectures had a notable impact. He was the teacher of Panaetius. An important controversy over method pitted him against the analogist school of Alexandria.

Cratinus, Athenian comic poet of the 5th c. B.C. Together with Eupolis and Aristophanes, he was among the most renowned authors of Old Comedy.

Cratippus of Pergamum, Peripatetic philosopher of the 1st c. B.C. He taught at Mytilene and Athens. Cicero in the *De Divinatione* informs us of his notions about dreams.

Crinagoras of Mytilene, epigrammatic poet of the 1st c. B.C., notable chiefly for his links with the circle of Augustus.

Cypria, an epic poem of the Trojan Cycle that sang in eleven books about the events that took place before the *Iliad.* Known to us (and probably also to Roman scholars) only through prose summaries.

Dares of Phrygia, presumed author of a history of the Trojan War that survives in the late (5th c.?) Latin novel *De Excidio Troiae.* His case is parallel to that of **Dictys of Crete.**

Democritus of Abdera, great thinker of the 5th c. B.C., famous particularly for his atomistic theories, which survived longer at Rome than elsewhere because of the Epicureans.

Demophilus, comic writer of the 3d c. B.C. We know about him only that his comedy *Onagos* ("The Ass-Driver") is the model for Plautus's *Asinaria.*

Demosthenes, 384–322 B.C., considered by posterity, including the Romans, as the greatest Attic orator. He is important also for the development of Roman oratory, of Cicero in particular (who derives from him the title *Philippics*).

Dexippus, Attic historian of the 3d c. A.D., notable as a source for the Gothic wars waged by the Empire in the period A.D. 238–74.

Dicaearchus of Messina, Peripatetic philosopher of the 4th c., pupil of Aristotle. He is notable also for his political, literary, and geographical interests, which make him an authoritative source.

Dictys of Crete, shadowy author of a novel on the war at Troy, probably composed in the 2d–3d c. A.D. A fragment is extant, as is the popular Latin version owed to a Lucius Septimius (4th c. A.D.).

Dio. *See* **Cassius Dio.**

Dio of Prusias, 1st–2d c. A.D., sophist and traveling rhetorician, pupil of Musonius and teacher of Favorinus.

Diodorus Siculus, active in the Caesarian and Augustan age, author of a universal history *(Bibliotheca)* in forty books, from the origins to 54 B.C. The history is partly preserved, partly known through summaries or extracts. He used Roman sources as well as Greek.

Diogenes of Oenoanda, 2d c. B.C. A philosophical inscription that he had engraved in his hometown is extant in fragments and useful for the study of Epicureanism.

Dionysius the Areopagite, Athenian of the 1st c. A.D., converted by Paul to Christianity. Philosophical writings marked by a bold fusion of Christianity and neo-Platonism circulated under his name (5th–6th c.?).

Dionysius of Halicarnassus, literary critic, rhetorician, and historian, who taught at Rome in the Augustan period. In 7 B.C. he published a *History of Rome,* from its origins to 264 B.C., in twenty books (filling in the period prior to the start of Polybius's classic work). Approximately half the work is preserved, and other parts can be reconstructed. He was also important as a grammarian and scholar of poetic style (especially in his treatise *De Compositione Verborum*).

Dionysius Periegetes, active under Hadrian (reigned A.D. 117–38). He composed a description of the earth in hexameters, which was used as a geographical text for school.

Dionysius Thrax ("the Thracian"), grammarian of the 2d c. B.C. who had an immense influence on grammatical instruction. His influence was introduced at Rome especially through Remmius Palaemon.

Dioscorides of Anazarbus (in Cilicia), 1st c. A.D., author of *On the Materia Medica,* which exercised a great influence in the pharmaceutical and medical field until modern times. The strong similarities between Dioscorides' work and the *Naturalis Historia* of Pliny the Elder (several decades later) are commonly explained by the use of the same Greek sources (Sestius Niger); it is believed that Pliny did not read Dioscorides.

Diphilus of Sinope, one of the best Attic comic writers, a representative (along with Menander and Philemon) from the first rank of New Comedy (4th c. B.C.). He seems to have been one of the chief models of Plautus (he is attested as the model of the *Casina,* the *Rudens,* and the *Vidularia*).

Duris of Samos, 4th–3d c. B.C., historian and scholar, a pupil of Theophrastus. His histories narrated events from 370 to 282 B.C. His work, which was strongly moralistic, influenced Nepos and Livy.

Empedocles of Agrigentum, 5th c. B.C., philosopher, scientist, and healer, author of two (?) poems in hexameters containing cosmological revelations and metempsychosis, *On Nature* and *Purifications.* The fragments of his works are numerous, the reconstruction controversial. He was still esteemed and used as a model for didactic poetry by Lucretius.

Epaphroditus of Chaeronea, a well-educated freed slave, went to Rome (1st c. A.D.), where he possessed a formidable library and brought out editions of Greek classics using Alexandrian techniques.

Ephorus of Cyme, 4th c. B.C., historian, pupil of the orator Isocrates. His history in twenty-nine books, which came down to the time of Philip of Macedon, was reused by **Diodorus Siculus** (q.v.), for one.

Epicharmus, 6th–5th c. B.C., great Sicilian comic poet, in the tradition of Doric comedy, specializing in mythological parodies and scenes of ordinary life. Also valued were the anthologies of maxims drawn from his works, which inspired in Ennius a work entitled *Epicharmus.*

Epictetus of Hierapolis (in Phrygia), 1st c. A.D. A Stoic thinker, he was a freed slave who was active at Rome and was later included in Domitian's banishment of the philosophers. His meditations are known to us through his pupil Arrian.

Epicurus of Samos, 341–270 B.C., famous founder of the philosophical school that takes its name from him. The Herculaneum papyri are one of the chief sources on Epicureanism, which deeply influenced Roman culture from the 1st c. B.C. (Lucretius) to the 1st c. A.D.

Eratosthenes of Cyrene, 3d c. B.C., philologist, geographer, didactic poet, and tireless scholar in a large number of scientific fields. He succeeded Apollonius of Rhodes in the Library at Alexandria. His self-description as "philologist" would prove influential.

Euhemerus of Messina, 4th–3d c. B.C., utopianist, known especially for his theories about the human origin of the gods. His success is evidenced by Ennius's *Euhemerus.*

Euphorion of Chalcis, Alexandrian poet of the 3d c. B.C., librarian at Antioch, author of many short mythological poems written in an original and difficult style. He influenced Roman neoteric poetry, in particular Gallus, it seems.

Eupolis, 5th c. B.C., great poet of Old Comedy, known at Rome only indirectly as an author of proverbial aggressiveness.

Euripides, 5th c. B.C., the last of the three great tragedians, is, along with Menander, the Greek dramatist best known and most imitated at Rome. All the archaic Roman tragedians reworked at least some of his plays; but his presence is also strong in the love poetry of the 1st c. B.C., in epic (Virgil, Ovid, Statius), and in Seneca's drama.

Eusebius of Caesarea, 3d–4th c. A.D., the great founder of ecclesiastical history. He is, among other things, the author of the *Chronicles,* which we possess in Jerome's Latin version.

Favorinus of Arles, 2d c. A.D., a brilliant and extremely successful orator connected to Fronto, Herodes Atticus, and Gellius. Although Gallic by birth, he preferred to write in Greek.

Flavius Josephus. *See* **Josephus Flavius**.

Galen of Pergamum, died A.D. 199, court doctor in the Rome of Marcus Aurelius and author of an immense body of medical and philosophical writings. During the Middle Ages and down to the Renaissance Galen's was the chief text of medical instruction, enjoying a reputation comparable to Aristotle's; even now he can be considered the founder of experimental physiology and systematic medicine.

Gregory of Nazianzus, 4th c. A.D., an outstanding rhetorician and a poet who was very skillful at clothing Christian theological subjects in classicizing forms.

Gregory of Nyssa, 4th c. A.D., friend of **Gregory of Nazianzus** (q.v.) and, like him, a champion of Christian orthodoxy. He was in contact with Jerome, upon whom he exerted a notable influence.

Hegesias of Magnesia, 3d c. B.C., rhetorician and historian often identified (sometimes polemically) as a typical representative of the Asian style.

Heliodorus of Emesa, 3d or 4th c. A.D., author of the *Aethiopica,* which many consider to be the best Greek novel. His personal connections with the cult of the Sun god are evident even in the novel.

Hellanicus of Mytilene, 5th c. B.C., active historian and antiquarian who was, among other things, one of the first to recount the saga of Aeneas in Italy.

Hephaestion of Alexandria, 2d c. A.D., important metrician, whose works are preserved for us in a compendium.

Heraclitus of Ephesus, 6th–5th c. B.C., philosopher of interest not only for his thought but also for the involved style of his formulations (which won him the epithet "obscure"). He maintained that everything "is" to the extent that it transforms itself into something else, in an eternal becoming that constitutes reality at the very moment at which it destroys that reality; *panta hrei,* "all things are in flux," is the most well-known phrase summarizing his theory.

Hermagoras of Temnos, rhetorician of the 2d c. B.C., important especially for his systematic classifications. He was a source for Quintilian.

Hermes Trismegistus, Greek name corresponding to the Egyptian "very great Toth," under which many religious, magical, and philosophical writings *(Hermetica)* circulated in the imperial period. With their superficial exoticism, they resemble Egyptian and, more generally, Eastern doctrines.

Hermesianax of Colophon, 3d c. B.C., Alexandrian poet known only in meager fragments. He was the author of mythological elegies linked (we do not know how) to the name of his beloved lady Leontion.

Hermogenes of Tarsus, 2d–3d c. A.D., important source for the history of rhetoric and stylistic doctrines.

Herodas, 3d c. B.C., notable Alexandrian poet of *Mimiambi,* mimes composed in the choliambic meter. He was a fine stylist who tended towards sketches of simple, ordinary life.

Herodes Atticus, Roman consul in A.D. 143, assigned (like Fronto) to educate Marcus Aurelius and Lucius Verus. He was a rich philanthropist and representative of the Second Sophistic.

Herodian, historian of the 3d c. A.D., author of a Roman history going from A.D. 180 to 238. The history is not very penetrating but useful, given the scarcity of sources for the period.

Herodian of Alexandria, 2d c. A.D., the last distinguished grammarian of the Alexandrian tradition.

Herodotus of Halicarnassus, 5th c. B.C., universally regarded as the "father of history" (the description is Cicero's). He had great influence (far more than Thucydides) on the tradition of ancient historiography.

Hesiod of Cyme (or "of Ascra," as he is designated much more often), ca. 8th and 7th c. B.C., considered the founder of didactic poetry *(Theogony, Works and Days, Eoiai)* and often set beside Homer. Studied and greatly revalued in the Alexandrian period, he directly influenced Roman poetry of the Augustan period, Virgil in particular.

Hipparchus, 2d c. B.C., perhaps the greatest astronomer of antiquity. His extraordinary authority, based on theories and discoveries that remain valid today, nonetheless had the negative consequence of causing the abandonment of the heliocentric theory, though it was widely held in Greek science: Hipparchus was a decided supporter of the theory that set the Earth at the center of the universe.

Hipponax, an iambic and parodic poet of the 6th c. B.C., well represented in papyrus fragments. He influenced Latin poetry, particularly Horace's *Odes* and *Epodes.*

Historia Apollonii Regis Tyrii, an anonymous late Roman novel (5th–6th c. A.D.) that presupposes a Greek original of the 2d–3d c. A.D., when the Greek novel had its greatest flourishing.

Homer, conventional name with which one indicates the author of the *Iliad* and the *Odyssey,* texts that are actually the cumulative result of various strata, though the original nucleus is commonly placed in the 8th c. B.C. His literary success was a constant in all of Roman literary history from Andronicus's version of the *Odyssey* onwards. Throughout the period of classical Latin he was a school author, and his immense popularity fell off only in the late period, when the study of Greek declined in the West. In the meantime substitute novels of his work establish themselves, "Troy Romances" like those of Dares the Phrygian and Dictys of Crete.

Hyperides, Attic orator of the 4th c. B.C., much admired (second only to Demosthenes) in the Greco-Roman oratorical tradition.

Iamblichus, 2d c. A.D., author of the novel *Babylonian Stories* (known solely from an epitome and fragments).

Ibycus of Rhegium, 6th c. B.C., lyric poet of Magna Graecia whose name is traditionally associated with that of **Stesichorus** (q.v.).

Iliad, Little, epic poem of the Trojan Cycle attributed to Lesches.

Iliupersis, epic poem of the Trojan Cycle attributed to Arctinus or Lesches. It was a source for the second book of Virgil's *Aeneid.*

Irenaeus of Lyon, 2d c. A.D., a father of the church and author of a *Confutation of the Heretics,* which is preserved in a Latin version.

Isocrates, 436–338 B.C., Athenian orator, central figure of his period and important for the development of oratory, prose writing in general, and education. He was an important presence in the ideal of *eloquentia,* developed by Cicero.

Josephus Flavius, 1st c. A.D., important historian of the Jews from their origins to the time of Nero and historian of the Jewish wars of Vespasian and Titus; he wrote a *Jewish War* in Greek, which was translated into Latin by the so-called Hegesippus. He was also the author of an attack on anti-Semitism, the *Contra Apionem.*

Julian, called **the Apostate,** Roman emperor from A.D. 360 to 363. The author of speeches and also of Menippean satires, he was the ascetic representative of a neo-Platonic, anti-Christian monotheism.

Leonidas of Tarentum, 3d c. B.C., admired as a poet of epigrams that were both realistic and sophisticated at the same time. Often considered the best Alexandrian epigrammatist, he was also imitated by the Roman poets (e.g., Propertius).

Lesches. *See Iliad, Little.*

Libanius of Antioch, 4th c. A.D., a phenomenally prolific rhetorician and prose writer and a friend of the emperor Julian. He left a vast collection of speeches and letters.

Lollianus, 2d c. A.D.?, author of a sensational adventure novel called *Phoinikika* (the papyrus fragments were published only in 1972), the closest example in Greek to what we call "commercial," or popular, fiction.

"Longinus," name transmitted, but probably in error, as that of the author of a fascinating literary treatise, the *Peri Hypsous* ("On the Sublime"), composed, it seems, in the first half of the 1st c. A.D. The work has a notable place in the history of modern as well as ancient esthetics.

Longus, 2d c. A.D., mysterious author of a charming novel in four books, *Daphnis and Chloe.* The work contains a subtle erotic atmosphere, a feeling for nature, and a relative scarcity of adventures and reversals of fortune. The whole is toned down to a Theocritus-like bucolic picture.

Lucian of Samosata, 2d c. A.D., rhetorician and storyteller in a delightfully humorous vein. He introduced new tendencies into dialogue, parody, and Menippean satire. In the corpus of his writings is found a work that is not by him but may derive from some lost narrative work of his, *Lucius, or the Ass,* which for us is evidence for the lost model of Apuleius's novel. *See also* **Lucius of Patrae.**

Lucillius, gifted epigrammatic poet of the Neronian era (A.D. 54–68), active at Rome too and a frequent model for Martial (occasional poems, jests, satiric epigram).

Lucius of Patrae, presumed author of a novel, *Metamorphoses.* The particulars agree with those of *Lucius, or the Ass,* attributed to **Lucian of Samosata** (q.v.), and the notice leads to the complicated problem of the sources of Apuleius's *Metamorphoses.*

Lycophron of Chalcis, poet of the 3d c. B.C. who wrote tragedies especially and was the representative of a difficult and hermetic Alexandrianism. Extant is the *Alexandra,* a large mythological poem in iambic trimeters that contains, among other things, a prophecy of Roman history (which some think is an interpolation, a prophecy *ex eventu* of the 1st c. B.C.).

Lydus, John, in the 6th c. A.D. a teacher of Latin at Constantinople. Some of his antiquarian works rely on good sources, including Roman ones, from the Republic and the Empire.

Lysias, Attic orator of the 5th–4th c. B.C. He was admired as a model of style, especially in the Hellenistic-Roman period, when Atticism brought back elegant simplicity.

Marcus Aurelius Antoninus, A.D. 121–80, Roman emperor. A Stoic thinker, he is important in the history of Greek literature for the twelve books of reflections *To Himself,* which he composed in the course of hard military campaigns.

Maximus of Tyre, 2d c. A.D., a sophist (i.e., traveling lecturer) active at Rome in the reign of Commodus.

Meleager of Gadara, 1st c. B.C., an epigrammatic and satiric poet who collected the first nucleus of what was to become the **Anthologia Palatina** (q.v.).

Menander, 342/341–291/290 B.C., the greatest poet of New Comedy, also the principal model of Latin comic drama and in particular of Plautus's *palliata (Bacchides, Cistellaria, Stichus, Aulularia)* and those of Caecilius and Terence *(Andria, Eunuchus, Heautontimoroumenos, Adelphoe).* The rediscovery of many papyrus fragments during this century made possible a new understanding of his art and produced several unexpected comparisons with the Roman transformations (especially of the *Dis Exapaton* with Plautus's *Bacchides).* His works are also important as models of love poetry and the novel, and in the florilegia of moral maxims *(sententiae).*

Menander of Laodicea, 3d c. A.D., Greek rhetorician and theoretical writer about the encomiastic genre of literature. The Latin panegyrists were inspired by him.

Menippus of Gadara, 3d c. B.C., a freed slave, a Cynic philosopher important in the history of the diatribe, and the founder of a satiric genre that (through Varro's *Menippean Satires*) is indissolubly linked to his name. He was the first, we are told, to experiment with satiric forms mixing prose and verse (cf. Petronius and the *Apocolocyntosis*), and in the 2d c. A.D. he still influenced **Lucian of Samosata** (q.v.).

Mimnermus of Colophon, an elegiac poet of the 7th c. B.C. He dealt with various subjects, but he is famous in the Hellenistic-Roman period chiefly as a love poet, a precursor of true love elegy.

Moschus of Syracuse, 2d c. B.C., Alexandrian poet of bucolic subjects and author of the epyllion *Europa.* He is one of the minor models of neoteric and bucolic Roman poetry in the 1st c. B.C.

Musonius Rufus of Volsinii, 1st c. A.D., Stoic philosopher, teacher of Epictetus and many Romans. He had difficult relations with Nero and Vespasian.

Nechepso and **Petosiris,** shadowy Egyptian priests under whose name an important astrological text circulated from the 2d c. B.C. on.

Neoptolemus of Parium, end of the 4th c. B.C., a poet and grammarian who wrote two epic poems (one on Dionysus) and various grammatical works, among them a *Poetica,* which is one of the models of Horace's *Ars Poetica.*

Nicander of Colophon, probably 2d c. B.C., important Alexandrian poet of didactic epic. His *Theriaka* (on poisonous serpents and animals) and *Alexipharmaka* ("Antidotes") are extant. The titles of various lost works (*Metamorphoses, Georgics,* and a poem on bees) suggest that he was used by Latin poets of the first rank (Virgil, Ovid, Aemilius Macer).

Nicolaus of Damascus, 1st c. B.C., a prolific author and historian of the court of Herod the Great. He is known above all for a laudatory biography of Augustus and an immense universal history.

Ninus, Romance of, perhaps 2d c. B.C., known in papyrus fragments, the earliest Greek novel now known and the one most closely tied to the historical-biographical tradition.

Nonnus of Panopolis, perhaps 5th c. A.D., author of the very long epic *Dionysiaka* and for us, along with Claudian, the chief figure of late antique epic. He makes intense use of Alexandrian (and Roman, according to some) mythological poetry.

Oppian, 2d–3d c. A.D., perhaps identical with **Oppian of Apamea** (q.v.). He wrote a didactic poem on fishing.

Oppian of Apamea, 2d c. A.D. He dedicated to Caracalla a didactic poem on hunting, in four books.

Origen, Christian theologian of the 3d c. A.D., to whom is owed the first great attempt to organize a solid philosophical and theological thought based on Scripture and the ecclesiastical tradition. His theories, imbued with Platonism and neo-Platonism, had great influence on Christian speculation, Greek and Latin, but they were also the cause of heated controversies (including a famous dispute between Rufinus, an admirer and follower of Origen, and Jerome, who came to regard Origen's position as heretical).

Panaetius of Rhodes, a Stoic philosopher of the 2d c. B.C., active at Rome as well as in the Greek world. He was closely tied to Scipio Aemilianus and the cultural milieu that is usually called the "Scipionic circle." He was a crucial figure in the ideological revival of Roman culture from the 2d to the 1st c. B.C. and a model for Cicero, especially in the essay *De Officiis.*

Parmenides of Elea, a philosopher of the 5th c. B.C., important for a didactic poem in hexameters, which contributed to the tradition of the didactic genre.

Parthenius of Nicaea, a Roman prisoner of war during the Third Mithridatic War. He arrived at Rome in 73 B.C. and then had a crucial role in making Alexandrian poetic taste better known. His relations with Gallus and Virgil are attested. He composed mythological elegies in the tradition of Callimachus and Euphorion and also a prose collection of rare love myths (*Erotika Pathemata*), dedicated to the love poet Cornelius Gallus for his use.

Paul of Tarsus, 1st c. A.D., commonly known as St. Paul, the greatest propagator of the Christian message in the Hellenistic-Roman world. His *Letters,* of capital importance for the formation of Christian theology, were variously translated into Latin.

Phanocles, Alexandrian poet, 3d–2d c. B.C., who composed elegies on the pederastic loves of mythological figures.

Philemon, 4th–3d c. B.C., great poet of Attic New Comedy. He was very much imitated at Rome and very entertaining (he was Plautus's model in *Mercator, Trinummus,* and probably *Mostellaria*).

Philinus of Agrigentum, 3d c. B.C., pro-Carthaginian historian and a source of Polybius for the First Punic War.

Philitas, or **Philetas, of Cos,** 4th–3d c. B.C., famous Alexandrian poet of mythological-erotic elegies. He is often cited by the Latin elegiac poets as a forerunner, along with Callimachus, of the true elegiac tradition.

Philo of Larissa, 2d–1st c. B.C., Academic philosopher active at Rome as well as in Greece. One of Cicero's teachers, he was used by Cicero as a source in some philosophical works (*Academica Priora, Lucullus,* etc.).

Philodemus of Gadara, 1st c. B.C., Epicurean philosopher active at Herculaneum and Naples. His instructional works are well represented in the papyri from Herculaneum and are among the principal sources for the Epicurean school. He was probably connected to Virgil, who from his youth frequented the Epicurean milieus of Naples. He was also significant as an epigrammatic love poet. He participated in Roman public life, and he may have influenced Varius Rufus's *De Morte.*

Philostratus, name borne by several members of a family of writers of the 2d–3d c. A.D. who are difficult to distinguish from one another. Among the works transmitted under this name, especially interesting are the *Life of Apollonius of Tyana,* a novelistic and hagiographic biography of a man who lived in the 1st–2d c. A.D. (see entry for him above), and the *Images,* rhetorical exercises in description, applied to works of art.

Phlegon of Tralles, 2d c. A.D., freedman of Hadrian who collected notices of Roman antiquities and *mirabilia* from various peoples.

Phocylides of Miletus, 6th c. B.C., elegiac poet of a didactic-moralizing approach, close to **Hesiod of Cyme** and **Theognis of Megara** (qq.v.). He was very popular in the following centuries.

Phrynichus, Athenian poet of the 6th–5th c. B.C., considered one of the founders of tragedy. He staged the *Capture of Miletus* only a couple of years after the event itself.

Phylarchus, historian of the 3d c. B.C. who lived at Athens. He was the author of a work narrating events from 272 to 220 B.C. He gave much room to pursuing effects and displaying his rhetorical skill. He was a source of Polybius and Plutarch (who pass a severe judgment on him, however) and, among the Latins, of Pompeius Trogus and (to some extent) Livy.

Physiologus, anonymous collection of marvels of natural history perhaps from the 2d c. A.D. It was later translated into Latin *(Physiologus)* and was extremely popular in the Middle Ages.

Pindar of Cynoscephalae, 518–438 B.C., the greatest Greek choral lyric poet. He was very much studied in the Alexandrian age and had a fitful influence—his style was justly regarded as inimitable—on Augustan poetry (Virgil and especially Horace in the *Odes*).

Plato, 427–347 B.C., the extremely famous Athenian philosopher who influenced Roman culture both through his own writings and through the evolution of his school, the Academy.

Plotinus, A.D. 205–70, the founder of neo-Platonism and author of a large number of extant works. He was long active at Rome, where he inspired an intellectual circle. From him arises the pagan philosophy that was to be dominant in the

Roman world down to the total suppression of the non-Christian centers of study in the 5th c.

Plutarch of Chaeronea, 1st–2d c. A.D., author of ethical and religious writings and biographer. He shows in his *Parallel Lives* (paired biographies of illustrious Greeks and Romans) a tendency to balance the recognition of the successes of Rome with the recovery of the ancient Greek historical heritage. His *Quaestiones Romanae* is a valuable repertory of Roman antiquities.

Pollux, sophist of the 2d c. A.D., active at Athens. He left us an encyclopedic compilation of notable interest especially for the history of theatrical antiquities.

Polybius of Megalopolis, 2d c. B.C., famous as a historian for his intelligent analysis of Rome's rise to global power. Achaean ambassador to Rome, and later included among the thousand Achaean hostages who after the defeat of Pydna were handed over to the Romans, he was close to Scipio Aemilianus and his cultural milieu. His *Histories,* which cover the period 220–146 B.C. (from Hannibal to the destruction of Carthage), are a vital source for the later Greek and Roman historians (e.g., Livy among the preserved historians).

Porphyry of Tyre, 3d c. A.D., a pupil of Plotinus at Rome and editor of his works. His vast philosophical-religious writings contributed powerfully to the spread of neo-Platonism.

Posidippus of Cassandrea, 3d c. B.C., a minor poet of New Comedy who seems to have been taken up by the Roman comic poets.

Posidonius of Apamea, 2d–1st c. B.C., philosopher and scientist. He spent a number of years at Rome and exercised a profound influence upon Cicero; he also affected the most varied poets, thinkers, historians, and naturalists of the period of Caesar, Augustus, and the early Empire. He wrote important *Histories,* from the end of Polybius (146 B.C.) to the dictatorship of Sulla, which took well-defined positions in the Roman political and ideological debate.

Pseudo-Callisthenes, linked to the name of Callisthenes (the historian of Alexander, 4th c. B.C.) by the late tradition of the *Romance of Alexander,* represented in Latin by Julius Valerius (3d c. A.D.).

Ptolemy, Claudius, 2d c. A.D., under the Empire the greatest authority on astronomy and geography. In later ages his name remained linked to the geocentric conception of **Hipparchus** (q.v.); he was important also as a source for astrological notions *(Tetrabiblos).* He was also popular in Arabic translation *(Almagest).*

Quintus of Smyrna, epic poet of the 4th c. A.D. He composed in fourteen books a continuation of the *Iliad (Posthomerica),* which presupposes many literary sources, Greek and perhaps also Latin (Virgil, Ovid).

Rhianus of Crete, epic poet of the 3d c. B.C. who composed many poems on historical subjects (themes of war, geographic and ethnographic themes). The genre probably influenced the formation of the Latin historical epic.

Rhinthon of Tarentum, 3d c. B.C. He distinguished himself in a comic genre, labeled in various ways ("hilarotragedy," Phlyax farce, or later, *fabula Rhinthonica*), that was based on crude parodies of tragic subjects and may have influenced the development of Italian farce and the Roman comic theater.

Sappho of Lesbos, 7th–6th c. B.C., famous poetess whose Aeolic language and meters made her an object of study for the Alexandrians, who collected the texts in a standard edition. She is a living presence in Catullus's love poetry (the epithalamia, poems 61 and 62, and the inspired recreation of poem 51; the name Lesbia is another indication of her influence), then in Horace's lyrics and in Ovid, who in one of the *Heroides* bases himself on the rich tradition of biographical legends that grew up around Sappho.

Satyrus of Callatis, 3d c. B.C., a grammarian and scholar of Peripatetic tendency who played an important part in the formation of the biographical genre that was later taken up at Rome.

Septuagint, the translation of the sacred scriptures from Hebrew and Aramaic into Greek, done by several hands at different times and completed, it seems, before the beginning of the Christian era. The work, which owes its name to a supposed original commission of seventy, or seventy-two, Hebrew scholars, very soon became the road of access to the Old Testament for Greek-speaking Christians. Until Jerome, the Latin versions were based on this text, without direct use of the original Semitic languages.

Sibylline Oracles, collections in hexameters of Sibylline responses, circulated repeatedly in Greco-Roman antiquity. A famous legend tells that the king of Rome, Tarquinius Priscus, entrusted a copy, which became the official one, to a suitable Roman priestly college. This "official" collection was several times destroyed and forged anew. The collection we possess is a late compilation, interpolated with Jewish-Hellenistic and Christian materials.

Simias of Rhodes, 4th c. B.C., versifier and grammarian known chiefly as the initiator of the *technopaegnia,* poems like *The Egg,* which graphically mimic the shape of the object to be described.

Simonides of Ceos, 6th–5th c. B.C., lyric and elegiac poet admired for his style and sentiments. Some of his tones survive in Horace's lyric poetry.

Siro, 1st c. B.C., Epicurean philosopher active in Naples. The young Virgil belonged to his circle. Cicero, who said he was his friend, praised the richness of Siro's learning.

Solon of Athens, 7th–6th c. B.C., great legislator and politician. He was also an elegiac poet who wrote political and ethical verse.

Sophocles, 497–406 B.C., the model of tragic style in Roman poetry. Many adaptations from Sophocles can be pointed to with some certainty, despite the small number of Sophoclean tragedies that have reached us entire (seven) and the fragmentary state of archaic Roman tragedy. The Roman use of Euripides' "modern" theater, however, is even more extensive.

Sophron of Syracuse, 5th c. B.C., apparently the first poet to give regular form to the "realistic" and everyday tradition of the mime.

Sotades of Maronea, 3d c. B.C., an iambic poet who invented the sotadean verse and developed a genre of free-and-easy epic parody. He was taken up by Ennius in the *Sota* and influenced a tradition of comic drama performed by effeminate men *(kinaidologoi).*

Stesichorus, 6th c. B.C. He left a much-admired collection of lyric poems on narrative subjects and influenced the revival of mythological poetry.

Strabo of Amasea, 1st c. B.C.–1st c. A.D., the greatest authority of his day in the field of geography. His historical work is lost, but his geographical work is preserved. He is distinguished for his pro-Roman cultural orientation.

Suda, a Byzantine dictionary of an encyclopedic nature compiled in the 10th c. A.D. It is a veritable mine of information on classical literature.

Teles, 3d c. B.C., Cynic philosopher, popularizing representative of the diatribe tradition, which would influence Latin satire and philosophy.

Terpander of Antissa (on the island of Lesbos), 7th c. B.C., the almost mythic progenitor of the melic poetry of **Sappho of Lesbos** and **Alcaeus of Mytilene** (qq.v.).

Theocritus, 3d c. B.C., principal model of Greek and Latin bucolic poetry. His verse circulated in the 1st c. B.C. in editions published by Alexandrian scholars, who were probably also active at Rome. His collection of thirty idylls (as the grammarians call the individual poems), after various minor attempts at pastoral poetry, inspired the *Bucolics* of Virgil; these, together with Theocritus's originals, fixed the basic shape of the European pastoral tradition.

Theognis of Megara, elegiac poet of the 6th c. B.C., author of a collection of poems in elegiac couplets (the so-called *Sylloge*) that poses various problems on account of the heterogeneity of the poems that make it up; the chief nucleus consists of moral precepts given to a young man, Cyrnus.

Theon, Aelius, 1st–2d c. A.D., rhetorician and author of the oldest collection of *progymnasmata,* rhetorical exercises, to have reached us. The collection is important for the history of rhetoric and declamation.

Theophanes of Mytilene, 1st c. B.C., political adviser to Pompey and historian (of questionable objectivity) of his undertakings.

Theophrastus, 4th–3d c. B.C., the successor of Aristotle. He enjoyed a vast renown chiefly for his scientific writings, which are, for instance, among the principal sources, direct and indirect, of the *Naturalis Historia.* He is also present, as a "pure" philosopher, in Cicero and Seneca.

Thucydides, 5th c. B.C., the most highly valued ancient historian but not necessarily the one most followed. His example of historiography is difficult to imitate, on account of both the profundity of his treatment of the problems and his very personal style. Herodotus and Isocrates had a wider influence, in Rome as in Greece.

Timaeus of Tauromenium, 4th–3d c. B.C., author of a *History* in thirty-eight books, from the Greek origins to the beginning of the First Punic War. He was much esteemed and much used, at least until the 1st c. A.D., especially as a source for Sicilian history and for Italian history in general.

Timagenes, 1st c. B.C., rhetorician and historian, and personal friend of Pollio. He wrote a *History of the Kings* that was used by Pompeius Trogus.

Tyrannio the Elder, 1st c. B.C., grammarian of the Alexandrian school brought to Rome by Lucullus. Important as a teacher, he was a friend of Cicero, Caesar, and Atticus, and he took an interest in Latin as well as Greek. He was concerned with the Greek manuscripts brought to Rome by Sulla (including the works of Aristotle).

Tyrannio the Younger, 1st c. B.C., freedman of Cicero's widow, a Greek grammarian active at Rome and, among other things, the teacher of Strabo.

Tyrtaeus of Sparta, 7th c. B.C., poet of warlike elegies and thus the initiator, along with **Callinus of Ephesus** (q.v.), of one strand of Greek elegy.

Xenophanes of Colophon, 6th c. B.C., an original poet-philosopher who distinguished himself especially for his polemical poetry (called *Silloi*), which contained critical revisions of mythology and traditional theology.

Xenophon, 5th–4th c. B.C. He reached the apogee of his popularity in the Roman period, not so much in his capacity as a historian as in his capacity as a narrator and popularizer of ethical-political ideals, employing a style of thought that was practical and respectful of the constituted powers. Cicero and Sallust show in various ways the effect of his approach.

Xenophon of Ephesus, probably 2d c. A.D., author of the erotic novel *Ephesiaka*.

Zeno of Citium, philosopher of the 4th–3d c. B.C., founder of the Stoa. He is important above all for his ethical doctrines (Stoicism).

Zeno of Sidon, 2d–1st c. B.C., an Epicurean philosopher. He had Cicero as an auditor (who used him in the *De Natura Deorum*) and Philodemus of Gadara as a pupil.

Zenodotus of Ephesus, 4th–3d c. B.C., Alexandrian philologist. He was the first director of the Library of Alexandria and one of the pioneers of Homeric exegesis.

Zoilus of Amphipolis, 4th c. B.C., Cynic thinker known especially for his attacks against Plato and even against Homer, which won him the nickname *Homeromastix,* "Scourge of Homer."

Zosimus, 5th–6th c. A.D., pagan historian of the Empire from Augustus to 410.

Appendix 3 Roman Culture: Politics, Society, Ideology

Abstinentia *See* **System of the virtues**.

Ambitio / ambitus The term derives from *ambire* ("go about," hence "solicit," almost "court") and designates the means by which a politician obtains the *gratia* ("favor" and therefore "influence") that is necessary for his activity. *Ambire* soon took on the special sense of the "round of the electorate" made by the candidate for a magistracy in order to solicit support for upcoming elections. *Ambitio* is a normal activity for the Romans, and Cicero, for one, defends its legitimacy; despite this, the term increasingly takes on a pejorative connotation, and in Sallust, for instance, it almost always designates a behavior that is marked by a demagogic passion for popularity and thus is blameworthy as a source of corruption. Originally *ambitus* does not seem to have been distinguished in meaning from *ambitio,* but in the last century of the Republic *ambitio* took on a general and abstract value, while *ambitus* indicated more concretely the various forms of electoral corruption and thus became a technical term of jurisprudence; hence the various laws *de ambitu,* which tried to oppose corruption.

Amicitia The concept of friendship (in Greek, *philia*) developed by Greek philosophical thought (especially Plato, Aristotle, Epicurus) involves more than anything the affective relation, established on an ethical basis, that obtains between two persons. The practice of Roman *amicitia,* however, is radically different and cannot be understood without keeping in mind the conditions under which the **political struggle** (q.v.) in the Republic took place. The Roman politician is primarily the head of a faction who makes use of a vast network of family and personal relations for the purpose of obtaining offices and furthering his own supporters. Thus *amicitia* and *inimicitia* in Roman society are often, not relations between private individuals, but situations codified and almost institutionalized: *amicitia* binds individuals of like social status together in power groups (whereas **clientela** subordinates the individuals from the lower classes to individuals from the ruling classes). It is important to note that the concept also finds an application in the field of international law, where one uses *amicus populi Romani* to define a people, or its leader, which has chosen to place itself within the political orbit of the Empire.

From early times, almost from the age of the Scipios, Roman intellectuals began to be disturbed by the inadequacy of this model of friendship when it was compared with the new sensibility that the refinement of manners and the penetration of Greek philosophy had helped to foster. The tendency emerged with difficulty, since the need for disinterested and satisfying friendships, that is, ones based on similarity of manners, moral choices, tastes, clashed with the need not to lose the political aspect of *amicitia,* which was an important cement of the ruling classes. Cicero's *Laelius de Amicitia* is the most significant attempt to resolve these divergent tendencies.

Auctoritas / dignitas The notion of *auctoritas*—the word is part of the oldest legal and religious stock in the Latin lexicon: cf. *augere, auctor, augur, augustus*—expresses the ability to exercise a leading function in political life through one's own influence or one's ancestry. It is based on a complex of factors: family traditions, personal qualities, the experience acquired with age, material power, the extent and strength of the bonds of **amicitia** and **clientela,** and so on. *Auctoritas* increases with military undertakings, but it grows especially in proportion as one advances along the **cursus honorum.** From the point of view of the one who acknowledges it and submits to it, *auctoritas* is based on the conviction that he who wields it possesses qualities that render him worthy to play a leading role; it presupposes a voluntary allegiance and submission, based on the relationship of **fides.** Thus *auctoritas* usually is not expressed through commands, but through advice and opinion (*sententia* is the technical term for the advice expressed in the Senate; *consilium* is the general word) or even through exemplary behavior, which others feel themselves bound to imitate.

The concept of *dignitas,* closely connected to that of *auctoritas,* expresses not only the right to have one's eminence recognized but, at the same time, the complex of obligations, governed by **fides,** that follow from it. For the Roman aristocrat, it is a duty and a point of honor to try to maintain and enhance his own *dignitas,* defending it against the attacks of those who would challenge it. Thus Caesar claimed to have started the civil war chiefly in order to safeguard his own *dignitas;* his story showed how this ideal of pursuing *dignitas* could conceal within itself the risk of elevating the individual above the state. Some, like Cicero, would try to take appropriate cautionary measures, indicating the necessity that the *dignitas* of the members of the aristocracy should not be put ahead of that of the Senate and the *res publica.*

Boni The term *bonus,* which in its political meaning originally designates the aristocratic landowners, who are distinguished by their military valor, undergoes a significant enlargement especially in Cicero's political thought. In his usage, the *boni* are the members of the well-to-do classes, who have taken the side of defending the constitutional order and are hostile to the agitations of the **populares.** The term thus takes on a moral as well as a political-social connotation: *bonus* is the man who has ethical qualities that oppose the *furor* of the subversives and who at the same time owns property that is threatened by that *furor.* The *bonus* is inspired by *iustitia* in everything he does; he possesses **fides** and the other qualities that a member of the ruling class needs in order to exercise political or administrative functions; he never wavers in support for the policy of the Senate. Towards the end of the Republic, therefore, the term *boni* indicated essentially the members of a middle class, which included levels of the senatorial order, the equestrian class, and the upper levels of the populace, and which found itself in the middle between the greater senatorial families of the **nobilitas** and the poorest of the plebs.

Clientela *See* **Patronage.**
Cognomen *See* **Gens.**
Comitas / severitas *Comitas* indicates an attitude of amiable and smiling courtesy, of complete agreeableness in relation with others. It often appears aimed at the winning of approval. Equally often, it is a behavior that is not practiced on an equal footing with its

recipient but instead "descends" from the man of higher social status to the man of lower social status; for example, it is the way of acting that distinguishes certain military leaders in relation to their soldiers. *Comitas* is part of the cluster of "modern" values that emerge with the culture of **humanitas** and **urbanitas**. The archaizing tradition of the **mos maiorum** evidently prefers an attitude of *severitas* in relation to inferior individuals or social groups: austere, stern strictness and an inflexibility in regard to oneself as much as to others. Traditionalists, not without reason, see concealed within *comitas* the dangers of demagoguery and subversion: going along with the wishes of the people and the soldiers may serve to create a personal power based on a mass following of a sort that could endanger the institutions of society. And yet, at least from the last decades of the *res publica* on, the path of *severitas* proves to be hardly practicable, since it is based on a purely repressive idea of domination; it threatens to destroy the hegemony of the ruling class, which is rooted in the consent of the lower classes. The need to temper the opposing demands is expressed in several ethical formulations that were especially dear to Cicero and other authors of the time, such as *comitas non sine severitate* or *comitate condita gravitas*.

Concordia ordinum	*See* **Senatus.**
Consilium	*See* **Auctoritas.**
Constantia	*See* **System of the virtues.**
Cursus honorum	The term indicates the order in which the different Roman magistracies are

held; after the preliminary military service, the usual sequence was quaestorship, praetorship, consulate, censorship. If one held the tribunate of the plebs or the aedileship, this normally occurred after the quaestorship. For a combination of reasons, neither the tribunate nor the aedileship was made obligatory. At the beginning of the second century B.C., having held the praetorship was a necessary prerequisite for the consulate. The skipping of the quaestorship, which was already quite unusual, was prohibited by Sulla. In 180 B.C. the *lex Villia annalis* regulated the *cursus honorum* still more strictly. A yet more binding scheme was put into effect at the beginning of the principate, when the vigintivirate became a prerequisite for the quaestorship, and the military tribunate was usually held between these two magistracies. The office of provincial governor and the new nonmagisterial offices, such as *praefectus* or *curator,* were usually held at fixed points in this overall scheme.

Decorum	*See* **System of the virtues.**
Dignitas	*See* **Auctoritas.**
Equites	*See* **Senatus.**
Existimatio	*See* **Gloria.**
Fides	It is likely that the original idea of *fides* was legal ("guarantee") rather than

moral; yet although the concept would always have a great importance in the field of law, the moral idea would become predominant in the system of Roman values, in which *fides* would play a central role. In very general terms, *fides* can be defined as the value that establishes and assures the relation between two parties, the "trust" of one in the other. Although always based on the reciprocity of the commitment, *fides* takes on different characteristics and contents according to the status of the two parties. It thus maintains relations between equals (as in marriage, in **amicitia,** in international alliances and treaties, and in all legal relations generally); yet the relation can also be asymmetrical, as in **patronage** (the *patronus* must not fail in his obligations to protect the client, and the *cliens* must lend his services and show the proper devotion to his patron), between victor and vanquished (the victor who accepts the surrender commits himself to moderation and clemency), between hegemonic state and client state, and so on.

Because of its role in the Roman system of thought, the concept was also given religious sanction. A tradition attributes to Numa Pompilius the introduction of the cult of *Fides* as a divinity; a temple was erected to her in the third century B.C. on the Capitoline beside the temple of Jupiter.

Frugalitas

The term, which derives from *frux*, properly indicates the style of life of the diligent farmer who lives from the fruits of his own harvest. As the early rural traditions grew more remote from Rome and as society was transformed by the influx of wealth and luxury goods, the concept of *frugalitas* came to form part of the **mos maiorum**. People began to see in it the model that needed to be restored if the crisis of the *res publica* was to be resolved; they celebrated the example of commanders such as Cincinnatus, who went from plowing to warfare and then returned to plowing. While the *homo frugi ac diligens* acquired normative character in legal literature as a criterion by which to evaluate someone's ability to administer an estate, Cicero in his philosophical work strove to modernize the concept of *frugalitas* by assimilating it to Greek ethical concepts. *Frugalitas* slowly became primarily an inner attitude, retaining only a dim echo of its rural origins and no longer designating a concrete style of life, a process brought to completion in certain passages of Seneca's *Epistles*.

Gens

According to the theory that is most widely accepted today, the *gens* ("household" or "clan"; the term is etymologically connected with *gignere*) was the set of family groups that recognized themselves as linked by descent from a common ancestor. At Rome every citizen had a personal name *(praenomen)*; a *nomen*, which denoted the *gens* to which he belonged; and a *cognomen*, which indicated the family or group of families within the *gens*—for instance, Publius *(praenomen)* Cornelius *(nomen)* Scipio *(cognomen)*. From the earliest times, the *gens* had religious rites *(sacra)* in common and possessed a common place of burial. Closely tied to the *gens* by the relation of **patronage**, but not full members of it, were the *clientes*. The theory is no longer accepted that at the origins of the Roman state the plebeians were the clients of the patricians; the division between plebeians and patricians probably originated in distinctions of rank and wealth, and, like the patricians, the plebeians were themselves organized in *gentes*, and, like them, they had *clientes*.

The *gentes* never had an official role in the state and never performed specific public or political tasks, apart from supervising various cults and ceremonies. Nonetheless, given the conditions under which the **political struggle** was waged at Rome, the *gentes* came to play a very important political and social role outside the institutions: their extensive connections and client relations allowed them to control segments of the citizenry and secured ample support for those who undertook a political career. Dynastic marriages between members of different *gentes* had the character of a political alliance.

Gloria / existimatio

According to the principles of the **mos maiorum,** the political or military *virtus* of the Roman aristocrat demanded recognition by his fellow citizens, and this recognition was, so to speak, the reward for it; this is the traditional concept of *gloria*. It was almost a hereditary possession of the great families, transmitted across generations and increasing or diminishing depending on whether the individual proved himself equal to his ancestors or not. The concept of *gloria* experienced a grave crisis with the upheavals of the last century of the *res publica*, when it became evident that recognition from the collectivity—which is the content of the *gloria*—was too often owed to the demagogic skills of those who fawned on the people in order to create a mass base for a personal, potentially abusive power. To Cicero principally is due the distinction between *vera* and *falsa* (or *popularis*) *gloria*: *vera gloria* was the heritage of the few who in their political action remained faithful to the ideals that had made Rome great in the past; they were indifferent to the opinion of the many and were inclined to brave the dislike of a corrupt populace. The traditional concept of *gloria* finally became empty in the *Somnium Scipionis* at the end of the *De Republica,* where transient earthly glory is derided as a petty aspiration and instead the metaphorical reward of heavenly bliss is held out to those politicians who in their lives pursued the ideal of greatness for their country.

Gloria, linked especially to political and military achievements, remains a prerogative of the ruling aristocracy. The term *existimatio* is used to express the general notion of "good repute," which can be applied in various fields and arises particularly from the diligence shown in a demanding commitment, for example, in the activity of a lawyer or even in many economic or semi-economic activities, such as the care of one's personal affairs, at which Cicero's friend Atticus excelled.

Gravitas

The term *gravitas* ("weight") combines within itself a series of meanings. Externally it is manifested in a dignified attitude, composed of seriousness, reserve, and self-control before unforeseen circumstances. In regard to intellect, it designates the knowledge of life and human affairs that derives from years of experience. In regard to ethics, it describes a conduct of life that is marked by dignity, austerity, and moral strictness. In this last sense the term is close to **severitas,** which describes more specifically the exterior aspect of an austere and strict person, one who lacks all inclination to pleasure or happiness. *Gravitas* presupposes harmony between one's actions and inmost sentiments, that is, the steady agreement with one's conscience and the unquestioned loyalty to one's principles that are expressed in the concept of *constantia.*

Humanitas

The concept of *humanitas* may have some roots in Athenian culture, but it is for the most part a Roman development. Even before the term *humanitas* was coined, some of the fundamental ideas that would form part of it found ample resonance in the Scipionic age, especially in the plays of Terence and the literary works of Lucilius. But the notion of *humanitas* was developed chiefly in the culture of the last decades of the Republic, by Cicero more than anyone else. In his writings *humanitas* was a style that distinguished the more open members of the aristocracy, and it took shape as a set of refined manners, tact, sensitivity, and literary education. For these aristocrats *humanitas* was deployed especially in private life, when they were at leisure from their duties towards the state; but it also had an important role in the behavior of those (e.g., the Atticus portrayed by Cornelius Nepos) who chose to refrain from public life in order to devote themselves exclusively to their own private interests. *Humanitas* brings grace and easy dealings with others; it thus helps to smooth every kind of relation between persons.

Under the Empire, the concept of *humanitas* acquired a new content, which in the end modified its meaning radically. Now *humanitas* corresponded to Greek *philanthropia* ("love for mankind"), a quality that characterized the indulgent, paternalistic relation of the **princeps** or his officials to the citizens and the peoples subject to the imperial administration.

Imperator	*See* **Princeps.**
Industria	*See* **System of the virtues.**
Inimicitia	*See* **Amicitia.**
Largitio	*See* **Liberalitas.**

Liberalitas	The term originally characterized the style of life suitable to the free man, as opposed to the slave. Soon, however, to this general meaning (for which an approximate translation might be "courtliness") was added the more specialized one of "generosity" or "munificence." *Liberalitas* often presupposes a position of superiority towards the recipient of the kindness; it is expressed, for instance, in being responsible for the debts of relatives, friends, or even clients and in committing one's credit and prestige in order to assist persons of one's circle. Yet the term may also designate a typically political and purposeful generosity, used to win the favor and support of the recipient. Then it became almost a synonym of *largitio,* which was more often used when one wanted to indicate a corrupting, demagogic generosity, like that of the candidates for office towards those who might vote for them (organization of festivals, games, and spectacles; distribution of money and basic necessities).
Magnitudo animi	*See* **System of the virtues.**
Metus hostilis	This is a concept the most consistent use of which is found in Sallust's historical works (though recently its strong presence has been identified in Varro as well), but it is far older at Rome, going back to the culture of the Scipionic age, and it probably has roots in Greek thought. It identifies one of the chief reasons why the crisis of the *res publica* came about and why the bloody civil wars flared up in the very midst of the peace and prosperity that followed the victory over Carthage: after that victory there was no longer that "fear of external enemies" that had long compelled the Roman citizens to remain united for their common salvation. In origin, the concept of *metus hostilis* was a political weapon in the hands of noble groups who were opposed to a policy of Mediterranean expansion that seemed excessively radical to them (and that was probably favored by the commercial and financial classes, who wanted the great competing commercial centers in the Mediterranean to be suppressed). We know that after his victory over Hannibal, Scipio Africanus tried to halt that policy—which called for peace on very harsh terms— with the argument that the presence of a strong adversary would preserve in the Romans the fear that was required to keep them on the path of prudence and order and to prevent them from growing arrogant by virtue of their prosperity. The concept was used again by Scipio Nasica in controversy with Cato on the eve of the Third Punic War, when the suitability of decisively destroying Carthage was under discussion. The aristocratic groups opposed to radical expansionism probably had a presentiment that such a policy, in a more or less distant future, would put an end to the domination of the oligarchy; in their fear of this outcome, they may have preferred to continue sharing the domination of the Mediterranean with other oligarchies.
	Moving away from its historical origins, the concept of *metus hostilis* becomes a commonplace of moral historiography and a universal key to interpreting the crisis of the *res publica*. The *Histories* of Sallust himself (where the pessimism is greater than in his earlier monographs), although they retain the idea of the *metus Punicus,* identify an earlier element of the crisis in the loss of the *metus hostilis* towards the Etruscans, which led to the breaking out of discord between patricians and plebeians and thus to the first injuries to the citizen body.
Mos maiorum	Roman culture shows, with few exceptions, a constant veneration of the "custom of the ancestors." The moral and intellectual heritage of the tradition is regarded as the base on which Rome's very power as an empire rests. As for its content, the *mos maiorum* is a jumble of concepts, values, and traditional usages; they are sometimes diverse and even contradictory in origin and meaning, but they all agree in

the fundamental purpose of halting any innovation whatever (which traditionalist thought regards as the result of capriciousness and as a potential threat to the solidarity of the constituted order). Hence the predominantly negative connotation of words such as *novus, novitas,* and so on, in the Roman ethical-political vocabulary; the expression *rebus novis studere,* for instance, indicates the activity of those planning to overthrow the state.

The traditionalism expressed in the *mos maiorum* is essentially that of archaic agrarian society: ethical concepts such as *industria, labor, pudor,* **pietas, frugalitas,** and so on, have their roots in this. On account of the revolution in customs brought on by imperial expansion and the influx of wealth, these concepts were soon on a collision course with the newer, more modern values, connected to the needs of an affluent society, that were trying to establish themselves. In fact, a head-on collision with the *mos maiorum* never took place. The modern morality did not put itself forward as a radical alternative to the old; rather, it attempted to bring it up to date by preserving some fundamental aspects. This is even true for that area of Roman cultural production—neoteric and elegiac poetry—in which the beginnings of impatience and of challenge to the *mos maiorum* are felt in the liveliest way. Cicero attempted to compromise in another way: he selected and carefully filtered elements of Greek thought, purging them of the most dangerously enlightened aspects, and strove to set them in the cultural complex of the *mos maiorum;* his aim was to modernize it without shaking its foundations as the guarantor of social stability.

Negotium / otium

The term *negotium* indicates basically the time and the activities devoted to the service of the state: politics, oratory (which is the tool of politics), and military service. *Otium* designates the time free from these commitments; and naturally there are more and less dignified ways for a member of the ruling class to fill his *otium*. Abandoning oneself to unmanly or indolent forms of inactivity is expressed by *ignavia, inertia, socordia,* or *desidia*. Roman culture attaches greater importance to those forms of *otium* that preserve some more or less indirect connection to *negotium* and that permit, for example, the intellectual understanding of the activity that is realized in the *negotia*. A good way for the politician to employ his *otium* was to devote himself to historiography; yet Cicero had difficulty in justifying to his fellow citizens philosophical thought, even though it preserved an organic link with the ethical-political problems of the *res publica*.

Nobilitas

The term indicates the few families that under the Republic constituted the oligarchy which in effect governed Rome (*nobiles* = "persons well known" for their important role in the state). After the plebeians had obtained complete legal equality with the patricians, this oligarchy comprised families of both plebeian and patrician origin, though the patricians were fewer in number, and patrician status conferred extra social distinction. The families of the *nobilitas* held a kind of monopoly on the magistracies: given the conditions under which the **political struggle** took place in Rome, their network of **clientelae** and **amicitiae** gave them a large advantage in elections.

Although never given strictly legal codification, the term *nobilis* in the end took on an increasingly exclusive meaning: in the last century of the Republic, it referred only to those who had consuls among their ancestors; that is, it was not sufficient that they had held lower magistracies, such as the praetorship. Although the nobility tended to regard the consulate as a prerogative of their own, to be jealously guarded, from time to time a **novus homo** of senatorial origin or, more rarely, of nonsenatorial origin (e.g., Cicero) succeeded in winning the supreme magistracy, usually thanks to the support of factions of the *nobilitas*. These *novi homines* were perfectly integrated into the oligarchy, and thus they assured its vitality through change. Under the Empire the term *nobilis*, once it had become a pure label of social distinction, was ordinarily applied to the descendants of the consuls of the *res publica*.

Nomen	*See* **Gens**.
Novus homo	In republican times the term has two meanings, which need to be kept apart:

in a more general sense it indicates the first member of a family to enter the Senate; in a more specific sense, the first to reach the consulate and thereby to enter the restricted circle of the **nobilitas**. Particularly rare was the case of one who succeeded in reaching the Senate without coming from a family of senatorial rank. This usually happened only with the support of groups of the *nobilitas* itself; Cato the Censor and Cicero are two of the most well-known instances. The career of the *novus homo* (in the second, more specific, meaning of the term) followed a particular model: during his own rise he tended to emphasize his *virtus*, comparing it to that of the founders of the families of the *nobilitas*, whose degenerate descendants he disparaged. After reaching the consulate, the *homo novus* tended to be integrated into the *nobilitas* and to defend the prerogatives of the order he had just joined, hoping thus for a social recognition equal to that of the more ancient *nobiles*, a stratagem that worked well for Cato, thanks in part to his longevity, and much less well for Cicero.

Obsequium	*See* **Patronage**.
Officia amicitiae	*See* **Officium**.
Officium	The term, which probably derives from *opificium* (cf. *opifex*, and *officina* from

*opificina), seems originally to have indicated the execution of an artisan's work. Soon, however, upon this concrete and material meaning there was superimposed the more abstract meaning of "rules governing an activity," "obligations entailed by a function." In particular, *officium* became specialized to designate the obligations deriving from a given function, activity, or social status; thus, one speaks of *officium consulis*, *officium praetoris*, *officium matronarum* (the dutiful behavior on the part of a married woman), and so on. The concept of *officia amicitiae* is very important, since, given the peculiar characteristics of Roman **amicitia**, it indicates the obligations deriving from the relation of mutual assistance that ought to obtain between *amici* or even in **patronage**.

Beginning with Cicero, *officium* began to develop an important role also in the technical terminology of philosophy, where it served to translate the Greek *kathekon* ("suitable action," "duty" in the vocabulary of the Stoics).

Optimates/	Latin texts quite often tend to overlap the concepts of **boni** and *optimates*; never-
populares	theless, a distinction appears possible and allows us to identify the *optimates* as

aristocratic groups concerned to maintain the power of the Senate chiefly for reasons of privilege and caste. The *optimates* often exercised political hegemony over the *boni*, skillfully using them as a mass to be manipulated. Precisely this dominating function brought it about that in the late Republic the term *optimates* often served to designate the political party that opposes the *populares*. The propaganda of the aristocratic, or at least the conservative, party painted a dark picture of the *populares* and their political action, emphasizing especially the negative connotations from the moral point of view: one hears them often speaking of the *furor* of the *populares*, who are branded as *improbi* or *mali* (in opposition to *boni*, *pii*, etc.). Leaving aside all distortion, the *populares* were something quite different from a democratic party in the modern sense of the term. The leaders of the *populares* were themselves generally aristocrats who demagogically, for the sake of personal power, exploited the needs of the underprivileged classes. If it is impossible to speak of an organic program for the *populares,* of a coherent project aiming at the improvement of society, still one must note a certain continuity in their legislative proposals, for instance, in fiscal (relief or cancellation of debts) or agrarian (land redistribution) matters. This is a sign of a constant tendency to appeal to the problems that were most keenly felt by the proletariatized segment of the population and of a programmatic hostility to the policy of the Senate, which is the only true common denominator of the *populares.*

Ordo	*See* **Senatus.**
Otium	*See* **Negotium.**
Patronage/	Patronage, which was very ancient in Roman society, is the relation of protec-
clientela	tion established by a man of power with persons of more modest social status

(clientes), from whom he receives in exchange submission and devotion *(obsequium),* active support in political contests, and so on. The ability to count on a substantial following of clients obviously contributed to the social prestige of the *patronus;* he, for his part, provided the client with aid in different kinds of emergencies, particularly assuring him legal assistance in court. The relation of clientship was regulated by the bond of **fides,** which was sanctioned already in the Laws of the Twelve Tables (which provided for weighty sanctions against the *patronus* who failed in his commitments to his *cliens*). The freed slave *(libertus)* automatically became the client of his former master, towards whom he retained a certain number of duties, which were fixed by law.

During the Republic the bond joining the victorious general to the peoples he had defeated was also understood as a relation of clientship; the same was true in the case of a foreign community that chose an influential Roman citizen to support its interests at Rome.

The institution of clientship deteriorated seriously under the Empire. Clients found themselves reduced more and more to the rank of common parasites, bound in a relation of humiliating dependency to patrons who more than anything liked to display their own magnificence; then clients were seen crowding the atria of the houses of the wealthy expecting the gift of a kind of salary *(sportula,* at first a dinner, then a modest sum of money), a condition denounced especially by the satiric poets, such as Martial and Juvenal.

Pietas

The adjective *pius,* probably to be connected with the verb *piare* ("to purify"), seems to have had originally the meaning "pure of heart." *Pietas* thus indicates the moral purity obtained by fulfilling one's duties towards the gods and other men, first of all towards one's blood relations. In this sense, the concept of *pietas* would also preserve strong religious connotations, evidence of its archaic character. The concept is linked to the forms of life associated with the pre-state community, which was governed by the gentilician organization. These religious connotations also serve to distinguish *pietas* from the duty *(officium)* that derives from exclusively social relations. The role of family relations in the political and social life of Rome, together with the need of a religious sanction for the imperial domination of the Roman state, explains how *pietas* continued to be for several centuries a central concept in the system of Roman ethical values. There is no need to recall how Virgil put the figure of *pius Aeneas* at the center of his imperial poem.

Political struggle

The nineteenth century's experience of parliamentary parties led historians to project onto the contrast between **optimates** and **populares** the contrast between conservatives and liberals, identifying therewith two parties in the modern sense, with opposing programs: the party of the *optimates* was conservative, whereas the party of the *populares* was based on vast projects for reforming the state and society. In our century, however, especially in England and Germany, as a reaction to this interpretation the so-called prosopographical method, which is based on minute study of the lives of the persons engaged in the political struggle, their family connections, **amicitia, clientela,** and so on, has established itself. According to this interpretation, ancient Rome did not have parties in the modern sense of the term, equipped with organic programs. Political alliances were not stable but were formed for an occasion, on the basis of the programs proposed by the candidates for the magistracies; the politician was more than anything the leader of a faction, and domination was concentrated for the most part in the hands of a few great families *(nobilitas)*. To break their power, their rivals were generally forced to seek the support of the tribunes of the plebs, proposing measures that seemed to gratify the people. The demagogic agitation for the purpose of securing the support of the masses is the sole common denominator of the policy of the *populares*.

This interpretation, which starts from the (correct) need to reject an anachronistic view of the ancient parties, nonetheless requires some clarification. Private gangs cannot be considered the chief driving force of the political struggle; rather, they presuppose a struggle in which vast forces are in play: the creation of the military and the urban proletariat as a result of the great conquests, the nearly total disappearance of small-scale farming, and the concentration of immense estates in the hands of a few. Behind the personal groups, more or less large social strata are in motion, whose needs, however, do not get expressed in stable and organic programs; the *potentes* can thus at different times rely on the needs of different strata of the population.

Populares   *See* **Optimates.**

Praenomen   *See* **Gens.**

Princeps/   The term *princeps,* which properly signifies, in a very general sense, "he who
imperator   holds the first position," is used to designate both chronological priority in an enterprise *(princeps consilii* = "promoter of a project"; in this sense the term is practically synonymous with *auctor)* and primacy, that is, a man's excellence and superiority in a given field *(princeps ingenii, princeps eloquentiae, princeps philosohiae,* etc.). In the political lexicon, *princeps* frequently serves to express the notion of "leader." It is applied to ruling men, who possess *auctoritas* in the highest degree; thus, in the plural the word indicates the most eminent figures in the Senate. Cicero was probably thinking of a restricted elite of such persons when in the *De Republica* he developed the theory of the *princeps,* in which some mistakenly have wanted to see a prefiguration of the principate of a single man, that is, a prefiguration of the role played in the state by Augustus. Augustus finally chose the term *princeps* because it lacked autocratic resonances and thus seemed to him to indicate more exactly his constitutional position (which only formally respected the limits of the republican constitution but in fact violated them; cf. Tacitus, *Annals* 1.1: *cuncta discordiis civilibus fessa nomine principis sub imperium accepit,* "under the name of *princeps* he took command of an entire world that had been wearied by civil warfare"). It should be noted that under the Empire *princeps* was never an official title: the emperor assumed it at the moment of his accession to the throne, without its conferral being sanctioned by the Senate; and it does not appear in the official titles of documents and inscriptions.

From Augustus onwards the term *imperator* is practically synonymous with *princeps. Imperator* emphasizes the military authority of the "first citizen" and his link to the armies; Octavian used it almost as a *praenomen (imperator Caesar)*, thus furnishing an example to his successors.

Probitas	*See* **System of the virtues.**
Rusticitas	*See* **Urbanitas.**
Senatus/equites	These are the two highest classes, or *ordines*, of Roman citizens. In the republican

period the senators constituted the political governing class, within which one should distinguish the **nobilitas,** an aristocracy usually engaged in defending its privileges and made up of those whose ancestors held the highest magistracies. The Roman aristocracy was not an aristocracy of blood, but of office. Belonging to the senatorial order was not hereditary but depended on having held certain magistracies, and it was theoretically possible for the son of a senator to fall back into the equestrian order. Still, in practice the magistracies were open only with difficulty to those whose ancestors did not form part of the senatorial class, and the consulship was jealously guarded by the members of the **nobilitas** as a virtually hereditary prerogative.

Immediately below the senatorial order was the equestrian, composed in large part of landowners (the bourgeoisie of Italy). From the Punic Wars on, the highest strata of the equestrian class directed their energies towards economic and commercial activities; the *societates publicanorum,* made up chiefly of *equites,* held contracts for collecting taxes in the conquered countries and derived immense profits from them. Towards the end of the Republic, disputes arose with particular frequency between political leadership and economic interests, in effect between the senatorial order and the equestrian; the latter was often dominated by its wealthiest and most influential members, who were actively engaged in the *societates publicanorum.* A program of *concordia ordinum* was formulated by Cicero at the time of his consulate, in 63: this proposed a kind of alliance among all the well-to-do classes (substantially the senatorial and equestrian orders) in order to halt the dangers of subversion from below. Nonetheless, it was in fact the Augustan principate that met the needs of the Italian bourgeoisie: taking over the political leadership of the state, it allowed that class to devote itself freely to its own economic activities. Under the Empire the *equites* continued to devote themselves to business of various kinds. From their *ordo* would often come the most diligent officials of the imperial bureaucracy.

Sententia	*See* **Auctoritas.**
Severitas	*See* **Comitas.**
Societates publicanorum	*See* **Senatus.**
Sportula	*See* **Patronage.**
System of the virtues	The principal *virtutes* that make up the system of values of the **mos maiorum**

are treated individually in this glossary. It is worthwhile to mention here a few others that also had a share in constituting the ethical model in which the Roman ruling class recognized itself. *Abstinentia* was the ability, necessary for strength of character, to resist the lure of pleasures of every sort; the term refers specifically to "clean" behavior in handling public money. *Constantia* indicates strength of character, the ability to be consistent with oneself in every situation, without allowing oneself to be carried away by exaltation or despondency; it was clearly one of the qualities required especially in one who was to command others. *Decorum* indicated the behavior that was suitable and appropriate for the different occasions; it was a virtue popularized especially by Cicero's *De Officiis. Industria* was the untiring activity that the member of the Roman aristocracy deployed in various areas of life, as lawyer, politician, and military commander. *Probitas* designated the behavior of the respectable person, of pure and transparent character. *Magnitudo animi,* finally, was the ability to think and operate on a large scale; the virtue of the Roman people as conqueror, and particularly one of the outstanding virtues of its ruling groups, it is analyzed in Cicero's *De Officiis.*

Urbanitas/ rusticitas

Urbanitas is a concept that from certain points of view is not far removed from **humanitas:** it indicates elegance of manners and clothing, affable and courteous behavior, fine and witty spirit, and, not least, a correct manner of speaking, which does not allow provincial accents or inflections—all characteristics of those who lived, and preferably were born, in the City *par excellence,* Rome.

The opposite of *urbanitas* is *rusticitas* (Athenian culture had opposed *asteiotes,* "urbanity," to *agroikia,* "rusticity"), a "roughness of countryfolk" expressed in crude sensitivity, rough manners, shabby clothing, and miserly frugality. The opposition of *urbanitas* and *rusticitas* is a result of the new style that became widespread in civilian life after the influx of great wealth from the conquered territories. Nonetheless, the ideology of *urbanitas* avoided, apart from sporadic instances of nonconformity, serious conflict with the archaic values, which were rooted in the traditional agrarian morality and expressed in the **mos maiorum,** aiming rather at a difficult mediation. The rejection of *rusticitas* was surrounded by much caution: the ruling class feared that an unconditioned acceptance of the modern way of life and of the new values that derived from it might create a limitless expansion of consumption and threaten the bases, both ethical and economic, on which the traditional arrangement of society rested.

Virtue

See **System of the virtues.**

Appendix 4 Terms of Rhetoric, Metrics, and Literary Criticism

Acrostic	Poetic composition in which the initial letters of the verses (or more rarely, the final letters), when read vertically, form names or words. From Greek *acros,* "extreme," and *stichos,* "verse."
Actio	Last of the five major divisions of the rhetorical art; it refers to the ways of delivering the speech (recitation, gesture, etc.).
Adespotos	Said of a text whose author is unknown, not attributable with certainty.
Adonian	Verse used in Aeolic poetry as the end of the Sapphic strophe; it is equivalent to the last two feet of the dactylic hexameter and derives its name from a metrical invocation to the god Adonis: *O ton Adonin* ($-\cup\cup-\underset{\smile}{}$).
Adynaton	Rhetorical figure that, in order to indicate the impossibility—even the merely subjective impossibility—of a certain event's taking place, puts that event in relation to another event, natural or historical, that is impossible or, as it were, paradoxical. Example: "Deer will graze in the sky . . . , and the exiled Parthian will drink in the Arar, the German in the Tigris, before his image will leave our heart" (Virgil). From the Greek verb *dynamai,* "I am able," with negative prefix.
Alexandrian (-ism)	Derived from Alexandria, the Hellenistic metropolis of Egypt, the term is applied, in a literary sense, to a historic phase of Greek poetry and culture (whose characteristic authors are Theocritus, Apollonius of Rhodes, and especially Callimachus), in the period from the beginning of the third century B.C. to the end of the second.
Alliteration	Repetition of the same consonant at the beginning of a word, or less correctly, repetition of the same vowel. Example: *o Tite, tute, Tati, tibi tanta, tyranne, tulisti* (Ennius).
Allusion	In literature, the echo of an earlier model, with which the new text compares itself.
Anadiplosis	Repetition of the last word of a verse or phrase at the beginning of the following verse or phrase. Example: "This you will make beautiful for Gallus, / for Gallus, love for whom . . . " (Virgil).
Anapest	Foot consisting of two shorts and a long ($\cup\cup-$) used in certain types of Latin dramatic verse.
Anaphora	Repetition of words or groups of words in initial position (of a phrase or, in poetry, of a verse). Example: *terruit urbem, terruit gentis* (Horace).
Anastrophe	Inversion of the usual word order. Example: *haec inter* for *inter haec.*
Anticlimax	Descending gradation (*see* **Climax**).
Antilogy	Speech that maintains a thesis opposed to another; the composition of opposing speeches, in antilogical pairs, was a common rhetorical exercise.
Antiphrasis	Properly speaking, the use of a positive term to indicate a negative idea, and vice versa. More generally, in literary terminology, a procedure of composition that

starts off with literary precedents (*see* **Intertextuality**) and reuses them by inverting the sign. From Greek *anti,* "against," and *phrasis,* "expression."

Aphorism	Brief maxim of general validity.
Aposiopesis	Literally, "falling silent"; the deliberate interruption of a phrase, which leaves to the listener the task of completing it. Example: *quos ego . . .* (Virgil, *Aeneid* 1.135).
Aprosdoketon	Properly speaking, the "unexpected" appearance in discourse of something for which the listener is not prepared. This is a typical procedure of some literary forms (epigram, satire) in which an unforeseen addition or conclusion surprises the reader, who was expecting a different outcome of the discourse. From the unexpected shift an effect of **distancing** (q.v.) is produced, mostly with comic intent.
Archaism	Term, form, or construction belonging to a stage of the language that is regarded as past or no longer used (lexical, morphological, syntactic archaisms).
Archetype	Image that can be regarded as universally valid, within a given culture or for mankind in general. In textual criticism, the version of a text to which all the witnesses we know may go back, directly or indirectly.
Aside	In the theater, remark that by convention is regarded as not heard by the other characters present on the stage. It may be explicitly addressed to the public.
Assonance	*See* **Homophony.**
Asyndeton	Series of lexical units or clauses placed beside one another without conjunctions. Example: *veni, vidi, vici.*
Boustrephedon writing	The most ancient type of writing, which in alternate lines proceeds from right to left and from left to right; it takes its name from the "turning of the oxen" when plowing the soil. It is attested in archaic Latin inscriptions as well as in Greek.
Caesura	A particular relation between the semantic units—the words joined to form the verses—and the metrical units. Properly speaking, one has a caesura (from *caedo,* "cut") every time that the end of a word "cuts" the foot or the meter; but in fact every type of verse has its special places in which the caesura is regularly found, giving a rhythmic regularity and a particular architecture to the verse. *See also* **Diaeresis.**
Canticum	In general, any type of song, sung aria; a technical term for the sung parts of dramatic works, in contrast to the recited parts and, in particular, to the parts recited without musical accompaniment. In the Roman *palliata* the *cantica* are predominantly solos of individual actors. They have complicated and variegated metrical forms, by contrast with the standard verses used in the recited parts (senarii and septenarii). *See also* **Deverbia.**
Catalectic	*Catalexis* means "suspension, cessation," and a verse is therefore called catalectic in which something is suppressed at the end, one or two syllables.
Catastrophe	"Reversal"; the change of situation and fortune of the characters that leads to the dénouement of the plot in classical tragedy.
Catharsis	"Purification"; the effect of freedom from the passions that, according to the well-known Aristotelian theory, tragic poetry produces in its audience.
Cento	Poem formed by "scraps," quotations of classical texts; the skill lies in producing a coherent whole and new meanings different from those of the original contexts from which the quotations are taken.
Chiasmus	Crossed arrangement of elements of the phrase that correspond to one another, forming the scheme *a b b a.* Example: *satis eloquentiae, sapientiae parum* (Sallust).
Choliamb	Literally, "limping iamb"; particular form of the iambic trimeter that gives an irrational long in the penultimate syllable of the verse (which for that reason is

called "limping"); thus in the final foot, instead of ∪— there is ——. It was also called "hipponactean," because it was first used by the Greek poet Hipponax (sixth century B.C.). In the Hellenistic age it was taken up by Callimachus and by Herodas, who used it in his mimiambs. At Rome it pleased the taste of the pre-neoterics and the neoterics (Laevius, Cinna, Calvus, Catullus). After Catullus—and modeled chiefly on his technique—choliambs are found again in Persius, Petronius, Martial, and Ausonius. The poems written in this meter have a comic-satiric tone for the most part.

Clausula In general, the final part of a verse, sentence, or speech. Classical rhetoric carefully controls the quantitative sequences placed at the end of the phrase or its members, and this care is confirmed by the practice of the artistic prose writers (e.g., Cicero, Petronius, Tacitus). One can thus distinguish preferred clausulae from undesirable clausulae in the various authors. In late antiquity the clausula gives way to the **cursus** (q.v.), paralleling the loss of feeling for syllable length.

Climax An ascending progression produced, for instance, when words of increasing length are juxtaposed *(uri vinciri verberari)*, or words of increasingly strong meaning; it is often combined with repetition and verbal parallelism. The descending progression is called **anticlimax** (q.v.).

Colon, cola Literally "member," "members"; section of the verse or the prose period that is felt as characterized by its own independent rhythm, for instance, the **hemistich** (q.v.); it is important in the structure of Ciceronian prose.

Concinnitas Pursuit of balance in the artistic structure of the period (typical, for instance, of Cicero's style); it has to do with the distribution of the words and the compositional architecture of the discourse. *See also Inconcinnitas.*

Connotation The opposite of **denotation** (q.v.); the meaning a word may take on or develop in a certain context in addition to its standard (denotative) meaning.

Contaminatio In modern philology, the procedure of fusing together two or more models; the currency of the term derives from the poetics of Terence, who defends against his critics the legitimacy of this operation, which he carried out on the Greek originals of his works.

Controversia Typical rhetorical exercise that trains students to debate a judicial case in hypothetical situations.

Corpus Group of texts or documents that have been transmitted to us together; or the set of texts linked by being the work of a single author or being attributed (even falsely) to a single author.

Couplet Strophe of two verses; the most well-known case is the elegiac couplet, comprising a hexameter and a pentameter. Also called "distich."

Cursus Phenomenon of medieval literary prose that takes up the heritage of the **clausula** (q.v.) in an altered linguistic context, basing itself now on rhythmic-accentual features (as in modern English), and no longer on quantitative.

Dactyl Foot of three syllables and four tempi (—∪∪). The commonest verse made up of dactyls is the **dactylic hexameter** (q.v.).

Dactylic hexameter Standard verse of Greek and Latin epic poetry composed of six dactylic feet the last of which is **catalectic** (q.v.). The dactyl may be replaced (theoretically, in any position) by a spondee. The resulting scheme is: —∪∪—∪∪—∪∪—∪∪—∪∪—∪. The hexameter combines with the **pentameter** (q.v.) to make up the elegiac couplet *(see* **Couplet**).

Denotation The opposite of **connotation** (q.v.); the principal and in some ways stable meaning of a word, recognized as such by a given linguistic community.

Deverbia	Conversational parts of Roman comedy, distinguished in particular from the *cantica,* the sung parts (see *Canticum*).
Diaeresis	In metrics, a regular pause in the verse that does not "cut" (as with the **caesura,** q.v.) a verse in the middle; the so-called "bucolic" diaeresis, for instance, falls between the fourth and fifth feet in the dactylic hexameter. Example: *arma virumque cano, Troiae qui / primus ab oris.*
Dispositio	The second of the five large divisions into which the art of rhetoric is divided; it has to do with the order in which the arguments and the subjects are presented. Such an order may be either natural (i.e., sticking to the logic and the usage of everyday communication) or artificial (i.e., elaborated, disarranged for artistic reasons, of effectiveness or persuasion).
Distancing	Artistic procedure that produces a shift from the usual and automatic aspects of ordinary life, reviving our perception of reality.
Distich	*See* **Couplet.**
Eclogue	Greek term used by the Latin grammarians to indicate the individual poems in which Virgil's *Bucolics* are articulated (thus one should properly talk of "the book of the *Bucolics*" but "the first, the second eclogue," though this distinction is often ignored). A corresponding term in Greek literature is **idyll** (q.v.), which, however, also had currency in a wider sense.
Ekphrasis	Greek rhetorical term for set-piece descriptions. It is especially used for literary descriptions of works of art, a subject of which Hellenistic-Roman literature was very fond (e.g., the bedcover with the story of Ariadne in Catullus's poem 64, Aeneas's shield in Virgil, etc.).
Elision	*See* **Synaloephe.**
Ellipsis	Rhetorical figure that consists in the suppression of an element of the phrase.
Elocutio	Third part of rhetorical technique: skillful choice and combination of the words that form the discourse (the corresponding Greek word is *lexis*). It is the level of literary practice that comes close to our concept of "style."
Enallage	A rhetorical figure not easily defined, and very important especially in poetic language. It is based on an exchange of functions between parts of the discourse, as, for instance, in *ibant obscuri sola sub nocte* (Virgil), in which, properly speaking— that is, in the language of ordinary communication—*obscuri* would be expected as an attribute of the night, and *sola* as an attribute of the persons moving about in that night.
Enjambment	Effect produced when the phrase continues beyond the limit of the verse, for example, when a **syntagma** (q.v.) is divided between the end of one verse and the beginning of the following, as in *innumerabilis / annorum series* (Ovid).
Epicedion	Poem on the death of a beloved person (or animal, e.g., Catullus's sparrow).
Epideictic	Oratory used to demonstrate one's own abilities and lacking in practical aim (therefore different from political and judicial oratory).
Epinician	In the division of the poetic genres of classical Greece, occasional poetry written to celebrate victories (Pindar's epinicians in honor of the victors in the Olympic games, etc., are famous).
Epiphoneme	Concluding comment, often of a sententious and generalizing character. Example: *tantum religio potuit suadere malorum* (Lucretius).
Epitaph	Greek term for a funeral eulogy, which may be represented by a prose speech or a poem.
Epithalamium	Poem intended for the celebration of a wedding, Catullus 61, for instance.
Epithet	Modifying adjective; when it expresses general qualities that are unconnected to

	the immediate context of the phrase (e.g., "the swift ship," said of a ship at anchor), one speaks of a "decorative" or "ornamental" epithet *(ornans)*.
Epode	Literally, "song that comes afterwards," "additional song." The name is used in metrics and in ancient poetry with various meanings; properly, it is the verse or *colon* that acts as a **clausula** (q.v.) to a metrical period. As a literary term it designates the second (shorter) verse following a longer verse and forming a couplet with it. Thus, in Archilochus and Horace the couplet consists for the most part of an iambic trimeter followed by an iambic dimeter. The book that later grammarians called *Epodes* Horace himself called *Iambi* to indicate both the predominant meter and the "iambic" character (i.e., the aggressive and satiric spirit, the tone of personal invective or moral resentment; this was the traditional character of the iambic genre, though with many different shades of meaning and different stylistic stances, at times more impetuous, at times more reflective).
Epyllion	A Greek word, composed of the term *epos* plus the suffix *-yllion,* which has diminutive value. In modern usage, it is applied to brief epic poems of the Alexandrian period, such as the *Hecale* of Callimachus or, at Rome, poem 64 of Catullus; this is not, however, an ancient sense of the word.
Eschatological	Referring to the final, otherworldly moments of the life of human beings and of the universe (death, the Underworld, etc.). From Greek *eschatos,* "final," and *logos,* "discourse."
Ethos	In Greek, "character" or "emotion"; in rhetoric the term is used as the opposite of *pathos* (q.v.) and indicates the production of effects that are not passionate and dramatic but more moderate, directed towards creating approval and provoking pleasure.
Ethopoeia	Representation of the *ethos* (understood as character) of a given person. It also indicates a type of rhetorical or literary activity that consists in giving voice to a historical, mythological, or fictitious character.
Excerpta	Passages detached from the continuous text of an author and presented independently.
Explicit	Literally "comes to an end," with "the book" understood, a term used in manuscripts, then employed to indicate in general the final word or words of a text; the opposite is *incipit* (q.v.).
Fabula	In Latin the word covers not only our "fable" but practically all types of fiction: myths and legends, novels, and texts for the stage, whether comic or dramatic. In modern literary criticism *fabula* indicates the abstract and linear description of a work's narrative content; thus its opposite is "plot" or "story," which indicates the work's concrete narrative structure organized from a particular point of view.
Figure	Corresponds to Greek *tropos*. To identify, describe, and classify the various kinds of figure is the principal task of classical rhetoric.
Figura etymologica	Employment in close proximity, and for the purpose of emphasis, of two or more terms from the same root. Example: *emit morte immortalitatem,* "he purchases deathlessness with his death" (Quintilian).
Foot	Unit of measure in Greco-Latin verse made up of a set of certain quantities; for example, the **dactyl** ($-\smile\smile$), the **spondee** ($--$), the **iamb** ($\smile-$), and the **trochee** ($-\smile$) (qq.v.).
Galliambic	Verse that has taken its name from the Galli, the priests of the goddess Cybele; in Latin known especially because of Catullus's poem 63.
Geminatio	Immediate repetition of the same word or group of words.

Gloss	(1) A difficult term (because it is archaic, rare, or dialectal, etc.) that is studied by grammarians or learned poets (e.g., the Alexandrians [*see* **Alexandrian**]). (2) A note, placed between one line and another of the text or out in the margin, that explains difficult locutions or comments on the content of a passage. An independent collection of glosses, arranged alphabetically, is a glossary.
Glyconic	Verse used for the most part in lyric poetry, in strophic sequences. Example: *Dianae sumus in fide* (Catullus).
Gnome	*Sententia,* maxim of instructive and general character.
Hapax legomenon	Literally "said once," meaning a word found only once in a given language or author or text.
Hemistich	Literally, "half-verse"; in the **dactylic hexameter** (q.v.), for instance, the verse is divided into two hemistichs by the main **caesura** (q.v.). Example: *Tityre, tu patulae / recubans sub tegmine fagi* (Virgil).
Hendiadys	Expression that replaces the group [noun + adjective] or [noun + complement] with two coordinated nouns. Example: *pateris libamus et auro,* "we make libations with the cups and with gold," used by Virgil in the sense of *libamus pateris aureis,* "we make libations with cups of gold." From the Greek *hen dia duoin,* "one thing by means of two."
Hexameter	*See* **Dactylic hexameter**.
Hiatus	Prosodical phenomenon in metrics, the opposite of **synaloephe** (q.v.); the two vowels—the final of one word and the initial of the following—that normally, when they meet, give way to synaloephe maintain their prosodical value and their syllabic independence. Example: *evolat infelix et femineo ululatu* (the final *o* of *femineo* does not enter into synaloephe with the beginning *u* of *ululatu*).
Homoeoptoton	Effect produced by the similarity of endings that occur together, as in *sparsis hastis longis* (Ennius), or at the end of parallel *cola* (q.v.). It belongs within the more general term **homoeoteleuton** (q.v.).
Homoeoteleuton	Effect produced by the similarity of final phonemes in words that are close to one another, as in *veni, vidi, vici,* or at the end of parallel *cola* (q.v.).
Homophony	Similarity or identity in sound of different words.
Hymn	Song in honor of a divinity; it may be intended for a ritual, liturgical situation, or it may be a purely literary development of mythical and religious themes.
Hyperbaton	Figure based on word order that separates from one another two terms normally joined in a continuous **syntagma** (q.v.). Example: *inter **audaces** lupus errat **agnos*** (Horace); or ***multa gracilis puer in rosa** (Horace)*.
Hyperbole	Rhetorical figure based on exaggeration.
Hypermetron	Verse that apparently has an extra syllable; in fact, the syllable enters into **synaloephe** (q.v.) with the first syllable of the following line. Example: *sors exitura et nos in aetern(um) / exilium impositura cumbae* (Horace).
Hypotaxis	Literally, "subordination"; syntactic structure by which the clauses of the period are arranged in a relation of logical and temporal dependence. Hypotaxis, which is the most common procedure in artistic prose (see Cicero), is opposed to parataxis, a style of writing in which two or more phrases are arranged one beside the other, juxtaposed as equivalent and not interdependent (*loquens ridet* is hypotactic, in contrast with the paratactic form *loquitur et ridet;* or *illum vivere credo* in contrast with *ille vivit, credo;* or *cum omnia periissent, ego perii* in contrast with *omnia perierunt, (et) ego perii*).
Hysteron proteron	Literally, "following preceding"; rhetorical figure that consists in inverting the logical or foreseeable sequence of two elements. Example: *moriamur et in media arma ruamus* (Virgil).

Iamb	Foot formed from a short syllable and a long syllable (∪—). Iambic verse is generally considered the verse form closest to the rhythm of ordinary language, and for that reason it is among those preferred in comedy. Use of the form by such poets as Archilochus and Hipponax led to the designation *iambi* being applied to poetry with aggressive and realistic content.
Iconic	Any type of sign that offers an image of its own significance.
Iconography	The collection of testimonia related to a theme, a person, or something similar, in visual art (e.g., the iconography of Augustus is the way that he is portrayed on coins, monuments, etc.).
Ictus	Metrical beat produced by the alternation of accented and unaccented syllables. The tendency today (though many Anglo-American scholars would disagree) is to deny its existence in classical meter, which appears to be based on a purely quantitative alternation of longs and shorts.
Idyll	From the Greek *eidyllion* ("vignette," approximately), the term used by the Greek grammarians to indicate the individual poems in Theocritus's collection (similar to the use of **eclogue** for Virgil and his *Bucolics*). Given the predominantly pastoral content of Theocritus's poetry, "idyll" and "idyllic" have also come to refer to content, indicating a certain type of poetic subject (natural scenery, idealization of the pastoral life, etc.).
Incipit	Literally, "begins," with "the book" understood; a term found in Latin manuscripts and used today as a technical term to indicate the first words of a text. It is the opposite of *explicit* (q.v.).
Inconcinnitas	Rejection of the principles of *concinnitas* (q.v.); pursuit of a style that is asymmetrical and unpredictable, especially in reaction to the classical Ciceronian architecture.
In medias res	Beginning in the middle of a story in order then to go back to the earlier parts, as in the *Odyssey*. The technique corresponds, in *dispositio* (q.v.), to an artificial rather than a natural order of narrative.
Intertextuality	Phenomenon by which, in literature, each new text enters into a network of relations with other, already written texts (recalling them, imitating them, parodying them, in short, presupposing them).
Inventio	Art of finding arguments, the first part of the rhetorical art; *inventio* has at its disposal a large repertory of *loci communes,* topoi (*see* **Topos**).
Isocolon	Parallelism and balanced correspondence among the *cola* (q.v.) of a period.
Iunctura	Collocation of words with an original and innovative effect that distances itself from the usual language by drawing new connotations from the individual words that make it up.
Litotes	Affirmation of something by denying its contrary; used especially of understatement (e.g., "not bad").
Locus amoenus	A classical **topos** (q.v.), the representation of an agreeable, idealized countryside, where the serenity of nature cancels the problems of society and history.
Locus communis	("commonplace") *See* **Topos**.
Melic	A form of poetry in Greece originally intended to be sung with musical accompaniment; it was often also accompanied by dance and was composed of elements of different rhythm and length. The Alexandrian grammarians often used, in addition to "melic poetry," "lyric poetry" (i.e., poetry sung to the sound of the lyre, since the lyre had once been the most important of the accompanying instruments); thus the philologists drew up a select list of the "Nine Lyric Poets" (Pindar, Bacchylides, Sappho, Anacreon, Stesichorus, Simonides, Ibycus, Alcaeus, and Alcman). In Augustan literature *lyricus* became the usual Latin term: Horace hopes to

be included among the *lyrici vates;* Ovid always uses *lyricus,* not *melicus,* and so do Quintilian, Pliny, and Seneca. The modern use of the term "lyric" derives from Latin literature (Quintilian and Horace becoming the preferred authors in the Italian Renaissance).

Memoria	The fourth part of rhetorical technique: the orator's ability to entrust to his mind the speech that he has worked out in anticipation of the delivery (*see* **Actio**).
Menippean	Kind of satire that goes back to the work of the Greek polemicist Menippus of Gadara (second century B.C.) and was later practiced by Varro; it had profound influence on Petronius and particularly on Seneca (the *Apocolocyntosis*) and Lucian of Samosata. So far as we can tell from surviving examples, the Menippean was characterized by a deliberately inharmonious mixture of prose and verse (*see* **Prosimetron**), seriousness and comedy (*see* **Spoudogeloion**), popular realism and sophisticated quotation or literary parody.
Metaphor	Rhetorical figure of primary importance, a substitution based on a similarity, as, for instance, "the evening of life" for "old age." In general, metaphor substitutes terms, whereas **simile** (q.v.) matches terms.
Metonymy	Rhetorical figure of primary importance, a substitution based on a relation of contiguity, as, for instance, *vulnera dirigere,* "hurl wounds" (Virgil), for "hurl javelins." The differences between metonymy and **metaphor** (q.v.) present notable problems to scholars of rhetoric and poetics.
Metrics	From the Greek *metron,* "measure"; the science that measures the **rhythm** (q.v.). In Greek and Latin poetry, metrics, which is based on the alternation of long and short syllables, presupposes **prosody** (q.v.).
Metron	The irreducible unit of measure of a given verse (terms such as "dimeter," "trimeter," and "tetrameter" indicate the number of such units contained in a verse). In certain cases the notion of metron coincides with that of **foot** (q.v.), as in the case of the dactylic meters, such as the **hexameter** (q.v.); in others it coincides with the set of two feet (dipody), as in the case of the iambic and trochaic meters.
Mime	"Imitation" of everyday life; a text intended for the stage, or for reading, that represents ordinary persons and situations. It may be a refined poetic genre (as often in Alexandrian poetry) or a form of farcical, commercial spectacle (the tendency that prevails in the end at Rome). *See also* **Pantomime**.
Neologism	A word not previously attested, one that does not appear in earlier texts.
Ode	Lyric poem, of varying metrical and strophic form; the content also varies, though it is predominantly erotic or ethical-civil. Originally, in Greek, the word referred to the combination of poetry with music and song; at Rome the term *carmen* came to be preferred.
Onomatopoeia	Effect of imitating natural sounds by linguistic means, by alliteration and phonic iteration, for instance. In poetry, the rhythm too may aid this expressive procedure.
Ordo	The linear arrangement of words or contents; rhetoric contrasts *ordo artificialis* and *ordo naturalis,* according to whether this arrangement does or does not appear natural and predictable.
Oxymoron	Figure based on the juxtaposition of antithetic words that seem to exclude one another. Examples: *symphonia discors,* "a discordant harmony" (Horace); *strenua inertia,* "a restless torpor" (Horace).
Paeon	Metrical foot consisting of three short syllables and a long.
Panegyric	Public discourse in celebration of an illustrious person.
Pantomime	A kind of ballet, a spectacle of music and dance very popular in the Rome of the

	first century A.D. It could be based on well-known mythological subjects and supported by a written script.
Parataxis	Relation of coordination between two or more phrases; the opposite of **hypotaxis** (q.v.).
Paronomasia	Juxtaposition of words having some phonic resemblance; the basis of plays on words.
Pathos	Violent, dramatic, intensely emotional effect, distinguished by degree of intensity from *ethos* (q.v.); consciously sought through strategies of style and content by an orator or poet.
Pentameter	Dactylic verse used only when paired with the **hexameter** (q.v.), to form the elegiac couplet (*see* **Couplet**). It can be considered the doubling of a **hemistich** (q.v.) of a hexameter: $-\cup\cup-\cup\cup-//-\cup\cup-\cup\cup-$.
Peripeteia	Passage of characters from one situation to another, a basic element in plots (of tragedy, comedy, novel, etc.).
Phalaecean	Verse of eleven syllables, generally used for poetry of a light and occasional content (it is often found in Catullus's *nugae*).
Pherecratean	Verse named from the Athenian comic poet Pherecrates, used at Rome in lyric strophes and associated with other verses. Example: *O Hymen Hymenaee* (Catullus).
Phoneme	Minimum isolable unit in the stream of speech, and lacking meaning in itself. Example: /p/.
Phonostylistics	Study of the formal messages that poetry transmits by the play of signifiers that constitutes the phonic structure. **Onomatopoeia** (q.v.) is only one particular instance of the effects studied by phonostylistics.
Plurilingualism	Openness in literary style to a plurality of linguistic levels and registers; the opposite tendency, which is selective and uniform, may be called "monolingualism."
Poeticism	Term belonging to the poetic language.
Poikilia	"Variety" of themes, metrical structures, and especially style and language within a conscious poetics. A Greek term, from the verb *poikillo,* "to variegate."
Polymetrics	Poems composed in varying meter.
Polyptoton	Repetition of a word in different grammatical cases. Example: *pectora pectoribus rumpunt* (Virgil).
Polysemy	Plurality of significances in a word or an entire sentence.
Polysyndeton	Marked succession of conjunctions between several terms or sentences (*see also* **Asyndeton**).
Praeteritio	Rhetorical figure by which one communicates that which one makes a show of wanting not to say. Example: "Why recall the ships burnt along the Erycian coast?" (Virgil).
Proem	Form of beginning typical of the epic poem.
Prosimetron	Literary form characterized by a frequent (not episodic) alternation of prose and verse; often associated with the **Menippean** (q.v.).
Prosody	In Greek, properly speaking, "modulation of the voice"; in Latin it corresponds in certain aspects to *accentus,* from *ad* and *cantus.* It is the part of phonetics that deals with the quantity of syllables and the accentuation of words. The term reveals the originally melodic nature that the accent had in both Greek and Latin. The study of prosody is fundamental, in that Latin versification, like Greek, was based on the alternation of long and short syllables according to certain schemes.
Prosopography	Systematic, historical study of the persons of a given era, nationality, class, or status.
Prosopopoeia	Device used to impersonate and give voice to a character or an abstraction (e.g., the State, or Nature).

Pseudepigraphic	Said of a work attributed to a certain author in error or by conscious falsification.
Quadrivium	*See* **Trivium**.
Recensio	From *recenseo*, "collect, review"; first stage in the task of critically constructing the text, consisting in collecting, describing, and evaluating the manuscripts that transmit it.
Rhetoric	The art of the word and its effects, articulated in the classical period into five large areas: *inventio, dispositio, elocutio, memoria,* and *actio* (qq.v.).
Recognition	Typical situation (analyzed by Aristotle) in the dénouement of dramatic works, either tragedy or comedy: the revelation of the true nature or origin of a person.
Rhythm	Measure that regulates and makes perceptible the flow of a continuous movement (the beating of the heart or the ticking of a clock, if we interpret it as ticktock, in two tempi). It is perceptible both in prose and in verse. In Latin it is based on the quantitative alternation of longs and shorts; Latin metrics of the classical period is based on this.
Sapphic ode	Poem consisting of Sapphic strophes (three hendecasyllables followed by an adonian). It is called thus because it was favored by Sappho, but in fact it is a metrical form belonging to Aeolic lyric in general (Alcaeus also uses it). Taken up by the Hellenistic poets, it was introduced into Latin by Catullus (poems 11 and 51) and was much used by Horace, who imposed some particular restrictions on it; Seneca also used it (in some choral passages of his tragedies), as did Statius, Paulinus of Nola, Prudentius, and others.
Scazon	*See* **Choliamb**.
Scholium	Annotation that explains and comments on a word or a passage of an ancient text. The scholia may be transmitted together with the text on which they comment or in independent collections.
Semantics	Study of the meanings of words and their development.
Senarius	Latin verse composed of six feet, especially the iambic senarius; it corresponds to the Greek iambic trimeter, which, however, as the name says, is organized, not by individual feet, but by dipodies, or metra, and is regulated by notably different structural principles.
Septenarius	Latin verse of seven feet, trochaic or iambic. The trochaic septenarius, which along with the senarius is the commonest verse in Roman drama, corresponds to the Greek trochaic tetrameter catalectic (four dipodies minus one foot = seven feet), with perceptible differences in the metrical-verbal structure.
Sermo cotidianus	Language used in normal, everyday communication.
Sermo familiaris	Language spoken in unofficial, informal relations, but in educated, high social classes; it is thus distinct from the *sermo vulgaris* (q.v.).
Sermo vulgaris	Language spoken by the people, uneducated language as distinct from the literary language and also from the *sermo familiaris* (q.v.). Our evidence of it comes to us in a filtered manner or is occasional and fragmentary (inscriptions, Pompeian graffiti, glosses, comparison with the Romance languages; also some literary texts, especially Petronius's *Satyricon* and certain works of late antiquity).
Simile	Basic rhetorical figure that juxtaposes two realities and compares them; the simile may produce, by substitution, **metaphor** (q.v.).
Sotadean	Ionic verse that takes its name from the licentious and mordant Hellenistic poet Sotades. Occasional sotadeans are found in the fragments of Ennius and Varro, as well as in comedy and, later, in Petronius and Martial; they are often parodistic.
Spondee	Foot of two long syllables, and thus of four tempi (– –), equivalent to the **dactyl** (q.v.), with which it alternates in hexameter verse.

Spondeiazon	Hexameter that, unusually, has a **spondee** instead of a **dactyl** (qq.v.) in the fifth foot. Example: *saxa per et scopulos et depressas convalles* (Virgil). Far rarer are hexameters made up entirely of spondees. Example: *olli respondit rex Albai Longai* (Ennius).
Spoudogeloion	The "serio-comic" style used by the Greek philosopher Menippus and in the **Menippean** satire (q.v.) in which a joking formulation and comic treatment are given to philosophical arguments.
Stemma	Genealogical tree of the tradition of a text, which textual criticism reconstructs, if possible, by means of the *recensio* (q.v.) of the manuscript witnesses.
Styleme	Stylistic preference; nexus or syntactic construction that may be regarded as indicative of the style of an author, genre, or literary tradition.
Suasoria	Rhetorical exercise; analysis of the possible courses of action to be taken in a fictitious situation. Example: Alexander the Great deliberates whether to continue his march towards the East.
Sympotic	Literally, "convivial"; said of poetry that is intended for hearing at a party (symposium) or that sings of subjects connected to this situation.
Synaloephe	Fusion between two vocalic syllables—the end of one word and the beginning of the next—that, for metrical purposes, results in a single syllable; if synaloephe does not take place, one has **hiatus** (q.v.). This phenomenon is less correctly called "elision."
Synecdoche	Rhetorical figure that can be considered a particular type of **metonymy** (q.v.); the substitution occurs between two terms one of which includes the other, in a relation of part and whole, class and subclass.
Synesthesia	Literally, "simultaneous perception"; phenomenon, typical of poetic language, by which different sense spheres are associated, for example, hearing and sight.
Syntagma	Syntactic construction, combination of elements (two or more) in the stream of speech.
Tetrameter	Sequence of four metra to form a verse. The most common tetrameter is the trochaic tetrameter catalectic, which later, among the Romans, became the trochaic septenarius or *versus quadratus*.
Threnody	From the Greek *threnos,* "dirge"; funeral lament.
Topos	A commonplace; stable and conventional motif that is part of the arsenal of rhetoric or literature and can be memorized, employed on various occasions, and readapted and transformed.
Tricolon	Syntactic construction composed of three *cola* (q.v.) that correspond syntactically. Example: "Vice has defeated modesty; unbridledness, fear; madness, reason" (Cicero).
Trimeter	A Greek verse form composed of three metra; the iambic trimeter consists of three dipodies, that is, of six iambs joined in pairs (*see* **Senarius**).
Trivium	In the Middle Ages the three liberal arts—grammar, dialectic, rhetoric—were called the "arts of the trivium" (or simply "the trivium"); they were regarded as the arts of discourse, as opposed to the scientific arts, or "arts of the quadrivium"—arithmetic, music, geometry, astronomy. The set of the trivium and the quadrivium constituted in the Middle Ages the typical canon of school studies. They were regularized in a kind of encyclopedia of knowledge by the works of Boethius and Cassiodorus (but the classification of the liberal arts, which included the trivium and quadrivium together, goes back to Plato).
Trochee	Foot formed by a long syllable and a short syllable ($-\cup$); it is part of some common dramatic verse forms, for instance, in Greek, the trochaic tetrameter catalectic (four trochaic dipodies minus a trochee), of which the Latin equivalent is the trochaic septenarius.

Trope	Greek term for a rhetorical figure, the basic object of rhetoric. Tropes are, for example, **metaphor, metonymy,** and **synecdoche** (qq.v.).
Urbanitas	Pure and elegant quality of the Latin spoken at Rome, as opposed to the language of the country *(rusticitas)* or the barbarized Latin spoken by foreigners and affected by external influences.
Xenia	Literally, "hospitality gifts" ; epigrammatic little poems that are offered as a sign of friendship and accompany a gift.
Zeugma	Figure that places two terms in a grammatical relation that properly fits only one. Example: *pacem an bellum gerens* (Sallust; only *bellum gerere,* "to wage war," and not *pacem gerere,* is normal phraseology in Latin).

Index of Names

The names that are followed by their full Latin equivalents in parentheses or, when the Latin equivalents are identical, by an asterisk, are those of people who are treated as authors of Latin literature. The index also includes the names of anonymous works. The page numbers of the main treatment (or treatments) of Latin authors are printed in boldface type; for Greek authors, Appendix 2 should also be consulted. The index includes significant references to Roman and Greek writers, neglecting most historical figures and all characters found in literary works.

Cato. *See* Valerius Cato

Cato the Censor (Marcius Porcius Cato Censorius), 19, 24, 68, 70, 72, 73, 75, 78, 83, 85–90, 241, 369, 612

Cato the Elder. *See* Cato the Censor

Cato the Younger. *See* Cato of Utica

Cato of Utica, 182, 238

Catullus (Gaius Valerius Catullus), 142–53, 221, 324

Catullus*, mimographer, 403

Celsus (Aulus Cornelius Celsus), 388–89

Censorinus*, 549, 616–17

Cethegus (Marcus Cornelius Cethegus), 68

Chalcidius*, 632

Charisius, grammarian (Flavius Sosipater Charisius), 626

Chirius Fortunatianus. *See* Fortunatianus

Choerilus of Iasus, 78

Chronograph of 354, 646

Cicero (Marcus Tullius Cicero), 110, 135, 136, 175–207, 210, 212, 221, 226, 231, 235, 238, 243, 373–74, 514, 527, 557–58, 715

Cicero, brother of orator (Quintus Tullius Cicero), 108–9, 203

Cincius, antiquarian, 70

Cincius Alimentus (Lucius Cincius Alimentus), 69–70

Cinna, neoteric poet (Gaius Helvius Cinna), 141–42

Ciris, 432

Claudian (Claudius Claudianus), 658–61, 706

Claudius, emperor (Tiberius Claudius Nero Germanicus), 401

Claudius Mamertinus, panegyrist (Flavius Claudius Mamertinus), 633

Claudius Marius Victorius (Claudius Marius Victorius Massiliensis), 709

Claudius Quadrigarius (Quintus Claudius Quadrigarius), 122, 368

Clitarchus, 122, 384

Cluvius Rufus*, 542

Codex Gregorianus, 616

Codex Hermogenianus, 616

Codex Iustinianus, 713

Codex Repetitae Praelectionis, 714

Codex Theodosianus, 702

Coelius Antipater (Lucius Coelius Antipater), 121

Columella (Lucius Iunius Moderatus Columella), 389–90

Commentator Cruquianus, 318

Commodian*, 606–8

Consentius*, grammarian, 700

Copa, 432

Corbulo (Gnaeus Domitius Corbulo), 542

Cordus. *See* Cremutius Cordus

Corippus (Flavius Cresconius Corippus), 720

Cornelius Celsus. *See* Celsus

Cornelius Gallus. *See* Gallus

Cornelius Nepos*, 143, 209, 210, 221–23, 547

Cornelius Severus*, 430

Cornelius Sisenna. *See* Sisenna

Cornelius Sulla. *See* Sulla

Cornutus, Stoic philosopher (Lucius Annaeus Cornutus), 286, 468, 478

Corpus Iuris Civilis, 713

Corpus Tibullianum, 330–31

Coruncanius (Tiberius Coruncanius), 394

Crassicius (Lucius Crassicius Pasicles Pansa), 576

Crassus, orator (Lucius Licinius Crassus), 119–20

Crates of Mallus, 94, 124, 572

Cremutius Cordus (Aulus Cremutius Cordus), 383

Culex, 432

Curiatius Maternus*, 418

Curtius Rufus (Quintus Curtius Rufus), 383–84

Cyprian (Thascius Caecilius Cyprianus), 604–6

Cyprianus Gallus*, 709

Damasus*, pope, 662–63

"Dares the Phrygian," 705

Decimus Laberius. *See* Laberius

De Excidio Troiae Historia, 705

Demophilus, 57

Demosthenes, 188, 199

De Ponderibus et Mensuris, 638

De Rebus Bellicis, 637

De Viris Illustribus, 646

Dicaearchus, 190, 213

Dicta Catonis. See *Disticha Catonis*

"Dictys Cretensis," 652–53

Digesta, 713

Diogenes, 70

Diomedes*, grammarian, 626

Dionysius of Halicarnassus, 575

Dionysius Thrax, Greek grammarian, 125, 573

Diphylus, 57, 93, 96

Dirae, 431

Disticha Catonis, 90, 612–23

Hegesias of Magnesia, 120
Hegesippus*, 652
Helenius Acron. *See* Acron
Helvius Cinna. *See* Cinna
Hemina. *See* Cassius Hemina
Herbarium, 637
Herennius, critic of Virgil, 285
Herennius Modestinus*, jurist, 616
Hermas, 597, 598
Hermesianax, 322
Herodes Atticus, 521
Hesiod, 80, 350
Hilary of Poitiers (Hilarius Pictaviensis), 643–44
Hirtius (Aulus Hirtius), 230
Historia Alexandri Magni, 653
Historia Apolloni Regis Tyrii, 653
Historia Augusta, 650–52
Historia de Origine Francorum, 705
Historia Tripertita, 646
Homer, 40–42, 45, 80, 276–77, 463–64
Honorius. *See* Julius Honorius
Horace (Quintus Horatius Flaccus), 116, 214, 256, 292–319, 467, 471
Hortensius (Quintus Hortensius Hortalus), 120, 150, 179, 180
Hosidius Geta*, 286, 611
Hostius, 110, 331
Hydatius*, 704
Hyginus (Gaius Iulius Hyginus), 285, 286, 386, 576
Hyginus*, mythographer, author of *Fabulae*, 386

Ilias Latina, 437
Institutiones, 713–14
Invectiva in Ciceronem, 243
Invectiva in Sallustium, 243
Isidore of Seville (Isidorus Hispalensis), 549, 720–21
Isocrates, 199, 200
Itala. See *Vetus Itala*
Itinerarium Alexandri, 653
Itinerarium Antonini, 638
Itinerarium Egeriae. See *Peregrinatio Aetheriae*
Itinerarium Hierosolymitanum, 638

Januarius Nepotianus. *See* Nepotianus
Jerome (Sophronius Eusebius Hieronymus), 681–85
Johannes Lydus, 549
John Cassian. *See* Cassian
Jordanes (Iordanis), 716
Julian. *See* Salvius Julianus

Julian of Eclanum (Iulianus Aeclanensis), 704
Julius Agricola. *See* Agricola
Julius Capitolinus (Iulius Capitolinus), 650
Julius Caesar. *See* Caesar
Julius Caesar Strabo (Gaius Iulius Caesar Strabo Vopiscus), 108–9, 186
Julius Honorius (Iulius Honorius), 701
Julius Hyginus. *See* Hyginus
Julius Naucellius. *See* Naucellius
Julius Obsequens (Iulius Obsequens), 652
Julius Paris (Iulius Paris), 381
Julius Paulus, jurist (Iulius Paulus), 616
Julius Romanus, grammarian (Iulius Romanus), 615
Julius Solinus. *See* Solinus
Julius Valerius (Iulius Valerius Alexander Polemio), 653
Julius Victor, rhetorician (Gaius Iulius Victor), 517, 629
Junianus Justin. *See* Justin, epitomator of Trogus
Junius Gracchanus (Marcus Iunius Gracchanus), 124
Justin, epitomator of Trogus (Marcus Iunian[i]us Iustinus), 379, 551–52
Justin, martyr, 601
Juvenal (Deciumus Iunius Iuvenalis), 467–68, 474–79
Juvencus (Gaius Vettius Aquilinus Iuvencus), 644–45

Labeo (Marcus Antistius Labeo), 395–96
Laberius (Decimus Laberius), 128
Labienus (Titus Labienus), 382
Lactantius (Lucius Caelius Firmianus Lactantius), 640–42
Lactantius Placidus*, 481, 487
Laelius (Gaius Laelius), 92, 119
Laevius*, 139, 140
Lampadio. *See* Octavius Lampadio
Laus Pisonis, 436
Laws of the XII Tables, 16–17, 20, 394
Licinius Calvus. *See* Calvus
Licinius Crassus. *See* Crassus
Licinius Imbrex*, 125
Licinius Macer (Gaius Licinius Macer), 122, 368
Licinius Mucianus (Gaius Licinius Mucianus), 500
Life of Anthony, 654
Livius (Titus Livius), 367–76, 492–93, 533, 538

Livius Andronicus (Lucius Livius Andronicus), 13, 26, **39–42**

Lucan (Marcus Annaeus Lucanus), **440–51**, 463

Lucceius, 203

Lucian of Samosata, 562–63

Lucifer of Cagliari (Lucifer Caralitanus), 642

Lucilius (Gaius Lucilius), 35, 74, 98, 112–16, 201, 298–300, 302

Lucilius, friend of Seneca, 413–15

Lucillius, epigrammatist, 507, 508

Lucius Acilius*, 573

Lucius Septimius*, 652–53

Lucius of Patrae, 562

Lucretius (Titus Lucretius Carus), 155–73, 199, 271–72, 314, 429, 471

Luscius of Lanuvium (?Lavinius Luscius Lanuvinus), 99, 125

Lutatius Catulus (Quintus Lutatius Catulus), 123, 137, 138–39

Lydia. See *Dirae*

Lygdamus*, 330

Lysias, 120

Macer. *See* Aemilius Macer; Licinius Macer

Macrobius (Ambrosius Theodosius Macrobius), 549, **629–32**, 691

Maecenas (Gaius Maecenas), 256, **258–59**, 262–63, 273, 292, 433

Mago, writer on agriculture, 499

Mamercus Scaurus (Mamercus Aemilius Scaurus), 417

Mamertinus. *See* Claudius Mamertinus

Manilius (Marcus Manilius), 428–29

Marcellus Empiricus*, 701

Marcomannus, rhetorician, 629

Marcus Aurelius, emperor (Marcus Annius Verus; as emperor, Marcus Aurelius Antoninus), 580

Marianus*, *poeta novellus*, 589

Marius Sacerdos. *See* Sacerdos

Marius Victorinus (Gaius Marius Victorinus), 642–43

Martial. *See* Gargilius Martial

Martial (Marcus Valerius Martialis), 505–10

Martianus Capella (Martianus Minneus Felix Capella), 217, **700–701**

Martin, saint, bishop of Tours, 695

Martin of Braga (Martinus Bracarensis), 720

Masurius Sabinus*, 396

Maternus. *See* Curiatius Maternus

Matius (Gnaeus Matius), 139–40

Maximian, elegiac poet (Marcus Aurelius Valerius Maximianus), 717

Maximus of Turin (Maximus episcopus Taurinensis), 704

Medicina Plinii, 502, **637**

Mela. *See* Pomponius Mela

Melissus (Gaius Melissus), 37

Memmius, friend of Catullus and Lucretius, 143, 156, 157–58

Menander, 33, 52, 56, 57, 66–67, 93, 95, 96, 98

Menander of Laodicea, 632

Menippus of Gadara, 215–16, 461

Merobaudes (Flavius Merobaudes), 707

Messalinus, 330

Messalla (Marcus Valerius Messalla Corvinus), 256, **260–61**, 326, 340

Messalla. *See* Vipstanus Messalla

Mettius Pompusianus, 374

Minucius Felix (Marcus Minucius Felix), **603–4**

Moretum, 432–33

Mucianus. *See* Licinius Mucianus

Mulomedicina Chironis, 637

Naevius (Gnaeus Naevius), 26, 31, 34, 43–47, 79, 81, 111, 493, 573

Namatianus. *See* Rutilius Namatianus

Naucellius (Iunius [or Iulius?] Naucellius), 661

Nazarius*, panegyrist, 633

Nemesianus (Marcus Aurelius Olympius Nemesianus), 436, **613–14**

Nepos. *See* Cornelius Nepos

Nepotianus (Ianuarius Nepotianus), 381

Nero, emperor, 402, 436–37, 441

Nerva, emperor, 535–36

Nicaeus*, pupil of Servius, 478

Nicander of Colophon, 160, 270, 350

Nicetes Sacerdos, 525

Nicomachi, family of, 374, 632

Nicomachus Flavianus (Virius Nicomachus Flavianus), 645

Nigidius Figulus (Publius Nigidius Figulus), 220–21

Nonius Marcellus*, 113, **626–27**

Notitia Dignitatum, 702

Novatianus*, anti-pope, 606

Novellae, 714

Novius*, 127

Numitorius, 285

Obsequens. *See* Julius Obsequens

Octavia, 419–20

Octavian/Octavian Caesar. *See* Augustus

Octavius, critic of Virgil, 285

Octavius Lampadio (Gaius Octavius Lampadio), 124, **573**

Opillus. *See* Aurelius Opillus

Optatianus Porfyrius (Publilius Optatianus Porfyrius), 645

Orbilius (Lucius Orbilius Pupillus), 292

Orientius*, 709

Origen, 682–83, 694

Origo Gentis Romanae, 646

Orosius (Paulus Orosius), 702–3

Otho, emperor, 537

Ovid (Publius Ovidius Naso), 257, 328, 330, **340–64**, 406, 429

Pacuvius (Marcus Pacuvius), **104–5**, 106–9

Palaemon. *See* Remmius Palaemon

Palladius (Palladius Rutilius Taurus Aemilianus), 637–38

Panaetius, 73, 74, 94, 196–97

Panegyrici, 632–34

Panegyricus Messallae, 330–31

Papinian, jurist (Aemilius Papinianus), 615

Parthenius of Nicaea, 136, 141–42, 324–25, 353

Passio Perpetuae et Felicitatis, 599–600

Passiones, 599

Paul the Deacon (Paulus Diaconus), 387, 718

Paulinus of Milan, biographer of Ambrose (Paulinus Mediolanensis), 704

Paulinus of Nola (Meropius Pontius Paulinus Nolanus), 667–70, 695–96

Paulinus of Pella (Paulinus Pellaeus), 709

Paulinus of Périgueux (Paulinus Petricordiensis), 709

Paulus Diaconus. *See* Paul the Deacon

Paulus Festus. *See* Paul the Deacon

Pelagius*, 623–24

Pelagonius*, 637

Pentadius*, 609

Peregrinatio Aetheriae, 638

Perellius Faustus, critic of Virgil, 285

Periochae, 374, 647

Persius (Aules Persius Flaccus), 467, **468–74**

Pervigilium Veneris, 609–10

Peter of Pisa, 718

Petronius (Petronius Arbiter), **453–65**, 540–41

Petrus Chrysologus*, 704

Phaedrus*, author of fables, 433–35

Philitas, 322

Philodemus of Gadara, 157, 158

Phylarchus, 372

Pictor. *See* Fabius Pictor

Piso. *See* Calpurnius Piso Frugi

Plato, 189, 190, 191

Plautus (Titus Maccius Plautus), 32, 33, 34, 35, **49–63**, 66, 94, 98, 100, 214, 216

Pliny the Elder (Gaius Plinius Secundus), **497–503**, 534

Pliny the Younger (Gaius Plinius Caecilius Secundus), 505, 520, **525–29**

Plotinus, 691–92

Plotius Gallus (Lucius Plotius Gallus), 120

Plotius Sacerdos. *See* Sacerdos

Plutarch, 223, 548

Polemio. *See* Julius Valerius

Pollio. *See* Asinius Pollio

Polybius, 74, 93–94, 190, 369

Pompeius*, grammarian, 700

Pompeius Festus. *See* Festus

Pompeius Trogus. *See* Trogus

Pomponius, author of Atellan farces (Lucius Pomponius), 127

Pomponius, jurist (Sextus Pomponius), 585

Pomponius Mela*, 391–92

Pomponius Secundus (?Publius ?Calvisius Sabinus Pomponius Secundus), 417–18

Pontius*, deacon, 606

Porcius Latro, 340

Porcius Licinus*, 139

Porphyrio, commentator on Horace (Pomponius Porphyrio), 318, 579

Porphyry, neo-Platonic philosopher, 691–92, 715

Posidonius of Apamea, 212, 533

Possidius*, biographer of Augustine, 704

Postumius Albinus*, 70

Priapea, 465–66

Priapea of *Appendix Vergiliana*, 433

Priscian*, grammarian, 713

Proba*, 663

Probus, grammarian (Marcus Valerius Probus), 101, 172, 286, 318, 473, **578–79**

Proculus*, 396

Propertius (Sextus Propertius), 250–51, 323, **331–38**, 347

Prosper of Aquitaine (Prosper Tiro), 703–4

Prudentius (Aurelius Prudentius Clemens), **664–67**, 669–70

Publilius Syrus*, 129

Quadrigarius. *See* Claudius Quadrigarius

Querolus sive Aulularia, 670–71

Quintilian (Marcus Fabius Quintilianus),
512–18, 527
Quodvultdeus, 704

Rabirius*, 430
Remius Favinus, 638
Remmius Palaemon (Quintus Remmius
Palaemon), 512, 513, 577
Reposianus*, 610
Rhetorica ad Herennium, 120
Romance of Alexander, 384, 653
Rufinus of Aquileia (Tyrannius Rufinus),
694
Rufius Festus*, 647
Rutilius Namatianus (Rutilius Claudius
Namatianus), 705–7
Rutilius Rufus (Publius Rutilius Rufus),
123

Sabinus, friend of Ovid, 359
Sabinus. *See* Masurius Sabinus
Sacerdos, grammarian (Marius Plotius
Sacerdos), 615
Sallust (Gaius Sallustius Crispus), 234–44,
250, 373, 533
Sallust, author of *Empedoclea* (Gnaeus Sallus-
tius), 160, 235
Salvianus*, 703
Salvius Julianus, jurist (Lucius Octavius
Cornelius Salvius Iulianus Aemilianus),
585
Sammonicus. *See* Serenus Sammonicus
Sappho, 150, 305
Scaevola the Augur (Quintus Mucius Scae-
vola Augur), 395
Scaevola the Pontifex (Quintus Mucius
Scaevola Pontifex), 17, 395
Scaurus. *See* Aemilius Scaurus
Scipio Aemilianus (Publius Cornelius
Scipio Aemilianus Africanus Numanti-
nus), 73, 92, 119
Scipio Africanus (Publius Cornelius Scipio
Africanus Maior), 68, 78, 90
Scipios, family and "circle" of, 73–74,
119
Scribonius Largus*, 389
Sedulius*, 709
Sempronius Asellio*, 121
Sempronius Tuditanus (Gaius Sempronius
Tuditanus), 122
Seneca (Lucius Annaeus Seneca), 217, 408–
24, 485, 513, 514, 515
Seneca the Elder (Lucius Annaeus Seneca),
383, 404–5

Septimius Serenus, *poeta novellus,* 589
Serenus. *See* Septimius Serenus
Serenus Sammonicus*, antiquarian writer,
613
Serenus Sammonicus (Quintus Serenus
Sammonicus), writer on medicine, 613
Servilius Nonianus (Marcus Servilius Noni-
anus), 383
Servius (Maurus [Marius] Servius Honora-
tus), 549, 628–29
Severus. *See* Cornelius Severus; Sulpicius
Severus
Sextilius Ena*, 430
Sidonius Apollinaris (Gaius Sollius Mo-
destus Apollinaris Sidonius), 707–9
Silius Italicus (Tiberius Catius Asconius Sil-
ius Italicus), 491–95
Simias of Rhodes, 589
Siro, 157, 262
Sisenna (Lucius Cornelius Sisenna), 122–
23, 240, 460, 561
Solinus (Gaius Iulius Solinus), 502,
617–18
Sophocles, 41, 42, 78
Sotades of Maronea, 76
Statius (Publius Papinius Statius), 481–88.
See also Caecilius Statius
Stilo (Lucius Aelius Stilo Praeconinus), 62,
124, 210, 572–73
Sueius*, 140
Suetonius (Gaius Suetonius Tranquillus),
528, 546–50
Sulla (Lucius Cornelius Sulla Felix), 123
Sulpicia, niece of Messalla, 326, 330
Sulpicia, poetess praised by Martial, 437
Sulpiciae conquestio, 661
Sulpicius Apollinaris, grammarian (Gaius
Sulpicius Apollinaris), 579
Sulpicius Galba (Servius Sulpicius
Galba), 68
Sulpicius Rufus, jurist (Servius Sulpicius
Rufus), 395
Sulpicius Rufus, orator (Publius Sulpicius
Rufus), 120
Sulpicius Severus*, 623, 694–96
Symmachi, family of, 374, 632
Symmachus, orator (Quintus Aurelius Sym-
machus Eusebius), 634–36
Syrus. *See* Publilius Syrus

Tacitus (Cornelius Tacitus), 516, 527,
530–44, 648–49
Terence (Publius Terentius Afer), 31, 66,
73, 92–202

Terentianus Maurus*, 611–12

Terentius Varro. *See* Varro

Tertullian (Quintus Septimius Florens Tertullianus), 601–3

Testamentum Porcelli, 616

Theocritus, 254, 264–65, 266

Theodorus Priscianus*, 637

Theophrastus, 96

Theopompus, 379

Thrasea Paetus (Publius Clodius Thrasea Paetus), 542

Thucydides, 170, 230, 241, 373, 378

Tiberianus*, 645

Tiberius, emperor, 401

Tiberius Donatus (Tiberius Claudius Donatus), 628

Tibullus (Albius Tibullus), 326–29

Timaeus, 89

Timagenes, 379, 384

Tiro, 202

Titinius*, author of *togatae,* 125

Titius (Gaius Titius), 108–9

Trabea (Quintus Trabea), 125

Trajan, emperor (Marcus Ulpius Traianus Germanicus Dacicus), 525

Trebellius Pollio*, 650

Trogus (Pompeius Trogus), 378–80

Tuditanus. *See* Sempronius Tuditanus

Turpilius, author of *palliatae* (Sextus Turpilius), 125

Turpio. *See* Ambivius Turpio

Tyrannio the Elder, 124

Ulpian, jurist (Domitius Ulpianus), 615–16

Vacca*, biographer of Lucan, 441

Valerius Aedituus*, 139

Valerius Antias*, 122, 368

Valerius Cato (Publius Valerius Cato), 140–41, 574–75

Valerius Flaccus (Gaius Valerius Flaccus Balbus Setinus), 488–91

Valerius Maximus*, 381–82

Valerius Messalla. *See* Messalla

Valerius Probus. *See* Probus

Valgius Rufus (Gaius Valgius Rufus), 330, 426

Varius Rufus (Lucius Varius Rufus), 108, 258, 263, 417, **429**

Varro (Marcus Terentius Varro), 50–51, 62, 209, **210–20**, 391, 547

Varro of Atax (Publius Terentius Varro Atacinus), 110–11, **141**

Vegetius (Flavius Vegetius Renatus), 637

Velleius Paterculus*, 380–81

Venantius Fortunatus (Venantius Honorius Clementianus Fortunatus), 722–23

Vennonius*, 122

Verrius Flaccus*, 172, 356, **386–87**

Vespa*, 610–11

Vettius Philocomus*, 124

Vetus Afra, 598

Vetus Itala, 598

Vetus Latina, 598

Vibius Sequester*, 638

Victor of Vita (Victor Vitensis), 719–20

Victorinus. *See* Marius Victorinus

Victorinus of Poetovium (Victorinus Poetovionensis), 606

Vipstanus Messalla*, 542

Virgil (Publius Vergilius Maro), 82, 171, 213, 250, **262–90**, 370, 389, 431, 436, 444, 445–46, 493–94, 631

Vitruvius (Vitruvius Pollio), **387–88**, 390

Volcacius Sedigitus*, 66, 77, 100, **139**, 573

Volcatius Gallicanus*, 650

Volusius, 110

Zeno of Verona (Zeno Veronensis), 642

The Library of Congress has cataloged the hardover edition of this book as follows:

Conte, Gian Biagio, 1941–
   [Letteratura latina. English]
   Latin literature : a history / Gian Biago Conte ; translated by
Joseph B. Solodow ; revised by Don Fowler and Glenn W. Most.
     p. cm.
   Translation of : Letteratura latina.
   Includes bibliographical references (p.) and index.
   ISBN 0-8018-4638-2 (acid-free)
   1. Latin literature—History and criticism.   2. Rome—
Civilization—Historiography.   3. Rome in literature.   I. Title.
PA6008.C6613   1994
870.9´001—dc20   93-20985

ISBN 0-8018-6253-1 (pbk.)